D1573112

Contemporary Authors®

NEW REVISION SERIES

ISSN 0275-7176

Contemporary Authors®

A Bio-Bibliographical Guide to
Current Writers in Fiction, General Nonfiction,
Poetry, Journalism, Drama, Motion Pictures,
Television, and Other Fields

DANIEL JONES
JOHN D. JORGENSON
Editors

NEW REVISION SERIES
volume **70**

GALE

DETROIT · LONDON

STAFF

Daniel Jones and John D. Jorgenson, *Editors, New Revision Series*

Thomas Wiloch, *Sketchwriting Coordinator and Online Research Specialist*

Tim Akers, Catherine V. Donaldson, Jeff Hunter, Jerry Moore, Deborah A. Schmitt, Polly A. Vedder, Tim White, and Kathy Wilson, *Contributing Editors*

Bruce Boston, Mary Gillis, Joan Goldsworthy, Anne Janette Johnson, Judson Knight, David Kroeger, Robert Miltner, Jani Prescott, Trudy Ring, Bryan Ryan, Susan Salter, Pamela L. Shelton, Charles Wagner, Shanna Weagle, and Tim Winter-Damon, *Sketchwriters*

James P. Draper, *Managing Editor*

Victoria B. Cariappa, *Research Manager*

Tamara C. Nott, Tracie A. Richardson, Cheryl L. Warnock, and Robert Whaley, *Research Associates*

Wendy K. Festerling and Corrine A. Stocker, *Research Assistants*

Library of Congress Catalog Card Number 81-640179
ISBN 0-7876-2039-4
ISSN 0275-7176

Printed in the United States of America

10 9 8 7 6 5 4 3 2 1

Contents

Indexing note: All *Contemporary Authors New Revision Series* entries are indexed in the *Contemporary Authors* cumulative index, which is published separately and distributed twice a year.

As always, the most recent *Contemporary Authors* cumulative index continues to be the user's guide to the location of an individual author's listing.

Preface

The *Contemporary Authors New Revision Series* (*CANR*) provides updated information on authors listed in earlier volumes of *Contemporary Authors* (*CA*). Although entries for individual authors from any volume of *CA* may be included in a volume of the *New Revision Series, CANR* updates only those sketches requiring significant change. However, in response to requests from librarians and library patrons for the most current information possible on high-profile writers of greater public and critical interest, *CANR* revises entries for these authors whenever new and noteworthy information becomes available.

Authors are included on the basis of specific criteria that indicate the need for a revision. These criteria include a combination of bibliographical additions, changes in addresses or career, major awards, and personal information such as name changes or death dates. All listings in this volume have been revised or augmented in various ways and contain up-to-the-minute publication information in the Writings section, most often verified by the author and/or by consulting a variety of online resources. Many sketches have been extensively rewritten, often including informative new Sidelights. As always, a *CANR* listing entails no charge or obligation.

The key to locating an author's most recent entry is the *CA* cumulative index, which is published separately and distributed twice a year. It provides access to all entries in *CA* and *CANR*. Always consult the latest index to find an author's most recent entry.

For the convenience of users, the *CA* cumulative index also includes references to all entries in these Gale literary series: *Authors and Artists for Young Adults, Authors in the News, Bestsellers, Black Literature Criticism, Black Writers, Children's Literature Review, Concise Dictionary of American Literary Biography, Concise Dictionary of British Literary Biography, Contemporary Authors Autobiography Series, Contemporary Authors Bibliographical Series, Contemporary Literary Criticism, Dictionary of Literary Biography, Dictionary of Literary Biography Documentary Series, Dictionary of Literary Biography Yearbook, DISCovering Authors, DISCovering Authors: British, DISCovering Authors: Canadian, DISCovering Authors: Modules* (including modules for Dramatists, Most-Studied Authors, Multicultural Authors, Novelists, Poets, and Popular/Genre Authors), *Drama Criticism, Hispanic Literature Criticism, Hispanic Writers, Junior DISCovering Authors, Major Authors and Illustrators for Children and Young Adults, Major 20th-Century Writers, Native North American Literature, Poetry Criticism, Short Story Criticism, Something about the Author, Something about the Author Autobiography Series, Twentieth-Century Literary Criticism, World Literature Criticism, World Literature Criticism Supplement,* and *Yesterday's Authors of Books for Children.*

A Sample Index Entry:

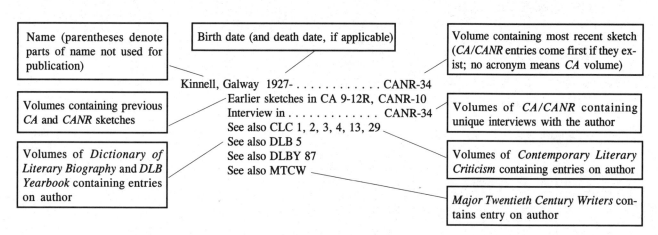

For the most recent *CA* information on Kinnell, users should refer to Volume 34 of the *New Revision Series,* as designated by "CANR-34"; if that volume is unavailable, refer to CANR-10. If CANR-10 is also unavailable, refer to CA 9-12R, published in 1974, for Kinnell's first revision entry.

How Are Entries Compiled?

The editors make every effort to secure new information directly from the authors. Copies of all sketches in selected *CA* and *CANR* volumes previously published are routinely sent to listees at their last-known addresses, and returns from these authors are then assessed. For deceased writers, or those who fail to reply to requests for data, we consult other reliable biographical sources, such as those indexed in Gale's *Biography and Genealogy Master Index,* and bibliographical sources, such as *Magazine Index, Newspaper Abstracts, LC MARC,* and a variety of online databases. Further details come from published interviews, feature stories, book reviews, online literary magazines and journals, author web sites, and often the authors' publishers supply material.

* Indicates that a listing has been compiled from secondary sources believed to be reliable, but has not been personally verified for this edition by the author sketched.

What Kinds of Information Does an Entry Provide?

Sketches in *CANR* contain the following biographical and bibliographical information:

- **Entry heading:** the most complete form of author's name, plus any pseudonyms or name variations used for writing

- **Personal information:** author's date and place of birth, family data, ethnicity, educational background, political and religious affiliations, and hobbies and leisure interests

- **Addresses:** author's home, office, or agent's addresses, plus e-mail and fax numbers, as available

- **Career summary:** name of employer, position, and dates held for each career post; resume of other vocational achievements; military service

- **Membership information:** professional, civic, and other association memberships and any official posts held

- **Awards and honors:** military and civic citations, major prizes and nominations, fellowships, grants, and honorary degrees

- **Writings:** a comprehensive, chronological list of titles, publishers, dates of original publication and revised editions, and production information for plays, television scripts, and screenplays

- **Adaptations:** a list of films, plays, and other media which have been adapted from the author's work

- **Work in progress:** current or planned projects, with dates of completion and/or publication, and expected publisher, when known

- **Sidelights:** a biographical portrait of the author's development; information about the critical reception of the author's works; revealing comments, often by the author, on personal interests, aspirations, motivations, and thoughts on writing

- **Biographical and critical sources:** a list of books and periodicals in which additional information on an author's life and/or writings appears

Related Titles in the *CA* Series

Contemporary Authors Autobiography Series complements *CA* original and revised volumes with specially commissioned autobiographical essays by important current authors, illustrated with personal photographs they provide. Common topics include their motivations for writing, the people and experiences that shaped their careers, the rewards they derive from their work, and their impressions of the current literary scene.

Contemporary Authors Bibliographical Series surveys writings by and about important American authors since World War II. Each volume concentrates on a specific genre and features approximately ten writers; entries list works written by and about the author and contain a bibliographical essay discussing the merits and deficiencies of major critical and scholarly studies in detail.

Available in Electronic Formats

CD-ROM. Full-text bio-bibliographic entries from the entire *CA* series, covering approximately 101,000 writers, are available on CD-ROM through lease and purchase plans. The disc combines entries from the *CA*, *CANR*, and *Contemporary Authors Permanent Series* (*CAP*) print series to provide the most recent author listing. It can be searched by name, title, subject/genre, nationality/ethnicity, personal data, and as well as advanced searching using boolean logic. The disc is updated every six months. For more information, call 1-800-877-GALE. *CA* is also available on CD-ROM from SilverPlatter Information, Inc.

Online. The *Contemporary Authors* database is made available online to libraries and their patrons through online public access catalog (OPAC) vendors. Currently, *CA* is offered through Ameritech Library Services' Vista Online (formerly Dynix).

GaleNet. *CA* is available on a subscription basis through GaleNet, a new online information resource that features an easy-to-use end-user interface, the powerful search capabilities of the BRS/Search retrieval software, and ease of access through the World Wide Web. For more information, call 1-800-877-GALE.

Magnetic Tape. *CA* is available for licensing on magnetic tape in a fielded format. The database is available for internal data processing and nonpublishing purposes only. For more information, call 1-800-877-GALE.

Suggestions Are Welcome

The editors welcome comments and suggestions from users on any aspects of the *CA* series. If readers would like to recommend authors for inclusion in future volumes of the series, they are cordially invited to write the editors; call toll-free at 1-800-347-GALE; fax at 1-248-699-8054; or email at john.jorgenson@gale.com or dan.jones@gale.com.

CA Numbering System and Volume Update Chart

Occasionally questions arise about the *CA* numbering system and which volumes, if any, can be discarded. Despite numbers like "29-32R," "97-100" and "157," the entire *CA* print series consists of only 164 physical volumes with the publication of *CA* Volume 167. The following charts note changes in the numbering system and cover design, and indicate which volumes are essential for the most complete, up-to-date coverage.

CA First Revision	• 1-4R through 41-44R (11 books) *Cover:* Brown with black and gold trim. There will be no further First Revision volumes because revised entries are now being handled exclusively through the more efficient *New Revision Series* mentioned below.
CA Original Volumes	• 45-48 through 97-100 (14 books) *Cover:* Brown with black and gold trim. • 101 through 167 (67 books) *Cover:* Blue and black with orange bands. The same as previous *CA* original volumes but with a new, simplified numbering system and new cover design.
CA Permanent Series	• *CAP*-1 and *CAP*-2 (2 books) *Cover:* Brown with red and gold trim. There will be no further *Permanent Series* volumes because revised entries are now being handled exclusively through the more efficient *New Revision Series* mentioned below.
CA New Revision Series	• *CANR*-1 through *CANR*-70 (70 books) *Cover:* Blue and black with green bands. Includes only sketches requiring significant changes; **sketches are taken from any previously published *CA*, *CAP*, or *CANR* volume**.

If You Have: You May Discard:

If You Have:	You May Discard:

CA First Revision Volumes 1-4R
  through 41-44R **and** *CA Permanent Series*
Volumes 1 and 2
	CA Original Volumes 1, 2, 3, 4
	    Volumes 5-6 through 41-44

CA Original Volumes 45-48 through 97-100 **and** 101 through 167	**NONE:** These volumes will not be superseded by corresponding revised volumes. Individual entries from these and all other volumes appearing in the left column of this chart may be revised and included in the various volumes of the *New Revision Series*.
CA New Revision Series Volumes *CANR*-1 through *CANR*-70	**NONE:** The *New Revision Series* does not replace any single volume of *CA*. Instead, volumes of *CANR* include entries from many previous *CA* series volumes. All *New Revision Series* volumes must be retained for full coverage.

A Sampling of Authors and Media People
Featured in This Volume

Ingmar Bergman

One of the most acclaimed directors of the twentieth century, Bergman is known for films which deal thematically with his own concerns: loneliness, the human spirit, the search for God, innocence, love. His work has been widely praised and has influenced many American directors, including Woody Allen. In addition to his films, Bergman is also venerated for his work in the theatre. His works include *The Seventh Seal, Persona, The Magic Lantern: An Autobiography,* and the Academy Award-winning *Fanny and Alexander.*

Alejo Carpentier

Carpentier was a Cuban journalist, editor, and author widely admired and emulated in Latin America. His fiction typically examined aspects of the development of Latin American life and culture. Though he never gained a large reading audience in the United States, critics praise Carpentier's encyclopedic knowlege, often ranking him with major Latin American authors such as Gabriel Garcia Marquez and Jorge Luis Borges. His works include *The Kingdom of This World* and *Explosion in a Cathedral.*

Joanna Cole

Cole is an American author of children's nonfiction and fiction. Critics praise Cole's ability to remain accurate while also writing in a style accessible to younger audiences, making complex and technical ideas easily understood. Cole's works have garnered numerous awards including many citations as best or notable books from the American Library Association, *Horn Book,* and *School Library Journal.* Her works include the "Animal Births," "Animal Bodies," "Gator Girls," and "Magic School Bus" series.

Wes Craven

Craven is an American film director known for his popular horror movies. Known for incorporating psychological phenomena in his films, Craven's work has led to his being dubbed the "Sultan of Slash" by critics. In addition to films, Craven has also directed numerous television projects, including many episodes of *The Twilight Zone* series. His other works include *Last House on the Left, The Hills Have Eyes, A Nightmare on Elm Street,* and the popular self-satirizing horror films, *Scream* and *Scream 2.*

Ariel Dorfman

Dorfman is an Argentinian-born novelist, dramatist, poet, and short story writer known for works that probe the despair of exile and dictatorship. Dorfman worked and lived in Chile until 1973, when he was exiled after the Allende government was defeated by the Pinochet military regime. Critics praise Dorfman's works for their political relevance and emotional impact, and for blending political and artistic concerns. His works include *Widows, Last Waltz in Santiago and Other Poems of Exile and Disappearance,* and the popular *Death and the Maiden.*

Primo Levi

Levi was an Italian Jew and concentration camp survivor whose apparent suicide is largely considered the result of his growing despair at the fading significance of the Holocaust from one generation to the next. Levi was considered one of the premiere chroniclers of the horrifying conditions endured by the Jews during the World War II years. Though he never intended to be a writer, Levi felt compelled to tell the story of the Holocaust and its effects in such works as *Survival in Auschwitz: The Nazi Assault on Humanity* and *The Reawakening.*

Joe McGinniss

McGinnis is an American nonfiction writer noted for an intense, personal involvement with the topics of his works. Critics praise McGinniss' insight and concise prose, lauding his ability to deal with controversial and emotionally charged stories. His works include *Fatal Vision,* a comprehensive account of the murder conviction of Dr. Jeffrey MacDonald, and *Cruel Doubt,* the story of Bonnie Von Stein, whose son had arranged to murder both his mother and step-father.

John Nichols

Nichols is an American author best known for his "New Mexico" trilogy, *The Milagro Beanfield War, The Magic Journey,* and *The Nirvana Blues,* which chronicles one town's metamorphosis from a quiet, traditional city into a commercial metropolitan area. Critics praise Nichols' social novels, some favorably comparing *The Milagro Beanfield War* to John Steinbeck, William Faulkner or Gabriel Garcia Marquez.

George Plimpton

Plimpton is an American journalist known as much for his eclectic interests as he is for his writing. An athlete, a comedian, a musician, and an actor as well as a writer, Plimpton has also edited the prestigious literary periodical, the *Paris Review*. His works include *Paper Lion*, a book about his experiences with the Detroit Lions football team, *The Curious Case of Sidd Finch*, a sports novel, and also collections of interviews from the *Paris Review*.

Denise Robins

Robins was a best-selling author of romance novels who published more than 200 novels during her long and prolific career. Her works have sold more than 100 million copies, and involve nearly every type of romantic entanglement imaginable, according to one critic. Though many of her works involve divorce and extra-marital affairs, her later works also involve themes of female independence and freedom. Her works include *The Marriage Bond, Put Back the Clock, The Crash*, and *Come Back, Yesterday*.

Jack Williamson

Williamson is an American science fiction writer praised by critics for helping to legitimize science fiction writing by utilizing a more literary approach to the genre. Lauded by critics for his skill at characterization, Williamson was given the Grand Master Award for lifetime achievement from the Science Fiction Writers of America in 1976. His works include *The Legion of Space* and the Hugo Award-winning *Wonder's Child: My Life in Science Fiction*.

Tom Wolfe

One of the most celebrated contemporary writers, Wolfe gained fame during the 1960s with his *The Kandy-Kolored Tangerine-Flake Streamline Baby*, an analysis and satire of American trends and pop culture. Critics laud Wolfe's social insights and his inventive prose, and he is widely considered among the premier literary journalists of the century. In addition to his journalistic works, Wolfe is also a celebrated novelist, whose works include the American Book Award-winning *The Right Stuff*, and *The Bonfire of the Vanities*.

A

AHLBERG, Allan 1938-

PERSONAL: Born June 5, 1938, in England; married Janet Hall (an illustrator), July, 1969; children: Jessica. *Education:* Sunderland Teacher Training College, Certificate in Education.

ADDRESSES: *Home*—Leicester, England. *Agent*—Penguin Books Ltd., 27 Wrights Lane, London W8 5TZ, England.

CAREER: Worked at various jobs, including postman, soldier, grave digger, schoolteacher, and plumber's mate; writer, 1975—.

AWARDS, HONORS: Commendation from Library Association (England), 1977, for *Burglar Bill;* Kate Greenaway Medal from Library Association (England), 1979, selected by the Notable Children's Book Committee of the Association for Library Service to Children, 1979, and named to the International Board on Books for Young People (IBBY) 1980 Honors List, all for *Each Peach Pear Plum: An "I Spy" Story;* Other Award from Children's Rights Workshop, 1980, for *Mrs. Plug the Plumber;* Best Books of the Year Award, *School Library Journal,* 1981, for *Funnybones; Peek-a-boo!* was a 1981 selection of the Notable Children's Book Committee of the Association for Library Service to Children, and recipient of *Parents Magazine* Best Book for Babies Award, 1985; commendation from Library Association (Great Britain), 1982, Best Books of the Year Award, *School Library Journal,* 1983, Teacher's Choice Award, National Council of Teachers of English, 1983, and citation, Notable Children's Book Committee of the Association for Library Service to Children, 1983, all for *The Baby's Catalogue;* Emil/

Kurt Maschler Award, 1986, Children's Book Award of the Federation of Children's Book Groups, 1986, Golden Key (Holland), 1987, Prix du Livre pour la Jeunesse (France), 1987, all for *The Jolly Postman; or, Other Peoples Letters;* Silver Paint Brush (Holland), 1988, for *Funnybones;* Signal Poetry Award, 1990, for *Heard It on the Playground.*

WRITINGS:

FOR YOUNG PEOPLE; ILLUSTRATED BY WIFE, JANET AHLBERG

The Old Joke Book, Kestrel Books (London), 1976, Viking (New York City), 1977.
Burglar Bill, Greenwillow (New York City), 1977.
The Vanishment of Thomas Tull, Scribner (New York City), 1977.
Jeremiah in the Dark Woods, Kestrel Books, 1977, Viking, 1978.
The One and Only Two Heads, Collins (London), 1979.
Two Wheels, Two Heads, Collins, 1979.
Son of a Gun, Heinemann (London), 1979.
Little Worm Book, Granada (London), 1979, Viking, 1980.
Funnybones, Greenwillow, 1980.
The Ha Ha Bonk Book, Penguin, 1982.
The Baby's Catalogue, Little, Brown (Boston), 1982.
The Jolly Postman; or, Other People's Letters, Little, Brown, 1986.
The Cinderella Show, Viking Kestrel, 1986, Penguin, 1987.
The Clothes Horse and Other Stories, Viking Kestrel (London), 1987, Viking Kestrel (New York City), 1988.
Starting School, Viking Kestrel, 1988.

Bye Bye Baby: A Sad Story with a Happy Ending,
    Little, Brown, 1989, published as *Bye Bye, Baby:*
    A Baby Without a Mommy in Search of One, 1990.
The Jolly Christmas Postman, Little, Brown, 1991.
The Bear Nobody Wanted, Viking, 1992.
It Was a Dark and Stormy Night, Viking, 1993.
The Jolly Pocket Postman, Little, Brown, 1995.

*"BRICK STREET BOYS" SERIES; ILLUSTRATED BY JANET
    AHLBERG*

Here Are the Brick Street Boys, Collins, 1975.
A Place to Play, Collins, 1975.
Sam the Referee, Collins, 1975.
Fred's Dream, Collins, 1976.
The Great Marathon Football Match, Collins, 1976.

*"DAISYCHAIN" SERIES; ILLUSTRATED BY JANET AHLBERG,
    EXCEPT AS NOTED*

Ready, Teddy, Go!, Heinemann, 1983.
Summer Snowman, Heinemann, 1983.
That's My Baby!, Heinemann, 1983.
Which Witch?, Heinemann, 1983.
Clowning About, illustrated by Andre Amstutz,
    Heinemann, 1984.
The Good Old Dolls, illustrated by Amstutz,
    Heinemann, 1984.
Monster Munch, illustrated by Amstutz, Heinemann,
    1984.
Rent-a-Robot, illustrated by Amstutz, Heinemann,
    1984.
One True Santa, Heinemann, 1985.

"SLOT BOOKS" SERIES; ILLUSTRATED BY JANET AHLBERG

Playmates, Viking Kestrel (London), 1984, Viking
    Kestrel (New York City), 1985.
Yum, Yum, Viking Kestrel (London), 1984, Viking
    Kestrel (New York City), 1985.

*"FOLDAWAYS" SERIES; ILLUSTRATED BY COLIN
    MCNAUGHTON*

Circus, Houghton, 1984.
Families, Houghton, 1984.
Monsters, Houghton, 1984.
Zoo, Houghton, 1984.

"FUNNYBONES" SERIES; ILLUSTRATED BY AMSTUTZ

The Black Cat, Greenwillow, 1990.
The Pet Shop, Heinemann, 1990, Mulberry Books
    (New York City), 1993.

Dinosaur Dreams, Greenwillow, 1991.
Mystery Tour, Greenwillow, 1991.
Skeleton Crew, Greenwillow, 1992.
Bumps in the Night, Heinemann, 1991.
Give the Dog a Bone, Heinemann, 1991.
The Ghost Train, Greenwillow, 1992.

"HAPPY FAMILY" SERIES

Master Salt the Sailor's Son, illustrated by Amstutz,
    Puffin (New York City), 1980, published in
    "Wacky Family" series, Golden Press (New
    York City), 1982.
Miss Jump the Jockey, illustrated by Amstutz, Puf-
    fin, 1980.
Mr. Biff the Boxer, illustrated by J. Ahlberg, Puffin,
    1980, published in "Wacky Family" series,
    Golden Press, 1982.
Mr. Cosmo the Conjurer, illustrated by Joe Wright,
    Puffin, 1980.
Mrs. Plug the Plumber, illustrated by Wright, Puffin,
    1980, published in "Wacky Family" series,
    Golden Press, 1982.
Mrs. Wobble the Waitress, illustrated by J. Ahlberg,
    Puffin, 1980, published in "Wacky Family" se-
    ries, Golden Press, 1982.
Master Money the Millionaire, illustrated by
    Amstutz, Puffin, 1981.
Miss Brick the Builder's Baby, illustrated by
    McNaughton, Puffin, 1981, published in "Wacky
    Family" series, Golden Press, 1982.
Mr. and Mrs. Hay the Horse, illustrated by
    McNaughton, Puffin, 1981, published in "Wacky
    Family" series, Golden Press, 1982.
Mr. Buzz the Beeman, illustrated by Faith Jaques,
    Puffin, 1981, published in "Wacky Family" se-
    ries, Golden Press, 1982.
Mr. Tick the Teacher, illustrated by Jaques, Puffin,
    1981.
Mrs. Lather's Laundry, illustrated by Amstutz, Puf-
    fin, 1981, published in "Wacky Family" series,
    Golden Press, 1982.
Master Bun the Baker's Boy, illustrated by Fritz
    Wegner, Puffin, 1988.
Miss Dose the Doctor's Daughter, illustrated by
    Wegner, Puffin, 1988.
Mr. Creep the Crook, illustrated by Amstutz, Puffin,
    1988.
Mrs. Jolly's Joke Shop, illustrated by McNaughton,
    Viking Kestrel, 1988.

Also author of *Miss Dirt the Dustman's Daughter,*
illustrated by Tony Ross, 1996; and *Mrs. Vole the
Vet,* illustrated by Emma Chichester Clark, 1996.

"HELP YOUR CHILD TO READ" SERIES

Bad Bear, illustrated by Eric Hill, Granada, 1982.
Double Ducks, illustrated by Hill, Granada, 1982.
Fast Frogs, illustrated by Hill, Granada, 1982.
Poorly Pigs, illustrated by Hill, Granada, 1982, Rand McNally (Chicago), 1984.
Rubber Rabbit, illustrated by Hill, Granada, 1982.
Silly Sheep, illustrated by Hill, Granada, 1982.
Hip-Hippo-Ray, illustrated by Amstutz, Granada, 1983, Rand McNally, 1984.
King Kangaroo, illustrated by Amstutz, Granada, 1983.
Mister Wolf, illustrated by Amstutz, Granada, 1983.
Spider Spy, illustrated by Amstutz, Granada, 1983.
Tell-Tale Tiger, illustrated by Amstutz, Granada, 1983.
Traveling Moose, illustrated by Amstutz, Granada, 1983.
Fast Frog and Friends: Help Your Child to Read Collection (includes *Bad Bear, Double Duks, Fast Frogs, Poorly Pigs, Rubber Rabbit,* and *Silly Sheep*), illustrated by Hill, Dragon, 1984.

"RED NOSE READERS" SERIES; ILLUSTRATED BY COLIN MCNAUGHTON

Bear's Birthday, Walker Books (London), 1985.
Big Bad Pig, Random House (New York City), 1985.
Fe Fi Fo Fum, Random House, 1985.
Happy Worm, Random House, 1985.
Help!, Random House, 1985.
Jumping, Walker Books, 1985.
Make a Face, Walker Books, 1985.
So Can I, Walker Books, 1985.
Blow Me Down!, Walker Books, 1986.
Crash! Bang! Wallop!, Random House, 1986.
Look Out for the Seals!, Walker Books, 1986.
Me and My Friend, Random House, 1986.
One, Two, Flea!, Walker Books, 1986.
Push the Dog, Random House, 1986.
Shirley's Shops, Random House, 1986.
Tell Us a Story, Walker Books, 1986.

Also author of *Put on a Show!,* 1996, and *Who Stole the Pie?,* 1996.

CHILDREN'S VERSE

Cops and Robbers, illustrated by J. Ahlberg, Heinemann (London), 1978, Greenwillow, 1979.
Each Peach Pear Plum: An "I Spy" Story, illustrated by J. Ahlberg, Kestrel Books, 1978, Viking, 1979, reprinted, 1991.

Peek-a-boo!, illustrated by J. Ahlberg, Viking, 1981 (published in England as *Peepo!,* Kestrel Books, 1981).
Please Mrs. Butler (see also below), illustrated by Wegner, Kestrel Books, 1983.
The Mighty Slide, illustrated by Charlotte Voake, Viking Kestrel, 1988.
Heard It in the Playground (see also below), illustrated by Wegner, Viking, 1989.

OTHER

(With John Lawrence) *The History of a Pair of Sinners: Forgetting Not Their Ma Who Was One Also* (verse), Granada, 1981.
Ten in a Bed (stories for children), illustrated by Amstutz, Granada, 1983.
Woof! (novel), illustrated by Wegner, Penguin, 1986.
Mrs. Butler Song Book (based on poems from *Please Mrs. Butler* and *Heard It in the Playground*), music by Colin Matthews, illustrations by Wegner, Viking, 1992.
The Better Brown Stories, illustrated by Fritz Wegner, Viking, 1995.
The Mysteries of Zigomar: Poems and Stories, illustrated by John Lawrence, Candlewick Press, 1997.
The Giant Baby, illustrated by Wegner, Viking, 1984.

SIDELIGHTS: British author Allan Ahlberg is recognized throughout England and the United States for his numerous picture books, comic tales, and rhyming stories for children. His work has garnered several top awards, including a Greenaway Medal for *Each Peach Pear Plum.* Ahlberg collaborates with a number of illustrators, such as Andre Amstutz, Colin McNaughton, Faith Jaques, Eric Hill, and Fritz Wegner. However, he is perhaps most recognized as working with his wife, Janet, an illustrator. Once, seven books by the husband and wife team were included among a list of fifty-one titles which the British government recommended as preparation for national curriculum tests. Part of their success, according to Aidan Chambers in *Horn Book,* stems from the sense of unity in their work: "Their books certainly possess that integrated relationship between words and pictures usually achieved only when writer and illustrator are the same—one person." "The story flows from the words into the pictures and back again. The story in the pictures is a counterpoint . . . to the story in the words," described Ahlberg in Douglas Martin's *The Telling Line.*

After working as a school teacher for almost a decade, Ahlberg decided to pair with his wife Janet, then a free-lance designer of educational visual-aids, to create picture books. After eighteen month and several rejection slips, the "Brick Street Boys" series was accepted for publication by Collins. These first books are parodies of "Dick and Jane" readers, which the Ahlbergs designed to assist older children with reading difficulties who did not want to be stigmatized for reading "baby books." "Here is Sam. Here is Fred. Here is the ball. Fred kicks the ball. Sam kicks the ball. Fred kicks Sam. Here is the referee" reads the text of one of the "Brick Street Boys" books. Following these comic-strip style books, the Ahlbergs have collectively produced more than one hundred books for children.

While the Ahlbergs have written a broad range of children's books, their works are similarly based on lighthearted fun, clear morals, and happy endings. Not only does good triumph over evil, but adversity itself is never overwhelming. In *Burglar Bill,* for instance, Bill steals such commonplace items as a toothbrush and a can of beans until one day when he is robbed himself. Seeing how unpleasant it is to have things stolen, Bill changes his ways. The Ahlbergs' picture books—including *The Baby's Catalogue, Each Peach Pear Plum,* and *Peek-a-Boo!*—fasten on the simplicity and joy of everyday objects and events while revealing a world of fascinating sights for preschoolers. As Eric Hadley noted in *Twentieth-Century Children's Writers,* an Ahlberg book is "wholesome and decent" and does not "present a troubled world or set out to disturb." As a *Times* contributor notes, "[The books by the Ahlbergs] are . . . refreshingly free from the standards of the po-faced ideologues who pontificate on children's books."

Classic fairy-tale characters like the three bears and Little Red Riding Hood are included in some of the Ahlbergs' stories. In *Each Peach Pear Plum,* preschoolers can scan the vibrant, detailed illustrations to find such celebrated figures as Jack and Jill, Little Book Peep, Tom Thumb, and Robin Hood. The boy detective in *Jeremiah in the Dark Woods* embarks on a journey that introduces him to three bears and takes him past a field of giant beanstalks. And *The Jolly Postman; or, Other People's Letters* features a postman delivering mail to famous characters like Cinderella, the Bid Bad Wolf, and Goldilocks. The latter has been especially popular with readers and critics alike, as reflected in Chris Powling's comments in *Books for Keeps:* "Once in a while a picture-book arrives that's so brilliant, so broad in its appeal, it seems to be a summation of the state-of-the-art. For me, *The Jolly Postman* is just such a book. As a matching of word and image it's a virtuoso performance; as a feat of design it's without a flaw."

Whether they are parodying the conventions of established genres and the fairy-tale tradition of wicked witches, dark forests, and beautiful princesses, as in *The Jolly Postman* and *Ten in a Bed,* or writing fanciful children's stories of their own creation, such as *The Vanishment of Thomas Tull* and *Burglar Bill,* the Ahlbergs invoke a warm, humorous nostalgia in their books. In Allan Ahlberg's collection of poems for junior school children, *Heard It in the Playground,* the setting is a primary school with no real sense of period, but full of observed details—wooden coat-pegs, marbles, the broad expanse of polished hallway floors, the class hamster—that render it timeless and never-changing. In the *Times Literary Supplement,* George Szirtes describes the setting as "a stage we pass through in which the differences between individual lives are reduced and blurred. We are communal but nuclear; we the class, we the teachers, and we the parents waiting at the school gates. Ahlberg's sympathy extends to all three sides in the eternal triangle."

A unique aspect of the Ahlbergs' partnership is the great attention to detail that they bring to their work, being active in many steps of a book's production. From creating the book "dummy" and deciding upon the visual interplay between illustration and text, to the selection of paper, novel design elements (such as punch-outs or bound-in envelopes) and typeface, the Ahlbergs' use of new technology has been, according to Martin, "restrained and individual." An innovative illustrator, Janet employs a great deal of hand-lettered elements within her drawings, and her illustrations are characterized by their use of margin artwork, which threads through or clusters around hand-lettered texts, sometimes replacing words altogether. "There are precedents for a lot of these techniques in children's books from many lands and long ago," Martin continues, "but the Ahlbergs have combined and added to them with great virtuosity and inventiveness, bringing fresh variations and insights to each subsequent book." Humor and a bit of irreverence, has made them one of the most popular of "bookmakers" for young people. As Aiden Chambers writes in *Horn Book,* "Their books are dramatic, not because they pack them with thrills and spills or popeyed goings on but because they know how to select from life and make a pattern of what they select that changes everydayness from dull routine to an excitement."

BIOGRAPHICAL/CRITICAL SOURCES:

BOOKS

Martin, Douglas, *The Telling Line,* Julia MacRae Books, 1989.
Twentieth-Century Children's Writers, St. James Press (Detroit), 1989.

PERIODICALS

Booklist, October 1, 1992; May 1, 1994; January 1, 1996.
Books for Keeps, January, 1987.
Commonweal, November 11, 1977.
Globe and Mail (Toronto), July 14, 1990.
Horn Book, December, 1982; September, 1996.
Junior Bookshelf, December, 1979.
Listener, November 8, 1979.
Los Angeles Times Book Review, May 31, 1981.
New Statesman, November 28, 1975; November 21, 1980; December 4, 1981; December 3, 1982.
New York Times Book Review, April 10, 1977; April 22, 1979; April 29, 1979; May 20, 1979; March 1, 1981; August 14, 1988; February 11, 1990.
Observer (London), July 19, 1981; December 6, 1981; November 29, 1992.
Publishers Weekly, February 28, 1994; November 27, 1995.
Punch, November 17, 1982.
Quill & Quire, February, 1995.
Saturday Review, May 28, 1977; May 26, 1979.
School Library Journal, September, 1981; July, 1995; February, 1996.
Spectator, July 16, 1977; December 11, 1993; December 10, 1994.
Times (London), March 5, 1980; November 29, 1986; October 1, 1988; March 8, 1991, p. 18.
Times Educational Supplement, November 23, 1979; January 18, 1980; March 7, 1980; June 20, 1980; November 21, 1980; January 2, 1981; July 24, 1981; November 20, 1981; November 19, 1982; March 11, 1983; June 3, 1983; September 30, 1983; January 14, 1994.
Times Literary Supplement, March 25, 1977; December 1, 1978; March 28, 1980; November 21, 1980; September 18, 1981; March 26, 1982; November 26, 1982; July 22, 1983; November 30, 1984; August 15, 1986; November 28, 1986; April 3, 1987; October 9, 1987; April 1, 1988; September 9, 1988; November 24, 1989.

Tribune Books (Chicago), November 16, 1986.
Washington Post Book World, February 11, 1979.
Wilson Library Bulletin, June, 1994.*

* * *

AI 1947-
(Florence Anthony)

PERSONAL: Born Florence Anthony, October 21, 1947, in Albany, TX; name changed to Ai. *Education:* University of Arizona, B.A., 1969; University of California, Irvine, M.F.A., 1971.

ADDRESSES: Home—1028 South Ash Ave., No. 8, Tempe, AZ 85281.

CAREER: Poet. Visiting poet at Wayne State University, 1977-78, and George Mason University, 1986-87; writer-in-residence, Arizona State University, 1988-89; University of Colorado at Boulder, visiting associate professor, 1996-97. Has also worked as an antiques dealer in New York City and elsewhere, and as a jewelry designer.

AWARDS, HONORS: Guggenheim fellow, 1975; Radcliffe (now Bunting) Institute fellow, 1975; Massachusetts Arts and Humanities fellowship, 1976; Lamont poetry selection, Academy of American Poets, 1978; National Endowment for the Arts fellowship, 1978, 1985; Ingram Merrill Award, 1983; St Botolph Foundation grant, 1986; American Book Award, Before Columbus Foundation, 1987, for *Sin.*

WRITINGS:

POETRY

Cruelty, Houghton (Boston), 1973.
Killing Floor (Lamont poetry selection), Houghton, 1979.
Sin, Houghton, 1986.
Fate, Houghton, 1991.
Greed, Norton (New York City), 1993.

OTHER

Black Blood (novel), Norton, 1997.

Contributor of articles and poems to magazines, including *American Poetry Review, Antaeus, Caprice, Paris Review, Poetry, Ms.,* and *Zone.*

A collection of Ai's manuscripts is housed at the New York Public Library.

SIDELIGHTS: In the volumes of verse she has published since her first collection, *Cruelty,* was released in 1973, poet Ai has remained on the cutting edge of feminist poetry. Dubbed "All woman—all human" by confessional poet Anne Sexton, Ai was credited by a *Times Literary Supplement* reviewer as capturing within her dramatic monologues "the cruelty of intimate relationships and the delights of perverse spontaneity—e.g. the joy a mother gets from beating her child." Alicia Ostriker countered Sexton's summation of Ai, writing: "'All woman—all human'; she is hardly that. She is more like a bad dream of Woody Allen's, or the inside story of some Swinburnean Dolorosa, or the *vagina-dentata* itself starting to talk. Woman, in Ai's embodiment, wants sex. She knows about death and can kill animals and people. She is hard as dirt. Her realities—very small ones—are so intolerable that we fashion female myths to express our fear of her. She, however, lives the hard life below our myths."

Ai uses the dramatic monologue to depict individuals that Duane Ackerson characterized in *Contemporary Women Poets* as "people seeking transformation, a rough sort of salvation, through violent acts." The speakers in her poems are not the poet but individuals—usually women, but occasionally men—isolated in their individual struggles by poverty, by small-town life, or by living on a remote farm. Ai's characters speak such lines as "I see your stomach is flat as an iron. / You've done it, as you warned me you would" ("Abortion"), or, "The street coughs blood / in a linen handkerchief, / as I strut down to the river" ("The Suicide"). As Ostriker noted, the speakers of such lines "count for nothing more than that of a slaughtered goat, where desire is like the smell of fresh meat. Each is savage, each is victim. . . . Their cruelty is theirs because it is nature's." In her volumes *Fate* and *Greed,* the latter published in 1993, Ai substitutes real individuals for the anonymous, troubled speakers of her earlier works. Here readers confront the inner worlds of former F.B.I. director J. Edgar Hoover, missing-and-presumed-dead Union leader Jimmy Hoffa, musician Elvis Presley, and actor James Dean: all dead and each in their own way out of sync with social or ethical "norms." Noting that Ai "reinvents" each of her subjects within her verse, Ackerson added that, through each monologue, what these individuals say, "returning after death, expresses more about the American psyche than about the real figures, and Ai intends it this way." In "Miracle in Manila," published in *Greed,* a now-dead Ferdinand Marcos watches his self-indulgent wife Imelda mimic the crucifixion, then, "after a transfusion, a facial, / and a manicure . . . proclaim herself "the only candidate / who can rise from the dead."

Aiming her poetic barbs directly at prejudices and societal ills of all types, Ai speaks from the perspective of one who has experienced her share of struggles, particularly with regard to her racial heritage. She detailed her feelings on race when she wrote in the article "On Being 1/2 Japanese, 1/8 Choctaw, 1/4 Black, and 1/16 Irish": "People whose concept of themselves is largely dependent on their racial identity and superiority feel threatened by a multiracial person. The insistence that one must align oneself with this or that race is basically racist. And the notion that without a racial identity a person can't have any identity perpetuates racism. . . . I wish I could say that race isn't important. But it is. More than ever, it is a medium of exchange, the coin of the realm with which one buys one's share of jobs and social position. This is a fact which I have faced and must ultimately transcend. If this transcendence were less complex, less individual, it would lose its holiness."

BIOGRAPHICAL/CRITICAL SOURCES:

BOOKS

Contemporary Literary Criticism, Gale (Detroit), Volume 4, 1975.
Contemporary Women Poets, St. James Press (Detroit), 1997.

PERIODICALS

American Poetry Review, November, 1994, p. 23.
Kenyon Review, winter, 1995, p. 150.
Kirkus Reviews, August 15, 1973.
New York Times Book Review, February 17, 1974.
Publishers Weekly, September 27, 1993, p. 46.
Times Literary Supplement, March 29, 1974.
Ms., June, 1974; June, 1978.

*   *   *

ALEXANDER, Meena 1951-

PERSONAL: Born February 17, 1951, in Allahabad, India; came to the United States in 1979; daughter of

George and Mary Alexander; married David Lelyveld; children: Adam Kuruvilla, Svati Mariam. *Education:* University of Khartoum, B.A. (with first-class honors), 1969; University of Nottingham, Ph.D., 1973.

ADDRESSES: Home—541 West 113th St., No. 4C, New York, NY 10025. *Office*—Department of English, Hunter College, City University of New York, 695 Park Ave., New York, NY 10021.

CAREER: University of Khartoum, Khartoum, Sudan, tutor in English, 1969; University of Delhi, Delhi, India, lecturer in English, 1974; Jawaharlal Nehru University, Delhi, lecturer in English and French, 1975; Central Institute of English and Foreign Language, Hyderabad, India, lecturer in English, 1975-77; University of Hyderabad, Hyderabad, lecturer, 1977-79, reader in English, 1979; Sorbonne, Paris, visiting fellow, 1979; Fordham University, Bronx, NY, assistant professor of English, 1980-87; Hunter College, City University of New York, New York City, assistant professor, 1987-89; associate professor, 1989-91, professor of English, 1992—; Columbia University, New York City, lecturer in writing program, 1990—; Lecturer at University of Stirling, 1973, and Osmania University, 1978; visiting fellow at Centre de Recherches en Litterature et Civilization Nord-Americaines, Sorbonne, University of Paris, autumn, 1979; visiting assistant professor at University of Minnesota—Twin Cities, summer, 1981; writer in residence at Center for American Culture Studies, Columbia University, 1988; MacDowell Colony fellow, 1993; poet-in-residence, American College, Madurai, India, 1994; Arts Council of England international writer-in-residence, 1995.

AWARDS, HONORS: National Endowment for the Humanities travel grant, 1985; New York State Council for the Arts grant, 1988.

WRITINGS:

POETRY

The Bird's Bright Ring, Writers Workshop (Calcutta, India), 1976.
Without Place, Writers Workshop, 1977.
I Root My Name, United Writers (Calcutta, India), 1977.
Stone Roots, Arnold-Heinemann (New Delhi, India), 1980.

House of a Thousand Doors, Three Continents (Washington, DC), 1989.
The Storm: A Poem in Five Parts, Red Dust (New York City), 1989.
Night-Scene: The Garden, Red Dust, 1992.
River and Bridge, Rupa (New Delhi, India), 1995.
The Shock of Arrival: Reflections on Postcolonial Experience, South End Press (Boston, MA), 1996.

NOVELS

Nampally Road, Mercury House (San Francisco), 1991.
Manhattan Music: A Novel, Mercury House, 1997.

PLAYS

In the Middle Earth, Enact (New Delhi, India), 1977.

OTHER

The Poetic Self: Towards a Phenomenology of Romanticism, Arnold-Heinemann, 1979, Humanities Press (Atlantic Highlands, NJ), 1981.
Women in Romanticism: Mary Wollstonecraft, Dorothy Wordsworth, and Mary Shelley, Macmillan (New York City), 1989.
Fault Lines (memoir), Feminist Press (New York City), 1992.

Contributing author to *New York Times Magazine.*

SIDELIGHTS: Poet, novelist, teacher, scholar, and memoirist, Meena Alexander draws from her international experiences growing up in India, being educated in England, and finally moving to the United States. As a result, her work exhibits the influences of a multilingual and multicultural background. Her poetry, characterized by Aruna Srivastava in *Contemporary Women Poets* as "a highly Imagistic poetry" which is marked by a tension between "different traditions of poetry, history, myth, and language," falls largely into two periods. The first period includes the poems published in India, including *The Bird's Bright Ring* which explores the consequences of British rule in India, and ends with *House of a Thousand Doors,* her first book published in the US, and one which Alexander told Srivastava she thinks of "as a beginning" because of its "sense of newness, of the persistent difficulty of another landscape, another life, becomes in those poems part of a search for a precarious truth." Here, Alexander develops the grandmother figures which serve as bridges between generations, time, and cultures.

The second period begins with *The Storm* and continues through *Night-Scene, The Garden,* poems which Alexander told Srivastava "form part of a poetic autobiography." In this second period, Alexander's poetry also becomes more fervently feminist, expanding upon the grandmother images to include mother-daughter relationships as well, and offering her own persona as a voice for the mute and disempowered: "Women of Delhi / You do not see how centuries of dream are flowing from your land / And so I sing knowing poetry to be like bread." Yet Alexander sees herself also as spokesperson for the disassociated and the displaced, trying to connect the fragmentation of the late twentieth century into a workable whole where the "bitten self cast back / into its intimate wreckage" will eventually discover itself to be "poised, apart, particular / lovely and rare."

Meena Alexander's memoir *Fault Lines* drew great critical acclaim. She told *CA:* "In *Fault Lines,* I move back and forth between India, the Sudan, and New York City. I have lived in the city since 1979 and it provides the framework within which I remember, within which I write, fabricate, make fictive worlds." As a result, as Lisa Nussbaum notes in *Library Journal,* the book crosses over the "fault lines" which are created by "the shifting ground of loyalties and identities" that develop from living on different continents and in different cultures, yet, Alexander "draws continuously on the silken threads that make up who she is and how she sees the world." Alexander recounts the difficulties in discovering a consistency of voice and theme from her diverse cultural experiences, though what emerges is a voice which Lauren Glen Dunlap in *Belles Lettres* calls "a treasure." In *Fault Lines,* Alexander writes of how "Multiple birth dates ripple, sing inside me, as if a long stretch of silk were passing though my fingers," and of how "As I make up a katha, a story of my life, the lives before me, around me, weave into a net without which I would drop ceaselessly." The image of the threads woven into a net, of multicultural experiences woven into a sustaining and sustainable life, offer readers, as Susheela N. Rao writing in *World Literature Today* notes, "an excellent record of a sensitive young Indian woman writer whose poetic expression is the consummate product of colorful experiences with many cultures and countries."

BIOGRAPHICAL/CRITICAL SOURCES:

BOOKS

Alexander, Meena, *Fault Lines: A Memoir,* Feminist Press (New York City), 1993.
Contemporary Poets, 6th edition, St. James Press (Detroit), 1996.
Contemporary Women Poets, St. James Press, 1997.
Reworlding: Writers of the Indian Diaspora, Greenwood Press (Westport, CT), 1993.

PERIODICALS

Amerasia Journal, fall, 1993, p. 103; fall, 1996, p. 164.
Belles Lettres, summer, 1993, p. 43.
Booklist, March 15, 1993, p. 1289.
Chicago Tribune, May 25, 1997, section 14, p. 1.
Chronicle of Higher Education, March 14, 1997, p. B8.
Library Journal, March 1, 1993, p. 86; March 1, 1997, p. 100.
Los Angeles Times Book Review, January 27, 1991, p. 7.
Ms., March, 1993, p. 65; January/February, 1994, p. 71.
Publisher's Weekly, December 14, 1990, p. 62; March 1, 1993, p. 50; October 21, 1996, p. 76; February 10, 1997, p. 68.
Small Press, summer, 1993, p. 59.
Times Literary Supplement, April 9, 1993, p. 22.
Washington Post, April 6, 1997, p. 9.
Wilson Library Bulletin, September, 1993, p. 113.
World Literature Today, autumn, 1994, p. 883.*

*   *   *

ANDREWS, Wayne 1913-1987
(Montagu O'Reilly)

PERSONAL: Born September 5, 1913, in Kenilworth, IL; died of a heart attack, August 17, 1987, in Paris, France; son of Emory Cobb (a businessman) and Helen (Armstrong) Andrews; married Elizabeth Anderson Hodges, June 12, 1948; children: Elizabeth Waties. *Education:* Harvard University, A.B., 1936; Columbia University, graduate study, 1946-48, Ph.D., 1955. *Politics:* Democrat. *Religion:* Episcopalian.

CAREER: New York Historical Society, New York City, curator of manuscripts, 1948-56; Charles Scribner's Sons, New York City, editor, trade department, 1956-63; Wayne State University, Detroit, MI, Archives of American Art Professor, 1964-87. Architectural photographer.

MEMBER: Societe Chateaubriand (Paris).

WRITINGS:

(Under pseudonym Montagu O'Reilly) *Pianos of Sympathy,* New Directions (New York City), 1936.

The Vanderbilt Legend, Harcourt (New York City), 1941.

Battle for Chicago, Harcourt, 1946.

(Under pseudonym Montagu O'Reilly) *Who Has Been Tampering with These Pianos?,* New Directions, 1948.

Architecture, Ambition and Americans: A Social History of American Architecture, Harper (New York City), 1955, revised edition, Free Press (New York City), 1978.

(Editor) *Best Short Stories of Edith Wharton,* Scribner (New York City), 1958.

(Editor) Theodore Roosevelt, *Autobiography,* Scribner, 1958.

Architecture in America: A Photographic History from the Colonial Period to the Present, Atheneum (New York City), 1960, revised edition, 1979.

(Editor with Thomas W. Cochran) *Concise Dictionary of American History,* Scribner, 1962.

Germaine: A Portrait of Madame de Stael, Atheneum, 1963.

Architecture in Michigan: A Representative Photographic Survey, Wayne State University Press (Detroit), 1967, reprinted, 1981.

Architecture in Chicago and Mid-America: A Photographic History, Atheneum, 1968.

Architecture in New York: A Photographic History, Atheneum, 1969, reprinted, Syracuse University Press (Syracuse, NY), 1995.

Siegfried's Curse: The German Journey from Nietzsche to Hesse, Atheneum, 1972.

Architecture in New England, Stephen Greene Press (Brattleboro, VT), 1973.

American Gothic: Its Origins, Its Trials, Its Triumphs, Random House (New York City), 1975.

Pride of the South: A Social History of Southern Architecture, Atheneum, 1979.

(With Claude Fraegnac) *The Great Houses of Paris,* Vendome Press (New York City), 1979.

Voltaire, New Directions, 1981.

The Surrealist Parade, New Directions, 1990.

SIDELIGHTS: Wayne Andrews, who was for many years a professor of art and architecture at Wayne State University in Detroit, led a wide and varied career in publishing. As a young man, he was an ardent student of the French language and culture and during trips to Paris made the acquaintance of some of the leading figures of the Surrealist movement. While at Harvard and Columbia, he wrote his own brand of Surrealist prose, work that can be found in two books published under the pseudonym Montagu O'Reilly, *Pianos of Sympathy* and *Who Has Been Tampering with these Pianos?* Yet, Andrews was perhaps best known for his surveys in words and photographs of American architecture, both from a national perspective and in works focused on regional architecture.

In books such as *Architecture, Ambition and Americans: A Social History of American Architecture* and its supplement, *Architecture in America: A Photographic History from the Colonial Period to the Present,* Andrews offered introductory overviews of American architecture, the author's own photographs, and explanatory captions. Although Andrews included much on the familiar work of twentieth-century standouts like Frank Lloyd Wright and the architects at McKim, Mead, and White, he also introduced the reader to many buildings that were unfamiliar and unusual, according to a *Nation* reviewer.

In later books, Andrews directed his insights and camera toward regional architecture. Andrews followed *Architecture in Michigan: A Representative Photographic Survey,* his overview of the little-known architecture of his adopted home state, with *Architecture in Chicago and Mid-America: A Photographic History,* an examination of one of twentieth-century America's centers for architecture. As William Alex noted in the *New York Times Book Review,* "The work of the Chicago School and [Frank Lloyd] Wright, plus that of [Ludwig] Mies van der Rohe, create for this book a core of significant [architecture]." Because the book provided little in the way of textual descriptions and analyses, *Book World* reviewer C. W. Condit called "Andrews' handsomely bound and printed book . . . strictly a pictorial album calculated to offer little more than a pure visual experience." The reviewer explained, "There are no plans, no functional and structural analyses, no details, no exposition of historical development." Even so, Condit concluded, "Andrews has put together a book that can only give pleasure to anyone with a taste for the building arts."

Through *Architecture in New England,* Andrews explored the "relationships between social, cultural, economic, and intellectual trends in New England life, and the architecture that has been an outgrowth," B. F. Tolles pointed out in the *New England Quarterly.* Though faulted in some circles for its limited textual analysis, a reviewer for *Choice* maintained, "Andrews' photographs fulfill everything an architectural historian desires; a large and emphatic image of inherent structure; qualities of sculptural form and textural surfaces: complementing shadow and foliage; [and] stylistic niceties." Tolles commented, "It well deserves to be brought to the attention of academic historians and sophisticated readers of historical and fine arts nonfiction." The reviewer added that "the volume should serve as an important vehicle in heightening public awareness of historic preservation aims, needs, and accomplishments."

In addition to his books on architecture, Andrews wrote biographies and social and cultural histories. *Germaine: A Portrait of Madame de Stael* and *Voltaire* profile two influential figures from eighteenth- and nineteenth-century French letters. *Siegfried's Curse: The German Journey from Nietzsche to Hesse* traces, as Andrews explained in the book, "the reactions of the writers and intellectuals who prophesied or witnessed this national suicide; how individuals behave under unholy circumstances." *The Surrealist Parade,* Andrews's last book, presents a "cunningly brief and amusingly opinionated personal history of Surrealism," Richard Burgin commented in the *New York Times Book Review.* "In precise but evocative prose," Burgin continued, the book "describes the intense visions and camaraderie, as well as the foibles and feuds, of the most famous writers and artists associated with the movement—from Apollinaire and Ernst to Dali and Magritte." According to Eric Basso in *Small Press,* this insider's view of Surrealism "successfully recreates what must have been one of the headiest and most immediately rewarding periods in the history of art and literature." Central to the book is Andrews's profile of Andre Breton, the founder of the movement. For Burgin, Andrews "manages deftly to balance his criticism of this magnetic leader with a well-informed admiration for the legacy of his parade."

BIOGRAPHICAL/CRITICAL SOURCES:

BOOKS

Laughlin, J., editor, *New Directions in Prose and Poetry,* New Directions, 1986.

PERIODICALS

Booklist, January 15, 1961, p. 286.
Book World, October 13, 1968, p. 4.
Choice, October, 1973, p. 1174.
Christian Science Monitor, November 23, 1960, p. 11.
Journal of Aesthetics, fall, 1968, p. 118.
Library Journal, September 15, 1963, p. 3202; May 1, 1973, p. 474.
Nation, December 24, 1960, p. 509.
New England Quarterly, September, 1973, p. 487.
New Yorker, November 16, 1963, p. 245.
New York Times Book Review, November 17, 1968, p. 70; July 1, 1990, p. 8.
Review of Contemporary Fiction, spring, 1991, p. 334.
Saturday Review, October 19, 1963, p. 38.
Small Press, February, 1991, p. 22.

OBITUARIES:

PERIODICALS

Chicago Tribune, September 13, 1987.
New York Times, August 25, 1987.*

*   *   *

ANGELL, Roger 1920-

PERSONAL: Born September 19, 1920, in New York, NY; son of Ernest and Katharine Shepley (maiden name, Sergeant) Angell; married Evelyn Ames Baker, October, 1942 (divorced, 1963); married Carol Rogge, October, 1963; children: (first marriage) Caroline S., Alice; (second marriage) John Henry. *Education:* Harvard University, A.B., 1942.

ADDRESSES: Home—1261 Madison Ave., New York, NY 10028. *Office*—New Yorker, 25 West 43rd St., New York, NY 10036.

CAREER: Curtis Publishing Company, New York City, editor and writer for *Magazine X,* 1946-47;

Holiday, New York City, senior editor, 1947-56; *New Yorker,* New York City, fiction editor and general contributor, 1956—. *Military service:* U.S. Army Air Forces, 1942-46; served in Pacific theater.

MEMBER: Authors Guild (vice-president, 1975-81 and 1984-89; member of national council, 1975—), Authors League of America, PEN, Century Association, Coffee House.

AWARDS, HONORS: George Polk Award for commentary, 1981.

WRITINGS:

The Stone Arbor and Other Stories, Little, Brown (Boston), 1960.
A Day in the Life of Roger Angell (humorous sketches), Viking (New York City), 1970, revised edition published as *A Day in the Life of Roger Angell: Parodies and Other Pleasures,* Penguin (New York City), 1990.
The Summer Game, Viking, 1972.
Five Seasons: A Baseball Companion, Simon & Schuster (New York City), 1977.
Late Innings: A Baseball Companion, Simon & Schuster, 1982.
(Author of text) Walter Iooss, Jr., photographer, *Baseball* (pictorial), Abrams (New York City), 1984.
Season Ticket: A Baseball Companion, Houghton (Boston), 1988.
Once More around the Park: A Baseball Reader, Ballantine (New York City), 1991.
(Contributor) Miro Weinberger and Dan Riley, editors, *The Yankees Reader,* Houghton, 1991.
(Editor) *Nothing But You: Love Stories from the New Yorker,* Random House (New York City), 1997.

Contributor to anthologies, including *This Great Game,* edited by Doris Townsend, Prentice-Hall (Englewood Cliffs, NJ), 1971, and *Birth of a Fan,* edited by Ron Fimrite, Macmillan (New York City), 1993. Author of introduction, *A Baseball Century: The First 100 Years of the National League,* edited by Jeanne McClow, Macmillan, 1976.

SIDELIGHTS: Of Roger Angell, Herbert Mitgang writes in the *New York Times* that he "makes baseball sound like an art form; he demonstrates that writing about it is an art form, too." It's a sentiment that's been echoed by many in the years since the publication of *The Summer Game,* Angell's first collection of elegant essays on baseball. Angell's ensuing books

include *Five Seasons, Late Innings, Season Ticket,* and *Once More around the Park,* and have confirmed his status as what Joel Conarroe (among others) describes as "our laureate of the pastime" in the *New York Times Book Review.*

"Angell is that rare baseball fan who has been able to make a career out of his pleasure," mused Steven P. Gietschier in *Dictionary of Literary Biography.* "Without abandoning the wonder, the affection, and the detachment that characterize a fan's kinship to baseball, Angell has fashioned a string of remarkable essays that explore the sport in consistently new ways. His work possesses a grace and elegance previously unknown in sports journalism and has earned a lasting place in the literature spawned by the national pastime."

The son of Katharine Shepley Sergeant and the stepson of E. B. White, Angell is a fiction editor at the *New Yorker,* where most of his baseball essays originally appeared. These literary roots set him apart in the field of sports writing. Mark Harris asserts in *Tribune Books* that Angell "sounds like no other baseball journalist." In a *Newsweek* article entitled "Angell of the Base Paths," David Lehman makes note of what he calls Angell's "poetic resonance" and quotes Angell: "If I was influenced by anyone, I guess it was by my stepfather, E. B. White. . . . He suffered writing but made it look easy."

According to Gary Dretzka in the *Los Angeles Times Book Review,* the very nature of Angell's assignments sets him apart from fellow baseball writers: "The *New Yorker* magazine's comparatively loose deadlines allow him to write for the ages," Dretzka tells us, "not just the next morning's box score scanners." Such deadlines have allowed for what Conarroe describes as Angell's "unhurried pace," noting: "Even the individual sentences suggest a leisurely approach to life. Mr. Angell is addicted to dashes and parentheses—small pauses or digressions in the narrative like those moments when the umpire dusts off home plate or a pitcher rubs up a new ball—that serve to slow an already deliberate movement almost to a standstill."

Characteristic of Angell's writing is his seemingly natural rapport with those whose lives revolve around baseball. As Art Hill of *Sports Illustrated* sees it, "One of the most appealing aspects of [the author's] reporting is the air of . . . innocence he takes with him when he talks to baseball people, whether it be in a World Series locker room or on a lazy spring afternoon at a training camp in Arizona or Florida. You don't get informative answers from players and managers unless you ask the right questions, but Angell makes it look easy—and the reader's sense of identification is enhanced by the perception, false but compelling, that he could have done it by himself with hardly any effort, given the opportunity."

To some, like Mim Udovitch in the *Village Voice,* there is a gentility in Angell's writing style that doesn't match the reality of the sport or its fans. In the *Washington Post Book World,* George Robinson suggests that there is something of the "windy" or the "gaudy" in Angell's *Once More around the Park,* but adds that "Angell is the Babe Ruth of baseball prose stylists, and you have to excuse the little lapses as the price of the thrills he can provide." In Robinson's opinion, "Angell has a reputation like the 1927 Yankees—the greatest ever, an untouchable."

Christopher Lehmann-Haupt in the *New York Times* likens Angell to a baseball player who is "no star of the brightest magnitude," but one who "does it all well and makes it all look easy. And reading all his pieces together makes one realize how well he's been playing throughout the years." Others liken the experience of reading Angell's work to the experience of attending a game. For Conarroe, "The next best thing to being at a baseball game is reading Roger Angell." Mitgang, reviewing *Once More around the Park* for the *New York Times,* writes: "To read it is like watching a game unfold in its own good time over a long afternoon, hoping it will go into extra innings and last until sundown."

For many, as Harris notes, Angell is "the ideal critic, free of jealousy, of partisan anger, of the temptation to assert his superiority to the athlete with abusive advice on how to play the game. He writes with respect of every player he mentions, making the game larger than winning and losing, bigger than persons or teams, a triumph of art and grace." In Wilfrid Sheed's opinion, expressed in the *New York Review of Books,* "Angell was born to write about baseball; it consumes him, as artists are consumed." "The degree of his caring about baseball, I think, is what makes Angell so special," says Hill. "Quite apart from his tremendous technical knowledge and his sharp eye for a significant, generally unnoticed detail, he obviously loves the game unstintingly."

Still, that great love has suffered because of the greed that has tainted modern baseball. In a *Dictio-*

nary of Literary Biography essay, Howard Good proclaimed that "a certain somberness has crept into Angell's prose" since the 1980s. Good further noted that the pieces Angell has written since his 1991 collection, *Once More around the Park,* have sometimes sounded "heavy-hearted," and concluded that "the 254-day players' strike that snatched away the 1994 pennant race and wiped out the World Series for the first time in ninety years served only to further alienate Angell's affections." Angell's feelings about the strike were expressed in "Hardball," described by Gietschier as "an evenhanded but passionate analysis of the sport's seemingly intractable labor-management war. Angell did not expect either side in the dispute to care much about what he had to offer in the way of suggestions to resolve their differences, but he did hope they would understand his concerns as one of the millions of fans who would have to decide whether or not to go back to the ballparks when the strike was settled: 'I'll probably want to go,' he concluded, 'but right now—and here's another baseball first—I'm not too sure about that.'" And yet, by 1995, Angell had written another essay urging fans—or former fans—to get out to the ballparks, support the game, and enjoy it.

"Angell belongs on any list of the 'all-time greatest' baseball writers," concluded Good. "He has avoided the cardinal sin of sportswriting (and sports movies)—the tendency to represent the games people play, or pay others to play for them, as a character test. His writing embodies the most endearing qualities of baseball itself: a complex harmony of parts; a leisurely, meditative pace; and a capacity to startle and delight."

BIOGRAPHICAL/CRITICAL SOURCES:

BOOKS

Berkow, Ira, *Red: A Biography of Red Smith,* McGraw-Hill (New York), 1987.
Coffin, Tristram Potter, *The Old Ball Game: Baseball in Folklore and Fiction,* Herder & Herder (New York City), 1971.
Contemporary Literary Criticism, Volume 26, Gale (Detroit), 1986.
Dictionary of Literary Biography, Gale, Volume 171: *Twentieth-Century American Sportswriters,* 1996, Volume 185: *American Literary Journalists, 1945-1995, First Series,* 1997.
Gill, Brendan, *Here at the New Yorker,* Random House, 1975.

Good, Howard, *Diamonds in the Dark: America, Baseball and the Movies,* Scarecrow (Metuchen, NJ), 1997.

Guttman, Allen, *A Whole New Ball Game,* University of North Carolina Press (Chapel Hill), 1988.

Lardner, *Some Champions,* edited by Matthew J. Bruccoli and Richard Layman, Scribners (New York), 1976.

Lehmann-Haupt, Christopher, *Me and Dimaggio: A Baseball Fan Goes in Search of His Gods,* Simon & Schuster, 1986.

Shannon, Mike, *Diamond Classics: Essays on 100 of the Best Baseball Books Ever Published,* McFarland & Co. (Jefferson, NC), 1989.

Smith, Leverett Y., Jr., *The American Dream and the National Game,* Popular Press (Bowling Green, OH), 1975.

PERIODICALS

Aethlon, fall, 1987, pp. 35-54.

Journal of American Culture, winter, 1982, pp. 52-56.

Journal of Popular Culture, fall, 1986, pp. 17-27.

Los Angeles Times Book Review, April 3, 1988, p. 10.

Massachusetts Review, summer, 1975, pp. 550-557.

Michigan Quarterly Review, summer, 1986, pp. 568-581.

National Review, October 14, 1977.

Newsweek, May 10, 1982; April 11, 1988, p. 74.

New York Review of Books, September 23, 1982, pp. 45-48.

New York Times, March 16, 1991.

New York Times Book Review, June 11, 1972; May 15, 1977, pp. 1, 32-34; May 23, 1982; March 20, 1988, p. 9.

People, July 26, 1982, pp. 81-83.

Publishers Weekly, July 10, 1972, p. 22.

SABR Review of Books, number 3, 1988, pp. 43-52.

Sports Illustrated, May 17, 1982.

Time, May 16, 1977; May 10, 1982.

Tribune Books (Chicago), March 6, 1988, p. 1.

Village Voice, April 23, 1991, p. 67.

Washington Post, October 10, 1984.

Washington Post Book World, June 5, 1977; May 23, 1982; March 27, 1988, p. 1; April 7, 1991, p. 11.

Writing on the Edge, fall, 1992, pp. 133-150.*

*   *   *

ANNIXTER, Paul
   See STURTZEL, Howard A(llison)

ANSLINGER, Harry Jacob 1892-1975

PERSONAL: Born May 20, 1892, in Altoona, PA; died in 1975; son of Robert John and Christina (Fladtt) Anslinger, *Education:* Pennsylvania State University, student, 1913-15; American University, LL.B., 1930. *Politics:* "Unaffiliated." *Religion:* Protestant.

CAREER: Served in U.S. Government, 1918-63, under nine presidents; held consular posts in The Netherlands, Germany, Venezuela, and the Bahamas, 1918-26; Treasury Department, chief of Division of Foreign Control, 1926-29, assistant commissioner of prohibition, 1929-30, commissioner, Bureau of Narcotics, 1930-63. U.S. representative at League of Nations conferences on narcotics, and on United Nations Narcotic Drugs Commission.

MEMBER: Police, pharmaceutical, and allied associations; Dacor House (Washington, DC).

AWARDS, HONORS: Proctor Gold Medal, 1952; selected as one of ten outstanding career men in federal government service by National Civil Service League, 1958; Alumni Recognition Award, American University, 1959; distinguished alumnus award, Pennsylvania State University, 1959; LL.D., University of Maryland; Remington Medal; Alexander Hamilton Medal.

WRITINGS:

(With William F. Tompkins) *The Traffic in Narcotics,* Funk, 1953.

(With Will Oursler) *The Murderers: The Story of the Narcotic Gangs,* Farrar, Straus, 1961.

(With J. Dennis Gregory) *The Protectors: The Heroic Story of the Narcotics Agents, Citizens, and Officials in Their Unending, Unsung Battles against Organized Crime in America and Abroad,* Farrar, Straus, 1964.

Contributor of articles to *Reader's Digest, Saturday Evening Post, FBI Bulletin, United Nations Bulletin,* and police and detective magazines.

SIDELIGHTS: Harry Jacob Anslinger served for many years as the American government's chief law enforcement officer in the fight against illegal drugs. Anslinger was the commissioner of the Treasury Department's Bureau of Narcotics from its inception in 1930 until his retirement in 1963. He also authored several books in which he presented the story of police efforts to curb the import and use of dangerous drugs.

In *The Traffic in Narcotics,* Anslinger and co-author William F. Tompkins outline the basics of the drug problem in America and detail possible methods of slowing the drug traffic and reducing the number of addicts. The reviewer for *Kirkus* called the book "a sober survey of addiction and the many areas which it affects," while the critic for the *U. S. Quarterly Book Review* found that "the general reader, desirous of informing himself on the basics of drug addiction, may well resort to this book." Meyer Berger in the *New York Times* noted that "it will be useful to the student of sociology, to law enforcement officers and to legislators, but it's not the kind of thing to curl up with for an afternoon of good cheer." *The Murderers: The Story of the Narcotic Gangs,* written by Anslinger and Will Oursler, presents a number of case histories in which narcotics officers fight the smuggling efforts of drug gangs. V. W. Peterson in the *Chicago Sunday Tribune* found that "case histories are presented in an interesting manner along with valuable data regarding the entire narcotics problem and methods of control." E. T. Smith in *Library Journal* called *The Murderers* a book "every thoughtful American should read," while A. R. Lindesmith in the *Nation* judged "the cops-and-robbers stories which abound in the book . . . interesting and sometimes exciting, viewed purely as entertainment. As realistic and accurate representations of the narcotics problem and of law enforcement they leave much to be desired."

Anslinger looked back at his long career in *The Protectors: The Heroic Story of the Narcotics Agents, Citizens, and Officials in Their Unending, Unsung Battles Against Organized Crime in America and Abroad,* written with J. Dennis Gregory. R. G. Mundy in *America* called the book "worth-while reading for anyone interested in the law-enforcement aspects of a grave social problem," while R. L. Hayne in *Library Journal* noted that "the book is especially interesting now because of current criticism and re-evaluation of the program Mr. Anslinger administered." Writing in *Book Week,* Nelson Algren summed up *The Protectors* as "a series of recollections of the cloak-and-dagger heroics by the men [Anslinger] worked with these 30 years, men he feels have protected American civilization, though the question still stands who that civilization needed protection from more—addicts or Anslinger's heroes."

BIOGRAPHICAL/CRITICAL SOURCES:

PERIODICALS

America, May 23, 1964, p. 110.
American Sociological Review, October, 1954, p. 19.
Booklist, March 15, 1954, p. 50.
Book Week, June 14, 1964, p. 6.
Chicago Sunday Tribune, January 10, 1954, p. 2; January 7, 1962, p. 4.
Christian Century, April 22, 1964, p. 81.
Christian Science Monitor, April 8, 1954, p. 9.
Kirkus, October 1, 1953, p. 21; September 1, 1961, p. 29.
Library Journal, November 15, 1961, p. 86; April 15, 1964, p. 89.
Nation, January 13, 1962, p. 194.
New York Times, April 11, 1954, p. 31.
New York Times Book Review, January 21, 1962, p. 26.
San Francisco Chronicle, January 14, 1962, p. 35.
Saturday Review, January 27, 1962, p. 45.
U.S. Quarterly Book Review, June, 1954, p. 10.*

* * *

ANTHONY, Florence
See AI

* * *

ARMSTRONG, Richard 1903-
(Cam Renton)

PERSONAL: Born June 18, 1903, in Northumberland, England; married, 1926, wife's name Edith; children: John.

CAREER: Worked in a large steel-works as an errand-boy, greaser and laborer, and crane driver, 1916-19; served in the merchant navy, 1919-36; held a variety of jobs in London, including work on a small newspaper; full-time writer, 1956—.

AWARDS, HONORS: Carnegie Medal, 1948, for *Sea Change*; first prize in the *New York Herald Tribune* Festival of Books, 1956, for *Cold Hazard.*

WRITINGS:

Mystery of Obadiah (illustrated by Marjorie Sankey), Dent (London), 1943.

Sabotage at the Forge (illustrated by L. P. Lupton), Dent, 1946, reprinted, 1962.

The Northern Maid, Dent, 1947, reprinted, Lythway Press, 1972.

Sea Change (illustrated by M. Leszczynski), Dent, 1948, reprinted, 1960.

The Whinstone Drift (illustrated by M. A. Charlton), Dent, 1951.

Passage Home, Dent, 1952.

Wanderlust: Voyage of a Little White Monkey (illustrated by Frederick Crooke), Faber (London), 1952.

Danger Rock (illustrated by Leszczynski), Dent, 1955, published as *Cold Hazard* (illustrated by C. Walter Hodges), Houghton (Boston, MA), 1956.

The Lost Ship: A Caribbean Adventure (illustrated by Edward Osmond), Dent, 1956, Day (New York City), 1958.

No Time for Tankers (illustrated by Reg Gray), Dent, 1958, Day, 1959.

The Lame Duck (illustrated by D. G. Valentine), Dent, 1959, published in America as *Ship Afire!* (a Literary Guild selection), Day, 1959.

Another Six, Blackwell (Oxford, England), 1959.

Sailor's Luck, Dent, 1959, reprinted, Lythway Press, 1974.

Before the Wind, Blackwell, 1959.

Horseshoe Reef (illustrated by Valentine), Dent, 1960, Duell, Sloan (New York City), 1961.

Out of the Shallows (illustrated by Valentine), Dent, 1961.

Trial Trip (illustrated by Valentine), Dent, 1962, Criterion Books (New York City), 1963.

(Under pseudonym Cam Renton) *The Ship Stealers* (illustrated by Val Biro), Friday Press (Pennhurst, Kent, England), 1963.

Island Odyssey (illustrated by Andrew Dodds), Dent, 1963, published as *Fight for Freedom: An Adventure of World War II* (illustrated by Don Lambo), McKay (New York City), 1966.

Storm-Path, Dent, 1964.

(Under pseudonym Cam Renton) *Big Head* (illustrated by B. S. Biro) Friday Press, 1964.

The Big Sea (illustrated by Dodds; Literary Guild selection), McKay, 1965.

Grace Darling, Maid and Myth, Dent, 1965.

Greenhorn (illustrated by Roger Payne), Nelson (London), 1965.

The Secret Sea (illustrated by Yukio Tashiro), McKay, 1966.

A History of Seafaring: The Early Mariners, Benn (London), 1967, Praeger (New York City), 1968.

The Mutineers (illustrated by Gareth Floyd; Literary Guild selection), McKay, 1968.

A History of Seafaring: The Discoverers, Benn, 1968, Praeger, 1969.

A History of Seafaring: The Merchantmen, Praeger, 1969.

(Editor) *Treasure and Treasure Hunters,* David White (New York City), 1969.

The Albatross (illustrated by Anderson), McKay, 1970.

Themselves Alone: The Story of Men in Empty Places, Houghton, 1972.

Powered Ships: The Beginnings, Benn, 1975.

SIDELIGHTS: Richard Armstrong spent the bulk of his thirty-year writing career producing seafaring adventures for young readers. Armstrong, a self-taught author, drew upon his own experiences in the merchant navy to craft coming-of-age tales that highlight the danger and responsibilities inherent in the sea-going life. *Dictionary of Literary Biography* contributor Lisa A. Wroble declared that Armstrong won readers with his "vivid details, captivating plots, and believable characters." However, in the midst of the action, Armstrong also taught important life lessons: "the main character and the reader learn something about discipline, maturity, and making decisions, as well as the forging of steel and the sailing of ships," wrote Wroble.

Born and raised in northern England, Armstrong dropped out of school at thirteen to go to work in a steel mill. Four years later he joined the merchant navy and traveled all over the world on ships. He began writing while at sea and continued when he returned to civilian life. His apprenticeship as an author was a lengthy one—he published his first book, *The Mystery of Obadiah,* when he was forty. *The Mystery of Obadiah* follows the adventures of three boys as they seek a mysterious criminal in an abandoned mine in northern England. The story's setting closely resembles Armstrong's childhood home in Northumberland and contains episodes drawn from his own experiences.

In books such as *Sea Change, Cold Hazard, Horseshoe Reef,* and *Ship Afire!* Armstrong reveals the details of life aboard a ship and the workings of the ship itself, while also spinning a yarn in which a young sailor assumes leadership duties in a time of hardship or danger. In the prize-winning *Cold Haz-*

ard, for instance, a seaman apprentice named Jim must deal with the consequences of having allowed his ship to founder on a submerged iceberg. Jim and a few of his mates, inadvertently left behind as the ship is abandoned, must struggle to survive on a deserted island until they can attempt a landfall in their tiny lifeboat. *The Lost Ship: A Caribbean Adventure* recounts the bravery of two apprentice seamen who are rescued from the water by a sailing schooner captained by a mysterious German. *Chicago Sunday Tribune* correspondent Polly Goodwin called *The Lost Ship* "a whopping good sea yarn . . . by a master storyteller."

Wroble noted: "Despite a lack of formal education, Armstrong displays a wealth of knowledge and sensitivity as a writer. His scenes and settings are not painted backdrops but credible and concrete. The dialogue is vivid and descriptive, carrying the story along." The critic went on to observe that, although the sea provides a vehicle for almost all of Armstrong's novels, "the characters and events of the various books are . . . noticeably different." Indeed, as his career extended into the 1960s and early 1970s, the author worked with delinquent boys in order to enrich his experience of the changing circumstances among young people. The result was "realistic, hard-hitting" stories—to quote a *Library Journal* critic—and a continued audience for his work.

A *Christian Science Monitor* reviewer declared Armstrong "a master at creating a suspenseful narrative," whose works offer "dramatic proof of the courage men can draw upon when the urge to be free is their driving-power." Wroble concluded: "Whatever theme or plot Armstrong uses, his reader will be entertained by an adventurous story and will perhaps realize he has gained knowledge of the sea and of himself."

BIOGRAPHICAL/CRITICAL SOURCES:

BOOKS

Dictionary of Literary Biography, Volume 160: *British Children's Writers, 1914-1960,* Gale (Detroit), 1996.

PERIODICALS

Chicago Sunday Tribune, March 2, 1958, p. 8.
Choice, July, 1969, p. 690; June, 1970, p. 596.
Christian Science Monitor, May 10, 1956; November 3, 1966, p. B11; May 23, 1968, p. 7.
Library Journal, September 15, 1966, p. 4346; May 15, 1968, p. 2118.
New York Herald Tribune, April 13, 1958.
New York Times, February 16, 1958, p. 34.
New York Times Book Review, April 30, 1961, p. 30.
Times Literary Supplement, January 29, 1960, p. 59; May 19, 1966, p. 437.*

*   *   *

ATHEARN, Robert G(reenleaf) 1914-1983

PERSONAL: Born August 30, 1914, in Kremlin, MT; died in 1983; son of Fred D. and Clarinda (Lomen) Athearn; married Claire B. Raney, 1942; children: Frederic James, Dana Leigh. *Education:* University of Minnesota, B.S., 1936, M.A., 1938, Ph.D., 1947.

CAREER: University of Colorado, Boulder, 1947-83, professor of United States history, 1956-83. *Military service:* U.S. Coast Guard, 1942-45, became lieutenant junior grade.

MEMBER: American Historical Association, Organization of American Historians, Western History Association (president, 1964-65).

AWARDS, HONORS: Ford Foundation fellowship, 1954-55; Fulbright fellowship in Great Britain, 1960-61; various awards for *Westward the Briton, High Country Empire,* and *Forts of the Upper Missouri;* award for distinguished career as writer on the American West, American Association for State and Local History, 1971.

WRITINGS:

Thomas Francis Meagher: An Irish Revolutionary in America, University of Colorado Press (Boulder), 1949.
Westward the Briton, Scribner (New York City), 1953.
William Tecumseh Sherman and the Settlement of the West, University of Oklahoma Press (Norman), 1956.
(Editor) *Soldier in the West: The Civil War Letters of Alfred Lacey Hough,* University of Pennsylvania Press (Philadelphia), 1957.

(With Carl W. Ubbelohde) *Centennial Colorado: Its Exciting Story,* Chambers, 1959.

High Country Empire: The High Plains and Rockies, McGraw (New York City), 1960.

Rebel of the Rockies: A History of the Denver and Rio Grande Western Railroad, Yale University Press (New Haven, CT), 1962.

The American Heritage New Illustrated History of the United States, sixteen volumes (with foreword by John F. Kennedy, introduction by Allan Nevins), Dell (New York City), 1963.

(With Robert E. Riegel) *America Moves West,* Holt (New York City), 1964.

Forts of the Upper Missouri, Prentice-Hall (Englewood Cliffs, NJ), 1967.

Union Pacific Country, Rand McNally (Chicago), 1971.

The Coloradans, University of New Mexico Press (Albuquerque), 1976.

In Search of Canaan: Black Migration to Kansas, 1879-1880, Regents Press of Kansas, 1978.

Contributor of about forty articles and 125 reviews to magazines.

SIDELIGHTS: Robert G. Athearn, a longtime professor of U.S. history at the University of Colorado, did much to bring little-known aspects of the history of the American West to the attention of scholars and general readers alike. In his 1953 book, *Westward the Briton,* Athearn mined the writings of over three hundred British visitors who traveled in the American West between 1869 and 1900. As a reviewer for the *New Yorker* commented, "The author . . . is the first to make a thorough study of this unusual chapter in the annals of British globe-trotting, and he has turned up an immense amount of obscure material, much of which has little in common with the celebrated observations of such biliously belligerent reporters as Kipling, Stevenson, and Wilde." As a result, in the opinion of George Dangerfield of the *Saturday Review,* "Professor Athearn has given us many valuable and delightful insights into a vanished way of life." Even so, as Dangerfield added, "He has told us even more about the British than he has about the West." In the end, observed Clarence Gorchels in *Library Journal,* "This is a book of history, and it is also a volume rich in human-interest, humor, and candor."

In *High Country Empire: The High Plains and Rockies,* published in 1960, Athearn explored the history of the states touched by the Missouri River and in so doing attempted to discover how U.S. expansion into this region affected the nation as a whole. Again, Athearn offered historical information that was not readily available. "This is the first adequate history of the High Country Empire I have ever found," wrote Hal Borland in the *Saturday Review.* He continued, "This is vivid, vigorous history, rich with incident, solid with research, firm with informed opinion." A reviewer for the *San Francisco Chronicle* characterized the book as "a very great mass of scholarly knowledge [that] expands, illuminates, and makes all alive within the major framework." And, in the opinion of Harlan Trott of the *Christian Science Monitor,* "Professor Athearn's depth of historical knowledge and perspective ties the story of this high country empire together so that it is socially and economically meaningful." Yet, as G. M. Gressley pointed out in *Library Journal,* the appeal of this book was not just in its historical detail. "Mr. Athearn is not only a good historian," wrote the reviewer, "he is an exceptionally able writer. His sparkling narrative—filled with quotable anecdotes and general perceptive insights—is a delight to read."

The year 1972 saw the publication of *Union Pacific Country,* another history in which Athearn broke new ground. "No one has done before what Athearn has in this volume," commented a reviewer for *Choice.* "He has utilized company records and a variety of other sources to write a very attractive and readable, but scholarly account, of the impact of the Union Pacific and its branch lines on the country it served from the 1860's to the 1890's." W. T. Jackson also noted the quality of Athearn's research, but emphasized that *Union Pacific Country* was "a book that will be widely read and enjoyed." In the view of R. C. Overton, writing in the *Journal of American History,* "This is social history at its best." The reviewer concluded, "This is certainly the most valuable history we have of the Union Pacific, and a consistently well-written one at that. I suspect that [it] will become, as it deserves to be, the authoritative work."

BIOGRAPHICAL/CRITICAL SOURCES:

PERIODICALS

American History Review, April, 1963, p. 837; April, 1972, p. 590.

Best Sellers, December 15, 1967, p. 371.

Choice, December 1971, p. 1377.

Christian Science Monitor, July 7, 1960, p. 7.

Journal of American History, March, 1972, p. 1029.

Kirkus Reviews, June 1, 1953, p. 352.
Library Journal, July, 1953, p. 1228; June 1, 1960, p. 2163; September 15, 1967, p. 3038.
New Yorker, September 26, 1953, p. 149.
New York Herald Tribune Book Review, August 30, 1953, p. 5; May 15, 1960, p. 8.
New York Times, August 23, 1953, p. 12.
New York Times Book Review, May 1, 1960, p. 10.
San Francisco Chronicle, September 20, 1953, p. 9; August 7, 1960, p. 21.
Saturday Review, October 10, 1953, p. 14; June 25, 1960, p. 23.
Times Literary Supplement, October 16, 1953, p. 664.*

*   *   *

ATWATER, Montgomery Meigs 1904-1976

PERSONAL: Born October 21, 1904, in Baker City, OR; died June, 1976; son of Maxwell W. (a mining engineer) and Mary (a writer and designer; maiden name, Meigs) Atwater; married Joan Hamill, May, 1956; *Education:* Harvard University, B.S., 1926.

CAREER: Author and avalanche specialist. With U.S. Forest Service from the end of World War II until 1964. *Military service:* U.S. Army, 1942; supervised a military ski and winter warfare school; commanded a reconnaissance unit in Europe.

WRITINGS:

Government Hunter (illustrated by Fred C. Rodewald), Macmillan (New York City), 1940.
Flaming Forest (illustrated by R. Farrington Elwell), Little, Brown (Boston), 1941.
Ski Patrol, Random House (New York City), 1943.
Hank Winton, Smokechaser (illustrated by E. Joseph Dreany), Random House, 1947.
(With Sverre Engen) *Ski with Sverre: Deep Snow and Packed Slope Ski Technique,* New Directions (New York City), 1947.
Smoke Patrol, Random House, 1949.
Avalanche Patrol, Random House, 1951.
Rustlers on the High Range, Random House, 1952.
(With F. C. Koziol) *The Alta Avalanche Studies,* United States Forest Service, 1953.
(With Koziol) *Avalanche Handbook,* United States Forest Service, 1953.
Cattle Dog, Random House, 1954.
The Trouble Hunters, Random House, 1956.

The Ski Lodge Mystery, Random House, 1959.
Snow Rangers of the Andes, Random House, 1957.
The Avalanche Hunters (introduction by Lowell Thomas), Macrae Smith, 1968.
The Forest Rangers, Macrae Smith, 1969.

SIDELIGHTS: An expert on avalanches who worked for many years with the United States Forest Service, Montgomery Meigs Atwater wrote adventure stories based on his own professional experiences. According to E. L. Buell in the *New York Times,* "If the United States Forest Service has any medals to bestow it certainly ought to consider Lieutenant Atwater for his books in which he sets forth, without fanfare but with convincing authority, the long-range service which that department renders to the country."

In the novels *Ski Patrol, Smoke Patrol* and *Avalanche Patrol,* Atwater fictionalized the work done by members of the Forest Service in their efforts to protect the country's parks. In *Ski Patrol,* Atwater tells the story of a college ski champion who helps capture a criminal in the mountains. M. A. Herr in *Library Journal* found the book to contain "much interesting information about forest service" and a "swiftly moving plot and good adventure." *Ski Patrol* contains, Robert Berry of *Book Week* writes, "a treasure chest of information on wild life and skiing." *Smoke Patrol* follows the career of a young man who joins the Forest Service's firefighting unit, while *Avalanche Patrol* details a forester's work as head of a ski resort.

Both *Avalanche Patrol* and *Ski Lodge Mystery* feature the character Brad Davis solving mysteries against a backdrop of mountains and wildlife adventure. The reviewer for the *Saturday Review of Literature* noted of *Avalanche Patrol* that "knowledge of the country, a contagious enthusiasm for skiing, and an ability to create convincing characters make this an unusually good adventure tale." M. S. Libby in the *New York Herald Tribune Book Review* believed that *Ski Lodge Mystery* "works up to a good climax of avalanche danger and relentless feuding on dangerous mountains."

BIOGRAPHICAL/CRITICAL SOURCES:

PERIODICALS

Booklist, June 1, 1943; September 15, 1949; May 1, 1951.
Book Week, May 23, 1943.

Kirkus, June 1, 1949; December 1, 1950; January 15, 1959.

Library Journal, July, 1943; October 15, 1949; June 1, 1951; May 15, 1959.

New York Herald Tribune Book Review, May 13, 1951, p. 17; May 10, 1959, p. 31.

New York Times, July 11, 1943, p. 14; January 22, 1950, p. 18; April 15, 1951, p. 18; May 10, 1959, p. 26.

Saturday Review of Literature, November 12, 1949; May 12, 1951.

Weekly Book Review, June 6, 1943, p. 8.

Wisconsin Library Bulletin, October, 1943.*

*   *   *

AVERY, Al
  See MONTGOMERY, Rutherford George

*   *   *

AYER, Frederick, Jr. 1917-1974

PERSONAL: Born 1917 in Topsfield, MA; died Jaanuary 4, 1974, in Tucker's Town, Bermuda; married Ann Moody; children: David, Ruth. *Education:* Harvard University, B.A., 1937, LL.B., 1941.

CAREER: Federal Bureau of Investigation, Washington, DC, special agent and chief of personnel of European theatre of operations, 1941-45; attorney in Boston, MA, 1945-52; Office of the Secretary of the Air Force, Washington, DC, special assistant for intelligence, 1953-60; attorney in Washington, DC, 1961-74. Republican candidate for attorney general of Massachusetts, 1950.

WRITINGS:

Yankee G-Man (autobiography), Regnery, 1957.
Walter, the Improbable Hound, Regnery, 1959.
Where No Flags Fly (novel), Regnery, 1961.
Before the Colors Fade: Portrait of a Soldier, George S. Patton, Jr., Houghton (Boston), 1964.
The Man in the Mirror (novel), Regnery, 1965.

SIDELIGHTS: Frederick Ayer, Jr., worked with the Federal Bureau of Ivnestigation, Air Force intelli-

gence, and as a private attorney. This varied background is reflected in his books of fiction and nonfiction.

Ayer's autobiography, *Yankee G-Man,* covers his years as a special agent with the FBI in Europe during the Second World War. Richard Blakesley of the *Chicago SUnday Tribune* called the memoir "an amazingly frank account of almost unbelievable experiences. Ayer is a topnotch writer." The reviewer for the *Springfield Republican* found that "Ayer tells his story with good humor but with considerable respect for the men he worked with and against."

In *Before the Colors Fade: Portrait of a Soldier, George S. Patton, Jr.,* Ayer wrote of his famous uncle, a leader of the American military in World War II. Retired Army Brigadier General S. L. A. Marshall reviewed *Before the Colors Fade* for the *New York Times Book Review:* "In a very real sense [Ayer] grew up in his famous uncle's shadow. During the campaigns in Europe, Ayer was present doing counterintelligence duty. Anecdotal material from that period, heart-to-heart conversations between uncle and nephew during drinking bouts amid Patton's greatest campaigns, enrich the story and reveal the general's character as nothing else has done." R. U. Ricklefs in *America* claimed that "the book allows one to see a Patton that millions of his contemporaries never even knew existed."

Ayer's fiction includes two suspense novels of international intrigue. In *Where No Flags Fly* he tells the story of an American scientist whose supposed defection to the Soviets allows him into Russian military circles where he can unearth vital intelligence information. Robert Kirsch in the *New York Times Book Review* found that Ayer's "skill as a novelist never equals his mastery of intelligence procedures," while the critic for the *Springfield Republican* praised the "wealth of colorful and authentic detail" to be found in the novel. V. P. Hass in the *Chicago Sunday Tribune* wrote that *Where No Flags Fly* "builds a tremendous head of susepnse steam."

The Man in the Mirror also draws on Ayer's experience in military intelligence, telling the story of a top presidential aide who is kidnapped by foreign agents and replaced with a look-alike substitute. While P. L. Buckley in *National Review* found the book's conclusion to be "fast and satisfying," D. B. Hughes in *Book Week* dubbed it "jsut another suspense yarn."

Ayer is credited with laying the groundwork that led to the solution of the 1948 murder of Columbia Broadcasting System correspondent George Polk.

BIOGRAPHICAL/CRITICAL SOURCES:

BOOKS

Ayer, Frederick, Jr., *Yankee G-Man*, Regnery, 1957.

PERIODICALS

America, July 4, 1964.
Atlantic, September, 1964.
Best Sellers, July 1, 1964; July 1, 1965.
Booklist, November 15, 1957; November 1, 1960.
Book Week, June 21, 1964, p. 5; July 11, 1965, p. 19.
Chicago Sunday Tribune, December 8, 1957; September 18, 1960, p. 3.
Christian Science Monitor, August 8, 1964, p. 9.
Kirkus, August 15, 1957.
Library Journal, November 1, 1960; September 15, 1964; November 1, 1965.
National Review, September 8, 1964; August 24, 1965.
New Yorker, July 25, 1964.
New York Review of Books, August 20, 1964.
New York Times Book Review, November 13, 1960, p. 46; June 21, 1964, p. 6.
Saturday Review, July 11, 1964; July 17, 1965.
Springfield Republican, December 8, 1957, p. C10; September 18, 1960, p. D5.

OBITUARIES:

PERIODICALS

New York Times, January 5, 1974.*

*   *   *

AYER, Jacqueline 1930-

PERSONAL: Born May 2, 1930, in New York, NY; married Frederic Ayer; children: Margot, Elizabeth. *Education:* Attended Art Students League, New York, NY, Syracuse University for two years, and Ecole des Beaux Arts, Paris, France.

CAREER: Writer and illustrator. Fashion illustrator in Paris, France; International Basic Economy Corp.,

fabric and fashion designer, started a small division called Design Thai, 1960-66; consultant and head fashion designer in London, England, 1966—. Has exhibited work at American Institute of Graphic Arts.

AWARDS, HONORS: Gold medal from the Society of Illustrators.

WRITINGS:

SELF-ILLUSTRATED

Nu Dang and His Kite, Harcourt (New York City), 1959.
A Wish for Little Sister, Harcourt, 1960.
The Paper-Flower Tree: A Tale from Thailand, Harcourt, 1962.
Little Silk, Harcourt, 1970.
Oriental Costume, Studio Vista, 1974.

ILLUSTRATOR

Petr Pavlovich Ershov, *Humpy,* translation by William C. White, Harcourt, 1966.
Grimm Brothers, *Rumpelstiltskin,* Harcourt, 1967.
William Somerset Maugham, *Princess September,* Harcourt, 1969.

SIDELIGHTS: Jacqueline Ayer's self-illustrated children's books are marked by their Asian themes, rhythmic prose and colorful illustrations. According to a reviewer for *Kirkus,* Ayer has a "lively familiarity with the oriental atmosphere and a decorative gift which is highly pleasing in its ingenious use of design and color."

Setting her books in Thailand, Ayer tells simple folktales involving young children. In *Nu Dang and His Kite,* for example, a young boy loses his kite and must go on a quest to discover its whereabouts. R. M. Burk in the *Chicago Sunday Tribune* calls the book "a delightful taste of languid, exotic Siam," while E. L. Buell in the *New York Times* praises "the rhythmic, fluent prose" and the "skillfully composed" drawings which are "full of detail, delicate in line but bold with the hot colors of the Orient."

A Wish for Little Sister concerns a little girl in Bangkok who is given a wish for her birthday and must choose the wish wisely. The *Saturday Review* critic finds that "the plot is almost superfluous to this brilliant glimpse of Thailand." The *Horn Book* reviewer cites Ayer's "beautiful drawings, many of them accented with brilliant colors, which give a feeling of the variety and atmosphere of the fascinating city."

In *The Paper-Flower Tree* a little girl hopes that by planting a seed from her paper tree she will grow a new tree. The *Wisconsin Library Bulletin* critic notes that the story of faith is "told in rhythmic, sensitive prose and pictured in colorful line drawings." The *Horn Book* reviewer calls *The Paper-Flower Tree* "a charming and entirely childlike tale."

Little Silk follows the life of a toy doll from her beginnings in rural Thailand a century ago to her present young owner in crowded Hong Kong. The *Horn Book* critic notes that "the simple picture-book story serves as the vehicle for delightfully animated drawings of an Oriental way of life." W. M. Levy in *Library Journal* calls *Little Silk* a "gentle story" and "a quiet but successful picture book."

BIOGRAPHICAL/CRITICAL SOURCES:

BOOKS

Illustrators of Children's Books: 1957-1966, Horn Book, 1968.

Klemin, Diana, *The Art of Art for Children's Books,* Clarkson Potter, 1966.

PERIODICALS

Booklist, June 15, 1959; April 15, 1960; May 1, 1962.
Chicago Sunday Tribune, May 10, 1959, p. 8; May 13, 1962.
Christian Science Monitor, May 10, 1962.
Commonweal, May 22, 1959.
Horn Book, April, 1959; April, 1960; June, 1962; October, 1970.
Kirkus, April 15, 1959; January 15, 1960; February 15, 1962.
Library Journal, May 15, 1959; May 15, 1960; June 15, 1962; February 15, 1971.
New York Herald Tribune Book Review, July 26, 1959, p. 9; May 8, 1960.
New York Herald Tribune Books, May 13, 1962.
New York Times, May 17, 1959, p. 30.
New York Times Book Review, May 8, 1960, p. 30.
San Francisco Chronicle, July 29, 1962, p. 25.
Saturday Review, June 18, 1960; October 24, 1970.
Springfield Republican, August 9, 1959, p. D4; March 20, 1960, p. D5; May 6, 1962, p. D4.
Times Literary Supplement, October 22, 1971.
Wisconsin Library Bulletin, July, 1960; July, 1962.

B

BAGWELL, Philip S(idney) 1914-

PERSONAL: Born February 16, 1914, in Ventnor, Isle of Wight, England; son of Philip William (a bookseller) and Nellie (Aldrich) Bagwell; married Rosemary Burnley Olney (a social worker), July 16, 1953; children: Susan, Alison Jane, Richard Philip. *Ethnicity:* "English." *Education:* University of Southampton, B.Sc. (with second class honors) and Cambridge Teacher's Certificate, 1936; London School of Economics and Political Science, Ph.D., 1950. *Politics:* Christian Socialist.

ADDRESSES: Home—14 Brent Way, Finchley, London N3 1AL, England. *Office*—Department of History, Polytechnic of Central London, 309 Regent St., London W1, England.

CAREER: University of London, College of Estate Management, London, lecturer, 1949-51; Polytechnic of Central London (now University of Westminster), London, 1951—, became professor of history, 1972-77, part-time teacher, 1977—, professor emeritus, 1977—. Visiting lecturer, London School of Economics and Political Science, University of London, 1975—. Member of house committee, Rehabilitation Centre for Alcoholics, London. *Military service:* British Army, Royal Corps of Signals, 1940-45; became sergeant; mentioned in dispatches.

MEMBER: Economic History Society, Society for the Study of Labour History (secretary, 1965-70).

WRITINGS:

The Railwaymen, Volume 1: *A History of the National Union of Railwaymen,* Fernhill, 1963,

Volume 2: *The Beeching Era and After,* Allen & Unwin (London), 1982.

The Railway Clearing House in the British Economy: 1842-1922, Augustus Kelley (London), 1968.

(With G. E. Mingay) *Britain and America, 1850-1939: A Study of Economic Change,* Praeger (New York City), 1970.

The Transport Revolution from 1770, Batsford (London, England), 1974, revised edition published as *The Transport Revolution, 1770-1988,* Routledge & Kegan Paul (London), 1988.

Industrial Relations in Nineteenth-Century Britain, Irish University Press (Blackrock, Ireland), 1974.

End of the Line?: The Fate of Public Transport under Thatcher, Verso Books, 1984.

Outcast London: A Christian Response, Epworth Press (London), 1987.

Doncaster: Town of Train Makers, Doncaster, 1991.

(With Joan Lawley) *From Prison Cell to Council Chamber: Philip W. Bagwell, 1885-1958,* William Sessions (York, England), 1994.

The Transport Crisis in Britain, Spokesman Books (Nottingham, England), 1996.

SIDELIGHTS: Philip S. Bagwell told *CA:* "The early chapters of the book, *From Prison Cell to Council Chamber: Philip W. Bagwell, 1885-1958,* contain information about my early life."

*   *   *

BAILEY, Alice Cooper 1890-1978

PERSONAL: Born December 9, 1890, in San Diego, CA; died February, 1978; daughter of Henry Ernest (a judge and first secretary of Territory of Hawaii) and Mary Ellen (Porter) Cooper; married George William Bailey (member of advisory board, Electrical & Electronics Engineers, Inc.), June 16, 1913; children: Mary Alice (Mrs. Luke Hamilton Montgomery), George William, Jr., Richard Briggs. *Education:* Attended Wellesley College, Oahu College, College of Hawaii (now University of Hawaii), and Boston Conservatory of Music; Honolulu Normal School, life diploma in teaching. *Politics:* Republican. *Religion:* Episcopalian.

CAREER: Writer. Lecturer on Hawaii and Robert Louis Stevenson. Weston School Committee, member, 1931-39, chair, 1939-40.

MEMBER: Women's National Book Association, National League of American Pen Women (state president for Massachusetts, 1946-50, Hawaii, 1954-56; president of Honolulu branch, 1952-54), New England Woman's Press Club (past vice-president), Hawaiian Historical Society, Friends of Iolani Palace (Honolulu), Boston Authors Club (president, 1941-43), Weston Community League (life member), Weston Historical Association, Concord Antiquarian Museum, Concord Woman's Club, Friends of the Concord Public Library.

AWARDS, HONORS: Second prize, National League of Pen Women, for *Footprints in the Dust.*

WRITINGS:

Katrina and Jan, P. F. Volland, 1923.
The Skating Gander, P. F. Volland, 1926.
Kimo, the Whistling Boy of Hawaii, P. F. Volland, 1927.
Sun Gold, Houghton (Boston), 1930.
Footprints in the Dust, Longmans, Green, 1936.
The Hawaiian Box Mystery, Longmans, Green, 1960.
To Remember Robert Louis Stevenson, McKay (New York City), 1966.

Contributor to *Travel, American Girl, Child Life,* and *Story Parade.* All of Bailey's galley proofs are part of the de Grummond Collection in the library of the University of Southern Mississippi. One book and all her magazine stories for teen-agers have been transcribed into Braille.

SIDELIGHTS: Alice Cooper Bailey's novels for young adults are set in the Hawaiian islands, where she has lived since the age of six weeks.

Sun Gold is the story of two young people, Jerry and Cynthia, who move to from New England to Hawaii after their mother dies. Their efforts to make a living in their new home forms the impetus of the plot. According to the *Boston Transcript* critic, "all the characters are well drawn and consistent." H. T. Follett in the *Saturday Review of Literature* calls the book "refreshing in its simplicity and appropriateness: it belongs to the islands quite naturally."

Footprints in the Dust is a mystery story set at an abandoned coffee plantation in Hawaii. Again, critics praised Bailey's mix of interesting story with colorful background. J. W. Maury in *Books* notes the "excellent character portrayal and a well developed plot, all in an exotic setting." The *Springfield Republican* critic particularly highlights the "excellent descriptions of tropical scenery and of Hawaiian life and customs."

In *The Hawaiian Box Mystery* Bailey tells a suspenseful tale set at a Hawaiian ranch and involving teen-aged girls who must solve a mystery and, in doing so, resolve a family problem as well. E. L. Buell in the *New York Times Book Review* calls the novel "a generously detailed story set against the brilliant backdrop of life in the islands." P. A. Whitney in the *Chicago Sunday Tribune* believes that Bailey "has handled a common growing-up problem with understanding and wisdom."

Bailey is an expert on the life and works of author Robert Louis Stevenson, a figure whose travels she traced in the book *To Remember Robert Louis Stevenson.* Visiting places where Stevenson lived and worked, Bailey also interviewed remaining family members and friends of the author to create "an affectionate pilgrimage," as Alice Dalgliesh writes in *Saturday Review.* A. B. Myers in the *New York Times Book Review* finds some "irrelevancies" in the book, but believes that Bailey's "conversation with Anne Ide (Cockran), the girl born on Christmas Day to whom Robert Louis Stevenson gave his own birthday, is a compensation."

At one time Bailey's father owned fifty-two coral atolls in the South Pacific; she inherited title to one-sixth of two islands she has never seen. Her father's office was in Iolani Palace and she has donated all her Hawaiian possessions, including bronze seals and candelabra, to the committee restoring that landmark. Her present home is a pre-revolutionary house on Concord's famous Historic Mile, within walking distance of the homes of Ralph Waldo Emerson, Louisa

May Alcott, and Nathaniel Hawthorne. Bailey's first two books, Dutch folktales, brought a note of appreciation from Queen Wilhelmina.

BIOGRAPHICAL/CRITICAL SOURCES:

PERIODICALS

Books, November 15, 1936, p. 32.
Boston Transcript, December 10, 1930, p. 6; February 7, 1931, p. 1.
Chicago Sunday Tribune, May 8, 1960, p. 15.
Horn Book, September, 1936.
Kirkus, February 15, 1960.
Library Journal, June 15, 1960; April 15, 1966.
New York Herald Tribune Book Review, May 8, 1960.
New York Times Book Review, June 12, 1960, p. 40; March 20, 1966, p. 26.
Saturday Review, May 14, 1966.
Saturday Review of Literature, December 27, 1930.
Springfield Republican, November 29, 1936, p. E7.
Times Literary Supplement, November 21, 1936, p. 963.*

*   *   *

BAILEY, Ralph Edgar 1893-1982

PERSONAL: Born September 24, 1893, in East Greenwich, RI; died April, 1982; son of George E. (a businessman) and Luella (Haley) Bailey; married Margaret Helen Suba, April 1, 1917; children: Brewster Burrows. *Education:* Attended East Greenwich Academy, 1909-13. *Politics:* Independent. *Religion:* Protestant Episcopal.

CAREER: Writer. *Providence News,* Providence, RI, journalist, 1914-37; public relations writer for Republican State Central Committee of Rhode Island, Providence, 1938-40; *Boston Traveler,* Boston, MA, journalist, 1941-62. *Military service:* National Guard, with Rhode Island Cavalry on Mexican border, 1916.

MEMBER: Boston Authors Club (member of board of directors, 1948-52).

WRITINGS:

Argosies of Empire, Dutton (New York City), 1947.
Sea Hawks of Empire: Eastward to the Indies for Trade and Treasure, 1500-1700, Dutton, 1948.
Tim's Fight for the Valley, Dutton, 1951.

Tony Sees It Through, Dutton, 1953.
Indian Fighter: The Story of Nelson A. Miles, Morrow (New York City), 1965.
Fighting Sailor: The Story of Nathaniel Fanning, Morrow, 1967.
Guns Over the Carolinas: The Story of Nathanael Greene, Morrow, 1967.
Fight for Royal Gorge, Morrow, 1968.
Wagons Westward: The Story of Alexander Majors, Morrow, 1969.

SIDELIGHTS: Ralph Edgar Bailey wrote biographies and fiction about outstanding historical figures of the past. His *Argosies of Empire* and *Sea Hawks of Empire* tell fictionalized stories of early naval explorers around the world. Bailey also wrote several biographies of Americans who played a part in the colonial and frontier periods of American history.

In *Argosies of Empire* Bailey recounts the history of naval exploration from the world's earliest trade routes to the sixteenth century, providing fictionalized stories of the great sea captains who opened up new territories for human exploration. *Sea Hawks of Empire* is a novelized story of John Davis, whose adventures incorporate actual historical details from the sixteenth to eighteenth centuries. A *Kirkus* reviewer noted that the book contains "lots of interesting and little-known historical material dresed up with some fictional characters," and found that "the freshness of the material and the light it throws on the period makes it worthwhile."

Bailey once told *CA:* "Of my published books, *Argosies* and *Sea Hawks* are a romanticized history of international trade, from the Phoenicians down to the Portuguese, Dutch and English, and are required reference reading in their fields in many high school libraries."

Bailey's biographies of historical figures won praise for their ability to present sympathetic portraits. In *Indian Fighter: The Story of Nelson A. Miles,* Bailey tells of the American soldier who captured Geronimo, forced Crazy Horse to surrender, and won a truce with Chief Joseph. Noting Bailey's "just and sympathetic treatment of the Indian," the *Best Sellers* critic nonetheless found the book to be a "heavy recitation of facts and figures." But Marjorie Stephenson in *Library Journal* praised the "vigorous masculine prose" of the book and believed that "Bailey's understanding of the tragedy of the Indian elevates this above the usual western." Kenneth Hufford in the *Christian Science Monitor* concluded that *Indian Fighter* is a "readable biography and an intriguing introduction to the Indian Wars."

Fighting Sailor: The Story of Nathaniel Fanning and *Guns Over the Carolinas: The Story of Nathanael Greene* focus on two flamboyant characters of the American Revolution. Fanning was a privateer who worked with the French navy to capture British shipping during the war. A *Best Sellers* critic cited the book as a "tale of battle and sailing ships" which also recounts the "little known struggle of America on the high seas during the Revolution." Greene was a pacifist Quaker who felt that America's cause was just and worth supporting. J. K. Meyers in *Library Journal* praised Bailey for "being highly selective and skillful in the inclusion of supporting detail."

BIOGRAPHICAL/CRITICAL SOURCES:

BOOKS

Mildred B. Flagg, *Notable Boston Authors,* Dresser, 1965.

PERIODICALS

Best Sellers, September 15, 1965; October 1, 1966; December 1, 1967; October 1, 1968.
Booklist, January 1, 1948; November 1, 1948.
Christian Science Monitor, November 4, 1965, p. B10.
Kirkus, August 1, 1947; September 15, 1948.
Library Journal, December 1, 1947; November 1, 1948; November 15, 1965; January 15, 1967; October 15, 1967; November 15, 1968.
New York Times Book Review, January 12, 1966, p. 18; November 5, 1967, p. 28; November 17, 1968.
Saturday Review of Literature, November 15, 1947; November 13, 1948.
Springfield Republican, November 7, 1948, p. B7.*

*   *   *

BAKER, (Mary) Elizabeth (Gillette) 1923-

PERSONAL: Born November 14, 1923, in Rochester, NY; daughter of Charles L. and Ruth (Otis) Gillette; married Morton H. Baker, 1947; children: Margaret, Maria, Stephen. *Education:* University of Rochester, A.B., 1945.

ADDRESSES: Home—284 Heath's Bridge Rd., Concord, MA 01742.

CAREER: Writer. Houghton Mifflin Co., Boston, MA, worked in advertising department, 1945-48.

AWARDS, HONORS: Weekly Reader fellowship to Bread Loaf Writers' Conference, 1959.

WRITINGS:

Tammy Camps Out, Houghton (Boston), 1958.
Treasures of Rattlesnake Hill, Houghton, 1959.
Fire in the Wind, Houghton, 1961.
Tammy Climbs Pyramid Mountain, Houghton, 1962.
Tammy Goes Canoeing, Houghton, 1966.
Stronger Than Hate, Houghton, 1969.
Tammy Camps in the Rocky Mountains, Houghton, 1970.
This Stranger, My Son, Houghton, 1971.

SIDELIGHTS: Elizabeth Baker has garnered her critical praise for her novels of light adventure and mystery set in the natural world and aimed at middle-grade readers.

Tammy Camps Out introduces the young heroine of several Baker novels. In this initial outing, Tammy is trapped with her brother in a landslide while camping with her family in the woods. It is up to her to blaze a trail back to camp to get help. "Tammy learns—the hard way—to build campfires and overcome her fears of the wild," writes Helen Perdue in *Library Journal.* The *Horn Book* critic particularly enjoys the book's "atmosphere of woods and river," and the reviewer for the *Christian Science Monitor* calls it "very well done." Tammy returns in *Tammy Climbs Pyramid Mountain,* in which the young girl goes on a climbing trip to New Hampshire. The *Horn Book* reviewer notes the "firsthand detail of rocks and trail, equipment and food [which] gives immediacy to the story." "Baker intertwines her tale of appealing real-life adventure with hints of mountain climbing and a smattering of nature lore," writes the *Christian Science Monitor* critic.

In addition to her stories about Tammy, Baker also wrote light mysteries for young readers. One such book is *Treasures of Rattlesnake Hill,* which finds a mystery surrounding an old land title in the Berkshire Hills of Massachusetts. Baker, according to the *Saturday Review* critic, writes "convincingly about new friendships, outdoor pleasures, and indoor explorations." The *Kirkus* critic calls the book "a singularly sunny story." "Adventure, mystery, and family fun make the kind of story to hold the interest of boys and girls," claims D. M. Blasco in *Library Journal.*

BIOGRAPHICAL/CRITICAL SOURCES:

PERIODICALS

Booklist, July 15, 1958.
Chicago Sunday Tribune, May 7, 1961, p. 7.
Christian Science Monitor, May 8, 1958, p. 13; November 5, 1959, p. B4; May 11, 1961, p. B3.
Horn Book, June, 1958.
Kirkus, March 15, 1958; August 1, 1959; January 1, 1961.
Library Journal, June 15, 1958; November 15, 1959; April 15, 1961.
New York Times Book Review, May 14, 1961, p. 21.
San Francisco Chronicle, November 8, 1959, p. 16.
Saturday Review, April 16, 1960.

* * *

BAKER, Laura Nelson 1911-

PERSONAL: Born January 7, 1911, in Humboldt, IA; daughter of Laurithz Wogen (a farmer) and Johanna (Torkelson) Nelson; divorced; children: Timothy Lee. *Education:* Attended University of Minnesota, 1929-31. *Politics:* Democrat.

ADDRESSES: Agent—Curtis Brown Ltd., 575 Madison Ave., New York, NY 10022.

CAREER: Writer. Unity Settlement House, Minneapolis, MN, house secretary, 1947-49; *Richfield News,* Richfield, MN, editor, 1949-53; University of California, Berkeley, Bancroft Library, supervisor of manuscript reading room, 1955-57.

AWARDS, HONORS: First prize for editorial in weekly newspaper class, 1952, first prize for fiction, 1953, 1954, all from National Press Women.

WRITINGS:

The Red Mountain, Itasca Press, 1946.
The Friendly Beasts, Parnassus (Oakland, CA), 1957.
(With Adrien Stoutenburg) *Snowshoe Thompson,* Scribner (New York City), 1957.
(With Stoutenburg) *Wild Treasure,* Scribner, 1958.

(With Stoutenburg) *Scannon, Dog with Lewis and Clark,* Scribner, 1959.
The Special Year, Knopf (New York City), 1959.
Torkel's Winter Friend, illustrated by Juliette Palmer, Abelard (New York City), 1961.
(With Stoutenburg) *Beloved Botanist,* Scribner, 1961.
Other Brother, Abelard, 1962.
Somebody, Somewhere, Knopf, 1962.
(With Stoutenburg) *Dear, Dear Livy: The Story of Mark Twain's Wife,* Scribner, 1963.
The Dahlbe Family Horse (juvenile), illustrated by Paul E. Kennedy, Dial (New York City), 1964.
Those Who Care, illustrated by Herbert Danska, Little, Brown (Boston), 1964.
Because of Anne, Knopf, 1965.
(With Stoutenburg) *Explorer of the Unconscious: Sigmund Freud,* Scribner, 1965 (published in England as *Freud: Explorer of the Unconscious,* R. Whiting, 1967).
Cousin Tryg, Lippincott (Philadelphia), 1966.
Go Away, Ruthie, Knopf, 1966.
A Tree Called Moses, illustrated by Penelope Naylor, Atheneum (New York City), 1966.
O Children of the Wind and Pines, illustrated by Inez Storer, Lippincott, 1967.
Here by the Sea, Lippincott, 1968.
Cowboy Pete, Lippincott, 1968.
Wild Peninsula: The Story of Point Reyes National Seashore, introduction by Stewart L. Udall, illustrated by Earl Thollander, Atheneum, 1969.
From Whales to Snails, illustrated by John Pimlott, Atheneum, 1970.
Ground Afire: The Story of the Death Valley National Monument, Atheneum, 1971.
(With Stoutenburg) *Listen, America: A Life of Walt Whitman,* Scribner, 1971.

Contributor of short stories and articles to *Christian Science Monitor, Woman's Day, Seventeen, American Girl,* and other publications. Work appears in several anthologies.

SIDELIGHTS: In her fiction for children and young adults, Laura Nelson Baker dealt with many of the issues common in the literature of young people: coming of age, coping with family problems, and finding one's place among friends and in the wider social context. Yet, Baker's nonfiction for young people often reveals fresh approaches to material. In *A Tree Called Moses,* Baker combined a history of the American continent from ancient times with the theme of ecology by recounting the life of a giant sequoia tree that continues to grow in California. As

J. R. Scott pointed out in *Library Journal,* "Known events are recounted in an engrossing manner," and the author "makes an eloquent plea for conservation." Scott found that the book should be "useful for book talks, curriculum enrichment, and . . . to awaken pride in our national heritage."

In another original approach to nonfiction, *O Children of the Wind and Pines,* Baker researched the writings of Jesuit missionaries in Canada to tell the story of Jean de Brebeuf. Father de Brebeuf traveled from France to the land of the Hurons in Canada in the early seventeenth century. While living among the Hurons, de Brebeuf composed the first Christmas carol written in North America, "Jesus Ahatonhia." In her book, Baker captured the uneasy coming together of cultures evident in the events surrounding the priest's attempts to teach the song to a young orphaned Huron girl. Ann Currah admitted in a *Library Journal* review that "The elements for a moving, unusual plot with a Christmas theme are here," but she added that the book lacked "a spark of inspiration to bring the story alive."

BIOGRAPHICAL/CRITICAL SOURCES:

PERIODICALS

Best Sellers, October 1, 1968, p. 275.
Book World, November 3, 1968, p. 26.
Christian Science Monitor, November 12, 1970, p. B5.
Library Journal, April 15, 1964, p. 1864; September 15, 1966, p. 4324; October 15, 1966, p. 5137; November 15, 1968, p. 4410; March 15, 1971, p. 1113.
New York Times Book Review, December 13, 1959, p. 24; May 17, 1964, p. 26; November 6, 1966, p. 58; December 4, 1966, p. 68; March 9, 1969, p. 26.
San Francisco Chronicle, November 8, 1959, p. 18.

* * *

BALABAN, John B. 1943-

PERSONAL: Born December 2, 1943, in Philadelphia, PA; son of Phillip and Alice (Georgies) Balaban; married Lana Flanagan (a teacher), November 27, 1970; children: Tally (daughter). *Education:* Pennsylvania State University, B.A. (with highest honors), 1966; Harvard University, A.M., 1967.

ADDRESSES: Home—720 North Thomas, State College, PA 16803. *Office*—Department of English,

CAREER: Pennsylvania State University, University Park, instructor, 1970-73, assistant professor, 1973-76, associate professor, 1976-82, professor of English 1982-92; University of Miami, Miami, FL, professor of English and director of Master of Fine Arts Program, 1992—. Fulbright senior lecturer in Romania, 1976-77; Fulbright distinguished visiting professor in Romania, 1978. Has given poetry readings at colleges and universities throughout the United States and in England, as well as on radio programs. Member of board of directors, Columbia University Translation Center, 1981—. Poetry judge for Academy of American Poets, 1978—, Pennsylvania Counci of the Arts, 1979, and Poetry Society of America, 1980. *Military service:* Instructor in literature and descriptive linguistics, International Voluntary Services, University of Can Tho, South Vietnam, 1967-68, and field representative, Committee of Responsibility to Save War-Injured Children, 1968-69, as alternative to military service.

MEMBER: PEN American Center, Association of Asian Scholars, Association of Literary Translators, Poetry Society of America.

AWARDS, HONORS: Woodrow Wilson fellowship from Harvard University, 1966-67; Chris Awar at Columbus Film Festival, 1969, for *Children of an Evil Hour;* Fulbright-Hays travel grant to Vietnam, 1971-72; National Endowment for the Humanities younger humanist fellowship, 1972; Pennsylvania State University Faculty Researc fellowships, 1974, 1977, 1984, and 1986; PEN American Center and Columbia University translation fellowship, 1974; Lamont Award from Academy of American Poets, 1974, and National Book Award for poetry nomination, 1975, both for *After Our War;* Translation Award from Columbia University Translation Center, 1977; National Endowment for the Arts fellowships, 1978 and 1985; Steaua Prize from Romanian Writers' Union, 1978; National Endowment for the Humanities grant, 1980; Vaptsarov Medal from Union of Bulgarian Writers, 1980; Pennsylvania Council on the Arts Creative Writing fellowship, 1983-84.

WRITINGS:

Children of the Evil Hour (film), Committee of Responsibility Inc., 1969.

Vietnam Poems (chapbook), Carcanet (South Hinksey, England), 1970.

(Editor and translator) *Vietnamese Folk Poetry*, Unicorn Press (Greensboro, NC), 1974.

After Our War (poems), University of Pittsburgh Press (Pittsburgh), 1974.

Letters from across the Sea/Scrisori de Peste Mare, Dacia Press (Cluj, Romania), 1978.

(Editor and translator) *Ca Dao Vietnam: A Bilingual Anthology of Vietnamese Folk Poetry*, Unicorn Press, 1980.

Blue Mountain (poems), Unicorn Press, 1982.

Coming Down Again (novel), Harcourt (San Diego), 1985, revised edition, Simon & Schuster (New York City), 1989.

The Hawk's Tale (juvenile), Harcourt, 1988.

(With Geoffrey Clifford) *Vietnam: The Land We Never Knew*, Chronicle (San Francisco), 1989.

Words for My Daughter, Copper Canyon Press (Poet Townsend, WA), 1991.

Remembering Heaven's Face: A Moral Witness in Vietnam, Poseidon (New York City), 1991.

(Editor with Nguyen Qui Duc) *Vietnam*, Whereabouts Press, 1996.

Locusts at the Edge of Summer (poems), Copper Canyon Press, 1997.

Contributor to several poetry anthologies. General editor, with Teo Savory, of Unicorn Press translation series of lesser known poets, 1984—. Contributor of poems, translations, and reviews to periodicals, including *Sewanee Review, New England Review, Southern Review, Nation, Poetry Now, College English, Translation Review, America Scholar, New York Times, Ploughshares, Triquarterly,* and *Life.*

ADAPTATIONS: *Ca Dao Vietnam: A Bilingual Anthology of Vietnamese Folk Poetry* was filmed as *Ca Dao Vietnam: Vietnamese Folk Poetry* in 1982.

SIDELIGHTS: John Balaban draws upon his experiences as a conscientious objector who worked in Vietnam as a university instructor and hospital field representative to write nonfiction, fiction and poetry. As Ronald Baughman explains in the *Dictionary of Literary Biography,* "Balaban's central subjects and themes emanate from his moral belief in taking decisive action to oppose human violence, particularly war."

Balaban's poetic work includes original poems and translations of Vietnamese folk poetry. His original work often revolves around his beliefs about American violence and is centered on the Vietnam War of two decades ago. In his memoir *Remembering Heaven's Face,* Balaban describes his own perspective to be "a moral witness in Vietnam," a perspective he maintains throughout his written work. The collection *Ca Dao Vietnam: A Bilingual Anthology of Vietnamese Folk Poetry* gathers together examples of a Vietnamese oral poetic tradition that stretches back several centuries. "I saw collecting these poems and translating them as the only sensible political act I could perform," Balaban explains in *Remembering Heaven's Face.*

Speaking of Balaban's first collection of poems, *After Our War,* Baughman notes that the poet "employs classical allusions to demonstrate the corruption of contemporary figures compared to their more heroic, classical models." One of Balaban's images, Baughman writes, is of four "American generals on horseback who, like the biblical Four Horsemen of the Apocalypse, personify the evils of war." In a more recent collection, *Locusts at the Edge of Summer,* Balaban finds America to be a land of violence in which "Late at night, when radio waves skip across States, / you can hear ricochets from Maine to L.A." The *Publishers Weekly* critic notes that Balaban "sometimes adopts a bitter, sneering stance toward ordinary people."

Balaban's skill as a poet, dexterity with language, and familiarity with South-East Asia all contribute to making his first novel, *Coming Down Again,* a success. The novel, an adventure story set in Vietnam toward the conclusion of U.S. involvement in the war there, tells of two Americans who are captured by a warlord for smuggling hashish and the efforts of their friend John Lacey to free them. Lacey's "personal creed of moral action," notes Baughman, "leads him to rescue his friends and their bisexual Vietnamese lover, Mai. With the aid of a mountain warlord, Lacey engineers a prison break." The book is praised by a *New Yorker* reviewer, who calls it "a Conradian novel, with a Conradian theme of integrity, a novel rich in language of action and of description." In the *Birmingham News* Philip D. Beidler also calls *Coming Down Again* "Conradian" and applauds Balaban's vivid depiction of the novel's setting. "The novel is alive with the strange, garish beauty of the landscape," he writes. "The air is dense with the smells, the sounds, and, perhaps most arrestingly of all . . . the language." *Los Angeles Times* contributor Douglas Sun comments favorably on the "unusual evocative power" of Balaban's prose.

"Balaban's poetry and prose," Baughman concludes, "collectively form an important statement of one who is committed to clarifying, as best he can, the painful morass of the Vietnam War. His convictions about opposing the war led him to act with a moral purpose. Perhaps his most important act, however, is to inform his readers . . . of what he saw and did, to examine the worst possibilities, and yet, through an ongoing moral struggle, to achieve some measure of good."

BIOGRAPHICAL/CRITICAL SOURCES:

BOOKS

Beidler, Philip D., *Re-Writing America: Vietnam Authors in Their Generation,* University of Georgia Press (Athens), 1991, pp. 145-205.
Dictionary of Literary Biography, Volume 120: *American Poets since World War II, Third Series,* Gale (Detroit), 1992.
Gilman, Owen W. and Lorrie Smith, editors, *America Rediscovered: Critical Essays on Literature and Film of the Vietnam War,* Garland Press (New York City), 1990, pp. 313-331.
Jason, Philip K., editor, *Fourteen Landing Zones: Approaches to Vietnam War Literature,* University of Iowa Press (Iowa City), 1991, pp. 49-66.

PERIODICALS

Birmingham News, July 28, 1985.
Christian Century, February 3, 1993, p. 123.
Christian Science Monitor, October 8, 1982.
Los Angeles Times, August 9, 1985.
New Yorker, August 26, 1985.
New York Review of Books, October 10, 1991.
Poetry, April, 1978.
Publishers Weekly, January 15, 1996, p. 457; April 28, 1997, p. 72.

*   *   *

BALDWIN, Hanson W(eightman) 1903-1991

PERSONAL: Born March 22, 1903, in Baltimore, MD; died of heart failure, November 13, 1991, in Roxbury, CT; son of Oliver Perry (managing editor of Baltimore *Sun*) and Caroline (Sutton) Baldwin; married Helen Bruce, June 8, 1931; children: Barbara, Elizabeth. *Education:* United States Naval Academy, B.S., 1924.

CAREER: Baltimore *Sun,* Baltimore, MD, police reporter, 1928. *New York Times,* New York City, reporter, 1929-37; military and naval correspondent, 1937-68; covering military activity in such places as the South Pacific, North Africa, Normandy, and Asia, military editor, 1942-68. *Military service:* U.S. Navy, 1920-27, served in Europe and the Caribbean; became lieutenant junior grade.

MEMBER: United States Naval Academy Alumni Association (former president); life member of board of trustees, George C. Marshall Research Foundation.

AWARDS, HONORS: Pulitzer Prize for journalism, 1942; Syracuse University School of Journalism distinguished service medal, 1944; honorary doctorates from Drake University and Clarkson Institute of Technology.

WRITINGS:

(Editor with Wayne Francis Palmer) *Men and Ships of Steel,* Morrow (New York City), 1935.
The Caissons Roll: A Military Survey of Europe, Knopf (New York City), 1938.
(Editor with Shepard Stone) *We Saw it Happen: The News Behind the News That's Fit to Print,* Simon & Schuster (New York City), 1938.
Admiral Death: Twelve Adventures of Men against the Sea, Simon & Schuster, 1939.
United We Stand!: Defense of the Western Hemisphere, McGraw (New York City), 1941, published in England as *Defense of the Western World,* Hutchinson (London), 1941.
The American Navy: What We Should Know about It, Allen & Unwin (New York City), 1941, 2nd edition published as *What the Citizen Should Know about the Navy,* Norton (New York City), 1942, 3rd edition published as *What You Should Know about the Navy,* Norton, 1943.
Strategy for Victory, Norton, 1942.
(Author of commentary) *The Navy at War: Paintings and Drawings by Combat Artists,* Morrow, 1943.
The Price of Power, Harper for the Council on Foreign Relations, 1948.
Power and Politics: The Price of Security in the Atomic Age, Claremont College (Claremont, CA), 1950.
Great Mistakes of the War, Harper (New York City), 1950.
Sea Fights and Shipwrecks: True Tales of the Seven Seas, Hanover House (Bayside, NY), 1955.

Middle East in Turmoil, Foreign Policy Association (New York City), 1957.

The Great Arms Race: A Comparison of U.S. and Soviet Power Today, Praeger (New York City), 1958.

World War I: An Outline History, Harper, 1962.

The New Navy, Dutton (New York City), 1964.

Battles Lost and Won: Great Campaigns of World War II, Harper, 1966.

Strategy for Tomorrow, Harper, 1970.

The Crucial Years: 1939-1941, Harper, 1976.

Tiger Jack, Old Army Press (Ft. Collins, CO), 1979.

Also contributor to *Harper's, Reader's Digest, Saturday Evening Post, New York Times Magazine, National Review,* and other periodicals.

SIDELIGHTS: The late Hanson W. Baldwin was a journalist and commentator for the *New York Times* who specialized in military issues. A graduate of the United States Naval Academy, Baldwin joined the staff of the *New York Times* in 1929 and became a military correspondent on the eve of World War II. His reportage extended over the following decades to encompass not only the Second World War, but also the Korean War, the Cold War, the Vietnam War, and the crisis situation in the Middle East. From 1935 into the mid-1970s, he published a number of books on pertinent military and historical subjects, culled from his journalism and lectures. In the *Saturday Review of Literature,* Fletcher Pratt noted that Baldwin "has an English prose style that allows him to be informative without didacticism, and energetic without inaccuracy; and he has a mind which allows him to hunt the essential fact through forests of detail and bring it back alive."

In 1941 Baldwin published one of his most important books, *United We Stand!: Defense of the Western Hemisphere.* The book describes U.S. military strength on the eve of America's intervention in World War II and predicts how the country will perform should it enter the war. A reviewer for *Living Age* magazine wrote of the work: "At a time when the American people are on the brink of making probably the most momentous decision in the nation's history, Mr. Baldwin's matter-of-fact survey and resume of American strength may be described as obligatory reading. It is not short of an ultimatum." *New York Times* correspondent S. F. Williamson stated: "To say that he has made a clear-headed, dependable analysis is merely to say, 'Hanson Baldwin has come through again.' But this time he offers something more, a guidebook to a

sound, effective, long-range military policy, and a handbook of useful military information for a bewildered people about to decide their own destiny—and duty."

In the post-war period Baldwin emerged as one of the most important—and powerful—civilian voices on U.S. military issues. He supported the buildup of U.S. nuclear weapons during the Cold War and viewed the Soviet leadership as a significant threat to world security. In books such as *Power and Politics: The Price of Security in the Atomic Age* and *The Great Arms Race: A Comparison of U.S. and Soviet Power Today,* he outlined what he saw as America's successes and failures in the ongoing arms race. "Mr. Baldwin's *Power and Politics* is a rational book produced in an irrational era," declared Hermit Eby in *Christian Century.* "It is also a book which gives one a world overview in a very short reading span. The fact that Hanson Baldwin is a military expert makes his rationality doubly impressive." S. T. Possony, reviewing *The Great Arms Race* in the *Annals of the American Academy,* contended that Baldwin "deserves much credit for an outstanding accomplishment. His research is meticulous, his judgment is realistic and balanced, his skill in compressing an enormously complicated material into a highly readable book of 116 short pages is truly enviable, and his message salutary. Hanson Baldwin has merited the praise of many grateful readers."

Baldwin retired from the *New York Times* in 1968 but continued writing and lecturing about American military strength through much of the 1970s. In 1970 he published *Strategy for Tomorrow,* his suggestions for the United States' defense needs—and his analysis of the changing threats to world peace—in the 1970s and 1980s. The book also contains his analysis of what went wrong in Vietnam and what could be done to stabilize the situation in Southeast Asia. In *Library Journal,* L.E. Spellman observed that *Strategy for Tomorrow* proved that Baldwin "hasn't lost his deft touch with matters military. . . . This work is proof of [his] perceptive grasp of humankind and the world situation today." In *National Review,* G. F. Eliot noted that *Strategy for Tomorrow* "is indispensable reading for any American who is interested in his country's future. . . . Let us hope that it may also be widely read and studied in all our institutions of higher learning."

All of Baldwin's books are characterized by an ability to render technical information into an understandable format for the general reader. As S. L. A.

Marshall put it in the *New York Times,* "Though not written in words of one syllable, [Baldwin's work] contains nothing that is beyond grasp by the average citizen." In the *Saturday Review,* Frank Altschul concluded: "As an acknowledged expert in a highly technical field, [Mr. Baldwin] has the knack of assembling and translating into terms that even the layman can understand a wealth of material. . . . No one will come away from [his books] with an enhanced sense of complacency."

BIOGRAPHICAL/CRITICAL SOURCES:

PERIODICALS

Annals of the American Academy, January, 1959, p. 650.
Atlantic, June 1, 1941, p. 458.
Books, May 4, 1941, p. 5.
Chicago Sunday Tribune, April 16, 1950, p. 6; October 16, 1955, p. 6; August 31, 1958, p. 4.
Christian Century, May 28, 1941, p. 20.
Christian Science Monitor, July 14, 1958, p. 7.
Library Journal, April 15, 1941, p. 355; October 1, 1958, p. 2742; July, 1966, p. 3411; July, 1970, p. 2491.
Living Age, June, 1941, p. 388.
Nation, May 10, 1941, p. 561.
National Review, December 13, 1966, p. 1277; November 28, 1967; November 17, 1970, p. 1221.
New Republic, May 26, 1941, p. 732.
Newsweek, April 22, 1968.
New York Herald Tribune Book Review, April 2, 1950, p. 10; August 17, 1958, p. 7.
New York Times, May 4, 1941, p. 1; April 2, 1950, p. 18; September 25, 1955, p. 3; July 13, 1958, p. 7.
New York Times Book Review, October 9, 1966, p. 6; September 13, 1970, p. 3.
San Francisco Chronicle, April 3, 1950, p. 16; September 18, 1955, p. 21.
Saturday Review, July 26, 1958, p. 28; September 26, 1970, p. 34.
Saturday Review of Literature, May 17, 1941, p. 14; September 16, 1950, p. 13.
Time, April 28, 1941, p. 88; September 26, 1955, p. 102.
Times Literary Supplement, August 2, 1941, p. 374.

OBITUARIES:

PERIODICALS

Chicago Times, November 14, 1991, section 2, p. 13.

Los Angeles Times, November 18, 1991, p. A22.
New York Times, November 14, 1991, p. D24.
Washington Post, November 14, 1991, p. D11.*

* * *

BANNING, Margaret Culkin 1891-1982

PERSONAL: Born March 18, 1891, in Buffalo, MN; died January 4, 1982, in Tryon, NC; daughter of William Edgar and Hannah (Young) Culkin; married Archibald T. Banning Jr. (lawyer), October 1, 1914; married LeRoy Salsich (corporation president), November 15, 1944; children: (first marriage) Mary, Archibald Tanner III. *Education:* Vassar College, A.B., 1912; Russell Sage College, fellowship for research, 1913; Chicago School of Philanthropy, certificate, 1914. *Politics:* Republican. *Religion:* Roman Catholic.

CAREER: Writer. Chair, Commission on Education of Women, American Council on Education; trustee, Duluth Public Library, 1930-82; trustee, Vassar College, 1937-45; member of advisory board, Women's Medical College of Pennsylvania.

MEMBER: American Association of University Women (past president of Duluth branch), League of Women Voters, Authors League of America, League of American Penwomen, PEN, Junior League (honorary member of Duluth branch), Arts Club (Chicago), Cordon Club (Chicago), Duluth Woman's Club, Northland Country Club (Duluth), Tryon Country Club, Tryon Riding and Hunt Club (Tryon, NC), Pen and Brush Club, Cosmopolitan Club (New York, NY), Phi Beta Kappa.

WRITINGS:

This Marrying, Harper (New York City), 1920.
Half Loaves, Harper, 1921.
Spellbinders, Harper, 1922, reprinted, Lighthouse (Los Angeles, CA), 1976.
Country Club People, Harper, 1923, reprinted, Lighthouse, 1976.
A Handmaid of the Lord, Harper, 1924.
The Women of the Family, Harper, 1926.
Pressure, Harper, 1927.
Money of Her Own, Harper, 1928.
Mixed Marriage, Harper, 1930.
The Town's Too Small, Harper, 1931.
Path of True Love, Harper, 1932.

The Third Son, Harper, 1933.
The First Woman, Harper, 1934.
The Iron Will, Harper, 1935.
Letters to Susan, Harper, 1936.
The Case for Chastity, Harper, 1937.
Too Young to Marry, Harper, 1938.
Enough to Live On, Harper, 1939.
Out in Society, Harper, 1940.
Salud: A South American Journal, Harper, 1940.
Letters from England, Harper, 1942.
Conduct Yourself Accordingly, Harper, 1944.
The Clever Sister, Harper, 1947.
Give Us Our Years, Harper, 1949.
Fallen Away, Harper, 1951.
The Dowry, Harper, 1955.
Echo Answers, Harper, 1960, second edition, Manor, 1968.
The Quality of Mercy, Harper, 1963.
The Vine and the Olive, Harper, 1964.
I Took My Love to The Country, Harper, 1966.
Mesabi, Harper, 1969.
The Splendid Torments, Harper, 1976.
Such Interesting People, Harper, 1979.

Also contributor of short stories and essays on American life and activities to magazines, including *Reader's Digest.* Member of editorial board, *Writer.*

SIDELIGHTS: Margaret Culkin Banning published her first novel in 1920 and her last in 1979, completing more than forty full-length books and four hundred short stories in between. Banning was not only a prolific writer of fiction and nonfiction primarily for female readers, she was also an author who chose controversial topics and covered them with sensitivity. An advocate of women's rights, she wrote stories and novels about serious career women and how their jobs affected their relationships with men. Her sense of social and religious duty led her to craft fiction about marriages between Catholics and Protestants, birth control, responsible parenting, and challenges to religious faith. A *New York Times* reviewer once called Banning "a craftsman of sure skill and unpretentious smoothness of style," and "a person of intelligence acutely aware of the unresolvable elements inherent in [her themes.]"

Banning was a practicing Roman Catholic. She was also a college-educated professional who wrestled with such issues as birth control and nontraditional family structures. A review of her novels reveals work that was ahead of its time: a 1920 effort, *This Marrying,* is about a woman who breaks ties with her middle-class family to seek fulfillment in a career; a

1930 novel, *Mixed Marriage,* is about the conflicts in a marriage between a Catholic woman and a Protestant man; and a 1955 novel, *The Dowry,* is about a woman who earns more money than her husband. Through these and other controversial stories, Banning established a reputation as a women's writer who "pulls no punches—she doesn't even roll with the punches," to quote Olive Carruthers in the *Chicago Sunday Tribune.* Carruthers added: "Nor is there any whitewash mixed in the colors with which [Banning] paints her picture."

Banning's books are "problem" novels in which her characters wrestle with philosophical and moral issues. Nevertheless, most critics found the author's talents sufficient to the task of breathing real life into the stories. In a *Boston Transcript* review of *This Marrying,* for instance, a reviewer wrote: "The success of the story lies not in an original plot, nor even in an unusual manner of telling the story, but rather in a certain freshness and joy in the experience of it all." According to P. O. Marsh in the *Christian Science Monitor,* *The Dowry* "is not a crusading book—it is primarily a good, absorbing story, relying on the interplay of characters and their emotions rather than on swift action and complicated plot." In a *Saturday Review of Literature* piece on *Fallen Away,* A. F. Wolfe praises the book as "an illumination of life and an authoritative commentary on our society." The critic concluded: "On that level, Mrs. Banning has never spoken more eloquently."

By virtue of her second marriage to an iron mining company president, Banning became acquainted with the lives of the upper class in the American Midwest and with the ironworkers as well. Her 1969 novel *Mesabi* was a thematic departure which chronicled life in the iron mines and among the mining families. As the years passed, however, she continued to concentrate on the issues that seemed most pressing to her, especially the Catholic church's stand on birth control and how faithful practitioners could reconcile themselves to it. Her 1964 title *The Vine and the Olive* tackles the problem again, as a young married couple seek advice from various priests and bishops within the church. In *Book Week,* R. V. Cassill noted of *The Vine and the Olive:* "Credit the author with the limited intent of putting before us the typical positions currently taken on this issue, subordinating minor dialectic qualifications by personifying them in minor characters, and using the movement of the story as agenda to give order to the sequence of adversary contentions."

Banning published her last novel in 1979 and was working on another when she died in North Carolina at the age of ninety. Her publishing career spanned six decades, a record made even more remarkable by the fact that Harper & Row served as publisher for almost all of her books. In a *New York Times* review of *This Marrying,* the critic summed up the essence of the author's longtime popularity: "The book is so distinctly pleasing, and is written with such unmistakable sincerity, that one passes over the blemishes—very trifling, after all—and gives himself up to the quiet enjoyment of a work that maintains its interest throughout without any strain or outbreak of violent emotion."

BIOGRAPHICAL/CRITICAL SOURCES:

PERIODICALS

America, June 27, 1964, p. 872.
Best Sellers, June 1, 1964, p. 108.
Booklist, July, 1920, p. 345.
Book Week, August 2, 1964, p. 14.
Boston Transcript, May 15, 1920, p. 10.
Chicago Sunday Tribune, September 31, 1951, p. 4; February 20, 1955, p. 4.
Christian Century, October 3, 1951, p. 1130.
Christian Science Monitor, February 17, 1955, p. 1.
Critic, October, 1964, p. 76.
Kirkus Reviews, May 1, 1944, p. 212; January 15, 1950, p. 37; June 15, 1951, p. 307.
New York Herald Tribune Book Review, April 16, 1950, p. 19; September 9, 1951, p. 6; March 13, 1955, p. 6; May 24, 1964, p. 40.
New York Times, June 27, 1920, p. 17; December 21, 1930, p. 8; April 2, 1950, p. 22; September 9, 1951, p. 23; February 20, 1955, p. 24.
Saturday Review of Literature, September 15, 1951, p. 15.
Springfield Republican, May 2, 1920, p. 13A; March 27, 1955, p. 8C.
Times Literary Supplement, September 24, 1931, p. 732.
Weekly Book Review, August 20, 1944, p. 16.

OBITUARIES:

PERIODICALS

AB Bookman's Weekly, February 15, 1982.
Chicago Tribune, January 7, 1982.
New York Times, January 6, 1982.
Publishers Weekly, January 22, 1982.
Time, January 18, 1982.*

BARKER, A(rthur) J(ames) 1918-1981

PERSONAL: Born September 20, 1918, in Yorkshire, England; died June 10, 1981, in Cape Town, South Africa; son of John Robert Marlow and Caroline Frances (Roe) Barker; married Dorothy Jeanna Hirst (marriage dissolved, 1968); married Alexandra Franziska Roderbourg, 1969; children: (first marriage) Timothy Marlow. *Education:* Attended Staff College, Quetta, India, 1944, and Royal Military College of Science, 1948-50. *Politics:* Conservative. *Religion:* Humanist.

CAREER: Career officer in British Army, 1936-58; commissioned in East Yorkshire Regiment; served as Infantry officer in Africa, 1940-41, Burma, 1942-44, and Malaya, 1952-54, as staff officer in Burma-India, 1945-46, Palestine and Egypt, 1947, and Malaya, 1956-58, and in other posts in northwestern Europe; retired with rank of lieutenant colonel, 1958; United Kingdom Atomic Energy Authority, London, England, administrator and editor of scientific reports, 1959-68; writer, 1968-81.

MEMBER: Royal Society of Arts (fellow), PEN, Authors Guild, Royal United Service Institution, Society for Army Historical Research, British Atlantic Committee (associate).

AWARDS, HONORS: NATO research fellowship, 1968.

WRITINGS:

Principles of Small Arms, Gale & Polden, 1952.
The March on Delhi, Faber (London), 1963.
Suez: The Seven Day War, Praeger (New York City), 1964.
Eritrea 1941, Faber, 1966.
The Bastard War: The Mesopotamian Campaign of 1914-1918, Dial (New York City), 1967, published in England as *The Neglected War: Mesopotamia, 1914-1918,* Faber, 1967.
Townshend of Kut: A Biography of Major-General Sir Charles Townshend, Cassell (London), 1967.
The Civilizing Mission: A History of the Italo-Ethiopian War of 1935-1936, Dial, 1968.
German Infantry Weapons of World War II, Arco, 1969, revised edition, Hippocrene (New York City), 1976.
Pearl Harbor, Ballantine (New York City), 1969.
British and American Infantry Weapons of World War II, Arco, 1969, revised edition, Leventhal (London), 1973.

The Vainglorious War: 1854-56, Weidenfeld & Nicolson (London), 1970, published as *The War against Russia: 1854-1856,* Holt (New York City), 1971.

(With John Walter) *Russian Infantry Weapons of World War II,* Arco (New York City), 1971.

The East Yorkshire Regiment, Leo Cooper (London), 1971.

Midway: The Turning Point, Ballantine, 1971.

The Suicide Weapon, Ballantine, 1971.

The Rape of Ethiopia, 1936, Ballantine, 1971.

Fortune Favours the Brave, Leo Cooper, 1973.

Shotguns and Shooting edited by Robert K. Brown and Peter C. Lund, Paladin Press (Boulder, CO), 1973.

Bloody Ulster, Ballantine, 1973.

Yamashita, Ballantine, 1973.

Six Day War, Ballantine, 1974.

Behind Barbed Wire, Batsford (London), 1974, published as *Prisoners of War,* Universe Books (New York City), 1975.

The October War: Yom Kippur, 1973, Ballantine, 1974.

Weapons and Armour (juvenile), Paul Hamlyn (London), 1974.

Famous Military Battles (juvenile), Paul Hamlyn, 1974.

Redcoats: The British Soldier in America, Dent (London), 1976.

(Author of introduction) *Soviet Army Uniforms and Insignia, 1945-1975,* Hippocrene, 1976.

(Translator) Janusz Piekalkiewicz, *Arnheim 1944: Germany's Last Victory,* International Publications, 1977.

Dunkirk: The Great Escape, Dent, 1977.

Panzers at War, Scribner (New York City), 1978.

(With James Sidney Lucas) *The Battle of Normandy: The Falaise Gap,* Holmes & Meier (New York City), 1978, published in England as *The Killing Ground: The Battle of the Falaise Gap, August 1944,* Batsford, 1978.

Japanese Army Handbook, Hippocrene, 1979.

Afrika Korps, Quality Books, 1979.

Arab-Israeli Wars, Ian Allan, 1980, Hippocrene, 1981.

Contributor of articles to *Royal United Service Institutional Journal, Army Quarterly,* and other military journals.

SIDELIGHTS: In histories written for both popular and scholarly consumption, one-time British Army officer A. J. Barker chronicled many of the twentieth century's lesser-known battles and wars in Europe, North Africa, and the Middle East; these conflicts continued to shape global politics for many years after the fighting stopped.

In *Suez: The Seven Day War,* Barker explored the 1956 conflict that followed the Egyptian nationalization of the waterway that linked the Mediterranean Sea with the Red Sea, providing Europe with vital shipping routes to the Middle East, East Africa, and Asia. After Egypt took control of the canal, Israel, Britain, and France all declared war, pushing to seize and reopen the waterway. Pressure from the United States, the Soviet Union, and the United Nations eventually ended the fighting. "Mr. Barker readably and clearly describes the military operation," wrote a reviewer for the *Economist.* "Colonel A. J. Barker's book . . . tells the military story from the British side in complete and unvarnished form, so thoroughly that it need not be done again," added J. C. Campbell in the *Saturday Review.* As E. P. Stickney pointed out in *Library Journal,* "The expedition disclosed serious shortcomings in the British military machine." And for his part, in uncovering these faults and the efforts of other armies in the conflict, "Colonel Barker keeps an efficient grasp on the general strategic intentions . . . of the allied high command," noted a *Times Literary Supplement* contributor. "He also succeeds in the difficult task of harmonizing into one narrative the stories of what were in effect two separate but simultaneous descents upon the canal, one British and one French."

World War I saw the British fighting in Europe against the Germans and at the same time in the Middle East against the Turks. Barker profiled the war on this front in *The Bastard War: The Mesopotamian Campaign of 1914-1918.* In this account of the military operations, Barker wrote "with skill, precision, and a fine handling of significant detail," E. V. Sutherland commented in *Library Journal.* As a result, observed Sutherland, the book "presents a compelling picture of what happens to soldiers in the field when the national strategy is ill-defined and the higher military direction unimaginative and inept." Yet, although he did not shy away from critical judgments of the British effort, "this story is all the more impressive because Mr. Barker pictures it soberly and with a minimum of reproach," Cyril Falls maintained in the *New York Times Book Review.*

BIOGRAPHICAL/CRITICAL SOURCES:

PERIODICALS

American History Review, February, 1968, p. 865; June, 1969, p. 1584.

Book Week, February 14, 1965, p. 5.

Bulletin of the Atomic Scientists, May, 1969, p. 51.
Choice, July, 1968, p. 660; September, 1969, p. 887.
Economist, January 16, 1965, p. 227; December 7, 1968, p. 56; November 21, 1970, p. 7.
Library Journal, May 15, 1967, p. 1925; October 15, 1968, p. 3782; December 15, 1970, p. 4256.
Nation, February 22, 1965, p. 200.
New Statesman, January 22, 1965, p. 116; December 22, 1967, p. 879.
New Yorker, August 14, 1971, p. 88.
New York Times Book Review, September 10, 1967, p. 52; March 7, 1971, p. 16.
Saturday Review, April 17, 1965, p. 55.
Times (London), January 7, 1965, p. 6.
Times Literary Supplement, November 16, 1967, p. 1082; February 20, 1969, p. 179; December 4, 1970, p. 1416.

OBITUARIES:

PERIODICALS

Times (London), June 23, 1981.*

* * *

BARKER, Shirley Frances 1911-1965

PERSONAL: Born April 4, 1911, in Farmington, NH; died November 18, 1965, in Concord, NH; daughter of Will Tilden and Alta (Leighton) Barker. *Education:* University of New Hampshire, B.A., 1934; Radcliffe College, A.M., 1938; Pratt Institute Library School, B.L.S., 1941. *Politics:* Republican.

CAREER: New York Public Library, New York, NY, librarian, mainly in American history department, 1940-44, 1946-53; professional writer, 1954-65.

MEMBER: Daughters of the American Revolution, Business and Professional Women's Club, many historical societies, Phi Beta Kappa.

AWARDS, HONORS: Younger Poets Award, Yale University, 1933.

WRITINGS:

The Dark Hills Under (poems), Yale University Press (New Haven, CT), 1933.

Peace, My Daughters, Crown (New York City), 1949.
Rivers Parting, Crown, 1950.
A Land and a People (poems), Crown, 1952.
Fire and Hammer, Crown, 1953.
Tomorrow the New Moon, Bobbs (New York City), 1955.
Liza Bowe, Random House (New York City), 1956.
Swear by Apollo, Random House, 1958.
The Trojan Horse, Random House, 1959.
The Last Gentleman, Random House, 1960.
Corner of the Moon, Crown, 1961.
The Road to Bunker Hill, Duell, Sloan & Pearce (New York City), 1962.
Strange Wives, Crown, 1963.

Assistant editor, *New Hampshire Profiles,* 1955-56.

SIDELIGHTS: Shirley Frances Barker was a poet and novelist who rarely strayed far from her native New England. Born and raised in New Hampshire, she set much of her poetry and a number of her novels in that state, commenting upon the New England character and the forces of history at work in the region. A *Kirkus* reviewer praised Barker's work for its "pace, vitality, atmosphere, [and] authentic people who live and move and shape their destinies."

Barker published her first volume of poetry while still an undergraduate at the University of New Hampshire. *Dark Hills Under* was a release under Yale University's "Series of Younger Poets" imprint, and it carried a warm foreword by celebrated poet Stephen Vincent Benet. In *Books,* Ruth Lechlitner described the verses as "conventional in form and traditional in content, in so far as the writer speaks from her environment and deals almost exclusively with the New England scene." The critic added that Barker "handles particularly well the narrative ballad . . . and her feeling for New England's dark hills and flinty acres is less strongly defined than her appreciation of the New England character." *New York Times* correspondent E. L. Walton wrote: "Shirley Barker writes very well. She handles the sonnet, the ballad, the dramatic poem, the long narrative, with skill. She has an interesting and new attitude toward New England and New Englanders."

Such a promising debut notwithstanding, Barker waited sixteen years for the publication of her next book. In the meantime she worked as a librarian at the New York Public Library, immersing herself in the American history section. Not surprisingly, when she began writing again, her work mined the information she could access at the library. What followed were a number of historical novels, many set in New England during the colonial and revolutionary eras. In *Swear by Apollo,* for instance, a young New Hampshire native returns to Edinburgh to study medicine just prior to the Revolutionary War. In the *New York Times,* A. F. Wolfe called *Swear by Apollo* "a pungent draught of romance fermented in the supernatural," noting further that Barker's primary achievement "is to evoke a Gaelic half-world of fused shadow and substance." *The Last Gentleman,* published in 1960, revolves around a beautiful widow who must choose between suitors—and also between loyalty to the crown and the revolutionary fervor brewing in New Hampshire. A *Kirkus* reviewer maintained that, in *The Last Gentleman,* Barker "spins a goodly yarn against a warm and sympathetically drawn background, and gives the reader a sense of history in the making and characters that are more than two dimensional."

The success of Barker's novels enabled her to return to New Hampshire, where she died in 1965. She wrote practically to the end of her life, and her stories—while catering to certain aspects of the romance novel—also offered authentic historical detail. A *Booklist* critic concluded that Barker's work was characterized by "interesting and unusual side lights on the social history of the times."

BIOGRAPHICAL/CRITICAL SOURCES:

PERIODICALS

Booklist, July 15, 1958, p. 625.
Books, November 19, 1933, p. 23.
Chicago Sunday Tribune, June 19, 1960, p. 3.
Kirkus Reviews, February 1, 1958, p. 93; April 15, 1960, p. 336.
New York Herald Tribune Book Review, January 7, 1951; December 23, 1956, p. 6; August 31, 1958, p. 7; July 10, 1960, p. 6.
New York Times, October 22, 1933, p. 10; August 24, 1958, p. 26.
Saturday Review, September 6, 1952, p. 29; December 1, 1956, p. 36; September 13, 1958, p. 43.
Springfield Republican, September 21, 1952, p. 26.
Times Literary Supplement, December 7, 1933.*

*   *   *

BARRETT, Julia
 See KESSLER, Julia Braun

BECKER, Robin 1951-

PERSONAL: Born March 7, 1951, in Philadelphia, PA; daughter of Benjamin (a realtor) and Ann (a realtor; maiden name, Weiner) Becker. *Education:* Boston University, B.A., 1973, M.A., 1976.

ADDRESSES: Home—215 Academy St., Boalsburg, PA 16827. *Office*—Department of English, Pennsylvania State University, 103 Burrowes Building, University Park, PA 16802-6200.

CAREER: Massachusetts Institute of Technology, Cambridge, lecturer in creative writing and humanistic studies, 1977-93, assistant professor of exposition and rhetoric, 1983-87; Pennsylvania State University, University Park, visiting professor, 1993-94, associate professor of English and Women's Studies, 1994—. Kent State University, visiting professor, 1992; writer-in-residence, Wyoming Council on the Arts, Sheridan, and the Writers' Place, Madison, WI, both 1991; Central High School, Philadelphia, *American Poetry Review* scholar-in-residence, 1994. Member, board of trustees, Cummington School of the Arts, 1976-83; member, board of directors, Associated Writing Programs, 1992-95. Co-coordinator of reading series at New Words (bookstore), 1981-83.

MEMBER: Modern Language Association of America, Poetry Society of America, Associated Writing Programs.

AWARDS, HONORS: Massachusetts Artists Foundation fellowship, 1985; Cambridge River Festival Poetry prize, 1986; *Prairie Schooner* Readers' Choice Awards, 1989; National Endowment for the Arts grant, 1989; Anna Davidson Rosenberg award, 1990; Mary Ingraham Bunting Fellowship, Radcliffe College, 1995-96; Pushcart Prize nomination, 1995, 1997, and 1998; Lambda Literary Prize, 1997, for *All-American Girl*; Faulkner Award, *Prairie Schooner* magazine, 1998.

WRITINGS:

(With Helena Minton and Marilyn Zuckerman) *Personal Effects,* Alice James Books (Cambridge, MA), 1976.
Backtalk, Alice James Books, 1982.
Giacometti's Dog, University of Pittsburgh Press (Pittsburgh), 1990.
All-American Girl, University of Pittsburgh Press, 1996.

Contributor of poetry and short fiction to numerous anthologies and textbooks, including *The Things That Divide Us,* Seal (Seattle), 1985, *Naming the Waves: Contemporary Lesbian Poetry,* Virago (London), 1988, *Dog Music: Contemporary Poems about Dogs,* St. Martin's (New York City), 1996, and *Poetry: An Introduction,* Bedford Books (Boston), 1998. Also contributor of essays and book reviews to *American Poetry Review, Boston Globe, Prairie Schooner, Women's Review of Books,* and other journals

Poetry editor, *Bay Windows,* 1983-85, and *Women's Review of Books,* 1986—.

WORK IN PROGRESS: A selection of narrative poems and sequences tentatively titled *From the Queer Diaspora;* also at work on several reviews and essays.

SIDELIGHTS: Poet and educator Robin Becker is noted for verse that is approachable and engaging for even the casual reader. Listening to conversations about one's former lover during a dinner party; drowning one's sorrows in a shopping trip that buries emotions beneath "things"; or joining an old friend in reminiscing about the past during a day-long bicycle trip: such are the subjects of Becker's poetry. Considered "as engaging and immediate as the best conversation," by *Contemporary Women Poets* essayist Kathleen Aguero, Becker's "strongest work moves toward reconciling apparent contradicions enabling a sense of life's possibilities to coexist with an awareness of human frailty." A contributor of poems to hundreds of periodicals, Becker has also published four poetry collections, among them *Backtalk, Giacometti's Dog,* and *All-American Girl.*

Writing in the *Village Voice Literary Supplement,* critic J. Kates called *Backtalk,* an "energetic" poetry collection. "The title and the poems themselves predicate an active listener as well as a speaker with a lively eye for imagery," Kates explained, adding that Becker is "at her best when she is directly involved in sassy and veracious backtalk with her imagined listener."

In Becker's third collection of verse, *Giacometti's Dog,* her subject ranges from the sensual ("The Bath") to the metaphysical ("Birch Trees"). In this book, as well as in her fourth collection, *All-American Girl,* the author's lesbianism becomes increasingly overt, and her use of imagery calling on each of the five senses also becomes more pronounced. In these later volumes, the poet "uses vivid detail to

root large concerns in the specifics of our lives," maintained Aguero. "Richly populated by friends, lovers, family, Becker's poems chronicle a search for community," as well as a quest for the meaning of love. Indeed, many of Becker's poems are thematically similar, prompting a *Publishers Weekly* critic to note that while the verses in *All-American Girl* are "intense, and a few . . . are stirring, . . . too many focus on similar events from similar emotional perspectives."

Becker once told *CA:* "I am very much influenced by women writers, particularly those whose work became readily available in the early 1970s—Adrienne Rich, Denise Levertov, Maxine Kumin, Susan Griffin, Audre Lorde. University teaching has been a compatible match with my writing career, allowing me long periods of time in which to write."

BIOGRAPHICAL/CRITICAL SOURCES:

BOOKS

Contemporary Women Poets, St. James Press (Detroit), 1997.

PERIODICALS

Booklist, August, 1990, p. 2149.
Publishers Weekly, May 4, 1990, p. 65; December 18, 1995, p. 52.
Village Voice Literary Supplement, June, 1982.
Women's Review of Books, July, 1996, pp. 40-41.

* * *

BELTING, Natalia Maree 1915-1997

PERSONAL: Born July 11, 1915, in Oskaloosa, IA; died December 17, 1997; daughter of Paul Everette and Anna Maree (maiden name, Hanselman) Belting. *Education:* Attended Coe College, 1932-33; University of Illinois, B.S., 1936, M.A., 1937, Ph.D., 1940. *Religion:* Presbyterian. *Avocational interests:* Baking, gardening, wood carving, the Indians of Illinois.

ADDRESSES: Office—Department of History, University of Illinois, Urbana, IL 61801.

CAREER: University of Illinois at Urbana-Champaign, 1942—, began as instructor, associate professor of history, 1973—. Supply preacher in rural Presbyterian churches, Illinois.

MEMBER: Authors Guild, Wildlife Federation, Delta Zeta, Phi Alpha Theta.

AWARDS, HONORS: Named Illinois Author of the Year by Illinois State Association of Teachers of English, 1979.

WRITINGS:

(With P. E. Belting) *The Modern High School Curriculum,* Garrard, 1940.

Kaskaskia under the French Regime, University of Illinois Press, 1948, reprinted Polyanthos, 1975.

Pierre of Kaskaskia, Bobbs-Merrill, 1951.

Moon Is a Crystal Ball, Bobbs-Merrill, 1952.

In Enemy Hands, Bobbs-Merrill, 1953.

Three Apples Fell from Heaven, Bobbs-Merrill, 1953.

Cat Tales, Holt, 1959, published in England as *King Solomon's Cat: Folk Tales from around the World,* Rapp & Whiting, 1968.

Indy and Mr. Lincoln, Holt, 1960.

Verity Mullens and the Indian, illustrated by Leonard Everett Fisher, Holt, 1960.

Elves and Ellefolk: Tales of the Little People, illustrated by Gordon Laite, Holt, 1961.

The Long-Tailed Bear, Bobbs-Merrill, 1961.

The Sun Is a Golden Earring, illustrated by Bernarda Bryson, Holt, Rinehart and Winston, 1962.

The Calendar Moon, Holt, 1964.

The Earth Is on a Fish's Back, Holt, 1965.

The Stars Are Silver Reindeer, illustrated by Esta Nesbitt, Holt, Rinehart and Winston, 1966.

Christmas Folk, illustrated by Barbara Cooney, Holt, Rinehart and Winston, 1969.

Winter's Eve, illustrated by Alan E. Cober, Holt, Rinehart and Winston, 1969.

Summer's Coming In, illustrated by Adrienne Adams, Holt, Rinehart and Winston, 1970.

The Land of the Taffeta Dawn, illustrated by Joseph Low, Dutton, 1973.

Our Fathers Had Powerful Songs, illustrated by Laszlo Kubinyi, Dutton, 1974.

Whirlwind Is a Ghost Dancing, illustrated by Leo and Diane Dillon, Dutton, 1974.

Moon Was Tired of Walking on Air, illustrated by Will Hillenbrand, Houghton Mifflin (Boston), 1992.

WORK IN PROGRESS: Transcribing and editing a dictionary of Illinois language, compiled by a Jesuit missionary in 1712.

SIDELIGHTS: Natalia Maree Belting's books for children retell folk tales and songs from around the world, garnering high praise for their rhythmic, often poetic, narratives. In works such as *Elves and Ellefolk,* Belting presents little-known stories from places such as Scandinavia, Polynesia, Africa, and elsewhere while her *Summer's Coming In* offers a new approach to the history of the English people through a look at its celebrations and rituals. Reviewers note that her readable, sometimes humorous, sometimes moving, stories make history accessible to young people and offer instructors an unusual approach to social studies curricula.

Elves and Ellefolk presents tales of the small, magical people who form a part of the mythology of many cultures throughout the world. "There are as many races and kinds of the Little People as there are of men, and some of the least familiar have been gathered here," noted a reviewer for the *Horn Book.* Belting includes stories of various lengths and complexity, making her book useful in a variety of situations, from reading aloud to younger children to resources for social studies and creative writing workshops for older children, reviewers noted. All are "fresh and original," according to Inger Boye in *Library Journal,* and "told in the picturesque language of an old teller of tales." Similarly, Belting offered stories and poems from a wide array of sources in her *Calendar Moon,* resulting in a work that is both "historically interesting as well as poetically spellbinding," *Library Journal* critic Ellen Rudin averred.

Calendar Moon collects folklore relating to the moon; in Belting's *The Earth is on a Fish's Back,* the author presents legends that explain how the world came to be as it is. Primarily drawn from Native American sources, all of the stories "are appropriate for creative and comparative activities associated with social studies," contended a reviewer in the *Horn Book.* In *The Stars Are Silver Reindeer,* Belting does for the stars what she had earlier done for the moon. "Harmony of text and illustrations mark a beautifully conceived and creative picture book for all ages," wrote Della Thomas in *Library Journal.*

In two other works, *Christmas Folk* and *Summer's Coming In,* Belting confined herself to English sources. Thus, *Christmas Folk* describes the festivities and rituals surrounding the Christmas season as it was celebrated in Queen Elizabeth I's day, when it lasted from the end of November to the beginning of January. In *Summer's Coming In,* Belting depicts a slightly later era through its annual celebration of spring. Stories from a much earlier era are retold in *The Land of the Taffeta Dawn,* in which Belting offers a vision of China through the tales brought back by the Viking traders.

Belting dove into American history for the sources of two of her picture books. In *Verity Mullens and the Indian,* which is set in colonial Plymouth, a young girl's dog becomes lost in the forest and is found by a friendly Indian, who returns him to his owner. "Such a delightful book!" enthused E. S. Dutton in *Chicago Sunday Tribune,* emphasizing the readability and humor of Belting's historical narrative. Belting's *Indy and Mr. Lincoln* retells the tale of the future president's humorous encounter with a pet pig in New Salem, Indiana. "This very funny story has a rhythmical style and genuine folk-tale flavor that make it fine for reading aloud," remarked Polly Goodwin in *Chicago Sunday Tribune,* a judgment echoed by other reviewers.

Belting's books for young people often showcase folk tales and legends little known in the West. As a reteller of traditional stories, Belting is prized for her lyrical prose, which recommends her works for both reading aloud and for older children to read on their own. Several critics have endorsed her anthologies for an adult readership interested in folklore. In addition, the author's theme-based collections such as *Christmas Folk* and *Calendar Moon,* are considered ideal books for expanding and enriching social studies curricula.

BIOGRAPHICAL/CRITICAL SOURCES:

PERIODICALS

Booklist, July 1, 1961.
Book Week, December 27, 1964, p. 13.
Book World, December 21, 1969, p. 8.
Chicago Sunday Tribune, April 17, 1960, p. 6; November 6, 1960, p. 16; May 14, 1961, section 2, p. 9.
Christian Science Monitor, May 11, 1961, p. 3B; April 3, 1971, p. 19.
Horn Book, August, 1961; February, 1965; August, 1965; December, 1969; August, 1973; August, 1974.
Kirkus Reviews, March 1, 1960; September 15, 1960; February 15, 1961.
Library Journal, May 15, 1960; November 15, 1960; May 15, 1961; January 15, 1965; June 15, 1965; July, 1966; July, 1970; September 15, 1973; September 15, 1974.

New York Herald Tribune Book Review, March 6, 1960, p. 10.
New York Herald Tribune Lively Arts, November 20, 1960, p. 40; May 14, 1961, section 12, p. 5.
New York Times Book Review, May 8, 1960, p. 26; February 15, 1965, p. 26; September 11, 1966.
San Francisco Chronicle, June 26, 1960, p. 27; November 13, 1960, p. 19.
Saturday Review, May 7, 1960; November 12, 1960; December 12, 1964; September 18, 1965.
Springfield Republican, March 20, 1960, p. 5D; April 30, 1961, p. 5D.*

*   *   *

BENET, Laura 1884-1979

PERSONAL: Name is pronounced *ben-nay;* born June 13, 1884, at Fort Hamilton, Brooklyn, NY; died February 17, 1979, in New York, NY; daughter of James Walker (an army officer) and Frances Neill (maiden name, Rose) Benet. *Education:* Emma Willard School, graduate, 1903; Vassar College, A.B., 1907. *Politics:* Democrat. *Religion:* Protestant Episcopal.

CAREER: Spring Street Settlement, New York City, Settlement, New York City, settlement worker, 1913-16; Children's Aid Society, New York City, placement worker, 1917; Red Cross Sanitary Commission, Augusta, GA, inspector, 1917-19; St. Bartholomew's Mission, New York City, worker, 1924-25; *New York Evening Post,* New York City, assistant editor of book page, 1926-28; *New York Evening Sun,* New York City, assistant to book page editor, 1928-29; *New York Times,* New York City, substitute review editor, 1930; writer, 1930-79. Air raid warden during World War II.

MEMBER: Poetry Society of America, PEN, Women Poets, Craftsman Group, Pen and Brush Club (honorary).

AWARDS, HONORS: Medal from National Poetry Center, 1936; poetry prizes from *Lyric* and *Voices;* D.Litt, Moravian College, 1967.

WRITINGS:

POETRY

Fairy Bread, Thomas Seltzer, 1921.
Noah's Dove, Doubleday, 1929.

Basket for a Fair, Doubleday, 1934.
Is Morning Sure?, Odyssey, 1947.
In Love with Time, Wake-Brook, 1959.
Bridge of a Single Hair, Branden, 1974.

FICTION

Goods and Chattels, Doubleday, 1930, reprinted, Books for Libraries Press, 1970.
The Hidden Valley (juvenile), Dodd, 1938.
Roxana Rampant (juvenile), Dodd, 1940.
Come Slowly, Eden, Dodd, 1942.

BIOGRAPHY

The Boy Shelley, illustrated by James MacDonald, Dodd, 1937, reprinted, 1964.
Enchanting Jenny Lind, Dodd, 1939, reprinted, 1964.
Young Edgar Allan Poe, illustrated by George Gillett Whitney, Dodd, 1941, reprinted, 1963.
Washington Irving, Explorer of American Legend, illustrated by Harve Stein, Dodd, 1944.
Thackeray, of the Great Heart and Humorous Pen, Dodd, 1947.
Coleridge, Poet of Wild Enchantment, Dodd, 1952.
Stanley, Invincible Explorer, Dodd, 1955.
The Mystery of Emily Dickinson, Dodd, 1974.

OTHER

Caleb's Luck (juvenile), Grosset, 1942.
Horseshoe Nails, illustrations by Harvey Kidder, Holt, 1943, reprinted, 1965.
Barnum's First Circus, and Other Stories (juvenile), 1949.
Famous American Poets, Dodd, 1950.
(Author of biographical introduction) *Tales by Edgar Allan Poe,* Dodd, 1952.
(Author of biographical introduction) *Thackeray's Henry Esmond,* Heritage, 1952.
Famous American Humorists, Dodd, 1959.
Famous Poets for Young People, Dodd, 1964.
Famous English and American Essayists, Dodd, 1966.
Famous Storytellers for Young People, Dodd, 1968.
Famous New England Authors, Dodd, 1970.
When William Rose, Stephen Vincent, and I Were Young, Dodd, 1976.

SIDELIGHTS: Laura Benet was a social worker, newspaper editor, poet, novelist, and biographer. After her retirement from social work, Benet worked for several New York newspapers, including the *New York Evening Post.* In addition to writing children's books, novels, and literary biographies, Benet was also a poet, and the author of two books on her brothers, Stephen Vincent and William Rose Benet. Her several volumes of poetry include *Is Morning Sure?,* of which L.T. Nicholl wrote in the *Saturday Review of Literature:* "This volume, perhaps not so even in quality as Laura Benet's three earlier books of poetry, nevertheless goes deeper in its best work."

Benet's highly regarded biographies of classic authors such as William Makepeace Thackeray, Percy Bysshe Shelley, and Edgar Allan Poe are noted for their sympathetic treatment of their subjects. "There is an exuberance here that is in keeping with the rebellious spirit of Shelley," noted E. A. Groves in a *Library Journal* review of Benet's biography *The Boy Shelley.* Similarly, in a *Books* review of *Young Edgar Allan Poe,* M.L. Becker contended that "Poe is presented, with a sympathy that never slops over, as a genius." And a *Kirkus Reviews* critique of Benet's *Washington Irving, Explorer of American Legend* dubbed it "a biography as winning as the man about whom it was written."

In addition to her clear understanding of her artistic subjects, Benet's biographies are credited with providing her audience with a portrait of the artists' times through her detailed research. "Besides a new knowledge of Thackeray, high school readers will gain from the book a comprehensive picture of the early Victorian literary scene," wrote a critic of *Thackeray of the Great Heart and Humorous Pen* in the *New York Times.* Although some critics faulted the author for confining her narratives to the younger years of her subjects' lives, an element that marks these works as intended for a young adult audience, some noted that Benet's perceptive, well-paced, biographies would fill the needs of an adult audience as well. Such was the judgment of a critic for the *Saturday Review,* who considered Benet's *Coleridge, Poet of Wild Enchantment* "so thoughtful and mature that it might well be published as an adult book."

BIOGRAPHICAL/CRITICAL SOURCES:

PERIODICALS

Atlantic, December, 1937.
Booklist, December 1, 1937; January 1, 1942; December 15, 1944; December 1, 1947; September 1, 1952.
Books, November 14, 1937, p. 31; December 14, 1941, p. 9.

Book Week, January 21, 1945, p. 11.

Catholic World, December, 1937; December, 1944.

Christian Science Monitor, January 11, 1945, p. 10; August 16, 1947, p. 10.

Commonweal, November 21, 1947.

Horn Book, November, 1937; January, 1938; January, 1942; January, 1948.

Kirkus Reviews, October 15, 1944.

Library Journal, November 1, 1937; November 15, 1937; December 15, 1941; December 1, 1944; December 1, 1947; August, 1952.

New York Herald Tribune Weekly Book Review, November 16, 1947, p. 43.

New York Times, November 12, 1944, p. 16; August 3, 1947, p. 10.

San Francisco Chronicle, November 30, 1947, p. 7.

Saturday Review of Literature, December 4, 1937; November 11, 1944; August 9, 1947; November 15, 1947; November 15, 1952.

Weekly Book Review, November 12, 1944, p. 18.

OBITUARIES:

New York Times, February 19, 1979.*

*   *   *

BERESFORD, Anne 1929-

PERSONAL: Born September 10, 1929, in Redhill, Surrey, England; daughter of Richmond (a film representative) and Margaret (a musician; maiden name, Kent) Beresford; married Michael Hamburger (a poet), 1951 (divorced, 1970, remarried 1974); children: Mary Anne, Richard, Claire. *Education:* Attended Central School of Speech Training and Dramatic Art, 1944-46. *Politics:* "Socialist."

ADDRESSES: Home—Marsh Acres, Middleton, Saxmundham, Suffolk IP17 3NH, England.

CAREER: Writer. British Broadcasting Corp. (BBC), London, broadcaster, 1960-70; high school drama teacher in Wimbledon, England, 1969-73; Arts Educational School, London, drama teacher, 1973-76. Poetry Workshop of Cockpit Theatre, London, teacher, 1970-72; teacher of drama and elocution in London. Actress, 1948-70.

MEMBER: Poetry Society of Great Britain, Inner London Education Authority.

WRITINGS:

POETRY

Walking without Moving, edited by Edward Lucie-Smith, Turret (London), 1967.

The Lair, Rapp & Whiting (London), 1968, Transatlantic, 1971.

The Courtship, Unicorn Bookshop (Brighton, England), 1972.

Footsteps on Snow, Agenda Editions (London), 1972.

Modern Fairy Tale, Sceptre Press (Knotting, Bedfordshire), 1972.

The Curving Shore, Agenda Editions, 1975.

Unholy Giving, Sceptre Press, 1978.

Songs a Thracian Taught Me, M. Boyars (London), 1980.

The Sele of the Morning, Agenda Editions, 1988.

Snapshots from an Album 1884-1895, Katabasis (London), 1992.

Charm with Stones, Claudia Gehrke (Germany), 1993.

Landscape with Figures, Agenda Editions, 1994.

Duet for Three Voices and Coda, Dedalus Press (London), 1997.

Selected Poems, Agenda Editions, 1997.

OTHER

(Translator) Vera Lungu, *Alexandros: Selected Poems,* Agenda Editions, 1975.

Author of radio plays, (with husband, Michael Hamburger) *Struck by Apollo,* 1965, and *The Villa,* 1968.

SIDELIGHTS: Born in England in 1929, poet Anne Beresford began taking herself seriously as a writer in 1961, when, at the age of thirty-three, she "sent some poems to Christopher Middleton and he wrote back telling me to go on writing. Since everyone in my family is a musician, it seemed more natural for me to choose the stage or music for a career rather than writing. But poetry was one of the things that made life worth living. It has always been so, and will always be so—for me at any rate." Since that time, Beresford has published several collections of her verse, among them *Footsteps on Snow, Unholy Giving,* and the 1994 work *Landscape with Figures.*

Beresford's oeuvre has been characterized by critics as subtle, and she has been referred to more than once as a mystic poet. In the *Dictionary of Literary Biography,* essayist William Cookson noted of

Beresford's work that its "quiet subtlety . . . stems from her attempts to define moments and states of mind, those aspects of consciousness and daily life which are most difficult to describe in words." Citing such works as "The Duke's Book of Hours," a 1975 poem sequence from *The Curving Shore,* Cookson also cited the presence of such foundational elements as legend, fairy tale, and myth in Beresford's works. While admitting that her subtlety sometimes borders on fragility and a lack of power, the reviewer added that "this weakness is at times offset by a clarity and simplicity of imagery which evoke much."

When asked by *CA,* Beresford labelled the influences upon her work as "varied," adding that "it's hard to say whether the poets I admire have influenced my writing." Her advice to young writers: "read everything and anything, and to study those poets you most admire."

"One of my favorite pastimes is walking in the country near where we live," Beresford continued. "Some of my images certainly come from the countryside. And others come from my odd, and at times, macabre, imagination."

BIOGRAPHICAL/CRITICAL SOURCES:

BOOKS

Contemporary Women Poets, St. James Press (Detroit), 1997.
Dictionary of Literary Biography, Volume 40: *Poets of Great Britain and Ireland since 1960,* Gale (Detroit), 1985.

PERIODICALS

Library Journal, January 15, 1981, p. 151.
Publishers Weekly, January 9, 1991, p. 70.
Queen's Quarterly, September, 1971.
Times Literary Supplement, October 13, 1972; July 9, 1976; April 10, 1981, p. 416.

*   *   *

BERGMAN, (Ernst) Ingmar 1918-
(Ernest Riffe; Buntel Eriksson, a joint pseudonym)

PERSONAL: Born July 14, 1918, in Uppsala, Sweden; son of a chaplain to the Royal Court of Stockholm; married Else Fisher (a dancer), 1943; married Ellen Lundstroem (a dancer), 1945 (divorced, 1950); married Gun Grut (a journalist), 1950; married Kaebi Laretei (a pianist), 1959 (separated, 1965); married Ingrid von Rosen, 1971; children: (first marriage) Lena; (second marriage) Eva, Jan, Anna, Mats; (third marriage) Ingmar; (fourth marriage) Daniel; one other child. *Education:* Attended University of Stockholm.

ADDRESSES: Home—Titurelstrasse 2, D-8000 Munich 8, Germany.

CAREER: Writer, director, and producer of motion pictures, teleplays, and stage productions. Director with Maaster Olofsgaarden, 1938-40, and Student Theater in Stockholm, 1941; Svensk Filmindustri, 1942-69, began as scriptwriter and editor, artistic adviser, 1961-69; director of Haelsingborg City Theater, 1944-46, Gothenburg City Theater, 1947-52, Malmoe City Theater, 1952-59, Royal Dramatic Theater in Stockholm, 1963-66, and Munich Residenzteater, 1977-82. Founder of film production companies Cinematograph, Sweden, 1968, and Personafilm, Munich, West Germany (now Germany), 1977.

AWARDS, HONORS: Grand Prix du Cinema, Cannes Film Festival, 1946, for *Hets;* Sao Paolo Film Festival prize, 1954, for *Gycklarnas afton;* comedy prize, Cannes Film Festival, 1956, for *Sommarnattens leende;* special award, Cannes Film Festival, 1957, and Joseph Bernstein Award for best foreign import, 1958, both for *Det sjunde inseglet;* Golden Bear award, International Berlin Film Festival, 1957, for *Smultronstaellet;* director's prize, Cannes Film Festival, 1958, for *Naera livet;* Gold Plaque, Swedish Film Academy, 1958; Academy Award for best foreign language film, Academy of Motion Picture Arts and Sciences, 1960, for *Jungfrukaellan,* and 1961, for *Saasom i en spegel;* co-recipient (with Charles Chaplin) of Erasmus Prize, Netherlands, 1965; awards for best director and for best film, National Society of Film Critics, 1967, for *Persona;* National Society of Film Critics award, 1968, for *Skammen;* Irving G. Thalberg Memorial Award, Academy of Motion Picture Arts and Sciences, 1971; award for best director, National Society of Film Critics, 1971, for *En passion;* award for best screenwriter, National Society of Film Critics, and awards for best screenwriter, best director, and best film, New York Film Critics, all 1972, all for *Viskningar och rop;* D.Phil., Stockholm University, 1975; Goethe Prize, 1976; Great Gold Medal,

Swedish Academy of Letters, 1977; best director award, New York Film Critics, 1983, and Academy Award for best foreign language film, 1984, both for *Fanny and Alexander;* decorated Commander of the Legion of Honor, 1985; Lillian Gish prize, 1995; numerous other film awards.

WRITINGS:

PROSE

A Project for the Theatre, edited and introduced by Frederick J. Marker and Lise-Lone Marker, Ungar (New York City), 1983.

Laterna Magica, Norstedt (Stockholm), 1987, translated by Joan Tate as *The Magic Lantern: An Autobiography,* Viking (New York City), 1988.

Bilder, Norstedt, 1990, translated by Marianne Ruuth as *Images: My Life in Film,* Arcade (New York City), 1994.

Den Goda Viljan (novel), Norstedt, 1991, translated by Joan Tate as *The Best Intentions,* Arcade, 1993.

Sondagsbarn (novel), Norstedt, 1993, translated by Tate as *Sunday's Children,* Arcade, 1994, published as *Sunday's Child,* Harvill (London), 1994.

Enskilda Samtal (novel), Norstedt, 1996, translated by Tate as *Private Confessions,* Arcade, 1997.

Also author of *Four Stories,* 1977.

SCREENPLAYS

(And assistant director) *Hets,* Svensk Filmindustri, 1944, English-language version released as *Frenzy* and as *Torment,* 1944.

(Adapter and director) *Kris* (based on the play *Moderdyret* by Leck Fisher), Svensk Filmindustri, 1945, English-language version released as *Crisis,* 1946.

(Adapter, with Herbert Grevenius, and director) *Det regnar paa vaar kaerlek* (based on the play *Bra mennesker* by Oskar Braathen), Sveriges Folkbiografer, 1946, English-language version released as *It Rains Our Love,* 1946.

Kvinna utan ansikte, Svensk Filmindustri, 1947, English-language version released as *Woman without a Face,* 1947.

(Adapter and director) *Skepp till Indialand* (based on the play by Martin Soederhjelm), Sveriges Folkbiografer, 1947, English-language version released as *A Ship to India* and *Land of Desire,* 1947.

(Co-adapter and director) *Hamnstad* (from a story by Olle Laensberg), Svensk Filmindustri, 1948, English-language version released as *Port of Call,* 1948.

(Co-author) *Eva,* Svensk Filmindustri, 1948.

(And director) *Faengelse,* Terrafilm, 1949, English-language version released as *Prison* and as *The Devil's Wanton,* 1949.

(And director) *Till glaedje,* Svensk Filmindustri, 1949, English-language version released as *To Joy,* 1949.

(With Grevenius, and director) *Sommarlek,* Svensk Filmindustri, 1950, English-language version released as *Summer Interlude* and as *Illicit Interlude,* 1950.

(With Grevenius) *Fraanskild,* Svensk Filmindustri, 1951, English-language version released as *Divorced,* 1951.

(And director) *Kninnors vantan,* Svensk Filmindustri, 1952, English-language version released as *Waiting Women* and as *Secrets of Women,* 1952.

(Adapter with P. A. Fogelstroem, and director) *Sommaren med Monika* (based on a novel by Fogelstroem), Svensk Filmindustri, 1952.

(And director) *Gycklarnas afton* (title means "Sunset of the Clown"), Sandrews, 1953, English-language version released as *The Naked Night* and as *Sawdust and Tinsel,* 1953.

(And director) *En lektion i kaerlek,* [Sweden], 1954, English-language version released as *A Lesson in Love,* 1954.

(And director) *Kvinnodroem,* Sandrews, 1955, English-language version released as *Journey into Autumn* and as *Dreams,* 1955.

(And director) *Sommarnattens leende* (also see below), Svensk Filmindustri, 1955, English-language version released as *Smiles of a Summer Night,* 1955.

(With Alf Sjoeberg) *Sista paret ut,* Svensk Filmindustri, 1956, English-language version released as *Last Couple Out,* 1956.

(Adapter and director) *Det sjunde inseglet* (from Bergman's play, *Traemalning;* also see below), Svensk Filmindustri, 1956, translated by Lars Malmstrom and David Kushner as *The Seventh Seal,* Simon & Schuster (New York City), 1960, revised edition, Lorrimer (London), 1984.

(And director) *Smultronstaellet* (also see below), Svensk Filmindustri, 1957, translated by Malmstrom and Kushner as *Wild Strawberries,* Simon & Schuster, 1960.

(With Ulla Isaksson, and director) *Naera livet* (also see below), Svensk Filmindustri, 1958, English-language version released as *The Magician* and as *The Face,* 1958.

(Adapter and director) *Djaevunes oega* (adapted from a Danish radio play), Svensk Filmindustri, 1960, English-language version released as *The Devil's Eye,* 1960.

Four Screenplays of Ingmar Bergman, translated by Malmstrom and Kushner, Simon & Schuster, 1960, published as *Four Screenplays of Ingmar Bergman: Smiles of a Summer Night, The Seventh Seal, The Magician,* [and] *Wild Strawberries,* 1989.

(And director) *Saasom i en spegel* (also see below), Svensk Filmindustri, 1961, English-language version released as *Through a Glass Darkly,* 1961.

(With Erland Josephson, under joint pseudonym Buntel Eriksson, and director) *Lustgaarden,* Svensk Filmindustri, 1961, English-language version released as *The Pleasure Garden,* 1961.

(And director) *Nattvardsgaesterna* (also see below), Svensk Filmindustri, 1962, English-language version released as *Winter Light* and as *The Communicants,* 1962.

(And director) *Tystnaden* (also see below), Svensk Filmindustri, 1963, English-language version released as *The Silence,* 1963.

En filmtrilogi: Saasom i en spegel, Nattvardsgaesterna, Tystnaden, PAN/Norstedt, 1963, translation by Paul Britten Austin published as *A Film Trilogy: Through a Glass Darkly, Winter Light, The Silence,* translated from the Swedish by Paul Britten, Orion Press (Columbus, OH), 1967, published as *Three Films by Ingmar Bergman,* Grove (New York City), 1970, published as *A Film Trilogy: Through a Glass Darkly, The Communicants (Winter Light),* [and] *The Silence,* Marion Boyars (New York City), 1988.

(With Josephson, under joint pseudonym Buntel Eriksson, and director) *Foer att inte tala om alla dessa kvinnor,* Svensk Filmindustri, 1964, English-language version released as *Now about These Women* and as *All These Women,* 1968.

(And director) *Persona* (also see below), Svensk Filmindustri, 1966.

(And director) *Vargtimmen* (also see below), Svensk Filmindustri, 1966, English-language version released as *The Hour of the Wolf,* 1968.

(And director) *Skammen* (also see below), Svensk Filmindustri, 1967, English-language version released as *Shame,* 1968.

(And director) *Riten,* Svensk Filmindustri/Cinematograph, 1969, English-language version released as *The Rite* and as *The Ritual,* 1969.

En passion (also see below), Svensk Filmindustri/Cinematograph, 1969, English-language version released as *A Passion* and as *A Passion of Anna,* 1969.

(And director) *Faaroedokument* (documentary), Cinematograph, 1969, English-language version released as *Faro Document,* 1969.

(And director) *Beroeringen* (also see below), [Sweden], 1970, English-language version released as *The Touch,* Cinematography/ABC Pictures, 1970.

(Adapter and director) *The Lie* (television screenplay; from a play by Bergman), British Broadcasting Corp. (BBC-TV), 1972.

(And director) *Viskningar och rop* (also see below), Cinematograph, 1972, English-language version released as *Cries and Whispers,* 1972.

Persona; and Shame: The Screenplays of Ingmar Bergman, Marion Boyars, 1972, as *Persona and Shame: Two Screenplays,* 1984.

Filmberaettelser, three volumes, PAN/Norstedt, 1973.

Scener ur ett iiktenshap (originally produced for Swedish television; also see below), Norstedt, 1973, translation by Alan Blair published as *Scenes from a Marriage,* Pantheon (New York), 1974.

(And director) *Ansikte mot ansikte* (co-produced by Bergman for BBC-TV; also see below), Cinematograph, 1976, translation by Blair published as *Face to Face,* Pantheon, 1976.

Four Stories by Ingmar Bergman: The Touch, Cries and Whispers, The Hour of the Wolf, The Passion of Anna, translation by Blair, Doubleday (New York City), 1976.

(And director) *Ormens aegg* (originally released in West Germany as *Das Schlangenei;* English-language version produced by Paramount, 1977), Norstedt, 1977, translation by Blair published as *The Serpent's Egg,* Pantheon, 1977.

Hoestsonaten (originally released in West Germany as *Herbstsonate;* English-language version released 1978; also see below), PAN/Norstedt, 1978, translation by Blair published as *Autumn Sonata,* Pantheon, 1978.

The Marriage Scenarios (contains *Scenes from a Marriage, Face to Face,* and *Autumn Sonata*), translation by Blair, Pantheon, 1978.

(And director and narrator) *Faaroe-dokument 1979* (documentary; English-language version released as *Faro 1979*), Cinematograph, 1980.

(And director) *Aus dem Leben der Marionetten,* [West Germany], 1980, translation by Blair published as *From the Life of the Marionettes,* Pantheon, 1980.

Fanny och Alexander (originally produced for Swedish television; Svensk Filminstitut, 1982; English-language version released 1981), Norstedt, 1982, translation by Blair published as *Fanny and Alexander,* Pantheon, 1982.

(And director) *After the Rehearsal* (television screenplay), Cinematograph, 1984.

Also author of other screenplays and teleplays, including *Dokument Fanny och Alexander* (documentary; also director), 1986; *Karins ansikte* (*Karin's Face;* based on pictures of Bergman's mother from his personal photo album; also director), 1986; *Den Goda viljan* (*The Best Intentions;* television mini-series; based on Bergman's autobiographical novel), 1991; *Markisinnan de Sade* (also director), 1992; *Sondagsbarn* (*Sunday's Children;* based on Bergman's novel of the same title), 1992; *Sista skriket* (*The Last Gasp;* teleplay; also director), 1995; *Enskilda samtal* (*Private Confessions;* television mini-series; based on Bergman's novel of the same title), 1996; and *Larmar och gor sig till* (*In the Presence of a Clown;* teleplay; also director), 1997.

PLAYS

Rakel och biografvaktmaestaren (title means "Rachel and the Cinema Doorman"; also see below), produced in Gothenburg, Sweden, 1945.

Dagen slutar tidget (title means "The Day Ends Early"; also see below), produced in Gothenburg, 1947.

Mig till skraeck (title means "To My Terror"; also see below), produced in Gothenburg, 1947.

Jack hos skadespelarna (title means "Jack among the Actors"), Albert Bonniers, 1948.

Moraliteter (title means "Morality Plays"; contains *Rakel och biografvadtmaestaren, Dagen slutar tidget,* and *Mig till skraeck*), Albert Bonniers, 1948.

Hets (title means "Torment"; adapted from his screenplay of the same title), produced in Oslo, Norway, 1948.

Mordet i barjaerna (title means "Murder at Baryaerna"), produced in Malmoe, Sweden, 1952.

Traemalning (title means "Wood Painting: A Morality Play"), produced in Stockholm, Sweden, 1955.

(Adapter) August Strindberg, *A Dream Play,* translated by Michael Meyer, Secker & Warburg (London), 1972.

Scenes from a Marriage (adapted from his screenplay), produced in Munich, 1981, adaptation with Rita Russek produced in London, 1990.

Also author of *Kaspers doed* (title means "Death of Punch"), produced in 1942, and *Staden* (title means "The City"), produced for radio in 1951. Author of unproduced plays, including *Resamrater* (title means "Travel Companions"), *Stationen* (title means "Station"), *De Ensamma* (title means "Lonely Ones"), *Trivolet* (title means "The Fun Fair"), *Fullmanen* (title means "Full Moon"), *Dimman* (title means "The Fog"), and *Om en moerdare* (title means "About a Murder").

OTHER

Contributor of essays to numerous film journals and periodicals, including *Cinemathek, Svenska radiopjaeser, Biografbladet, Tulane Drama Review,* and, under pseudonym Ernest Riffe, *Chaplin.*

WORK IN PROGRESS: Trolosa, a screenplay to be directed by Liv Ullman, to be filmed in the fall of 1999.

ADAPTATIONS: The musical *A Little Night Music,* by Steven Sondheim and Hugh Wheeler, was suggested by a film by Bergman.

SIDELIGHTS: Throughout his career as an internationally renowned filmmaker and screenwriter, Swedish director Ingmar Bergman has imbued his work with the concerns, fears, and hopes of his own life. "Films would seem to be the most personal part of Bergman's life," asserts John Osborne in the *New York Review of Books.* "Certainly his personal life is openly reflected in them." As in his movies, Bergman's 1988 autobiography, *The Magic Lantern,* reveals the importance of this link, while also employing a highly subjective writing technique that is similar to the style he uses in many of his screenplays. "*The Magic Lantern* is constructed much like a Bergman film," acknowledges London *Times* contributor David Thompson; "real memories [are] intermingled with fantasized encounters and flashes forward to the last few years [of his life]." This stylistic approach has led *Time* reviewer Richard Schickel to call *The Magic Lantern* "one of the finest self-portraits of an artist written in our time." But "what Bergman is [also] saying," adds Schickel, "is that however acutely his art reflected his sense of life, it was much more important to him as a refuge from life. It was the place where he could at least briefly impose order on life's terrible confusions, find for himself a sustaining moment of peace and grace."

An unhappy, sickly child, Bergman was the son of a strict Lutheran minister, who often locked his son in a closet or forced him to wear a dress as punishment for even the most insignificant transgressions. The psychological effects of this abusive treatment made a strong impression on Bergman, and for this reason the film director "never—presumably could not—shut the window to his childhood," notes Lloyd Rose in the *Voice Literary Supplement.* Becoming rebellious, Bergman adulated German chancellor Adolf Hitler for a short time, until he was confronted with the shocking truth of the Nazi concentration camps. This realization led the young Bergman to feel "despair" and "self-contempt," as he reveals in his autobiography. But as a student at the University of Stockholm, he finally found a certain release from his frustrations in the writings of Swedish playwright and novelist August Strindberg. As quoted by Charles Champlin in the *Los Angeles Times,* Bergman said that Strindberg "expressed things I'd experienced and which I couldn't find words for." The expressionistic style of Strindberg's writing would thereafter have a profound influence on the director's work.

Although Bergman is best known for his films, he reveals in the autobiographical *The Magic Lantern* that, like Strindberg, his real love is for the stage. Indeed, he has worked for several playhouses in Sweden, including a position as chief director of Sweden's prestigious Royal Dramatic Theatre. But "from a strictly professional point of view," admits Bergman in his autobiography, "my years as a theatre director were wasted." The plays that he has written for the stage have not achieved the acclaim his films have, and are relatively unknown today. "Yet," Champlin asserts, "it's obvious that his writing for the theatre was an immensely useful preparation for the kind of intimate, intense drama of characters and relationships that Bergman was to write for the screen." Arlene Croce declares in *Commonweal* that the filmmaker "has in fact created a theater of the film."

Bergman began his film career in 1943, when he left college for a position with Svensk Filmindustri. According to Peter Harcourt in his *Six European Directors: Essays on the Meaning of Style,* "the problems of loneliness, humiliation, and of the essential isolation of the human spirit" have dominated the director's work since that time. *Film Quarterly* critic Eugene Archer writes that the filmmaker's "early films [are] strange, exceedingly personal, and deeply provocative, sometimes deriving from the Protestant environment of his own childhood." Works like *Tor-*

ment and *Summer with Monika* are "dramas of adolescent revolt," continues Archer. They also project Bergman's early pessimistic view of human nature, as well as a "preoccupation with youth and the vulnerability of innocence," remarks *Ingmar Bergman* author Robin Wood. For example, in *Torment,* a student is abused by a sadistic teacher, who, it is later revealed, murdered the student's girlfriend. The film ends with the boy forsaking society to become an outcast. A similar ending occurs in *Summer with Monika,* in which a young boy and girl become lovers and leave the city for the northern woods of Sweden. "Bergman's youthful pessimism is climaxed by *Faengelse* (Prison)," observes Archer, "which depicts modern life as a total hell from which there can be no salvation because man has lost the ability to believe in God."

However, the films of Bergman's early period are not all pessimistic. *Smile of a Summer Night,* in Archer's appraisal, is "a delightful comedy of manners in the tradition of the French boudoir farce." But the critic also notes that, like most of the director's movies, it "is subject to a dual interpretation, and an underlying serious meaning is readily apparent." The comedic aspects of the film are balanced by themes concerning the loss of love, frustration, and humiliation. *The Naked Night,* a much more gloomy film about a couple's loss of dignity in their search for reconciliation, echoes the themes presented in *Smiles of a Summer Night.* These two completely different films also share in common the "analysis of the human condition, of man's attitude toward the great abstract questions," according to Joern Donner in his *The Personal Vision of Ingmar Bergman.*

Several of these first films have been praised by critics, 1950's *Summer Interlude* being the point where Archer believes Bergman "attained complete maturity as a director." The movie is about a summer romance that is overshadowed by a sense of disaster. Bergman's films after *Summer Interlude,* according to Archer, "are, without exception, masterful in their evocations of mood and movement, the principle ingredients of cinematic style." However, in his book *Cinema Eye, Cinema Ear: Some Key Film-Makers of the 'Sixties,* John Russell Taylor argues that *Prison* is really the director's first early significant work. "[*Prison*] has all the marks of a key work in his career," Taylor opines, "wildly bundling together any number of themes which are to recur later. . . . Moreover, it is the first of Bergman's films which demonstrate any real desire . . . to experiment with the medium, to use it positively as a means of expression in itself, rather than recording with competence but no special aptitude." Taylor also feels that *Smiles of a Summer Night* is important in that "for the first time, and virtually for the last, all Bergman's diverse talents [are seen] together in a single film."

Despite the quality of these productions, Bergman did not receive significant international recognition until the release of the 1956 film *The Seventh Seal*. By this time, the director had gathered about him a small troupe of actors, actresses, and behind-the-scenes people who would regularly work with him throughout his career, often filming at Bergman's favorite location, the Faeroe Islands north of Britain. Liv Ullmann, Max von Sydow, Gunnar Bjoernstrand, Bibi Andersson, Ingrid Thulin, and Harriet Andersson often appear as stars in Bergman's films; Bergman also relied on the talents of photography directors Sven Nykvist and Gunnar Fisher for thirty-two of his films. With this capable staff, and with the enthusiastic support of Svensk Filmindustri, Bergman began a new phase in his career with *The Seventh Seal* that is notable for its artistic freedom. *The Seventh Seal* and a number of the films that followed it also delineate a period that is dominated by one theme: mankind's search for God.

Bergman's preoccupation with this theme goes back to his childhood and the Protestant indoctrination he received from his father. Bergman "absorbed his [father's] chill upbringing into his marrow," attests Rose. "There's never been a director . . . more Protestant. Carried to its (theo)logical extreme, Protestantism is as absurd as something out of [Samuel] Beckett. It completely jettisons cause and effect. God may save you or He may damn you, but your actions have nothing to do with it . . . and if God—by an act of divine judgement totally beyond your comprehension—decides to let you burn, tough luck. As a director, Bergman is often accused of being mysterious and indecipherable. At least he comes by it honestly."

In *The Seventh Seal* Bergman's search for God comes to life in a medieval knight's quest for meaning after the Crusades. "The film," explains Birgitta Steene in *Scandinavian Studies,* "illustrates [the] gradual alienation of man from God by depicting in the crusader a human being at first engaged in a holy enterprise but at last willing to sell his soul to the Devil—could he only find him! For the Devil, he argues with insane logic, must know God since he only exists in

opposition to God." But the knight's doubts are not the characteristic concerns of a medieval man, according to Steene, who notes that "he is closer to a modern skeptic whose burning need of faith cannot be fulfilled because he refuses to accept a god who does not give intellectual proof of his existence."

Some reviewers have criticized Bergman's presentation of modern concerns within a medieval motif. *Encounter* contributor Caroline Blackwood, for example, objects to the filmmaker's use of "all the old morbid medieval metaphors which formed the staple fare of silent German movies of the twenties." Blackwood also finds it difficult "to see anything very 'illuminating' in Bergman monotonously repeating that all knowledge and learning are instruments of the Devil." Many other reviewers, though, share the sentiment of Peter Cowie's *Sweden Two* assessment: *The Seventh Seal* is a "triumphant blend of literary antecedent and visual metaphor that makes [it] such a profound and ambitious film, unequaled in the Swedish cinema as an exercise in tempered expressionism."

Another accomplishment of *The Seventh Seal,* says Steene, is that it "sets up a dichotomy, which is to remain a basic one in Bergman's production, between a god who is a silent monster and torturer of man, and a god who is a lover of life." Several of the Bergman films that followed express one side or the other of this dichotomy. *Wild Strawberries,* for example, represents "the culmination and fulfillment of the Christian side of Bergman," according to Wood, for "the presence of a benevolent deity seems to permeate the film." Although *Wild Strawberries* is not as overtly religious as *The Seventh Seal,* a positive message about God's presence is expressed when the protagonist, Isak Borg, is made to realize through a series of dreams that he has been a cold and heartless person. Seeing the error of his ways, Isak decides to return home and asks his parents to forgive him for neglecting them. "It is significant that the Bergman film embodying the Christian virtues of love, forgiveness, humility, should be centrally concerned with forgiveness between parents and children," notes Wood, who concludes that "Isak Borg's relationship to Bergman himself is obvious."

Another production with a positive affirmation of God is *Through a Glass Darkly.* In this case, the director clearly presents God as a god of love. This "intensely personal work," as Cowie calls it in a *Films and Filming* article, concerns a self-involved father and the lack of communication he has with his children. By the end of the movie, there is a reconciliation between the father and his son when the father asserts that God is love. Symbolically, this conclusion is significant because, as Steene points out, "from the children's point of view the father has become connected, if not identified with their image of God." Although critics like Wood consider *Through a Glass Darkly* to be an "extremely important" film for the director, the reviewer also believes it to be "extremely unsatisfactory." The movie's conclusion, elaborates Wood, "is beyond question the worst ending in mature Bergman" because "the consistent undermining of the father throughout the film suggests Bergman's lack of confidence in his last words. They are indeed mere words." Nevertheless, this movie is significant since, as Harcourt suggests, it marks the beginning of a period in the director's career in which he attempts to bring his audience "closer to fewer and fewer people, perhaps with deliberate ambition to 'illuminate the human soul.'"

As in *Through a Glass Darkly, Winter Light* involves a father-child relationship; but it also extrapolates the situation by involving characters outside the family. In this case, a minister, Tomas Ericsson, is unable to prevent the suicide of a fisherman because his parents' inability to show Tomas affection has left him incapable of showing love for others. Again, the parents in the film represent God; and Tomas's failure to communicate with God causes him to isolate himself from others. There is, however, some hope in *Winter Light* in Tomas's resolve to cling to his religious faith despite his tenuous belief in God. However, in Bergman's *The Silence* (originally titled *God's Silence*), God's presence is completely abrogated. Unlike *Through a Glass Darkly* and *Winter Light,* the father in *The Silence* is dead when the plot begins. Bergman examines the consequences of the father's (i.e., God's) total absence through the use of language, which is "related to Bergman's religious questioning and his portrayal of the father-child relationship," according to Steene in *Cinema Journal.* "When God dies away," Steene concludes, "language looses its communicative and healing power." The film illustrates this theme by isolating its characters—two sisters and their nephew—in a country whose people speak a language they do not understand. The final scene underlines the theme when one of the character's efforts to read a list of translations is drowned out by the noise of a passing train.

With the completion of *The Silence,* Bergman dropped his obsession with theology, considering his films on the subject "bogus," according to Roger Manvell in *International Dictionary of Films and Filmmakers.* By this time, surmises Schickel in a *Life* review, "Bergman has . . . accepted [God's] death and, indeed, seems to find that event no longer worthy of comment. His absence is now simply one of the terms of our existence." With the trilogy comprised of *Persona, The Hour of the Wolf,* and *Shame,* the director focuses more on another of his favorite subjects: the artistic character. Compared to Bergman's films about God, Stanley Kauffman describes *Persona* in his *Figures of Light: Film Criticism and Comment* as "a successful work of art," the early trilogy being "masterfully made, but introspectively remote rather than dramatized."

Persona is about an actress who suddenly, inexplicably refuses to speak. All attempts by her nurse to encourage the actress to speak fail; but the experience results in the nurse's realization that she, like the actress, has been wearing a mask that conceals her true self. Vernon Young, author of *Cinema Borealis: Ingmar Bergman and the Swedish Ethos,* is somewhat less enthusiastic about *Persona* than Kauffman, comparing its artistic value to *The Hour of the Wolf.* "Any expectation that *Persona* was more than a skirmish in [Bergman's] inconclusive battle with the duplicity of the artist was certainly frustrated by *The Hour of the Wolf.*" Young remarks. "[*The Hour of the Wolf*] is pure dementia . . . in it Bergman explores nothing; this is wholly a disintegration product, replying to no serious question." In *The Hour of the Wolf* an artist is plagued by demons. Whether the demons are real or not is never explained, nor is any reason given for the artist's torture. Because nothing is fully explained, reviewers like Young consider the movie too obscure, although others such as *Film Quarterly* contributor Ernest Callenbach praise Bergman as being "personally brave in the sense of being willing to work with dangerous psychic material."

Reviews of *Shame* have generally been much more positive than for *The Hour of the Wolf.* This time, Bergman places two artists in the middle of a war and describes their futile efforts to remain neutral for the sake of their art. *Shame* stirred some controversy among Bergman's compatriots, who felt the movie was a sarcastic comment on Sweden's neutrality during both World Wars. But a number of critics have praised *Shame* for its unique view on war. "*Shame* is in fact quite remarkable among war films," attests Callenbach, "and takes its place among a tiny honorable handful that may be considered genuinely antiwar." In Wood's book, the author offers even higher tribute: "*Shame* is Bergman's masterpiece to date [1969] and one of the greatest films of the last decade."

An important element in Bergman's films has always been the role of his female characters, who, explains *Film Quarterly* contributor Joan Mellen, "sometimes serve Bergman to express his agony over our ultimate inability to derive meaning from life." Beginning with the director's *A Passion,* women play an increasingly important part in his films. "It wasn't until *A Passion* that I really got to grips with the man-woman relationship," Bergman is quoted as saying in Manvell's essay. In this essay Bergman also states that his later films illustrate his "ceaseless fascination with the whole race of women." Besides his use of expressionism, this is an aspect of Bergman's work that bears an affinity with Strindberg. But whereas Strindberg became bitter after his second divorce, Bergman's divorces have not changed his views about women. Strindberg and Bergman "differ markedly in tone," observes Champlin: "Bergman usually compassionate, however candid in his depictions, Strindberg more often misogynistic."

Two films that explore this theme as it pertains to the institution of marriage are *A Passion* and *Scenes from a Marriage.* One of Bergman's most experimental works in terms of photography, the use of color, and the manner in which he interrupts the film with interpretive narratives by the actors, *A Passion* delves into the relationships of two men and two women who are isolated on an island. When they become involved in one another's lives, their fears and insecurities are revealed. Harcourt believes that, up to this point in the filmmaker's career, *A Passion* is the most complete movie involving "the essential isolation of the human spirit." Several critics, such as Schickel, feel that in this film "the art of Ingmar Bergman reaches its pinnacle. Though it is one of his rare color films, it is in every important way his most austere and elliptical work, a thing of silences and enigmas that nevertheless makes very clear the tragic vision of life that possesses its author." *Scenes from a Marriage* also deals with man-woman relationships. Originally made for television, some reviewers have complained that it has a soap opera quality that, as *Esquire* contributor John Simon reports, makes it "too commonplace." Disagreeing with this opinion, Simon avers that the married couple in the film "are not platitudes; they are encyclopedias" meant to represent all of us. *Film Quarterly* contributor Marsha Kinder is also enthusiastic

about *Scenes from a Marriage,* calling it "emotional dynamite." The movie, she concludes, achieves "a depth of characterization previously thought possible only in the novel."

With *Cries and Whispers,* a movie about the relationships between four women, Bergman examines the nature of women in the greatest depth yet. According to *Massachusetts Review* contributor Julian C. Rice, "Bergman defines his principal theme [in *Cries and Whispers*] as a concern with the 'wholeness inside every human being.' This 'wholeness' is the basis upon which relationships with other human beings are formed." But some critics, like Mellen, object to this film's portrayal of women, claiming that Bergman "provides one of the most retrograde portrayals of women on the contemporary screen." Other reviewers, however, believe this interpretation misses the point of the film. In *Salmagundi,* Robert Boyers remarks that the suffering of Bergman's female characters in *Cries and Whispers* is not indicative of any misogynistic feelings on the director's part. Bergman, writes Boyers, no more punishes women "than he punishes men who are cold and all but indifferent to their functions as integrated human beings." Robert E. Lauder similarly asserts in *Christian Century* that "the truth of the matter is that the filmmaker is involved in a love-hate relationship with women and men—and indeed with himself." As quoted by *Times Literary Supplement* critic S. S. Prawer, Bergman explains that *Cries and Whispers* is really "a first attempt at circumscribing the image I have of my mother. . . . Mama was the overwhelming experience of my childhood."

The conclusion of *Cries and Whispers* foreshadows the optimism of Bergman's later movie, *Face to Face.* "*Cries and Whispers,*" remarks Rice, "suggests that wholeness and communication are indeed possible, if only for fleeting redemptive moments." However, according to Lauder, in *Face to Face* there is a "clear presence of hope." But this increasing tone of optimism in Bergman's work was destroyed for a time when the director suffered the greatest humiliation of his life. Having entrusted his finances to dishonest advisers, in 1976 the filmmaker unwittingly found himself the subject of a tax scandal that led him to a nervous breakdown. Eventually cleared of the charges, Bergman nevertheless exiled himself to West Germany. It is here that the director filmed his nightmarishly violent and skeptical film about pre-Hitler Germany, *The Serpent's Egg.* The film was an immense critical failure, however, largely due to its overly-grim nature and because the political statement it makes demonstrates, as *Film Quarterly* contributor Ronald S. Librach notes, that politics is not "Bergman's strongest intellectual suit."

After *The Serpent's Egg* Bergman got back on his feet with *Autumn Sonata* and *From the Life of the Marionettes,* produced in Norway and West Germany respectively. These films return to the director's concern with interpersonal relationships, while focusing on "very few characters in an elementary situation," says Gilberto Perez in a *New York Arts Journal* article on *Autumn Sonata.* "Bergman," Perez comments further, "feels he's getting down to the essential of the human condition," by limiting the scope of these later productions. With the completion of these movies, the filmmaker decided to return to his homeland, where he filmed what he vowed would be his last motion picture for the screen. The result was Bergman's longest movie yet, *Fanny and Alexander,* a three-hour-long multigenerational work containing virtually all of the themes expressed in the director's previous films.

This major effort, says its creator in a London *Times* article by Michiko Kakutani, represents "the sum total of my life as a filmmaker." "*Fanny and Alexander,*" observes Kakutani, "is at once a nostalgic reinvention of the director's own childhood and a mature summation of his work. All the familiar Bergman themes and motifs are here—the humiliation of the artist, the hell and paradise of marriage, the quest for love and faith-but they are infused, this time, with a new tenderness and compassion. . . . Bergman seems to have achieved a measure of distance from and acceptance of his own past." *New York Times* critic Vincent Canby also recognizes this new, uncharacteristic mood of Bergman's, calling it "something that, in Bergman, might pass for serenity." Among critics, *Fanny and Alexander* has been generally well received, although a few, like *Washington Post* reviewer Gary Arnold, feel that "the movie has a text that tends to ramble and gush . . . and the host's powers of invention frequently go on the fritz." *Los Angeles Times* contributor Sheila Benson, however, writes that the film is "so lavish, so detailed and so satisfying that we want it to go on forever."

Fears that Bergman's career had come to an end with the production of *Fanny and Alexander* were soon dispelled with the release of the short television drama, *After the Rehearsal. After the Rehearsal,* did not violate Bergman's promise to cease making mov-

ies for the theater, since the director never said anything about the television media. His next project, *The Best Intentions,* was also made for television. Although written by Bergman, it is directed by Bille August, a Danish director. The movie is about the ten years of the filmmaker's parents' marriage before he was born. With *Best Intentions* Bergman finally accepts his parents, portraying them with more sympathy than ever before. "Until I wrote this manuscript," said the dramatist to Steve Lohr of the *New York Times,* "I never really knew how complicated their lives were. . . . We always regret that we did not ask our parents more, really get to know them while they were alive." "If [this] sounds like a belated reconciliation with his parents," remarks Lohr, "it may be. But Mr. Bergman is at pains to emphasize to anyone listening that he has perhaps mellowed with age, but that the inner turmoil that has been a hallmark of both the man and the artist is still intact. 'The anger and the creativity are so closely intertwined with me,' he said. 'And there's plenty of anger left.'"

Whereas *The Magic Lantern* deals primarily with the particulars of Bergman's life, *Images: My Life in Film* deals directly with his films. In it, drawing on notebooks, plot summaries, and at times quoting at length from *The Magic Lantern* and other previously published work, Bergman discusses all of his 45 films. The book is arranged thematically rather than chronologically, which several reviewers find confusing. "The text," according to *Washington Post* reviewer Adam Hochschild, "is a curious, unsatisfying mishmash." This confusion is mediated somewhat by an extensive and detailed (more than fifty pages) filmography of Bergman's work. Also included are over one hundred pages of photographs from Bergman's films, which Michael Meyer of the *New York Review of Books* describes as "perhaps the book's most valuable feature." *Images* is not a book actually written by Bergman; rather it consists of the transcription of sixty hours of interviews with Bergman conducted by film critic Lasse Bergstrom. Bergstrom subsequently deleted his own questions, edited and reorganized the text, and submitted it to Bergman for final approval. Hochschild notes: "Bergman the painstaking craftsman—as much so with words as with film—would never have produced something so rambling and uneven." Although most critics agree with the negative aspects of Hochschild's assessment, most also find much that is worthwhile in *Images.* Meyer, characterizing *Images* as a "prolonged self-indictment" like most of Bergman's films, feels "there is much to fascinate, and the rewards outweigh the disappointments."

Philip French in the *Observer Review* notes that *Images* provides interesting background on Bergman's successful relationships with his actors and goes on to state that "Bergman's students and admirers will find this superbly illustrated book fascinating, for the revelations of his sources (mostly dreams and childhood memories), the accounts of his working process, and the painful honesty." Despite his criticisms, Hochschild agrees that *Images* "does let slip some clues to Bergman's astounding creativity," and "nearly every page reveals . . . his intense loyalty to his actors." In contrast, David Caute of the *Spectator* warns: "Beware Bergman on Bergman. In recent years he has been conducting his own autopsy nonstop and with the publication of *Images* there are disturbing confirmations of the recycling."

Discussing a 1996 retrospective of Bergman's films at Chicago's Film Center, *Chicago Tribune* movie critic Michael Wilmington concludes: "He remains a powerful cinematic presence in the "90's—because even though he no longer directs films, he still writes them. . . . [In] his twilight years, Bergman's life and work recall his surrogate Isak Borg (the dreamy old man. . .in *Wild Strawberries*). . . . As in those marvelous closing scenes of *Wild Strawberries,* he makes you weep, smile. Like all great artists, his store of pain and joy—right to the end—seems rich, deep and inexhaustible."

BIOGRAPHICAL/CRITICAL SOURCES:

BOOKS

Bergman, Ingmar, *The Magic Lantern: An Autobiography,* Viking (New York), 1988.
Bergman, Ingmar, *Images: My Life in Film,* Arcade (New York), 1994.
Bjoerkman, Stig, Torsten Manns, and Jonas Sima, editors, *Bergman on Bergman: Interviews with Ingmar Bergman,* Simon & Schuster (New York), 1973.
Contemporary Literary Criticism, Gale (Detroit), Volume 16, 1981, Volume 72, 1992.
Cowie, Peter, *Sweden 2,* A. S. Barnes, 1970.
Donner, Joern, *The Personal Vision of Ingmar Bergman,* Indiana University Press, 1964.
Donner, Joern, *The Films of Ingmar Bergman,* Dover, 1972.
Film and Dreams: An Approach to Bergman, edited and introduced by Vlada Petric, Redgrave (South Salem, NY), 1981.
Gibson, Arthur, *The Silence of God: Creative Response to the Films of Ingmar Bergman,* Harper, 1969.

Harcourt, Peter, *Six European Directors: Essays on the Meaning of Film Style,* Penguin Books, 1974.
Jones, G. William, editor, *Talking with Ingmar Bergman,* Southern Methodist University Press, 1983.
Kael, Pauline, *Reeling,* Little, Brown, 1976.
Kaminsky, Stuart M., and Joseph F. Hill, editors, *Ingmar Bergman: Essays in Criticism,* Oxford University Press, 1975.
Kauffman, Stanley, *Figures of Light: Film Criticism and Comment,* Harper, 1971.
Lyon, Christopher, editor, *The International Dictionary of Films and Filmmakers,* Volume 2, St, James Press (Chicago), 1984.
Oliver, Roger W., editor, *Ingmar Bergman: An Artist's Journey on Stage, on Screen, in Print,* Arcade, 1995.
Schickel, Richard, *Second Sight: Notes on Some Movies, 1965-1970,* Simon & Schuster, 1972.
Simon, John, *Ingmar Bergman Directs,* Harcourt, 1972.
Slayton, Ralph Emil, *Ingmar Bergman's "The Seventh Seal": A Criticism,* University Microfilms (Ann Arbor, MI), 1973.
Sontag, Susan, *Styles of Radical Will,* Farrar, Straus, 1969.
Steene, Birgitta, *Ingmar Bergman,* Twayne, 1968.
Taylor, John Russell, *Cinema Eye, Cinema Ear: Some Key Film Makers of the Sixties,* St. Martin's Press, 1964.
Wood, Robin, *Ingmar Bergman,* Praeger, 1969.
Young, Vernon, *Cinema Borealis: Ingmar Bergman and the Swedish Ethos,* David Lewis, 1971.

PERIODICALS

America, January 24, 1976.
Chicago Tribune, February 20, 1981; July 5, 1983; September 11, 1988; January 18, 1996, section 5, p. 9A; January 28, 1996, section 7, p. 1.
Christian Century, October 27, 1976.
Cinema Journal, fall, 1970.
Commonweal, March 11, 1960.
Cue, December 28, 1968.
Encounter, April, 1961.
Esquire, January, 1975.
Film Literature Quarterly, spring, 1980.
Film Quarterly, summer, 1959; summer, 1968; fall, 1969; fall, 1973; winter, 1974-75.
Films and Filming, January, 1963.
Film Society Review, January, 1972.
Globe and Mail (Toronto), August 23, 1986.
Life, April 26, 1968.
Listener, April 5, 1979.

Los Angeles Times, January 15, 1974; June 29, 1983; June 20, 1984; September 16, 1987; September 18, 1988.

Massachusetts Review, winter, 1975.

New Statesman & Society, October 22, 1993, p. 40.

Newsweek, November 24, 1975; April 12, 1976; September 26, 1988.

New York, April 12, 1976.

New York Arts Journal, Number 13, 1979.

New York Review of Books, October 27, 1988; June 9. 1994, p. 17.

New York Times, January 22, 1978; January 27, 1978; June 17, 1983; July 3, 1983; June 21, 1984; September 7, 1988; September 6, 1989; April 30, 1995, section 2, pp. 1, 30; May 5, 1995, pp. C1, C20.

New York Times Book Review, February 21, 1965; August 4, 1974; September 18, 1988; May 23, 1993, section 7, p. 7; January 30, 1994, section 7, p. 7; March 27, 1994, section 7, p. 10; January 12, 1997, section 7, p. 11.

New York Times Magazine, December 7, 1975.

Observer Review, March 27, 1994, p. 21.

Quarterly Review of Film Studies, February, 1977.

Salmagundi, winter, 1978.

Scandinavian Studies, February, 1965.

Sight and Sound, winter, 1962-63; summer, 1965; summer, 1978.

Spectator, June 4, 1988; February 19, 1994, pp. 26-27.

Take One, March-April, 1972.

Time, November 13, 1972; April 12, 1976; January 30, 1978; September 26, 1988.

Times (London), July 6, 1983; May 19, 1988; June 24, 1989.

Times Literary Supplement, September 26, 1969; February 28, 1975; June 24, 1977; June 17, 1988.

Tulane Drama Review, December, 1960.

Voice Literary Supplement, March, 1989.

Washington Post, June 30, 1983; July 1, 1983; August 22, 1984; August 24, 1984; July 9, 1995, p. G4.

Washington Post Book World, September 25, 1988; February 13, 1994, p. 5.*

*   *   *

BISHOP, Leonard 1922-

PERSONAL: Born October 17, 1922, in New York, NY; son of Edward and Essie (maiden name, Milembach) Bishop; married Linda Allen, August 12, 1955; children: Matthew, Michael. *Education:* Attended public schools in New York, NY, but dropped out before completing high school.

ADDRESSES: Home—1608 Felton St., San Francisco, CA. *Agent*—Harold D. Cohen, 580 Fifth Ave., New York, NY.

CAREER: Prior to 1950, traveled throughout the country, working as draftsman, prizefighter, teacher, actor, flagpole painter, salesman, carpenter, waiter, short-order cook, construction worker, and lecturer; full-time writer, 1950—. Has taught creative writing at Columbia University, New York University, Windham College, and University of California Extension.

WRITINGS:

Down All Your Streets, Dial, 1952.

Days of My Love, Dial, 1953.

Creep Into Thy Narrow Bed, Dial, 1954.

The Butchers, Dial, 1956.

The Angry Time, Fell, 1960.

Make My Bed in Hell, Gold Medal Books, 1962.

Against Heaven's Hand, Random House, 1963.

The Everlasting, Poseidon, 1982.

Dare to Be a Great Writer: 329 Keys to Powerful Fiction, Writer's Digest Books, 1988.

Contributor to magazines, including *Esquire* and *New World Writing.*

WORK IN PROGRESS: A biography of Louis R. Lurie.

SIDELIGHTS: Leonard Bishop is noted for his extreme, sometimes sensational plots, to which he brings an attention to detail, particularly in dialogue, that contributes to the realism of his narratives. Blanche Gelfant compared Bishop's work to James T. Farrell's "ecological novel of manners that reveals the . . . intimate insider's knowledge of an everyday way of life." Thus, in novels such as *Days of My Love* and *The Butchers,* Bishop garnered praise for his realistic portrayals of life in the big city. In *Days of My Love,* the author presents the story of an immigrant family, "lost, but seeking in the stone jungle of the American city," according to Benjamin Appel in the *Saturday Review.* "The character pictures are sharply drawn," commented H. L. Roth in the *Library Journal,* "particularly that of the penurious, domineering wife and her little husband." Likewise, in *The Butchers,* in which a young man from the slums becomes involved with racketeers in his bid to become a professional boxer, Bishop "brings his characters furiously alive and sweeps the reader along on ever higher waves of tension and violence," according to Milton Rugoff in the *New York Herald Tribune Book Review.* And in a mixed review of Bishop's *Creep into Thy Narrow Bed,* a novel which centers on a struggling actor who gets swept into an abortion racket in his desperation for money, David Dempsey wrote in the *New York Times:* "The author respects his people and, in spite of their melodramatic machinations, makes them come to life."

Bishop has occasionally been faulted for attempting too large a subject and thus failing in the smaller details of individual characterization. The *New Yorker* review of *Down All Your Streets,* a family drama set during the Great Depression, remarked that though the novel is "written with vigor and enthusiasm," it nevertheless lacks insight into a single character. Not all critics felt that this was the book's great flaw, however. Bishop has captured more negative attention from the critics for his liberal use of slang and obscenity, and for his gloomy subject matter, than for any lack in his characterizations. "A depressing book," wrote R. W. Henderson in *Library Journal* of *Down All Your Streets,* "perhaps of interest as 'documentary,' but not for public libraries." Likewise, in Robert Molloy's review of *The Butchers* for the *Chicago Sunday Tribune,* the critic wrote: "The book is a dogged chronicle of brutality and depravity, written without restraint. If you want another journey to the end of the night, here it is." Nevertheless, some critics who commented negatively on Bishop's penchant for the seemy side of life found his stories irresistably compelling. "You may not like it," wrote Maxwell Geismar in the *Saturday Review* of *Down All Your Streets,* "you may find it positively unpleasant—but the chances are you will go on reading it, as I did, to the bitter end."

The Leonard Bishop Collection is held at Boston University.

BIOGRAPHICAL/CRITICAL SOURCES:

BOOKS

Burke, W. J., and Will D. Howe, *American Authors and Books: 1640 to the Present Day,* third revised edition by Irving Weiss and Anne Weiss, Crown, 1972.

Fuller, Edmund, *Man in Modern Fiction,* Random House, 1958.

Gelfant, Blanche, *The American City Novel,* University of Oklahoma Press, 1954.

Reginald, Robert, *Science Fiction and Fantasy Literature, 1975-1991,* Gale, 1992.

PERIODICALS

America, January 11, 1964.
Best Sellers, December 1, 1963.
Book Week, November 17, 1963, p. 32.
Chicago Sunday Tribune, April 27, 1952, p. 4; March 22, 1953, p. 5; July 29, 1956, p. 8.
Library Journal, March 1, 1952; March 1, 1953; December 15, 1963; January 1, 1964.
New York Herald Tribune Book Review, August 5, 1956, p. 5.
New York Times, April 6, 1952, p. 30; March 8, 1953, p. 26; June 6, 1954, p. 25; July 29, 1956, p. 4.
New Yorker, April 5, 1952.
Saturday Review, April 19, 1952; March 21, 1953; July 3, 1954; September 22, 1956.

*   *   *

BLANCH, Lesley 1907-

PERSONAL: Born in 1907 in London, England; married Romain Gary (a writer), 1945 (divorced, 1963).

ADDRESSES: Home—Roquebrune Village, 06500 Cap Martin, France.

CAREER: Writer.

MEMBER: Royal Society of Literature (fellow).

WRITINGS:

Round the World in Eighty Dishes: The World through the Kitchen Window for Armchair Travellers and Young Enthusiasts, J. Murray (London), 1956.
The Wilder Shores of Love (biography), Simon & Schuster (New York City), 1954.
(Editor and author of introduction) Harriette Wilson, *Game of Hearts,* Simon & Schuster, 1955.
The Sabres of Paradise (biography), Viking (New York City), 1960.

Under a Lilac-Bleeding Star (travel book), J. Murray, 1964.

The Nine Tiger Man (novel), Collins (London), 1965.

Journey Into the Mind's Eye: Fragments of an Autobiography, Collins, 1968, Atheneum (New York City), 1969.

Pavilions of the Heart (biography), Weidenfeld & Nicolson (London), 1974.

Farah, Shabanou of Iran, Queen of Persia (biography), Collins, 1978.

Pierre Loti: The Legendary Romantic, Harcourt (San Diego), 1983, published in England as *Pierre Loti: Portrait of an Escapist,* Collins, 1983.

From Wilder Shores: The Tables of My Travels, J. Murray, 1989.

SIDELIGHTS: Lesley Blanch has written numerous books, including biographies, travel narratives, and novels. In one of her earliest books, *The Wilder Shores of Love,* she offered portraits of four nineteenth-century European women who figured prominently in the history of the Near East and North Africa. *New Statesman & Nation* reviewer V. S. Pritchett had reserved praise for the book, judging Blanch an "uneven writer" who "occasionally gushes," but ultimately approving of *The Wilder Shores of Love* as "a deeply absorbing book." R. P. Corsini took a better view of Blanch's writing style, referring in *Saturday Review* to her "sinuous, rich, and many-hued prose." "Splendid reading," summarized H. M. Champness in *Spectator.*

In *The Sabres of Paradise,* Blanch told the story of Shamyl, the Great Imam, the nineteenth-century ruler of the region known as the Caucasus, and his fight against Russian occupation. Richard West called the book "profound and exhilarating" in his *Guardian* review, and credited it with transforming "an obscure war into a universal saga." Numerous reviewers found the book to be an excellent primer on the Russian character, and Robert Payne in the *New York Times Book Review* stated that he could "imagine no better introduction to modern Russia." Advising that *The Sabres of Paradise* was "a really massive book," he went on to say that "there is not a word too much." Blanch "has told the story of Shamyl with great wealth of detail, lovingly, with a proper sense of his place in Russian history."

Blanch reflected on her own preoccupation with "Russianness" in *Journey into the Mind's Eye: Fragments of an Autobiography.* Described by Arthur Marshall in *New Statesman* as "factual-fantastical, evocative, witty . . . moving" and "pleasurable," the book begins with her childish fantasies about Russia and ends with her description of a journey she eventually made on the trans-Siberian railway. "She jams her limpid narrative with jewels from a life-time of reading and memories recalled with a breathtaking accuracy of detail," declared P. D. Zimmerman, who further praised the book as providing "brilliant and exotic snatches of Russian history."

BIOGRAPHICAL/CRITICAL SOURCES:

PERIODICALS

Atlantic, November, 1960; June, 1965; February, 1969.

Best Sellers, April 1, 1969.

Booklist, November 1, 1954; March 1, 1961.

Book Week, June 27, 1965, p. 22.

Chicago Sunday Tribune, December 12, 1954, p. 6; November 13, 1960, p. 4.

Christian Science Monitor, November 10, 1955, p. B6; December 29, 1960, p. 7; February 13, 1969, p. 5.

Economist, November 9, 1968.

Guardian, October 28, 1960, p. 6.

Horn Book, February, 1956.

Kirkus Reviews, June 1, 1954; September 1, 1955; August 1, 1960.

Library Journal, August, 1954; February 15, 1956; September 15, 1960; April 1, 1964; March 1, 1965; February 15, 1969.

Nation, November 6, 1954.

New Statesman, January 3, 1964; June 4, 1965; November 29, 1968.

New Statesman & Nation, October 9, 1954.

Newsweek, March 29, 1965; January 20, 1969.

New York Herald Tribune Book Review, September 5, 1954, p. 1; November 13, 1955, p. 35; October 16, 1960, p. 5.

New York Times, September 5, 1954, p. 3; December 25, 1955, p. 12.

New York Times Book Review, October 16, 1960, p. 3; March 29, 1964, p. 7; April 4, 1965, p. 33; February 23, 1969, p. 6.

New Yorker, September 25, 1954; April 17, 1965; March 22, 1969.

San Francisco Chronicle, March 11, 1956, p. 22; October 14, 1960, p. 29.

Saturday Review, November 6, 1954; October 22, 1960; April 10, 1965.

Spectator, September 10, 1954, p. 320; October 7, 1960, p. 530.

Time, September 13, 1954; October 17, 1960.

Times Literary Supplement, October 1, 1954, p. 623; October 14, 1960, p. 658; January 2, 1964, p. 5; November 21, 1968, p. 1303.

* * *

BLANKFORT, (Seymour) Michael 1907-1982

PERSONAL: Born December 10, 1907, in New York, NY; died as a result of head injuries suffered in an accidental fall, July 13, 1982, in Los Angeles, CA; son of Henry and Hannah (Goldstein) Blankfort; married second wife, Dorothy V. Stiles (an agent), July 22, 1950; children: (previous marriage) Susan Camiel, Ellen Blankfort Clothier. *Education:* University of Pennsylvania, B.A., 1929; Princeton University, M.A., 1930.

CAREER: Bowdoin College, Brunswick, ME, instructor in psychology, 1929; Princeton University, Princeton, NJ, instructor in psychology, 1931; New Jersey Reformatory, Rahway, psychologist, 1933; Theatre Union, New York, NY, producer and director, 1933-36. Free-lance novelist and dramatist, 1933-82; screenwriter for Hollywood studios, 1939-82. Lecturer, New York University Extension, 1934-35. Board member, Brandeis Institute, 1953-82; trustee, Los Angeles County Museum of Art. *Military service:* U.S. Marine Corps, 1942-45; became captain.

MEMBER: Authors League, Dramatists Guild, Writers Guild of America (president, 1967-69), Academy of Motion Picture Arts and Sciences (member of board of governors, 1970-80).

AWARDS, HONORS: Academy award nomination and Screen Writers Award for Best Script, both 1951, for *Broken Arrow;* Daroff Award, 1952, for *The Juggler;* Commonwealth Club Gold Medal, 1965, for *Behold the Fire;* S. Y. Agnon Award, Hebrew University, 1978.

WRITINGS:

PLAYS

(Adaptor) Friedrich Wolf, *Sailors of Cattaro* (first produced in New York City at Civic Repertory Theater, December 10, 1934), Samuel French (New York City), 1935.

(With Michael Gold) *Battle Hymn* (first produced in New York City at Experimental Theater, May 22, 1936), Samuel French, 1936.

The Crime (first produced in New York City at Civic Repertory Theater, March 1, 1936), New Theater League, 1936.

The Brave and the Blind (first produced in New York City, March 21, 1937), New Theater League, 1937.

(With wife, Dorothy V. Stiles) *Monique* (first produced on Broadway at John Golden Theater, October 22, 1957), Samuel French, 1955.

Also author of *The Spaniard,* 1954.

SCREENPLAYS

Blind Alley, Columbia, 1939.
Adam Had Four Sons, Columbia, 1941.
Texas, Columbia, 1941.
Flight Lieutenant, Columbia, 1942.
An Act of Murder, Universal, 1948.
Dark Past, Columbia, 1949.
Broken Arrow, Twentieth Century-Fox, 1950.
Halls of Montezuma, Twentieth Century-Fox, 1951.
My Six Convicts, Columbia, 1952.
Lydia Bailey, Twentieth Century-Fox, 1952.
The Juggler (also see below), Columbia, 1953.
The Caine Mutiny, Columbia, 1954.
Untamed, Twentieth Century-Fox, 1955.
Tribute to a Bad Man, Metro-Goldwyn-Mayer, 1956.
The Vintage, Metro-Goldwyn-Mayer, 1957.
The Plainsman, Universal, 1965.

Author of films for television, including *A Pelican in the Wilderness,* ABC, 1963, *The Other Man,* NBC, 1968, and *Fire in the Sky,* NBC, 1978.

NOVELS, EXCEPT AS INDICATED

I Met a Man, Bobbs-Merrill (New York City), 1937.
The Brave and the Blind, Bobbs-Merrill, 1940.
A Time to Live, Harcourt (San Diego), 1943.
The Widow Makers, Simon & Schuster (New York City), 1946.
The Big Yankee: The Life of Colonel Carlson of the Marine Raiders (biography), Little, Brown (Boston), 1947.
The Juggler, Little, Brown, 1952.
The Strong Hand, Little, Brown, 1956.
Goodbye, I Guess, Simon & Schuster, 1962.

Behold the Fire: A Novel Based on Events That Took Place between 1914 and 1918 in London, Cairo, Constantinople, Jerusalem, and Some of the Villages of Palestine, New American Library (New York City), 1965.

I Didn't Know I Would Live So Long, Scribner (New York City), 1973.

Take the A Train, Dutton (New York City), 1978.

An Exceptional Man, Atheneum (New York City), 1980.

Also author of *A Cry From a Red Field.*

OTHER

(Author of introduction) Maurice Tuchmand and Anne Carnegie Edgerton, *The Michael and Dorothy Blankfort Collection,* Los Angeles County Museum of Art (Los Angeles), 1982.

Michael Blankfort (sound recording), Phoenix House (Tempe, AZ), between 1978 and 1981.

SIDELIGHTS: Michael Blankfort worked as an educator, psychologist, screenwriter, playwright, and novelist. After brief careers as a college instructor and prison psychologist, Blankfort turned to producing and directing plays, and in 1937 was hired by producer David O. Selznick as a screenwriter. Among Blankfort's screenwriting credits are *The Caine Mutiny, The Plainsman,* and *Broken Arrow,* for which he received an Academy Award nomination in 1951. Many of Blankfort's novels are based in fact and contain settings and elements connected with periods of war. At the time of his death, Blankfort had just completed his fourteenth novel, *A Cry From a Red Field.*

Blankfort "made excellent use of his skill as a playwright and his knowledge of human nature gained as a university instructor in psychology" when writing his first novel, *I Met a Man,* according to *New York Times* reviewer Drake de Kay. Set in 1915 Germany, this "first rate story with never a dull moment," described *Books* contributor F. T. Marsh, is about the friendly relationship between two men, a German officer and an American working for the British secret service and disguised as a German.

The Brave and the Blind deals with the Spanish Civil War and with it, proclaimed L. B. Salomon in the *Nation,* "Mr. Blankfort has done a truly remarkable job: basing his main events on the historical facts of the siege, he peoples the Alcazar entirely with characters imagined by himself. . . . The few dozen men

and women who are brought into sharp focus have the tangible, matter-of-fact reality of next door neighbors." However, *New York Times* critic Harold Straus complained: "There is no central character here, and it may be this which has weakened an otherwise impressive novel." Despite earning mixed reviews, generally critics concluded something similar to what a *New Yorker* contributor stated: "A deeply felt book, [*The Brave and the Blind* is] written with considerable power."

The Juggler, another of Blankfort's books earning mixed but overall favorable reviews, concerns the internal struggles of a famous juggler who survived a German concentration camp and fled to Israel to establish a new life. The story is written with "lean, rhythmic prose," and, according to Rose Feld in the *New York Herald Tribune Book Review,* it "demands respect on every count . . . especially for its masterly portrait of a new nation and of an exile who didn't know he had come home." Although Frederic Morton believed the protagonist to be unnatural at times, he saw the book as having only "minor flaws in an otherwise vivid novel" and recognized in his *New York Times* review: "Mr. Blankfort is gifted with a fine sympathy that can conjure onto his canvas some moving specimens of the newest of all nationalities—the Israeli."

Set in an earlier period, *Behold the Fire: A Novel Based on Events That Took Place between 1914 and 1918 in London, Cairo, Constantinople, Jerusalem, and Some of the Villages of Palestine* involves "a small group of Jewish pioneers living in Turkish controlled Palestine during World War I" and, according to S. L. Simon in *Library Journal,* it "is told with a good deal of color. The characters are well drawn, the action is frequently suspenseful, and the novel moves along at a good pace." "Although the interest flags somewhat toward the middle of the book," wrote a *Best Sellers* critic, "one is bound to be caught up in this taut dramatic tale replete with entirely believable selfless acts of heroism. . . . There is the pervading presence of an unquenchable thirst for freedom."

Blankfort once told *CA:* "Having written plays, movies and novels, learning from each, I find my home in the novel. Indeed, I wrote novels even while I was writing movies. It is not that I believe that one craft and art is superior to the others. Rather it is a matter of temperament. I have always enjoyed writing, but with the novel there is a kind of super-satisfaction, even an occasional ecstasy. I have no illusions either about my literary position or my popularity, but if I have brought into the minds of a few others some insights of human behavior, I'll have managed well enough."

BIOGRAPHICAL/CRITICAL SOURCES:

PERIODICALS

Best Sellers, June 1, 1965.
Books, November 7, 1937; May 26, 1940.
Chicago Sun Book Week, March 23, 1947.
Christian Century, July 28, 1965.
Christian Science Monitor, April 26, 1947.
Commonweal, May 10, 1940; April 16, 1943.
Library Journal, September 15, 1965.
Nation, May 18, 1940; April 10, 1943; April 12, 1947.
New Republic, May 3, 1943; December 9, 1946; March 10, 1947.
New York Herald Tribune Book Review, March 2, 1952.
New York Herald Tribune Weekly Book Review, March 2, 1947; July 20, 1947.
New York Times Book Review, July 11, 1965.
New York Times, November, 14, 1937; May 5, 1940; April 4, 1943; November 17, 1946; March 9, 1947; July 27, 1947; March 9, 1952; June 30, 1978.
New Yorker, May 11, 1940; May 29, 1952.
San Francisco Chronicle, November 24, 1946.
Saturday Review of Literature, May 11, 1940; December 7, 1946; October 11, 1947; May 24, 1952.
Springfield Republican, April 4, 1943.
Washington Post, July 22, 1978.
Weekly Book Review, April 11, 1943; November 24, 1946.

OBITUARIES:

PERIODICALS

Chicago Tribune, July 16, 1982.
Los Angeles Times, July 19, 1982.
New York Times, July 16, 1982.
Washington Post, July 16, 1982.*

*   *   *

BLANTON, (Martha) Catherine 1907-

PERSONAL: Born March 3, 1907, in San Angelo, TX; daughter of Buford Ransome (a railroad conduc-

tor) and Elizabeth (George) Blanton. *Education:* Attended public schools, Tucson, AZ. *Politics:* Democrat. *Religion:* Methodist.

CAREER: Writer.

MEMBER: American Civil Liberties Union, American Association for the United Nations, Wesleyan Service Guild (vice-president), Fellowship of Reconciliation, Indoor Sports Club (for physically handicapped, vice-president), Tucson Writers Club (charter member).

WRITINGS:

The Three Miracles (juvenile novel), Day, 1946.
Pedro's Choice (juvenile novel), Whittlesey House, 1948.
Trouble on Old Smokey, Whittlesey House, 1951.
Hold Fast to Your Dreams, Messner (New York City), 1955.
The Gold Penny, Day, 1957.
What a Break!, Friendship (New York City), 1962.

SIDELIGHTS: Catherine Blanton's first two novels are set in Mexico. Her debut novel, *The Three Miracles,* is about a Mexican boy, his stubborn donkey, and a selfish, crippled American's quest to Mexico City for a miracle from the Lady of Guadeloupe. "This slight story with amusing pictures in color carries a simple moral, easily understood by young children," remarked a Horn Book reviewer. *Pedro's Choice,* Blanton's second novel for preteens, is about an aspiring matador who changes his career interest to a farmer after seeing his pet bull in the arena. "This warm and touching story is beautifully handled both by the writer and the illustrator," stated a *Commonweal* critic. "The anti-bullfight angle is new and handled very well. Animal lovers will rejoice and young converts will be made," concluded S. J. Johnson in *Library Journal.*

Moving the setting north of Mexico, Blanton's third novel, *Trouble on Old Smokey,* involves an American family whose homeland is made into a wild animal preserve by the government. It is "a heart-warming story with good characterization, a convincing plot and a real feel of the mountain country in the midst of the Great Smokies," wrote J. D. Lindquist and S. M. Andrews in *Horn Book.* Other reviewers concurred, such as *Saturday Review of Literature*'s M. G. Davis, who remarked: "Its strength lies in the true picture that it gives of the mountain people, especially of Sunny [the story's protagonist] and his mother." Similarly, a *New York Times* critic, stated: "Miss Blanton has drawn here a moving portrait of a boy standing halfway between the traditions of his people and a new world. She shows the independence of the mountain people and their fierce love for that rugged, beautiful country. Yet Sunny and his parents are individuals, not types, and one follows their story to its happy outcome with sympathy and rising suspense."

Hold Fast to Your Dreams, Blanton's fourth novel deals with an African-American girl's confrontations with issues of prejudice and segregation. "Blanton has handled [the] issues deftly and fairly and woven them skillfully into the story," concluded *Library Journal* contributor Augusta Baker. However, a critic for the *New York Times* believed that "this is a theme of interest to many young girls, but Miss Blanton's treatment is only partially successful." In the story, according to L. S. Betchels *New York Herald Tribune Book Review:* "The author balances heartbreak with high school friendships, teen-age matters, and gay parties so that this will be read first as a girls' story and second for its better understanding of some young Americans' problems."

Severely disabled by polio shortly after she was three years old, Miss Blanton explained: "My physical disability, rather than a handicap, has served as a spur, leaving me with a wholesome discontent and I must constantly be at the business of trying to shape lives." She was encouraged by her teachers to write, "but it was not until my late teens that I considered it seriously. With little or no help in the beginning, I learned to write by writing, writing, writing."

BIOGRAPHICAL/CRITICAL SOURCES:

PERIODICALS

American Junior Red Cross News, November, 1948.
Chicago Sunday Tribune, November 25, 1951.
Commonweal, November 19, 1949.
Home Quarterly, January, February, March, 1954.
Horn Book, March, 1947; November, 1948; December, 1951.
Library Journal, January 1, 1949; January 1, 1952; April 15, 1955.
New York Herald Tribune Weekly Book Review, November 10, 1946; October 14, 1951; May 22, 1955.
New York Times, September 23, 1951; April 24, 1955.

Saturday Review of Literature, November 9, 1946; November 13, 1948; October 20, 1951.
Springfield Republican, November 7, 1948.
Trails for Juniors, August 4, 1957.*

* * *

BLIGHT, Rose
See GREER, Germaine

* * *

BLIVEN, Bruce 1889-1977

PERSONAL: Born July 27, 1889, in Emmetsburg, IA; son of Charles Franklin (a farmer) and Lilla Cordelia (Ormsby) Bliven; died from complications from a broken hip, May 27, 1977, in Palo Alto, CA; married Rose Frances Emery, May 17, 1913; children: Bruce, Jr. *Education:* Stanford University, A.B., 1911. *Politics:* Independent. *Avocational interests:* Reading, music, theatre, walking.

CAREER: San Francisco Bulletin, San Francisco, CA, member of editorial staff, 1909-12; advertisement writer and free-lance writer, 1912-14; University of Southern California, Los Angeles, director of department of journalism, 1914-16; *Printer's Ink,* New York City, member of editorial staff, 1917-19; *New York Globe,* New York City, member of editorial board, 1919-23; *New Republic,* New York City, managing editor, 1923-30, editor, 1930-55, member of editorial board, 1923-55; Stanford University, Stanford, CA, lecturer in communication and journalism, 1956-77. New York correspondent, *Manchester Guardian,* 1927-47. Member of board of directors of Foreign Policy Association of the United States, 1923-45, and Twentieth Century Fund, 1923-56.

MEMBER: National Association of Science Writers.

WRITINGS:

The Jewish Refugee Problem, League for Industrial Democracy (New York City), 1939.
The Men Who Make the Future, Duell, Sloan & Pearce (New York City), 1942.
(Editor with A. G. Mezerik) *What the Informed Citizen Needs to Know,* Duell, Sloan & Pearce, 1945.

(Editor) *Twentieth Century Unlimited,* Lippincott (Philadelphia), 1950.

Preview for Tomorrow: The Unfinished Business of Science, Knopf (New York City), 1953.

The World Changers, John Day (New York City), 1965.

Five Million Words Later (autobiography), John Day, 1970.

A Mirror for Greatness: Six Americans, McGraw (New York City), 1976.

OTHER

The Jewish Problem (microfilm), League for Industrial Democracy (New York City), 1939.

Contributor of articles to national magazines, including *New Republic, Reader's Digest, Harper's, Saturday Evening Post, Atlantic, Ladies' Home Journal, McCall's, Redbook, American Heritage,* and *New York Times Magazine.*

SIDELIGHTS: Bruce Bliven, called by the *New York Times* a "champion of liberalism," was best known for his editorship of the *New Republic.* "The editor's chair of that small but very influential weekly was an ideal vantage point for witnessing the history of our times," in the words of a *New Yorker* writer. From that seat, Bliven worked to bring about social change "through statements of belief and ideals, both in print and from the speaker's podium, and through constant research and consistent intellectual striving to develop clear formulas for liberal political and economic agendas," declared Peyton Brien in *Dictionary of Literary Biography.*

Bliven grew up in the Midwest, the son of a farm family. He showed an interest in writing and literature when he was quite young, and devoured all the reading material available to him in his small town. At the age of ten he won two national essay contests for children. During high school, he founded a student newspaper, and his short stories were printed in the town's newspaper. During college, he served as a correspondent to the *San Francisco Bulletin.* After completing his studies, Bliven worked in advertising for a while, then took on the job of organizing and directing a department of journalism at the University of Souther California. He sidelined as music and theater critic for two Los Angeles newspapers.

In 1917 Bliven took a position on the editorial staff of the advertising trade journal *Printers' Ink,* and he and his family moved to New York City. Bliven was soon teaching writing classes at New York University. In 1919, he was invited to become chief editorial writer at the *Globe* newspaper. Brien observed: "Among his more important writings for the paper was an article in which Bliven proposed an urban development and taxation method, which he believed could, through subsidies, encourage development of new housing projects and a decrease in the cost to the builder without any actual loss of city or state revenues." This influential article led to a meeting with the state's governor and the passage of legislation putting Bliven's plan into effect. That legislation profoundly influenced the demographics of New York City and New York State, and led to a great deal of significant construction.

Bliven eventually became managing editor of the *Globe,* a position he held until moving to the *New Republic* in 1923. Bliven spent the next thirty years at the magazine. Brien explained that although the magazine never had a circulation of more than about 35,000 a week, "this number does not reflect the magazine's impact upon the county. Its well-thought-out and intensively researched editorials and Bliven's public lectures, both aimed at encouraging moderate to left-wing political factions, are credited with having influenced the national thinking on hundreds of political and social issues of the day." Though small, the magazine's readership was made up of people in influential, powerful positions—including clergymen, educators, editors and reporters, high-ranking politicians, and social workers.

Bliven once told *New York Times* interviewer Stephen V. Roberts, "The essence of liberalism is a desire to have an open mind, a desire to have an open society, a desire to know the fundamental truth, a desire that as many people as possible should have a better life. . . . I don't know of any better ambition for society." Musing on the ways journalism could help the cause of liberalism, Bliven said, "you make people conscious of themselves, of where they stand in relation to the world, where they stand in relation to history, what is possible to be done, and then they do it, with heartbreaking slowness. But the world does move, eventually, it moves."

BIOGRAPHICAL/CRITICAL SOURCES:

BOOKS

Bliven, Bruce, *Five Million Words Later,* John Day, 1970.

Dictionary of Literary Biography, Volume 137: *American Magazine Journalists, 1900-1960, Second Series,* Gale (Detroit), 1994.

Seideman, *The New Republic: A Voice of Modern Liberalism,* Praeger (New York City), 1986.

PERIODICALS

Library Journal, November 1, 1970.
New Republic, January 9, 1971, pp. 32-36.
New Yorker, January 23, 1971.
New York Times, July 27, 1969, p. 33.
New York Times Book Review, November 29, 1970, p. 64.

OBITUARIES:

PERIODICALS

AB Bookman's Weekly, June 27, 1977.
New York Times, May 29, 1977.
Time, June 13, 1977.
Washington Post, May 29, 1977.*

*   *   *

BLOCH, Chana 1940-

PERSONAL: Born March 15, 1940, in New York, NY; daughter of Benjamin (a dentist) and Rose (Rosenberg) Faerstein; married Ariel A. Bloch (a professor), October 26, 1969 (divorced, 1996); children: Benjamin Daniel, Jonathan Max. *Education:* Cornell University, B.A., 1961; Brandeis University, M.A., 1963, M.A., 1965; University of California, Berkeley, Ph.D., 1975. *Religion:* Jewish.

ADDRESSES: Home—12 Menlo Pl., Berkeley, CA 94707. *Office*—Department of English, Mills College, Oakland, CA 94613. *Agent*—Georges Borchardt, 136 East 57th Street, New York, NY 10022. *E-mail*—chana@mills.edu.

CAREER: Hebrew University of Jerusalem, Jerusalem, Israel, instructor in English literature, 1964-67; Mills College, Oakland, CA, instructor, 1973-75, assistant professor, 1975-81, associate professor, 1981-86, chair of English department, 1986-89, professor of English literature, 1987—, director, creative writing program, 1993—, W. M. Keck Professor, 1996-99.

MEMBER: Modern Language Association of America, Poetry Society of America, American Literary Translators Association, Association of Literary Scholars and Critics.

AWARDS, HONORS: Discovery Award for poetry, 1974; Graves Award, Pomona College, 1976-77; translation award, Columbia University's Translation Center, 1978, for *A Dress of Fire;* National Endowment for the Humanities fellowship, 1980-81; Book of the Year award, Conference on Christianity and Literature, 1986, for *Spelling the Word: George Herbert and the Bible;* Writers award, Poets and Writers Exchange, 1988; National Endowment for the Arts poetry fellowship, 1989-90; Felix Pollak Prize in Poetry, 1998, for *Mrs. Dumpty.*

WRITINGS:

POETRY

The Secrets of the Tribe, Sheep Meadow Press (New York City), 1980.
The Past Keeps Changing, Sheep Meadow Press, 1992.
Mrs. Dumpty, University of Wisconsin Press (Madison), 1998.

Poetry represented in anthologies, including *A Geography of Poets,* 1978; *Voices within the Ark,* 1980; and *The Pushcart Prize, VI,* 1981. Contributor of poetry to periodicals, including the *Atlantic Monthly, Nation,* and the *New Yorker.*

OTHER

(Translator) Dahlia Ravikovitch, *A Dress of Fire: Selected Poetry,* Menard, 1976.
Spelling the Word: George Herbert and the Bible, University of California Press (Berkeley), 1985.
(Translator and editor with Ariel Bloch) Ravikovitch, *The Window: New and Selected Poems,* Sheep Meadow Press, 1989.
(Translator and editor, with Stephen Mitchell) Yehuda Amichai, *The Selected Poetry,* Harper (New York City), 1986, revised and expanded, University of California Press, 1996.
(Translator, with Ariel Bloch, and author of introduction) *The Song of Songs,* Random House (New York City), 1995.

WORK IN PROGRESS: "Translation of Yehuda Amichai's *Open Closed Open,* with Chana Kronfeld."

Contributor of translations (from Yiddish and Hebrew) to literary journals and popular magazines, including *Atlantic Monthly, New Yorker, Playboy, American Poetry Review, Iowa Review, Poetry, Tikkun,* and *Judaism.*

SIDELIGHTS: A professor of English literature at Mills College, Chana Bloch is also a poet and literary critic. In addition to poetry collections *The Secrets of the Tribe, The Past Keeps Changing,* and *Mrs. Dumpty,* she has authored several noted works of criticism focusing on biblical writings, including the 1985 work *Spelling the Word: George Herbert and the Bible,* and an introduction to her co-translation of the *Song of Songs* published in 1995 as *The Song of Songs: A New Translation.*

As she noted in a commentary published in *Contemporary Women Poets,* Bloch writes about the double-edged sword that one confronts in intimate relationships. Her first poetry volume, 1980's *The Secrets of the Tribe,* focuses on her many roles as a woman: daughter, wife, and as a female Jew, a "member of the tribe." She makes parallels between her own life and the book of Genesis, "creating a world where the mythological enters unobtrusively into the suburbs," according to *Contemporary Women Poets* essayist Cynthia Davidson. What was once paradise resolves itself into the commonplace, as the poet notes in "Exile" when she writes of the ten lost tribes: "they found work, married, grew smaller,/started to look like the natives/in a landscape nobody chose./Soon you couldn't have picked them out of a crowd."

The Past Keeps Changing recounts Bloch's personal battle with cancer, as well as her husband, Ariel Bloch's, struggle with depression. Her poems here also reflect "the ways in which we (often unwittingly) shape the lives of our children," Bloch noted; "and the strains of a long marriage, particularly in the face of crisis." As Davidson notes, the verse in *The Past Keeps Changing* shows a progression: "movement away from mythological and historical backgrounds . . . to freer constructs of [Bloch's] own immediate reckoning . . . and other particular experiences of a woman's rich and varied life."

Together with her former husband, Bloch made a new translation of the biblical "Song of Songs" that treats the ancient Hebrew verse as an original love poem rather than a pastiche of unrelated ancient texts, as some scholars have viewed it. The Blochs' work was praised by *Commentary* contributor Hillel Halkin as "blessed with what the King James [version] lacks and the great and mysterious Hebrew poem has throughout: a breathlessness, a swift running from short phrase to short phrase that perfectly reflects the erotic excitement of the lovers who are the poem's two principle figures." And Sidra DeKoven Ezrahi adds her praise in *Tikkun,* maintaining that the Blochs' translation restores the poem's "original colors and contours from under the patina of centuries of interpretation," with "colors [that] appear to be brighter and more dazzling than centuries of gazing had rendered them."

Speaking of *Mrs. Dumpty,* Bloch told *CA:* "*Mrs. Dumpty* is a memoir-in-verse about 'a great fall,' the dissolution of a long and loving marriage. The poems speak about the familiar strains in a marriage of many years—aging, dependency, the erosion of feeling—as compounded by the ravages of a spouse's mental illness. I write not only about horrors like electroshock therapy but about the aftershocks of history as well—in this case, the trauma of Hitler's Germany, which continues to take its toll on the second generation. Although they tell a story of disintegration, these poems are not simply documentary or elegiac. What interests me is the inner life: how we are formed by our losses and those of our parents, how we learn what we need to know through our intuitions and confusions, how we deny and delay and finally discover who we are. *Mrs. Dumpty* chronicles a process of inner transformation in which 'the end of safety,' with all its attendant terrors, proves to be the beginning of freedom."

BIOGRAPHICAL/CRITICAL SOURCES:

BOOKS

Contemporary Women Poets, St. James Press (Detroit), 1997.
Mavor, Anne, *Strong Hearts, Inspired Minds: 21 Artists Who Are Mothers Tell Their Stories,* Rowanberry Books (Portland, OR), 1996.

PERIODICALS

American Book Review, January/February, 1982; October/November, 1993.
Bloomsbury Review, March/April, 1987.
Commentary, November, 1995, p. 117.
Literature and Medicine, spring, 1995, pp. 87-104.
Nation, December 6, 1986.
New York Times Book Review, April 15, 1979; August 3, 1986, p. 14.

San Francisco Review of Books, January/February, 1981.

Santa Barbara Review, spring, 1996, pp. 11-25.

Tikkun, July/August, 1996, p. 65.

* * *

BOAS, Louise Schutz 1885-1973

PERSONAL: Born October 22, 1885, in Providence, RI; died March, 1973; daughter of Rudolph Gibbs and Esther (Beekman) Schutz; married Ralph Philip Boas (a writer), September 6, 1911 (deceased); children: Ralph Philip, Jr., Marie (Mrs. A. Rupert Hall). *Education:* Brown University, A.B., 1907, A.M., 1908.

CAREER: Professor and lecturer at colleges, 1910-29; Wheaton College, Norton, MA, professor of English, 1929-52, professor emeritus, 1952-73.

MEMBER: Boston Athenaeum (proprietor), Friends of Brown University Library, Life Friend of the Bodleian Library (Oxford University), Life Friend of the London Library, American Association of University Women, Phi Beta Kappa.

WRITINGS:

(With husband, Ralph P. Boas) *Leading Facts for New Americans,* American Book Co. (New York City), 1923.

(With Ralph P. Boas) *Cotton Mather: Keeper of the Puritan Conscience,* Harper (New York City), 1928.

Great Rich Man: Life of Sir Walter Scott, Longmans, Green (New York City), 1929.

Elizabeth Barrett Browning, Longmans, Green, 1929.

Women's Education Begins, Wheaton College Press (Norton, MA), 1935, reprinted, Arno (New York City), 1971.

Harriet Shelley: Five Long Years, Oxford University Press (Oxford, England), 1962, reprinted, Greenwood Press (Westport, CT), 1979.

(Author of introduction) Thomas Taylor, Platonist, *A Vindication of the Rights of Brutes,* Scholar's Facsimilies and Reprints (Delmar, NY), 1966.

Contributor of articles and letters to *Notes and Queries* (London), *Explicator, Times Literary Supplement,* and other journals.

SIDELIGHTS: Louise Schutz Boas taught English at Wheaton College in Massachusetts and, sometimes with her husband and sometimes alone, published biographies of literary and political figures. Her publishing career spanned some forty-three years, beginning in the early-1920s and continuing until the mid-1960s, and most of her works were praised for their qualities of scholarship and stylish prose.

In 1929, Boas and her husband released a biography entitled *Cotton Mather: Keeper of the Puritan Conscience.* The book drew positive responses from both sides of the Atlantic. "In these pleasantly written pages psychology is skillfully used to explain the seeming contradictions of Cotton Mather's neurotic character," wrote *Nation* contributor V. L. Parrington. K. A. Porter, reviewing the book for the *New York Evening Post,* declared: "So far as is humanly possible the authors have spared this hapless man. They wished to be scrupulously fair to him, and they have been. . . . The result is a very fine biography of Cotton Mather." *New York World* correspondent Arthur Strawn commented: "to anyone who wants an insight into the Puritan mind, its dignity and its pitiful delusions, this book will give it, and with it a highly illuminating picture of the intimate life of the times, presented with charm, understanding and illuminating scholarship." From England a *Times Literary Supplement* reviewer concluded: "This volume studies the man in all his distances and guises, employing critical acumen, literary art, and psychological analysis."

Within the same time period Boas published two books under her solo authorship: *Elizabeth Barrett Browning* and *Great Rich Man: The Romance of Sir Walter Scott.* The biography of Elizabeth Barrett Browning charts her ascent from isolated semi-invalid to poet and vibrant wife of another noted poet, Robert Browning. "Mrs. Boas writes the story well," noted H. F. Whicher in *Books.* "She is supremely good in the art of portraiture. . . . Of the love story itself she can write with a sure sympathy that never degenerates into sentimental ecstasies." To quote Margaret Wallace in the *New York Evening Post, Elizabeth Barrett Browning* "is a swift and amusing study, true to the facts, and, in general, faithful enough to its probabilities." An *Outlook* contributor observed: "Mrs. Boas' excellent biography is the progress of a luminous, gentle soul, literally from darkness into light—from a tomb-like chamber into a 'world of men.'"

Mixed reviews greeted *Great Rich Man: The Romance of Sir Walter Scott.* S. A. Coblentz in the *New*

York Times called the biography "interesting," but added: "The amount of research and understanding revealed by the book is small; there is no evidence of a comprehension of Scott's character or of an appreciation of his work; and the inconsistencies in the author's statements are glaring." Conversely, a *Christian Science Monitor* reviewer wrote that Walter Scott's life "is an oft-told story, familiar enough in its main features. But Mrs. Boas makes it live again in bright, vivid colors. . . . This is frankly romance which is not fiction, but appreciative reconstruction of the actual."

One of Boas's best known books is *Harriet Shelley: Five Long Years,* the history of Harriet Westbrook's ill-fated marriage to Percy Bysshe Shelley and her suicide at age twenty-one. By concentrating on Harriet Shelley's perspective, Boas brought a new slant to scholarship on Percy Shelley—and reviewers noticed her point of view. "In the many biographies of Percy Bysshe Shelley his first wife, Harriet, has never been given a proper hearing," maintained F. E. Faverty in the *Chicago Sunday Tribune.* "This biography is more than a vindication of Harriet, however. It is a full scale reconstruction of her last exciting years." Wrote G. M. Matthews in *Spectator:* "It is a great pity . . . that this readable and welcome rehabilitation of Harriet should depend largely on discrediting the other side. . . . But when all criticisms are made, the book is well worth reading and will permanently restore to Harriet the importance she deserves." A *Times Literary Supplement* piece on *Harriet Shelley* concluded: "A portrait of Harriet Westbrook has to be a study of the ebullient youth of Shelley from a new angle. Mrs. Boas adds richness and perspective by combining two new angles. . . . Her approach is one of common sense, if not impartiality. . . . In turning a senseless melodrama into human tragedy Mrs. Boas has drawn a portrait of Harriet that is consistent, appealing and understandable."

BIOGRAPHICAL/CRITICAL SOURCES:

PERIODICALS

Booklist, December, 1929, p. 115; May, 1930, p. 309.
Books, March 16, 1930, p. 18.
Boston Transcript, March 19, 1930, p. 3.
Chicago Sunday Tribune, March 25, 1962, p. 8.
Christian Science Monitor, January 18, 1930, p. 7.
Churchman, December 22, 1928, p. 20.
Dial, May, 1929, p. 438.

Nation, January 30, 1929, p. 137; July 9, 1930, p. 45.
New Republic, April 16, 1930, p. 252.
New Yorker, April 21, 1962, p. 182.
New York Evening Post, November 3, 1928, p. 8; February 22, 1930, p. 9.
New York Times, February 16, 1930, p. 30; March 2, 1930, p. 11; May 12, 1935, p. 18.
New York Times Book Review, April 29, 1962, p. 4.
New York World, February 3, 1929, p. 10.
Outlook, January 30, 1929, p. 190; March 5, 1930, p. 386.
Saturday Review of Literature, June, 1929, p. 1146.
Spectator, February 9, 1962, p. 180.
Springfield Republican, March 9, 1930, p. E7.
Times Literary Supplement, February 14, 1929, p. 108; February 9, 1962, p. 90.*

*   *   *

BOASE, T(homas) S(herrer) R(oss) 1898-1974

PERSONAL: Born August 31, 1898, in Dundee, Scotland; died April 14, 1974; son of Charles Millet and Anne (Ross) Boase. *Education:* Oxford University, M.A., 1925.

CAREER: Hertford College, Oxford University, Oxford, England, fellow and tutor, 1922-37; University of London, London, professor of art history and director of Courtauld Institute of Art, 1937-47; Oxford University, president of Magdalen College, 1947-68, vice-chancellor of the university, 1958-60. Temporary civil servant, British Air Ministry, in Cairo, Egypt, and United Kingdom, 1939-43; chief representative in Middle East, British Council, 1943-45. Trustee of National Gallery, 1947-53, Shakespeare Birthplace Trust, beginning 1949, and British Museum, 1950-69; governor of Rugby School, 1951-63, Shakespeare Memorial Theatre, beginning 1952; commissioner for "Exhibition of 1851," beginning 1956. *Military service:* British Army, Oxford and Bucks Light Infantry, 1917-19; became lieutenant; received Military Cross.

MEMBER: British Archaeological Association (president, 1969-72), British Academy (fellow), American Philosophical Society (foreign member), Oxford and Cambridge Club (London).

AWARDS, HONORS: D.C.L., Oxford University; LL.D., University of St. Andrews, University of

Melbourne, and Rockefeller Institute; D.Litt., University of Durham and University of Reading.

WRITINGS:

Boniface VIII, Constable (London), 1933.
St. Francis of Assisi, Duckworth (London), 1936, reprinted, Indiana University Press (Bloomington), 1968.
(Editor) *Oxford History of English Art,* Oxford University Press (Oxford, England), 1949.
English Art, 1100-1216, Clarendon Press (Oxford, England), 1953.
Christ Bearing the Cross: Attributed to Valdes Leal at Magdalen College, Oxford: A Study in Taste, Oxford University Press, 1955.
English Art, 1800-1870, Clarendon Press, 1959.
Castles and Churches of the Crusading Kingdom (photographs by Richard Cleave), Oxford University Press, 1967.
(Contributor of critical essay) *The Sculpture of David Wynne, 1949-1967,* M. Joseph (London), 1968.
Kingdoms and Strongholds of the Crusades, Thames & Hudson (London), 1971.
Death in the Middle Ages: Mortality, Judgment and Remembrance, McGraw (New York City), 1972.
(Author of text) Arthur Boyd, *Nebuchadnezzar: 34 Paintings and 18 Drawings by Arthur Boyd,* Thames & Hudson, 1972.
(Editor) Hammelmann, Hanns A., *Book Illustrators in Eighteenth-Century England,* Yale University Press (New Haven, CT), 1975.
(Editor and contributor) *The Cilician Kingdom of Armenia,* Scottish Academy Press (Edinburgh), 1978.
Giorgio Vasari: The Man and the Book, St. Martin's (New York City), 1979.

Editor, *Journal of the Warburg and Courtauld Institutes.*

SIDELIGHTS: T. S. R. Boase was an administrator at Oxford University and an authority on English art history. While serving as president of Oxford's Magdalen College, Boase also edited the multi-volume *Oxford History of English Art* and wrote two of its volumes himself. The two volumes that appeared from his pen reflect his wide-ranging interests: one covered the twelfth century, the other the years 1800-1870. In a *Spectator* review of *English Art, 1100-1216,* a critic wrote that Boase "rises magnificently to the exacting task of incorporating the latest results of research in different fields, dealing fully and at the highest level of scholarship, with every

aspect of artistic activity: architecture as well as sculpture and painting." A *Times Literary Supplement* reviewer also found *English Art, 1100-1216* "quite admirable," adding: "The reader will find in the volume a complete and up-to-date statement of modern views on the Romanesque period from the Norman Conquest . . . to the early thirteenth century. . . . The author is careful in his assessments, without ever being betrayed into the extravagant or unsubstantiated hypotheses to which some medieval art-historians are prone."

Boase's *English Art, 1800-1870* was also widely and thoroughly reviewed, with most critics praising the author for his authoritative treatment of a difficult period in English art. "This first comprehensive history of British art in the nineteenth century is a notable piece of pioneering work," declared Alan Bowness in *Spectator.* "Such an authoritative general book has long been badly needed. . . . Mr. Boase is an enthusiast for his subject, and doesn't in consequence get depressed by the mediocrity of much of what he has to write about." To quote A. C. Ritchie in the *Yale Review,* "While the present book breaks little new ground, it is an unusually detailed, smoothly written, and occasionally, a gently humorous account of one of the most baffling seventy years in the history of the visual arts in Britain." A contrasting opinion was offered by Basil Taylor in *New Statesman.* Taylor found *English Art, 1800-1870* "dull, shallow, and impercipient," noting that the book "does not suggest any particular enthusiasm which is not also second-hand." Conversely, *Manchester Guardian* contributor Eric Newton stated: "No historian could have been more competent to undertake the task and no period could be more calculated to defeat the competence of any historian. . . . None the less, one cannot imagine a more adequate solution of a difficult problem."

After retiring from Oxford, Boase turned to another field of study, publishing *Castles and Churches of the Crusading Kingdom, Kingdoms and Strongholds of the Crusades, St. Francis of Assisi,* a biography, and *Death in the Middle Ages: Mortality, Judgment and Remembrance.* These volumes of medieval history and architecture were also well received among the critics. *Library Journal* correspondent M. L. Garvey, for instance, called *St. Francis of Assisi* "a small masterpiece . . . a gracious retelling of the fact and fable that make up the legend." In *Art Bulletin,* Robert Branner praised *Castles and Churches of the Crusading Kingdom* for its "straightforward text that is both well informed and readable." The critic added: "The very latest archaeological information is included, but at no point does the text slip away from the reader. This takes a rare gift and a mellowness, and Boase has both." A *Choice* reviewer deemed *Death in the Middle Ages* "recommended for ideas it might develop in intelligent students"—just the sort of comment that might well please any Oxford don.

Boase died in 1974 with several of his projects nearing completion at the time. These were published posthumously over the next five years. A *New York Herald Tribune Book Review* correspondent hailed Boase for his pioneering work on "activity in the arts from the first century to the present against a background of history."

BIOGRAPHICAL/CRITICAL SOURCES:

PERIODICALS

Art Bulletin, September, 1968, p. 292.
Canadian Forum, March, 1954, p. 282.
Choice, January, 1968, p. 1232; December, 1972, p. 1338.
Christian Century, June 16, 1954, p. 738; October 4, 1967, p. 1255.
Class World, September/October, 1973, p. 53.
Library Journal, October 1, 1959, p. 3024; November 15, 1967, p. 4143; August, 1968, p. 2853.
Manchester Guardian, November 17, 1953, p. 4; June 19, 1959, p. 4.
New Statesman, August 1, 1959, p. 138.
New York Herald Tribune Book Review, December 6, 1959, p. 15.
Saturday Review, November 25, 1967, p. 36.
Spectator, February 5, 1954, p. 162; July 31, 1959, p. 147.
Times Literary Supplement, November 6, 1953, p. 704; July 24, 1959, p. 429; August 29, 1968, p. 926.
Virginia Quarterly Review, winter, 1973, p. 43.
Yale Review, March, 1960, p. 464.*

*   *   *

BOLT, Carol 1941-
    (Carol Johnson)

PERSONAL: Born August 25, 1941, in Winnipeg, Manitoba, Canada; daughter of William Victor (a carpenter) and Marjorie (a teacher; maiden name, Small) Johnson; married David Bolt (an actor), June

19, 1969; children: Alexander. *Education:* University of British Columbia, B.A., 1961.

ADDRESSES: Agent—Great North Agency, 345 Adelaide St., W., Toronto, Ontario, Canada M5V 1R5.

CAREER: Worked in Canada as statistical researcher for Dominion Board of Statistics, London School of Economics, Market Facts of Canada Ltd., and Seccombe House, 1961-72; Playwrights Cooperative (now Playwrights Canada), Toronto, Ontario, dramaturge, 1972-73, head of management committee, 1973-74; playwright. Dramaturge at Toronto Free Theatre, 1973; writer in residence at University of Toronto, 1977-78. Member of Advisory Arts Panel of Toronto, 1974-75.

MEMBER: Playwrights' Union of Canada.

AWARDS, HONORS: Grants from Canada Council, 1967, 1972, and Ontario Arts Council, 1972, 1973, 1974, and 1975; Silver Jubilee Award, 1978.

WRITINGS:

PLAYS

(Under name Carol Johnson) *I Wish,* first produced in Toronto, 1966.
Daganawida, first produced in Toronto, 1970.
The Bluebird, first produced in Toronto, 1973.
Pauline, first produced in Toronto, 1973.
Maurice (first produced in Toronto, Ontario, 1974), published in *Performing Arts in Canada,* winter, 1974.
Shelter (first produced in Toronto, 1974), Playwrights Press, 1975.
Cyclone Jack (first produced in Toronto, 1972), published in *A Collection of Canadian Plays,* Volume IV, Simon & Pierre, 1975.
Finding Bumble, first produced in Toronto, 1975.
Bethune, first produced in Gravenhurst, Ontario, 1976.
Okey Doke, first produced in Kingston, ON, 1976.
Norman Bethune: On Board the Empress of Asia, first produced in 1976.
Desperadoes, first produced in Toronto, 1977.
Constance Brissenden, editor, *Playwrights in Profile: Carol Bolt* (contains *Buffalo Jump,* first produced as *Next Year Country* in Regina, Saskatchewan, 1971, produced as *Buffalo Jump* in Toronto, 1972; *Gabe,* first produced in Toronto, 1973; *Tangleflags,* first produced in Toronto, 1973; and *Red Emma: Queen of the Anarchists,* first produced in Toronto, 1974), Playwrights Press, 1976.

One Night Stand (first produced in 1977), Playwrights Press, 1977.

T.V. Lounge, first produced in Toronto, 1977.

Deadline, first produced in Toronto, 1979.

My Best Friend Is Twelve Feet High (first produced in 1972), Dreadnaught Press, 1978, published in *Kids' Plays,* Playwrights Press, 1980.

Star Quality (first produced in 1980), Britain-America Repertory Company, 1981.

Escape Entertainment: A Comedy (first produced in Toronto, 1981), Playwrights Canada (Toronto), 1982.

Love or Money, first produced in Blyth, ON, 1981.

TELEVISION SCRIPTS

Valerie, Canadian Broadcasting System (CBC), 1971.

A Nice Girl like You, CBC, 1974.

Distance, CBC, 1974.

Red Emma, CBC, 1976.

Cyclone Jack, CBC, 1977.

One Night Stand, CBC, 1978.

The Move, CBC, 1978.

In a Far Country, CBC, 1981.

Mayor Charlotte, CBC, 1982.

I Don't Care, CBC, 1983.

Also author of scripts for *Edison Twins* and *Evergreen Raccoons* television series, CBC, 1983-85.

RADIO SCRIPTS

Guy and Jack, CBC, 1970.

Fast Forward, CBC, 1976.

Silent Pictures, CBC, 1983.

Tinsel in My Stetson, CBC, 1984.

Unconscious, CBC, 1986.

Dancing with Each Other, CBC, 1987.

OTHER

Drama in the Classroom, Playwrights Canada, 1986.

ADAPTATIONS: Red Emma was adapted as an opera and staged by the Canadian Opera Company in Toronto in 1995.

SIDELIGHTS: Carol Bolt has shaped, according to Sandra Souchotte and Constance Brissenden in *Contemporary Dramatists,* "a unique form of social documentary using factual reference material to gain access to an imaginative Canadian mythology. Her best early plays are cohesive, rich in entertainment and dramatic values, politically inspired but romantically motivated, and imbued with a keen, sometimes riotous sense of social injustice." Cynthia Diane Zimmerman in the *Dictionary of Literary Biography* calls Bolt "a pioneer of Canadian theater, a founding member of the Playwright's Union of Canada, and consistently active on behalf of the theater community."

Typical of Bolt's work is *Red Emma, Queen of the Anarchists,* a play based on the real-life radical Emma Goldman, "a young, idealistic woman given to histrionic poses and flamboyant gestures," as Souchotte and Brissenden write. Zimmerman notes that the play's "intention is unabashedly romantic. The work does not engage the ethics of radical political action; rather, its preoccupation is with the charismatic adventuress, with the urgency of her passion for politics and emotional entanglements." The play "marked a breakthrough in [Bolt's] career," concludes Zimmerman. "*Red Emma* opened to wide critical acclaim." In 1995, *Red Emma* was adapted as an opera by Gary Kulesha of the Canadian Opera Company.

BIOGRAPHICAL/CRITICAL SOURCES:

BOOKS

Brissenden, Constance, editor, *Playwrights in Profile: Carol Bolt,* Playwrights Co-op (Toronto), 1976.

Contemporary Dramatists, 5th edition, St. James Press (Detroit), 1993.

Dictionary of Literary Biography, Volume 60: *Canadian Writers since 1960, Second Series,* Gale (Detroit), 1987.

Zimmerman, Cynthia and Robert Wallace, editors, *The Work: Conversations with English-Canadian Playwrights,* Coach House Press (Toronto), 1982, pp. 264-276.

PERIODICALS

Canadian Drama, spring, 1978, pp. 64-67.

Maclean's, December 11, 1995, p. 71.

*   *   *

BRANDON, Sheila
  See RAYNER, Claire (Berenice)

BRAUN, Hugh 1902-

PERSONAL: Born December 28, 1902, in London, England. *Avocational interests:* Middle East (once took part in excavations in Iraq for Oriental Institute of Chicago), horses, riding.

ADDRESSES: Agent—Curtis Brown Group Ltd., 1 Craven Hill, London W2 3EW, England.

CAREER: Practicing architect in England, specializing in country homes, historical styles, and restorations, 1931—; architect in Australia, 1958-60. *Military service:* British Army, Royal Engineers, 1939-45.

MEMBER: Society of Antiquaries of London (fellow), Royal Institute of British Architects (fellow).

WRITINGS:

The English Castle, Batsford, 1936.
The Story of the English House, Batsford, 1940.
Maltese Architecture, Times of Malta, 1944.
The Centuries Look Down, Richards Press, 1947.
Works of Art in Malta, H.M.S.O., 1948.
The Story of English Architecture, Faber (London), 1950.
Old London Buildings, Convoy Press, 1951.
An Introduction to English Mediaeval Architecture, Faber, 1951, 2nd edition, Praeger (New York City), 1968.
Historical Architecture, Faber, 1953.
The Restoration of Old Houses, Faber, 1954.
Old English Houses, Faber, 1962.
Parish Churches: Their Architectural Development in England, Transatlantic (Albuquerque, NM), 1970.
English Abbeys, Faber, 1971.
Cathedral Architecture, Crane, Russak (New York City), 1972.
Elements of English Architecture, David & Charles (North Pomfret, VT), 1973.
A Short History of English Architecture, Faber, 1976.

Contributor to archaeological journals and magazines interested in Georgian architecture.

SIDELIGHTS: Hugh Braun is the author of many significant books on English architecture. In *The English Castle,* he provided detailed architectural comment on specific castles in England, and he also gave a rich account of castle life and the rise and fall of feudalism. Though the book contained a wealth of information, it never became muddled, according to *New Statesman & Nation* reviewer John Betjeman. He wrote: "Mr. Braun's enthusiastic way of writing, his anti-Puritan prejudice and his skilful selection of what must have been an overwhelming array of facts help the text along." A *Christian Science Monitor* cited Braun's "commendable care and scholarship." Pointing out the book's value for architects, the writer added: "For the historian, the book will be fascinating; whole periods come alive under the author's pen." Braun used the same approach in a later book, *English Abbeys.* In that volume, he took a look at the design and construction of specific abbeys and also provided a social history of the church in England.

Braun was again well-reviewed after the publication of *The Story of the English House.* The book began with a photograph of a prehistoric hut and traced English housing all the way up to twentieth-century public housing. The *Times Literary Supplement* reviewer called it "a clear and interesting account of the development of the dwelling-house in England." Osbert Lancaster, writing in *Spectator,* drew attention to Braun's considerable skill as a writer: "He is invariably interesting, and his final chapter, wherein the whole of modern domestic architecture from Nash to Mendelssohn is wittily dealt with in half-a-dozen pages . . . represents a *tour de force* that can have few parallels in the whole *corpus* of architectural criticism."

BIOGRAPHICAL/CRITICAL SOURCES:

PERIODICALS

Booklist, July, 1936.
Books, September 15, 1940, p. 18.
Choice, March, 1972.
Christian Science Monitor, June 25, 1936, p. 18; August 10, 1940, p. 10.
Library Journal, October 15, 1971.
Manchester Guardian, May 26, 1936, p. 7; June 7, 1940, p. 7.
New Statesman & Nation, June 20, 1936.
New York Times, July 12, 1936, p. 22.
Spectator, August 2, 1940.
Springfield Republican, July 22, 1936, p. 10.
Times Literary Supplement, June 6, 1936, p. 479; July 6, 1940, p. 331; November 26, 1971, p. 1488.*

BREUER, Bessie 1893-1975

PERSONAL: Born October 19, 1893, in Cleveland, OH; died September 26, 1975; married Henry Varnum Poor III (an artist; deceased); children: Anne Poor Kahler, Peter Varnum. *Education:* Attended University of Missouri.

CAREER: Writer. Reporter for *St. Louis Times,* St. Louis, MO; editor, *New York Tribune,* New York, NY; national director of publicity, American Red Cross; staff member, *Ladies' Home Journal;* editor, *Charm* (magazine). *Military service:* Worked in Office of War Information during World War II.

AWARDS, HONORS: O. Henry Memorial Award, 1944, for short story "Home Is a Place."

WRITINGS:

Memory of Love, Simon & Schuster (New York City), 1935.
The Daughter, Simon & Schuster, 1938.
The Bracelet of Wavia Lea (short story collection), Sloane, 1947.
The Actress, Harper (New York City), 1957.
Take Care of My Roses, Atheneum (New York City), 1961.

Also author of play, *Sundown Beach,* produced at Actors Studio. Work appears in anthologies, including *Prize Stories: The O. Henry Awards,* 1944. Contributor of short stories and articles to *New Yorker, Harper's, Pictorial Review* and *Harper's Bazaar.* Breuer's novels have been translated for European publication.

ADAPTATIONS: Memory of Love was filmed as *In Name Only,* starring Cary Grant and Carole Lombard.

SIDELIGHTS: Bessie Breuer's novels and stories display an insight into the "shallow, sophisticated life of the fashionable beach and the smart hotel," as A. F. Wolfe noted in *Saturday Review of Literature.* Virgilia Peterson in the *New York Times Book Review* described Breuer's typical female characters as being "fluttering, wind-driven, lethal creatures."

In *Memory of Love,* a man sadly remembers an intense love affair that ended badly. "Breuer," wrote the critic for *Nation,* "has managed to condense into her short book such a terrific sense of the agonizing, yearning power of half-fulfilled love that it is more

affecting than a dozen well-executed novels." Currie Cabot in *Saturday Review of Literature* claimed that "Breuer's novel has an intensity and sharpness of life that is rare indeed." E. H. Walton in *Forum* called *Memory of Love* "an original and galvanizing book. Once read it will not be lightly forgotten."

The Daughter follows a troubled mother and daughter as they travel across America and Europe before settling for a few short weeks in a small Florida town. R. C. Feld in *Books* described *The Daughter* as "a powerful book, cxccllcnt in portraiture but repellent in portrait. It has the angular and piercing grace of the poetry of Auden and it probes and shatters conventional beauty with demoniac laughter." Although noting that the novel showed some "unevenness in the craftsmanship," Mina Curtiss in *Nation* claimed that "as a social document it says more to me, both explicitly and by implication, about the Florida landscape, about North versus South, rich versus poor, drunks, intellectuals, the whole contemporary American scene, than that much more adeptly written book *To Have and Have Not.*" Lucia Alzamora in *Saturday Review of Literature* found the book "a fully written, carefully though, deeply felt novel" and praised Breuer's "brilliant, unabashed writing."

The Actress concerns Joanna Trask, "an ambitious but insecure young woman who, in her professional and personal relationships, is confused and baffled by lack of script and direction," as Rose Feld explained in the *New York Herald Tribune Book Review.* While P. G. Anderson in *Library Journal* dubbed Trask "lifeless, dull in spite of her unconventionalities, superficial and boring," Kay Boyle in the *New York Times* found that "it is the human being's constant capacity for renewal which the author confirms in this rewarding book."

Take Care of My Roses tells the tragic story of Alma Salter, a highly emotional woman who takes her own life. The story is told by Ida, Alma's jealous housekeeper. The *Booklist* reviewer found the novel to be "subdued yet intense," while Peterson praised the story's "beautifully deft and prismatic manner."

BIOGRAPHICAL/CRITICAL SOURCES:

PERIODICALS

Atlantic Bookshelf, April, 1935.
Booklist, October 15, 1961.
Books, January 13, 1935, p. 3; April 17, 1938, p. 8.

Boston Transcript, May 7, 1938, p. 1.

Chicago Daily Tribune, January 12, 1935, p. 10.

Chicago Sunday Tribune, October 6, 1957, p. 4; November 12, 1961, p. 11.

Forum, March, 1935.

Kirkus, September 15, 1947; August 1, 1957; July 15, 1961.

Library Journal, October 15, 1957; September 15, 1961.

Nation, January 30, 1935; April 20, 1938.

New Republic, April 27, 1938.

New Yorker, November 8, 1947.

New York Herald Tribune Book Review, October 6, 1957, p. 3.

New York Herald Tribune Weekly Book Review, November 9, 1947, p. 6.

New York Times, January 13, 1935, p. 6; May 1, 1938, p. 6; November 23, 1947, p. 32; October 6, 1957, p. 4.

New York Times Book Review, October 1, 1961, p. 4.

San Francisco Chronicle, November 5, 1961, p. 31.

Saturday Review of Literature, January 12, 1935; April 16, 1938; November 29, 1947.

Springfield Republican, February 10, 1935, p. E7; May 1, 1938, p. E7; December 28, 1947, p. B7.

Time, April 18, 1938.

Times Literary Supplement, October 3, 1935, p. 613; January 14, 1939, p. 23.

Wilson Bulletin, October, 1938.

OBITUARIES:

PERIODICALS

New York Times, September 28, 1975.*

* * *

BREWSTER, Dorothy 1883-1979

PERSONAL: Born 1883, in St. Louis, MO; died April 17, 1979, in Lancaster, PA; daughter of William Morris and Lillie (Higbee) Brewster. *Education:* Barnard College, A.B., 1906; Columbia University, A.M., 1907, Ph.D., 1913.

CAREER: Barnard College, New York City, assistant in English, 1908-11; Bryn Mawr College, Bryn Mawr, PA, reader in English, 1914-15; Columbia University, New York City, 1915-50, began as instructor, became associate professor of English.

MEMBER: Modern Language Association of America, Women's Faculty Club (Columbia University), English-Speaking Union (New York).

WRITINGS:

Aaron Hill: Poet, Dramatist, Projector, Columbia University Press (New York City), 1913.

(With Angus Burrell) *Dead Reckonings in Fiction,* Longmans, Green (London), 1924.

(Editor) *A Book of Modern Short Stories,* Macmillan (New York City), 1928.

(With Burrell) *Adventure or Experience: Four Essays on Certain Writers and Readers of Novels,* Columbia University Press, 1930, reprinted, Arno (New York City), 1967.

(With Burrell) *Modern Fiction,* Columbia University Press, 1934.

(Editor) *Contemporary Short Stories,* Macmillan, 1937.

East-West Passage, Allen & Unwin, 1954.

Virginia Woolf's London, Allen & Unwin, 1959, New York University Press (New York City), 1960.

Virginia Woolf, New York University Press, 1962.

(With Burrell) *Modern World Fiction,* Littlefield, 1963.

Doris Lessing, Twayne (New York City), 1965.

William Brewster of the Mayflower: Portrait of a Pilgrim, New York University Press, 1968.

SIDELIGHTS: A specialist in modern fiction and short-story writing, Dorothy Brewster was a longtime member of the English faculty at Columbia University and the author of literary biographies and books on American literature.

Dead Reckonings in Fiction and *Modern Fiction* gather literary essays that Brewster wrote with colleague Angus Burrell. Modern fiction writers, including Chekhov, D. H. Lawrence and May Sinclair, are profiled in *Dead Reckonings in Fiction* and their fictional works examined in light of the authors' own experiences. Raymond Weaver in *Bookman* judged the book to be "a thrilling departure among books of literary criticism." The critic for the *Boston Transcript* believed that "this book of interpretations should prove worth reading as throwing upon the writers' efforts the additional illumination of two intelligent admirers." *Modern Fiction* focuses on novelists whose works represent specific trends in contemporary literature. Although he found some faults in the authors' approach to literature, especially their Freudian interpretations, Arthur

Livingston in *Nation* nonetheless praised the "elegance" of the writing and found Brewster and Burrell to be "agile, original, ingenious thinkers." "If the promotion of more and happier contacts between good authors and their readers is a measure of excellence in criticism," wrote J. H. Foster in *Library Quarterly,* "then *Modern Fiction* deserves warm praise."

Brewster's *Virginia Woolf's London* examines the role played by the city in the novels of Virginia Woolf. R. R. Rea in *Library Journal* called the study "a book of unique merit as literary criticism." The *Kirkus* reviewer found *Virginia Woolf's London* "a charmingly written book," while E. C. Dunn in the *New York Herald Tribune Book Review* dubbed it a "small but important book." Aileen Pippett of the *New York Times Book Review* explained that Brewster "writes with the modest sobriety of a scholar whose function is to stand aside while pointing out to students what they are supposed to see."

BIOGRAPHICAL/CRITICAL SOURCES:

PERIODICALS

Booklist, February, 1935.
Bookman, December, 1924.
Books, March 31, 1935, p. 10.
Boston Transcript, November 19, 1924, p. 7.
Catholic World, February, 1935.
Choice, June, 1966.
Guardian, November 27, 1959, p. 15.
Kirkus, December 15, 1959.
Library Journal, April 15, 1960.
Library Quarterly, April, 1935.
Literary Review, December 6, 1924, p. 4.
Nation, January 22, 1914; February 13, 1935.
New Republic, December 17, 1924.
New York Herald Tribune Book Review, April 24, 1960, p. 4.
New York Times, November 2, 1913; January 27, 1935, p. 18.
New York Times Book Review, May 8, 1960, p. 7.
New York World, November 30, 1924, p. E9.
Pratt, summer, 1935, p. 25.
Saturday Review, May 21, 1960; April 2, 1966.
Spectator, February 14, 1914.
Times Literary Supplement, January 15, 1960, p. 35.

OBITUARIES:

PERIODICALS

New York Times, April 28, 1979.*

BRICK, John 1922-1973

PERSONAL: Born January 1, 1922, in Newburgh, NY; died October 15, 1973; son of John T. and Elizabeth (Connell) Brick; married Mary Yakim, December 4, 1943; children: John W., Martha E., Janice A. (Mrs. Dennis Schreckengast). *Education:* Attended New York University and Columbia University. *Avocational interests:* Reading and fishing.

CAREER: Export Trade, New York City, managing editor, 1945-49; fulltime writer, 1950-60; *Life,* Book Division, New York City, staff writer, 1960-61; University of Toledo, Toledo, OH, assistant to the president, 1962-63; U.S. Senate Permanent Investigating Subcommittee, Washington, DC, professional staff member, 1963-73. *Military service:* U.S. Army Air Forces, World War II.

MEMBER: Authors Guild (vice-president).

AWARDS, HONORS: Farrar, Straus regional fellowship, 1950, for *Troubled Spring.*

WRITINGS:

Troubled Spring, Farrar, Straus (New York City), 1950.
The Raid, Farrar, Straus, 1951.
Homer Crist, Farrar, Straus, 1952.
The Rifleman, Doubleday (New York City), 1953.
The King's Rangers, Doubleday, 1954.
They Ran for Their Lives, Doubleday, 1954.
Eagle of Niagara (juvenile), Doubleday, 1955.
Jubilee, Doubleday, 1956.
Panther Mountain, Doubleday, 1958.
The Strong Men, Doubleday, 1959.
Gettysburg, Popular Library (New York City), 1960.
The Raid (juvenile), Duell, Sloan & Pearce, 1960.
Yankees on the Run (juvenile), Duell, Sloan & Pearce, 1961.
Tomahawk Trail (juvenile), Duell, Sloan & Pearce, 1962.
Captives of the Senecas (juvenile), Duell, Sloan & Pearce, 1963.
The Richmond Raid, Doubleday, 1963.
Ben Bryan, Morgan Rifleman, Duell, Sloan & Pearce, 1963.
Rogues' Kingdom, Doubleday, 1965.
They Fought for New York (juvenile), Putnam (New York City), 1965.
On the Old Frontier, Putnam, 1966.

Staff writer on *Life Picture Atlas* and *Life Nature Library*. Contributor of short stories to magazines.

ADAPTATIONS: The screen rights to Brick's first novel, *Troubled Spring,* were purchased by Metro-Goldwyn-Mayer.

SIDELIGHTS: John Brick's historical novels were set in the New York state of the nineteenth century. *Troubled Spring,* Brick's first novel, tells of a Union soldier during the Civil War who returns home to the farmlands of upper New York after spending time in the Confederate prison camp at Andersonville. He finds his girlfriend has married his brother, and his hometown has prospered on wartime profits. The critic for *Christian Science Monitor* noted "the soberness of the account and the honesty of the revolt against war." The reviewer for *Kirkus* pointed out the "taut narration and dramatic values." Lloyd Wendt, in his review for the *Chicago Sunday Tribune,* wrote: "Few pleasures rival that of a first meeting with a fine story-teller, and an acquaintance with John Brick is a great delight."

Homer Crist follows the career of a nineteenth century farmboy who grows up to become a United States congressman. The critic for the *New York Herald Tribune Book Review* called the book "much more than merely another historical chronicle." Edmund Fuller in the *Chicago Sunday Tribune* found that "Brick writes well of bitter family dissensions, of marital frustrations, and of the political arena."

The Rifleman and *King's Rangers* are set in New York state during the period of the American Revolution. *The Rifleman* is the story of Tim Murphy, a frontiersman who fought in the Revolution. "Brick has re-created a violent, turbulent, wandering roisterer, always the hero," according to the critic for the *New York Herald Tribune Book Review.* Richard Match in the *New York Times* called the book "an able and entertaining historical novel about one of the 'lost men of American history.'" *King's Rangers* is told from the point of view of British loyalists who fought in the forests of New York during the Revolution. As the critic for the *New York Herald Tribune Book Review* noted, Brick "succeeded very well in conveying the atmosphere of the times, the motives which impelled the revolutionary and Tory alike, and the customs and habits of the day." Henry Cavendish in the *New York Times* praised the book as "a finely woven account of the fratricidal days when families were divided and neighbor was split from neighbor."

BIOGRAPHICAL/CRITICAL SOURCES:

PERIODICALS

Booklist, December 1, 1952; May 1, 1953; March 1, 1954; December 15, 1954.
Bookmark, May, 1953; February, 1954; October, 1954.
Catholic World, August, 1953.
Chicago Sunday Tribune, April 23, 1950, p. 3; December 21, 1952, p. 7; April 19, 1953, p. 5; February 7, 1954, p. 3; September 12, 1954, p. 5.
Christian Science Monitor, May 13, 1950, p. 8.
Kirkus, April 15, 1950; September 15, 1952; March 1, 1953; December 1, 1953; July 1, 1954.
Library Journal, November 1, 1952; February 1, 1954.
New Yorker, November 29, 1952.
New York Herald Tribune Book Review, June 18, 1950, p. 17; November 30, 1952, p. 14; May 10, 1953, p. 13; May 2, 1954, p. 15.
New York Times, May 21, 1950, p. 27; January 4, 1953, p. 23; April 26, 1953, p. 28; February 14, 1954, p. 26; October 10, 1954, p. 37.
San Francisco Chronicle, April 25, 1954, p. 18.
Saturday Review, June 6, 1953; April 17, 1954.
Springfield Republican, May 24, 1953, p. C7.*

*   *   *

BRIGGS, Peter 1921-1975

PERSONAL: Born April 15, 1921, in St. Paul, MN; died July 18, 1975; son of Allan and Winifred (Douglas) Briggs; divorced; children: Andy. *Education:* University of Chicago, B.A., 1942.

CAREER: Worked in book advertising department at A. S. Barnes, and as promotion manager at Columbia University Press, Henry Holt, G. P. Putnam's Sons, John Day & Co., and Coward McCann, 1946-51; *Ladies' Home Journal,* New York City, articles editor, 1951-63; freelance writer, 1963-75. *Military service:* U.S. Navy, World War II; became ensign.

WRITINGS:

Water: The Vital Essence, Harper (New York City), 1967.
Men in the Sea, Simon & Schuster (New York City), 1968.

The Great Global Rift, Weybright (New York City), 1969.

Science Ship: A Voyage Aboard the Discoverer, Simon & Schuster, 1969.

Rivers in the Sea, Weybright, 1969.

Mysteries of the Sea, McKay (New York City), 1969.

Mysteries of Our World: Unanswered Questions about the Continents, the Seas, the Atmosphere, the Origins of Life, McKay, 1969.

Buccaneer Harbor: The Fabulous History of Port Royal, Jamaica, Simon & Schuster, 1970.

Laboratory at the Bottom of the World, McKay, 1970.

200,000,000 Years Beneath the Sea, Holt (New York City), 1971.

What Is the Grand Design?: The Story of Evolving Life and the Changing Planet on Which It Is Lived, McKay, 1973.

Will California Fall into the Sea?, McKay, 1973.

Rampage: The Story of Disastrous Floods, Broken Dams, and Human Fallibility, McKay, 1973.

Population Policy: The Social Dilemma, British Book Center, 1974.

SIDELIGHTS: Peter Briggs wrote a number of nonfiction books on scientific subjects, particularly on marine biology and oceanography. In several works, he recounted his own participation in seafaring research activities.

Briggs's *Men in the Sea* contains brief biographies of nine pioneering oceanographers and the story of the research submarine Alvin, which located a lost hydrogen bomb off the coast of Spain in 1966. Zena Sutherland in *Saturday Review* called the book "as stimulating as any adventure story," while "the stories of the exploits and explorations of the sea are spiced with danger, courage, and innovation." E. B. Garside in the *New York Times Book Review* opined: "Anyone with the least desire to become oriented in oceanography . . . will profit from the author's knowledgeable acquaintance."

Science Ship: A Voyage Aboard the Discoverer shares the highlights of Briggs's three-week cruise aboard a Coast Guard research ship. Told in diary fashion, the narrative was labeled "pleasant, quiet, vastly informative" by the critic for the *Christian Science Monitor*. A similar sea voyage is the subject of *200,000,000 Years Beneath the Sea*. Briggs accompanied the Glomar Challenger research vessel in 1968 as it engaged in the earliest deep sea drilling in the world, gathering in the process evidence for the theory of continental drift. "In popular language, this volume explains the activities and importance of the cruises of the Glomar Challenger," P. D. Thomas explained in *Library Journal*. The critic for the *New York Times Book Review* found that Briggs "knows his subject and has written about it very well."

Briggs turned to history with the book *Buccaneer Harbor: The Fabulous History of Port Royal, Jamaica*, an account of a major pirate stronghold in Jamaica in the seventeenth century. After a notorious run as a criminal headquarters, Port Royal suffered an earthquake which drove much of the small city into the sea. W. M. Levy in *Library Journal* called *Buccaneer Harbor* a "clear account of the spectacular demise" and "historically sound."

BIOGRAPHICAL/CRITICAL SOURCES:

PERIODICALS

Best Sellers, March 1, 1968; May 1, 1970.
Christian Science Monitor, May 15, 1969, p. 15.
Economist, September 2, 1972.
Library Journal, January 15, 1967; October 15, 1968; November 15, 1969; September 15, 1970; August, 1971.
New York Times Book Review, July 7, 1968, p. 16; February 6, 1972, p. 40.
Saturday Review, August 24, 1968.*

*   *   *

BRIGGS, Raymond Redvers 1934-

PERSONAL: Born January 18, 1934, in London, England; married Jean Taprell Clark (a painter), 1963. *Education:* Attended Wimbledon School of Art and Slade School of Fine Art. *Avocational interests:* Reading, gardening, growing fruit, and modern jazz.

ADDRESSES: Home—Sussex, England.

CAREER: Illustrator and author of books for children, 1957—. Part-time faculty member at Brighton College of Art, 1961—. *Military service:* British Army.

MEMBER: Society of Industrial Artists, Dairy Farmer's Association.

AWARDS, HONORS: Kate Greenaway Medal, runner-up, 1964, for *Fee Fi Fo Fum,* and winner, 1966, for *Mother Goose Treasury.*

WRITINGS:

SELF-ILLUSTRATED CHILDREN'S BOOKS

Midnight Adventure, Hamish Hamilton (London), 1961.

The Strange House, Hamish Hamilton, 1961.

Ring-a-Ring o' Roses, Coward (New York City), 1962.

Sledges to the Rescue, Hamish Hamilton, 1963.

The White Land: A Picture Book of Traditional Rhymes and Verses, Coward, 1963.

Fee Fi Fo Fum: A Picture Book of Nursery Rhymes, Coward, 1964.

(Editor) *The Mother Goose Treasury,* Coward, 1966.

Jim and the Beanstalk, Coward, 1970.

Father Christmas, Coward, 1973.

Father Christmas Goes on Holiday, Coward, 1975.

Fungus the Bogeyman, Hamish Hamilton, 1977.

When the Wind Blows, Schocken Books (New York City), 1982.

The Tin-Pot Foreign General and the Old Iron Woman, Hamish Hamilton, 1984.

The Party, Little, Brown, 1985.

(With Mitsumasa Anno) *All in a Day,* Philomel Books (New York City), 1986.

The Bear, Random House (New York City), 1994.

The Man, Random House, 1995.

"SNOWMAN" SERIES

The Snowman, Random House, 1978.

Building the Snowman, Little, Brown (Boston), 1985.

Dressing Up, Hamish Hamilton, 1985.

Walking in the Air, Little, Brown, 1985.

Snowman Pop-up, Hamish Hamilton, 1986.

The Snowman Storybook, Random House, 1990.

The Snowman Tell-the-Time Book, Hamish Hamilton, 1991.

The Snowman: Things to Touch and Feel, See and Sniff, Random House, 1994.

ILLUSTRATOR

(With others) Julian Sorell Huxley, *Wonderful World of Life,* Doubleday (New York City), 1958.

Ruth Manning-Sanders, *Peter and the Piskies,* Oxford University Press (London), 1958, Roy (New York City), 1966.

Alfred Leo Duggan, *Look at Castles,* Hamish Hamilton, 1960, published as *The Castle Book,* Pantheon (New York City), 1961.

A. L. Duggan, *Arches and Spires,* Hamish Hamilton, 1961, Pantheon, 1962.

Jacynth Hope-Simpson, editor, *Hamish Hamilton Book of Myths and Legends,* Hamish Hamilton, 1964.

William Mayne, *Whistling Rufus,* Hamish Hamilton, 1964, Dutton (New York City), 1965.

Manning-Sanders, editor, *Hamish Hamilton Book of Magical Beasts,* Hamish Hamilton, 1965, published as *A Book of Magical Beasts,* Thomas Nelson (Camden, NJ), 1970.

James Aldridge, *The Flying 19,* Hamish Hamilton, 1966.

Bruce Carter, *Jimmy Murphy and the White Duesenberg,* Coward, 1968.

Carter, *Nuvolari and the Alpha Romeo,* Coward, 1968.

Nicholas Fisk, *Lindbergh: The Lone Flier,* Coward, 1968.

Fisk, *Richtofen: The Red Baron,* Coward, 1968.

Mayne, editor, *The Hamish Hamilton Book of Giants,* Hamish Hamilton, 1968, published as *William Mayne's Book of Giants,* Dutton, 1969.

Michael Brown, *Shackleton's Epic Voyage,* Coward, 1969.

Elfrida Vipont Foulds, *The Elephant and the Bad Baby,* Coward, 1969.

Showell Styles, *First up Everest,* Coward, 1969.

James Reeves, *The Christmas Book,* Dutton, 1970.

Ian Serraillier, *The Tale of Three Landlubbers,* Hamish Hamilton, 1970, Coward, 1971.

Virginia Haviland, editor, *The Fairy Tale Treasury,* Coward, 1972.

Manning-Sanders, editor, *Festivals,* Heinemann (London), 1972, Dutton, 1973.

OTHER

When the Wind Blows (screenplay; based on Briggs' book of the same title), Film Four, 1986.

ADAPTATIONS: The Snowman was filmed by Weston Woods Studios in 1982.

SIDELIGHTS: Raymond Redvers Briggs uses the medium of children's picture books for his radical social commentary. Focusing on such subjects as nuclear war, nationalism, racial intolerance and government wrong-doing, Briggs offsets the harsh, controversial messages of his stories with cartoon-like formats and visual humor. A critic in *Books for Your*

Children praises Briggs' "glorious early picture books for very young children," while noting that "it is his lively picture strip books that have been most innovative."

Perhaps Briggs' most popular books are those in the Snowman series, in which the author presents a snowman who comes to life and his adventures with the little boy who created him. "Here there is no hint of social criticism," remarks Suzanne Rahn in *Lion and the Unicorn.* The *Publishers Weekly* critic finds the first book in the series, *The Snowman,* to be "incomparably sweet, touching and funny . . . with all the depth and breadth of a novel." A reviewer for the *Economist* calls it Briggs' "great classic."

In *Fungus the Bogeyman* Briggs' creates an entire imaginary world alternative to the everyday world. It is, according to Rahn, "Briggs's most deeply fantastic book for children and his most startling." As Geoff Fox describes it in the *Times Educational Supplement,* "the story of *Fungus the Bogeyman* is little more than a thread we follow through the underworld which is Bogeydom. Here live Fungus, his wife Mildew, little Mould and the whole bogey community, relishing the 'fetid darkness,' dirt, slime and smells." Russell Davies, writing in the *Times Literary Supplement,* notes that *Fungus the Bogeyman* is "an obsessive monologue on decay" and finds it "peculiarly disgusting" for its "anal-erotic preoccupations." But Margery Fisher, writing in *Growing Point,* concludes that *Fungus the Bogeyman* "is in fact a highly intellectual book."

Briggs' turns to nuclear holocaust in *When the Wind Blows,* the story of a quiet retired couple, the Bloggs, as they face atomic war. As Christopher Lehmann-Haupt puts it in his review for the *New York Times,* "Armageddon comes, and we are in a place to which no picture book has ever taken us before." The Bloggs carry on gamely in the face of socictal breakdown following a nuclear strike by the Soviet Union, seemingly oblivious to both the disaster's source or consequences. Penelope Mesic in the *Bulletin of the Atomic Scientists* notes that "it would make devastating reading for anyone so young or innocent as to lack a protective cynicism. . . . The tone of the narrative is bitterly ironic."

In *The Man* Briggs' presents the story of a young boy confronted by an unwanted guest—a miniature man, naked, cold, and hungry, who demands to be cared for. While young John seeks to please his demanding, rude guest, and keep him secret from his parents, the man disrupts his life with his thoughtless behavior. The visitor, writes Peter F. Neumeyer in *Horn Book,* "arrives, says he's cold, demands food, urinates, warms himself, bathes, eats again, demands toilet paper, and climbs to the roof to defecate. . . . Aside from his stench of carnality, Briggs's Man is by turns arrogant, vain, peremptory, maudlin, whining, frightened. He is xenophobic . . . and racist." The story, Susan Dove Lempke explains in *Booklist,* "touches on subjects ranging from politics and religion to philosophy." "Though the characters' conversations touch on some worthy issues (self-image, identity, tolerance and diversity), it's a lot for kids to sort out," writes the critic for *Publishers Weekly.*

BIOGRAPHICAL/CRITICAL SOURCES:

BOOKS

Children's Literature Review, Volume 10, Gale (Detroit), 1986.
Hopkins, Lee Bennett, *Books Are by People,* Citation, 1969.
Moss, Elaine, *Picture Books for Young People,* Thimble Press, 1981, pp. 31-35.

PERIODICALS

Booklist, February 1, 1974, pp. 595, 598; January 1, 1976, p. 622; November 1, 1978, p. 474; February 1, 1995, p. 1008; February 1, 1996, p. 931.
Book Report, September-October, 1983, p. 55.
Books and Bookmen, November, 1984, pp. 22-23.
Books for Your Children, autumn, 1976, p. 6; autumn-winter, 1980, pp. 22-23; summer, 1982, p. 21; autumn-winter, 1982, pp. 32-33.
Book Week, January 19, 1964, p. 16.
Book Window, winter, 1978, p. 13; spring, 1980, p. 22.
Boston Review, September, 1985, p. 27.
British Book News, January, 1985, p. 47.
British Book News Children's Supplement, autumn, 1980, p. 12; autumn, 1982, p. 3.
Bulletin of the Atomic Scientists, February, 1983, pp. 39-40.
Bulletin of the Center for Children's Books, February, 1983, p. 103.
Catholic Library World, September, 1979, pp. 91-92.
Children's Book Review, December, 1973, p. 170.
Commonweal, May 24, 1963; November 15, 1963; November 6, 1964; November 20, 1970.

Economist, December 1, 1984, p. 110; November 26, 1994, p. 101.

Growing Point, April, 1963, p. 130; September, 1970, p. 1577; December, 1973, p. 2301; December, 1975, p. 2774; July, 1978, pp. 3368-3369; November, 1978, p. 3425; May, 1980, pp. 3708-3709.

Horn Book, December, 1964; February, 1971, p. 42; December, 1973, p. 583; February, 1980, pp. 96-103; March-April, 1995, p. 182; May-June, 1996, p. 315.

Junior Bookshelf, July, 1963, p. 129; October, 1970, p. 277; December, 1973, pp. 377-378; August, 1974, pp. 195-196; April, 1976, pp. 80-81; August, 1980, pp. 166-167.

Kirkus Reviews, September 15, 1970, p. 1027.

Library Journal, October 15, 1962; November 15, 1963; November 15, 1964.

Lion and the Unicorn, Volumes 7 and 8, 1983-84, pp. 5-19.

New Statesman, November 6, 1970.

New Yorker, November 24, 1962.

New York Times, September 14, 1982, p. C7.

New York Times Book Review, November 11, 1962, p. 62; November 10, 1963; November 8, 1970.

Observer, October 2, 1977, p. 25; November 27, 1977, p. 29.

Publishers Weekly, November 5, 1973, pp. 12-13; October 9, 1978, p. 76; November 14, 1994, p. 66; October 2, 1995, p. 73.

Saturday Review, October 24, 1970.

School Library Journal, March, 1971, p. 116; October, 1975, pp. 78-81.

Signal, September, 1973, p. 163; January, 1979.

Times Educational Supplement, November 18, 1977, p. 35; May 23, 1980, p. 29; October 31, 1980, p. 24; June 11, 1982, p. 41; November 19, 1982, p. 36.

Times Literary Supplement, November 23, 1962, p. 905; November 28, 1963, p. 972; November 26, 1964, p. 1064; October 16, 1969; October 30, 1970, p. 1261; December 2, 1977, p. 1412; October 3, 1984, p. 1139.

Voice of Youth Advocates, June, 1983, p. 101.

Wilson Library Bulletin, April, 1979, p. 576; March, 1980, pp. 456-457.

* * *

BRIGHT, John M. 1908-1995

PERSONAL: Born September 25, 1908, in Chattanooga, TN; died in 1995; son of John (a business-

man) and Elizabeth (Nall) Bright; married Carrie Lena McMullen, July 28, 1938; children: Charles Crawford, Robert Nall. *Education:* Presbyterian College, B.A., 1928; Union Theological Seminary, Richmond, VA, B.D., 1931, Th.M., 1933; Johns Hopkins University, Ph.D., 1940. *Religion:* Presbyterian.

CAREER: Ordained Presbyterian minister, Atlanta, GA, 1935. First Presbyterian Church, Durham, NC, assistant pastor, 1936-37; Catonsville Presbyterian Church, Baltimore, MD, pastor, 1937-40; Union Theological Seminary, Richmond, VA, professor of Hebrew and interpretation of Old Testament, beginning 1940. *Military service:* U.S. Army, served overseas as chaplain, 1943-46; became captain.

MEMBER: Society of Biblical Literature and Exegesis, American Oriental Society, Biblical Colloquium.

AWARDS, HONORS: D.D. degree from Presbyterian College, 1947; Abingdon-Cokesbury Award for *The Kingdom of God,* 1953.

WRITINGS:

The Kingdom of God: The Biblical Concept and Its Meaning for the Church, Abingdon (Nashville), 1953.

(Contributor) *The Interpreter's Bible,* Abingdon, 1953.

Early Israel in Recent History Writing, S.C.M. Press, 1956.

A History of Israel, Westminster (Philadelphia), 1959.

Jeremiah, Doubleday (Garden City, NY), 1965.

The Authority of the Old Testament, Abingdon, 1967.

Covenant and Promise: The Prophetic Understanding of the Future in Pre-Exilic Israel, Westminster, 1976.

Contributor to *Interpreter's Dictionary of the Bible, Hastings Dictionary of the Bible, Religion in Geschichte und Gegenwart,* and to professional journals.

SIDELIGHTS: John M. Bright was a prominent theologian whose books dealt with biblical interpretation as well as the history of Isreal.

Bright's first book, *The Kingdom of God: The Biblical Concept and Its Meaning for the Church,* concerned the idea of the Kingdom of God as found in both the Old and New Testaments, tracing the development of the idea from Abraham to St. John. The *Library Journal*'s E. H. Weeks recommended the book "for public libraries with mature readers interested in theology, for ministers, and for college, university, and theological libraries." W. E. Garrison in *Christian Century* found: "Bright's development of his thesis often brings to mind the great sweep of Augustine's philosophy of history—and this is high praise."

History of Israel begins in prehistory and continues through the Old Testament. The *Booklist* critic noted that Bright's history gives "equal attention to political and religious events." While A. A. Greenbaum in *Library Journal* called the book "a much-needed, up-to-date handbook aimed at the English-speaking student," the critic for the *Times Literary Supplement* believed it to be a work of "high scholarly excellence." James Mullenburg in *Christian Century* described *History of Israel* as "a book which no student of the Bible can afford to ignore. . . . The book is written in a clear, lively and engaging style."

In *The Authority of the Old Testament* Bright dealt with the fundamental questions of biblical authority, aiming his discussion at ministers who might handle the topic in sermons. As the *Times Literary Supplement* critic explained, Bright "is constrained to propose a method which does not impair the authority of the Old Testament and at the same time draws from it a message applicable to the convinced Christian." "Bright's work," N. C. Habel wrote in *Christian Century,* "is a brilliant and powerful summons for new works in biblical theology." The *Choice* reviewer concluded that *The Authority of the Old Testament* "is a serious study of importance to anyone concerned with the role and authority of the Hebrew scriptures within the Christian church."

BIOGRAPHICAL/CRITICAL SOURCES:

PERIODICALS

Booklist, February 15, 1960.
Bookmark, November, 1953.
Chicago Sunday Tribune, December 13, 1953, p. 8.
Choice, April, 1968.
Christian Century, October 21, 1953; October 12, 1960; November 15, 1967.
Guardian, November 4, 1960.
Kirkus, November 1, 1953; December 1, 1959.
Library Journal, November 15, 1953; November 1, 1959.
New York Times, October 25, 1953, p. 46.

Times Literary Supplement, September 9, 1960, p. 581; February 1, 1968, p. 115.*

* * *

BRIGHT, Robert (Douglas, Sr.) 1902-1988 (Michael Douglas)

PERSONAL: Born August 5, 1902, in Sandwich, MA; died of cancer, November 21, 1988, in San Francisco, CA; son of Edward and Blanche (Denio) Bright; married Katherine Eastman Bailey; children: two. *Education:* Princeton University, B.A., 1923.

CAREER: Author and illustrator. Reporter and editor for newspapers, including *Baltimore Sun* and *Paris Time;* also worked in advertising.

WRITINGS:

The Travels of Ching, W. R. Scott (New York City), 1943.
The Life and Death of Little Jo, Doubleday (New York City), 1944, published as *Little Jo,* Cresset Press (London), 1948.
The Intruders, Doubleday, 1946.
The Olivers: The Story of an Artist and His Family, Doubleday, 1947.
Me and the Bears, Doubleday, 1951.
Richard Brown and the Dragon, Doubleday, 1952.
(With Dorothy Brett) *Hurrah for Freddie!,* Doubleday, 1953.
Miss Pattie, Doubleday, 1954.
I Like Red, Doubleday, 1955.
The Spirit of the Chase (illustrated by Mircea Vasiliu), Scribner, 1956.
The Friendly Bear, Doubleday, 1957, reprinted, 1971.
My Red Umbrella, Morrow (New York City), 1959.
(Under pseudonym Michael Douglas) *Round, Round World* (poems), Golden Press (New York City), 1960.
My Hopping Bunny (poems), Doubleday, 1960.
Which Is Willy?, Doubleday, 1962.
Gregory: The Nosiest and Strongest Boy in Grangers Grove, Doubleday, 1969.

"GEORGIE" SERIES

Georgie, Doubleday, 1944.
Georgie to the Rescue, Doubleday, 1956.
Georgie's Halloween, Doubleday, 1958.

Georgie and the Robbers, Doubleday, 1963.
Georgie and the Magician, Doubleday, 1966.
Georgie and the Noisy Ghost, Doubleday, 1971.
Georgie Goes West, Doubleday, 1973.
Georgie's Christmas Carol, Doubleday, 1975.
Georgie and the Buried Treasure, Doubleday, 1979.
Georgie and the Baby Birds, Doubleday, 1983.
Georgie and the Runaway Balloon, Doubleday, 1983.
Georgie and the Ball of Yarn, Doubleday, 1983.
Georgie and the Little Dog, Doubleday, 1983.

ADAPTATIONS: Georgie and *Georgie to the Rescue* were filmed. Composer J. Donald Robb adapted *The Life and Death of Little Joe* as an opera which premiered in Albuquerque, NM.

SIDELIGHTS: Robert Bright was most widely known as the author and illustrator of more than twenty books for children. He was especially known for his numerous stories about Georgie the Ghost, ranging from *Georgie* in 1944 to *Georgie and the Little Dog* in 1983. Although, as Patrick Groff noted in *Twentieth-Century Children's Writers,* Bright's work "is seldom referred to in any serious discussion of children's literature," his books have always enjoyed "enthusiastic endorsements from young children."

The Georgie books "are pleasant distortions of reality about a wise and brave but altogether gentle little ghost, named Georgie, who resides, unknown to them, with a rather docile and witless old couple," explained Groff. Georgie began life in stories Bright told his own children. He then drew pictures to accompany the stories—"scrawly and droll" pictures, according to E. L. Buell in the *New York Times.* According to a critic for the *Saturday Review of Literature,* "the pictures, in a dark, mysterious blue ink, are quite as amusing as the story and quite as pleasantly ghostly." Writing in the *New York Herald Tribune Book Review,* M. S. Libby noted one reason for Georgie's popularity with young readers. He has, she wrote, "an endearing shyness shared and appreciated by many of the very young who love to hear of his doings." Georgie's heroics were also popular. In each book, Georgie "heroically undertakes to set to rights some villainous action or unfortunate mishap," Groff explained.

BIOGRAPHICAL/CRITICAL SOURCES:

BOOKS

Twentieth-Century Children's Writers, 4th edition, St. James Press (Detroit), 1995.

PERIODICALS

Booklist, July 1, 1953; June 15, 1955; April 15, 1956; September 15, 1956.
Bookmark, November, 1955.
Book Week, February 13, 1944; October 15, 1944.
Boston Globe, November 29, 1944.
Chicago Sunday Tribune, May 10, 1953; June 3, 1956, p. 4; August 26, 1956; October 26, 1958.
Christian Science Monitor, May 14, 1953; July 28, 1955; October 23, 1958.
Horn Book, June, 1953; August, 1955; June, 1956.
Kirkus, August 15, 1944; April 15, 1953; June 1, 1955; March 1, 1956; July 1, 1956.
Library Journal, September 15, 1944; June 1, 1953; June 15, 1955; June 1, 1956; August, 1956; January 15, 1959.
New Yorker, February 19, 1944; November 24, 1956.
New York Herald Tribune Book Review, July 17, 1955; May 13, 1956, p. 12; August 12, 1956; October 19, 1958.
New York Times, February 6, 1944; September 10, 1944; May 10, 1953; April 29, 1956, p. 32; September 2, 1956; October 26, 1958.
San Francisco Chronicle, July 24, 1955; May 20, 1956, p. 17; September 16, 1956.
Saturday Review, October 17, 1953; April 21, 1956; August 25, 1956; October 25, 1958.
Saturday Review of Literature, February 12, 1944; October 21, 1944.
Weekly Book Review, February 6, 1944.

OBITUARIES:

PERIODICALS

New York Times, December 3, 1988.
Washington Post, December 5, 1988.*

*   *   *

BRIN, David 1950-

PERSONAL: Born October 6, 1950, in Glendale, CA; son of Herbert (an editor) and Selma (a teacher) Brin; married Cheryl Ann Bringham (a doctor of cosmochemistry), March, 1991. *Education:* California Institute of Technology, B.S. (Astronomy), 1972; University of California, San Diego, M.S., 1979, Ph.D. (Applied Physics and Space Science), 1981. *Avocational interests:* Backpacking, music, science, and "general eclecticism."

ADDRESSES: Home—11625 Montana, Number 9, Los Angeles, CA 90049-4676. *Office*—Heritage Press, 2130 South Vermont Ave., Los Angeles, CA 90007. *Agent*—Richard Curtis Associates, Inc., 164 East 64th St., New York, NY 10021.

CAREER: Hughes Aircraft Research Laboratories, Newport Beach and Carlsbad, CA, electrical engineer in semiconductor device development, 1973-77; managing editor, *Journal of the Laboratory of Comparative Human Cognition,* 1979-80; Heritage Press, Los Angeles, book reviewer and science editor, 1980—. San Diego State University, teacher of physics and writing, 1982-85; post-doctoral research fellow, California Space Institute, La Jolla, CA, 1983-86; Westfield College, University of London, visiting artist, 1986-87.

MEMBER: Science Fiction Writers of America (secretary, 1982-84), Planetary Society, British Interplanetary Society.

AWARDS, HONORS: John W. Campbell Award nomination, 1982, for best new author; Balrog Award, 1984, for *The Practice Effect;* Locus Award, Locus Publications, 1984, for *Startide Rising,* and 1986, for *The Postman,* and 1988, for *The Uplift War;* Nebula Award, Science Fiction Writers of America, 1984, for *Startide Rising;* Hugo Award, World Science Fiction Convention, 1984, for *Startide Rising,* and 1985, for the short story "The Crystal Spheres", and 1988, for *The Uplift War;* John W. Campbell Memorial Award, 1986, for *The Postman.* American Library Association Best Books for Young Adults citation, 1986, for *The Postman;* Nebula Award nomination, Science Fiction Writers of America, 1986, for *The Postman,* and 1988, for *The Uplift War;* Hugo Award nomination, World Science Fiction Convention, 1986, for *The Postman.*

WRITINGS:

Sundiver (futuristic murder mystery), Bantam (New York City), 1980.
Startide Rising (science fiction novel; first printed in a shorter version in *Analog* magazine as the novella *The Tides of Kithrup*), Bantam, 1983, revised hardcover edition, Phantasia Press (West Bloomfield, MI), 1985.
The Practice Effect (novel), Bantam, 1984.
The Postman, Bantam, 1985.
(With Gregory Benford) *Heart of the Comet,* Bantam, 1986.

The River of Time (short stories, contains "The Crystal Spheres"), Dark Harvest, 1986.
The Uplift War (novel, sequel to *Startide Rising*), Phantasia Press, 1987.
Dr. Pak's Preschool (novella, illustrated by Alan Giana), Cheap Street (New Castle, VA), 1989.
Earth, Bantam, 1990.
Glory Season (novel), Bantam, 1993.
Brightness Reef: Book One of the New Uplift Trilogy, Bantam, 1995.
Infinity's Shore: Book Two of the New Uplift Trilogy, Bantam, 1996.
Heaven's Reach: The Final Book of the New Uplift Trilogy, Bantam, 1998.
The Transparent Society: Will Technology Force Us to Choose between Privacy and Freedom, Addison-Wesley (Reading, MA), 1998.

Also author with T. Kuiper of *Extraterrestrial Civilization* (non-fiction/science), 1989; author with Poul Anderson, Breg Bear, and Gregory Benford of *Murasaki,* 1993; and author of *Otherness: Collected Stories by a Modern Master of Science Fiction,* 1994, and *Earthclan,* 1986.

OTHER

Contributor to *Far Frontiers,* Baen, 1985; and *Thinking Robots, an Aware Internet, and Cyberpunk Librarians: The 1992 LITA President's Program: Presentations by Hans Moravec, Bruce Sterling, and David Brin,* Library of Information Technology (Chicago), 1992; Also contributor of articles and stories to scientific journals, including *Astrophysical Journal,* and popular magazines, including *Analog* and *Asaac Asimov's Science Fiction Magazine.*

ADAPTATIONS: A film adaptation of *The Postman,* directed by and starring Kevin Costner, was released by Warner Bros. in 1997. The novella *The Loom of Thessaly* has been recorded on audio cassette by Off-Centaur Press.

SIDELIGHTS: When *Sundiver,* the first novel by astrophysicist David Brin, was published, few if any science fiction fans were familiar with its author's name. But his second book, *Startide Rising,* quickly gained Brin fame as one of the genre's best young writers. Sweeping the field's major awards, this 1983 novel won the Hugo for its popularity among readers, and the Nebula for impressing the critics. Brin also won numerous other awards, including the John

W. Campbell Memorial Award for Best Novel for *The Postman,* one of his contributions to mainstream fiction.

Though Brin's first two novels were most commended by the science-fiction community, the ideas and ethical concerns they explore have earned them recognition from outside the genre, say reviewers Debra Rae Cohen of *Voice Literary Supplement* and Donald M. Hassler of *Science Fiction and Fantasy Book Review.* At home on both sides of that boundary, the novels also provide "space opera characteristics," notes Hassler. Both *Sundiver* and *Startide Rising* are set in the Progenitors universe, which teems with inhabited galaxies and their numerous races, complicated by conflicts and technological problems on an epic scale. The most intelligent races in its five galaxies believe they were "uplifted" to sapience through the efforts of an elder but now-missing species, and that it is their duty to use genetic engineering to raise other species to the status of participants in their culture. "Some of these 'Galactics' are moderates; other races appear fanatical to a beleaguered humanity," Brin once told *CA.* Without the presumably necessary aid of patrons, humans had achieved the ability to travel in space and to "uplift" dolphins and chimpanzees. Such audacity must be checked, believe the "fanatics," who fight each other for the right to "adopt" the humans into a remedial retraining program.

Brin further explained to *CA* his thoughts when creating his Progenitor universe: "I wanted to explore [genetic engineering, specifically] the ethical problems involved in changing more sophisticated creatures such as dolphins or apes, to give them the capabilities to become fellow-citizens in our culture. Do we have the right to meddle with species that have their own dignity? There are serious ethical questions about this whole matter of uplift, of being patrons of a client species. We'll face these questions in the real world in just a few years. . . . .I [also] wanted to come up with a scenario in which a civilization would be possible in the galaxy which would have conservation of so-called 'nursery worlds' like the earth as a paramount objective. . . . . It's basically a 'gedanken-experiment' or thought experiment. One role of SF is to explore the limits of an idea."

Sundiver introduces this universe; *Startide Rising,* taking place two centuries later, shows the Earth ship *Streaker* pursued by aliens and grounded on the water-world planet of Kithrup for repairs. The few

humans aboard are observers of the ship's crew, a team of uplifted dolphins who speak in a poetic language akin to haiku, which Brin indicated to *CA* was derived primarily from his imagination—"it comes straight from the back of [my] skull." "Each of Brin's dolphins is a distinct and unique individual, without ever losing an essential dolphinity," writes Stephen B. Brown in a *Washington Post Book World* review. In Brown's opinion, "the care and empathy with which Brin describes the relationships between his aquatic characters elevates this book into a substantial achievement." Brown commends the author for skillfully weaving "the byzantine intrigues of . . . various dolphin factions" while consistently developing "the idea that a viable human/dolphin collaboration can be something greater than each race on its own."

"Brin's toying with the vision of evolution is probably the strongest feature in both books," Hassler remarks. Brin's "notion of managed development" as opposed to natural selection, "which by contrast seems blind, [and] inefficient," says Hassler, allows the author to examine ethical problems that result from the subordination of uplifted species to their patrons, and the universal search for the Progenitors, the supposed first species, as well. Hassler comments, "Such tales of origins and the running debate between [Charles] Darwin and [Erich] Von Daniken are truly sublime." Whereas most reviewers praised *Startide Rising*'s fast-paced action and complex plot, *Minneapolis Tribune* contributor D. R. Martin expressed his wish that "someone—Brin or his editor—had tightened things up along the way." Brin revised the book extensively for its hardcover printing in 1985, a reissue *Publishers Weekly* dubbed "an SF event."

Because he feels that the creation of fictional worlds can foster egotistic and "self-indulgent" writing, Brin explained to *CA* interviewer Jean W. Ross that he limits himself to write no more than two books in a row about any given universe. Consequently, he interrupted the telling of the story of the search for the Progenitors with a third novel in a lighter vein. In *The Practice Effect,* he gives indulgence full play, venting "all the bad puns" that don't belong, as he told Ross, in the "more serious work." "*The Practice Effect* [is] a light adventure-fantasy and romance which is accessible to bright children," Brin relayed to *CA,* "I decided to have some fun with a strict formula piece that was completely self-indulgent. . . . It's a romp, it's fun."

Accordingly, reviewers find *The Practice Effect* an enjoyable time-travel romance in the tradition of Mark Twain's *A Connecticut Yankee in King Arthur's Court.* Perhaps not surprisingly, in an interview with *CA* Brin named Twain one of the "many . . . old masters" who greatly influence him. Like Twain's "Yankee," Brin's Dennis Nuel enters a strange world, rescues a princess, defeats a formidable enemy and contributes to progress by virtue of skills that would be considered quite ordinary at home. This formula has been used often since Twain wrote the prototype, say reviewers, but Brin gives it a new twist: Nuel finds himself in a world where repeated use improves objects instead of wearing them out. Sequences showing what many simple objects become as the result of "practice" (flint knives become super-sabers; a zipper becomes a saw) are interlaced with Nuel's adventures "which can only be called rollicking," writes Baird Searles in *Isaac Asimov's Science Fiction Magazine.* Adding to the fun are sometimes slant references to "the great moments of SF history," notes the reviewer, who believes that "the high spirits and inventiveness" of the practice "more than compensate" for the plot's occasional "repetitiveness" and the author's somewhat "collegiate" humor.

Brin gives a new treatment to another branch of fiction with *The Postman,* his portrayal of life in North America after nuclear world war. Unlike other post-apocalypse novels that bemoan total destruction, *The Postman* depicts what Brin told Ross is "the real horror of such a war"—the prospect of surviving in a holocaust-ravaged environment. As Brin explained to *CA:* "The real horror, to me, is not death and destruction. We've had that all our lives, and for thousands of years. If the curtain is all coming down, a la *On the Beach,* then it's all over; nobody suffers anymore. But it strikes me as more likely that some of our descendants would survive even the worst nuclear war, and they would probably go back to living like Michael Landon in 'Little House on the Prairie.' But they would not be as happy as our pioneer forebears. They would be fundamentally scarred forever because of one fact: they would know how close we came to a sane, decent, better world, and that might-have-been would haunt them."

"The world Brin draws [in *The Postman*] is terrifying," says *Los Angeles Times Book Review* contributor Ronald Florence, referring to the power-hungry paramilitary bands that tyrannize people who live in small, unprotected settlements. Stripped by the bandits, protagonist Gordon Krantz finds a mail carrier's remains and borrows the dead postman's uniform. Thereafter, the villagers see him "as a symbol of civilization," relates *Washington Post Book World*'s Gregory Frost. Maintaining ever-larger lies about his identity, Krantz accepts the role of public servant and civil authority they ascribe to him. The story develops "Brin's premise that people need something bigger than survival to believe in," notes a *New York Times Book Review* contributor. *Analog*'s Tom Easton finds it a recommendable demonstration of "the value of myths." Like other reviewers, Frost notes several "weaknesses" he later deems "minor," and praises the "mythic dimension" Brin brings to almost every element of the novel."

When discussing the benefits of writing fiction of different lengths, Brin described why *The Postman* has "a mythical tone": "I feel I get different things from the three different lengths. The short stories are attempts at epiphanies, at making a ringing note that will hang in the reader's ear, like the effect Joyce achieved in his smaller works. It's like a painting; you take it all in. My large novels, on the other hand, tend to be very complicated. They're explorations of many ideas, woven together trying to make a complex tapestry. In between is the length known as the novella, which happens to be my favorite. This length allows one to explore a mythic theme that one can't afford to muddy up with all sorts of complexities. This is the length that I believe is right for legend. And I think this helps explain why *The Postman,* of all of my novels, has more of a mythic feel to it; it actually is made up of three separate novellas." *The Postman* was later adapted into a motion picture, directed by and starring actor Kevin Costner; it was released in 1997.

If these books—*Sundiver, Startide Rising, The Practice Effect,* and *The Postman*—prove that Brin finds the science fiction category a bit too confining, his next book, *The Heart of the Comet,* say Chicago *Tribune Books* reviewers James and Eugene Sloan, confirms his place among those writers "who are busy putting the hard science back into science fiction." Works in the genre drifted toward "softer" speculation and fantasy during the past decade, John R. Cramer reports in the *Los Angeles Times.* However, he notes with pleasure, that then-NASA scientist Brin and co-author Gregory Benford present "accurate physics and biology" when narrating the conditions that threaten a crew of scientists as they ride Halley's Comet to the farthest point of its range and try to move it into an orbit closer to earth. Recounting his long distance collaboration with Gregory

Benford, Brin described to *CA* how the book was organized: "We carefully outlined the book, divided it up among three points of view represented by three characters whose scenes alternated through the book. Benford took one character and wrote all of that person's scenes; I took another character and all of his scenes. We took turns with the third. It resulted in a very different voice for each character. It was a most intriguing, interesting experiment, and, I feel, a successful one." Applause from the critics included the Sloans's remark that *Heart of the Comet* "may well be the masterpiece of [the hard science revival]. . . . Light years ahead of [Carl] Sagan's rival effort, this book is what science fiction is."

In *The Uplift War,* Brin goes back to the universe of his first two novels for a closer look at uplifted chimpanzees as they relate to humans in the struggle to rebuild an ecologically damaged planet while trying to resist alien invaders. "It's a very large book— 220,000 words—and not so much a sequel as a parallel volume [to *Startide*]," Brin explained to *CA:* "I had a good time with the book. It's more fun than *Startide,* less ethereal. The apes get a little gritty at times. There's a scene in which a riot breaks out in a blue-collar, working chimps' bar. I think readers might like that." Brin's message, observes Easton, is the positive value of a sense of humor. "Humans and neochimps and Tymbrimi [a race of alien pranksters] together defeat [their attackers] and score massive points in the Uplift culture with the aid of one of the grandest jokes in galactic history," relates Easton, who finds Brin's handling of the Uplift concept enjoyable, his plots satisfying, and his ideas "beautifully" developed.

1993 would see the publication of *Glory Season,* a novel "Brin begins by sticking his neck out a country mile," states Tom Easton in an *Analog* review. The novel is heavily influenced by feminist theory: in an outlying colony called Stratos, which has become a woman-centered world, the female inhabitants have been engineered according to their original creators' ideal genetic standards and provided with the ability to clone themselves as a means of reproduction. However, men are still needed in order to create the biological diversity necessary to help the species adapt to change: to eliminate total reliance on cloning, mating continues on a limited basis, its frequency determined by the seasons. This continued reliance on males becomes one of the frictions in Stratos society, as an element of radical women wish to eliminate their presence altogether. Others want things to remain as they are; still others want men to

have a more equal role in society. When Renna, a male representative from the colonizing planet, arrives to inform the Stratonians that they will soon be visited by their creators and that their society must become more egalitarian, these social tensions erupt.

"There is violence and death, pursuit and discovery, betrayal and maturation, immense enjoyment and final satisfaction, all in the service of a thoughtful approach to the question of intergender relations," comments Easton, comparing *Glory Season* favorably with Ursula LeGuin's classic *Left Hand of Darkness.* While noting that the novel, which weighs in at 557 pages, is overly lengthy, *Washington Post Book World* critic Marin Morse Wooster praises *Glory Season* as a "cool and confident reexamination of a perennial science-fiction theme" and calls it "one of the most important sf novels of the year." Brin followed *Glory Season* with a three-volume series of books featuring the world he created in *Sundiver: Brightness Reef, Infinity's Shore,* and *Heaven's Reach,* the last published in 1997.

BIOGRAPHICAL/CRITICAL SOURCES:

BOOKS

Contemporary Literary Criticism, Volume 34, Gale (Detroit), 1985.

PERIODICALS

Amazing, January, 1984.
Analog: Science Fiction/Science Fact, November, 1983; July, 1984; March, 1986; November, 1987; November, 1990; November, 1993; January, 1995; February, 1996; March, 1997.
Booklist, September, 1, 1987; August, 1994; September 1, 1995.
Book World, October, 19, 1986.
Chicago Tribune Book World, March, 23, 1986.
Fantasy Review, September, 1985; July, 1987.
Information Technology and Libraries, March, 1994.
Isaac Asimov's Science Fiction Magazine, December, 1983; July, 1984.
Locus, June, 1990; July, 1990; August, 1990; February, 1991; March, 1991; July, 1991; April, 1993; May, 1993; October, 1993; February, 1994; July, 1994; October, 1994; February, 1995.
Los Angeles Times, December 16, 1985; April 1, 1986.
Los Angeles Times Book Review, December 15, 1985; January 12, 1986; May 20, 1990.

Magazine of Fantasy and Science Fiction, March, 1986; March, 1996.

Minneapolis Tribune, December 25, 1983.

New York Times Book Review, November 24, 1985; July 8, 1990; July 14, 1991; June 13, 1993.

Publishers Weekly, August 12, 1983; September 6, 1985; October 11, 1985; January 10, 1986; June 13, 1986; March 27, 1987; April 2, 1993; September 4, 1995; November 18, 1996.

San Jose Mercury News, March 11, 1984.

School Library Journal, January, 1992; December, 1990.

Science Fiction and Fantasy Book Review, September, 1983; November, 1983.

Science Fiction Chronicle, December, 1985; March, 1987; June, 1987; September, 1987; February, 1996.

Science Fiction Review, August, 1984.

Voice Literary Supplement, December, 1983.

Washington Post Book World, April 22, 1984; December 22, 1985; July 25, 1993.*

* * *

BRINDZE, Ruth 1903-1984

PERSONAL: Born July 18, 1903, in New York, NY; died November, 1984; married Albert W. Fribourg (a lawyer). *Education:* Graduated from Columbia University. *Avocational interests:* Reading, writing, cooking, gardening, and sailing.

CAREER: Writer. Worked on various newspaper staffs.

AWARDS, HONORS: New York Herald Tribune Children's Book Festival Prize, 1945, for *The Gulf Stream;* Honorable mention in Children's Science Book category, from New York Academy of Sciences, 1975, for *Look How Many People Wear Glasses: The Magic of Lenses.*

WRITINGS:

How to Spend Money: Everybody's Practical Guide to Buying, Vanguard (New York City), 1935, published as *How to Spend Money: How to Get Your Money's Worth,* Garden City Publishing, 1938.

Not to Be Broadcast: The Truth about the Radio, Vanguard, 1937, reprinted, Da Capo Press (New York City), 1974.

Johnny Get Your Money's Worth (illustrated by Emery I. Gondor), Vanguard, 1938.

Seamanship below Deck, Harcourt (New York City), 1939.

Daily Bread and Other Foods (illustrated by Harry Daugherty), Row, Peterson, 1941.

Stretching Your Dollar in Wartime, Vanguard, 1942.

You Can Help Your Country Win (illustrated by Gondor), Vanguard, 1943.

The Gulf Stream (illustrated by Helene Carter; Junior Literary Guild selection), Vanguard, 1945.

Boating Is Fun (illustrated by Kurt Wiese), Dodd (New York City), 1949.

The Story of Our Calendar (illustrated by Carter), Vanguard, 1949.

The Story of the Totem Pole (illustrated by Yeffe Kimball), Vanguard, 1951.

The Story of Gold (illustrated by Robert Bruce), Vanguard, 1955.

The Experts' Book of Boating (illustrated by Fred Wellbrock), Prentice-Hall (Englewood Hills, NJ), 1959.

All about Undersea Exploration, Random House (New York City), 1960.

The Story of the Trade Winds (illustrated by Hilda Simon), Vanguard, 1960.

All about Sailing the Seven Seas, Random House, 1962.

All about Courts and the Law (illustrated by Leonard Slonevsky), Random House, 1964.

The Rise and Fall of the Seas: The Story of the Tides (illustrated by Felix Cooper), Harcourt, 1964.

Investing Money: The Facts about Stocks and Bonds, Harcourt, 1968.

The Sea: The Story of the Rich Underwater World, Harcourt, 1971.

Charting the Oceans, Vanguard, 1973.

Hurricanes: Monster Storms from the Sea, Atheneum (New York City), 1973.

Look How Many People Wear Glasses: The Magic of Lenses, Atheneum, 1975.

SIDELIGHTS: Ruth Brindze wrote many nonfiction books for children and adults. Among her titles is *The Story of the Totem Pole,* a book the critic for *Saturday Review of Literature* called "a valuable record of early Indian art and literature." L. S. Bechtel in the *New York Herald Tribune Book Review* believed that Brindze did "a superb job" on *The Story of the Totem Pole.*

In several books, Brindze focused on the sea. *All about Undersea Exploration* is a science book for young readers in which Brindze presents "gripping stories of man's ventures into the dark, mysterious crushing pressures of the oceanic abyss," as the *Horn Book* reviewer noted. *Gulf Stream* tells the story of how this ocean current has played an important role in exploration, travel, and international trade. A. M. Jordan in *Horn Book* called the book "a fascinating account," while the critic for *Kirkus* found that the "text is lively and sparkles with historical bright spots."

BIOGRAPHICAL/CRITICAL SOURCES:

PERIODICALS

Best Sellers, November 15, 1964.
Booklist, May 1, 1942; July 1, 1945; December 15, 1951; March 1, 1961; April 15, 1961.
Bookmark, May, 1942; August 1, 1945.
Books, April 12, 1942.
Book Week, June 27, 1943; July 15, 1945.
Cleveland Open Shelf, May, 1942.
Commonweal, November 6, 1964.
Horn Book, July, 1945; October, 1960; April, 1961; December, 1964.
Journal of Home Economics, September, 1942.
Kirkus, July 15, 1945; August 15, 1960.
Library Journal, August, 1945; December 1, 1951; January 15, 1961; October 15, 1964.
Nation, September 5, 1942.
New Yorker, December 8, 1945; December 1, 1951.
New York Herald Tribune Book Review, November 11, 1951.
New York Herald Tribune Lively Arts, February 26, 1961.
New York Times, July 11, 1943; June 24, 1945; November 18, 1951.
New York Times Book Review, November 1, 1964.
Pratt, December, 1942.
Saturday Review, February 25, 1961.
Saturday Review of Literature, November 10, 1945; November 10, 1951.
Survey, August, 1942.
Weekly Book Review, July 11, 1943; May 20, 1945.*

*   *   *

BRINNIN, John Malcolm 1916-1998

PERSONAL: Born September 13, 1916, in Halifax, Nova Scotia, Canada; died June 26, 1998; brought to United States in 1920; son of John Thomas and Frances (Malcolm) Brinnin (American citizens).

Education: Attended Wayne State University, 1936; University of Michigan, B.A., 1941; Harvard University, additional study, 1941-42.

CAREER: Vassar College, Poughkeepsie, NY, instructor, 1942-47; Dodd, Mead & Co., New York City, associate editor, 1948-50; University of Connecticut, Storrs, associate professor of English, 1951-62; Boston University, Boston, MA, professor of English, 1961-78, professor emeritus, 1978-98. Poet-in-residence, Stephens College, 1947. Director, Young Men's and Young Women's Hebrew Association's Poetry Center (New York City), 1949-56; U. S. State Department lecturer and delegate in Europe, 1954, 1956, and 1961.

MEMBER: Connecticut Academy of Arts and Sciences, Signet Society.

AWARDS, HONORS: Avery Hopwood Award, University of Michigan; Jeanette Sewell Davis Prize, *Poetry* magazine, 1939; Levinson Prize, 1943; received gold medal, Poetry Society of America, 1955, for distinguished service; Centennial Medal for distinction in literature, University of Michigan, 1963; National Institute of Arts and Letters grant, 1968.

WRITINGS:

POEMS

The Garden Is Political, Macmillan (New York City), 1942.
The Lincoln Lyrics, New Directions (New York City), 1942.
No Arch, No Triumph, Knopf (New York City), 1945.
The Sorrows of Cold Stone: Poems, 1940-1950, Dodd (New York City), 1951, reprinted, Greenwood Press, 1971.
The Selected Poems of John Malcolm Brinnin, Little, Brown (Boston), 1963.
Skin Diving in the Virgins and Other Poems, Delacorte (New York City), 1970.

OTHER

Dylan Thomas in America: An Intimate Journal, Little, Brown, 1955, reprinted, 1971.
The Third Rose: Gertrude Stein and Her World, Little, Brown, 1959.
William Carlos Williams: A Critical Study, University of Minnesota Press (Minneapolis), 1961.

Arthur: The Dolphin Who Didn't See Venice (juvenile), Little, Brown, 1961.

William Carlos Williams (pamphlet), University of Minnesota Press, 1963.

The Sway of the Grand Saloon: A Social History of the North Atlantic, Delacorte (New York City), 1972.

Sextet: T. S. Eliot and Truman Capote and Others, Delacorte, 1981.

Beau Voyage: Life Aboard the Last Great Ships, Congdon & Lattes (New York City, 1981.

Truman Capote: Dear Heart, Old Buddy, Delacorte, 1986, published as *Truman Capote: A Memoir,* Sidgwick & Jackson (London), 1987.

Grand Luxe: The Transatlantic Style, Holt (New York City), 1988.

Travel and the Sense of Wonder, Library of Congress (Washington, DC), 1992.

EDITOR

(With Kimon Friar) *Modern Poetry: American and British,* Appleton (New York City), 1951.

A Casebook on Dylan Thomas, Crowell (New York City), 1960.

Emily Dickinson: Poems, Dell (New York City), 1960.

(With Bill Read) *The Modern Poets: An American-British Anthology,* McGraw (New York City), 1963, 2nd edition, 1970.

Selected Operas and Plays of Gertrude Stein, University of Pittsburgh Press (Pittsburgh), 1970.

(With Read) *Twentieth Century Poetry, American and British (1900-1970): An American-British Anthology,* McGraw, 1971.

Contributor of numerous articles and stories to periodicals.

SIDELIGHTS: "Although he is most deservedly known for his poetry, John Malcolm Brinnin's broad range of literary activities stamps him as a man of letters," according to Philip L. Gerber in the *Dictionary of Literary Biography.* "Besides producing six volumes of verse, he earned reputations as editor, anthologist, social historian, and literary biographer."

Discussing his philosophy of poetry, Brinnin wrote in *Poets on Poetry* that he was always "less interested in understanding a poem than in feeling it. What moved me then, as now, was the language and the music of language, the perception of the sheer poetic thing, without reference to the ideas which it is meant to serve or to promote. . . . In other words, poetry for me was, from the very beginning, not a vehicle, nor an agent, nor a means to salvation, but the liveliest art, the most gloriously useless and the most necessary."

Gerber pointed out that Brinnin as a poet has always shown an "interest in, and command of, form. . . . Although he is equally at home in the free-verse tradition . . . , Brinnin's free verse has never pretended to a spontaneous pouring-out of emotion on the page. Rather, his free verse is much like Eliot's, always tightly controlled, explicitly cadenced, and more often than not moving to the tune of sporadic unpatterned rhymes."

Reviewing *The Selected Poems of John Malcolm Brinnin* for *Library Journal,* B. W. Fuson noted: "Brinnin's range of experience and sensibility is amazing: these poems run the gamut from macabre to hilarious, savagely pessimistic to warmly sympathetic . . . , nostalgic to prophetic. . . . Brinnin's status as a major modern American poet should be more widely recognized." In a review of *Skin Diving in the Virgins and Other Poems,* P. H. Marvin in *Library Journal* described Brinnin as "one of the few poets who is perfectly predictable as to the high quality of each new volume. In a sense none of Brinnin's poems fail, for his style is distinguished, his mastery of his own poetic conventions is complete, and the limits he sets for himself are precise."

In two nonfiction books, *Dylan Thomas in America* and *Truman Capote: Dear Heart, Old Buddy,* Brinnin offers memoirs of two leading literary figures and personal friends. K. A. Porter wrote in the *New York Times* of Brinnin's *Dylan Thomas in America* that it is "a very honorable attempt to set [Brinnin's] share of the record straight." In doing so, Brinnin revealed much about Thomas's darker side, including his problems with alcohol. "It is a book of unusual frankness," as W. T. Scott noted in the *New York Herald Tribune Book Review.* "It is not so in any scandalous or malicious sense. It has, rather, an uncompromising, fierce honesty." Reviewing the memoir for *Nation,* M. L. Rosenthal summed up: "Brinnin's book is invaluable."

In *Truman Capote: Dear Heart, Old Buddy* Brinnin remembers his long friendship with novelist Capote in a memoir "delightful in its fund of anecdotal lore," as David Lehman in *Newsweek* stated. While Capote's own decline into alcoholism is only briefly described in the book, because the two friends saw less of each other during those years, the book does cover the earlier, more successful period in depth. "Brinnin's ability to think like a biographer, write like a novelist, and analyze like a critic," wrote Bernard F. Dick in *World Literature Today,* "has resulted in a reminiscence written with such grace and eloquence that it produces a dual reaction: one responds to it as one does to a novel, yet one reflects on it as one does on something that is undeniably true."

Gerber concluded: "Urbane, sophisticated, literate, witty, contemplative, formalist—any and all of these terms suit the talents of John Malcolm Brinnin, both in prose and in verse."

BIOGRAPHICAL/CRITICAL SOURCES:

BOOKS

Contemporary Poets, fifth edition, St. James Press (Detroit), 1991.
Dictionary of Literary Biography, Volume 48: *American Poets, 1880-1945, Second Series,* Gale (Detroit), 1986.
Nemerov, Howard, editor, *Poetry and Fiction,* Rutgers University Press, 1963.
Nemerov, editor, *Poets on Poetry,* Basic Books, 1966.

PERIODICALS

Atlantic, January, 1956; December, 1971.
Best Sellers, December 15, 1971.
Booklist, December 15, 1955.
Book Week, February 25, 1945, p. 4; October 27, 1963, p. 25.
Book World, November 28, 1971, p. 9.
Chicago Sunday Tribune, November 27, 1955, p. 4.
Christian Science Monitor, June 6, 1963, p. 11; September 5, 1963, p. 11.
Horn Book, October, 1963.
Kirkus, January 15, 1945; September 15, 1955.
Library Journal, October 15, 1955; August, 1963; July, 1970; January 15, 1972.
Music & Letters, May, 1995, p. 314.
Nation, August 1, 1942, p. 97; February 13, 1943; December 17, 1955.
New Republic, March 29, 1943; April 2, 1945; November 13, 1971.
New Statesman, September 27, 1963.
New Yorker, November 27, 1971.
New York Herald Tribune Book Review, November 20, 1955, p. 1.

New York Times, February 25, 1945, p. 10; July 22, 1951, p. 12; November 20, 1955, p. 5.
New York Times Book Review, December 22, 1963, p. 4; January 9, 1972, p. 30.
Poetry, February, 1943, pp. 622-626; April, 1945, pp. 32-35; March, 1972.
Prairie Schooner, fall, 1974, pp. 201-221.
Publishers Weekly, December 11, 1981, pp. 6-7.
San Francisco Chronicle, July 22, 1951, p. 17; November 27, 1955, p. 12.
Saturday Review, November 19, 1955; February 1, 1964; January 29, 1972, p. 12.
Saturday Review of Literature, March 24, 1945; December 29, 1951, p. 10.
Time, January 3, 1972.
Times Literary Supplement, August 4, 1972, p. 920.
U. S. Quarterly Booklist, June, 1945.*

*   *   *

BRINTON, Henry 1901-1977
(Alex Fraser)

PERSONAL: Born July 27, 1901, in Wolverhampton, Staffordshire, England; died June 1, 1977; son of Henry Brinton; married Helen Cross Reid Fraser, 1941; children: John Richard, Julie Caroline, Alix Veronica. *Education:* Attended school at Haileybury, England. *Avocational interests:* Astronomy, sailing.*

CAREER: Involved for many years in social and political work. Author and lecturer. Principal, Ministry of Labour. Member of regional health board, National Health Service.

MEMBER: Royal Astronomical Society (fellow), British Astronomical Association, PEN.

WRITINGS:

Christianity or the New Paganism?, Muller, 1938.
Christianity and Spain, United Editorials, 1939.
Vengeance Is Dear, Temple, 1946.
The Context of the Reformation, Hutchinson (London), 1968.

FICTION

Death to Windward, Hutchinson, 1952.
One Down and Two to Slay, Hutchinson, 1953.
Now Like to Die, Hutchinson, 1954.

Drug on the Market, Macmillan (New York City), 1954.

Coppers and Gold, Macmillan, 1955.

Ill Will, Hutchinson, 1956.

An Apple a Day, Washburn, 1957.

An Ordinary Day, Hutchinson, 1959, published as *Apprentice to Fear,* Macmillan, 1961.

Rude Awakening, Hutchinson, 1961.

Purple 6, Walker (New York City), 1962.

Can Death Be Sleep?, Hutchinson, 1965.

Gunpowder Treason, Lutterworth, 1968.

JUVENILES

(With Patrick Moore) *Navigation,* Methuen (London), 1961.

The Telephone, John Day, 1962.

Exploring Spain, Weidenfeld & Nicolson (London), 1962.

(With Moore) *Exploring Maps,* Odhams (London), 1962, Hawthorne (New York City), 1967.

(With Moore) *Exploring Time,* Odhams, 1962.

Measuring the Universe, Roy (New York City), 1962.

Sound, John Day, 1963.

(With Moore) *Exploring the Weather,* Transatlantic (New York City), 1964.

Spain, Soccer, 1964.

(With Moore) *Exploring Other Planets,* Odhams, 1965, Hawthorne, 1967.

(With Moore) *Exploring Earth History,* Odhams, 1967.

Man in Space, Dufour, 1969.

Astronomy for Beginners, Pelham, 1970.

UNDER PSEUDONYM ALEX FRASER

Three Wives, Bles, 1956.

Constables Don't Count, Bles, 1957.

Death Is So Final, Bles, 1958, Roy, 1962.

Bury Their Dead, Roy, 1959.

High Tension, Bles, 1960.

The Dark Places, Bles, 1961.

SIDELIGHTS: Henry Brinton wrote mystery novels under his own name and the pseudonym Alex Fraser. Brinton's mysteries were often what Riley Hughes in *Catholic World* described as "those extremely casual, wonderfully written British pieces of mystery-making." The effect of the novel *Coppers and Gold,* according to L. G. Offord of the *San Francisco Chronicle,* "is one of good nature and literacy amid confusion." Reviewing the novel *Bury Their Dead,* James Sandoe in the *New York Herald Tribune Book Review* noted that Brinton "sustains interest rather through his observation of country mores than in his evocation of another locked room." Speaking of the detective character in the novel *Drug on the Market,* Anthony Boucher opined: "Strang is one of the more charmingly civilized of recent detective-creations."

In *Purple-6,* Brinton turned from the more traditional mystery story he had been writing to pen a fast-moving thriller. The story concerns a possible Soviet missile launch against England and the scientists who must determine the authenticity of the alleged attack and take measures to counter it. "What life is like under threat of thermonuclear annihilation only minutes away by ballistic missiles is the subject," wrote Taliaferro Boatwright in the *New York Herald Tribune Books.* Boatwright summed up: "What develops is plausible and even exciting." E. A. McGinnis in *Best Sellers* found: "The entire account is for the most part well written and the author very successfully brings out the personality of his characters."

BIOGRAPHICAL/CRITICAL SOURCES:

PERIODICALS

Best Sellers, January 1, 1963.

Booklist, March 1, 1958.

Catholic World, April, 1957.

Chicago Sunday Tribune, April 20, 1958, p. 3.

Guardian, December 18, 1959, p. 6.

Kirkus, December 1, 1956; November 15, 1960.

Manchester Guardian, March 20, 1959, p. 10.

New Statesman, May 11, 1962.

New York Herald Tribune Book Review, February 10, 1957, p. 12; January 12, 1958, p. 11; August 7, 1960, p. 12.

New York Herald Tribune Books, December 9, 1962, p. 13.

New York Herald Tribune Lively Arts, January 15, 1961, p. 39.

New York Times, February 10, 1957, p. 26; January 12, 1958, p. 25.

New York Times Book Review, July 17, 1960, p. 28; January 22, 1961, p. 26; November 18, 1962, p. 68.

San Francisco Chronicle, March 3, 1957, p. 23; March 2, 1958, p. 31.

Saturday Review, July 6, 1957; January 28, 1961.

Times Literary Supplement, March 1, 1957, p. 134; November 13, 1959, p. 664.*

BRITT, Albert 1874-1969

PERSONAL: Born November 26, 1874, in Utah, IL; died February 18, 1969, in Worcester, MA; son of Edward (a farmer) and Sarah (Foster0 Britt; married Dorothy Wellington, September 10, 1921; children: Sarah, Priscilla (Mrs. George W. Knowlton IV). *Education:* Knox College, A.B., 1898; Columbia University, graduate study, 1898-1901.

CAREER: Public Opinion, New York City, editor, 1900-06; *Railroad Man's Magazine,* New York City, editor, 1906-09; *Outing,* New York City, editor, 1909-24; Knox College, Galesburg, IL, president, 1925-36; Scripps College of the Associated Colleges of Claremont, Claremont, CA, professor of American history, 1936-56.

AWARDS, HONORS: Litt.D., Park College, 1925; LL.D., Lawrence College, 1936; L.H.D., Knox College, 1937.

WRITINGS:

Wind's Will, Moffett Yard, 1910.
Boys' Own Book of Modern Adventurers, Macmillan (New York City), 1921.
Boys' Own Book of Frontiersmen, Macmillan, 1923.
Lincoln for Boys and Girls, Frank-Maurice, 1925.
The Great Biographers, McGraw (New York City), 1934.
Great Indian Chiefs: A Study of Indian Leaders in the Two Hundred Year Struggle to Stop the White Advance, McGraw, 1938.
(With Donald R. Richberg) *Only the Brave Are Free,* Caxton, 1958.
Ellen Browning Scripps: Journalist and Idealist, Scripps College Press (Claremont, CA), 1961.
The Hungry War: An Account of the American Revolution, Barre, 1961.
Toward the Western Ocean, Barre, 1963.
An America That Was: What Life Was Like on an Illinois Farm Seventy Years Ago, Barre, 1964.
Turn of the Century, Barre, 1967.

Contributor to *Saturday Evening Post, Harper's,* and *Yale Review.*

SIDELIGHTS: After some twenty-five years as the editor of magazines, including the popular travel magazine *Outing,* Albert Britt moved on to pursue an academic career. He served as president of Knox College for eleven years, and then became a history professor at Scripps College. Britt's books include popular histories and biographies for a general audience, as well as two books of memoirs.

Britt's *The Great Biographers* grew out of a course he taught at Knox College in the history of written biography. Beginning with the earliest known examples of the form, Britt's study analyzed the common themes and approaches biographers had used through the ages to write of their subjects. S. A. Coblentz in the *New York Times* found the book to be "an interesting and valuable outline of biography," while the critic for the *Saturday Review of Literature* believed that, with his coverage of English and American biographers in particular, "Britt's strength and independence of judgment become enjoyable."

In *Great Indian Chiefs: A Study of Indian Leaders in the Two Hundred Year Struggle to Stop the White Advance,* Britt profiles eight prominent Indian leaders, including Pontiac, Sitting Bull and Tecumseh. The critic for the *New York Times* claimed that Britt "has gone a long way toward giving us a real understanding of these men. . . . He writes here to . . . present unbiased human pictures. He has succeeded admirably in that task." A. W. Hoopes in *Social Studies* believed that *Great Indian Chiefs* "should be in every library and private collection dealing with the American Indian."

Britt turned to the American Revolution in *The Hungry War: An Account of the American Revolution,* a recounting of the struggle for independence for younger readers. Although aimed at a young audience, the *Springfield Republican* critic noted that "it is so well done and so comprehensively covers all the essential facts about the Revolution, that it should appeal to many adult readers as well." Bernhard Knollenberg in the *New England Quarterly* found the book to be "well-organized and well-written" and "enlightening and entertaining reading for the youngsters. . . . I know of none better in its field."

An America That Was: What Life Was Like on an Illinois Farm Seventy Years Ago and *Turn of the Century* focused on Britt's own remembrances of life in his childhood home of Illinois at the end of the nineteenth century. *An America That Was* presents Britt's remembrances of the period from 1875 to 1900, ending with his college years and before he went into journalism. R. W. Henderson in *Library Journal* called the book "a moving picture of the pioneer farmer." Paul Pickrei of *Harper* called *An*

America That Was "a charming testament to a long-gone way of life, but it is also a sturdy witness to human resilience."

Covering a host of figures who made up the popular culture of the time—including the publisher S. S. McClure and cartoonist Peter Finley Dunn—Britt's *Turn of the Century* includes both a personal reminiscence of his early life and snapshot anecdotes of some of the prominent individuals of the time. The *Choice* critic found it to be "most useful when discussing journalism history," while H. W. Allen in the *Journal of American History* noted that "the book offers an evening's pleasant readings."

BIOGRAPHICAL/CRITICAL SOURCES:

PERIODICALS

Booklist, June 15, 1938.
Books, October 23, 1938, p. 22.
Boston Transcript, May 14, 1938, p. 1.
Canadian History Review, September, 1938.
Choice, May, 1967.
Harper, July, 1964.
Journal of American History, March, 1967.
Library Journal, August, 1961; November 1, 1964.
New England Quarterly, June, 1962.
New Yorker, April 30, 1938.
New York Times, April 5, 1936, p. 2; May 8, 1938, p. 16.
Pratt, autumn, 1936, p. 37.
Saturday Review of Literature, May 16, 1936.
Social Education, October, 1938.
Social Studies, October, 1938.
Springfield Republican, August 8, 1936, p. 6; July 24, 1938, p. E7; July 30, 1961, p. D4.*

* * *

BROAD, C(harlie) D(unbar) 1887-1971

PERSONAL: Born December 30, 1887, in Harlesden, Middlesex, England; died March 11, 1971; son of Charles Stephen (a vintner) and Emily (Gomme) Broad. *Education:* Trinity College, Cambridge, degree in philosophy (with first class honors), 1910.

CAREER: Assistant to professor of logic at St. Andrews University in St. Andrews, Scotland; lecturer at University College in Dundee, Scotland; Bristol University, Bristol, England, professor of

philosophy, 1920-c. 1922; Trinity College, Cambridge, England, fellow and lecturer in moral science, c. 1922-33, Knightbridge Professor of Moral Philosophy, 1933-53. Visiting lecturer at Trinity College, Dublin, Ireland, 1929, University of Michigan, 1953-54, University of California, Los Angeles, 1954, and Columbia University, 1960.

MEMBER: American Academy of Arts and Sciences (fellow), British Academy (fellow), Society for Psychical Research (president, 1935-36, 1959-60), Aristotelian Society (president, 1927-28, 1954-55).

AWARDS, HONORS: Several honorary degrees, including Litt.D. from Cambridge University.

WRITINGS:

Perception, Physics, and Reality: An Enquiry Into the Information That Physical Science Can Supply about the Real, Putnam (New York City), 1914.
Scientific Thought, Harcourt (New York City), 1923, reprinted, Humanities, 1969.
The Mind and Its Place in Nature, Harcourt, 1925, Routledge & Kegan Paul, 1962.
The Philosophy of Francis Bacon: An Address Delivered at Cambridge on the Occasion of the Bacon Tercentenary, 5 October 1926, Cambridge University Press, 1926, Octagon, 1976.
Five Types of Ethical Theory, Harcourt, 1930.
Examination of McTaggart's Philosophy, two volumes, Cambridge University Press, 1933-38, reprinted, Octagon, 1976.
Ethics and the History of Philosophy: Selected Essays, Routledge & Kegan Paul, 1952, reprinted, Hyperion Press, 1979.
Religion, Philosophy, and Psychical Research: Selected Essays, Harcourt, 1953.
Lectures on Psychical Research, Incorporating the Perrott Lectures Given in Cambridge University in 1959 and 1960, Humanities, 1962.
Induction, Probability, and Causation: Selected Papers, D. Reidel, 1968.
Broad's Critical Essays in Moral Philosophy, edited by David R. Cheney, Humanities, 1971.
Leibniz: An Introduction edited by C. Lewy, Cambridge University Press, 1975.
Kant: An Introduction, edited by Lewy, Cambridge University Press, 1978.

Contributor to *Mind* and *Hibbert Journal,* and proceedings of British Academy, Society for Psychical Research, and Aristotelian Society.

SIDELIGHTS: C. D. Broad was concerned with the importance of the senses and the ultimate reality of the objects in our perceptions. His first two books, *Perception, Physics, and Reality* and *Scientific Thought,* discuss this concept in depth. Broad also wrote extensively about psychic phenomena. Broad summed up his function as a philosopher in his book, *Scientific Thought.* "If I have any kind of philosophical merit," he wrote, "it is neither the constructive fertility of an Alexander, nor the penetrating critical acumen of a Moore; still less is it that extraordinary combination of both with technical mathematical skill which characterises Whitehead and Russell. I can at most claim the humbler (yet useful) power of stating things clearly and not too superficially."

Broad's first volume of philosophy, *Perception, Physics, and Reality,* is a revision of his Trinity College, Cambridge, fellowship thesis. The book met with glowing reviews. An *Athenaeum* critic proclaimed: "One would almost wish to term Mr. Broad's volume 'palatable philosophy,' it is written in so easy and attractive a style, and shows such excellent common sense. . . . He may be congratulated upon the success with which he brushes down some ancient cobwebs." Similarly, A. Wolf commented in the *Hibbert Journal* that "there can be no doubt that we are indebted to Mr. Broad for a very searching investigation into some of the most important problems of philosophy, and no serious student of philosophy can afford to overlook this treatise."

Scientific Thought, Broad's next endeavor, also met with an enthusiastic reception. A reviewer for the *Times Literary Supplement* praised the work as a "closely-reasoned and particularly lucid book" and added that it "is certain to take a chief place in the discussions of the philosophical problem which at the present time is of central interest—that of the nature and import of the new concepts of the physical universe which are being adopted in science as the result of recent experimental work devised by mathematicians and physicists." C. J. Keyser of the *Literary Review of the New York Evening Post* asserted that the "book is an exceedingly valuable contribution to Critical Philosophy."

Broad's *Mind and Its Place in Nature* caused a commotion in philosophical circles because it included evidence of psychic phenomena, which indicated the possibility of human life after death. The book received generally favorable reviews, although critics were skeptical of Broad's conclusions regarding psychic phenomena. Durant Drake remarked in the *Journal of Philosophy* that "the reader needs a good wind to follow the argument through its intricate windings to its rather abrupt and baffling end. But [Broad] makes his definitions so precise, and so refines his distinctions, that no one can fail to understand exactly what he means or to follow even his most intricate arguments." Writing in the *Nation and Atheneum,* Bertrand Russell agreed: "It may be doubted whether his results are definitive. Nevertheless, his book is full of accurate thought and useful distinctions to a degree which is surpassed by very few philosophers."

For a later volume, *Five Types of Ethical Theory,* Broad was again applauded for his clear, analytical thinking and writing. Henry Hazlitt declared in *Nation* that "Broad has many of the more important merits of a fine philosophical writer. . . . He is a rigorous and acute logician, quick to smell and pounce upon a fallacy or an ambiguity." C. E. M. Joad in the *Nation and Atheneum* concurred: "Broad's may be described as the surgical method. He is for ever dividing thought and cutting it up, introducing distinctions which are usually ignored, and pointing out ambiguities which others have failed to detect."

In *Religion, Philosophy, and Psychical Research,* Broad expanded on the subject he introduced in *Mind and Its Place in Nature* with favorable results. Huston Smith of *Christian Century* contended that "if I could name three topics on which I would like to hear one of the best trained and clearest minds of our generation discourse, I think they would be religion, politics, and psychical research." "The reader who can appreciate cogent argument in a lucid style, relieved by flashes of mordant wit, will enjoy himself and will incidentally learn a number of interesting facts about psychical research," according to Martha Kneale in the *Manchester Guardian.*

Broad followed this volume with the more comprehensive work, *Lectures on Psychical Research.* G. A. Miller of *Scientific American* was doubtful of Broad's argument for psychic phenomena. "It is uncomfortable to find oneself in disagreement with so gifted and persuasive an author. The most any skeptic must grant when he closes this book is not that paranormal phenomena exist but merely that we cannot prove they do not exist." On the other hand, a *Times Literary Supplement* reviewer felt the book was "admirable" and its "clarity of thought, its detailed precision of treatment, and its exact and impartial examination of all that is meant, involved and implied by psychical research could hardly be bettered."

BIOGRAPHICAL/CRITICAL SOURCES:

PERIODICALS

American Journal of Sociology, September, 1930.
Annals of the American Academy, July, 1953.
Athenaeum, July 18, 1914.
Booklist, November, 1923.
Boston Transcript, June 2, 1923, p. 2.
Catholic World, May, 1953.
Choice, March, 1970.
Christian Century, June 3, 1953.
Hibbert Journal, January, 1915.
International Journal of Ethics, July, 1930.
Journal of Philosophy, December 6, 1923; October 14, 1926; January 29, 1970.
Literary Review of the New York Evening Post, January 5, 1924, p. 424.
Manchester Guardian, March 20, 1953, p. 4.
Nation, December 24, 1914; April 9, 1930.
Nation and Athenaeum, November 28, 1925; April 12, 1930.
Nature, April 15, 1915; June 30, 1923.
New Statesman, May 26, 1923; October 17, 1925; January 11, 1963.
New Statesman and Nation, February 28, 1953.
New York Herald Tribune Books, July 18, 1926, p. 10.
New York Times, July 1, 1923, p. 20.
Pittsburgh Monthly Bulletin, December, 1930.
St. Louis, March, 1926.
Saturday Review of Literature, March 17, 1923; March 6, 1926.
Science, November 20, 1914.
Scientific American, November, 1963.
Spectator, April 29, 1923.
Springfield Republican, June 6, 1926, p. F7.
Times Literary Supplement, March 15, 1923, p. 172; October 1, 1925, p. 632; May 15, 1930, p. 406; February 20, 1953, p. 6; May 15, 1953, p. 321; January 11, 1963, p. 20.*

* * *

BROOKES, Edgar Harry 1897-

PERSONAL: Born February 4, 1897; son of Job Harry and Emily Elizabeth (Thomas) Brookes; married Heidi Genevieve Baurquin, 1925; married Edith Constance Moe; children: (first marriage) Arthur, Charles, Rosemary Brookes Rittman, David, Heidi. *Education:* University of South Africa, M.A., 1920, D.Litt., 1924. *Religion:* Anglican.

CAREER: University of Pretoria, Transvaal, South Africa, professor, 1920-33; Adams College, Adams Mission Station, South Africa, principal, 1934-45; Parliament of South Africa, Cape Town, senator, 1937-52; University of Natal, Pietermaritzburg, South Africa, professor of history and political science, 1953-62. *Military service:* Special Service, 1914-15; became sergeant.

MEMBER: South African Institute of Race Relations (president, 1930-31, 1955-56, 1960).

AWARDS, HONORS: Royal African Society medal for dedicated service in Africa; LL.D., University of Cape Town, 1958, and Queen's University, Kingston, Ontario, 1962; D.Litt., University of Natal, 1966.

WRITINGS:

History of Native Policy in South Africa, Nesionale Press, 1924.
The Colour Problems of South Africa, Lovedale, 1934, reprinted, Negro Universities Press, 1980.
South Africa in a Changing World, Oxford University Press (London), 1954.
(With Nathan Hurwitz) *Native Reserves of Natal,* Oxford University Press, 1957.
(With J. B. Macaulay) *Civil Liberty in South Africa,* Oxford University Press, 1959, Greenwood Press (Westport, CT), 1973.
The Commonwealth Today, University of Natal Press (Pietermaritzburg), 1959.
The City of God and the Politics of Crisis, Oxford University Press, 1960.
Power, Law, Right and Love: A Study in Political Values, Duke University Press, 1963.
(With Amry Vandenbosch) *The City of God and the City of Man in Africa,* University of Kentucky Press, 1964.
(With Colin de B. Webb) *A History of Natal,* University of Natal Press, 1964.
Three Letters from Africa, Pendle Hill (Wallingford, PA), 1965.
History of the University of Natal, University of Natal Press, 1965.
Freedom, Faith, and the Twenty-First Century, Ryerson, 1966.

America in Travail, Pendle Hill, 1968.
Apartheid: A Documentary Study of Modern South Africa, Routledge & Kegan Paul, 1968.
White Rule in South Africa, 1830-1910: Varieties in Governmental Policies Affecting Africans, University of Natal Press, 1974.
A South African Pilgrimage, Raven Press (Johannesburg), 1977.

Also author of *The Universal Church in Its South African Setting: Four Lectures Delivered at the Federal Theological Seminary of Southern Africa,* 1966.

SIDELIGHTS: Edgar Harry Brookes served as a member of the South African parliament and as professor of history and political science at the University of Natal. His books concern South Africa's history, its political and racial problems, and its standing in the modern world.

Brookes's *Civil Liberty in South Africa,* co-written with J. B. Macaulay, examines the erosion of civil liberties in South Africa brought on, so the authors argue, by the system of apartheid. C. R. Nixon in *American Political Science Review* calls *Civil Liberty in South Africa* "an essential book" because "it brings into sharp focus those changes in the civil liberties of South Africans which are occurring in the effort to maintain white dominance." As G. M. Carter notes in *American Sociology Review,* "No one who reads this work can again be free of the nagging awareness that to limit the civil liberties of any group in the community is to imperil those of all."

Power, Law, Right and Love: A Study in Political Values is a study of human relationships from a religious perspective. T. R. Adam in *America* calls the work "a courageous attempt to link the political process to the meaning of life," while the critic for the *Times Literary Supplement* finds it to be "an attempt to define in precise, academic language the moral objections to racial oppression by whomsoever it is practised."

Brookes again draws upon his religious faith in *The City of God and the City of Man in Africa,* co-written with Amry Vandenbosch. Looking at the rise of African nationalism during the 1950s and 1960s, the authors discuss the possibilities of dramatic societal changes brought about by religious faith. Concluding that individuals must live according to their faith, doing what they feel is morally right in their daily lives, Brookes sees this method as being the best to achieve a better Africa. The critic for *Christian*

Century notes that "the authors take a highly positive view of African nationalism and African spirituality and counsel the West to heed both before it is too late."

BIOGRAPHICAL/CRITICAL SOURCES:

PERIODICALS

America, November 9, 1963.
American Political Science Review, December, 1959; March, 1965.
American Sociology Review, June, 1958; December, 1959.
Annals of the American Academy, September, 1958.
Choice, February, 1970.
Christian Century, May 27, 1964.
Foreign Affairs, April, 1960.
Library Journal, December 15, 1968.
New Statesman, June 6, 1959.
Spectator, June 5, 1959, p. 821.
Times Literary Supplement, June 12, 1959, p. 351; December 26, 1963, p. 1069.

* * *

BROOKS, Paul 1909-

PERSONAL: Born February 16, 1909, in New York, NY; son of Ernest (an architect) and Jeanne (Marion) Brooks; married Susan Anderson Moller, June 24, 1931; children: Elizabeth Sweetser (Mrs. John W. Harris), Douglas (deceased), Samuel Jameson, Susan (Mrs. John D. Morris), Kate. *Education:* Harvard University, A.B. (cum laude), 1931.

ADDRESSES: Home—5 Silver Hill Rd., Lincoln Center, MA 01773.

CAREER: Houghton Mifflin Co., Boston, MA, editorial reader, 1931, assistant editor, managing editor, editor-in-chief and director of company, 1943-67, vice-president, 1968-69. Trustee, Trustees for Conservation; member of national council, Nature Conservancy. *Military service:* Chief of book section, U.S. Office of War Information, 1945.

MEMBER: American Academy of Arts and Sciences (fellow), Massachusetts Audubon Society (director, 1943-47), Sierra Club (director), Signet Associates (president, 1964-65), Phi Beta Kappa (president of Harvard chapter, 1978-79), St. Botolph Club, Tavern

Club, Saturday Club, Examiner Club (Boston), Century Association (New York).

AWARDS, HONORS: John Burroughs Medal of American Museum of Natural History, and the Sarah Chapman Francis Medal of the Garden Club of America, both for *Roadless Area,* 1965; H.L.D. from University of Massachusetts, 1973; Walter A. Starr Award from Sierra Club.

WRITINGS:

Roadless Area, Knopf (New York City), 1964.
The Pursuit of Wilderness, Houghton (Boston), 1971.
The House of Life: Rachel Carson at Work, Houghton, 1973.
Trial by Fire: Lincoln, Massachusetts, and the War of Independence, Lincoln 1975 Bicentennial Commission, 1975.
The View from Lincoln Hill: Man and the Land in a New England Town, Houghton, 1976.
(Author of introduction) Ansel Adams, *Yosemite and the Range of Light,* New York Graphic Society, 1979.
Speaking for Nature: How Literary Naturalists from Henry Thoreau to Rachel Carson Have Shaped America, Houghton, 1980.
The Old Manse and the People Who Lived There, Trustees of Reservations, 1983.
Two Park Street: A Publishing Memoir, Houghton, 1986.
(Editor with Thomas B. Adams) *The Saturday Club, 1957-1986,* Saturday Club (Boston), 1988.
The People of Concord: One Year in the Flowering of New England, Globe Pequot Press (Chester, CT), 1990.

Contributor to *Atlantic, Harper's, Horizon,* and other magazines. Contributing editor, *Audubon Magazine* and *Living Wilderness.*

SIDELIGHTS: During his long career with the publishing house of Houghton Mifflin, Paul Brooks promoted writings about the natural world. He was the editor of environmentalist Rachel Carson's *Silent Spring,* which he acknowledges "as one of those rare books that change the course of history." Brooks's *The House of Life: Rachel Carson at Work* is based on Carson's papers and published work. Brooks has also written several books on the environment.

"[Rachel Carson] is responsible for one of the great revolutions of history—the Ecological Movement," F. J. MacEntee of *Best Sellers* explains in a review of *The House of Life.* "Very few people could even define the word ten years ago; now it is a household word, as well it should be, for the Greek root meaning of ecology is 'house,' hence the book's title. . . . The present volume has a twofold purpose: to present a selection of Rachel Carson's best writing, and to show—in her own words—how she achieved what she did." *Saturday Review*'s David McCord remarks that "what Mr. Brooks has produced is not a personal biography . . . but a strong, unsentimental yet affectionate study of a professional biologist who had the genius, the passion, and the sensitive ear to write exquisite prose." Josephine Johnson in the *New York Times Book Review* calls *The House of Life* "a rich and readable work" and "deeply moving."

Many critics admire and respect Brooks' ability to capture the breathtaking beauty of nature. His book *Roadless Area* gathers together descriptions of trips made by Brooks and his wife to such places as Alaska, Baja California, and Kenya. The *Atlantic*'s Edward Weeks observes that Brooks "writes with humor, vividly and with strong conviction." *Roadless Area,* S. F. Olson comments in the *New York Times Book Review,* "is a treasure for all who feel deeply about wild unsettled places. It is also a powerful warning to take heed—before we find that we have lost such places of joy and spiritual meaning forever."

In *The Pursuit of Wilderness* Brooks describes several efforts to save wilderness areas threatened by development. Weeks writes that this "is a most timely exposure of how close we have come to losing three unique preserves in Alaska, the Everglades, and the North Cascades." Brooks' book *The Pursuit of Wilderness* "is beautiful for two reasons," writes MacEntee, "the sheer lyricism of much of the prose and more pragmatically, the fact that national concern for environment is catching on. . . . Even if you are not an ardent conservationist, or even a lukewarm one, reading this book will leave you considerably enriched."

In *Speaking for Nature: How Literary Naturalists from Henry Thoreau to Rachel Carson Have Shaped America,* Brooks examines the role American nature writers have played in celebrating the environment. His study includes many lesser known writers over the past century, as well as poets and fiction writers whose environmental works proved popular with the reading public. Joseph Kastner in the *New York Times Book Review* describes the book as "a brisk and illuminating survey," while R. W. Bradford in

American Literature writes that "Brooks does his job well" and "gives good attention to women writers."

BIOGRAPHICAL/CRITICAL SOURCES:

PERIODICALS

American Literature, November, 1981.
Atlantic, October, 1964; July, 1971; April, 1972.
Best Sellers, June 15, 1971; April 1, 1972.
Book World, March 26, 1972, p. 6.
Choice, July/August, 1972.
Christian Science Monitor, August 25, 1964, p. 9; May 10, 1972, p. 11.
Horn Book, August, 1972.
Library Journal, July, 1971; April 1, 1972; October 1, 1980.
New York Times Book Review, September 20, 1964, p. 12; April 30, 1972, p. 30; January 4, 1981, p. 7.
Saturday Review, March 25, 1972.

* * *

BROOK-SHEPHERD, (Frederick) Gordon 1918-
(Gordon Shepherd)

PERSONAL: Born March 24, 1918, in England; son of Alfred (an architect) and Doreen (Pearson) Brook-Shepherd; married Baroness Sochor, June, 1948; children: Clive Anthony, Nicola. *Education:* Cambridge University, B.A. (first class honors), 1939. *Politics:* Leftwing Conservative. *Religion:* Church of England. *Avocational interests:* Shooting, fishing, skiing, tennis, music.

ADDRESSES: Home—5 South Ter., Knightsbridge, London S.W. 7, England. *Office—Sunday Telegraph,* 135 Fleet St., London E.C.4, England. *Agent—* Brandt & Brandt, 101 Park Ave., New York, NY 10017.

CAREER: Daily Telegraph, London, England, foreign correspondent, 1949-60; *Sunday Telegraph,* London, diplomatic editor, 1960-65, assistant editor, 1965-75, deputy editor, 1975—. *Military service:* British Army, General Staff, World War II; became lieutenant colonel.

MEMBER: Royal Central Asian Society, Royal Institute of International Affairs, PEN, Travellers Club and Roehampton Club (both London).

WRITINGS:

Russia's Danubian Empire, Praeger, 1954.
The Austrian Odyssey, St. Martin's, 1957.
(With Kurt Peter Karfeld) *Austria in Color* (includes text by Brook-Shepherd), Oesterreichische Staatsdruckerei, 1957.
Where the Lion Trod, St. Martin's 1960.
Dollfuss (biography), St. Martin's 1961, published as *Prelude to Infamy: The Story of Chancellor Dollfuss of Austria,* Obolensky, 1962.
The Anschluss, Lippincott, 1963 (published in England as *Anschluss: The Rape of Austria,* Macmillan, 1963).
Eagle and Unicorn (novel), Weidenfeld & Nicolson, 1966, published as *The Eferding Diaries,* Lippincott, 1967.
The Last Hapsburg, Weybright & Talley, 1968.
Between Two Flags: The Life of Baron Sir Rudolf von Slatin Pasha, Widenfeld & Nicolson, 1972, Putnam, 1973.
Uncle of Europe: The Social and Diplomatic Life of Edward VII, Harcourt, 1976.
The Storm Petrels: The First Soviet Defectors, 1928-1938, Collins, 1977, pbulished as *The Storm Petrels: The Flight of the First Soviet Defectors,* Harcourt, 1978.
November 1918, Little, Brown, 1981.
Archduke of Sarajevo: The Romance and Tragedy of Franz Ferdinand of Austria, Little, Brown, 1984, published as *Victims of Sarajevo: The Romance and Tragedy of Franz Ferdinand and Sophie,* Harville Press (London), 1984.
Royal Sunset: The European Dynasties and the Great War, Doubleday, 1987.
The Storm Birds: Soviet Postwar Defectors, Weidenfeld & Nicolson, 1989, Holt, 1990.
The Last Empress: The Life and Times of Zita of Austria-Hungary, 1892-1989, Harper, 1991.
The Austrians: A Thousand-Year Odyssey, Carroll & Graf, 1997.

Contributor to *Holiday, Atlantic Monthly, Esquire,* and other periodicals.

SIDELIGHTS: Gordon Brook-Shepherd is a respected scholar of Austrian history. Having lived in Austria for some fifteen years following World War II, a period which allowed him to meet many of the country's most prominent citizens, Brook-Shepherd has an intimate knowledge of Austria and its people that has served him well in writing his biographies and histories.

Among Brook-Shepherd's biographies is *Prelude to Infamy,* which concerns Austrian Chancellor Dollfuss, who was murdered during the Nazi putsch of 1934. G. A. Craig in *New York Herald Tribune Books* writes: "Brook-Shepherd's discussion of the evolution of Dollfuss' policy is both interesting and perceptive . . . his account of Dollfuss' tragic end is entirely absorbing." "Brook-Shepherd must be given credit," E. S. Pisko states in the *Christian Science Monitor,* "for shedding light on Austria's struggle and on its doomed helmsman in the throes of a hurricane."

In *Between Two Flags* Brook-Shepherd writes of Baron Sir Rudolf von Slatin Pasha, an Austrian who made England his home and served in the British Army in the Sudan. During World War I, Slatin turned on his British friends and offered his services to the Turks. "This is the first full-scale biography of Slatin," writes J. A. Casada in *Library Journal,* "and it does full justice to the Viennese cosmopolitan. . . . The research is thorough . . . and the author's writing style makes reading this work a real treat." The critic for the *Economist* finds that "the wide and careful research has resulted in a well-rounded portrait of Slatin and many insights into the age in which he lived."

Archduke of Sarajevo: The Romance and Tragedy of Franz Ferdinand of Austria is the story of the Austrian archduke whose assassination launched the First World War. "The first biography of the Archduke written in English," as Joseph W. Constance notes in *Library Journal,* Brook-Shepherd's account examines a figure who, had he lived another three years, would have ascended to the Austro-Hungarian throne. Given his reformist tendencies, Ferdinand may have been able to defuse the nationalistic tensions which led to the First World War. Constance finds the book to be "a pleasantly written work that makes solid use of the major primary sources." Barbara W. Tuchman, reviewing the book for the *New York Times Book Review,* calls it "a very worthwhile biography."

In 1997 Brook-Shepherd published *The Austrians: A Thousand-Year Odyssey,* a massive work which draws upon his extensive knowledge of the country as well as his previous written works. An "engrossing, elegantly written history," writes the critic for *Publishers Weekly, The Austrians* is a "dramatic, lively narrative." Gilbert Taylor of *Booklist* labels the book "a solidly informative and well-written work," while Randall L. Schoeder in *Library Journal*

was most impressed by Brook-Shepherd's "lively writing style."

BIOGRAPHICAL/CRITICAL SOURCES:

PERIODICALS

America, March 16, 1985.
Best Sellers, February 1, 1967; April 1, 1969.
Booklist, April 1, 1997, p. 1277.
Choice, September, 1973.
Christian Science Monitor, May 24, 1962, p. 9; January 26, 1967, p. 11.
Economist, April 13, 1963; January 20, 1973.
Foreign Affairs, July, 1962.
Library Journal, August, 1963; March 1, 1967; May 15, 1973; June 15, 1984; April 1, 1997, p. 105.
New Statesman, November 24, 1961; April 12, 1963; September 9, 1966; January 26, 1973.
New York Herald Tribune Books, April 8, 1962, p. 13.
New York Times Book Review, April 18, 1963, p. 3; February 5, 1967, p. 48; July 29, 1984, p. 24.
Publishers Weekly, February 17, 1997, p. 200.
Saturday Review, September 7, 1963.
Spectator, November 24, 1961.
Springfield Republican, April 8, 1962, p. D4.
Times Literary Supplement, November 17, 1961, p. 815; March 22, 1963, p. 195; June 29, 1973, p. 734.
Yale Review, October, 1963.

*   *   *

BROWN, Bill
See Brown, William L(ouis)

*   *   *

BROWN, Joe David 1915-1976

PERSONAL: Born May 12, 1915, in Birmingham, AL; died in 1976; son of William Samuel (a newspaper publisher) and Lucille (Lokey) Brown; married Mildred Harbour, October 24, 1935 (divorced, 1943); married Frances O'Reilly, June 30, 1945; children: Joe David, Jr., Tedd H., Gilbreth. *Education:* Attended University of Alabama. *Politics:* Independent. *Religion:* Protestant. *Avocational interests:* Hunting and fishing.

CAREER: Worked on newspapers in Alabama and Missouri, 1935-39; *New York Daily News,* New York City, feature writer, 1939-46; *Time* and *Life,* New York City, foreign correspondent in New Delhi, Paris, London, Moscow, 1949-57; freelance writer, 1957-76. *Military service:* U.S. Army, parachutist with 517th Combat Team, 1942-45; became second lieutenant; received battlefield commission, Purple Heart, and Croix de Guerre with palm (France).

WRITINGS:

NOVELS

Stars in My Crown, Morrow (New York City), 1946.
The Freeholder, Morrow, 1949.
Kings Go Forth, Morrow, 1956.
Glimpse of a Stranger, Morrow, 1968.
Addie Pray (Literary Guild selection), Simon & Schuster (New York City), 1971, published as *Paper Moon,* New American Library (New York City), 1972.

NONFICTION

(With the editors of *Life*) *India,* Time-Life (New York City), 1961, revised edition, 1969.

EDITOR

The Hippies, Time-Life, 1967.
Can Christianity Survive?, Time-Life, 1967.
Sex in the 60's: A Candid Look at the Age of Mini-Morals, Time-Life, 1967.

OTHER

Stars in My Crown (film based on his novel of same title), Metro-Goldwyn-Mayer, 1949.

Short stories anthologized in *Best Post Stories, Literature in America,* and *This Is Your War.* Contributor of short stories and articles to national magazines, including *Saturday Evening Post, Sports Illustrated,* and *Colliers.*

ADAPTATIONS: Kings Go Forth was filmed by United Artists in 1958; *Addie Pray* was filmed by Paramount under the title *Paper Moon* in 1973.

SIDELIGHTS: Joe David Brown wrote several novels that drew upon his own experiences growing up in America's South and his wartime experience in Europe during the Second World War. Three of his novels—*Stars in My Crown, Kings Go Forth* and *Addie Pray*—were adapted as successful films.

Brown's first novel, *Stars in My Crown,* is set in a small Georgia town and revolves around a minister and his inseparable grandson. David Tilden in the *New York Herald Tribune Weekly Book Review* found the story to be "a sentimental and nostalgic portrait," while the critic for *Kirkus* found that it revealed "a sympathetic understanding of human nature." Therese de Grace in the *New York Times* was impressed by "the considerable charm of this first novel."

In *Kings Go Forth,* Brown drew on his own wartime experiences to write the story of two American soldiers in Europe during the Second World War who vie for the same girl. Ruth Telser in the *San Francisco Chronicle* judged the book "a short, tense novel of psychological suspense." W. K. Harrison in the *Library Journal* believed that "women will appreciate the sensitively told romance," while the *Time* critic believed "the scenes of military conflict flare across the pages as vividly as tracers stabbing the night sky."

Addie Pray is the story of a young orphan girl who works with an older conman to swindle Depression-era farmers in the American South. Reviewing *Addie Pray* in *Time,* Martha Duffy observed, "Brown has a special feeling for the Depression-era South [and] for the likes of his protagonist. . . . Addie's speech . . . is vulgar, pungent country talk, which adds greatly to the book's easygoing charm." Earl Tannenbaum of *Library Journal* called *Addie Pray* "a latter-day rogue story." "The characters' hairbreadth escapes and sense of accomplishment as their schemes succeed make it easy for the reader to identify with the lovable rascals," Tannenbaum concluded.

BIOGRAPHICAL/CRITICAL SOURCES:

PERIODICALS

Best Sellers, May 15, 1968.
Booklist, November 15, 1947; September 1, 1949.
Chicago Sunday Tribune, April 15, 1956, p. 4.
Christian Science Monitor, September 15, 1949, p. 15.
Kirkus, September 1, 1947; July 1, 1949; February 1, 1956.
Library Journal, August, 1949; April 15, 1956; January 15, 1968; September 15, 1971.
New Yorker, August 21, 1971.

New York Herald Tribune Book Review, November 20, 1949, p. 20.
New York Herald Tribune Weekly Book Review, October 19, 1947, p. 20.
New York Times, October 19, 1947, p. 18; September 18, 1949, p. 37; May 13, 1956, p. 28.
New York Times Book Review, March 24, 1968, p. 28; August 8, 1971, p. 20.
San Francisco Chronicle, May 27, 1956, p. 25.
Saturday Review, April 7, 1956.
Saturday Review of Literature, December 3, 1949.
Springfield Republican, October 23, 1949, p. A19.
Time, April 9, 1956; March 15, 1968; July 26, 1971.*

* * *

BROWN, John Mason 1900-1969

PERSONAL: Born July 3, 1900, in Louisville, KY; died in 1969; son of John Mason (a lawyer) and Carrie (Ferguson) Brown; married Catherine Screven Meredith, February 11, 1933; children: Preston, Meredith Mason. *Education:* Harvard University, A.B. (cum laude), 1923.

CAREER: Theatre Arts Monthly, New York City, associate editor and drama critic, 1924-28; *New York Evening Post,* New York City, drama critic, 1929-41; *New York World Telegram,* New York City, drama critic, 1941-42; *Saturday Review,* New York City, associate editor, 1944-45, author of column, "Seeing Things," 1944-64, editor-at-large, 1955-69. American Laboratory Theater, staff lecturer, 1925-31; teacher of courses on the theater at University of Montana, summers of 1923, 1929, 1931, at Yale University, 1932, at Bread Loaf Writers' Conference, Middlebury College, summers of 1935, 1936, and at Harvard University, summers of 1937-40. Public lecturer throughout United States, beginning in 1928. Conductor of Columbia Broadcasting System program, "Of Men and Books," 1944-47, American Broadcasting Co. television program, "Critic-at-Large," 1948-49; panelist on Columbia Broadcasting System television program, "The Last Word," 1957-59. Book-of-the-Month Club judge, 1956-69. Harvard College, overseer, 1949-55; trustee of Metropolitan Museum of Art, 1951-56, of New York Society Library, 1950-69, and of Recordings for the Blind. *Military service:* U.S. Naval Reserve, lieutenant, 1942-44; served on staff of Vice-Admiral Alan G. Kirk during invasions of Sicily and Normandy; received Bronze Star.

MEMBER: New York Drama Critics Circle (president, 1941-42, 1945-49), PEN (president, 1947-48), National Institute of Arts and Letters, Council on Foreign Relations, Century Association, Phi Beta Kappa, Harvard Club.

AWARDS, HONORS: L.H.D., Williams College, 1941; D.Litt., University of Montana, 1942, Clark University, 1947, University of Louisville, 1948, Hofstra College, 1954, Long Island University, 1963.

WRITINGS:

The Modern Theater in Revolt, Norton (New York City), 1929.
Upstage: The American Theatre in Performance, Norton, 1930.
(Editor with Montrose Moses) *American Theatre as Seen by Its Critics,* Norton, 1934.
Letters from Greenroom Ghosts, Viking (New York City), 1934.
The Art of Playgoing, Norton, 1936.
Two on the Aisle, Norton, 1938.
(With others) *George Pierce Baker, a Memorial,* Dramatists, 1939.
Broadway in Review, Norton, 1940.
Inside Out, Dodd (New York City), 1942.
Accustomed as I Am, Norton, 1942.
To All Hands, McGraw (New York City), 1943.
Many a Watchful Night, McGraw, 1944.
Seeing Things, McGraw, 1946.
Seeing More Things, Whittlesey House, 1948.
Beyond the Present, Ampersand, 1948.
Morning Faces, Whittlesey House, 1949.
(Editor) *The Portable Charles Lamb,* Viking, 1949.
Still Seeing Things, McGraw, 1950.
As They Appear, McGraw, 1952.
Daniel Boone, the Opening of the Wilderness, Random House (New York City), 1952.
Through These Men, Harper (New York City), 1956.
(Editor) *Ladies' Home Journal Treasury,* Simon & Schuster (New York City), 1956.
Dramatis Personae, (contains complete text of *The Modern Theatre in Revolt*), Viking, 1963.
The Worlds of Robert E. Sherwood: Mirror of His Times, 1896-1939, Harper, 1965.
The Ordeal of a Playwright: Robert E. Sherwood and the Challenge of War, edited and with introduction by Norman Cousins, Harper, 1970.

Also author of introduction to several books, including Hiram K. Moderwell, *The Theater of Today,* Dodd, 1927; Bennett A. Cerf and V. H. Cartmell, editors, *Sixteen Famous British Plays,* Garden City Publishers, 1942; Margaret Webster, *Shakespeare Without Tears,* McGraw, 1942; and Joseph Hennessey, editor, *The Portable Woollcott,* 1946.

SIDELIGHTS: Theatre critic John Mason Brown had an enthusiastic reading audience and an immense popularity as a lecturer. Several collections of Brown's theatrical reviews, reprinting his judgments first published in New York newspapers, were popular with the reading public. *Two on the Aisle: Ten Years of the American Theatre in Performance* was, according to R. H. Gaines in the *New York Times,* "as readable, witty and worth-while a compendium of comment on the modern stage as you are likely to come across." The collection proved Brown to be, according to E. N. Jenckes in the *Springfield Republican,* "a discerning critic and able writer." James Gray in the *Saturday Review of Literature* believed: "If all other records were lost, *Two on the Aisle* would give a future historian an adequate and interesting idea of what liberal opinion toward dramatic art, and dramatic art itself, had been."

Seeing Things, Seeing More Things and *Still Seeing Things* gathered together examples of Brown's weekly column "Seeing Things" from the *Saturday Review.* Brown wrote the column for twenty years, commenting not only on plays but on theatre personalities, films, and related topics. The *Kirkus* reviewer noted that *Seeing Things* showed Brown to have "a sophistication balanced with a real effort of evaluation, a charm of style that is often brightened by a precise humor." Irwin Edman in the *Saturday Review of Literature* described Brown's collection as "a sort of philosophical running commentary, a philosophy of life in these various aspects of it which impinge on Mr. Brown's lively and delicate sensibilities."

Brown's fellow critics were at times divided as to his precise merits. George Freedley in *Library Journal* called his selected critical writings, *Dramatis Personae,* "one of the great theater books of this century." Yet John Simon in the *New York Times Book Review* said of the same collection: "What is most lacking is discrimination." At the time of Brown's death, Norman Cousins wrote: "He was first of all a man of taste, a presiding fact about his criticism that everyone connected with the theater came to recognize and respect. . . . His writings in [*The Saturday Review*] widened progressively until they embraced the world of the creative arts as a whole . . . combining the public interest in the topical with the critic's interest in the generic and the historical."

BIOGRAPHICAL/CRITICAL SOURCES:

BOOKS

Stevens, George, *Speak for Yourself: The Life of John Mason Brown,* Viking, 1974.

PERIODICALS

American Literature, November, 1971.
Atlantic, November, 1946; September, 1965.
Booklist, January, 1935; November 1, 1938; January 1, 1945; October 1, 1946; October 15, 1948; November 15, 1952; December 15, 1952.
Bookmark, November, 1952.
Books, November 25, 1934.
Book Week, December 24, 1944, p. 1; September 15, 1946.
Boston Globe, December 27, 1944, p. 15.
Chicago Sun, October 31, 1948.
Chicago Sunday Tribune, November 16, 1952, p. 14.
Christian Century, December 27, 1944.
Christian Science Monitor, December 15, 1944, p. 14; October 5, 1946, p. 16; November 6, 1952, p. 11.
Cleveland Open Shelf, December, 1938, p. 22; September, 1946, p. 18.
Commonweal, October 15, 1948.
Harper, January, 1971.
Kirkus, November 1, 1944; August 1, 1946; July 15, 1948; August 1, 1952.
Library Journal, October 15, 1948; September 15, 1952; October 1, 1952; June 1, 1963; February 1, 1971.
Manchester Guardian, October 25, 1946, p. 3.
Nation, December 19, 1934; October 15, 1938.
New Republic, January 1, 1945.
Newsweek, March 31, 1969.
New Yorker, December 9, 1944; October 18, 1952.
New York Herald Tribune Weekly Book Review, October 10, 1948, p. 5; October 26, 1952, p. 3; November 16, 1952, p. 11.
New York Times, November 18, 1934, p. 11; October 30, 1938, p. 5; December 3, 1944, p. 7; September 15, 1946, p. 6; September 26, 1948, p. 28; October 19, 1952, p. 34; March 17, 1969.
New York Times Book Review, July 14, 1963, p. 26; September 19, 1965.
Pratt, winter, 1939, p. 25.
San Francisco Chronicle, September 12, 1946, p. 12; September 22, 1948, p. 18; October 28, 1952, p. 19.

Saturday Review, November 15, 1952; June 8, 1963; March 29, 1969.
Saturday Review of Literature, December 15, 1934; October 15, 1938; December 2, 1944; September 21, 1946; October 9, 1948.
Springfield Republican, October 15, 1938, p. 6; December 17, 1944, p. D4; November 14, 1948, p. C7.
Theatre Arts, November, 1938; January, 1945; October, 1946; October, 1948.
Time, March 28, 1969.
Times Literary Supplement, October 26, 1946, p. 522.
Variety, March 19, 1969.
Washington Post, March 17, 1969.
Weekly Book Review, December 3, 1944, p. 1; September 15, 1946, p. 4.*

* * *

BROWN, John Russell 1923-

PERSONAL: Born September 15, 1923, in Bristol, England; son of Russell Alan (a butcher) and Olive Helen (Golding) Brown; married Hilary Sue Baker (a potter), April, 1961; children: Alice Amelia, Sophia Clemence, Jasper James Mallord. *Education:* Keble College, Oxford, B.A., 1949, B.Litt., 1952; University of Birmingham, Ph.D., 1960.

ADDRESSES: Office—Department of Theatre Arts, State University of New York, Stony Brook, NY, 11794; and National Theatre, South Bank, London SE1, England.

CAREER: University of Birmingham, Birmingham, England, 1955-71, began as lecturer, became senior lecturer in English literature, 1955-63, professor of drama and theater arts and head of department, 1963-71; University of Sussex, Falmer, Brighton, Sussex, England, professor of English, 1971-82; State University of New York at Stony Brook, professor, 1982—. Reynolds Lecturer, University of Colorado, 1957; Folger Library fellow, Washington, DC, 1957, 1963; Mellon Professor of Drama, Carnegie Institute (now Carnegie-Mellon University), 1964; Jones Lecturer, University of Liverpool, 1972; Robb Lecturer, University of Auckland, 1979. Visiting professor, University of Zurich, Switzerland, 1970-71; university lecturer, University of Toronto, 1971. Director, Orbit Theatre Company, 1971—; associate director, National Theatre, 1973—. Theatre Museum, London,

England, member of advisory council, 1975—, chairman, 1980—. Member of the drama panel of the Arts Council of Great Britain, 1978-82; member of advisory council of Victoria and Albert Museum, 1980—. *Military service:* Royal Navy, 1942-46; became sub-lieutenant.

WRITINGS:

(Editor) Shakespeare, *The Merchant of Venice,* Methuen (London), 1955.
Shakespeare and His Comedies, Methuen, 1957, 2nd edition, Barnes & Noble (New York City), 1962.
(Editor) John Webster, *The White Devil,* Methuen, 1960.
Shakespeare: The Tragedy of Macbeth, Edward Arnold (London), 1962.
(Editor) Webster, *The Duchess of Malfi,* Methuen, 1965.
(Editor) Shakespeare, *Henry V,* New American Library (New York City), 1965.
Shakespeare's Plays in Performance, Edward Arnold, 1966, St. Martin's (New York City), 1967.
A University and the Theatre: An Inaugural Lecture Delivered in the University of Birmingham on 26th October 1967, University of Birmingham (Birmingham, England), 1968.
Drama, Heinemann (London), 1968.
(Editor) *Modern British Dramatists: A Collection of Critical Essays,* Prentice-Hall (Englewood Cliffs, NJ), 1968, revised edition published as *Modern British Dramatists: New Perspectives,* 1984.
Effective Theatre: A Study with Documentation, Heinemann, 1969.
(Editor) *Shakespeare: Antony and Cleopatra, a Casebook,* Aurora Publishers (Nashville), 1970.
Shakespeare's Dramatic Style: Romeo and Juliet, As You Like It, Julius Caesar, Twelfth Night, Macbeth, Heinemann, 1970, Barnes & Noble, 1971.
(Editor) *Drama and the Theatre with Radio, Film and Television: An Outline for the Student,* Routledge (London), 1971.
Theatre Language: A Study of Arden, Osborne, Pinter and Wesker, Taplinger (New York City), 1972.
Free Shakespeare, Heinemann, 1974.
Shakespeare in Performance: An Introduction through Six Major Plays, Harcourt (New York City), 1976.
(Editor) Christopher Marlowe, *Tamburlaine the Great: Parts One and Two,* Collins (London), 1976.

Discovering Shakespeare: A New Guide to the Plays, Columbia University Press (New York City), 1981.

Shakespeare and His Theatre, Lothrop (New York City), 1982.

(Editor) *Focus on Macbeth,* Routledge, 1982.

A Short Guide to Modern British Drama, Barnes & Noble, 1983.

The Complete Plays of the Wakefield Master, in a New Version for Reading and Performance, Heinemann, 1983.

(Editor) Shakespeare, *The Life of Henry V, with New Dramatic Criticism and an Updated Bibliography,* New American Library, 1988.

(Editor) *Shakescenes: Shakespeare for Two,* Applause Books (New York City), 1992.

William Shakespeare: Writing for Performance, St. Martin's, 1996.

What Is Theatre?, Focal Press (Boston), 1997.

(Editor) *The Oxford Illustrated History of Theatre,* Oxford University Press (New York City), 1997.

General editor, "Stratford-upon-Avon Studies" and "Stratford-upon-Avon Library."

SIDELIGHTS: John Russell Brown is a respected scholar of Shakespearian theatre whose studies, drawing upon his own experience in the theatre, are written for those who are staging Shakespeare's plays rather than studying them as works of written literature. A critic for the *Virginia Quarterly Review* notes: "Brown is perceptive and his theatrical approach justifies itself time and again in close and subtle readings of the text."

In *Shakespeare's Plays in Performance* Brown evaluates the relationships between Shakespeare's plays and both the actors performing them and the audience viewing them, focusing on recent British performances of Shakespeare. According to the reviewer for the *Times Literary Supplement,* the "strongest impression left by this book is its author's practical experience of the theatre, his understanding of its needs and its possibilities. Thus, he can also offer actors and directors a method of approaching the plays that will yield fruitful rewards." As the *Choice* critic notes: "The book will please those who prefer theatrical criticism to literary criticism."

Shakespeare's Dramatic Style: Romeo and Juliet, As You Like It, Julius Caesar, Twelfth Night, Macbeth again examines Shakespeare's dramatic works from the perspective of actors and directors wishing to stage the texts. Describing Brown as "a man who knows how to read Shakespeare," J. H. Crouch in *Library Journal* calls Brown's *Shakespeare's Dramatic Style* a book of "refined logic and (often) inspired interpretation." The *Choice* critic finds that Brown gives "both the experienced and the novice reader of Shakespeare an opportunity to understand the plays by helping him see what takes place in the 'theatre of the mind.'"

BIOGRAPHICAL/CRITICAL SOURCES:

PERIODICALS

Choice, December, 1967; June, 1971; July/August, 1973.

Library Journal, April 1, 1968; June 1, 1971; December 1, 1972.

Times Literary Supplement, January 5, 1967, p. 10; December 29, 1972, p. 1569.

Virginia Quarterly Review, winter, 1968; summer, 1968.

Yale Review, December, 1967.

*   *   *

BROWN, Marion Marsh 1908-

PERSONAL: Born July 22, 1908, in Brownville, NE; daughter of Cassius Henry and Jenevie (Hairgrove) Marsh; married Gilbert S. Brown (a lawyer), 1937 (deceased); children: Paul Marsh. *Education:* Peru State Teachers College (now Peru State College), Peru, NE, A.B., 1927; University of Nebraska, M.A., 1930; University of Minnesota, graduate study. *Politics:* Republican. *Religion:* Presbyterian.

ADDRESSES: Home—2615 North 52nd St., Omaha, NE 68104.

CAREER: Writer. Teacher of English and speech in public high schools in Nebraska, 1928-36; Peru State Teachers College (now Peru State College), Peru, NE, assistant professor of English, 1935-37; Municipal University of Omaha (now University of Nebraska at Omaha), Omaha, NE, associate professor, 1953-64, professor of English, 1965-67.

MEMBER: American Association of University Women (past president), National Pen Women, National Council of Teachers of English, Nebraska Council of Teachers of English, Nebraska Writers'

Guild (past president), Phi Delta Gamma, Sigma Tau Delta, Kappa Delta Pi, Zeta Tau Alpha.

AWARDS, HONORS: Distinguished Service Award, Peru State College, 1979.

WRITINGS:

Young Nathan (Junior Literary Guild selection), Westminster (Philadelphia), 1949.
Swamp Fox (Boys' Clubs of America selection), Westminster, 1950.
Frontier Beacon, Westminster, 1953.
Broad Stripes and Bright Stars (Children's Book Club selection), Westminster, 1955.
Prairie Teacher, Bouregy, 1957.
Learning Words in Context, Chandler Publishing (New York City), 1961, revised edition, Harper (New York City), 1974.
A Nurse Abroad, Bouregy, 1963.
(With Ruth Crone) *The Silent Storm* (Junior Literary Guild selection), Abingdon, 1963.
Stuart's Landing, Westminster, 1968.
(With Crone) *Willa Cather: The Woman and Her Works,* Scribner (New York City), 1970.
Marnie, Westminster, 1971.
The Pauper Prince: A Story of Hans Christian Andersen, Crescent Publications (Los Angeles), 1973.
The Brownville Story, Nebraska Historical Society, 1974.
(With Crone) *Only One Point of the Compass: Willa Cather in the Northeast,* Archer Editions (Danbury, CT), 1980.
Homeward the Arrow's Flight, Abingdon (Nashville), 1980.
Dream Catcher: The Life of John Neihardt, Abingdon, 1983.
Sacagawea: Indian Interpreter to Lewis and Clark, Children's Press (Chicago), 1988.
Singapore, Children's Press, 1989.
Susette La Flesche: Advocate for Native American Rights, Children's Press, 1992.

Contributor of about 200 short stories and articles to magazines.

SIDELIGHTS: Marion Marsh Brown has written biographies of heroic figures from America's colonial and frontier days, including Nathan Hale, Francis Marion, John Neihardt and Sacagawea. Her work—usually aimed at a teenaged reading audience—has been particularly praised for its realistic characters. *Young Nathan* tells the story of Revolutionary War hero Nathan Hale, beginning with his school years and leading to his death during the American Revolution. The critic for *Kirkus* calls the book "a beautifully written fictionalized biography," while Esther Gorey in *Library Journal* notes that the story is "so real it seems as though one of our own friends were being marched off to the gallows."

In *Swamp Fox* Brown tells the heroic story of Francis Marion, an American general during the Revolutionary War who led a ragtag group of soldiers in a guerilla war against the British in South Carolina. Because of his ability to strike unexpectedly and then disappear, Marion earned the nickname Swamp Fox. Writing in *Library Journal,* Elizabeth Burr finds that Brown's book makes an "admirable contribution to the understanding of the Revolutionary period." L. S. Bechtel in the *New York Herald Tribune Book Review* writes: "The style is frequently sentimental, but the tale is full of action and will make Marion's campaign real."

Homeward the Arrow's Flight concerns the life story of Susan La Flesche, an Omaha Indian woman who became a medical doctor in the nineteenth century. Her sister, Susette La Flesche, was an activist in the Native American Rights movement. For Susan to become a doctor at the time she did was unusual, as few women or Indians were admitted into medical schools at the time. The critic for the *Bulletin of the Center for Children's Books* notes that Brown's "writing style is ornate, occasionally fulsome, but the facts are interesting enough to alleviate such weaknesses." M. J. Porter in *Voice of Youth Advocates* calls *Homeward the Arrow's Flight* "a good book for a reader looking for a new biographical topic."

Brown once told *CA:* "One of my editors once said that I write for 'the young in heart, age nine to ninety.' Although I have directed a large portion of my writing to young people in middle school through high school, it is true that adults read and enjoy my books. I hope this says I have something to say which is of value. "I have always enjoyed young people and believe that I understand some of their growing-up problems. So, through my writing, I have tried to help them confront their problems from a sound value base, and to give them a feeling of continuity with the past which I believe is essential in developing maturity."

BIOGRAPHICAL/CRITICAL SOURCES:

PERIODICALS

Best Sellers, October 15, 1963.
Booklist, October 1, 1949; February 15, 1951; June 15, 1953.
Bookmark, November, 1949.
Book Week, November 10, 1963, p. 34.
Bulletin of the Center for Children's Books, November, 1980.
Christian Century, December 18, 1963.
Commonweal, November 15, 1963.
Horn Book, September, 1949.
Kirkus, August 1, 1949; September 1, 1950; February 15, 1953.
Library Journal, October 15, 1949; October 1, 1950; April 15, 1953; September 15, 1963.
New York Herald Tribune Book Review, January 21, 1951, p. 10; April 12, 1953, p. 16.
New York Times, January 22, 1950, p. 18.
New York Times Book Review, January 26, 1964, p. 26.
Voice of Youth Advocates, February, 1981.

* * *

BROWN, Mark H(erbert) 1900-1988

PERSONAL: Born July 6, 1900, in Wellman, IA; died February 16, 1988; son of William John (a farmer) and Harriett (Varney) Brown; married Alice Mildred Hansell (a teacher), June 9, 1934; children: John Herbert, Judith Harriett (deceased). *Education:* Iowa State College of Agriculture and Mechanic Arts (now Iowa State University of Science and Technology), B.S., 1924, M.S., 1930, Ph.D., 1932 *Religion:* Protestant.

CAREER: U. S. Department of Agriculture, Soil Conservation Service, soil scientist in various parts of the country, 1934-54; Trails End Farm, Alta, IA, farmer, 1954-88. *Military service:* U.S. Army, 1918. U.S. Army Air Forces and U.S. Air Force, active duty as Intelligence officer, 1942-53, Reserve service, 1953-62; became lieutenant colonel; received Bronze Star Medal, 1945.

AWARDS, HONORS: Buffalo Award, New York Posse of the Westerners, for best nonfiction western book of 1955, *The Frontier Years: L. A. Huffman, Photographer of the Plains.*

WRITINGS:

(With William Reid Felton) *The Frontier Years: L. A. Huffman, Photographer of the Plains,* Holt (New York City), 1955.
(With Felton) *Before Barbed Wire: L. A. Huffman, Photographer on Horseback,* Holt, 1956.
The Plainsmen of the Yellowstone: A History of the Yellowstone Basin, Putnam (New York City), 1961.
The Flight of the Nez Perce, Putnam, 1967.

Contributor to periodicals.

SIDELIGHTS: Mark H. Brown specialized in books about the American West. With William Reid Felton, Brown co-wrote two books on Western photographer L. A. Huffman. Huffman was official photographer at an army post in the Montana Territory in 1878, and his photographs captured early images of the area's Native Americans, frontier towns, buffalo hunters, and homesteaders. In *Frontier Years: L. A. Huffman, Photographer of the Plains* Brown and Felton present over 120 of Huffman's photographs which trace "the end of a frontier civilization," as E. W. Foell wrote in the *Christian Science Monitor.* Along with the photographs is a "running commentary" by Brown and Felton which provides "a wealth of fascinating detail," according to J. K. Hutchens in the *New York Herald Tribune Book Review.* Walter Prescott Webb, writing in the *Saturday Review,* called *Frontier Years* "a classic on the American West. I do not use the word classic lightly. . . . This one has a quality of content and a texture that make it unique." Foell also found the book "in every sense a classic."

In *Before Barbed Wire: L. A. Huffman, Photographer on Horseback,* Brown and Felton gather Huffman's photographs of range life among the cowboys of Montana. Peter Pollack in the *Chicago Sunday Tribune* praised the "clearly written, perfectly annotated, and authenticated text" which Brown and Felton wrote to accompany the photographs. Ross Santee in the *New York Herald Tribune Book Review* judged the text to be "done with clarity and simplicity."

Brown's solo effort, *The Plainsmen of the Yellowstone: A History of the Yellowstone Basin* traces the history of the region from the earliest French explorers to the Sioux Indian uprising of the late-nineteenth century. The *Booklist* reviewer described the book as an "extensive, carefully researched work [which] contains a wealth of information." Although the *Kirkus* critic called *The Plainsmen of the Yellowstone* "unevenly written and awkwardly arranged," he admitted that "professional historians . . . will value it for its quotations from little-known sources and for its excellent bibliography." G. W. Gressley in *Library Journal* believed that "the merits of the work . . . are substantial and . . . should guarantee the purchase by every library which desires to have a basic Western Americana collection."

In *The Flight of the Nez Perce* Brown tells of the epic nineteenth-century march of the Nez Perce Indians from their reservation in Idaho to the Canadian border, fighting American troops along the way. Brown, a former Army intelligence officer, wrote his account from an intelligence perspective, examining all the evidence behind the conflict between the Nez Perce and the American government and criticizing the way the army conducted itself during the prolonged campaign. J. N. Goodsell in the *Christian Science Monitor* claimed: "Brown's recounting of the Nez Perce story is better than earlier accounts." H. E. Smith of *Library Journal* admitted that "this will likely be the definitive history of the Nez Perce War for many years." N. S. Momaday in the *New York Times Book Review* called Brown's history "thorough and thoroughly readable."

BIOGRAPHICAL/CRITICAL SOURCES:

PERIODICALS

American Historical Review, July, 1967.
Booklist, November 15, 1955; November 15, 1956; October 15, 1961.
Book Week, January 29, 1967, p. 1.
Chicago Sunday Tribune, November 6, 1955, p. 6; November 18, 1956, p. 3; September 24, 1961, p. 4.
Christian Science Monitor, December 8, 1955, p. 8; December 20, 1956, p. 7; February 23, 1967, p. 11.
Journal of American History, June, 1967.
Kirkus, August 15, 1955; August 15, 1960.
Library Journal, December 1, 1955; September 15, 1961; December 15, 1966.
New Yorker, March 11, 1967.
New York Herald Tribune Book Review, October 30, 1955, p. 2; December 9, 1956, p. 4.
New York Times Book Review, March 19, 1967, p. 55.
San Francisco Chronicle, January 14, 1962, p. 35.

Saturday Review, November 26, 1955; November 24, 1956.
Time, December 17, 1956.*

* * *

BROWN, Marvin L(uther), Jr. 1920-

PERSONAL: Born September 1, 1920, in Philadelphia, PA; son of Marvin L. and Helen (DePue) Brown; married Elizabeth Dodge, July 16, 1943; children: Elizabeth F. (Mrs. Walter R. Tucker), Helen D. P.O. Box 607, Garner, NC 27529. *Education:* Haverford College, A.B., 1943; University of Pennsylvania, A.M., 1947, Ph.D., 1951. *Religion:* Episcopalian.

ADDRESSES: Office—Department of History, North Carolina State University, Raleigh, NC 27607.

CAREER: Haverford College, Haverford, PA, instructor in history, 1949; North Carolina State University, Raleigh, instructor, 1949-51, assistant professor, 1951-57, associate professor, 1957-59, professor of history, 1959—. Fulbright research professor at University of Vienna, 1955-56; visiting professor at Duke University, 1961, 1968. *Military service:* U.S. Marine Corps, 1942-46. U.S. Marine Corps Reserve, 1942-63; retired as major.

MEMBER: American Historical Association, Society for French Historical Studies.

WRITINGS:

(Editor and translator) *American Independence through Prussian Eyes: A Neutral View of the Peace Negotiations of 1782-1783: Selections from the Prussian Diplomatic Correspondence,* Duke University Press (Durham, NC), 1959.
The Baroness von Riedesel and the American Revolution: Journal and Correspondence of a Tour of Duty, 1776-1783, University of North Carolina Press (Chapel Hill), 1965.
(Editor with Evelyn M. Acomb) *French Society and Culture Since the Old Regime,* Holt (New York City), 1966.
The Comte de Chambord: The Third Republic's Uncompromising King, Duke University Press, 1967.

(Editor with Nancy N. Barker) *Diplomacy in an Age of Nationalism: Essays in Honor of Lynn Marshall Case,* Nijhoff (The Hague), 1971.

Heinrich von Haymerle: Austro-Hungarian Career Diplomat, 1828-1881, University of South Carolina (Columbia), 1973.

(With Harold T. Parker) *Major Themes in Modern European History: An Invitation to Inquiry and Reflection,* three volumes, Moore Publishing (Durham), 1974.

Louis Veuillot: French Ultramontane Catholic Journalist and Layman, 1813-1883, Moore Publishing, 1977.

(Editor) Frederick A. Seelig, *One Marine Mustang's Memoirs: Fifty Months with Defense Batallions in the Pacific, 1940-1945,* Vantage Press (New York City), 1997.

Editor of *French Historical Studies,* 1958-63.

SIDELIGHTS: Marvin L. Brown has written and edited a number of volumes about European and American history of the eighteenth and nineteenth centuries.

In *American Independence through Prussian Eyes* and *The Baroness von Riedesel and the American Revolution* Brown presents European correspondence from the period of the American Revolution which reveals fresh information on how European nations not involved in the conflict viewed the affair. *American Independence through Prussian Eyes* contains some 248 letters written by Prussian king Frederick the Great to his diplomats about the peace negotiations between England and American in 1782 and 1783. The letters, according to F. E. Hirsch in *Library Journal,* "throw new light on the history of American independence and on Frederick the Great's diplomacy." W. M. Wallace in the *American Historical Review* claims that "the letters are sufficiently revealing to satisfy all but the most exacting scholars of the period." *The Baroness von Riedesel and the American Revolution* contains letters written by the wife of General von Riedesel, who commanded the German mercenary troops fighting with George Washington during the American Revolution. In these letters, the baroness gives her perspective on life in Colonial America during the Revolution. The critic for *Virginia Quarterly Review* notes: "It is the best woman's view we have of the American Revolution." J. A. Schutz in *American Historical Review* calls the book an "unusually intimate journal. . . . [Brown] has done a careful editing job."

BIOGRAPHICAL/CRITICAL SOURCES:

PERIODICALS

American Historical Review, October, 1959; July, 1965; April, 1968.
Choice, April, 1968; September, 1973.
Journal of American History, June, 1965.
Library Journal, October 15, 1958.
New England Quarterly, December, 1959; December, 1965.
Times Literary Supplement, September 14, 1973, p. 1048.
Virginia Quarterly Review, spring, 1965.

*   *   *

BROWN, Norman O(liver) 1913-

PERSONAL: Born September 25, 1913, in El Oro, Mexico; son of Norman C. (a mining engineer) and Marcarita Brown; married Elizabeth Potter, October 1, 1938; children: Stephen R., Thomas N., Rebecca M., Susan E. *Education:* Balliol College, Oxford, B.A., 1936; attended University of Chicago; University of Wisconsin, Ph.D., 1942.

ADDRESSES: Office—Department of Humanities, Cowell College, University of California, Santa Cruz, CA 95060.

CAREER: Nebraska Wesleyan University, Lincoln, professor of languages, 1942-43; Wesleyan University, Middletown, CT, 1964-68, began as assistant professor of classics, became J. A. Seney Professor of Greek; former Wilson Professor of Classics and Comparative Literature, University of Rochester, Rochester, NY; University of California, Santa Cruz, 1971—, member of humanities faculty. *Military service:* Office of Strategic Services, 1943-46.

MEMBER: American Philological Association.

AWARDS, HONORS: Commonwealth Fund fellow, 1936-38; Ford Foundation teaching fellow, 1953-54; Guggenheim fellow, 1958-59.

WRITINGS:

Hermes the Thief: The Evolution of a Myth, University of Wisconsin Press (Madison), 1947.

(Translator and author of introduction) Hesiod, *Theogony,* Liberal Arts Press (New York City), 1953.

Life against Death: The Psychoanalytical Meaning of History, Wesleyan University Press (Middletown, CT), 1959.

Love's Body, Random House (New York City), 1966.

Closing Time, Random House, 1973.

Apocalypse and/or Metamorphosis, University of California Press (Berkeley), 1991.

SIDELIGHTS: Norman O. Brown is known for several provocative books of philosophical speculation. In *Life Against Death: The Psychoanalytical Meaning of History,* Brown draws on Freudian concepts in an attempt to write a history of the human race. As Maurice Richardson explains in the *New Statesman,* "*Life Against Death* is a running dive off the Freudian springboard into history's deep end. It is a fascinating book, discursive, inconsequent, sometimes preposterous, but full of interesting ideas, product of a learned man in a tight place, one of those rare genuine stimulators." J. E. Dittes in *Yale Review* writes: "Brown . . . takes us on an admittedly exciting Peter Pan-like tour of many different realms," while P. A. Bertocci in *Christian Century* warns: "To be so facile with ideas, to be so loose in the use of terms, is only to detract from the basic impact that this book could have made as a provocative rather than provoking, and scholarly, work."

Love's Body is a discussion of the role of erotic love in human history, seeing a constant struggle between eroticism and civilization as the key to humankind's dilemma. As the critic for *Time* sums it up, Brown "seems to advocate the complete abolition of 20th century civilization. If all trappings of civilization were put aside, he believes all repressions would go with them." W. S. Schlamm in *National Review* finds that Brown's frequent aphorisms should more rightly be called "bcforisms: it's all been said before, by Nietzsche and Freud, only more wittily, more poetically, and with more scholarship." Allan Angoff in *Library Journal* claims that even if *Love's Body* "sometimes seems overlearned, it will prove stimulating to the patient reader."

Closing Time is an interweaving of quotations from James Joyce's *Finnegan's Wake* with excerpts from the works of eighteenth-century philosopher Giambattista Vico. Brown provides interconnecting commentaries to draw comparisons between Vico's theoretical ideas and those expressed in Joyce's novel. E. W. Said in the *New York Times Book Review* praises *Closing Time* for "the freedom of its text and organization, and for the pleasure of its learning and intellectual performance." T. J. Galvin in *Library Journal* calls the book "an extraordinary tour de force."

BIOGRAPHICAL/CRITICAL SOURCES:

BOOKS

Shepherd, William C., *Symbolical Consciousness: A Commentary on Love's Body,* Scholars Press (Missoula, MT), 1976.

PERIODICALS

American Scholar, winter, 1966-67.
Book Week, July 10, 1966, p. 5.
Christian Century, June 24, 1959; July 20, 1966.
Commentary, February, 1967; March, 1967.
Commonweal, December 23, 1966.
Harper, November, 1966.
Library Journal, April 15, 1959; July, 1966; July, 1973.
National Review, October 18, 1966.
New Republic, September 22, 1973.
New Statesman, September 19, 1959.
New York Review of Books, May 4, 1967.
New York Times, July 15, 1966.
New York Times Book Review, July 24, 1966, p. 3; September 9, 1973, p. 31.
Saturday Night, July, 1967.
Shenandoah, summer, 1967.
Spectator, December 4, 1959, p. 831.
Time, July 15, 1966.
Times Literary Supplement, October 16, 1959, p. 595.
Tri-Quarterly, spring, 1968.
Yale Review, June, 1959.

*   *   *

BROWN, Pamela (Beatrice) 1924-1989

PERSONAL: Born December 31, 1924, in Colchester, Essex, England; died January 26, 1989; daughter of Frederick Leonard and Sepha (Sale) Brown; married Donald Masters, June 24, 1949 (died, 1963); children: Verity Madeleine, Juliet Maxine Sepha. *Education:* Attended county schools in England and Royal Academy of Dramatic Art.

CAREER: Writer. Worked in theatre, films and broadcasting before 1950; British Broadcasting Corp., London, producer, 1950-55; Scottish Television, Glasgow, Scotland, producer, 1956-57; Granada Television, London and Manchester, 1956-57; Granada Television, London and Manchester, England, producer, 1958-63.

MEMBER: National Book League, Arts Theatre Club.

WRITINGS:

The Swish of the Curtain, Thomas Nelson, 1941, Winston, 1943, revised edition, Brockhampton Press, 1971.
Maddy Alone, Thomas Nelson, 1945, Hutchinson Library Service, 1972.
Golden Pavements, Thomas Nelson, 1947.
Blue Door Venture, Thomas Nelson, 1949, Hutchinson Library Service, 1972.
To Be a Ballerina and Other Stories, Thomas Nelson, 1950.
Family Playbill, Thomas Nelson, 1951, published as *Family Troupe,* Harcourt, 1953.
The Television Twins, Thomas Nelson, 1952.
Harlequin Corner, Thomas Nelson, 1953, Meredith (New York City), 1969.
The Windmill Family, Thomas Nelson, 1954, Crowell, 1955.
Louisa, Crowell, 1955.
Maddy Again, Thomas Nelson, 1956.
The Bridesmaids, Brockhampton Press, 1956, McKay, 1957.
Backstage Portrait, Thomas Nelson, 1957.
Showboat Summer, Brockhampton Press, 1957.
Understudy, Thomas Nelson, 1958.
First House, Thomas Nelson, 1959.
As Far as Singapore, Brockhampton Press, 1959, Taplinger, 1961.
The Other Side of the Street, Brockhampton Press, 1965, Follett (Chicago), 1967.
The Girl Who Ran Away, Brockhampton Press, 1968.
A Little Universe, Brockhampton Press, 1970.
Summer Is a Festival, Brockhampton Press, 1972.
Looking After Libbey, Brockhampton Press, 1974.
Every Day Is Market Day, Hodder & Stoughton (London), 1977.

Brown's books were translated into the major European languages and Japanese.

SIDELIGHTS: Pamela Brown became a successful children's author while still a teenager herself, using her own fascination with the theater as the basis for her 1941 novel, *The Swish of the Curtain.* Proceeds from the book enabled her to attend the Royal Academy of Dramatic Art, after which she worked as an actress during the 1940s. From 1950 to 1963 she was a television producer, first with the British Broadcasting Corporation and later with Scottish Television and Granada Television.

The Swish of the Curtain concerns a group of children who organize a theatrical company in pre-war England. The *Times Literary Supplement* critic remarked: "For an author only fifteen years old Pamela Brown has extraordinary smoothness and vigour." F. B. Sloan in the *Christian Science Monitor* found that Brown "relates the story with lively and humorous touches and succeeds in making her characters come alive."

Also based on Brown's theatrical experience was *Family Troupe,* the story of an English theatrical family in Victorian times. The reviewer for *Horn Book* noted: "It has much to recommend it as an amusing period story, with never a dull moment, by an author who is thoroughly informed in the ways of the theater." F. N. Chrystie in the *New York Times* praised *Family Troupe* as "a clearly detailed picture of theatrical life in the nineteenth century, peopled with recognizable characters and sparked with a sense of drama."

Back-Stage Portrait concerns a teenaged girl who joins her uncle's theater in Wales to work as assistant stage manager. Jane Cobb in the *New York Times* admitted that the lead character "has a pleasant time, as will the book's readers—particularly those who are stage-struck." S. B. Bellows in the *Christian Science Monitor* found that the novel "gives what is probably an authentic portrait of the back-stage activities in a small English repertory company."

Brown turned from the theatre to a London tenement for the setting of her novel *The Other Side of the Street.* In this story, teenaged Linda wants to raise enough money to move her poor family into their own house. Madalynne Schoenfeld in *Library Journal* praised the book's "glossy image of lower middle class London life." Zena Sutherland in *Saturday Review* found that the novel possessed "a sophistication of tone consisting in part of the treatment of child characters as interesting, and in part of the writing style itself, vigorous yet polished." The critic for the *Chicago Tribune Book World* wrote of *The Other Side of the Street,* "The vital, gritty quality and the sturdy realism that many English books for children possess, but which often are lacking in their American counterparts, are found in good measure in this excellent story."

BIOGRAPHICAL/CRITICAL SOURCES:

BOOKS

Twentieth-Century Children's Writers, 2nd edition, St. Martin's, 1983.

PERIODICALS

Booklist, April 1, 1943; April 1, 1957.
Book Week, November 7, 1943, p. 9.
Book World, February 11, 1968, p. 15.
Chicago Sunday Tribune, July 12, 1953, p. 11; February 17, 1957, p. 9; August 24, 1958, p. 6.
Christian Science Monitor, September 23, 1943, p. 10; October 17, 1957, p. 11; May 8, 1958, p. 14; May 11, 1961, p. B7; February 1, 1968, p. 7.
Horn Book, April, 1953; April, 1968.
Kirkus, January 15, 1953; July 1, 1955; January 15, 1957; July 15, 1957; February 1, 1961.
Library Journal, October 15, 1943; March 15, 1953; October 15, 1955; June 15, 1957; July, 1958; November 15, 1967.
New York Herald Tribune Book Review, May 3, 1953, p. 8; October 9, 1955, p. 10; March 31, 1957, p. 8.
New York Times, July 12, 1953, p. 18; October 23, 1955, p. 36; April 28, 1957, p. 44; October 13, 1957, p. 51; July 20, 1958, p. 24.
New York Times Book Review, March 19, 1961, p. 42.
San Francisco Chronicle, May 11, 1958, p. 23.
Saturday Review, November 12, 1955; January 27, 1968.
Springfield Republican, April 12, 1953, p. C8.
Times Literary Supplement, December 27, 1941, p. 658; December 4, 1959.
Weekly Book Review, August 1, 1943, p. 6.

OBITUARIES:

PERIODICALS

Times (London), February 1, 1989.*

BROWN, Stuart Gerry 1912-1991

PERSONAL: Born April 13, 1912, in Buffalo, NY; died October 1, 1991, in Honolulu, HI; son of Charles H., Jr. and Edith (Warner) Brown; married Katharine DuB. Franchet, September 15, 1934 (divorced, 1940); married Mildred Geneva Kraus, August 22, 1941; children: (first marriage) Antoinette; (second marriage) Thomas Stuart, Stuart Gerry, Jr. *Education:* Amherst College, A.B., 1934; Princeton University, Ph.D., 1937. *Politics:* Democrat.

CAREER: University of Wisconsin, Madison, instructor in English, 1937-40; Grinnell College, Grinnell, IA, associate professor of English, 1940-43, professor of English and philosophy, 1943-47; Syracuse University, Syracuse, NY, professor of citizenship and American culture, 1947-58, Maxwell Professor of American Civilization, 1958-65; University of Hawaii, Honolulu, visiting professor, 1961-62, 1964-65, professor of American studies, beginning 1965. Visiting professor, Australian National University, Royal Military College, 1971.

MEMBER: American Studies Association (member of executive council, 1950-54).

AWARDS, HONORS: Grants from Rockefeller Foundation, American Philosophical Society, Alfred P. Sloan Foundation, and Chinn Ho Foundation.

WRITINGS:

The First Republicans: Political Philosophy and Public Policy in the Party of Jefferson and Madison, Syracuse University Press, 1954, reprinted, Greenwood Press (Westport, CT), 1976.
(With C. Peltier) *Government in Our Republic,* Macmillan (New York City), 1960, 4th edition, 1971.
Memo for Overseas Americans, Syracuse University Press, 1960.
Conscience in Politics: Adlai E. Stevenson in the 1950s, Syracuse University Press, 1961.
Thomas Jefferson, Washington Square Press (New York City), 1964.
Adlai E. Stevenson, A Short Biography: The Conscience of the Country, Barron's Woodbury Press (Woodbury, NY), 1965.
The American Presidency: Leadership, Partisanship, and Popularity, Macmillan, 1966.
Alexander Hamilton, Washington Square Press, 1967.

(With W. Fiser and J. Gibson) *Government in the United States,* Ronald, 1967.

The Presidency on Trial: Robert Kennedy's 1968 Campaign and Afterwards, University Press of Hawaii (Honolulu), 1972.

(With R. Farmer) *Government: The American System,* Macmillan, 1973.

EDITOR

(With Wallace Stegner and Claude Simpson) *An Exposition Workshop,* Little, Brown (Boston), 1939.

(With Wright Thomas) *Reading Poems: An Introduction to Critical Study,* Oxford University Press (New York City), 1941.

We Hold These Truths, Harper (New York City), 1941, 2nd edition, 1948.

Great Issues, Harper, 1948.

The Social Philosophy of Josiah Royce, Syracuse University Press, 1950.

(With Thomas) *Reading Prose,* Oxford University Press, 1952.

The Religious Philosophy of Josiah Royce, Syracuse University Press, 1952.

The Autobiography of James Monroe, Syracuse University Press, 1959.

(With H. Bragdon and S. McCutchen) *Frame of Government,* Macmillan, 1962.

Process of Government, Macmillan, 1963.

Revolution, Confederation, and Constitution, Appleton (New York City), 1971.

Great Issues: The Making of Current American Policy, Books for Libraries Press (Freeport, NY), 1971.

OTHER

Contributor of articles and reviews to professional journals. Politics editor, *Encyclopedia International,* 1962-64.

SIDELIGHTS: Stuart Gerry Brown wrote a number of studies of the American presidency and those men who have sought to serve in that office. Several of Brown's studies focused on the early years of the American Republic and the people and forces which shaped our political culture. *First Republicans: Political Philosophy and Public Policy in the Party of Jefferson and Madison,* for example, is a condensed history of the first three decades of American politics as embodied in the lives and political philosophies of

Thomas Jefferson and James Madison. R. D. Ronsheim, writing in the *New England Quarterly,* observed that Brown's book makes a good case that "the leaders of the party were both libertarians and nationalists." C. G. Bowers in the *Annals of the American Academy* called the study "an admirable and authoritative book that all Americans would do well to read."

Brown turned again to the early days of the American Republic in his biography *Thomas Jefferson,* part of the "Great American Thinkers" series. Presenting not only an account of Jefferson's life, the book also examines the political ideas of the Founding Father and discusses his ideas in relation to the ideas of other leading thinkers of the time. Jack VanDerhoof in *Library Journal* judged the book to be "carefully done" and a "good and solid introductory" volume on its subject. The critic for the *Journal of American History* dubbed the study "well written, interesting, lively, and . . . accurate in fact and thoughtful in interpretation."

In his studies focusing on more recent political events, Brown wrote two books on Adlai Stevenson, a two-time presidential candidate for the Democratic Party. Brown knew Stevenson well, having interviewed him a number of times and having access to many of the politician's private papers for his studies. In *Conscience in Politics: Adlai E. Stevenson in the 1950s,* Brown examined the political style and speechmaking of Stevenson as presented in the politician's public writings and lectures. The critic for *Booklist* called it "thought-provoking though partisan," while Godfrey Sperling in the *Christian Science Monitor* labeled Brown "the enthusiastic Stevenson advocate" and found that "one would not have to be a disciple of this two-time Democratic standard bearer to enjoy this book." Martin Peretz summed up in *Commonweal:* "Professor Brown has written a partisan portrait, an almost elegiac evocation of Adlai Stevenson. . . . It is a work of tribute and affection, and one without facade."

In *Adlai E. Stevenson, A Short Biography: The Conscience of the Country* Brown presented a biography of the popular politician which K. Natwar-Singh in the *Saturday Review* found to be "obviously a labor of love, although as a study of Adlai E. Stevenson, it is inadequate and patchy." W. B. Johnson in *Book Week* noted that Brown "has written with insight and perception."

BIOGRAPHICAL/CRITICAL SOURCES:

PERIODICALS

American Historical Review, April, 1962; October, 1966.
American Political Science Review, June, 1962.
Annals of the American Academy, March, 1955; September, 1962; November, 1966; September, 1972.
Best Sellers, May 15, 1972.
Booklist, January 1, 1962.
Book Week, February 20, 1966, p. 3.
Choice, October, 1966.
Christian Century, February 7, 1962.
Christian Science Monitor, November 15, 1961, p. 13; June 9, 1966, p. 9.
Commonweal, December 22, 1961.
Foreign Affairs, July, 1962.
Journal of American History, September, 1966.
Library Journal, January 15, 1962; March 15, 1966; August, 1966; March 15, 1972.
New England Quarterly, June, 1955.
New York Times Book Review, November 26, 1961, p. 3.
Saturday Review, January 1, 1966.
Social Education, March, 1962.
U. S. Quarterly Book Review, March, 1955.

OBITUARIES:

PERIODICALS

Washington Post, October 5, 1991, p. C6.*

* * *

BROWN, Wenzell 1912-1981

PERSONAL: Born May 10, 1912, in Portland, ME; died in 1981; son of Cecil Preston and Isabel (Wenzell) Brown. *Education:* Rollins College, A.B., 1932; attended King's College, London, 1932-33; Columbia University, M.A., 1940.

CAREER: Taught in public schools in Puerto Rico, 1937-39; Lingnan University, Canton, China, assistant professor, 1940-42; security promotion specialist, U.S. Treasury Department, 1943-44; Morris College, Sumter, SC, associate professor, 1967-69; Barber-Scotia College, Concord, NC, professor, 1969-71; PATH Program, New York City, consult-

ant, 1973-74; assistant to director of Rafael Hernandez Senior Citizen Center, beginning 1974. Professor, American International College, summers, 1953-54, 1966.

MEMBER: Mystery Writers of America, PEN.

AWARDS, HONORS: American-Scandinavian Foundation research fellow in Denmark, 1950; Edgar Allan Poe Award, Mystery Writers of America, 1958, for *Women Who Died in the Chair;* Freedoms Foundation Award.

WRITINGS:

Hong Kong Aftermath, Smith & Durrell, 1943.
Dynamite on Our Doorstep: Puerto Rican Paradox, Greenberg, 1945.
Murder Seeks an Agent, Green Publishing Co., 1945.
Angry Men, Laughing Men: The Caribbean Caldron, Greenberg, 1947.
Dark Drums, Appleton (New York City), 1950, reprinted, Warner Books (New York City), 1977.
They Called Her Charity, Appleton, 1951 (published in Australia as *Purloined Flame,* Invincible Press, 1953).
Self-Defense, A. S. Barnes, 1951.
Introduction to Murder: The Unpublished Facts behind the Notorious Lonely Hearts Killers, Martha Beck and Raymond Fernandez, Greenberg, 1952, published as *The Lonely Hearts Killers,* P. Collier, 1965.
Run, Chico, Run, Gold Medal (New York City), 1952.
Monkey on My Back, Greenberg, 1953.
(With Israel Beckhardt) *The Violators,* Harcourt (New York City), 1954.
The Big Rumble, Popular Library, 1955 (also published as *Jailbait Jungle*).
They Died in the Chair, Popular Library, 1958, published as *Women Who Died in the Chair: The Dramatic True Stories of Six Women Who Committed the Deadliest Sin,* P. Collier, 1958.
Bedeviled: The True Story of the Interplay of the Aggressor and the Victim in Sexual Attacks, Monarch, 1961.
The Murder Kick, Gold Medal, 1961.
Women of Evil, Monarch, 1963.
How to Tell Fortunes with Cards, Sterling (New York City), 1963.
Sherry, Monarch, 1964.
The Golden Witch, Monarch, 1964.
Kept Women, Lancer Books, 1966.
Possess and Conquer, Warner Books, 1975.

Also author of *Prison Girl,* Pyramid Books. Contributor to anthologies, including *Alfred Hitchcock's Tales to Keep You Spellbound,* Davis Publications (New York), 1976. Contributor to several magazines, including *Look, Reader's Digest, Saturday Review,* and *Saint.*

SIDELIGHTS: Wenzell Brown's books often focused on the criminal or sordid aspects of modern life. He published accounts of Japanese prisoner of war camps, murder cases, and the poverty to be found in the Caribbean.

Brown's *Hong Kong Aftermath* is the story of the Stanley prison camp run by the Japanese in Hong Kong during World War II. Here, prisoners of war from America, Britain and Russia were held in conditions of terrible hardship. Max Hill in the *New York Times* calls Brown's account "an excellent book, because it can serve as a guide for those among us who still consider the Japanese a kindly, civilized people." Joseph Newman in the *Weekly Book Review* notes that, although "there have been a number of books on the fall of Hong Kong and the indescribable treatment of foreign nationals seized there by the Japanese," Brown's report on the camp is "perhaps the most informative and best written." The *New Yorker* critic concludes by calling *Hong Kong Aftermath* "one of the most moving and unsparingly truthful of the personal-experience books, written with skill and power."

Introduction to Murder: The Unpublished Facts behind the Notorious Lonely Hearts Killers, Martha Beck and Raymond Fernandez is a detailed account of a pair of murderous criminals who preyed on women who joined their lonely hearts club. Despite the nature of the crimes described, the reviewer for the *New York Herald Tribune Book Review* finds that Brown's reporting is "careful and restrained." "Brown tells the story factually and objectively," writes the critic for the *New Yorker,* "and the reader may easily conclude that his protagonists were far more suitable candidates for a lunatic asylum than for the electric chair."

Brown based several of his books on his first-hand experience working and travelling in the Caribbean. In *Dynamite on Our Doorstep: Puerto Rican Paradox,* Brown documents the problems of poverty and disease plaguing the Caribbean island. "This book," writes Edmund Wilson in the *New Yorker,* "is a piece of reporting of a rare and valuable kind. Mr. Brown is not only unsparing in his record of the miseries of the island; he is able to do justice to its extraordinary scenery and its flamboyant flora and fauna." Harold Fields in the *Saturday Review of Literature* notes that Brown "chooses to present the picture, state a few facts, guide the reader's thinking, and let him draw his own conclusions. For that, for the interesting stories and experiences that are related, for the excellent drawings, this book is to be commended."

In *Angry Men, Laughing Men: The Caribbean Caldron,* Brown writes of his travels throughout the Caribbean, with sections devoted to the individual countries he visited. Lorenzo Medrano in the *Chicago Sun Book Week* finds that "the book is charmingly populated with prostitutes, drunkards, killers, beggars. . . . The result is as savory and as hard to digest as one of those dishes from the Dutch Indies." "Brown relates his own experiences and describes the beauties and ugliness of the islands with a candor and honesty that win respect," according to Henrietta Hardman in the *New York Times.*

Brown based some of his fiction on his knowledge of the Caribbean as well. In *Dark Drums,* he fictionalizes the life of Kate Donley, whose rise to power in eighteenth century Jamaica was achieved through violence, voodoo and treachery. Richard Blakesley in the *Chicago Sunday Tribune* calls *Dark Drums* "an exciting, sometimes fearsome novel," while the reviewer for the *Springfield Republican* labels it "an exciting story. . . . Brown has spun a tale of violence, intrigue and strange cults in this novel of colonial Jamaica." Brown's *They Called Her Charity* is an historical novel set on St. Thomas in the Virgin Islands during its days as a buccaneer haven. The reviewer for *Kirkus* admits that the story contains "tropical color, violent battle, hot-headed argument and passion." Henry Cavendish in the *New York Times* believes that "the book is far more than a historical romance of blood and thunder. Cruelty is raised to a tragic level and the action becomes symbolic of an indecisive character groping blindly for the truth."

BIOGRAPHICAL/CRITICAL SOURCES:

PERIODICALS

Booklist, October 1, 1943; May 1, 1947.
Book Week, August 15, 1943, p. 6; December 2, 1945, p. 20.
Chicago Sun Book Week, August 10, 1947, p. 7.
Chicago Sunday Tribune, October 29, 1950, p. 2; November 18, 1951, p. 15.

Commonweal, December 7, 1945.

Foreign Affairs, October, 1947.

Kirkus, October 1, 1950; October 1, 1951.

Library Journal, November 1, 1945.

New Yorker, August 14, 1943; December 29, 1945; April 26, 1952.

New York Herald Tribune Book Review, October 29, 1950, p. 24; July 13, 1952, p. 10.

New York Times, August 8, 1943, p. 7; April 20, 1947, p. 32; June 8, 1947, p. 26; December 2, 1951, p. 53; April 20, 1952, p. 32.

San Francisco Chronicle, April 13, 1947, p. 21; April 12, 1952, p. 12.

Saturday Review of Literature, August 14, 1943; November 10, 1945; April 19, 1947; February 24, 1951.

Springfield Republican, Decemebr 17, 1950, p. A30.

Weekly Book Review, August 15, 1943, p. 14; November 11, 1945, p. 5.*

* * *

BROWN, William L(ouis) 1910-1964
(Bill Brown)

PERSONAL: Born April 5, 1910, in Myrtle Point, OR; died September 28, 1964; son of Louis E. Brown (a life insurance representative) and Viola May (Davis) Brown; married Gertrude E. (Rosalie) Moore (an author), June 30, 1942; children: Deborah Ann, Celia Jeanne Camas Eve. *Education:* Attended University of Oregon, 1930-31, and Mexico City College, 1950. *Politics:* Republican.

CAREER: Coos Bay World, Coos Bay, OR, reporter, 1934-38; *300 Magazine,* San Francisco, CA, editor, 1940-42; California Division of Beaches and Parks, Lagunitas, CA, ranger, 1953-64. Teacher of creative writing, adult education, Marin County and Sonoma County, CA. Member of Fairfax City Park Commission, 1960-62. *Military service:* U.S. Army Air Forces, 1942-44; became sergeant.

AWARDS, HONORS: Commonwealth Club of California silver medal for best juvenile book, 1953, for *Roaring River.*

WRITINGS:

UNDER NAME BILL BROWN

Roaring River, Coward (New York City), 1953.

Uncharted Voyage, Coward, 1955.

People of the Many Islands, Coward, 1958.

The Rain Forest, Coward, 1962.

UNDER NAME WILLIAM L. BROWN; WITH WIFE, ROSALIE BROWN

Forest Firemen, Coward, 1954.

Whistle Punk, Coward, 1956.

Boy Who Got Mailed, Coward, 1957.

Big Rig, Coward, 1959.

Department Store Ghost, Coward, 1961.

Tickly and the Fox, Lantern, 1962.

Contributor to periodicals.

SIDELIGHTS: Bill Brown drew upon his own travels in such places as the Himalayas and the South Pacific to write adventure stories. With his wife, Rosalie Brown, he also wrote lighter, more humorous stories for young readers.

Roaring River, based on Brown's experiences while stationed in India during the Second World War, tells of a young geology student who accompanies an older adventurer on an exploration into the Indian jungle. The two companions share a mutual dislike which is only worsened by the hardships of their journey. The critic for *Saturday Review* found that "the background of the story—the description of the country—the river, the canyons, the jungles—is excellent." L. S. Bechtel in the *New York Herald Tribune Book Review* wrote: "The violence of the jungle matched by that of the human relations when under pressure of fear makes an interesting theme."

Among the stories Brown wrote with his wife are *The Boy Who Got Mailed, Big Rig,* and *The Department Store Ghost. The Boy Who Got Mailed* tells the fanciful tale of a young boy who wants to travel to his Aunt Jane's house but is stopped by a blizzard. Reasoning that the mail always gets through, he convinces his local postmaster to mail him to his aunt. With postage stamps stuck to his forehead and labels reading "Do Not Bend," Peter is sent by mail bag on a humorous cross-country adventure. The critic for the *Chicago Sunday Tribune* wrote: "This book is lots of fun for reading aloud." Phyllis Fenner in the *New York Times* predicted: "I believe that this is a story that will leave children breathless from laughter."

In *Big Rig,* a truck driver in the American West finds that a small mouse has been chewing on his cargo and determines to find the creature and stop his damaging activities. Instead, he and the mouse become friends and even save a party of school children when they become trapped in a blizzard. The critic for *Saturday Review* found that "what could easily have been the outrageous mixture of fantasy gimmick and dry information results in an entirely successful book." C. H. Bishop in *Commonweal* called the story "very funny and full of truckdriving lore," while the reviewer for the *Christian Science Monitor* judged it "a lively story."

The Department Store Ghost tells of the founder of a department store returning as a ghost on the store's one hundredth anniversary. At first angry with how things have changed in the store's operations, "Grandpa finds a happy niche in the running of the store he founded," as Charlotte Jackson explained in the *San Francisco Chronicle*. "Children will be amused," wrote M. S. Libby in the *New York Herald Tribune Lively Arts,* "especially when Grandpa blows a fuse and starts a wild confusion during the birthday celebration." The critic for *Kirkus* called the story "an original way of contrasting old ways and new in running a department store."

BIOGRAPHICAL/CRITICAL SOURCES:

PERIODICALS

Booklist, April 15, 1953; October 1, 1956; June 15, 1962.
Chicago Sunday Tribune, November 11, 1956, p. 11; November 17, 1957, p. 22.
Christian Science Monitor, August 23, 1956, p. 7; November 5, 1959, p. B4.
Commonweal, November 13, 1959.
Horn Book, June, 1953.
Kirkus, January 1, 1953; July 1, 1956; October 15, 1957; July 15, 1959; November 1, 1960; March 1, 1962.
Library Journal, October 15, 1956; November 15, 1957; November 15, 1959; February 15, 1961; May 15, 1962.
New York Herald Tribune Book Review, April 12, 1953, p. 16; November 18, 1956, p. 26.
New York Herald Tribune Lively Arts, April 23, 1961, p. 32.
New York Times, March 1, 1953, p. 32; November 17, 1957, p. 52.
New York Times Book Review, April 23, 1961, p. 32.
San Francisco Chronicle, November 15, 1953, p. 2; November 8, 1959, p. 18; May 14, 1961, p. 27; May 13, 1962, p. 26.
Saturday Review, September 19, 1953; March 19, 1960.*

*   *   *

BRUFF, Nancy
See GARDNER, Nancy Bruff

*   *   *

BRUMBAUGH, Robert Sherrick 1918-1992

PERSONAL: Born December 2, 1918, in Oregon, IL; died July 14, 1992; son of Aaron J. and Ruth (Sherrick) Brumbaugh; married Ada Z. Steele, June 5, 1940; children: Robert Conrad, Susan Christianna, Joanna Pauline. *Education:* University of Chicago, A.B., 1938, M.A., 1938, Ph.D., 1942.

CAREER: Bowdoin College, Brunswick, ME, assistant professor of philosophy, 1946-48; Indiana University, Bloomington, assistant professor of philosophy, 1948-50; Yale University, New Haven, CT, assistant professor, 1951-54, associate professor, 1955-60, professor of philosophy, beginning 1961. *Military service:* U.S. Army, 1943-46.

MEMBER: Metaphysical Society of America (counsellor, 1961-65; president, 1965-66), American Philosophical Association, American Association of University Professors (chapter president, 1961-62; member of national council, 1975-78), Society for Ancient Greek Philosophy, Connecticut Academy of Arts and Sciences, Phi Beta Kappa.

WRITINGS:

(With Newton Phelps Stallknecht) *The Spirit of Western Philosophy,* Longmans, Green (New York City), 1950.
(With Stallknecht) *The Compass of Philosophy: An Essay in Intellectual Orientation,* Longmans, Green, 1954.
Plato's Mathematical Imagination, Indiana University Press (Bloomington), 1954.
(Editor and translator) *Plato on the One: The Hypotheses in the Parmenides and Their Interpretation,* Yale University Press (New Haven, CT), 1961.

(Editor with Rulon Wells) *The Plato Manuscripts,* Yale University Press, 1962, new edition published as *The Plato Manuscripts: A New Index,* 1968.

Plato for the Modern Age, Collier (New York City), 1962.

(With Nathaniel M. Lawrence) *Philosophers on Education: Six Essays on the Foundations of Western Thought,* Houghton (Boston), 1963.

The Philosophers of Greece, Crowell (New York City), 1965.

Ancient Greek Gadgets and Machines, Crowell, 1966.

(Editor) *Six Trials,* Crowell, 1969.

(With Lawrence) *Philosophical Themes in Modern Education,* Houghton, 1973.

The Most Mysterious Manuscript: The Voynich Roger Bacon Cipher Manuscript, Southern Illinois University Press (Carbondale), 1978.

Whitehead, Process Philosophy and Education, State University of New York Press (Albany), 1982.

Unreality and Time, State University of New York Press, 1984.

Platonic Studies of Greek Philosophy: Form, Arts, Gadgets, and Hemlock, State University of New York Press, 1989.

Western Philosophic Systems and Their Cyclic Transformations, Southern Illinois University Press, 1992.

Contributor to journals.

SIDELIGHTS: Robert S. Brumbaugh was a prominent scholar of Greek philosophy who wrote introductory books on the subject as well as advanced treatises. Brumbaugh's *Plato for the Modern Age* provides a brief biography of the Greek philosopher and a discussion of his ideas in relation to current philosophical debate. Writing in *Classical World,* G. R. Morrow found that "any one who has studied the difficult problems raised by [Plato's] late dialogues will find Brumbaugh's treatment of them immensely suggestive." J. W. Lenz in the *Yale Review* noted that *Plato for the Modern Age* "has many merits," including "a very good account of the background and development of Plato's thought" and a "freshness and imagination" in dealing with Plato's major doctrines.

An introductory text explaining the development of ancient Greek thought and the philosophers who contributed to this development, *The Philosophers of Greece* is "a lucid, easily understood introduction," according to the critic for *Library Journal.* The *Yale*

Review critic claimed: "Both the general reader who may question the practical achievements of the philosophic enterprise and the student of philosophy who is seeking an orientation to the classical philosophies of Greece would surely profit from this volume."

Brumbaugh once told *CA:* "One very important thesis that I hope to demonstrate in my writing about philosophy and education is that many of the undesirable features of twentieth century life, which are popularly thought of as 'bad luck,' are rather consequences of bad metaphysics. Given a generally accepted 'common sense' that is out of phase with reality, it is no surprise to find institutions and policy decisions unrealistic and unsuccessful."

BIOGRAPHICAL/CRITICAL SOURCES:

BOOKS

Benson, Garth D. and Bryant E. Griffith, editors, *Process, Epistemology, and Education: Recent Work in Educational Process Philosophy: Essays in Honour of Robert S. Brumbaugh,* Canadian Scholars' Press (Toronto), 1996.

Hendley, Brian P., editor, *Plato, Time, and Education: Essays in Honor of Robert S. Brumbaugh,* State University of New York Press, 1987.

PERIODICALS

Atlantic, November, 1966.
Christian Century, November 13, 1969.
Classical World, April, 1963; April, 1965.
Library Journal, October 1, 1962; February 15, 1965; November 1, 1966; January 15, 1970.
Yale Review, December, 1963; October, 1965.*

*   *   *

BRUNDAGE, Burr Cartwright 1912-1993

PERSONAL: Born December 15, 1912, in Buffalo, NY; died April 16, 1993; *Education:* Amherst College, A.B. (with honors), 1936; University of Chicago, Ph.D., 1939. *Avocational interests:* Speaks French and Spanish, and has a reading knowledge of Italian, German, Latin, Egyptian Hieroglyphic (Old, Middle and New Kingdoms), Demotic, Hebrew, Coptic, Quechua and Nahuatl.

CAREER: MacMurray College, Jacksonville, IL, instructor in history, 1939-41; Office of Coordinator of InterAmerican Affairs, Washington, DC, area officer, 1941-42; Carleton College, Northfield, MN, assistant professor, 1942-43; Department of State, Washington, DC, political desk officer for Chile, 1943-47; Cedar Crest College, Allentown, PA, professor of history, and head of department, 1947-61; Eckerd College, St. Petersburg, FL, professor of history, 1961-78, professor emeritus, 1978-93.

AWARDS, HONORS: Three research grants for travel to Peru and Mexico from the Board of Higher Education, Presbyterian Church; Six grants for Pre-Columbian research from the Research Committee of Florida Presbyterian College; American Philosophical Society research grant for the study in Mexico of Aztec religion.

WRITINGS:

The Juniper Palace (poems), A. B. Bookman, 1951, revised edition, with introduction by Giles Gunn, Valkyrie Press (St. Petersburg, FL), 1976.

The Empire of the Inca, University of Oklahoma Press (Norman), 1963.

Lords of Cuzco: A History and Description of the Inca People in Their Final Days, University of Oklahoma Press, 1963.

A Rain of Darts: The Mexican Aztecs, University of Texas Press (Austin), 1972.

No Chance Encounter (poems), Valkyrie Press, 1974.

Two Earths, Two Heavens: An Essay Contrasting the Aztecs and the Incas, University of New Mexico Press (Albuquerque), 1975.

The Fifth Sun: Aztec Gods, Aztec World, University of Texas Press, 1979.

The Phoenix of the Western World: Quetzalcoatl and the Sky Religion, University of Oklahoma Press, 1982.

The Jade Steps: A Ritual Life of the Aztecs, University of Utah Press (Salt Lake City), 1985.

The King Who Cast No Shadow, University Press of America (Lanham, MD), 1986.

Contributor to *Christian Scholar, History, Historian, American Historical Review,* and *Journal of Near Eastern Studies.*

SIDELIGHTS: Burr Cartwright Brundage wrote a number of books on the Aztec and Incan peoples of South and Central America. He was, as a *Choice* critic noted, "a recognized authority on Mesoamerica." Brundage's *Empire of the Inca* is a comprehensive history of the Incan people from their earliest beginnings to their conquest by Spanish forces in the sixteenth century. Alfred Kidder in *Science* called the book "an excellent and very readable history. . . . This is an important and most welcome addition to the literature on the Inca, and one that can be read with pleasure by anyone with an interest in the American Indian."

Brundage's *Lords of Cuzco: A History and Description of the Inca People in Their Final Days* covers the final generation of the Incan royal family in their losing battle with the conquering Spanish. Although he admitted that "ethno-historians are likely to argue a long time over this volume," Woodrow Borah in the *American Historical Review* called *Lords of Cuzco* "a possible account [of the Incan demise], boldly and brilliantly done." Robert Silverberg, writing in *Saturday Review,* dubbed the volume "a major contribution to our understanding of a vanished culture."

Brundage examines the Aztec people of ancient Mexico in *A Rain of Darts: The Mexican Aztecs, The Fifth Sun: Aztec Gods, Aztec World* and *The Phoenix of the Western World: Quetzalcoatl and the Sky Religion.* Calling Brundage "an excellent historical researcher," the critic for *Choice* labelled *A Rain of Darts* "a remarkable historical narrative." *The Fifth Sun* and *The Phoenix of the Western World* both deal with Aztec religious beliefs and ceremonies. The *Choice* reviewer called *The Fifth Sun* "a very well-written book." Although, the reviewer continued, some of Brundage's "views might be seen as controversial, his arguments, which are based on careful readings of such conquest sources as Sahagun and Duran, are well made and well supported." P. W. Silvernail in the *Library Journal* found "particularly intriguing" Brundage's "comparisons of primitive mythologies, made possible by his depth of understanding and ability to conjecture on extant sources."

The Phoenix of the Western World is an examination of the Aztec god Quetzalcoatl, a feathered serpent who was central to their sky religion. As the *Choice* reviewer noted, Brundage's book "is the most comprehensive English study of Quetzalcoatl." Writing in *Archaeology,* Jamake Highwater found: "Quetzalcoatl is depicted in this impassioned and insightful book as the emblematic core of a whole religion which sheds enormous light on a much misunderstood and often belied civilization."

BIOGRAPHICAL/CRITICAL SOURCES:

PERIODICALS

American Historical Review, July, 1964; June, 1968; February, 1983.
Archaeology, November/December, 1982.
Choice, July/August, 1973; September, 1979; September, 1982.
Library Journal, November 15, 1963; July, 1973; June 1, 1979; January 1, 1982.
New York Times Book Review, December 8, 1963, p. 41.
Saturday Review, November 25, 1967.
Science, January 3, 1964.*

* * *

BRUSSEL, James Arnold 1905-1982

PERSONAL: Born April 22, 1905, in New York, NY; died October, 1982; son of A. Stanley and Rose (Schwarzwald) Brussel; married Audrey Schuman, March 7, 1957; children: John, Judith. *Education:* University of Pennsylvania, B.S., 1926, M.D., 1929; postgraduate study at Columbia University and New York Psychiatric Institute. *Religion:* Hebrew. *Avocational interests:* Brussel was a tympanist with the New York Doctors' Orchestral Society and the Queens Symphony Orchestra.

CAREER: Beth Israel Hospital, New York City, intern, two years; Department of Mental Hygiene, New York City, employee, 1931-69, assistant commissioner, 1952-69. Certified by American Board of Psychiatry and Neurology in both specialties; certified mental hospital administrator. Consultant, Veterans Administration Hospital, Samson, NY, 1946-48, and New York State Social Welfare Department. *Military service:* U.S. Army, Medical Corps, 1940-46, 1951-52; chief of neuropsychiatric service at various Army hospitals and aboard hospital ship.

MEMBER: American College of Physicians (fellow), American Medical Association, American Psychiatric Association, American Association for the Advancement of Science, New York Academy of Medicine, New York State and County Medical Societies.

AWARDS, HONORS: American Physicians Literary Guild prizes.

WRITINGS:

The Rorschach Psychodiagnostic Method, New York State Hospital Press, 1942, revised edition, 1950.
Just Murder, Darling (novel), Scribner (New York City), 1959.
The Layman's Guide to Psychiatry, Barnes & Noble (New York City), 1961, 2nd edition, 1967.
(With others) *Medical Aid Encyclopedia for the Home,* Stravon, 1965, published as *The New Illustrated Medical Aid Encyclopedia,* Royal Publishers (Nashville), 1987.
Mother's Encyclopedia, Parents Institute, 1965.
The Layman's Dictionary of Mental Health, Barnes & Noble, 1965.
The Layman's Dictionary of Psychiatry, Barnes & Noble, 1967.
Casebook of a Crime Psychiatrist, Geis (New York City), 1968.
The Physician's Concise Handbook of Psychiatry, Brunner (New York City), 1969.
(With Theodore Irwin) *Instant Shrink: How to Become an Expert Psychiatrist in Ten Easy Lessons,* Cowles (New York City), 1971.
(With Irwin) *Understanding and Overcoming Depression,* Hawthorn (New York City), 1973.
(With others) *Basic Health Care and Emergency Aid,* Varsity Co. (Nashville), 1984.

Contributor to *Encyclopedia Americana,* 1948-60, and *World Encyclopedia.* Contributor of articles to *New Yorker, Life and Health, Catholic Digest, New York Times, Cosmopolitan, Medical Economics, Daily Telegraph,* and other magazines, newspapers, and professional journals. Contributor of cartoons to such publications as *Judge* and *Army.*

SIDELIGHTS: James Arnold Brussel was a New York City psychiatrist whose work involved him in a number of criminal cases. Brussel's specialty was the criminal profile, in which the psychiatrist can work his way back from a crime's known facts to determine what kind of criminal personality would have committed the crime. Brussel was called in to assist police in many investigations of murder and bombing cases, including the Boston Strangler.

Brussel's *Casebook of a Crime Psychiatrist* recounts some of his more interesting criminal cases. C. M. Curtis in the *Atlantic* noted that the book "offers a number of fascinating insights into the behavior of the Boston Strangler and other murderous celebrities." M. A. Forslund in the *Library Journal* believed that "anyone interested in famous or unusual crimes will enjoy reading it."

Brussel also drew upon his investigative experience to write a mystery novel, *Just Murder, Darling.* Critical opinion was generally positive, with James Sandoe in the *New York Herald Tribune Book Review* finding the story to be "told with a dry savagery which might have been too harsh for us if it weren't related through a disarming mockery."

BIOGRAPHICAL/CRITICAL SOURCES:

PERIODICALS

Atlantic, January, 1969.
Kirkus, May 1, 1959.
Library Journal, September 1, 1959; September 15, 1968.
New York Herald Tribune Book Review, August 2, 1959, p. 9.
New York Times Book Review, August 9, 1959, p. 19.
San Francisco Chronicle, August 30, 1959, p. 17.
Saturday Review, September 19, 1959; November 30, 1968.*

*   *   *

BRUUN, (Arthur) Geoffrey 1898-1988

PERSONAL: Born October 20, 1898, in Montreal, Quebec, Canada; died of a kidney ailment, July 13, 1988, in Ithaca, NY; son of Ernest Theodore and Irene (Jukes) Brunn; married Margarete Herta Hill, 1929; children: Olga Bruun Staneslow and Doris Erika. *Education:* University of British Columbia, B.A., 1924; Cornell University, Ph.D., 1927. *Religion:* Unitarian Universalist. *Avocational interests:* Poetry, travel.

CAREER: New York University, New York, NY, 1927-41, started as instructor, professor of history, 1938-41; Sarah Lawrence College, Bronxville, NY, professor of history, 1943-44; Columbia University, New York, NY, professor of history, 1945-47; writer and lecturer, beginning 1949. Visiting professor at University of British Columbia, 1949, Cornell University, 1952, Mount Holyoke College, 1955, 1963, Smith College, 1957-58, University of Illinois, 1963-65. *Military service:* British Royal Air Force, 1918, cadet, appointed honorary second lieutenant.

MEMBER: American Historical Association, American Association for the Advancement of Science, American Geographical Association.

WRITINGS:

The Enlightened Despots, Holt (New York City), 1929.
Saint-Just: Apostle of the Terror, Houghton (Boston), 1932.
(With Wallace K. Ferguson) *A Survey of European Civilization,* Houghton, 1936.
Europe and the French Imperium, 1799-1814, Harper (New York City), 1938.
Clemenceau, Harvard University Press (Cambridge, MA), 1943.
Europe in Evolution, 1415-1815, Houghton, 1945.
The World in the Twentieth Century, Heath, 1948, 5th edition, 1967.
(With Henry Steele Commager) *Europe and America Since 1492,* Houghton, 1954.
Revolution and Reaction, 1848-1852, Van Nostrand (New York City), 1958.
Nineteenth-Century European Civilization, Oxford University Press (New York City), 1959.
(With Michael R. Martin) *A Graphic Guide to World History,* Holt, 1959.

Contributor of book reviews to various newspapers and magazines.

SIDELIGHTS: Geoffrey Bruun, a historian who specialized in French history, taught at New York University beginning in 1927, moved to Sarah Lawrence College in 1943, and served as professor of history at Columbia University from 1945 to 1947. He was known for his biographies of prominent French historical figures and studies of European history. As W. S. Lynch noted in the *Saturday Review of Literature,* Bruun was "the author of several first-rate and important historical studies" and was "one of the most competent American historians in his field of study."

In *Saint-Just: Apostle of the Terror* Bruun profiled Antoine de Saint-Just, who played a major role in the bloodshed of the French Revolution and the short-lived dictatorship established by Robespierre. The critic for the *Nation* found Bruun's study to be "interesting and historically sound" and noted that the author "treats Saint-Just with far more tolerance than the majority of unsympathetic historians." Albert Guerard in *Books* called the biography "a model of crisp historical narrative; it would have satisfied Voltaire."

Bruun focused on a more contemporary figure in his *Clemenceau,* a biography of Georges Clemenceau, French leader of the First World War. Jacques Barzun in the *New Republic* had much praise for the work, claiming that "Bruun has done an immense amount of research; he has bound together background and foreground with the skill of an old master; he has written in swift yet unhurried prose a book of which every page contains a fact, a maxim, a connection worth noting." The critic for *Commonweal* believed that "from the moment that this book exists on the market it has become an unavoidable necessity for anyone concerned with [the First World War]." It is, the critic concluded, "absolutely necessary to read this biography."

Bruun's more general studies of European history included *Europe in Evolution, 1415-1815* and *The World in the Twentieth Century.* The first volume covers four hundred years of European history and details the major trends, events and personalities of those tumultuous centuries. L. B. Packard in the *American Historical Review* found the ambitious book to be "a fresh, vigorous introduction to the evolution of modern Europe" done with "particular skill." Speaking of *The World in the Twentieth Century,* G. S. Greene in *Social Studies* found that Bruun presented "a rational synthesis and integration of dominant world forces today." J. C. McLendon of *Social Education* wrote: "The social studies teacher, as a student of contemporary history, will do well to become acquainted with Bruun's book."

Bruun's study of the height of French imperialism, *Europe and the French Imperium, 1799-1814,* retells the story of Napoleon's conquests. The critic for *Christian Science Monitor* praised Bruun for his "gift for combining a vivid readability with a skillful selection of relevant facts." Crane Brinton in the *Saturday Review of Literature* found "the refreshing thing is that Mr. Bruun makes generalizations, that he writes clearly and calmly, avoiding dullness as effectively as flippancy, and that he gives his reader ample material for reflection and dissent."

BIOGRAPHICAL/CRITICAL SOURCES:

PERIODICALS

American Historical Review, January, 1946.

Booklist, July 1, 1938; December 15, 1943; July 1, 1948.
Books, December 18, 1932, p. 4; June 26, 1938, p. 5.
Boston Transcript, September 17, 1932, p. 1.
Christian Century, June 8, 1938; December 29, 1943.
Christian Science Monitor, May 18, 1938, p. 18.
Commonweal, December 10, 1943.
Nation, December 21, 1932.
New Republic, August 17, 1938; December 6, 1943.
New York Times, September 4, 1938, p. 2; December 5, 1943, p. 4.
Saturday Review of Literature, May 7, 1938; November 20, 1943.
School & Society, March 27, 1948.
Social Education, December, 1948.
Social Studies, November, 1948.
Springfield Republican, December 12, 1943, p. E7
   Times Literary Supplement, July 9, 1938, p. 459.
Weekly Book Review, September 23, 1945, p. 20.

OBITUARIES:

PERIODICALS

New York Times, July 17, 1988.*

* * *

BRYSON, Bernarda 1905-
(Bernarda Bryson Shahn)

PERSONAL: Born March 7, 1905, in Athens, OH; daughter of Charles Harvey (an editor and publisher) and Lucy (a Latin professor; maiden name, Weethee) Bryson; married Victor Luster Parks, 1927 (divorced, 1930); married Ben Shahn (the artist), 1935 (died, 1969); children: (second marriage) Jonathan, Susanna Shahn Watts (deceased), Abby Shahn Slamm; stepchildren: Judith Shahn Dugan, Ezra. *Education:* Attended Ohio University, 1922-25, Ohio State University, 1926, Western Reserve University (now Case Western Reserve University), 1927, and New School for Social Research. *Politics:* "Generally Democrat." *Religion:* Protestant.

ADDRESSES: Home—Roosevelt, NJ.

CAREER: Illustrator for *Fortune, Harper's, Scientific American,* and other magazines. Columbus Gallery of Fine Arts School, Columbus, OH, instructor in etching and lithography, 1931.

MEMBER: Authors League, Society of Illustrators.

AWARDS, HONORS: Book of the Year, American Institute of Graphic Arts, 1962, for *The Twenty Miracles of Saint Nicolas,* and 1967, for *Gilgamesh, Man's First Story.*

WRITINGS:

(Self-illustrated) *The Twenty Miracles of Saint Nicolas,* Little, Brown (Boston), 1960.
(Self-illustrated) *The Zoo of Zeus,* Grossman, 1964.
(Self-illustrated) *Gilgamesh, Man's First Story,* Holt (New York City), 1967.
Ben Shahn, Abrams (New York City), 1973.
(Contributor of essay) *The Dreyfuss Affair: The Ben Shahn Prints,* Crossroads Books (Cincinnati), 1984.
The Vanishing American Frontier: Bernarda Bryson Shahn and Her Historical Lithographs Created for the Resettlement Administration of FDR, Wien American (New York City), 1995.

Contributor to *Penrose Annual, Graphis,* and *Image.* Editor of *Southside Advocate,* 1929-31; art columnist for *Ohio State Journal.*

ILLUSTRATOR

Charlton Ogburn, *The White Falcon,* Houghton (Boston), 1955.
Rutherford Platt, *The River of Life,* Simon & Schuster (New York City), 1956.
Lives in Science, Simon & Schuster, 1957.
Jane Austen, *Pride and Prejudice,* Macmillan (New York City), 1962.
Natalia M. Belting, *The Sun Is a Golden Earring,* Holt, 1962.
Emily Bronte, *Wuthering Heights,* Macmillan, 1963.
Pauline Clarke, *The Return of the Twelves,* Coward (New York City), 1963.
Belting, *Calender Moon,* Holt, 1964.
Norma Keating, *Mr. Chu,* Macmillan, 1965.
Frank R. Stockton, *The Storyteller's Pack: A Frank R. Stockton Reader,* Scribner (New York City), 1968.
Carl Withers, *The Grindstone of God,* Holt, 1970.

Also illustrator of *Bright Hunter of the Skies* and *The Son of the Sun.*

SIDELIGHTS: Bernarda Bryson's award-winning children's books *The Twenty Miracles of Saint Nicholas* and *Gilgamesh, Man's First Story* present traditional tales for children with the author's own illustrations.

The Twenty Miracles of Saint Nicholas gathers twenty traditional tales concerning the well-known saint of the third century. The book, according to the critic for *Kirkus,* is "a veritable treasury of strange and wondrous happenings told with delicacy and conviction. A book which will become a permanent member of the child's library." "Children," writes Olga Hoyt in the *New York Times Book Review,* "will be spellbound by these stories." Bryson's illustrations also drew praise. E. L. Heins in *Library Journal* calls it "a work of graphic art that all libraries will want." "If a book of real distinction and lasting quality is sought for a holiday gift," the *Horn Book* critic believes, "there could be no better choice."

Gilgamesh, Man's First Story recounts the ancient Sumerian legend of King Gilgamesh's quest, a story which is the oldest recorded in human history. "The present *Gilgamesh* is a powerful rendering of the legend, done with beauty and style," writes Shulamith Oppenheim in the *New York Times Book Review.* John Greenway in *Book World* notes that Bryson "tells the tale with prose redolent of that time of gold in Sumer. . . . She has conveyed the same magic in her magnificent illustrations." Zena Sutherland in the *Saturday Review* also praises Bryson's illustrations, calling them "remarkably handsome and varied, beautiful in color, design, and technique."

BIOGRAPHICAL/CRITICAL SOURCES:

PERIODICALS

Atlantic, December, 1960.
Booklist, December 1, 1960.
Book World, November 5, 1967, p. 8.
Chicago Sunday Tribune, December 4, 1960, p. 33.
Commonweal, November 18, 1960; November 10, 1967.
Horn Book, December, 1960; December, 1967.
Kirkus, August 1, 1960.
Library Journal, September 15, 1960; November 15, 1967.
New York Herald Tribune Lively Arts, December 11, 1960, p. 39.
New York Times Book Review, November 6, 1960, p. 44; November 12, 1967, p. 42.

San Francisco Chronicle, November 13, 1960, p. 17.
Saturday Review, December 17, 1960; November 11, 1967.
Springfield Republican, December 25, 1960, p. D4.

* * *

BUCK, Margaret Waring 1910-

PERSONAL: Born June 3, 1910, in Brooklyn, NY; daughter of Charles A. (draftsman) and Mary (Atwater) Buck. *Education:* Attended Art Students League and other art schools in New York City. *Avocational interests:* Ceramics, especially small animal sculpture, bird watching, nature.

ADDRESSES: Home—19 Clift St., Mystic, CT.

CAREER: Writer and artist.

WRITINGS:

Animals Through the Year, Rand McNally, 1941.
Country Boy, Abingdon (Nashville), 1947.
In Woods and Fields, Abingdon, 1950.
In Yards and Gardens, Abingdon, 1952.
In Ponds and Streams, Abingdon, 1955.
Pets from the Pond, Abingdon, 1958.
Small Pets from Woods and Fields, Abingdon, 1960.
Along the Seashore, Abingdon, 1964.
Where They Go in Winter, Abingdon, 1968.
How They Grow, Abingdon, 1972.

SIDELIGHTS: Margaret Waring Buck has produced a number of self-illustrated books explaining how animals live in the wild. The typical Buck nature book contains detailed black-and-white drawings of the plants, animals, insects and birds to be found in a particular outdoors location, along with an explanatory text ideal for young naturalists who are beginning to learn about the subject.

Among Buck's best received works are *In Woods and Fields, In Yards and Gardens* and *In Ponds and Streams. In Woods and Fields* contains descriptions and illustrations for several hundred animals, plants, insects, and birds. J. W. McGill in the *New York Times* believes that the book is "an invaluable companion," while Millicent Taylor in the *Christian Science Monitor* calls it "an intimate little volume that should help guide a child to observe more beauty and

to be more considerate." Speaking of *In Yards and Gardens,* N. S. Chasteen in *Library Journal* writes that "a nine- or ten-year-old can use it himself with very little help." Polly Goodwin in the *Chicago Sunday Tribune* labels the same book "a fascinating fund of information on the outside world close by and a persuasive eye opener to its delights." *In Ponds and Streams* "is an excellent reference book, written in simple, clear language," according to the critic for *Saturday Review.* Iris Vinton in the *New York Times* finds: "Young nature lovers beginning to delight in identifying living and growing things will find *In Ponds and Streams* a useful guide."

BIOGRAPHICAL/CRITICAL SOURCES:

PERIODICALS

Atlantic, June, 1955.
Booklist, June 1, 1947; March 15, 1950; April 1, 1952; April 15, 1955.
Bookmark, April, 1950; May, 1952.
Book Week, May 10, 1964, p. 33.
Chicago Sun Book Week, May 25, 1947, p. 5.
Chicago Sunday Tribune, April 23, 1950, p. 16; April 27, 1952, p. 14.
Christian Science Monitor, April 29, 1950, p. 6; May 15, 1952, p. 10; May 12, 1955, p. 11; May 7, 1964, p. B9.
Cleveland Open Shelf, May, 1950.
Commonweal, May 22, 1964.
Horn Book, May, 1950; April, 1952; April, 1955.
Kirkus, March 15, 1947; February 15, 1950; February 15, 1952; February 1, 1955.
Library Journal, April 15, 1947; May 1, 1950; May 1, 1952; May 15, 1955; April 15, 1964.
New York Herald Tribune Book Review, April 27, 1947, p. 8; April 9, 1950, p. 8; April 6, 1952, p. 8; May 15, 1955.
New York Times, May 11, 1947, p. 22; March 5, 1950, p. 22; June 8, 1952, p. 30; July 24, 1955, p. 18.
Saturday Review, May 10, 1952; May 14, 1955.
Saturday Review of Literature, March 11, 1950.
Springfield Republican, September 14, 1947, p. B5; March 26, 1950.

* * *

BUCKLE, (Christopher) Richard (Sandford) 1916-

PERSONAL: Born August 6, 1916; son of C. G. (an army officer) and R. E. (Sandford) Buckle. *Educa-*

tion: Attended Balliol College, Oxford. *Avocational interests:* Caricature, light verse.

ADDRESSES: *Home*—Roman Rd., Gutch Common, Semley, Shaftesbury, Dorsetshire, England.

CAREER: Writer and designer of exhibitions. Founder of *Ballet* magazine, 1939. *Observer*, London, England, ballet critic, 1948-55; *Sunday Times*, London, ballet critic, 1959-75. Member of advisory council, Theatre Museum; ballet adviser to Canada Council, 1962. Has organized art exhibitions at museums in Canada and England. *Military service:* British Army, Scots Guards, 1940-46; served in Italy; mentioned in dispatches.

WRITINGS:

John Innocent at Oxford, Chatto & Windus (London), 1939.
(Editor and author of introduction) *Katherine Dunham: Her Dancers, Singers, Musicians,* Ballet Publications (London), 1949.
The Adventures of a Ballet Critic, Cresset (London), 1953.
In Search of Diaghilev, Sidgwick & Jackson, 1955.
Modern Ballet Design: A Picture Book with Notes, A. & C. Black (London), 1955.
Family Tree (play), produced in Worthing, England, 1956.
The Prettiest Girl in England, J. Murray, 1958.
(Editor) Lydia Sokolova, *Dancing for Diaghilev,* Macmillan (New York City), 1961, published as *Dancing for Diaghilev: The Memoirs of Lydia Sokolova,* Mercury House (San Francisco), 1989.
(Author of introduction) *Epstein Drawings,* Faber, 1962.
Harewood: A Guide-book to the Yorkshire Seat of Her Royal Highness, the Princess Royal, and the Earl of Harewood, English Life Publications (Derby, England), 1962.
Jacob Epstein, Sculptor, World Publishing, 1963.
Nijinsky, Weidenfeld & Nicolson (London), 1971, 2nd edition, 1976.
(Author of introduction and notes) Valentine Gross, *Nijinsky on Stage: Action Drawings,* Studio Vista (London), 1971.
Costumes and Curtains from the Diaghilev and de Basil Ballets, Sotheby Parke-Bernet (London), 1972.
(Editor) *U and Non-U Revisited,* Debrett's Peerage (London), 1978.

(Editor) Cecil Beaton, *Self Portrait with Friends: The Selected Diaries of Cecil Beaton, 1926-1974,* Times Books (New York City), 1979.
Diaghilev, Atheneum (New York City), 1979.
Buckle at the Ballet, Atheneum, 1980.
The Most Upsetting Woman (autobiography), Collins (London), 1981.
In the Wake of Diaghilev (autobiography), Holt (New York City), 1983.
George Balanchine: Ballet Master, Random House (New York City), 1989.

Also author of *The Shakespeare Exhibition, 1954-1964,* 1964; *Monsters at Midnight: The French Romantic Movement as a Background to the Ballet Giselle,* 1966; and *The Message: A Gothick Tale of the A-1,* 1969. Also author of play, *Gossip Column,* 1953. Contributor to magazines, including *Books and Bookmen.*

SIDELIGHTS: Long-time ballet critic Richard Buckle has written about the arts, theatre and ballet. His major works are biographies of leading figures in the arts, which have won critical praise for their diligent research.

In Search of Diaghilev tells of Buckle's work to assemble the Diaghilev Exhibition at the Edinburgh Festival in 1954. The book recounts the travels he made and the people he met along the way. While George Freedley in *Library Journal* calls the book "a major contribution to ballet history," the critic for the *Christian Science Monitor* finds the book to be "an exhibition in itself" because of the many illustrations included. "But the text is as important as the illustrations," the critic concludes. "It makes pictures of its own."

Nijinsky is a biography of the famous ballet dancer and an evaluation of his career. Buckle interviewed family members as well as others in the field of ballet who knew the dancer to create what Dorothy Nyren in *Library Journal* calls the "definitive biography of Nijinsky." the critic for the *Economist* complains that the biography "is far too long," but concedes that Buckle "has been immensely industrious" in his research and admits that "ballet lovers prepared to pay the high price of the book will find much to interest them."

In *Jacob Epstein, Sculptor* Buckle writes another biography of a leading artist, including over 400 examples of the artist's works as well. Louis Barron in *Library Journal* calls *Jacob Epstein, Sculptor* "one of the outstanding art books of last year," while the critic for the *Times Literary Supplement* labels it a "massive and compendious tome." Richard McLanathan in the *New York Times Book Review* concludes that "this thoughtfully conceived volume by Richard Buckle . . . provides a handsome visual chronicle of Jacob Epstein's career in a fashion both appealing and impressive."

BIOGRAPHICAL/CRITICAL SOURCES:

PERIODICALS

Best Sellers, October 15, 1972.
Chicago Tribune Book World, September 30, 1979.
Christian Science Monitor, August 8, 1956, p. 9; December 13, 1972, p. 15.
Commentary, May, 1964.
Economist, November 13, 1971.
Guardian, September 28, 1962, p. 6.
Kirkus, September 1, 1962.
Library Journal, March 1, 1956; August, 1956; December 1, 1962; February 15, 1964; September 1, 1972.
Nation, December 22, 1962; December 28, 1964; November 20, 1972.
New Statesman and Nation, February 11, 1956; August 28, 1964.
Newsweek, December 30, 1963; October 9, 1972.
New York Times Book Review, January 5, 1964, p. 7; October 8, 1972, p. 27.
Saturday Review, September 8, 1962; December 5, 1964; October 7, 1972.
Spectator, December 23, 1955, p. 876.
Theatre Arts, August, 1956; October, 1956.
Times Literary Supplement, December 16, 1955, p. 756; January 20, 1956, p. 32; August 3, 1962, p. 552; February 6, 1964, p. 110; January 14, 1972, p. 35.
Washington Post Book World, December 30, 1979.

*   *   *

BUCKLEY, Jerome Hamilton 1917-

PERSONAL: Born August 30, 1917, in Toronto, Ontario, Canada; naturalized U.S. citizen, 1948; son of James O. and Madeline (Morgan) Buckley; married Elizabeth Jane Adams, 1943; children: Nicholas, Victoria, Eleanor. *Education:* University of Toronto, B.A., 1939; Harvard University, M.A., 1940, Ph.D., 1942. *Politics:* Democrat. *Religion:* Episcopalian.

ADDRESSES: Home—191 Common St., Belmont, MA 02178. *Office*—Widener Library, Harvard University, Cambridge, MA 02138.

CAREER: University of Wisconsin—Madison, 1942-54, began as instructor, became professor of English; Columbia University, New York City, professor of English, 1954-61; Harvard University, Cambridge, MA, professor of English, 1961-75, Gurney Professor of English Literature, 1975—. Summer and visiting professor at numerous universities.

MEMBER: International Association of University Professors of English, Modern Language Association of America, Academy of Literary Studies, American Academy of Arts and Sciences, Tennyson Society (vice-president).

AWARDS, HONORS: Guggenheim fellowship, 1946-47, 1964; Christian Gauss Prize; Phi Beta Kappa book award, 1952.

WRITINGS:

William Ernest Henley: A Study in the "Counter-Decadence" of the Nineties, Princeton University Press (Princeton, NJ), 1945, reprinted, Octagon Books (New York City), 1971.
The Victorian Temper: A Study in Literary Culture, Harvard University Press (Cambridge, MA), 1951, 2nd edition, 1969.
(Editor with George Benjamin Woods) *Poetry of the Victorian Period,* Scott, Foresman (New York City), 1955, revised edition, 1965.
(Editor) *Poems of Tennyson,* Houghton (Boston), 1958.
Tennyson: The Growth of a Poet, Harvard University Press, 1960.
(Co-editor) *Masters of British Literature,* Houghton, 1962.
(Editor) Tennyson, *Idylls of the King,* Houghton, 1963.
The Triumph of Time: A Study of the Victorian Concepts of Time, History, Progress, and Decadence, Harvard University Press, 1966.
(Compiler) *Victorian Poets and Prose Writers,* Appleton (New York City), 1966, 2nd edition, AHM Publishing, 1977.
(Editor and author of introduction) *The Pre-Raphaelites,* Random House (New York City), 1968.
Season of Youth: The Bildungsroman from Dickens to Golding, Harvard University Press, 1974.

(Editor) *The Worlds of Victorian Fiction,* Harvard University Press, 1975.

The Turning Key: Autobiography and the Subjective Impulse since 1800, Harvard University Press, 1984.

(Editor and author of introduction) *The Pre-Raphaelites,* Academy Chicago (Chicago), 1986.

(Editor) Charles Dickens, *David Copperfield: Authoritative Text, Backgrounds, Criticism,* Norton (New York City), 1990.

Also co-editor of *Twelve Hundred Years,* 1949. Contributor to encyclopedias. Contributor of articles and reviews to journals. Advisor to *Victorian Studies, Victorian Poetry, Clio,* and *Review.*

SIDELIGHTS: Jerome Hamilton Buckley is known for his studies of both individual authors and of larger literary trends.

In *The Victorian Temper: A Study in Literary Culture* and *The Triumph of Time: A Study of the Victorian Concepts of Time, History, Progress, and Decadence,* Buckley focuses on the Victorian period to present the prevalent attitudes of the time and their relationship with the literature then created. Carlos Baker, reviewing *The Victorian Temper* in the *New York Times,* finds that Buckley's "diagnosis of the Victorian temper is one of the wisest and sanest available in the field of cultural evaluation." Similarly, the *New Yorker* critic labels the book "an intelligent work of social and literary history." In *The Triumph of Time,* according to L. W. Griffin in *Library Journal,* Buckley "considers eruditely an intriguing topic: the Victorians' unprecedented awareness of time. . . . A thoughtful, well-written book on an important topic in an equally important period."

Buckley's *Season of Youth: The Bildungsroman from Dickens to Golding* examines a popular genre which has received relatively little critical attention: the coming-of-age novel. The study examines a number of classic works of the type and compares their handling of similar themes. Buckley's "commentaries are graceful, informed, and perceptive," writes Keith Cushman in *Library Journal,* "and there is a genuine value in looking at these familiar novels in the context of their shared genre." The critic for *Choice* praises Buckley for "his usual penetrating insight and clarity of expression" and believes that *Season of Youth* "will unquestionably become a standard critical work."

In *Tennyson: The Growth of a Poet* Buckley combines a biography of the famous poet with a comprehensive study of Tennyson's body of work. "Perhaps the outstanding merit of Buckley's important work is that it is the first to fully and persuasively set forth Tennyson's claim to be regarded on every count as one of the supreme poets of the language," writes E. D. H. Johnson in *Modern Philology. Saturday Review*'s T. H. Johnson finds that Buckley's study "enhances the stature of a poet who, without originality, made his art superbly the instrument of vision and of voice." DeLancey Ferguson in the *New York Herald Tribune Lively Arts* notes that "one need not learn a special vocabulary in order to understand [Buckley's book]; psychoanalytical terminology and the jargon of the New Criticism are alike absent." G. N. Ray in the *New York Times Book Review* calls *Tennyson: The Growth of a Poet* "an able, thorough, and carefully meditated book that will wear well. Indeed, it should remain for a good many years the standard survey of Tennyson's poetry." Similarly, Johnson concludes: "Buckley has written the most authoritative study of Tennyson's poetry which has yet appeared."

BIOGRAPHICAL/CRITICAL SOURCES:

BOOKS

Lockridge, Laurence S., John Maynard and Donald D. Stone, editors, *Nineteenth-Century Lives: Essays Presented to Jerome Hamilton Buckley,* Cambridge University Press (New York City), 1989.

PERIODICALS

Booklist, October 1, 1951.
Book Week, December 2, 1945.
Choice, October, 1974.
Christian Century, December 12, 1945.
Christian Science Monitor, September 13, 1951.
Library Journal, October 15, 1945; September 1, 1951; December 1, 1960; September 15, 1966; June 15, 1974.
Modern Philology, November, 1961.
New Republic, January 7, 1946.
New Yorker, September 22, 1951.
New York Herald Tribune Lively Arts, January 8, 1961.
New York Times, November 25, 1945; September 9, 1951.
New York Times Book Review, January 1, 1961; October 30, 1966.

Saturday Review, January 28, 1961.
Saturday Review of Literature, December 22, 1945;
    October 13, 1951.
Spectator, April 21, 1961.
Springfield Republican, September 9, 1951.
Time, October 15, 1945.
Times Literary Supplement, August 11, 1961.

* * *

BURNET, (Frank) Macfarlane 1899-1985

PERSONAL: Born September 3, 1899, in Traralgon,
Victoria, Australia; died of cancer, August 31, 1985,
in Melbourne, Australia; son of Frank (a bank manager) and Hadassah (Mackay) Burnet; married Edith
Linda Marston Druce, July 10, 1929 (died November
10, 1973); married Hazel Foletta Jenkin, January 16,
1976; children: Elizabeth (Mrs. Paul Dexter), Ian,
Deborah (Mrs. John Giddy). *Education:* University
of Melbourne, M.B. and B.S., both 1923, M.D.,
1924; University of London, Ph.D., 1928.

CAREER: Melbourne Hospital, Melbourne, Australia, resident pathologist, 1923-24; Lister Institute,
London, England, Beit fellow in medical research,
1926-27; Walter & Eliza Hall Institute for Medical
Research, Melbourne, Australia, assistant director,
1928-31, 1934-44, director, 1944-65, Rowden White
research fellow in microbiology, 1966-67; National
Institute for Medical Research, Hampstead, England,
visiting worker, 1932-33; writer, 1967-85. University of Melbourne research professor, 1944-66, professor emeritus and guest professor, 1966-85.
Dunham lecturer at Harvard University, 1944;
Croonian lecturer for Royal Society; Herter lecturer
at Johns Hopkins University, 1950; Abraham Flexner
lecturer at Vanderbilt University, 1958. Member of
World Health Organization medical research advisory committee in Geneva, 1957-60; chair of medical
research advisory committee in Papua New Guinea,
1962-69; chair of board of trustees of Commonwealth Foundation (London), 1966-69.

MEMBER: Australian Academy of Science (president, 1965-69), Royal Australian College of Physicians (fellow), Australian Medical Association, Royal
Society (fellow), Royal College of Physicians (fellow), Royal College of Surgeons (honorary fellow),
Pathological Society of the United Kingdom, National Academy of Sciences (United States; foreign

associate), American College of Physicians (fellow),
American Academy of Arts and Sciences (foreign
member), Swedish Royal Academy of Science.

AWARDS, HONORS: Sc.D. from Cambridge Univer-
sity, 1946; Royal Society, Royal Medal, 1947,
Copley Medal, 1959; knighted, 1951, named knight
commander of the British Empire, 1969; Emil von
Behring Prize, University of Marburg, 1952; Lasker
Award, American Public Health Association, Lasker
Foundation, 1952, for contribution to the understand-
ing of virus disease; Order of Merit, 1958; Galen
Medal in Therapeutics, Society of Apothecaries,
1958; co-winner of Nobel Prize for Medicine, 1960;
D.Sc. from Oxford University, 1968.

WRITINGS:

Biological Aspects of Infectious Disease, Cambridge
    University Press (London), 1940, second edition
    published as *Natural History of Infectious Dis-
    ease,* 1953, fourth edition (with D. O. White),
    1972.
Virus as Organism, Harvard University Press (Cam-
    bridge, MA), 1945.
Viruses and Man, Penguin, 1953, second edition,
    1955.
*2000 A. D.: A Biologist's Thoughts on the Next Forty
    Years,* Adult Education Board of Tasmania
    (Hobart), 1959.
The Clonal Selection Theory of Acquired Immunity,
    Vanderbilt University Press (Nashville, TN),
    1959.
*The Integrity of the Body: A Discussion of Modern
    Immunological Ideas,* Harvard University Press,
    1962.
Biology and the Appreciation of Life, Australian
    Broadcasting Commission (Sydney), 1966.
Changing Patterns: An Atypical Autobiography,
    Heinemann (Melbourne), 1968, American
    Elsevier (New York City), 1969.
Cellular Immunology, Cambridge University Press,
    1969.
Dominant Mammal: The Biology of Human Destiny,
    Heinemann, 1970, St. Martin's (New York
    City), 1972.
Immunological Surveillance, Pergamon (Elmsford,
    NY), 1970.
Genes, Dreams, and Realities, Basic Books (New
    York City), 1971.
Walter and Eliza Hall Institute, 1915-1965,
    Melbourne University Press (Carlton, Victory),
    1971.

Auto-Immunity and Auto-Immune Disease: A Survey for Physician or Biologist, F. A. Davis (Philadelphia), 1972.

(With others) *Man and His Australian Environment,* Ormond (Melbourne), 1973.

Intrinsic Mutagenesis: A Genetic Approach to Aging, J. Wiley (New York City), 1974.

The Biology of Aging, Oxford University Press (Wellington), 1974.

Immunology, Aging, and Cancer: Medical Aspects of Mutation and Selection, W. H. Freeman (San Francisco), 1976.

(Author of introductions and additional material) *Immunology: Readings from Scientific American,* W. H. Freeman (San Francisco), 1976.

Endurance of Life: The Implications of Genetics for Human Life, Melbourne University Press, 1978.

Credo and Comment: A Scientist Reflects, Melbourne University Press (Carlton), 1979.

(Contributor) *Biological Foundations and Human Nature,* edited by Miriam Balaban, Academic Press (New York City), 1983.

Also author of other books on technical subjects.

SIDELIGHTS: A microbiologist and virologist, Macfarlane Burnet shared the 1960 Nobel Prize in medicine for his work in immunology. In announcing the award, the Swedish Academy noted Burnet's pioneer research on the human immuneresponse system, which helped to eliminate one of the major obstacles in human tissue and organ transplant. Also renowned for his work on the nature of viruses, Burnet discovered that influenza existed as a mutating virus adapting to human immunities, and his studies on the genetic material of viruses form the basis for current theories linking viruses to cancer. In 1952 the American Public Health Association honored Burnet with the prestigious Lasker Award, citing his contribution to the understanding of virus disease. Among Burnet's other awards and honors were the Copley Medal and Royal Medal from the Royal Society and Germany's exalted scientific award, the Emil von Behring Prize. He was knighted in 1951 and made knight commander of the British Empire in 1969.

Burnet spent much of his career as the director of the Walter and Eliza Hall Institute for Medical Research at the Royal Melbourne Hospital. Additionally, he taught biology, zoology, and comparative anatomy at such institutions as the University of Melbourne and Harvard University. Burnet retired from teaching and research in 1965 and served as the president of the Australian Academy of Science from 1965 to 1969.

His many writings include *Biological Aspects of Infectious Diseases, Virus as Organism, Immunological Surveillance, Intrinsic Mutagenesis: A Genetic Approach to Aging,* and his autobiography *Changing Patterns: An Atypical Autobiography.*

Burnet's autobiography *Changing Patterns,* an "eminently enjoyable volume," according to *Library Journal* reviewer J. J. Taylor, is "written . . . objectively and volubly . . . [and] the tediousness of more 'typical' autobiographies is neatly avoided." A less impressed *Choice* critic classified it as a "technical" work with "large portions [that] are rather dull" and contended that it is "good for a study of the author but it is not the popular handling of ideas in medicine and microbiology during the years 1917-67 that it asserts." A contrasting review by R. E. Billingham in *Science* praised this "delightful biologist's book": "[Burnet] has written an extremely honest, as well as readable, analytical account of his 50 years' highly productive life as a medical scientist. . . . Through Burnet's eyes . . . we review the exciting changes in the scientific aspects of medicine and approaches to biological research . . . that have come about during his career. . . . [As well as] his views about the impact of science . . . on human affairs of the future."

The future predictions and general attitude Burnet presented in *Genes, Dreams, and Realities* were not very well received. Extremely pessimistic, more than one critic expressed complaints. A *Choice* contributor contended that "a major defect of this challenging and provocative book [written to the educated layman] is its complete lack of references to support its pessimistic views of the future value of all that may be encompassed by the term 'molecular biology.'" Although most of the book, specifically the parts which detail Burnet's "own subjects," is "lucid and authoritative and a pleasure to read," according to an *Economist* critic the portion of the book "discussing mental disease, population, the limits of therapy, the future of biological science and indeed of the world . . . reveals a pessimism that becomes grating." Echoing the comments made in *Economist,* a reviewer for the *Times Literary Supplement* cited this example: "[Burnet] can see 'no hope for any revolutionary improvement in the cure of cancer.' This is a molecular biological statement that no molecular biologist would feel able to venture, so slight is our real understanding of the problem."

Prior to his death in 1985, Burnet once wrote: "Two autobiographical books, *Changing Patterns* and

Walter and Eliza Hall Institute present personal pictures of my own scientific development and the growth of an Australian laboratory. Since my retirement, I have written extensively on aspects of human biology in the board sense, mostly as lectures to professional groups of various sorts. [*Dominant Mammal: The Biology of Human Destiny*] summarized my 1970 attitudes without attracting much attention. [*Endurance of Life: The Implications of Genetics for Human Life*] is more ambitious and more controversial, with a strong bias toward stressing the importance of genetics in all behavioral as well as structural aspects of the human being. The social implications of such a viewpoint are already becoming evident."

BIOGRAPHICAL/CRITICAL SOURCES:

BOOKS

Burnet, Macfarlane, *Changing Patterns,* Heinemann, 1968, American Elsevier, 1969.

Burnet, *Walter and Eliza Hall Institute, 1915-1965,* Melbourne University Press, 1971.

Norry, Roy, *Virus Hunter in Australia: The Story of Sir Macfarlane Burnet,* illustrated by Don Angus, Nelson (Melbourne), 1966.

Sexton, Christopher, *The Seeds of Time: The Life of Sir Macfarlane Burnet,* Oxford (New York City), 1991.

PERIODICALS

Choice, October, 1970; May, 1972

Economist, August 21, 1971

Lancet, Volume I, 1965.

Library Journal, July, 1970; July, 1972

Science, March 12, 1971

Scientific America, January, 1973.

Times Literary Supplement, December 25, 1969; October 22, 1971; April 7, 1972.

OBITUARIES:

PERIODICALS

Chicago Tribune, September 4, 1985.

Detroit Free Press, September 4, 1985.

New York Times, September 3, 1985.

Times (London), September 2, 1985.

Washington Post, September 2, 1985.*

BURRIDGE, Kenelm (Oswald Lancelot) 1922-

PERSONAL: Born October 31, 1922, in St. Julians, Malta; son of William (a professor) and Jane (Torregiani) Burridge; children: Julian Langford. *Education:* Oxford University, B.A., 1948, diploma in anthropology, 1949, M.A., 1950, B.Litt., 1950; Australian National University, Ph.D., 1953.

ADDRESSES: Home—Apt, 4, 2265 Acadia Rd., Vancouver, British Columbia, Canada V6T 1R7. *Office*—Department of Anthropology and Sociology, University of British Columbia, Vancouver, British Columbia, Canada.

CAREER: University of Baghdad, Baghdad, Iraq, professor of anthropology, 1953-56; Oxford University, Oxford, England, lecturer in ethnology, 1956-68; University of British Columbia, Vancouver, professor of anthropology, 1968—, head of anthropology and sociology department, 1973—. Visiting lecturer at University of Western Australia, 1968. *Military service:* Royal Navy; became lieutenant.

MEMBER: American Anthropological Association, Canadian Sociological and Anthropological Association, Royal Society of Canada, Royal Anthropological Institute of Great Britain and Ireland.

AWARDS, HONORS: Research fellow at University of Malaya, 1953-56; Guggenheim fellow, 1972-73; S.S.H.R.C. fellow and Killam fellow, both 1979-80.

WRITINGS:

Mambu: A Melanesian Millenium, Methuen, 1967, reprinted, Princeton University Press (Princeton, NJ), 1995.

Tangu Traditions: A Study of the Way of Life, Mythology, and Developing Experience of a New Guinea People, Clarendon Press (Oxford, England), 1969.

Encountering Aborigines, A Case Study: Anthropology and the Australian Aboriginal, Pergamon Press (New York City), 1973.

New Heaven, New Earth: A Study of Millenarian Activities, Schocken (New York City), 1969, reprinted Blackwell (Oxford, England), 1986.

Someone, No One: An Essay on Individuality, Princeton University Press, 1979.

In the Way: A Study of Christian Missionary Endeavors, UBC Press (Vancouver, British Columbia), 1991.

SIDELIGHTS: Anthropology is frequently defined as the comparative study of humankind. The word comparative carries special significance for many contemporary cultural anthropologists, including Kenelm Burridge, a professor who has published works such as *In the Way: A Study of Christian Missionary Endeavors, Someone, No One: An Essay on Individuality,* and *Mambu: A Melanesian Millenium.* Burridge believes that a culture must be judged by how well it serves its own people's needs, and not be arbitrarily criticized through another's standards. Nevertheless, it is vital to realize a culture's relevance to every other society. Burridge takes this position in *Encountering Aborigines, A Case Study: Anthropology and the Australian Aboriginal.* Though suggested by the title, his work is not totally devoted to the aborigine; rather, it is "concerned with the way the anthropological enterprise has been shaped by the context of Western civilization, as that enterprise is revealed through its praxis among the Aborigines," explained Philip L. Newman in *Science.*

Burridge begins *Encountering Aborigines* with a cumulation of much of the published information available on the migratory tribe to date. He then draws generalizations on the society as a whole, leading directly into "motives" or "themes" applicable to any culture. The aborigine is seen as "everyman," reacting in his own unique way to the basic biological and sociological stimuli faced by all humankind. By not taking into account alien cultures such as this one, Burridge insists we cannot ultimately understand our own. And to gain this intrinsic knowledge, the overwhelming conceit in the virtue of our own morals and traditions with its condescending opinion of other cultures must be eradicated.

Burridge's "critique of evolutionary theory [in *Encountering Aborigines*] is particularly interesting in terms of his general thesis," praised Newman. However, "most of the standard works on the history of anthropological theory [are not mentioned]," noted a *Choice* critic, complaining: "Burridge's command of Aboriginal data seems limited, although 'extensive field work' is claimed. A convoluted and ponderous style makes for obscurity and leads Burridge into errors." Nevertheless, Newman contended: "Burridge can count the book a success insofar as it moves its reader into a greater awareness of whence he came intellectually and where, possibly, he might go."

Burridge sees the unfortunate trend of anthropology today leaning toward "professionalism" rather than "humanism." Cultures are statistically and categorically analyzed with little apparent regard for inherent motivating factors. Rituals and routines alike are duly recorded, but the spirit of the people themselves never emerges. As in most human endeavor, however, a reversal is in sight. Burridge believes the current attitude will soon run its course, with a more humanistic approach resulting.

Critics of *Tangu Traditions: A Study of the Way of Life, Mythology, and Developing Experience of a New Guinea People* praised the methodology Burridge used in exploring the Tangu people. "Besides adding to what we know of [the Tangu] culture, it presents an interesting and innovative mode of analysis. . . . Both substantively and methodologically the book is a valuable addition to a library collection in anthropology," claimed a *Choice* contributor. A *Times Literary Supplement* reviewer lauded: "Here we have an ideal combination of the empiricism of British anthropology and the metaphysics of French structuralism. Following from his field research in the early 1950s, Dr. Burridge has found and developed a theoretical framework that has resulted in this most important contribution to social anthropology so far. He has tackled one of the most complex aspects of the discipline but with undoubted competence and with invaluable results."

Another Burridge accomplishment, *New Heaven, New Earth: A Study of Millenarian Activities* "is a thoughtful, provocative, and exiting book that will encourage a fresh approach not only to millenarian activities but to the question of dynamics generally," according to *Pacific Affairs* contributor D. G. Bettison. In this work Burridge reviews and criticizes existing literature as well as providing his own theories; it "presents a model of the social process responsible for that type of millennial movement in which transition to a money economy presents a crucial challenge to male integrity," described A. F. C. Wallace in *American Anthropology.* Burridge "is intent on using millenarian activities as a test case in the search for a new objective validity to the interpretation of social relations," explained Bettison. "Although the model is too narrow for application to all revitalization movements, it permits a penetrating analysis of some movements," maintained Wallace. "When Burridge turns to the task of explanation, he does this in a way that is singularly appropriate for the present stage of sociological and anthropological enquiries," judged Alasdair MacIntyre in a 1970 *Encounter* review, concluding: "This is one of the most interesting books in the field of the human sciences for some time."

BIOGRAPHICAL/CRITICAL SOURCES:

PERIODICALS

American Anthropology, October, 1970.
Choice, September, 1970; May, 1974.
Encounter, March, 1970.
Pacific Affairs, summer, 1970.
Science, June 28, 1974.
Times Literary Supplement, March 5, 1970.*

*   *   *

BURTON, Hal
    See BURTON, Harold Bernard

*   *   *

BURTON, Harold Bernard 1908-1992
    (Hal Burton)

PERSONAL: Born April 15, 1908, in Minneapolis, MN; died March, 1992; son of Barney and Josephine (Deutsch) Burton; married Henrietta Kimberly Ward, September 24, 1948; children: Mary Ward and Frederick Barney (twins). *Education:* Attended University of Wisconsin—Madison, 1927. *Politics:* Republican. *Religion:* Episcopalian. *Avocational interests:* Travel (South America, Europe).

CAREER: New York Daily News, New York City, editorial writer, 1934-41; *Newsday,* Garden City, NY, chief editorial writer, 1958-68, book editor, 1968-76. Chair of New York governor's commissions on skiing, 1938-41, 1955-57; commissioner of Adirondack Mountain Authority, 1957-68. *Military service:* U.S. Army, Infantry, 1942-45; served in Italy; became captain; mentioned in British dispatches.

MEMBER: National Ski Association (member of board of directors, 1939-41), American Alpine Club, Adirondack Mountain Club, Keene Valley Country Club.

AWARDS, HONORS: Named recreationist of the year by New York State Conservation Council, 1969;

named honorary director of Olympic Winter Games in Lake Placid, NY, 1980.

WRITINGS:

UNDER NAME HAL BURTON

The Walton Boys and Gold in the Snow, Whitman Publishing (Racine, WI), 1948.
The Walton Boys and Rapids Ahead, Whitman Publishing, 1950.
The Walton Boys in High Country, Whitman Publishing, 1952.
The Real Book about Treasure Hunting, (juvenile; illustrated by Jean Michener), Garden City Books, 1953.
The City Fights Back: A Nation-Wide Survey of What Cities Are Doing to Keep Pace with Traffic, Zoning, Shifting Population, Smoke, Smog and Other Problems; Narrated and Edited from Material Developed by the Central Business District Council of the Urban Land Institute, Citadel Press (Secaucus, NJ), 1954.
(Editor) *Great Acting: Laurence Olivier, Sybil Thorndike, Ralph Richardson, Peggy Ashcroft, Michael Redgrave, Edith Evans, John Gielgud, Noel Coward,* Hill & Wang (New York City), 1967.
(Editor) *Acting in the Sixties: Richard Burton, Harry H. Corbett, Albert Finney, John Neville, Eric Porter, Vanessa Redgrave, Maggie Smith, Robert Stephens, Dorothy Tutin,* British Broadcasting Corp. (London), 1970.
The Ski Troops, Simon & Schuster (New York City), 1971.
The Morro Castle: Tragedy at Sea, Viking (New York City), 1973.

Also author of *The Walton Boys,* 1975, and *Hal,* 1977. Contributor to popular magazines, including *Saturday Evening Post.*

SIDELIGHTS: Editor and ski enthusiast Harold Bernard Burton, better known as Hal Burton, contributed to popular magazines as well as publishing a variety of books, both fiction and non-fiction. In addition to authoring works such as *The Ski Troops* and several "*Walton Boys*" books, he edited two publications focused on acting, *Great Acting: Laurence Olivier, Sybil Thorndike, Ralph Richardson, Peggy Ashcroft, Michael Redgrave, Edith Evans, John Gielgud, Noel Coward,* and *Acting in the Sixties: Richard Burton, Harry H. Corbett, Albert Finney, John Neville, Eric Porter, Vanessa*

Redgrave, Maggie Smith, Robert Stephens, Dorothy Tutin. Also among his literary accomplishments is *The Real Book About Treasure Hunting,* "a 'fun education' book" comprised of both fact and fiction which its juvenile readers "will enjoy . . . heartily," declared Iris Binton in the *New York Times.*

In his work for the *New York Daily News,* Burton first addressed the 1934 Morro Castle tragedy—the pre-dawn raging fire on a cruiseliner which killed many passengers and destroyed the ship just off the coast of New Jersey. Burton later produced *The Morro Castle: Tragedy at Sea,* "a suspenseful, minute-by-minute account of the events of that tragic morning," in which, according to *Best Sellers* contributor K. J. Cox, the author "has interestingly recorded the facts . . . enabling a clarification and sequencing of the events as they occurred." Cox reported that Burton "thoroughly researched the incident and, through the use of interviews with survivors, he captures the personal fear and heroism that characterized the Morro Castle disaster."

BIOGRAPHICAL/CRITICAL SOURCES:

PERIODICALS

Best Sellers, July 15, 1973.
Booklist, October 1, 1953.
Kirkus Reviews, July 1, 1953.
Library Journal, April 15, 1973; November 15, 1973.
New Yorker, November, 1941.
New York Times, December 27, 1953.
San Francisco Chronicle, June 21, 1954.
Springfield Republican, November 14, 1954.*

*   *   *

BUTLER, William 1929-

PERSONAL: Born in 1929, in Portland, OR; married Lindsley Cameron; children: one son. *Avocational interests:* Composing music, traveling, hiking.

CAREER: Production and program director, Pacifica Radio stations; lecturer in literature, Bennington College, Bennington, VT; newspaper cartoonist, Tokyo, Japan; lecturer in English, Kita-Kyushu University, Fukuoka, Japan.

WRITINGS:

NOVELS

The Butterfly Revolution (juvenile), P. Owen (London), 1961, Putnam (New York City), 1967.
The Experiment, P. Owen, 1961.
The Tyburn Talent (juvenile), Brown, Watson, 1961.
The House at Akiya, P. Owen, 1963, Scribner, 1969.
Mr. Three, P. Owen, 1964, Putnam, 1966.
Cire Perdue, P. Owen, 1965.
The Ring in Meiji, Putnam, 1965.
A Danish Gambit, P. Owen, 1966.
Spying at the Fountain of Youth, P. Owen, 1968.
A God Novel, Scribner (New York City), 1969.
Man in a Net, P. Owen, 1971.
The Pseudologia, P. Owen, 1971.
The Bone House, P. Owen, 1972.

Contributor to periodicals, including *Harper's, Cornhill, Paris Review,* and *Harpers Bazaar.*

ADAPTATIONS: A Danish Gambit was adapted into a play by John McGrath, *Bakke's Night of Fame,* Davis-Poynter (London), 1973.

SIDELIGHTS: William Butler is the author of many novels first published during the 1960s and early-1970s in England as well as the United States. A visitor and at one time a resident of Japan, Butler has portrayed Japan and Japanese culture and history in some of his novels. Taking place in both Europe and Japan, critics of *A God Novel* applauded the "spiritual quest" aspect of the story about four strangers of American, Indian, and Lebanese backgrounds who try to return a golden crown stolen from a statue of the Virgin Mary; however, as Martin Levin complained in the *New York Times Book Review,* the "tangled little book is . . . sparse in invention and metaphor." "[This] is a frankly religious book, a spiritual thriller which employs a perverse kind of psychology for its movement," declared *Book World* contributor Paul Theroux, who claimed that only as "surface complexity" is the book "an intelligently observed novel . . . [attempting] to give large questions a dramatic form." Theroux faulted: "The characters are from backgrounds as far-flung as the action. . . . [They] have extremely elusive idenitities, and their presences are not so strong." R. W. Henderson judged in *Library Journal:* "Mythological allusions, symbolism, and a mood of mysticism make the book hard to follow, but it could be rewarding to those who care to give it a thoughtful reading."

The Ring in Meiji is "a nine-cycled epic about mid-nineteenth-century Japan and the incursions of western commerce and politics," described a *Times Literary Supplement* contributor. "In every way this novel is a big book. . . . Butler knows his history of Japan and the geography of the country. . . . One learns much . . . about the character of the people of Japan with roots in a long not always peaceful quest," wrote R. F. Grady in *Best Sellers*. Less positively, Francis Hope assessed in *New Statesman:* "[Butler's] Japanese family, neatly exemplifying pro- and anti-western tendencies, are sometimes too consciously and exhibitonistically Japanese, too like a couloured anatomy chart for first-year students, to draw one deeply into their lives. And although he can describe some things very well—particularly the scenes of violence which erupt without warning from time to time—his prose is in general clotted, tortuous and scarred with inversions." Conversely, D. J. Pearce judged in *Library Journal* that *The Ring in Meiji* is "tightly written and finely conceived," declaring: "[This novel] uses the locale well and accurately and portrays this time of Japanese development and the foreigners involved in it with sensitivity to character and imagination in language. . . . It is a fine, well-written novel with a skillful blend of fiction and historical fact."

In *The House at Akiya,* a New York firm representative moves with his family to Akiya, a small town outside of Tokyo, where he purchases a house that the locals think is haunted. "Written with an economy the is a pleasure to read," *Book World*'s L. J. Davis described the book as a "finely wrought, disturbing short novel . . . at once a kind of ghost story and at the same time a highly intellectualized, brooding tale of cultural collision." Davis lauded the novels "perfect symmetry, its beautiful compactness, [and] the rare intelligence of the thing," suggesting, "[Perhaps] the book is too well-made and therefore brittle. . . . I admire [it], but I wish that it had ravelled somewhere." "Butler must be credited with having produced a rare thing, a tale about Japan that is neither facetious nor condescending, and only occasionally and very slightly sentimental," praised Edward Seidensticker in the *New York Times Book Review*. However, Seidensticker claimed the novel falls short of "the highest marks" of a "Gothic tale," the conditions where "one is pulled under the spell of its horrid happenings to the extent that one accepts them despite their improbability." Seidensticker specifies: "So bland and matter-of-fact is the narrative that one is left asking questions." *Commonweal* critic Richard Elman contended that "Butler's restraint is not the absence of emotion. It is the mood through which that absence is noticed and felt." Elman heralded *The House at Akiya* as Butler's best work, proclaiming: "I have been deeply moved by the novels of William Butler for quite a number of years. . . . [This is] his masterpiece. It is a sparse, intense, queer work or art about the disintegration of a personality."

BIOGRAPHICAL/CRITICAL SOURCES:

PERIODICALS

America, November 29, 1969.
Best Sellers, June 15, 1965; November 15, 1969.
Book World, November 23, 1969; September 13, 1970.
Christian Science Monitor, July 22, 1965.
Commonweal, December 5, 1969.
Library Journal, June 15, 1965; October 15, 1969; September 1, 1970.
New Statesman, January 22, 1965.
New Yorker, June 26, 1965.
New York Times Book Review, December 21, 1969; August 23, 1970.
Times Literary Supplement, January 28, 1965; February 27, 1969.
Washington Post Book World, November 23, 1969; September 13, 1970.*

C

CADY, Edwin Harrison 1917-

PERSONAL: Born November 9, 1917, in Old Tappan, NJ; son of Edwin Laird and Ethel (Harrison) Cady; married Norma Mae Woodard, 1939; children: Frances (Mrs. Edward Hitchcock), Elizabeth (Mrs. Larry Saler). *Education:* Ohio Wesleyan University, A.B., 1939; University of Cincinnati, A.M., 1940; University of Wisconsin, Ph.D., 1943. *Religion:* Episcopalian.

ADDRESSES: Home—Box 168, RFD 4, Hillsborough, NC 27278. *Office*—Perkins Library 329, Duke University, Durham, NC 27706.

CAREER: University of Wisconsin, Madison, instructor in English, 1944-45; Ohio State University, Columbus, instructor in English, 1946; Syracuse University, Syracuse, NY, assistant professor, 1946-47, associate professor, 1947-53, professor of English, 1953-59; Indiana University, Bloomington, James H. Rudy Professor of English, 1959-73; Duke University, Durham, NC, professor of English, 1973-75, Andrew W. Mellon Professor in the Humanities, 1975—. Smith-Mundt Visiting Professor of American Literature at University of Uppsala and University of Stockholm, 1951-52; Fulbright lecturer at Japanese universities and Kyoto Seminar in American Studies, summer, 1967; lecturer at other universities. Center for Editions of American Authors, Modern Language Association of America, founding member, 1962-63, member of executive committee, 1964-68; consultant to numerous scholarly organizations; member of U.S. National Commission for UNESCO, 1969-71; Indiana University, chair of athletics committee and faculty representative to Big Ten Athletic Conference and National Collegiate Athletic Conference (NCAA), 1962-73; Duke University, chair of Athletics Council and faculty representative to Atlantic Coast Conference and NCAA, 1977-79. *Military service:* Served in American Field Service, Italy, 1943-44; U.S. Navy, 1945.

MEMBER: Modern Language Association of America (chair of American literature section, 1979), Phi Beta Kappa, Phi Gamma Delta, Omicron Delta Kappa.

AWARDS, HONORS: Guggenheim fellow, 1954-55, 1975-76; Litt.D. from Ohio Wesleyan University, 1964, and Oklahoma City University, 1967.

WRITINGS:

The Gentleman in America: A Literary Study in American Culture, Syracuse University Press (Syracuse, NY), 1949, reprinted, Greenwood Press (Westport, CT), 1969.

The Road to Realism: The Early Years, 1837-1885, of William Dean Howells (also see below), Syracuse University Press, 1956, reprinted, Greenwood Press, 1986.

The Realist at War: The Mature Years, 1885-1920, of William Dean Howells (also see below), Syracuse University Press, 1958, reprinted, Greenwood Press, 1986.

William Dean Howells: Dean of American Letters (contains *The Road to Realism* and *The Realist at War*), Syracuse University Press, 1958.

Stephen Crane, Twayne (New York City), 1962, revised edition, 1980.

John Woolman: The Mind of the Quaker Saint, Washington Square Press (New York City), 1965, revised edition, 1966.

The Light of Common Day: Realism in American Fiction, Indiana University Press (Bloomington), 1971.

The Big Game: College Sports and American Life, University of Tennessee Press (Knoxville), 1978.

Young Howells & John Brown: Episodes in a Radical Education, Ohio State University Press (Columbus), 1985.

EDITOR AND AUTHOR OF INTRODUCTION

Literature of the Early Republic, Rinehart, 1950, second edition, Holt (New York City), 1969.

(With Lars Ahnebrink) *An Anthology of American Literature, 1620-1900,* Svenska Bokforlaget, 1953.

(With Lester G. Wells) *Stephen Crane's Love Letters to Nellie Crouse,* Syracuse University Press, 1954.

(With Frederick J. Hoffman and Roy Harvey Pearce) *The Growth of American Literature,* two volumes, American Book Co. (New York City), 1956.

W. D. Howells, *The Rise of Silas Lapham,* Houghton (Boston), 1957.

Corwin K. Linson, *My Stephen Crane,* Syracuse University Press, 1958.

W. D. Howells, *The Shadow of a Dream* [and] *An Imperative Duty,* College & University Press, 1962.

(With David L. Frazier) *The War of the Critics over William Dean Howells,* Row, Peterson, 1962.

William Cooper Howells, *Recollections of Life in Ohio from 1813 to 1840,* Scholars' Facsimiles & Reprints (Delmar, NY), 1963.

(With David F. Hiatt) W. D. Howells, *Literary Friends and Acquaintances,* Indiana University Press, 1968.

Nathaniel Hawthorne, *The Scarlet Letter,* C. E. Merrill, 1969.

EDITOR

(With Harry Hayden Clark) *Whittier on Writers and Writing: The Uncollected Critical Writings of John Greenleaf Whittier,* Syracuse University Press, 1950, reprinted, Books for Libraries (Freeport, NY), 1971.

(Compiler) *The American Poets, 1800-1900,* Scott, Foresman (Glenview, IL), 1966.

Literature of the Early Republic, Holt (New York City), 1969.

W. D. Howells as Critic, Routledge (Boston), 1973.

(Compiler with Norma W. Cady) *Critical Essays on W. D. Howells, 1866-1920,* G. K. Hall (Boston), 1983.

EDITOR WITH LOUIS J. BUDD

(With Carl L. Anderson) *Toward a New American Literary History: Essays in Honor of Arlin Turner,* Duke University Press (Durham, NC), 1980.

On Mark Twain, Duke University Press, 1987.

On Whitman, Duke University Press, 1987.

On Emerson, Duke University Press, 1988.

On Melville, Duke University Press, 1988.

On Faulkner, Duke University Press, 1989.

On Dickinson, Duke University Press, 1990.

On Hawthorne, Duke University Press, 1990.

On Henry James, Duke University Press, 1990.

On Frost, Duke University Press, 1991.

On Humor, Duke University Press, 1992.

On Howells, Duke University Press, 1993.

On Poe, Duke University Press, 1993.

CONTRIBUTOR

(With William M. Gibson) *The Situation of English,* Modern Language Association of America (New York City), 1963.

Hawthorne Centenary Essays, Ohio State University Press, 1964.

Lewis Leary, editor, *The Teacher and American Literature,* National Council of Teachers of English (Urbana, IL), 1965.

Ray B. Browne, editor, *New Voices in American Studies,* Purdue University Studies (West Lafayette, IN), 1966.

Clarence Gohdes, editor, *Essays on American Literature in Honor of Jay B. Hubbell,* Duke University Press, 1967.

Robert Merideth, editor, *American Studies: Essays on Theory and Method,* C. E. Merrill (Columbus, OH), 1968.

American Literature: A Critical Survey, Volume I, American Book Co., 1968.

Hennig Cohen, editor, *Landmarks of American Writings,* Basic Books (New York City), 1969.

(With Elizabeth C. Saler) James Woodress, editor, *Essays Mostly on Periodical Publishing in America: A Collection in Honor of Clarence Gohdes,* Duke University Press, 1973.

(Author of introduction) *Stephen Crane: Tales, Sketches, and Reports,* University Press of Virginia (Charlottesville), 1973.

Literature and Ideas in America: Essays in Memory of Harry Hayden Clark, Ohio University Press, 1975.

Contributor of numerous articles to scholarly journals. Member of board of editors, Syracuse University Press, 1948-59, Indiana University Press, 1962-67, and *College English,* 1962-63; *American Literature,* member of board of editors, 1961-63, associate editor, 1963-75, managing editor, 1976-79, chair of board of editors, 1979—; editor of "Studies in the Bobbs-Merrill Papers" issue of *Indiana University Bookman,* March, 1967.

SIDELIGHTS: Edwin Harrison Cady is the editor and author of numerous nonfiction books focusing on various literary figures and movements. Frequently recognized for his works about William Dean Howells, Cody authored what a *New Yorker* critic recognized as a "definitive, if dully written, biography" of Howells, published in two separate books. Although noting that the second volume, *The Realist at War: The Mature Years, 1885-1920, of William Dean Howells,* was "intelligent and interesting," Alfred Kazin, a *New York Times* reviewer, complained that the "biography is essentially the history of [Howells'] publications, and in this second volume Mr. Cady really does little more than go through Howells' literary opinions, year by year." Although *Saturday Review* critic Granville Hicks could also "imagine a better biography . . . more searching, more incisive, written with greater distinction," Hicks pleasantly stated the second volume was not "anticlimactic" and "grateful[ly]" recognized Cady's 1958 contribution.

Cady's 1949 debut book, *The Gentleman in America: A Literary Study in American Culture,* proves through "an interesting survey of certain aspects of American literature" that "social patterns in reality [have not] been as equalitarian as [the] political campaign speeches," according to a *Christian Century* critic who cited Cady's chapter on Howells as one of his best. "Cady sets himself a problem: to discover how the concept of the gentleman was adapted to the changing culture of the United States from the time of the Puritans," explained Robert Halsband in the *Saturday Review of Literature.* "He examines the writings of non-literary figures . . . as well as of men of letters. . . . Most of his discussion seems to center in New England."

Presenting another literary topic, Cady's 1971 *The Light of Common Day: Realism in American Fiction*

was discussed at length at the 1972 MLA Convention. "In all of [the] essays, Cady affirms his faith in literature as 'a means of communion' between reader and author and between reader and reader. . . . His eloquent commentaries on a variety of literary texts give proper meaning and dignity to both of those terms," described *Library Journal* contributor Robert Regan, concluding that the work is "an important volume." "Although Cady's book is frankly personal, it supports its conclusions with responsible argument and should provoke discussion among teachers and students," maintained a *Choice* critic. Similarly, R. S. Moore lauded in *American Literature:* "Cady despite his admission that the essays are expressions more of 'experience and conviction than of scholarship,' is a 'responsible' and lucid critic who [with *The Light of Common Day*] has made a constructive contribution to the definition of realism and to the criticism of American fiction."

BIOGRAPHICAL/CRITICAL SOURCES:

PERIODICALS

American Literature, May, 1972.
Booklist, November 15, 1956; January 15, 1959.
Chicago Sunday Tribune, December 2, 1956.
Choice, April, 1972.
Christian Century, December 14, 1949.
Library Journal, November 1, 1956; October 15, 1971.
New Yorker, November 1, 1958.
New York Times, November 2, 1958.
Saturday Review, September 27, 1958.
Saturday Review of Literature, December 3, 1949.*

* * *

CALITRI, Charles J(oseph) 1916-1984

PERSONAL: Born June 20, 1916, in New York, NY; died November, 1984; son of Antonio and Esther (Leinkram) Calitri; married Elaine Beck, 1942; children: Robin, Stephan. *Education:* New York University, B.S., 1939, M.A., 1948. *Religion:* Jewish. *Avocational interests:* Boating, fishing.

CAREER: High school teacher of English in New York, NY, 1948, 1960, Oceanside, NY, 1951-52; Hofstra College (now University), Hempstead, Long Island, NY, assistant professor of education. National Defense Education Act Summer Institute for

Teachers of the Disadvantaged, director, 1965-66. *Military service:* U.S. Army Air Forces, 1941-46; became first lieutenant.

MEMBER: National Council of Teachers of English, New York State College Committee for the Disadvantaged.

WRITINGS:

Rickey, Scribner (New York City), 1952.
(Editor with Frank Jennings) *Stories,* Harcourt (New York City), 1957.
Strike Heaven on the Face, Crown (New York City), 1958.
Father, Crown, 1962.
(With Bertram D. Brettschneider) *The Goliath Head: A Novel about Caravaggio,* Crown, 1972.

SIDELIGHTS: Charles Calitri's first novel, *Rickey,* received high critical praise. The book tells of the murder trial of a fifteen-year-old boy and explores the negative parental and environmental influences that contributed to his crime. According to R. W. Henderson writing in *Library Journal:* "This first novel, of powerful dramatic intensity, is written with genuine social consciousness. Absorbing as a tale, it arouses many questions concerning juvenile delinquency [and] family life." A. J. Winterbottom of the *New York Times* touted *Rickey* both as a mystery thriller and as a novel of psychological detection, while Mary Ross of the *New York Herald Tribune Book Review* called it "an unusual novel that could only have been written by a man who likes and deeply understands people, especially young people." Echoing the consensus, Martin Rice of the *Saturday Review* deemed it a book "of absorbing interest and power that excites our compassion and deepens our understanding."

Calitri's second novel, *Strike Heaven on the Face,* was far less well-received by critics. A new high school dean hears rumors of a sex club operating at the school. As he attempts to uncover the truth, his job is threatened and he meets opposition from friends, faculty, and even his own wife. However, if he is to live up to his moral responsibility as a parent and educator, he must persevere. Richard Sullivan of the *Chicago Sunday Times* commented: "I'm sure *Strike Heaven on the Face* is well intended. But stylistically and structurally—indeed even in its fundamental conception—it is flimsy stuff." A reviewer

for *Kirkus* condemned the book as both "sordid" and "salacious." Edmund Fuller of *Saturday Review* contended that Calitri's "method, his story structure and details . . . remain sensational and inflammatory in the unsolved problems of an unsuccessful and ill-advised novel." However, R. H. Glauber of the *New York Herald Tribune Book Review* praised *Strike Heaven on the Face* as a "powerful and shocking story" that "bristles with taut dialogue." Glauber goes on to credit it with being "one of the bitterest and at the same time most moving tributes to the teaching profession in many a year."

Father, Calitri's third novel, tells the story of a young man's journey to a small Italian village where his father had once served as a parish priest. The father later abandoned the priesthood and came to New York, where he married an Orthodox Jew. The protagonist and narrator of the novel was raised as a Jew. The book explores his search for understanding and a reconciliation of both his Jewish and Catholic heritages. Writing in *Commonweal,* T. P. McDonnell called *Father* "a novel of unusual proportions and of more than usual insight," while at the same time criticizing the material of the book as cliched. Frances O'Brien of *Saturday Review* observed: "Calitri writes very well about Montefumo and its lusty inhabitants. . . . He draws his minor characters with convincing realism and his story is deftly plotted."

BIOGRAPHICAL/CRITICAL SOURCES:

PERIODICALS

Chicago Sunday Tribune, October 26, 1958, p. 16; May 13, 1962, p. 9.
Commonweal, June 22, 1962, p. 334.
Kirkus, July 1, 1952; September 1, 1958, p. 674.
Library Journal, August, 1952, p. 1302; November 15, 1958; March 15, 1962.
New York Herald Tribune Book Review, August 17, 1952, p. 6; November 9, 1958, p. 11; March 18, 1962, p. 7.
New York Times, August 17, 1952, p. 14; October 26, 1958, p. 56.
New York Times Book Review, April 22, 1962, p. 22.
San Francisco Chronicle, September 2, 1952, p. 23.
Saturday Review, August 16, 1952, p. 15; November 1, 1958, p. 21; March 17, 1962, p. 28.
Springfield Republican, September 14, 1952, p. C16.*

CALL, Hughie Florence 1890-1969

PERSONAL: Born April 20, 1890, in Trent, TX; died, 1969; daughter of John Hicks (a physician and state health officer of Texas) and Kethleen (Best) Florence; married Thomas Jesse Call (a sheep rancher; died, 1946); children: Leigh, Andrew. *Education:* Educated in public schools in border towns of Texas and by tutors. *Politics:* Republican. *Religion:* Episcopal.

CAREER: Freelance writer.

MEMBER: Theta Sigma Phi.

WRITINGS:

Golden Fleece (autobiography), Houghton (Boston, MA), 1942, reprinted, illustrated by Paul Brown, University of Nebraska Press (Lincoln), 1981.
Rising Arrow, illustrated by Jacob Landau, Viking (New York City), 1950.
Peter's Moose, illustrated by Robert MacLean, Viking, 1955.
The Little Kingdom, illustrated by Gloria Kamen, Houghton, 1964.
The Shorn Lamb, Houghton, 1969.

Contributor to *Reader's Digest, American, Woman's Home Companion, Saturday Evening Post, This Week* and *Country Beautiful.*

SIDELIGHTS: Hughie Call's first book, the autobiographical *Golden Fleece,* recounts thirty years of her life as a sheep rancher's wife in Montana. Reviewing *Golden Fleece* for the *New York Times,* Hal Borland stated: "A thoroughly readable book that is local history as well as autobiography. It makes no pretense of being literature, but it does tell of an American way of life with gusto, a sense of humor and a richness of human understanding that entitle it to a solid place among the regional books." Struthers Burt of *Books* contended that *Golden Fleece* was so "concise, well selected, informative, and easy to remember" that one could "almost start running sheep" after reading it.

In addition to *Golden Fleece,* Call wrote four juvenile novels, all reflecting western life as she experienced it. *Rising Arrow* tells the story of two boys,

the twelve-year-old narrator Jack and his younger brother Dan, who spend a year on their uncle's sheep ranch. A reviewer for *Christian Science Monitor* noted: "Jack tells the story so invitingly that young readers will be wishing that they had sheepman uncles in Montana." A reviewer for *Horn Book* praised both the novel's storytelling and its "solid characterization." In *Peter's Moose,* a young boy befriends and raises a motherless moose calf. According to Robert Kraske of the *New York Times Book Review:* "The story line is slender but strong and there are moments of tenderness, light suspense and a satisfying, exciting climax."

The Little Kingdom is both a juvenile novel and a reminiscence. Call tells the story from the perspective of her own daughter growing up on a sheep ranch in Montana, relating her experiences with her family, the sheepherders, and both the domestic and wild animals that inhabit the ranch land. A reviewer for *Library Journal* observed: "There is a great feeling of western living here and amusing anecdotes of the many animal pets on the farm as well as a rather sturdy philosophy for facing tragedy. It does not have the literary stature of Gunther's *Death Be Not Proud* . . . but it is direct, sincere, not overly sentimental, and should evoke a warmhearted response from high school readers."

BIOGRAPHICAL/CRITICAL SOURCES:

PERIODICALS

Atlantic, October, 1942.
Booklist, October 1, 1942; May 15, 1955; July 1, 1961.
Bookmark, November, 1942.
Books, September 6, 1942, p. 2.
Christian Science Monitor, November 21, 1942, p. 12; May 12, 1955, p. 10; May 11, 1961, p. B5.
Cleveland Open Shelf, November, 1942, p. 23.
Horn Book, June, 1955, p. 183; June, 1961.
Kirkus, February 15, 1955; January 15, 1961.
Library Journal, September 1, 1942; June 15, 1955; June 15, 1961; June 15, 1964.
New York Herald Tribune Book Review, July 17, 1955, p. 8; May 14, 1961.
New York Times, September 6, 1942, p. 5; July 10, 1955, p. 17.
New York Times Book Review, June 25, 1961, p. 21; August 23, 1964, p. 23.
Saturday Review, August 20, 1955; July 22, 1961.
Saturday Review of Literature, September 12, 1942.*

CAPERS, Gerald Mortimer, Jr. 1909-

PERSONAL: Born May 30, 1909, in New Orleans, LA; son of Gerald Mortimer (printer) and Vivia (Deane) Capers; married Roberta (college professor), December 27, 1962. *Education:*Southwestern at Memphis, B.A., 1930; Yale University, Ph.D., 1936. *Avocational interests:* Hunting and fishing. Paddled canoe from the source of the Mississippi River to New Orleans, 1937. Reads Latin, French and Spanish.

ADDRESSES: IIome—244 Vinet, Ncw Orlcans, LA 70121. *Office*—Newcomb College, Tulane University, New Orleans, LA 70118.

CAREER: Yale University, New Haven, CT, instructor in history, 1936-40; Tulane University, New Orleans, LA, 1940—, chair of history department, 1941—, professor, beginning 1948. *Military service:* U.S. Air Corps, 1942-45; became captain.

MEMBER: Mississippi Valley Historical Association, Southern Historical Association, American Association of University Professors, Phi Beta Kappa, Omicron Delta Kappa.

AWARDS, HONORS: American Council of Learned Societies Fellow, 1952; Guggenheim Fellow, 1959.

WRITINGS:

Biography of a River Town: Memphis, Its Heroic Age, University of North Carolina Press (Chapel Hill), 1939.
Stephen A. Douglas, Defender of the Union, Little, Brown (Boston, MA), 1959.
John C. Calhoun, Opportunist: A Reappraisal, University of Florida Press (Gainesville), 1960.
Occupied City: New Orleans under the Federals, University of Kentucky Press (Lexington), 1965.
The Mississippi River Before and After Mark Twain, Exposition Press (Hicksville, NY), 1977.

Contributor to professional journals and encyclopedias.

SIDELIGHTS: Gerald M. Capers brings his avocational interest in river travel to bear on his scholarly works, writing about the evolution of river towns in the South and some of the special circumstances that can affect local politics. Capers's doctoral thesis, for instance, was published as *Biography of a River Town: Memphis, Its Heroic Age.* The book follows the history of Memphis from the years prior to its habitation through its development as a major portal to the West. "Posing the local scene before the national one, using local instance to illuminate the national epic, Mr. Capers' compact study is a model of what the biography of a city should be," notes a reviewer in the *Christian Science Monitor.* E. S. Morgan likewise praises the work in the *Boston Transcript,* observing that for Capers, "local history is national history placed under a microscope, and the insights thus revealed are illuminating to general reader and professional historian alike."

While serving as a history professor at Tulane University, Capers wrote *Occupied City: New Orleans under the Federals,* a treatment of the Civil War's effect upon the port of New Orleans. In his *American History Review* piece on the book, H. L. Trefousse declares: "Capers' conclusions are unequivocal. . . . He has demonstrated that the relative failure of New Orleans to keep pace with other cities had nothing to do with the Civil War and Reconstruction. . . . The time has . . . arrived for a summary of the extant works on New Orleans during the Civil War. This is a task the author has done well, especially in his treatment of economic affairs." A *Choice* reviewer maintains that the book "should not be relegated to regional literature, for it treats the earliest reconstruction experience—that of New Orleans. . . . It is well written."

As a biographer, Capers was especially acclaimed for his title *Stephen A. Douglas: Defender of the Union.* Capers's work helps Douglas to emerge from the shadow of Abraham Lincoln and take his rightful position as a prominent nineteenth century statesman. To quote R. J. Graf in the *Chicago Sunday Tribune, Stephen A. Douglas* is "a splendid example of what objective and intelligent historical writing can be. In 200 pages the dramatic essentials of the 1850s have been compressed with little loss of vitality or extent of the conflicts." In *Library Journal,* W. A. Heaps styles the book "an inspiring and well-told story of a truly dedicated American, and a valuable addition to biographical collections."

BIOGRAPHICAL/CRITICAL SOURCES:

PERIODICALS

American History Review, January, 1940, p. 412; July, 1966, p. 1450.
Booklist, June 15, 1939, p. 346; March 1, 1959, p. 367.

Boston Transcript, June 10, 1939, p. 3.
Chicago Sunday Tribune, February 22, 1959, p. 2.
Choice, September, 1966, p. 569.
Christian Science Monitor, May 20, 1939, p. 16.
Library Journal, January 1, 1959, p. 91.
Springfield Republican, March 8, 1959, p. 4D.
Tulane Alumni Magazine, spring, 1961.*

* * *

CARAMAN, Philip 1911-

PERSONAL: Born August 11, 1911, in London, England; son of R. A. Caraman. *Education:* Attended Stonyhurst College, 1923-30; Campion Hall, Oxford, M.A.

ADDRESSES: Home—114 Mount St., London W1, England.

CAREER: Roman Catholic priest; member of Society of Jesus. Editor, *Month,* 1948-63.

MEMBER: Royal Society of Literature (fellow).

WRITINGS:

(Translator) John Gerard, *Autobiography of an Elizabethan* (also see below), Longmans, Green (London), 1951.

(Editor) J. Keating, *Retreat Notes,* Gill & Sons (London), 1952.

(Translator) Gerard, *Autobiography of a Hunted Priest,* Pellegrini & Cudahy, 1952.

(Editor) *Saints and Ourselves,* Kenedy, Volume I, 1953, Volume II, 1955, Volume III, 1958.

(Editor and author of introduction) F. C. Devas, *What Law and Letter Kill,* Burns, 1953.

(Editor and author of introduction) Devas, *Law of Love,* Kenedy, 1954.

(Translator) William Weston, *Autobiography from the Jesuit Underground,* Farrar, Straus (New York City), 1955 (published in Canada as *Autobiography of an Elizabethan,* Longmans, Green, 1955).

(Editor and author of foreword) R. H. Benson, *Come Rack! Come Rope!,* Kenedy, 1957.

Henry Morse, Priest of the Plague, Farrar, Straus, 1957.

(Editor with J. J. Dougherty) *Holy Bible for the Family,* Longmans, Green, 1958.

The Other Face: Catholic Life under Queen Elizabeth I, Longmans, Green, 1960, Sheed (New York City), 1961.

(Editor and author of introduction) Ronald Knox, *Pastoral Occasional Sermons,* Burns, 1960.

(Editor and author of introduction) Ronald Arbuthnott Knox, *Pastoral Sermons,* Sheed, 1960.

(Editor with James Walsh) *The Fulton J. Sheen Sunday Missal,* Hawthorn (New York City), 1961.

Saint Angela: The Life of Angela Merici, Foundress of the Ursulines (1474-1540), Longmans, Green, 1963, Farrar, Straus, 1964.

(Editor and author of introduction) Ronald Arbuthnott Knox, *University and Anglican Sermons: Together with Sermons Preached on Various Occasions,* Burns & Oates, 1963, published as *University Sermons: Together with Sermons Preached on Various Occasions,* Sheed, 1964.

Henry Garnet (1555-1606) and the Gunpowder Plot, Farrar, Straus, 1964.

(Editor) *The Years of Siege: Catholic Life from James I to Cromwell,* Longmans, Green, 1966.

C. C. Martindale: A Biography, Longmans, Green, 1967.

Norway, Longmans, Green, 1969, Eriksen, 1970.

The Cure d'Ars, Catholic Truth Society (London), 1969.

(Contributor) Marina Chavchavadze, editor, *Man's Concern with Holiness,* Hodder & Stoughton (London), 1970.

The Lost Paradise: An Account of the Jesuits in Paraguay, 1607-1768, Sidgwick & Jackson (London), 1975, published as *The Lost Paradise: The Jesuit Republic in South America,* Seabury (New York City), 1976.

Praying Together, Catholic Truth Society, 1976.

Saint Cuthbert Mayne, Catholic Truth Society, 1978.

Saint Nicholas Owen: Maker of Hiding Holes, Catholic Truth Society, 1980.

The University of the Nations: The Story of the Gregorian University, Paulist Press (Ramsey, NJ), 1981.

Saint Philip Howard, Catholic Truth Society, 1985.

Margaret Clitherow, Catholic Truth Society, 1986.

The Jesuit Republic of Paraguay, Catholic Truth Society, 1986.

The Lost Empire: The Story of the Jesuits in Ethiopia, University of Notre Dame Press (South Bend, IN), 1986.

Ignatius Loyola: A Biography of the Founder of the Jesuits, Harper (San Francisco, CA), 1990.

The Western Rising, 1549: The Prayer Book Rebellion, Westcountry Books (Tiverton, Devon), 1994.

A Study in Friendship: Saint Robert Southwell and Henry Garnet, Institute of Jesuit Sources (St. Louis, MO), 1995.

Tibet: The Jesuit Century, Institute of Jesuit Sources, 1997.

Contributor to *Tablet, Downside Review, Times Literary Supplement,* and other periodicals.

SIDELIGHTS: Father Philip Caraman, a member of the Society of Jesus, has spent his career documenting various aspects of Jesuit history and theology. Caraman is best known for his works on English Catholicism during the Elizabethan and Reformation periods, with special attention to Henry Garnet, a priest who was executed in 1606. An *Economist* reviewer wrote of Caraman's work: "Since most history in English of the Tudor and Stuart period is written from the Protestant viewpoint, Father Caraman's studies of Roman Catholic life at this time are a valuable corrective to the traditional interpretation."

In 1964 Caraman published *Henry Garnet (1555-1606) and the Gunpowder Plot,* a detailed biography of the martyred Jesuit and his times. "This is easily one of the five most interesting books that I have read in the last ten years," declared Paul Kiniery in *Best Sellers.* "Henry Garnet grips you after the fashion of a good detective story. . . . One's respect for Father Garnet is unbounded; one's contempt for Elizabeth I and James I is equally unbounded, after reading this excellent book which required fourteen painstaking years for its production." *Critic* reviewer Edmund Wehrle likewise found much to praise in the work. "The author has, as often as possible, allowed Garnet to tell in his own words the story of English Catholicism during and just after the reign of Queen Elizabeth I," Wehrle noted. "What Father Caraman has done is to vindicate this devoted and sincere priest. Moreover, he has given us an incredibly vivid picture of Catholic life at the time of Elizabeth." A *Times Literary Supplement* reviewer commended the book as "an important contribution for the student of religious controversy, while for the layman the exciting incidents Father Caraman marshalls with such skill into his easy-flowing narrative give his book the quality of a first-rate adventure story."

In the ensuing years Caraman has authored numerous titles about Jesuit activities all around the world, including a comprehensive biography of the Society's founder, Father Ignatius Loyola. In a review of *The University of the Nations: The Story of the Gregorian*

University, Colman McCarthy of the *Washington Post* wrote: "With modesty, Caraman says that he is writing 'popular history.' Which is what is needed. The Gregorian, for too long, has been known only to scholars. It ought to be as known and appreciated, as Oxford, Harvard and Fribourg. With this fine work, perhaps it will be."

BIOGRAPHICAL/CRITICAL SOURCES:

PERIODICALS

America, May 22, 1965, p. 778.

Best Sellers, May 15, 1965, p. 83.

Catholic World, November, 1953, p. 160; June, 1957, p. 240.

Commonweal, September 18, 1953, p. 594; February 28, 1964, p. 674.

Critic, June, 1965, p. 74.

Economist, January 23, 1965, p. 348.

New Statesman, December 4, 1964, p. 890.

New Statesman & Nation, May 11, 1957, p. 617.

New Yorker, July 3, 1965, p. 76.

Spectator, June 28, 1957, p. 856.

Times Literary Supplement, October 2, 1953, p. 633; May 10, 1957, p. 287; February 27, 1964, p. 180; December 24, 1964, p. 1167; April 18, 1986.

Virginia Quarterly Review, summer, 1965, p. 90.

Washington Post, September 1, 1981.

*   *   *

CARDUS, Neville 1889-1975

PERSONAL: Born April 2, 1889, in Manchester; England; died February 28, 1975, in London, England; married Edith Honorine King, 1921 (died, 1968). *Education:* Attended free lectures at University of Manchester, 1904-1912. *Avocational interests:* Walking, conversation, and "anything not in the form of a game or sport."

CAREER: Shrewsbury School, Manchester, England, assistant cricket coach and secretary to the headmaster, 1912-1916; *Manchester Guardian,* Manchester, reporter, music writer, and cricket correspondent, 1916-27, music critic, 1927-40; *Morning Herald,* Sydney, Australia, music critic and cricket writer, 1941-47; *Sunday Times,* London, England, staff member, 1948-49; *Manchester Guardian,* Manchester, music critic, 1951-75.

MEMBER: National Liberal Club, Garrick Club, Lancashire County Cricket Club (president, 1970-71).

AWARDS, HONORS: Wagner Medal from City of Bayreuth, 1963; Commander of the British Empire, 1964; Knighted by Queen Elizabeth II, 1967; honorary member, Manchester College of Music, 1968; International Press Club special award, 1970; honorary member, Royal Academy of Music, 1972.

WRITINGS:

A Cricketer's Book, G. Richards (London), 1922.

Days in the Sun: A Cricketer's Journal, G. Richards, 1924, new edition, Hart-Davis (London), 1948.

(Editor) Samuel Langford, *Musical Criticisms,* Oxford University Press (Oxford, England), 1929.

The Summer Game: A Cricketer's Journal, Cayme Press, 1929, new edition, Hart-Davis, 1948.

Cricket, Longmans, Green (London), 1930, new edition, 1949.

Good Days: A Book of Cricket, J. Cape (London), 1934, new edition, Hart-Davis, 1948.

(Contributor) Thomas Moult, editor, *Bat and Ball,* Arthur Baker, 1935.

(Author of introduction) Wilhelm Mueller, *Die schonen Muellerin, Schubert,* Die schonen Muellerin Society (London), 1935.

Australian Summer, J. Cape, 1937, new edition, Hart-Davis, 1949.

Music for Pleasure, Angus & Robertson (London), 1942.

Ten Composers, J. Cape, 1945, enlarged edition published as *A Composers Eleven,* J. Cape, 1958, published as *Composers Eleven,* Braziller (New York City), 1959, reprinted, Books for Libraries Press (Freeport, NY), 1970.

English Cricket, Collins (London), 1945.

Autobiography, Collins, 1947, 3rd edition, 1961, reprinted, Greenwood Press (Westport, CT), 1975.

The Essential Neville Cardus, edited by Rupert Hart-Davis, J. Cape, 1949, revised edition published as *Cardus on Cricket: A Selection from the Cricket Writings of Sir Neville Cardus,* edited and introduced by Hart-Davis, Souvenir Press (London), 1977.

Second Innings (autobiography), Collins, 1950.

Cricket All the Year, Collins, 1952.

(Editor and contributor) *Kathleen Ferrier: A Memoir,* Hamish Hamilton (London), 1954, Putnam (New York City), 1955, 3rd edition, Hamish Hamilton, 1969.

Close of a Play, Collins, 1956.

Talking of Music, Macmillan (London), 1957, reprinted, Greenwood Press, 1975.

Sir Thomas Beecham: A Memoir, Collins, 1961.

The Playfair Cardus, Dickens Press, 1963.

Gustav Mahler: His Mind and His Music, St. Martin's (New York City), 1965.

The Delights of Music: A Critic's Choice, Gollancz (London), 1966.

(Compiler with John Arlott) *The Noblest Game: A Book of Fine Cricket Prints,* Harrap (London), 1969.

Full Score, Cassell (London), 1970.

(Author of foreword) Robin Daniels, *Blackpool Football: The Official Club History,* R. Hale (London), 1972.

What Is Music?, edited by Margaret Hughes, illustrated by Richard Hook, White Lion (London), 1977.

Cardus in the Covers, Souvenir Press, 1978.

Play Resumed with Cardus, Souvenir Press, 1979.

A Fourth Innings with Cardus, Souvenir Press, 1981.

The Roses Matches, Souvenir Press, 1919-1939, Souvenir Press, 1982.

Cardus on Music: A Centenary Collection, Hamish Hamilton, 1988.

SIDELIGHTS: As both a music critic and one of England's leading authorities on cricket, Neville Cardus "richly fulfilled his two-fold ambition," according to his London *Times* obituary. The article noted: "He had no formal training in either field. . . . He could talk as well as he wrote and was as welcome in exalted music circles as among cricketers in a pub. No compliment pleased him more than that he had made many people wish they had actually been at a cricket match or actually attended a concert. He wrote on cricket as a cricketer; on music as a listener."

Cardus was raised in the slums of Manchester by an aunt who he said "joined the oldest of professions and became an ornament of it." He never knew his father. Cardus spent his youth working at odd jobs instead of attending school, reading independently according to his whim. He once said: "I am a terribly uneducated man. I took a terrible lot of risks. I suppose now I would have been given a grant and probably would have gone to university and I would probably never have known as much as I know now."

After serving as a cricket coach at the Shrewsbury School, Cardus joined the journalists' ranks in 1917 as a reporter and critic of music hall shows. He found a niche when his newspaper, the *Manchester Guardian,* sent him to Lancashire to report on the cricket season. His writings on cricket, studded as they were with allusions to music and poetry, became quite popular with readers, and before long he had adopted the pseudonym "Cricketer." He might have enjoyed a long career writing only about the sport, but in 1920 he became an assistant music critic at the *Guardian*. By 1927 he was chief music critic.

According to a *Kirkus Reviews* critic, Cardus's writings on music provide "a pleasant balancing of genius and ability, delicacies and permanence, music as an emotion and an art." For nearly a half century Cardus's voice was one of the most respected in British music criticism, and he ably represented the popular, journalistic viewpoint. Wrote a *Library Journal* correspondent: "Although the author has published twice as many books on cricket as on music, one should not infer that this places him in the second rank of music critics. He is among the finest." And a *New Yorker* contributor praised the author's "marvellous ability to convey his favorites' best qualities and to enlist his readers' affections beside his own."

Cardus was not detached from his subject matter. He formed close friendships with composers and performers, including Sir Thomas Beecham, Sir John Barbirolli, Artur Schnabel, and Claudio Arrau. A particular favorite was contralto Kathleen Ferrier, whom he eulogized in a 1955 title he edited, *Kathleen Ferrier.* In *New Statesman & Nation,* Andrew Porter declared of the work: "This is a moving book. . . . All who knew her, loved her; the 'inner glow of her nature' shines reflected from these pages and from the photographs."

Toward the end of his life Cardus received some of Britain's highest honors, including a knighthood bestowed by Queen Elizabeth II. After his death in 1975 his work continued to find its way into print, with Souvenir Press releasing a number of cricket volumes and Hamish Hamilton a collection of his music criticism. A *Christian Science Monitor* reviewer recommended Cardus's critical writings, noting that "aspiring critics . . . may learn many valuable lessons in the art of rendering a judgment that loses nothing in scholarship and gains much in . . . the warmth of human kindness."

BIOGRAPHICAL/CRITICAL SOURCES:

BOOKS

Brookes, Christopher, *His Own Man: The Life of Neville Cardus,* Methuen (London), 1985.

Cardus, Neville, *Autobiography,* Collins, 1947, 3rd edition, 1961, reprinted, Greenwood Press, 1975.
Cardus, Neville, *Second Innings* (autobiography), Collins, 1950.
Daniels, Robin, *Conversations with Cardus,* Gollancz (London), 1976.

PERIODICALS

Chicago Sunday Tribune, September 11, 1955, p. 12.
Choice, February, 1967, p. 1134.
Christian Science Monitor, January 30, 1958, p. 5.
Economist, December 4, 1965, p. 1096.
Kirkus Reviews, August 1, 1955, p. 579; October 1, 1957, p. 763.
Library Journal, August, 1955, p. 1709; December 1, 1957, p. 3111; May 15, 1959, p. 1607; August, 1966, p. 3734.
Manchester Guardian, September 28, 1954, p. 4; November 29, 1957, p. 12; August 15, 1958, p. 4.
Music Library Association Notes, March, 1958, p. 217; June, 1967, p. 742.
New Statesman, August 23, 1958, p. 228; April 30, 1965, p. 690.
New Statesman & Nation, December 11, 1954, p. 798.
New Yorker, February 8, 1958, p. 135; June 13, 1959, p. 132.
New York Times, September 11, 1955, p. 16; June 28, 1959, p. 6.
Spectator, November 19, 1954, p. 657; January 17, 1958, p. 82.
Springfield Republican, March 9, 1958, p. 17C.
Times Literary Supplement, October 15, 1954, p. 652; January 10, 1958, p. 16; April 22, 1965, p. 306; November 6, 1969; November 20, 1970; June 26, 1981; May 20, 1983.
Virginia Quarterly Review, spring, 1967, p. 88.

OBITUARIES:

PERIODICALS

AB Bookman's Weekly, March 17, 1975.
New York Times, March 1, 1975.
Times (London), March 1, 1975.*

*   *   *

CARMER, Carl (Lamson) 1893-1976

PERSONAL: Born October 16, 1893, in Cortland, NY; died September 11, 1976, in Bronxville, NY;

son of Willis Griswold (a superintendent of schools) and Mary (Lamson) Carmer; married Elizabeth Black (an artist and illustrator), December 24, 1928. *Education:* Hamilton College, Ph.B., 1914, Ph.M., 1917; Harvard University, M.A., 1915.

CAREER: Syracuse University, Syracuse, NY, instructor in English, 1915-16; University of Rochester, Rochester, NY, assistant professor of English, 1916-17; Hamilton College, Clinton, NY, chair of public speaking department, 1919; University of Rochester, assistant professor of English, 1919-21; University of Alabama, Tuscaloosa, associate professor, 1921-24, professor of English, 1924-27; *New Orleans Morning Tribune,* New Orleans, LA, columnist, 1927; *Vanity Fair,* New York City, assistant editor, 1928-29; *Theatre Arts Monthly,* New York City, associate editor, 1929-33; full-time writer and folklorist, 1933-76. *Military service:* U.S. Army, Field Artillery, World War I; became first lieutenant; served with U.S. Army Air Forces during World War II; received War Department certificate for distinguished service in combat areas.

MEMBER: Society of American Historians (councillor), Authors Guild (former president), Poetry Society of America (former president), American Center PEN (former president), New York State Historical Association (vice-president of board of trustees), New York State Folklore Society (honorary vice-president), Edward MacDowell Association (former president), Phi Beta Kappa, Psi Upsilon, Pilgrims Club, Century Association.

AWARDS, HONORS: Litt.D., Elmira College, 1937; L.H.D., Hamilton College, 1941; Litt.D., Susquehanna University, 1944; LL.D., University of Buffalo, 1962; *New York Herald Tribune* Children's Book Festival award for *Windfall Fiddle;* cited for contributions to children's literature by New York State Association for Curriculum Development; adopted by Wolf Clan of the Seneca Nation.

WRITINGS:

(With Edwin Francis Shewmake) *College English Composition,* Johnson, 1927.
French Town (poetry), privately published, 1930, 2nd edition, Pelican (New Orleans, LA), 1968.
Deep South (poetry), Farrar & Rinehart (New York City), 1930.
Stars Fell on Alabama (Literary Guild selection), Farrar & Rinehart, 1934, 4th edition, University of Alabama Press (University), 1985.

Listen for a Lonesome Drum, Farrar & Rinehart, 1936, reprinted, Syracuse University Press (Syracuse, NY), 1995.
The Hurricane's Children, illustrated by wife, Elizabeth Black Carmer, Farrar & Rinehart, 1937, reprinted, McKay (New York City), 1967.
The Hudson, Farrar & Rinehart, 1939, revised edition, Grosset (New York City), 1968, reprinted, Fordham University Press (Bronx, NY), 1992.
Gennessee Fever (Literary Guild selection), Farrar & Rinehart, 1941, reprinted, McKay, 1971.
(Collector and narrator) *America Sings,* Knopf (New York City), 1942.
(Editor) *Songs of the Rivers of America,* Farrar & Rinehart, 1942.
(Editor and author of introduction) *The War against God,* Henry Holt (New York City), 1943.
The Jesse James of the Java Sea, Farrar & Rinehart, 1945.
Taps Is Not Enough (verse drama), Henry Holt, 1945.
(Editor with C. Van Doren) *American Scriptures,* Boni & Gaer, 1946.
For the Rights of Man, Hinds, 1947, reprinted, Books for Libraries (Freeport, NY), 1969.
Dark Trees in the Wind: A Cycle of York State Years, illustrated by John O'Hara Cosgrove, Sloane, 1949, reprinted, McKay, 1965.
Rebellion at Quaker Hill: A Story of the First Rent War, Winston (Philadelphia, PA), 1954.
The Screaming Ghost, and Other Stories, Knopf, 1956.
American Folklore and Its Old-World Backgrounds, Compton (New York City), 1956.
(Editor) *Cavalcade of America,* Crown (New York City), 1956.
Pets at the White House, Dutton (New York City), 1959, revised edition, 1962.
(Editor) *The Tavern Lamps Are Burning: Literary Journeys through Six Regions and Four Centuries of New York State* (anthology), McKay, 1964, reprinted, Fordham University Press, 1996.
My Kind of Country: Favorite Writings about New York, McKay, 1966, reprinted, Syracuse University Press, 1995.
The Farm Boy and the Angel, Doubleday (Garden City, NY), 1970.

JUVENILE

Wildcat Furs to China, Knopf, 1945, reprinted, McKay, 1969.
Eagle in the Wind, Aladdin, 1948.

Too Many Cherries, Viking (New York City), 1949.

Hurricane Luck (Children's Book Club selection), Aladdin, 1949.

Windfall Fiddle, illustrated by Arthur Conrad, Knopf, 1950.

A Flag for the Fort, Messner (New York City), 1952.

(Compiler with Cecile Matschat) *American Boy Adventure Stories,* Winston (New York City), 1952.

(Editor) *A Cavalcade of Young Americans,* Lothrop (New York City), 1958.

Henry Hudson: Captain of the Ice-Bound Seas, illustrated by Cosgrove, Garrard (Champaign, IL), 1960.

The Hudson River, Holt, 1962, revised edition, Grosset, 1968.

(With wife, Elizabeth Carmer) *Francis Marion: Swamp Fox of the Carolinas,* illustrated by William Plummer, Garrard, 1962.

(With E. Carmer) *The Susquehanna from New York to the Chesapeake,* Garrard, 1964.

(With E. Carmer) *Captain Abner and Henry Q,* illustrated by Ted Schroeder, Garrard, 1965.

(With E. Carmer) *Tony Beaver: Griddle Skater,* illustrated by Mimi Korach, Garrard, 1965.

(With E. Carmer) *Mike Fink and the Turkey Shoot,* illustrated by Korach, Garrard, 1965.

(With E. Carmer) *Pecos Bill and the Long Lasso,* illustrated by Korach, Garrard, 1968.

The Boy Drummer of Vincennes, illustrated by Seymour Fleishman, Harvey House (Irvington-on-Hudson, NY), 1972.

The Pirate Hero of New Orleans, illustrated by Marilyn Hirsh, Harvey House, 1975.

Also author of booklet, *The Years of Grace, 1808-1958,* 1958. Writer and narrator of documentary films for motion pictures and television; writer for radio programs, *Your Neck of the Woods* and *American Scriptures;* adaptor of scripts for *Melody Time;* collector and editor of four albums of folk songs, Decca Records. Editor, "Rivers of America" series, Holt, and "Regions of America" series, Harper. Contributor to *American Heritage* and other publications.

SIDELIGHTS: A regional writer who managed to find a national audience for his work, the late Carl Carmer took as his subject the picturesque Hudson River and surrounding countryside in New York State. In fiction and nonfiction alike, Carmer explored the region, revealing its folklore, its history, its geography, and its most notable citizens. "Carmer is at the very top of his field among regional writers, and he is rather more as well," noted *Saturday Review* correspondent J. K. Hutchens. "He is a poet, an historian, a folklorist, a storyteller, something of a mystic, and frequently he is all five at once." A *Library Journal* contributor noted that throughout Carmer's work, "you cannot escape the author's genuine awareness and love for his native state. His ability to transfer this affection comes through his gifts as a narrator."

Among Carmer's best known books is *The Hudson,* which originally appeared in 1939 as part of the "Rivers of America" series. Still in print today, the title was praised by S. H. Holbrook in *Books* as "a highly entertaining volume, best in its digging up really important history which in the past has for some unknown reason been relegated to files of old newspapers and to the columns of historical quarterlies." *New York Times* reviewer Horace Reynolds observed: "Carmer has the common touch. He's as much interested in the people as in the patroons, more interested in folkways than in war and politics. Marrying history to travel and biography to geography, he has given us a splendid impressionistic picture of one of the great valleys of America." Concluded J. P. Gavit in the *Saturday Review of Literature:* "A corking book this. . . . I commend it with enthusiasm, both as fruit of evidently long and exhaustive research *con amore* in documents and by first-hand investigation, and as exceptionally charming writing." Carmer also published a juvenile version of the book as *The Hudson River,* acclaimed in the *Library Journal* as "an interesting, accurate and a most readable history of the 'Great River of the Mountain.'"

Carmer began collecting regional folklore early on in his career, publishing *Stars Fell on Alabama* soon after leaving a teaching position in that state. His many volumes of New York lore include ghost stories, tall tales, and simpler accounts of actual occurrences. Again, many of these compilations remain in print today, although they were first released decades ago. In a piece on *Dark Trees to the Wind: A Cycle of York State Years, New York Herald Tribune Book Review* contributor S. H. Adams maintained: "The effect is that of an old-time panorama accompanied and explained with the charm and persuasiveness of a master narrator. . . . The author has caught [York Staters'] looks and actions, their eccentricities and habits, their way of thought and way of life and fixed it in a consistently vivid record." A *New York Times* critic concluded: "Reading Mr. Carmer's gracefully phrased, yarn-crammed book, one is reminded of the inexhaustible variety of York State life in particular, of American life in general."

Carmer's fiction ranged more widely than his nonfiction, but some of his best-known juveniles were also set in the Hudson Valley. In *Windfall Fiddle,* for instance, a boy living in a small New York town longs for a fiddle so desperately that he spends a summer working hard in order to buy one. L. S. Bechtel noted of the book in the *New York Herald Tribune Book Review:* "It is a 'period piece' of the 1890's, but so full of action and humor that modern boys will forget its actual date." Likewise, E. L. Buell suggested in the *New York Times* that *Windfall Fiddle* "is full of color of the period and the setting, but, better still, it is a story of people. And a grand crowd they are, too, individualistic, wise and humorous." *Too Many Cherries,* another popular Carmer offering, was cited in *Kirkus Reviews* for its "original story, with regional as well as occupational flavor." In the *Saturday Review of Literature,* M. G. Davis concluded of the same title: "This is a story of America. . . . vigorous and honest . . . Here is a fine Christmas present for some lucky boy."

BIOGRAPHICAL/CRITICAL SOURCES:

BOOKS

Clegg, Ernest, *The History, Lore, and Legend of the Rivers of America and of Its People, Told in a Series of Books Edited by Stephen Vincent Benet and Carl Carmer,* Farrar & Rinehart (New York City), 1942.
Murrow, Edward R., *This I Believe,* Simon & Schuster (New York City), 1954.
Parks, Gordon, *Camera Portraits,* F. Watts (New York City), 1948.

PERIODICALS

Annals of the American Academy, January, 1940, p. 243.
Booklist, September 1, 1962, p. 40.
Books, July 2, 1939, p. 1.
Book Week, January 13, 1946, p. 4.
Chicago Sunday Tribune, November 16, 1952, p. 4.
Christian Science Monitor, August 26, 1939, p. 10; January 26, 1946, p. 15; December 22, 1949, p. 16; July 29, 1950, p. 6.

Kirkus Reviews, October 15, 1945, p. 465; August 15, 1949, p. 428; September 15, 1949, p. 531; February 15, 1950, p. 101; August 15, 1952, p. 504; March 1, 1956, p. 168; April 15, 1962, p. 388.
Library Journal, December 15, 1945, p. 1189; December 15, 1949, p. 1916; May 15, 1962, p. 2022; October 1, 1966, p. 4664.
New Yorker, July 1, 1939, p. 66; January 5, 1946, p. 74; November 26, 1949, p. 134.
New York Herald Tribune Book Review, November 6, 1949, p. 4; May 7, 1950, p. 7; October 11, 1953.
New York Herald Tribune Weekly Book Review, October 2, 1949, p. 8.
New York Times, June 25, 1939, p. 3; January 6, 1946, p. 5; November 6, 1949, p. 27; May 28, 1950, p. 22; July 15, 1956, p. 20; May 27, 1962, p. 28; September 12, 1976.
New York Times Book Review, November 13, 1949, p. 26; November 27, 1949, p. 26; May 17, 1970; January 28, 1973, p. 8.
San Francisco Chronicle, November 16, 1949, p. 22; August 26, 1956, p. 21.
Saturday Review of Literature, July 1, 1939, p. 5; December 6, 1941; January 19, 1946, p. 38; November 12, 1949, p. 25; December 17, 1949, p. 15; May 13, 1950, p. 36; January 29, 1955; December 24, 1966, p. 45.
Time, July 3, 1939, p. 54.
Weekly Book Review, January 6, 1946, p. 8.*

*   *   *

CARPENTIER (Y VALMONT), Alejo 1904-1980 (Jacqueline)

PERSONAL: Born December 26, 1904, in Havana, Cuba; died of cancer, April 24, 1980, in Paris, France; son of Jorge Julian Carpentier y Valmont (an architect; also known as Georges); married Lilia Esteban Hierro. *Education:* Attended Universidad de Habana.

CAREER: Journalist, editor, educator, musicologist, and author. Worked as a commercial journalist in Havana, Cuba, 1921-24; *Cartels* (magazine), Havana, editor-in-chief, 1924-28; Foniric Studios, Paris, France, director and producer of spoken arts programs and recordings, 1928-39; CMZ radio, Havana, writer and producer, 1939-41; Conservatorio Nacional, Havana, professor of history of music,

1941-43; traveled in Haiti, Europe, the United States and South America in self-imposed exile from his native Cuba, 1943-59; Cuban Publishing House, Havana, director, 1960-67; Embassy of Cuba, Paris, cultural attache, 1966-80.

AWARDS, HONORS: Prix du Meilleur Livre Etranger (France), 1956, for *The Lost Steps* (*Los pasos perdidos*); Cino del duca Prize, 1975; Prix Medici, 1979.

WRITINGS:

FICTION

Ecue-yambo-o!, Espana, 1933.
Viaje a la semilla, Ucar & Garcia, 1944; translation published as *Journey Back to the Source*, 1970.
El reino de este mundo, Ibero Americana, 1949, translation by Harriet de Onis published as *The Kingdom of This World*, Knopf (New York City), 1957.
Los pasos perdidos, Ibero Americana (Mexico City), 1953, enlarged edition, Editorial de Arte y Literatura (Havana), 1976, translation by de Onis published as *The Lost Steps*, Knopf, 1956, new edition with introduction by J. B. Priestly, Knopf, 1967.
El acoso, Losada (Buenos Aires), 1956, new edition with introduction by Mercedes Rein, Biblioteca de Marcha (Montevideo), 1972; translation published as *Manhunt* in *Noonday*, Volume 2, 1959, translation by Alfred MacAdam published as *The Chase*, Farrar, Straus (New York City), 1990.
Guerra del tiempo: Tres Relatos y una novela (contains "El camino de Santiago" [also see below], "Viaje a la semilla," "Semejante a la noche," and *El acoso*), General (Mexico City), 1958, translation by Frances Partridge published as *The War of Time*, Knopf, 1970.
El siglo de las luces, General, 1962, translation by John Sturrock published as *Explosion in a Cathedral*, Little, Brown (Boston, MA), 1963.
El camino de Santiago (short story), Galerna (Buenos Aires), 1967.
(With others) *Cuentos cubanos de lo fantastico y lo extraordinario*, UNEAC (Havana), 1968, published as *Cuentos cubanos*, Laia (Barcelona), 1974.
"Viaje a la semilla" y otros relatos (short stories), Editorial Nascimento (Santiago), 1971.
Concierto barroco: Novela, Siglo XXI (Mexico City), 1974, reprinted, Editorial de la Universidad de Puerto Rico (San Juan), 1994.

El recurso del metodo: Novela, Editorial Arte y Literatura (Havana), 1974, translation by Partridge published as *Reasons of State*, Knopf, 1976.
Dos novelas (contains *El reino de este mundo* and *El acoso*), Editorial Arte y Literatura, 1976.
Cuentos, Arte y Literatura, 1977.
La consagracion de la primavera: Novela, Siglo Veintiuno, 1979.
El arpa y la sombra, Siglo Veintiuno, 1979, reprinted, Ediciones de la Universidad de Alcala, 1994.
Cuentos completos, French & European Publications, 1980.
Los confines del hombre, edited by Felix Baez-Jorge, Siglo Veintiuno Editores (Mexico), 1994.
El amor a la ciudad, Santillana (Madrid), 1996.

OTHER

Poemes des Antilles (poetry), [Paris], 1929.
Dos poemas afro-cubanos (deux poemes afro-cubains), Senart, 1930.
La musica en Cuba (music history), Fondo de cultura economica (Mexico), 1946.
Tristan y Isolda en Tierra Firme, Nacional, 1949.
El derecho de asilo, illustrations by Marcel Berges, General, 1962.
Tientos y diferencias (essays), Universidad Nacional Autonoma (Mexico City), 1964, 3rd enlarged edition, Arca (Montevideo), 1973.
Literatura y conciencia politica en America Latina (essays), Corazon, 1969.
Papel social del novelista, Hombre Nuevo (Buenos Aires), 1969.
(Author of text) *La ciudad de las columnas* (architectural study of Havana), photographs by Paolo Gasparini, Lumen (Barcelona), 1970.
Los convidados de plata, Sandino (Montevideo), 1972.
Novelas y relatos, Union de Escritores y Artistas de Cuba (Havana), 1974.
America Latina en su musica, UNESCO (Havana), 1975.
Letra y solfa, edited by Alexis Marquez Rodriguez, Sintesis Dosmil (Caracas), 1975, reprinted, Editorial Letras Cubanas (Havana), 1993.
El acoso [and] El derecho de asilo (collection), Editora Latina (Buenos Aires), 1975.
Cronicas (collection of articles), Arte y Literatura, 1975.
El periodista: Un cronista de su tiempo, Granma (Havana), 1975.

Razon de ser: Conferencias, Rectorado (Caracas), 1976.

Vision de America (essays), Nemont (Buenos Aires), 1976.

Afirmacion literaria americanista, Universidad Central (Caracas), 1978.

Bajo el signo de La Cibeles: Cronicas sobre Espana y los espanols, 1925-1937, edited by Julio Rodrigeuz Puertolas, Nuestra Cultura (Madrid), 1979.

El adjetivo y sus arrugas, Galerna, 1980.

Ese musico que llevo dentro, three volumes, edited by Zoila Gomez Garcia, Letras Cubanas (Havana), 1980.

La novela latinoamericana en visperas de un nuevo siglo y otros ensayos (essays), Siglo Veintiuno, 1981.

Obras completas, nine volumes, Siglo Veintiuno, 1983-86.

Ensayos, Letras Cubanas, 1984.

Historia y ficcion en la narrativa hispanoamericana, Monte Avila (Caracas), 1984.

Conferencias, Letras Cubanas, 1987.

Tientos, diferencias y otros ensayos, Plaza & Janes (Barcelona), 1987.

Author of oratorio, *La Passion noire,* first performed in Paris in the 1920s. Also author of libretti; author of two sound recordings, both produced by Casa de las americas, *Alejo Carpentier narraciones* (cassette), and *Alejo Carpentier lee sus narraciones.* Former columnist for *El Nationale* (Caracas). Contributor of articles on politics, literature, and musicology to numerous publications, including *Revolutions Surrealist.* Former editor, under pseudonym "Jacqueline," of fashion section of Havana publication; former editor, *Iman* (Paris).

SIDELIGHTS: Although considered a major literary force in his native Latin America, Cuban Alejo Carpentier did not achieve widespread recognition with the American reading public. His prose examines historico-political factors as they relate to Latin American life and cultural development. In his writing, "Carpentier searches for the marvelous buried beneath the surface of Latin American consciousness, where African drums still beat and Indian amulets rule; in depths where Europe is only a vague memory of a future still to come," asserted Roberto Gonzalez-Echevarria in his *Alejo Carpentier: The Pilgrim at Home.* Gonzalez-Echevarria continued: "On the one hand, Carpentier maintains that the baroque nature of Latin American literature stems from the necessity to name for the first time realities that are outside the mainstream of Western culture. On the other, he states that what characterizes Latin American reality is its stylelessness, which results from its being an amalgam of styles from many cultural traditions and epochs: Indian, African, European, Neoclassical, Modern, etc."

Saturday Review contributor G. R. McMurray praised Carpentier as "a mature, imaginative artist, one of the first to universalize in fiction the Latin American experience." Indeed, Carpentier is said to have had an influence on such other notable Latin American authors as Gabriel Garcia Marquez and Carlos Fuentes. To quote Gonzalez-Echevarria in the *Dictionary of Literary Biography,* Carpentier's works provide "a model of how to write fiction in Latin America that is based on the history of the New World."

Born in Cuba in 1904, Carpentier was the son of a French father and a Russian mother who had only recently arrived on the island. His family was affluent, and he grew up immersed in his father's library, speaking French at home and Spanish in the streets with his friends. His association with Cubans of African, Indian, and Spanish origin influenced Carpentier profoundly as he sought to combine the European and American worlds of his childhood. Gonzalez-Echevarria wrote in the *Dictionary of Literary Biography:* "Carpentier never succeeded in synthesizing the mixture of cultures from which he sprang, and perhaps it is to this failure that one can attribute the tension behind his creative impulse."

After spending part of his teen years touring France and Russia—and attending a prestigious private school in Paris—Carpentier returned to Cuba to enroll at the University of Havana, where he planned to study music and architecture. His education ended abruptly when his father deserted the family in 1922. Forced by economic necessity to find a job, Carpentier became a journalist, and in only two years he had become editor-in-chief of *Carteles,* an avant-garde weekly magazine.

As political tensions escalated in the 1920s, Carpentier joined the student movement to oust dictator Gerardo Machado y Morales. His literary and political efforts led to his arrest and forty-day imprisonment, and upon his release he discovered that he was blacklisted and still under suspicion. A French poet, Robert Desnos, helped Carpentier escape to France, and the author spent eleven years in Paris, immersing himself in the study of American history and culture. Carpentier was quoted in the *Dictionary of Hispanic Biography* as saying of this period: "America was seen as an enormous nebula that I tried to understand, because I felt vaguely that my work originated there, that it was going to be profoundly American." Gonzalez-Echevarria observed in the *Dictionary of Literary Biography:* "Years later Carpentier would attempt to substitute the Spanish America that he discovered in book in Paris for another experienced firsthand. This effort was, perhaps, together with his attempt to define himself culturally, the essence of Carpentier's spiritual and artistic life."

Active in the French avant-garde, Carpentier continued to contribute to Cuban periodicals, and it was while he was in Paris that he published his first novel, *Ecue-yamba-o!* The book did not fare well with critics, and it would be more than a decade before Carpentier tried again to publish fiction. In the meantime he enjoyed a comfortable existence as a journalist, lecturer, and radio writer.

In 1939 Carpentier returned to Havana, and it was there—as well as in another self-imposed exile in Venezuela—that he began to create the important works of his career. His triumphant re-entry into Cuba in 1959 as a supporter of Fidel Castro brought him a controversial position of privilege within that regime. To quote Gonzalez-Echevarria in the *Dictionary of Literary Biography:* "Carpentier probably saw in the Cuban revolution the culmination of a kind of theodicy similar to the one present in many of his books, a synthesis of politics and art, the unity of a desire for a utopia and its realization in history. Inspired perhaps by the feeling that life ultimately imitates art, Carpentier did not care to test too severely the connection of such lofty ideals with the practice of politics, and he looked the other way."

Carpentier's relative obscurity in the United States may have been related to his position in Cuba, or else to the broad spectrum of knowledge he displayed in his writing. Commented Gene H. Bell in the *New Boston Review:* "Out of a dozen or so major [South American] authors (Borges and Garcia Marquez are the best-known here), Alejo Carpentier remains the one least recognized in these parts. . . . Some readers may be put off by Carpentier's displays of learning, an encyclopedism that ranges over anthropology, history, geography, botany, zoology, music, folk and classical, the arts, visual and culinary, and countless forgotten novels and verse—in all an erudition easily rivaling that of Borges." Yet despite

Carpentier's immense scholarship, Bell perceived a universal quality in the author's writing, noting, "Precisely because of . . . national differences, however, Carpentier's novel[s] (like those of Fuentes or Garcia Marquez) can furnish already interested Americans more insight into the social dislocations of the Southern continent than many a Yankee Poli Sci professor could."

Most critics familiar with Carpentier's work applauded the scholarly qualities that Bell enumerated, yet others criticized these very elements. The *New York Times Book Review*'s Alexander Coleman commented that Carpentier's early books were "often pretty heavy going, what with their tiresome philosophizing and heavily laid-on historical panoplies." Alan Cheuse concurred in *Review,* observing that some "readers may have decided that indeed the reasons for Carpentier's failure to capture an audience here are the same reasons put forth by the earliest reviewers: that his fiction is too 'erudite,' that he is more a 'cultural historian' than a novelist, . . . or that he is a 'tiresome philosophizer.'" However, Paul West remarked, also in *Review,* that "Carpentier is a master of both detail and mass, of both fixity and flux." West continued, "He can not only describe: he can describe what no-one has seen; and, best, he seems to have the hypothetical gift of suggesting, as he describes."

Carpentier's writing encompasses numerous styles and techniques. The *New York Review of Book*'s Michael Wood remarked that Carpentier "is interested not in myth but in history, and his method is to plunge us circumstantially into an earlier period, before, during, and after the First World War." Cheuse noted: "Intelligence and erudition are certainly present . . . in Carpentier's fiction. But so are sex, violence, political uproar, war, revolution, voyages of exploration, naturalist extravaganzas, settings ranging from ancient Greece to contemporary New York City, and characters running the gamut from the simple Haitian protagonist of *The Kingdom of This World* to the worldly wise, word-weary Head of State [in *Reasons of State*], . . . all of this comprising a complex but highly variegated and appealing fictional matrix."

Carpentier's themes often illustrate an awareness of broad social issues. Bell noted in the *New Boston Review* that "Carpentier's fiction regularly depicts individuals swept—often against their wishes—into the larger social struggle; they thereby become participants in history and embody the conflicts of their times." Gonzalez-Echevarria asserted in *Alejo Carpentier: The Pilgrim at Home* that "the plot in Carpentier's stories always moves from exile and fragmentation toward return and restoration, and the overall movement of each text is away from literature into immediacy." Gonzalez-Echevarria further explained the historical relevance of Carpentier's themes: "The persistence of the structure and thematics of fall and redemption, of exile and return, of individual consciousness and collective conscience, stems from a constant return to the source of modern Latin American self-awareness."

Many critics found *Reasons of State* and *The Lost Steps* among Carpentier's best efforts. *Reasons of State (El recurso del metodo)* deals with a Francophile South American dictator attempting to rule the fictitious Nueva Cordoba from his Paris home, periodically returning to his country to control revolutionary outbreaks. Bell stated: "This is no drama of the individual soul, but an imaginative evocation of the material and cultural forces of history." He added: "*Reasons of State* is not a psychological study in tyranny. . . . Carpentier rather places the Dictator (who is actually something of a cultural-historical caricature) within a broader global process, shows how the petty brutalities of South American politics ultimately interlock with European and, later, U.S. interests."

Reviewers saw *Reasons of State* as a departure in style from earlier Carpentier books. The *New York Times Book Review*'s Coleman commented: "*Reasons of State* is something different—a jocular view of imaginative idealism, repressive power and burgeoning revolution, all done with breezy panache. Once again Carpentier has shown how canny and adept a practitioner he can be in mediating between the many realms which his own life has touched upon." Bell concurred, noting that the novel "exhibits a new lightness of touch, a wry and rollicking humor."

Carpentier's *The Lost Steps (Los pasos perdidos)* "is considered his masterpiece," wrote Ruth Mathewson in the *New Leader*. The novel, which contains autobiographical elements, "represents an attempt at unification and synthesis, if only because it is centered on a continuous and reflexive narrative presence," suggested Gonzalez-Echevarria in *Alejo Carpentier: The Pilgrim at Home*. Like his other novels which deal with historical analysis, *The Lost Steps* also exhibits historical aspects. Gregory Rabassa observed in the *Saturday Review* that "Carpentier digs into the past: it almost seems as if he cannot get away from

it, even in his novel *The Lost Steps,* which is contemporary in time but is really a search for origins—the origin first of music and then of the whole concept of civilization."

In an overall summation of Carpentier's work presented in *Alejo Carpentier: The Pilgrim at Home,* Gonzalez-Echevarria stated: "History is the main topic in Carpentier's fiction, and the history he deals with— the history of the Caribbean—is one of beginnings or foundations." Gonzalez-Echevarria concluded in his book-length work that, "in a sense, as in *The Lost Steps,* Carpentier's entire literary enterprise issues from the desire to seize upon that moment of origination from which history and the history of the self begin simultaneously—a moment from which both language and history will start, thus the foundation of a symbolic code devoid of temporal or spatial gaps."

Carpentier was serving as Cuba's cultural attache to France—and had just finished the first novel of a planned trilogy—when he succumbed to cancer at his home in Paris on April 24, 1980. He is buried in Cuba at the Necropolis de Colon.

BIOGRAPHICAL/CRITICAL SOURCES:

BOOKS

Acosta, Leonardo, *Musica y epica en la novela de Alejo Carpentier,* Letras Cubanas (Havana), 1981.

Chao, Ramon, *Palabras en el tiempo de Alejo Carpentier,* Argos Vergara (Barcelona), 1984.

Contemporary Literary Criticism, Gale (Detroit, MI), Volume 8, 1978; Volume 11, 1979; Volume 38, 1986.

Dictionary of Hispanic Biography, Gale, 1996, pp. 177-80.

Dictionary of Literary Biography, Volume 113: *Modern Latin American Fiction Writers, First Series,* Gale, 1992, pp. 96-109.

Flores, Angel, *Spanish American Authors: The Twentieth Century,* H. W. Wilson (New York City), 1992, pp. 168-72.

Garcia-Carranza, Araceli, *Biobibliografia de Alejo Carpentier,* Letras Cubanas, 1984.

Giacoman, Helmy F., editor, *Homenaje a Alejo Carpentier,* Las Americas, 1970.

Gonzalez, Eduardo, *Alejo Carpentier: El tiempo del hombre,* Monte Avila (Caracas, Venezuela), 1978.

Gonzalez Echevarria, Roberto, *Alejo Carpentier: The Pilgrim at Home,* Cornell University Press (Ithaca, NY), 1977.

Gonzalez Echevarria and Klaus Mueller-Bergh, *Alejo Carpentier: Bibliographical Guide,* Greenwood Press (Westport, CT), 1983.

Harss, Luis, and Barbara Dohmann, *Into the Mainstream,* Harper (New York City), 1967.

Hispanic Literature Criticism, Gale, 1994.

Janny, Frank, *Alejo Carpentier and His Early Works,* Tamesis (London), 1981.

King, Lloyd, *Alejo Carpentier, Caribbean Writer,* University of the West Indies Press (St. Augustine, Trinidad), 1977.

Marques Rodriguez, Alexis, *La obra narrativa de Alejo Carpentier,* Universidad Central (Caracas), 1970.

Marques Rodriguez, *El barroco y lo real maravilloso en la obra de Alejo Carpentier,* Siglo XXI (Mexico City), 1982.

Mazziotti, Nora, editor, *Historia y mito en la obra de Alejo Carpentier,* Garcia Cambeiro (Buenos Aires, Argentina), 1972.

Mueller-Bergh, Klaus, editor, *Asedios a Carpentier,* Universitaria (Santiago, Chile), 1972.

Rodriguez Monegal, E., *Narradores de esta America,* Alfa (Montevideo), 1963.

Sentata aniversario de Alejo Carpentier, La Habana, 1975.

Shaw, Donald L., *Alejo Carpentier,* Twayne (Boston, MA), 1985.

Speratti-Pinero, Emma S., *Pasos hallados en El reino de este mundo,* Colegio de Mexico (Mexico City), 1981.

Vila Selma, Jose, *El "ultimo" Carpentier,* Mancomunicadad del Cabildo, 1978.

PERIODICALS

Books Abroad, spring, 1959.
Bulletin of Hispanic Studies, Volume 57, 1980, pp. 55-66.
Casa de las Americas, Volume 131, 1982, pp. 117-22.
Cuba, Volume 3, number 24, 1964, pp. 30-33.
Hispanic Review, summer, 1981, pp. 297-316.
Latin American Research Review, Volume 16, number 2, 1981, pp. 224-45.
Modern Language Notes, March, 1979, pp. 386-93.
New Boston Review, fall, 1976.
New Leader, July 5, 1976.
New Statesman, May 28, 1976.
New York Review of Books, December 9, 1976.
New York Times Book Review, May 2, 1976.

PMLA, spring, 1963; September, 1963, pp. 440-48.
Review, fall, 1976.
Revista Iberoamericana, Volume 40, number 86, 1974, pp. 65-86; Volume 41, numbers 92-93, 1975, pp. 297-442; January-June, 1981, pp. 95-128; April-September, 1983, pp. 293-322; Volume 154, 1991, pp. 151-60.
Saturday Review, March 21, 1970, p. 42; May 29, 1976.
Studies in Short Fiction, winter, 1971.
Times Literary Supplement, January 8, 1970, p. 39.
UNESCO Courier, January, 1972; June, 1973.

OBITUARIES:

PERIODICALS

New York Times, April 26, 1980.
Times (London), April 26, 1980.*

* * *

CARRICK, Carol (Hatfield) 1935-

PERSONAL: Born May 20, 1935, in Queens, NY; daughter of Chauncey L. (a salesman) and Elsa (Schweizer) Hatfield; married Donald Carrick (an artist), March 26, 1965 (died June 26, 1989); children: Christopher, Paul. *Education:* Hofstra University, B.A., 1957.

ADDRESSES: Home—High St., Edgarton, MA 02539.

CAREER: Coronet, New York City, staff artist, 1958-60; H. Allen Lightman (advertising agency), New York City, staff artist, 1960-61; freelance artist, 1961-65; writer for children, 1965—.

AWARDS, HONORS: Children's Book of the Year award from Library of Congress, 1974, for *Lost in the Storm,* 1980, for *The Climb,* and 1983, for *Patrick's Dinosaurs;* Children's Book of the Year from Child Study Association, 1974, for *Lost in the Storm,* 1975, for *The Blue Lobster,* 1976, for *The Accident,* 1979, for *A Rabbit for Easter* and *Some Friend!,* 1980, for *The Climb,* 1981, for *The Empty Squirrel, The Accident,* and *Ben and the Porcupine,* 1983, for *What a Wimp!* and *Two Coyotes,* 1985, for *Beach Bird* and *Stay Away from Simon!,* and 1987, for *The Foundling;* Children's Book Showcase from the Children's Book Council, 1975, for *Lost in the*

Storm, 1976, for *The Blue Lobster: A Life Cycle,* and 1978, for *The Washout;* Outstanding Science Trade Book for Children from the National Science Teachers Association and the Children's Book Council, 1975, for *The Blue Lobster,* and 1980, for *The Crocodiles Still Wait;* New York Academy of Sciences Children's Science Book Award Junior Honor Book, 1975, and one of the Best Children's Books of the Season from *Saturday Review,* 1976, both for *The Blue Lobster;* Children's Choice from the International Reading Association and the Children's Book Council, 1975, for *The Blue Lobster,* 1978, for *The Sand Tiger Shark,* 1979, for *Octopus* and *Paul's Christmas Birthday,* and 1982, for *The Empty Squirrel; The Crocodiles Still Wait* was selected one of the *New York Times*'s Best Books of the Year, 1980; New York English-Speaking Union Books-across-the-Sea Ambassador of Honor Book, 1982, for *Ben and the Porcupine; Stay Away from Simon!* was selected one of *School Library Journal*'s Best Books of the Year, 1985, and *What Happened to Patrick's Dinosaurs?,* 1986; *Stay Away from Simon!* was selected one of the New York Public Library's Children's Books, 1985; *What Happened to Patrick's Dinosaurs?* was selected one of the *New York Times*'s Notable Books, 1986; California Young Readers Medal from the California Reading Association, 1989, for *What Happened to Patrick's Dinosaurs?*

WRITINGS:

JUVENILES; ILLUSTRATED BY HUSBAND, DONALD CARRICK

The Old Barn, Bobbs-Merrill (New York City), 1966.
The Brook, Macmillan (New York City), 1967.
Swamp Spring, Macmillan, 1969.
The Pond, Macmillan, 1970.
The Dirt Road, Macmillan, 1970.
A Clearing in the Forest, Dial (New York City), 1970.
The Dragon of Santa Lalia, Bobbs-Merrill, 1971.
Sleep Out, Seabury (New York City), 1973, Clarion Books (New York City), 1988.
Beach Bird, Dial, 1973.
Lost in the Storm, Seabury, 1974.
Old Mother Witch, Seabury, 1975.
The Blue Lobster: A Life Cycle, Dial, 1975.
The Accident, Seabury, 1976.
The Sand Tiger Shark, Seabury, 1977.
The Highest Balloon on the Common, Greenwillow (New York City), 1977.
The Foundling, Seabury, 1977.
Octopus, Seabury, 1978.

The Washout, Seabury, 1978.
Paul's Christmas Birthday, Greenwillow, 1978.
A Rabbit for Easter, Greenwillow, 1979.
Some Friend!, Houghton (Boston), 1979.
What a Wimp!, Clarion Books, 1979.
The Crocodiles Still Wait, Houghton, 1980.
The Climb, Clarion Books, 1980.
Ben and the Porcupine, Clarion Books, 1981.
The Empty Squirrel, Greenwillow, 1981.
The Longest Float in the Parade, Greenwillow, 1982.
Two Coyotes, Clarion Books, 1982.
Patrick's Dinosaurs, Clarion Books, 1983.
Dark and Full of Secrets, Clarion Books, 1984.
Stay Away from Simon, Clarion Books, 1985.
What Happened to Patrick's Dinosaurs?, Clarion Books, 1986.
The Elephant in the Dark, Clarion Books, 1988.
Left Behind, Clarion Books, 1988.
Big Old Bones: A Dinosaur Tale, Clarion Books, 1989.
Aladdin and the Wonderful Lamp, Scholastic Books, Inc. (New York City), 1989.
In the Moonlight, Waiting, Clarion Books, 1990.

OTHER

Norman Fools the Tooth Fairy, illustrated by Lisa McCue, Scholastic (New York City), 1992.
Whaling Days, woodcuts by David Frampton, Clarion Books, 1993.
Two Very Little Sisters, illustrated by Erika Weihs, Clarion Books, 1993.
Banana Beer, illustrated by Margot Apple, A. Whitman (Morton Grove, IL), 1995.
Valentine, illustrated by Paddy Bouma, Clarion Books, 1995.
Melanie, illustrated by Alisher Dianov, Clarion Books, 1996.
Patrick's Dinosaurs on the Internet, illustrated by David Milgrim, Clarion Books, 1999.

Carrick's books have been translated into Swedish, Finnish, Danish, German, and Japanese; a collection of her manuscripts is kept in the University of Minnesota's Kerlan Collection.

ADAPTATIONS: The Accident (videocassette), Barr Films, 1985; *The Foundling* (videocassette), Grey Haven Films, 1986, (cassette), Houghton, 1990; *Patrick's Dinosaurs* (cassette), Houghton, 1987, and videocassette; *What Happened to Patrick's Dinosaurs?* (cassette), Houghton, 1988; *Old Mother Witch* (videocassette), Phoenix, 1989; *Sleep Out* (cassette),

Houghton, 1989; *Lost in the Storm* (cassette), 1990. Some of Carrick's work has been adapted to film.

SIDELIGHTS: A winner of numerous children's literature awards, Carol Carrick is the author of fiction and nature books. Carrick grew up in Queens, New York, at a time when ponds and woods could still be found in New York City's suburbs. Her family lived near a pond where she found tadpoles, turtles, and, in the surrounding trees, cocoons, all of which she would often take home and try to raise. It was the happiness she found in walking through this next-door natural setting that inspired her later in life to write her nature books, including her acclaimed work, *The Blue Lobster: A Life Cycle.* When she was a child, however, nature books for children were rare; she could not find any books to tell her how to raise her little pets, so most of them died. "Those early disappointments caused me a lot of grief," Carrick once commented to *CA,* "and prompted me to make my nature books as accurate as possible."

The career that Carrick originally chose was not writing. She studied art while in college, working as an artist for several years before meeting her husband. Carol offered to write the text for a children's book Donald had been commissioned to illustrate, even though she had never written a book before. Neither Donald nor Carol had any experience in writing for children, and initially only knew they wanted to write some type of nature-related book. The two collaborators eventually created *The Old Barn.* "I don't have a great sense of fantasy, so I never really thought of myself as a writer," she once said. "After our first book I never believed there would be another one. As a matter of fact, I fear that every book is the last book for me."

Following *The Old Barn,* Carrick and her husband eventually produced over 35 books. They collaborated for over two decades, until Donald died of cancer in 1989. Despite this personal and professional loss, Carrick has continued to write for children. Disclosing some of the changes following her husband's death, Carrick stated in *Something about the Author, Autobiography Series (SAAS):* "It has been difficult to go on without [Donald]. And it has been difficult to share my new books with other artists, artists I have never met. Now my published book comes in the mail as a stranger. I recognize only its title. Someone else, like a cowbird, has left an egg in my nest, and this hatchling doesn't look like the rest of my chicks. Apprehensively, I turn the pages for the first time. But slowly, I warm up to

them. I am beginning to recognize these offspring as my own."

Greatly influenced by her personal life, Carrick's writing has evolved with the changes in her family. She married Donald before they first started work on *The Old Barn,* and by the time they finished they had reached the next milestone in their lives. "We signed our first contract when I was in the hospital having our first baby," Carrick recalls in *Junior Literary Guild.* With the addition of two sons to the family, Carrick's interests in writing subjects began to switch from nature stories to stories about children. They were a good source of inspiration for her writing, and Carrick admits that she stole material from her family life and their little day-to-day adventures. "*The Empty Squirrel,* for example, concerns a boy who nurses a fish back to health because his mother didn't want to cook it," relates Carrick in her interview. "That really happened to us."

"I have always needed the security of knowing my characters and setting well, either through a great deal of research or my own experience," declared Carrick in *SAAS,* "So, it felt comfortable in my story *Sleep Out* to use my own son [Christopher] in the setting of Greenwich Village, where we lived, and at our cabin in Vermont. . . . I also wrote about our second son, Paul, whose character was slightly younger: *Paul's Christmas Birthday, A Rabbit for Easter, The Empty Squirrel,* and *The Highest Balloon on the Common.* As Paul grew into picture book age, Don's illustrations of boys began to look like him." Carrick further described in *SAAS,* "As the boys grew to junior high age. . . . [they had important] issues that were too complex for picture books. . . . I started my first attempts at chaptered books by writing the parts I felt familiar with. Then I developed the characters and plotline. These problems of friendship, bullying, and being different didn't have easy answers. For some reason, I left the main character feeling hopeful and positive in *Some Friend!, What a Wimp!, Stay Away from Simon,* and *The Elephant in the Dark,* and resisted ending each story with the kind of wrap-up 'feel good' conclusion that is so tempting."

When Carrick's sons grew older than her characters, she ran out of raw material for her writing. "If I had had a daughter, I probably would have gone into writing a teenage book because she would have rekindled things from my childhood." Instead, Carrick wrote her first historical book, *Stay Away from Simon!,* which is set in the nineteenth century and gave the author an ideal opportunity to exercise the meticulous research skills she had first honed with her nature books.

Carrick's favorite books are *Patrick's Dinosaurs* and *What Happened to Patrick's Dinosaurs?* because their element of fantasy made them the most fun to write. She hopes to write more books like these in the future, as well as more nature books. Without her husband to illustrate them, though, Carrick feels her books will never be quite the same. "Donald was skilled at drawing a wide range of subjects: children, nature, humor. To find somebody else who can do all of those thing," she concludes, "is unlikely."

BIOGRAPHICAL/CRITICAL SOURCES:

BOOKS

Something about the Author, Autobiography Series, Volume 18, Gale (Detroit), 1994.

PERIODICALS

Booklist, August, 1985; September 15, 1988; November 15, 1988; February 15, 1989; March 1, 1989; October 15, 1989; March 1, 1990; September 1, 1990; December 15, 1990; November 1, 1991; May 1, 1992; May 1, 1993; October 1, 1993; April 1, 1995; September 15, 1996.
Children's Literature in Education, Volume 11, number 3, 1980; June, 1995.
Christian Science Monitor, July 5, 1985.
Five Owls, January, 1990.
Horn Book, January, 1986; September, 1988; January, 1989; May, 1989; May, 1990; May, 1993; June, 1995.
Junior Literary Guild, September, 1979; March, 1981; April/September, 1986; April/September, 1988.
New York Times Book Review, May 4, 1975; July 7, 1977; April 30, 1978; November 13, 1983; April 27, 1986; February 5, 1989; September 30, 1990.
Publishers Weekly, April 25, 1986; October 31, 1986; March 20, 1987; August 14, 1987; November 13, 1987; June 24, 1988; March 10, 1989; November 10, 1989; January 25, 1991; May 24, 1991; February 17, 1992.
School Library Journal, November, 1984; April, 1985; May, 1986; December, 1988; March, 1989; May, 1989; October, 1989; July, 1990; November, 1991; April, 1992; May, 1993; March, 1994; April, 1995; May, 1995; November, 1996.
Wilson Library Bulletin, September, 1988.*

CARRIGHAR, Sally 1898-1985

PERSONAL: Born February 10, 1898, in Cleveland, OH; died October, 1985. *Education:* Attended Wellesley College.

CAREER: Writer and naturalist. Wrote for various motion picture companies, 1923-28, and for radio, 1928-38.

AWARDS, HONORS: Guggenheim fellowship for field work in the Arctic.

WRITINGS:

One Day on Beetle Rock, Knopf (New York City), 1944, reprinted, University of Nebraska Press (Lincoln), 1978.
One Day at Teton Marsh, Knopf, 1947, reprinted, University of Nebraska Press, 1979.
Icebound Summer, Knopf, 1953.
As Far as They Could Go (play), [Fairbanks, Alaska], 1956.
Moonlight at Midday, Knopf, 1958.
Wild Voice of the North, Doubleday (Garden City, NY), 1959 (published in England as *A Husky in the House,* M. Joseph [London], 1959).
The Glass Dove (novel), Doubleday, 1962.
Wild Heritage, Houghton (Boston, MA), 1965.
Home to the Wilderness (autobiography), Houghton, 1973.
The Twilight Seas, Weybright, 1975 (published in England as *Blue Whale,* Gollancz [London], 1978).

Also author of screenplay, *One Day at Teton Marsh* (adapted from the book by Carrighar), Walt Disney, 1966. Contributor of articles to magazines, including *Saturday Evening Post, Atlantic Monthly,* and *Reader's Digest.*

SIDELIGHTS: At a time when most nature writers were men, Sally Carrighar forged a writing career for herself by undertaking numerous books about animal behavior. Her subjects ranged widely, from the Sierra Nevada mountains to the wilds of Alaska, but critics almost unanimously viewed her as a sensitive and talented wildlife enthusiast. "Miss Carrighar is a woman of intelligence and taste," noted Harold Bloomquist in *Library Journal.* "Not only is her writing delightful, but it is effective." In another *Library Journal* piece, Aaron Fessler wrote: "Carrighar has earned for herself the esteem of her fellow naturalists as well as the deep affection of her numerous readers for her many beautifully written accounts of animal life."

Carrighar was introduced to nature at an early age—she spent her childhood at her grandparent's home in Ohio where her playground was the outdoors. From those grandparents she gained her deep-seated interest in animals and plants, and as a result, much of her life has been spent in the appreciation and study of nature—several summers in the Canadian woods, with a guide who taught her how to track wild animals, and trips into northern Michigan, the Rockies and the Ozarks, where she spent six months as a guide at a fishing lodge.

In 1937 she turned to writing about her experiences. Material for her first book was collected after spending months at Beetle Rock in Sequoia National Park, in the Sierra Nevada Mountains, where she spent her time learning about every part of the living world around her. *One Day at Beetle Rock* was the outcome, and it was widely acclaimed. A *New York Times* reviewer called the work "a book of rare distinction, at once a record of objective facts, of deep feeling without sentimentality and intense and subtle perception expressed in beauty. The reader must, indeed, be hardened whom it does not lead into the paths of nature study, whether these paths are familiar or explored for the first time." And a *Book Week* critic also praised it: "The book is beautifully written, but there is more here than mere beautiful writing. With a skillful, expansive style the author succeeds in imparting the 'feel' of nine diverse lives, each as different from the others as though they existed in different worlds. Each chapter is a new experience for the reader, each animal a new study in actions and emotions."

One Day at Beetle Rock proved an auspicious literary debut for Carrighar. Alan Devoe, in the *Saturday Review of Literature,* stated that the work "is one of the small, fine company of books that are not merely popular animal stories, or merely scientific studies of animals, but animal literature." In the *Weekly Book Review,* E. W. Teale declared: "The volume is far more than a surpassingly good first book. It is far more than a find which discerning readers will cherish. It is an event in nature-literature publishing. 'One Day on Beetle Rock' is a front-row addition to any shelf of nature classics."

Carrighar's next book, *One Day at Teton Marsh,* focused on the habits and behavior of marsh animals

when caught in an equinoctial storm. Illustrated by George and Patritia Mattson, the book was another critical success, "both beguiling to look at and to read and own," wrote David McCord. Another reviewer, William Beebe, held that "For a minimum of anthropomorphism, and in faithful representation of activities possible in a day in the life of each of these creatures, Miss Carrighar's book deserves a place near the top of fictional natural history." Noted J. H. Jackson: "Wise, observant, patient, able to set down what she sees and learns in simple, admirable prose, Miss Carrighar is like no one else who has ever written about animals, birds and insects. Better still, she has the kind of sensitivity that doesn't need a conflict on man-scale in order to produce tension. . . . She can build a drama even—well, even around a mosquito."

Thanks to a Guggenheim fellowship, received as a result of her studies of natural animal behavior, Carrighar was able to take up the study of the Eskimos and wild animals of the Arctic. She stayed nine years, part of the time in Unalakleet, a primitive, isolated village, supporting herself through writing when her fellowship ran out. From her years in the Arctic came *Icebound Summer, Moonlight at Midday,* and *Wild Voice of the North.*

With *Icebound Summer,* critics were again struck by the virtues of Carrighar's prose and her special sensitivity to animal life. "Her writing is delicate and precise," noted P. L. Adams, "and she has a fine touch with the physical maneuvers of her subjects and the look of the country itself, the visual effects of cold, sunlight, wind, and water." W. M. Teller found that "Throughout her book Miss Carrighar inspires confidence in her accuracy as a wildlife observer. But she does more—she communicates her excitement and fervor. Her stories are informed with drama, pathos and surprise." T. M. Longstreth concluded: "Few first books have founded a reputation unanimously as did Sally Carrighar's 'One Day on Beetle Rock.' Few second books uphold a reputation better than 'One Day at Teton Marsh.' When a third book is finest yet, congratulations and purchases are in order, for we have fame in the making."

The Alaskan people themselves are treated in *Moonlight at Midday,* offering both a description and an analysis of the problems brought to the Arctic by Western civilization. Though R. L. Neuberger thought that "more thorough analyses of Alaska's economic plight" had already been written, he conceded that "as an interpreter and analyst of those fetching native residents, the Eskimos, Sally Carrighar is without any superior." Added F. H. Guidry: "With humor, warmth, good taste, and scientific thoroughness . . . Miss Carrighar covers a broad range of questions that any newcomer to the region might ask."

The third book of Carrighar's Alaskan period, *Wild Voice of the North,* presents what *New York Herald Tribune Book Review* correspondent Rose Feld called "a highly personal and deeply moving story" about the author's seven-year association with Bobo, an Eskimo lead dog. Living in a house of the gold-rush days, Carrighar weathered an Alaskan winter in Nome and learned to communicate with her companion "by inflection of voice as well as through Bobo's intuition and insight," Feld remarked. She also "has a good deal to say about lemmings, huskies, Eskimos and life in the North," commented a writer for *Kirkus Reviews.* "And she says it in a prose in which the cooly scientific is balanced by the haunting warmth and loneliness left in the wake of a profound and unique friendship." J. A. Arndt in the *Christian Science Monitor* commented that *Wild Voice of the North* "is not an animal book for children but a thought-provoking, sensitive account of the relationship of this Eskimo dog—part wolf—to other dogs and to human beings. . . . All who make animals their friends will read her account with sympathy."

In her novel, *The Glass Dove,* Carrighar tells of Sylvia MacIntosh's efforts to run a station on the underground railroad during the American Civil War. Sylvia's task is complicated, however, by a romance with a suspected Confederate spy. According to Henry Cavendish, "The narrative, tho more leisurely than brisk, is packed with suspense thruout," whereas William Hogan found the book "tough going; the characters surprisingly lifeless." But P. P. Stiles observed that the story "examines the subtle intricacies of human nature—specifically the origins of a selfish love. . . . Characterizations are delicate and skillful." Another reviewer, Henrietta Buckmaster, remarked that "The resolution is not glib; it sustains the quite probing tone of the whole book. This is one of the best things that can be said about this good book, that however melodramatic are the events, the human beings invariably move at a level of complete credibility and also with moral strength."

In 1965 Carrighar returned to her naturalist concerns with *Wild Heritage.* The book purports to show "how

close is our behavior to that of other animals and how much we can discover from them about ourselves," she wrote. Reviewing the title in the *Atlantic,* Edward Weeks thought that the book "is delightfully written, packed with episodes one pauses to enjoy for a second time, and well illustrated. . . . The chapter on sex . . . is the most fascinating and provocative portion of Wild Heritage, and here, as throughout her text, Miss Carrighar supplements her own findings with the absorbing testimony she has garnered from other behaviorists. . . . The passages she selects are not only colorful; they tend to corroborate a central line of reasoning." As Marston Bates explained in the *New York Times Book Review,* Carrighar "is in rebellion against the school of thought, most fashionable early in the century, which regards animals as machines, without feelings or insights. . . . I think that [she] tends to overstress the cooperative aspects of the system of nature; but many other writers have overstressed conflict."

Eight years later, Carrighar's autobiography, *Home to the Wilderness,* drew this response from H. T. Anderson in *Best Sellers:* "I have just finished reading [one] of the most fascinating autobiographies to come my way in quite some time. . . . A great portion of Sally Carrighar's life was spent living in baroque hostility with her mother. For reasons profound, disturbing, and tragic, the child was hated by a mother who was unquestionably paranoic. Even a dog was taken away from her while she was very young, her mother admonished, 'You have to be learned not to be loved.' . . . The book chronicles monstrous, disturbing cruelty that ends in triumph. . . . From poverty to attempted suicide to psychoanalysis to the point of becoming an extraordinarily perceptive if not mystical writer of the world of nature—this author writes from the deepest level and withholds nothing."

Another work of fiction published in 1975, *The Twilight Seas,* depicts the life of a blue whale from birth to death. "Inspired by the grace and playfulness of these creatures, the writing at times becomes almost as liquid and as graceful as the blue whale itself," remarked John Ruppe. "In attempting to disclose the animal's point of view, its probable 'thought patterns,' as one might say, there is of course the danger of making the creature think like a human. I am always impressed, however, by the subtlety and delicacy with which Miss Carrighar copes with the problem." Reviewer V. M. Gilboy commented that this "is a very beautifully written book—a real delight to read. Miss Carrighar certainly has a wonderful knowledge of the ways of the oceans and the living beings within them. She spent many months of research and of correspondence with whale scientists at oceanographic institutes from Oslo to San Diego and the result is apparent in this work."

BIOGRAPHICAL/CRITICAL SOURCES:

BOOKS

Blain, Virginia, Patricia Clements, and Isobel Grundy, *The Feminist Companion to Literature in English,* Yale University Press (New Haven, CT), 1990.

Carrighar, Sally, *Home to the Wilderness* (autobiography), Houghton (Boston, MA), 1973.

Mainiero, Lina, editor, *American Women Writers: A Critical Reference Guide from Colonial Times to the Present,* Ungar (New York City), 1979.

PERIODICALS

Atlantic Monthly, February, 1945, p. 137; November, 1947; August, 1953; April, 1965, p. 150.

Best Sellers, April 1, 1965, p. 18; May 15, 1973, p. 78; May, 1975.

Book Week, April 18, 1965, p. 4; November 19, 1944, p. 8.

Chicago Sunday Tribune, April 1, 1962.

Christian Science Monitor, July 23, 1953; October 23, 1958; December 7, 1959, p. 13; March 22, 1962; May 7, 1975.

Kirkus Reviews, September 1, 1944, p. 390; September 15, 1959, p. 724.

Library Journal, March 15, 1962; June 1, 1965, p. 2568; June 15, 1973, p. 1910; October 15, 1974, p. 2752.

New York Herald Tribune Book Review, September 28, 1947; July 19, 1953; August 2, 1953; October 26, 1958; December 6, 1959, p. 8.

New York Times, December 10, 1944, p. 7; July 19, 1953; October 26, 1958.

New York Times Book Review, July 19, 1953; March 28, 1965, p. 4.

San Francisco Chronicle, September 25, 1947; July 28, 1953; November 9, 1958; February 9, 1960, p. 27; March 7, 1962.

Saturday Review, March 20, 1965, p. 29.

Saturday Review of Literature, February 24, 1945, p. 29.

Springfield Republican, February 11, 1945, p. 4D.

Weekly Book Review, November 26, 1944, p. 5.*

CHENEY, Glenn Alan 1951-

PERSONAL: Born September 6, 1951, in Melrose, MA; son of Theodore Albert Rees (an author and educator) and Dorothy (Bates) Cheney (a homemaker); married Solange Aurora Cavalcante (a secretary), May 24, 1978; children: Ian Alan. *Ethnicity:* "English/Welsh/Scottish/Irish." *Education:* Fairfield University, B.A., 1974, M.A., 1982, Universidade Federal de Minas Gerais (Brazil), M.A., 1990, Vermont College, M.A., 1991. *Politics:* Green Party. *Religion:* "Personal." *Avocational interests:* Gardening, beekeeping, writing, beer brewing.

ADDRESSES: Home and office—P.O. Box 284, 18 Parkwood Rd., Hanover, CT 06350. *E-mail*—cheney@compuserve.com; fax: 860-822-1212.

CAREER: English teacher in Sao Paulo and Minas Gerais, Brazil, 1975, 1978-80; teacher of English as a foreign language for English Language Services at University of Bridgeport, 1977; American Heart Association, Norwalk, CT, director of public information, 1980-82; freelance writer and photographer, 1981—; Grey & Davis Advertising, New York City, public relations account executive, 1982-85; Cheney & Associates, Hanover, CT and Belo Horizonte, MG, Brazil (public relations, editorial services, translation, photography, writing and production of newsletters), partner, 1985—; Institute for Children's Literature, Redding Ridge, CT, correspondence-course instructor, 1988-91; adjunct professor, Norwalk Community College, 1988, Albertus Magnus College, 1989, and Fairfield University, 1988-94; Connecticut College, visiting instructor, 1994—. Executive editor and writer for Jay Nisberg & Associates; writer and researcher for Xerox Learning Systems. Chairperson, Sprague Public Library, 1995—.

AWARDS, HONORS: Notable Trade Book acknowledgement, American Association of Social Studies Teachers, for *Television in American Society;* nominated for Pushcart Prize XVII, for short story, "Henney's Tubes;" awarded second place, Arts and Entertainment Reporting, New England Press Association, 1991; gold medal (shared), International Radio Festival, for "Tuning in the U.S.A.," 1991; honorable mentions, Writer's Digest, Fiction Contest, 1991, for "Bail," Article Contest, 1992, for "Reflections on a Radioactive Zone," and Poetry Contest, 1992, for "Cave Lux(e)"; awarded Book for the Teen Age, New York Library Association, 1994, for *Drugs, Teens and Recovery: Seven Real-Life Stories,* and 1997, for *They Never Knew: The Victims of Nuclear Testing;* named among Quick Picks for YA Readers, American Library Association, 1996, for "Teens and Disabilities."

WRITINGS:

Life in Caves (novel), Royal Fireworks Printing Co., 1994.
Acts of Ineffable Love (collected short stories), Shetucket Press, 1995.
Journey to Chernobyl: Encounters in a Radioactive Zone, Academy Chicago Publishers, 1995.
Why Didn't I Go (two-story chapbook), Dark Valley Press (grand Junction, CO), 1995.

YOUNG ADULT BOOKS

El Salvador: Country in Crisis, F. Watts (New York City), 1982, revised edition, 1990.
Mohandas Gandhi, F. Watts, 1983.
Television in American Society, F. Watts, 1983.
Revolution in Central America, F. Watts, 1983.
The Amazon, F. Watts, 1984.
Mineral Resources, F. Watts, 1984.
Revolution in Central America, F. Watts, 1985.
Responsibility, F. Watts, 1985.
The Mariana Scouts in the Valley of Spirits, McGraw-Hill (Sao Paulo, Brazil), 1986.
The Mariana Scouts in Amazonia, McGraw-Hill (Sao Paulo), 1987.
Chernobyl: The Ongoing Story of the World's Deadliest Nuclear Disaster, Macmillan (New York City), 1993.
Drugs, Teens and Recovery: Seven Real-Life Stories, Enslow Publishers (Hillside, NJ), 1993.
Teens with Disabilities: Real Life Stories of Meeting the Challenges, Enslow Publishers, 1994.
They Never Knew: The Victims of Nuclear Testing, F. Watts, 1996
Nuclear Proliferation, F. Watts, 1998.

OTHER

Author of scripts, "Tuning in the U.S.A.," a series of radio dramas teaching English as a foreign language, for worldwide broadcast on Voice of America, and for sale by Macmillan Publishing.

Translator (Portuguese to English) of "Economics" (a feature article for Brazilian-American Chamber of Commerce Directory); Danilo Azevedo, *The Fifth Key* (one-act play by Brazilian playwright); *Local*

Area Networks and High Level Protocol, McGraw-Hill (Sao Paulo).

Also contributor to *The Random House Handbook of Business Terms* (all definitions of financial and economic terms), Random House, 1989; *Grolier's Popular Science Annuals* (articles on Nobel Prizes, the Census, Chernobyl, and environmental issues), 1991, 1992, 1993; and *Grolier's World Geography* series (introductions to regional chapters).

Editorial contribution to *No Guarantees,* by Chris Campbell (revising and editing memoirs), Macmillan.

Contributor of stories and poetry to periodicals, including, *Anathema Review, Bellingham Review, Blueline, Bottomfish, Colorado North Review, Maple Twig, Oxford Magazine, Potato Eyes, Potomac Review, Sundog: The Southeast Review, Verve,* and *Yankee Brew News.*

Contributor of columns to periodicals, *Tax Notes* (weekly, on FASB meetings), and *Accounting Today* (biweekly, on FASB activities).

Contributor of articles to newspapers and periodicals, including *Accounting Today, Area Development, Atom Mind, Business Digest of Greater New Haven, E Magazine, Eyecare Business, Fairfield Citizen-News, Journal of Accountancy, Small Business Controller,* and *Tea & Coffee Trade Journal.*

Occasional editor of the news desk for *Journal of Accountancy.*

WORK IN PROGRESS: "A novel; a brief history of very early America."

SIDELIGHTS: "In 1974 I hitchhiked from Connecticut to Brazil," Cheney once told *CA.* "This trip gave me a basic understanding of and deep sympathy with the situation of the people in Latin America, and led to my first book, *El Salvador: Country in Crisis.*

"In 1977 I traveled around northern Africa, crossing the Sahara and finally getting very sick in Ouagadougou, Upper Volta.

"In 1979 I went to Brazil and married a Brazilian girl I had met in Bridgeport, Connecticut, where I had been teaching English. We stayed in Brazil for two years, then returned to Bridgeport. Now we are planning to return to Brazil as soon as I publish a healthy novel. Then I will be a very free free-lancer, living on a farm in Brazil while having the income of books published in the United States—a nice plan.

"I suppose that is the primary motivation behind my writing: freedom. A long time ago I figured out that if I wrote for a living, I could live anywhere in the world. At the slightest whim or urge, I could get up and go live somewhere else. No boss, government, or social pressure could force me to do anything I couldn't run away from—another nice plan.

"Look at the fringe benefits: fame, respect, virtual immortality, and big bucks to boot. Can you beat that?

"Somebody beat it. I live in a tiny apartment in Queens. No one has heard of me. Respect is still a dream. The books I've put my name on have shelf lives of an estimated eighteen months. Last year I qualified for food stamps. So I took a job at a public relations agency. My boss, my government, and my peers have me pretty well squared away. But I still write. It doesn't do me any good, but it keeps life from being a complete waste of time. And you can't beat that."

Cheney more recently told *CA:* "I've been writing since I was a child. I could not stop any more than I could stop thinking. In fact, my writing has become my mode of thought. By a mysterious process I do not understand, language leads me to thoughts, conclusions, ideas, stories, and discoveries. It all starts with words.

"I write all kinds of things: long and short fiction, creative nonfiction, traditional journalism, essays, lots of letters to editors, the occasional poem. I wish these projects more often led to publication and a paycheck. I wish I had more time to focus on a project that interests me rather than dashing off to a project that someone is willing to pay for—inevitably a project less worth writing.

"But I can't complain. This is a great profession, a noble craft, a sacred art. It satisfies my curiosity. It leaves me independent. I work at home—or wherever I happen to be. I like to think that the product of my effort leaves the world a little better than it used to be.

"My profession also gives me license to pursue any studies or travels that pique my interest. For the sake of a solid career, I suppose I should have pursued a Ph.D. As a writer, however, I wanted an education that was wide rather than deep. I've ended up with a B.A. in philosophy, an M.A. in communication, an M.A. in English (from a university in Brazil), and an M.F.A, in writing.

"My career as a writer began just as I finished graduate studies in human communication with a concentration in professional writing. Through a contact at a publishing house, I started writing books for young adults. Over the next decade, I'd write a dozen of them. Some I wrote after a hard and unsatisfying day at a public relations agency. Sometimes I worked on two or three books at a time.

"The book that satisfied me most was *Journey to Chernobyl: Encounters in a Radioactive Zone.* I did the research during a very intense and challenging month in Russia and Ukraine during the very weeks when the Soviet Union fell apart. I arrived in Kiev with the name of one contact, but for the first few days I couldn't find her. Yet within hours of my arrival I was talking with people who had witnessed the Chernobyl disaster and its aftermath. I ended up writing not only the young adult book I'd been asked to write but also an odd travelogue. Unlike any other book about Chernobyl, it looked at how the disaster affected people. The story alternated between horrific human drama and a humorous account of myself stumbling around the shambles of the Evil Empire.

"*Journey* is a good example of the new genre known as creative nonfiction or literary journalism. It uses the devices of fiction—characters, tension, scenes, voice, drama, plot—to portray the real world. The product is nonfiction that grips the reader, generates emotion and shows a truth beyond the reach of traditional journalism. Until my father wrote a book about this new genre (*Writing Creative Nonfiction,* Theodore A. Rees Cheney, Ten-Speed Press), I always assumed that the novel was the genre of great art. As it turns out, the novel may be close to passe.

"Nevertheless, I'm working on a novel. I'm also tinkering with a history of the Pilgrims. I'm also working on my biweekly article about the exciting world of accounting. Yesterday I wrote a letter to an editor, and, today, if I get time, I'll write another. I don't know if I'll take out my poem about my bees—I'm a beekeeper—and work on it, but I might. In the next few weeks I have to update a manuscript of a book about nuclear proliferation. I also owe a few people some letters.

"Such is my life as a writer. It's good."

CHESTERSON, Denise
  See ROBINS, Denise (Naomi)

*   *   *

CHETWYND, Berry
  See RAYNER, Claire (Berenice)

*   *   *

CHIN, Marilyn (Mei Ling) 1955-

PERSONAL: Born January 14, 1955, in Hong Kong; daughter of George (a restaurant owner) and Rose Chin; married Charles Moore, 1993. *Education:* University of Massachusetts at Amherst, B.A., 1977; University of Iowa, M.F.A., 1981. *Politics:* Democrat.

ADDRESSES: Home—9644 Plimpton Rd., La Mesa, CA 91941. *Office*—Department of English and Comparative Literature, San Diego State University, San Diego, CA 92182-8140.

CAREER: University of Iowa, Iowa City, translator and editor in International Writing Program, 1978-82; San Diego State University, San Diego, CA, assistant professor of creative writing, 1988-96, professor of English and Asian American studies, 1996—, director, Living Writers Series, 1989—. Visiting assistant professor, University of California, Los Angeles, 1990, and University of California— San Diego, 1993.

MEMBER: Poets and Writers, Associated Writing Programs.

AWARDS, HONORS: National Book Council award, 1982; Mary Roberts Rinehart Award, 1983; Virginia Center for the Creative Arts fellowship, 1983; Stamford University Stegner fellow, 1984-85; National Endowment for the Arts grant, 1984-85, 1991; Centrum fellowship, 1987; MacDowell Colony fellowship, 1987; Gjerassi Foundation fellowship, 1989; Yaddo fellowship, 1990-94; Josephine Miles Award, PEN, 1994, 1995; Pushcart Prize, 1994, 1995, 1997.

WRITINGS:

(Translator) Gozo Yoshimasu, *Devil's Wind: A Thousand Steps or More,* Oakland University Press, 1980.
(Translator with Pen Wenlan and Eugene Eoyang) Eugene Eoyang, editor, *Selected Poems of Ai Qing,* Indiana University Press, 1982.
(Editor) *Writing from the World,* University of Iowa Press, 1985.
Dwarf Bamboo (poems), Greenfield Review Press (Greenfield Center, NY), 1987.
(Editor) *Dissident Song: A Contemporary Asian American Anthology,* University of California Press (Santa Cruz), 1991.
The Phoenix Gone, the Terrace Empty, Milkweed Editions (Minneapolis), 1994.

Work represented in anthologies, including *Two Hundred Contemporary Poets,* edited by David Ray, Swallow Press, 1981; and *Breaking Silence: An Anthology of Contemporary Asian American Poets,* Greenfield Review Press, 1984. Contributor of poems to periodicals, including *Ploughshares, Caliban, MELUS, New Letters, Yellow Silk, Massachusetts Review,* and *Ms.* Co-editor of *Iowa Review,* 1984.

WORK IN PROGRESS: Short stories; translating the work of contemporary Chinese poets.

SIDELIGHTS: Born in Hong Kong and raised in the American Northwest, poet and educator Marilyn Chin distills her experiences both as an Asian American and as a politically attuned woman into verse that is direct and often confrontational. "The pains of cultural assimilation infuse her . . . poems," according to *Contemporary Women Poets* essayist Anne-Elizabeth Green, who notes that in the collections *Dwarf Bamboo* and *The Phoenix Gone, the Terrace Empty* "Chin struggles passionately and eloquently in the pull between the country left behind and America—the troubled landscape that is now home."

Chin's exploration of East-to-West cultural assimilation carries harsh political overtones. In her "How I Got That Name: An Essay on Assimilation" from her 1994 collection *The Phoenix Gone, the Terrace Empty,* she writes of her father's seduction by Western culture and values: a "petty thug," he "obsessed with a bombshell blonde/transliterated 'Mei Ling' to 'Marilyn,'" thus dooming his dark-haired daughter to bear for life the name of "some tragic white woman/ swollen with gin and Nembutal." Other verses reflect upon the scars borne by diverse Asian Americans, including women whose value as a human being has been reduced to their novelty as a sex object ("Homage to Diana Toy") or even of the second-generation of Asian Americans about whom Chin writes in "I'm Ten, Have Lots of Friends, and Don't Care," included in her first collection of verse, 1987's *Dwarf Bamboo.*

Reviewing *The Phoenix Gone* in *The Progressive,* Matthew Rothschild comments that Chin "has a voice all her own—witty, epigraphic, idiomatic, elegiac, earthy. . . . she covers the canvas of cultural assimilation with an intensely personal brush." The poet's intensity has also been noted by a *Publishers Weekly* critic, who notes of the same volume that Chin's "stalwart declaration" provides her verse with a "grounded force, line to line; and her imagery, simple and spare, lifts up those same lines." Chin herself explained in *Contemporary Women Poets:* "I believe that my work is daring, both technically and thematically. . . . My work is seeped with the themes and travails of exile, loss and assimilation. What is the loss of country if it were not the loss of self?"

BIOGRAPHICAL/CRITICAL SOURCES:

BOOKS

Contemporary Women Poets, St. James Press (Detroit), 1997.
Lim, Shirley Geok-lin, *Reading the Literatures of Asian America,* Temple University Press (Philadelphia), 1992.

PERIODICALS

New York Times, September 26, 1994, p. 11.
Progressive, May, 1994, p. 49.
Publishers Weekly, February 28, 1994, p. 79.

*   *   *

COLE, Joanna 1944-
    (Ann Cooke)

PERSONAL: Born August 11, 1944, in Newark, NJ; daughter of Mario and Elizabeth (Reid) Basilea; married Philip A. Cole (an artist and retired psychotherapist), October 8, 1965; children: Rachel Elizabeth. *Education:* Attended University of Massachusetts at Amherst and Indiana University—Bloomington; City College of New York (now of the City University of New York), B.A., 1967.

ADDRESSES: *Office*—c/o Scholastic, Inc., 555 Broadway, New York, NY 10012-3999.

CAREER: New York City Board of Education, New York City, elementary school librarian and instructor, 1967-68; *Newsweek,* New York City, letters correspondent, 1968-71; Scholastic, Inc., New York City, associate editor of See-Saw Book Club, 1971-73; Doubleday & Co., Garden City, NY, senior editor of books for young readers, 1973-80; full-time writer, 1980—.

MEMBER: Authors Guild, Authors League of America, Society of Children's Book Writers and Illustrators, American Association for the Advancement of Science.

AWARDS, HONORS: Many of Cole's science books have been named Outstanding Science Trade Books for Children by the National Science Teachers Association/Children's Book Council; Child Study Association of America's Children's Books of the Year, 1971, for *Cockroaches,* 1972, for *Giraffes at Home* and *Twins: The Story of Multiple Births,* 1973, for *My Puppy Is Born* and *Plants in Winter,* 1974, for *Dinosaur Story,* 1975, for *A Calf Is Born,* and 1985, for *Large as Life Daytime Animals Life Size, Large as Life Nighttime Animals Life Size,* and *The New Baby at Your House;* Children's Book Showcase selection, Children's Book Council, 1977, for *A Chick Hatches;* New York Academy of Sciences Children's Science honor book, 1981, and Children's Choice selection, International Reading Association-Children's Book Council (IRA-CBC), 1982, both for *A Snake's Body;* Golden Kite Honor Book Award, Society of Children's Book Writers, and Notable Children's Book selection, Association for Library Service to Children, both 1984, both for *How You Were Born;* Irma Simonton Black Award for Excellence in Children's Literature, 1986, for *Doctor Change; Boston Globe-Horn Book* Honor Book for Nonfiction, 1987, for *The Magic School Bus at the Waterworks.*

IRA/CBC Children's Choice award, 1990, for *The Magic School Bus inside the Earth;* Eva L. Gordon Award, American Nature Study Society, 1990, for body of science and nature writing; *Washington Post/* Children's Book Guild Award for Nonfiction, 1991, for body of work; David McCord Children's Literature Citation, Framingham (MA) State College and the Nobscot Council of the International Reading Association, 1994, for significant contribution to excellence in children's literature. Also recipient of state children's book awards, including Colorado Children's Choice Award and Washington State Children's Choice Award, both for *The Magic School Bus at the Waterworks.* Many of Cole's books have received best or notable book citations from the American Library Association, *Horn Book,* and *School Library Journal.*

WRITINGS:

NONFICTION FOR CHILDREN

Cockroaches, illustrated by Jean Zallinger, Morrow (New York City), 1971.

(Under pseudonym Ann Cooke) *Giraffes at Home,* illustrated by Robert Quackenbush, Crowell (New York City), 1972.

(With Madeleine Edmondson) *Twins: The Story of Multiple Births,* illustrated by Salvatore Raciti, Morrow, 1972.

Plants in Winter, illustrated by Kazue Mizumura, Crowell, 1973.

Fleas, illustrated by Elsie Wrigley, Morrow, 1973.

Dinosaur Story, illustrated by Mort Kunstler, Morrow, 1974.

Saber-Toothed Tiger and Other Ice-Age Mammals, illustrated by Lydia Rosier, Morrow, 1977.

(With Jerome Wexler) *Find the Hidden Insect,* Morrow, 1979.

Cars and How They Go, illustrated by Gail Gibbons, Crowell, 1983.

The New Baby at Your House, photographs by Hella Hammid, Morrow, 1985, revised, photographs by Miller, 1998.

Cuts, Breaks, Bruises, and Burns: How Your Body Heals, illustrated by True Kelly, Crowell, 1985.

Large as Life Daytime Animals Life Size, paintings by Kenneth Lilly, Knopf (New York City), 1985, published with *Large as Life Nighttime Animals Life Size* as *Large as Life Animals in Beautiful Life-Size Paintings,* 1990.

Large as Life Nighttime Animals Life Size, paintings by Lilly, Knopf, 1985, published with *Large as Life Daytime Animals Life Size* as *Large as Life Animals in Beautiful Life-Size Paintings,* 1990.

Hungry, Hungry Sharks: A Step Two Book, illustrated by Patricia Wynne, Random House (New York City), 1986.

Evolution, illustrated by Aliki, Crowell, 1987.

Asking about Sex and Growing Up: A Question-and-Answer Book for Boys and Girls, illustrated by Alan Tiegreen, Morrow, 1988.

A Gift from Saint Francis: The First Creche, illustrated by Michele Lemieux, Morrow, 1989.

Your New Potty, illustrated by Miller, Morrow, 1989.

Your Insides, illustrated by Paul Meisel, Putnam & Grosset (New York City), 1992.

(With Stephanie Calmenson) *Crazy Eights and Other Card Games,* illustrated by Tiegreen, Morrow, 1994.

You Can't Smell a Flower with Your Ear!: All about Your Five Senses, illustrated by Mavis Smith, Grosset & Dunlap (New York City), 1994.

Spider's Lunch: All about Garden Spiders, illustrated by Ron Broda, Grosset & Dunlap, 1995.

Riding Silver Star, photographs by Miller, Morrow, 1996.

The Any Day Book, Morrow, 1997.

(With Calmenson) *The Rain or Shine Activity Book: Fun Things to Make or Do,* illustrated by Tiegreen, Morrow, 1997.

(With Calmenson and Michael Street) *Marbles: 101 Ways to Play,* illustrated by Tiegreen, Morrow, 1998.

"ANIMAL BIRTHS" NONFICTION SERIES FOR CHILDREN; PHOTOGRAPHS BY WEXLER; EXCEPT AS NOTED; PUBLISHED BY MORROW

My Puppy Is Born, 1973, revised edition, photographs by Margaret Miller, 1991.

A Calf Is Born, 1975.

A Chick Hatches, 1976.

A Fish Hatches, 1978.

How You Were Born, 1984, revised edition, photographs by Miller, 1993.

My New Kitten, photographs by Miller, Morrow, 1995.

"ANIMAL BODIES" NONFICTION SERIES FOR CHILDREN; PHOTOGRAPHS BY WEXLER; EXCEPT AS NOTED; PUBLISHED BY MORROW

A Frog's Body, 1980.

A Horse's Body, 1981.

A Snake's Body, 1981.

A Cat's Body, 1982.

A Bird's Body, 1982.

An Insect's Body, photographs by Wexler and Raymond A. Mendez, 1984.

A Dog's Body, photographs by Jim and Ann Monteith, 1986.

The Human Body: How We Evolved, illustrated by Walter Gaffney-Kessell and Juan Carlos Barberis, 1987.

"MAGIC SCHOOL BUS" SERIES; ILLUSTRATED BY BRUCE DEGEN; PUBLISHED BY SCHOLASTIC (NEW YORK CITY)

The Magic School Bus at the Waterworks, 1986, special edition, Scholastic/New York City Department of Environmental Protection, 1990.
The Magic School Bus inside the Earth, 1987.
The Magic School Bus inside the Human Body, 1989.
The Magic School Bus Lost in the Solar System, 1990.
The Magic School Bus on the Ocean Floor, 1992.
The Magic School Bus in the Time of the Dinosaurs, 1994.
The Magic School Bus inside a Hurricane, 1995.
The Magic School Bus inside a Beehive, 1996.
The Magic School Bus and the Electric Field Trip, 1997.
The Magic School Bus Shows and Tells: A Book about Archaeology, 1997.
The Magic School Bus Explores the Senses, 1999.

"THE CLOWN-AROUNDS" FICTION SERIES FOR CHILDREN; ILLUSTRATED BY JERRY SMATH, PUBLISHED BY PARENTS MAGAZINE PRESS (NEW YORK CITY)

The Clown-Arounds, 1981, reprinted, 1994.
The Clown-Arounds Have a Party, 1982, reprinted, 1995.
Get Well, Clown-Arounds!, 1982, reprinted, 1993.
The Clown-Arounds Go on Vacation, 1983, reprinted, 1993.
Sweet Dreams, Clown-Arounds, 1985, reprinted, 1993.

"THE GATOR GIRLS" FICTION SERIES FOR CHILDREN; WITH CALMENSON; ILLUSTRATED BY MUSINGER; PUBLISHED BY MORROW

The Gator Girls, 1995.
Rockin' Reptiles, 1997.
Get Well, Gators!, 1998.

FICTION FOR CHILDREN

Cousin Matilda and the Foolish Wolf, A. Whitman (Niles, IL), 1970.
The Secret Box, illustrated by Joan Sandin, Morrow, 1971.
Fun on Wheels, illustrated by Whitney Darrow, Jr., Morrow, 1976, revised, illustrated by Don Gauthier, Delmar (Albany, NY), 1990.
Golly Gump Swallowed a Fly, illustrated by Bari Weissman, Parents Magazine Press, 1981, reprinted, 1992.

Aren't You Forgetting Something, Fiona?, illustrated by Ned Delaney, Parents Magazine Press, 1983, reprinted, 1994.
Bony-Legs, illustrated by Dirk Zimmer, Four Winds (New York City), 1983.
Doctor Change, illustrated by Donald Carrick, Morrow, 1986.
Monster Manners, illustrated by Jared Lee, Scholastic, 1986, reprinted, 1995.
This Is the Place for Me, illustrated by William Van Horn, Scholastic, 1986.
Monster Movie, illustrated by Lee, Scholastic, 1987.
Norma Jean, Jumping Bean, illustrated by Lynn Munsinger, Random House (New York City), 1987.
Mixed-Up Magic, illustrated by Kelly, Hastings House (New York City), 1987.
Animal Sleepyheads: 1 to 10, illustrated by Jeni Bassett, Scholastic, 1988.
(With husband, Philip Cole) *Hank and Frank Fix up the House,* illustrated by Van Horn, Scholastic, 1988.
The Missing Tooth, illustrated by Marilyn Hafner, Random House, 1988.
(With P. Cole) *Big Goof and Little Goof,* illustrated by M. K. Brown, Scholastic, 1989.
Buster Cat Goes Out, illustrated by Rose Mary Berlin, Western Publishing (Racine, WI), 1989.
It's Too Noisy!, illustrated by Kate Duke, Crowell, 1989.
Who Put the Pepper in the Pot?, illustrated by Robert W. Alley, Parents Magazine Press, 1989.
Bully Trouble: A Step Two Book, illustrated by Hafner, Random House, 1989.
Monster Valentines, illustrated by Lee, Scholastic, 1990.
Don't Call Me Names!, illustrated by Munsinger, Random House, 1990.
Don't Tell the Whole World!, illustrated by Duke, Crowell, 1990.
How I Was Adopted: Samantha's Story, illustrated by Maxie Chambliss, Morrow, 1995.
(With Calmenson) *Bug in a Rug: Reading Fun for Just-Beginners,* Alan illustrated by Tiegreen, Morrow, 1996.
Monster and Muffin, illustrated by Karen Lee Schmidt, Grosset & Dunlap, 1996.
I'm a Big Brother, illustrated by Chambliss, Morrow, 1997.
I'm a Big Sister, illustrated by Chambliss, Morrow, 1997.

CHILDREN'S ANTHOLOGIES

(Selector and author of introduction) *Best-Loved Folktales of the World,* illustrated by Jill Karla Schwarz, Doubleday (New York City), 1982.

(Selector and author of introduction) *A New Treasury of Children's Poetry: Old Favorites and New Discoveries,* illustrated by Judith Gwyn Brown, Doubleday (Garden City, NY), 1983.

(Compilor) *Anna Banana: 101 Jump Rope Rhymes,* illustrated by Tiegreen, Morrow, 1989.

CHILDREN'S ANTHOLOGIES; COMPILOR WITH CALMENSON

The Laugh Book: A New Treasury of Humor for Children, illustrated by Hafner, Doubleday, 1986.

The Read-Aloud Treasury: Favorite Nursery Rhymes, Poems, Stories & More for the Very Young, illustrated by Ann Schweninger, Doubleday (New York City), 1988.

Miss Mary Mack and Other Children's Street Rhymes, illustrated by Tiegreen, Morrow, 1990.

Ready, Set, Read!: The Beginning Reader's Treasury, illustrated by Anne Burgess and others, Doubleday, 1990.

The Scary Book, illustrated by Chris Demarest and others, Morrow (Garden City, NY), 1991.

The Eentsy, Weentsy Spider: Fingerplays and Action Rhymes, illustrated by Tiegreen, Morrow (New York City), 1991.

Pat-a-Cake and Other Play Rhymes, illustrated by Tiegreen, Morrow, 1992.

Pin the Tail on the Donkey and Other Party Games, illustrated by Tiegreen, Morrow, 1993.

Six Sick Sheep: 101 Tongue Twisters, illustrated by Tiegreen, Morrow, 1993.

Give a Dog a Bone: Stories, Poems, Jokes, and Riddles about Dogs, illustrated by John Speirs, Scholastic, 1994.

Why Did the Chicken Cross the Road?: And Other Riddles Old and New, illustrated by Tiegreen, Morrow, 1994.

A Pocketful of Laughs: Stories, Poems, Jokes, and Riddles, illustrated by Hafner, Doubleday, 1995.

Ready, Set, Read—and Laugh!: A Funny Treasury for Beginning Readers, Doubleday, 1995.

Yours Till Banana Splits: 201 Autograph Rhymes, illustrated by Tiegreen, Morrow, 1995.

OTHER

The Parents TM Book of Toilet Teaching, Ballantine, Morrow, 1983.

(With Calmenson) *Safe from the Start: Your Child's Safety from Birth to Age Five,* Facts on File (New York City), 1989.

On the Bus with Joanna Cole: A Creative Autobiography, Heinemann (Portsmouth, NH), 1996.

Also contributor of articles to *Parents.*

ADAPTATIONS: An animated series for PBS-TV based on the "Magic School Bus" books, for which Cole and illustrator Degen serve as consultants, began in 1994 and features the voices of Lily Tomlin as Ms. Frizzle, Robby Benson, Carol Channing, and Malcolm-Jamal Warner; some programs in the "Magic School Bus" television series are original storylines that were later adapted to books by various authors, including Linda Beech, Patricia Relb, and Nancy E. Krulik; the "Magic School Bus" series is also available in a CD-ROM version by Microsoft Home and Scholastic, Inc.; the "Magic School Bus" series was used as the basis of the American Library Association's 1994 reading program, "Reading Is a Magic Trip"; cassette recordings have been made for *Bony-Legs,* Random House, 1985, and *Monster Movie* and *Dinosaur Story,* both for Scholastic, 1989.

SIDELIGHTS: A writer of fiction and nonfiction for children, Joanna Cole is best known for the science books she has created, such as her series on animal anatomy and her "Magic School Bus" books. A thorough researcher, the author has been praised by critics for her scientific accuracy, but her books are widely considered effective because of her frank and easily understood explanations that bring complicated, technical subjects within reach of younger audiences. Her "Magic School Bus" books, among others, combine humor and science to help children learn about the world around them.

Cole first discovered the pleasures of writing when she was in grade school. "I discovered in the fifth grade what I liked to do; write reports and stories, make them interesting and/or funny and draw pictures to go along with the words," she once told *CA.* "Except for the pictures, I still do that. I remember grade school very clearly when I sat at my desk, happily interested in whatever subject I was writing about. Science was my favorite. Our teacher, Miss Bair, would assign us to read a science trade book every week. And each week, she would choose one student to do an experiment and report on it to the class. I would have done an experiment every week if she had let me. Grade school was very important to me, much more influential than my later education. Maybe that's why as an adult I ended up writing books for children."

After receiving her bachelor's degree from the City College of the City University of New York, Cole pursued her interest in books by working variously as a librarian, teacher, and editor. It was during her first job at an elementary school that she was inspired by an article about cockroaches in the *Wall Street Journal.* Realizing that this was a subject she had never read about in school, Cole decided to write about it herself. The first publisher she submitted her manuscript to rejected the idea, but the author had more luck when she sent her book to the publishing house of William Morrow, where editor Connie C. Epstein helped Cole hone her skills in science writing.

Many of Cole's nonfiction works focus on the life sciences. In her series on animals' bodies, Cole introduces young readers to the anatomy of such animals as horses, frogs, dogs, birds, cats, and snakes. This series concludes with *The Human Body: How We Evolved,* which explains how archaeologists have pieced together the evolutionary history of mankind and how human anatomy compares to that of apes, chimpanzees, gorillas, and others of our primate cousins.

Accuracy is an important consideration in such works. According to a *School Library Journal* article by Epstein, the author feels that "accuracy is harder to achieve in books for the very young than in those for older readers, because so much must be left out in order to keep the text sufficiently simple." In addition to the extensive research that Cole does for each book, she tries to confer with experts in whatever subject she happens to be doing at the time. "Cole prefers to discuss the project with the expert directly, as his general point of view may be even more valuable to her than his factual check," notes Epstein. "When the rare error does creep in, . . . it is usually one that has been repeated in several supposedly trustworthy sources." Cole has emphasized, however, that she is not interested in presenting only the bare facts of a subject. She told *CA* that her main goal is to "share with kids the things I find out about how the world works and that fascinates me."

In her science writing Cole has always been aware of how children's feelings affect their reactions to factual material. Her series on animals' births, which includes *A Calf Is Born, My Puppy Is Born,* and *My New Kitten,* explain the physiology of birth with

candor and accuracy. Cole is careful to include the gentle care baby mammals need to grow, which mirrors children's own experience. Similarly, a number of her books focus on child development. These titles—*How You Were Born, The New Baby at Your House, Your New Potty, Asking about Sex and Growing Up,* and *How I Was Adopted: Samantha's Story*—help families share facts and feelings about key issues in children's lives.

In her popular "Magic School Bus" series, including *The Magic School Bus at the Waterworks, The Magic School Bus inside the Earth, The Magic School Bus inside the Human Body,* and *The Magic School Bus Lost in the Solar System,* Cole has combined science and imaginative fun into stories that have been warmly received by critics and readers alike. The adventures involve a class of school children led by their eccentric teacher Ms. Frizzle. The humorous illustrations by Bruce Degen and the unlimited possibilities for travel in a bus that can dig through the earth, shrink to microscopic size, or blast off into space result in lively reading. "Just as 'Sesame Street' revolutionized the teaching of letters and numbers by making it so entertaining that children had no idea they were actually learning something, so the 'Magic School Bus' books make science so much fun that the information is almost incidental," writes Katherine Bouton in the *New York Times Book Review.* Bouton declares that these books offer "the freshest, most amusing approach to science for children that I've seen."

Cole based the character of Ms. Frizzle on her favorite science teacher, Miss Bair, although she later told *CA,* "Miss Bair did not dress at all like Ms. Frizzle!" The kids in the "Magic School Bus" books may grumble a bit about the adventures they experience, but in their hearts they love "the Friz" and are proud to be in her class. "In 'The Magic School Bus' books I use the same criteria as I do in all my science books," Cole explained. "I write about ideas, rather than just facts. I try to ask an implicit question—such as, How do our bodies get energy from the food we eat? or How do scientists guess what dinosaurs were like? Then I try to answer the question in writing the book." The success of Cole's "Magic School Bus" books has carried over to television, where PBS has turned them into an animated series; Cole and illustrator Degen serve as consultants.

Although Cole is more often recognized for her science books, she is also the author of a number of stories for children, has compiled anthologies of children's literature, and has written books for adults on parenting and child development. Discussing her fiction writing, which she sometimes bases on old folktales, Cole related: "In so many folktales, the hero wins, not because he is strong, but because he is able to reach out to others for help, something the greedy, selfish villain cannot do. The hero can also change and develop, and so he can accomplish things at the end of the story that seemed impossible at the beginning. The same thing happens with children as they grow, and that is one reason why children love folktales so much."

"It is also a main theme of my life; I consistently try to do things in my writing and in my life that are all but impossible. On one level, I am pleased with my work; on another level, dissatisfied. My response to this situation is simply to keep trying and keep doing; that's the only way to grow." The author told *CA* that her favorite fiction work for children is *Bony-Legs:* "I have a warm spot for *Bony-Legs* because I wrote it for my daughter when she was four." Of her life in general, Cole commented: "I lived in New York City for over twenty years. My daughter was born there and my husband and I consider ourselves New Yorkers. But at one point we felt we needed to move to the country, and now we have a barn, eight guinea pigs, a dog, and lots of trees. I'm very happy."

BIOGRAPHICAL/CRITICAL SOURCES:

BOOKS

Children's Literature Review, Volume 5, Gale (Detroit), 1983.

PERIODICALS

Appraisal: Science Books for Young People, spring, 1973; spring, 1975; spring, 1978; winter, 1980; winter, 1981; winter, 1982.
Booklist, April 15, 1994; August, 1994; October 15, 1994; January 1, 1995; February 15, 1995; March 1, 1995; April 15, 1995; June 1, 1995; August, 1995; October 1, 1995; February 1, 1996; April 1, 1996; September 1, 1996; April 1, 1997; March 1, 1997; August, 1997.
Bulletin of the Center for Children's Books, July-August, 1986; November, 1986; February, 1987; January, 1988; March, 1988; June, 1988; December, 1992.
Christian Science Monitor, September 26, 1996.
Entertainment Weekly, August 19, 1994.

Horn Book, October, 1980; February, 1982; May, 1995; November, 1995; May-June, 1996; September, 1996; November, 1996.
Junior Bookshelf, December, 1996.
Los Angeles Times Book Review, March 22, 1987; February 28, 1988; July 30, 1989; December 17, 1989; September 30, 1990.
New York Times Book Review, February 7, 1988; January 1, 1995.
Publishers Weekly, April 18, 1984; July 4, 1994; October 2, 1995; September 2, 1996.
School Library Journal, December, 1971; February, 1973; January, 1980; May, 1982; March, 1987; November, 1992; December, 1992; April, 1993; June, 1994; September, 1994; April, 1995; September, 1995; March, 1996; May, 1996; June, 1996; October, 1996; November, 1996; April, 1997.
Science Books and Films, December, 1979; March-April, 1982.
Washington Post Book World, April 10, 1983; September 8, 1984; October 14, 1990.

OTHER

Riding the Magic School Bus with Joanna Cole and Bruce Degen (videotape), Scholastic, 1993.*

*　*　*

COLEMAN, Jonathan (Mark) 1951-

PERSONAL: Born September 26, 1951, in Hattiesburg, MS; son of Frederic (a retailer) and Sylvia (a retailer; maiden name, Berkowitz); married Kathryn Court (a publisher), July 8, 1978 (divorced February, 1989); married Eileen S. Dinan (a management consultant), May 30, 1992. *Education:* University of Virginia, B.A. (with distinction), 1973. *Avocational interests:* Basketball, softball, squash, reading, movies.

ADDRESSES: Home—801 Park St., Charlottesville, VA 22902. *Office*—English Department, University of Virginia, Charlottesville, VA 22903. *Agent*—Owen Laster, William Morris Agency, 1350 Avenue of the Americas, New York, NY 10019.

CAREER: New Review (magazine), London, England, editorial assistant, 1974, U.S. representative, 1975; Alfred A. Knopf, Inc., New York City, publicity writer, 1975-77; Simon & Schuster, Inc., New

York City, associate editor, 1977-78, senior editor, 1978-81, member of editorial board, 1980-81; Columbia Broadcasting System, Inc. (CBS-TV), New York City, associate producer of network news, 1981-83; nonfiction writer, 1983—; University of Virginia, Charlottesville, lecturer in advanced nonfiction writing, 1986—; writer.

MEMBER: American PEN.

AWARDS, HONORS: Edgar Allan Poe Award nominee, Mystery Writers of America, 1986, for *At Mother's Request;* special mention, Best American Sportswriting, 1992, for a piece about Little League.

WRITINGS:

At Mother's Request: A True Story of Money, Murder, and Betrayal, Atheneum (New York City), 1985.
Exit the Rainmaker, Atheneum, 1989.
Long Way to Go: Black and White in America, Atlantic Monthly Press (New York City), 1997.

Contributor to various periodicals, including the *New York Times Book Review* and *Time.*

ADAPTATIONS: At Mother's Request: A True Story of Money, Murder, and Betrayal was adapted by Richard DeLong Adams into a four-hour miniseries starring Stefanie Powers and Doug McKeon, broadcast by CBS-TV, in 1987.

SIDELIGHTS: Jonathan Coleman is a chronicler of real-life stories that revolve around atypical human behavior and circumstances. In his books, he explores occurrences that, due to their bizarre nature, fascinate him. His works delve into topics ranging from the motives for greed and murder, to the reasons behind desertion. Alluding to the common focus on people's unusual actions that permeates his writings, Coleman told Chris Goodrich of *Publishers Weekly,* "that's what obsesses me—why people snap, cross a line, and do something that affects a h—- of a lot of other people." The author's chosen subjects have proved of interest to both the public and critics as well. His first volume, *At Mother's Request: A True Story of Money, Murder, and Betrayal,* became a hardcover and paperback bestseller and spawned a television miniseries. His second book, *Exit the Rainmaker,* also rose to bestseller status in paperback. Reviewers, in turn, have lauded Coleman for his presentation of information in a clear, interesting, and concise manner.

Born in 1951 in Allentown, Pennsylvania, Coleman has worked as a writer and editor for much of his professional career. Holding posts at Knopf, Simon & Schuster, and finally Columbia Broadcasting System (CBS-TV) network news, the author developed a growing interest in unusual real-life stories. After a stint as an associate news producer at CBS-TV, Coleman decided to try his hand as a true-crime writer, penning his first book, *At Mother's Request,* in 1985. Coleman actually began to investigate the story in the early 1980s, researching the 1978 slaying of Utah auto parts magnate Franklin James Bradshaw. His examination included some 250 interviews with people associated with the case. Coleman's goal was to illuminate the motives behind the shooting of Bradshaw by his seventeen-year-old grandson, Marc Schreuder, who was ultimately sentenced to prison for second-degree murder. The author also sought to expose the role played by Marc's mother, Frances Schreuder, who was eventually convicted of first-degree murder for pressuring her son to kill her father.

In a 1989 interview with *CA,* Coleman described *At Mother's Request:* "This [story] is [about] a human tragedy . . . this was a family that was destroyed. . . .It's a sad family and a very sad story. I get asked a lot: "What do we learn from it?" I think there's a lot to be learned from it. . . . But to me what the Bradshaw story is really about is how the adults we become are so clearly shaped by the kind of childhoods we had. That's why I found Alice Miller's book *Prisoners of Childhood* [an acclaimed psychoanalytical study of negligent parenting and its effect on children] so useful, not only in the conclusion but in all my thinking about the story. *At Mother's Request* is also about the ways a family can be torn asunder and what it means to have an absentee father who has good intentions but can't follow through—and when he tries to, it's too late. It's about the fierce rivalries that can exist between siblings and what parents will do to their own children as a way of getting back at their parents."

At Mother's Request opens with the murder, then recaps relevant events prior to the slaying as well as those incidents leading to the arrests of Frances and her son several years after Bradshaw's death. Information regarding the duo's subsequent trials and convictions is also included. In addition, Coleman provides background data illuminating the Bradshaw/ Schreuder family's apparent history of mental illness—Frances's brother Robert was lobotomized due to schizophrenia while her eldest son Larry served a prison sentence for trying to kill his college room-mate with a hammer. Finally, Coleman explains the initial mystery surrounding the seventy-six-year-old Bradshaw's death in his Salt Lake City warehouse and exposes the millionaire as a workaholic, neglect-ful, penny-pinching father. The author discusses the paranoia and dominance to which Frances subjected her family and the fear of disinheritance that moti-vated her.

When preparing his manuscript for *At Mother's Re-quest,* Coleman examined police records, court tran-scripts, personal testimonies, high school yearbooks, letters, and other documents to explain the unusual circumstances involved in the case. He also attended Frances's trial. The author maintains suspense in the book by keeping the identity of the murderer secret as he describes the crime: "Bradshaw was surprised to see his visitor. They talked for fifteen minutes or so about things that mutually concerned them. Feel-ing he might be unable to shoot him face to face, the visitor hoped Bradshaw would turn around for a sec-ond—all that he would need. When Bradshaw finally did, the gunman fired one bullet, at close range, into his back, and then, as the old man was slumped on the green linoleum floor, another into the back of his head."

Coleman's work in *At Mother's Request* was praised by various critics. Some reviewers lauded his objec-tivity in presenting the details surrounding Frances's alleged insatiable quest to become a New York so-cialite, her failed attempt to contract a hit man to commit the murder, and her procrastination in paying off a thirty-seven-hundred-dollar debt to a confidante who, in turn, implicated the Schreuders in the mur-der. A few critics acknowledged the plausibility of Coleman's psychological appraisals at the book's conclusion, including his assertion that the murderers hoped to be caught since they failed to dispose of the .357 magnum used in the slaying. Several reviewers also commented on the book's speculative ending—that through the murder, Frances was really acting out what she perceived to be *her* mother Berenice's request.

Impressed with Coleman's cogent presentation of a vast amount of information, some critics compared his work in *At Mother's Request* to that of twentieth-century writer Truman Capote's 1966 *In Cold Blood.* Coleman's volume, an Edgar Allan Poe Award nomi-nee, was judged "wealthy in character and detail," by John Katzenbach in the *Washington Post Book World.* He further deemed the story "a masterwork

of reporting." *Newsweek*'s Walter Clemons called the work "harrowing and convincing," suggesting that Coleman's "slow-but-sure recounting of police pro-cedures makes even a search for vanished airline records absorbing."

While on a book tour promoting *At Mother's Re-quest,* Coleman contemplated his next volume, re-calling the mysterious disappearance of a Maryland college president that he reported for CBS News in 1982. Knowing that the forty-seven-year-old former Charles County Community College president Dr. Julian Nance Carsey had surfaced in Texas, Coleman decided that the story could not be told effectively without an interview with the educator. Carsey, Coleman discovered, had not fled as a result of his involvement in any impropriety, nor had he been kidnapped. Instead, Carsey reportedly felt over-whelmed by stress, sought to begin life anew, and decided to avoid the conventional good-byes and resignations by leaving without advance notice. Thus, he sent six cryptic letters and one postcard to family and colleagues, vanishing with twenty-eight thousand dollars from a secret account he maintained at a bank.

To learn more, Coleman ventured abroad to meet Carsey, who was teaching at military bases, and was nearly denied an interview by the skeptical instruc-tor. The author, however, managed to gain Carsey's confidence and obtained information which served as the foundation for *Exit the Rainmaker*—Coleman's 1989 book named after both a local production of N. Richard Nash's 1954 play (in which Carsey had a role) and the former president's keen ability to be successful in his ventures. Delving into Carsey's flight from his seventeen-year job, Coleman's study probes the educator's personal life and fourteen-year childless marriage. In addition, the author explores Carsey's image as a charismatic, prosperous, and influential man who had many friends, while charting the effects of the president's departure on his family and associates.

Exit the Rainmaker also illuminates the new life Carsey established for himself as Jay Martin Adams in Texas. Coleman notes that under the alias, Carsey purchased a struggling bar and began a new relation-ship with a woman said to be much different from his wife. In summation, Coleman attempts to explain Carsey's motives for his actions—reasons that range from the disintegration of his marriage, to the college's growing financial difficulties, to his in-creasing dependence on alcohol. Describing his overall findings to the *New York Times,* Coleman explained: "Jay came of age before the women's movement, which also raised men's consciousness, telling them it was O.K. to express their feelings. Jay came out of the Eisenhower era. If something was troubling you, you didn't talk about it. He was the man in the gray flannel suit."

Exit the Rainmaker received mixed reviews from critics. Katzenbach, this time writing for the *New York Times Book Review,* contended that Coleman used the "same thoroughgoing techniques" he applied in *At Mother's Request* when compiling his second book. "The result," the critic offered, "is a book rife with detail, but unfortunately drained of mystery." While some critics perceived Coleman's second work as "meandering," *Los Angeles Times Book Review*'s Thomas Cahill reasoned that the author discloses Carsey's motivations "with the tenacity of a scientist, the patience of a novelist, and the instincts of a hunter." And in a review for the *Washington Post,* John Jerome called *Exit the Rainmaker* a "dogged examination," concluding that the book "finally illuminates . . . how utterly banal the act of desertion is." In the *Publishers Weekly* interview, Coleman explained to Goodrich: "Carsey did what a lot of people only dream of doing. . . . When Carsey left that life, thinking he could invent himself all over again, he found out you really can't. . . . [His story] suggests that you take yourself wherever you go."

"I think there's a lot to be gleaned from [*Rainmaker* and *At Mother's Request*]," commented Coleman in his 1989 interview with *CA,* "[They are] both stories about families, and that's what my main interest is: families and human behavior. In Jay Carsey's case, in *Rainmaker,* I'm interested in families on more than one level: The family he came out of, why he didn't want to have his own. I went back to Jay's childhood to try to figure out what made him constantly need to have the approval of others and what made it so hard for him to articulate emotion. In *At Mother's Request* I had to go back to Frances's childhood in order to understand the mother she had become. In going back to that childhood, I came face to face with Berenice Bradshaw. I had no idea when I started the book just how potent and important a figure she was going to become in the story."

"I want to write things that cause discussion," Coleman proclaimed in his 1989 *CA* interview, delineating: "*Rainmaker* has been controversial, I think, because it's so much more mainstream. *At Mother's*

Request was less controversial than troubling. I do think that all of us at some time or another have murderous impulses, and I think that we look at a story like this—a moneyed family that disintegrates—and feel reassured because it didn't happen to us. It's reassuring to some people to realize that it doesn't matter if you have a lot of money; you can still have problems."

For his third book, 1997's *Long Way to Go: Black and White in America,* Coleman delves into a broader controversial topic: the continued existence of racism in the United States. Calling the book "grounded and accessible" in a review for *Time,* Romesh Ratnesar set forth Coleman's conclusions: "[White people] 'can either give up on the idea of racial harmony and just go on . . . or [try] to find ways to change hearts and minds.'" Interviewing many residents in the segregated city of Milwaukee, Wisconsin during the 1980s, Coleman attempts to answer this question: Why do economic and social issues still divide the races in America? "Coleman seeks out both black and white dissenters from racial orthodoxy and gives them a fair hearing," noted James Traub in the *New York Times Book Review,* in discussing the author's somewhat liberal approach to the racism issue. While commenting favorably on the author's conclusion—that U.S. society needs to break through the barriers still constructed by racial issues—Traub maintained: "What apparently has not occurred to Coleman . . . is that the obsessive focus on racism and injury, the vigilant patrolling of the borders of racial identity, is part of the problem rather than part of the solution. He is absolutely right in thinking that ordinary people need to break out of the shell of racial isolation and talk to one another. But perhaps they need to talk about something other than race."

Coleman once told *CA:* "I never intended to become a writer. Even now, I consider myself to be a reluctant one. When I left CBS News to write *At Mother's Request,* I did so because my instinct, as a former book editor, told me that the story could only be fully understood as a book. Had I still been a book editor, I would have been tireless in my efforts to persuade one of my authors to undertake it. But I was no longer in that position, so I took the project on, having no idea whether I could actually do what I had contractually obligated myself to do.

"As much as I thought I was sensitive to and understood the psyches of writers, I didn't completely realize what it meant to be one until I found myself in that position. The way I look at it is this: You're usually in a state of anxiety, feeling lonely and inse- cure much of the time. The only way I am able to combat that feeling is by approaching each day with what I like to call the 'lunchpail approach': trying to achieve a certain amount each day, every day, just like 'normal people.' And I never, ever, romanticize what I do. It's a job—hard, painstaking, and decid- edly unglamorous. If I viewed it any other way, I'd never get it done. I'm proud of what I've achieved. I hope my work will last. But. . . . [I try to] to balance my work with my life. Like everyone else."

BIOGRAPHICAL/CRITICAL SOURCES:

BOOKS

Coleman, Jonathan, *At Mother's Request: A True Story of Money, Murder, and Betrayal,* Ath- eneum, 1985.
Coleman, *Exit the Rainmaker,* Atheneum, 1989.
Coleman, *Long Way to Go: Black and White in America,* Atlantic Monthly Press, 1997.

PERIODICALS

Christian Science Monitor, October 25, 1989.
Detroit Free Press, September 17, 1989.
Detroit News, August 4, 1985, p. 2F.
Los Angeles Times Book Review, July 14, 1985, p. 1; January 19, 1986, p. 8; October 8, 1989, p. 12; September 23, 1990, p. 14.
Newsweek, June 17, 1985, p. 80.
New York, August 28, 1989, p. 62.
New York Times, May 19, 1985; May 28, 1985; September 17, 1989, section 21, p. 10.
New York Times Book Review, June 16, 1985, p. 3; January 26, 1986, p. 38; September 10, 1989, p. 30; January 26, 1996, p. 38; September 7, 1997, p. 14.
People, September 27, 1982, pp. 57-59.
Publishers Weekly, May 17, 1985, p. 102; July 14, 1989, p. 62; September 8, 1989, pp. 52-53; July 20, 1990, p. 56; July 7, 1997, p. 54.
Time, June 17, 1985, p. 74; September 25, 1989, p. 82; September 8, 1997, p. 63.
Times Literary Supplement, January 31, 1986, p. 121.
Tribune Books (Chicago), June 30, 1985, p. 25.
USA Today, June 28, 1985, p. 5D.
Virginia Quarterly Review, summer, 1990.
Wall Street Journal, June 18, 1985.
Washington Post, September 5, 1989.
Washington Post Book World, May 26, 1985, p. 1.*

COLES, Robert (Martin) 1929-

PERSONAL: Born October 12, 1929, in Boston, MA; son of Philip Winston (an engineer) and Sandra (Young) Coles; married Jane Hallowell (a teacher), July 4, 1960; children: Robert Emmet, Daniel Agee, Michael Hallowell. *Education:* Harvard University, A.B., 1950; Columbia University, M.D., 1954. *Poli- tics:* Independent. *Religion:* Episcopalian. *Avocational interests:* Tennis, skiing.

ADDRESSES: Home—P.O. Box 674, Concord, MA 01742. *Office*—Harvard University Health Services, 75 Mt. Auburn St., Cambridge, MA 02138.

CAREER: University of Chicago clinics, Chicago, IL, intern, 1954-55; Massachusetts General Hospital, Boston, resident in psychiatry, 1955-56; McLean Hospital, Belmont, MA, resident in psychiatry, 1956-57; Massachusetts General Hospital, member of alcoholism clinic staff, 1957-58; Metropolitan State Hospital, Boston, supervisor in children's unit, 1957- 58; Judge Baker Guidance Center—Children's Hospi- tal, Roxbury, MA, resident, 1957-58, fellow in child psychiatry, 1960-61; Lancaster Industrial School for Girls, Lancaster, MA, psychiatric consultant, 1960- 62; Massachusetts General Hospital, Boston, member of psychiatric staff, 1960-62; Harvard University Medical School, Cambridge, MA, clinical assistant in psychiatry, 1960-62, research psychiatrist, 1963—, lec- turer in general education, 1966—, professor of psy- chiatry and medical humanities, 1978—; Southern Regional Council, Atlanta, GA, research psychia- trist, 1961-63; writer, 1966—.

Consultant to Ford Foundation, Southern Regional Council, and Appalachian Volunteers; member of board of trustees, Robert F. Kennedy Memorial; member of board of Field Foundation, Institute of Current World Affairs, Reading Is Fundamental, American Freedom from Hunger Foundation, Na- tional Rural Housing Coalition, Twentieth Century Fund, National Sharecroppers Fund, Lyndhurst Foundation, and National Advisory Committee on Farm Labor. *Military service:* U.S. Air Force, 1958- 60; chief of neuropsychiatric service, Keesler Air Force Base, Biloxi, MS.

MEMBER: American Psychiatric Association, Ameri- can Orthopsychiatric Association, Group for the Advancement of Psychiatry, American Academy of Arts and Sciences (fellow), Phi Beta Kappa, Harvard Club (New York and Boston).

AWARDS, HONORS: Atlantic grant, 1965, in support of work on *Children of Crisis: A Study in Courage and Fear;* National Educational Television award, 1966, for individual contribution to outstanding programming; Family Life Book Award, Child Study Association of America, Ralph Waldo Emerson Award, Phi Beta Kappa, Anisfeld-Wolf Award in Race Relations, *Saturday Review,* Four Freedoms Award, B'nai B'rith, and *Parents' Magazine* Medal, all 1968, all for *Children of Crisis;* Hofheimer Prize for research, American Psychiatric Association, 1968; Pulitzer Prize, 1973, for Volumes II and III of *Children of Crisis;* McAlpin Award, National Association of Mental Health, 1973; MacArthur Foundation fellowship, 1981-86; Sarah Josepha Hale Award, Friends of the Richard Library (Newport, NH), 1986; Robert F. Kennedy Book Award honorable mention citation, 1987, for *The Political Life of Children.*

WRITINGS:

Children of Crisis, Little, Brown (Boston), Volume 1: *A Study in Courage and Fear,* 1967, Volume 2: *Migrants, Sharecroppers, Mountaineers,* 1971, Volume 3: *The South Goes North,* 1971, Volume 4: *Eskimos, Chicanos, Indians,* 1978, Volume 5: *Privileged Ones: The Well-Off and the Rich in America,* 1978.

Dead End School, illustrated by Norman Rockwell, Little, Brown, 1968.

Still Hungry in America, with introduction by Edward M. Kennedy, World Publishing, 1969.

The Grass Pipe (juvenile), Little, Brown, 1969.

The Image Is You, Houghton (Boston), 1969.

(With Maria W. Piers) *The Wages of Neglect,* Quadrangle, 1969.

Uprooted Children: The Early Lives of Migrant Farmers (Horace Mann lecture, 1969), University of Pittsburgh Press (Pittsburgh, PA), 1970.

(With Joseph H. Brenner and Dermot Meagher) *Drugs and Youth: Medical, Psychiatric, and Legal Facts,* Liveright (New York City), 1970.

Erik H. Erikson: The Growth of His Work, Little, Brown, 1970.

The Middle Americans, photographs by Jon Erikson, Little, Brown, 1971.

(With Daniel Berrigan) *The Geography of Faith,* Beacon Press (Boston), 1971.

Saving Face, Little, Brown, 1972.

(Editor, with Jerome Kagan) *Twelve to Sixteen: Early Adolescence* (essays), Norton (New York City), 1972.

Farewell to the South, Little, Brown, 1972.

A Spectacle unto World, Viking (New York City), 1973.

Riding Free, Atlantic-Little, Brown, 1973.

The Old Ones of New Mexico, University of New Mexico Press (Albuquerque, NM), 1973.

Doris Ulmann: The Darkness and the Light, Aperture (Millerton, NY), 1974.

The Buses Roll, Norton, 1974.

Irony in the Mind's Life: Essays on Novels by James Agee, Elizabeth Bowen, and George Eliot, University Press of Virginia (Charlottesville), 1974.

Headsparks, Little, Brown, 1975.

William Carlos Williams: The Knack of Survival in America, Rutgers University Press (New Brunswick, NJ), 1975.

Mind's Fate: Ways of Seeing Psychiatry and Psychoanalysis, Little, Brown, 1975.

A Festering Sweetness: Poems of American People, University of Pittsburgh Press, 1978.

(With wife, Jane Hallowell Coles) *Women of Crisis,* Delacorte (New York City), Volume 1: *Lives of Struggle and Hope,* 1978, Volume 2: *Lives of Work and Dreams,* 1980.

The Last and First Eskimos, New York Graphic Society (Boston), 1978.

Walker Percy: An American Search, Atlantic-Little, Brown, 1978.

Flannery O'Conner's South, Louisiana State University Press (Baton Rouge), 1980.

Dorothea Lange: Photographs of a Lifetime, Aperture, 1982.

(Editor) William Carlos Williams, *The Doctor Stories,* New Directions (New York City), 1984.

(With Geoffrey Stokes) *Sex & the American Teenager,* Harper (New York City), 1985.

The Moral Life of Children, Atlantic Monthly Press, 1986.

The Political Life of Children, Atlantic Monthly Press, 1986.

Simone Weil: A Modern Pilgrimage, Addison-Wesley (Reading, MA), 1987.

Dorothy Day: A Radical Devotion, Addison-Wesley, 1987.

Harvard Diary: Reflection on the Sacred & the Secular, Crossroads (Los Angeles), 1988.

The Red Wheelbarrow: Selected Literary Essays, University of Iowa Press (Iowa City), 1988.

Times of Surrender: Selected Essays, University of Iowa Press, 1988.

Learning by Example: Stories and the Moral Imagination, Houghton, 1989.

Rumors of Separate Worlds (poems), University of Iowa Press, 1989.

The Spiritual Life of Children, Houghton, 1990.

(Essayist) Pamela Fong, *Breaking the Cycle: Survivors of Child Abuse and Neglect,* Norton, 1991.

Their Eyes Meeting the World: The Drawings and Paintings of Children, edited by Margaret Sartor, Houghton, 1992.

Anna Freud: The Dream of Psychoanalysis, Addison-Wesley, 1992.

Conversations with Robert Coles, edited by Jay Woodruff and Sarah Carew Woodruff, University Press of Mississippi (Jackson), 1992.

A Robert Coles Omnibus, University of Iowa Press, 1993.

The Call of Service: A Witness to Idealism, Houghton, 1993.

The Story of Ruby Bridges, illustrated by George Ford, Scholastic, Inc. (New York City), 1995.

The Ongoing Journey: Awakening Spiritual Life in At-Risk Youth, Boys Town Press, 1995.

The Mind's Fate: A Psychiatrist Looks at His Profession, Little, Brown, 1995.

Doing Documentary Work, Oxford University Press (New York City), 1997.

(With Robert E. Coles, Daniel A. Coles, and Michael H. Coles) *The Youngest Parents: Teenage Pregnancy as it Shapes Lives,* photographs by Jocelyn Lee and John Moses, Norton, 1997.

Also author of *The Call of Stories,* 1989, and *The Moral Intelligence of Children.*

CONTRIBUTOR

Charles Rolo, editor, *Psychiatry in American Life,* Little, Brown, 1963.

Erik H. Erikson, editor, *Youth: Change and Challenge,* Basic Books (New York City), 1963.

Talcott Parsons and Kenneth Clark, editors, *The Negro American,* Houghton, 1966.

Jules Masserman, editor, *Science and Psychoanalysis,* Volume 9, Grune (New York City), 1966.

James L. Sundquist, *On Fighting Poverty,* Basic Books, 1969.

Philip Kelley and Ronald Hudson, editors, *Diary by E. B. B.: The Unpublished Diary of Elizabeth Barrett Browning, 1831-1832,* Ohio University Press (Athens), 1969.

John H. Fandberg, editor, *Introduction to the Behavioral Sciences,* Holt (New York City), 1969.

Ross Spears and Jude Cassidy, *Agee: His Life Remembered,* Holt, 1985.

Helen Levitt, *In the Street: Chalk Drawings and Messages, New York City, 1938-1948,* Duke University Press (Durham, NC), 1987.

Contributor to numerous periodicals and professional journals, including *Atlantic Monthly, New Yorker, New Republic, New York Review of Books, Book Week, Partisan Review, Harper's, Saturday Review, New York Times Book Review, Yale Review, American Journal of Psychiatry,* and *Commonweal.*

OTHER

Contributing editor, *New Republic,* 1966—; member of editorial board, *American Scholar,* 1968—, *Contemporary Psychoanalysis,* 1969-70, and *Child Psychiatry and Human Development,* 1969—.

SIDELIGHTS: Robert Coles has spent his professional life exploring and illuminating the inner world of children. His numerous works on child psychology include the Pulitzer Prize-winning series *Children in Crisis,* a study of childhood development under stressful circumstances. Coles was trained as a psychiatrist, but he tempers his scientific conclusions with humanism, recognizing and celebrating the individual within the group or the trend. As Jonathan Kellerman puts it in the *Los Angeles Times Book Review,* the author "has seemingly ignored the delineation between the academic and the popular, producing books that are scholarly, yet accessible, writing with warmth, clarity and grace that set him apart in a field notorious for jargon-laden puffery."

A native of the Boston area, Coles attended college at Harvard University. As an undergraduate he came under the influence of several notable scholars, chief among them physician-poet William Carlos Williams. The association with Williams proved momentous for Coles; in a 1989 interview with *CA,* Coles declared Williams' influence: "[I became] so involved with him that my own interests began to echo his." Just as Williams had, Coles decided to train as a doctor. He received his medical education at Columbia University, specializing in child psychiatry, and the studies he undertook in the early 1960s began to reflect his thorough grounding in literature and the humanities. *New York Times Book Review* correspondent Helen Bevington writes that Coles "reminds one of Williams, with the same moral imagination, the kindness and compassion—though without the truculent manner, the toughness, the profanity, the anger, the scorn of intellectuals that marked the man he came to revere." Bevington continues: "The main lesson Williams the doctor taught [Coles] was always to listen to his patient, not only listen to his story but confide to him one's own, since only through stories can one person fully enter another's life.

Slowly . . . Dr. Coles learned to let the patient be the teacher, without hurrying to a diagnosis."

As an author, Coles also departs from standard academic practice by allowing his subjects to tell their own stories and by listening to them over many years as their circumstances change. In the *New York Times Book Review,* Neil Postman remarks that Coles "is to the stories that children have to tell what Homer was to the tale of the Trojan War. . . . He is at his best when he is listening to children talk, recording their talk and then transforming their talk into a kind of narrative poetry." Coles' books, Postman adds, are "a major contribution to our understanding of how children become socialized. . . . But these books, like the *Iliad,* are not about conclusions. They are about the myths, prejudices, worries and observations from which children generate their opinions and loyalties."

Talking about the *Children of Crisis* series, Coles explained to *CA* in 1989: "My task was to be a mediator of sorts between two worlds—a translator, I've been called, correctly, and also maybe a storyteller. Instead of being the social science theorist or the psychoanalytic clinician, I think I became the one who listens to what is happening in the lives of people, listens to their stories as they're told, and then relates those stories to others as best he can as a writer. . . . the primary intent of the *Children of Crisis* series—and of the two recent books that I consider part of that series, *The Moral Life of Children* and *The Political Life of Children*—is to convey to the ordinary reader some sense of the way children think and feel by conveying the stories they have to tell." Coles credits his wife as a major force shaping his perspectives and procedures used in researching of the series' initial book, *A Study in Courage and Fear,* and thus influencing subsequent books: "I think the whole effort would have fallen flat on its face if my wife hadn't taken on as a project to wean me away from a certain kind of professional decorum, if not arrogance. . . . she got me to relax and take off my necktie and sit on the floor with people, to eat with them and watch television with them and become part of their lives. . . . I was simply trying to be amidst events and let them in their own ways teach me and perhaps give me a kind of language for apprehending them"

Coles' monumental *Children of Crisis,* series evolved from events the author witnessed while present in the deep South in the early 1960s during the first tense moments of integration. He was astounded by the courage some black children showed as they entered integrated schools through crowds of jeering, hostile adults. Volume I of *Children in Crisis,* titled *A Study in Courage and Fear,* documents the feelings of these black youngsters as they face threats and insults. The work was hailed as a sensitive portrayal of the effects of discrimination on its youngest victims. Coles followed this study with similar ones on migrant workers, Eskimos and Indians, Appalachian children, and children of the wealthy.

Coles' work on the *Children of Crisis* series and other studies in child psychology earned him a prestigious MacArthur fellowship in 1981. The fellowship provided a monthly stipend that allowed Coles to undertake his research on an international basis. In 1986 he released two books, *The Political Life of Children* and *The Moral Life of Children,* that drew on interviews in South Africa, Brazil, Northern Ireland, Poland, Southeast Asia, Nicaragua, French-speaking Canada, and a number of American locales. In her review of both works, *Washington Post Book World* contributor Katherine Paterson writes: "Children tend not to say what we want to hear when we want to hear it, but, to the patient, perceptive adult who takes them seriously, their words are eloquent, disturbing, transforming. Most of us are not good listeners, but the moral and political life of our nation would take a giant leap forward if we were to pay close attention to this man who is."

The MacArthur fellowship also allowed Coles to pursue other interests, including biographies of Catholic altruists Dorothy Day and Simone Weil, essays, book reviews, lectures, and literary criticism. In the *Times Literary Supplement,* Iain Bamforth commends Coles for his "conviction that appreciation of literature is a useful adjunct to the study of medicine." Coles, adds the critic, "lends a cautionary voice to what is otherwise understated or overlooked in a profession which tends, like many others, to talk only to itself." *National Review* contributor Thomas Molnar likewise concludes that in his essays Coles "leaves the reader with the impression of a decent and religious man with common-sensical views."

Coles' fascination with the human spirit, particularly that ability to transcend self-interest and act for the sole benefit of others, prompted his 1993 work, *The Call of Service: A Witness to Idealism.* Examining what he terms man's "moral hunger" and "the phenomenology of service" that is its outward manifestation, Coles describes his personal experiences with the numerous individuals he has met and come to know over the years: from Vista workers, to personal heroes William Carlos Williams and Dorothy Day, to his own parents. As such, *The Call of Service* is also memoir, revealing what it is to be a middle-class American attempting to eliminate the inequalities that permeate U.S. society through countless hours spent teaching and gaining understanding of others. Coles "tries to understand the volunteers," comments Chicago's *Tribune Books* commentator James North—"to investigate what combination of religion, ethics, even patriotism. . . motivates these people to donate their time and energy, sometimes for years on end." Francine du Plessix Gray notes in a *New York Times Book Review* appraisal that *The Call of Service* "is flawed by Dr. Coles' habitual reliance on oral history [and] by the drabness of his interviewees' responses." However, E. J. Dionne Jr. maintains in the *Washington Post Book World* that "by allowing so many to speak of their experiences, Coles slowly and quietly explodes almost any preconceptions readers might have about what motivates idealists."

Coles' presentation of children's speech has been an issue for more than one critic. In a 1989 *CA* interview, Cole commented on his philosophy and practice in reproducing children's speech for his books: "I listen to particular children sometimes for as long as five or six years, to the recurrent themes and topics that they bring up; and I keep recording, either with a tape recorder or in notes, what they have to say. Then my job becomes one of pulling together many conversations and remarks into a rather limited presentation in the pages of what becomes a book. It's a distillation and a condensation, a "reading" of a particular life through an examination of the spoken words—and of the pictures drawn or painted. . . . What a novelist does is try to highlight a certain moment. That's what I try to do too, so I pick those remarks of the children that I think are most convincing, or illustrative of certain themes, or dramatic or provocative. . . . I'm trying to be as suggestive as I can in the selections I come up with so that the reader can glimpse something about some kind of essence in a particular child, something of a quintessential psychological and moral and even spiritual 'reality' in that child."

In addition to writing both nonfiction and several volumes of poetry, Coles has served as professor of psychiatry and medical humanities at Harvard University since 1978, where his curriculum includes literature classes for students of medicine, law, and

architecture. In fact, writes Fitzhugh Mullan in the *Washington Post Book World,* the most consistent theme in Coles' work "is the importance of the humanities in our lives." The reviewer continues: "It is literature in all its forms—the interview, the child's story, the poem and the novel—that preoccupies Coles [because] . . . it is the humanities that recognize the individual and resist the tendency toward the average that is celebrated by statisticians." Kellerman concludes that in his own writings, Coles has blended scientific inquiry and literary form to great effect. Kellerman calls the author "a master chronicler, providing few answers but asking his questions so eloquently that his writings emerge as classic portrayals of social upheaval and its effect upon the young."

BIOGRAPHICAL/CRITICAL SOURCES:

BOOKS

Coles, Robert *The Mind's Fate: A Psychiatrist Looks at His Profession,* Little, Brown, 1995.
Coles, Robert, *The Call of Service: A Witness to Idealism,* Houghton, 1993.
Hilligoss, Susan, *Robert Coles,* Twayne (New York City), 1997.
Woodruff, Jay, and Sarah Carew Woodruff, editors, *Conversations with Robert Coles,* University Press of Mississippi, 1992.

PERIODICALS

American Spectator, March, 1989.
Art News, March, 1993.
Booklist, April 15, 1985; November 15, 1985; January 15, 1986; March 15, 1989; January 1, 1990; November 15, 1990; November 1, 1992; January 15, 1995; November 15, 1996.
Boston Review, February, 1986.
Chicago Tribune, April 24, 1979; May 13, 1986; March 24, 1989.
Choice, November, 1986; December, 1986; November, 1987; February, 1988; June, 1991.
Christian Century, February 27, 1991; December 1, 1993.
Christian Science Monitor, May 2, 1968; February 12, 1991; February 4, 1993; December 9, 1993.
Commentary, September, 1990.
Commonweal, March 13, 1987; November 6, 1987; March 9, 1990; March 8, 1991.

Kirkus Reviews, July 15, 1993; November 15, 1996; February 15, 1997.
Library Journal, January 1, 1972; March 1, 1978.
Los Angeles Times, June 20, 1985.
Los Angeles Times Book Review, February 9, 1986; September 13, 1987; October 3, 1993.
Maclean's, March 17, 1986.
National Review, June 2, 1989.
New Republic, August 31, 1987.
New Yorker, February 10, 1986; January 7, 1991.
New York Review of Books, March 9, 1972.
New York Times, January 10, 1979; October 20, 1984.
New York Times Book Review, June 11, 1978; January 19, 1986; September 6, 1987; January 3, 1988; December 25, 1988; February 26, 1989; April 30, 1989; November 25, 1990; June 9, 1991; October 6, 1991; May 10, 1992; December 13, 1992; November 21, 1993; February 12, 1995; September 10, 1995.
People, December 24, 1990.
Publishers Weekly, March 29, 1985; December 20, 1985; May 1, 1987; May 15, 1987; March 18, 1988; July 15, 1988; October 21, 1988; January 20, 1989; February 3, 1989; September 15, 1989; October 26, 1990; November 16, 1990; January 4, 1991; September 27, 1991; November 29, 1991; January 20, 1992; September 21, 1992; July 12, 1993; December 19, 1994; July 10, 1995; July 29, 1996; November 18, 1996.
Saturday Review, November 21, 1970.
School Library Journal, August, 1988; March, 1995; June, 1996; December, 1986.
Sewanee Review, October, 1989; April, 1995.
Time, February 14, 1972; July 15, 1974; March 17, 1986; January 21, 1991.
Times Literary Supplement, November 21, 1980; July 7, 1989.
Tribune Books (Chicago), November 9, 1980; December 1, 1985; December 23, 1990; October 13, 1991; October 17, 1993.
USA Today, January 17, 1986.
USA Weekend, October 15-17, 1993.
U. S. News & World Report, December 3, 1990.
Village Voice, August 27, 1985; December 24, 1985..
Virginia Quarterly Review, autumn, 1986; spring, 1989; summer, 1990; summer, 1992; winter, 1994.
Wall Street Journal, November 15, 1993.
Washington Post, June 4, 1985.
Washington Post Book World, June 29, 1980; February 2, 1986; May 8, 1988; October 10, 1993.*

COLLIER, Gaydell M(aier) 1935-

PERSONAL: Born June 28, 1935, in Long Island, NY; daughter of Harry (a building manager) and Jean (Gaydell) Maier; married Roy Hugh Collier (a rancher), December 27, 1955; children: Sam Patrick, Frank Robert, Jenny Gay, Fred Melder. *Education:* Attended Middlebury College, 1953-55, and University of Wyoming, 1955-56.

ADDRESSES: Home—Backpocket Ranch, Rural Route 364 Farrall Rd., Sundance, WY 82729-9520. *Office*—Crook County Library, P.O. Box 910, Sundance, WY 82729.

CAREER: Freelance writer and editor, 1962—. Member of library staff at University of Wyoming, 1970-73, head of circulation department, 1973-74; owner and manager of Backpocket Ranch Bookshop, 1977—; Crook County (WY) Library System, director, 1985—. Member of board of trustees of Albany County Public Library, 1967-72, and of Vore Buffalo Jump Foundation, 1992—; member of Wyoming State Advisory Council on Libraries, 1971-72.

MEMBER: Western Writers of America, Women Writing the West, Wyoming Writers, Wyoming Library Association, Bearlodge Writers.

AWARDS, HONORS: Wyoming Library Association award, 1974, for outstanding dedication and contributions to Coe Library, Albany County Library as trustee, to WLA Library section, and to the world of books, 1974; book of the month selection, Classic Book Club, 1979, and Best Nonfiction Book, Wyoming Writers, 1980, both for *Basic Training of Horses;* Wyoming Writers Contest awards, first place, traditional poetry, and third place, non-fiction (essay), both 1981, first place, Christmas card poem, 1982, third place, short story, 1983, and second place, Wyoming essay, 1990; Creative Non-Fiction Weekend Anthology, Casper College, 1989; named Wyoming Librarian of the Year, 1990; honorable mention, Wyoming Arts Council, literature fellowship, 1992.

WRITINGS:

(Editor) John Gorman, *The Western Horse: Its Types and Training,* fifth edition (Collier was not associated with earlier editions), Interstate (Danville, IL), 1967.

(With Eleanor Prince) *Basic Horsemanship, English and Western: A Complete Guide for Riders and Instructors,* Doubleday (New York City), 1974.

(With Prince) *Basic Training for Horses: English and Western,* Doubleday, 1979, paperback edition, 1989.

Basic Horse Care, Doubleday, 1979, paperback edition, 1989.

(Editor with Linda Hasselstrom and Nancy Curtis) *Leaning into the Wind,* Houghton (Boston), 1997.

OTHER

Contributor to anthologies, including *Sportsource,* edited by Bob Anderson, World Publications, 1975; *Windsingers,* Wyoming Writers fiction anthology, 1984; *Visions of Wyoming,* Casper Star Tribune (essays), 1993; *Western Horse Tales* (Western Writers of America anthology), edited by Don Worcester, Republic of Texas Press, 1994.

Contributor of articles and reviews to magazines and newspapers, including *Christian Science Monitor, Discovery, Horse of Course, National Wildlife, Poets & Writers, Science News, Science World, Smithsonian,* and *Westering.* Member of advisory board of *WLA Roundup* (Wyoming Library Association), 1973.

Contributor of book reviews to periodicals, including *Library Journal* (reviewed for 12 years), *The Roundup Quarterly* (Western Writers of America), *The Leader* (NOLS), and others.

SIDELIGHTS: Gaydell Collier told *CA:* "I grew up surrounded by books—floor-to-ceiling bookcases in the dining room and books in every room of the house. Today, as a writer, editor, library director, and bookstore owner, I'm still surrounded by books.

"But my main source of inspiration comes from nature—from the wisdom of animals, from the infinite beauty and variety of the Western landscape. I believe that it is in the appreciation and understanding of beauty that our lives are ultimately expressed.

"One great source of pleasure for me (along with my family) has been to encourage others to write—and then to stand in awe as I watch their progress (I'm thinking especially of such writers as Page Lambert, Kathleen O'Neal Gear, and W. Michael Gear). Working with the many women who wrote for *Leaning into the Wind* has proved to me that the bud of

beauty in every one of us can flower beyond all expectation."

Collier's *Basic Horse Care* was published in a German translation edition by Albert Mueller Verlag, in 1992.

*   *   *

COOKE, Ann
  See COLE, Joanna

*   *   *

CRACE, Jim 1946-
  (James Turton)

PERSONAL: Born March 1, 1946, in Brocket Hall, Lemsford, Hertfordshire, England; son of Charles Sydney (an insurance agent) and Edith Grace (a homemaker; maiden name, Holland) Crace; married Pamela Ann Turton (a teacher), January 3, 1975; children: Thomas Charles, Lauren Rose. *Education:* Birmingham College of Commerce, London, B.A. (with honors), 1968. *Politics:* "Libertarian Socialist." *Religion:* "Atheist." *Avocational interests:* "Family and garden; tennis and politics."

ADDRESSES: Home—Moseley, Birmingham, England.

CAREER: Sudanese Educational Television, Khartoum, volunteer producer and writer, 1968-69; Kgosi Kgari Sechele Secondary School, Molepolole, Botswana, teacher of English, 1969-70; freelance radio and feature journalist, 1970-86; full-time novelist, 1986—. Midlands Arts Centre, writer-in-residence, 1981-83; Birmingham Festival of Readers and Writers, founder and director, 1983; West Midlands Arts, chair of literature panel, 1984-85.

MEMBER: International PEN, National Union of Journalists, Labour Party, Campaign for Nuclear Disarmament, Anti-Apartheid.

AWARDS, HONORS: Arts Council of Great Britain major writing bursary, 1976; West Midlands Arts writing award, 1980; Whitbread Award for first novel, David Higham Prize for Fiction, and *Guardian* Fiction Prize, all 1986, and Premio Antico

Fattore, 1987, all for *Continent;* GAP International Award for Literature, Echoing Green Foundation, 1989, for *The Gift of Stones.*

WRITINGS:

Continent (stories), Harper (New York City), 1986, reprinted, Ecco Press (Hopewell, NJ), 1997.
The Gift of Stones (novel), Scribner (New York City), 1988.
Arcadia (novel), Atheneum, (New York City), 1991.
Signals of Distress (novel), Farrar, Straus (New York City), 1995.
Quarantine (novel), Farrar, Straus, 1997.

Author of radio plays *Salateen* and *The Bird Has Flown,* BBC-Radio. Contributor to *Introduction Six,* Faber, 1977; contributor to periodicals, including the *Sunday Times, Telegraph Sunday Magazine,* and the *Times Literary Supplement.*

SIDELIGHTS: Jim Crace is known for his original fiction probing the social and political nature of human beings. Although his works are often remarkable for their unique settings—*Continent* takes place on an imaginary continent and *The Gift of Stones* is set in a prehistoric era—the books' scenery becomes subordinate to Crace's examination of communal behavior. "I'm not interested in truths, [or in] drawing an accurate picture of the real world," Crace told Robin Pogrebin in the *New York Times Book Review.* "I'm interested in exploring the verities of the human condition. . . . I believe that in some respects, if you hit the [nail] of storytelling right on the head, then you can come up with lies which are more powerful than any truth."

Crace's first book, *Continent,* portrays an invented and unnamed continent modeled after the Third World. A collection of seven loosely connected stories, the work contains vignettes that demonstrate how development impinges on old-world ways, often exploiting the continent's natives. Nevertheless, Crace once told a *CA* interviewer that the work was never meant to be a polemic, or even to represent his own opinions. "With *Continent* I wasn't writing about what I knew—political views that I'd already formed about the relationship between the Western World and the Third World, or between the new ways of mankind and the old," he explained. "I was writing about what I was interested in and what I still wanted to debate and discover. So that book poses questions rather than answers them; I find that a

much more interesting way of approaching narrative than writing political tracts."

Robert Olen Butler describes the essence of *Continent* in the *New York Times Book Review:* "Tradition and progress, superstition and rationalism, the primal and the mercantile struggle for the souls of men." In one story, for example, a city-educated young man returns to his small village and contemplates how to carry on his father's business of selling milk with supposed magical properties. The son decides to continue marketing the milk as magical, determining that preying on the villager's superstitious nature can be quite profitable. In another story, electricity is introduced to a town by way of a ceiling fan in a local establishment. The fan packs so much power, though, that it knocks bystanders against walls while the urbanized installer of the appliance stands safely in the "calm" of the fan directly beneath. And, in the story "Sins and Virtues," a calligrapher, whose antiquated signs are suddenly in great demand in the United States, is urged by his government to produce new masterpieces for export. Elderly and exhausted, the craftsman is unable to produce signs in his former manner and resorts to submitting forgeries of his own work for sale; notes the calligrapher, "The quest for Meaning in Form belongs to an age long past."

Continent was hailed enthusiastically by reviewers. Calling the book "brilliant, provocative and delightful," Butler writes: "One of the basic tasks of fiction is to strip down and rearrange experience in order to distance the reader from habitual reactions to surface reality and thereby, paradoxically, draw him closer to a deeper reality. Mr. Crace . . . does this splendidly." Crace was not only applauded for creating a fictional landscape that highlights social and political realities, but also for composing lucid and lyrical prose. While John Melmoth in his *Times Literary Supplement* article deems the stories of *Continent* "sparsely and elegantly constructed," Brian Stonehill observes in the *Los Angeles Times Book Review* that "Crace's language is alive, a distinctive voice, an engaging character in itself. Life not only is the subject of, but is subject to, his artful words. We welcome his new-found 'Continent' to our maps."

Crace moves from an imaginary present-day setting to an actual historical one with his second work of fiction, *The Gift of Stones.* Set in the late-Stone Age, the book depicts a community whose livelihood rests on its stone-crafting skills. The villagers' flint tools and weapons are so superior that trading them sustains the community fully, thereby affording it seclusion from outside influences and dangers. Visions of the outside world, though, are brought to the village by a storyteller who, rendered useless as a laborer when he lost one arm as a boy, travels in search of adventures with which to embellish his tales. During his travels he befriends a young woman, Doe, and her daughter. When the three return to the storyteller's village, they find the community in economic turmoil. Doe is then mysteriously killed by a bronze-headed spear, thus foretelling the village's demise in the face of technological advancement. The community disbands under the leadership of the storyteller. "Formerly," observes Richard Eder in the *Los Angeles Times Book Review,* "the storyteller's fictions had simply been their entertainment; now they are prophecy and all they have left."

The setting and plot of *The Gift of Stones,* reviewers note, is secondary to Crace's efforts to explore themes of art and technological progress. The author himself once told *CA:* "I was interested in what happens when a community is robbed of the certainty of wealth and occupation that is provided by having jobs." The resulting novel "is not a 'you are there' experience, but a contemplative one," comments Jane Smiley in the *New York Times Book Review.* "The setting . . . is, rather than an attempt to create a world, a conceit that provides the author scope for his meditation. The reader seeking to be swept into the past will be disappointed." Describing how the author conveys his themes, *Chicago Tribune Books* contributor Perry Glasser notes, "Crace writes allegory. Every carefully shaped event advances an idea and illuminates one more facet of the argument. *The Gift of Stones* is not about people, but about imaginative art, storytelling in particular, and the complicated relationship between art and the realm of commerce that at once supports and despises its artists." And *Times Literary Supplement* writer Richard Deveson offers another interpretation of Crace's intentions: "He suggests . . . that the artist may . . . be the true progressive, and that it is the imagination, rather than economics, that will teach a society how to regenerate itself."

The Gift of Stones earned overwhelming appreciation from critics. "One of Crace's virtues is to make a deep imprint with light steps," remarks Eder. "The implications of his novel are complex, but they grow out of simplicity." Commenting on the author's prose, Glasser points out that "Crace's language, crackling with sensory detail and intensely imagined, achieves the kind of effortless ease that comes only

with extraordinary work and care. . . . Poetry lurks in this prose." And Smiley avers that "*The Gift of Stones* is a work to be read and savored, full of thought, but also full of the concrete world . . . a prose poem where the natural world is new and powerfully evoked."

The success of *Continent* and *The Gift of Stones* allowed Crace to devote himself full-time to fiction after having worked as a scriptwriter with the British Broadcasting Corporation and as a journalist for two decades. Crace told *Publishers Weekly* that, although he is a disciplined worker who spends at least five hours a day in his office—and who sets a 5,000-word per-week goal for himself—he still views himself as an adventurer. "I am not like some writers who have a flow-chart on their walls before they start writing," he said. "I definitely fly by the seat of my pants."

Crace once elaborated in *CA:* "One of the key pieces of advice which colors the way I write is something I read many years ago from a Chinese poet called Wei T'ai. He said that poetry presents 'the thing' in order to convey the feeling. 'If a writer wishes to set heaven and earth in motion and call up the spirits, then he should be precise about the thing and reticent about the feeling or the emotion,' In other words, the writer ought to describe the coffin and not the grief. This has been advice that I have applied to fiction. I don't want to define for the reader the heights or depths of emotion that he or she should feel, but to provide the raw materials that will elicit that response independently from the reader. That's one of my narrative methods."

That method informs Crace's 1995 novel *Signals of Distress,* a tale set in a small, English fishing village in 1836. The story begins with a storm that grounds an ocean-going American vessel on a sandbar near fictitious Wherrytown. Simultaneously, a moralistic entrepreneur named Aymer Smith arrives via steamboat, preparing to tell the local kelpers that he no longer needs their services in the production of soap and is hoping to find a wife. The zealous Smith soon comes into conflict with the American ship's captain after he sets the captain's slave, Otto, free, giving the African *carte blanche* to run away during a snow storm without food or sufficient clothing. Calling Crace "one of the brightest lights in contemporary British fiction," *New York Times Book Review* correspondent Charles Johnson describes *Signals of Distress* as "a quiet tale of strangers thrown together by caprice, emigrants, business scions, paupers, street toughs and former slaves who, before their paths diverge, find their lives are unintentionally and irreversibly linked."

As is often the case with Crace's fiction, the actual historical details in *Signals of Distress* are less important than the tone of the narrative and the interplay of the characters. "The point of my fiction is to adopt a tone of voice and use language and make things up which sound authentic, that are more real than real," the author once explained to *CA*. This technique proved useful in *Signals of Distress,* a novel "in which history is reimagined, viewed through a late 20th century microscope," according to *Chicago Tribune Books* reviewer William O'Rourke. The reviewer adds: "Crace's novel has the look of miniaturized Dickens, revved up and sleeked down for the 1990s. . . . Crace's cast is to a man (and woman) vivid and compelling."

The notices on *Signals of Distress* have not been universally positive. Although Tim Parks comments in *Spectator* that Crace's "blend of period pastiched terse modern prose is excellent and engaging, with the set piece descriptions—the shipwreck, the night fishing, the snowstorm— particularly strong," the critic contends, "what promised to be an excellent plot crumbles away in a series of costume sideshows, beautifully written, but somehow inconsequential, even when lives are at stake. In short, the book fails to focus." Conversely, in the *Times Literary Supplement,* T. J. Binyon asserts that *Signals of Distress* "is an intriguing work; more approachable, being less schematic, than Crace's three earlier books." And *Library Journal* contributor Barbara Hoffert concludes that the book is "real, vivid and indelible . . . a quiet, thoughtful work that pulls the reader in powerfully."

Crace admitted in *Publishers Weekly* that the success of his fiction has "seemed like the resolution of a lot of unspoken dreams," dating back to his student days when his father encouraged him to write. "There are five impulses which form the basis of my fiction," he explained in a *CA* interview: "one, the simple pleasures of invention, of convincingly merging the real and the concocted, the mundane and the bizarre; two, an admiration for the disciplines of good journalism—clarity and depth of expression, orderliness of structure and design; three, a preoccupation with international issues and politics, and a disdain for the domestic; four, an instinctive preference for restrained and dispassionate prose which avoids sentiment and declamation but which takes its power from the narrative itself and not from authorial intervention; and five, a 'fear-of-self' hostility towards politi-

cal repression, conservatism, racism, sexism, Puritanism, officialdom, and rules."

BIOGRAPHICAL/CRITICAL SOURCES:

PERIODICALS

Boston Globe, November 1, 1992, p. B40.
Commonweal, June 18, 1993, p. 26.
Guardian (London), September 30, 1986.
Library Journal, August, 1995, p. 114.
Los Angeles Times Book Review, April 12, 1987, p. 4; April 9, 1989, p. 3; October 4, 1992, p. 3; January 28, 1996, p. 9.
New Republic, May 6, 1996.
New Statesman & Society, September 2, 1994, pp. 36-37.
New York Review of Books, December 3, 1992, p. 14.
New York Times Book Review, June 28, 1987, p. 30; July 16, 1989, p. 12; October 18, 1992, p. 11; September 24, 1995, p. 20; February 9, 1997, p. 32.
Observer (London), October 12, 1986, p. 29; September 4, 1988, p. 41; September 11, 1994.
Publishers Weekly, July 10, 1995, p. 42; October 2, 1995, pp. 49-50; November 6, 1995, p. 59.
Spectator, March 21, 1992, p. 34; September 3, 1994, pp. 36-37.
Times (London), October 16, 1986.
Times Literary Supplement, October 3, 1986, p. 1113; September 2, 1988, p. 952; March 13, 1992, p. 22; September 2, 1994, p. 12.
Tribune Books (Chicago), April 16, 1989, p. 6; November 15, 1992, p. 3; December 31, 1995, pp. 3, 7; March 9, 1997, p. 8.
Village Voice, June 30, 1987, p. 58.
Washington Post, June 4, 1987; December 1, 1992, p. C2.*

*   *   *

CRAVEN, Wes(ley Earl) 1939-

PERSONAL: Born August 2, 1939, in Cleveland, OH; son of Paul (a factory worker) and Caroline (a secretary; maiden name, Miller) Craven; married Bonnie Susan Broecker, June, 1964 (divorced, 1970); married Millicent Eleanor Meyer (a flight attendant), July 25, 1982 (divorced, 1985); children: (first marriage) Jonathan, Jessica. *Education:* Wheaton College, B.A., 1963; Johns Hopkins University, M.A., 1964.   *Politics:* Egalitarian. *Avocational interests:* Flying, playing classical guitar, art, cinema, jazz and classical music, carpentry, gardening, traveling.

ADDRESSES: Office—Wes Craven Films, Metro-Goldwyn-Mayer Television, 10000 West Washington Blvd., Suite 3016, Culver City, CA 90232. *Agent*—Lin Radner, International Creative Management, 8942 Wilshire Blvd., Beverly Hills, CA 90211.

CAREER: Writer, director, and producer for films and television. Westminster College, New Wilmington, PA, professor of humanities, 1964-65; Clarkson University, Potsdam, NY, professor of humanities, 1965-67; taught high school in Madrid, Spain, and Waddington, NY, 1967-68; also worked as a messenger and a post-production assistant for a film production house and as synch-up assistant to filmmaker Sean Cunningham. Director of films, including *Deadly Friend,* Warner Brothers, 1986; *The Serpent and the Rainbow,* Universal, 1988; *Vampire in Brooklyn,* Paramount, 1995; Scream, *Woods Entertainment/Dimension Films,* 1996; and *Scream 2,* Craven/Maddelena Films/Konrad Pictures/Dimension Films/Miramax, 1997. Other film work includes editor for *You've Got to Walk It Like You Talk It or You'll Lose That Beat,* JER Pictures, 1971; appearance as Man Neighbor in *Shocker,* Universal, 1989; and adviser for *Bloodfist II,* Concorde, 1990. Director of television productions, including "A Little Peace and Quiet," "Wordplay," "Shatterday," "Chameleon," "The Road Not Taken," "Her Pilgrim's Soul," and "Dealer's Choice," all episodes for *Twilight Zone* (series), Columbia Broadcasting System, Inc. (CBS-TV), 1985; *Stranger in Our House* (movie), National Broadcasting Company, Inc. (NBC-TV), 1978; *Invitation to Hell* (movie), CBS-TV, c. 1982; *Chiller* (movie), American Broadcasting Companies, Inc. (ABC-TV), c. 1983; and *Casebusters* (movie), ABC-TV, 1986. Other television work includes executive producer for *The People Next Door* (series), CBS-TV, 1989; and appearance in *Fear in the Dark* (documentary), Arts & Entertainment, 1991. Also see below.

MEMBER: Writers Guild of America, Directors Guild of America, Screen Actors Guild.

AWARDS, HONORS: Best picture award, London Film Festival, 1978, and Sitges International Fantasy Film Festival Honors, 1978, both for *The Hills Have Eyes;* Madrid Film Festival, most popular film, 1980, for *Deadly Blessing,* and best director, 1988;

Critic's Choice Award, French Science Fiction and Horror Film Festival, 1984, best horror film nomination, Academy for Science Fiction, Fantasy, and Horror, 1984, and best horror film award, Avoriaz International Festival of Fantasy and Science Fiction Films, 1985, all for *A Nightmare on Elm Street;* grand prize, Avoriaz International Festival of Fantasy and Science Fiction Films, 1992, for *The People under the Stairs.*

WRITINGS:

SCREENPLAYS

(And director and editor) *Last House on the Left,* American International, 1972.
(And director and editor) *The Hills Have Eyes,* Vanguard, 1978.
(With Glenn M. Benest and Matthew Barr; and director) *Deadly Blessing,* United Artists, 1981.
(And director) *Swamp Thing,* Embassy, 1982.
(And director) *A Nightmare on Elm Street,* New Line Cinema, 1984.
(And director) *The Hills Have Eyes: Part II,* VTC, 1985.
(With Bruce Wagner; and executive producer) *A Nightmare on Elm Street Part III: Dream Warriors,* New Line Cinema, 1987.
(And director and executive producer) *Shocker,* Universal, 1989.
(And director and executive producer) *The People under the Stairs,* Universal, 1991.
(And director) *Wes Craven's New Nightmare,* New Line Cinema, 1994.

FOR TELEVISION

(With Richard Rothstein; and director) *Invitation to Hell* (movie), ABC-TV, 1984.
(With J. D. Feigelson; and director) *Chiller* (movie), CBS-TV, 1985.
The Twilight Zone (series pilot), CBS-TV, 1985.
(And director and executive producer) *Night Visions* (movie), NBC-TV, 1990.
(And executive producer) *Nightmare Cafe,* NBC-TV, 1992.

OTHER

Writer for cabaret comedy.

ADAPTATIONS: Bob Italia has adapted *A Nightmare on Elm Street* and several other Craven films into novels, all published by Abdo & Daughters, Minneapolis.

WORK IN PROGRESS: A film, *Fiddlefest,* about an inner-city violin teacher; a remake of the 1962 horror film *Carnival of Souls,* with Craven as executive producer; a novel, *The Fountain Society.*

SIDELIGHTS: With films such as *Last House on the Left, The Hills Have Eyes, A Nightmare on Elm Street, Scream,* and *Scream 2,* writer and director Wes Craven has established himself as one of the most innovative and successful creators of horror films. Dubbed "The Sultan of Slash" and "The Guru of Gore" by reviewers, Craven goes beyond traditional horror standards of violence and bloodshed by frequently incorporating dreams and other psychological phenomena into his presentations, a strategy that allows even the most innocuous settings to become arenas for terror. Craven achieved one of his greatest successes in the creation of Freddy Krueger, the homicidal bogeyman who stalks and kills his young suburban victims in their dreams in *A Nightmare on Elm Street.* A box-office hit, the film inspired a number of sequels and a syndicated television show. In 1996 and 1997, Craven made yet another mark on popular culture by directing Kevin Williamson's scripts for *Scream* and *Scream 2,* movies that made fun of the conventions of horror films.

Born in 1939, Craven grew up in a strict Baptist, working-class family in Cleveland, Ohio. His fundamentalist parents considered most Hollywood movies "too sexual, too violent and too anti-Christian for their children to see," Craven told *Newsweek* writer Jeff Giles in 1997. Craven added that he is uncertain if his affinity for horrific subjects was a reaction to his upbringing. "(T)here was stuff I needed to work out," Giles quoted him as saying. "And I don't know if it was rage from a youth that was so oppressed." After high school Craven left home to attend the religiously affiliated Wheaton College, where he received a degree in English and psychology—and where some of his stories for the college literary magazine were deemed immoral by school authorities. He went on to study at Johns Hopkins University, earning a master's degree in philosophy and writing. After teaching for three years as a humanities professor, Craven decided to pursue his interest in filmmaking. Craven once commented to *Authors & Artists for Young Adults* (*AAYA*): "My interest in filmmaking really came out of left field. There was a sort of a buzz of *cinema verite,* filmmaking being written about a lot in things like *Evergreen Magazine* at the time when I found myself fascinated by it. Maybe it was due to my being disallowed films as a youngster, or the fact that my friend's father with

whom I spent so much time while my mother worked was an avid filmmaker (home movies). I can't explain quite where it came from, but I basically decided to make a career move into films and left teaching."

After working a string of odd jobs around movie production houses, Craven met filmmaker Sean Cunningham, who later created the "Friday the 13th" series of movies. Craven explained to *AAYA* how Cunningham gave him the opportunity to work on his first film: "Sean was the first guy to hire me for something other than messenger. I kept the dailies for a little feature he was doing. We worked on that for about ten months and at the end of that time had a friendship. So when Sean got the offer to make a scary feature film, he said, 'Why don't we do it together?' and offered me the job of writing, directing, and cutting it. . . . I was on the absolute ground floor of making a film. I had never gone to film school, never even read a book on making a film. I knew nothing about coverage, screen directing, lenses and really just learned by doing."

The result of this collaboration was *Last House on the Left,* a 1972 film loosely based on director Ingmar Bergman's re-interpretation of a medieval ballad, *The Virgin Spring.* Craven's contemporary version of the story focuses on two teenage girls on their way to a rock-and-roll concert. They encounter a group of four ex-convicts who abduct, torture, rape, and kill the girls. Wandering through the woods where the killings took place, the murderers eventually find lodging in a suburban house, convincing the owners that they have been stranded because of car trouble. The homeowners happen to be the parents of one of the murdered girls and, when they discover evidence of what their house guests have done, enact their own grisly revenge on the killers. Although made on a relatively low budget, the film was successful with horror-film audiences and has remained a cult movie favorite. Roger Ebert described *Last House on the Left* in *Film Comment* as "a neglected American horror exploitation masterpiece on a par with [George Romero's] *Night of the Living Dead.* . . . Its very artlessness, its blunt force, makes it work." Robin Wood in *Film Comment* considered the violence of *Last House on the Left* to be an expression of larger social issues and stated: "No act of violence in the film is condoned, yet we are led to understand *every* act as the realization of potentials that exist within us all, that are intrinsic to our social and personal relationships."

Craven attributes the basis for the type of violence found in *Last House on the Left* to the violence inherent in human and family relations as well as modern American society, particularly as expressed in the events of the Vietnam War. Craven told Wood, "The family is the best microcosm to work with. . . . It's very much where most of our strong emotions or gut feelings come from. . . . I grew up in a white working-class family that was very religious, and there was an enormous amount of secrecy in the general commerce of our getting along with each other. . . . A lot of things were not spoken of or talked about. . . . As I got older I began to see that as a nation we were doing the same thing."

Craven uses family life as a starting point for another successful if not equally violent film, *The Hills Have Eyes*. On a holiday drive through the desert, members of a suburban family find themselves stranded when their car breaks down. Their troubles increase when they realize they are in the territory of a cannibalistic mutant people who are both violent and hungry. Most of the family is slaughtered, and those who survive have been severely compromised; the movie insinuates that in their fight to protect themselves, the remaining family members have become as uncivilized and violent as their attackers.

Craven described to *AAYA* his interest in portraying the type of violence seen in his first two films: "I'm interested in frightening people on a deep level, not just making them jump. My first two films blew away the cliches of handling violence. Before, screen violence had been neat and tidy; I made it painful and protracted and shocking and very human. And I made the people who were doing the killing human."

After the less profitable ventures *Deadly Blessing* and *Swamp Thing*, Craven found box-office success with *A Nightmare on Elm Street*. The film incorporates many of Craven's favorite elements: lack of communication between adolescents and adults, the unique horrors of suburban life, the fine line between dreams and reality, and some very creative killing. The film begins with four teenagers all having similar dreams, or rather nightmares, about a horribly scarred man with a hand equipped with long, razor-sharp blades. The villain, Freddy Krueger, was once arrested for committing a series of child murders in the Elm Street neighborhood and burned to death by a mob of angry parents when he was released on a legal technicality. Freddy has returned to take revenge on his killers by murdering their adolescent children from within their dreams. One by one the teenagers are pursued and caught in their dreams by Freddy, resulting in their very violent and bloody deaths in the real world. Only one, Nancy, manages to avoid Freddy by staying awake.

A Nightmare on Elm Street was generally praised as an intelligent and suspenseful horror film. Many credited the film's success to Craven's ability to place the events of the film in deceptively familiar territory. In a review for the *Washington Post*, Paul Attanasio wrote, "Craven . . . has a remarkable feel for the habits and humor of teen-agers; the sharp eye and ear with which he sketches his protagonists' early scenes, as they trick their parents into allowing them to slumber-party together, grounds the horror in everyday life." David Robinson in the London *Times* also appreciated the fact that the teenagers in the horror film "are, for once, real characters, not plasticized dollies." Other reviewers cited the psychological aspect of Craven's movie as a key to its effectiveness. *New Statesman* critic Frances Wheen called *A Nightmare on Elm Street* "a most elegant shocker," stating that the movie's plot "is simplicity itself [and] doubly effective because it recalls one's own half-forgotten childhood fears." Attanasio, summing up Craven's technique of combining graphic violence and dreamlike sequences of terror and suspense, described *A Nightmare on Elm Street* as "halfway between an exploitation flick and classic surrealism."

Busy with his next releases, the unsuccessful *The Hills Have Eyes: Part II* and *Deadly Friend*, Craven did not work on the first sequel to *A Nightmare on Elm Street*. He did, however, return to the movie series as executive producer and coauthor of *A Nightmare on Elm Street Part III: Dream Warriors,* a film directed by Chuck Russell. The plot features the heroine of the first *Nightmare* film, Nancy, who, several years after her original run-ins with Freddy, has become a dream disorder specialist. She arrives at a psychiatric clinic to treat seven suicidal teenagers who are all having the threatening dreams involving Freddy Krueger with which she is so familiar. While Nancy and the teenagers try to protect themselves and devise a plan to destroy Freddy, he continues to inflict creative and gory deaths on unfortunate victims, including, eventually, Nancy herself. Reviewers, often expressing lack of satisfaction with the plot as a whole, generally agreed that the dream sequences and the elaborate, and often humorous, forms of torture that Freddy devises were the strength of the film. Janet Maslin of the *New York Times* declared that "the film's dream sequences are ingenious, and they feature some remarkable nightmare images and special effects." The critic also proclaimed that while many of the film's characters were disappointing, "the real star is Freddy himself. . . . Freddy taunts his victims a lot more vocally and colorfully than most of his horror-film comrades." Other critics also enjoyed the comic aspects of *Nightmare*'s sequels, which *Los Angeles Times* reviewer Kevin Thomas termed "burlesques of the original." Noting a prominent theme carried over from the first *Nightmare* release, Thomas also lauded the manner in which the film "proceeds with a kind of nightmare logic while suggesting almost subliminally that youngsters must learn to stand up for themselves, even in their dreams."

A later project of Craven's, *The Serpent and the Rainbow,* also deals with psychological phenomena in its exploration of the voodoo religion and its practice of creating zombies. The movie, which received favorable reviews, was directed by Craven and written by Richard Maxwell. Filming primarily in Haiti, Craven and his crew observed voodoo rituals firsthand, after which some crew members reportedly had unusual psychological experiences such as hallucinations and temporary amnesia. Craven told *Chicago Tribune* reporter Rick Kogan that he was interested in the topic of voodoo because it represents "a totally different psychic environment. . . . It is a full-blown religion, a religion in the round. To believers, people can fly." His success in making a larger film dealing with the more mysterious potentials of the mind was encouraging to the filmmaker. In his interview with Kogan, Craven commented that "I'd like to push toward larger films, more adult and complex movies because, I'm more adult and complex, by and large. . . . I think I've made a film that flows. Watching it is like riding on a river, passing one amazing thing after another. I've shown what I can do."

Shocker was Craven's next attempt at a larger film. In writing and directing *Shocker,* Craven tried to create a horror figure that would surpass all others, including his own Freddy Krueger. The result was Harold Pinker, a television repair man and mass murderer who, when killed in the electric chair for his crimes, is transformed into an equally homicidal spirit that moves and acts through electrical currents, possessing human bodies and various appliances and machines, particularly televisions, as he stalks his prey. The Pinker character and the film as a whole, however, did not spark the interest of theater-goers or generate the positive reviews that *A Nightmare on Elm Street* had. While many were impressed by the special effects, some critics felt that the film was overly complex and did not have a cohesive plot. Michael Wilmington in a review in the *Los Angeles Times* asserted that "*Shocker* is crammed with dazzling bursts of macabre technique" in its many dream sequences, but suggested "it's in those dreams, strung through the entire movie, where *Shocker* goes wrong." *Washington Post* contributor Richard Harrington assessed that "Craven relies too much on dreams to advance and justify his plot" and found that "for the longest time, *Shocker* is low voltage, just another gathering of slasher cliches. Toward the end, though, it comes to life thanks to an extended special effects package that is only hinted at earlier." Critics were most impressed with Craven's use of images from contemporary media as a backdrop for Pinker's violent actions. Wilmington suggested that "Craven is working over our paranoia of the media and especially TV: the way it manipulates us, takes over our lives, and the endless cornucopia of horrors—wars, crimes, disasters—that pour through its receivers." Stephen Holden, writing in the *New York Times,* acknowledged Craven's references to such larger social issues, but also noted the use of humor and satire in the film: "If the movie's metaphors are as obvious and as portentous as the heavy metal music that punctuates the action, *Shocker* at least has the feel of a movie that was fun to make."

The People under the Stairs, Craven's 1991 release, also met with mixed reviews. The film focuses on a ghoulish couple, Man and Woman, wealthy slumlords who kill and save the bodies of anyone who happens to come calling at their mansion. In the basement reside other unwilling guests, a clan of kidnapped boys who have had their ears, eyes, and tongues removed for learning too much about the secret activities of the homeowners. When a young boy from the ghetto, Fool, decides to rob the couple, he uncovers their secret captives and attempts to set them free. While disappointed with the movie, Dave Kehr in the *Chicago Tribune* did note Craven's attempt to bring up a more political issue, specifically the relationship between the rich and poor, in his film: "Though his basic dramatic format remains the same [as his other films], helpless children struggling to escape the clutches of crazed parental figures, there's an unmistakable social dimension to the imagery this time." The reviewer concluded, "With a bit more shape and follow-through, *The People under the Stairs* might have been a minor classic, yet even in its half-formed state its raw ambition is impressive."

In his interview for *AAYA,* Craven acknowledged that he has tried to instill his films with intellectual concerns as well as with the suspense and terror that has made him such a popular filmmaker: "A true idea grasps the perceiver on any of . . . infinite levels. The best stories deal with a simple and pure inner truth about the human condition. They could be studied for centuries by scholars, written about in reams of books, or be appreciated by the audience as a great yarn. An intellectual person can see *Nightmare on Elm Street* as a study of consciousness and another can see it as a hell of a ride. They are both right. If there's one thing I'd like to see them come away with from my films it is the idea that there is hope. The world is what you imagine it to be. You imagine your own solutions, defenses, even attacks on the Freddy Kruegers of life."

Craven altered his direction with *Scream,* released in late 1996. His tongue-in-cheek treatment of the horror genre resulted in a box office hit and focused attention on screenwriter Kevin Williamson. "Poised on the knife edge between parody and homage, Wes Craven's *Scream* is a deft, funny, shrewdly unsettling tribute to slasher-exploitation thrillers," wrote Owen Glieberman in *Entertainment Weekly. People* reviewer Tom Gliatto described *Scream* as "a quick, cheap, knowingly funny thriller in which the murderer and his teenage victims were all well-versed in the cliches of the genre." *Time*'s Richard Corliss was not so impressed, though, saying that "Craven began his career by imitating better directors and kept at it until he was mature enough to imitate himself." *Scream*'s ticket sales of more than $100 million guaranteed the making of a sequel, *Scream 2,* also written by Williamson, and released at the end of 1997.

In *Scream 2,* Sidney, the teenage heroine terrorized in *Scream,* has gone to college, where murders similar to those in the first film are taking place. Apparently a movie called *Stab,* based on Sidney's experiences, has given a killer ideas. This film-within-a-film is a source of *Scream 2*'s humor, as are frequent discussions by the college students about the poor quality of horror-movie sequels. "While the original was a send-up of slasher conventions, *Scream 2*— starring most of the survivors of *Scream*—is a takeoff on the follow-up efforts of Leatherface, Freddy Krueger, and friends," noted David Hochman in *Entertainment Weekly. Variety* reviewer Leonard Klady found *Scream 2* "(v)isceral, witty and appropriately redundant" and added that the movie has a "chilling underlying message" about the influence of popular culture. Not all critics thought *Scream 2*

lived up to its predecessor; *People*'s Gliatto, for instance, contends that nothing in the film approached "the shock of *Scream*'s famous opening scene or the surprise of its conclusion." In his *Newsweek* article, though, Jeff Giles asserts that while "not as streamlined" as *Scream,* the sequel is, nevertheless, "a hell of a movie—a thrilling marriage of Zeitgeisty satire and timeless scare tactics."

Despite his success with horror films, Craven has indicated he plans to work outside the genre, at least for a while. He has signed with Miramax to do three films, including a documentary on an inner-city music teacher. Craven also signed a contract with Simon & Schuster for publication of his first novel, *The Fountain Society,* a scientific thriller. "It's a vindication," he told Hochman, "when people acknowledge that you can do more than just horror." Giles quoted Craven as saying he was "profoundly ambivalent" toward the horror genre. "When I think about it in the most positive way," Craven added, "I say, 'For whatever reasons, you have a real gift for this, and you're exploring a certain dark territory that is as valid as anything else.'"

BIOGRAPHICAL/CRITICAL SOURCES:

BOOKS

Authors & Artists for Young Adults, Volume 6, Gale (Detroit), 1991, pp. 25-37.
Contemporary Theatre, Film, and Television, Volume 6, Gale, 1989.

PERIODICALS

Chicago Tribune, February 23, 1988; November 5, 1991, section 2, p. 8.
Entertainment Weekly, April 19, 1996; January 10, 1997; February 21-28, 1997; July 11, 1997, p. 6; November 28, 1997, p. 28.
Film Comment, July/August, 1978, p. 49; March/April, 1980, p. 24; September/October, 1989.
Los Angeles Times, February 27, 1987; October 18, 1989; October 27, 1989; November 18, 1989.
Maclean's, December 29, 1997, p. 105.
New Statesman, September 6, 1985, p. 33.
Newsweek, December 15, 1997, p. 70.
New York Times, February 27, 1987; October 28, 1989, p. A16; October 14, 1994; October 27, 1995; January 2, 1997.
People, November 13, 1989, p. 159; December 22, 1997, p. 22; January 12, 1998, p. 25.
Time, December 30-January 6, 1997.

Times (London), August 30, 1985.

Variety, October 13, 1997, p. M5; December 8, 1997, p. 111.

Washington Post, January 23, 1985; March 2, 1987; November 2, 1989; November 6, 1991, p. B1.*

D-F

DANIELS, Max
   See GELLIS, Roberta L(eah Jacobs)

* * *

DANIELS, Robert V(incent) 1926-

PERSONAL: Born January 4, 1926, in Boston, MA; son of Robert Whiting and Helen (Hoyt) Daniels; married Alice M. Wendell, July 2, 1945; children: Robert H., Helen L., Irene L., Thomas L. *Education:* Harvard University, A.B., 1945, A.M., 1947, Ph.D., 1951. *Politics:* Democrat.

ADDRESSES: Home—195 South Prospect St., Burlington, VT 05401.

CAREER: Harvard University, Cambridge, MA, research fellow, Russian Research Center, 1950-51; Massachusetts Institute of Technology, Cambridge, research associate, Center for International Studies, 1951-52; Bennington College, Bennington, VT, member of social science faculty, 1952-53, 1957-58; Indiana University at Bloomington, assistant professor of Slavic studies, 1953-55; Columbia University, New York, NY, research associate, 1955-56; University of Vermont, Burlington, assistant professor, 1956-64, professor of history, 1964-88, professor emeritus, 1988—, chairman of department, 1964-69, director of experimental program, 1969-71; Vermont State Senate, Montpelier, VT, senator, 1973-82, assistant minority leader, 1977-82. Chairman of Platform Committee, Vermont Democratic Party, 1963-66, 1970-72, 1976-80. Member of Chittenden County Democratic Committee, beginning 1959, board of visitors,

U.S. Air Force Academy, 1965-67, and Burlington Democratic City Committee, beginning 1965. Alternate delegate, Democratic Party National Convention, 1968, and 1980; member of Democratic National Platform Committee, 1980. *Military service:* U.S. Naval Reserve, 1944-46, served on U.S.S. Albany; became ensign.

MEMBER: American Historical Association, American Association for the Advancement of Slavic Studies (member of board of directors, 1968-71; president, 1992), American Association of University Professors, Northeast Slavic Association (president, 1971-72), Vermont Historical Society (trustee, 1968-71).

AWARDS, HONORS: International relations research grant, Rockefeller Foundation, 1961-62, 1963-64; senior fellow, National Endowment for the Humanities, 1971-72; research fellow, Russian Research Center, Harvard University, 1971-72; Guggenheim fellow, 1980-81.

WRITINGS:

The Conscience of the Revolution: Communist Opposition in Soviet Russia, Harvard University Press (Cambridge, MA), 1960, new edition, Westview Press (Boulder, CO), 1988.
(Editor) *A Documentary History of Communism,* Random House (New York City), 1960.
The Nature of Communism, Random House, 1962.
Understanding Communism, Singer, 1964.
Russia, Prentice-Hall (Englewood Cliffs, NJ), 1964.
(Contributor) W. Cahnman and A. Boskoff, editors, *Sociology and History,* Free Press of Glencoe, 1964.

Russia, Prentice-Hall, 1965.

(Editor) *The Stalin Revolution: Fulfillment or Betrayal of Communism?,* Heath (Boston), 1965, 2nd edition, 1972.

(Editor) *Marxism and Communism: Essential Readings,* Random House, 1965.

Studying History: How and Why, Prentice-Hall, 1966, 3rd edition, 1981.

Red October: The Bolshevik Revolution of 1917, Scribner (New York City), 1967.

(Contributor) *The Soviet Union under Brezhnev and Kosygin,* Van Nostrand, 1971.

(Editor) *The Russian Revolution,* Prentice-Hall, 1972.

(Editor) *The Stalin Revolution: Foundations of Soviet Totalitarianism,* Heath, 1972, published as *The Stalin Revolution: Foundations of the Totalitarian Era,* 1990.

Fodor's Europe Talking, McKay, 1975.

(Editor with Paul Cocks and Nancy Whittier Heer, and contributor) *The Dynamics of Soviet Politics,* Harvard University Press, 1976.

(Editor) *A Documentary History of Communism,* University Press of New England (Hanover, NH), 1984.

Russia, the Roots of Confrontation, Harvard University Press, 1985.

Is Russia Reformable?: Change and Resistance from Stalin to Gorbachev, Westview Press, 1988.

Year of the Heroic Guerrilla: World Revolution and Counterrevolution in 1968, Basic Books (New York City), 1989.

(Senior editor) *The University of Vermont: The First Two Hundred Years,* University Press of New England, 1991.

Trotsky, Stalin and Socialism, Westview Press, 1991.

The End of the Communist Revolution, Routledge (New York City), 1993.

(Editor) *A DOcumentary History of Communism in Russia, from Lenin to Gorbachev,* University Press of New England, 1993.

(Editor) *A Documentary History of Communism and the World, from Revolution to Collapse,* University Press of New England, 1994.

Soviet Communism from Reform to Collapse, Heath, 1995.

Russia's Transformation: Snapshots of a Crumbling System, Rowman & Littlefield (Lanham, MD), 1997.

Contributor to *Encyclopedia Americana* and *Encyclopaedia Britannica.* Contributor of articles to scholarly journals and general periodicals.

SIDELIGHTS: Robert V. Daniels has written extensively about the Soviet Union and Russian Communism. His many books examine the history of Russia, the Russian Revolution of 1917, the Stalinist creation of a totalitarian regime, and the final collapse of the communist system in the early 1990s.

In *The Conscience of the Revolution: Communist Opposition in Soviet Russia,* Daniels documents the history of the many resistance groups which fought against the totalitarian regime of the Soviet Union; many of these groups are little-known in the West. Focusing primarily on the Communist regime's first decade in power, when total control had not yet been established and some open debate was still possible, Daniels' book "is extensively documented from published Soviet sources and from the Trotsky Archive at the Houghton Library," as A. M. Cienciala of *Canadian Forum* explains. W. B. Ballis, analyzing the study for the *Annals of the American Academy,* finds that Daniels' "insights and massive documentation give this book special distinction." Robert Conquest, reviewing the book for the *Spectator,* admits that Daniels "disarms me by the clarity, thoroughness and readability of his account." "Daniels has written an outstanding book," the critic for *Current History* writes. "It is superbly documented, lucidly written, and analyzed with sophistication and insight."

Daniels seeks to define Russian Communism in *The Nature of Communism,* a book that Harry Schwartz in the *New York Times Book Review* labels "the best single volume on the nature and origins of modern communism. . . . The specialist will find new insights in this book; the curious intelligent layman can pick it up and be confident that he has a sane guide." While the reviewer for *Kirkus* finds *The Nature of Communism* "a brilliant and authoritative interpretation," Hans Rogger in *Current History* calls it "stimulating, sound, fair, and enlightening."

In *Russia* Daniels presents a history of the Russian nation from its earliest beginnings to the mid-twentieth century, showing that many of the totalitarian excesses of the Soviet Union have their roots in earlier Russian history. As S. H. Baron notes in *American History Review,* Daniels places "particular emphasis on the continuities between tsarist and Soviet Russia." Baron sums up: "There can be little doubt that Daniels has written one of the very best brief introductions to the USSR." Oleg Ivsky in *Library Journal* judges the work to be an "excellently written study."

Narrowing his focus to the year 1917, the year of the Communist takeover of Russia, Daniels' book *Red October: The Bolshevik Revolution of 1917* is "one of the best books to date on the Russian Revolution," according to P. E. Leinbach in *Library Journal.* Arguing against the idea of mass support for the revolution, or its historical inevitability, Daniels presents instead a carefully rendered version of the actual day-by-day events of the revolution, seeking to show its nature by showing the course of its development. "The conclusions that may be drawn from a work such as [this] have quite enough significance for anyone concerned with the broader meanings of 1917," as H. L. Roberts states in the *New York Times Book Review.*

As a participant in U.S.-Soviet cultural exchange, Daniels traveled to the Soviet Union in 1966 and 1976.

BIOGRAPHICAL/CRITICAL SOURCES:

PERIODICALS

American History Review, April, 1961; October, 1965.
American Political Science Review, June, 1961.
Annals of the American Academy, March, 1961.
Booklist, March 15, 1962.
Book World, November 5, 1967, p. 5.
Canadian Forum, July, 1961.
Canadian History Review, June, 1961.
Chicago Sunday Tribune, March 25, 1962, p. 2.
Choice, March, 1968.
Current History, January, 1961; June, 1962.
Economist, February 17, 1968.
Foreign Affairs, January, 1961; July, 1962.
Kirkus, December 15, 1961.
Library Journal, September 1, 1960; September 15, 1960; March 15, 1962; February 1, 1965; September 15, 1967.
Nation, March 25, 1961.
New York Herald Tribune Books, March 4, 1962, p. 11.
New York Herald Tribune Lively Arts, November 20, 1960, p. 45.
New York Times Book Review, November 20, 1960, p. 34; February 25, 1962, p. 14; November 26, 1967, p. 60.
Political Science Quarterly, June, 1961; March, 1970.
San Francisco Chronicle, August 28, 1960, p. 23.
Social Sciences, January, 1966; April, 1973.
Spectator, May 5, 1961.

Times Literary Supplement, October 13, 1961, p. 677; May 16, 1968, p. 498.

* * *

DAVYS, Sarah
See MANNING, Rosemary (Joy)

* * *

DESANI, G(ovindas) V(ishnoodas) 1909-

PERSONAL: Born July 8, 1909, in Nairobi, Kenya; immigrated to United States, 1970, naturalized citizen, 1979; son of Vishnoodas Manghirmal (a merchant) and Rukmani (Chabria) Desani. *Education:* Privately educated.

ADDRESSES: Office—Department of Philosophy, University of Texas, Austin, TX 78712. *Agent*—Stephen Greenberg, 1306 Guadalupe St., Austin, TX 78701-1629.

CAREER: Journalist, 1928-35; correspondent, *Times of India,* Reuters, and Associated Press, 1935-45; British Government, London, England, lecturer on Indian affairs for Ministry of Information, 1940-46; lecturer and writer, 1946-68; University of Texas at Austin, professor of philosophy, 1969-79; professor emeritus, 1979—. Lecturer on antiquities, Bombay Baroda and Central India Railway, late 1930s. BBC broadcaster, 1930s-40s. Visiting Professor of Religion and Distinguished Visiting Professor of Religion, Boston University, 1979 and 1981. Lecturer, Imperial Institute, Council for Adult Education in the British Armed Forces, London and Wiltshire County Councils, and Royal Empire Society.

AWARDS, HONORS: Fulbright-Hays Lecturer, 1968.

WRITINGS:

All About Mr. Hatterr, F. Aldor (London), 1948, published as *All About H. Hatterr, a Gesture,* Farrar, Straus (New York City), 1951, published as *All About H. Hatterr: A Novel,* introduction by Anthony Burgess, McPherson (New Paltz, NY), 1986.
Hali (prose poem), with a foreword by T. S. Eliot and E. M. Forster, Saturn Press (London), 1951,

Lancer Books (New York City), 1972, reissued with other writings in *Hali and Collected Stories,* McPherson (Kingston, NY), 1991.
Mainly Concerning Kama and Her Immortal Lord, Indian Council on Cultural Relations (New Delhi), 1973.

Columnist and special contributor, *Illustrated Weekly of India* (Bombay), 1962-68.

WORK IN PROGRESS: Writing and editing of *Indian Diaries* (1950-1960); editing a collection of his *Illustrated Weekly* articles.

SIDELIGHTS: "Modern Indian writing in English, as practised now, may be traced back to G. V. Desani's *All About H. Hatterr,*" says Vijay Nambisan in the *Indian Review of Books.* Published in 1948, Desani's comic novel caused a stir in the British publishing world and became known as an important Anglo-Indian work. T. S. Eliot praised it for its style and tempo. R. D. Graff in the *New York Times* considers *All About H. Hatterr* "a rewarding feast of fish and fowl, fiction and philosophy, hilarity and hope."

"Like many important novels, it is a sort of *Bildungs-roman,*" writes Anthony Burgess in the introduction to *All About H. Hatterr: A Novel.* The hero, H. Hatterr, is born of a European sailor and a Malaysian woman, and is later adopted by a Scottish missionary. He seeks wisdom from India's seven sages, but constantly bungles the mission. H. Hatterr's "adventures with sages and women reveal him as a hilarious compound of the sensual and the spiritual," explains Vasant A. Shahane in *World Literature Today.* He is "grotesque, crazy, absurd, part holy man, part rogue, part mystic, part Everyman." Patricia T. O'Conner in the *New York Times Book Review* describes H. Hatterr as "a truth seeker and ne'er-do-well whose virtue is surpassed perhaps only by his naive ineptitude."

Another distinguishing characteristic of H. Hatterr is his unconventional use of English. "H. Hatterr is, on the surface, a grotesque autodidact who has built up a remarkable vocabulary with the aid of an English dictionary and a French and a Latin primer," continues Burgess. Perry D. Westbrook, in *Contemporary Novelists,* also mentions the hero's use of language. "H. Hatterr's incessant flow of vulgarisms, cynicisms, sarcasms, and malapropisms reflects the vulgarity-cum-naivety of his character as a 20th-century everyman."

Phillip Toynbee considers *All About H. Hatterr* "a comic masterpiece." He believes G. V. Desani "stands astride the two cultures, the Eastern and Western, belonging to neither, and therefore able to look at both with the incredulous eye of the outsider." Westbrook mentions that "the fact that H. Hatterr enjoys the absurdity of life, at least as he leads it, serves to raise him somewhat above the stature of a mere buffoon and to give the reader the sense that the author's purpose is one of life-affirmation."

BIOGRAPHICAL/CRITICAL SOURCES:

BOOKS

Contemporary Novelists, St. James Press (Detroit), 1996.
Desani, G. V., *All About H. Hatterr: A Novel,* introduction by Anthony Burgess, McPherson, 1986.
Ramanujan, Molly, *G. V. Desani: Writer and Worldview,* Arnold Heinemann (New Delhi), 1984.
Singh, Khushwant, and Peter Russell, editors, *A Note . . . on G. V. Desani's "All About H. Hatterr" and "Hali,"* Szeben, 1952.

PERIODICALS

Book World, December 21, 1986, p. 12.
Chicago Sunday Tribune, July 1, 1951, p. 5.
Independent, August 2, 1993, p. 12.
India Review of Books, October, 1997.
Kirkus Reviews, February 1, 1951, p. 70.
Library Journal, March 15, 1951, p. 516.
Nation, June 16, 1951, p. 572.
New Pages, spring, 1987, p. 10.
New York Times, June 18, 1951, p. 10.
New York Times Book Review, February 8, 1987, p. 38.
Time, June 18, 1951, p. 110.
World Literature Today, spring, 1987, p. 353.
World Literature Written in English, November, 1974.*

*   *   *

DOMINGUEZ, Jorge Ignacio 1945-

PERSONAL: Born June 2, 1945, in Havana, Cuba; immigrated to the United States in 1960, naturalized citizen, 1966; son of Jorge J. (a business executive) and Lilia (De La Carrera) Dominguez; married Mary

Alice Kmietek (a teacher), December 16, 1967; children: Lara, Leslie. *Education:* Yale University, B.A., 1967; Harvard University, M.A., 1968, Ph.D., 1972.

ADDRESSES: Office—Center for International Affairs, Harvard University, 1737 Cambridge St., Cambridge, MA 02138; fax 617-495-8292.

CAREER: Harvard University, Cambridge, MA, assistant professor, 1972-77, associate professor, 1977-79, professor, 1979-93, Frang G. Thomson professor of government, 1993-96, Clarence Dillon professor of international affairs, 1996—. Director, Center for International Affairs; Harvard University associated fellow, Inter-American Dialogue; member, Center for International Affairs, 1972—, Latin American Scholarship Program of American Universities, and Council on Religion and International Affairs; past president, Institute of Cuban Studies; past chair (2 terms), Harvard University Committee on Latin American and Iberian Studies.

MEMBER: Inter-American Dialogue, Council on Foreign Relations; Latin-American Studies Association (chair of national convention program, 1977-79; member of board of trustees, 1980-85; president, 1982-83; chair, 1982), Latin-American Scholarship Programs of American Universities (former board chair).

AWARDS, HONORS: Distinguished Fulbright Visiting Professor, El Colegio De Mexico, 1983, 1988; winner of Peabody Award, for "Crisis in Central America: A Four-Part Special Report."

WRITINGS:

Cuba: Order and Revolution, Harvard University Press (Cambridge, MA), 1978.
(With N. S. Rodley, B. Wood, and R. Falk) *Enhancing Global Human Rights,* McGraw (New York City), 1979.
Insurrection or Loyalty: The Breakdown of the Spanish-American Empire, Harvard University Press, 1980.
(With K. Deutsch and H. Heclo) *Comparative Government: Politics of Industrialized and Developing Nations,* Houghton (Boston), 1981.
To Make a World Safe for Revolution: Cuba's Foreign Policy, Harvard University Press, 1989.
(With James A. McCann) *Democratizing Mexico: Public Opinion and Electoral Choices,* Johns Hopkins University Press (Baltimore, MD), 1996.

EDITOR

Cuba: Internal and International Affairs, Sage (Beverly Hills, CA), 1982.
Economic Issues and Political Conflict: U.S.-Latin American Relations, Butterworth (Woburn, MA), 1982.
Mexico's Political Economy: Challenges at Home and Abroad, Sage, 1982.
(With R. Hernandez) *U.S.-Cuban Relations in the 1990s,* Westview Press (Boulder, CO), 1989.
(With R. Pastor and D. Worrell) *Democracy in the Caribbean,* Johns Hopkins University Press, 1993.
(And chapter co-author) *Essays on Mexico, Central and South America: Scholarly Debates from the 1950s to the 1990s,* seven volumes, Garland Publishing (New York City), 1994.
(With A. Lowenthal) *Constructing Democratic Governance: Latin America and the Caribbean in the 1990s,* Johns Hopkins University Press, 1996.
(With M. Lindenberg) *Democratic Transitions in Central America,* University of Florida Press (Gainesville), 1997.
Technopols: Freeing Politics and Markets in Latin America in the 1990s, Pennsylvania State University Press (University Park), 1997.

OTHER

Series editor for "Crisis in Central America: A Four-Part Special Report," FRONTLINE, Public Broadcasting System, including "The Yankee Years," "Castro's Challenge," "Revolution in Nicaragua," and "Battle for El Salvador," 1985. Chief editorial advisor for MEXICO, Public Broadcasting System, including "Revolution," "From Boom to Bust," and "End of an Era," 1988. Contributor to *Handbook of Political Science.* Contributor to political science and law journals. Contributing editor, *Foreign Policy;* member of editorial boards, *Mexico, Cuban Studies* (and co-editor), *Political Science Quarterly,* and *Revista de Ciencias Sociales.*

WORK IN PROGRESS: Mexican elections; U.S.-Latin American relations; Cuban politics; co-writing *The Politics of U.S.-Latin American Economic Relations* and *The International Implications of Mexico's Internal Affairs.*

SIDELIGHTS: Jorge Ignacio Dominguez once told *CA:* "I like to vary my work from internal to international affairs and from historical to contemporary. My books and articles reflect this range."

DORFMAN, Ariel 1942-

PERSONAL: Born May 6, 1942, in Buenos Aires, Argentina; naturalized Chilean citizen, 1967; exiled from Chile, 1973; came to United States, 1980; son of Adolfo (an economist, engineer, and adviser to the government of Argentina) and Fanny (a Spanish literature teacher; maiden name, Zelicovich) Dorfman; married Maria Angelica Malinarich (an English teacher and social worker), January 7, 1966; children: Rodrigo, Joaquin. *Education:* University of Chile, Licenciado en filosofia con mencion en literatura general (summa cum laude), 1967.

ADDRESSES: Home—Durham, NC; and Santiago, Chile. *Office*—Center for International Studies, 2122 Campus Dr., Box 90404, Duke University, Durham, NC 27708-0404. *Agent*—Andrew Wylie, 250 West 57th St., Suite 2106, New York, NY 10017.

CAREER: University of California, Berkeley, research scholar, 1968-69; University of Chile, Santiago, Chile, professor of Spanish-American studies, 1970-73; Sorbonne, University of Paris, Paris, France, maitre des conferences reemplacant of Spanish-American literature, 1975-76; University of Amsterdam, Amsterdam, Holland, chief research scholar at Spaans Seminarium, 1976-80; Woodrow Wilson Center for International Scholars, Washington, DC, fellow, 1980-81; Institute for Policy Studies, Washington, DC, visiting fellow, 1981-84; Duke University, Durham, NC, visiting professor during fall semesters, 1984-89, research professor of literature and Latin American studies, 1989-96, Walter Hines Page research professor of literature and Latin American studies, 1996—. Visiting professor at University of Maryland, College Park, 1983. Coproducer of film *Death and the Maiden,* Canal Productions/Fine Line Features, 1994. Guest on television and radio news programs, including *All Things Considered, Nightline, This Week with David Brinkley, Crossfire, This Morning, Nightwatch,* and *Larry King Live;* lecturer.

MEMBER: International PEN, National Writers' Union, Sociedad de Escritores Chilenos, Drama Guild, Academie Universelle des Cultures, Academic Freedom Committee Human Rights Watch.

AWARDS, HONORS: Award for best screenplay from Chile Films, 1972, for unproduced film *Balmaceda;* Premio Ampliado Sudamericana from *La Opinion* (Buenos Aires newspaper), 1973, for *Moros en la costa;* New American Plays award from Kennedy Center-American Express, 1988, for the play *Widows;* Roger L. Stevens Award, 1991, for extraordinary playwrighting; Sir Laurence Olivier Award for best play in London, 1992; 29th Dong Award for best play of the season, 1992-93, for *Death and the Maiden;* named Literary Lion, New York Public Library, 1992; honorary degrees: L.H.D., Illinois Wesleyan University, 1989, Litt.D., Wooster College, 1991, L.H.D., Bradford College, 1993.

WRITINGS:

NOVELS

Moros en la costa (title means "The Coast Is Not Clear in Chile"), Sudamericana, 1973, translation by George R. Shivers published as *Hard Rain,* Readers International, 1990.
Viudas (also see below), Siglo XXI, 1981, translation by Stephen Kessler published as *Widows,* Pantheon Books, 1983.
La ultima cancion de Manuel Sendero, Siglo XXI, 1983, translation by Dorfman and Shivers published as *The Last Song of Manuel Sendero,* Viking, 1987.
Mascara, Viking, 1988.
Konfidenz, Planeta (Buenos Aires), 1994, English edition, Farrar, Straus (New York City), 1995.
The Nanny and the Iceberg, Farrar, Straus, 1999.

OTHER

El absurdo entre cuatro paredes: El teatro de Harold Pinter (criticism; title means "Enclosures at the Absurd: Harold Pinter's Theatre"), Universitaria, 1968.
Imaginacion y violencia en America (essays; title means "Imagination and Violence in Latin America"), Universitaria, 1970.
(With Armand Mattelart) *Para leer al Pato Donald,* Siglo Vientiuno Argentina, 1972, translation by David Kunzle published as *How to Read Donald Duck: Imperialist Ideology in the Disney Comic,* International General, 1975, 2nd edition, 1984.
Ensayos quemados en Chile: Inocencia y neocolonialismo (essays; title means "Essays Burnt in Chile: Innocence and Neocolonialism"), Ediciones de la Flor, 1974.
(With Manuel Jofre) *Superman y sus amigos del alma* (essays; title means "Superman and His Cronies"), Galerna, 1974.
Culture et resistance au Chili (essays; title means "Culture and Resistance in Chile"), Institut d'Action Culturelle, 1978.

La ultima aventura del Llanero Solitario (essays; title means "The Last Adventure of the Lone Ranger"), Universitaria Centroamericana (Costa Rica), 1979.

Cria Ojos (short stories; also see below), Nueva Imagen, 1979, translation by Dorfman and Shivers published as *My House Is on Fire* (includes "Reader"), Viking, 1990.

(Contributor) *El intelectual y el estado, Venezuela-Chile* (essays; title means "The Intellectual and the State, Venezuela-Chile"), University of Maryland, 1980.

Pruebas al canto (poems; title means "Soft Evidence"), Nueva Imagen, 1980.

Reader's nuestro que estas en la tierra: Ensayos sobre el imperialismo cultural (essays; title means "Our Readers That Art on Earth"), Nueva Imagen, 1980, translation by Clark Hansen published as *The Empire's Old Clothes: What the Lone Ranger, Babar, and Other Innocent Heroes Do to Our Minds* (includes three previously unpublished essays in English), Pantheon Books, 1983.

Missing (poems), translated by Edie Grossman, Amnesty International British Section, 1982.

Hacia liberacion del lector latinoamericano (essays), Ediciones del Norte, 1984.

Patos, elefantes y heroes: La infancia como subdesarrollo (essays; title means "On Ducks, Elephants, and Heroes"), Ediciones de la Flor, 1985, revised edition, Planeta, 1997.

Dorando la pildora (stories; title means "The Medicine Goes Down"), Ediciones del Ornitorrinco, 1985.

Los suenos nucleares de Reagan (nonfiction), Editorial Legasa, 1986.

Pastel de choclo (poetry), Sinfronteras, 1986, translation by Dorfman and Grossman published as *Last Waltz in Santiago and Other Poems of Exile and Disappearance* (includes selected poems originally published in *Missing*), Penguin, 1988.

Widows (two-act play based on Dorfman's novel of the same name; first produced in Williamstown, MA, at the Williamstown Theatre Festival, 1988; revised version, cowritten with Tony Kushner, produced in 1991), Nick Hern Books, 1996.

Some Write to the Future: Essays on Contemporary Latin American Fiction (criticism), translated by Ariel Dorfman and George Shivers, Duke University Press, 1991.

Cuentos casi completos (short stories), Ediciones Letra Buena (Buenos Aires), 1991.

Death and the Maiden (drama), Viking, 1992.

La obra de Ariel Dorfman: ficcion y critica, (collection), Editorial Pliegos (Madrid), 1992.

Teatro (play collection), Ediciones de la Flor (Buenos Aires), 1992.

Traverse Theatre Presents the World Premier of Reader (play; based on Dorfman's short story of the same title), Nick Hern Books (London), 1995.

(With son, Rodrigo Dorfman) *Prisoners in Time* (teleplay), British Broadcasting Corporation, 1995.

The Resistance Trilogy, Nick Hern Books, 1998.

Heading South, Looking North: A Bilingual Journey (nonfiction; biographies of exiled Chilean writers), Farrar, Straus and Giroux, 1998.

Author of plays, with son Rodrigo Dorfman, *Mascara* (based on Ariel Dorfman's novel of the same title), staged in both Germany and the United States, 1998, and *Who's Who,* staged in Germany, 1998. Also author and director, with son, Rodrigo Dorfman, of film short *My House Is on Fire,* 1997; also author of unproduced screenplay *Balmaceda,* 1972. Contributor of articles, stories, and editorials to periodicals, including *Harper's, Nation, New York Times, Los Angeles Times, Village Voice, Washington Post,* and *New York Times Sunday Magazine.*

WORK IN PROGRESS: A second part of *Heading South, Looking North,* to be titled *Heading North, Looking South;* a novella, *Therapy.*

ADAPTATIONS: Death and the Maiden was adapted as a motion picture, written by Dorfman and Rafael Yglesias, directed by Roman Polanski, starring Sigourney Weaver and Ben Kingsley, Canal Productions/Fine Line Features, 1994.

SIDELIGHTS: Argentinean-born author, journalist, and scholar Ariel Dorfman is best known for his opposition to political oppression in Chile. Since his 1973 expulsion from his adopted country for his outspoken resistance to the harsh policies of dictator Augusto Pinochet, Dorfman has produced poetry, nonfiction, short stories, and three acclaimed novels that probe the terror of dictatorship and the despair of exile. According to Robert Atwan in the *New York Times Book Review,* Dorfman's fiction displays his "ability to create methods of storytelling that enact, not merely record, a political vision, [and] that fuse both the political and the literary imaginations."

Dorfman was born in Argentina in 1942 to a family well acquainted with the pain of exile: his Jewish grandparents had escaped the pogroms in Eastern Europe, and his father, an economist, fled Argentina and took a job in New York City at the United Nations when Dorfman was two years old. Dorfman and his family spent ten years in the United States before they returned to South America, settling in Chile in 1954. Although initially averse to leaving New York, Dorfman grew to love his new country; he completed his education, married, and in 1967 became a naturalized Chilean citizen.

Dorfman established himself in Chile as a writer, publishing his first novel, *Moros en la costa,* and several nonfiction studies. These included a critical analysis of the works of English playwright Harold Pinter, a book of essays on the Latin American novel, and a 1972 collaboration with Armand Mattelart titled *Para leer al Pato Donald,* which was widely reviewed in English. Translated as *How to Read Donald Duck: Imperialist Ideology in the Disney Comic,* the book is an examination of the ways Donald Duck and other Disney characters subtly transmit capitalist ideology to their Latin American audiences, with whom the cartoons are extremely popular. A later study translated as *The Empire's Old Clothes: What the Lone Ranger, Babar, and Other Innocent Heroes Do to Our Minds* presents Dorfman's analysis of how American children's literature and popular culture also project dominant values.

Dorfman worked as an activist, journalist, and writer in Chile until 1973, when Salvador Allende's democratically elected Marxist government was overthrown by Pinochet in a U.S.-supported coup, resulting in Allende's death and the expulsion of thousands of intellectuals, writers, clergymen, and politicians from the country. After receiving death threats and witnessing the burning of his books in Santiago, Dorfman was expelled from Chile. Devastated by the loss of his citizenship and appalled by the intimidation and violence perpetrated on his countrymen by the Pinochet regime, Dorfman, after a brief stay in Argentina, settled in France. There he worked for the Chilean resistance movement in Paris and later taught Spanish-American literature at the Sorbonne.

After a period of two years during which his distress over his country's turmoil blocked his creativity and left him unable to write, Dorfman composed a group of poems expressing his thoughts about the atrocities—which included torture, murder, and abductions—he knew were still occurring in his homeland. The poems, which were published in an English collection titled *Missing* in 1982, center on *desaparecidos,* people deemed subversive by the Chilean government and abducted ("disappeared") by secret agents. In the collection Dorfman describes the effects this practice has upon the families of the dis-

appeared; one poem conveys the conflicting emotions of parents who receive word from a prison camp veteran that their son—whom they feared dead—is still alive but being tortured. "I discovered a way in which I could become a meeting ground of the living and the dead—a way to give voice to the missing, which was also a metaphor for the whole country and what had been irretrievably lost," Dorfman later told Leslie Bennetts of the *New York Times.* "All of my poems are ways of giving voices to those who have disappeared and those who are left behind; I am a bridge between them. Words become a way of returning to your country—a cemetery, but also a resurrection ground."

Dorfman left France in 1976 for a position as chief research scholar at the University of Amsterdam, remaining there until 1980, when he accepted a Woodrow Wilson fellowship in Washington, D.C. He returned to fiction writing, voicing his deep concern for the disappeared in a second novel, *Viudas (Widows).* Knowing that its highly sensitive subject would probably prevent the book's publication in Chile, he devised an elaborate scheme to have *Viudas* printed first in Europe. Using the pseudonym Eric Lohmann, Dorfman included in the manuscript a foreword—which claimed to be written by Lohmann's son—explaining that the book's author was a World War II Danish resistance fighter who had set the story in Greece in order to have it safely published in his homeland. *Viudas*'s foreword also stated that Lohmann had been killed by the Nazi secret police just days after the book's completion, and that Lohmann's son had only recently found and published the manuscript. Dorfman then planned to have the novel published first in Danish, French, or German and subsequently issued at home as a Spanish translation of the European novel. "That double distancing—of mediation through an author who was not me and a country which was not my own—allowed me to write an allegory which is simultaneously realistic, [and] a literary solution to the problem of how to write about overwhelming horror and sorrow," the author explained in an interview with Peggy Boyers and Juan Carlos Lertora in *Salmagundi.* At the last minute, however, Dorfman's Spanish-language publisher backed out; the novel was ultimately released, under Dorfman's real name, by the Mexican firm Siglo XXI in 1981.

Translated in 1983, *Widows* is set in a Greek village under the control of Nazi soldiers during World War II and centers on Sofia Angelos, a village peasant woman whose husband, father, and son have been disappeared by the military regime. Given no information about their menfolk's safety or whereabouts, Sofia and the other peasant women—whose male relatives have also been abducted—rise in opposition to the soldiers when Sofia claims an unidentifiable corpse that has washed up on the river bank is her father and demands the right to bury him.

Widows was acclaimed for its political relevance as well as for its powerful portrayal of the grief and emotional strain that disappearances put on the families of the missing. Alan Cheuse, for example, in his *New York Times Book Review* critique, compared the book's intensity and scope to that of such Greek tragedies as *Antigone* and *The Trojan Women,* and praised *Widows*'s "emotional amplitude and political resonance." Noting especially its "sharply observed details of the bereaved . . . who suffer . . . painfully," Cheuse asserted that the reader "moves [through the novel] as if in a dream of outrage among its tombs of love." *Times Literary Supplement* contributor Nicholas Rankin also admired Dorfman's work, applauding the way the author bypassed the "realist clutter of local detail" in order to create "a tragedy of universal application."

Dorfman followed *Widows* with the 1983 *La ultima cancion de Manuel Sendero,* a lengthy novel that explores the larger implications of repression and exile through several complexly interwoven narratives. "There's fantasy," Dorfman said of the book in an interview with Richard J. Meislin in the *New York Times Book Review,* "but also the very harsh terror of reality. Writers of Latin American literature, especially my generation, are constantly being pulled between two poles: what you would call the dictatorship of everyday life and the imagination of things that might come and might be." Translated as *The Last Song of Manuel Sendero,* the work unfolds through several perspectives, mainly that of unborn fetuses who have been organized into a revolt—in the form of a mass refusal to emerge from their mothers' wombs. Much of the novel contains the generation's discussions about whether it is better to shun a world full of violence and fear, or to risk birth in order to solve human problems. The babies, according to Dorfman, also serve as the book's principal metaphor. "They are the utopia that are inside each of us," the author affirmed in a *Los Angeles Times* interview with Mona Gable. "There are millions of people who are born and never born—they don't leave any change in the world. To read the novel means I want people to come away with a sense of what is unborn inside them." Other narratives in *The Last Song of Manuel Sendero* include the realistic dialogue between David and Felipe, exiled Chilean cartoonists living in Mexico and collaborating on a comic strip for their fellow expatriates; the lives of characters within David and Felipe's comic strip; and notes and scholarly commentary from a course in "Prehistoric Amerspanish III," given thirty thousand years in the future.

Critical response to *The Last Song of Manuel Sendero* was generally favorable, with reviewers commenting both on the book's complexity and on Dorfman's success in blending his political and artistic concerns. Judith Freeman, for example, in the *Los Angeles Times Book Review,* stated: "This is a demanding book, but for those who make the effort it requires, the result is a ride on a parabolic roller coaster of timely and humanitarian thought." Earl Shorris's *New York Times Book Review* critique expressed a similar assessment, noting that "after the complications of plot and puzzle have done their work, the richness of invention breaks through." Concluded Pat Aufderheide in the *Boston Review:* "every page, every insistent act of imagination is an act of resistance against the death-in-life of political oppression and the life-on-hold of exile."

In 1983, ten years after Dorfman was forced to leave Chile, Pinochet's government softened its attitude somewhat towards many of the nation's exiles, and Dorfman was allowed to return to the country temporarily; he began to split his time between living in Santiago and teaching as a visiting professor at North Carolina's Duke University. He persisted, however, in voicing his criticism of Pinochet's dictatorial policies during the next five years, both in articles and editorials in American and international publications as well as during appearances on American news programs. Although Dorfman has been given permission to return to Chile, unsettling incidents (such as Chilean news reports announcing Dorfman's death and Dorfman's unexplained detention and expulsion from the Santiago airport after which he was temporarily refused entry into the country in 1987) have made his full-time residence there unlikely as long as Pinochet remains in power.

In the late 1980s Dorfman published another volume of poetry titled *Last Waltz in Santiago and Other Poems of Exile and Disappearance* and *My House Is on Fire,* a translation of earlier short stories. He also completed the thriller *Mascara* in 1988. Written in English and considered the least overtly political of Dorfman's novels, the story centers on personal identity as it is created, controlled, changed, and escaped by three characters—an anonymous loner who works as a photographer for an obscure government agency, an amnesiac woman with multiple personalities, and a manipulative plastic surgeon—whose monologues form the book's three sections. *Mascara* was well received by critics, who admired its compelling narration, suspenseful plot, and ambiguous ending, and compared it to the fiction of German novelists Guenter Grass and Franz Kafka. *Mascara,* noted Atwan, "is an intricately layered book [that] can be read as an ominous fairy tale, a literary horror story, a post-modern version of Jekyll and Hyde. But the book is also a parable of human identity and paranoia engendered by authoritarian politics."

Dorfman's *Some Write to the Future,* published in 1991, is a collection of his essays (some previously published) on contemporary Latin American fiction. His prose themes of violence and repression surface within critical reviews of the works of writers such as Garcia Marquez, Borges, and Arguedas. Mark I. Millington, writing for the *Modern Language Review,* found the essays "constrained" both "by their not having been revised"so as to take advantage of more current thinking, as well as Dorfman's own tendency "to work *with* the grain of the texts under analysis, so that there is a slight lack of critical edge." However, the "sense of [Dorfman's] emotional and ideological involvement. . .makes for enjoyable reading." Other critics, such as D. A. N. Jones in the *London Review of Books,* reviewed *Some Write to the Future* with an eye to this emotional involvement of Dorfman's rather than as a critical work. Commenting on his interpretation of Garcia Marquez's *Chronicle of a Death Foretold* Jones noted, "The sombre Dorfman does try to offer an optimism of the will, as well as a pessimism of the intellect."

Dorfman returned to playwriting in 1992 with his critically acclaimed piece, *Death and the Maiden.* A powerful story centered on three characters, it takes place in a country recently returned to a democratic government after an era of fearsome repression. Paulina is the wife of a lawyer asked to serve on a commission investigating the crimes under the previous government, including her own brutal rape by a doctor. Through her husband, she meets the man she believes raped her. She kidnaps him and decides to place him on trail for his crimes in her own home. The play, which was staged in London and New York, was later produced as a film by Roman Polanski. The story's juxtaposition of politics and ethics was hailed by critics. John Butt in the *Times*

Literary Supplement noted that "More than one critic has commented on. . .the way it unwinds with a remorseless inevitability that recalls the finest classical tragedy" and concluded "Such praise hardly seems exaggerated." Ilan Stavans, writing for *World Literature Today,* mirrored Butt's comments, finding *Death and the Maiden* to have "the taste of a tautly constructed classic."

Konfidenz, Dorfman's 1994 novel, is a story told almost entirely through dialogue. As a result, it "reveals some of the possibilities as well as some of the hazards of the mode," remarked Sven Birkert in the *New York Times Book Review.* The conversation is between Barbara and Leon/Max. Barbara has come to Paris believing that her lover Martin, who is engaged in the resistance movement, is in danger. Leon/Max identifies himself as a political friend of Martin's but seems to know the intimate details of Barbara's life. As their conversation and relationship deepen, they elaborate on Dorfman's themes of identity and trust.

Critics noted that while the tightly woven tale engages readers initially, the suspense fades as the novel progresses. Michael Kerrigan stated in the *Times Literary Supplement,* "Instead of building on the complex and dramatic situation with which he began, Dorfman unpacks it piece by piece, rendering it less complex, less dramatic with each chapter." Birkert continued, "We begin to feel the law of diminishing returns assert itself. We listen less intently and let our attention begin to drift." Kate Kellaway, writing for *The Observer,* commented, "The novel aims for the menace of Genet, but keeps being brought down by something cheaper and more ordinary, a touch of Francois Sagan or of Marguerite Duras on a bad day." Still, Dorfman's attempts at something out of the ordinary were appreciated. "The originality of Dorfman's technique is welcome proof that the experimental nature of contemporary Latin American fiction is not on the wane," declared Marie Arana-Ward in the *Washington Post Book World.* "With [this novel] Dorfman steps confidently from the realm of Latin American storyteller into the arena of a world novelist of the first category."

Despite the uncertainty about his permanent return to Chile, Dorfman continues to protest—through his writing and in person—repression and brutality in his homeland and elsewhere. Denouncing violence and offering hope through his writing that the situation in Chile will improve, Dorfman remains optimistic. "My literature *should* be the literature of despair," Dorfman concluded to Geoffrey Stokes in the *Voice*

Literary Supplement, "but always, not because I desire it, but because it comes out, I find myself telling the story of human beings who have managed to rescue dignity from the midst of terror."

Dorfman wrote *CA:* "My writing has been haunted, ever since I can remember, by twin obsessions, a central paradox that I cannot be rid of: on the one hand, the glorious potential and need of human beings to tell stories; and, on the other, the brutal fact that in today's world, most of the lives that should be telling these stories are generally ignored, ravaged and silenced.

"My life has been fortunate, inasmuch as I have been able to dedicate my existence to reaching others through my imagination; and unfortunate because a great part of that life, like the life of so many others in the twentieth century of ours, has been spent under the shadow of innumerable tyrannies that thrive by denying people the possibility of communicating with each other.

"And yet, as of late, I have come to the conclusion that my writing may not be determined exclusively by the exploration, at the personal and the historical levels, of the two opposite experiences of liberation and domination, but that there is another struggle going on simultaneously in my life and in my work: the attempt to overcome distance, question its corrosion, defeat it. Wondering, all these years, how to achieve closeness. Even while recognizing that too much closeness can also be dangerous. Embraces can smother: being too near anybody, anything, too deep inside a community. We may lose ourselves in closeness—just like in distance. So that I have had to learn to use distance, use exile, use the perspective of the uprooted, to understand what otherwise I would perhaps not even have been able to see, let alone deal with.

"The struggle with distance must have begun at my birth, but as I don't remember that initial leap into life, it is with banishment that this story really starts: when, hardly more than two years old, I left my native Argentina to go to the United States in 1945. I adopted my new country as a foster homeland and its language, English, as my protector; but distance was following me, it lay in wait, and ten years later, when my father had to flee McCarthy and go to Chile, I found myself suddenly returned to Spanish and Latin America, with literature as my one secure ally against the currents and outrages of geography and death, my connection to a community that had been marginalized from history and power. Seduced by Chile and its language and by an upcoming revo-

lution, I eventually disowned English and the United States, hoping that I could will myself into becoming monolingual, intact, immobile, hoping that distance would leave me alone. It did not: the democratically elected government of Salvador Allende was overthrown in 1973 and, like my father before me, I had to escape a dictatorship. I had to accept that I would not be able to live and die in one land forever, accept, in fact, that the word 'forever' was not meant for me: except inasmuch as I marked a page with words that could withstand the vagaries and ambiguities of a body that can be expelled one day, arrested another, welcomed on yet a different day, literature as a home in the midst of migration. The migration of words through a text bridging that other distance, with other members of this errant humanity, bringing me closer to them, allowing me to persist inside heads and hearts that I suspect exist, out there, in here, waiting to create a community of interconnected language and imagination. Political distance defeated by closeness; closeness facilitated by aesthetic distance.

"Divided and joined by politics and literature: like my work itself, my books, my plays, my films, my poems. Trying to go back home in the only way I now know, in a way that I carry with me every place I travel, in the disturbances and joyful turbulence I create in others, returning to men and women what they unknowingly have offered me, the nearby voices beyond frontiers they have loaned to my distance all these years.

"The culmination of this search has probably been *Heading South, Looking North: A Bilingual Journey.* By writing a memoir and figuring out how my life had ended up being so different from what I had planned, trying to come to terms with how and why I had survived the 1973 military takeover that fractured my existence and tore my country asunder, by looking at my two languages and cultures and continents, I feel that I have liberated myself to write in a different way, though probably always obsessed by the same themes of memory and justice, duality and resistance."

A full interview with Dorfman appears in *CA,* Volume 130.

BIOGRAPHICAL/CRITICAL SOURCES:

BOOKS

Contemporary Literary Criticism, Gale (Detroit), Volume 48, 1988, Volume 77, 1993.
Hispanic Literature Criticism, Volume 1, Gale, 1994.

PERIODICALS

Booklist, April 15, 1992, p. 1496.
Books Abroad, June 27, 1978.
Boston Review, April, 1987.
Chasqui XX, May, 1991.
Chicago Tribune, March 18, 1987.
Chicago Tribune Book World, July 17, 1983.
Globe and Mail (Toronto), March 4, 1989.
Harper's, December, 1989.
Index on Censorship, June, 1991.
Library Journal, April 15, 1992, p. 89.
London Review of Books, November 5, 1992, p. 30.
Los Angeles Magazine, March, 1994.
Los Angeles Times, August 7, 1987; August 16, 1987; September 16, 1987.
Los Angeles Times Book Review, June 12, 1983; April 5, 1987; October 30, 1988; January 28, 1990, pp. 3, 10.
Modern Language Review, April, 1993, p. 501.
Nation, February 11, 1978; September 24, 1983; October 18, 1986.
New Republic, May 11, 1992.
New Statesman and Society, July 10, 1992, p. 40.
New Yorker, March 30, 1992, p. 69.
New York Times, February 17, 1987; April 14, 1988; October 8, 1988.
New York Times Book Review, May 8, 1983; July 24, 1983; February 15, 1987; November 6, 1988; December 31, 1989; August 11, 1991, p. 20; December 25, 1994, p. 10.
Observer (London), June 28, 1992, p. 66; February 19, 1995, p. 19.
Publishers Weekly, October 21, 1988, pp. 39-40.
Salmagundi, spring/summer, 1989.
Spectator, July 26, 1975.
Times Literary Supplement, June 11, 1971; December 9, 1983; February 28, 1992, p. 22; June 26, 1992, p. 22; February 24, 1995, p. 20.
Voice Literary Supplement, September, 1982; April, 1987.
Washington Post, August 25, 1988.
Washington Post Book World, June 12, 1983; April 5, 1987; January 21, 1990; February 19, 1995.
World Literature Today, summer, 1993, p. 596.

* * *

DOUGLAS, Michael
  See BRIGHT, Robert (Douglas, Sr.)

DUFFY, Carol Ann 1955-

PERSONAL: Born December 23, 1955, in Glasgow, Scotland; daughter of Francis (an engineer) and Mary (Black) Duffy. *Education:* University of Liverpool, B.A. (with honors), 1977. *Politics:* Socialist.

ADDRESSES: Home—London, England. *Agent*—Penny Tackaberry, Tessa Sayle Agency, 11 Jubilee Pl., London SW3 3TE, England.

CAREER: Writer, 1977—. *Ambit* (magazine), London, poetry editor, 1983—; North Riding College, Scarborough, visiting fellow, 1985; Southern Arts, Thamesdown, writer-in-residence, 1987-88.

AWARDS, HONORS: C. Day Lewis fellow of poetry, Greater London Arts Association, 1982; first prize, British Broadcasting Corp. (BBC), poetry competition, 1983, for "Whoever She Was"; Eric Gregory Award, British Society of Authors, 1984; Scottish Arts Council award, 1986, for *Standing Female Nude*; first prize, Peterloo Poets' "Poems about Painting" competition, 1986, for "The Virgin Punishing the Infant"; Somerset Maugham award, 1988; Dylan Thomas award, 1989.

WRITINGS:

POETRY

Fleshweathercock and Other Poems, Outposts (Walton-on-Thames, Surrey), 1974.
Fifth Last Song, Headland (Wirral, Merseyside), 1982.
Standing Female Nude, Anvil Press Poetry (London), 1985.
Thrown Voices, Turret (London), 1986.
Selling Manhattan, Anvil Press Poetry, 1987.
The Other Country, Anvil Press Poetry, 1990.
Mean Time, Anvil Press Poetry, 1993.
Selected Poems, Penguin (London), 1994.

PLAYS

Take My Husband (two-act), produced in Liverpool, England, 1982.
Cavern of Dreams (two-act), produced in Liverpool, 1984.
Loss (one-act), broadcast on BBC-Radio, 1986.
Little Women, Big Boys (one-act), produced in London, 1986.

OTHER

(Editor) *Home and Away,* Southern Arts (Thames-down), 1988.
(Editor) *I Wouldn't Thank You for a Valentine: Poems for Young Feminists,* illustrated by Trisha Rafferty, Viking, 1992.
(Editor) *Stopping for Death: Poems of Death and Loss,* illustrated by Rafferty, Holt, 1996.

SIDELIGHTS: The author of several collections of poetry and a number of stage plays, as well as editor of several verse anthologies, award-winning British poet Carol Ann Duffy is noted for what *Contemporary Women Poets* contributor Michael Donaghy calls "an impressive range of styles . . . from love lyrics . . . to razor-sharp political satire." In many of her books—particularly her early collections—Duffy employs the technique of the dramatic monologue, a method whereby each of the poet's fictional narrators speaks in his or her own voice, without "commentary" by the outsider-poet. Creating the thoughts and words of individual speakers from all walks of life, and focusing particularly on the voices of women—Duffy is noted for her feminist point of view—the poet "coax[es] pathos and a rarefied music from the sentence fragments" of even her most disoriented subjects, in the opinion of Donaghy.

A graduate of the University of Liverpool, Duffy published her first volume of poetry, *Fleshweathercock and Other Poems,* in 1973 while still in high school. Her first major collection was 1985's *Standing Female Nude,* which showcased Duffy's ability to bring to life even the most unusual personalities through her dramatic monologue. Through evocative soliloquies, Duffy engages the reader, seducing him or her to eventual acceptance of the perspective of the speaker. Noting the startling effect of this technique upon the reader who often finds they have begun to identify with individuals of questionable moral values, as Duffy deliberately causes to happen through her choice of characters, Donaghy notes that the poet "exploits the effect created by this tension" she creates in the reader sympathetic to the speaker yet in conflict with the moral code implicit "in poems spoken by murderers and crypto-Nazis." In "Education for Leisure," for instance, the reader is drawn to the speaker until he begins to divulge the inner motivations for his evening stroll: "Today I am going to kill something. Anything . . . ." Additional collections by Duffy include *Selling Manhattan, The*

Other Country, and *Mean Time.* A career-spanning volume, *Selected Poems,* was published in 1994.

In addition to Duffy's original writings, she has also edited several collections of poetry written by others. *I Wouldn't Thank You for a Valentine: Poems for Young Feminists,* published in 1993, showcases the poet's feminist stance through its themes of female empowerment and independence. Her 1996 edited collection, *Stopping for Death: Poems of Death and Loss,* focuses on a far different topic. Within the volume's eighty poems, written by such authors as Emily Dickinson, Wilfred Owen, Christina Rossetti, Alice Walker, W. H. Auden, and Anne Sexton, Duffy confronts the tragic aspects of the end of life, but balances this perspective with views of death as a threshold to a better place. Characterizing the volume as containing "a vision . . . that gives readers a deeper understanding of the impact of loss," *School Library Journal* critic Saron Korbeck praises *Stopping for Death* as "not at all grim." While noting that some of the individual works in the collection are "difficult," *Booklist* contributor Hazel Rochman lauds Duffy's editorship in selecting verses from around the world, and commends the poems' ability "to lift the spirit with their truthful feeling and words that sing."

BIOGRAPHICAL/CRITICAL SOURCES:

BOOKS

Contemporary Women Poets, St. James Press (Detroit), 1997.

PERIODICALS

Bete Noir, number 6, 1989.
Booklist, August, 1996, p. 1893.
Kirkus Reviews, June 15, 1996, p. 897.
London Review of Books, July 6, 1995, pp. 20-21.
Observer, April 23, 1995, p. 21.
Times Literary Supplement, March 3, 1995, p. 24; July 7, 1995, p. 32.
Voice of Youth Advocates, October, 1996, p. 238.
Women's Review of Books, May, 1995, p. 12.*

*   *   *

ERIKSSON, Buntel
See BERGMAN, (Ernst) Ingmar

FRASER, Alex
  See BRINTON, Henry

                    *   *   *

FRAZEE, Steve (Charles) 1909-1992
  (Dean Jennings)

PERSONAL: Born September 28, 1909, in Salida, CO; died August 21, 1992; son of Charles William and Laura Bclle (Blcvins) Frazee; married Patricia Thomass, September 2, 1937; children: Eric, Linda. *Education:* Western State College of Colorado, A.B., 1937. *Avocational interests:* Whitewater boating, fishing, philately.

ADDRESSES: Home—Box 534, Salida, CO 81201. *Agent*—Scott Meredith Literary Agency, Inc., 845 Third Ave., New York, NY 10022.

CAREER: Worked at heavy construction and mining, 1926-36, 1941-43; La Junta High School, La Junta, CO, instructor in journalism, 1937-41; full-time writer, 1946-92. Director, Salida Building and Loan Association; building inspector, City of Salida, 1950-63. Member of advisory council, San Isabel National Forest, 1959-92.

MEMBER: Western Writers of America (president, 1954; vice-president, 1962), Fib Ark (commodore, 1959), American Canoe Association, American White Water Association, Colorado Authors League.

AWARDS, HONORS: Ellery Queen's Mystery Magazine prize, 1953; Western Heritage Award for short story, "Legal and Proper," 1960; first annual short story award of the Cowboy Hall of Fame, 1961.

WRITINGS:

(Under pseudonym Dean Jennings) *Range Trouble,* Phoenix Press (New York City), 1951.
Shining Mountains, Rinehart (New York City), 1951.
Pistolman, Lion (New York City), 1952.
Utah Hell Guns, Lion, 1952.
The Sky Block, Rinehart, 1953.
Lawman's Feud, Lion, 1953.
Sharp the Bugle Calls, Lion, 1953, reprinted as *Gold at Kansas Gulch,* Fawcett (New York City), 1958.
Spur to the Smoke, Permabooks (New York City), 1954.

The Gun-Throwers (short stories), 1954.
Cry Coyote, Macmillan (New York City), 1955.
Many Rivers to Cross, Gold Medal (New York City), 1955.
Tumbling Range Woman, Pocket Books (New York City), 1956.
He Rode Alone, Gold Medal, 1956.
High Cage, Macmillan, 1957.
Running Target (also see below), Gold Medal, 1957.
Desert Guns, Dell, 1957, published in England as *Gold of the Seven Saints,* Consul (London), 1961.
Rendezvous, Macmillan, 1958.
High Hell, Fawcett, 1958.
Walt Disney's Zorro (novelization of television play), Whitman (Racine, WI), 1958.
Smoke in the Valley, Gold Medal, 1959.
A Day to Die, Avon (New York City), 1960.
The Alamo, Avon, 1960.
Hellsgrin, Rinehart, 1960.
First through the Grand Canyon (juvenile), Winston (Philadelphia), 1960.
More Damn Tourists, Macmillan (New York City), 1960.
Year of the Big Snow (juvenile), Holt (New York City), 1962.
Bragg's Fancy Woman, Ballantine (New York City), 1966, published in England as *A Gun for Bragg's Woman,* Panther (London), 1967.
Killer Lion (juvenile), Whitman, 1966.
Lassie: The Mystery of the Bristlecone Pine (juvenile), Whitman, 1967.
Outcasts, Popular Library (New York City), 1968.
Where Are You?: All about Maps (juvenile), Meredith (New York City), 1968.
Flight 409, Avon, 1969.
Fire in the Valley, Lancer Books (New York City), 1972.
Lassie: Lost in the Snow (juvenile), Golden Press (New York City), 1979.
Lassie: The Secret of the Smelter's Cave (juvenile), Golden Press, 1979.
Lassie: Trouble at Panter's Lake (juvenile), Golden Press, 1979.
The Best Western Stories of Steve Frazee, edited by Bill Pronzini and Martin H. Greenberg, Southern Illinois University Press (Carbondale), 1984.

Contributor to anthologies, including *The Killers,* edited by Peter Dawson, Bantam (New York City), 1955, *Gunfight at the OK Corral and Other Western Adventures,* Avon, 1957, and *The Warriors,* edited by Bill Pronzini and Martin H. Greenberg, Doubleday (New York City), 1985. Also author, with others, of screen adaptation of his novel *Running Target,* 1957.

Collections of Frazee's manuscripts are housed at the University of Wyoming and the University of Kentucky.

ADAPTATIONS: Seven motion pictures and fifteen television programs have been based on Frazee's stories, including *Many Rivers to Cross,* MGM, 1955, *Running Target,* United Artists, 1957, *Wild Heritage,* Universal, 1958, *Gold of the Seven Saints,* Warner, 1961, and *The Alamo,* starring John Wayne.

SIDELIGHTS: Steve Frazee was not one of the most famous authors of westerns, but according to *Twentieth-Century Western Writers* contributor Bill Pronzini, he was one of the best. In that critic's opinion, "during the 1950's, no one wrote better popular western novels and stories than Steve Frazee." Many contemporary book reviewers also heartily endorsed Frazee's work. *Shining Mountains,* published in 1951, was an adventure story concerning a group of former soldiers—Confederate and Union—who joined forces during a gold rush in Colorado. A *San Francisco Chronicle* writer declared that the book "challenges while it entertains." *Hellsgrin,* published in 1960, was rated "first-class" by Nelson Nye in the *New York Times Book Review,* and praised for its "crisp narrative" by James Sandoe in the *New York Herald Tribune Book Review.* L. G. Offord, reviewer for the *San Francisco Chronicle,* found this western mystery "decidedly different, and absorbing." In addition to his adult novels, Frazee wrote many popular books for young readers.

Pronzini asserted: "It may safely be said that few contemporary writers can match Frazee for evocative, lyrical descriptions of wide-open spaces and of the awesome power of nature. Other of his attributes include flawless characterization, particularly when it involves the clash of human passions; believable dialogue; and the ability to create and sustain damp-palmed suspense. His work deserves more critical attention than it has thus far received, and it is to be hoped that this neglect will one day be rectified."

BIOGRAPHICAL/CRITICAL SOURCES:

BOOKS

Twentieth-Century Western Writers, St. James Press (Chicago), 1991.

PERIODICALS

Booklist, June 15, 1951; November 1, 1953; July 15, 1960.

Christian Science Monitor, May 12, 1960, p. 5B.
Kirkus Reviews, July 15, 1953; December 15, 1959; January 1, 1960.
Library Journal, April 15, 1951; May 15, 1960.
New Yorker, October 24, 1953.
New York Herald Tribune Book Review, September 27, 1953, p. 19; February 14, 1960, p. 15.
New York Times, September 27, 1953, p. 34.
New York Times Book Review, March 13, 1960, p. 33.
San Francisco Chronicle, July 29, 1951, p. 17; October 25, 1953, p. 23; March 13, 1960, p. 21.
Wilson Library Bulletin, September, 1960.*

* * *

FRENCH, Ashley
See ROBINS, Denise (Naomi)

* * *

FRIDAY, Nancy 1937-

PERSONAL: Born August 27, 1937, in Pittsburgh, PA; daughter of Walter (a financier) and Jane (Colbert) Friday; married W. H. Manville (a writer), October 20, 1967 (marriage ended); married Norman Pearlstine (an editor), July, 1988. *Education:* Attended Wellesley College.

ADDRESSES: Home—1108 Southard St., Key West, FL 33040. *Agent*—Betty Anne Clarke, International Creative Management, 20 West 51st St., New York, NY 10019.

CAREER: San Juan Island Times, San Juan, Puerto Rico, reporter, 1960-61; editor, *Islands in the Sun* (magazine), 1961-63; freelance writer, 1963—.

WRITINGS:

NONFICTION

My Secret Garden: Women's Sexual Fantasies, Trident, 1973.
Forbidden Flowers: More Women's Sexual Fantasies, Pocket Books, 1975.
My Mother/My Self: The Daughter's Search for Identity, Delacorte, 1977.

Men in Love: Men's Sexual Fantasies; The Triumph of Love over Rage, Delacorte, 1980.

Jealousy, Perigord, 1985.

Women on Top: How Real Life Has Changed Women's Sexual Fantasies, Simon & Schuster (New York City), 1991.

The Power of Beauty, HarperCollins (New York City), 1996.

ADAPTATIONS: Women on Top was adapted for audiocassette by Simon & Schuster Audioworks, 1991.

SIDELIGHTS: Nancy Friday entered the ranks of "pop-psychology" in the early 1970s with her books *My Secret Garden: Women's Sexual Fantasies* and *Forbidden Flowers: More Women's Sexual Fantasies.* Though non-scientific, both books broke ground as forums for women who might not otherwise suspect that their fantasies could be shared by others. But even before these works were published, Friday had been researching questions on the theme of mother-daughter relationships in contemporary times. In 1978, after interviewing three hundred mothers and daughters nationwide, Friday published perhaps her best-known book to date, *My Mother/My Self: The Daughter's Search for Identity.*

A quick bestseller, *My Mother/My Self* generated controversy because of the frank and often disturbing conclusions the author offered. "In effect, Friday is saying that our mothers molded us to fit the pre-liberation ideal of woman, and thus burdened us with the task of freeing ourselves," according to Amy Gross, writing in a *Village Voice* review. "She is also saying that until we do free ourselves, we will define happiness in terms of the symbiotic relationship we had with mother, no matter how unhappy that was." Gross faults *My Mother/My Self* for the author's "demands that we accept her every point as the truth about our lives," adding that in this book Friday's "focus is on the psychologically pathological. Her focus is on rage." But to *New York Times Book Review* critic Doris Grumbach, *My Mother/My Self* is "rich in anecdote, memories, testimonials, confessions, opinions by experts. What [the author] tells us that we inherit from our mothers much of what we are: our physical selves, our capacities, our whole baggage of repressions, insecurities and guilts," continues Grumbach. "Friday instructs us to look at ourselves not so much as the victims of a discriminatory patriarchy, but of an inevitable and unavoidable and destructive maternalism."

Friday followed *My Mother/My Self* with *Men in Love: Men's Sexual Fantasies; The Triumph of Love over Rage.* Similar in format to her first two books (the author solicited responses by including a mailing address within the two volumes) *Men in Love* includes two hundred male fantasies culled from three thousand letters. As the book was being released, Friday predicted it would be more controversial than her previous works because "people found it easy to talk about [female fantasies]; they're easily dismissed as trivial. This time you're dealing with *men,* the bedrock of society, you're talking about the deepest vulnerabilities of the so-called powerful sex," as Friday told John F. Baker in a *Publishers Weekly* interview. In the same article, the author revealed that *Men in Love* deals with "very powerful, primitive feelings, which arouse deep anxiety. The way I see it, the fantasies and feelings don't need an intellectual response; they need a gut-level deeply felt reaction, and that's how I treat them."

A number of critics fault Friday's analytics in *Men in Love.* *Newsweek's* Peter S. Prescott, for one, reports that the volume features a "stupefying quantity of testimony to various agitated states of mind interleaved with brief essays in which the author repeats what we have just read and ventures her interpretations. . . . Her thesis, that men's love of women is filled with rage, is pretty enough, but entirely unsupported by any of the evidence she has assembled." But Prescott does confess his "affection for this woman. Her charm, surely has much to do with her lack of credentials, with her distrust of statistical method, with her conviction that she has become in our society a liberating force, and with her refusal to disbelieve whatever her excited informers tell her to be true. I particularly like her just-folks prose style," the critic adds.

Jealousy, Friday's 1985 publication, postulates that jealousy and envy, two emotions that may seem synonymous, are in fact vastly different. The author makes an important distinction in this respect, says Susan Wood of *Washington Post Book World.* Jealousy "arises from a fear of losing something we have," while envy "is a desire to have something someone else has," as Wood relates. "Envy is by far the most destructive emotion and it is envy that is most often at work when we spoil what we love."

Again, critical reaction proved mixed. *Los Angeles Times* reviewer Carolyn See, taking the negative viewpoint, calls *Jealousy* "long, too long, way too long" at 524 pages, and adds that the author's "own diligent work habits may have finally betrayed her. She may have worked so long on 'Jealousy' that her . . . finger has slipped off the pulse of the nation: While she was working the temper of the times may have changed." Noting a passage in the book's introduction, where Friday describes a lustful encounter with a man who "introduced her [later on] to *huevos rancheros,*" See remarks that "no woman in the 1980s—when the rest of the nation is contemplating monogamy, children, 'the new chastity' and the sinister specter of AIDS—can hope to establish authority and credibility with tales of picking up other women's underwear and eating Mexican breakfasts." Wood, while sharing See's opinion that the book's length "might seem daunting," nonetheless adopts a more positive viewpoint overall. In *Jealousy,* she says, "nearly every page is readable, intelligent and full of insight and information. Most of all, *Jealousy* is big in importance. Relatively little has been written on the subject, certainly for the general reader, and Friday is convincing in her argument of jealousy's central role in our lives and the ways in which our lack of understanding, even our denial of the 'green-eyed monster' often cripples our most intimate relationships."

In 1991 Friday produced *Women on Top: How Real Life Changed Women's Sexual Fantasies,* another volume of female sexual fantasies collected anonymously via mail. Though heralding a transformation in women's sexuality, notably from submission to dominance as the title suggests, the book received criticism for its highly graphic and sensational content. Noting persistent references to bondage and bestiality, Margaret Carlson summarizes Friday's findings in a *Time* magazine review, "Women nowadays, it seems, aren't so much dominant as mutually sadistic." "Friday is so enraptured with the logistics of who is doing what to whom," Andrea Stuart writes in a *New Statesman and Society* review, "that she fails to achieve any analytical sophistication."

Friday followed with *The Power of Beauty,* in which she asserts the profound and undeniable effect of female physical appeal in society and among women themselves. Caryn James notes in the *New York Times* that Friday "suggests that women do themselves a disservice by pretending looks don't matter, and she urges men and women not only to acknowledge beauty's power but also to use it." While railing against "Matriarchal Feminism," a term Friday uses to describe those who advocate a superior or hostile position toward men, she advocates the introduction of supportive competition among women and an end to envy.

BIOGRAPHICAL/CRITICAL SOURCES:

BOOKS

Friday, Nancy, *My Mother/My Self: The Daughter's Search for Identity,* Delacorte, 1977.
Friday, *Jealousy,* Perigord, 1985.
Friday, *The Power of Beauty,* HarperCollins, 1996.

PERIODICALS

Chicago Tribune Book World, May 18, 1980.
Esquire, March, 1980; June, 1995, pp. 58, 76.
Los Angeles Times, November 26, 1985.
Los Angeles Times Book Review, December 8, 1991, p. 6.
Ms., May, 1980.
Nation, May 31, 1980.
New Statesman and Society, December 6, 1991, p. 46.
Newsweek, March 17, 1980; November 4, 1991, p. 54.
New York Review of Books, May 13, 1976.
New York Times, December 30, 1977; July 23, 1996, p. B3.
New York Times Book Review, October 7, 1973; February 12, 1978; February 22, 1981; October 6, 1985.
People Weekly, December 19, 1977; January 13, 1992, p. 26.
Publishers Weekly, February 28, 1980; October 18, 1991, p. 44; May 13, 1996, p. 64.
Time, December 2, 1991, p. 78.
Times Literary Supplement, October 24, 1975.
Vanity Fair, November, 1991, p. 216.
Village Voice, November 28, 1977.
Washington Post Book World, August 19, 1973; March 23, 1980; September 29, 1985.*

G

GARDNER, Nancy Bruff 1915-
(Nancy Bruff)

PERSONAL: Born November 15, 1915, in Fairfield County, CT; daughter of Austin J. (a broker) and Alice (Birdsall) Bruff; married Edwin Thurston Clarke, March 11, 1937 (died, 1962); married Esmond B. Gardner (a banker), July 20, 1963; children: (first marriage) Thurston B., Penelope. *Education:* Attended Sorbonne, University of Paris.

ADDRESSES: Home—150 East 72nd St., New York, NY. *Agent*— Lerniger Literary Agency, 437 Fifth Ave., New York, NY.

CAREER: Novelist and poet.

WRITINGS:

UNDER NAME NANCY BRUFF

The Manatee, Dutton (New York City), 1945.
My Talon in Your Heart (poems), Dutton, 1946.
Cider from Eden, Dutton, 1947.
Beloved Women, Messner, 1949 (published in England as *Love is Not Love,* Laurie, 1950).
The Fig Tree, Obolensky, 1965.
The Country Club, Bartholomew House (New York City), 1969.

SIDELIGHTS: Nancy Gardner writes novels under the name Nancy Bruff. Bruff's *The Manatee* is the story of a Nantucket whaling captain whose sadistic nature was formed during his fateful first voyage. A *Kirkus* reviewer finds that "the picture of the times and of Nantucket, as the whaling industry collapsed, is very well done." But William De Bois in the *New York Times* claims that *The Manatee* "would serve a class in novel-writing well, as a truly remarkable example of what not to do." Mary Ross, writing in the *Weekly Book Review,* notes that *The Manatee* "is lively reading, with fast action, exotic detail and bizarre incident."

Cider from Eden is the story of Chloe Van Fleet, who abandons her husband and children for South America and a life of romance. A *Kirkus* reviewer notes that "the plot is hastily stitched together and superficial," while a critic for the *New Yorker* claims that Bruff "does her earnest and dogged best to startle the lending-library set." B. V. Winebaum of the *New York Times* notes: "Bruff is concerned with the baser manifestations of sex" and *Cider from Eden* contains "adultery on desertion, impotence on lust, madness on immorality, and so on."

Bruff's 1949 novel, *Beloved Woman,* tackles a controversial subject. Mary Robbin begins an anonymous correspondence with a secret admirer, only to discover that the admirer is her black porter. Although a critic for the *New Yorker* believes "the expressed sentiments on behalf of our common humanity are entirely admirable [they] never quite parallel the real sentiments of real people." But C. M. Brown in the *Saturday Review of Literature* points out how "Bruff traces [her characters'] sorrows with form, deep sympathy, and brilliance."

BIOGRAPHICAL/CRITICAL SOURCES:

PERIODICALS

Atlantic, January, 1946.
Booklist, November 1, 1945.

Book Week, October 21, 1945, p. 5; March 24, 1946, p. 13.

Chicago Sun Book Week, March 23, 1947, p. 8.

Christian Science Monitor, May 12, 1949, p. 15.

Kirkus, September 1, 1945; February 15, 1946; January 1, 1947; March 1, 1949.

Library Journal, October 15, 1945; March 1, 1947.

New Yorker, October 27, 1945; March 15, 1947; May 7, 1949.

New York Herald Tribune Weekly Book Review, March 30, 1947, p. 29; October 2, 1949, p. 20.

New York Times, October 21, 1945, p. 30; March 16, 1947, p. 43; April 24, 1949, p. 30.

San Francisco Chronicle, March 16, 1947, p. 10.

Saturday Review of Literature, November 17, 1945; March 23, 1946; July 23, 1949.

Springfield Republican, October 28, 1945, p. D4; March 21, 1946, p. 6.

Time, March 17, 1947.

Weekly Book Review, October 21, 1945, p. 10.*

*   *   *

GEBHARD, Paul H(enry) 1917-

PERSONAL: Born July 3, 1917, in Rocky Ford, CO; son of Paul Adam (a cattle buyer) and Eva (Baker) Gebhard; married Agnes E. West, May 19, 1939 (divorced); married Joan C. Huntington, July 24, 1982; children: (first marriage) Mark, Jan, Karla. *Education:* Attended University of Arizona, 1937-38; Harvard University, B.S. (cum laude), 1940, M.A., 1942, Ph.D., 1947.

ADDRESSES: Home—3772 Hickory Hill Dr., Nashville, IN 47448. *Office*—Department of Anthropology, Indiana University, Bloomington, IN 47405.

CAREER: Institute for Sex Research, Bloomington, IN, research associate, 1946-55, executive director, 1956-82; Indiana University, Bloomington, IN, instructor, 1947-53, assistant professor, 1953-61, associate professor, 1961-65, professor of anthropology, 1966-86, professor emeritus, 1986—.

MEMBER: International Academy of Sex Research, American Anthropological Association (fellow), American Association for the Advancement of Science, Society for the Scientific Study of Sexuality, Indiana Academy of Science (fellow), Sigma Xi.

WRITINGS:

(With Kinsey, Pomeroy, and Martin) *Sexual Behavior in the Human Female,* Saunders (Philadelphia, PA), 1953.

(With Pomeroy, Martin, and Christenson) *Pregnancy, Birth and Abortion,* Harper-Hoeber, 1958.

(With Gagnon, Pomeroy, and Christenson) *Sex Offenders: An Analysis of Types,* Harper (New York City), 1965.

(With Raboch and Giese) *Der Sexualitaet der Frau,* Rowohlt, 1968.

(With Johnson) *The Kinsey Data,* Saunders, 1979.

Contributor of about seventy journal articles and book chapters from 1941-97.

*   *   *

GELLIS, Roberta L(eah Jacobs) 1927-
(Max Daniels, Priscilla Hamilton, Leah Jacobs)

PERSONAL: Born September 27, 1927, in Brooklyn, NY; daughter of Morris B. (a chemist) and Margaret (Segall) Jacobs; married Charles Gellis (a teacher), April 14, 1946; children: Mark Daniel. *Education:* Hunter College (now Hunter College of the City University of New York), B.A., 1946; Brooklyn Polytechnic Institute, M.S., 1951; New York University, M.A., 1958. *Politics:* Democratic ("vaguely"). *Religion:* Jewish.

ADDRESSES: Home—P.O. Box 483, Roslyn Heights, Long Island, NY 11577. *Agent*—Lucienne Diver, Spectrum Literary Agency, 111 Eighth Ave., New York, NY 10011. *E-mail*—robertagellis@juno.com; fax: 516-484-0871.

CAREER: Freelance writer and editor. Foster D. Snell, Inc., New York City, chemist, 1947-54; McGraw-Hill, New York City, editor, 1954-56; New York University, New York City, teaching assistant in English, 1956-58; Hudson Laboratories, New York City, microbiologist, 1961-63.

MEMBER: Authors Guild, Authors League of America, Pen and Brush Club, Science Fiction and Fantasy Writers of America, Romance Writers of America, Novelists, Inc.

AWARDS, HONORS: Lifetime Achievement Award, Romance Writers of America; several awards from the *West Coast Review of Books, Romantic Times,* and other publications.

WRITINGS:

Knight's Honor, Doubleday (New York City), 1964.
Bond of Blood, Doubleday, 1965.
(Under name Leah Jacobs) *The Psychiatrist's Wife,* New American Library (New York City), 1966.
Sing Witch, Sing Death, Bantam (New York City), 1975.
The Dragon and the Rose, Playboy Press (Chicago), 1977.
The Sword and the Swan, Playboy Press, 1977.
(Under pseudonym Max Daniels) *Space Guardian,* Pocket Books (New York City), 1978.
(Under pseudonym Max Daniels) *Offworld,* Pocket Books, 1979.
(Under pseudonym Priscilla Hamilton) *Love Token,* Playboy Press, 1979.
A Tapestry of Dreams, Berkley Publishing (New York City), 1985.
The Rope Dancer, Berkley Publishing, 1986.
Fires of Winter, Jove, 1987.
Masques of Gold, Jove, 1988.
A Delicate Balance, Leisure Books, 1993.
Dazzling Brightness, Pinnacle (New York City), 1994.
Shimmering Splendor, Pinnacle, 1995.
Enchanted Fire, Pinnacle, 1996.

"ROSELYNDE CHRONICLE" SERIES

Roselynde, Playboy Press, 1978.
Alinor, Playboy Press, 1978.
Joanna, Playboy Press, 1978.
Gilliane, Playboy Press, 1979.
Rhiannon, Playboy Press, 1981.
Sybelle, Jove, 1983.

"HEIRESS" SERIES

The English Heiress, Dell (New York City), 1980.
The Cornish Heiress, Dell, 1981.
The Kent Heiress, Dell, 1982.
Fortune's Bride, Dell, 1983.
A Woman's Estate, Dell, 1984.

"ROYAL DYNASTY" SERIES

Winter Song, Playboy Press, 1982.
Siren Song, Playboy Press, 1981.

Fire Song, Jove (New York City), 1984.
A Silver Mirror, Jove, 1989.

OTHER

Contributor to *Irish Magic: Four Tales of Romance and Enchantment from Four Acclaimed Authors,* Kensington (New York City), 1995, and *Irish Magic II: Four Unforgettable Novellas of Love and Enchantment,* Kensington, 1997.

WORK IN PROGRESS: "An historical mystery; another historical mystery; and *Bull God,* a mythological novel."

SIDELIGHTS: Roberta L. Gellis is a well-respected author of historical romances. Jean Mason, a contributor to *Romance Reader,* named Gellis "one of the pioneers of the romance genre," and identified her "strong characterizations, attention to historical detail, and intriguing plots" as reasons for her success. In Mason's opinion, Gellis is "the standard of excellence" in the romance field.

Barbara E. Kemp, a contributor to *Twentieth-Century Romance and Historical Writers,* concurred that Gellis is a strong writer. She advised that when a reader picks up a Roberta Gellis novel, "one should be prepared to enter a historical world of great vitality. Her stories are carefully researched and are loaded with details of the life and manners of the period. . . . There is a wealth of detail that immerses the reader in another time and place. Although that same detail might seem overwhelming at times, Gellis creates such real characters that they bring all the facts into focus and make history a living thing rather than a collection of dry dates and events. The underlying love stories serve to point out how historical events affect individuals."

Gellis has degrees in chemistry and has worked as a chemist and microbiologist; her writing had its genesis in her interest in medieval history and literature. As she explained in *Publishers Weekly:* "I always was a dichotomy in college. While I was getting my degree in chemistry, I took all my electives in English literature. I took medieval literature, and I always had a strong interest in writing. I even wrote as a child."

Most of Gellis's novels are set in the medieval period, and her books are notable for their accurate portrayal of the era. She has been faulted by some commentators, however, for creating numerous heroines who are strong and very much in control. Questioned about this by Mason, Gellis replied: "Strong women were surprisingly common in the medieval period. You don't hear much about them in the chronicles or history books, of course: Nicolaa de la Hay is mentioned and Hadwissa . . . Queen Eleanor herself. But in addition there were hundreds and hundreds of women whose men were always away at war or conducting legal cases. These women were left in charge of the property and managed it and defended it in the men's absence."

Discussing the heroines of Gellis's "Roselynde" series, Kemp noted: "Gellis makes it clear that she is dealing with extraordinary, rather than average, women. It is to her credit that she is able to portray such strong women so believably. It would be a mistake, however, to think that these women dominate their male companions. The women may be the central focus, but the men are their equals. They too are extraordinary: fiercely independent, passionate, and devoted to duty and honour." Kemp concluded that Gellis "excels in developing vibrant characters and integrating their stories with the historical period's events. . . . Gellis's view of men and women as individuals who are equal, who are able to maintain their individuality and equality in their male-female relationships, sets a different tone in the historical romance genre and places Gellis well ahead of many other authors in terms of quality."

In an interview for *Love's Leading Ladies,* Gellis remarked: "What influences my writing most, I think, was reading medieval literature and being enchanted by people who believe in honor and true love, although naturally, being human beings, they were as dishonorable and faithless then as people are now. The difference is that they had ideals, even if they did not live up to them; and when they did not live up to them, they knew they had done wrong and sometimes, tried to do better." Gellis once told *CA,* "I hope to give my readers a feeling for history—a thing lived and made by people, not a string of dry dates and facts."

BIOGRAPHICAL/CRITICAL SOURCES:

BOOKS

Falk, Kathryn, *Love's Leading Ladies,* Pinnacle Books, 1982.
Twentieth-Century Romance and Historical Writers, St. James Press (Detroit), 1994.

PERIODICALS

Publishers Weekly, November 13, 1981.
Romance Reader, July 3, 1997.*

*   *   *

GIOIA, (Michael) Dana 1950-

PERSONAL: Surname is pronounced "*Joy*-a"; born December 24, 1950, in Los Angeles, CA.; son of Michael (a cab driver and owner of a shoe store) and Dorothy (a telephone operator; maiden name, Ortiz) Gioia; married Mary Hiecke (a businesswoman), February 23, 1980; children: Michael (deceased), Theodore, one other son. *Education:* Stanford University, B.A. (with high honors), 1973, M.B.A., 1977; Harvard University, M.A., 1975. *Religion:* Roman Catholic.

ADDRESSES: Agent—Glen Hartley Agency, 25 West 19th St., New York, NY 10011.

CAREER: General Foods Corp., White Plains, NY, 1977-92, manager of new business development, 1977-87, marketing manager, beginning 1988, became vice president; freelance writer, 1992—. Member of board of directors of Wesleyan University Writers Conference, 1985—.

MEMBER: International PEN, Poetry Society of America (member of board of governors, 1988—).

AWARDS, HONORS: Listed in *Esquire 1984 Register* of "men and women under forty who are changing America"; Frederick Bock Prize in Poetry from *Poetry,* 1986; Poetry Book Society (London) main selection, 1991; Poet's Prize, 1992; *Publishers Weekly* Best Books award, 1992; American Literary Translator's award, 1992.

WRITINGS:

POETRY

Two Poems, Bowery (New York City), 1982.
Daily Horoscope, Windhover (Iowa City), 1982, enlarged edition, Graywolf Press (St. Paul, MN), 1986.
Letter to the Bahamas, Abattoir (Omaha, NE), 1983.
Summer, Aralia Press (West Chester, PA), 1983.

Journeys in Sunlight, Ex Ophidia (Cottondale, AL), 1986.

Words for Music, Parallel (Tuscaloosa, AL), 1987.

The Gods of Winter, Graywolf Press, 1991.

(With Robert McDowell) *The Diviners: A Book Length Poem,* Story Line Press (Brownsville, OR), 1995.

EDITOR

Weldon Kees, *The Ceremony and Other Stories,* Graywolf Press, 1984.

(With William Jay Smith) *Poems from Italy* (text in English and Italian), New Rivers Press (St. Paul, MN), 1985.

(With Alastair Reid) *The Printed Poem: The Poem as Print,* Press at Colorado College, 1985.

(With Michael Palma) *New Italian Poets* (anthology), Story Line Press, 1990.

(With William Logan) *Certain Solitudes: On the Poetry of Donald Justice,* University of Arkansas Press (Fayetteville), 1997.

OTHER

(Author of introduction) Weldon Kees, *Two Prose Sketches,* Aralia Press, 1984.

(Translator) Eugenio Montale, *Mottetti: Poems of Love,* Graywolf Press, 1990.

Can Poetry Matter?: Essays on Poetry and American Culture, Graywolf Press, 1992.

(With X. J. Kennedy) *An Introduction to Poetry,* HarperCollins College Publishers (New York City), 1994.

(Compiler, with Kennedy) *Literature: An Introduction to Fiction, Poetry, and Drama,* Harper-Collins College Publishers, 1995.

(Compiler, with Kennedy) *An Introduction to Fiction,* HarperCollins College Publishers, 1995.

(Translator) Seneca, *The Madness of Hercules,* Johns Hopkins University Press (Baltimore, MD), 1995.

Contributor of poems and reviews to magazines, including the *New Yorker, Kenyon Review, Hudson Review,* and *Poetry. Sequoia,* editor, 1971-73, poetry editor, 1975-77; *Inquiry,* literary editor, 1977-79, poetry editor, 1979-83.

SIDELIGHTS: Dana Gioia is "probably the most interesting poet to have emerged in the United States since the 1980s," in the estimation of *Contemporary Poets* writer William Oxley. Gioia realized that writing was his vocation while he was a student at

Stanford University. After graduating with high honors from that school, he went on to do postgraduate work at Harvard, where he studied with such luminaries as Robert Fitzgerald and Elizabeth Bishop. While at Harvard, Gioia's dedication to literature increased, but he became disillusioned with the academic world and what he perceived as its dry, detached attitude toward poetry. While maintaining his determination to be a poet, Gioia also decided to go on to Stanford Business School, where he earned a master's degree in business administration. Next, he took a job at the giant General Foods conglomerate. Gioia eventually became a vice president at General Foods, and, in his early years there, his associates were unaware that he was also a poet. He would work for ten to twelve hours at the office, then return home to write for a few more hours. "My seemingly constrained life gave me a sort of imaginative freedom that allowed me to grow as an artist," he was quoted as saying in a *New York Times* article by Paul Helou.

The "heart of his art," according to Oxley, is "its program . . . to make accessible transcendent reality through the commonplace. His poetry is calmly and unobtrusively measured. . . . Gioia keeps it simple." His poems usually focus on the details of life, yet they are frequently metaphysical as well. Discussing Gioia's first major collection, *Daily Horoscope,* Lewis Turco noted in *Dictionary of Literary Biography:* "[His] handling of the blank-verse mode is skillful throughout. . . . Gioia's emotional range . . . is wide, extending from the memorial to the humorous, but his forte is the elegiac." In *The Gods of Winter,* which was dedicated to his son who died from Sudden Infant Death Syndrome (SIDS), "there is a touch of anguish," found Oxley, "a darkening of tone, an intensification of feeling, bringing his poetry closer to lyrical spontaneity."

Turco mused: "Gioia is unusual because, unlike many of those poets who teach, he knows precisely what he is doing in his poetry and shows it through a masterful handling of the various levels of his poems. Unlike many of his academic peers, he is able to articulate his theory and practice in intelligent and constructive criticism, nearly a lost art among contemporary poets."

Gioia once told *CA:* "Though most of my poems use rhyme or meter, they rarely follow 'traditional' patterns. I love traditional forms, but I find them slightly dangerous. Their music can become so seductive that one loses touch with contemporary speech (which is, to my judgment, the basis for all genuine poetry). I am fascinated by the way rhyme and meter can create a sense of verbal tension in a poem that heightens every nuance of sound and sense. But I prefer to go after that effect either by experimenting with new forms or by playing with the rules of traditional patterns to achieve something slightly unexpected—I try to surprise myself as well as the reader.

"The Beat and Confessional poets were the strongest influences on me. Their unfailing verbosity and heroic self-absorption proved a constant inspiration—showing me everything I *didn't* want to do. One cannot overestimate the importance of negative examples at certain points in literary history when sensibilities shift. Growing up in California during the 1960s and 1970s, I knew what the early modernists must have felt in late Victorian America. Like them, one faced an exhausted tradition—in this case modernism itself now in arteriosclerotic old age—smugly dominant, academically entrenched, and in its current practitioners utterly boring. Although I then had little sense of what direction my own poetry might take, I knew what it must reject. Certainly my interest in form and narrative was encouraged by my milieu's insistence that they were impossible materials for serious poetry. Yet is seemed obvious—at least to a working-class kid like me—that form and narrative still had immense vitality in the popular arts like movies and rock music. I suspect that when high culture becomes tired and insular, popular culture usually has the remedy somewhere close at hand."

A collection of Gioia's manuscript is housed in the Berg Collection of the New York Public Library.

BIOGRAPHICAL/CRITICAL SOURCES:

BOOKS

Contemporary Poets, St. James Press (Detroit), 1996.
Dictionary of Literary Biography, Volume 120: *American Poets since World War II, Third Series,* Gale (Detroit), 1992.
McDowell, Robert, editor, *Poetry after Modernism,* Story Line Press, 1991.

PERIODICALS

Business Month, March, 1990.
Coda, November/December, 1985.

Commentary, February, 1993, p. 61.
Connoisseur, March, 1989.
Esquire, December, 1984.
Forbes, March 21, 1988, pp. 170-72.
New York Times, August 16, 1992.
New York Times Book Review, November 30, 1986, p. 17.
Sewanee Review, winter, 1989, pp. 73-96.
Writers' Digest, February, 1998, p. 10.*

*   *   *

GLANVILLE, Brian (Lester) 1931-

PERSONAL: Born September 24, 1931, in London, England; son of James Arthur and Florence (Manches) Glanville; married Elizabeth Pamela de Boer Manasse, March 19, 1959; children: Mark Brian James, Toby John and Elizabeth Jane (twins), Josephine Sarah. *Education:* Attended Charterhouse School, 1945-49. *Avocational interests:* Playing soccer.

ADDRESSES: Home—160 Holland Park Ave., London W. 11, England. *Agent*—John Farquharson Ltd., 162-168 Regent St., London W1R 5TB, England.

CAREER: Journalist and writer, 1949—. Sports columnist, *Sunday Times,* London, 1958—; soccer columnist, *New York Times.* Manager of football (soccer) club, the Chelsea Casuals, in London. Literary adviser, The Bodley Head Ltd., London, 1958-62.

AWARDS, HONORS: Berlin Film Festival prize for Broadcasting Corp. television documentary, 1963, for *European Centre Forward;* British Film Academy Award, 1967, for documentary; Thomas Coward Memorial Award, 1982.

WRITINGS:

(With Cliff Bastin) *Cliff Bastin Remembers,* Ettrick Press (London), 1950.
(Editor) *Footballer's Who's Who,* Ettrick Press, 1951.
Arsenal Football Club, Convoy (London), 1952.
The Reluctant Dictator, Laurie (London), 1952.
Henry Sows the Wind, Secker & Warburg (London), 1954.
Soccer Nemesis, Secker & Warburg, 1955.
Along the Arno, Secker & Warburg, 1956, Crowell (New York City), 1957.

The Bankrupts, Doubleday (New York City), 1958.

(With Jerry Weinstein) *World Cup,* R. Hale (London), 1958.

(With Jack Kelsey) *Over the Bar,* Paul (London), 1958.

After Rome, Africa, Secker & Warburg, 1959.

Soccer Round the Globe, Abelard Schuman (London), 1959.

A Bad Streak, and Other Stories, Secker & Warburg, 1961.

Diamond, Farrar, Straus (New York City), 1962.

(Editor) *The Footballer's Companion,* Eyre & Spottiswoode (London), 1962.

The Director's Wife, and Other Stories, Secker & Warburg, 1963.

The Rise of Gerry Logan, Secker & Warburg, 1963, Delacorte (New York City), 1965.

Know about Football, Blackie (London), 1963.

Goalkeepers Are Crazy: A Collection of Football Stories, Secker & Warburg, 1964.

World Football Handbook (annual), Hodder & Stoughton (London), 1964, Mayflower (London), 1966-72, Queen Anne Press (London), 1974.

The King of Hackney Marshes, and Other Stories, Secker & Warburg, 1965.

A Second Home, Secker & Warburg, 1965, Delacorte, 1966.

A Roman Marriage, M. Joseph (London), 1966, Coward, 1967.

The Artist Type, Jonathan Cape (London), 1967, Coward, 1968.

People in Sport, Secker & Warburg, 1967.

Soccer: A History of the Game, Its Players, and Its Strategy, Crown (New York City), 1968, published as *Soccer: A Panorama,* Eyre & Spottiswoode (London), 1969.

The Olympian, Coward, 1969.

A Betting Man (stories), Coward, 1969.

A Cry of Crickets, Coward, 1970.

The Puffin Book of Football, Penguin (London), 1970, revised edition, 1984.

Goalkeepers Are Different Hamish Hamilton (London), 1971, Crown, 1972.

Money Is Love, Doubleday, 1972 (published in England as *The Financiers,* Secker & Warburg, 1972).

Brian Glanville's Book of World Football, Dragon (London), 1972.

(With others) *Penguin Modern Stories 10,* Penguin, 1972.

The Thing He Loves, and Other Stories, Secker & Warburg, 1973.

The Sunday Times History of the World Cup, Times Newspapers (London), 1973, published as *History of the Soccer World Cup,* Macmillan (New York City), 1974, revised edition published as *The History of the World Cup,* Faber (London), 1984.

The Comic, Secker & Warburg, 1974, Stein & Day (New York City), 1975.

Soccer 76, Queen Anne Press, 1975.

The Dying of the Light, Secker & Warburg, 1976.

Target Man, Macdonald & Jane's (London), 1978.

The Puffin Book of Footballers, Penguin, 1978, revised edition published as *Brian Glanville's Book of Footballers,* 1982.

A Book of Soccer, Oxford University Press (New York City), 1979.

Never Look Back, M. Joseph, 1980.

Kevin Keegan, illustrated by Michael Strand, Hamish Hamilton, 1981.

The Puffin Book of Tennis, Penguin, 1981.

A Visit to the Villa (play), produced in Chichester, Sussex, 1981.

(With Patrick Garland and Roy Hudd) *Underneath the Arches* (play; produced in Chichester, Sussex, 1981, produced in London, 1982), Weinberger (London), 1984.

The Puffin Book of the World Cup, Penguin, 1984.

(With Kevin Whitney) *The British Challenge,* Muller (London), 1984.

Love Is Not Love, and Other Stories, Blond (London), 1985.

Kissing America, Blond (London), 1985.

(Editor) *The Joy of Football,* Hodder & Stoughton, 1986.

The Catacomb, Hodder & Stoughton, 1988.

Champions of Europe: The History, Romance, and Intrigue of the European Cup, Guinness (Enfield, Middlesex, England), 1991.

Also author of television documentary *European Centre Forward,* 1963, of screenplay, *Goal!,* 1967, and of radio plays *The Diary,* 1987, and *I Could Have Been King,* 1988. Author of scripts for British Broadcasting Corp. television program, *That Was the Week That Was.* Contributor of short stories and articles to *Mademoiselle, Gentleman's Quarterly,* and other magazines.

SIDELIGHTS: A sportswriter, novelist, and author of short stories Brian Glanville "has made the previously unexamined world of the professional footballer (soccer player) a subject of serious fiction," writes James J. Schramer in the *Dictionary of Literary Biography.* "But he has done more than write the standard sports book for male adolescents . . . ; he has captured the speech cadences of working-class Britons, giving voice to their aspirations and dreams. He has recreated the world from which have come both soccer's most rabid fans and its most skillful players." Writing in *Contemporary Novelists,* Trevor Royle notes: "Glanville's mastery of language and skillful handling of dialogue convey subtle shifts of feeling, and they also constantly change his and the reader's focus on this kaleidoscopic world. Above all, Glanville shows that he is one of the few contemporary novelists capable of tackling and expressing the values, or lack of them, in our rapidly changing society."

Glanville's best-known novel is probably *The Olympian,* the story of the making of an Olympic runner. But as Glanville states in his essay for the *Contemporary Authors Autobiography Series (CAAS):* "Of the many novels I have published in the States, *The Olympian* was best received, and far better understood than it was in England. Its protagonist is a runner, but as the shrewd Joe Garagiola remarked to me on the *Today Show,* 'This book isn't about track, is it?' Americans, especially then, seemed to me much more open, generous, and receptive than their English counterparts—reviewers who saw little and could be told nothing. Garagiola at one pole, Mark Schorer at another, responded warmly to *The Olympian,* whose ultimate subject, reworking a classical myth, is indeed not 'track' at all but the predicament of people in a Faustian world."

The book has been exceptionally well received by critics, many of whom believe that it is the author's finest work. Bill Perkins of the *National Observer* calls it "one of the best sports novels of all time" and goes on to say that Glanville "tells his story with a variety of techniques, all of which work wonderfully. Parts are told by Ike [the runner] in his simple Cockney style, parts in third person, parts through newspaper clippings and sports announcers, and parts by an articulate friend who serves as the drama's Greek chorus." Pete Axthelm, in his *Newsweek* review, explains that Glanville's "satirical gifts in themselves make the book a worthwhile portrait of a fascinating and little-understood field. But he provides much more. His tale is brilliantly told. . . . And it is also as serious an effort as anyone has made to explore the tortures and indecisions of the totally dedicated athlete."

Thomas Lask of the *New York Times* writes that *The Olympian* "takes a median position, equidistant from the mythic, fantasy-serving character of Bernard Malamud's *The Natural* and from the hard-line naturalism of Budd Schulberg's *The Harder They Fall."* Richard Schickel, in a review for *Harper's,* calls *The Olympian* "a sober, suspenseful, carefully crafted and controlled work that penetrates to the center of the athletic enigma. Which is this: you ask a quite ordinary personality who has, by chance, been endowed with some extraordinary physical capacity . . . and ask him to develop it, arduously, painfully, at the expense of life's ordinary amenities to absolutely freakish levels."

BIOGRAPHICAL/CRITICAL SOURCES:

BOOKS

Contemporary Authors Autobiography Series, Volume 9, Gale (Detroit), 1989.
Contemporary Literary Criticism, Volume 6, Gale, 1976.
Contemporary Novelists, 6th edition, St. James Press (Detroit), 1996.
Dictionary of Literary Biography, Volume 139: *British Short-Fiction Writers, 1945-1980,* Gale, 1994.
Walsh, William, *A Human Idiom,* Chatto & Windus (London), 1965.

PERIODICALS

Best Sellers, May 1, 1970.
Books, October, 1969; April, 1970.
Harper's, August, 1969.
London Magazine, April, 1961.
National Observer, July 21, 1969.
New Statesman, November 17, 1967.
Newsweek, June 23, 1969.
New York, April 18, 1970.
New York Times, May 22, 1969; June 13, 1969.
New York Times Book Review, June 29, 1969.
Punch, October 18, 1967.
Times Literary Supplement, July 17, 1969; October 24, 1980.

* * *

GLOAG, Julian 1930-

PERSONAL: Born July 2, 1930, in London, England; son of John Edwards (a writer) and Gertrude Mary (Ward) Gloag; married Elise Piquet, 1963 (divorced, 1966); married Danielle J. H. Haase-Dubosc (a university professor), September 4, 1968 (divorced,

1981); children: (second marriage) Oliver Toby Jacques, Vanessa Agnes Judith. *Education:* Magdalene College, Cambridge, B.A., 1953, M.A., 1958.

ADDRESSES: Home—4 place du 18 juin 1940, 75006 Paris, France. *Agent*—Georges Borchardt, Inc., 136 East 57th St., New York, NY 10022; Scott Simon Ltd., 43 Dought St., London WC1N 2LF, England; Michelle Lapautre, 6 rue Jean Carries, 75007 Paris, France.

CAREER: Chamber's Encyclopaedia, London, England, researcher, 1954-56; Ronald Press, New York City, assistant editor, 1956-59; freelance writer, 1959-61; Hawthorn Books, New York City, editor, 1961-63; freelance writer, 1963—. *Military service:* British Army, rifleman, 1949-50.

MEMBER: Royal Society of Literature (fellow), Royal Society of Arts (fellow), Authors Guild, Authors League of America, Garrick Club.

WRITINGS:

NOVELS

Our Mother's House, Simon & Schuster (New York City), 1963.
A Sentence of Life, Simon & Schuster, 1966.
Maundy, Simon & Schuster, 1969.
A Woman of Character, Random House (New York City), 1973.
Sleeping Dogs Lie, Dutton (New York City), 1980.
Lost and Found, Linden Press (New York City), 1981.
Blood for Blood, Holt (New York City), 1985.
Only Yesterday, Holt, 1987.
Love as a Foreign Language, Sinclair Stevenson (London), 1991.

OTHER

(Editor) John Gloag, *The American Nation: A Short History of the United States* (nonfiction), revised edition (Gloag not associated with first edition), Cassell (London), 1955.
Only Yesterday (television play; based on his novel), 1986.
The Dark Room (television play), 1988.

A collection of Gloag's manuscripts is housed at the Mugar Memorial Library at Boston University.

ADAPTATIONS: Our Mother's House was filmed by Metro-Goldwyn-Mayer and Filmways in 1967.

SIDELIGHTS: Novelist Julian Gloag, whose father was an acclaimed British architecture critic, has established his own literary reputation as a suspense writer with a penchant for the macabre. "Gloag is a novelist with quite remarkable gifts of observation," writes Christopher Smith in *Contemporary Novelists.* "His portrayals of human life, whether in Britain or in France, which he has made his home in recent years, are thoroughly persuasive and his characters come across as human beings who are compellingly convincing both in their psychology and in the marvelously accurate dialogue in which they express themselves and, no less significantly, betray their inner selves."

Gloag's first novel, the bestselling *Our Mother's House,* is a gruesome tale of seven children left alone by the death of their mother. The children, Smith writes, "seek to hide her death from the authorities and the prying neighbors. They do so for fear of being consigned to an orphanage." Through his delicate, but unsentimental, characterization of the children, Gloag traces what *Best Sellers* critic G. M. Casey calls "the intricate intermingling of innocence and evil." Dorrie Pagones says the characters "bring to mind the boys in William Golding's *Lord of the Flies*" in her *Saturday Review* critique. Smith, too, sees a similarity with the children who revert to primitivism in Golding's *Lord of the Flies,* noting that "when problems arise, the children gather at the tabernacle they have erected over the grave which they laboriously dug for their mother's corpse, and consult her spirit. The uneasy situation is disturbed by the return of the dead woman's husband, which, far from resolving problems, leads at first to further disaster before finally law and order is restored." Writing in the *TV Guide,* Judith Crist praises the "taut truth" of Gloag's depiction. "Gloag's characters are persons, not symbols," Casey concludes, "and their very vitality is a tribute to their creator's skill as a novelist."

In the suspenseful *A Sentence of Life,* Gloag tells the story of Jordan Maddox, a publishing house employee who is suspected of murdering his secretary. Although innocent, Maddox's refusal to tell the whole truth when questioned by police entangles him in a dangerous situation. Smith writes: "Whichever way he turns, however hard he tries to escape from suspicion, evidence keeps on turning up which seems to point unambiguously the finger at him. An extra dimension is added by a number of flashbacks which, far from clearing Jordan, appear to lend credibility to the detective's suspicions about his motives and actions."

Characterization is the strong point of Gloag's psychological suspense story entitled *Sleeping Dogs Lie*. The book opens with psychiatrist Hugh Welchman talking to Alex Brinton, a new patient who has recently developed a phobia about descending the stone staircase at his college. Through his questioning, Welchman forces Alex to confront his past, but instead of banishing his patient's fears, the psychiatrist is pulled into the nightmare. "Welchman is a brilliant creation," states Evan Hunter in the *New York Times Book Review*. "A dedicated, gently probing professional, his frame of reference is entirely psychological; the smallest detail, the slightest gesture is noted in clinical terms. . . . But oh how relentlessly *human* he is as well. In fact, the triumph of Julian Gloag's intricate tale is that Welchman must eventually come to grips with his own ghosts as well as those that are haunting his young patient." Concludes the *New Yorker* critic, "*Sleeping Dogs Lie* is a psychological study of almost gothic ferocity, stirring and shattering—a dazzle of literary brilliance."

Blood for Blood begins as a murder mystery but gradually becomes a more sinister mystery altogether. "At first," writes Smith," "it seems that the issue is simply one of discovering who murdered the barrister Vivian Winter with such excessive violence. Gradually, though, we learn more and more about the character from his friend Ivor Speke, a minor writer with a past complicated by personal tragedies, and we eventually realize that Vivian was not at all what he seemed to be at the outset, but instead something disturbingly different. . . . Initial sympathies are gently transformed as the focus subtly changes from the classic question of who committed the crime to the more intriguing problem of deciding who the characters really are."

Only Yesterday turns from Gloag's usual focus on mystery and the macabre to tell the story of a middle-aged son announcing to his elderly parents that he has quit his job and is divorcing his wife. Smith describes the novel as "short, with its plot reduced to a bare minimum, but with every character evoked with a host of idiosyncrasies that ring true, and set against the precisely detailed background of a comfortable London suburb. . . . There is a good deal of gentle humor, but that only adds to what has rightly been hailed by the critics as a brilliant portrayal of old age and what the realization of old age

and death must mean both to the elderly and to younger generations."

BIOGRAPHICAL/CRITICAL SOURCES:

BOOKS

Authors in the News, Volume 1, Gale (Detroit), 1976.
Contemporary Novelists, 6th edition, St. James Press (Detroit), 1996.

PERIODICALS

Best Sellers, May 15, 1963.
Chicago Tribune Book World, July 27, 1980; July 26, 1981.
Milwaukee Journal, June 24, 1973.
New Yorker, October 13, 1980; August 3, 1981.
New York Times Book Review, May 12, 1963; March 9, 1969; May 27, 1973; July 20, 1980; July 26, 1981.
Saturday Review, June 22, 1963; February 22, 1969.
Times Literary Supplement, June 26, 1969; December 12, 1980; October 23, 1981.
TV Guide, July 15, 1972.
Washington Post Book World, July 28, 1981.

*   *   *

GODFREY, (William) Dave 1938-

PERSONAL: Born August 9, 1938, in Winnipeg, Manitoba, Canada; son of Richmond (a lawyer) and Marguerite (a teacher; maiden name, Hutcheson) Godfrey; married Ellen Swartz, 1963; children: Jonathan Kofi, Rebecca, Samuel. *Education:* Attended Harvard University, 1957, and University of Toronto, 1957-58; University of Iowa, B.A., 1960, M.F.A., 1963, Ph.D., 1966; Stanford University, M.A., 1963; attended University of Chicago, 1965.

ADDRESSES: Office—Department of English, University of Victoria, Victoria, BC, Canada V8W 2Y2.

CAREER: Adisadel College, Cape Coast, Ghana, lecturer in African literature and English and acting head of department, 1963-65; University of Toronto, Trinity College, Toronto, Ontario, assistant professor of English, 1966-68, 1969-74, writer-in-residence at Erindale College, 1973-74; York University, Downsview, Ontario, visiting professor of English, 1974-75; University of Toronto, Trinity College, visiting professor of English, 1975-76, coordinator of Canadian literature minor program; York University, associate professor of humanities, 1976-77; University of Victoria, Victoria, British Columbia, head of creative writing department, 1977-82, professor of English, 1982—. Editor, Press Porcepic Ltd., Victoria, 1972—. Co-founder, editor, and president of House of Anansi, 1966-70; senior editor of New Press, 1969-73.

MEMBER: Association of Canadian Publishers (president, 1972-73), Association for the Export of Canadian Books (founding director, 1972—), Inter-Provincial Association for Telematics and Telidon (vice-president, 1982—).

AWARDS, HONORS: President's medals from University of Western Ontario, 1964, for story "Gossip: The Birds That Flew, the Birds That Fell," and 1966, for article "Letter from Africa to an American Negro" and story "The Hard-Headed Collector"; Canada Council grants, 1965 and 1968-69; Governor-General's award, 1970, for *The New Ancestors*.

WRITINGS:

Death Goes Better with Coca-Cola (stories), House of Anansi Press (Toronto), 1967, 3rd edition, 1976.
(Editor with Bill McWhinney) *Man Deserves Man: CUSO in Developing Countries,* Ryerson (Toronto), 1967.
(With Clark Blaise and Lewis Stein) *New Canadian Writing 1968,* Clarke Irwin (Toronto), 1969.
The New Ancestors (novel), New Press (Toronto), 1970.
(Editor with Mel Watkins) *Gordon to Watkins to You—A Documentary of the Battle for Control of Our Economy,* New Press, 1970.
(Editor with Robert Fulford and Abe Rotstein) *Read Canadian: A Book about Canadian Books,* Lorimer (Toronto), 1972.
I Ching Kanada (prose poems), Press Porcepic (Erin, Ontario), 1976.
Dark Must Yield (stories), Press Porcepic, 1978.
(Editor with Douglas Parkhill) *Gutenberg Two,* Press Porcepic, 1979, 4th edition, 1984.
The Telidon Book, Press Porcepic, 1981, Reston (Reston, VA), 1982.
(With Sharon Sterling) *The Elements of CAL: The How-to Book on Computer-Aided Learning,* Reston, 1982.

(With Jack Brahan) *Computer-Aided Learning Using the NATAL Language,* Press Porcepic, 1984.
(Editor) Harold A. Innis, *Empire and Communications,* Press Porcepic, 1986.

Contributor to anthologies, including *Great Canadian Short Stories,* edited by Alec Lucas, Dell, 1971, *Power Corrupted,* edited by A. Rotstein, New Press, 1971, and *Canadian Anthology,* edited by Carl F. Klink and Reginald Watters, Gage, 1976. Contributor of twenty short stories and of articles and reviews to periodicals, including *Tamarack Review, Canadian Literature, Saturday Night, Impulse,* and *Canadian Forum.* General editor of "Canadian Writers" series, McClelland & Stewart, 1968-72. Editor of *Canadian Poetry Annual,* 1976—. Fiction editor of *Canadian Forum,* 1971-72; editor of *Porcepic,* 1972—; member of editorial board, *CIPS* (magazine).

SIDELIGHTS: "In both its form and content Dave Godfrey's fiction reflects the nationalistic political stance that colors his career," writes Robert Lecker in *Contemporary Novelists.* "As an emerging writer in the 1960s, Godfrey initiated several attempts to define Canadian literary consciousness through policies affecting the publishing industry and through fiction that addressed the issue of foreign influence in Canada. His activities in publishing, including the founding of House of Anansi Press, New Press, and Press Porcepic." As Peter Buitenhuis notes in the *Dictionary of Literary Biography,* Godfrey's "literary, teaching, and political activities have as their common goal creating those conditions under which the writer in Canada can best flourish."

According to Lecker, Godfrey's "experimental, nationalistic stance is suggested by the title of his first collection of stories, *Death Goes Better with Coca-Cola,* a book that explores the connection between American Coca-Cola culture and death—a death that Godfrey writes against in a series of densely-textured tales about various forms of life-giving liberation." "Aggression," writes Buitenhuis, "against animals, other humans, and of one culture against another may be said to be what *Death Goes Better with Coca-Cola* is about."

In his only novel, *The New Ancestors,* Godfrey draws on his own experience as a teacher in Ghana. Telling the story of an African dictator and his people's struggle to free themselves from his control, the novel focuses on the re-emergence of belief in lost tribal gods, the "new ancestors" of the title. "Although the book is set abroad," Lecker believes, "it is clear that Godfrey saw in an African struggle for independence important parallels with Canada's desire for a similar independence from foreign control. Thus the novel can be read in allegorical terms. But it can also be appreciated for Godfrey's experiments with perspective, in that the story is told from four vastly different viewpoints which must be interpreted individually and collectively before the tragic story can emerge." Buitenhuis finds that "the novel presents a rich and evocative tapestry of life on the African continent, a portrayal so rich in detail that it sometimes overshadows the drama and significance of events played out against this backdrop. At the end the reader is left uncertain about the meanings of all these events—which is perhaps one of Godfrey's intentions." Lecker sums up *The New Ancestors* as "a brilliant Canadian *nouveau roman.*"

In *I Ching Kanada,* Godfrey adapts the traditional Chinese book used in divination as a means to explore Canadian cultural heritage. In a series of 64 prose poems, Buitenhuis explains, Godfrey explores "different aspects of Canada's past and present: the myths and legends of the native peoples, the original settlement from the American colonies in the east, the western settlements, and the encroachment of American economic and cultural interests." "The book presents no final message or overall coherence," Lecker writes, "because Godfrey is interested in exploring the relationship between chance and the movement toward nationhood. If the meditations are also seen as reflections on selfhood, as some commentators have suggested, then *I Ching Kanada* becomes a metafictional text through which Godfrey reveals himself, his fiction, and the relationship he sees between the two."

Buitenhuis concludes that "as an artist [Godfrey] uses his ability to welcome and put to use new ideas. As a social commentator, he is highly sensitive to the role that the arts can play in social change. Underlying all his work is a passionate desire to make Canada culturally, politically, and economically independent. No small part of the credit for the movement toward these goals is due to his efforts in writing, publishing, editing, and crusading."

Godfrey once told *CA:* "I am most interested in that portion of literature where myth meets social realities; literary dogma concerning the purity of fantasy or of realism does not interest me. The Canadian environment has influenced me greatly although I write mainly about people from cultures other than my own. A good part of my twenties was spent traveling about the U.S. and Africa. I strive for great complexity in my writing because that is how I find life; I do not believe the writer has the duty to simplify or interpret life for his readers; his major tasks are to be as intelligent as possible and to take flights of imagination into bodies, minds and situations other than his own."

BIOGRAPHICAL/CRITICAL SOURCES:

BOOKS

Cameron, Donald, *Conversations with Canadian Writers,* Macmillan (Toronto), 1973.
Contemporary Novelists, 6th edition, St. James Press (Detroit), 1996.
Dictionary of Literary Biography, Volume 60: *Canadian Writers since 1960, Second Series,* Gale (Detroit), 1987.
Gibson, Graeme, *Eleven Canadian Novelists,* Anansi, 1972.
Moss, John, *Sex and Violence in the Canadian Novel,* McClelland & Stewart (Toronto), 1977.

PERIODICALS

Ariel, July, 1973, pp. 5-15.
Canadian Forum, March, 1968; October, 1968; February, 1969; April, 1971.
Canadian Literature, winter, 1977, pp. 15-26, 27-40; summer, 1983, pp. 72-80.
Ellipse, autumn, 1970.
Journal of Canadian Fiction, Volume 4, number 1, 1975, pp. 96-110.
Modern Fiction Studies, autumn, 1976, pp. 375-385.
Mysterious East, December, 1970.
Nation, September 6, 1971.
Quill & Quire, April, 1981, pp. 16-17.
Saturday Night, June, 1968.
Studies in Canadian Literature, winter, 1977, pp. 82-92.

*   *   *

GORDON, Suzanne 1945-

PERSONAL: Born November 2, 1945, in New York, NY; daughter of Dan M. (a physician) and Blanche Gordon; married Peter Fehler (a carpenter), August 8, 1973. *Education:* Cornell University, B.A., 1967; Johns Hopkins University, M.A., 1969.

ADDRESSES: Home and office—Oakland, CA. *Agent*—David Obst, 1910 N St. N.W., Washington, DC 20036.

CAREER: Substitute teacher in Baltimore, MD, public schools, 1969-70; United Press International, Baltimore, reporter and photographer, 1970. Editor and translator for French journalist Philippe de Villers.

WRITINGS:

(With G. E. de Villiers) *Poetry: Now and Then,* Macmillan (New York City), 1968.
In This Temple: A Guide Book to the Lincoln Memorial, Museum Press, 1973.
Black Mesa: The Angel of Death, John Day (New York City), 1973.
Lonely in America, Simon & Schuster (New York City), 1975.
Off Balance: The Real World of Ballet, photographs by Earl Dotter, Pantheon (New York City), 1983.
A Talent for Tomorrow: Life Stories of South African Servants, photographs by Ingrid Hudson, Ravan Press (Johannesburg, South Africa), 1985.
Under the Harrow: Lives of White South Africans Today, Heinemann (London), 1988.
Prisoner's of Men's Dreams: Striking out for a New Feminine Future, Little, Brown (Boston), 1991.
Life Support: Three Nurses on the Front Lines, introduction by Claire M. Fagin, Little, Brown, 1997.

EDITOR

(With David McFadden) *Economic Conversion: Revitalizing America's Economy,* Ballinger (Cambridge, MA), 1984.
(With Patricia Benner and Nel Noddings) *Caregiving: Readings in Knowledge, Practice, Ethics, and Politics,* University of Pennsylvania Press (Philadelphia), 1996.
(With Ellen D. Baer and Claire M. Fagan) *Abandonment of the Patient: The Impact of Profit-Driven Health Care on the Public,* Springer (New York City), 1996.

OTHER

Contributor of articles, poems, and short stories to *Earth, Washington Post, Newsweek, Sundance, Ms.,* and *Ramparts.* Contributor to *Raising Hell: How the Center for Investigative Reporting Gets the Story,* compiled by David Weir and Dan Noyes, Addison-Wesley, 1983.

SIDELIGHTS: In *Prisoner's of Men's Dreams: Striking Out for a New Feminine Future,* investigative reporter Suzanne Gordon examines how women's entry into the workplace has undermined what she calls the "transformative feminism" of the 1960s. It is Gordon's contention, supported by interviews with successful business and professional women, that the values of caring and compassion inherent in this feminism have failed to humanize the power structure of the capitalist system. Rather, capitalism has changed the women who have become a part of its power structure so that their values are no different than men with whom they are competing; namely, their goals are self-centered and turn primarily on the accumulation of wealth, power, and prestige. Gordon feels that the women's movement needs to regroup and rededicate itself to a feminism based more on caring than on competition, more on collective action for the betterment of all than on individual aspiration. She calls for feminists to support a "National Care Agenda," the particulars of which would include universal health care, affordable housing, increased financing of public education, one-month paid vacations, and a return to the 40-hour work week. Ellen Franklin Paul, writing in *Reason,* is highly critical both of Gordon's thesis and her suggested solutions. Paul argues that Gordon misunderstands the value of the free marketplace and believes that the programs she suggests pose a threat to personal freedom. Erika Munk, in the *New York Times Book Review,* grants the "humane impulses" behind *Prisoner's of Men's Dreams,* but feels that the book suffers on several counts: a failure to clearly define "caring," an inadequate exploration of the role of men in the problems discussed, and ultimately, a kind of romanticism that ignores the lessons of history.

In *Life Support: Three Nurses on the Front Lines* Gordon presents both a book about the lives and work of contemporary registered nurses and a critical assessment of our health care system. Gordon conducted in-depth interviews with three nurses working at a Boston hospital. A *Publishers Weekly* reviewer notes: "Profiling a variety of cases the three worked on, Gordon lets the nurses speak for themselves, effectively illustrating their commitment to their profession and involving readers in real-life drama." Arguing that quality nursing is essential to the quality of our health care, Gordon goes on to point out that for-profit hospitals and managed care systems are in the process of eliminating registered nurses exclusively for economic reasons, replacing them with unlicensed "care technicians" or general hospital staff. She also examines in critical detail the philosophies and methodologies of contemporary health care in America. *Washington Post* reviewer Beryl Lieff Benderly is lavish in her praise of *Life Support: Three Nurses on the Front Lines.* She calls it "a beautiful, profound and profoundly important book." "Heeding its counsel," Benderly contends, "would do more to improve our nation's health care, decrease suffering and control costs than all the . . . panels . . . reports . . . studies and . . . reviews that the nation could possibly undertake."

BIOGRAPHICAL/CRITICAL SOURCES:

PERIODICALS

Booklist, November 15, 1973, p. 308.
Boston Globe, April 29, 1997, p. D1.
Chicago Tribune, March 23, 1997, section 14, p. 3.
Choice, October, 1975, p. 1058; July-August, 1983, p. 1606.
Kirkus Reviews, January 1, 1997, p. 36.
Library Journal, February 1, 1997, p. 99.
Nation, May 14, 1983, pp. 610-11.
New Statesman, August 26, 1988, pp. 36, 38.
New York Review of Books, January 16, 1992, p. 13-17.
New York Times Book Review, February 29, 1976, p. 5; May 1, 1997, p. 67; August 12, 1984, p. 32; January 13, 1991, p. 20.
Publishers Weekly, July 2, 1973, p. 74; January 20, 1997, p. 388.
Reason, December, 1991, pp. 33-34.
Village Voice, June 14, 1983, p. 28.
Washington Post, May 26, 1997, p. C1; August 5, 1997, p. Z11.

*   *   *

GOVER, (John) Robert 1929-
(O. Govi)

PERSONAL: Born November 2, 1929, in Philadelphia, PA; son of Bryant Addison and Anna (Wall) Gover; married Mildred Vitkovich (a nurse-anesthetist), March 15, 1955 (divorced, 1966); married Jeanne-Nell Gement, December 23, 1968; children: (second marriage) Bryant. *Education:* University of

Pittsburgh, B.A., 1953. *Politics:* Anarchist. *Avocational interests:* "Digging people, the various styles they live in and the range of 'realities' they believe in."

ADDRESSES: Home—K8 River's Bend, Carney's Point, NJ 08069.

CAREER: Reporter for various small daily newspapers in Pennsylvania and Maryland, 1954-60; also employed as a construction worker and bookstore salesman, and operator of a beach shop near Convention Hall, Atlantic City, NJ, 1960; freelance writer, 1961—.

MEMBER: Authors Guild, PEN.

WRITINGS:

NOVELS

One Hundred Dollar Misunderstanding (first in a trilogy), Ballantine (New York City), 1961, with a new introduction by Herbert Gold, Grove (New York City), 1980.
The Maniac Responsible, Grove, 1963.
Here Goes Kitten (second in the trilogy), Grove, 1964.
Poorboy at the Party, Simon & Schuster (New York City), 1966.
J.C. Saves (last in the trilogy), Simon & Schuster, 1968.
Going for Mr. Big, Bantam (New York City), 1973.
(Under pseudonym O. Govi) *To Morrow Now Occurs Again,* Ross Erikson (Santa Barbara, CA), 1975.
(Under pseudonym O. Govi) *Getting Pretty on the Table,* Capra Press (Santa Barbara, CA), 1975.

OTHER

(Editor) *The Portable Walter* (anthology of prose and poetry of Walter Lowenfels), International Publishers (New York City), 1968.
Bring Me the Head of Rona Barrett (stories), M. Hargraves (San Francisco), 1981.
Voodoo Contra, Samuel Weiser (York Beach, ME), 1985.

Contributor to periodicals.

SIDELIGHTS: According to George Perkins in *Contemporary Novelists,* Robert Gover's work is often "formula fiction: shake up the characters, move them to a new starting point, put them in motion, follow the formula, and you have another book. . . . Yet there is an honesty in Gover, a vision of the life about him and a quality of writing that raises him above the level of either the pulp pornographer or the slick composer of bestsellers. However much he taxes the reader's impatience with shallow characterizations, absurd plot manipulations, gratuitous sex, and moral implications that are occasionally downright silly, he is at times an accomplished satirist. One must only imagine his books in the form of Classic Comics, illustrated by cartoonists for *Mad Magazine,* to be made aware how sure is his touch of the particular grotesque exaggeration that comically, or cruelly, reveals a specific truth. His are not realistic novels, but verbal comic strips, sharing a good many of the virtues and faults of such a paradigm of the genre as Norman Mailer's *An American Dream.* In large measure he is a moralist—disgusted at times, bitter and angry at others, but always subordinating the matter to the message. And the message is always the same: the Anglo-Saxon American power structure has created a society in which sex and violence are so perversely twisted together that there is no place for honest respect and affection between individuals, classes, or races."

Gover once told *CA:* "I have tended to avoid public exposure or publicity about myself; I'd prefer to have my work succeed or fail on its own, keeping myself free to think and do the unexpected without the need to explain. If, later in life, my work has counted for something, I'd very much enjoy being honored . . . [My] major vocational interest is human nature and the suicidal course our species is on, how we got on it and how we might get off it.

BIOGRAPHICAL/CRITICAL SOURCES:

BOOKS

Contemporary American Novelists, edited by Harry T. Moore, Southern Illinois University Press, 1964.
Contemporary Novelists, 6th edition, St. James Press (Detroit), 1996.
Hargraves, Michael, *Robert Gover: A Descriptive Bibliography,* Meckler (Westport, CT), 1988.

PERIODICALS

L'Express, August 30, 1962.
New York Times Book Review, August 25, 1968.

GOVI, O.
See GOVER, (John) Robert

*   *   *

GRAHAM, Robert
See HALDEMAN, Joe (William)

*   *   *

GRAY, Harriet
See ROBINS, Denise (Naomi)

*   *   *

GREER, Germaine 1939-
(Rose Blight)

PERSONAL: Born January 29, 1939, near Melbourne, Australia; daughter of Eric Reginal (a newspaper advertising manager) and Margaret May Mary (Lanfrancan) Greer; married Paul de Feu (a journalist), 1968 (divorced, 1973). *Education:* University of Melbourne, B.A., 1959; University of Sydney, M.A., 1961; Newnham College, Cambridge, Ph.D., 1967. *Politics:* Anarchist. *Religion:* Atheist.

ADDRESSES: Home—Tuscany, Italy. *Agent*—Curtis Brown Ltd., 162-68 Regent St., London W1R 5TA, England.

CAREER: Taught at a girls' school in Australia; University of Warwick, Coventry, England, lecturer in English, 1967-73; founder and director of Tulsa Centre for the Study of Women's Literature, 1979-82; director of Stump Cross Books, 1988—; special lecturer unofficial fellow, Newnham College, Cambridge, 1989—; writer. Has been an actress on a television comedy show in Manchester, England.

AWARDS, HONORS: J. R. Ackerly Prize, Internationazionale Mondello, 1989, for *Daddy, We Hardly Knew You;* honorary degree from University of Griffith, 1996.

WRITINGS:

The Female Eunuch, MacGibbon & Kee, 1970, McGraw, 1971.

The Obstacle Race: The Fortunes of Women Painters and Their Work, Farrar, Straus, 1979.

Sex and Destiny: The Politics of Human Fertility, Harper, 1984.

Shakespeare (literary criticism), Oxford University Press, 1986.

The Madwoman's Underclothes: Essays and Occasional Writings, Picador, 1986, Atlantic Monthly Press, 1987.

(Editor with Jeslyn Medoff, Melinda Sansone, and Susan Hastings) *Kissing the Rod: An Anthology of Seventeenth-Century Women's Verse,* Farrar, Straus, 1989.

Daddy, We Hardly Knew You, Viking Penguin, 1989.

The Change: Women, Aging, and the Menopause, Hamish Hamilton (London), 1991.

Slip-Shod Sibyls: Recognition, Rejection, and the Woman Poet, Viking, 1995.

Contributor to *River Journeys,* Hippocrene Books, c. 1985. Contributor to periodicals, including *Esquire, Listener, Oz, Spectator,* and, under pseudonym Rose Blight, *Private Eye.* Columnist, *London Sunday Times,* 1971-73. Co-founder of *Suck.*

SIDELIGHTS: Germaine Greer's writings, which include *The Female Eunuch, The Obstacle Race: The Fortunes of Women Painters and Their Work, Sex and Destiny: The Politics of Human Fertility,* a literary study titled *Shakespeare,* and the essay collection *The Madwoman's Underclothes,* have earned her both praise and disparagement from mainstream, academic, and feminist critics. The praise has typically been offered for her scholarly insight—which is perhaps most notable in *Shakespeare* and her study of great but unrecognized women artists, *The Obstacle Race*—and the criticism for her refusal to routinely espouse whatever literary or feminist ideas are most popular at a given time.

Greer had become a media success upon the American publication of *The Female Eunuch* in 1971. Such celebrity was consistent with her roles as a television performer and as a self-avowed London "groupie" (her enthusiasm for jazz and popular music had brought her into contact with musicians and other members of Britain's underground culture); but critics seized upon her slick and frankly sexual image as counterproductive to the feminist cause she espoused. While *The Female Eunuch* climbed the best-seller charts in both the United States and England and *Vogue* magazine hailed her as "a super heroine," many members of the women's liberation movement questioned her authority. While *Newsweek* described her as "a dazzling combination of erudition, eccentricity and eroticism," some feminist writers wondered whether an indisputably attractive Shakespearean scholar could speak with understanding about the plight of women in general.

Nevertheless, *The Female Eunuch* sold. It was made a Book-of-the-Month Club alternate and a Book Find Club selection and was ultimately translated into twelve languages. During a United States promotional tour in the spring of 1971, Greer furthered her message on television and radio talk shows, in *Life* magazine, and in a well-publicized debate with Norman Mailer, a novelist and self-confirmed "male chauvinist."

Greer's basic argument, as explained in the book's introduction, is that women's "sexuality is both denied and misrepresented by being identified as passivity." She explains that women, urged from childhood to live up to an "Eternal Feminine" stereotype, are valued for characteristics associated with the castrate—"timidity, plumpness, languor, delicacy and preciosity"—hence the book's title. From the viewpoint of this primary assumption, Greer examines not only the problems of women's sexuality, but their psychological development, their relationships with men, their social position, and their cultural history. What most struck early critics of the book was that she considered "the castration of our true female personality. . . not the fault of men, but our own, and history's." Thus *Newsweek* considered Greer's work "women's liberation's most realistic and least anti-male manifesto"; and Christopher Lehmann-Haupt called it "a book that combines the best of masculinity *and* femininity."

In 1989 she published a more personal book than her previous volumes, *Daddy, We Hardly Knew You,* which records her painstaking investigations into the life and personality of her father, Reginald "Reg" Greer, after his death in 1983. Greer's "quest" to reconstruct her father's lineage leads to an international tour through the landscape and archives of Britain, Australia, South Africa, India, Tuscany, Malta, and finally Tasmania, where she discovers her father's humble upbringing as a foster child whose lifelong reticence was intended to bury his illegitimate origin. According to Jill Johnston in the *New York Times Book Review,* the story of Reg Greer "is a very sad story, which his daughter glosses with her rage and transcends with her vast knowledge of all sorts of things." The paucity of information produced by her frustrating research is supplemented by expansive digressions that portray the land and people encountered on her travels, including an entire chapter entitled "Sidetrack" that documents various physical and historical aspects of the Australian continent. Nancy Mairs describes the book in the *Los Angeles Times Book Review* as "part childhood reminiscence, part travelogue, part genealogy, part history, part social commentary." As the author can no longer view her father as a "hero" or "prince in disguise," Johnston concludes, "In the end Germaine Greer can't reconcile her father's lack of love with her understanding of the fear that made him lie to conceal his lowly origins."

Greer produced a forceful indictment of modern youth culture with *The Change: Women, Aging, and the Menopause,* renaming the later female life stage "climacteria" and invoking the term "anophobia" to describe the irrational fear and hostility directed toward older women. As Joan Frank observes in the *San Francisco Review of Books,* Greer identifies menopause as "a real and crucial transition in a woman's life for which no—repeat, *no*—reliable information, clear role models, rites of passage, historic or cultural sanctions exist as they do for comparable transitions: birth, the onset of menarche, marriage, childbirth, and death." Gleaning evidence from diverse and unlikely sources such as "historical accounts, memoirs, correspondence from the court of Louis XIV, old medical textbooks, anthropology tracts, novels, and poems both familiar and obscure," as Natalie Augier notes in the *New York Times Book Review,* Greer "talks with unvarnished candor about the invisibility of the middle-aged woman in our own culture, the unfairness of a system that lionizes the silver-haired male while scorning his female counterpart as beyond use, pathetic, desiccated, desexualized, a crone." Katha Pollitt remarks in a *New Yorker* review that Greer's version of post-menopausal life is "so charming, so seductively rendered—especially when it's contrasted with the situation of the wistful wives, desperate party girls, and breast-implanted exercise addicts which for her constitutes the only alternative—that the reader may find herself barely able to wait." Greer views menopause as "a liberation, an unwanted liberation," as quoted by Sarah Boxer in the *New York Times Book Review.*

In *Slip-Shod Sibyls: Recognition, Rejection, and the Woman Poet,* Greer challenges the validity of feminist revisionism and the status of celebrated female poets in the Western canon, including Sappho, Aphra Behn, Christina Rossetti, and Elizabeth Barrett Browning. Carol Rumens writes in a *Times Literary Supplement* review, "Though Greer admits we should carry on reclaiming women's work, she believes that 'to insist on equal representation or positive discrimination so that She-poetry appears on syllabuses in our schools and universities is to continue the system of false accounting that produced the double standard in the first place.'" Camille Paglia notes in the *Observer Review,* "the absence of pre-modern female poets from the curriculum," in Greer's view, "is not entirely due to sexism but rather to a lack of quality." Citing the life and work of Sylvia Plath and Anne Sexton, Greer similarly dismisses contemporary female poetry for its futile, and often fatal, narcissism. According to Greer, as Margaret Anne Doody summarizes in the *London Review of Books:* "The 20th century merely adds to the heap of sickly, self-regarding and self-destructive female poets. Lacking education, training in the Great Tradition, certainty about voice or subject-matter—and in the absence of any sense of how the culture of publicity and publication can work—woman writers of poetry over three centuries have exhibited themselves delving into their emotions. Poetry with them constantly becomes a morbid exercise." Furthermore, Greer contends that women poets were often responsible for their own artistic shortcomings. Fleur Adcock writes in a *New Statesman and Society* review that Greer suggests such female writers "took bad advice; they fell for flattery; they wrote fast and without revising sufficiently; and they failed to understand 'what was involved in making a poem.'" Praising *Slip-Shod Sibyls* and Greer's significant contribution to feminist criticism, Paglia concludes, "When the history of modern women is written, Germaine Greer will be seen as one who, like Jane Austen, permanently redefined female intellect."

BIOGRAPHICAL/CRITICAL SOURCES:

PERIODICALS

Chicago Tribune Books, January 11, 1990, p. 6.
Detroit News, May 9, 1971.
Globe and Mail (Toronto), February 25, 1984; October 17, 1987; April 29, 1989; August 5, 1989.
Life, May 7, 1971.
Listener, October 22, 1970.
London Review of Books, December 14, 1995, p. 14-5.
Los Angeles Times, March 7, 1984; November 26, 1987.

Los Angeles Times Book Review, September 6, 1987; April 8, 1990.

National Review, January 18, 1993, p. 49.

New Republic, January 31, 1994, p. 29.

New Statesman and Society, March 24, 1989, pp. 36-7; October 6, 1995, pp. 37-8.

Newsweek, March 22, 1971; November 16, 1992, p. 79.

New Yorker, April 16, 1990, p. 116; November 2, 1992, p. 106.

New York Times, April 20, 1971; November 1, 1979; March 5, 1984; April 23, 1984.

New York Times Book Review, October 11, 1987; January 28, 1990; October 11, 1992, pp. 1, 33.

Observer (London), October 11, 1970.

Observer Review, October 8, 1995, p. 14.

Publishers Weekly, May 25, 1984; December 1, 1989, p. 42; August 24, 1992, p. 66.

San Francisco Review of Books, January, 1992, p. 6.

Time, April 16, 1984; October 26, 1992, p. 80.

Times (London), March 20, 1986; October 23, 1986; March 20, 1989; March 25, 1989.

Times Literary Supplement, June 17, 1988; March 17, 1989; October 13, 1995, p. 29.

Washington Post, November 22, 1979; January 24, 1990.

Women's Review of Books, January, 1993.*

*   *   *

GRUMBACH, Doris (Isaac) 1918-

PERSONAL: Born July 12, 1918, in New York, NY; daughter of Leonard William and Helen Isaac; married Leonard Grumbach (a professor of physiology), October 15, 1941 (divorced, 1972); children: Barbara, Jane, Elizabeth, Kathryn. *Education:* Washington Square College, A.B., 1939; Cornell University, M.A., 1940. *Politics:* Liberal. *Religion:* Episcopalian.

ADDRESSES: Home—Sargentville, ME. *Agent*—c/o Tim Seldes, Russell and Volkening, 50 W. 29th St., New York, NY 10001.

CAREER: Writer. Metro-Goldwyn-Mayer, New York City, title writer, 1940-41; *Mademoiselle,* New York City, proofreader and copy editor, 1941-42; Time Inc., associate editor of *Architectural Forum,* 1942-43; Albany Academy for Girls, Albany, NY, English

teacher, 1952-55; College of Saint Rose, Albany, instructor, 1955-58, assistant professor, 1958-60, associate professor, 1960-69, professor of English, 1969-73; *New Republic,* Washington, DC, literary editor, 1973-75; American University, Washington, DC, professor of American literature, 1975-85. Visiting University fellow, Empire State College, 1972-73; adjunct professor of English, University of Maryland, 1974-75. Literary critic; *Morning Edition,* National Public Radio, book reviewer, beginning 1982. Board member for National Book Critics Circle and PEN/Faulkner Award; judge for writing contests. *Military Service:* U.S. Navy, Women Accepted for Volunteer Emergency Service, 1941-43.

MEMBER: PEN, American Association of University Professors, Phi Beta Kappa.

WRITINGS:

The Spoil of the Flowers, Doubleday (New York City), 1962.

The Short Throat, the Tender Mouth, Doubleday, 1964.

The Company She Kept (biography), Coward (New York City), 1967.

Chamber Music, Dutton (New York City), 1979.

The Missing Person, Putnam (New York City), 1981.

The Ladies, Dutton, 1984.

The Magician's Girl, Macmillan (New York City), 1987.

Coming into the Endzone, Norton, 1991.

Extra Innings: A Memoir, Norton, 1993.

Fifty Days of Solitude, Beacon Press (Boston), 1994.

The Book of Knowledge: A Novel, Norton, 1995.

Life in a Day, Beacon Press, 1996.

Also author of introductions and forwards for books. Contributor to books, including *The Postconcilor Parish,* edited by James O'Gara, Kennedy, 1967, and *Book Reviewing,* edited by Silvia E. Kameran, Writer, Inc., 1978. Columnist for *Critic,* 1960-64, and *National Catholic Reporter,* 1968—; author of nonfiction column for *New York Times Book Review,* 1976—, column, "Fine Print," for *Saturday Review,* 1977-78, and fiction column, *Chronicle of Higher Education,* 1979—. Contributing editor, *New Republic,* 1971-73; book reviewer for *MacNeil-Lehrer Newshour,* Public Broadcasting Service (PBS). Contributor of reviews and criticism to periodicals, including the *New York Times Book Review, Chicago Tribune, Commonweal, Los Angeles Times, Nation, Washington Post, Washington Star,* and *New Republic.*

SIDELIGHTS: Doris Grumbach, a biographer and respected literary critic, is the author of several novels with historical, biographical, and autobiographical elements. Early in her career, Grumbach worked as a title writer, copy and associate editor, literary editor, and an English teacher; her career as a novelist did not begin until her early forties. In an essay for *Contemporary Authors Autobiography Series (CAAS),* the author recalls the time when she sought to have her first book published: "The manuscript was in a typing-paper box, wrapped in a shopping bag from the A. & P., and taped shut with scotch tape. I left it with the receptionist, remembering too late that I had not put my name and address on the outside of the box. I expected, as one does with an unlabeled suitcase at the airport, never to see it again. Two weeks later I got a phone call from an editor at Doubleday telling me they wished to publish the novel. Two years later they published a second novel." These first two books, *The Spoil of the Flowers,* about student life in a boarding house, and *The Short Throat, the Tender Mouth,* about life on a college campus three months before Hitler's march on Poland, "were by a beginner at a time in my life when I no longer should have been a beginner," Grumbach relates in *CAAS.* "There are some good things, I believe, in both novels: had I much time ahead of me now, I would rewrite them and resubmit them for publication."

Grumbach's third book, *The Company She Kept,* is a literary biography of the acerbic novelist Mary McCarthy. This book became the subject of a threatened lawsuit before its publication and of a volatile critical debate after its release. *The Company She Kept* parallels events and characters in McCarthy's novels with those in her life. "The fiction of Mary McCarthy is autobiographical to an extraordinary degree, in the widest sense of autobiography," Grumbach explains in the foreword to the book. "In the case of Mary McCarthy there is only a faint line between what really happened to her, the people she knew and knows, including herself, and the characters in her fictions." To prepare the biography, Grumbach spent a year reading McCarthy's work and criticism of it and interviewed the author extensively at her Paris home. Difficulties with McCarthy arose, Grumbach says, when McCarthy, who suggested she read the galleys of the book to catch any factual errors, protested against some of the information Grumbach had included in the manuscript.

In a *New York Times Book Review* article on her dispute with McCarthy, Grumbach reports that McCarthy voluntarily provided her with intimate biographical details in conversation and in a detailed memorandum. McCarthy's anger over their inclusion therefore came as a surprise, says Grumbach. "I was unprepared for the fury of her response when she saw the galleys . . . and realized that I had used the autobiographical details she had, as she said, given me," comments Grumbach. "She had said, once, that it felt strange to have a book written about one, 'a book that includes you as a person, not just a critical analysis of your writings.' Now she insisted that the *curriculum vitae* had been sent to be 'drawn upon,' not used, although just how this was to be done continues to be a mystery to me. . . . [McCarthy's] feeling was that the tapes and her letters to me had been intended solely for 'your own enlightenment.'"

For all the attendant publicity, however, *The Company She Kept* was not well-received by the literary establishment. Stephanie Harrington writes in *Commonweal:* "To anyone who has read *The Company She Kept* . . . the newspaper stories that followed the book's publication must have seemed too preposterous to be anything but a desperate attempt by the publisher's publicity department to drum up business for a clinker." A *Times Literary Supplement* contributor, who describes *The Company She Kept* as "sparkily written and often critically sharp," feels that Grumbach falls short of her stated goal of "weaving one fabric of [the] diverse threads of McCarthy's biography and her fiction." Grumbach, says the reviewer, "never fully succeeds in dramatizing the complex interactions that go into such a process; [therefore, *The Company She Kept*] is likely to end up as required reading for gossips." Ellen Moers in the *New York Times Book Review* does not argue the validity of Grumbach's attempt to find the fact in Mary McCarthy's fiction—the process of "set[ting] out to name names," as Moers calls it—but instead claims that Grumbach misreads McCarthy and thus arrives at erroneous conclusions. To Grumbach's statement that "there is only a faint line" between fact and fiction for McCarthy, Moers responds: "This simply cannot be true. The husbands in McCarthy fiction . . . are such dreary mediocrities, her artist colonies and political oases are so bare of talent or distinction, her suites of college girls are so tediously third-rate—only a powerful imagination could have made such nonentities out of the very interesting company that Mary McCarthy actually kept."

Saturday Review critic Granville Hicks, however, does not find Grumbach's approach in *The Company*

She Kept objectionable and approves of her straightforward manner in tackling it. "Although there is nothing novel about finding Miss McCarthy in her books, critics are usually cautious about identifying characters in fiction with real people, and I am grateful for Mrs. Grumbach's refusal to beat around that particular bush."

In the wake of the harsh reviews *The Company She Kept* received, Grumbach tried to deflect some of the criticism from herself by explaining the circumstances leading to her decision to write the McCarthy biography. Explaining in the *New York Times Book Review* that she was asked to write the book on McCarthy, rather than instigating the project herself, Grumbach states, "An editor asks, somewhere in the inner room of a dim New York restaurant, would you do a book on Her? And because you do not ordinarily eat and drink such sumptuous lunches in the proximate company of so many successful-looking people, and because you need the money, and because after all, She *is* a good writer (you've *always* thought this) and apparently a *fascinating* woman, you say yes, I will." Comments Harrington: "Mrs. Grumbach's apologia in the *Times* . . . [indicates] that it was foolhardy to expect a serious piece of work in the first place when she only decided to take on Mary McCarthy because an editor asked 'somewhere in the inner room of a dim New York restaurant, would you do a book on Her?'" Recognizing the shortcomings of *The Company She Kept,* Grumbach summarizes her difficulties with the book in the *New York Times Book Review:* "The value of the whole experience lies, for me," she says, "in the recognition of how difficult, even well-nigh impossible, it is to write a book that deals with a living person. It does not matter in the least that the living person is willing to assist the writer (beware the Greeks bearing . . .) in conversation or letter; the fact remains, the law being what it is, the subject can give with one hand, take back with the other, and in this process of literary Indian-giving the writer is virtually helpless."

Ten years after publishing *The Company She Kept* and fifteen years after writing her novels, *The Short Throat, the Tender Mouth* and *The Spoil of the Flowers,* Grumbach returned to fiction. Her first novel after the hiatus was *Chamber Music,* written as the memoirs of ninety year-old Caroline MacLaren, widow of a famous composer and founder of an artists' colony in his memory. Released with a 20,000 copy first printing and a $20,000 promotional campaign, *Chamber Music* won the popular and critical acclaim that eluded Grumbach's earlier books. Peter Davison in the *Atlantic Monthly* calls the book "artful, distinctive, provocative, [and] compassionate." *Chamber Music,* writes Victoria Glendinning in the *Washington Post Book World,* "is a book of originality and distinction." *Chamber Music* is the story of "the chamber of one heart," says Caroline MacLaren in the introduction to her memoirs.

The novel's plot revolves around the subjugation of Caroline to her husband Robert and to Robert's music. Their marriage is a cold and barren one and *Chamber Music* charts its course through Robert's incestuous relationship with his mother, his homosexual affair with a student, and, finally, to his agonizing death in the tertiary stage of syphilis. Especially noted for its sensitive handling of its delicate subject matter and for its characterizations, *Chamber Music* is called by the *New York Times*'s John Leonard, "one of those rare novels for adults who listen." The characters in *Chamber Music,* Leonard continues, "are all stringed instruments. The music we hear occurs in the chamber of Caroline's heart. It is quite beautiful." With her third novel, Grumbach "makes us hear the difficult music of grace," says Nicholas Delbanco in the *New Republic.*

Although *Chamber Music*'s "revelations of sexuality are meant to shatter," as one *Publishers Weekly* contributor comments, and the passage on Robert's illness gives "a clinical description so simply precise, so elegantly loathsome, that it would do nicely either in a medical text or in a book on style," as Edith Milton observes in the *Yale Review,* it is the contrast between *Chamber Music*'s action and its language that gives the novel its impact. While much of the material in *Chamber Music* is meant to shock, the language is genteel and full of Victorian phrases. "What gives the main part of this book its polish and flavor is the contrast between matter and manner," says Glendinning. "Clarity and elegance of style account . . . for the distinction of *Chamber Music,*" writes Eleanor B. Wymard in *Commonweal,* and other critics have high praise for Grumbach's writing. A *Washington Post Book World* reviewer claims the book's language is "as direct and pure as a Hayden quartet," and Abigail McCarthy in *Commonweal* states that *Chamber Music* has "the classical form, clarity, and brilliance of a composition for strings." Because it is Caroline's story, the novel adopts her voice—a voice that is "slightly stilted, slightly vapid, of the genteel tradition," one *Atlantic* contributor observes. Asserts Milton: "The novel is wonderfully written in [Caroline's] voice to evoke a time gone by, an era vanished. . . . The prose, understated, beautiful in its economies, supports a story of almost uncanny bleakness."

In her short preface to *Chamber Music,* Grumbach states that the novel's characters "are based vaguely upon persons who were once alive" but stresses that the book is fiction. "*Chamber Music* is a thinly, and strangely, fictionalized variation on the life of Marian MacDowell, [composer] Edward MacDowell's widow, who . . . founded an artist's colony in New Hampshire. . . . The names are changed; though not by much considering what else changes with them," says Milton. Gail Godwin, writing in the *New York Times Book Review,* suspects that the parallels between the MacDowells and the MacLarens "handicap . . . [Grumbach's] own possibilities for creating a fictional hero who might have come to life more vividly." However, other critics, including Glendinning, find that "the illusion of authenticity is strengthened by the inclusion of real people." "Robert MacLaren himself is given a semihistorical glamour by the parallels between his career and that of . . . Edward MacDowell—the two share teachers, musical styles, even a Boston address, and MacDowell's widow did indeed found an artist's colony in his name," writes Katha Pollitt. "Such details give Caroline's memoirs the piquancy of a historical novel."

Franny Fuller, the protagonist of Grumbach's novel *The Missing Person,* is also patterned after an actual figure. Franny, a 1930s movie star and sex symbol, closely resembles actress Marilyn Monroe. Written as a series of vignettes interweaving the events of Franny's career with an ongoing commentary by a gossip columnist, *The Missing Person* traces the actress's life from her sad beginnings in Utica, New York, through her rise to stardom, and finally to her disappearance from both Hollywood and the public consciousness. "Here, with certain sympathetic changes, is quite visibly another tale about the sad life of Marilyn Monroe," observes the *New York Times*'s Herbert Mitgang. "Missing person," says Cynthia Propper Seton in the *Washington Post Book World,* refers to "this sense that one is all facade, that there is no self inside." Franny is supposed to serve as a prototype for all the "missing persons" who are, "above all, missing to themselves," claims Herbert Gold in the *New York Times Book Review.* "There seems evidence," McCarthy writes in *Commonweal,* "that Doris Grumbach may initially have thought of Franny Fuller's story as a feminist statement in that women like Franny whom America 'glorifies and elevates' are sex objects made larger

than life. But if so, as often happens in the creative process, she has transcended the aim in the writing. The creatures of the Hollywood process she gives us, men as well as women, are all victims."

Grumbach, in a prefatory note to the novel, comments on the nature of the book. "This novel is a portrait, not of a single life but of many lives melded into one, typical of the women America often glorifies and elevates, and then leaves suspended in their lonely and destructive fame," she says. Still, comments Richard Combs in a *Times Literary Supplement,* "there is no prize for guessing that the novel's heroine is Marilyn Monroe." The close correlation between Marilyn Monroe's and Franny's lives is disturbing to many critics. "The question that poses itself about a book like this is, Why bother? If you must write about Marilyn Monroe then why not do so in fiction or otherwise?," asks James Campbell in the *New Statesman.* "Real names thinly disguised are a bore." Combs believes Grumbach's reliance on the facts of Marilyn Monroe's life hinders her ability to substantiate the point she makes in the preface. "The more the real Hollywood shows through [in the novel], the less satisfying the portrait becomes," Combs says. "The author's assumption . . . seems to be that since Hollywood put fantasy on an anonymous, mass-production basis, the results can be freely arranged by the inspired do-it-yourselfer. . . . But in refantasizing the fantasy factory, Mrs. Grumbach allows herself the license of fiction without taking on the responsibility . . . to find revised truth in the revised subject."

"It is hard for [Franny] to have a separate imaginary existence in the mind of the reader," states McCarthy. "But this flaw, if it is one, is more than compensated for by the writer's evocation of the scene against which Franny moves—tawdry, wonderful Hollywood at its peak." Indeed, Grumbach is praised for her fine writing and for "the adroit structure of the novel," as Gold calls it. "There is in this prose a certain leanness, a sparseness that separates most of the characters into a chapter each, surrounded by an implied emptiness. Instead of the usual crowded Hollywood narrative, [*The Missing Person*] has the melancholy air . . . of an underpopulated landscape," writes Combs. Seton comments on Grumbach's ability to capture the tone and feeling of old Hollywood films and newsreels in her writing. "Doris Grumbach's special gift lies in her ability to suit the style and structure of her novels to the world in which she writes," McCarthy says. "*The Missing Person* is itself like a motion picture—a pastiche of scenes centered on the star, complete with flashbacks, close-ups and fade-outs."

Grumbach switches her topic from the rise then demise of a 1930s starlet in *The Missing Person,* to the public ostracism then acceptance of two aristocratic lesbian lovers of the eighteenth century in her novel *The Ladies.* "Grumbach compellingly recreates the lives of two women who so defied convention and so baffled their contemporaries that they became celebrities," lauds Catharine R. Stimpson in the *New York Times Book Review.* The story relates Grumbach's concept of how Eleanor Butler and Sarah Ponsonby, two Irish aristocrats known as "the Ladies of Llangollen," shocked the community with their lesbian relationship but were eventually accepted and visited by such noteworthy individuals as Anna Seward, the Duke of Wellington, and Walter Scott. Stimpson notes the book "eloquently documents the existence of women who lived as they wished to, instead of as society expected them to."

As Grumbach relates, Lady Eleanor, feeling the lack of love from her parents because she wasn't a boy, becomes the boy in her behavior and dress. Always looking to fill her need for acceptance and love, Eleanor falls in love with the orphan, Sarah Ponsonby, who is being sexually harassed by her guardian. Eleanor attempts to rescue Sarah, but the two are caught before they get far. A second attempt prompts the families to allow the couple to leave together, but under the condition that Lady Eleanor is banned from Ireland forever. After a few years of wandering, Eleanor and Sarah settle with a former servant and create their own haven in Wales. Eleanor and Sarah "seemed to each other to be divine survivors, well beyond the confines of social rules, two inhabitants of an ideal society. . . . They had uncovered a lost continent on which they could live, in harmony, quite alone and together," writes Grumbach in *The Ladies.* Eventually, visited by other aristocrats, they become more secure within the outer community, however, problems arise in their relationship as their greed and fame alters their lives.

The Ladies met with good reviews. Stimpson, while recognizing Grumbach's pattern of blurring biography and fiction, praises the book noting that "*The Ladies* is boldly imagined, [and] subtly crafted." Comparing Grumbach's work with the likes of Virginia Woolf and Charlotte Perkins Gillman, Sandra Gilbert claims in the *Washington Post Book World* that Grumbach has "recounted their story with grace and wit," and applauds "the sureness with which

Grumbach accumulates small details about the lives of her protagonist and the tough but loving irony with which she portrays their idiosyncrasies." She observes, though, that while the protagonists' "road to reposeful Llangollen is strewn with obstacles for the runaway ladies. . . . All ends well once the weary travelers arrive in friendship's vale." Thus Gilbert maintains that "if there is anything problematic about *The Ladies,* it is that all seems to go almost too well" in the novel and "like Grumbach's earlier *Chamber Music,* seems here and there to flirt with the conventions of an increasingly popular new genre: The Happy Lesbian novel."

The title for Grumbach's next novel, the *The Magician's Girl,* is borrowed from Sylvia Plath's poem "The Bee Meeting." In this story Grumbach writes about three women who were college roommates and grew up during the twenties and thirties. In episodic fashion, the stories of Minna, Liz, and Maud are related from their childhood to their sixties, and from their hopes and dreams to their reality. Pretty, shy Minna marries a doctor, has a son, and becomes a history professor. After surviving years in a loveless marriage, at the age of sixty she finally develops a loving relationship with a young man in his twenties. Not long after they meet and she experiences this fulfillment, she is killed in a car accident. Maud, the daughter of a nurse and army sergeant, marries a handsome man whom she eventually rejects, has twins whom she neglects, and spends most of her time writing poetry. Her poetry is good but she destroys it all, except for the copies she sends to Minna in her letters; she commits suicide before realizing the true success of her writings. Liz, the only survivor, lives with her partner in a lesbian relationship, achieving fame as a photographer. Summarizing the book's theme, Anita Brookner in her review for the *Washington Post Book World,* states that the formulaic stories about these three women demonstrates "the way early beginnings mature into not very much, for despite the achievements that come with age, a sense of disillusion persists." Brookner asserts that Grumbach asks more questions about women's lives than she answers in her story, including the question, "Is that all?," and surmises that this may be more important than the answers. In conclusion, she praises *The Magician's Girl* as "a beautifully easy read, discreet and beguiling, and attractively low-key. It is an honorable addition to the annals of women's reading."

The reviews for *The Magician's Girl* were mixed. Several critics faulted Grumbach for too closely describing the lives of Sylvia Plath and Diane Arbus as the characters of Maud and Liz respectively. Other critics found Grumbach's writing weak in definition and description. *Times Literary Supplement*'s Marianne Wiggins finds events "unlocated in time" and places "without a sense of period." She asserts that it is written "as if the text were a rehearsal for a talent contest," and considers this especially disconcerting since she regards Grumbach as the "master of the quick sketch" and points out that generally "when her narrative shifts to describing the specific, it soars." In contrast, Paula Deitz in the *New York Times Book Review* commends Grumbach's attention to detail in *The Magician's Girl*. She deems that the characters described "are all rich images, informed with the magic conveyed by the small details that reveal the forming of these lives." Deitz further maintains that "*The Magician's Girl* is most disturbing, and therefore at its best, in its acute awareness of the pains endured unflinchingly by the young." *Christian Science Monitor*'s Merle Rubin summarizes: "What is most poignant about this novel is that its special aura of serenity tinged with sadness comes not from the pains and losses the characters endure, although there are many of these, but from the conviction it conveys that life, for all its sorrows, is so rich with possibilities as to make any one life—however long—much too short."

Grumbach shares feelings, events, and remembrances of the year she turned seventy in her 1991 autobiography, *Coming into the End Zone: A Memoir*. "What is most delightful about *Coming into the End Zone*—[is] the wry, spry, resilient, candid recording of present happenings and suddenly remembered past happenings which fill almost every page with anecdotes and reflections," exclaims *Washington Post Book World*'s Anthony Thwaite. Grumbach comments on a wide range of topics, including contemporary annoyances such as phrases like "the computer is down," the death of several friends from the complications of acquired immunodeficiency syndrome, her dislikes of travel, her move to rural Maine, her memories of being fired from the *New Republic,* and Mary McCarthy's last curt comment to her. "The best moments are the passages in which the author seems least to be writing for posterity, merely trying to capture herself on the page, moments when the need to maintain a public persona gives way to the vulnerability of the private person, sometimes even to the young girl still inside this old woman," declares Carol Anshaw in the *Tribune Books*. "The book that Ms. Grumbach intended as a confrontation with death winds up being a celebration of life," comments Noel Perrin in the *New York*

Times Book Review, adding that "it is a deeply satisfying book." "Grumbach's reflections record—with honesty, fidelity, much important and unimportant detail, and with much grace and informal wit—her feelings of the time. I know no other book like it," hails Thwaite. He concludes: "This is a book to grow old with even before one is old. The best is yet to be."

Grumbach continues her reminiscences in *Extra Innings: A Memoir*. Reviewers disagree about how satisfactorily the author presents her experiences. In *Washington Post Book World,* Diana O'Hehir defines a memoir as a grab bag and, directing her comments to Grumbach, writes: "I felt yours wasn't enough of a grab bag. Not enough gossip about people. Not enough detail about you, not enough specific detail about relationships, family." However, Kathleen Norris presents her view in the *New York Times Book Review* that the book is "more of a hodgepodge" than *End Zone*. Norris maintains that "for all its recounting of ordinary events, *Extra Innings,* like *End Zone,* is a document still too rare in literary history, an account of a woman who has lived by words. Ms. Grumbach wittily chronicles the absurdities and ambiguities of the modern American writer's life."

In *The Book of Knowledge* Grumbach introduces four central characters as adolescents the summer before the great stock market crash of 1929, then touches on each of their lives into adulthood, through the Great Depression and World War II. Two of the characters are a brother and sister who become intimate, sexually and emotionally, that summer. The other two are the vacationing son and daughter of a wealthy stockbroker, with whom the brother and sister become friends. All strive for selfhood in various fashions; and the two young men eventually have a homosexual relationship. Nina Mehta writes in *Tribune Books* that "Grumbach cuts right to sexuality, condemning her main characters to lives stunted by their inability to deal honestly with their sexual feelings." According to Julia Markus of the *Los Angeles Times Book Review*, "the stories of [the four] and their families are told and interwoven with great irony, subtlety and beauty." Markus concludes that "with masterful conciseness and with her own unique haunting force, Doris Grumbach has brilliantly delineated the tragedy of an entire generation."

But other reviewers fault Grumbach for not delving into the foursome. Grumbach makes "a lot of tendentious commentary about puberty and the chasteness of homosexual inclinations," points out Mehta, "but what's most disheartening . . . is the book's lack of insight." Mehta maintains that "by neglecting to ventilate her characters' lives with even a breeze of introspection, Grumbach gives them less personality, less psychological weight, than they deserve." Sara Maitland asserts in the *New York Times Book Review:* "Ms. Grumbach prods at her four central characters with a sharp stick, but when they turn over, she withdraws her authorial attention in disgust." Maitland decries that the reader is "never shown the painful workings through of . . . personal choices that we are *told* the characters have to endure."

BIOGRAPHICAL/CRITICAL SOURCES:

BOOKS

Contemporary Authors Autobiography Series, Volume 2, Gale (Detroit), 1985.
Contemporary Literary Criticism, Gale, Volume 13, 1980, Volume 22, 1982, Volume 64, 1991.

PERIODICALS

America, June 2, 1979.
American Spectator, January, 1982.
Atlantic Monthly, March, 1979.
Booklist, October 1, 1993.
Christian Science Monitor, February 26, 1987, p. 22.
Commonweal, October 6, 1967; June 22, 1979; January 15, 1982.
Library Journal, March 1, 1979.
Listener, August 9, 1979.
London Review of Books, August 20, 1992.
Los Angeles Times Book Review, July 16, 1995, p. 3.
Ms., April, 1979.
Nation, March 28, 1981, pp. 375-76.
National Review, June 8, 1979.
New Republic, March 10, 1979.
New Statesman, August 17, 1979; August 28, 1981.
Newsweek, March 19, 1979.
New Yorker, April 23, 1979.
New York Times, March 13, 1979; July 20, 1989.
New York Times Book Review, June 11, 1967; March 25, 1979; March 29, 1981, pp. 14-15; September 30, 1984, p. 12; February 1, 1987, p. 22; September 22, 1991; November 21, 1993, p. 11; October 21, 1993; October 2, 1994; June 25, 1995, p. 19.
Observer, August 12, 1979.
Publishers Weekly, January 15, 1979; February 13, 1981.
Sewanee Review, January, 1995.

Spectator, August 11, 1979.
Time, April 9, 1979.
Times Literary Supplement, December 7, 1967; November 30, 1979; September 11, 1981; July 12, 1985; June 19, 1987, p. 669.
Tribune Books (Chicago), September 29, 1991; August 13, 1995, p. 6.
Village Voice, August 24, 1987.
Washington Post Book World, March 18, 1979; February 10, 1980; April 5, 1981, pp. 9, 13; September 30, 1984, p. 7; January 4, 1987, pp. 3, 13; September 8, 1991; October 24, 1993, p. 5; October 10, 1996.
Women's Review of Books, December, 1993; December, 1995.
Yale Review, autumn, 1979.*

* * *

GUBAR, Susan (David) 1944-

PERSONAL: Born in 1944.

ADDRESSES: Office—Department of English, Indiana University, Bloomington, IN 47405-1101.

CAREER: Professor of English at Indiana University, Bloomington.

AWARDS, HONORS: National Book Critics Circle Award nomination, with Sandra M. Gilbert, for outstanding book of criticism, 1979, for *The Madwoman in the Attic: The Woman Writer and the Nineteenth-Century Literary Imagination; Ms.* Magazine Woman of the Year citation, 1986, for co-editing *The Norton Anthology of Literature by Women.*

WRITINGS:

(Editor and author of introduction with Sandra M. Gilbert) *Shakespeare's Sisters: Feminist Essays on Women Poets,* Indiana University Press, 1979.
(With Gilbert) *The Madwoman in the Attic: A Study of Women and the Nineteenth-Century Literary Imagination,* Yale University Press, 1979.
(Editor with Gilbert) *The Norton Anthology of Literature by Women: The Tradition in English,* Norton, 1985, 2nd edition, 1996.
(With Gilbert) *No Man's Land: The Place of the Woman Writer in the Twentieth Century,* Yale University Press, Volume 1: *The War of the*

Words, 1988, Volume 2: *Sexchanges,* 1989, Volume 3: *Letters from the Front,* 1994.

(Editor with Joan Hoff) *For Adult Users Only: The Dilemma of Violent Pornography,* Indiana University Press, 1989.

(Editor with Jonathan Kamholtz) *English Inside and Out: The Places of Literary Criticism,* Routledge & Kegan Paul, 1992.

(With Gilbert) *Masterpiece Theatre: An Academic Melodrama,* Rutgers University Press (New Brunswick, NJ), 1995.

(With Gilbert and Diana O'Hehir) *Mothersongs: Poems for, by, and about Mothers,* Norton (New York City), 1995.

Contributor to periodicals, including *New York Times Book Review.*

SIDELIGHTS: Literary theorist Susan Gubar, along with her frequent collaborator Sandra M. Gilbert, has produced a number of groundbreaking works of literary criticism that focus on the work of women writers. In their 1979 classic, *The Madwoman in the Attic,* Gubar and Gilbert argue that nineteenth-century women writers were forced to write within the confines of a male-dominated literary tradition that equated the pen with the penis. Viewed as trespassers in the domain of male writers, women who took up the pen risked being condemned as unfeminine. At the same time, female authors—such as Jane Austen, Charlotte and Emily Bronte, Mary Shelley, George Eliot (Mary Ann Evans), and Emily Dickinson—who attempted to defy the male tradition or explore a new viewpoint received ridicule as "lady novelists" or "female poetasters." Consequently, maintain the authors, women writers became both fearful that they lacked true artistic expression and angry because they felt trapped within the powerful patriarchal structure. Repressing their rage and fear, women writers of the nineteenth century began to subvert the male tradition in which they wrote, clandestinely developing a literary style distinctly their own.

New Leader's Phoebe Pettingell labels the authors' "close textual readings . . . insightful and valuable." LeAnne Schreiber notes in the *New York Times Book Review* that in developing a "complex and compelling understanding of the subterfuges that have made the work of women such as Emily Bronte and Mary Shelley seem puzzling and odd," Gubar and Gilbert present "the first persuasive case for the existence of a distinctly female imagination." Carolyn G. Heilbrun of the *Washington Post Book World* concurs, deeming *The Madwoman in the Attic* "a pivotal

book, one of those after which we will never think the same again."

The *Norton Anthology of Literature by Women: The Tradition in English (NALW)* "is a landmark not only in feminism but in the study of literature," asserts Laura Shapiro in *Newsweek.* She states that the book makes "possible, for the first time, a realistic perspective on literary achievement." The tome, which "showcases a wealth of acknowledged treasures," focuses on the work of women writers throughout history to the present. Shapiro adds, "Many of their [the editors'] choices have no bearing on feminism as such, but all of them reflect the editors' belief, expressed in their introduction, that women's writing reveals a relationship to the world that is necessarily different from men's." Julia Epstein observes in the *Washington Post Book World* that the *Norton Anthology of Literature by Women* "resoundingly endorses a centuries-old tradition of women's writing and a matrilineal evolution of styles and subjects. Its publication, therefore, bears witness to the coming of age of feminist literary scholarship."

In addition, Epstein remarks, "*NALW* also redraws boundaries, shifting the usual period designations in a way better suited to women's history, considering a range of genres often dismissed (letters, diaries, polemics) and broadening the English-speaking world to embrace geographically diverse writers from India to New Zealand, Canada to Australia." In the *Los Angeles Times Book Review,* Diane Middlebrook describes the book as "a capacious and readable volume. . . . It is encyclopedic." She further explains, "Organized chronologically, this collection demonstrates that women have participated vigorously in every period, trend, fashion, experiment and genre of writing in English. The editors themselves, however, are adroitly contemporary in their own outlook." Middlebrook concludes that "the most obvious strength of this anthology, though, is its representation of modern and contemporary female writers."

The first volume, *The War of the Words,* of *No Man's Land: The Place of the Woman Writer in the Twentieth Century* is "a thoroughly provocative (and provocatively thorough) revisioning of the genesis of modernism. The central premise of *No Man's Land*— that the radical departures that characterize such classics as *The Waste Land, Ulysses* and *The Waves* derive from context of sexual as well as social, political and economic conflict—is developed by means of a thematic overview of late nineteenth-century and early twentieth-century texts that showcase women's attempts to assert their right not to primacy but to a place in the predominantly masculine world of letters," claims Janice Kulyk Keefer in the Toronto *Globe & Mail.* Kulyk Keefer admires the authors' treatment of misogyny and their attention to female linguistic issues, yet she finds "problematic" their attempts to define what they term "the female affiliation complex," a female-oriented historical literary tradition. She concludes that Gubar and Gilbert "have produced a challenging and engaging introduction to a central feature of the cultural movement that continues to shape our century."

Wendy Lesser hails *The War of the Words* in the *Washington Post Book World* as a "fascinating, controversial, and ambiguous study of the post-Victorian period." The critic questions both the authors' "specific interpretation of texts" and their perception of "the extent to which men as a class have banded together as a literary mafia." She admires, however, their writing: "Their prose is fluid and accessible, yet intelligent and pointed; they mingle analytic remarks with expository summaries in a way that shows both respect and consideration for the reader." Barbara Hardy comments in the *Times Literary Supplement* that "*No Man's Land* figures a crisis of male impotence and aggression, a woman's projected utopia, and the territory of contemporary conflicts and confusions. The revisionary word-play acts out a central theme, that of men and women struggling both with and for language." She adds, "Although it sprawls through time, space and hosts of examples, *The War of the Words* is not really a large, loose, baggy monster, but sharply attentive to the business of illustrating extremes of anxiety and confidence, aggression and submission, and making them into a pattern."

About *Sexchanges,* the second volume of *No Man's Land,* Walter Kendrick of the *New York Times Book Review* writes that it "is not so much a sequel to *The War of the Words* as a supplement to it, another layer of brush strokes on a still unfinished canvas." Kendrick believes that if *No Man's Land* as a whole "achieves its . . . goal, it will set the direction of feminist criticism for the next generation of students and scholars." The reviewer further comments that "success seems likely, because Ms. Gilbert and Ms. Gubar write with facility and have a knack for subsuming complex problems under easily memorable labels."

Letters from the Front, Volume 3 in the *No Man's Land* series, covers the period from the 1930s to the present. Analyzing the works of writers such as Virginia Woolf, Marianne Moore, Edna St. Vincent Millay, and Zora Neale Hurston, Gubar and Gilbert "read women's 20th-century literary productions as letters from the shifting fronts of the 'sex war,'" comments Mark Hussey in the *New York Times Book Review.* While commending parts of the volume, Hussey notes that the authors' "tendency to see everything in terms of war and conflict often makes for simplistic analysis." Helen Carr, reviewing *Letters from the Front* in the *New Statesman & Society,* concurs, remarking that "much of the critical account is a relentlessly reductive or strained reading of texts to wrench out images of violence and prove their point." While declaring that the volume "has nothing like the panache and drive" of *The Madwoman in the Attic,* Carr exclaims that *No Man's Land* "helps to make clear the rich and varied contribution made by women writers to the modernist movement."

BIOGRAPHICAL/CRITICAL SOURCES:

BOOKS

Cain, William E., editor, *Making Feminist History: The Literary Scholarship of Sandra M. Gilbert and Susan Gubar,* Garland (New York City), 1994.

PERIODICALS

Globe & Mail (Toronto), February 13, 1988.
Harper's, December, 1979.
Los Angeles Times Book Review, May 12, 1985, p. 1.
Ms., February, 1980; January, 1986, p. 59.
New Leader, February 25, 1980.
New Republic, March 10, 1986, p. 30; February 19, 1990, p. 27.
New Statesman & Society, October 7, 1994, p. 45.
Newsweek, July 15, 1985, p. 65.
New York Review of Books, December 20, 1979; May 31, 1990, p. 23.
New York Times Book Review, December 9, 1979; April 28, 1985, p. 13; February 7, 1988, p. 12; February 19, 1989, p. 9; November 6, 1994, p. 27.
Publishers Weekly, March 27, 1995, p. 79.
Times Literary Supplement, August 8, 1980; June 3, 1988, p. 621; January 12, 1990, p. 32; May 28, 1993, p. 11.
Washington Post Book World, November 25, 1979; June 2, 1985, p. 10; January 17, 1988, p. 4.
Yale Review, winter, 1980.*

H-J

HACKING, Ian 1936-

PERSONAL: Born February 18, 1936, in Vancouver, British Columbia, Canada; son of H. E. and Margaret (MacDougall) Hacking; married Nancy Cartwright (a professor); children: Jane Frances, Daniel, Rachel. *Education:* University of British Columbia, B.A., 1956; Cambridge University, B.A., 1958, M.A., Ph.D., 1962.

ADDRESSES: Office—Institute of History and Philosophy of Science, University of Toronto, Toronto, Ontario, Canada, M5S 1K7.

CAREER: Peterhouse College, Cambridge University, Cambridge, England, fellow, 1962-64; University of British Columbia, Vancouver, associate professor of philosophy, 1964-69; Cambridge University, university lecturer in philosophy and fellow of Peterhouse, both 1969-75; Stanford University, Stanford, CA, fellow at Center for Advanced Study in the Behavioral Sciences, 1974, Henry W. Stuart professor of philosophy, 1975-82; University of Toronto, Toronto, Ontario, professor, 1982—.

WRITINGS:

The Logic of Statistical Inference, Cambridge University Press (New York City), 1965.

A Concise Introduction to Logic, Random House (New York), 1971.

Emergence of Probability, Cambridge University Press, 1975.

Why Does Language Matter to Philosophy?, Cambridge University Press, 1975.

(Editor) *Scientific Revolutions,* Oxford University Press (New York City), 1981.

Representing and Intervening: Introductory Topics in the Philosophy of Natural Science, Cambridge University Press, 1983.

(Editor) *Exercises in Analysis: Essays by Students of Casimir Lewy,* Cambridge University Press, 1985.

The Taming of Chance, Cambridge University Press, 1990.

Rewriting the Soul: Multiple Personality and the Sciences of Memory, Princeton University Press (Princeton, NJ), 1995.

SIDELIGHTS: Reviewing Ian Hacking's *The Taming of Chance* for *American Historical Review,* Bruce Kuklick characterizes Hacking as "one of a small group of innovative and talented philosophers investigating conceptual problems in science and mathematics from a wide-ranging historical perspective." In *The Taming of Chance,* Hacking continues the exploration begun in his earlier work, *Emergence of Probability.* Both books deal with the history of ideas: specifically, how attitudes towards the influence of chance in both society and nature have evolved over the last four centuries. In the earlier work Hacking demonstrated how probabilistic reasoning, as opposed to a deterministic view of reality, developed in the seventeenth century. In *The Taming of Chance,* he tackles the eighteenth and nineteenth centuries, arguing that the gathering of numbers and the growth of statistical analysis both in the natural world and in all fields of human endeavor have led philosophers of the twentieth century to abandon a mechanistic view of the world in favor of one based on chance and percentages. Writing in *Isis,* Timothy L. Alborn notes that *The Taming of Chance* derives much of its content from previous work in probabilistic theory, yet feels that "Hacking sees farther. . . . by an agile ability to synthesize the rich array of secondary material . . . by wielding a vibrant writing style . . . and by employing a kind of documentational parsimony." In contrast, although Kuklick praises the range and quality of Hacking's scholarship he is critical of his writing style, finding that "the random zigs and zags in Hacking's account . . . make his philosophical points hard to follow." "The struggle," Kuklick concludes, "is nonetheless worthwhile."

In *Rewriting the Soul*, Hacking shifts his interest from the history of philosophical ideas to the history of psychological ones. The book deals with the concept of multiple personality disorder (MPD) and its link to repressed memories and childhood sexual abuse. However, Hacking is not so much concerned with the validity of MPD as a psychological diagnosis nor in its determining factors as he is in discovering what has caused MPD to be accepted by psychiatrists and in the public consciousness as a valid phenomenon. Hacking traces the history of MPD diagnosis from its appearance in nineteenth-century France and America, through its disappearance in favor of schizophrenia in the first part of the twentieth century, to its current popularity, particularly as a defense in criminal cases. He examines the debates that have raged around MPD and the ethics involved in psychiatric diagnosis. Alasdair Palmer, writing in the *Spectator*, calls *Rewriting the Soul* "a remarkable testament to the ways in which prejudice and irrationality can come to be built into institutions and medical practice." Greg A. Eghigian, in the *American Journal of Sociology*, sees the book as "successful in introducing the topic of multiple personality and showing the uses to which history and philosophy can be put in studying contemporary social problems." Yet more than an historical exposition, *Rewriting the Soul* is about our own changing concepts of identity and memory, with MPD portrayed as a new frame of reference for defining the self. Hacking's concern and warning is that "The outcome of multiple personality therapy is a type of false consciousness. . . . It is contrary to our best vision of what it is to be a human being."

BIOGRAPHICAL/CRITICAL SOURCES:

BOOKS

Honderich, Ted, editor, *The Oxford Companion to Philosophy*, Oxford University Press (New York City), 1995.

PERIODICALS

American Historical Review, February, 1992, p. 157.
American Journal of Sociology, January, 1996, pp. 1150-52.
Choice, June, 1991, pp. 1651-52.
Ethics, July, 1996, pp. 845-848.
Isis, Volume 63, number 2, 1992, pp. 366-67.
London Review of Books, May 3-16, 1984, p. 5; May 23, 1991, pp. 6-8.
Philosophy, March 9, 1984, p. 258.
Poetics Today, fall, 1994, pp. 467-78.
Spectator, August 12, 1995, pp. 33-31.
Times Literary Supplement (London), November 1, 1985, p. 1246; December 14, 1990, p. 1340.

* * *

HALDEMAN, Joe (William) 1943-
(Robert Graham)

PERSONAL: Born June 9, 1943, in Oklahoma City, OK; son of Jack Carroll (a hospital administrator) and Lorena (Spivey) Haldeman; married Mary Gay Poetter (a teacher), August 21, 1965. *Education:* University of Maryland, B.S., 1967; University of Iowa, M.F.A., 1975; also attended American University and University of Oklahoma. *Politics:* "Skeptic." *Religion:* "Skeptic." *Avocational interests:* Classical guitar, bicycling, woolgathering, strong drink, travel, gardening.

ADDRESSES: Home and office—5412 N.W. 14th Ave., Gainesville, FL 32605. *E-mail*—joe.haldeman-@genie.geis.com. *Agent*—Ralph Vicinanza, 111 Eighth Ave., #1501, New York City, NY 10011.

CAREER: Freelance writer, 1970—. University of Iowa, teaching assistant, 1975; former editor of *Astronomy;* has taught writing at University of North Florida and other schools; Massachusetts Institute of Technology, adjunct professor, 1983—. *Military service:* U.S. Army, 1967-69; became combat engineer; served in Vietnam; wounded in combat; received Purple Heart and other medals.

MEMBER: Authors Guild, Science Fiction Writers of America (treasurer, 1970-72; chair of Grievance Committee, 1979-80; president, 1992-94), L-5 Society, National Space Institute, Writers Guild, Poets and Writers.

AWARDS, HONORS: Hugo Award, World Science Fiction Convention, 1975, Nebula Award, Science Fiction Writers of America, 1975, and Locus Award, *Locus* magazine, 1975, all for *The Forever War;* Hugo Award, World Science Fiction Convention, 1976, and Locus Award, *Locus* magazine, 1976, both for best short story, for "Tricentennial"; Ditmar Award, 1976; Galaxy Award, 1978, for *Mindbridge;* Rhysling Award, Science Fiction Poetry Association, 1984, 1990; Nebula Award, Science Fiction Writers of America, 1990 and 1993; Hugo Award, World Science Fiction Convention, 1991, Nebula Award, Science Fiction Writers of America, 1991, and Locus Award, *Locus* magazine, 1991, all for story, "None So Blind"; Hugo Award, World Science Fiction Convention, 1995, for *The Hemingway Hoax;* Homer Award, 1995.

WRITINGS

SCIENCE FICTION NOVELS

The Forever War, St. Martin's (New York City), 1974.

Mindbridge, St. Martin's, 1976.

Planet of Judgment (a Star Trek novel), Bantam (New York City), 1977.

World without End: A Star Trek Novel, Bantam (New York City), 1979.

(With brother, Jack C. Haldeman) *There Is No Darkness,* Ace (New York City), 1983.

Tool of the Trade, Morrow (New York City), 1987.

Buying Time, introduction by James Gunn, illustrated by Bryn Barnard, Easton Press (Norwalk, CT), 1989, published in Britain as *The Long Habit of Living,* New English Library (London).

The Hemingway Hoax, Morrow, 1990.

None So Blind, Morrow, 1996.

The Forever Peace, Ace Books (New York City), 1997.

"WORLDS" TRILOGY; SCIENCE FICTION NOVELS

Worlds: A Novel of the Near Future, Viking (New York City), 1981.

Worlds Apart, Viking, 1983.

Worlds Enough and Time: The Conclusion of the Worlds Trilogy, Viking, 1992.

ADVENTURE NOVELS; UNDER PSEUDONYM ROBERT GRAHAM

Attar's Revenge, Pocket Books (New York City), 1975.

War of Nerves, Pocket Books, 1975.

WAR NOVELS

War Year, Holt Reinhart (New York City), 1972, original version, Pocket Books, 1978.

1968: A Novel, Hodder and Stoughton (London, England), 1994, Morrow, 1995.

SHORT STORY COLLECTIONS

All My Sins Remembered, St. Martin's, 1977.

Infinite Dreams, St. Martin's, 1978.

Dealing in Futures: Stories, Viking Press, 1985.

More than the Sum of His Parts, Pulphouse (Eugene, WA), 1991.

Vietnam and Other Alien Worlds (with essays and poetry), New England Science Fiction Association Press (Framingham, MA), 1993.

PLAYS

The Devil His Due, published in *Fantastic* (New York City), August, 1974; produced at the University of Iowa Film Workshop.

The Moon and Marcek, published in *Vertex* (Los Angeles), August, 1974.

The Forever War, produced in Chicago, 1983.

EDITOR

Cosmic Laughter: Science Fiction for the Fun of It, Holt Reinhart (New York City), 1974.

Study War No More: A Selection of Alternatives, St. Martin's (New York City), 1977.

Nebula Award Stories 17, Holt Reinhart, 1983.

(With Martin H. Greenberg and Charles G. Waugh) *Body Armor: 2000,* Ace (New York City), 1986.

(With Greenberg and Waugh) *Supertanks,* Ace, 1987.

The Best of John Brunner, Ballantine (New York City), 1988.

(With Greenberg and Waugh) *Spacefighters,* Ace, 1988.

OTHER

(Author of introduction) Robert A. Heinlein, *Double Star,* Gregg (Boston, MA), 1978.

Work included in "best of" anthologies, including *The Best from Galaxy,* edited by Ejler Jakobbsen, Universal-Award, 1972; *Best SF: 1972,* edited by Harry Harrison and Brian Aldiss, Putnam, 1973; *The Best Science Fiction of the Year—1972,* edited by Terry Carr, Ballantine, 1973; *Best SF: 1973,* edited by Harrison and Aldiss, Putnam, 1974; *The Best from Galaxy,* Volume 3, Award, 1975; *Nebula Award Stories II,* Harper, 1975; *Best Science Fiction Stories,* Dutton, 1977; *Nebula Award Stories XII,* Harper, 1977; and *Annual World's Best SF,* DAW, 1978.

Contributor to major science fiction anthologies, including *Orbit Eleven,* edited by Damon Knight, Putnam, 1971; *Showcase,* edited by Roger Elwood, Harper, 1973; *Analog 9,* edited by Ben Bova, Doubleday, 1973; *Combat SF,* edited by Gordon Dickson, Doubleday, 1975; *Frights,* edited by Kirby McCauley, St. Martin's, 1976; *Close Up: New Worlds,* St. Martin's, 1977; *Time of Passage,* Taplinger, 1978; *The Endless Frontier,* Ace Books, 1979; *The Road to SF 3,* Mentor, 1979; *Thieve's World,* edited by Robert Asprin, Ace Books, 1979; *The Future at War,* Ace Books, 1980; and *Dark Forces,* edited by McCauley, Viking, 1980.

Contributor of numerous short stories and articles to *Analog, Galaxy, Isaac Asimov's SF Adventures, Magazine of Fantasy and Science Fiction, Omni, Playboy,* and other publications.

Haldeman's novels have been translated into French, Italian, German, Dutch, Japanese, Hebrew, Spanish, and Swedish.

SIDELIGHTS: In his award-winning science fiction novel *The Forever War,* Joe Haldeman combines his experiences as a soldier during the Vietnam War, in which he was severely wounded, with a realistic, scientifically accurate presentation. The novel tells of a war that stretches across intergalactic distances and long periods of time, the soldiers involved traveling to remote battlefields via black holes. Because the soldiers travel at faster-than-light speeds, they age far slower than the civilians for whom they fight. This difference in relative age—the soldiers a few years older, their society centuries older—results in an alienation between the soldiers and the people they defend.

"Haldeman exercises his literary license," James Scott Hicks writes in the *Dictionary of Literary Biography,* "to comment on, and ultimately to expunge from his memory, America's last ground war [Vietnam]." Hicks points out that Haldeman's first novel, *War Year,* based on his army diaries, deals with Vietnam directly. "But the demon of Vietnam," Hicks writes, "was not exorcised from Haldeman's soul by writing [*War Year*], and frontline combat became the subject of . . . *The Forever War.*"

Haldeman, Hicks believes, is particularly adept at presenting his "theme of quiet resentment felt by those waging war."

Because of his scientific training in physics and astronomy, Haldeman is particularly careful to present *The Forever War* as realistically and accurately as possible. "The technology involved in this interplanetary campaign," Martin Levin of the *New York Times Book Review* notes in his review of *The Forever War,* "is so sophisticated that the book might well have been accompanied by an operator's manual. But then, all the futuristic mayhem is plugged into human situations that help keep the extraterrestrial activity on a warm and even witty plane."

Among newer novelists in the field, Haldeman, Richard Geis of *Science Fiction Review* believes, "is one of the best realistic science fiction writers going; maybe *the* best." Hicks finds that "Haldeman confronts his readers with painful questions, but he asks them with no small literary skill and with careful attention to scientific credibility." "It's comforting to know," writes Algis Budrys of the *Magazine of Fantasy and Science Fiction,* "that the cadre of impressive talent among younger writers is not diminishing, and to think that people like Haldeman will be around for a long time to set high standards."

Haldeman's "Worlds" trilogy, published over a span of a dozen years, follows the exploits of Marianne O'Hara, who is, summarizes Michael Pavese in *Best Sellers,* "an intelligent, promiscuous (in space promiscuity is encouraged) New New York citizen." Born in space, she travels from her orbiting, manmade world to Earth, to engage in post-graduate studies at New York University, in the first book, *Worlds: A Novel of the Near Future.* It details her adventures and misadventures on twenty-second century Earth, a far poorer, more decadent, chaotic, and dangerous extension of contemporary society. It is a society rapidly nearing a total breakdown, with Marianne's space ship veritably riding the shockwave of nuclear devastation home to New New York. *Worlds Apart* details Marianne's career as an ambitious politician of the orbital worlds, who, thinking her former lover, Jeff Hawkings, has died in the nuclear holocaust, takes a pair of husbands. In addition, the book not only tracks Jeff's career, now peddling medications to devolved Earth tribes, it includes, notes Charles Platt in *Washington Post,* "a grab-bag of extraneous notions in between: a Manson-worshipping death cult, a starship with an anti-matter drive, a formalized menage-a-trois, a hijacked space shuttle, an expedition into regressed Florida, a new science of behavioral conditioning, and more." In the final book, *Worlds Enough and Time,* Marianne, her two husbands, and her cybernetic "twin sister," along with 10,000 other would-be colonists, venture forth in the starship *Newhome* to seek their destinies on an Earth-like planet in the Epsilon Eridani system. A *Publishers Weekly* reviewer lauded: "Haldeman shows his strengths here: the workings of *Newhome* are believably complex, the novel's scientific background is neither strained nor especially complicated, and the reader's attention is focused on O'Hara's character, her inner life and her interpersonal relationships."

In addition to the obvious recurring theme of war—both real and imagined—in many Haldeman's books, essayist Duncan Lunan notes another theme in the *St. James Guide to Science Fiction Writers.* Referring back to *The Forever War,* where the enemy aliens are controlled by a hive-mind, Lunan says, "*Mindbridge* was another examination of human contact with a hive-mind, while *All My Sins Remembered* was a damning indictment not merely of big government but also of the standard SF attitude toward individuality. SF used to be full of people who find out that they're really someone else (usually someone more powerful), and part of the problem in identifying with central characters is often they lack individuality." Says Lunan, "McGavin in *All My Sins Remembered* is a government agent, repeatedly given new identities through psychological conditioning and plastic surgery." Lunan adds, "he is an individual moved and controlled by an organisation which commands his loyalty but is beyond his control." The theme of individuals preyed upon and controlled by ultra-powerful agencies or corporate entities is also central to Haldeman's "Worlds" trilogy, as with the CIA and KGB in *Tool of the Trade,* and by the wealthy in *Buying Time.* And Sybil S. Steinberg says in *Publishers Weekly,* "Evoking painful nostalgia, . . . Haldeman uses bold language, powerful images and a graphic style to tell his emotional tale, in which concentrated, diary-like entries intensify the drama and despair."

Sue Martin, writing in *Los Angeles Times,* terms *The Hemingway Hoax* "A bright, short science fiction novel, . . . [this] quirky effort offers a unique solution to one of the enduring literary mysteries of our time: Just what DID happen to Ernest Hemingway's missing manuscripts, lost in 1922 at the Gare de Lyon in Paris?" She continues, "For Hemingway fans, Haldeman's answer is a hoot, and as different a theory as you can find." Marc Leepson, in a *Book World* review, described Haldeman's fictionalized but largely autobiographical *1968* as "a well-crafted, biting novel set in Vietnam."

Forever Peace is a sequel to the problems raised in Haldeman's acclaimed *Forever War.* In 2043, an American-led alliance has been battling with the third-world, Ngumi confederation, primarily, on the alliance's part, with "soldierboys"—killing machines controlled by brain-linked "mechanics," among them, the protagonist, physicist Julian Class. Meanwhile, the Jupiter Project, the most ambitious scientific experiment of all time, circles Jupiter—Julian's lover, Amelia, discovers it may endanger not only our solar system, but the universe, in a new "Big Bang." Among other complications, their attempt to stop the disaster runs afoul of an influential Christian cult, the Hammer of God, dedicated to bringing on the Endtime. A *Publishers Weekly* reviewer concludes: "As always, Haldeman, a Vietnam vet, writes with intelligence and power about the horrors of war, and about humanity's seeming inability to overcome its violent tendencies."

A full interview with Haldeman appears in *Contemporary Authors New Revision Series,* Volume 6.

BIOGRAPHICAL/CRITICAL SOURCES:

BOOKS

Dictionary of Literary Biography, Volume 7: *Twentieth-Century American Science Fiction Writers,* Gale (Detroit), 1981.
Gordon, Joan, *Joe Haldeman,* Starmont House (Mercer Island, WA), 1980.
St. James Guide to Science Fiction Writers, St. James Press (Detroit), 1996.

PERIODICALS

Algol, summer-fall, 1977; summer-fall, 1978.
Analog, March, 1978; September, 1978; July, 1979; November, 1982, p. 164-165; September, 1983, p. 164; March, 1984, p. 168; February, 1986, p. 182; December, 1986, p. 182; January, 1990, p. 308-309.
Best Sellers, December, 1976; February, 1978.
Bloomsbury Review, January/February, 1996, p. 3, 20.
Booklist, June 1, 1975.
Book World, July 2, 1995, p. C95.

Chicago Tribune, September 26, 1976; September 2, 1991, p. 10.

Chicago Tribune Book World, June 14, 1981.

Commonweal, October 27, 1972.

Destinies, November/December, 1978.

Foundation, May, 1978.

Futures, June, 1975.

Galaxy, December, 1976; March, 1978.

Library Journal, October 15, 1997, p. 97.

Los Angeles Times Book Reviews, October 30, 1983, p. 4; July 8, 1990, p. 9.

Magazine of Fantasy and Science Fiction, May, 1975; October, 1975; April, 1977; September, 1979; August, 1981, p. 55-56; March, 1984, Volume 66, number 3, p. 43-45.

New Republic, November 26, 1977.

New York Times Book Review, May 21, 1972; March 23, 1975; February 27, 1977; January 15, 1984, p. 29; February 10, 1985, p. 40; June 7, 1987, p. 18; July 2, 1989, p. 15; June 14, 1992, p. 24.

Observer (London), May 8, 1977.

Publishers Weekly, March 13, 1987, p. 70; December 7, 1990, p. 78; April 6, 1992, p. 54; April 17, 1995, p. 38; April 22, 1996, p. 64; August 25, 1997, p. 49.

Science Fiction Review, August, 1976; February, 1977; February, 1978.

Science Fiction Studies, Volume 21, 1994, p. 238-240.

Starlog, Volume 17, 1978.

Thrust, summer, 1979.

Times Literary Supplement, July 8, 1977.

Washington Post Book World, April 26, 1981; May 13, 1990, p. 8; May 31, 1992, p. 6; July 2, 1995, p. 4.*

*　　*　　*

HALEY, (Harry) Russell 1934-

PERSONAL: Born April 10, 1934, in Dewsbury, England; immigrated to Australia, 1961; immigrated to New Zealand, 1966; son of Harry (a salesman and amateur linguist) and Gertrude (Convey) Haley; married Jean Marjorie Kay (a resource consultant), April 2, 1959; children: Ian, Katherine. *Education:* University of Auckland, M.A. (with first class honors), 1970. *Politics:* Labour. *Religion:* None.

ADDRESSES: Home and office—90 Taylor's Rd., Auckland 4, New Zealand.

CAREER: Writer. Literary fellow at University of Auckland, 1985—. Worked as laboratory assistant, turf cutter, foreign exchange cashier, flexowriter operator, itinerant fruit picker, ditch digger, tractor assembler, gardener, university lecturer, telegraphist, groundsman, furniture salesman, tape librarian, weighbridge operator in a sugar mill, high school teacher, bus conductor, postman, and clerical worker. *Military service:* Royal Air Force, senior aircraftsman, 1952-54, wireless operator, 1953-54; served in Iraq.

MEMBER: International PEN.

WRITINGS:

The Walled Garden (poems), Mandrake Root (Auckland), 1972.

On the Fault Line and Other Poems, Hawk Press (Paraparaumu, New Zealand), 1977.

The Sauna Bath Mysteries and Other Stories, Mandrake Root, 1978.

Real Illusions: A Selection of Family Lies and Biographical Fictions in Which the Ancestral Dead Also Play Their Part, Victoria University Press (Wellington, New Zealand), 1984, New Directions (New York City), 1985.

The Settlement (novel), Hodder & Stoughton (London), 1986.

Hanly: A New Zealand Artist, Hodder & Stoughton (Auckland, NZ), 1989.

(Editor with Susan Davis) *The Penguin Book of Contemporary New Zealand Short Stories,* Penguin (New York City), 1989.

Beside Myself (novel), Penguin, 1990.

RADIO PLAYS

Journey to Understanding, Australian Broadcasting Commission, 1965.

Day in the Ozone, Australian Broadcasting Commission, 1967.

Bach Life, Radio New Zealand, 1979.

Three Priests for Michael Convey, Radio New Zealand, 1980.

The Scarlet Blackbird, Radio New Zealand, 1981.

I'll Plant You a Kowhai, Radio New Zealand, 1981.

The Devonport Mutiny, Radio New Zealand, 1982.

OTHER

Also author of *The Transfer Station,* 1989.

SIDELIGHTS: "*The Sauna Bath Mysteries and Other Stories* established Russell Haley's reputation as a pioneering writer of postmodernist experimental fiction with affinities with writers such as Nabakov, Beckett, John Barth, Robert Coover, and Thomas Pynchon," writes Janet Wilson in *Contemporary Novelists.* "This has been confirmed in the achievement of his two novels, *The Settlement* and *Beside Myself,* and the series of interlinked stories that are collected in *The Transfer Station.* These extend the narrative strategies of his short stories, such as the classic 'Barbados—A Love Story,' into ambitious performances in which he collapses the boundaries between fiction and reality, overlapping dream, memory, and experience and undermining epistemological certainties."

Haley's novel *The Settlement* concerns Walter Lemanby, who finds himself a patient in either a convalescent home or an asylum after suffering a severe fall. Wilson notes: "Images of menacing control abound—mysterious installations, searchlights, helicopters, curfews, nameless uniformed assailants. They point either to civil unrest or to the existence of a centralized, totalitarian state that represses the individual; they are reinforced in the plot in the sinister, masked figure of Dr. Grimshaw." Haley disrupts his own narrative by admitting some fifty pages into the story that he is the "secret collaborator within this text" and beginning his story again. Wilson notes: "Haley's foregrounding of the process of writing through metafictional games that stress the artifice of illusion and the fictional nature of subjectivity, however, rarely lapses into linguistic solipsism. His narratorial self-consciousness is both artful and endearing. Walter's struggles to familiarize himself with an alien world, to reorder experience by labeling his landscape, are intensely personal if not moving."

Haley once told *CA:* "My motivation is obscure, but to make a place and a name must be important, even if it's a scratch on a decayed wall. Our circumstances are always financially appalling. Travel, dreams, reading, and memory are the vital sources of my writing, and the work is always thrown out of conventional alignment by the fact that I am an immigrant/emigrant. Carl Jung is a prod and Samuel Beckett a luminous example. *Real Illusions* is probably a key work since it has traveled, if a little diffidently, beyond the frontiers of the country in which I live and work."

BIOGRAPHICAL/CRITICAL SOURCES:

BOOKS

Contemporary Novelists, 6th edition, St. James Press (Detroit), 1996.

PERIODICALS

New York Times Book Review, May 5, 1985.

*   *   *

HALL, Willis 1929-

PERSONAL: Born April 6, 1929, in Leeds, England; son of Walter (a fitter) and Gladys (Gomersal) Hall; married second wife, Valerie Shute, 1973; children: Peter, Macer, Daniel, James. *Education:* Attended Cockburn High School, Leeds, England.

ADDRESSES: Home—64 Clarence Rd., St. Albans, Hertfordshire, England. *Agent*—London Management, 235-241 Regent St., London W1A 2JT, England.

CAREER: Writer. *Military service:* British Regular Army, 1947-52; served as radio playwright for Chinese Schools Department of Radio Malaya.

MEMBER: Garrick Club, Savage Club, Lansdowne Club.

AWARDS, HONORS: Play of the Year Award, *Evening Standard,* 1959, for *The Long and the Short and the Tall.*

WRITINGS:

FOR CHILDREN

(With I. O. Evans) *They Found the World,* Warne (London), 1959.
The Royal Astrologers: Adventures of Father Mole-Cricket; or, The Malayan Legends, Heinemann (London), 1960, Coward (New York City), 1962.
Incredible Kidnapping, Heinemann, 1975.
The Summer of the Dinosaur, Bodley Head, 1977, published as *Henry Hollins and the Dinosaur,* illustrated by Maggie Ling, 1979.

The Last Vampire, illustrated by Babette Cole, Bodley Head, 1982.

The Irish Adventures of Worzel Gummidge, Severn House, 1984.

The Inflatable Shop, illustrated by Ling, Bodley Head, 1984.

The Return of the Antelope (also see below), illustrated by Rowan Barnes Murphy, Bodley Head, 1985.

Dragon Days, illustrated by Alison Claire Darke, Bodley Head, 1985.

The Antelope Company Ashore, Bodley Head, 1986.

Spooky Rhymes, 1987.

The Antelope Company at Large, Bodley Head, 1987.

Dr. Jekyll and Mr. Hollins, Bodley Head, 1988.

The Vampire's Revenge, illustrated by Tony Ross, Bodley Head, 1993.

The Vampire's Christmas, illustrated by Tony Ross, Bodley Head, 1994.

PUBLISHED PLAYS

Final at Furnell (radio play; broadcast in 1954), M. Evans, 1956.

(With Lewis Jones) *Poet and Pheasant* (radio play; broadcast in 1955), Deane, 1959.

The Long and the Short and the Tall (produced in Edinburgh, Scotland, 1958; produced in London, 1959; produced in New York, 1962; also see below), Heinemann, 1959, Theatre Arts, 1961.

The Play of the Royal Astrologers (produced in Birmingham, England, 1958; produced in London, 1968), Heinemann, 1960.

A Glimpse of the Sea: Three Short Plays (contains *A Glimpse of the Sea,* one act, produced in London, 1959; *The Last Day in Dreamland,* one act, produced in London, 1959; and *Return to the Sea,* television play, broadcast in 1959), M. Evans, 1960.

The Day's Beginning: An Easter Play, Heinemann, 1963.

The Gentle Knight (radio play; broadcast in 1964), Blackie, 1966.

The Railwayman's New Clothes (television play; broadcast in 1971), S. French (New York City), 1974.

Kidnapped at Christmas (produced in London, 1975), Heinemann, 1975.

Walk On, Walk On (produced in Liverpool, 1975), S. French, 1976.

A Right Christmas Caper (produced in 1977), S. French, 1978.

Treasure Island (musical; based on novel by Robert Louis Stevenson; produced in 1985), S. French, 1986.

Wind in the Willows (musical; based on story by Kenneth Grahame; produced in 1985), S. French, 1986.

Jane Eyre: A Play (based on novel by Charlotte Bronte), S. French, 1994.

The Three Musketeers (based on novel by Alexandre Dumas), S. French, 1995.

PUBLISHED PLAYS; WITH KEITH WATERHOUSE

Billy Liar (adaptation of novel by Waterhouse; produced in London, 1960; produced in New York, 1963; also see below), Norton (New York City), 1960.

Celebration: The Wedding and the Funeral (produced in Nottingham, England, then London, 1961), M. Joseph, 1961.

England, Our England (musical; produced in London, 1962), M. Evans, 1964.

The Sponge Room [and] *Squat Betty* (the former: one act, produced in Nottingham, 1962, produced in New York, 1964; the latter: one act, produced in London, 1962, produced in New York, 1964), M. Evans, 1963.

All Things Bright and Beautiful (produced in Bristol, England, 1962; produced in London, 1962), M. Joseph, 1963.

Come Laughing Home (produced as *They Called the Bastard Stephen* in Bristol, 1964; produced as *Come Laughing Home* in Wimbledon, England, 1965), M. Evans, 1965.

Say Who You Are (produced in London, 1965), M. Evans, 1967, published as *Help Stamp Out Marriage* (produced in New York, 1966), S. French, 1966.

(Also translators) *Saturday, Sunday, Monday* (adaptation of play by Eduardo de Filippo; produced in London, 1973; produced in New York), Heinemann, 1974.

Who's Who (produced in Coventry, England, 1971; produced in London, 1973), S. French, 1974.

Children's Day (produced in Edinburgh, 1969; produced in London, 1969), S. French, 1975.

Worzel Gummidge (musical; adaptation of television series based on characters created by Barbara Euphan Todd; produced in 1981; also see below), S. French, 1984.

UNPUBLISHED PLAYS

Chin-Chin (adaptation of play, *Tchin-Tchin,* by Francois Billetdoux), produced in London, 1960.

(With Robin Maugham) *Azouk* (adaptation of play by Alexandre Rivemale), produced in Newcastle upon Tyne, 1962.

(Co-author) *Yer What?* (revue), produced in Nottingham, 1962.

The Love Game (adaptation of play by Marcel Archard), produced in London, 1964.

(With Waterhouse) *Joey, Joey* (musical), produced in London, 1966.

(With Waterhouse) *Whoops-a-Daisy,* produced in Nottingham, 1968.

(With Waterhouse) *The Card* (musical; adaptation of novel by Arnold Bennett), produced in Bristol, then London, 1973.

Christmas Crackers, produced in London, 1976.

Stag-Night, produced in London, 1976.

Filumena (adaptation of work by de Filippo), produced in 1977.

The Water Babies (musical; based on work by Charles Kingsley), produced in 1987.

(With Waterhouse) *Budgie* (musical), produced in 1989.

Author of screenplays, including *The Long and the Short and the Tall,* 1961; (with Waterhouse) *Whistle down the Wind,* 1961; (with Waterhouse) *A Kind of Loving,* 1961; *The Valiant,* 1962; (with Waterhouse) *Billy Liar* (adapted from novel by Waterhouse), 1963; *West Eleven,* 1963; (with Waterhouse) *Man in the Middle,* 1964; (with Waterhouse) *Pretty Polly,* 1968; and *Lock Up Your Daughters,* 1969.

Author of television plays, including *Air Mail from Cyprus,* 1958; *On the Night of the Murder,* 1962; *By Endeavour Alone,* 1963; (with Waterhouse) *Happy Moorings,* 1963; *How Many Angels,* 1964; *The Ticket,* 1969; *They Don't All Open Men's Boutiques,* 1972; *The Villa Maroc,* 1972; *Song at Twilight,* 1973; *Friendly Encounter,* 1974; *The Piano-Smashers of the Golden Sun,* 1974; *Illegal Approach,* 1974; *Midgley,* 1975; *Match-Fit,* 1976; and *The Road to 1984.*

Author of radio plays, including: *The Nightingale,* 1954; *Furor at Furnell,* 1955; *Frenzy at Furnell,* 1955; *Friendly at Furnell,* 1955; *Fluster at Furnell,* 1955; *One Man Absent,* 1955; *A Run for the Money,* 1956; *Afternoon for Antigone,* 1956; *The Long Years,* 1956; *Any Dark Morning,* 1956; *Feodor's Bride,* 1956; *One Man Returns,* 1956; *A Ride on the Donkeys,* 1957; *The Calverdon Road Job,* 1957; *Harvest the Sea,* 1957; *Monday at Seven,* 1957; *Annual Outing,* 1958; *The Larford Lad,* 1958; and

(with Leslie Halward) *The Case of Walter Grimshaw,* 1958.

Writer for television shows, including *Inside George Webley,* 1968; *Queenie's Castle,* 1970; *Budgie,* 1971-72; *The Upper Crusts,* 1973; *Three's Company,* 1973; *Billy Liar,* 1973-74; *The Fuzz,* 1977; *Worzel Gummidge,* 1979; *The Danedyke Mystery,* 1979; *Stan's Last Game,* 1983; *The Bright Side,* 1985; and *The Return of the Antelope,* 1986.

Work represented in anthologies, including *The Television Playwright: Ten Plays for BBC Television,* edited by Michael Barry, Hill & Wang, 1960; *Modern Short Plays from Broadway and London,* edited by Stanley Richards, Random House, 1969; *Drama Study Units,* edited by John Foster, Heinemann, 1975; and *Prompt Three,* edited by Alan Durband, Hutchinson, 1976.

OTHER

(With Michael Parkinson) *The A to Z of Soccer,* Pelham, 1970.

(With Bob Monkhouse) *The A to Z of Television,* Pelham, 1971.

My Sporting Life, Luscombe, 1975.

Editor of books, including (with Waterhouse) *Writers' Theatre,* Heinemann, 1967; (with Parkinson) *Football Report: An Anthology of Soccer,* Pelham, 1973; *Football Classified: An Anthology of Soccer,* Luscombe, 1975; and *Football Final,* Pelham, 1975.

ADAPTATIONS: The Return of the Antelope was adapted as a picture book by Mary Hoffman, illustrated by Faith Jaques, Heinemann, 1985.

SIDELIGHTS: Willis Hall is a prolific author of works for both adults and children. Plays written by Hall include numerous published and produced works, including the award-winning *The Long and the Short and the Tall* and stage adaptations of classic books such as *Jane Eyre* and *The Three Musketeers.* Working frequently with co-writer Keith Waterhouse—the pair has collaborated on such works as *Billy Liar, Come Laughing Home,* and *All Things Bright and Beautiful*—Hall often sets his adult fictions in the northern English towns where he grew up. In addition to plays for radio, television, film, and the stage, Hall has adapted the works of several novelists, including Waterhouse, Charlotte Bronte, and Eduardo de Filippo, into popular plays. Beginning in the mid-1980s, his work as a writer for television provided the inspiration for several popular fantasy books for children that feature unique plots, humorous dialogue, and likeable characters.

Hall's "Antelope" series for young readers, which is set during the final years of the nineteenth century, had its origins in a television series that began running in England in 1986. Each of the "Antelope" stories features a shipwrecked group of miniature people—descendants of the Lilliputians discovered by Lemuel Gulliver in Jonathan Swift's *Gulliver's Travels*. Befriended by a pair of children, the three tiny newcomers attempt to lay claim to their discovery (the island of Great Britain), then attempt to find a new boat to return them to their native Lilliput. Hall's series features suspenseful plots and a creepy villain. In the first installment, 1985's *Return of the Antelope*, the evil Harwell Mincing, proprietor of a local freak show, is determined to add the diminutive crew of the *Antelope II* to his collection, although his efforts are constantly foiled by the watchful children Gerald and Philippa. "The story of the castaways proceeds with coincidence and surprise and an open ending assures interested readers that there are more adventures to come," according to a *Growing Point* reviewer.

The Antelope Company Ashore finds the short-statured trio—Spelbush, Fistram, and Brelca, by name—safely hidden in the house of Gerald and Philippa's grandfather, a renowned Victorian photographer by the name of Garstanton. Unfortunately, Mincing is still lurking about in hopes of capturing the visitors, and he sets a series of elaborate traps to accomplish his evil goal. "The Lilliputians have been given enough personality to account for the amusing ambiguity of their position," noted *Growing Point*. "They address the children, who believe themselves to be protectors, in conceited, demanding and even aggressive tones," and when they are left alone in the house at the end of the book, other adventures for these "entrancing little people" will surely follow. And they do. In *The Antelope Company at Large*, Gerald, Philippa, and their grandfather have moved to the country; the Lilliputians now find new protectors in a boot-black named Ernest, and in Emily, an orphan. Protection is still needed, too, as Mincing continues his efforts at capturing the shipwrecked trio. While noting that the stories contain numerous adventures, a *Junior Bookshelf* reviewer contended that the narrative relies on "pictures and all sorts of technical tricks to point out the contrast between miniature folk and humans. . . ; without these aids it falls flat." However, a critic in *Growing*

Point disagreed, writing that "the humor of relative size and the irony of human personalities displayed in miniature make good reading and the domestic and social life of Edwardian England is as always sharply and precisely suggested."

A number of Hall's books for middle school-aged readers feature the Hollins family, which includes Henry Hollins, a young lad who somehow always seems to end up in the most amazing situations. In 1977's *Summer of the Dinosaur*—republished in 1988 as *Henry Hollins and the Dinosaur*—Henry finds a dinosaur egg and takes it home, with humorous results. *The Last Vampire*, published in 1983, finds Henry and his family trekking through Europe, where, lost, they come upon a town terrorized by the mysterious Count Alucard, last of the family Dracula. With a foreboding castle, packs of howling wolves, and suspicious, garlic-carrying villagers, Hall's tale quickly draws readers into mystery. Equally unsurprising to readers familiar with Hall's magic-laced adventure stories, 1985's *Dragon Days* finds Henry transported back in time; from the stage of a local magician where he is assisting with an illusion, he finds himself in Camelot, whisked there by Merlin the Magician himself. Followed by his doting and umbrella-toting mother and a sword-swallower called Great Alma, Henry must help King Arthur save the dragons from certain extinction at the hands of zealous dragon hunters. While Fiona Ross commented in *School Librarian* that "the style of the writing is slick and self-conscious, too sophisticated perhaps for most primary children," a *Junior Bookshelf* critic called *Dragon Days* "a very entertaining book with a sparkling text." Added a reviewer in *Growing Point*: "this tall-story deserves attention for its spry topical humour . . . and for a deftly concealed message about our own reckless behaviour towards wild life."

Other novels that feature the outrageous escapades of the popular Hollins family include *The Inflatable Shop, Dr. Jekyll and Mr. Hollins,* and *The Vampire's Christmas,* the latter published in 1995 in *The Inflatable Shop*. On vacation at a sea-side resort, eleven-year-old Henry is among four people who happen to be in a toy shop when the inflatable toys are filled with hydrogen gas instead of air. With the small building now airborne and floating out to sea, the quick-thinking boy tosses a message-bearing bottle over the side in. In 1988's *Dr. Jekyll and Mr. Hollins,* Henry's father visits a London doctor for medicine for his back, only to find that the pills he is accidentally given result in radical mood swings—

he turns into a terrible, hairy-armed monster. And *The Vampire's Christmas* reunites readers with Count Alucard, whose attempts to travel among human holiday-goers are foiled when he is offered garlic-based salad dressing one night at dinner and his extreme distaste for the stuff causes suspicions regarding his true nature. Enter Henry Hollins, who rescues the Count from the revealing situation and reunites him with the rest of his family, in a series of "amazing adventures [that] will appeal to children of junior age who enjoy fantasy and the idea of an incompetent vegetarian vampire," according to a *Junior Bookshelf* critic.

The Incredible Kidnapping, a chapter book for young readers published in 1975, was based on a play by Hall. In the novel, two looney prisoners named Crosby and Gilbert decide to escape from their cells on Christmas Eve, but the police dispersed to round the convicts back up, led by the curmudgeonly Detective Constable Brummett, prove to be even crazier than their quarry. Despite the interference of an obnoxious child, a slew of disguises, chases, and assorted other subterfuges, the prisoners end up spending Christmas Day curled up in their cells. While noting wryly that "some humour has always flourished at the dangerous edges of bad taste," *Times Literary Supplement* reviewer Nicholas Tucker maintained that Hall "takes risks, and comes through well" in his humorous escapade through the underworld. "*The Incredible Kidnapping* is a very funny book," added Tucker; "would that there were more like it."

While children's books have been the focus of Hall's more recent works, plays comprise the bulk of his oeuvre. Beginning as a writer for radio, Hall saw his first work for the stage, a 1958 comedy set in a Malaysian military outpost called *The Long and the Short of It,* achieve popularity on stages in Edinburgh, London, and New York City. From successful stage works, including 1960's *Chin-Chin,* his long-running adaptation of Francois Billetdoux's *Tsin-Tsin,* Hall quickly moved to the lucrative world of television, writing original teleplays including 1964's *How Many Angels* and 1976's *Match-Fit,* as well as contributing to such popular television series as *Three's Company* and *The Bright Side.* Working together with Waterhouse, who, like Hall, grew up in Yorkshire, he has published several popular dramatic works, including 1960's *Billy Liar,* which was later adapted as a television play, and *Worzel Gummidge,* a musical based on a popular British television series created by Barbara Euphan Todd. In

addition to writing for the television series, Hall also produced the spin-off novel, *The Irish Adventures of Worzel Gummidge,* published in 1984.

BIOGRAPHICAL/CRITICAL SOURCES:

PERIODICALS

Growing Point, April, 1976, p. 2851; March, 1985, p. 4405; March, 1986, pp. 4570-71; May, 1987, pp. 4796-97; May, 1988, pp. 4975-77.
Junior Bookshelf, April, 1976, p. 103; February, 1983, p. 41; June, 1985, p. 127; February, 1986, pp. 33-34; December, 1986, p. 263; February, 1988, p. 47; December, 1988, p. 290; February, 1989, p. 22; February, 1995, p. 19.
School Librarian, March, 1983, pp. 34-35; December, 1984, p. 350; September, 1985, p. 237.
School Library Journal, November 1993, p. 155.
Times Literary Supplement, December 5, 1975.*

*   *   *

HAMILTON, Hervey
See ROBINS, Denise (Naomi)

*   *   *

HAMILTON, Priscilla
See GELLIS, Roberta

*   *   *

HARDWICK, Elizabeth (Bruce) 1916-

PERSONAL: Born July 27, 1916, in Lexington, KY; daughter of Eugene Allen and Mary (Ramsey) Hardwick; married Robert Lowell (a poet), July 28, 1949 (divorced, 1972); children: Harriet. *Education:* University of Kentucky, A.B., 1938, M.A., 1939; Columbia University, graduate study, 1939-41.

ADDRESSES: Home—15 West 67th St., New York, NY 10023.

CAREER: Writer. Adjunct associate professor of English, Barnard College, New York City, and founder and advisory editor, *New York Review of Books.*

MEMBER: American Academy and Institute of Arts and Letters.

AWARDS, HONORS: Guggenheim fellowship in fiction, 1948; George Jean Nathan Award for dramatic criticism (first woman recipient), 1966; National Academy and Institute of Arts and Letters award in literature, 1974; National Book Critics Circle Award nomination, 1980, for *Sleepless Nights;* Gold Medal for criticism, American Academy of Arts and Letters, 1993; Iva Sandrof Award for Lifetime Achievement in Publishing, National Book Critics Circle, 1995.

WRITINGS:

The Ghostly Lover (novel), Harcourt (New York City), 1945.

The Simple Truth (novel), Harcourt, 1955.

(Editor) *The Selected Letters of William James,* Farrar, Straus (New York City), 1960.

A View of My Own: Essays in Literature and Society, Farrar, Straus, 1962.

Seduction and Betrayal: Women and Literature (essays), Random House, 1974.

Sleepless Nights (novel), Random House (New York City), 1979.

Bartleby in Manhattan and Other Essays (essays), Random House, 1984.

(Editor with Robert Atwan) *The Best American Essays 1986,* Ticknor & Fields (New York City), 1986.

(Editor) *The Selected Letters of William James,* Doubleday, 1993.

Sight Readings: Essays on Writers, Biographies about Them, and Public Happenings Here and There, Random House, 1998.

Work appears in numerous anthologies, including two volumes of *O. Henry Memorial Award Prize Stories* and six volumes of *The Best American Short Stories* series. Editor, *Rediscovered Fiction by American Women: A Personal Selection* series, Ayer, 1977—. Contributor to periodicals, including *Partisan Review, New Yorker, Yale Review, New York Review of Books* and *Harper's.*

SIDELIGHTS: An accomplished essayist and novelist, Elizabeth Hardwick is perhaps best known "primarily for brilliant literary and social criticism, which has graced the pages of many of the country's leading liberal journals, most notably the *Partisan Review* and the *New York Review of Books,"* according to Joseph

J. Branin, in a *Dictionary of Literary Biography* article on Hardwick.

Hardwick's first novel, *The Ghostly Lover,* focuses on Marian Coleman who, according to Carol Simpson Stern in *Contemporary Novelists,* "learns that she cannot settle for the comforts of a man, it offers telling glimpses into her life, the life of her restless parents, the hot, lazy days in the South, the grubby days studying in New York, and the dreams of the ghostly men who pursue her." "Throughout the novel, Marian is presented as a profoundly lonely young person," notes Branin. "[She] longs for connection and intimacy with another person but finds it impossible to break through the separateness of the characters in the novel. She is especially disappointed with her mother, whom she adores from a distance."

As Branin reports, *The Ghostly Lover* garnered mixed critical reaction. But soon after its publication, Hardwick was contacted by Philip Rahv, an editor of the avant-garde *Partisan Review,* to become a contributor. "She accepted the offer eagerly and thus began her long and successful career as a social and literary critic," Branin writes. As Hardwick's reputation as a writer grew, so did her fame outside the editorial offices. She married the poet Robert Lowell in 1949, a union that lasted until 1972, when Lowell divorced Hardwick to marry Caroline Blackwood, an Irish writer. "In 1977, the last year of his life, Lowell returned to Hardwick," relates Branin. "They summered together in Castine, Maine, before Lowell died of heart failure in New York." Hardwick tells a *New York Times* reporter that her former husband was "the most extraordinary person I have ever known, like no one else—unplaceable, unaccountable."

Hardwick's published works include a second novel, *The Simple Truth,* a story of speculation and accusation surrounding a sensational murder trial. "Tightly plotted, probing the motives behind a frightful act, the novel examines the death of a beautiful college girl, Betty Jane Henderson, who died in her boyfriend's rooming-house, after hours," explains Stern. "The trial of the boyfriend, Rudy, dominates the book. It is examined from numerous perspectives, most important those of two curious onlookers, the affable, married Mr. Parks and the middle-aged, married Anita Mitchell who is drawn to the case to investigate the working of the unconscious. The truth about the act, late at night, in a rooming-house where two lovers frolicked and struggled, ultimately emerges, but equally as interesting is the picture of the psyches of the characters who become caught up in the trial."

The author's third novel, *Sleepless Nights,* "is a difficult work to classify," comments Branin. One possible definition may be "autobiographical": the fiction centers on a writer named Elizabeth, who grew up in Kentucky and moved to Manhattan. In the course of the story the narrator "remembers certain people and places from her past. . . . [Her] compassion for her old acquaintances and her careful observations as she brings these memories to life give the work its power and unity," Branin states. "The autobiographical component of the novel is openly confronted, and handled effectively," writes Stern. "Roaming like an insomniac from one recollection to another, the book continually surprises us with its fleeting memories of rooms we have all known, feelings we have felt, losses we have never remedied." Stern observes that "the book is a queer blend of autobiography and fiction. Hardwick's decision to create a persona with her own name heightens our sense of how life informs fiction. The Elizabeth of this book is very nearly the Elizabeth Hardwick who lives, the woman who is a career journalist, writer, reviewer for *Partisan Review* and the *New York Review of Books,* and the ex-wife of the poet Robert Lowell. The memories and imaginings of the persona curl about the lives of deprived souls, of which Elizabeth is one."

Hardwick's essays and critical writings have garnered her a substantial reputation. Her 1974 collection, *Seduction and Betrayal: Women and Literature,* caught the attention of several critics, including Rosemary Dinnage, who remarks in a *Times Literary Supplement* article that the book "is so original, so sly and strange, but the pleasure in embedded in the style, in the way [the author] flicks the English language around like a whip." Hardwick's concern in *Seduction and Betrayal,* Dinnage goes on to say, "is to present her own angry and witty view of the sexes, and for this she has more scope with the fictional beings and the companions of writers than with the great creative women, for these less easily align themselves with the victims." Hardwick "is no hand-wringer," says *Books and Bookmen* critic Jean Stubbs. "She is a literary surgeon, admirably equipped to expose the nerves." And in the opinion of Joan Didion, writing in *New York Times Book Review.* "Perhaps no one has written more acutely and poignantly about the ways in which women compensate for their relative physiological inferiority, about the poetic and practical implications of walking around the world deficient in hemoglobin, deficient in respiratory capacity, deficient in muscular

strength and deficient in stability of the vascular and autonomic nervous systems."

By the time Hardwick's collection *Bartleby in Manhattan* came out, in 1984, she was almost universally acclaimed as a major essayist, prompting *New York Times* reviewer Christopher Lehmann-Haupt to remark, "one is interested in anything that Elizabeth Hardwick writes. That is a given." For this volume of social and literary musings, however, Lehmann-Haupt does have some reservations: "The subjects . . . give one a moment or two of pause. The atmosphere in the South during the civil rights movement of the 1960's? The significance of Martin Luther King, Jr. and of Lee Harvey Oswald and his family?. . . . It isn't so much that we've lost interest in these topics as that they've become as familiar to us by now as our fingers and our toes." Another reviewer finds more to recommend in *Bartleby in Manhattan.* "As these essays of the past 20 years show, Hardwick's [concerns] have two qualities that make her one of our finest critics: a heart that wants to be moved and a critical intelligence that refuses to indulge it," finds *Los Angeles Times Book Review* writer Richard Eder. "Much that she deals with produces more disquiet in her than reward; she looks for values in the fiery writing of the '60s and the distanced writing of the '70s and finds them poor or limited. Our reward is the record of her search." "Whatever her subject," says novelist Anne Tyler, acting as critic for *New Republic,* Hardwick "has a gift for coming up with descriptions so thoughtfully selected, so exactly right, that they strike the reader as inevitable." As Tyler also notes, "Mere aptitude of language, of course, is not sufficient. What makes *Bartleby in Manhattan* memorable is the sense of the author's firm character. 'Pull yourself together,' she says briskly to a racist who tells her he feels sick at the sight of an integrated crowd."

Hardwick "is the voice of toughminded gentility," says Joan Joffe Hall in a *New Republic* review from 1974. "She inspires confidence because she seems just like the reader, a shade smarter perhaps, able to turn the commonplace into revelation, talking in someone's living room with an earnest casualness beyond personality. It's the quality most of us aspire to."

BIOGRAPHICAL/CRITICAL SOURCES:

BOOKS

Contemporary Literary Criticism, Volume 13, Gale (Detroit), 1980.

Contemporary Novelists, 6th edition, St. James Press (Detroit), 1996.
Dictionary of Literary Biography, Volume 6: *American Novelists since World War II,* Gale, 1980.

PERIODICALS

American Book Review, March-April, 1985.
Atlantic, June, 1979.
Books and Bookmen, January, 1976.
Chicago Tribune, November 25, 1986.
Hudson Review, winter, 1974-75.
London Review of Books, November 17, 1983.
Los Angeles Times Book Review, May 29, 1983.
Nation, June 14, 1975.
New Republic, May 25, 1974; June 20, 1983.
New Statesman, August 17, 1979.
Newsweek, June 17, 1974; May 30, 1983.
New York Review of Books, January 27, 1974; April 29, 1979.
New York Times, April 2, 1982; May 24, 1983.
New York Times Book Review, May 5, 1974; June 12, 1983.
Sewanee Review, Volume 92, number 4, fall, 1984.
Times Literary Supplement, November 29, 1974.
Village Voice, May 7, 1979.
Washington Post Book World, May 12, 1974; May 29, 1983.
World Literature Today, spring, 1980.

*   *   *

HARRINGTON, William 1931-
(Megan Marklin)

PERSONAL: Born November 21, 1931, in Marietta, OH; son of William K. (an oil producer) and Virginia (Pickens) Harrington; first marriage ended in divorce, 1960s; married Diana C. Fitch, 1972 (divorced 1992); children: one son. *Education:* Marietta College, A.B., 1953; Duke University, M.A., 1955; Ohio State University, J.D., 1958.

ADDRESSES: Agent—Tod Chichak Agency, 400 E. 55th St., New York, NY 10022.

CAREER: Lawyer in private practice, Marietta, OH, 1958-62; Office of Ohio Secretary of State, Columbus, elections counsel, 1962-65; Ohio State Bar Association, Columbus, counsel, 1965-71; lawyer in private practice, Columbus, 1971-78; Mead Data

Central, senior attorney, 1978-80; author, 1980—. Also worked as a computer consultant and is a licensed pilot.

MEMBER: PEN, American Civil Liberties Union, Phi Beta Kappa, New York City Bar Association.

AWARDS, HONORS: Ohioana Book Award, 1967, for *Yoshar the Soldier;* Lit.D., Marietta College, 1986.

WRITINGS:

CRIME NOVELS

Which the Justice, Which the Thief, Bobbs-Merrill (Indianapolis), 1963.
The Power, Bobbs-Merrill, 1964, published as *The Gospel of Death,* M. Joseph (London), 1966.
Yoshar the Soldier, Dial (New York City), 1966, published as *One Over One,* McKay (New York City), 1970.
The Search for Elisabeth Brandt, McKay, 1968.
Trial, McKay, 1970.
The Jupiter Crisis, McKay, 1971.
Mister Target, Delacorte (New York City), 1973.
Scorpio 5, Coward McCann (New York City), 1975.
Partners, Seaview (New York City), 1980.
The English Lady, Seaview, 1982.
Skin Deep, Seaview/Putnam (New York City), 1983.
The Cromwell File, St. Martin's (New York City), 1986.
Oberst, Donald I. Fine (New York City), 1987.
For the Defense, Donald I. Fine, 1988.
Town on Trial, Donald I. Fine, 1994.

CRIME NOVELS; COLUMBO SERIES; PUBLISHED BY FORGE (NEW YORK CITY)

Columbo: The Grassy Knoll, 1993.
Columbo: The Helter Skelter Murders, 1994.
Columbo: The Hoffa Connection, 1995.
Columbo: The Game Show Killer, 1996.
Columbo: The Glitter Murder, 1997.
Columbo: The Hoover Files, 1998.

OTHER

(With Peter Young) *The 1945 Revolution,* Davis-Poynter (London), 1978.
Virus (novel), Morrow (New York City), 1991.
Endgame in Berlin (novel), Donald I. Fine, 1991.
(Under pseudonym Megan Marklin) *The Summoned,* Pocket Books, 1993.

(With Thomas McKenna) *Manhattan North Homicide* (nonfiction), St. Martin's, 1996.

Also ghostwriter of fourteen books for celebrities; author of seventeen books under several pseudonyms. Some of Harrington's work has been translated into Italian, Spanish, German, Hebrew, Turkish, Hungarian, and Japanese.

SIDELIGHTS: Attorney William Harrington intended his first novel, *Which the Justice, Which the Thief* (1963), as an answer to sensationalist media portrayals of courtroom activity. The lawyer and writer continued to write courtroom dramas or police procedurals, among them *Trial* (1970), and by 1980 he had left the legal practice to write full time. In the years that followed, he published political thrillers such as *Scorpio 5* (1975) in addition to his courtroom novels.

But legal thrillers, often with subdued narration that seemed to belie the "thriller" label, remained Harrington's mainstay. *Town on Trial* (1994) recalled his first novel in its use of a thoughtful, mild-mannered judge as narrator. *Publishers Weekly* noted that readers would be "charmed by narrator Bill McIntyre"; but it assessed the story, which concerns the murder of a Congressman and two others by a well-to-do art collector, as "bland and uninvolving work from the usually more reliable Harrington."

In a general description of Harrington's work, Jon L. Breen wrote in the *St. James Guide to Crime & Mystery Writers*: "The sweeping scope, tantalizing plot concepts, and explicit (sometimes bordering on exploitative) sex scenes of many of Harrington's novels make it easy to typecast him as another seeker after blockbuster bestsellerdom, but any implication he is a schlockmeister would be unfair. His books would have a better chance at the bestseller lists if he really were as conventional in his writing and plotting as the dustjacket blurbs sometimes suggest. His novels constantly ring surprising changes on standard situations and reflect an individual and thoughtful viewpoint."

Harrington, who has ghostwritten a number of books, co-wrote *Manhattan North Homicide* (1996) with detective Thomas McKenna. McKenna's three decades with the New York Police Department brought him into contact with a number of notable cases, such as the rape of the Central Park jogger and the preppie murder case, which are both presented in the book.

In 1992, Harrington was invited to work with a detective of another sort: the fictional Lieutenant Columbo, popularized by television actor Peter Falk beginning in the 1970s. Harrington's series of Columbo novels integrated elements of history, such as the assassination of President John F. Kennedy in 1963 and the Manson family murders of 1969, with fictional cases to which Columbo is assigned. As with the television series, these are not whodunits: readers learn the perpetrator's identity early in the story, and the suspense emerges from Columbo's dogged investigation of the case.

The title of *Columbo: The Grassy Knoll* (1993) refers to the theory that President Kennedy may have actually been shot by a gunman on a "grassy knoll" in Dealey Plaza, rather than by Lee Harvey Oswald. In the story, talk-show host Paul Drury is obsessed with the assassination and keeps extensive computer files on the subject. After he is murdered, Columbo discovers that his assassination files have been erased. "Does that mean a dead end?" asked Newgate Callendar in his *New York Times* review. "Don't be silly. Leave it to Lieutenant Columbo." A review in *Publishers Weekly* concluded that "Harrington. . . gets every note right. . . . Readers will clamor for sequels."

The next Columbo story, *The Helter Skelter Murders* (1994), also took a famous criminal case from the 1960s as its basis. The wife of millionaire Yussef Khoury, along with several others, is killed by intruders to the Khoury's Beverly Hills home, and police find the words "Helter Skelter" and "All Piggies Die" written in blood on the walls. The evidence seems to recall the grisly Tate-LaBianca murders of 1969, committed by members of the Charles Manson "family." It so happens that Mrs. Khoury's secretary was once a member of the Manson family, a fact which Khoury hastens to point out to Columbo. Columbo, according to *Publishers Weekly,* "bumbles his way straight through the film industry, posh retail trade, scuba-diving clubs and Manson Family lore to keep readers enthralled."

Columbo: The Hoffa Connection (1995) involves the real-life disappearance of union leader Jimmy Hoffa in 1975, along with a murder of a female rock star. The book received a less enthusiastic review from *Publishers Weekly* than its predecessors: "Columbo's tried-and-true TV shtick . . . just [doesn't] work in print."

Publishers Weekly was more positive in its review of *Columbo: The Game Show Killer* (1996), the first book in the series that did not involve a real-life criminal case. High-profile defense attorney Grant Kellogg convinces game-show hostess Erika Bjorling that the man who killed her daughter, Tammy, six years earlier was none other than Bjorling's ex-husband, western film star Tim Wylie. Kellogg offers her a plan to kill Wylie, get caught, go on trial—and make a fortune from a book deal and paid TV appearances. The only obstacle to his brilliant plan, of course, is Lt. Columbo. "The prose is thin . . . and there's barely a whiff of suspense," according to *Publishers Weekly,* "but readers will come away as satisfied as the tourists who gather to watch Old Faithful spout."

Columbo: The Glitter Murder (1997) and *Columbo: The Hoover Files* (1998) employ elements familiar to readers of the earlier books. *The Glitter Murder* is a Hollywood case, replete with glamour, sex, crime, and death. As with *The Hoffa Connection, Publishers Weekly* criticized Harrington's attempt to make a television character come alive on paper, observing that "Falk's charm is noticeably absent." *The Hoover Files* yet again resurrects historical facts, if not a criminal case. This time the real-life subject is former FBI director J. Edgar Hoover. Columbo is on the case of a former FBI agent who kills a reporter before she publishes her "expose on his beloved and allegedly crossdressing former boss," wrote a *Publishers Weekly* reviewer, who noted the book as a "seamless recreation and updating" of the televised Columbo.

Harrington once told *CA:* "I remain convinced that writing is the art of communication. If a reader must read my sentence or paragraph twice to understand me, I have failed to communicate. Obscurity in writing is an affectation. No matter how complex an idea or how subtle an emotion, the writer's goal must be to communicate it to another—with clarity. I have no right to demand that my reader struggle to understand me. Why should he? It is my job to communicate to him, not his to extract my thoughts from my turgid prose."

"A single man after two marriages and divorces, my typical workday is nine to about six-thirty, taking time out for lunch and often a brief post-lunch nap—seven days a week. It is my privilege to earn my living doing the thing I most love in all the world."

BIOGRAPHICAL/CRITICAL SOURCES:

BOOKS

St. James Guide to Crime & Mystery Writers, fourth edition, St. James (Detroit), 1996.

PERIODICALS

New Republic, October 16, 1971.
New York Times, April 3, 1972; April 3, 1982.
New York Times Book Review, February 26, 1969; April 12, 1970; December 19, 1971; May 30, 1982; December 19, 1993.
Observer Review, August 6, 1967.
Publishers Weekly, September 13, 1993, p. 97; April 11, 1994, p. 56; June 6, 1994, p. 58; June 12, 1995, p. 49; February 26, 1996, p. 93; June 17, 1996, p. 50; December 16, 1996, p. 45; November 10, 1997, p. 59.
Variety, December 17, 1969.*

*   *   *

HARROWER, Elizabeth 1928-

PERSONAL: Born February 8, 1928, in Sydney, New South Wales, Australia.

ADDRESSES: Home—5 Stanley Ave., Mosman, New South Wales 2088, Australia.

CAREER: Writer. Australian Broadcasting Commission, Sydney, member of staff, 1959-60; *Sydney Morning Herald,* Sydney, reviewer, 1960; Macmillan & Co. Ltd., Sydney, member of staff, 1961-67.

AWARDS, HONORS: Fellowships from Commonwealth Literary Fund, 1968, and Australian Council for the Arts, 1974.

WRITINGS:

Down in the City, Cassell (London), 1957.
The Long Prospect, Cassell, 1958.
The Catherine Wheel, Cassell, 1960.
The Watch Tower, Macmillan, 1966.

Work represented in anthologies, including *Summer's Tales 1,* Macmillan, 1964, *Modern Australian Writing,* Fontana, 1966, *Australian Writing Today,* Penguin, 1968, and *The Vital Decade,* Sun (Melbourne), 1968. Contributor to periodicals, including *Australian Letters, Overland,* and *Melbourne Herald.*

SIDELIGHTS: Elizabeth Harrower's "fictional universe," according to John Colmer in *Contemporary Novelists,* "is a world in which selfish men manipulate their women and material possessions in a vain attempt to achieve happiness; frustrated by their blind male egotism, they become subject to fits of smoldering violence and frequent relapses into bouts of alcoholism and morbid self-pity. The woman's role is to suffer, to pity, and to provide the innocent seeing eye for the narrative."

"In most of her work," Colmer believes, "Harrower combines sharp observation of individual life with a searching critique of Australian society. Although she lacks the resilient vitality of such English novelists as Margaret Drabble, her vision of a male-dominated society is depressingly authentic. She has been highly praised and compared favorably with Patrick White, but her unflattering, somewhat drab and disenchanted view of Australian life is now winning her the wide local readership her work certainly deserves."

BIOGRAPHICAL/CRITICAL SOURCES:

BOOKS

Burns, D. R., *The Directions of Australian Fiction, 1920-1974,* Cassell (Melbourne), 1975.
Contemporary Novelists, 6th edition, St. James Press (Detroit), 1996.
Geering, R. G., *Recent Fiction,* Oxford University Press, 1974.
Hetherington, John, *Forty-Two Faces,* Cheshire, 1962.
Taylor, A. and R. McDougall, editors, *(Un)common Ground,* CRNLE (Bedford Park, South Australia), 1990.

PERIODICALS

Australian Letters, December, 1961.
Books and Bookmen, December, 1966.
Hecate, Volume 9, numbers 1-2, 1983.
Observer, October 16, 1966.
Quadrant, November, 1979.
Southerly, Number 2, 1970; Number 4, 1990.
Times Literary Supplement, November 10, 1966.
Westerly, September, 1980.

*   *   *

HART, Josephine 1942(?)-

PERSONAL: Born c. 1942, in Mullingar, Ireland; married Paul Buckley (in publishing), 1972 (di-

vorced, 1983); married Maurice Saatchi (chairman of an advertising firm); children: (first marriage) Adam, (second marriage) Edward. *Education:* Attended Guildhall School of Music and Drama.

ADDRESSES: Home—London, England. *Agent*—Ed Victor, Ed Victor, Inc., 9255 Sunset Blvd., Suite 301, Los Angeles, CA 90069.

CAREER: Haymarket Publications, London, England, started in sales, became publishing director; theater producer; writer.

WRITINGS:

Damage (novel), Knopf (New York City), 1991.
Sin (novel), Knopf, 1992.
Oblivion (novel), Viking (New York City), 1995.

ADAPTATIONS: Damage has been adapted as an audiocassette, Random House, 1991, and as a film directed by Louis Malle, 1992.

WORK IN PROGRESS: Novels.

SIDELIGHTS: Josephine Hart realized substantial critical and commercial success with her first novel, *Damage.* "I'd always wanted to write," she told *People Weekly* magazine. "For years I paced around composing novels in my head. Everything was there; I just couldn't crash through the brick wall in front of me." But as she told the *New York Times,* "eventually it became more terrible not to write than to write." And when Hart finally produced her first book in 1991, it was, as *People Weekly* noted, "with spectacular results," winning enthusiastic recommendations from reviewers and a place on the *New York Times*'s best-seller list.

Damage is the story of a middle-aged family man who becomes obsessed with his son's attractive, intriguing fiancee. The protagonist-narrator, a member of British Parliament, eventually commences physical relations with the woman, who describes herself as emotionally damaged. Some of that damage, she reveals, stems from the death of her brother, who killed himself in despair over his unrequited love for her. The novel's central relationship—so passionate and erotic in its early stages—soon degenerates into more brutal expression. "The result," wrote Rhoda Koenig in *New York,* "is a climax that is somewhat operatic . . . , but its heartbreaking, confused consequences are real enough."

Upon publication in 1991, *Damage* won acclaim as a compelling, provocative novel. Koenig, in her *New York* assessment, hailed Hart's work as "that tricky thing, a novel of obsession." The reviewer contended that *Damage* is a daring literary venture. "Hart walks a wobbly line at times," Koenig observed, "but the intensity and observations of *Damage* sustain this nervy performance." Another enthusiast, *Detroit Free Press* reviewer Linnea Lannon, recommended *Damage* as "terrific fun." Hart's novel, she added, is a "short, chilling story of obsessive love."

Hart returned to the theme of obsession in her second novel, *Sin*. The story of an evil woman, Ruth, who conspires her whole life to ruin her "good" sister, Elizabeth, *Sin* contains Hart's trademark minimalist prose. Unlike its predecessor, however, *Sin* was not warmly received by critics, many of whom felt that the novel contained simplistic characters and a thin plot. "'Sin' sketches a world devoid of emotion," remarked Linda Gray Sexton in the *New York Times Book Review*. Added Sexton: "Ruth's strong and unemotional voice, which narrates throughout, chills us into numbness." Writing in the *Washington Post Book World*, Sally Emerson commented, "The chief problem of this flawed novel is that neither Ruth nor Elizabeth . . . is presented with any complexity or tenderness." *Los Angeles Times Book Review* contributor Thomas M. Hines was even more critical, calling the novel "a skeletal little outing with big pretensions." However, *New York Times* critic Michiko Kakutani, while admitting that "Hart's staccato prose frequently grows mannered," noted that "this portentous language somehow works to draw us into the novel's rarefied, heightened world." Kakutani concluded that *Sin* is "a novel that's a limited but highly efficient tour de force."

Hart continued her pattern of short, intensely drawn narratives with her third novel, *Oblivion*. Whereas Hart's first novel explored lust and her second, envy, *Oblivion* tackles the subject of death. The plot features a grieving young widower, Andrew Bolton, whose attempts to carry on with his job as a journalist and recreate a normal personal life are hampered by his longing for his dead wife. Andrew's life takes a turn when he receives an important work assignment: a rare interview with the famous playwright, Catherine Samuelson. In the interview, Samuelson discusses her latest play, which is a study of death and its consequence: oblivion. Samuelson's play becomes a story within the story of *Oblivion*, engaging Andrew in examining the loss of his wife and his complicated feelings toward his current girlfriend.

Reviewers were more generous toward the story than they were toward *Sin*. Writing in the Chicago *Tribune Books*, Victoria Jenkins stated that "Hart is extremely clever. Her work is stylish and remarkably assured." Noting that Hart's "fiction is marked by a brave attempt to tackle huge, dark topics" such as "lust, cruelty, [and] despair," *Spectator* reviewer Anne Chisholm commented, "Inside its modish carapace, a simple, deeply felt story is struggling for breath." Concluded Chisholm: "Finally, the impression is of a small but determined talent in pursuit of the biggest, scariest subject around."

Despite the considerable success of her debut novel and her subsequent efforts, Hart does not envision a particularly long career for herself as a writer. "I've only got about six or seven books in my head," she disclosed in the *Washington Post*. "The view from the window of the world that I see is very narrow and specific." She added: "When I've seen everything I've wanted to see, it will stop. . . . And then I will withdraw gracefully."

BIOGRAPHICAL/CRITICAL SOURCES:

BOOKS

Contemporary Literary Criticism, Volume 70, 1992.

PERIODICALS

Cosmopolitan, May, 1991, p. 258; August, 1992, p. 26.
Detroit Free Press, March 17, 1991, p. G8.
Entertainment Weekly, February 14, 1992, p. 50; September 18, 1992, p. 73.
Fortune, August 26, 1991, p. 114.
Glamour, April, 1991, p. 228.
Globe and Mail (Toronto), February 1, 1992, p. C7.
Harper's Bazaar, August, 1992, p. 42.
Hudson Review, Autumn, 1991, p. 500.
Interview, March, 1991, p. 70.
Library Journal, February 15, 1991, p. 220; July, 1992, p. 124.
Los Angeles Times Book Review, September 13, 1992, p. 1.
Mademoiselle, September, 1992, p. 56.
New Statesman and Society, March 22, 1991; September 25, 1992, p. 56.
Newsweek, March 25, 1991, p. 54.
New York, March 11, 1991, p. 86.
New Yorker, April 29, 1991, p. 104.
New York Times, April 13, 1991, p. 13; August 25, 1992, p. C16.

New York Times Book Review, March 24, 1991, p. 8;
    August 30, 1992, p. 16.
Observer (London), February 9, 1992, p. 63; September 13, 1992, p. 55.
People Weekly, June 3, 1991.
Publishers Weekly, December 21, 1990, p. 45; April
    5, 1991, p. 115; June 8, 1992, p. 51.
Spectator, March 21, 1993, p. 38; September 19,
    1992, p. 31; June 17, 1995, p. 45.
Time, March 25, 1991, p. 71; September 14, 1992,
    p. 74.
Times, (London), March 21, 1991, p. 22.
Times Literary Supplement, March 29, 1991, p. 18.
Tribune Books (Chicago), December 17, 1995, p. 3.
Washington Post, May 22, 1991, p. B1.
Washington Post Book World, March 17, 1991, p. 5;
    August 23, 1992, p. 4.*

* * *

HAU'OFA, Epeli 1939-

PERSONAL: Born December 7, 1939, in Papua New Guinea; son of missionaries; married wife, Barbara, 1966; children: two. *Education:* Attended University of New England, 1961-64, and McGill University, 1965-68; Australian National University, Ph.D., 1975.

ADDRESSES: Office—School of Social and Economic Development, University of the South Pacific, P.O. Box 1168, Suva, Fiji.

CAREER: University of Papua New Guinea, Port Moresby, senior tutor in sociology, 1968-70; University of the South Pacific, Suva, Fiji, research fellow, 1975-77; University of New South Wales, Kensington, Australia, visiting fellow, 1977; deputy private secretary to the King of Tonga, with office in Nuku'alofa, 1978-81; University of the South Pacific, director of Rural Development Centre in Nuku'alofa, 1981-83, reader in sociology, beginning 1983, currently professor of sociology. Visiting fellow at Centre for Pacific Studies, University of Auckland, 1985; consultant to World Bank and Asian Development Bank.

WRITINGS:

Our Crowded Islands, Institute of Pacific Studies, University of the South Pacific (Fiji), 1977.

Corned Beef and Tapioca: A Report on the Food Distribution Systems in Tonga, Development Studies Centre, Australian National University (Canberra), 1979.
Mekeo: Inequality and Ambivalence in the Village Society, Australian National University Press, 1981.
Tales of the Tikongs (stories), Longman Paul (Auckland), 1983, Penguin (New York City), 1988.
Kisses in the Nederends (novel), Penguin, 1987.

Co-founder and co-editor of *Faikava.*

SIDELIGHTS: Epeli Hau'ofa's fiction reflects a highly developed sense of the comic. The stories that comprise the *Tales of the Tikongs* describe the foibles and gentle follies of life on an imaginary South Pacific island so small it cannot be found on a map without the use of a microscope. "While Hau'ofa's stories often have a satiric relationship to actual events and persons in the South Pacific," writes Bruce King in *Contemporary Novelists,* "they show an amused appreciation of the trickster and swindler. At times satire is blended with a tolerance of extravagance, outrageousness, and absurdity which approaches moral anarchy and fun for its own sake."

Although primarily concerned with being humorous, Hau'ofa's "stories show the various ways European culture and politics have affected the South Pacific, leaving a conformist middle class and a corrupt elite, a legacy of church dominance, inappropriate forms of education and educational qualifications, and subservience to and dependence on foreigners. Although the islanders' way of life was not destroyed despite Christianity and colonialism, national independence led to increased dependence. At Independence the local rulers and their relatives change their English clothes for a melange of 'Afro-shirts and other Third World clothes' and take over from the colonial administration positions for which they are not trained or qualified. Mistrusting and feeling threatened by their own new university graduates, so that the skilled and talented flee the country, they fill the resulting vacancies with foreign experts, technical advisers, youthful volunteers, and the well-paid employees of United Nations organizations."

BIOGRAPHICAL/CRITICAL SOURCES:

BOOKS

Contemporary Novelists, 6th edition, St. James Press (Detroit), 1996.

HAUSER, Marianne 1910-

PERSONAL: Born December 11, 1910, in Strasbourg, France; became American citizen, 1944; married Frederic Kirshberger (a concert pianist; divorced, 1966); children: Michael.

ADDRESSES: Home—2 Washington Sq. Village, Apt. 13-M, New York, NY 10012. *Agent*—Perry Knowlton, Curtis Brown Ltd., 1 Astor Pl., New York, NY.

CAREER: Writer. Columnist for Swiss and French publications in various countries, 1934-39. Lecturer, Queens College of the City University of New York, 1962-79; has also taught at New York University and New School.

AWARDS, HONORS: Rockefeller fellowship; National Endowment for the Arts grant, 1977.

WRITINGS:

NOVELS

Monique, Ringier (Zurich), 1934.
Shadow Play in India, Zinnen (Vienna), 1937.
Dark Dominion, Random House (New York City), 1947.
The Living Shall Praise Thee, Gollancz (London), 1958, published as *The Choir Invisible,* Mc-Dowell, Obolensky (New York City), 1959.
Prince Ishmael, Stein & Day (New York City), 1963.
The Talking Room, Fiction Collective (New York City), 1976.
The Memoirs of the Late Mr. Ashley, Sun & Moon Press (Los Angeles), 1985.
Me and My Mom, Sun & Moon Press, 1993.

OTHER

A Lesson in Music (short stories), Texas University Press, 1964.

Contributor of short stories to *Harper's Bazaar, Mademoiselle, Carleton Miscellany, Parnassus, Denver Quarterly, Fiction International, Witness,* and other magazines, and of book reviews to *New York Times, New York Herald Tribune,* and *Saturday Review.* A collection of Hauser's manuscripts is housed at the University of Florida, Gainesville.

SIDELIGHTS: In all of Marianne Hauser's fiction, according to Sinda Gregory in *Contemporary Novel-*

ists, the author depicts an "inability to relate to a world of dizzying complexity and ambiguity through linguistic systems that reduce experience to simple binary categories." For Hauser, Gregory believes, reality "is a dynamic, multi-layered process for which the conventions of traditional realism—with its empirical biases and emphasis on causal relationships and logic—are ill-equipped to represent. This conviction has resulted in a series of novels and stories that weave together dream and waking reality, the known and unknown, the perverse and banal, and the poetic and idiomatic into darkly humorous fables of great emotional power, uniqueness, and universal relevancy."

The Talking Room, according to Gregory, is "among the most significant and original feminist novels of the past 20 years." As Hauser explains in her essay for the *Contemporary Authors Autobiography Series* (*CAAS*), "My protagonists in *The Talking Room* couldn't be more timely: an ill-matched lesbian couple and their daughter, a pregnant teenager—most likely a test-tube baby." Hauser reveals in *CAAS* that following her divorce in 1966, she "rented an apartment on Christopher Street, in earshot of the waterfront of lower Manhattan. Nostalgic wailings of the foghorn. But also a nightly pandemonium of rock-rolling sadomasochist tenants above, and the interminable scream of police or ambulance sirens. *The Talking Room* is informed by the same waterfront life. The Sapphic theme, intrinsic to the milieu, came as easily to my androgynous nature as any other sexual variant."

The story centers on the pregnant daughter's efforts to uncover her lineage. Mixing the daughter's own voice, those of her mother and her mother's lover, the conversations of their eccentric friends, and the voices from the radio, the novel is a complex and multi-layered narrative. In *The Talking Room,* Gregory believes, Hauser presents her belief in "the limitations of rationality and the ways that the search for one's self and one's origins are ultimately limited by the fact that the self is never a discrete entity but a plurality of different selves whose 'essences' are themselves shifting perpetually in a state of transformation."

BIOGRAPHICAL/CRITICAL SOURCES:

BOOKS

Contemporary Authors Autobiography Series, Volume 11, Gale (Detroit), 1990.

Contemporary Novelists, 6th edition, St. James Press (Detroit), 1996.

PERIODICALS

Publishers Weekly, October 4, 1993, p. 69.

*   *   *

HAYNES, John Earl 1944-

PERSONAL: Born November 22, 1944, in Plant City, FL; son of John Milner (an educator) and Sarah Elizabeth (Farmer) Haynes; married Janette Marie Murray (an educator), December, 1971; children: Joshua, Amanda, William. *Education:* Florida State University, B.A., 1966; University of Minnesota—Twin Cities, M.A., 1968, Ph.D., 1978. *Religion:* Anglican Catholic.

ADDRESSES: Home—10041 Frederick Ave., Kensington, MD 20895. *Office*—Manuscript Division, Library of Congress, Washington, DC 20540-4780.

CAREER: Library of Congress, Washington, DC, twentieth-century political historian in Manuscript Division, 1987—. *Military service:* U.S. Army Reserve, inactive, 1989—; major.

MEMBER: Historians of American Communism (president, 1992-93).

WRITINGS:

Dubious Alliance: The Making of Minnesota's DFL Party, University of Minnesota Press, 1984.
Communism and Anti-Communism in the United States: An Annotated Guide to Historical Writings, Garland Publishing (New York City), 1987.
(With Harvey Klehr) *The American Communist Movement: Storming Heaven Itself,* Twayne (New York City), 1992.
(With Klehr and Fridrikh Igorevich Firsov) *The Secret World of American Communism: Documents from the Soviet Archives,* Yale University Press (New Haven, CT), 1995.
Red Scare or Red Menace?: American Communism and Anti-Communism in the Cold War Era, Ivan R. Dee (Chicago), 1996.

(With Klehr and Kyriil Mikhailovich Anderson) *The Soviet World of American Communism,* Yale University Press, 1998.
(Editor) *Calvin Coolidge and the Coolidge Era: Essays on the History of the 1920s,* Library of Congress (Washington, DC), 1998.

Editor of *Historians of American Communism* (newsletter), 1982-92.

SIDELIGHTS: John Earl Haynes is a prominent scholar of the American communist movement. His books *The Secret World of American Communism: Documents from the Soviet Archives* and *The Soviet World of American Communism* were the first to draw on documentation from official Soviet archive sources not previously available to those in the West.

In *The Secret World of American Communism: Documents from the Soviet Archives,* Haynes and co-authors Haarvey Klehr and Fridrikh Igorevich Firsov use documents found in the archives of the former Soviet Union to draw a more accurate picture of Soviet influence on the American communist movement than previously available. The authors found that, contrary to what American Communist Party members had maintained for decades, the party was an instrumental part of Soviet espionage operations, was heavily financed by the Soviet Union, and was implicated in the deaths or disappearances of many former members and political rivals. Furthermore, the evidence for these charges, notes Eric Breindel in the *National Review,* was found in "the Comintern archive and in the archive of the CPUSA [Communist Party of the United States of America]. Both collections are located in Moscow." "Documents now available in Russia," notes Arthur M. Schlesinger, Jr., in the *New Republic,* "prove beyond any question that the American party functioned as an instrument of Soviet espionage." As Mark Falcoff put it in *Commentary,* "Now, surviving members of the party and, even more, their tenured apologists, will be forced to make their case in the face of documentary evidence of a kind they never expected to confront."

Particularly damaging to American communists was the new evidence for the party's involvement in the murder of exiled Soviet leader Leon Trotsky in Mexico. Although, as Breindel notes, the book's "research serves largely to confirm much that had already been alleged," it does prove that Trotsky's murder was "a joint undertaking between the Soviet secret police and the U.S. Party's underground networks."

American communist involvement with the murder of Soviet dissidents is more fully documented in *The Soviet World of American Communism,* in which Haynes, Klehr and Kyrill M. Anderson presented more documentation of Soviet influence on American communism, all of it drawn from official Soviet sources. The critic for *Booklist* points out the particular case of Lovett Fort-Whiteman, a black communist leader of the 1930s who disappeared when he went afoul of the party. He was, states the critic, but "one of as many as a thousand accused Trotskyists that the American party turned over to Soviet police." As Ronald Radosh explains in the *New Republic,* the authors "have provided definitive and overwhelming evidence that the American Communist Party was not a movement created by indigenous American radicals, but an organization controlled, financed, and run entirely by the leadership of the Communist Party of the Soviet Union." The *Publishers Weekly* critic calls *The Soviet World of American Communism* "another important volume for understanding the U.S., the U.S.S.R., and the 20th century."

Haynes told *CA:* "I enjoy the study of history because it allows me to understand how and why human history happened the way it did. I enjoy writing about it because, once I have come to an understanding of how and why something came about, I want to tell others. I find writing about communism and anti-communism interesting because the conflict over communism was one of the defining events of the twentieth century."

BIOGRAPHICAL/CRITICAL SOURCES:

PERIODICALS

Booklist, February 1, 1998, p. 883.
Commentary, June, 1995, p. 61.
Library Journal, February 15, 1998, p. 157.
Nation, June 12, 1995, p. 846.
National Review, June 12, 1995, p. 63.
New Republic, May 29, 1995, p. 36.
Publishers Weekly, January 26, 1998, p. 77.
Society, November-December, 1996, p. 101.

*   *   *

HAZZARD, Shirley 1931-

PERSONAL: Born January 30, 1931, in Sydney, Australia; daughter of Reginald (a government offi-

cial) and Catherine (Stein) Hazzard; married Francis Steegmuller (a novelist and biographer), December 22, 1963 (died October, 1994). *Education:* Educated at Queenwood College, Sydney, Australia.

ADDRESSES: Home—200 East 66th St., New York, NY 10021. *Agent*—McIntosh & Otis, Inc., 475 Fifth Ave., New York, NY 10017

CAREER: Writer. Worked for British Intelligence in Hong Kong, 1947-48, and for British High Commissioner's Office, Wellington, New Zealand, 1940-50; United Nations, New York, NY, general service category, Technical Assistance to Underdeveloped Countries, 1952-62, serving in Italy, 1957; Boyer lecturer, Australia, 1984, 1988.

MEMBER: American Academy and Institute of Arts and Letters.

AWARDS, HONORS: U.S. National Institute of Arts and Letters award in literature, 1966; National Book Award nomination, 1971; Guggenheim fellow, 1974; National Book Critics Circle Award, American Book Award nomination, and PEN/Faulkner Award nomination, all 1981, for *The Transit of Venus.*

WRITINGS:

Cliffs of Fall, and Other Stories, Knopf (New York City), 1963.
The Evening of the Holiday (novel), Knopf, 1966.
People in Glass Houses: Portraits from Organization Life (nonfiction), Knopf, 1967.
The Bay of Noon (novel), Atlantic-Little, Brown (Boston), 1970.
Defeat of an Ideal: A Study of the Self-Destruction of the United Nations (nonfiction), Atlantic-Little, Brown, 1973.
The Transit of Venus (novel), Viking (New York City), 1980.
Coming of Age in Australia (lectures), Australian Broadcasting Corp., 1985.
Countenance of Truth: The United Nations and the Waldheim Case (nonfiction), Viking, 1990.

Work appears in anthologies, including several volumes of *Winter's Tales* and *O. Henry Prize Stories.* Contributor to periodicals, including *New Yorker, Ladies' Home Journal* and *McCall's.*

SIDELIGHTS: Even before the publication of her best-selling novel *The Transit of Venus,* Shirley Hazzard's work met with unusual critical approval.

For example, Robie Macauley writes in the *New York Times Book Review* that Hazzard's *The Bay of Noon* is "one of those rare novels that tries to address itself to the reader's intelligence rather than his nightmares. Its assumptions are fine and modest: That the reader will enjoy a sense of place if that place is drawn for him so perfectly that it seems to breathe, that the reader will understand a story based on the interactions of personality rather than mere violence, that the reader will take pleasure in a style that is consciously elegant and literary." Laurence La Fore, also of the *New York Times Book Review,* asserts that "Shirley Hazzard's writing is like some electronic mechanism, enormously intricate in design and function, charged with great power, but so refined by skill that it may be contained in a small case and exhibit a smooth and shapely surface." A *Time* reviewer describes Hazzard's earlier prose as "so understated that it forces the reader to become uncommonly attentive. But mostly it is because she chooses her words with such delicacy and precision that even ordinary situations acquire poetic shadings." "*People in Glass Houses,*" writes Laurie Clancy in *Contemporary Novelists,* "is a brilliantly funny and scathing collection of eight interrelated stories concerning an unnamed "organization" which is transparently the United Nations."

It was with the release of *The Transit of Venus* that Hazzard gained a wider and more diverse readership. Writing in the *Chicago Tribune,* Lynne Sharon Schwartz remarks: "If the literary establishment were given to pageantry, [*The Transit of Venus*] ought to be welcomed with a flourish of trumpets. Last year John Gardner clamored for moral fiction: Here is a book that ventures confidently amid the abiding themes of truth, beauty, goodness, and love, and is informed, moreover, by stringent intelligence and lacerating irony. Hazzard spares no one, not even her reader." Clancy believes that "Hazzard's masterpiece and the basis of her reputation is undoubtedly *The Transit of Venus.* . . . The meticulous—sometimes almost too meticulous—craftsmanship of the novel and the elegance and subtle wit of the style are a delight and almost unique among contemporary Australian fiction writers."

New York Times Book Review critic Michiko Kakutani explains that "during the last decade and a half, Shirley Hazzard has achieved much critical acclaim for her fiction—fiction distinguished by its sculptured prose and its civilized portrayals of love and loss. Yet with her self-consciously literary style, the author . . . neither sought nor expected to cultivate a wider public. Considerably longer and more complex than her previous work, *The Transit of Venus* suddenly appeared on the Best Seller List."

Los Angeles Times critic Doris Grumbach writes that she was very moved by *The Transit of Venus.* She feels that it "is an impressive, mature novel, full and satisfying, by a novelist whose earlier work—two novels and two collections of stories . . . did not prepare us for this book. Without fear of exaggeration I can say it is the richest fictional experience I have had in a long time, so sumptuous a repast that it may not be to every reader's taste."

Although characterization plays a vital role in all of her writings, Hazzard exhibits particular skill in this area in *The Transit of Venus.* Webster Schott points out in the *Washington Post:* "Her purpose is to reveal [the characters] in the act of living and to make their pleasure, anguish and confusion rise out of their personalities as they respond to change. . . . All of *The Transit of Venus* is human movement, and seen from near the highest level art achieves."

New York Times Book Review critic Gail Godwin points out that "Hazzard has even managed to forge a sort of 'godlike grammar' to contain her ambitious design. This is reflected in her precise, frequently elliptical style and in a certain *distanced* outlook, the 'godlike' overview that spots the movements of people, then picks out and connects the salient details over fastmoving, curved sweep of time."

However, John Leonard suggests that Hazzard's skill not only lies in her characterizations but in her literary style in general. "Miss Hazzard writes as well as Stendhal," Leonard remarks in the *New York Times.* "No matter the object—a feeling, a face, a room, the weather—it is stripped of its layers of paint, its clots of words, down to the original wood; oil is applied; grain appears, and a glow. Every epigram and apostrophe is earned. A powerful intelligence is playing with a knife. It is an intelligence that refuses to be deflected by ironies; irony isn't good enough."

The feature that several critics have identified as the underlying factor of Hazzard's skillful characterization and literary style is her sensitivity. One such critic, Webster Schott, writes in the *Washington Post:* "Her perceptions of gesture, voice, attitude bespeak an omniscient understanding of human personality. The story she tells is, for the most part, so usual as to sound irrelevant. What she brings to it is virtually everything that story alone cannot tell about human lives." Agreeing with this premise, Lynne Sharon Schwartz remarks in the *Chicago Tribune* that "*The Transit of Venus* evidences the wisdom of one not only well traveled but well acquainted with truth and falsehood in their numberless guises. Interwoven with the story of Caro's and Grace's lives and loves are a devastating representation of British class structure, with barriers and loopholes clearly marked; an acerbic, satirical view of a governmental bureaucracy that scoops the marrow out of men and leaves them empty bone; a glimpse at underground activists struggling for fundamental political decencies in Latin America, as well as a survey of various modes of contemporary marriage."

Hazzard relayed her own opinion as to the reason for the success of *The Transit of Venus*. She tells Michiko Kakutani in an interview published in the *New York Times Book Review* that "I think there is a tendency now to write jottings about one's own psyche and then call it a novel. My book, though, is really a *story*—and that might have contributed to its success."

BIOGRAPHICAL/CRITICAL SOURCES:

BOOKS

Contemporary Literary Criticism, Volume 18, Gale (Detroit), 1981.
Contemporary Novelists, 6th edition, St. James Press (Detroit), 1996.
Dictionary of Literary Biography Yearbook: 1982, Gale, 1983.
Geering, R. G., *Recent Fiction,* Oxford University Press (Melbourne), 1974.

PERIODICALS

Australian Literary Studies, October, 1979.
Chicago Tribune, March 9, 1980.
Globe and Mail (Toronto), September 24, 1988.
Listener, October 19, 1967.
Los Angeles Times, March 9, 1980.
Meanjin, summer, 1970; December, 1970.
National Review, February 27, 1968.
New Statesman, October 20, 1967.
New Yorker, April 13, 1970.
New York Times, February 26, 1980.
New York Times Book Review, January 9, 1966; November 12, 1967; April 5, 1970; March 16, 1980; May 11, 1980; April 29, 1990.
Publishers Weekly, February 2, 1990, p. 70; March 9, 1990, p. 48.

Saturday Night, June, 1990, p. 59.
Saturday Review, January 8, 1966.
Texas Studies in Literature and Language, Volume 25, number 2, 1983.
Time, January 14, 1966; November 24, 1967.
Times Literary Supplement, July 7, 1966; October 19, 1967; May 7, 1970.
Village Voice, March 3, 1980.
Washington Post, March 9, 1980.
Washington Post Book World, April 8, 1990.

*   *   *

HEMPEL, Amy 1951-

PERSONAL: Born December 14, 1951, in Chicago, IL; daughter of Gardiner and Gloria Hempel. *Education:* Attended Whittier College, 1969-71, San Francisco State University, 1973-74, and Columbia University, 1981.

ADDRESSES: Home—New York, NY.

CAREER: Writer.

AWARDS, HONORS: Silver Medal, Commonwealth Club of California, 1986, for *Reasons to Live;* Pushcart Prize.

WRITINGS:

Reasons to Live (stories), Knopf (New York City), 1985.
At the Gates of the Animal Kingdom (stories), Knopf, 1990.
(Editor, compiler and contributor) *Unleashed: Poems by Writers' Dogs,* Crown (New York City), 1995.
Tumble Home: A Novella and Short Stories, Scribner (New York City), 1997.

Works represented in anthologies, including *Best American Short Stories,* 1986, and *Norton Anthology of Short Fiction.* Contributor to periodicals, including *Vanity Fair, Harper's, Mother Jones, Triquar-terly, Vogue, Interview,* and *New York Times Magazine;* contributing editor of *Vanity Fair,* 1985-86.

SIDELIGHTS: Amy Hempel has earned widespread distinction as the author of two acclaimed collections of short stories. Her first, *Reasons to Live,* is a rather brief volume of nearly one hundred thirty pages, yet it is comprised of fifteen tales. Critics have observed that these narratives, some numbering only one page in length, are written in an economical manner that nonetheless succeeds in conveying Hempel's quirky humor as well as her bleak world-view. Hempel's fictional realm is one of sadness and bittersweet consolations, and it is a world of natural catastrophe, automobile accidents, madness, and death. Among the more distinguished stories in *Reasons to Live* is "In the Cemetery Where Al Jolson Is Buried," where a woman desperately tries to distract her terminally ill friend by reciting various facts; "Tonight Is a Favor to Holly," which depicts the ironic existence of a woman devoted to what she calls "the beach life"; and "Nashville Gone to Ashes," about a veterinarian's widow who must take care of the animals she always resented in the wake of her husband's demise.

Upon its publication in 1985, *Reasons to Live* received attention as a provocative and disturbing story collection. Sheila Ballantyne, writing in the *New York Times Book Review,* declared that "at their best these stories are tough-minded, original and fully felt." Noting Hempel's minimalist technique, Ballantyne added, "In most of the stories that make up this collection, Amy Hempel has succeeded in revealing both the substance and intelligence beneath the surface of a spare, elliptical prose." More effusively, James Kaufmann reported in the *Washington Post* that "Hempel makes small and cryptic moments explode with suggestion." And *New York Times* critic Michiko Kakutani, who described *Reasons to Live* as a volume of "astringent" stories, affirmed that for Hempel "even the smallest act, the tiniest gesture. . . can be an act of courage." Kakutani also noted that Hempel portrays her characters "with charity and understanding."

In her next story collection, *At the Gates of the Animal Kingdom,* Hempel further refined her stylistically spare, narratively brief technique, thus prompting *New York Times Book Review* contributor Robert Towers to cast Hempel as a miniaturist rather than a minimalist. Hempel's fiction, Towers maintained, is marked "by an almost miraculous exactitude of observation and execution." Like the earlier book, *At the Gates of the Animal Kingdom* is concerned with people coping—or, at least, surviving—in a world of sadness and mayhem. "The Harvest," for instance, concerns a woman maimed in a motorcycle accident, and "The Day I Had Everything" relates the activities within an organization of women who lament the loss of loved ones and the unrelent-

ing nature of physical decay. In still another tale, "Lead Us Not into Penn Station," a narrator merely relates a day's observations and events in New York City—a wino bleeds, a man recalls fornicating with a household appliance, a blind man enters a bank and orders a sandwich—and then expresses their cumulatively overwhelming nature.

At the Gates of the Animal Kingdom, which appeared in 1990, confirmed Hempel's stature as a unique storyteller. "The stories," Elizabeth Tallent wrote in the *Los Angeles Times Book Review,* "are . . . smartly observed, cryptically titled, the prose as tight as if it fears spilling a single drop." And Towers, in a *New York Times Book Review* assessment, lauded "the elegance and compactness" of Hempel's style and added, "What one cherishes in Amy Hempel are . . . her quirky sensibility and the beautifully honed verbal craft she brings to bear on the situations and themes that have attracted her amused and rueful eye." Towers acknowledged that Hempel manages to produce stories of both humor and sadness. He declared that in *At the Gates of the Animal Kingdom,* "The combination of comedy and loss is pervasive." Philip Gourevitch made a similar observation in the *Washington Post,* commenting that "it is Hempel's great achievement in these stories that she always maintains compassion and keeps the laugh lines coming."

Hempel's minimalist style was again showcased in her 1997 novella, *Tumble Home.* The slim volume, which also contained stories as short as one paragraph long, gained the attention of *New York Times* reviewer Elizabeth Gleick, who found that "each story is written as if assembled from fragments of conversations or snatches of melody."

Gleick singled out pieces such as "Weekend," which examined the group dynamics of families vacationing at the beach, as fiction that "has much in common with poetry. Using only a few phrases, [Hempel] succeeds in evoking a mood or . . . even an entire summer at the shore." In "Housewife," the tale of an unfaithful married woman is told in a single sentence, prompting critic Claire Messud to declare in the *Washington Post Book World* that the author "unsettles our uncomfortable conceptions of 'story.'" (On the other hand, a *Kirkus Review* writer found the one-sentence story "just short and rather silly.")

The title novella of *Tumble Home* is a sort of free-association conversation in the form of a letter from young woman in a mental institution to the famous artist whom she may or may not have once met. In this longer work *Chicago Tribune* writer Andy Solomon found Hempel to be "at her most enigmatic and most lyrical." Solomon went on to note that "people attempting to find a plot in her fiction will be shocked. Even those attempting to find fiction in it will discover themselves in an exquisite but mysterious territory where, although the lines extend to the right margin, we sense ourselves in the presence of a poet."

Hempel moved from poetry-like fiction to poetry proper as editor of the 1995 collection *Unleashed: Poems by Writers' Dogs,* featuring works credited to the animal companions of such luminaries as Edward Albee, Maxine Kumin, John Irving, and Hempel herself. In Hempel's hands what "might have been nothing more than, well, doggerel—just another of those self-consciously cute cat and dog books that crowd the bookstore shelves" instead becomes "a summer treat, by turns endearingly funny and achingly tender," according to Polly Paddock in her *Chicago Tribune* review. Equally impressed was *New York Times* guest reviewer "Jacques," identified as the dog of novelist Daniel Pinkwater. While the critical canine noticed "a measure of contamination discernible in some of the selections, dogs talking about things no sensible [pooch] would ever think about," Jacques ultimately gave a paws-up to *Unleashed:* "I had a barking good time with this book. The compilers deserve to be given a croissant and have their ears scratched."

BIOGRAPHICAL/CRITICAL SOURCES:

BOOKS

Contemporary Literary Criticism, Volume 39, Gale (Detroit), 1986.

PERIODICALS

Chicago Tribune, June 30, 1995; June 22, 1997.
Esquire, June, 1995, p. 44.
Kirkus Reviews, March 15, 1997.
Los Angeles Times, April 4, 1985.
Los Angeles Times Book Review, March 11, 1990, pp. 2, 11.
Newsweek, April 28, 1997, p. 78.
New York Times, April 13, 1985.
New York Times Book Review, April 28, 1985; March 11, 1990, p. 11; June 4, 1995; July 27, 1997.
People, September 25, 1995, p. 43.

Tribune Books (Chicago), April 29, 1990, p. 6.
Washington Post, March 8, 1990.
Washington Post Book World, May 7, 1985; April 13, 1997.

*   *   *

HENISCH, Heinz K. 1922-
(Benjamin Spear)

PERSONAL: Born April 21, 1922, in Neudek, Germany; son of Leo (an attorney) and Fanny (Soicher) Henisch; married Bridget Ann Wilsher (a retired photo-historian and medievalist), February 6, 1960. *Education:* University of Bristol, B.Sc., 1940; University of Reading, B.Sc., 1942, Ph.D., 1949. *Avocational interests:* Computers, music, photography.

ADDRESSES: Home and office—346 West Hillcrest Ave., State College, PA 16803; fax 814-238-3577.

CAREER: Royal Aircraft Establishment, Farnborough, England, junior scientific officer, 1942-46; University of Reading, Reading, England, lecturer in physics, 1948-62; Pennsylvania State University, University Park, professor of physics, 1963-93, professor of the history of photography, 1974-93, associate director of Materials Research Laboratory, 1968-75, research professor emeritus of the history of photography, Department of Art History, 1993—, professor emeritus of physics, 1993—. Visiting scientist at Sylvania Electric Products, 1955-56; Samuel Newton Taylor Lecturer at Goucher College, 1973; lecturer at colleges and universities in Austria, Czechoslovakia, Israel, Mexico, Peru, Romania, Switzerland, Taiwan, Venezuela, and throughout the United States, as well as on television. Co-director of exhibition "Beauty in Science: Science in Art" at Central Pennsylvania Festival of the Arts, 1973, 1974; co-guest curator, with wife, of major photo-history exhibition at Palmer Museum of Art, 1988, and an exhibition of Henisch's own photographs, "People, Places, Patterns," at HUB Formal Gallery, University Park, August-September, 1989. Has attended international conferences all over the world; has eight patents, all on various aspects of semiconductor technology. Member of Volunteers in Technical Assistance; member of scientific advisory board of Tem-Pres Research, Inc., 1966-70. Chair of Pennsylvania State University Press committee, 1973-75. Consultant to Philco Corp., Polaroid Corp., Energy Conversion Devices, Inc., and Carborundum Co.

MEMBER: U.K. Institute of Physics (fellow), American Physical Society (fellow), Royal Photographic Society (fellow, since 1976), American Photographic Historical Society (fellow).

AWARDS, HONORS: Honorary fellow of A74 Group of Photographers, Warsaw, 1975; D.Sc. from University of Reading, U.K., 1979; elected to life fellowship, of Institute for the Arts and Humanistic Studies, Pennsylvania State University; Rudolf and Hertha Benjamin Award, American Photographic Historical Society, 1996, for The Painted Photograph, 1839-1914: Origins, Techniques, Aspirations.

WRITINGS:

Metal Rectifiers, Oxford University Press (Oxford, England), 1949.
(Editor) Semiconductor Materials, Butterworth & Co. (Woburn, MA), 1951.
Rectifying Semiconductor Contacts, Oxford University Press, 1957.
Electroluminescence, Pergamon (Elsevier, Oxford, England), 1962.
(Editor with others) Silicon Carbide, Pergamon, 1969.
Crystal Growth in Gels, Pennsylvania State University Press, (University Park, PA), 1970, paperback edition, Dover Press (New York City), 1997.
Semiconductor Contacts, an Approach to Ideas and Models, Oxford University Press, 1984, paperback edition, 1989.
Crystals in Gels and Liesegang Rings, Cambridge University Press (New York City), 1988.
Periodic Precipitation: A Microcomputer Analysis of Transport and Reaction Processes in Diffusion Media, with Software Development, Pergamon Press, 1990.
First Dance in Karlsbad ("a small volume of childhood memories"), Carnation Press (State College, PA), 1993, translated into German by H. Ullmann, Universitas Verlag/F. A. Herbig (Munich, Germany), 1996.

COAUTHOR OF PHOTOGRAPHY BOOKS WITH WIFE, B. A. HENISCH

Chipmunk Portrait, Carnation Press, 1970.
The Photographic Experience, Pennsylvania State University Press, 1988.
The Photographic Experience, 1839-1914; Images and Attitudes, Pennsylvania State University Press, 1994.

The Painted Photograph, 1839-1914: Origins, Techniques, Aspirations, Pennsylvania State University Press, 1996.
Positive Pleasures; Early Photography and Humor, Pennsylvania State University Press, 1998.

OTHER

Author of nearly 150 research papers. Also contributor to journals of photo-history and related fields, sometimes under pseudonym Benjamin Spear. Editor of "International Series of Monographs on Semiconductors," Pergamon, 1959-67; founding editor, Materials Research Bulletin (Pergamon Press), 1968-93, and History of Photography (Taylor and Francis, London; international quarterly), 1977-90; member of editorial board of Journal of the Physics of Chemical Solids, 1957—, Journal of Solid State Electronics, 1958—, Physica Status Solidi, 1961-63, Penn State Studies, 1963-66, and Progress in Crystal Growth and Assessment.

WORK IN PROGRESS: A book of essays, Toiling in the Groves; research on James Robertson, Victorian photographer, and on Cuthbert Bede, Victorian photo-humorist.

SIDELIGHTS: Heinz K. Henisch once told CA that he studies "science as an exercise in aesthetics, and science as literature."

Henisch updated CA: "Early in 1996, the considerable holdings of the B. & H. Henisch Photo-History Collection were transferred to the Rare Books Room of the Pattee Library."

Metal Rectifiers was published in a Russian translation, under the title, Semiconductor Rectifiers, 1950; Electroluminescence was published in a Japanese translation in 1963, and a Russian translation was published in 1964; Crystal Growth in Gels was published in a Japanese translation by Corona Publishing Co., Japan, 1972, and a Russian translation was published in 1973.

*   *   *

HIGGINS, Aidan 1927-

PERSONAL: Born March 3, 1972, in County Kildare, Ireland; son of Bartholomew Joseph and Lillian Ann (Boyd) Higgins; married Jill Damaris Anders,

November 25, 1955; children: Carl, Julien, Elwin. *Education:* Attended Clongowes Wood College.

ADDRESSES: Home—Muswell Hill, London, England.

CAREER: Writer. Laborer in light industry in and around London for about two years; brief career in advertising; John Wright's Marionette Co., puppeteer in Europe, South Africa, and Rhodesia, 1958-60; Filmlets, Johannesburg, South Africa, scriptwriter, 1960-61.

AWARDS, HONORS: Somin Trust Award, 1963, for *Felo de Se;* James Tait Black Memorial Prize, 1967, for *Langrishe, Go Down;* DAAD grant, 1969; Irish Academy of Letters Award, 1970; American-Irish Foundation grant, 1977; recipient of British Arts Council grants.

WRITINGS:

Killachter Meadow (stories), Grove (New York City), 1960, published in England as *Felo de Se,* Calder (London), 1960.
Langrishe, Go Down (novel), Grove, 1966.
Images of Africa: Diary (1956-60), Calder, 1971.
Balcony of Europe, Delacorte (New York City), 1973.
Scenes from a Receding Past, Calder, 1977.
(Editor and author of introduction) *A Century of Short Stories,* Cape (London), 1977.
Asylum, and Other Stories, Calder, 1978, Riverrun Press (New York City), 1979.
(Editor) Carl, Julien, and Elwin Higgins, *Colossal Gongorr and the Turkes of Mars,* Cape, 1979.
Bornholm Night-Ferry: A Novel, Allison and Busby (London), 1983.
Helsingor Station and Other Departures: Fictions and Autobiographies, 1956-1989, Secker & Warburg (London), 1989.
Ronda Gorge and Other Precipices: Travel Writings, 1959-1989, Secker & Warburg, 1989.
Lions of the Grunewald, Secker & Warburg, 1993.
Donkey's Years: Memories of a Life as Story Told, Secker & Warburg, 1995.
Samuel Beckett, Secker & Warburg, 1995.

Also author of several radio plays, including *Assassination,* 1973, *Imperfect Sympathies,* 1977, *Discords of Good Humour,* 1982, *Vanishing Heroes,* 1983, *Texts for the Air,* 1983, *Winter Is Coming,* 1983, *Tomb of Dreams,* 1984, *Zoo Station,* 1985, and *Boomtown,* 1990. Contributor to *X Magazine, Art &*

Literature, Evergreen Review, Les Letters nouvelles, Transatlantic Review, Malahat Review, and *Tri-Quarterly. Killachter Meadow* has been published in France, Germany, Italy, Holland, Portugal, and Denmark. A collection of Higgins's manuscripts are housed at the University of Victoria, British Columbia.

ADAPTATIONS: Harold Pinter adapted *Langrishe, Go Down* for BBC Television, 1978. The film starred Pinter, Jeremy Irons, and Judi Dench.

SIDELIGHTS: Aidan Higgins is "one of the best known of the younger Irish prose writers," John Montague once stated. Higgins has even been mentioned as a successor to the great Irish writers of the twentieth century, namely Frank O'Connor, Samuel Beckett, James Joyce, and Brian O Nuallain. Yet, Higgins has resisted being hemmed in by his origins and has revealed the influence of other literary figures such as Jorge Luis Borges and T. S. Eliot. As Peter G. W. van de Kamp points out in *Contemporary Novelists,* "In his attempt to escape the traditional constraints of Irish fiction, Aidan Higgins has emerged as an Irish internationalist, firmly grounded in his Irish experience and yet devoted to an extensive view." Reflecting this extensive view, Higgins's novels and short stories often involve Irish characters in foreign landscapes or in relationships with non-Irish characters.

The family "as a kind of collective neurosis, imprisoning its members inextricably in a welter of obsessions and delusions" is the subject of *Langrishe, Go Down,* as Bill Grantham writes in the *Dictionary of Literary Biography.* The novel focuses on the women of the Langrishe family, specifically "on the affair in 1932 between Imogen Langrishe, a spinster from a declining line of the Irish landed middle class, and Otto Beck, a German research student," Grantham explains. The setting is Ireland during the years leading up to World War II, and as Grantham observes, "While the action is confined to a debilitated section of Ireland and its culture, the dramatic sweep encompasses the vast upheavals on the European scene." This type of setting, a cloistered locale vexed by rumblings in the distance, is a device characteristic of Higgins's stories, according to Grantham. The critic describes it as a "depiction of localized, personal events being held in suspension by outside matters which at once appear beyond the reach of the characters of the story and yet hold them completely in thrall."

Langrishe, Go Down captures what Moynihan has termed "entropy, the slow running down of sequestered lives." A *Times Literary Supplement* reviewer writes: "Mr. Higgins clearly feels his responsibilities towards prose rather acutely, but his style is sustained not so much by ambition as by an unremitting attention, and although his particularities can verge on the gratuitous, they do make you see. The relation of the bits of the novel to the whole piece is not always convincing . . . but [the book] certainly reveals a promising talent." Moynihan states that Higgins "shows us, . . . entirely in terms of the phenomenal, that failing and decaying—the dissipation of physical, moral and psychic energy—entail the same, and the same amounts of, energy conversion as succeeding and flowering. As it is surveyed and occupied in this book the ground of the phenomenal is anything but barren, and life seen at dead level is anything but dead."

Balcony of Europe, set in Spain in the early 1960s, introduces the character of Dan Ruttle, an Irish painter married to a New Zealander. Ruttle moves in expatriate circles and the characters he meets form a "panorama of grotesques and misfits," Grantham explains, "all distillations of aspects of the European societies rent asunder by the war and finding it impossible to put back together what has been lost." In this context, Ruttle begins an affair with the American wife of a friend. In creating yet another isolated community where personal tensions are influenced by events happening on the larger scale, "plot is largely sacrificed for a number of cognitive tableaux," comments van de Kamp, "held together by cross-references and a distinctively idiosyncratic voice. As a result," the critic continues, "the novel is dominated by a technique of Beckettian repetitions, ellipses, and grammatical distortions to which are added spices of [Laurence] Sterne and numerous quotations from [William Butler] Yeats." Through this approach, "Higgins manages to produce a work again similar to a historical novel, but not quite in that category," Grantham suggests. "History itself is the issue here—its status, its theory, its influence."

Scenes from a Receding Past offers more of Dan Ruttle's personal history, following the Irish artist from his early childhood through his marriage to Olivia, the girl from New Zealand, past his experiences in Spain. The novel is "constructed primarily through the use of a montage effect: events and moments blend with newspaper reports, scorecards from cricket matches, and other ephemera from Ruttle's life," relates Grantham. Though not as well

received as Higgins's two previous novels, *Scenes from a Receding Past* provides a logical bridge between those works and *Bornholm Night-Ferry,* according to van de Kamp. The "epistolary form" of this novel, set in northern Europe, "enables Higgins to combine successfully post-modernism and his timeless gift for detail," adds the critic.

BIOGRAPHICAL/CRITICAL SOURCES:

BOOKS

Contemporary Novelists, 6th edition, St. James Press (Detroit), 1996.
Dictionary of Literary Biography, Volume 14: *British Novelists since 1960,* Gale (Detroit), 1983.
Higgins, Aidan, *Donkey's Years: Memories of a Life as Story Told,* Secker and Warburg, 1995.

PERIODICALS

Christian Century, April 1, 1967.
Irish University Review, autumn, 1973.
New Leader, September 25, 1967.
New York Times Book Review, April 16, 1967; January 28, 1973.
Review of Contemporary Fiction, spring, 1983.
Saturday Review, March 4, 1967.
Spectator, February 11, 1966.
Times Literary Supplement, March 3, 1966.

*   *   *

HINES, Barry (Melvin) 1939-

PERSONAL: Born June 30, 1939, in Barnsley, South Yorkshire, England; son of Richard Laurence (a miner) and Annie (Westerman) Hines; divorced; children: Sally, Thomas. *Education:* Attended Loughborough College of Education, teaching certificate, 1963. *Politics:* Socialist.

ADDRESSES: Home and office—323 Fulwood Rd., Sheffield, Yorkshire S10 3BJ, England. *Agent*—Lemon Unna and Durbridge Ltd., 24 Pottery Lane, London W11 4LZ, England.

CAREER: Teacher at schools in London, England, 1960-62, and Barnsley, England, 1963-68; West Riding County Council Education Authority, Wakefield, England, teacher, 1968-72; University of Sheffield, Yorkshire Arts fellow in creative writing, 1972-

74; Matlock College of Further Education, Derby-shire, East Midlands Arts fellow in creative writing, 1975-77; University of Wollongong, New South Wales, Australia, fellow in creative writing, 1979; Sheffield City Polytechnic, Arts Council fellow, 1982-84.

MEMBER: Royal Society of Literature (fellow), East Midlands Arts Association (fellow, 1975-77).

AWARDS, HONORS: Best British screenplay award from Writers Guild of Great Britain, 1970, for *Kes;* Society of Authors traveling scholarship, 1989; honorary fellow, Sheffield City Polytechnic, 1985.

WRITINGS:

NOVELS

The Blinder, M. Joseph (London), 1966.
A Kestrel for a Knave, M. Joseph, 1968.
First Signs, M. Joseph, 1972.
The Gamekeeper, M. Joseph, 1975.
The Price of Coal, M. Joseph, 1979.
Looks and Smiles, M. Joseph, 1981.
Unfinished Business, M. Joseph, 1983.
The Heart of It, M. Joseph, 1994.

PLAYS

Kes (produced in Oldham, Lancashire, 1979), Heine-mann (London), 1976.
The Price of Coal (produced in Nottingham, 1984), Hutchinson (London), 1979.
Billy's Last Stand, produced in London, 1985.
Two Men from Derby, produced in London, 1989.

SCREENPLAYS

(With Ken Loach) *Kes,* United Artists, 1969.
Looks and Smiles, 1981.

TELEVISION PLAYS

Billy's Last Stand, first broadcast by British Broad-casting Corp. (BBC), 1970.
Speech Day, first broadcast by BBC, 1973.
Two Men from Derby, first broadcast by BBC, 1976.
The Price of Coal (two films), first broadcast by BBC, 1977.
The Gamekeeper, first broadcast by Associated Tele-vision Ltd., December 10, 1980.
(With Loach) *A Question of Leadership* (documen-tary), first broadcast by Associated Television Ltd., 1981.

OTHER

Also author of the television plays, *Threads,* 1984; *Shooting Stars,* 1990; and *Born Kicking,* 1992. Work appears in anthologies, including *Dandelion Clocks,* M. Joseph, 1978, and *The Northern Drift,* Blackie (London), 1980. Contributor to *Argosy.*

SIDELIGHTS: The novels of Barry Hines focus on British working class characters. "Hines has found his own voice," remarks H. Gustav Klaus in *Contemporary Novelists.* "It is not only an angry voice denouncing class prejudice and class privilege, and attacking the shortcomings of the once celebrated affluent society. It has also a cautiously hopeful ring emanating from the creative, defiant, and ultimately invincible qualities which his working-class characters display, often against overwhelming opposition." "The best of Hines' writing . . . ," explains Peter Whittaker in *New Statesman & Society,* "is built on solid, unshowy foundations; a dogged, workmanlike celebration of the ordinary."

Among Hines' most popular works are *A Kestrel for a Knave* (adapted as the film *Kes*), *The Gamekeeper* and *The Price of Coal.* In *A Kestrel for a Knave* Hines follows a day in the life of an alienated working class boy told in a series of brief, often amusing episodes. The story conveys, Klaus writes, "not only a sense of the complete breakdown of communication between adults and the adolescent but also his consequent negative perception of social relations and institutions."

The Gamekeeper focuses on another working class character, this time an estate's gamekeeper whose job it is to raise pheasants. In raising the birds and protecting them from poachers, the gamekeeper insures that his employer can hunt the pheasants on his own. As Klaus comments, "this form of living in direct contact with natural processes cannot shed capitalist relations of property and domination."

The Price of Coal revolves around a royal visit to a nationalized coal mine. "The miners . . . are a singularly class-conscious and humorous breed," notes Klaus. Inspired in part by coal strikes in 1972 and 1974, the novel "goes to show how close to the thoughts and feelings of ordinary working people Hines has remained over the years," writes Klaus, "how loyal to his roots and faithful to his socialist humanist creed."

BIOGRAPHICAL/CRITICAL SOURCES:

BOOKS

Contemporary Novelists, 6th edition, St. James Press (Detroit), 1996.

Gray, Nigel, *The Silent Majority: A Study of the Working Class in Post-War British Fiction,* Barnes & Noble (New York City), 1973.

Hawthorn, Jeremy, editor, *The British Working-Class Novel in the Twentieth Century,* Arnold (London), 1984.

Paul, Ronald, *Fire in Our Hearts,* Gothenburg Studies in English (Gothenburg, Sweden), 1982.

PERIODICALS

New Statesman & Society, June 10, 1994, p. 38.

*   *   *

HIRSHFIELD, Jane 1953-

PERSONAL: Born February 24, 1953, in New York, NY; daughter of Robert L. (a clothing manufacturer) and Harriet (a secretary; maiden name, Miller) Hirshfield. *Education:* Princeton University, A.B. (magna cum laude), 1973. *Religion:* Zen Buddhist. *Avocational interests:* Horses, gardening, wilderness.

ADDRESSES: Home—367 Molino Ave., Mill Valley, CA 94941. *Office*—c/o HarperCollins, 10 East 53rd St., New York, NY 10022. *Email*—jhpac@pacbell.net; fax: 415-383-1852.

CAREER: University of San Francisco, lecturer in creative writing, 1991-98; University of California, Berkeley, visiting associate professor, 1995. Member of the faculties of numerous writers conferences and in-school programs, including California Poets in the Schools, 1979-85, Squaw Valley Art of the Wild Writers Conference, 1992—, Bennington College M.F.A. writing seminars, core faculty, 1999—, and Port Townsend and Napa Valley Writers Conferences; University of Cincinnati, Elliston Visiting Poetry Professor, 2000. Freelance editor, 1983—; translator.

MEMBER: PEN, Authors Guild, Poetry Society of America, Associated Writing Programs, Marin Arts Council, Marin Poetry Center, Lindisfarne Associa-

tion (fellow), Djerassi Resident Artists Program (board director), Phi Beta Kappa.

AWARDS, HONORS: Poetry Competition Prize, *Nation,* 1973; Poetry Prize, *Quarterly Review of Literature,* 1982, for *Alaya;* Yaddo fellowships, 1983, 1985, 1987, 1989, 1992, 1996; Guggenheim fellowship, 1985; Joseph Henry Jackson Award, San Francisco Foundation, 1986; Columbia University Translation Center Award, 1988, and Japan-U.S. Friendship Commission Prize for Literary Translation honorable mention, 1988, both for *The Ink Dark Moon: Poems by Ono no Komachi and Izumi Shikibu, Women of the Ancient Court of Japan;* Gordon Barber Award, Poetry Society of America, 1987; Poetry Medal, Commonwealth Club of California, and Pushcart Prize, both 1988, both for *Of Gravity & Angels;* Cecil Hemley Award, Poetry Society of America, 1988; Achievement Grant, Marin Arts Council, 1990; Dewar's Young Artists Recognition Award in Poetry, 1990; MacDowell Colony fellowship, 1994; Poetry Medal, Commonwealth Club of California, Poetry Center Book Award, both 1994, both for *The October Palace;* Bay Area Book Reviewers Award, 1995, for *The October Palace;* Rockefeller Foundation Bellagio Study Center fellowship, 1995.

WRITINGS:

POETRY

Alaya, Quarterly Review of Literature Poetry Series (Princeton, NJ), 1982.

Of Gravity & Angels, Wesleyan University Press (Middletown, CT), 1988.

The October Palace, HarperCollins (New York City), 1994.

The Lives of the Heart, HarperCollins, 1997.

Contributor to anthologies, including *The Pushcart Prize XIII: Best of the Small Presses,* Pushcart Press, 1988; *Deep Down,* Faber, 1988; *Touching Fire: Writings by Women,* Carrol & Graf, 1989; *Cries of the Spirit,* Beacon Press (Boston), 1990; *The Amicus Anthology of Contemporary Poetry,* Natural Resources Defense Council, 1990; *Beneath a Single Moon: Legacies of Buddhism in Contemporary American Poetry,* Shambhala, 1991; *A Hand-Span of Red Earth: An American Farm Poetry Anthology,* University of Iowa Press, 1991; *Changing Light,* HarperCollins, 1991; *To Woo & To Wed: Poets on Love and Marriage,* Simon & Schuster (New York City), 1992; *The Quarterly Review of Literature Fif-*

tieth Anniversary Anthology, Quarterly Review of Literature, 1993; *The Wesleyan Tradition: Four Decades of American Poetry,* Wesleyan University Press, 1993; *Claiming the Spirit Within,* Beacon Press, 1996; *What Will Suffice: Contemporary American Poets on the Art of Poetry,* Gibbs-Smith, 1997; *Poetry: An Introduction,* Bedford Books, 1997; and *Wild Song: Poems of the Natural World,* University of Georgia Press, 1998. Contributor to periodicals, including *American Poetry Review, Antaeus, Antioch Review, Atlantic, Five Points, New Republic, Southern Review, Georgia Review, Ironwood, Nation, New Yorker, Ontario Review, Paris Review, Ploughshares, Poetry, Sierra, Threepenny Review, Whole Earth Review, Wilderness,* and *Zyzzyva.*

OTHER

(Editor and translator, with Mariko Aratani) *The Ink Dark Moon: Poems by Ono no Komachi and Izumi Shikibu, Women of the Ancient Court of Japan,* Scribners (New York City), 1988, expanded edition, Random House (New York City), 1990.

(Editor and translator) *Women in Praise of the Sacred: 43 Centuries of Spiritual Poetry by Women,* HarperCollins, 1994.

Nine Gates: Entering the Mind of Poetry, HarperCollins, 1997.

SIDELIGHTS: Award-winning poet and translator Jane Hirshfield is the author of several collections of verse, many of which are influenced by her Zen Buddhist practice and her knowledge of classical Japanese verse. In addition to her own published collections, which include *Of Gravity & Angels* and *The Lives of the Heart,* Hirshfield has translated works by early women poets Ono no Komachi and Izumi Shikibu in her *The Ink Dark Moon,* as well as other woman-authored verse from the past in *Women in Praise of the Sacred: 43 Centuries of Spiritual Poetry by Women,* released in 1994. The Eastern and Western poetry that often inspires Hirshfield are short forms with a turning point or moment of insight. "Such moments arise in Hirshfield's own poetry," asserted *Common Boundary* reviewer Rose Solari. "There is a wholeness, a sense of completeness in her work."

Hirshfield published her first poem in 1973, shortly after graduating from Princeton University as part of that institution's first graduating class to include women. She then put aside her writing for nearly eight years to study at the San Francisco Zen Center.

"I felt that I'd never make much of a poet if I didn't know more than I knew at that time about what it means to be a human being," the poet told Solari. "I don't think poetry is based just on poetry; it is based on a thoroughly lived life. And so I couldn't just decide I was going to write no matter what; I first had to find out what it means to *live.*" While Hirshfield does not use Zen terminology in her verse, she once told *CA* that "it is my hope that the experience of that practice underlies and informs it as a whole. My feeling is that the paths of poetry and of meditation are closely linked—one is an attentiveness and awareness that exist in language, the other an attentiveness and awareness that exist in silence, but each is a way to attempt to penetrate experience thoroughly, to its core."

After completing her studies in Zen in the early 1980s, Hirshfield began to write and teach, earning numerous grants and awards throughout the remainder of the decade. Her work throughout her career has been inspired by a series of new influences, in both the Eastern and Western traditions: "Greek and Roman lyrics, the English sonnet, those foundation stones of American poetry [Walt] Whitman and [Emily] Dickinson, 'modern' poets from [T. S.] Eliot to [Anna] Akhmatova to [C. P.] Cavafy to [Pablo] Neruda—all have added something to my knowledge of what is possible in poetry," Hirshfield explained to *CA.* Equally influential have been classical Chinese poets Tu Fu, Li Po, Wang Wei, and Han Shan; classical Japanese Heian-Era poets Komachi and Shikibu; and such lesser known traditions and Eskimo and Nahuatl poetry.

Hirshfield's translation of love poems by Komachi and Shikibu, as well as her collection of poems *Of Gravity & Angels* appeared in 1988. The poems that comprise *Of Gravity & Angels* most often depict nature. "The beauty and reassurance of the natural world constantly infuses Hirshfield's work with freshness," remarked Frances Mayes in the *San Jose Mercury News.* In *Contemporary Women Poets,* essayist Allen Hoey also commented on the influence of poet James Wright on Hirshfield's work, particularly the poem "After Work." Several other critics remarked on the theme of transcendence in Hirshfield's verse. "Lyrical, attentive to color and light, precise in focus and in naming, this godless but holy book sanctifies the homely and the here-and-now," pronounced poet Emily Leider in the *San Francisco Chronicle.* "Concrete and wedded to the tactile world, the poems give off an other-worldly beauty and resonance." Concluded Mayes, "Hirshfield is a strong new talent. Her sensibility is lyric, and her intellect is as sharp as any ax in her toolshed."

In 1987 Hirshfield began collecting sacred verse by women after the poet and translator Stephen Mitchell asked for her help in compiling his anthology of sacred verse. "I had a feeling that women had always written about these things and that it was just a matter of finding them," she explained to Joan Smith of the *San Francisco Examiner.* "It was like a treasure hunt." The result of Hirshfield's research appeared in 1994 as *Women in Praise of the Sacred: 43 Centuries of Spiritual Poetry by Women,* a collection that spans the centuries from 2300 B.C. to the early-1900s and includes the work of seventy poets from many cultures, spiritual traditions, and social classes. "*The Ink Dark Moon* and *Women in Praise of the Sacred,* were each done in the effort to make more widely known the work of historical women poets whose words I found both memorable and moving, able to enlarge our understanding of what it is to be human," Hirshfield explained to *CA.* "They were also done to help counteract the lingering myth that there were no historical women writers of significance."

The October Palace, a poetry collection that also appeared in 1994, is, in the words of its creator, "about awareness, about waking up to the substance and sensuousness and depths and wideness of our existence." Encompassing an even more vast expanse of references than her previous collections—from Zen monks to modernist painters—Hirshfield's "knowledge never seems donned like a valedictory robe, . . . but [instead] serves to illuminate recesses of thought," according to Hoey. "I chose the word *October* because for me it means *transience,*" Hirshfield told *San Francisco Review of Books* critic Pam Houston. "I think the hardest thing people have to deal with in their lives is that everything changes." The poet viewed *The October Palace* as a response to the pressures of everyday life. "You can either fall into total grief or total joy—you never know which way it is going to go. The effort of this book is to accept the terms of the world, but it's not easy; it's never easy." Summing up *The October Palace,* Houston enthused, "[Hirshfield's] poems are honest and beautiful, sensuous and clean, as full of passion as they are full of grace, as risky as they are wise."

In addition to her verse publications, Hirshfield has also written *Nine Gates: Entering the Mind of Poetry,* a collection of prose pieces. Based on her lectures before writing conferences or adapted from essays

published in literary journals, Hirshfield's essays touch upon such subjects as originality, the nature of metaphoric mind, translation, and the psychological shadow. Praised by *Booklist* contributor Donna Seaman as an "enlightening volume [that] does exactly what Hirshfield hoped it would: it intensifies our response to poetry, hence to life," the nine essays cite numerous examples from familiar works written in English, as well as from Japanese works taken from translation (Hirshfield does not read Japanese). "With her feet firmly planted in both the Western and Eastern canons, Hirshfield delivers a thorough and timely collection on our relationships to poetry, our relationship to the world, and everything in between," maintained a *Publishers Weekly* reviewer in praise of *Nine Gates.*

Hirshfield once told *CA:* "My primary interest has always been the attempt to understand and deepen experience by bringing it into words. Poetry, for me, is an instrument of investigation and a mode of perception, a way of knowing and feeling both self and world. In one sense, then, I write for myself; but poetry is also a mode of being in which subjective and objective can approach and become each other—in the lyric poem, choices of outer description inevitably reveal inner being, while the most seemingly subjective expression touches the universal experiences of passion, grief, love, loss and the subtler experiences of both daily life and what, for lack of any better term, I will call metaphysical inquiry. The speaking voice of a poem during its composition is intensely private, but the finished work is nonetheless a way of bringing the fruit of my innermost thinking to others. I am interested in poems that find a clarity without simplicity; in a way of thinking and speaking that does not exclude complexity but also does not obscure; in poems that know the world in many ways at once—heart, mind, voice, and body."

BIOGRAPHICAL/CRITICAL SOURCES:

BOOKS

Contemporary Women Poets, St. James Press (Detroit), 1997.

PERIODICALS

American Poetry Review, July/August, 1988, p. 39.
Antioch Review, winter, 1995, pp. 121-22.
Artists Dialogue, October/November, 1994, pp. 2, 4.
Booklist, September 1, 1997.
Common Boundary, March, 1994, pp. 33-34, 39.

Hungry Mind Review, winter, 1994, p. 54; winter, 1997-98.

Library Journal, October 1, 1997, p. 86.

New York Times Book Review, July 3, 1994, p. 19.

Ploughshares, spring, 1998.

Publishers Weekly, August 11, 1997, p. 394.

San Francisco Chronicle, May 8, 1988.

San Francisco Examiner, May 4, 1994, pp. C1, C4.

San Francisco Review of Books, April/May, 1994, pp. 18-20.

San Jose Mercury News, January 22, 1989; June 25, 1994.

Village Voice, August 26, 1997.

Yale Review, April, 1995, pp. 147-52.

* * *

HOWARD, Mark
See RIGSBY, Howard

* * *

HOWARD, Vechel
See RIGSBY, Howard

* * *

HOWE, Fanny (Quincy) 1940-

PERSONAL: Born October 15, 1940, in Buffalo, NY; daughter of Mark DeWolfe (a lawyer) and Mary (a writer; maiden name, Manning) Howe; married Carl Senna, October 27, 1968 (divorced); children: Ann, Lucien, Danzy, Maceo. *Education:* Attended Stanford University, 1958-61. *Religion:* Roman Catholic.

CAREER: Employed in various jobs, 1961-68; Tufts University, Medford, MA, lecturer in creative writing, 1968-72; associated with Massachusetts Poetry-in-the-Schools program, 1973; Emerson College, Boston, MA, lecturer in creative writing, 1973-74; Columbia University, New York City, lecturer in creative writing, 1974-77; Massachusetts Institute of Technology, Cambridge, visiting writer, 1978-87; University of California, San Diego, professor, 1987—; University of California Study Center, London, England, associate director, 1993-95.

AWARDS, HONORS: McDowell Colony fellow, 1965, 1990; National Endowment for the Arts grant, 1970, 1991; Bunting Institute fellow, 1974; St. Botolph Award, 1976; Writers Choice award, 1984; *Village Voice* fiction award, 1988.

WRITINGS:

Forty Whacks (short stories; contains "Forty Whacks," "Rosy Cheeks," "The Last Virgin," "Plug Body," "The Other Side of Lethe," and "Dump Gull"), Houghton (Boston), 1969.

Eggs (poems), Houghton, 1970.

First Marriage (novel), self-illustrated, Avon (New York City), 1974.

Bronte Wilde (novel), Avon, 1976.

The Amerindian Coastline Poem, Telephone Books (New York City), 1976.

Holy Smoke (novel), illustrations by Colleen McCallion, Fiction Collective (New York City), 1979.

Poems from a Single Pallet, Kelsey Street Press, 1980.

The White Slave (novel), Avon, 1980.

The Blue Hills (young adult novel), Avon, 1981.

Alsace-Lorraine (poetry), Telephone Books, 1982.

Yeah, But (young adult novel), Avon, 1982.

In the Middle of Nowhere (novel), Fiction Collective, 1984.

Radio City (young adult novel), Avon, 1984.

For Erato: The Meaning of Life (poems), Tuumba Press (Berkeley, CA), 1984.

Taking Care (young adult novel), Avon, 1985.

The Race of the Radical (for children), Viking (New York City), 1985.

Robeson Street (poetry), Alice James Books (Boston), 1985.

Introduction to the World (poetry), The Figures (New York City), 1986.

The Lives of a Spirit (fiction), Sun & Moon Press (Los Angeles), 1986.

The Deep North, Sun & Moon Press, 1988.

The Vineyard, Lost Roads (Providence, RI), 1988.

Famous Questions: A Novel, Ballantine (New York City), 1989.

The End, Littoral Books, (Los Angeles) 1992.

The Quietist (poetry), O Books (Oakland, CA), 1992.

Saving History, Sun & Moon Press, 1992.

O'Clock (poetry), Reality Street (London), 1994.

One Crossed Out (poetry), Greywolf, 1997.
Nod, Sun & Moon Press, 1997.

SIDELIGHTS: Novelist and poet Fanny Howe is noted for an increasingly avant-garde creative output. Beginning her career in print with mainstream New York City publishers, Howe's work has become increasingly less commercial, and much of her more recent output has been made available through smaller presses. Grouped since the late-1970s with so-called "language poets," such as Lyn Hejinian, Charles Bernstein, and others, Howe's most well-known work is her long poem *The Lives of a Spirit,* which is based on the work of poet Rainer Maria Rilke and in which "the openness of the text, the sometimes dizzying abysses between the sentences, invite the reader to embark on a spiritual pilgrimage parallel to the authors'," according to *Contemporary Women Poets* contributor Burton Hatlen.

Forty Whacks, Howe's first book, is considered among her more popular mainstream early work. A volume of prose published in 1969, it contains six short stories dealing with troubled women. Some of the protagonists are murderers, others adulteresses, but as M. Ann Petrie pointed out in a *New Leader* review, "all are out of touch with themselves and the world—and they are lonely." The protagonists of short stories "Forty Whacks" and "The Other Side of Lethe" provide evidence of Petrie's observations. The main character of the title story reveals her detachment as she describes in her diary, in the cool language of psychoanalysis, her deliberate destruction of a couple's marriage. She rationalizes her actions, in an account *Nation* reviewer Shaun O'Connell judged "as tightly told as [Robert] Browning's dramatic monologues," and when she has achieved her goal, she decides she doesn't want the husband after all. Instead of being the "severely alive" person she believes she is, "she proves to be a very dead young woman," assessed Petrie. The heroine of "The Other Side of Lethe" is a woman left dispassionate by amnesia. Because she has forgotten the details of the death of her lover, whom she was convicted of murdering, she is unaffected by them. She relates the events, described O'Connell, "as though she were arranging flowers."

After Howe's marriage to fellow writer Carl Senna in 1968, her work became increasingly "eccentric," as Howe noted in an essay in the *Something about the Author Autobiography* series (SAAS). In a multi-racial marriage, exposed to a culture different from the

white, middle-class culture of her youth, Howe continued to write fiction and poetry, but found that "some world view was inexorably shifting in me, and I felt sidelined by conversations and remarks that would have slid by unnoticed before." The period between 1968 and 1988 was a fertile period for Howe as an author—she published thirteen novels and seven collections of poetry during this period—but socially her life became more sheltered.

Later works by Howe include the 1992 novel *Saving History,* and *One Crossed Out,* a collection of poetry published in 1997. Poetry and prose have merged increasingly throughout Howe's oeuvre, and *Saving History* exemplifies this merger: a long narrative work, it is broken by passages of verse. And in the twenty poems comprising *One Crosses Out,* Howe's poetry too is experimental. Characterized as "inventive" and "consistently surprising," her verses challenge the commonly held conventions of both "lyric and narrative through an idiosyncratic . . . understanding of how language inhabits things," in the words of *Library Journal* contributor Fred Muratori. Told from the viewpoint of May, a homeless women with a drug problem, the poems in *One Crossed Out* were cited by a *Publishers Weekly* critic as an "acquired taste." But, noted the critic, the work "can also reveal how a language of brutalized distress can be unexpectedly beautiful." As Howe herself explained in *Contemporary Women Poets,* "my poetry has continued to work as a response to the daily world and how strange it is in every aspect."

BIOGRAPHICAL/CRITICAL SOURCES:

BOOKS

Contemporary Women Poets, St. James Press, 1997.
Something about the Author Autobiography Series, Volume 27, Gale, 1997.

PERIODICALS

American Book Review, February, 1994, p. 14.
Library Journal, November 1, 1997, p. 77.
Nation, December 8, 1969.
New Leader, November 24, 1969.
New York Times Book Review, December 14, 1969; March 2, 1975; May 9, 1976; May 20, 1984.
Publishers Weekly, October 27, 1997, p. 72.
Sulphur, spring, 1994, p. 229.
Times Literary Supplement, March 5, 1971.
Village Voice, August 13, 1979.*

HUNTER, Stephen 1946-

PERSONAL: Born March 25, 1946, in Kansas City, MO; son of Charles Francis (a professor) and Virginia (an executive; maiden name, Ricker) Hunter; married Lucy Hageman (a teacher), September 13, 1969; children: James H., Amy E. *Education:* Northwestern University, B.S.J., 1968.

ADDRESSES: Home—10013 Cape Anne Dr., Columbia, MD 21046. *Office—Baltimore Sun,* 501 North Calvert, Baltimore, MD 21203.

CAREER: Baltimore Sun, Baltimore, MD, copy reader, 1971-73, book review editor, 1973-82, film critic, 1982—. *Military service:* U.S. Army, Infantry, 1968-70.

WRITINGS:

NOVELS

The Master Sniper, Morrow (New York City), 1980.
The Second Saladin, Morrow, 1982.
The Spanish Gambit, Crown (New York City), 1985, published as *Tapestry of Spies,* Dell (New York City), 1997.
Target, Warner Books (New York City), 1985.
The Day Before Midnight, Bantam (New York City), 1989.
Point of Impact, Bantam, 1993.
Dirty White Boys, Random House (New York City), 1994.
Black Light, Doubleday (New York City), 1996.

FILM CRITICISM

Violent Screen: A Critic's 13 Years on the Front Lines of Movie Mayhem, Bancroft Press (Baltimore, Md.), 1995.

Contributor to *Crawdaddy.*

SIDELIGHTS: A veteran journalist and longtime film critic with the *Baltimore Sun,* Stephen Hunter has captured the attention of readers as the author of action-packed, psychologically incisive thrillers.

Hunter's novel *The Spanish Gambit* focuses on one of the most infamous double agents of the twentieth century: Kim Philby, the Cambridge-educated British intelligence operative who spied for the Soviet Union and defected to that country in the early 1960s. Hunter's novel, which *Armchair Detective* critic

Jeanne F. Bedell hails as "more complex psychologically and richer in historical background than most espionage fiction," explores Philby's career as a *London Times* correspondent during the Spanish Civil War, and speculates on the circumstances surrounding his recruitment as a Soviet agent.

In *The Day Before Midnight,* a military-political thriller, a shadowy cadre of crack soldiers seizes control of an American missile base and threatens to launch an attack on the Soviet Union. *New York Times Book Review* critic Newgate Callendar acknowledges the novel's strengths as an entertainment, with its "nonstop action and mounting tension" but wondered, "What will authors do if, in a few years, the Russians are our friends?"

Hunter seems to have risen to the challenge. With the waning of the cold war and the collapse of the Soviet Union, he has taken his thrillers in a new direction, toward tales examining uniquely American characters and situations. He has achieved his greatest popular success, as well as his most enthusiastic critical reception, with the trilogy comprised of *Point of Impact, Dirty White Boys,* and *Black Light.* Like his previous novels, these have plenty of action, abundant graphic violence, and—one of Hunter's trademarks—meticulous descriptions of firearms. But all are set in contemporary America, and the evils found here are all essentially homegrown.

Bob Lee Swagger, the central character in *Point of Impact,* served as a Marine sniper in Vietnam, where he scored eighty-seven kills, earning the nickname "Bob the Nailer." With the war now twenty years in the past, Swagger, a taciturn, withdrawn man, lives in the mountains of rural Arkansas, where his chief pastimes are hunting and tending to his gun collection. His idyllic way of life is shattered when he is contacted and hired by RamDyne, a mysterious firm with ties to military intelligence. Ostensibly hired as a consultant to protect the president from assassination, Swagger soon realizes that he has been set up. He then finds himself the most-wanted man in America, pursued not only by the police and the F.B.I., but also by killers from RamDyne, who want him silenced. Forced underground and into flight, Swagger finds but one ally, an over-the-hill F.B.I. man who, like himself, is an expert marksman. His eventful, often bloody quest for justice and revenge ends with a dramatic court case. In a *New York Times Book Review* notice, Callendar writes, "More than a mere action novel, *Point of Impact* is superbly written. Mr. Hunter has made a fine effort to get into the mind of his protagonist." Christine E. Thompson in *Armchair Detective* calls *Point of Impact* an "excellent novel" delivering a "top-notch emotional experience."

Dirty White Boys, perhaps Hunter's most widely acclaimed novel, presents an elaborate cat-and-mouse game between a homicidal prison escapee and the Oklahoma highway patrolman who pursues him. In the novel's opening scenes, convicted killer Lamar Pye escapes from Oklahoma's maximum security McAlester State Penitentiary accompanied by his cousin Odell, a mentally retarded giant with a cleft palate, and Richard Peed, a scholarly, rather effeminate man whose sketches have captivated Lamar. Led by Lamar, this awkward trio cuts a swath of murder and mayhem across Oklahoma and Texas, eventually taking refuge in the farmhouse of a psychotic young woman who becomes their partner in crime, their helpmate, and Lamar's lover. Their chief antagonist is Oklahoma Highway Patrol Sergeant Bud Pewtie, a veteran cop and family man whose normal stolidity is disrupted by two obsessions: his adulterous affair with his partner's wife, and capturing Lamar Pye. *New York Times Book Review* contributor Marilyn Stasio hails *Dirty White Boys* as "an exhilarating crime novel" with a "big, mythic theme," and observed, "of all the killings in *Dirty White Boys* . . . , the death of the American family is the most monstrous." According to Daniel Woodrell in the *Washington Post Book World,* "Hunter is extremely knowledgable about small arms, criminal behavior, and law enforcement techniques. He writes very well, in direct and savory prose, poetically evocative and rough-and-tumble by turns."

With the publication of *Black Light,* Hunter revealed that his tenuously connected two previous novels were actually the first two parts of a genuine trilogy, which, as *Los Angeles Times Book Review* critic Dick Lochte notes, "[explores] the relationship between sons and fathers." The lawman father of Billy Lee Swagger, the hero of *Point of Impact,* killed the criminal father of Lamar Pye, the arch-fiend of the Dirty White Boys. In *Black Light,* Billy Lee Swagger returns, this time teaming up with Russell Pewtie, the son of Oklahoma Highway Patrolman Bud Pewtie. In *Dirty White Boys,* Russell Pewtie is a studious, Princeton-bound teenager; in *Black Light,* he is a young newspaperman helping Billy Lee Swagger investigate the four-decade-old murder of the latter's father, a crime found to have connections to, among other things, the C.I.A. and corrupt Arkansas politicians. According to *Los Angeles Times* critic

Lochte, "The result is a big, bristly bear of a book, edgy and violent. . . . Hunter has saved the best for last." The critic for *Publishers Weekly* believes that, with *Black Light,* "Hunter confirms his status as one of the most skilled hands in the thriller business."

BIOGRAPHICAL/CRITICAL SOURCES:

PERIODICALS

Armchair Detective, summer, 1993, pp. 23-24; fall, 1993, p. 118.
Baltimore Evening Sun, May 27, 1980.
Chicago Tribune Books, February 21, 1993, p. 7; November 20, 1994, p. 6.
Entertainment Weekly, December 23, 1994, p. 61.
Kirkus Reviews, September 1, 1994, pp. 1152-53.
Library Journal, November 15, 1995, pp. 76-77.
Los Angeles Times, December 13, 1985; June 23, 1996, p. 10.
New York Times Book Review, April 23, 1989, p. 33; February 28, 1993, p. 24; November 20, 1994, p. 44; June 9, 1996, p. 29.
People, January 23, 1995, p. 28; June 17, 1996, p. 32.
Publishers Weekly, September 19, 1994, p. 49; April 29, 1996, p. 51; May 27, 1996, p. 75.
Washington Post Book World, January 8, 1995, p. 4.

*   *   *

HYMAN, Trina Schart 1939-

PERSONAL: Born April 8, 1939, in Philadelphia, PA; daughter of Albert H. (in sales) and Margaret Doris (Bruck) Schart; married Harris Hyman (a mathematician and engineer), 1959 (divorced, 1968); children: Katrin. *Education:* Studied at Philadelphia Museum College of Art, 1956-59, Boston Museum School of the Arts, 1959-60, and Konstfackskolan (Swedish State Art School), Stockholm, 1960-61. *Politics:* None. *Religion:* "Unorthodox."

ADDRESSES: Home—Brick Hill Rd., Lyme, NH 03768.

CAREER: Artist and illustrator. Art director, *Cricket* Magazine, LaSalle, IL, 1972-79.

AWARDS, HONORS: Boston Globe-Horn Book honor for illustration, 1968, for *All in Free but Janey,* and 1978, for *On to Widecombe Fair;* Spring Book Festival Award, *Bookworld,* 1969, for *A Walk Out of the World,* and 1971, for *A Room Made of Windows; The Pumpkin Giant* was selected one of American Institute of Graphic Arts "Children's Books," 1970; Outstanding Books of the Year, *New York Times,* 1971, for *A Room Made of Windows;* Canadian Library Association award, 1973, for *The Marrow of the World; Boston Globe-Horn Book* award for illustration, 1973, for *King Stork;* Children's Book Showcase, Children's Book Council, 1975, for *Greedy Mariani and Other Folktales of the Antilles,* and 1976, for *Magic in the Mist; Boston Globe-Horn Book* honor for nonfiction, 1976, for *Will You Sign Here, John Hancock?;* Jewish Welfare Board National Jewish Book Award, 1982, for *The Night Journey;* Canadian Library Association award, 1983, for *The Marrow of the World;* Golden Kite Award for Illustration and Parents' Choice Award for Illustration, both 1983, and Caldecott Honor Book designation, American Library Association (ALA), 1984, all for *Little Red Riding Hood;* Best Illustrated Books of the Year, *New York Times,* 1984, and Randolph Caldecott Medal, ALA, 1985, both for *Saint George and the Dragon: A Golden Legend Adapted from Edmund Spenser's Faerie Queen;* Dorothy Canfield Fisher Award, 1987, for *A Castle in the Attic;* Caldecott Honor Book designation, ALA, 1990, for *Hershel and the Hanukkah Goblins;* Picture-Illustration honor, Golden Kite, 1988, for *Canterbury Tales,* and 1992, for *The Fortune-Tellers;* Best Illustrated Books, *New York Times,* 1992, and *Boston Globe-Horn Book* illustration honor, 1993, both for *Canterbury Tales;* Children's Literature Festival Award, Keene State College (New Hampshire), 1991, for body of work; Drexel Citation, School of Library and Information Science of Drexel University and the Free Library of Philadelphia, 1993, for body of work.

WRITINGS:

SELF-ILLUSTRATED

How Six Found Christmas, Little, Brown (Boston), 1969.
(Reteller) *The Sleeping Beauty, from the Brothers Grimm,* Little, Brown, 1977.
A Little Alphabet, Little, Brown, 1980.
Self-Portrait: Trina Schart Hyman, Addison-Wesley (Reading, MA), 1981.
(Reteller) Jakob Grimm and Wilhelm Grimm, *Little Red Riding Hood,* Holiday House (New York City), 1983.

The Enchanted Forest, Putnam (New York City), 1984.

ILLUSTRATOR

Hertha Von Gebhardt, *Toffe och den lilla bilen* (title means "Toffe and the Little Car"), Raben & Sjoegren, 1961.
Carl Memling, *Riddles, Riddles, from A to Z,* Western, 1963.
Melanie Bellah, *Bow Wow! Meow!,* Western, 1963.
Sandol S. Warburg, *Curl Up Small,* Houghton (Boston), 1964.
Eileen O'Faolain, *Children of the Salmon,* Little, Brown, 1965.
Ruth Sawyer, *Joy to the World: Christmas Legends,* Little, Brown, 1966.
Joyce Varney, *The Magic Maker,* Bobbs-Merrill (New York City), 1966.
Virginia Haviland, reteller, *Favourite Fairy Tales Told in Czechoslovakia,* Little, Brown, 1966.
Edna Butler Trickey, *Billy Finds Out,* United Church Press, 1966.
E. B. Trickey, *Billy Celebrates,* United Church Press, 1966.
Jacob D. Townsend, *The Five Trials of the Pansy Bed,* Houghton, 1967.
Elizabeth Johnson, *Stuck with Luck,* Little, Brown, 1967.
Josephine Poole, *Moon Eyes,* Little, Brown, 1967.
John T. Moore, *Cinnamon Seed,* Houghton, 1967.
Paul Tripp, *The Little Red Flower,* Doubleday (New York City), 1968.
Eve Merriam, reteller, *Epaminondas,* Follett, 1968, published as *That Noodle-Head Epaminondas,* Scholastic (New York City), 1972.
Varney, *The Half-Time Gypsy,* Bobbs-Merrill, 1968.
Johnson, *All in Free but Janey,* Little, Brown, 1968.
Norah Smaridge, *I Do My Best,* Western, 1968.
Betty M. Owen and Mary MacEwen, editors, *Wreath of Carols,* Scholastic, 1968.
Tom McGowen, *Dragon Stew,* Follett, 1969.
Susan Meyers, *The Cabin on the Fjord,* Doubleday, 1969.
Peter Hunter Blair, *The Coming of Pout,* Little, Brown, 1969.
Clyde R. Bulla, *The Moon Singer,* Crowell (New York City), 1969.
Ruth Nichols, *A Walk Out of the World,* Harcourt (San Diego), 1969.
Claudia Paley, *Benjamin the True,* Little, Brown, 1969.
Tripp, *The Vi-Daylin Book of Minnie the Mump,* Ross Laboratories, 1970.

Donald J. Sobol, *Greta the Strong,* Follett, 1970.

Blanche Luria Serwer, reteller, *Let's Steal the Moon: Jewish Tales, Ancient and Recent,* Little, Brown, 1970.

Mollie Hunter, *The Walking Stones: A Story of Suspense,* Harper (New York City), 1970.

McGowen, *Sir Machinery,* Follett, 1970.

Phyllis Krasilovsky, *The Shy Little Girl,* Houghton, 1970.

The Pumpkin Giant, retold by Ellin Greene, Lothrop (New York City), 1970.

Wylly Folk St. John, *The Ghost Next Door,* Harper, 1971.

Osmond Molarsky, *The Bigger They Come,* Walck, 1971.

Molarsky, *Take It or Leave It,* Walck, 1971.

Carolyn Meyer, *The Bread Book: All about Bread and How to Make It,* Harcourt, 1971.

Johnson, *Break a Magic Circle,* Little, Brown, 1971.

Greene, reteller, *Princess Rosetta and the Popcorn Man* (from *The Pot of Gold* by Mary E. Wilkins), Lothrop, 1971.

Eleanor Cameron, *A Room Made of Windows,* Little, Brown, 1971.

Eleanor Clymer, *How I Went Shopping and What I Got,* Holt (New York City), 1972.

Dori White, *Sarah and Katie,* Harper, 1972.

Nichols, *The Marrow of the World,* Atheneum (New York City), 1972.

Eva Moore, *The Fairy Tale Life of Hans Christian Andersen,* Scholastic, 1972.

Jan Wahl, *Magic Heart,* Seabury (New York City), 1972.

Krasilovsky, *The Popular Girls Club,* Simon & Schuster (New York City), 1972.

Paula Hendrich, *Who Says So?,* Lothrop, 1972.

Myra C. Livingston, editor, *Listen, Children, Listen: An Anthology of Poems for the Very Young,* Harcourt, 1972.

Carol Ryrie Brink, *The Bad Times of Irma Baumlein,* Macmillan (New York City), 1972.

Howard Pyle, *King Stork* (story first published in Pyle's collection, *The Wonder Clock*), Little, Brown, 1973.

Hans Christian Andersen, *The Ugly Duckling and Two Other Stories,* edited by Lillian Moore, Scholastic, 1973.

Phyllis La Farge, *Joanna Runs Away,* Holt, 1973.

Greene, compiler, *Clever Cooks: A Concoction of Stories, Recipes and Riddles,* Lothrop, 1973.

Brink, *Caddie Woodlawn,* revised edition, Macmillan, 1973.

Elizabeth Coatsworth, *The Wanderers,* Four Winds (Bristol, FL), 1973.

Eleanor G. Vance, *The Everything Book,* Western, 1974.

Doris Gates, *Two Queens of Heaven: Aphrodite and Demeter,* Viking (New York City), 1974.

Dorothy S. Carter, editor, *Greedy Mariani and Other Folktales of the Antilles,* Atheneum, 1974.

Charles Causley, *Figgie Hobbin* (poetry), Walker, 1974.

Charlotte Herman, *You've Come a Long Way, Sybil McIntosh: A Book of Manners and Grooming for Girls,* J. Phillip O'Hara (Merrick, NY), 1974.

J. Grimm and W. Grimm, *Snow White,* translated from the German by Paul Heins, Little, Brown, 1974.

Jean Fritz, *Why Don't You Get a Horse, Sam Adams?,* Coward, 1974.

Tobi Tobias, *The Quitting Deal,* Viking, 1975.

Margaret Kimmel, *Magic in the Mist,* Viking, 1975.

Jane Curry, *The Watchers,* Atheneum, 1975.

Louise Moeri, *Star Mother's Youngest Child,* Houghton, 1975.

Fritz, *Will You Sign Here, John Hancock?,* Coward, 1976.

Daisy Wallace, editor, *Witch Poems,* Holiday House (New York City), 1976.

Bill Sleator, *Among the Dolls,* Dutton (New York City), 1976.

Tobias, *Jane, Wishing,* Viking, 1977.

Spiridon Vangheli, *Meet Guguze,* Addison-Wesley (Reading, MA), 1977.

Norma Farber, *Six Impossible Things before Breakfast,* Addison-Wesley, 1977.

Betsy Hearne, *South Star,* Atheneum, 1977.

Patricia Gauch, *On to Widecombe Fair,* Putnam, 1978.

Hearne, *Home,* Atheneum, 1979.

Farber, *How Does It Feel to Be Old?,* Dutton, 1979.

Pamela Stearns, *The Mechanical Doll,* Houghton, 1979.

Barbara S. Hazen, *Tight Times,* Viking, 1979.

Wallace, editor, *Fairy Poems,* Holiday House, 1980.

J. M. Barrie, *Peter Pan,* Scribner (New York City), 1980.

Elizabeth G. Jones, editor, *Ranger Rick's Holiday Book,* National Wildlife (Vienna, VA), 1980.

Kathryn Lasky, *The Night Journey,* Warne (New York City), 1981.

Fritz, *The Man Who Loved Books,* Putnam, 1981.

J. Grimm and W. Grimm, *Rapunzel,* retold by Barbara Rogasky, Holiday House, 1982.

Margaret Mary Kimmel and Elizabeth Segel, *For Reading Out Loud! A Guide to Sharing Books with Children,* Delacorte (New York City), 1983.

Mary Calhoun, *Big Sixteen,* Morrow (New York City), 1983.

Astrid Lindgren, *Ronia, the Robber's Daughter,* Viking, 1983.

Charles Dickens, *A Christmas Carol: In Prose, Being a Ghost Story of Christmas,* Holiday House, 1983.

Myra Cohn Livingston, *Christmas Poems,* Holiday House, 1984.

(With Hilary Knight and others) Pamela Espeland and Marilyn Waniek, *The Cat Walked through the Casserole: And Other Poems for Children,* Carolrhoda (Minneapolis, MN), 1984.

Margaret Hodges, *Saint George and the Dragon: A Golden Legend Adapted from Edmund Spenser's Faerie Queen,* Little, Brown, 1984.

Elizabeth Winthrop, *The Castle in the Attic,* Holiday House, 1985.

Dylan Thomas, *A Child's Christmas in Wales,* Holiday House, 1985.

J. Grimm and W. Grimm, *The Water of Life,* retold by Rogasky, Holiday House, 1986.

Vivian Vande Velde, *A Hidden Magic,* Crown (New York City), 1986, Harcourt, 1997.

Livingston, compiler, *Cat Poems,* Holiday House, 1987.

Mark Twain, *A Connecticut Yankee in King Arthur's Court,* Morrow, 1988.

Geoffrey Chaucer, *Canterbury Tales,* adapted by Barbara Cohen, Lothrop, 1988.

(With Marcia Brown and others) Beatrice Schenk de Regniers, compiler, *Sing a Song of Popcorn,* Scholastic, 1988.

Swan Lake, retold by Margot Fonteyn, Harcourt, 1989.

Eric Kimmel, *Hershel and the Hanukkah Goblins,* Holiday House, 1989.

Hodges, *The Kitchen Knight: A Tale of King Arthur,* Holiday House, 1990.

Rogasky, compiler and editor, *Winter Poems,* Scholastic, 1991.

Lloyd Alexander, *The Fortune-Tellers,* Dutton, 1992.

Marion Dane Bauer, *Ghost Eye,* Scholastic, 1992.

Eric A. Kimmel, reteller, *Iron John,* Holiday House, 1994.

Kimmel, reteller, *The Adventures of Hershel of Ostropol,* Holiday House, 1995.

Rogasky, *The Golem: A Version,* Holiday House, 1996.

Hodges, adapter, *Comus,* Holiday House, 1996.

Angela Shelf Medearis, *Haunts: Five Hair-Raising Tales,* Holiday House, 1996.

Pyle, *Bearskin,* Morrow, 1997.

Katrin Tchana, reteller, *The Serpent Slayer and Other Stories of Strong Women,* Little, Brown, 1997.

Kathleen Abel, *A Smile So Big,* Harcourt, 1998.

All Kinds of Signs, Western, 1965.

Contributor of illustrations to textbooks and reference works; contributor to *Cricket* magazine.

ADAPTATIONS: Dragon Stew was adapted as a filmstrip with record, BFA Educational Media, 1975; *Tight Times* was filmed as a "Reading Rainbow" special, PBS-TV, 1983; *Little Red Riding Hood* was adapted as a filmstrip with cassette, Listening Library, 1984.

SIDELIGHTS: A highly regarded illustrator of scores of books for young people, Trina Schart Hyman is best known for her work with folklore and fairy tales. Praised by *Children's Books and Their Creators* contributor Christine C. Behr as "the gifted creator of many of the most beautiful princesses, gallant knights, gruesome monsters, and frightful hags ever to grace the pages of a picture book," Hyman has provided pictures for such classic stories as the works of the Brothers Grimm, J. M. Barrie's *Peter Pan,* Charles Dickens's *A Christmas Carol,* and Mark Twain's *A Connecticut Yankee in King Arthur's Court.* In addition, Hyman has teamed with many of the most celebrated of contemporary children's authors to produce a body of work that has garnered her a host of honors, among them the coveted Caldecott Medal. "The focus of my illustrations—largely because of the kinds of stories I choose to illustrate—is almost always on human beings," Hyman asserted in comments for *Children's Books and Their Creators.* "People—and this includes monsters and other fantastic creatures—are endlessly fascinating to me as subject matter. Facial expressions, body language, gestures of both action and repose can express a wealth of information. . . . The story within the story can nearly always be found in my illustrations."

While Hyman and her husband were living in Sweden, she got her first illustrating job. It took her nearly five months to read the manuscript, which was written in Swedish. She recalled that it "took nearly as long . . . to translate it as it did to draw the forty-six black and white illustrations." In 1963, one of Hyman's friends got a job as art director for adult books at Little, Brown Publishing. As a favor, she offered Hyman an illustrating job. Helen Jones, the children's book editor, saw Hyman's work and gave her another book to do. Jones later became Hyman's mentor. "I loved and respected her with all my heart," Hyman remembered. "She gave me courage and knocked some good sense into me at the same time."

In 1972, Hyman became art director for *Cricket* magazine, where she made valuable contacts with a large group of writers and illustrators. Over the years, Hyman has illustrated a wide variety of texts, from fairy tales to poetry collections. She has received special critical attention for her adaptations of *Snow White* and its successor, *Sleeping Beauty.* In both books, Hyman aimed for a pictorial narrative, where all the characters (even the minor ones) came alive. Hugh Crago, writing in the *Dictionary of Literary Biography,* claimed that "in this series of rich, somber paintings, where careful and often significant background detail never overwhelms the drama of foreground events, the longing, devotion, hatred, suspicion, and fear . . . are given full reign as never before in a version for young viewers."

Hyman's characteristic blending of realism, fantasy, and humor and her expressive, romanticized depictions of the human form have been cited by many commentators in reviews of her works. Praising Hyman's "masterful" pictures for Lloyd Alexander's *The Fortune-Tellers,* *School Library Journal* contributor Linda Boyles noted: "Expressive figures are dynamically placed against a West African landscape, in colors so rich and clear that they invite readers to touch the fabrics and breathe the air." Ellen Fader of *Horn Book* similarly praised the "visual feast" awaiting readers of the work. Reviewing Eric Kimmel's adaptation of *Iron John* by the Brothers Grimm, Carolyn Phelan of *Booklist* paid tribute to Hyman's "sensitivity to the expressiveness of the human form." Phelan added that "the characters reveal their hearts and minds in the illustrations as clearly as in the text."

Comus, Margaret Hodges's adaptation of John Milton's *Masque at Ludlow Castle,* features illustrations by Hyman that have been praised for effectively capturing the mood of the seventeenth-century tale. According to a *Publishers Weekly* reviewer, Hyman's illustrations greatly enhance the text "by cleverly suggesting a stage with curtain-opening imps, also furnishing a deeply gloomy and haunted wood, a horrifically comic mob of monsters and the bright dawn of a happy ending." Janice Del Negro, writing in *Booklist,* highlighted once again the artist's particular strength, asserting that "the faces of the characters

are beautifully rendered: Hyman's villains are truly evil, and her forces of good glow."

"One of the nicest things about being an artist is the ability to see things a little differently, a little more carefully, perhaps a little more imaginatively, than most other people do," Hyman noted in her Caldecott Medal acceptance speech. "To be able to see the possibilities in things; to see the magic in them, to see what it is that makes that thing inherently itself. And then, sometimes, to go beyond the surface of the thing and see what it is that the thing wishes to become: the cities that live in clouds, the landscapes that become human bodies, the human face that becomes an animal, the tree that becomes a woman."

BIOGRAPHICAL/CRITICAL SOURCES:

BOOKS

Dictionary of Literary Biography, Volume 61: American Writers for Children since 1960—Poets, Illustrators, and Nonfiction Authors, Gale (Detroit), 1987, pp. 108-115.
Hyman, Trina Schart, *Self-Portrait: Trina Schart Hyman,* Addison-Wesley (Reading, MA), 1981.
Kingman, Lee, compiler, *Illustrators of Children's Books: 1957-1966,* Horn Book (Boston), 1968.
Silvey, Anita, editor, *Children's Books and Their Creators,* Houghton (Boston), 1995, pp. 337-39.

PERIODICALS

Booklist, July, 1992, p. 1938; September 15, 1994, p. 134; November 1, 1994, p. 498; March 1, 1996, p. 1182; October 1, 1996, p. 335.
Horn Book, July-August, 1985, pp. 410-425; September-October, 1992, pp. 570-71.
New York Times Book Review, December 17, 1995, p. 28; November 10, 1996, p. 44.
Publishers Weekly, October 31, 1994, p. 63; February 19, 1996, p. 215.
School Library Journal, September, 1992, p. 196; October, 1994, p. 114; December, 1994, pp. 97-98; March, 1996, p. 196; October, 1996, p. 126.

*   *   *

JACOBS, Leah
  See GELLIS, Roberta L(eah Jacobs)

JACQUELINE
    See **CARPENTIER (Y VALMONT), Alejo**

* * *

JENNINGS, Dean
    See **FRAZEE, Steve (Charles)**

* * *

JILES, Paulette 1943-

PERSONAL: Born April 4, 1943 in Salem, MO; immigrated to Canada, 1969. *Education:* University of Missouri, B.A. (Spanish literature), 1969.

ADDRESSES: Agent—Liz Darhansoff Literary Agency, 1220 Park Avenue, New York, NY 10128.

CAREER: Writer. Canadian Broadcasting Corp. (CBC-Radio), Toronto, freelance reporter, 1968-69; journalism consultant to Native Canadian communication groups in Arctic region, 1973-83; David Thompson University, Nelson, British Columbia, instructor, 1983-84; Phillips Academy, Andover, MA, writer-in-residence, 1987-88; appeared in documentary film *Rose's House,* 1976.

AWARDS, HONORS: President's Gold Medal, 1973; Pat Lowther Memorial award, 1984; Gerald Lampert award, 1974; Governor General's Award, 1985, for *Celestial Navigation*; A.C.T.R.A. award, 1989, for *Money and Blankets.*

WRITINGS:

POETRY

Waterloo Express, Anansi (Toronto), 1973.
Celestial Navigations, McClelland & Stewart (Toronto), 1984.
The Jesse James Poems, Polestar Press (Winlaw, British Columbia), 1988.
Blackwater, Knopf (New York City), 1988.
Song to the Rising Sun, Polestar Press, 1989.
Flying Lessons: Selected Poems, Oxford University Press (Toronto), 1995.

NOVELS

Sitting in the Club Car Drinking Rum and Karma-Kola: A Manual of Etiquette for Ladies Crossing Canada by Train (novella), Polestar Press, 1986.
The Late Great Human Road Show, Talonbooks (Vancouver), 1986.
Cousins, Knopf, 1991.

OTHER

Rose's House (screenplay), Canadian National Film Board, 1976.
North Spirit: Travels among the Cree and Ojibway Nations and Their Star Maps, Doubleday Canada (Toronto), as *North Spirit: Sojourns among the Cree and Ojibway,* Hungry Mind (St. Paul, MN), 1995.

Also author of radio plays *My Mother's Quilt,* 1987, and *Money and Blankets,* 1988. Work represented in anthologies, including *Canada First,* edited by P. Anson, Anansi, 1970, and *Mindscapes.* Contributor of short stories to *Saturday Night.*

SIDELIGHTS: Novelist and poet Paulette Jiles has become well known in her adopted country of Canada for what *New York Times Book Review* contributor George Garrett calls "a realized sense of place—places really. . . . a real world with sharp corners and edges and with real people with muscles and bones, minds and spirits, hopes and memories, characters who cast shadows." Among her works are the novel *Cousins* and the poetry collections *Blackwater* and *Celestial Navigation,* the latter winning Canada's prestigious Governor General's award in 1985.

Jiles's first volume of poetry, 1973's *Waterloo Express,* met with an enthusiastic reception. Dennis Lee commented in *Saturday Night* that "the author is often presented in folk outline: she laments a string of busted love affairs, hits the road again and again to forget, and can talk as sardonic and lowdown as any blues momma. Yet the TNT and agony she drags around come crackling out in images of manic brilliance, controlled by a frequently superb ear." Linda Rogers of *Canadian Literature* was similarly impressed with Jiles' use of language. Her "images have a life of their own," Rogers explained, and "in visual terms, the poems are like the paintings of Marc Chagall. Gorgeous disconnected figures float by. . . . All the paraphernalia of life's circus is assembled in a giant mobile moving in the wind."

It was over a decade before Jiles' second book, *Celestial Navigation,* was published. Containing twenty-one poems from *Waterloo Express,* the volume also includes many newer poems, comprising a "collection that derives its dynamic energy from Jiles's skill with language," according to *Books in Canada* reviewer Judith Fitzgerald. "Whether she focuses on interpersonal relationships or interplanetary movements, all things flourish where she turns her eyes," the critic maintains. *Celestial Navigation,* which also includes several long, narrative prose poems, uses storytelling to create what *Canadian Poetry* essayist Susan J. Schenk calls "a distinctively female, profoundly personal response to experience. . . . The voice talking . . . is for Jiles a means of both displacing personal experience, locating it in the experiences of others, and revealing intensely personal thoughts and emotions."

Jiles' 1988 verse collection, *Blackwater,* was Jiles' first volume to be published in the United States, where she was born and raised. The collection incorporates her *Jesse James Poems,* a montage of poetry and contemporary newspaper articles, photographs, and other artifacts related to the outlaw gang that Garrett terms "a major achievement" through Jiles' ability to colorfully recreate, "with an eccentric linking of narrative points of view . . . the rowdy, bloody adventures and misadventures of the James boys." *Blackwater* also contains several short prose works, as well as Jiles' 1986 comic novella, *A Manual of Etiquette for Ladies Crossing Canada by Train,* which was published in Canada under the title *Sitting in the Club Car Drinking Rum and Karma-Kola.* A parody of the 1940s detective novels of Raymond Chandler and Dashiel Hammett, *A Manual of Etiquette* follows its heroine as she avoids the payment of $50,000 in overdue bills by fleeing across country.

Song to the Rising Sun contains both poetry and several of Jiles' radio scripts. The collection focuses on the poet's recollections of her youth, growing up in Missouri's Ozark Mountain region around a number of colorful—and talkative—friends, neighbors, and relatives. "The poet's voice sounds everywhere with a strong incantatory beat and a marked use of repetition," according to *Contemporary Women Poets* contributor Patience Wheatley. More recent works include *Flying Lessons: Selected Poems,* a 1995 collection that incorporates some poems from *Song to the Rising Sun* along with more recent work, and a novel, *Cousins,* published in 1991. Jiles has also published *North Spirit: Sojourns among the Cree and*

Ojibway, a 1995 nonfiction work that recounts her experiences while living among Canada's northern tribes in the 1970s and 1980s.

BIOGRAPHICAL/CRITICAL SOURCES:

BOOKS

Contemporary Literary Criticism, Volume 13, Gale (Detroit), 1980.
Contemporary Women Poets, St. James Press (Detroit), 1997.

PERIODICALS

Books in Canada, October, 1984, pp. 27-28; January/February, 1987, p. 15.
Canadian Forum, August, 1974; August/September, 1987, pp. 48-49.
Canadian Literature, summer, 1974; spring, 1988, pp. 209-11.
Canadian Poetry, spring/summer, 1987, pp. 67-79.
New York Times Book Review, October 23, 1988, p. 22.
Quill & Quire, December, 1986, p. 38.
Saturday Night, December, 1973; December, 1977.*

*   *   *

JOHNSON, Carol
   See BOLT, Carol

*   *   *

JORDAN, June 1936-
   (June Meyer)

PERSONAL: Born July 9, 1936, in Harlem, NY; daughter of Granville Ivanhoe (a postal clerk) and Mildred Maude (Fisher) Jordan (a nurse); married Michael Meyer, 1955 (divorced, 1966); children: Christopher David. *Education:* Attended Barnard College, 1953-55 and 1956-57, and University of Chicago, 1955-56. *Politics:* "Politics of survival and change." *Religion:* "Humanitarian."

ADDRESSES: Office—Department of Afro-American Studies, University of California, 3335 Dwinelle Hall, Berkeley, CA 94720. *Agent*—Victoria Sanders,

241 Avenue of the Americas, Suite 11H, New York, NY 10014.

CAREER: Poet, novelist, essayist, and writer of children's books. Assistant to producer for motion picture *The Cool World,* New York City, 1963-64; Mobilization for Youth, Inc., New York City, associate research writer in technical housing department, 1965-66; City College of the City University of New York, New York City, instructor in English and literature, 1966-68; Connecticut College, New London, teacher of English and director of Search for Education, Elevation, and Knowledge (SEEK Program), 1967-69; Sarah Lawrence College, Bronxville, NY, instructor in literature, 1969-74; City College of the City University of New York, assistant professor of English, 1975-76; State University of New York at Stony Brook, professor of English, 1982-89, director, Poetry Center and Creative Writing Program, 1986-89; University of California, Berkeley, professor of Afro-American studies and women's studies, 1989-93, professor of African-American studies, 1994—, founder and director of Poetry for the People, 1991—. Visiting poet-in-residence at MacAlester College, 1980; writer-in-residence at City College of the City University of New York; playwright-in-residence, New Dramatists, New York City, 1987-88, poet-in-residence, 1988. Visiting lecturer in English and Afro-American studies, Yale University, 1974-75; chancellor's distinguished lecturer, University of California, Berkeley, 1986; visiting professor, Department of Afro-American Studies, University of Wisconsin, Madison, summer 1988; poet-in-residence, Walt Whitman Birthplace Association, 1988. Has given poetry readings in schools and colleges around the country and at the Guggenheim Museum. Founder and co-director, Voice of the Children, Inc.; co-founder, Afro-Americans against the Famine, 1973—. Member of board of directors, Teachers and Writers Collaborative, Inc., 1978—, and Center for Constitutional Rights, 1984—; member of board of governors, New York Foundation for the Arts, 1986—.

MEMBER: American Writers Congress (member of executive board), PEN American Center (member of executive board), Poets and Writers, Inc. (director).

AWARDS, HONORS: Rockefeller grant for creative writing, 1969-70; Prix de Rome in Environmental Design, 1970-71; Nancy Bloch Award, 1971, for *The Voice of the Children; New York Times* selection as one of the year's outstanding young adult novels, 1971, and nomination for National Book Award, 1971, for *His Own Where—*; New York Council of the Humanities award, 1977; Creative Artists Public Service Program poetry grant, 1978; Yaddo fellowship, 1979; National Endowment for the Arts fellowship, 1982; achievement award for international reporting from National Association of Black Journalists, 1984; New York Foundation for the Arts fellow in poetry, 1985; MacDowell Colony fellowship, 1987; Nora Astorga Leadership award, 1989; PEN West Freedom to Write Award, 1991; Ground Breakers-Dream Makers Award, The Women's Foundation (San Francisco, CA), 1994; Lila Wallace Writers Award, *Reader's Digest,* 1995; The Critics Award and The Herald Angel Award, Edinburgh Arts Festival, 1995, for *I Was Looking at the Ceiling and Then I Saw the Sky;* President's Certificate of Service and Contribution to the Arts, Harvard University, 1997; Student's Choice Louise Patterson African American Award, University of California, Berkeley, 1998, for most outstanding African American faculty.

WRITINGS:

POETRY

Some Changes, Dutton (New York City), 1971.

New Days: Poems of Exile and Return, Emerson Hall (New York City), 1973.

Things That I Do in the Dark: Selected Poetry, Random House (New York City), 1977, revised, Beacon Press (Boston), 1981.

Okay Now, Simon & Schuster (New York City), 1977.

Passion: New Poems, 1977-1980, Beacon Press, 1980.

Living Room: New Poems, 1980-84, Thunder's Mouth Press (New York City), 1985.

High Tide—Marea Alta, Curbstone (Willimantic, CT), 1987.

Naming Our Destiny: New and Selected Poems, Thunder's Mouth Press, 1989.

Lyrical Campaigns: Selected Poems, Virago, 1989.

The Haruko: Love Poetry of June Jordan, Serpent's Tail (New York City), 1994.

Kissing God Goodbye: New Poems, Scribners (New York City), 1997.

FOR CHILDREN

Who Look at Me?, Crowell (New York City), 1969.

His Own Where— (young adult novel), Crowell, 1971.

Dry Victories, Holt (New York City), 1972.

Fannie Lou Hamer (biography), Crowell, 1972.

New Life: New Room, Crowell, 1975.

Kimako's Story, illustrated by Kay Burford, Houghton (Boston), 1981.

PLAYS

In the Spirit of Sojourner Truth, produced in New York City at the Public Theatre, May, 1979.

For the Arrow that Flies by Day (staged reading), produced in New York City at the Shakespeare Festival, April, 1981.

I Was Looking at the Ceiling and Then I Saw the Sky (opera libretto), music by John Adams, Scribners, 1995.

Composer of lyrics and libretto, *Bang Bang Ueber Alles,* 1985.

OTHER

(Editor) *Soulscript: Afro-American Poetry,* Doubleday (Garden City, NY), 1970.

(Editor, with Terri Bush) *The Voice of the Children* (reader), Holt, 1970.

Civil Wars: Selected Essays, 1963-1980 (essays, articles, and lectures), Beacon Press, 1981, revised edition with a new introductory essay, Scribner, 1996.

Bobo Goetz a Gun, Curbstone Press, 1985.

On Call: New Political Essays, 1981-1985, South End Press (Boston), 1985.

Moving towards Home: Political Essays, Virago (London), 1989.

Technical Difficulties: African-American Notes on the State of the Union, Pantheon (New York City), 1994.

(Editor with Lauren Muller) *June Jordan's Poetry for the People: A Revolutionary Blueprint,* Routledge (New York City), 1995.

Affirmative Acts: New Political Essays, Doubleday, 1998.

Portrait of a Poet as a Little Black Girl (memoir), Doubleday, in press.

Regular columnist to the *Progressive,* 1989-97. Also contributor to *Double Stitch: Black Women Write about Mothers and Daughters,* edited by Patricia Bell-Scott, HarperPerennial, 1992. Contributor of stories and poems, prior to 1969 under name June Meyer, to various periodicals, including *Esquire, Nation, Evergreen, Partisan Review, Black World, Black Creation, Essence, Village Voice, New York*

Times, and *New York Times Magazine.* Contributing editor to the *San Francisco Bay Guardian,* 1992-94.

SIDELIGHTS: June Jordan is an accomplished poet, novelist, playwright, and essayist. Called one of the most versatile and prolific late twentieth-century African American writers by *Contemporary Women Poets* contributor Saundra Towns, Jordan's written works, taken as a whole, "chart the artistic concerns of a poet who successfully maintains a sense of spiritual wholeness and the vision of a shared humanity," while frequently confronting and addressing a less-than-appealing reality.

Jordan grew up in Brooklyn, New York, where she was the only black student at Midwood High School. She then attended the Northfield School for Girls in Massachusetts, where her interest in writing was encouraged, although her constant exposure to white male poets undermined her confidence in her own abilities. Jordan's family also presented difficulties, since her father beat her regularly and her mother was complicit in the violence. In 1953 Jordan entered Barnard College, where she met Michael Meyer, a white student; the two were married in 1955. Jordan's *Civil Wars* offers a vivid glimpse of the author's problematic relationship with her husband and the problem of public intolerance of interracial marriages. Jordan and Meyer divorced in 1966, and Jordan took full responsibility for supporting their son, Christopher, who was born in 1958. During the early- to mid-1960s, Jordan worked as a research associate and writer for the Technical Housing Department of Mobilization for Youth in New York City. Then, in the fall of 1967, she began a teaching career at City College of New York, the first in a series of positions that led to her appointment as a tenured professor at the State University of New York at Stony Brook. Her first book, *Who Look at Me?,* was published in 1969.

A collection of essays published in periodicals between 1964 to 1980, 1981's *Civil Wars* is an important source of biographical information on Jordan, as it serves as a record of her development as a writer and addresses each of the author's main concerns: feminism, the black experience, children, and education, including her personal experience as a mother. The book is regarded as an autobiographical testament to Jordan's commitment to the black community. Toni Cade Bambara comments in a *Ms.* review of Jordan's *Civil Wars* that Jordan has written a "chilling but profoundly hopeful vision of living in the USA. Jordan's vibrant spirit manifests itself throughout this collection of articles, letters, journal entries, and essays. What is fundamental to that spirit is caring, commitment, a deep-rooted belief in the sanctity of life. . . . 'We are not powerless,' she reminds us. 'We are indispensable despite all atrocities of state and corporate power to the contrary.'" And as Patricia Jones points out in the *Village Voice:* "Whether speaking on the lives of children, or the victory in Nicaragua, or the development of her poetry, or the consequences of racism in film Jordan brings her faithfulness to bear; faith in her ability to make change. . . . You respect June Jordan's quest and her faith. She is a knowing woman."

Later essay collections by Jordan have included *On Call: New Political Essays, 1981-1985,* wherein the author turns to nonfiction to discuss a variety of international and domestic political subjects ranging from U.S. policy concerning Nicaragua to Israeli foreign policy in relation to South Africa. "What emerges, for Jordan," comments Dorothy Abbott in *Women's Review of Books* "is an affirmation of her faith in the possibility of a truly democratic society." In another essay collection, *Technical Difficulties: African-American Notes on the State of the Union,* Jordan articulates her progressive views on racial, sexual, and feminist issues. Joseph Jordan in *Antioch Review* remarks that the collection "aspires to capture Jordan's passion for justice, which is a constant and conscious part of her language."

As with *Civil Wars* and other of her essays, critics have also detected autobiographical elements in Jordan's young adult novel *His Own Where—,* which portrays Buddy and Angela, two teenaged lovers searching for a secure future in Harlem. Critics have emphasized the novel's concern with the physical, economic, and cultural structures of an urban environment, along with the significance of Black English as a valid and highly expressive means of communication. "The language [used in *His Own Where—*] moves freely, violating syntax to get to deeper levels of meaning," comments Sarah Webster Fabio in the *New York Times Book Review.* "At first the speech patterns might seem to create a barrier for the reader, but not for long."

Jordan writes for a variety of audiences, from young children to adults, and in genres that include poetry, fiction, essays, and plays. In all of her writings, she powerfully and skillfully explores the black experience in America. "The reader coming to June Jordan's work for the first time can be overwhelmed by the breadth and diversity of her concern, and by

the wide variety of literary forms in which she expresses them," writes Peter B. Erickson in the *Dictionary of Literary Biography.* "But the unifying element in all her activities is her fervent dedication to the survival of black people."

Chad Walsh writes of Jordan in the *Washington Post Book World:* "Exploring and expressing black consciousness, [Jordan] speaks to everyman, for in his heart of hearts every man is at times an outsider in whatever society he inhabits." Susan Mernit writes in *Library Journal* that "Jordan is a poet for many people, speaking in a voice they cannot fail to understand about things they will want to know." In a *Publishers Weekly* interview with Stella Dong, Jordan explains: "I write for as many different people as I can, acknowledging that in any problem situation you have at least two viewpoints to be reached. I'm also interested in telling the truth as I know it, and in telling people, 'Here's something new that I've just found out about.' I want to share discoveries because other people might never know the thing, and also to get feedback. That's critical."

Reviewers have generally praised Jordan for uniquely and effectively uniting in poetic form the personal, everyday struggle and the political oppression of blacks. For example, Mernit believes that Jordan "elucidates those moments when personal life and political struggle, two discrete elements, suddenly entwine. . . . [Jordan] produces intelligent, warm poetry that is exciting as literature." Honor Moore comments in *Ms.* that Jordan "writes ragalike pieces of word-music that serve her politics, both personal and public." And Peter B. Erickson remarks: "Given her total commitment to writing about a life beset on all sides, Jordan is forced to address the whole of experience in all its facets and can afford to settle for nothing less. Jordan accepts, rises to, the challenge."

Jordan sees poetry as a valid and useful vehicle to express her personal and political ideas while at the same time masterfully creating art. Among her verse collections have been *New Days: Poems of Exile and Return, Things That I Do in the Dark,* and *Naming Our Destiny: New and Selected Poems.* While combining humane concerns with somewhat strident political views, Honor Moore states in *Ms.* that Jordan "never sacrifices poetry for politics. In fact, her craft, the patterning of sound, rhythm, and image, make her art inseparable from political statement, form inseparable from content. [She] uses images contrapuntally to interweave disparate emotions."

Jordan's 1989 work, *Naming Our Destiny,* represents the range of the poet's political concerns and poetic techniques over three decades, while 1994's *The Haruko: Love Poems* presents poems concerned with the theme of love and the emotions of joy and loss that accompany it. Praising the strength and effectiveness of the voice manifested in the poems of the latter collection, Margaret Randall of the *American Book Review* comments: "She says exactly what she means to say, and says it so powerfully that the reader (or fortunate listener) hears each phrase: isolated, made specific, an essential part of the whole."

Jordan is also noted for the intense passion with which she writes about the struggles against racism. Susan McHenry remarks in *Nation* that "Jordan's characteristic stance is combative. She is exhilarated by a good fight, by taking on her antagonists against the odds. . . . However, Jordan [succeeds] in effectively uniting her impulse to fight with her need and 'I' desire to love." Jascha Kessler comments in *Poetry* that Jordan's literary "expression is developed out of, or through, a fine irony that manages to control her bitterness, even to dominate her rage against the intolerable, so that she can laugh and cry, be melancholic and scornful and so on, presenting always the familiar faces of human personality, integral personality." Kessler adds that Jordan "adapts her poems to the occasions that they are properly, using different voices, and levels of thought and diction that are humanly germane and not disembodied rages or vengeful shadows; thus she can create her world, that is, people it for us, for she has the singer's sense of the dramatic and projects herself into a poem to express its special subject, its individuality. Of course it's always her voice, because she has the skill to use it so variously: but the imagination it needs to run through all her changes is her talent." Faith and optimism are perhaps the two common threads that weave through all of Jordan's work, whether it be prose or poetry, for juvenile readers or for a more mature audience.

BIOGRAPHICAL/CRITICAL SOURCES:

BOOKS

Alexander, Amy, *Fifty Black Women Who Changed America,* Birch Lane Press, 1998.
Authors and Artists for Young Adults, Volume 2, Gale (Detroit), 1989.
Children's Literature Review, Volume 10, Gale, 1986.

Contemporary Literary Criticism, Gale, Volume 5, 1976, Volume 11, 1979, Volume 23, 1983.
Contemporary Women Poets, St. James Press (Detroit), 1997.
Dictionary of Literary Biography, Volume 38: *Afro-American Writers after 1955: Dramatists and Prose Writers,* Gale, 1985.
Twentieth-Century Children's Writers, third edition, St. James Press, 1989.

PERIODICALS

American Book Review, March, 1995, p. 1545; May, 1995, p. 26.
Antioch Review, summer, 1993, p. 459.
Belles Lettres, spring, 1995, p. 68.
Black Scholar, January-February, 1981.
Booklist, October 1, 1992; May 1, 1995, p. 1545.
Callaloo, Volume 9, number 1, 1986.
Choice, October, 1985.
Christian Science Monitor, November 11, 1971.
Chronicle of Higher Education, February 23, 1996, p. 87.
Essence, April, 1981; July, 1995, p. 56.
Kirkus Reviews, September 15, 1971; September 15, 1992, p. 1167.
Library Journal, December 1, 1980; November 1, 1989, p. 92; September 15, 1992; January, 1994; May 15, 1995, p. 73.
Los Angeles Times, September 3, 1986; January 21, 1993.
Ms., April, 1975; April, 1981.
Nation, April 11, 1981; January 29, 1990; July 5, 1993.
Negro Digest, February, 1970.
New Statesman, June 5, 1987, p. 38.
New York, July 31, 1995, p. 46.
New Yorker, May 29, 1995, p. 94.
New York Times, April 25, 1969.
New York Times Book Review, November 7, 1971, pp. 6, 34; April 20, 1972, pp. 13-14; October 9, 1977; August 9, 1981.
Partisan Review, 1969.
Poetry, February, 1973.
Progressive, May, 1994.
Publishers Weekly, February 21, 1972; May 1, 1981; January 17, 1994, p. 428.
Quarterly Black Review of Books, summer, 1994, p. 42.
San Francisco Examiner, December 7, 1977.
Saturday Review, April 17, 1971.
Village Voice, May 27-June 2, 1981.
Virginia Quarterly Review, winter, 1978.
Washington Post, October 13, 1977.

Washington Post Book World, July 4, 1971.
Wilson Library Bulletin, October, 1978.
Women's Review of Books, June, 1986, p. 6.

K

KAEL, Pauline 1919-

PERSONAL: Born June 19, 1919, in Petaluma, CA; daughter of Isaac Paul (a farmer) and Judith (Friedman) Kael; children: Gina James. *Education:* Attended University of California, Berkeley, 1936-40.

CAREER: Freelance writer, 1953—; Berkeley Cinema Guild and Studio, Berkeley, CA, manager, 1955-60; film critic in New York City for *Life* magazine, 1965, *McCall's* magazine, 1965-66, *New Republic,* 1966-67, and the *New Yorker,* 1968-79, 1980-91. Executive consultant on film projects for Paramount Pictures Corp., 1979-80. Lecturer on films to colleges and universities.

MEMBER: National Society of Film Critics (chair, 1970), New York Film Critics, Phi Beta Kappa.

AWARDS, HONORS: Guggenheim fellowship, 1964; George Polk Memorial Award for Criticism, 1970; National Institute of Arts and Letters Award, 1970; National Book Award, 1974, for *Deeper into Movies;* Front Page Awards, Newswomen's Club of New York, 1974 and 1983. L.L.D. from Georgetown University, 1972; D.Litt. from Columbia College (Chicago), 1972, Smith College, 1973, and Allegheny College, 1979; D.H.L. from Kalamazoo College, 1973, Reed College, 1975, and Haverford College, 1975.

WRITINGS:

I Lost It at the Movies, Little, Brown (Boston), 1965, reprinted as *I Lost It at the Movies: Film Writings, 1954-1965,* M. Boyars (New York City), 1994.

Kiss Kiss Bang Bang, Little, Brown, 1968.

Going Steady, Little, Brown, 1970, reprinted as *Going Steady: Film Writings, 1968-1969,* M. Boyars, 1994.

(With others) *The Citizen Kane Book: Raising Kane* (includes the shooting script by Herman J. Mankiewicz and Orson Wells, notes on the shooting script prepared by Gary Carey, and RKO cutting continuity from Orson Wells production of the film *Citizen Kane*), Little, Brown, 1971, reprinted *as The Citizen Kane Book,* Paladin (St. Albans), 1974, Limelight Editions (New York City), 1984.

(Contributor with Norman Mailer of critical essays) Bernardo Bertolucci, *Bernardo Bertolucci's Last Tango in Paris; The Screenplay,* Delacorte (New York City), 1973.

Deeper into Movies, Little, Brown, 1973.

Reeling, Little, Brown, 1976.

When the Lights Go Down, Holt (New York City), 1980.

5001 Nights at the Movies: A Guide from A to Z, Holt, 1982, revised edition, 1991.

Taking It All In, Holt, 1984.

State of the Art, Dutton (New York City), 1985.

Pauline Kael on Jonathan Demme: A Selection of Reviews Accompanying the Retrospective Jonathan Demme, an American Director: Presented by Walker Art Center, Minneapolis, 5-27 August 1988, Walker Art Center (Minneapolis), 1988.

Hooked, Dutton, 1989.

Movie Love: Complete Reviews 1988-1991, Dutton, 1991.

For Keeps, Dutton, 1994.

Contributor to *Partisan Review, Vogue, McCall's, Atlantic, Film Quarterly, Massachusetts Review, Sight and Sound, Modern Writing, New Republic, Second Coming, Harper's, Movie Goer, New York Times Book Review,* and other publications.

SIDELIGHTS: Until her retirement from the *New Yorker* in 1991, Pauline Kael was perhaps one of the country's most widely-read and respected film critics. Her books, beginning with 1965's *I Lost It at the Movies,* are primarily collections of her magazine columns which chronicle nearly thirty years of film history. Kael's entertaining writing style—sometimes scathing, frequently witty, always insightful—blends her enthusiasm for movies with a keen understanding of their impact on society. Anatole Broyard proclaimed in the *New York Times* that "reading a Pauline Kael review gives you a pretty good idea of the current state of our morality, our esthetics, [and] our politics. . . . Very few pictures are worth 1,000 of her words."

Although an avid moviegoer while she was growing up, Kael happened upon her career as a movie critic by chance. As a philosophy major at the University of California at Berkeley, she developed a passion for literature and the arts. After college, she tried her hand at writing plays, film scripts, and literary essays while working at various jobs in order to support herself and her daughter. She did regular broadcasts of movie reviews on KPFA listener-supported radio in Berkeley, and for several years she managed a movie theater in Berkeley. Her first published essay in San Francisco's *City Lights* was about movies, and she wrote for various journals in New York and London. In 1965, after publishing her first collection of essays, she moved to New York City and began writing reviews for magazines, including *Life* and *McCall's.*

When she landed a permanent position at the *New Yorker,* Kael was almost fifty: "There's no question in my mind that I could have done more as a writer had I gotten an earlier start, when I had all that crazy energy," she told Polly Frost and Ray Sawhill of *Interview* magazine. Fortunately for Kael, the *New Yorker* did not limit the length of her reviews, enabling her to thoroughly explore minute aspects of a film and digress as much as she pleased—a luxury critics at most other magazines were denied. Kael credits her background in the arts in making her an effective critic; she once told *CA* that her knowledge of literature, painting, music, and opera "all seemed to fuse" when she began writing about the movies.

At the time Kael entered the film criticism scene, it was a venue for erudite theorists who were deprecia-

tive of American movies and often preferred foreign directors like Federico Fellini and Michelangelo Antonioni, whose films were more popular among the literati than with the general public. Kael's regard for mainstream Hollywood movies stood in sharp contrast to theorists like Andrew Sarris, who promoted the *auteur* theory of filmmaking in which certain directors were revered as visionaries, but actors, writers, and cinematographers received little attention. Michael Olmert of *Book World* summarized Kael's style by saying that "her temperament and prose have led her to be the first to deflate cant, wherever she finds it—whether in the movies or in the film theorists themselves." "She anointed herself the liberator of American film criticism, freeing it from snooty academics who treated movies as weightless *divertissements,*" conferred Neal Gabler in *New York Times Book Review.* "Pauline Kael taught us how to stop worrying and love movies," Gabler concluded.

The publication of *I Lost It at the Movies* in 1965 propelled Kael into the spotlight as one of the country's premier film critics. Richard Schickel's review of her first book in the *New York Times Book Review* stated that she is "the sanest, saltiest, most resourceful and least attitudinizing movie critic currently in practice in the United States." Subsequent Kael publications continued to garner similar praise. Eliot Freemont-Smith of the *New York Times* noted that besides having "the niftiest title of the year," *Kiss Kiss Bang Bang* reveals Kael to be "the most interesting and invigorating film critic around and one of the most valuable social and cultural commentators that we have." *Deeper into Movies,* which won a National Book Award in 1974, further displays Kael's penchant for sexually-tinged titles and provides insightful opinions on the films of the early 1970s, an era many critics believe was one of the most creative periods in cinema history; it included such films as *M*A*S*H* and *The Last Picture Show.* Irving Howe in the *New York Times Book Review* quoted Kael's essay "Trash, Art, and the Movies" from *Going Steady* in explaining how she views movies within society: "Movies are, or could be, 'a great art form . . . [but] movies alone are not enough: a steady diet of mass culture is a form of deprivation [and] to study mass culture in the same terms as traditional art forms is to accept the shallowness of mass culture.'"

"Raising Kane," one of Kael's longest and best-known essays (it occupied the better portion of two issues of the *New Yorker* when originally published), is an enduring contribution to the field of film criticism. Published along with the shooting script of *Citizen Kane* as *The Citizen Kane Book,* the essay is hailed as a revisionist view of what many believe is the best movie ever made. Kael redistributes part of the credit for *Citizen Kane* from its director, Orson Welles, to its screenwriter, Herman Mankiewicz, and cinematographer, Gregg Toland. Though Kael does not deny Welles' genius, she presents compelling evidence of Mankiewicz's and Toland's previously overlooked contributions. For example, even though Welles received the Oscar for best screenplay, it was Mankiewicz who wrote the screenplay based on actual incidents from his relationship with newspaper magnate William Randolph Hearst. Regarding the famed "Rosebud" mystery of the film, as Michael Olmert of *Book World* summarized Kael's research: "It was Mankiewicz who had lost a bike—not a sled—as a child and who never got over it." Similarly, Kael demonstrates that the film noir style of *Citizen Kane* is due in large part to Toland, whose cinematography for the 1935 film, *Mad Love* starring Peter Lorre, presents many parallels to *Kane,* including near-identical sets, lighting, make-up, and placement of figures that all foreshadow his work with Welles. In addition, Kael notes that the "screeching white cockatoo, which isn't in the script of 'Kane' but appeared out of nowhere in the movie to provide an extra 'touch,' is a regular member of Lorre's household."

More than the story of one movie, Olmert called "Raising Kane" "an incredible tapestry of 1930s film history . . . [and] a gem of research and analytical insight." While giving credit where it is due, Kael is sympathetic to Welles, admitting that "no one has ever been able to do what was expected of Welles . . . all his actual and considerable achievements looked puny compared to what his destiny was supposed to be." Nevertheless, Mordecai Richler of the *New York Times Book Review* proclaimed Kael successful in "cutting Orson Welles down to size, denying his needlessly grandiose claim to having been solely responsible for everything that went into 'Kane.'"

Through her column, Kael tracked the careers of the industry's most visible directors, often praising Robert Altman, Brian De Palma, and Steven Spielberg. Her effusive praise for Bernardo Bertolucci's *Last Tango in Paris* in *Reeling* is an example of what some critics call her hyperbole: "The most powerfully erotic movie ever made. . . . A landmark in movie history . . . Bertolucci and Brando have al-

tered the face of an art form," quoted Robert Brustein in *New York Times Book Review.* Conversely, she provided vivid epithets for those actors and films she despised: "*Rain Man* is Dustin Hoffman humping one note on a piano for two hours and eleven minutes" quoted Diane Jacobs in *New York Times Book Review,* and *Gorillas in the Mist* is "a feminist version of *King Kong*—now it's the gorillas who do the screaming," quoted Mark Horowitz in the *Washington Post Book World.* Describing Yoda, a character from *The Empire Strikes Back,* Kael says the creature "looks like a wonton and speaks like a fortune cookie," according to Gerald Mast in *New York Times Book Review.* Also inherent in Kael's writing style are her self-created definitions of adjectives, as John Podhoretz explained in *American Scholar:* "*Messy,* as she uses it, means a movie that is not carefully put together and thus may have some real life to it. . . . *Good* in the Kaelian critical vocabulary is generally used as a means of damning with faint praise." However entertaining these perceptions may be, according to Gabler in *New York Times Book Review,* "her impressionism is also her limitation."

Criticism of Kael's views often stem from her unflinching support for a cause or an idea in the face of popular opposition. Her fondness for violent films like *Dressed to Kill* and *The Godfather* was initially justified for their "kinetic energy," but Podhoretz maintained that "after a while she seemed simply to enjoy the sight of destruction, human and otherwise." Kael's praise for comedies that critic Stephen Farber deems "moronic," like *Up in Smoke* and *Stripes,* encourages "the trend toward infantile moviemaking," Farber asserted in *New York Times Book Review.* Robert Sklar in the *New York Times Book Review* argued that Kael lacks "a clear sense of dialogue . . . between reviewer and reader, an admission that more than one response to a film is possible." Kael's frequent scorn for successful movies like *Dances with Wolves* prompted David Ansen in *Newsweek* to comment that "her tastes in the '80s were more often than not out of synch with the public."

Kael resigned briefly from her *New Yorker* position in the late 1970s to become an executive consultant on film projects for Paramount Pictures. Kael quickly decided that "it wasn't for me. In order to be effective, I would have had to spend too many years of my life there," she told *Village Voice* writer Arthur Bell. Discouraged by the politics of moviemaking, she returned to the *New Yorker* in

1980. Kael once told *CA* about the situation: "I read many very fine scripts out there that are not going to be filmed. . . . [A script] may go through five or six drafts until everything that was good in it is gone. A lot of the best work gets rewritten, and by the time it arrives on the screen it's a mess."

In the introduction to *Deeper into Movies,* Kael explains how she approaches a film: "I try to use my initial responses (which I think are probably my deepest and most honest ones) to explore not only what a movie means to me, but what it may mean to others: to get at the many ways in which movies, by affecting us on sensual and primitive levels, are a supremely pleasurable—and dangerous—art form." She told Polly Frost and Ray Sawhill of *Interview:* "I rarely try to think anything out ahead of time. I want it, paragraph by paragraph through the whole structure, to surprise me." Throughout the years, Kael has noticed the changing role films play in society. "In the '60s and '70s movies played an adversarial role in the culture. . . . Movies became sort of the enemy. Now they are definitely not the enemy. I wish they were," she told Frost and Sawhill. Kael says of people viewing films on VCRs, "there's no way of discussing a film when it's not affecting the whole culture at the same time. . . . and with VCRs movies don't stay in your mind the same way."

Movie Love contains Kael's *New Yorker* reviews from October 1988 until her retirement in February 1991. Charles Solomon declared in the *Los Angeles Times Book Review* that the book "provides welcome reading at a time when film criticism seems to have been reduced to 'A 10!' and 'Two thumbs up.'" Anthony Quinn noted in *New Statesman & Society:* "Certainly there is a difference between this collection and her writing of 20 years ago, but it's not a difference in quality: the Kael style perhaps became less academic, more relaxed, but it remained inimitably her own." He observed that the reviews reflect Kael's candidness, preference for some directors, and her "remarkable knack for identifying exactly what is wrong with certain actors." *Washington Post Book World*'s Mark Horowitz estimated that "more than half the reviews are cold-blooded demotion jobs of . . . overpraised hits." He added, "She is impervious to sentimentality and is the master of the unforgettable tag." He disclosed: "Even now, after nearly 40 years of moviegoing for hire, and despite all the disappointments, Kael remains a true enthusiast or, as she prefers, a movie lover, often unrequited, frequently betrayed, but faithful to the end."

In a review of *For Keeps,* Pat Dowell claimed in the *Washington Post Book World:* "Kael's writing has the power to change a reader's mind about a movie, and she is one of the few critics who produce works that will become just as much favorites as the movies they cover." *For Keeps* collects about a fifth of her writings from ten previously published books. David Ehrenstein commented in the *Los Angeles Times Book Review:* "There's a constant refrain running through *For Keeps;* a hymn of praise directed at films that 'don't take themselves too seriously.'" He lauded Kael as "a critic whose misfires are as fascinating as her bull's-eyes." In *Time* Richard Corliss summed up the book thus: "It's movie analysis with a serrated edge; film criticism as stand-up bawdry; intellectual improvisation that soars into the highest form of word jazz."

When Kael "first mounted her assault on the highbrows and the purists and discovered the art in Hollywood trash, it was the act of a cultural provocateur," wrote Ansen. Janet Maslin of the *New York Times,* in response to the announcement of Kael's retirement in 1991, quoted a fellow film critic's assessment of Kael's career: "A whole generation of film critics has had to respond to her either by imitating her or resisting her." Frost and Sawhill provided one explanation for why Kael's twice monthly *New Yorker* columns were the highlight of the magazine for many subscribers and why her books continue to be popular—she is so persuasive "that when you don't agree with her you can go around for days arguing with her in your head."

BIOGRAPHICAL/CRITICAL SOURCES:

BOOKS

Brantley, Will, editor, *Conversations with Pauline Kael,* University Press of Mississippi (Jackson), 1996.
Kael, Pauline, *Deeper into Movies,* Little, Brown, 1973.
Kael, *The Citizen Kane Book,* Little, Brown, 1971.
Slattery, William J., Claire Dorton, and Rosemary Enright, *The Kael Index: A Guide to a Movie Critic's Work, 1945-1991,* Libraries Unlimited (Englewood, CO), 1993.

PERIODICALS

American Film, November, 1991.
Artforum, September, 1993.
Atlantic Monthly, December, 1994.
Belles Lettres, summer, 1991; summer, 1994.

Book World, October 31, 1971; March 12, 1995.
Cristian Science Monitor, February 1, 1985.
Interview, April, 1989.
Los Angeles Times Book Review, September 22, 1991; October 9, 1994; October 13, 1996.
New Statesman & Society, July 6, 1990; February 14, 1992.
Newsweek, March 18, 1991.
New Yorker, December 19, 1994.
New York Review of Books, March 23, 1995.
New York Times, May 21, 1968; February 22, 1973; March 13, 1991.
New York Times Book Review, March 14, 1965; October 31, 1971; February 18, 1973; April 4, 1976; November 14, 1982; April 15, 1984; December 16, 1984; December 8, 1985; March 19, 1989; October 13, 1991.
Observer, December 1, 1985; December 7, 1986; June 7, 1987; January 31, 1988; July 1, 1990; October 10, 1993; January 30, 1994; February 6, 1994.
Publishers Weekly, September 27, 1985; September 9, 1988; August 22, 1994.
Spectator, April 4, 1987.
Theatre Crafts, August, 1985.
Time, November 7, 1994.
Times Educational Supplement, February 28, 1986; July 31, 1987; July 13, 1990; November 22, 1996.
Times Literary Supplement, July 24, 1987; September 7, 1990; November 15, 1991; April 29, 1994; January 17, 1997.
Tribune Books (Chicago), April 28, 1991; September 15, 1991.
Village Voice, August 8, 1989; June 9, 1980.
Washington Post Book World, January 26, 1992; March 12, 1995.
Yale Review, April, 1993.*

*   *   *

KANE, Julia
  See ROBINS, Denise (Naomi)

*   *   *

KESSLER, Julia Braun 1926-
  (Julia Barrett, a joint pseudonym)

PERSONAL: Born April 22, 1926, in New York, NY; daughter of Max (a contractor) and Hermina Klein (a homemaker) Braun; married Jascha Kessler (a writer), July 30, 1950; children: Margot Kessler Fullerton, Adam, William. *Ethnicity:* "Hungarian-Jewish." *Education:* University of Chicago, Ph.B., 1947; Columbia University, M.A., 1948. *Politics:* "Independent." *Religion:* Jewish. *Avocational interests:* History, music, art.

ADDRESSES: Home and office—218 16th St., Santa Monica, CA 90402; fax 310-393-0697. *E-mail*—jbraun@ucla.edu. *Agent*—Evan Marshall, 6 Tristam Pl., 22 South Park St., Pine Brook, NJ 07058.

CAREER: Encyclopedia Americana, New York City, research editor, 1949-50; University of Michigan, Ann Arbor, editor at Institute for Social Research, 1950-54; *Seventeen,* New York City, features editor, 1954-57; University of California, Los Angeles, adjunct associate professor of humanities, 1967-69; University of Southern California, Los Angeles, editorial consultant at Ethel Percy Andrus Gerontology Center, 1971-74; fulltime freelance writer, editor, and ghost writer, 1974—.

MEMBER: Authors Guild, PEN International.

WRITINGS:

Getting Even with Getting Old (nonfiction; a study of aging in America), Nelson Hall (Chicago, IL), 1980.
(With Gabrielle Donnelly, under joint pseudonym Julia Barrett) *Presumption: An Entertainment* (novel; a sequel to Jane Austen's *Pride and Prejudice,*) M. Evans (New York City), 1993, paperback edition, University of Chicago Press (Chicago, IL), 1995.
The Third Sister (novel; a continuation of Jane Austen's *Sense and Sensibility,*) Donald I. Fine/Penguin (New York City), 1996, paperback edition, MIRA, 1998.

Contributor of more than 250 magazine articles and newspaper features, including *East-West Network Periodicals, Family Circle, Geo, Human Behavior, Los Angeles Daily News, Los Angeles Herald Examiner, Los Angeles Times, Modern Maturity, San Francisco Chronicle,* and *Travel and Leisure.*

WORK IN PROGRESS: Novel, "tentatively entitled *Charlotte,* that is contracted and scheduled to appear in late 1998, with Penguin/Putnam." It is "yet another attempt (under the pseudonym, Julia Barrett) to answer one of those fascinating and recurring fictional questions left unanswered by Jane Austen in her short writing career."

SIDELIGHTS: Julia Braun Kessler told *CA:* "Mine has been an extensive career in writing, editing, and teaching. After completing college, I was lucky enough to get a first job as a research editor with the *Encyclopedia Americana,* where I was trained in every aspect of research. In that position, I was fortunate, in that it enabled me to learn to use every specialized library in New York City, an education in itself. In Ann Arbor at the Institute for Social Research, I wrote articles and edited monographs and books for a staff of social scientists. At *Seventeen* I did pieces on young musicians, teachers, nurses, and scientists. I was in charge of all cultural materials for that publication for several years.

"More recently, I taught humanities at the University of California, Los Angeles, and then served with the University of Southern California's Ethel Percy Andrus Gerontology Center. It was the latter experience that resulted in my work *Getting Even with Getting Old,* a book aimed at bringing forward in lay terms all the progress that specialists have made in regard to the aging process.

"Regarding the book *Presumption,* I would like to mention that this sequel was a lifetime notion of mine. The idea came from Jane Austen's own conclusion to her *Pride and Prejudice,* where she literally teases us with predictions of future lives for her characters. Still, I felt that, as an American, I could hardly undertake such an effort alone. Luckily I was introduced to Gabrielle Donnelly, a British writer now living in Los Angeles, and since she felt just as strongly in favor of the idea as I did, we decided to try it together.

"There is no question that, to those of us who love Austen's work, the fact that she wrote so few books is punishment. Our thought was not to try in any way to reproduce her great work, but only to see if some of those enchanting types of hers could be brought forth again so that we might find out what became of them and, by borrowing some of the lady's magic, work toward our own version of an Austen novel. The best thing about the reactions to *Presumption* has been that many have assured us that the book does manage to bring back some of the pleasures that readers remembered from the original."

KIRWAN, Laurence Patrick 1907-

PERSONAL: Born May 13, 1907, in London, England; son of Patrick and Mabel (Norton) Kirwan; children: (first marriage) Jennifer Preston; (step-children) Clare Monck Stevens, Nicholas Monck. *Education:* Merton College, Oxford, B. Litt., 1935; research fellow, Edinburgh University, 1937-39. *Politics:* Liberal. *Religion:* Roman Catholic. *Avocational interests:* Lawn tennis, travel.

ADDRESSES: Home—Flat 5, 152 Kings Rd., London, S.W. 7, England. *Office*—Royal Geographical Society, London, S.W. 7, England.

CAREER: Archaeologist. Former assistant director of the Egyptian Antiquities Department's archaeological survey of Nubia; former field director of Oxford University excavations in Sudan; Royal Geographic Society, London, director, and editor of *Geographical Journal. Military service:* British Army, Infantry, 1939-46; became lieutenant colonel; Territorial Army Reserve, 1946-57.

MEMBER: British Institute of History and Archaeology in East Africa (former president), Royal Geographical Society (fellow), Athenaeum Club (London).

AWARDS, HONORS: Campanion, Order of St. Michael and St. George; Knight Cross, Order of St. Olav, Norway; Territorial Decoration; knighted.

WRITINGS:

Excavations and Survey from Wadi Sebua to Adindan, Government Press (Cairo), 1935.
(With Walter B. Emery) *The Royal Tombs at Ballana and Qustul,* Government Press, 1938.
The Oxford University Excavations at Firka, Oxford University Press (Oxford), 1939.
The White Road: A Survey of Polar Exploration, Hollis & Carter (London), 1959, published as *A History of Polar Exploration,* Norton (New York City), 1961.
Rome Beyond the Southern Egyptian Frontier, Oxford University Press, 1977.

Also author of pamphlets, including *Oxford University Excavations in Nubia, 1934-35,* Egypt Exploration Society (London), 1935; *Recent Archaeology in British Africa,* Journal of the Royal African Society, 1938; *The Birth of Christian Nubia: Some Archaeological Problems,* Rivista degli studi orientali, 1987;

(with Mark Norman) *The Taharqa Shrine and Its Conservation,* Ashmolean Museum (Oxford), 1989; and *Some Roman Mummy Tickets,* Annales du Service des Antiquites de l'Egypte. Contributor of articles to *Ashmolean, Journal of the Royal African Society* and other newspapers and magazines. Editor, *Geographical Journal.*

SIDELIGHTS: A respected British Egyptologist, Laurence Patrick Kirwan has nonetheless won critical acclaim on both sides of the Atlantic for his book *A History of Polar Exploration.* Beginning with the earliest explorations of the Arctic region by the Vikings, Kirwan's study traces the history of both Arctic and Antarctic polar exploration through the 1950s. The book is, according to R. C. Cowen in the *Christian Science Monitor,* "authoritative history and an exciting adventure story."

A History of Polar Exploration was the first history of its kind to be published. Critics were especially impressed by Kirwan's ability to combine coverage of many different polar expeditions into a single narrative. Morris Zaslow in the *Canadian History Review* notes: "The histories of two regions a world apart have been quite successfully blended into a single account." D. B. Bagg in the *Springfield Republican* writes that the book is "a single coherent account with due attention to the adventurous and dramatic aspects as well as to the motives involved." "Modest in size, quiet in tone and admirable in its narrative sweep," writes Jeanette Mirsky in the *New York Herald Tribune Book Review,* "*A History of Polar Exploration* gives the grand design of motives and myths, methods and men involved both in the twenty-two centuries of Arctic venturing and in the short two-hundred-year-old Antarctic activity, and manages to relate these separate efforts."

BIOGRAPHICAL/CRITICAL SOURCES:

PERIODICALS

Booklist, June 1, 1960.
Canadian History Review, December, 1960.
Christian Science Monitor, March 17, 1960, p. 11.
Library Journal, April 1, 1960.
New Statesman, January 2, 1960.
New York Herald Tribune Book Review, July 10, 1960, p. 7.
Springfield Republican, April 17, 1960, p. D4.
Times Literary Supplement, January 15, 1960, p. 35.*

KIZER, Carolyn (Ashley) 1925-

PERSONAL: Born December 10, 1925, in Spokane, WA; daughter of Benjamin Hamilton (a lawyer and planner) and Mabel (a biologist and professor; maiden name, Ashley) Kizer; married Charles Stimson Bullitt, January 16, 1948 (divorced, 1954); married John Marshall Woodbridge (an architect and planner), April 11, 1975; children: (first marriage) Ashley Ann, Scott, Jill Hamilton. *Education:* Sarah Lawrence College, B.A., 1945; graduate study at Columbia University, 1945-46, and University of Washington, 1946-47; studied poetry with Theodore Roethke, University of Washington, Seattle, 1953-54. *Politics:* Independent. *Religion:* Episcopalian.

ADDRESSES: Home 19772 8th St. East, Sonoma, CA 95476.

CAREER: Poet, educator, and critic. *Poetry Northwest,* Seattle, founder and editor, 1959-65; National Endowment for the Arts, Washington, DC, first director of literary programs, 1966-70; University of North Carolina at Chapel Hill, poet-in-residence, 1970-74; Ohio University, Athens, McGuffey Lecturer and poet-in-residence, 1975; Iowa Writer's Workshop, University of Iowa, Iowa City, professor of poetry, 1976; University of Maryland, College Park, professor, 1976-77; Stanford University, Stanford, CA, professor of poetry, spring, 1986; Princeton University, Princeton, NJ, senior fellow in the humanities, fall, 1986; Fannie Hurst Professor of Literature at Washington University, St. Louis, MO, 1971; lecturer at Barnard College, spring, 1972; acting director of graduate writing program at Columbia University, 1972; visiting professor of writing, University of Arizona, Tucson, 1989, 1990, and University of California—Davis, 1991; Coal Royalty Chair, University of Alabama, 1995. Participant in International Poetry Festivals, London, 1960, 1970, Yugoslavia, 1969, 1970, Pakistan, 1969, Rotterdam, Netherlands, 1970, Knokke-le-Zut, Belgium, 1970, Bordeaux, 1992, Dublin, 1993, and Glasgow, 1994. Volunteer worker for American Friends Service Committee, 1960; specialist in literature for U.S. State Department in Pakistan, 1964-65. Member of founding board of directors of Seattle Community Psychiatric Clinic.

MEMBER: International PEN, Amnesty International, Association of Literary Magazines of America (founding member), Poetry Society of America, Poets and Writers, Academy of American Poets (chancellor), American Civil Liberties Union.

AWARDS, HONORS: Masefield Prize, Poetry Society of America, 1983; Washington State Governors Award, and San Francisco Arts Commission award, both 1984, both for *Mermaids in the Basement: Poems for Women*; award in literature, American Academy and Institute of Arts and Letters, 1985; Pulitzer Prize in poetry, 1985, for *Yin: New Poems*; Frost Medal, Poetry Society of America, Theodore Roethke Memorial Foundation Poetry Award, and President's Medal, Eastern Washington University, all 1988; D.Litt, Whitman College, 1986, St. Andrew's College, 1989, Mills College, 1990, and Washington State University, 1991.

WRITINGS:

POETRY

Poems, Portland Art Museum (Portland, OR), 1959.
The Ungrateful Garden, Indiana University Press (Bloomington), 1961.
Knock upon Silence, Doubleday (New York City), 1965.
Midnight Was My Cry: New and Selected Poems, Doubleday, 1971.
Mermaids in the Basement: Poems for Women (also see below), Copper Canyon Press (Port Townsend, WA), 1984.
Yin: New Poems (contains selections from *Mermaids in the Basement*), Boa Editions (Brockport, NY), 1984.
The Nearness of You: Poems for Men, Copper Canyon Press, 1986.
Harping On: Poems 1985-1995, Copper Canyon Press, 1996.

OTHER

(Editor, with Elaine Dallman and Barbara Gelpi) *Woman Poet—The West,* Women-in-Literature (Reno, NV), 1980.
(Editor) Robertson Peterson, *Leaving Taos,* Harper, 1981.
(Editor) Muriel Weston, *Primitive Places,* Owl Creek Press, 1987.
(Translator) *Carrying Over* (poetry), Copper Canyon Press, 1988.
(Editor) *The Essential John Clare,* Ecco Press (Hopewell, NJ), 1992.
Proses: Essays on Poems & Poets, Copper Canyon Press, 1993.
(Editor) *One Hundred Great Poems by Women,* Ecco Press, 1995.

Picking and Choosing: Essays on Prose, Eastern Washington University Press (Cheney), 1995.

Contributor to numerous anthologies, including *New Poems by American Poets,* Ballantine, 1957; *New Poets of England and America,* Meridian Publishing, 1962; *Anthology of Modern Poetry,* Hutchinson, 1963; *Erotic Poetry,* Random House, 1963; and *New Modern Poetry,* Macmillan, 1967.

Translator of *Sept Versants Sept Syllables* (title means "Seven Sides, Seven Syllables"). Also contributor to various periodicals, including *Poetry, New Yorker, Kenyon Review, Spectator, Paris Review, Shenandoah, Antaeus, Grand Street,* and *Poetry East.*

SIDELIGHTS: Although Carolyn Kizer's poetry collections are not vast in number, they bear witness to her much-praised meticulousness and versatility. Critics find that Kizer's subject matter has changed over the years, but not the caliber of her art; in 1985 her collection *Yin: New Poems*—twelve years in the making—won the Pulitzer Prize in poetry. Kizer is "a writer to treasure," maintains Elizabeth B. House in a *Dictionary of Literary Biography* essay. "She has created poetry that will endure. . . . Faced with the human inevitability of loss and destruction, Kizer, in both poetry and life, celebrates the joys of art, friendship, family, and good works. Undoubtedly, she has earned a secure niche in American letters."

"Like some people, Carolyn Kizer is many people," notes *Washington Post* reviewer Meryle Secrest. Kizer received her B.A. degree from Sarah Lawrence College in 1945 and then went on to do graduate work at both Columbia University and the University of Washington. During the mid-1950s, she studied poetry at the University of Washington under the tutelage of Theodore Roethke. Later, she co-founded the prestigious Seattle-based *Poetry Northwest,* a journal she edited from its inception in 1959 until 1965. In 1964 Kizer went to Pakistan as a U.S. State Department specialist and taught at various institutions, including the distinguished Kinnaird College for Women. Among her other activities, Kizer was the first director of literary programs for the newly created National Endowment for the Arts in 1966, a position she held until 1970. As literary director, she promoted programs to aid struggling writers and literary journals, and she worked to have poetry read aloud in inner city schools. In addition to teaching and lecturing nationwide, Kizer has translated Urdu,

Chinese, and Japanese poetry. According to Kizer, "what is so marvelous about living today is that it is possible to extend, like a flower, spreading petals in all directions," records Secrest.

House claims that, as a poet, Kizer deals equally well with subjects that have often been treated by women and those that have not. "Tensions between humans and nature, civilization and chaos," are topics no more and no less congenial to her than are love affairs, children, and women's rights." According to House, in Kizer's first two poetry collections, *The Ungrateful Garden* and *Knock upon Silence,* the poet employs grotesque imagery—"lice cozily snuggling in a captured bat's wing, carrion birds devouring the last pulp of hell-bound bodies," and other unsettling topics—but the poet is not fearful of femininity and sentimentality. Sometime in the past, Roethke composed a list of common complaints made against women poets that included such things as lack of sense of humor, narrow range of subject matter, lamenting the lot of women, and refusing to face up to existence. In *Alone with America: Essays on the Art of Poetry in the United States since 1950,* Richard Howard maintains that Kizer has first incurred and then overcome these complaints. "She does not fear—indeed she *wants*—to do all the things Roethke says women are blamed for, and indeed I think she does do them. . . . But doing them or not, being *determined* to do them makes her a different kind of poet from the one who manages to avoid the traps of his condition, and gives her a different kind of success," notes Howard.

The Ungrateful Garden, Kizer's first major collection, appeared in 1961. Devoted in large part to the examination of people's relationships to nature, it is a candid work, according to *Saturday Review* critic Robert D. Spector. Because "candor is hardly ever gentle, her shocking images are brutal," the critic continues. Kizer "abuses adult vanity by setting it alongside a child's ability to endure the removal of an eye. Pretensions to immortality are reduced to rubbish by 'Beer cans on headstones, eggshells in the [cemetery] grass.'" In the title poem and in one of her better-known pieces, "The Great Blue Heron," Kizer presents her belief that nature has no malevolence toward man, that the two simply exist side by side. In "The Great Blue Heron," according to House, "the heron is a harbinger of death, but [Kizer] never suggests that the bird is evil. As part of nature, he merely reflects the cycle of life and death that time imposes on all living creatures."

In *The Ungrateful Garden,* House also sees Kizer emphasizing the distance between humans and nature, and also the perils of modern governments quashing individual identity. Kizer demonstrates that a reprieve from the terrors of nature and government can be found in human relationships, and especially in poetry. In the poem "From an Artist's House," for example, the poet celebrates the unchanging nature of verse. On the whole, D. J. Enright of *New Statesman* feels there are "some remarkably good things in this strong-tasting collection, thick with catastrophes and fortitude."

Whereas *Poetry* critic William Dickey considers *The Ungrateful Garden* to showcase a poet "more concerned with the manner of [her poems'] expression than with the material to be expressed," *Saturday Review* contributor Richard Moore comments that Kizer's third poetry collection, *Knock upon Silence,* contains relaxed meters and simple diction: "There are no verbal fireworks, no fancy displays." As with much of Kizer's poetry, an Eastern influence is present in *Knock upon Silence,* with its calm, cool, sensitive verse. The collection consists of two long poems—"A Month in Summer" and "Pro Femina"—a section called "Chinese Imitations," and several translations of the eighth-century Chinese poet Tu Fu. "She's at the top of her form, which is to say, devastating in her observations of the human animal," writes Gene Baro in the *New York Times Book Review.* "How true, one thinks, when this poet writes about feminine sensibility or about love."

Of the two longer poems included in *Knock upon Silence,* "A Month in Summer" received mixed reviews. This diary of love gone sour, which contains both prose segments and occasional haiku, is viewed by Moore as the "weakest part of [Kizer's] book. . . . It is moving in places, witty in others; but there is also a tendency to be straggling and repetitive." In contrast, Bewley cites this piece as "the heart and triumph" of *Knock upon Silence:* "It manages to compress within a very few pages alive with self-irony and submerged humor, more than most good novelists can encompass in a volume."

The other long selection in *Knock upon Silence* "Pro Femina" is comprised of three conversational poems that discuss the role of the liberated woman in the modern world, particularly the woman writer. "Pro Femina" is a satiric piece keenly aware of the fact that women still confront obstacles related to their gender: "Keeping our heads and our pride while remaining unmarried; / And if wedded, kill guilt in its tracks when we stack up the dishes / And defect to the typewriter."

Kizer turns, in part, to different matters in her collection *Midnight Was My Cry: New and Selected Poems,* which contains several previously published poems and sixteen new ones. Though she remains dedicated to meter and Eastern restraint—"the poet's mind continually judges, restrains, makes passion control itself," writes Eric Mottram in *Parnassus*—her newer poems express an interest in the social and political problems of the contemporary world, especially those of the 1960s. These poems center on anti-segregation sit-ins, the Vietnam conflict, and the assassination of Senator Robert Kennedy. For *Poetry* contributor Richard Howard, Kizer has "reinforced her canon by some dozen first-rate poems, observant, solicitous, lithe."

Catching the literary world a little by surprise, Kizer published two poetry volumes in 1984, *Mermaids in the Basement: Poems for Women* and *Yin: New Poems. Mermaids in the Basement* received minor critical attention, perhaps because it contains several poems from her previous collections, including "A Month in Summer" and "Pro Femina," the latter one of her best-known poems satirizing as it does liberated women writers by mimicking the hexameter used by the ancient misogynist poet Juvenal. According to Patricia Hampl in the *New York Times Book Review,* "the craft for which . . . Kizer is known serves her well in [the poem] 'Thrall'; a remarkable compression allows her to review the entire disappointing history of her relationship with her father. . . . There is a great effort toward humor in these poems. But the tone is uneven; the humor, as well as the outrage, seems arch at times." *Yin,* in contrast, received a favorable critical reception from the outset, winning the Pulitzer Prize for poetry in 1985. "One could never say with certainty what 'a Carolyn Kizer poem' was—until now. . . . Now we know a Kizer poem is brave, witty, passionate, and not easily forgotten," proclaims *Poetry* critic Robert Phillips.

The word "yin" is Chinese for the feminine principle, and many of the poems in this award-winning collection focus on feminine perceptions and creativity. In her joint review of *Mermaids in the Basement* and *Yin,* Hampl considers the prose memoir in *Yin* titled "A Muse" to be "a real find. . . . This piece, about . . . Kizer's extraordinary mother, is not only a fascinating portrait, but a model of detachment and self-revelation." "A Muse" examines Kizer's childhood feelings about the ambitions her mother had for

her: "The poet describes a . . . mama smothering her precocious offspring with encouragement. . . . Only with the woman's death does the speaker's serious life as an artist begin," assesses Joel Conarroe in the *Washington Post Book World.* In addition, "Semele Recycled" is considered an imaginative treat with its description of a modern-day Semele symbolically torn apart at the sight of her lover and then made whole again.

Probably the most admired piece in the *Yin* collection is the poem "Fanny." Written in Roman hexameter, this 224-line poem is the proposed diary of Robert Louis Stevenson's wife, Frances (Fanny), as she nurses her husband during the last years of his life. Remarks Kizer in Penelope Moffet's *Los Angeles Times* review: "'Fanny' is about what happens to women who are the surrogate of gifted men. Women who look after the great writers, whether mothers, sisters, wives or daughters. What they do with their creativity, because they can't engage in open or active competition. I think 'Fanny' [is] a political poem, if you consider feminism a political issue, as I do." In addition, Conarroe claims "Fanny" is "Keatsian in the sensuousness of its imagery, the laughing of its odors and textures. Kizer gives a shattering sense of a woman's sacrifice and isolation while communicating vividly the terrible beauty of the woman's obsession with her husband's health." Whereas Suzanne Juhasz in *Library Journal* considers *Yin* a "mixed bag, or blessing," most reviewers agree with Phillips that *Yin* "is a marvelous book."

Kizer's *The Nearness of You* serves as a "companion piece" to *Mermaids in the Basement,* as it is a collection of poetry on men. According to Charles Libby in the *New York Times Book Review,* the collection "shows evidence that writing about the other sex involves different struggles than writing about one's own. Despite many local triumphs, the new collection is in many ways less striking, technically and psychologically more self-conscious [than *Mermaids in the Basement*]." In *Contemporary Women Poets,* essayist John Montague notes, with relief, that "In an era when a shrill feminism threatens to tilt the scales of past injustice, Kizer's view of the sexual universe contains polarity without hostility." Meanwhile Diane Wakoski, appraising *The Nearness of You* for the *Women's Review of Books,* finds the work somewhat uneven, but concludes that "What this book convinces me of, finally, is that Carolyn Kizer is a poet of occasion, of person and personality. When she becomes historical or formal, when she attempts either love-lyrics or story poems, she is mediocre at best. . . . But as the ambassador of goodwill in the poetry world . . . as the woman longing for a family of artists and intellectuals who will replace the one she lost in growing up and leaving her father—yes, yes, yes. Believable, strong, someone who deserves to be remembered."

Kizer's subsequent collection, *Harping On: Poems 1985-1995,* was not published until 1996. Christine Stenstrom, writing for *Library Journal,* notes of the volume that Kizer's "political poems satisfy less than those vividly recalling parents and friends in small masterpieces of verse narrative." In *Publishers Weekly,* a critic describes Kizer's voice as "distinctly irreverent," her politics "left-leaning," and noted of her poetry that "Kizer employs everything from slanted rhymes to venerable forms like the villanelle and pantoum with a chatty grace that makes the intricacy of her structures all but invisible." Commenting on the satire that wires its way throughout the poems in *Harping On, New Leader* reviewer Phoebe Pettingell maintains that while the poet comes across as a "clever, tough-minded, and erudite" harpy "exercising her slashing wit on her self as often as others," the poetry scene of the 1990s "needs her voice, whether hectoring, prophesying, seducing, or informing, to raise our consciousness with the eloquence of her subtle lyrics."

Kizer's essays and criticism have been gathered in several volumes, including 1994's *Proses: Essays on Poems and Poets.* Kate Fitzsimmons, reviewing the book for the *San Francisco Review of Books,* finds Kizer's writing to be engaging. "The joy Kizer experiences in reading other poets is infectious," Fitzsimmons exclaims. "Whether she is writing about the lives of poets or their poetry, her enthusiasm for their work is evident, nearly tactile." While Doris Lynch in *Library Journal* praises the effort, a *Publishers Weekly* reviewer is less impressed, commenting that if the book had been written by a more-obscure writer, "it would fade quickly into blessed obscurity."

Although the more pointed aspects of her verse are often couched in sarcasm and stylistic intricacy, Kizer considers herself a political poet. As she remarked to Moffet: "Because I do not feel that [it] is a steady undercurrent, just as feminism is, there are these parallel streams that I hope infuse everything that I do. And I find that stream getting more and more strong in my work. But I don't ever want to be hortatory or propagandistic." With regard to the quantity of poetic output—Kizer is not known for

being especially prolific herself—she had this to say to inexperienced poets: "I think a lot of younger poets get terrible anxiety that they'll be forgotten if they don't have a book all the time. Well, maybe they will be forgotten, but if they're any good they'll come back."

BIOGRAPHICAL/CRITICAL SOURCES:

BOOKS

Contemporary Authors Autobiography Series, Volume 5, Gale (Detroit), 1987.

Contemporary Literary Criticism, Gale, Volume 15, 1980, Volume 39, 1986.

Contemporary Women Poets, St. James Press (Detroit), 1997.

Dictionary of Literary Biography, Volume 169: *American Poets since World War II, Fifth Series,* Gale, 1996.

Howard, Richard, *Alone with America: Essays on the Art of Poetry in the United States since 1950,* Atheneum, 1969.

Kizer, Carolyn, *The Ungrateful Garden,* Indiana University Press, 1961.

Kizer, *Knock upon Silence,* Doubleday, 1965.

Malkoff, Karl, *Crowell's Handbook of Contemporary American Poetry,* Crowell, 1973.

Rigsbee, David, editor, *An Answering Music: On the Poetry of Carolyn Kizer,* Ford-Brown (Boston), 1990.

PERIODICALS

Approach, spring, 1966.

Hollins Critic, June, 1997.

Hudson Review, spring, 1972; summer, 1985, pp. 327-40.

Library Journal, July, 1984; November 1, 1993, p. 93; July, 1996, p. 120.

Los Angeles Times, January 13, 1985.

New Leader, February 254, 1997, p. 14.

New Statesman, August 31, 1962.

New York Review of Books, March 31, 1966.

New York Times Book Review, March 26, 1967; November 25, 1984; March 22, 1987, p. 23.

Parnassus, fall-winter, 1972.

Poetry, November, 1961; July, 1966; August, 1972; March, 1985; November, 1985.

Prairie Schooner, fall, 1964.

Publishers Weekly, October 18, 1993, p. 70; August 26, 1996, p. 94.

San Francisco Review of Books, October/November, 1994, p. 20.

Saturday Review, July 22, 1961; December 25, 1965.
Shenandoah, winter, 1966.
Tri-Quarterly, fall, 1966.
Village Voice, November 5, 1996.
Washington Post, February 6, 1968.
Washington Post Book World, August 5, 1984; February 1, 1987, p. 6.
Women's Review of Books, September, 1987, p. 6.
World Literature Today, summer, 1997.

* * *

KUZMA, Greg 1944-

PERSONAL: Surname is pronounced Koozma; born July 14, 1944, in Rome, NY. *Education:* Syracuse University, B.A., 1966, M.A., 1967.

ADDRESSES: Office—Department of English, University of Nebraska, Lincoln, NE 68508.

CAREER: University of Nebraska, Lincoln, assistant professor of English, 1969—; conducts poetry writing workshops.

AWARDS, HONORS: Independent Presses Editor's Recommended Book citation, 1997, for *Wind Rain and Stars and the Grass Growing.*

WRITINGS:

POETRY

Something at Last Visible, Zeitgeist, 1969.
Sitting Around, Lillabulero, 1969.
Eleven Poems, Portfolio, 1971.
The Bosporus, Hellric, 1971.
Harry's Things, Apple Magazine, 1971.
Song for Someone Going Away, Ithaca House (Ithaca, NY), 1971.
Good News: Poems, Viking (New York City), 1973, reprinted, Carnegie-Mellon University Press (Pittsburgh, PA), 1994.
A Problem of High Water, West Coast Poetry Review (Reno, NV), 1973.
The Buffalo Shoot: Poems, Basilisk, 1974.
The Obedience School, Three Rivers Press (Pittsburgh, PA), 1974.
A Day in the World, Abattoir (Omaha, NE), 1976.
Village Journal, Best Cellar (Rochester, NY), 1978.

A Horse of a Different Color, Illuminati (Los Angeles, CA), 1979.
For My Brother, Abattoir, 1981.
Everyday Life, Spoon River Poetry Press (Peoria, IL), 1983.
Of China and of Greece, Sunnyside (Lynn, MA), 1984.
Poems for the Dead, Best Cellar, 1984.
A Turning: A Sequence, Stormline Press (Urbana, IL), 1988.
Wind Rain and Stars and the Grass Growing, Orchises (Alexandria, VA), 1993.
Selected Poems, Carnegie Mellon University Press, 1996.
What Poetry Is All About, Orchises, 1997.

EDITOR

Gone Into if Not Explained: Essays on Poems by Robert Frost, Best Cellar, 1976.
Forty Nebraska Poets, Best Cellar, 1981.

OTHER

Contributor of poems to the *New Yorker, Nation, Poetry, Shenandoah, North American Review, Carleton Miscellany, Commonweal, Antioch Review, New York Quarterly,* and other magazines. Poetry-book review editor, *Prairie Schooner;* editor of *Pebble* and of Best Cellar Press pamphlet series.

SIDELIGHTS: Based at the University of Nebraska in Lincoln, Greg Kuzma has been teaching and writing poetry for more than three decades. Kuzma eschews confessional poetry for work that is frank and darkly humorous. His poems, in some cases, "represent ideal worlds, where the reader can find charm, intelligence, and sweetness; they are escapes, but civilized escapes," according to John R. Carpenter in *Poetry.* To quote Sam Hamill in *Margins,* Kuzma has found a voice that is "alert to landscape and rhythms of process, a landbound creature alive with the processes of living."

Kuzma began publishing poetry while he was in his twenties and has been producing creative works ever since. He also serves as editor of Best Cellar Press. In a *Shenandoah* review, Arthur Oberg wrote of the author: "[Kuzma] wants to engage us. He wants to witness and to bear witness to. He wants to recreate, rediscover, and rewrite. . . . Kuzma's poetry is fresh, sexual, and confident. . . . He writes a lyric that shows how much pleasure and surprise poetry can yield."

BIOGRAPHICAL/CRITICAL SOURCES:

BOOKS

Contemporary Literary Criticism, Volume 7, Gale
    (Detroit, MI), 1977, pp. 196-97.
Saunders, Mark, editor, *On Common Ground: The
    Poetry of William Kloefkorn, Ted Kooser, Greg
    Kuzma, and Don Welch,* Sandhills Press (Ord,
    NE), 1983.

PERIODICALS

Margins, March, 1975, pp. 66-69.
Poetry, March, 1971; December, 1974, pp. 169-70.
Shenandoah, winter, 1976, pp. 98-99.*

L

LANCASTER, Bruce 1896-1963

PERSONAL: Born August 22, 1896, in Worcester, MA; died June 20, 1963; son of Walter Moody and Sarah Jenkins (Hill) Lancaster; married Jessie Bancroft Payne, December 12, 1931. *Education:* Harvard University, A.B., 1919. *Politics:* Republican. *Religion:* Episcopalian.

CAREER: Businessperson in Worcester, MA, 1919-27; U.S. Department of State, foreign service officer in Kobe and Nagoya, Japan, 1927-33; Board of Governors, Society of New York Hospital, New York City, assistant secretary, 1934-38; author, mainly of historical novels, 1938-63. Trustee, Beverly Public Library, 1958-63. *Military service:* First Massachusetts Field Artillery, served on Mexican border, 1916. American Expeditionary Forces, Field Artillery, 1917-19; received five battle stars.

MEMBER: Company of Military Collectors and Historians (fellow), Authors League of America, PEN, Cambridge Historical Society, St. Botolph Club (Boston), Harvard Club (New York City).

WRITINGS:

The Wide Sleeve of Kwannon, Frederick A. Stokes, 1938, reprinted, Rivercity Press (Rivercity, MA), 1976.
Guns of Burgoyne, Frederick A. Stokes, 1939 (published in England as *Gentleman Johnny,* Heinemann [London], 1939), revised and condensed edition published as *Guns in the Forest,* Atlantic-Little, Brown (Boston, MA), 1952, reprinted as *Guns of Burgoyne,* Rivercity Press, 1975.

(With Lowell Brentano) *Bride of a Thousand Cedars,* Frederick A. Stokes, 1939.
For Us the Living, Federick A. Stokes, 1940, reprinted, Rivercity Press, 1983.
Bright to the Wanderer, Little, Brown, 1942, reprinted, Rivercity Press, 1983.
Trumpet to Arms, Atlantic-Little, Brown, 1944, reprinted, Aeonian Press (Leyden, MA), 1983.
The Scarlet Patch, Atlantic-Little, Brown, 1947.
No Bugles Tonight, Atlantic-Little, Brown, 1948.
Phantom Fortress, Atlantic-Little, Brown, 1950.
Venture in the East, Atlantic-Little, Brown, 1951.
The Secret Road, Atlantic-Little, Brown, 1952.
Blind Journey, Atlantic-Little, Brown, 1953.
From Lexington to Liberty: The Story of the American Revolution, Doubleday (Garden City, NY), 1955.
Roll, Shenandoah, Atlantic-Little, Brown, 1956.
The American Revolution (juvenile), Garden City Books (Garden City, NY), 1957.
(Author of narrative) *The American Heritage Book of the Revolution,* American Heritage Press (New York City), 1958, reprinted, 1985.
Night March, Little, Brown, 1958.
Ticonderoga: The Story of a Fort (juvenile), Houghton (Boston, MA), 1959.
The Big Knives, Little, Brown, 1964.

Contributor of articles and book reviews to *Atlantic* and *Saturday Review.* Editor, *Old-Time New England,* published by Society for the Preservation of New England Antiquities, 1951-56.

SIDELIGHTS: Bruce Lancaster was best known for his epic historical novels, most of which drew upon events in the American Revolutionary War or the American Civil War. Himself a decorated World War

I veteran, Lancaster immersed himself in the details of the prior conflicts and then crafted novels revealing specific battles or campaigns through the eyes of ordinary soldiers. "Bruce Lancaster writes well and convincingly on a foundation of solid fact," declared a *Christian Science Monitor* reviewer in 1948. "Without once descending to the lurid or the titillating, he succeeds in creating a novel completely absorbing."

Lancaster was particularly fond of the Revolutionary War period. In books such as *Guns of Burgoyne, The Secret Road,* and the posthumously-published *The Big Knives,* he freely mingled historical personages with fictional characters and authentic battle scenes with melodramatic love stories. In a *New York Times Book Review* piece about *The Secret Road,* Melville Heath characterized Lancaster as "a veteran craftsman at the top of his form . . . [who] mingles fact and fiction expertly as his breathless plot unfolds." Stephen Vincent Benet, writing in the *New York Herald Tribune Books,* likewise praised *Guns of Burgoyne* as "skillfully and movingly done. . . . Mr. Lancaster has given us a first-class story from the American past."

In his Civil War novels, Lancaster invariably takes the Union soldier as hero, although the soldier's military objectives might not always be met. In the *New York Times Book Review,* Hoffman Birney commended the author for bringing an affecting immediacy into his stories by using "ordinary" protagonists. "The reader is one of those men whom [the hero] molds from shambling recruits into blooded veterans who stood firm against shrapnel, musket-fire and bayonet," the critic stated. ". . . It is in such things that Mr. Lancaster's skill is found. 'The Scarlet Patch' is the story of many men who died and a few who lived; a tale of heroism without heroics. Both as a novel and as a re-creation of history it is a memorable achievement." Earl W. Foell concluded in the *Christian Science Monitor* that Lancaster "is an able popularizer of history . . . [who] displayed some talent for stirring fictional characters into serious historical chronicles without distorting the facts."

Lancaster's nonfiction titles included *From Lexington to Liberty: The Story of the American Revolution* and two juveniles, *The American Revolution* and *Ticonderoga: The Story of a Fort. New York Herald Tribune Book Review* correspondent Carl Carmer found *From Lexington to Liberty* "more vivid, more swift in narrative, more full of impressive detail than any [books] that come to mind. . . . Mr. Lancaster's

research has been prodigious, . . . his choice of material has been for the most part sound, . . . [and] his narrative contains well reasoned interpretations of historic events and moving anecdotes of human interest."

Lancaster once described his work pattern for *CA:* "I choose my period or setting first of all, then set about learning all that I can about it and the people who figured in it. Not until all of this is as solid as I can make it, do I begin the fictional part. . . . I have been as careful as is humanly possible to bring about a blending of fact and fiction without any distortion of fact." As soon as actual writing began, each day's work was read back to him by his wife. "This began with the first book," Lancaster explained, "and for me [it is] an essential part of the whole writing process."

BIOGRAPHICAL/CRITICAL SOURCES:

BOOKS

Contemporary Literary Criticism, Volume 36, Gale (Detroit, MI), 1986, pp. 241-46.

PERIODICALS

Best Sellers, May 15, 1964, pp. 74-75.
Christian Science Monitor, August 25, 1948, p. 18; September 12, 1956, p. 9; May 22, 1958, p. 15.
New York Herald Tribune Book Review, June 5, 1955, p. 5.
New York Herald Tribune Books, March 13, 1938, p. 4; March 26, 1939, p. 1; November 3, 1940, p. 2.
New York Herald Tribune Weekly Book Review, April 27, 1947, p. 10.
New York Times Book Review, March 26, 1939, p. 6; November 3, 1940, p. 5; April 20, 1947, p. 5; June 15, 1952, p. 5; July 3, 1955, p. 5.
Saturday Review, July 5, 1952, p. 18.
Saturday Review of Literature, August 21, 1948, pp. 11-12; March 25, 1950, p. 32.*

*   *   *

LAWRENCE, David 1888-1973

PERSONAL: Born December 25, 1888, in Philadelphia, PA; died of a heart attack, February 11, 1973, in Sarasota, FL; son of Harris (a tailor) and Dora Lawrence; married Ellanor Campbell Hayes, July 17, 1918 (died June 13, 1969); children: David, Mark, Nancy (deceased), Etienne. *Education:* Princeton University, B.A., 1910.

CAREER: Buffalo Express, Buffalo, NY, reporter, 1903-06; Associated Press correspondent at Princeton University, 1906-10, member of Washington, DC, staff, 1910-15; *New York Evening Post,* New York City, Washington correspondent, 1916-19; Consolidated Press Association, Washington, DC, president, 1919-33; *United States Daily,* Washington, DC, founder and president, 1926-33; *United States News,* Washington, DC, founder and president, 1946-48; *U.S. News and World Report,* Washington, DC, editor, 1948-73, president, 1948-59, chair of the board, 1959-73.

MEMBER: National Press Club, Metropolitan Club, Cosmos, Princeton Club, Sigma Delta Chi (fellow).

AWARDS, HONORS: Certificate of achievement from National Press Club, 1963; University of Missouri Honor Medal and induction into School of Journalism Hall of Fame, both 1965; Presidential Medal of Freedom conferred by President Richard M. Nixon, 1970; charter member, Washington Chapter, Sigman Delta Chi Hall of Fame.

WRITINGS:

The Truth about Mexico, New York Evening Post (New York City), 1917.
The True Story of Woodrow Wilson, Doran (New York City), 1924.
The Business Man and His Government, United States Daily (Washington, DC), 1929.
The Other Side of Government, Scribner (New York City), 1929.
Industry's Public Relations, American Management Association (New York City), 1930.
Beyond the New Deal, McGraw (New York City), 1934.
Stumbling Into Socialism and the Future of Our Political Parties, Appleton-Century (New York City), 1935.
Nine Honest Men, Appleton-Century, 1936.
Supreme Court or Political Puppets?, Appleton-Century, 1937.
Who Were the Eleven Million?, Appleton-Century, 1937.
Diary of a Washington Correspondent, H.C. Kinsey (New York City), 1942.

U.S. News and World Report: A Two-Way System of Communication, Newcomen Society (New York City), 1969.
The Editorials of David Lawrence, six volumes, U.S. News and World Report (Washington, DC), 1970.

Contributor of articles to numerous magazines, newspapers, and journals. Political columnist for the *Washington Star-News* and other newpapers.

SIDELIGHTS: David Lawrence was an important American journalist who is today best remembered as the founder and director of *U.S. News and World Report.* Lawrence began working for newspapers while still in high school and continued to immerse himself in the print medium literally until hours before his death, penning his last editorial shortly before suffering a fatal heart attack. A *New York Times* eulogized the Philadelphia native as "one of the nation's most highly respected and warmly regarded newspapermen, and it is as such that he would want to be remembered." Likewise, a *Washington Star-News* reporter wrote: "He was the newsman in the classic mold. His opinions were firm, but they never overrode the reporter's instinct to get to the bottom of the story. . . . One of the best things that can be said about the profession of journalism is that, very occasionally, it produces a David Lawrence."

Born in Philadelphia and raised in Buffalo, New York, Lawrence was the son of an immigrant tailor. During school vacations in his teen years he served as a cub reporter with the *Buffalo Express,* and as a college student at Princeton he "scooped" more experienced journalists by being the first to know of—and report about—Grover Cleveland's death. Also while at Princeton Lawrence became acquainted with Woodrow Wilson, and their relationship continued through Wilson's presidential campaign and on into Wilson's White House years. At that time Lawrence worked for the Associated Press as Washington correspondent, and though he and Wilson always retained cordiality for one another, their discourse was almost always kept on a professional level. Lawrence declared in his book *The True Story of Woodrow Wilson:* "In all the years of [my] acquaintance with Woodrow Wilson, no favor was sought and none given. No obligation was incurred, no political allegiance established. Most of the time it fell to [my] lot as a newspaper reporter to see behind the curtain of events." Indeed, Lawrence's objectivity led Wilson, on at least one occasion, to describe him as "a nuisance."

In 1916 Lawrence moved from the Associated Press to the staff of the *New York Evening Post,* where he refined his Capitol Hill coverage to include commentary on important national issues. Cabell Phillips was quoted in the *Dictionary of Literary Biography* on Lawrence's work: "His stint was to write the daily lead story out of Washington under his own by-line. This was not an uncommon assignment for Washington correspondents in those days. Lawrence, however, gave his stories a new twist by appending a shirttail of succinct interpretation. Not content to give simply the who, what, and where of Washington events, he gave the *why* also. He set the current happening in the larger canvas of what had gone before and what might reasonably be anticipated in the future." After leaving the *Post* in 1919, Lawrence inaugurated a wire service, the Consolidated Press Association, through which he supplied political commentary to a number of newspapers across America. He is therefore recognized as one of the nation's first syndicated columnists, and a pioneer of the political column.

The success of his Consolidated Press Association enabled Lawrence to open his own newspaper, the *United States Daily,* in 1926. He also served as a radio commentator and was one of the first journalists to have a regular broadcast, *Our Government,* on the National Broadcasting Company (NBC) network. In 1933 he decided to make his daily newspaper into a weekly, and the *United States News* was born. The publication changed to a magazine format in 1940, and its circulation—already at 85,000—increased threefold. After the Second World War Lawrence founded a corollary weekly, *World Report,* to cover international news. Within two years he consolidated the two periodicals under the title *U.S. News and World Report.*

Lawrence served as the editor of *U.S. News and World Report* from its first issue in 1948 until his death in 1973. From an initial circulation of 378,776, the magazine grew under his leadership to attract 1.94 million subscribers. In keeping with his view that the news should be delivered dispassionately and without commentary, Lawrence kept the contents of his end-page editorials to himself until they were published, and made sure they carried a caveat that they presented "the opinion of the Editor." The rest of the magazine was restricted to factual representation of events. Arthur Krock, quoted in the *Dictionary of Literary Biography,* noted that the reputation of *U.S. News and World Report* "was built on the unadorned presentation of facts on national and international affairs."

Lawrence's achievements with *U.S. News and World Report* led to many citations and honors, most significantly the 1970 Presidential Medal of Freedom, the nation's highest civilian award. The journalist continued to work through ill health and the death of his wife, completing his last editorial just hours before passing away from a heart attack at his winter home in Sarasota, Florida. *Dictionary of Literary Biography* contributor Ronald S. Marmarelli wrote: "As a reporter, columnist, publisher, and editor, David Lawrence stood at the top among his fellow journalists for more than sixty years. . . . His work throughout his career was motivated in large part by a personal fascination with public affairs and a commitment to the ideal that citizens must be provided every means possible for keeping informed about the affairs of the national and the world. His guiding belief was that there was a great need for 'enlightened public opinion, steadily and persistently' and that it was the task of journalists to provide the means for enlightenment."

BIOGRAPHICAL/CRITICAL SOURCES:

BOOKS

Allen, Robert S. and Drew Pearson, *Washington Merry-Go-Round,* Liveright (New York City), 1931.
Bulman, David, editor, *Molders of Opinion,* Bruce (Milwaukee, WI), 1945, pp. 121-31.
Clark, Delbert, *Washington Dateline,* Stokes (Washington, DC), 1941.
Dictionary of Literary Biography, Volume 29: *American Newspaper Journalists, 1926-1950,* Gale (Detroit, MI), 1984, pp. 158-67.
Fisher, Charles, *The Columnists,* Howell, Soskin (New York City), 1944.
Lawrence, David, *The True Story of Woodrow Wilson,* Doran (New York City), 1924.
Lawrence, *Diary of a Washington Correspondent,* Kinsey (New York City), 1942.
Marbut, F. B., *News from the Capital,* Southern Illinois University Press (Carbondale, IL), 1971.
Schlesinger, Arthur M., *The Coming of the New Deal,* Houghton (Boston, MA), 1958.

PERIODICALS

Everybody's, October, 1920, pp. 68-73.
New York Times, February 16, 1926, p. 13; June 9, 1931, p. 29.

Reader's Digest, January 1974, pp. 75-79.
U.S. News and World Report, July 24, 1978.

OBITUARIES:

Christianity Today, March 2, 1973.
National Review, March 2, 1973.
Newsweek, February 26, 1973.
New York Times, February 12, 1973.
Time, February 26, 1973, p. 46.
U.S. News and World Report, February 26, 1973, pp. 3, 93-98; March 5, 1973, pp. 82-84.
Washington Post, February 12, 1973.*

* * *

LEA, Sydney (L. Wright, Jr.) 1942-

PERSONAL: Born December 22, 1942, in Chestnut Hill, PA; son of Sydney L. W. (in business) and Jane (Jordan) Lea; married second wife, M. Robin Barone, July 9, 1983; children (first marriage): Creston, Erika; (second marriage): Jordan, Catherine, Sydney. *Education:* Yale University, B.A., 1964, M.A., 1968, Ph.D., 1972.

ADDRESSES: Office—New England Review and Bread Loaf Quarterly, Middlebury College, Middlebury, VT 05753.

CAREER: Dartmouth College, Hanover, NH, assistant professor, 1970-78, adjunct professor of English, 1978-80; Yale University, New Haven, CT, adjunct professor, 1980-86; Middlebury College, Middlebury, VT, associate professor of English, 1987—.

MEMBER: Modern Language Association of America, Committee of Small Magazine Editors and Publishers, Poets and Writers.

AWARDS, HONORS: Bread Loaf Writer's Conference, scholar, 1977, fellow, 1979; Lamont Award nomination, 1982, for *The Floating Candles;* Guggenheim Fellowship, 1987-88, for poetry; American writer in residence, Tyrone Guthrie Centre for the Arts; Rockefeller foundation fellowship.

WRITINGS:

Searching the Drowned Man (poems), University of Illinois Press (Urbana), 1980.

(Editor with Jay Parini and wife, M. Robin Barone) *Richard Eberhart: A Celebration,* Kenyon Hill (Hanover, NH), 1980.
Gothic to Fantastic: Readings in Supernatural Fiction (critical study), Arno (New York City), 1981.
The Floating Candles (poems), University of Illinois Press, 1982.
(Editor with Robert Pack and Jay Parini) *The Bread Loaf Anthology of Contemporary American Poetry,* University Press of New England (Hanover, NH), 1985.
The Blainville Testament (poetry chapbook), Tamarack Editions (Syracuse, NY), 1987, reprinted, Story Line Press (Brownsville, OR), 1992.
No Sign (poems), University of Georgia Press (Athens), 1987.
(Editor) *The Burdens of Formality: Essays on the Poetry of Anthony Hecht,* University of Georgia Press, 1989.
A Place in Mind (novel), Scribner (New York City), 1989, reprinted, Story Line Press, 1997.
Prayer for the Little City: Poems, Scribner, 1990.
Hunting the Whole Way Home, University Press of New England, 1994.
To the Bone: New and Selected Poems, University of Illinois Press, 1996.

Contributor to magazines, including *Atlantic, Chicago Review, Nation, New Republic, New Yorker,* and *Studies in Romanticism.* Editor of *New England Review and Bread Loaf Quarterly,* 1978—.

WORK IN PROGRESS: Editing an anthology on the poetry of Anthony Hecht; *Last of the Light,* a novel.

SIDELIGHTS: Sydney Lea's poetry and fiction reflects the dual inspirations of intellectualism and outdoorsmanship. In fact, Lea has described himself as a "borderliner," or one who visits the wilds with his head full of books. A Yale-educated professor and editor of the prestigious *New England Review and Bread Loaf Quarterly,* Lea fashions poetry from the voices he hears in the rural regions and the situations that lead to human interaction there. "Reading Lea, one gets the impression of two poets with antipodal concerns collaborating under a pseudonym," noted Norman German in the *Dictionary of Literary Biography.* "While his frustration with the distorting effects of language casts him as a semiotician trapped in a poet's body, his childlike capacity for wonder betrays him as a Wordsworthian mystic." The critic continued: "Lea's subjects include natural objects, moods, and processes, and, increasingly, the family. His themes involve undercut expectations, nature's grandeur and indifference, and language's inability to capture the essence of objects."

Lea was born and raised in the Chestnut Hill section of Philadelphia, but he spent a good deal of his youth at an uncle's farm in Ambler, Pennsylvania. An early immersion in outdoor sports such as hunting and fishing helped to set a pattern not only for his future avocational interests but for his artistic vision as well. Perhaps not surprisingly, he settled in New England as a mature poet and has worked there ever since, writing not only poetry, criticism, and fiction, but magazine pieces about hunting and dog-training. German declared that much of Lea's creativity reveals a "fascination with New England terrain and characters. . . . The dominant tone is wistfulness for people, places, and times that have passed, are passing, or will pass."

Though essentially Christian in his outlook, Lea often cultivates the impulses of spite and revenge in his poetry. German sees Lea as "especially focusing on people's judgmental nature and their tendency to pin a moral tale on every plain-donkey occurrence." The critic added: "Whatever brand of Christianity Lea professes, his poetic vision . . . waxes pantheistic. His personal philosophy, though, seems expansive enough to contain any apparent contradiction in views. In fact, one of the virtues of Lea's poetry, both early and late, is the way it camouflages polemical tensions and offers its wisdom plainly."

Similar concerns animate Lea's novel, *A Place in Mind,* in which an aging college professor reminisces about his younger days while fishing a favorite river. "In a series of lyrical, stunningly crafted flashbacks, [the protagonist] recalls barroom brawls, lusty affairs, travels to France and a crucial friendship, all over a span of 40-odd years," wrote Krysia Bereday in the *New York Times Book Review.* "Within this framework emerges a portrait of a lonely man trying to order his life by looking back on its disparate moments."

Sydney Lea told *CA:* "My chief interests are in the out of doors and in 'outdoorsy' people, especially oldtimers whose ilk is vanishing. I turned to poetry as the most suitable mode of recording not only natural facts (as a poet I'm as much interested in facts as anything), but also the cadences and locutions of the oldtimer. Having gotten that far with *Searching the Drowned Man,* I have tried to apply what I learned about fact and eloquence (and fact *as*

eloquence) to a wider range of places and concerns, including spiritual, and ultimately Christian ones."

BIOGRAPHICAL/CRITICAL SOURCES:

BOOKS

Dictionary of Literary Biography, Volume 120: *American Poets since World War II, Third Series,* Gale (Detroit, MI), 1992, pp. 180-85.

PERIODICALS

New York Times Book Review, October 1, 1989, p. 26.
Southern Review, spring, 1981; autumn, 1984.
Virginia Quarterly Review, autumn, 1980.

*   *   *

LEBOWITZ, Fran(ces Ann) 1951(?)-

PERSONAL: Born in Morristown, NJ; daughter of Harold and Ruth Lebowitz (furniture store proprietors).

ADDRESSES: Home—New York, NY.

CAREER: Writer. Visiting lecturer. Previously worked at a number of "colorful and picturesque" jobs in New York City, including bulk mailing, taxi driving, apartment cleaning, poetry reading, and selling advertising for *Changes* magazine.

WRITINGS:

Metropolitan Life, Dutton (New York City), 1978.
Social Studies, Random House (New York City), 1981.
The Fran Lebowitz Reader (includes *Metropolitan Life* and *Social Studies*), Vintage Books (New York City), 1994.
Mr. Chas and Lisa Sue Meet the Pandas (children's book), illustrated by Michael Graves, Knopf (New York City), 1994.

Former author of columns, "I Cover the Waterfront," in *Interview,* and "The Lebowitz Report," in *Mademoiselle,* 1977-79. Contributor of book and film reviews to *Changes* magazine.

WORK IN PROGRESS: A novel, tentatively titled *Exterior Signs of Wealth.*

SIDELIGHTS: As author of two bestselling books, *Metropolitan Life* and *Social Studies,* and a monthly column published for many years in *Interview* magazine, Fran Lebowitz has become recognized as a talented author of satirical essays on the trendy aspects of urban life. Descriptions of Lebowitz have run the gamut from "daring" by *New York Times* reviewer Anatole Broyard, and "right on the mark" by Jean Strouse in *Newsweek,* to "an unlikely and perhaps alarming combination of Mary Hartman and Mary McCarthy" by John Leonard in the *New York Times.* She has also been compared to various other humorists, notably Erma Bombeck, Dorothy Parker, and Oscar Wilde. "Fran Lebowitz is not only the funniest woman in America," Edmund White wrote in the *Washington Post Book World,* "she is also the guardian of the proprieties. Like all satirists she is a moralist, and like most moralists she is conservative. She is for the eternal verities of sleep, civilized conversation and cigarette smoking. The list of what she is against is somewhat longer."

"[Lebowitz] disapproves of virtually everything, particularly fads, trends, and the relaxation of social and personal restraints in general," remarked Vic Sussman in the *Washington Post Book World.* Scot Haller commented in the *Saturday Review:* "Chronicling the baroque customs and bizarre behavior of the American species near the end of the 20th century, Lebowitz sounds like Dorothy Parker in Gomorrah, or Emily Post in hysterics. From cafe society to the coffee-klatsch crowd, no social set or disorder escapes her infectious wrath." And finally, Paul Rudnick observed in *New Times* that Lebowitz's "pose is neither establishment lackey nor avant-garde artiste; she has followed the Noel Coward tradition of an intensely civilized, titillating frivolity. Her work is marvelously entertaining and intentionally superficial; any subversiveness is masked by a declaration of triviality. She can insult anyone she likes, as long as the offense is smothered in charm and wit. It is a remarkably difficult tightrope to navigate."

The daughter of furniture store owners, Lebowitz grew up in Morristown, New Jersey. From a very early age she loved to read, and this passion easily translated into a desire to write. "Until I was about 7, I thought books were just there, like trees," she recalled in the *New York Times.* "When I learned that people actually wrote them, I wanted to, too, because all children aspire to inhuman feats like flying. Most

people grow up to realize they can't fly. Writers are people who don't grow up to realize they can't be God."

Formal schooling proved a trial for Lebowitz, and as a teen she was expelled from high school. She quickly earned her equivalency degree and embarked for New York City where, at age twenty-one, she began writing B-movie reviews for Andy Warhol's *Interview* magazine. In the early 1970s she was given a column in *Interview,* which she styled "I Cover the Waterfront." It was there that her satirical pieces on life in New York first saw print. "My real audience was that old *Interview* audience," Lebowitz later commented in *Interview.* "It wasn't that I wrote for them; it's just that they were the same as me. That's a real audience—an audience isn't an audience you make up using demographics. . . . To have an audience that so understands what you do, it becomes, in a certain way, a collaborator because you can do your best in a natural way."

Lebowitz was therefore unprepared for the immense popularity of her first book, *Metropolitan Life,* which became a bestseller. "By the time my first book . . . came out in 1978, I had been writing regularly in *Interview* for seven years—every single month, a full-page column in a New York publication," she told *Interview.* "But when my book came out, no one had ever heard of me—by which I mean no one associated with any big newspaper or magazine or anything. I was considered this big discovery despite the fact that I thought . . . I was already a big success."

Metropolitan Life was generally greeted with overwhelmingly favorable reviews. Richard Locke, for example, described the book as a "remarkable collection of satirical pieces." Continued the critic in his *New York Times Book Review* article: "Though she is young in years, [Lebowitz's] book *Metropolitan Life* exhibits an exceptional ferocity and tone of camp authority that deserve attention. She may lack the mimetic range and dramatic flair of her distinguished elders—she tends toward the firm didactic statement or a desperate Basic English sneer—but she epitomizes the 70's New York know-it-all fashion-magazine/artistic world, and I confess I'm head over heels at her feet." And A. J. Anderson wrote in *Library Journal* of *Metropolitan Life:* "Unpredictable variety is the keynote of [Lebowitz's] musings; she discourses on everything from the pros and cons of children to digital clocks and pocket calculators, always projecting a light-hearted and sometimes nonsensical view of things."

One reviewer who did not agree with those who praised *Metropolitan Life* was Madora McKenzie. In a *Christian Science Monitor* review, McKenzie observed: "Apparently Miss Lebowitz wrote these pieces while sucking on lemon drops, because sour grapes crop up so often. . . . All her imagination and energies are devoted to exposing and ridiculing indignities and indemnities of life; she cannot seem to come up with any palatable alternatives." However, *Melus* essayist Don L. F. Nilsen cited Lebowitz for a "wide range of satiric targets" that make her "popular with both middle class and low class readers, who can identify with landlords who are able to provide 4,000 roaches per tenant. . . . In short, she writes excellent urban satire."

Lebowitz's second book, *Social Studies,* was greeted with nearly the same degree of enthusiasm as *Metropolitan Life.* Hall, again writing in *Saturday Review,* declared that, "for the most part, *Social Studies* is a textbook example of astute, acerbic social comedy. . . . The quick-witted, quick-tempered Lebowitz may be the funniest chronic complainer on the scene." Anatole Broyard commented in the *New York Times* that one of Lebowitz's most entertaining qualities is that "she never gets used to anything. She experiences customs and situations as if they were all done on purpose to her. And the funniest thing of all is that she's right."

Reviewing *Social Studies* for the *Los Angeles Times Book Review,* Elaine Kendall maintained that "most of the time [Lebowitz is] both original and brave, taking on subjects everyone would like to laugh at but few people dare—highly charged topics that arouse emotional response, some of it furious." Finally, Peter Grier stated in the *Christian Science Monitor* that in *Social Studies* Lebowitz "makes W. C. Fields look like St. Francis of Assisi. . . . Not everyone may think Fran Lebowitz is funny. . . . *Social Studies* might offend you. Then again, as Lebowitz says, 'Being offended is the natural consequence of leaving one's home.'"

In her *Los Angeles Times Book Review* article on *Social Studies,* Kendall speculated on why Lebowitz's form of satire is so successful while that of other writers fails. Kendall wrote: "Other satirists bite; Lebowitz nibbles. They're corrosive while she's

just tart." Even so, according to Glenn Collins in the *New York Times Book Review,* "Lebowitz's wit will not be appreciated by all of the people all of the time. . . . Fran Lebowitz is not exactly brimming over with human compassion. Hers is not an Up-With-People view." While this may be the case, Kendall stated that "the humorist who worries excessively about hurt feelings soon runs out of material and winds up doing trite monographs on smog, the only target with no organization dedicated to its defense. If you want to be funny for more than a week or so, you have to be willing to take chances and risk unpopularity."

In the 1990s Lebowitz continued working on an unfinished novel, as she had for many years. In the meantime, in 1994 she published her first book since *Social Studies:* the children's story *Mr. Chas and Lisa Sue Meet the Pandas.* Illustrated by noted architect Michael Graves, the story involves two children who unexpectedly discover two pandas hiding in their New York City apartment building. The pandas, named "Pandemonium" and "Don't Panda to Public Taste," express anxiety about being discovered and forced to live at the zoo. They decide to disguise themselves as dogs but then realize that to have decent lives as dogs they need to live in Paris. One of the children then attempts to persuade his father to take the pandas with him on a business trip to Paris, where, dressed like dogs, the pandas can live an exciting life. Reviewers recognized the dry wit and urban satire in the story but felt that the book would not be as appealing to children as it would be to their parents. Writing in the *New York Times Book Review,* for instance, Jon Katz remarked, "There is no harsh, vivid, unsettling or frightening moment in [the book.] In fact, nothing much happens at all." In a discussion with Melia Marden for *Interview,* Lebowitz commented that she had always wanted to write a children's book. She also admitted, "There are quite a few children's books that are really meant for adults. And I think that people expect my children's book to be that sort of book."

Success came very early to Lebowitz, who admits that she is a slow writer. "I've never met anyone who even comes close to me in laziness," she joked in the *New York Times.* "I would have made a perfect heiress. I enjoy lounging. And reading. The other problem I have is fear of writing. The act of writing puts you in confrontation with yourself, which is why I think writers assiduously avoid writing." Most of Lebowitz's income in the 1990s has been derived from lecture engagements.

In his *Washington Post Book World* piece about Lebowitz, Vic Sussman concluded: "Those unfamiliar with Lebowitz might think her a moralist, an elitist, a snob. She is all those. But she is an equal-opportunity snob, venting her disdain regardless of one's race, disability, sexual persuasion, or for that matter, species. Lebowitz is unashamedly Lebowitz, thank goodness, a funny, urbane, intelligent one-woman bulwark against cultural ticky-tack, creeping mellowness, and the excesses of what [H. L.] Mencken dubbed 'boobus Americanus.'"

BIOGRAPHICAL/CRITICAL SOURCES:

BOOKS

Contemporary Literary Criticism, Gale, Volume 11, 1979, Volume 36, 1986, pp. 247-51.
Walker, Nancy, and Zita Dresner, *Redressing the Balance: American Women's Literary Humor from Colonial Times to the 1980s,* University Press of Mississippi (Jackson), 1988.

PERIODICALS

Booklist, December 15, 1994, p. 758.
Bookviews, September, 1978.
Christian Science Monitor, March 15, 1978.
Crawdaddy, June, 1978.
Entertainment Weekly, November 4, 1994, p. 66.
Esquire, August, 1981.
Harper's, May, 1978; November, 1993, p. 34.
Interview, October, 1994, p. 30; November, 1994, p. 66.
Library Journal, April 1, 1978, August, 1981.
Los Angeles Times Book Review, August 30, 1981.
Melus, winter, 1996, p. 71.
Ms., May, 1978.
New Statesman, February 19, 1982.
Newsweek, April 10, 1978; September 14, 1981.
New Times, July 10, 1978.
New York, September 14, 1981.
New York Times, March 31, 1978; September 2, 1981; August 10, 1994.
New York Times Book Review, March 26, 1978; April 23, 1978; July 15, 1979; August 23, 1981; February 28, 1982; November 13, 1994, p. 55.
People, September 4, 1978.
Publishers Weekly, October 24, 1994, p. 62.
Saturday Review, April 15, 1978; August, 1981.
School Library Journal, February, 1995, p. 75.
Time, May 29, 1978.
Vogue, August, 1991, p. 168; June, 1992, p. 154; December, 1994, p. 214.

Washington Post Book World, April 30, 1978; June 5, 1978; August 30, 1981.*

* * *

LELCHUK, Alan 1938-

PERSONAL: Born September 15, 1938, in Brooklyn, NY; son of Harry and Belle (Simon) Lelchuk. *Education:* Brooklyn College (now Brooklyn College of the City University of New York), B.A., 1960; Stanford University, M.A., 1963, Ph.D., 1965; University of London, graduate study, 1963-64.

ADDRESSES: Office—Department of English, Dartmouth College, Hanover, NH. *Agent*—Georges Borchardt, Inc., 136 East 57th St., New York, NY 10022.

CAREER: Brandeis University, Waltham, MA, assistant professor of English, 1966-77, writer-in-residence, 1978-85; Dartmouth College, Hanover, NH, professor of English, 1985—. Senior editor, Steerforth Press, Canaan, VT, 1994—.

MEMBER: Authors Guild.

AWARDS, HONORS: Received Yaddo fellowships, 1968-69, 1971, 1973; MacDowell Colony fellowship, 1969; Guggenheim fellow, 1976-77; Mishkenot Sha'Ananim fellow, 1976-77.

WRITINGS:

American Mischief, Farrar, Straus (New York City), 1973.
Miriam at Thirty-Four, Farrar, Straus, 1974.
Shrinking: The Beginning of My Own End, Little, Brown (Boston, MA), 1978.
(Contributor) A. Edelstein, editor, *Images and Ideas in American Culture,* Brandeis University Press (Waltham, MA), 1979.
(Editor with Gershon Shaked) *Eight Great Hebrew Short Novels,* New American Library (New York City), 1983.
Miriam in Her Forties, Houghton (Boston), 1985.
On Home Ground, illustrated by Merle Nacht, Harcourt (New York City), 1987.
(Contributor) *Congregations: Contemporary Writers Read the Jewish Bible,* Harcourt, 1987.

(Contributor) *Testimony: Contemporary Writers Make the Holocaust Personal,* Times Books (New York City), 1989.

Brooklyn Boy: A Novel, McGraw-Hill (New York City), 1990.

(Contributor) *Facing America: Multikulturelle literatur der heutigen U.S.A.,* Rotpunkteverlag (Zurich, Switzerland), 1994, translation by Regina Rosenthal published as *Facing America: Multicultural Literature of Contemporary U.S.A., A Reader,* Wesleyan University Press, 1995.

Playing the Game: A Novel, Baskerville (Dallas, TX), 1995.

SCREENPLAYS

(With Jiri Weiss) *Tippy,* 1978.
(With Isaac Yeshurun) *What Ashley Wants,* 1987.
(With Bill Phillips) *Degrees of Honor,* 1993.

OTHER

Contributor to periodicals, including *New American Review, Modern Occasions, Partisan Review, New York Review of Books, Dissent, Works in Progress, New Republic, New York Times Book Review,* and *Transatlantic Review.* Associate editor of *Modern Occasions,* 1970-72. A collection of Lelchuk's papers can be found at Mugar Memorial Library, Boston University.

SIDELIGHTS: Alan Lelchuk's first novel, *American Mischief,* achieved notoriety for its author even before its publication. The novel first received attention because Bantam Books reportedly paid more than $250,000 for the paperback rights—a very high figure for a first book, especially in 1972. Then Lelchuk collided with Norman Mailer over a scene in the novel in which a character named Norman Mailer is murdered in an ignominious manner. At a meeting with Lelchuk and Farrar, Straus & Giroux representatives, Mailer complained that the scene was libelous and degrading to his character. At one point in the discussion, which grew heated, Mailer remarked, "Lelchuk, I don't want ever to meet you in an alley, because if I do, you're going to be nothing but a hank of hair and some fillings." For his part, Lelchuk argued that the importance of the scene had been blown out of proportion. "The scene is four pages out of 500 pages," he said, "and it obviously plays a small part in the whole texture of the book." Eventually, Lelchuk made some changes in the scene, but he insisted that the alterations were minor.

Notwithstanding highly favorable advance comments from Philip Roth, *American Mischief* received many unfavorable reviews. A *Time* critic, for example, declared: "*American Mischief* is another exploitive, topical novel. Lelchuk romps through the confusions and contradictions of today's beleaguered values . . . like a gratuitous looter in a cultural disaster area." Joseph Epstein, writing in the *Washington Post Book World,* believed that the novel is "as botched a piece of literature as has come along in some while. . . . Dialogue, plot and character are rudimentary. Everyone speaks exactly alike. . . . The plot itself, and especially the way the book ends, is slipshod and disappointing." In a *New York Times Book Review* critique, Alfred Kazin found Lelchuk to be "a lively enough writer of narrative, entertaining above all in his provocativeness." Yet Kazin went on to say that the novel is "too intellectual" and expresses "no point of view that gets to the reader." Eliot Fremont-Smith, in *Saturday Review,* also had a mixed response to the work. He considered the book "good and bad, immensely repetitive and boring," and "clever, funny, and fashionable." Not every critic proved hostile, however. In the *New York Times Book Review,* Samuel Shem deemed *American Mischief* "a sprawling, energetic, sexual and intellectual Jewish carnival."

Miriam at Thirty-Four, Lelchuk's second novel, also elicited some negative responses. In the *New York Times Book Review,* Sara Blackburn contended that Lelchuk's handling of female sexuality "leaves readers holding a bag of demonstration sex scenes and pretentious modern moralizing." In addition, Blackburn felt that the characters lack depth, and she concluded that "in presenting Miriam [the protagonist] and everyone in only one dimension—the sexual—Lelchuk has at once sensationalized and trivialized the culture and the character whose life he means to illuminate." On the other hand, William H. Pritchard noted in the *Hudson Review* that *Miriam at Thirty-Four* "is superb in its presentation of Greater Boston, particularly the 'accepted insanities' of Cambridge." But he suggested that this realistic presentation does not mesh well with the novel's "parables of self-destruction [or] self-fulfillment." A better reception awaited Lelchuk's sequel, *Miriam in Her Forties,* which Samuel Shem characterized as "a dense, fine-grained and trenchant slide show of modern life. . . . Mr. Lelchuk is a writer of intelligence, sexual sensibility and drive. 'Miriam' is a full-bodied portrait of a woman who lives hard in our heads. . . . Yet she lives with spirit. I expect we'll hear from her again."

Mixed reviews continued with the publication of *Shrinking: The Beginning of My Own Ending.* In *Saturday Review,* Robert Stephen Spitz commented that *Shrinking* "is a confusing, often brilliant work that is too grandiose in scope to command the force or focus necessary to substantiate any one of its many subplots." Robert Towers, writing in the *New York Times Book Review,* reacted more strongly. He objected that the book seems to plead for favorable treatment from critics, that it lacks wit, that "the writing is often slapdash," and that the book is a mixture of disparate elements, including "diatribes against critics and against stylistic distinction . . . , half-baked lectures on Melville and Babel, . . . transcripts of creative-writing classes, and remembered episodes from [the protagonist's] Brooklyn childhood." In contrast to this, Anthony R. Cannella, in *Best Sellers,* admired Lelchuk's ambition, integrity, and intelligence in tackling the "meaty topics" of "the relationships of life and art, literature and criticism, illusion and reality, genius and madness, psychiatry and religion, fiction and autobiography." And John Leonard of the *New York Times* discovered "fun and passion in *Shrinking,* as well as reasonably interesting counterpoint between the devices of art and psychiatry." Yet Leonard also cited the work for "hundreds of pages of tedium," observing: "Mr. Lelchuk careens from a comedy of literary manners to a seriousness so nervous and defensive that you want to give him a calming lollipop."

As any author might be, Lelchuk has been stunned and confused by the critical response to his work. "With their blend of blunt realism and frank language, erotic scenes and wayward intellectuals, provocative mix of class and race . . . [my novels] are not so easy to pigeonhole or categorize, or to use for tidy formulas about fiction," he wrote in an essay for *Contemporary Authors Autobiography Series.* "And my protagonists, bewildered intellectuals who try to steer between the Scylla of contemporary vulgarity and the Charybdis of ivory tower artificial purity are figures of contradictory desires. And since the prose generally is in the service of character and vision, and not the other way around, the novels tend to go against the grain of current terms of favor, like 'well-crafted novel' or 'stylish performance.'" Lelchuk admitted: "I've not tried very hard to conform to the prevailing fashions of our time, be it feminism or multiculturalism. On the contrary, playing the 'good boy' has never been my bag." The author expressed the opinion that some of his books "were simply misread and badly misrepresented."

One of the titles Lelchuk cited as "misread" is *Brooklyn Boy,* an imaginative part-fictional memoir of his own childhood in Brooklyn. *New York Times Book Review* correspondent Daniel Stern derided the work as "a poorly conceived confusion of realms," adding: "Buried any which way in this derivative, slapdash prose are the abortive beginnings of a Bildungsroman, the hints of an autobiography of a Jewish boy growing up in Brooklyn in the 1950's and 60's, and a prolonged, exhaustive love song to Brooklyn, to baseball in general and the Brooklyn Dodgers in particular. . . . For all its high intentions, 'Brooklyn Boy' does not read as successful serious fiction." Michiko Kakutani reacted more favorably to the book in her *New York Times* review. *Brooklyn Boy,* she wrote, "feels nostalgic, even elegiac, in tone. It's a paean to a lost time and world, an affectionate portrait of a sensitive young man, as yet unspoiled by ambition and disappointment. . . . There are moments when 'Brooklyn Boy' succeeds in communicating to the reader a sense of what it must have been like to grow up in a particular neighborhood, in a particular family, at a particular time, and for that, it is worthwhile."

Lelchuk's 1995 sports novel, *Playing the Game*—a tale of an Ivy League basketball team that advances to the NCAA Final Four—was hailed in *Publishers Weekly* for presenting "several compelling versions of many moral dilemmas faced by coaches and players." Led by a coach who quotes Emerson to his inner-city players, the novel follows the unlikely team to its eventual upset triumph. Bill Ott, reviewing the novel in *Booklist,* notes that tales of underdogs tend to follow a predictable pattern, but Lelchuk "manages to work some tantalizing variations on it. . . . [The coach] wins us over just as convincingly as he converts his inner-city charges to the glories of the passing game and the wisdom of the Transcendentalists."

BIOGRAPHICAL/CRITICAL SOURCES:

BOOKS

Contemporary Authors Autobiography Series, Volume 20, Gale (Detroit, MI), 1994, pp. 237-55.
Contemporary Literary Criticism, Volume 5, Gale, 1976.

PERIODICALS

Booklist, April 15, 1995, p. 1480.
Hudson Review, Volume 28, number 1, 1975.
Ms., April, 1975.

New York Review of Books, February 8, 1973.

New York Times, May 8, 1978; November 17, 1989, p. 40.

New York Times Book Review, February 11, 1973; November 17, 1974; May 21, 1978; November 3, 1985, p. 15; January 7, 1990, p. 24.

Publishers Weekly, March 20, 1995, p. 45.

Saturday Review, February 17, 1973; June 24, 1978.

Time, February 26, 1973.

Washington Post Book World, February 11, 1973.

World, February 13, 1973.

*   *   *

LERMAN, Rhoda 1936-

PERSONAL: Born January 18, 1936, in Far Rockaway, NY; daughter of Jacob (an accountant) and Gertrude (Langfur) Sniderman; married Robert Rudolph Lerman (a carpet distributor), September 15, 1957; children: Jill, Julia, Matthew. *Education:* University of Miami, Coral Gables, FL, B.A., 1957. *Politics:* "Traditional democrat, becoming conservative." *Religion:* Jewish.

ADDRESSES: Home—Shore Acres, Cazenovia, NY 13035.

CAREER: Syracuse University, Syracuse, NY, instructor in English and parapsychology. Former manager of rock and roll band.

WRITINGS:

NOVELS

Call Me Ishtar, Doubleday (Garden City, NY), 1973, reprinted, Syracuse University Press (Syracuse, NY), 1998.

The Girl That He Marries, Holt (New York City), 1976.

Eleanor, Holt, 1979.

The Book of the Night, Holt, 1984.

God's Ear, Holt, 1989, reprinted, Syracuse University Press, 1997.

Animal Acts, Holt, 1994.

NONFICTION

In the Company of Newfies: A Shared Life, Holt, 1996.

OTHER

Contributor to *Nickel Review* and *Syracuse New Times.*

SIDELIGHTS: Rhoda Lerman is a writer whose fiction tackles some of the deepest questions of religious faith and gender interaction while maintaining a humorous bent. The author's novels, to quote *Publishers Weekly* correspondent Suzanne Mantell, "are idiosyncratic affairs, wildly inventive, lusty and fabulistic, tackling subject matter that, however related at its core by humor feminism and mysticism, has a wide variety of surfaces." While no two of her books are alike, Lerman has been cited repeatedly for her prose style and her reliance on myth, theology, and anthropology to inform her stories. In the *New York Times Book Review,* Brett Singer wrote of Lerman: "Hers is a unique voice—wildly funny, achingly spiritual, profoundly Jewish and feminist at the same time."

Lerman was born on Long Island but grew up in Connecticut and Florida. For many years she has lived in the hamlet of Cazenovia, NY, where she raises purebred Newfoundland dogs. She began writing novels three decades ago after being inspired by helping to manage a rock and roll band. *Call Me Ishtar,* her debut novel, offers "a patchwork satire of patriarchy, sublimation and suburbia," according to Harriet Rosenstein in the *New York Times Book Review.* Told from the point of view of a suburban housewife who believes herself to be the incarnation of the goddess Ishtar, *Call Me Ishtar* includes ironic reflections on male-female relations, modern Judaism, and ancient mythology. Rosenstein applauded the work as "great fun and often wonderfully funny," adding: "It should probably be read slowly, as an anthology, and savored, as a promise. . . . It announces a writer of genuine talent. Rhoda Lerman is a find."

Lerman's next two books, *The Girl That He Marries* and *Eleanor,* were critical and commercial successes for the author. The subject matter of both—the politics of courtship and marriage—earned Lerman characterization as a feminist writer. *The Girl That He Marries,* a dark comedy, follows the efforts of a 30-year-old scholar to lure a man into marriage. *Village Voice* contributor Erica Abeel styled the work an "outrageous and hilarious account of the New York mating game" and "a nightmare vision of premarital transactions." Abeel continued: "Despite its bleak view of our mating habits, this novel is antically funny. Reality is canted through Rhoda Lerman's slyly irreverent sensibility, one of the most idiosyncratic in contemporary prose." In her *New York Times Book Review* piece on the novel, Alix Nelson wrote: "For those of us who've been waiting around for Alexander Portnoy to get his, author Rhoda Lerman here 'hulls him from the belly button like an overripe strawberry' to prove that writing well is the best revenge."

Lerman spent three years researching *Eleanor,* a fictional account of Eleanor Roosevelt and her troubled marriage to a future president. The story covers four years in Eleanor's life, from 1918 until 1921, and ends as she nurses her ailing husband through a crippling bout of polio. "What Rhoda Lerman has achieved in this re-creation of the crucial and personally troubled years in the life of a great American woman—a lonely and sensitive wife of a charming, unfaithful husband—is an imaginative success," noted Doris Grumbach in *The Chronicle of Higher Education.* "Lerman brings what has always been a stick figure in history to glowing, aching life." In *Harper's,* Frances Taliaferro cited the work for the author's "poetic, impressionistic version of Eleanor" that presents "a 'reality' truer and more haunting than the most scrupulous notes of the biographer." Taliaferro concluded: *"Eleanor* is distinguished historical fiction." *American Book Review* critic Susan Mernit likewise applauded *Eleanor* as a *"tour de force,"* praising "the strength of Rhoda Lerman's imagining, her careful integration of research and reportage into a fictional document." Observed the critic: "We can only applaud Lerman's total immersion in her character."

In a *Publishers Weekly* interview, Lerman suggested of her writing career: "It's been downhill since *Eleanor* into anonymity." She was referring to sales of her subsequent novels, which have never reached the popularity of *Eleanor* or *The Girl That He Marries.* Lerman offered a reason for her dwindling audience: "I keep reinventing my wheel and wiping out my fan club," she told the interviewer. What the "fan club" might not appreciate, however, the critics certainly do: most of Lerman's novels have received uniformly good notices and consistent praise.

One such later work is *God's Ear,* a fable in which a wealthy and successful Jewish insurance salesman is pressured by the will of God to become rabbi to his father's congregation deep in the American West. A *Kirkus Reviews* contributor maintained that in *God's Ear,* "Lerman effortlessly works an immense amount of Jewish learning and Hasidic lore into a novel that's moving, wise, and very, very funny." In a *Publishers Weekly* piece, a reviewer declared: "Lerman . . . proves herself mistress not only of side-splitting one-liners but also of pregnant perceptions about faith and virtue." In his *New York Times Book Review* essay on *God's Ear,* Singer concluded: "When Rhoda Lerman's wise words enter God's willing ear, the holy connection crackles so, I pity the poor birds resting their feet on the wire."

Lerman's next novel, *Animal Acts,* offers yet another thematic departure. The heroine, a wealthy but unhappy Long Islander, flees her husband and lover in the company of a trained gorilla she has found hiding in her van. The relationship between human and animal provides Lerman with a vehicle through which she explores the mental and cognitive differences between human males and females. *Booklist* correspondent Donna Seaman called *Animal Acts* "a cleverly provocative satire by an author who excels at physical description, slapstick, and pointed mystical speculation." A *Publishers Weekly* reviewer wrote: "Taut and darkly suspenseful, [*Animal Acts*] is also a thesis on the way men and women think, feel, and decode the world. . . . Lerman's writing has a sweetness and a desperation that sharpen her piquant questions about human existence."

A longtime interest in Newfoundland dogs led Lerman to write her first nonfiction title, *In the Company of Newfies: A Shared Life.* Lerman generally shares her estate with as many as eight large Newfoundlands, and she has a hired handler to help with them. Reflecting on her career in *Publishers Weekly,* the author was both humble and grateful. "It's fortunate that I can live as I do, have what I want now, and want what I have," she said. "I can still write what I want to write."

BIOGRAPHICAL/CRITICAL SOURCES:

BOOKS

Contemporary Literary Criticism, Volume 56, Gale (Detroit, MI), 1989, pp. 175-80.

PERIODICALS

American Book Review, February, 1980, p. 8.
Booklist, May 1, 1994, p. 1583; June 1, 1996, p. 1657.
Chronicle of Higher Education, April 16, 1979, pp. R12-R13.

Fantasy Review, January, 1984, p. 17.
Harper's, June, 1979, pp. 94, 98.
Kirkus Reviews, February 15, 1989, p. 238.
New York Times Book Review, November 25, 1973, p. 46; August 8, 1976, pp. 10-11; October 28, 1984, p. 27; July 2, 1989, p. 6; July 3, 1994.
Partisan Review, Volume 41, number 3, 1974, pp. 469-76.
Publishers Weekly, March 3, 1989, p. 86; May 2, 1994, p. 282; August 1, 1994, pp. 60-61; April 8, 1996, p. 48.
Village Voice, July 19, 1976, p. 35.
West Coast Review of Books, May, 1979, p. 23.

*   *   *

LERNER, Carol 1927-

PERSONAL: Born July 6, 1927, in Chicago, IL; daughter of Edwin August (in sales) and Elsie (Harders) Drath; married Ralph Lerner (a teacher), October 30, 1954; children: Joshua, Jesse. *Education:* University of Chicago, B.A., 1950, M.A., 1954. *Avocational interests:* Films.

ADDRESSES: Home—Chicago, IL. *Office*—c/o William Morrow & Company, Inc., 105 Madison Ave., New York, NY 10016.

CAREER: Writer and illustrator, 1977—.

AWARDS, HONORS: Award for special artistic merit from Friends of American Writers, 1979, for *On the Forest Edge.*

WRITINGS:

SELF-ILLUSTRATED CHILDREN'S BOOKS

On the Forest Edge, Morrow (New York City), 1978.
Flowers of a Woodland Spring, Morrow, 1979.
Seasons of the Tallgrass Prairie, Morrow, 1980.
A Biblical Garden, Morrow, 1982.
Pitcher Plants: The Elegant Insect Traps, Morrow, 1983.
A Forest Year, Morrow, 1987.
Moonseed and Mistletoe: A Book of Poisonous Plants, Morrow, 1988.
Plant Families, Morrow, 1989.
Dumb Cane and Daffodils: Poisonous Plants in the House and Garden, Morrow, 1990.

A Desert Year, Morrow, 1991.
Cactus, Morrow, 1992.
Plants That Make You Sniffle and Sneeze, Morrow, 1993.
Backyard Birds of Summer, Morrow, 1996.
My Backyard Garden, Morrow, 1998.
My Indoor Garden, Morrow, 1999.

ILLUSTRATOR

Glenda Daniel, *Dune Country,* Swallow Press, 1977.
Robert M. McClung, *Peeper: First Voice of Spring,* Morrow, 1977.
McClung, *Green Darner,* Morrow, 1980.
Daniel Sullivan and Jerry Sullivan, *A Naturalist's Guide to the North Woods,* Sierra Club, 1981.
McClung, *Sphinx: The Story of a Caterpillar,* Morrow, 1981.
Anita Holmes, *The 100-Year-Old Cactus,* Four Winds, 1982.
Millicent Selsam, *Tree Flowers,* Morrow, 1984.

SIDELIGHTS: Through Carol Lerner's pen comes images of woodland wildflowers, desert cacti and the myriad creatures whose interdependence helps keep their ecosystem thriving. A leading author and illustrator of young-adult nonfiction, Lerner creates books that combine the scientific with the informational to introduce an increasingly high-tech generation to the wonders of the natural world.

A native of Chicago, Lerner had graduated college, married and begun to raise two sons before she found her literary calling. She was inspired by her family's summer vacations to rural Michigan, which provided "a daily intimacy with nature that was different from anything we had known as city dwellers," as Lerner noted in an essay published in *Something about the Author Autobiography Series (SAAS).* "The beach and the bluff behind it offered a rich complement of animal and plant life, as well as exhilarating views of sky and water." Spurred by her sons' passion for the outdoors, Lerner began a course of nature studies at Chicago's Morton Arboretum.

One class—botanical illustration—struck Lerner as particularly challenging and rewarding. Her aptitude for depicting recreating plant and animal life became apparent as she began submitting illustrations for local guidebooks. The next step was publishing original works. "I knew nothing about gaining entry into children's publishing, except for the obvious fact that manuscripts have to be submitted to editors," she wrote in *SAAS.* "Had I known more, I might well have been intimidated by the difficulties of entering the field. As it was, I set about to write and illustrate a nonfiction book for kids."

Lerner produced a work on prairie plant life, but found publishing it a daunting task. While her book made the rounds of submissions and rejections, the artist did find assignments illustrating two books that were published in the mid-1970s, Glenda Daniel's *Dune Country* and Robert McClung's *Peeper: First Voice of Spring.* Finally, Lerner had her own book accepted, and *On the Forest Edge* was published in 1978. (Her original manuscript, now called *Seasons of the Tallgrass Prairie,* was released in 1980.)

On the Forest Edge was greeted with enthusiasm by reviewers like R. Gregory Belcher, who noted in *Appraisal: Children's Science Books* that Lerner had "written and illustrated most appealingly an introduction to ecology which will be accepted with ease and joy." Similarly, *School Library Journal* critic Anne Boes found the work "a pleasing addition to ecology collections that sheds light on a little-noticed but significant slice of forest life."

With *Flowers of a Woodland Spring,* Lerner "has again produced a very special book," wrote Diane Holzheimer in *Appraisal.* This study of "ephemerals"—flowers whose short-but-active lives of blooming, seeding, producing shoots and disappearing bring forest floors to vibrant life every spring—features intricate black-and-white line drawings interspersed with full-color plates. R. Gregory Belcher, in another *Appraisal* review, admitted that a book written for children could find an audience beyond the youth market: "It is too good for anyone to miss."

Lerner's most unusual book, *A Biblical Garden,* is also one of her most ambitious. Working mainly from historical sources, the author covers the characteristics, history and symbolic significance of twenty plants mentioned in the Old Testament. Figs, lentils, olives, papyrus and pomegranates all get their due in text and illustration, along with the biblical passage that refers to the subject. While *School Library Journal* contributor George Gleason found the "idea for the book is excellent," he also cited elements lacking in the work, notably "some comparison figure [in the illustrations] to give an idea of size." No such drawbacks were mentioned by a *Publishers Weekly* reviewer who concluded that "there should be no age limit on so informative and beautiful a book."

Since 1982 Lerner has produced a self-illustrated book at the rate of nearly one each year, with topics intended to entice junior readers: insect-eating plants, poisonous houseplants, desert life. In 1991 Lerner told *SAAS* that even after so many publications "I mean to stay with it. There's no point in stopping when you're having a good time."

BIOGRAPHICAL/CRITICAL SOURCES:

BOOKS

Children's Literature Review, Volume 34, Gale (Detroit), 1995.
Something about the Author Autobiography Series, Volume 12, Gale, 1991,

PERIODICALS

Appraisal: Children's Science Books, spring, 1979; spring, 1980; fall, 1980; spring, 1990; autumn, 1990.
Appraisal: Science Books for Young People, September, 1981; winter, 1982; winter, 1983; winter, 1988; spring, 1992.
Booklist, November 1, 1977; September 15 1978; December 15, 1980; February 15, 1990; November 1, 1991; October 15, 1992; November 15, 1994; February 15, 1996; March 15, 1998.
Bulletin of the Center for Children's Books, October, 1992; October, 1993.
Horn Book, May-June, 1987; May-June, 1989; March, 1990; September-October, 1991; January-February, 1993; January-February, 1994; March-April, 1995; May-June, 1996.
Kirkus Reviews, August 15, 1977; July, 1991; August 1, 1992; July 15, 1993.
Publishers Weekly, April 9, 1982.
School Library Journal, November, 1978; February, 1981; April, 1982; April, 1983; August, 1987; September, 1990; November, 1991; December, 1992.
Science Books & Films, November-December, 1987; October, 1991.
Voice of Youth Advocates, October, 1989.

*   *   *

LERNER, Gerda 1920-

PERSONAL: Born April 30, 1920, in Vienna, Austria; came to the United States in 1939; naturalized in 1943; daughter of Robert and Ilona (Neumann) Kronstein; married Carl Lerner (a film maker), 1941 (died, 1973); children: Stephanie, Daniel. *Education:* New School for Social Research, B.A., 1963; Columbia University, M.A., 1965, Ph.D., 1966. *Avocational interests:* Music, gardening, backpacking.

ADDRESSES: Office—Department of History, University of Wisconsin, 3221 Humanities Building, 455 North Park St., Madison, WI 53706.

CAREER: Professional writer and translator, 1941—; New School for Social Research, New York City, lecturer and historian, 1963-65; Long Island University, Brooklyn, NY, assistant professor, 1965-67, associate professor of American history, 1967-68; Sarah Lawrence College, Bronxville, NY, member of history faculty, 1968-80, director of graduate program in women's history, 1972-76, 1978-79; University of Wisconsin, Madison, Robinson-Edwards Professor of history, beginning 1980, director and co-director of graduate program in women's history, 1981-90. Member of Columbia University Seminar on American Civilization, and Seminar on Women and Society, 1972. Co-director, FIPSE grant for Promoting Black Women's History, 1980-83; educational director, summer institutes in women's history, Sarah Lawrence College, 1976 and 1979; project director, "Documenting the Midwest Origins of 20th Century Feminism," 1990-93.

MEMBER: Organization of American Historians (president, 1981-82), American Historical Association, American Association of University Women, American Studies Association, Authors League of America.

AWARDS, HONORS: Social Science Research Council research fellow, 1970-71; Robert H. Lord Award, Emmanuel College, 1974; National Endowment for the Humanities fellow, 1976; Ford Foundation fellow, 1978-79; Lilly Foundation fellow, 1979; Special Book award, The Berkshire Conference of Women Historians, 1980, for *The Majority Finds Its Past: Placing Women in History;* Guggenheim fellow, 1980-81; Organization of American Historians grant, 1980-83; Senior Distinguished Research Professor, University of Wisconsin Alumni Research Foundation, 1984-1990; Educational Foundation Achievement Award, American Association of University Women, 1986; Joan Kelly Award, American Historical Association, 1986, for best book in women's history, for *Women and History;* Lucretia Mott

Award, 1988; award for scholarly distinction, American Historical Association, 1992; Kathe Leichter-Preis, Austrian State Prize for Women's History and the History of the Labor Movement, both 1995; Austrian Cross for Science and Art, 1996; recipient of ten honorary degrees.

WRITINGS:

No Farewell (novel), Associated Authors (New York City), 1955.
(With husband, Carl Lerner) *Black Like Me* (screenplay; based on book of same title by John Howard Griffin), Walter Reade Distributors, 1964.
The Grimke Sisters from South Carolina: Rebels against Slavery, Houghton (Boston), 1967.
The Woman in American History (textbook), Addison-Wesley (Reading, MA), 1971.
(Editor) *Black Women in White America: A Documentary History,* Pantheon (New York City), 1972.
Women Are History: A Bibliography in the History of American Women, Sarah Lawrence College (New York City), 1975, fourth revised edition (with Marie Laberge), University of Wisconsin Press (Madison), 1986.
(Editor) *The Female Experience: An American Documentary,* Bobbs-Merrill (Indianapolis, IN), 1976.
A Death of One's Own, Simon & Schuster (New York City), 1978.
The Majority Finds Its Past: Placing Women in History, Oxford University Press (New York City), 1979.
Teaching Women's History, American Historical Association (Washington, DC), 1981.
Women and History, Volume 1: The Creation of Patriarchy, Oxford University Press, 1986.
Women and History, Volume 2: The Creation of Feminist Consciousness, From the Middle Ages to 1870, Oxford University Press, 1993.
Why History Matters: Life and Thought, Oxford University Press, 1997.
The Feminist Thought of Sarah Grimke, Oxford University Press, 1998.

Also author of *Dorothea Dix* and *Elizabeth Cady Stanton and Susan B. Anthony,* sound recordings, Pacifica Tape Library. Co-author, with Eve Merriam, of the musical, *Singing of Women,* 1956. Contributor of short stories to various literary magazines, and of articles and reviews to professional journals. Author of numerous professional translations.

SIDELIGHTS: A pioneer in the field of women's studies, Gerda Lerner has written extensively about the role of women in history and how traditional histories have failed to address specifically female issues. Using a variety of sources, Lerner frequently compares issues of race, class, and gender in her studies of women. Believed to have taught the first postwar college course in women's history, she has also helped establish several graduate programs in the field. Anne Lewis Osler in *Feminist Writers* explains: "Lerner's research, combined with her commitment to organize programs designed to train future generations of feminist scholars, helped establish women's history as an essential component of contemporary history curriculums in colleges and universities both in the United States and abroad." As Elizabeth Fox-Genovese describes her in the *New Republic*, Lerner "has played a unique role in making women's history the thriving field it has become; she has delineated its appropriate contours; searched for a method and a theory appropriate to its practice; unearthed the sources necessary to its writing; insisted not merely on its autonomy and integrity, but on its inescapable centrality to any worthy history of humankind."

Lerner's 1972 book *Black Women in White America: A Documentary History* chronicles 350 years of suffering by individuals who were often considered property not only by reason of their race, but of their gender. Reviewer Joyce Jenkins comments in *Saturday Review* that this "superb" book is "the first, to my knowledge, to treat in depth the grossly neglected segment of American history staked out by the book's title." Lerner uses numerous documents as well as newspaper items to report the troubles of these women from their own perspective, not that of a distanced observer. While Jenkins disputes some of the author's assertions, such as the supposedly recurrent theme of racial solidarity, she remarks that overall it "displays sharp insight into the long-range effects of this slave past." Feminist poet Adrienne Rich observes in the *New York Times Book Review* that, although as a white historian Lerner is "scrupulously restrained in her theorizing," in *Black Women in White America* she provides "a thorough historical framework in which the documents could be read and interpreted."

Moreover, Rich describes the documentary as an "indispensable complement" to Lerner's next work, *The Female Experience: An American Documentary*. Rich explains that this second documentary "expands [Lerner's] vision of history, while keeping the form begun earlier. "As with *Black Women in White America,* the book presents letters, diaries, newspaper clips, speeches, and other documents that had not been published previously. "More than any other compilation, " remarks Eve Merriam in *Ms.,* "all the many strands needed for comprehending the female experience are successfully interwoven. " More notable, however, is the author's presentation of her material; instead of following traditional divisions of history, which she claims do not represent important milestones for women, Lerner attempts to establish an order according to women's issues known as "historical periodization." As Rich explains, the author recognizes that "periods of history regarded as progressive for men have often been regressive for women. . . . 'Progress' has been defined from a male point of view." Merriam offers similar praise: "In *The Female Experience,* Lerner has lifted history out of its iron rigidity, out of its chronological framework—what a daring concept and how inexorable it seems now that she has done so."

The Majority Finds Its Past: Placing Women in History compiles many of Lerner's essays and speeches, including those of her theories of historical periodization, into one book. "By bringing these pieces together, " comments June Sochen in the *Washington Post Book World,* "Lerner gives us a good opportunity to see the development of her thought as she participated in the shaping of the discipline." Sochen criticizes some of Lerner's ideas, however, such as her tendency to see women's history and culture as independent from mainstream events: "Does the existence of a female culture operate outside history?. . . . The temptation of some women historians to portray all examples of female culture as subversive, alternative value-systems is questionable at best." Fox-Genovese, while she praises Lerner's work as ground-breaking, still faults the author's failure to consider religious and class issues as notable influences in women's history. These reservations aside, the critic finds that "committed to recreating the female perspective, Lerner nonetheless never sacrifices the specificities of income and race to an all-inclusive feminism. "

In *The Creation of Patriarchy,* volume one of *Women and History,* Lerner ventures into prehistory, attempting to trace the roots of patriarchal dominance. In doing so, Elizabeth Kamarck Minnich claims in *Ms.* that Lerner "gives us a grand historical framework that was impossible even to imagine before the enlightenment about women's place in the world provided by her earlier work." In the work, Lerner cites "historical, archeological, literary, and artistic evidence for the idea that patriarchy is a cultural invention, " describes Glenn Collins in the *New York Times.* Although the author herself acknowledges that this kind of evidence is "fragile, " Sarah B. Pomeroy still criticizes her use of these sources. "To construct a grandiose paradigm demonstrating the continually deteriorating position of women," the critic writes in the *New York Times Book Review,* "Mrs. Lerner considers societies as different as the Sumerians, Babylonians, . . . Hebrews, and Greeks as though they existed on a historical continuum and evolved directly from one another." This kind of evidence, remarks Pomeroy, "does not permit definitive conclusions." Contrarily, Minnich finds that Lerner uses "careful scholarship and ever more carefully refined theoretical concepts" to present her ideas about women and the evolution of patriarchy.

The Creation of Feminist Consciousness: From the Middle Ages to 1870 is the second volume of *Women and History.* In this book, the author reviews European culture from the seventh century through the nineteenth century, showing the limitations imposed by a male-dominated culture and the sporadic attempt to resist that domination. She examines in detail the educational deprivation of women, their isolation from many of the traditions of their societies, and the expressive outlet many women have found through writing. "Interwoven with the multitudes of fascinating examples that Lerner provides is, of course, the broader argument," advises Susan E. Henking in *America.* "Mysticism, motherhood and creativity have been available—and utilized—as routes to self-authorization for centuries. Glimmers of feminist consciousness appeared and disappeared in the interstices of patriarchal culture; feminism's lineage thus reaches much further back than has been traditionally understood. Yet it did not linger. Why?" Lerner examines the many reasons for this, and gives her thoughts on what is needed to continue the social progress for women. Lynn Hunt, a contributor to *Journal of Social History,* says of *The Creation of Feminist Consciousness,* "Its range and sympathetic detail make this an excellent one-volume overview of women writing about women's consciousness in the centuries before the organization of an explicit feminist movement." Evaluating both volumes of *Women and History,* Londa L. Schiebinger states in *Journal of Interdisciplinary History:* "Together they provide a powerful history of the insidious workings of patriarchy and the toll that being left out of history has taken on women and their creativity."

Although it is a personal narrative rather than a historical study, *A Death of One's Own* contains the same humanist perspective and development of ideas as the rest of Lerner's work. Written six years after her husband's death, the work recounts Gerda and Carl Lerner's attempts to deal with the knowledge that Carl was dying of a brain tumor. The two decide on a policy of openness and honesty, sharing their feelings as the cancer progresses, even if this policy conflicts with their individual needs. "There's little melodrama or self-pity in this," observes Alex Raksin in the *Los Angeles Times Book Review,* "only an extraordinarily personal evocation of [Lerner's] struggle to achieve peace of mind through realism rather than nihilism."

In writing the book, Lerner takes an approach similar to that of her other work; she uses various sources, such as diary entries, poems, and straight narrative to present her story. "In her deeply moving book," comments Joan Kron in *Ms.,* Lerner "has woven a tapestry: recollections of Carl's illness, her conflicting diary entries from the same period, and "fragments' of her life in Europe before she became a refugee from the Nazis." In doing so, she "strives to connect past and present, living and dead in a continuum of meaning," says Helen Yglesias in the *New York Times Book Review.*

Many reviewers express similar praises for *A Death of One's Own.* Yglesias comments that it is "a book that heartens and breaks the heart at the same time," even though Lerner "is no sentimentalist, and does not sensationally display the grim details." Anne Tyler writes in the *Washington Post Book World,* "Gerda Lerner's simple ability to cope—her endurance, her strength, her willingness to fight whenever fighting will help—is admirable. . . . But what I found awe-inspiring is the fact that through it all, she never loses the capacity to feel." Tyler also finds the book to be a "pageturner," and Kron similarly finds it involving. "When Carl Lerner finally dies," Kron writes, "one not only weeps for him, but for oneself with envy for such a relationship."

In *Why History Matters: Life and Thought,* Lerner fuses memoir and scholarly thought. This collection of essays begins with her recollections of life in post-World War I Austria and describes her family's flight from the advance of the Nazis and their subsequent relocation to the United States. Lerner relates how, as a teenager, she questioned the exclusion of women from full participation in synagogue, and eventually abandoned organized Judaism for over fifty years. She reflects on her experiences with anti-Semitism, her path to scholarly eminence, and all the things she lost when she rejected her Jewish heritage and her German background. "The result is an intensely moving and intellectually satisfying collection," approves Eleanor J. Bader in *Progressive*. Bader concludes: "*Why History Matters* underscores the importance of knowing our familial, ethnic, and societal histories. These are starting points toward a world without hierarchies, war, or economic inequity." Catharine R. Stimpson in the *Nation* writes: "As survivor and historian, Lerner warns us that we cannot survive and grow—as individuals or as a species—unless we have a full, accurate, enabling sense of the past. This triple sense of loss, pain and responsibility pervades her work. . . . *Why History Matters* records her heroic quest to respect differences among women, to work hard, if not always successfully, to avoid the false universal, and to offer a unifying vision of women's history and of America."

Through the perspective of her literary and scholarly career, Lerner "can be seen as a worthy," writes Fox-Genovese. "An historian to be sure, the most active and politically astute of the opening phase of the new women's history, but also a specially talented writer, an inspiring and demanding teacher, a model as well as a companion to younger female scholars, a forceful presence in her chosen profession."

BIOGRAPHICAL/CRITICAL SOURCES:

BOOKS

Feminist Writers, St. James Press (Detroit), 1996.
Lerner, Gerda, *A Death of One's Own,* Simon & Schuster, 1978.

PERIODICALS

America, December 4, 1993, p. 17; September 16, 1995, pp. 3-5.
Booklist, June 1, 1996, p. 1744; April 1, 1997, p. 1279.
Boston Globe, April 6, 1997, p. N17.
Journal of Interdisciplinary History, spring, 1995, pp. 671-72.
Journal of Social History, spring, 1995, pp. 675-77.
Kirkus Reviews, February 1, 1997, p. 202.
Library Journal, March 15, 1997, p. 74. *Life,* May 5, 1972.

Los Angeles Times Book Review, November 17, 1985.
Ms., May, 1977; October, 1978; September, 1980; May, 1986.
Nation, May 12, 1997, p. 34.
New Republic, December 1, 1979.
New Yorker, March 25, 1972.
New York Times, April 28, 1986; July 27, 1997, p. 20.
New York Times Book Review, March 20, 1977; August 6, 1978; April 20, 1986; May 2, 1993; December 4, 1994, p. 88; July 27, 1997, p. 20.
Progressive, March, 1994, pp. 18-22; May, 1997, p. 39.
Publishers Weekly, February 3, 1997, p. 83.
Saturday Review, May 6, 1972.
Voice Literary Supplement, November, 1995, p. 24.
Washington Post Book World, August 13, 1978; January 27, 1980.

*   *   *

LETTAU, Reinhard 1929-1996

PERSONAL: Born September 10, 1929, in Erfurt, Germany; naturalized U.S. citizen; son of Reinhard F. and Gertrude (Felsberg) Lettau; married Mary Gene Carter, September 4, 1954; children: Karen, Kevyn, Catherine. *Education:* Attended University of Heidelberg; Harvard University, Ph.D., 1960.

ADDRESSES: Home—1150 Cuchara Dr., Del Mar, CA. *Office*—Department of Literature, University of California, San Diego, P.O. Box 109, La Jolla, CA 92037.

CAREER: Smith College, Northampton, MA, instructor, 1957-59, assistant professor, 1959-63, associate professor of German literature and language, 1963-67; University of California, San Diego, La Jolla, CA, professor of German literature and creative writing, 1967—. Guest lecturer at University of Massachusetts, 1958, and Mt. Holyoke College, 1960; Hanser Verlag, Munich, Germany, scout, 1965—.

MEMBER: P.E.N., Modern Language Association of America, German Academy of Performing Arts, Group 47.

AWARDS, HONORS: Prize for best German radio play, 1978.

WRITINGS:

Schwierigkeiten beim Haeuserbauen (short stories; also see below), Hanser Verlag (Munich), 1962, translation by Ursule Molinaro published as *Obstacles,* Pantheon (New York City), 1965.

Auftritt Manigs (short prose), Hanser Verlag, 1963, translation by Molinaro and Ellen Sutton published, with Molinaro's translation of *Schwierigkeiten beim Haeuserbauen,* in England as *Obstacles,* Calder & Boyars (London), 1966.

(Editor) *Lachen mit Thurber,* Rowohlt (Hamburg), 1963.

Gedichte, Colloquium (Berlin), 1967.

(Editor) *Die Gruppe 47: Bericht, Kritik, Polemik: Ein Handbuch,* Luehterhand (Berlin), 1967.

Feinde, Hanser Verlag, 1968, translation by Agnes Book published as *Enemies,* Calder & Boyars, 1973.

Taglicher Faschismus: Amerikanische Evidenz aus 6 Monaten, Hanser Verlag, 1971.

Immer kuerzer werdende Geschichten und Gedichte und Portraets, Hanser Verlag, 1973.

(Editor) Franz Kafka, *Die Aeroplane in Brescia und andere Texte,* Fischer Verlag (Frankfurt am Main), 1977.

(Co-editor) *Love Poems of Karl Marx,* City Lights (San Francisco, CA), 1977.

Fruehstueckgespraeche in Miami (comedy; first produced in Giessen, West Germany, 1978), Hanser Verlag, 1977, translation by Lettau and Julie Pradi published as *Breakfast in Miami,* Riverrun Press (New York City), 1981.

Schwierigkeiten beim Haeserbauen: Auftritt Manigs, Hanser Verlag, 1979.

Zerstreutes Hinausschaun: vom Schreiben ueber Vorgaenge in direkter Naehe oder in d. Entfernung von Schreibtischen (essays), Hanser Verlag, 1980.

Der Irrgarten: Geschichten und Gespraeche, Reclam (Leipzig), 1980.

Zur Frage der Himmelsrichtungen, Hanser Verlag, 1988.

Flucht vor Gaesten: Roman, Hanser Verlag, 1994.

Also author of "Oscar Wilde's Trials," produced on German television, 1966. Translations of Reinhard Lettau's books have appeared in France, England, Spain, Italy, Poland, Sweden, Denmark, Norway, Finland, and China.

SIDELIGHTS: Reinhard Lettau takes as his themes the absurdities of everyday life and the human response to these absurdities. In works both satirical and grotesque, Reinhard challenges the commonplace and its attendent establishment thinking; his humorous works show the influence of both Franz Kafka and James Thurber. According to *Dictionary of Literary Biography* contributors Otto F. Best and David S. Roth, Lettau's stories and poems explore "the incongruity which results when objective reality conflicts with subjective perception. . . . His language is ready to escape into a new reality that displaces the reality originally referred to."

Born and raised in Germany, Lettau came to America to study comparative literature at Harvard after completing his undergraduate studies at the University of Heidelberg. After earning his Ph.D. at Harvard he remained in America as a professor and became a naturalized citizen. His ties to Germany continued strong, however, and he lent his intellectual strength to the German student movement of the late-1960s. By that time he had already published his challenging collection of stories, published in English translation as *Obstacles.*

Lettau's stories and poetry are marked by conciseness and brevity. To quote Best and Roth, the author's works reveal "use of a concentrated style to depict everyday events with such precision that hidden elements suddenly become obvious. The stories further attest to the author's refusal to accept unquestioningly the commonplace and the established." Lettau's political views are represented in such works as *Taeglicher Faschismus,* an appraisal of the fascist nature of the American press, and *Fruehstuecksgespraeche in Miami,* a play composed of vignettes featuring deposed Latin American dictators. Best and Roth noted that the play, translated as *Breakfast in Miami,* "ridicules dictators and the people who support them."

Best and Roth concluded: "The unifying element in these heterogeneous literary and political pieces is the author's determination to take language literally. Lettau's method of getting closer to the truth is an objective, unemotional use of language, following Karl Kraus's dictum that language is not the handmaiden but the mother of ideas."

BIOGRAPHICAL/CRITICAL SOURCES:

BOOKS

Dictionary of Literary Biography, Volume 75: *Contemporary German Fiction Writers, Second Series,* Gale (Detroit), 1988, pp. 190-92.

Harris, Christopher P., *Reinhard Lettau and His Use of the Grotesque,* University of Warwick (Coventry, England), 1972.

PERIODICALS

Basis, Number 1, 1970, pp. 89-98.
Furman Studies, Volume 21, number 4, 1974, pp. 7-12.
San Diego Union, April 28, 1979.
Times Literary Supplement, July 10, 1969; October 10, 1971.*

* * *

LEVI, Primo 1919-1987
(Damiano Malabaila)

PERSONAL: Born July 31, 1919, in Turin, Italy; died from a fall down a stairwell in an apparent suicide attempt, April 11, 1987, in Turin, Italy; son of Cesare (a civil engineer) and Ester (Luzzati) Levi; married Lucia Morpurgo (a teacher), September 8, 1947; children: Lisa, Renzo. *Education:* University of Turin, B.S. (summa cum laude), 1941. *Religion:* Jewish.

CAREER: Chemist and author. Partisan in Italian Resistance, 1943; deported to Auschwitz Concentration Camp in Oswiecim, Poland, and imprisoned there, 1943-45; SIVA (paints, enamels, synthetic resins), Settimo, Turin, Italy, technical executive, 1948-77.

AWARDS, HONORS: Premio Campiello (Venice literary prize), 1963 for *La Tregua,* and 1982, for *Se non ora, quando?;* Premio Bagutta (Milan literary prize), 1967, for *Storie Naturali;* Premio Strega (Rome literary prize), 1979, for *La chiave stella;* Premio Viareggio (Viareggio literary prize), 1982, for *Se non ora, quando?;* co-recipient (with Saul Bellow) of Kenneth B. Smilen fiction award from Jewish Museum in New York, 1985; Present Tense/Joel H. Cavior literary award, 1986, for *The Periodic Table.*

WRITINGS:

Se Questo e un Uomo, F. de Silva (Turin), 1947, fifteenth edition, Einaudi (Turin), 1975, translation published as *If This Is a Man,* Orion Press (New York City), 1959, published as *Survival in*

Auschwitz: The Nazi Assault on Humanity, Collier (New York City), 1961 (also see below), new edition, 1966 (published in England as *If This Is a Man,* Bodley Head [London], 1966), dramatic version in original Italian (with Pieralberto Marche), Einaudi, 1966.
La Tregua, Einaudi, 1958, eighth edition, 1965, translation published as *The Reawakening,* Little, Brown (Boston), 1965 (also see below; published in England as *The Truce: A Survivor's Journey Home From Auschwitz,* Bodley Head, 1965).
(Under pseudonym Damiano Malabaila) *Storie Naturali* (short story collection), Einaudi, 1967.
(With Carlo Quartucci) *Intervista Aziendale* (radio script), Radiotelevisione Italiana, 1968.
Vizio di Forma (short story collection), Einaudi, 1971.
Il sistema periodico, Einaudi, 1975, translation by Raymond Rosenthal published as *The Periodic Table,* Schocken (New York City), 1984, reprinted, Knopf (New York City), 1996.
Abruzzo forte e gentile: Impressioni d'occhio e di cuore, edited by Virgilio Orsini, A. Di Cioccio, 1976.
Shema: Collected Poems, Menard, 1976.
La chiave a stella (novel), Einaudi, 1978, translation by William Weaver published as *The Monkey's Wrench,* Summit Books (New York City), c. 1986.
La Ricerca della radici: Antologia personale, Einaudi, c. 1981.
Lilit e altri racconti, Einaudi, 1981, translation by Ruth Feldman published as *Moments of Reprieve,* Summit Books, c. 1986.
Se non ora, quando? (novel), Einaudi, 1982, translation by Weaver published as *If Not Now, When?,* introduction by Irving Howe, Summit Books, c. 1985.
(Translator) Franz Kafka, *Il processo,* c. 1983.
L'altrui mestiere, Einaudi, c. 1985.
Sommersi e i salvati (originally published in 1986), translation by Rosenthal published as *The Drowned and the Saved,* Summit Books, 1988.
Survival in Auschwitz [and] *The Reawakening: Two Memoirs,* Summit Books, 1986, reprinted, 1993.
Autoritratto di Primo Levi, Garzanti (Milan), 1987.
The Collected Poems of Primo Levi, translation by Feldman and Brian Swann, Faber & Faber (Winchester, MA), 1988.
The Mirror Maker, translation by Rosenthal, Schocken, 1989.
(With Tullio Regge) *Dialogo,* Princeton University Press (Princeton, NJ), 1989.
Other People's Trades, translation by R. Rosenthal, Summit Books, 1989.

The Sixth Day, and Other Tales, Summit Books, 1990, Penguin (New York City), 1990.
Conversazione con Primo Levi, Garzanti, 1991.

SIDELIGHTS: The suicide of Primo Levi, at age 68, was more than a shocking event. It was a definitive gesture by one of modern history's witnesses, a writer who had reportedly grown increasingly despondent over the fading significance of the Holocaust from generation to generation. For Levi—an Italian Jew and concentration-camp survivor—was considered one of the premier chroniclers of the hellish conditions endured by his people during the World War II years.

A year before Levi's death, writer David Denby examined the writer for a *New Republic* article, noting that he was the product of a family "with substantial roots in the tolerant soil of northern Italy. Thoroughly assimilated, Levi's family, like most Italian Jews, did not speak Yiddish but an eccentric and seemingly contradictory mixture of the Piedmontese dialect. . .and bits of Hebrew." Trained as a chemist, Levi found his career goals restricted by the emerging Fascist government. With war looming in the late 1930s Levi and his peers reacted by withdrawal; as he once wrote: "We proclaimed ourselves the enemies of Fascism, but actually Fascism had had its effect on us, as on almost all Italians, alienating us and making us superficial, passive and cynical."

But as the Nazi party took over Italy, Levi could no longer afford to be passive. He joined the partisans in 1943, a move that, as Levi has written, was doomed to failure: "We were cold and hungry, the most disarmed partisans in the Piedmont, and probably the most unprepared." Betrayed and arrested, Levi revealed his Jewish heritage to his interrogators, "partly out of fatigue, but partly out of a sudden surge. . .of haughty pride." He was sentenced to Auschwitz.

A *Haftling* (prisoner), Levi bore the number 174517 on his arm and was set to work at a rubber factory connected with the concentration camp. He spent a year at labor, experiencing firsthand the definitive catastrophe of 20th century humanity. Release came in January 1945 with the arrival of Red Army tanks. Levi was one of only three partisans to survive.

Though he had not aspired to be a writer before his internment, Levi was compelled to tell the story of the millions who perished. In 1947 he published his first book, *Se Questo e un Uomo* (*If This Is a Man*), which was published in America as *Survival in Auschwitz: The Nazi Assault on Humanity.*

This work, according to *American Journal of Sociology* contributor W. J. Cahnman, is "literally a report from hell: the detached, scientific, unearthly story of a man who descended to the nether word at Auschwitz and returned to the land of the living." (The themes of this book have been compared to the depiction of Dante's exploring hell in the epic poetry of *The Inferno.*) Survival, in Levi's experience, means learning from prisoners shrewd in the ways accommodation and appropriation in the prison camps. In Denby's view, Levi "becomes almost vivacious in describing these schemes, the complexity of which, in this setting, can be startling. The intimates of Auschwitz, who had no chance of surviving if they merely obeyed the rules and ate what was given them, appear to have produced a classical model of rational economic behavior out of nothing— out of pieces of wood and stone, scraps of metal, cloth, and bread."

In the end, *Survival in Auschwitz* "turns out to be, of all things, a book about the forms of civilization," declared Denby. "Levi describes the system of death and survival in the camp but he also presents a variety of relationships—economic spiritual, fraternal and even cultural—that can only be called the contours of a social world." Indeed, Levi's "lack of personal bitterness is almost unnatural, especially when it is realised that he wrote so soon after the German retreat brought him his freedom," notes G. F. Seddon in the *Manchester Guardian.* "Levi's more outstanding virtue is his compassionate understanding of how in these conditions men cease to be men, either give up the struggle or in devious ways win it, usually at the expense of their fellow men." In a 1985 interview published in the *Los Angeles Times,* Levi defended his scientific approach to recounting the horrors of the Holocaust: "It was my duty not to behave as a victim, not to wail and weep, but to be a witness, to give readers material for judgment. This is Divine Law, to be a witness, not to overstate or distort but to deliver and furnish facts. The final judge is the reader."

Sergio Pacifici points out in *Saturday Review* that like *If This Is a Man, The Reawakening,* which chronicles the author's return to Italy, is more than an intimate and accurate diary. "It is a plea for self-restraint and generosity in human relations that may well be heeded in our own critical times," he says.

"Levi's lucid and wise reflections on the nature of man deserve more than a mere hearing. *The Re-awakening* must take its honored place next to Carlo Levi's *Christ Stopped at Eboli,* Andre Schwartz-Bart's *The Last of the Just,* and *The Diary of Anne Frank.*"

After the successful publication of these first two memoirs, Levi continued to write about the Jewish Holocaust in a variety of works, including two award-winning novels, *La chiave a stella* (published in English as *The Monkey's Wrench*) and *Se non ora, quando?* (published in English as *If Not Now, When?*). Toward the mid-1980s, however, Levi became progressively despondent over what he felt was a general disregard for the immense suffering and loss the Jews experienced during World War II. For reasons not clearly understood, Levi ended his life in 1987 when he jumped down a stairwell in his native town of Turin, Italy. Levi's friend Italian newspaper editor Lorenzo Mundo told Steve Kellerman of the *New York Times* that during the months preceding his death, Levi "would come to visit me and his face looked so discouraged and helpless. He kept saying he was tired, physically and mentally. And he was terribly pessimistic about the destiny of the world and the fate of the spirit of man." Since Levi's death a number of his works have been translated into English, including *The Collected Poems of Primo Levi, The Mirror Maker, The Sixth Day, and Other Stories, Other People's Trades,* and *The Drowned and the Saved.*

Other People's Trades presents 43 essays on a variety of diverse scientific and personal subjects ranging from insect behaviors to computers to the patterns of human memory. Critics have praised the impressive range of knowledge, insight, and originality evidenced by the essays, often noting that the volume provides insight into Levi as a talented writer apart from his role as a witness of the Holocaust. Christopher Lehmann-Haupt of the *New York Times* notes that "the prevalent themes of these essays are the behavior of matter, its independence of human desires and the extent to which we project our fears onto the behavior of animals that are more or less indifferent to us." Leonard Michaels, writing in *New York Times Book Review,* emphasizes the sense of alienation that characterizes Levi's contemplation of the universe and humankind's relationship to the cosmos in *Other People's Trades.*

The Sixth Day and Other Tales surprised many readers who were familiar with Levi's nonfiction; the volume contains fantastical short fables that reveal the influence of futurism and surrealism. Writing in Chicago *Tribune Books,* Constance Markey argues that Levi's fiction is weak in comparison with his nonfiction writings about the Holocaust. She comments: "Rich in imagination, Levi is nonetheless uncomfortable with fiction, not to mention comedy." Richard Eder of the *Los Angeles Times,* however, notes the limitations of Levi's short fiction but also praises the stories as imaginative vehicles of social commentary that suggest both the influence of Levi's experience of the Holocaust and his scientific training.

The Mirror Maker combines both essays and stories, many of which Levi wrote during the last twenty years of his life for the newspaper *La Stampa* in Turin. Like *Other People's Trades,* the volume contains essays on a variety of scientific topics as well as stories that reveal Levi's interest in science fiction and the fantastic. Discussing *The Mirror Maker* in *The Sewanee Review,* Gabriel Motola comments: "Levi's most engaging stories and essays remain those that address ethical and moral questions raised by political considerations and by his literary readings and scientific studies." Levi's suicide remains the subject of speculative discussion; many critics examine his later writings in hopes of finding evidence of the author's motivation to kill himself. Critics such as Isa Kapp and Michiko Kakutani, for example, perceive a note of darkness and pessimism concerning the human condition in some of the later pieces included in *The Mirror Maker.* Kapp, writing in *The New York Times Book Review,* suggests that "Levi had many reasons for faith in humanity, for feeling himself lucky. Yet perhaps he imagined that the impact of his warnings, of his moral force, was evaporating." To Richard Eder, in a *Los Angeles Times Book Review* piece, Levi "wrote of life as an immortal principle, not an immortal possession. The stubborn radiance of his notion of what it means to be human is universally accessible but individually transient. It is because the mortal Levi, with whatever depressions and despairs he may have possessed, could write as he did that what he wrote is so valuable."

BIOGRAPHICAL/CRITICAL SOURCES:

BOOKS

Camon, Ferdinando, *Conversations with Primo Levi,* Marlboro Press (Marlboro, VT), 1989.
Contemporary Literary Criticism, Gale (Detroit), Volume 37, 1986, Volume 50, 1988.

Hughes, H. Stuart, *Prisoners of Hope: The Silver Age of the Italian Jews, 1924-1974,* Harvard University Press (Cambridge, MA), 1983, pp. 55-85.

Patruno, Nicholas, *Understanding Primo Levi,* University of South Carolina Press (Columbia), 1995.

Rosenfeld, Alvin H., *A Double Dying: Reflections on Holocaust Literature,* Indiana University Press (Bloomington), 1980, pp. 37-61.

Rudolf, Anthony, *At an Uncertain Hour: Primo Levi's War against Oblivion,* Menard Press, 1990.

Short Story Criticism, Volume 12, Gale, 1993.

Sodi, Risa B., *A Dante of Our Time: Primo Levi and Auschwitz,* P. Lang (New York City), 1990.

PERIODICALS

American Journal of Sociology, May, 1960, pp. 638-639.

American Scholar, winter, 1990, p. 142.

Christian Science Monitor, May 27, 1965, p. 9.

Commentary, October, 1985, pp. 41-47.

Georgia Review, summer, 1986, pp. 576-579.

Hudson Review, summer, 1986, pp. 329-333.

Isis, June, 1986, pp. 330-332.

Listener, April 14, 1977, pp. 491-492.

London Review of Books, December 19, 1985, p. 23.

Los Angeles Times Book Review, May 31 1987, p. 11; June 17, 1990, p. 3; May 14, 1993, p. 8.

Manchester Guardian, April 22, 1960; February 12, 1965.

Nation, August 3-10, 1985, pp. 86-88.

New Leader, November 26, 1984, pp. 16-17.

New Republic, July 28, 1986, pp. 27-33; May 11, 1987, p. 42.

New Statesman, March 19, 1960, p. 410; August 20, 1971, pp. 245-46.

New Statesman & Society, October 19, 1990, p. 32.

New Yorker, May 11, 1987, pp. 31-32.

New York Review of Books, January 17, 1985, pp. 8, 10; March 28, 1985, pp. 14-17.

New York Times, November 29, 1984, p. C21; April 12, 1987, p. 42; May 22, 1989, p. C18; December 12, 1989, p. C23.

New York Times Book Review, November 7, 1965, p. 85; December 23, 1984, p. 9; October 12, 1986, pp. 1, 40-41; July 5, 1987, p. 5; May 7, 1989, p. 14; February 4, 1990, p. 15.

Observer, January 26, 1965; December 21, 1986, p. 21; April 19, 1987, p. 23; October 22, 1989, p. 49; November 11, 1990, p. 67.

Partisan Review, winter, 1989, pp. 21-23.

PN Review, Volume 14, number 1, 1987, pp. 15-19.

Publishers Weekly, February 22, 1985, p. 151; May 11, 1990, p. 246.

Saturday Review, January 2, 1960, p. 23; May 15, 1965.

Scientific American, February, 1985, pp. 23, 27.

Sewanee Review, summer, 1990, pp. 506-514.

Stand, summer, 1991, pp. 74-83.

Technology Review, April, 1990, p. 77.

Tel Aviv Review, winter, 1990, pp. 149-165.

Times Literary Supplement, April 15, 1960; December 3, 1982; March 9, 1990, p. 248; November 23, 1990, p. 1271.

Tribune Books (Chicago), July 5, 1990.

Vanity Fair, January, 1988, pp. 78-84, 94.

Voice Literary Supplement, March, 1986, pp. 10-14.

Washington Post Book World, December 30, 1984, p. 7; May 19, 1985, pp. 3, 14.

World Literature Today, winter, 1977, p. 75; winter, 1983, pp. 83-84; spring, 1983, pp. 265-266.

OBITUARIES:

PERIODICALS

Chicago Tribune, April 13, 1987.

Cincinnati Post, April 14, 1987.

Detroit Free Press, April 12, 1987.

Fresno Bee, April 12, 1987.

International Herald Tribune, April 13, 1987.

Los Angeles Times, April 12, 1987.

New York Daily News, April 12, 1987.

New York Times, April 12, 1987; April 14, 1987.

Times, April 20, 1987.

Times (London), April 13, 1987.

Wall Street Journal, April 13, 1987.

Washington Post, April 12, 1987.*

*   *   *

LEVINE, Norman 1924-

PERSONAL: Born October 22, 1924, in Ottawa, Ontario, Canada; son of Moses Mordecai and Annie (Gurevich) Levine; married Margaret Payne, January 2, 1952 (died August 15, 1978); married Anne Sarginson, August 10, 1983; children: (first marriage) Cassie, Kate, Rachel. *Education:* McGill University, B.A. (with honors), 1948, M.A., 1949.

ADDRESSES: Home—45 Bedford Rd., St. Ives, Cornwall, England; and 103 Summerhill Ave., Toronto, Ontario, Canada. *Agent*—Dr. Ruth Liepman, Maienburgweg 23, Zurich, Switzerland.

CAREER: Writer. Head of English department, Barnstaple Boys Grammar School, 1953-54; first resident writer, University of New Brunswick, 1965-66. *Military service:* Royal Canadian Air Force, 1942-45; became flying officer.

AWARDS, HONORS: Canada Council fellowship, 1959; Canada Council arts award, 1969 and 1971.

WRITINGS:

Myssium (poetry), Ryerson Press, 1948.
The Tightrope Walker (poetry), Totem Press, 1950.
The Angled Road (novel), Werner Laurie, 1952.
Canada Made Me (travel), Putnam, 1958, reprinted, Deneau, 1979.
One Way Ticket (stories), Secker & Warburg, 1961.
(Editor) *Canadian Winter's Tales,* Macmillan, 1968.
From a Seaside Town (novel), Macmillan, 1970.
I Don't Want to Know Anyone Too Well (stories), Macmillan, 1971.
Selected Stories, Oberon Press, 1975.
I Walk by the Harbour (poetry), Fiddlehead Poetry Books, 1976.
In Lower Town, Commoners, 1977.
Thin Ice (stories), Deneau, 1979.
Why Do You Live So Far Away? (stories), Deneau, 1984.
Champagne Barn (stories), Penguin, 1984.
(Editor) Walter Kaye Bauer, *A Century of Musical Humor and Show Business Wit,* Plucked String Book (Arlington, VA), 1988.
Something Happened Here, Penguin Books (New York City), 1991.

Contributor of teleplays to the Canadian Broadcasting Co. (CBC) and the British Broadcasting Co. (BBC). Contributor of short stories to *Encounter, Vogue, Harper's Bazaar, Sunday Times Magazine, Daily Telegraph Magazine, Saturday Night,* and other periodicals. Levine's manuscripts are housed at York University, Toronto, and at the Harry Ransom Humanities Research Center, University of Texas at Austin.

SIDELIGHTS: Norman Levine first left his native Canada for England during World War II and flew missions for the Royal Canadian Air Force. After finishing a degree at Montreal's McGill University after the war, Levine would return to England permanently.

His experiences as an "outsider"—a Jew in Christian-oriented Canada, a Canadian in England, then later as an expatriate visiting his homeland—have provided the basis for Levine's autobiographical novels. With *The Angled Road* (1952), about a youth's migration from rural Canada to WWII England, the author established a style of prose that is sparse in construction, realistic in tone and emotionally detached. Perhaps too detached, in the opinion of *Canadian Forum* critic Alice Eedy, who wrote of *The Angled Road:* "The effects of the last scenes is one of flat autobiographical echoes. . . . More power, more light is needed, one feels, to release [Levine] from the confines of his own narrowness."

In 1956 Levine, who had settled in Cornwall, England with his wife and children, made a trip back to Canada, criss-crossing the country "from Halifax to Ucluelet on Vancouver Island," recounts Ira Bruce Nadel in a *Dictionary of Literary Biography* piece. "Instead of merely recording his responses to the surface, however, he confronted his past and in realistic descriptive pros analyzed the meaning of his departure." The resulting book, *Canada Made Me,* became one of Levine's best-known works. What was originally intended as a travelogue, according to Nadel, "quickly became a unique Canadian autobiography," with the author blending "the essence of the immediate with the truth of the past. Flashbacks and biographies of various individuals create an absorbing text, although his portrait of the country is unsympathetic. In Canada he sees optimism and energy replaced by unhappiness and boredom. The countryside is desolate, the cities barren."

Its acerbic portrait of Levine's homeland kept *Canada Made Me* off Canadian bookshelves until 1969, though 500 copies were distributed by a publisher in that country in 1958. Canadian book critics who caught an early glimpse of Levine's work found plenty to sink their teeth into. In *Canadian Historical Review,* Hector G. Kinloch suggested that given the book's pastiche of reminiscence, autobiography, social commentary and philosophy "perhaps a psychologist would be best fitted to decide the correct shelf on which to place this repulsively fascinating soul-baring of a professional odd man out fleeting through the mammon-choked sewers of Canada from his bourgeois tormentors." Desmond Pacey of *Canadian Forum* said he tasted a "sour grapes flavor" in *Canada Made Me,* adding that the book struck as the product "of a disappointed man who felt had not realized his own potential and was eager to blame his native country for his failure." The book's reissue in

1979 brought this impression from British critic Victoria Glendinning: "*Canada Made Me* is a very good book indeed. Quite apart from the autobiographical excursions, some of [Levine's] descriptions of things newly seen are startlingly effective: there is, for example, an extended account of a visit to a slaughterhouse in Winnipeg that is disturbing and unforgettable."

"I suppose we might as well call Norman Levine's *From a Seaside Town* a novel," began Phyllis Grosskurth's *Saturday Night* review in 1970, "but the facts from [the main character's] life bears so close a resemblance to the biographical blurb about Levine on the dust-jacket that the author seems to be having a little private joke about his fiction." This book indeed continues in the author's style of "write what you know" storytelling; it describes the travails of a Canadian-born writer, Joseph Grand, who suffers from personal and professional inertia from his life as a husband and father in a small coastal English town. Maurice Capitanchik lauded Levine in a *Books and Bookmen* article by calling *Seaside Town* a "deceptively modest tale of an intelligent fidget [that] is notable for the fact that Grand weaves his despair at his fate as a slightly successful writer into a convincing individual vision." Likewise, a *Times Literary Supplement* writer found that "one of the most pleasing things about the self-investigatory tone of *From a Seaside Town* is the air of wry apology with which it is assumed."

BIOGRAPHICAL/CRITICAL SOURCES:

BOOKS

Contemporary Authors Autobiography Series, Volume 23, Gale (Detroit), 1996.
Contemporary Literary Criticism, Volume 54, Gale, 1989.
Dictionary of Literary Biography, Volume 88: *Canadian Writers, 1920-1959*, Gale, 1989.
Heath, Jeffrey M., editor, *Profiles in Canadian Literature 4*, Dundurn (Toronto), 1982, pp. 29-36.

PERIODICALS

Books and Bookmen, September, 1972, pp. 32-33.
Books in Canada, December, 1979, pp. 8-9; February, 1980, pp. 24-25; June-July, 1984, pp. 16-17; November, 1984, pp. 23-24.
Canadian Forum, October, 1953, p. 163; March, 1962, p. 285.

Canadian Historical Review, March, 1960, pp. 75-76.
Canadian Literature, spring, 1962, pp. 70-71; summer, 1970, pp. 61-67; autumn, 1976, pp. 93-96; summer, 1984, pp. 69-81.
Fiddlehead, autumn, 1985, pp. 103-105.
Journal of Commonwealth Literature, Volume 23, number 1, 1988, pp. 61-75.
Maclean's, November 19, 1979, p. 58.
Montreal Star, September 26, 1970.
New Statesman, February 15, 1980, pp. 250-251.
Queen's Quarterly, winter, 1976, pp. 690-692; summer, 1976, pp. 217-230.
Quill & Quire, August, 1984, p. 30.
Saturday Night, December, 1970, pp. 36-37.
Times (London), July 19, 1970.
Times Literary Supplement, August 28, 1970, p. 941; December 3, 1971, p. 1497; March 14, 1980, p. 289.
Today, October 11, 1980, pp. 11-13.

* * *

LEVINSON, Deirdre 1931-

PERSONAL: Born October 24, 1931, in Llanelly, Wales; came to the United States in 1965; daughter of Judah (a cantor) and Miriam (Miller) Levinson; married Allen Bergson (a psychotherapist), June 4, 1968; children: Miranda, Tobias (deceased), Malachi (adopted). *Education:* St. Anne's College, Oxford, B.A., 1954, M.A., 1957, B.Litt., 1957. *Religion:* Jewish. *Avocational interests:* Works of art, "the past and future or futurelessness of the human race."

ADDRESSES: Home—220 West 93rd St., New York, NY 10025. *Office*—Department of English, Queens College of the City University of New York, Flushing, NY 11367. *Agent*—Peggy Caulfield, A. Watkins, Inc., 77 Park Ave., New York, NY 10016.

CAREER: Oxford University, St. Anne's College, Oxford, England, part-time tutor in Old English, 1955-56; University of Cape Town, Cape Town, South Africa, lecturer in English, 1957-62; street trader in London, 1962-63; University of Maryland, Overseas Program in England, instructor in English, 1963-64; Tougaloo College, Tougaloo, MS, instructor in English, 1965; New York University, New York City, instructor in English, 1965-68; Queens College of the City University of New York, Flushing, NY, lecturer in English, 1969—.

AWARDS, HONORS: National Endowment for the Arts award, 1973.

WRITINGS:

Five Years (novel), Deutsch (New York City), 1966.
Modus Vivendi (novel), Viking (New York City), 1984.

Contributor of stories to *Commentary.*

SIDELIGHTS: Deirdre Levinson's two novels draw upon personal experience and then detail lives and situations with humor and pathos. Levinson's first book, *Five Years,* illuminates the desperation of life in South Africa during the years of apartheid. The author once told *CA:* "My novel [*Five Years*] is based on my experience, emphatically political, of South Africa. In 1962 I travelled—on foot, and on passing vehicles—from South Africa up to East Africa and Sudan, then across the Sahara, to West Africa (Nigeria and Ghana)." The first-person novel follows its English-born heroine as she teaches in Cape Town and joins a revolutionary group called the Africa People's Organisation. The level of distrust she finds within that group—as personified by its leader, Mr. French—complicates her attempt to experience "total inclusiveness." *New Statesman* contributor Conor Cruise O'Brien praised *Five Years* as "laconically and brilliantly written, full of suffering and horror, simultaneous with comedy." O'Brien added: "*Five Years* is 'an experience of South Africa.' The reality of apartheid reaches one, drily, without rhetorical accompaniment, through a personality which feels it as a permanent assault." A *Times Literary Supplement* reviewer characterized *Five Years* as "an engrossingly well-written, serious novel by a new author whom we are sure to hear of again. Her concern is with people, and she will not exhaust it easily."

Twelve years passed before Levinson released her second novel, the grim but hopeful *Modus Vivendi.* The narrative revolves around Queenie Quesky Ansell, a literature teacher who loses her infant son to heart failure after taking amphetamines early in her pregnancy. "How one woman goes on living in the face of tragedy, guilt and despair is the theme of this powerful novel," noted a *Publishers Weekly* reviewer. "[Levinson's] distinctive, vibrant narrative voice propels the chronicle and makes us care about her and think about the implications of her accommodation to a life forever altered by dark knowledge and emotional pain."

Modus Vivendi was greeted with enthusiasm by most critics. In the *New York Times,* Christopher Lehmann-Haupt called the book a "fiercely eloquent, ironic novel" and declared the prose "so affecting that it's almost lonely to leave it. A spell is broken when it ends. You feel abandoned to the trickle of your own consciousness." In her *Washington Post Book World* review, Anne Tyler deemed the novel "a strangely dense and muffled book" with an "overblown style," but nonetheless remarked: "Deirdre Levinson has a special talent for single-stroke characterization." *New York Times Book Review* correspondent Carolyn See welcomed *Modus Vivendi* as "'women's material': life and death seen, not by whole countries scorched to ashes, but one infant boy suffocating—done to death by the negligence of his mother." See added: "Mrs. Levinson has been trained. Her learning, her defiant excellence in performance, turn a novel of 'men and women' into something as harsh and implacable as an Icelandic saga."

BIOGRAPHICAL/CRITICAL SOURCES:

BOOKS

Contemporary Literary Criticism, Volume 49, Gale (Detroit, MI), 1988, pp. 226-29.

PERIODICALS

Best Sellers, November, 1984, p. 288.
New Statesman, June 17, 1966, p. 885.
New York Times, August 6, 1984, p. C22.
New York Times Book Review, September 2, 1984, p. 11.
Publishers Weekly, June 8, 1984, p. 56.
Times Literary Supplement, July 7, 1966, p. 600.
Washington Post Book World, August 26, 1984, pp. 3-4.

*   *   *

LOWRY, Lois 1937-

PERSONAL: Born March 20, 1937, in Honolulu, HI; daughter of Robert E. (a dentist) and Katharine (Landis) Hammersberg; married Donald Grey Lowry (an attorney), June 11, 1956 (divorced, 1977); children: Alix, Grey, Kristin, Benjamin. *Education:* Attended Brown University, 1954-56; University of

Southern Maine, B.A. (English), 1972, also graduate study. *Religion:* Episcopalian.

ADDRESSES: Home—8 Lexington Avenue, Cambridge, MA 02138; and Sanbornton, NH. *Agent*—Claire Smith, Harold Ober Associates, 40 East 49th Street, New York, NY, 10017.

CAREER: Freelance writer and photographer, 1972—.

AWARDS, HONORS: Children's Literature Award, International Reading Association, 1978, for *A Summer to Die;* American Library Association Notable Book citation, 1980 for *Autumn Street;* American Book Award nomination (juvenile paperback category), 1983, for *Anastasia Again!;* Boston Globe-Horn Book award, Golden Kite Award, and Child study Award, Children's Book Committee of Bank street College, all 1987, all for *Rabble Starkey;* Newbery medal, National Jewish Book Award, and Sidney Taylor Award, National Jewish Libraries, all 1990, all for *Number the Stars.*

WRITINGS:

JUVENILE NOVELS; PUBLISHED BY HOUGHTON (BOSTON), EXCEPT AS NOTED

A Summer to Die, illustrated by Jenni Oliver, 1977.
Find a Stranger, Say Goodbye, 1978.
Anastasia Krupnik, 1979.
Autumn Street, 1980, published as *The Woods at the End of Autumn Street,* Dent (London), 1987.
Anastasia Again!, decorations by Diane de Groat, 1981.
Anastasia at Your Service, decorations by De Groat, 1982.
Taking Care of Terrific, 1983.
The One Hundredth Thing About Caroline, 1983.
Anastasia Ask Your Analyst, 1984.
Us and Uncle Fraud, 1984.
Anastasia on Her Own, 1985.
Switcharound, 1985.
Anastasia Has the Answers, 1986.
Rabble Starkey, 1987.
Anastasia's Chosen Career, 1987.
All about Sam, illustrated by De Groat, 1988.
Number the Stars, 1989.
Your Move, J.P.!, 1990.
Anastasia at This Address, 1991.
Attaboy, Sam!, illustrated by De Groat, 1992.
The Giver, 1993.
Anastasia, Absolutely, 1995.

See You Around, Sam!, illustrated by De Groat, 1996.
Stay!: Keeper's Story, illustrated by True Kelly, 1997.

OTHER

Black American Literature (textbook), J. Weston Walsh (Portland, ME), 1973.
Literature of the American Revolution (textbook), J. Weston Walsh, 1974.
A Day in the Life of a Waitress (Slide), J. Weston Walsh, 1977.
Values and the Family, J. Weston Walsh, 1977.
(Photographer) Frederick H. Lewis, *Here in Kennebunkport,* Durrell (Brattleboro, VT), 1978.
(Author of introduction) *Dear Author: Students Write about the Books that Changed Their Lives,* collected by Weekly Reader's Read Magazine, Conari (Berkeley, CA), 1995.
Looking Back: A Book of Memories, Houghton, 1998.

Author of introduction, *The Secret Garden,* by Frances H. Burnett, Bantam, 1987. Contributor of stories, articles, and photographs to periodicals, including *Redbook, Yankee,* and *Downeast.*

ADAPTATIONS: Number the Stars by Douglas W. Larche with Susan Elliot Larche is based on the novel by Lowry, Dramatic Pub. (Woodstock, IL), 1996.

SIDELIGHTS: Lois Lowry is a children's writer whose books have broad appeal. She "writes well in different modes and for all ages," according to a reviewer in *Language Arts,* and her novels frequently explore topical themes, such as an adopted child's search for her real mother or the loneliness facing the elderly. She once told *CA* that she gauges her success as a writer by her ability to "help adolescents answer their own questions about life, identity, and human relationships." In a *Publishers Weekly* interview, Lowry says that "kids are too sophisticated nowadays to enjoy a completely idealized view of human existence," noting that when she was a child certain books, such as *Catcher in the Rye,* were off-limits to readers her age because "there was a feeling that kids should be protected from—what?—real life." Lowry strives to create realistic characters who suffer some of the same problems as her readers and with whom they can identify; in *Publishers Weekly* she says that "when I'm writing I always think about that kid who lives inside me."

Born the daughter of an army dentist stationed at Pearl Harbor, Hawaii, Lowry moved to Pennsylvania at the outbreak of World War II to live with her mother's family. She lived in Japan briefly following the war before returning to the United States to attend boarding school and college. She left Brown University her sophomore year to get married. Lowry explained to *CA:* "That was the '50's, and that's what you did when somebody asked you to marry him; immediately you gave up your academic aspirations. Then I had four children by the time I was twenty-five." Eventually Lowry returned to college and began writing textbooks while she was a graduate student. For some time she was a professional photographer of children, and it did not occur to her to write children's books until she impressed an editor with a short story she had written for a magazine.

Her first novel, *A Summer to Die,* involves thirteen-year-old Meg Chalmers' adjustment to living in the country for a year while her English-professor father is on sabbatical. Meg's older sister, Molly, inspires in her both feelings of jealously and inferiority, until Molly is stricken with leukemia. Through her sister's fatal illness Meg matures and discovers strength. She befriends a young couple who invite her to witness the birth of their baby, and it is through these events Meg comes to understand cycles of life and death. The book is autobiographical from the standpoint that Lowry's own sister died from cancer while they were both in their twenties, but she says that "very little [of *A Summer to Die*] was factual, except the emotions."

Well-received by critics, *A Summer to Die* garnered praise for both its form and content. "The author skillfully integrates the subplot—the natural, home birth of Ben and Maria's baby—with Molly's death, and explores the meaning of mourning, loss and sorrow without being too heavy-handed or obvious," according to a reviewer in *Kliatt.* A *Horn Book* contributor calls the novel "not simply another story on a subject currently in vogue," but rather "a well-crafted reaffirmation of universal values." The writing is "beautifully unobtrusive, yet bracing and compelling" in a *Junior Bookshelf* reviewer's eyes, and a *Publishers Weekly* contributor proclaims *A Summer to Die* "a marvelous book and a help in understanding loss."

Memories of childhood, as well as experiences as a parent, have inspired some of Lowry's most popular

characters, especially the adolescent Anastasia Krupnik. "Until I was about twelve I thought my parents were terrific, wise, and wonderful, beautiful, loving, and well-dressed," she confesses to *CA,* "By age twelve and a half they turned into stupid, boring people with whom I did not want to be seen in public. . . . That happens to all kids, and to the kids in my books as well." The precocious Anastasia is confronted with crises ranging from dealing with her weird parents (her father keeps his poetry manuscripts in the refrigerator crisper in case the house burns down) to being the only one in her class who cannot climb the rope in gym; with each volume of the series she reaches a new level of maturity.

Originally written as a short story for a magazine, Lowry decided to expand the devilish Anastasia character after growing so fond of her. As Lowry tells *CA:* "I did not intend to make [her] into a series . . . [but] I have the feeling that she's going to go on forever—or until I get quite sick of her, which hasn't happened yet. I'm still very fond of her and her whole family." As a ten-year-old in the first installment of the series, Anastasia deals with the impending birth of a sibling and her anguish over her name. In *Anastasia Again!* she must adjust to her parents decision to move from Cambridge, Massachusetts to a large Victorian house in the suburbs—a move she originally protests. Subsequent volumes address such pressing issues as Anastasia's belief that she needs psychotherapy because of all the "different personalities seething inside," and her concern over her raging hormones. Carrie Carmichael sums up the focus of the Anastasia novels in *New York Times Book Review,* "Lois Lowry addresses every teenager's fear: being weird."

Lowry depicts another family, the Tates, in several of her other books, such as *The One Hundredth Thing About Caroline, Switcharound,* and *Your Move, J.P.!.* "In her 'Tate' [novels], Lowry has created equally endearing characters who enjoy close family ties," describes Laura M. Saidman in *Twentieth-Century Young Adult Writers,* "Caroline, eleven, her thirteen year-old brother, J.P., and mother, Joanna Tate, affirm the single-parent family's ability to solve problems with humor and love." Commenting on the different books, Saidman writes: "[In] *The One Hundredth Thing About Caroline.* . . . The siblings explore the mysteries of their world, creating zany situations. In the sequel, *Switcharound,* Caroline and J.P. spend the summer with their father and stepmother, and their [three] children. . . . Caroline and J.P. resolve their differences to survive their summer visit. In *Your Move, J.P.!,* first love creates havoc in J.P.'s life."

Lowry confronts more serious topics in several of her other works. In *Find a Stranger, Say Goodbye,* Lowry tells the story of Natalie Armstrong, an adopted girl who is searching for her natural parents. *Rabble Starkey* is about a twelve-year old girl who grows up without a father and watches her best friend's mother go insane. In *Switcharound* Caroline and her brother J.P. are sent, against their will, to spend the summer in Des Moines with their father and his new wife, and are duped into babysitting and baseball coaching duties much to their dismay. "Young readers are bound to identify with these injustices of childhood," says Kristiana Gregory, writing in *Los Angeles Times Book Review,* "and also the warmth within a caring family." *Publishers Weekly* contributor Amanda Smith states that Lowry's "conviction that teenagers must be prepared to live in a sophisticated world is a major influence on her work," which is "elegant and witty . . . tempered with compassion and often with humor."

Autumn Street, one of Lowry's darker visions of childhood, is partly autobiographical. In it, Elizabeth Lorimer recounts the year she was six and moved to her grandfather's house in Pennsylvania at the start of World War II, just as Lowry had herself. Elizabeth recalls her guilt over the death of her sadistic neighbor, Noah Hoffman, and the murder of her housekeeper's grandson. Elizabeth contracts a serious case of pneumonia and falls into a coma; she regains consciousness on her birthday, the first day of spring. A reviewer in the *New Yorker* characterizes the work as "a fine novel about the twilight zone between early childhood and the first dawning of adult understanding." Though these dark themes suggest a work that is more suitable for adults than juveniles, Lowry does not object to the publisher's decision to market it as a children's book. "Publishers, for whatever reason, feel that they have to put an age level on a book," Lowry tells *CA.* "It does cross those boundaries. . . . I'm glad special people come along and find *Autumn Street* and it becomes special to them."

Lowry won the prestigious Newbery Medal in 1990 for *Number the Stars,* an historical account of Nazi-occupied Denmark during World War II. Ten-year-old Annemarie Johansen's family becomes involved

in the resistance movement by shuttling Denmark's Jews in to neutral Sweden, thereby saving them from imprisonment in concentration camps. Annemarie's best friend, Ellen Rosen, is Jewish, and poses as her sister to avoid detection by the Germans during their journey to safety. Though Edith Milton, writing in the *New York Times Book Review,* states that "the book fails to offer . . . any sense of the horror that is the alternative if the Johansens' efforts to save Ellen and her family fail," Newbery Committee Chair Caroline Ward notes in *School Library Journal,* "Lowry creates suspense and tension without wavering from the viewpoint of Annemarie, a child who shows the true meaning of courage." *Los Angeles Times Book Review* contributor Carolyn Meyer regards the book as "poignant because it may have happened just this way."

The Giver is a science fiction novel set in the future in a place where life is strictly structured and unfettered of emotional and physical wants and concerns. When children reach age twelve, they are assigned their life's work. The central character, Jonas, is selected to be the Receiver of Memories. During his training he discovers there are truths no one else knows or experiences, and he ponders what he should do with this newfound knowledge. Ann Flowers writes in *Horn Book* that "the air of disquiet is delicately insinuated. And the theme of balancing the values of freedom and security is beautifully presented." Karen Ray maintains in the *New York Times Book Review* that "despite occasional logical lapses, *The Giver* [is] a powerful and provocative novel."

Lowry once explained to *CA* that writing children's books is not as easy as it looks. "An awful lot of people believe the myth that it's easy to write for kids, so they think they can sit down and do it on Sunday afternoon after the dishes are done. People who think that are wrong. They should spend their time *reading* books for young people. A lot of them think they can write for young people but they haven't read what's being written, so they aren't familiar with it. I think, in general, anybody who wants to write anything should *a,* read a lot and *b,* write a lot, and quit worrying about who's going to buy it. It seems to be a part of the current generation, which is very impatient, to want to sit down and write something and sell it. If they'd concentrate on the writing instead of the selling, they'd probably end up a lot better off. But it's tough to convince them of that. Instant gratification seems to be very important these days."

BIOGRAPHICAL/CRITICAL SOURCES:

BOOKS

Authors and Artists for Young Adults, Gale (Detroit), Volume 5, 1990.

Chaston, Joel D., *Lois Lowry,* Twayne Publishers (New York City), 1997.

Children's Literature Review, Volume 6, Gale, 1984.

Dictionary of Literary Biography, Volume 52: *American Writers for Children since 1960: Fiction,* Gale, 1987.

Markham, Lois, *Lois Lowry,* Learning Works (Santa Barbara, CA), 1995.

Something about the Author Autobiography Series, Volume 3, Gale, 1986.

Twentieth-Century Young Adult Writers, First Edition, St. James (Detroit), 1994.

PERIODICALS

Booklist, September 1, 1982; April 15, 1993; October 1, 1996.

Christian Science Monitor, January 14, 1980.

Five Owls, September, 1993.

Horn Book, August, 1977; June, 1978; December, 1979; August, 1980; October, 1981; December, 1982; June, 1983; May, 1989; March, 1990; July, 1993; November, 1993; September, 1996.

Junior Bookshelf, August, 1979; August, 1980.

Kirkus Review, March 1, 1978; December 15, 1979; June 15, 1980.

Kliatt, April, 1979; April, 1982.

Language Arts, October, 1977; May, 1982; March, 1983.

Locus, July, 1993.

Los Angeles Times Book Review, August 27, 1989.

New Yorker, December 1, 1980.

New York Times Book Review, September 18, 1977; February 28, 1982; April 11, 1982; August 5, 1984; September 14, 1986; May 21, 1989; October 31, 1993.

Publishers Weekly, June 29, 1977; May 15, 1978; March 26, 1979; September 24, 1979; April 11, 1980; July 27, 1984; February 21, 1986; March 13, 1987.

School Library Journal, May, 1977; May, 1978; October 1979; January, 1980; April, 1980; March, 1981; October, 1981; November, 1982; November, 1984; August, 1985; August, 1988; October, 1996.

Times Literary Supplement, March 28, 1980.

Voice of Youth Advocates, August, 1993.

Washington Post Book World, May 9, 1993.

Wilson Library Bulletin, October, 1993.*

* * *

LUARD, Nicholas 1937-
(James McVean)

PERSONAL: Born June 26, 1937, in London, England; son of James McVean and Susan (Spencer) Luard; married Elizabeth Baron Longmore (a wildlife painter), February 25, 1963; children: Caspar, Francesca, Poppy, Honey. *Education:* Attended Winchester College, 1951-54, and Sorbonne, University of Paris, 1954-55; Cambridge University, M.A., 1960; University of Pennsylvania, M.A., 1961.

ADDRESSES: Home—10 Wilbraham Pl., London SW1, England. *Agent*—Jonathan Clowes Ltd., 22 Prince Albert Road, London NW1 7ST, England.

CAREER: Writer. Worked in theatre and publishing; also associated with North Atlantic Treaty Organization (NATO). Co-founder of *Private Eye* magazine. Founder of Establishment theatre club. Referendum Party candidate for British Parliament, 1997. *Military service:* Coldstream Guards, 1955-57; became second lieutenant.

MEMBER: John Muir Trust (founder and chairman), Gaia Trust (chairman), World Wildlife Federation (council member), Wilderness Trust (member, board of trustees).

WRITINGS:

NOVELS

The Warm and Golden War, Secker & Warburg (London), 1967, Pantheon (New York City), 1968.

The Robespierre Serial, Harcourt (New York City), 1975.

Travelling Horseman, Weidenfeld & Nicolson (London), 1975.

The Orion Line, Secker & Warburg, 1976, Harcourt, 1977.

(Under pseudonym James McVean) *Blood Spoor,* Dial (New York City), 1978.

The Dirty Area, Harcourt, 1979.

The Shadow Spy, Harcourt, 1979.

(Under pseudonym James McVean) *Seabird Nine*, Coward, McCann (New York City), 1981.

(Under pseudonym James McVean) *Titan*, Macdonald (London), 1984.

Gondar, Simon & Schuster (New York City), 1988.

Kala, Century Hutchinson (London), 1990.

Himalaya, Century (London), 1992.

Sanctuary, Hodder & Stoughton (London), 1994.

Silverback, Hodder & Stoughton, 1996.

OTHER

(With Dominick Elwes) *Refer to Drawer* (humor), A. Barker (London), 1964.

The Last Wilderness: A Journey across the Great Kalahari Desert, Simon & Schuster (New York City), 1981.

Andalucia: A Portrait of Southern Spain, Century, 1984.

Wildlife Parks of Africa, Joseph (London), 1985, Salem House (Salem, NH), 1986.

Landscape in Spain, with photographs by Michael Busselle, Pavilion (London), 1988.

SIDELIGHTS: Nicholas Luard has produced a diverse body of work encompassing military and espionage thrillers, fantasy novels, and travel books. Luard "is a man of parts," proclaimed Sally Ann Melia in an essay for the *St. James Guide to Fantasy Writers*. Luard is also a linguist, a conservationist, and a sometime-politician, having run unsuccessfully for a seat in Parliament in 1997.

Luard's first novel, *The Warm and Golden War*, is about a photographer, down on his luck, who becomes involved with soldiers of fortune. *Spectator* reviewer William Buchan pronounced the novel "an absorbing and original story," although occasionally marred by mixed metaphors and turgid prose. Luard has followed that book with numerous other novels of intrigue, such as *The Orion Line*, concerning a 1970s British intelligence agent investigating events that happened in World War II.

Spectator's Patrick Cosgrave found this novel's theme familiar, but Luard's handling of it "sensitive, exciting, and often brilliant." He also noted "the influence of Hemingway" in *The Orion Line*. Luard also has written thrillers with an environmental focus, under the pseudonym James McVean.

Since 1988 Luard has published several fantasy novels. Melia classified them as "a type of fantasy that draws on the myths of deepest, darkest Africa and is reminiscent of nothing so much as updated Rider-Haggard romance." She pronounced Luard "one of a new breed of writers . . . producing great colorful epics drawing on the lore of distant places and times gone by."

Luard's first fantasy epic was *Gondar*, about a nineteenth-century Scottish explorer in Africa who tries to help a deposed queen regain her position as the ruler of a land called Gondar. "Their tale is told in the expansive style of the great escapist saga-novel," commented Melia. She found the book "beautifully written, with breathtaking landscapes and richly described towns and villages" and pronounced the primary characters "confidently drawn." Melia thought another of Luard's fantasy efforts, *Kala*, suffered from insufficient development of its title character, a woman brought up by hyenas in Africa, then exploited by British stage impresarios as a novelty act. "We cannot get inside the skin of Kala," Melia remarked.

Luard's third novel in this genre, *Himalaya*, concerns a woman who happens upon an isolated group of people, the Yeti, after becoming separated from her fellow explorers in Nepal. Rival factions of the Yeti are at war; in telling their story the book changes "from an epic mountain quest . . . to something reminiscent of Jean Auel's prehistoric 'loin-cloth-ripper' *Clan of the Cave Bear* (1980), and the narrative becomes rather too stereotyped," Melia complained. She considered *Himalaya* Luard's "least successful" fantasy work, but one with good points, such as the descriptions of the mountains and valley landscape. She summed up Luard's career as a fantasy writer by saying, "His works set a new standard, his undoubted story-telling talent combining the tradition of great tales with the colours of a very real Africa, and reviving forgotten myths."

That "very real Africa" has been the subject of some of Luard's travel books as well. In *The Last Wilderness: A Journey across the Great Kalahari Desert*, Luard describes one of the most forbidding areas in the world, so dry that rivers evaporate, and with temperatures ranging from sub-freezing in the winter to 120 degrees in the summer. The Kalahari Bush people once inhabited the area, but most of them have been pushed out by such encroachments as mining and big-game hunting. "In making his journeys in the Kalahari Nicholas Luard fulfilled an ambition conceived while he was still a schoolboy," noted Eric Newby in a *Spectator* review. Newby pronounced Luard "a gifted writer" and enthused over his descriptions of the country and of the people who are remaking the Kalahari—people including Peace Corps volunteers and religious missionaries as well as hunters and mining engineers. The critic cared little, however, for Luard's travel companions, characterizing them as "raffish, hard-drinking, Restoration-type fellows who appear to have contributed nothing to the expedition except banal comments."

Spain is another focus of Luard's travel narratives. *Andalucia: A Portrait of Southern Spain* gives an account of Cordoba, Seville, Granada, Ronda, and other places in the region. But Simon Courtauld, critiquing the book for *Spectator,* thought Luard ignored a large part of Andalucia, spending little or no time on such noteworthy spots as Huelva, Almeria, and Jaen. He also found Luard's writing sometimes marred by cliche and exaggeration. He did, however, praise Luard's depictions of Andalucian peasants and the region's natural features. "Mr. Luard's book, within the limits which he ought to have set himself and accepted, has much to recommend it," opined Courtauld.

BIOGRAPHICAL/CRITICAL SOURCES:

BOOKS

St. James Guide to Fantasy Writers, St. James Press (Detroit), 1996.

PERIODICALS

New York Times Book Review, April 6, 1975.
Spectator, July 28, 1967, p. 105; January 17, 1976; October 16, 1976, p. 23; July 25, 1981, pp. 19-20; June 2, 1984, pp. 25-26.*

—*Sketch by Trudy Ring*

* * *

LUZI, Mario 1914-

PERSONAL: Born October 20, 1914, in Florence, Italy; son of Margherita (Papini) Luzi; married Elena Monale (a teacher), June 20, 1942; children: Gianni. *Education:* University of Florence, D.Ph., 1936. *Religion:* Catholic.

ADDRESSES: Home—Bellariva 20, Florence, Italy 50136.

CAREER: Poet. University of Florence, Florence, Italy, professor of French literature, 1938—.

AWARDS, HONORS: Premio Marzotto Narrative o Poesia, 1957, for *Onore del vero;* Premio Taormina, 1964, for *Nel magma.*

WRITINGS:

Un'illusione platonica e altri saggi (essays), Edizioni di Rivoluzione (Florence), 1941, enlarged edition, M. Boni (Bologna), 1972.
Biografia a Fbe, Vallecchi (Florence), 1942.
Un brindisi (poetry), G. C. Sansoni (Florence), 1946.
L'inferno e il limbo (essays), Marzocco (Florence), 1949, enlarged edition, Casa editrice II Saggiatore (Milan), 1964.
Primizie del deserto (poetry), Schwarz (Milan), 1952.
Studio su Mallarme, G. C. Sansoni, 1952.
Aspetti della generazione napoleonica: e Ed altri soggi di litteratura francese (essays), Guanda (Parma), 1956.
Onore del vero (poetry), N. Pozza (Venice), 1957.
(Editor) *L'idea simbolista,* Garzanti (Milan), 1959.
Il giusto dell vita (poetry), Garzanti, 1960, second edition, 1971.
Lo stile di Constant, II Saggiatore, 1962.
Nel magma (poetry), Garzanti, 1963, 2nd edition, All'Insegna del Pesce d'Oro (Milan), 1964, enlarged edition, Garzanti, 1966.
Dal fondo delle campagne (poetry), Einaudi (Torino), 1965.
Tutto in questione (essays), Vallecchi, 1965.
(Editor) *Faraoni* (memoirs of Enzo Faraoni), Galleria Pananti (Florence), 1969.
(Author of text with Mario de Micheli) *Cento opere di Carlo Carra,* Galleria d'arte moderna Fratelle Falsetti (Prato), 1971.
Su fondamenti invisibili (poetry), Rizzoli (Milan), 1971.
(With Carolo Cassola) *Poesia e Romanzo* (poetry), Rizzoli, 1973.
Ipazia (one-act play), Scheiwiller, 1973, enlarged edition, Rizzoli, 1979.
Vicissitudine e forma (essay), Rizzoli, 1974.
In the Dark Body of Metamorphosis and Other Poems, translation by Isidore Lawrence Salomon, Norton, 1975.
Al fuoco della controversia, Garzanti, 1978.
Tutte le poesie, two volumes, Garzanti, 1979.
Trame, Rizzoli, 1982.
Il sizenzio, la voce, Sansoni, 1984.

Discorso naturale, Garzanti, 1984.

Per il battesimo dei notri frammenti, Garzanti, 1985.

Hystrio, Rizzoli, 1987.

Scritti, Arsenale, 1989.

Corale della citta di Palermo per Santa Rosalia, San Marco Giustiniani, 1989.

L'alta, la cupa fiamma: Poesie, 1935-1985, Rissoli, 1990.

Frasi e incisi di un canto salutare, Garzanti, 1990.

Il purgatorio, la notte lava la mente, Costa & Nolan, 1990.

After Many Years: Selected Poems, Dedalus Press (Dublin), 1990.

De quibus, Zanetto, 1991.

Le parole agoniche della poesia, Alfabetica, 1991.

Io, Paula, la commediante, Garzanti, 1992.

For the Baptism of Our Fragments, Guernica (Montreal), 1992.

La luce: dal Paradiso di Dante, Galleria Pegaso, 1994.

Viaggio terrestre e celeste di Simone Martini, Garzanti, 1994.

Felicita turbate, Garzanti, 1995.

Cantami qualcosa pari alla vita, Nuova Compagnia, 1996.

La porta del cielo: conversazioni sul cristianesimo, Piemme, 1997.

Sperdute nel buio: 77 critiche cinematografiche, Archinto, 1997.

Ceneri e ardori, Garzanti, 1997.

Also author of *Reportage: un poemetto; seguito dal, Taccuino di viaggio in Cina 1980,* 1984. Contributor to *Corriere della Sera* and *Il Giornale Nuovo.*

SIDELIGHTS: One of Europe's most respected modern writers, Mario Luzi has "always been at the centre of modern Italian poetry," as Bruce Merry commented in *Modern Language Review.* Agrees *Dictionary of Literary Biography* writer Laura Baffoni-Licata, Luzi emerges as "one of the most creative, morally charged voices in the contemporary Italian poetic scene."

Luzi knew from early on that he was destined to devote his life to the written word. "I was an ordinary child," he told interviewer Mario Rosi in an article for *UNESCO Courier,* "even if I sometimes had interests that were not shared by all my chums." At the age of nine, Luzi produced his first poem, sensing "an almost physical need—a need to transfer the living element of the grass and the park where I was playing on to paper." As a boy he was taken by the epic poetry of Dante, whose *Divine Comedy* sparked Luzi's imagination for mystical and forbidden places. As he would recall in a biography years later, he had other early influences: "[Marcel] Proust, some short stories by Thomas Mann, and above all *Dadelus* by [James] Joyce impressed me greatly and gave me, among other things, the conviction that those were the true philosophers of our time."

After graduating from the University of Florence with a degree in French literature, Luzi would become a proponent of what was known as the "hermetic" movement—a period of fruitful and expressive writing from poets based, like him, in Florence. "The literary tradition of Dante's city was not the only reason why [the best poets congregated] there," Luzi remarked in Rosi's article. "During the Fascist period Florence was an 'oasis,' a place 'apart' in Italian life. Because of its marginal relationship with the country's main political and economic centres, it enjoyed a degree of cultural freedom that encouraged the emergence of innovative movements."

According to Baffoni-Licata, "Luzi's literary beginnings (1935-1940) are deeply entrenched in the hermetic movement. His poetic discourse, however, reveals immediately a new personal and lyrical voice that offers a subtle perspective, open to a judgment free of critical apriorisms." Baffoni-Licata points to *La barca*—"the source of all may later work," as Luzi commented—as an example of "the quest of a poet who slowly abandons his self-oriented search to attempt to join the flow of the world. The metaphors of the boat and of flowing, present throughout the collection, are particularly evident in the poem 'Alla vita' (To Life): *Friends from the boat one can see the world / and within it a truth that proceeds / intrepid, a deep breath / from the ends to the beginning.*"

With *La barca* and subsequent works, Baffoni-Licata continued, Luzi "never considered poetry in escape or evasion from reality but rather a deep and intense search. In his verse there is no perfection or isolation, but most the suffering of the word and, at the same time, the awareness of the impossibility of redeeming such suffering with his art."

Luzi's poems have been published in thirty languages, leading interviewer Rosi to wonder about the effect of translation on poetry. Luzi replied that the language barrier "complicates matters and is certainly a limitation. I realize that any translation is debatable, that the legitimacy of the choices made can always be questioned, and that translation is always to some extant inadequate or unfaithful. But no one, I'm glad to say, has ever been able to prevent translation from going on. And anyway, surely the whole point of poetry is that it transcends its original context, overcomes the language barrier, and carries its massage beyond the source from which it sprang."

BIOGRAPHICAL/CRITICAL SOURCES:

BOOKS

Contemporary Literary Criticism, Volume 13, Gale (Detroit), 1980.
De Vita, Ugo, *Semina: conversazione con Mario Luzi,* Edizioni Nuova Cultura (Rome), 1997.
Dictionary of Literary Biography, Volume 128: *Twentieth-Century Italian Poets,* Gale, 1993.
Forti, Marco, *Le proposte della poesia e nuove proposte,* Mursia, 1971, pp. 234-247.
Giunta, Elio, *Mario Luzi: Poeta del fluire,* Pitre (Palermo), 1977.
Landi, Michela, *Mario Lunzi: fidele a la vie,* L'Harmattan, 1995.
Luisi, Luciano and Christina Becatelli, *Mario Luzi: Una vita per la cultura,* Poligrafici (Cassino), 1983.
Macri, Oreste, *Realta del simbolo,* Vallecchi (Florence), 1968, pp. 149-176.
Mariani, Gaetano, *Il lungo viaggio verso la luce,* Liviana (Padua), 1982.
Panicali, Anna, *Saggio su Mario Luzi,* Garzinti, 1987.
Pautasso, Sergio, *Mario Luzo: Storia di una poesia,* Rizzoli (Milan), 1981.
Quiriconi, Giancarlo, *Il fuoco e la metamorfosi: La sconessa totale di Mario Luzi,* Cappelli (Bologna), 1980.
Raboni, Giovanni, *Poesia degli anni sessanta,* Riuniti (Rome), 1976, pp. 29-39.
Ramat, Silvio, *La pianta della poesia,* Vallecchi (Florence), 1972, pp. 365-375.
Salvi, Sergio, *Il Metro di Luzi,* Leonardi (Bologna), 1967.
Scarpati, Claudio, *Mario Luzi,* Mursia (Milan), 1970.
Serrao, Achille, editor, *Atti del Convegno di Studi,* Ateneo (Rome), 1983.
Squarotti, Giorgio Barberi, *Poesia e narrativa del secondo Novecento,* Mursia, 1967, pp. 75-85.
Zagarrio, Giuseppe, *Luzi,* Nuova Italia (Florence), 1968.

PERIODICALS

Anello che non Tiene: Journal of Modern Italian Literature, fall, 1988, pp. 17-30.
Approdo Letterario, Number 61, 1973, pp. 87-90.
Communita, Number 7, 1954, pp. 49-55.
Espresso, September 5, 1971, pp. 16-18; December 17, 1978, pp. 22-24.
Michigan Quarterly Review, winter, 1975.
Modern Language Review, April, 1973.
New York Review of Books, April 17, 1975.
Rivista di Letterature Moderne e Comparate, June, 1980, pp. 129-155.
Sigma, May-December, 1981, pp. 157-165.
Times Literary Supplement, January 24, 1975.
UNESCO Courier, April, 1997, p. 4.

* * *

LYNCH, Patricia (Nora) 1898-1972

PERSONAL: Born June 7, 1900, in Cork City, Ireland; died September 1, 1972; daughter of Timothy Patrick (in business) and Nora (Lynch) Lynch; married Richard Michael Fox (an author), October 31, 1922. *Education:* Educated at convent school, and at secular schools in Ireland, Scotland, England, and Belgium.

CAREER: Author of children's books. *Christian Commonwealth,* London, staff member, 1918-20.

MEMBER: PEN (Dublin; delegate to PEN Congress in Vienna), Irish Women Writers Club.

AWARDS, HONORS: Silver Medal, Aonac Tailtean, for *The Cobbler's Apprentice;* London Junior Book Club annual award, for *The Turf-Cutter's Donkey;* Irish Women Writers' Club annual award, for *Fiddler's Quest.*

WRITINGS:

The Green Dragon, Harrap, 1925.
The Cobbler's Apprentice, Harold Shaylor, 1930.
The Turf-Cutter's Donkey: An Irish Story of Mystery and Adventure, Dent, 1934, Poolbeg (Swords, Ireland), 1988.
The Turf-Cutter's Donkey Goes Visiting: The Story of an Island Holiday, Dent, 1935, published in

America as *The Donkey Goes Visiting: The Story of an Island Holiday,* Dutton, 1936.

King of the Tinkers, Dutton, 1938.

The Turf-Cutter's Donkey Kicks Up His Heels, Dutton, 1939.

The Grey Goose of Kilnevin, Dent, 1939, Dutton, 1940.

Fiddler's Quest, Dent, 1941, Poolbeg, 1994.

Long Ears, Dent, 1943.

Knights of God: Stories of the Irish Saints (Children's Book Club selection), Hollis & Carter, 1945, Regnery, 1955, new edition published as *Knights of God: Tales and Legends of the Irish Saints,* Bodley Head, 1967, Holt, 1969.

Strangers at the Fair, and other Stories, Browne & Nolan, 1945.

A Story-Teller's Childhood (autobiographical), Dent, 1947, Norton, 1962.

The Mad O'Haras, Dent, 1948, published in America as *Grania of Castle O'Hara,* L.C. Page & Co. 1952.

Lisbeen at the Valley Farm, and Other Stories, Gayfield Press, 1949.

The Seventh Pig, and Other Irish Fairy Tales, Dent, 1950, new edition published as *The Black Goat of Slievemore, and Other Irish Fairy Tales,* 1959.

The Dark Sailor of Youghal, Dent, 1951.

The Boy at the Swinging Lantern, Dent, 1952, Bentley, 1953.

Tales of Irish Enchantment, Clonmore & Reynolds, 1952, published as *Enchanted Irish Tales,* illustrated by Alan Nugent, Mercier Press (Cork, Ireland), 1989.

Delia Daly of Galloping Green, Dent, 1953.

Orla of Burren, Dent, 1954.

Tinker Boy, Dent, 1955.

The Bookshop of the Quay, Dent, 1956.

Fiona Leaps the Bonfire, Dent, 1957.

Shane Comes to Dublin, Criterion, 1958.

The Old Black Sea Chest: A Story of Bantry Bay, Dent, 1958.

Jinny the Changeling, Dent, 1959.

The Runaways, Basil Blackwell, 1959.

Sally from Cork, Dent, 1960, Poolbeg Press, 1990.

Ryan's Fort, Dent, 1961.

The Golden Caddy, Dent, 1962.

The House by Lough Neagh, Dent, 1963.

Holiday at Rosquin, Dent, 1964.

The Twisted Key, and Other Stories, Harrap, 1964.

Mona of the Isle, Dent, 1965.

The Kerry Caravan, Dent, 1967.

Back of Beyond, Dent, 1967.

"BROGEEN" SERIES, ALL PUBLISHED BY BURKE PUBLISHING, EXCEPT AS INDICATED:

Brogeen of the Stepping Stones, Kerr-Cross Publishing Co., 1947.

Brogeen Follows the Magic Tune, 1952, Macmillan (New York City), 1968.

Brogeen and the Green Shoes, 1953.

Brogeen and the Bronze Lizard, 1954, Macmillan (New York City), 1970.

Brogeen and the Princess of Sheen, 1955, illustrated by Martin Gale, Dolmen (Portaloise, Ireland), 1986.

Brogeen and the Lost Castle, 1956.

Cobbler's Luck (short stories), 1957.

Brogeen and the Black Enchanter, 1958.

The Stone House at Kilgobbin, 1959.

The Lost Fisherman of Carrigmor, 1960.

The Longest Way Round, 1961.

Brogeen and the Little Wind, 1962, Roy, 1963.

Brogeen and the Red Fez, 1963.

Guests at the Beech Tree, 1964.

SIDELIGHTS: In the literary world created by Patricia Lynch, children embark on amazing adventures where they meet leprechauns, magical animals and historical heroes of Ireland. Indeed, Lynch was noted in her day for both her scope of children's fables and the rich heritage of Irish legend and Celtic magic that imbues her stories.

In her youth, Lynch was moved from place to place to follow her father's business; later, after losing her father, Lynch settled in her native Ireland, eventually marrying another writer, Richard Michael Fox. As befitting her past, said *Dictionary of Literary Biography* writer Judith Gero John in a chapter on the novelist, themes of loss and searching appear in all Lynch's works: "Sometimes the children are miserable at home and must find new homes; sometimes they reunite with their scattered families."

The first Lynch book to gain critical and popular success was *The Turf-Cutter's Donkey* (1935), in which young siblings Eileen and Seamus are followed through several fantastical stories—as in the one where a leprechaun repairs Eileen's boots "and instills in them the power that allows her to jump great distances," as John described. On its publication, critic E. L. Buell of the *New York Times* remarked that "if the book lacks the inner significance, the final touch of inspired madness which distinguishes the best of fantasy, it has, nevertheless, more than its quota of charm." The title-creature of *The*

Turf-Cutter's Donkey—itself a magical donkey, of course—appears in the book *The Turf-Cutter's Donkey Kicks up His Heels.*

A more introspective Lynch was on display with *Fiddler's Quest,* where "there is no magic other than the spell of the story itself," according to John. Young Sheila is pulled out of school by her father, who is preparing to sail to America to seek his fortune. Unable to take Sheila with him, the father puts her on a ship bound for Dublin, where it is believed she will find her grandfather. The girl copes with her journey with the help of her violin, which she hopes to play for her grandfather, a master Irish fiddler. Beyond its merits as a children's story, said a *Book Week* reviewer, *Fiddler's Quest* "will appeal to anyone who likes realistic characters and appreciates the charm that hangs over Ireland and its people." Violins also provide the motivation in *King of the Tinkers,* which combines make-believe and reality in the tale of a boy who heads into Ireland's mountain country to retrieve his father's prized violin from the hands of the magical tinkers. With this book, said a *Boston Transcript* writer, Lynch "is rapidly ascending towards the first rank in dispensing Irish lore in truly engaging form."

In 1947, the author "produced three books that define and reserve her place in the worlds of both Irish literature and children's books," in John's words. "*The Cobbler's Apprentice* received the Silver Medal at the Aonac Tailteann festival. Lynch's autobiography, A *Story-Teller's Childhood,* offered adult readers and critics a blueprint by which to examine all of [her] works. . . .[And 1947 also brought] the first of Lynch's Brogeen books, *Brogeen of the Stepping Stones.*"

A shoemaker leprechaun, Brogeen loves to travel into the human world. "He collects companions; sometimes he has a pig, but more often he is accompanied by a tiny elephant named Trud," explained John. "In several stories he is bothered by a strange man named the Black Enchanter, who turns out to be neither black nor too much of an enchanter. The Brogeen books offer many readers a chance to view Ireland's fairyland and long for a brief visit to the [leprechaun's homeland] the Fort of Sheen." Brogeen and his friends appeared in a total of 13 collected volumes between 1947 and 1963.

In her penchant for combining the worlds of fantasy and reality, John concluded, Lynch performed a valuable service for her young readers. "The fear of being left alone, abandoned, and hungry are the fears that haunt childhood. Lynch's books frequently admit that life is hard but that even if the worst happens, there are wonderful people to meet and exciting adventures to be had on the road to a new home."

BIOGRAPHICAL/CRITICAL SOURCES:

BOOKS

Dictionary of Literary Biography, Volume 160: *British Children's Writers, 1914-1960,* Gale (Detroit), 1996.
Lynch, Patricia, *A Story-Teller's Childhood,* Dent, 1947.

PERIODICALS

Atlantic Bookshelf, October, 1935.
Booklist, September, 1935; January 1, 1938; July 15, 1943; May 15, 1962.
Books, November 3, 1935, p. 9.
Books and Bookmen, February, 1970.
Book Week, July 18, 1943, p. 10.
Boston Transcript, October 22, 1938, p. 2.
Catholic World, December, 1935.
Chicago Sunday Tribune, May 6, 1962, p. 4.
Christian Science Monitor, July 12, 1962, p. 7.
Commonweal, November 29, 1935.
Horn Book, October, 1935; November, 1938; July, 1943.
Junior Bookshelf, March, 1943; March, 1949.
Library Journal, November 15, 1938; July, 1943; July, 1969, May, 1970.
Manchester Guardian, September 30, 1938, p. 6.
New Yorker, December 4, 1943.
New York Herald Tribune Books, May 20, 1962, p. 10.
New York Times, August 4, 1935, p. 11; November 13, 1938, p. 11; August 15, 1943, p. 7.
Spectator, December 2, 1938.
Springfield Republican, December 1, 1935, p. E7; December 4, 1938, p. E7; June 27, 1943, p. E7; May 20, 1962, p. D4.
Times Literary Supplement, December 10, 1938, p. 789; December 1, 1961; May 25, 1967.
Weekly Book Review, June 27, 1943, p. 7.*

* * *

LYNTON, Ann
See RAYNER, Claire (Berenice)

LYTLE, Andrew (Nelson) 1902-1995

PERSONAL: Born December 26, 1902, in Murfreesboro, TN; died December 12, 1995, in Monteagle, TN; son of Robert Logan (a farmer and lumberman) and Lillie Belle (Nelson) Lytle; married Edna Langdon Barker, June 20, 1938 (deceased); children: Pamela (Mrs. James Law), Katherine Anne (Mrs. Talbot Wilson), Lillie Langdon. *Education:* Sewanee Military Academy, graduate; Exeter College, Oxford, student, 1920; Vanderbilt University, B.A., 1925; Yale University, School of Drama, student, 1927-29.

CAREER: Southwestern College, Memphis, TN, lecturer in American history, 1936; University of the South, Sewanee, TN, lecturer in history and managing editor of *Sewanee Review,* 1942-43, lecturer in creative writing, 1961-68, professor of English, beginning 1968, editor of *Sewanee Review,* beginning 1961. University of Iowa, Iowa City, School of Writing, lecturer, 1946, acting head, 1947. Lecturer, University of Florida, 1948-61. Lecturer at writers' workshops and conferences at Universities of North Carolina, Oklahoma, Colorado, Utah, Oregon, Florida, Dallas, and at Eastern Kentucky State College, Morehead College, Converse College, Vanderbilt University, Cumberland College, and Jacksonville University. Chairman of humanities seminar, International Seminar at Harvard University, 1958.

MEMBER: Association of Literary Magazines of America (chairman of admissions committee), South Atlantic Modern Language Association.

AWARDS, HONORS: Guggenheim fellowships for creative work in fiction, 1940-41, 1941-42, 1960-61; *Kenyon Review* fellowship for fiction, 1956; National Foundation on Arts and Letters grant, 1966-67; Litt.D., Kenyon College, 1965, University of Florida, 1970.

WRITINGS:

Bedford Forrest and His Critter Company (biography), Minton, Balch, 1931, revised edition with introduction by Lytle, McDowell, Obolensky, 1960.
The Long Night (novel), Bobbs-Merrill (Indianapolis), 1936.
At the Moon's Inn (novel), Bobbs-Merrill, 1941.
A Name for Evil (novel), Bobbs-Merrill, 1947.
The Velvet Horn (novel), McDowell, Obolensky, 1957.

A Novel, a Novella, and Four Stories, McDowell, Obolensky, 1958.
The Hero with the Private Parts (literary criticism), Louisiana State University Press (Baton Rouge), 1966.
(Editor) *Craft and Vision: The Best Fiction from the "Sewanee Review,"* Delacorte (New York City), 1971.
A Wake for the Living: A Family Chronicle, Crown (New York City), 1975.
The Lytle-Tate Letters: The Correspondence of Andrew Lytle and Allen Tate, edited by Thomas Daniel Young and Elizabeth Sarcone, University Press of Mississippi (Jackson), 1987.
Southerners and Europeans: Essays in a Time of Disorder, Louisiana State University Press, 1988.
From Eden to Babylon: The Social and Political Essays of Andrew Nelson Lytle, edited by M. E. Bradford, Regnery (Washington, DC), 1990.
Kristin: A Reading, University of Missouri Press (Columbia), 1992.

Contributor to books, including *I'll Take My Stand: The South and the Agrarian Tradition,* Harper, 1930, Herbert Agar and Allen Tate, editors, *Who Owns America?,* Houghton, 1936, and to *White Folks Primer, American Harvest, Introduction to Literature,* and other anthologies. Contributor to literary reviews.

SIDELIGHTS: "William Faulkner is an undisputed fact of our literature," began Robert V. Weston in a *Southern Review* article. "Andrew Lytle is a neglected, little-understood figure, who is in some danger of suffering a total eclipse."

While Lytle was a peer of Faulkner, Robert Penn Warren and other Southern-based luminaries, he remains today something of a background figure in discussions of the century's most influential genre writers. This, Weston felt, does Lytle an injustice: "In terms of literary significance, of quality and value, Lytle stands up surprisingly well against the Goliath of Southern fiction. His position is not exactly that of a David, but just as David was able to accomplish a great deal with a few well-chosen stones, so Lytle has managed with little more than three books to project an imaginative vision that turns out to be even larger than Yoknapatawpha County."

Born in 1902 in Tennessee, Lytle literally grew up with the 20th century, establishing himself early as someone with a literary air. In fact, the young Lytle was known "for walking down the street talking to himself—imagining scenes in internal dramas," according to a profile by J. O. Tate published in *Dictionary of Literary Biography Yearbook.* After graduating from Vanderbilt University in 1925, Lytle began a literary odyssey that took him from Yale to New York's Greenwich Village. But he would return to his roots in Tennessee, where the author would produce his best-known works.

A proponent of the Southern Agrarian movement, which advocated farming and warned of the dangers of industrialization, Lytle published his first nonfiction book, *Bedford Forrest and His Critter Company,* in 1931. At that time, "young southerners were fired by the outrageousness of American history and in response gave a new life to it," said Tate. "Lytle's [*Bedford Forrest*] must be seen today a probably the most orally inflected of all modern books about the Civil War, for its author had grown up with Forrest's name 'in the air'—the hero had saved [the author's hometown of] Murfreesboro. He had known old soldiers who had ridden with Forrest and had even spoken with the general's sister. Lytle's Forrest is the epic hero who defended his community, and the betrayal of Forrest by his superiors explains why the South lost the war."

The historical novel *The Long Night,* also set in the Civil War years, was hailed by Hamilton Basso in 1936 as "the best fictional performance of the Southern Agrarians." In his *New Republic* review, Basso went on to note that some scholars compare Lytle's writing to that of the Russian legend Fyodor Dostoevski. But, said Basso, Lytle's book "deserves more substantial praise than that. The emotion in this book is not terror, there is nothing Doestoevskian about it, it is simply a very good story about a man who sets out to avenge the murder of his father."

Lytle's best-known fictional work was his fourth and last such effort *The Velvet Horn,* "a novel that was clearly intended as a magnum opus," as Tate remarked. Certainly, the essayist continued, *The Velvet Horn* "is a tour de force of language and technique, and beyond that a Jungian and Shakespearean exploration of individuation and sexuality, innocence and guilt, the local and the universal." As described by *Dictionary of Literary Biography* writer James Kilgo, the two stories that make up *The Velvet Horn* "are those of young Lucius, which occurs in the novel's present, and his mother Julia, which belongs to the past. As Julia's brother and Lucius' uncle, [protagonist Jack Cropleigh] knows both stories and functions

for the reader as what Lytle calls 'the hovering bard' who alone among the characters has enough information to make sense of the various fragments." The setting is a gothic, drought-ravaged Southland; as the novel begins, uncle and nephew search the hills for water. There Lucius meets a mountain family's daughter, with resulting images of seduction, suicide, alcoholism, and eventually murder.

Southern Review critic Robert V. Weston praised *The Velvet Horn* as having "more variety of style and pace" than previous Lytle fictions: "There are portions which are straightforward, rapid narrative; there are lengthy conversations in Tennessee mountain dialect that is as flawless as the Mississippi delta dialect in Faulkner. There are scenes of action so dramatically shaped that they could be staged. And throughout it all, through the careful use of allusive imagery, we are alerted to deeper implications of meaning than those which meet the eye."

When not publishing books, Lytle taught creative writing and was editor of the acclaimed *Sewanee Review.* Lytle, who had raised three daughters with his wife, lived a life of courtly Southern manners; visitors to his Tennessee home (called Log Cabin) were served bourbon out of silver cups and enjoyed biscuits made by the author himself. The occasion of his death in 1995 brought the reminiscence from friend and author Madison Smart Bell, published in *Dictionary of Literary Biography Yearbook.* To Bell, Lytle "was the author of more than one masterpiece of fiction, but perhaps his life was his greatest work."

BIOGRAPHICAL/CRITICAL SOURCES:

BOOKS

Bradford, M. E., editor, *The Form Discovered: Essays on the Achievement of Andrew Lytle,* University and College Press of Mississippi, 1973.

Contemporary Literary Criticism, Volume 22, Gale (Detroit), 1982.

Dictionary of Literary Biography, Volume 6: *American Novelists since World War II,* Gale, 1980.

Dictionary of Literary Biography Yearbook: 1995, Gale, 1996.

Kramer, Victor A., *Andrew Lytle, Walker Percy, Peter Taylor: A Reference Guide,* G. K. Hall (Boston), 1983.

Lucas, Mark, *The Southern Vision of Andrew Lytle,* Louisiana State University Press, 1986.

Madden, David, editor, *Rediscoveries,* Crown, 1971, pp. 17-28.

Rubin, Louis D., Jr., editor, *A Bibliographical Guide to the Study of Southern Literature,* Louisiana State University Press, 1969, p. 243.

Wright, Stuart T., *Andrew Nelson Lytle: A Bibliography, 1920-1982,* University of the South (Sewanee, TN), 1982.

PERIODICALS

Atlantic, September, 1958.

Chattahoochee Review, summer, 1988.

Critique, winter, 1967-68, pp. 53-68.

Georgia Review, summer, 1968, pp. 208-221.

Michigan Quarterly Review, summer, 1972, pp. 186-190.

Mississippi Quarterly, fall, 1970.

New Republic, September 30, 1936, p. 231; August 25, 1947, p. 31.

New York Times, August 31, 1958.

New York Times Book Review, September 6, 1936, p. 9.

San Francisco Chronicle, August 10, 1947.

Saturday Review, August 17, 1957, pp. 13-14.

Sewanee Review, winter, 1971, pp. 130-139; fall, 1975, pp. 730-736.

Southern Literary Journal, fall, 1974, pp. 67-77.

Southern Review, January, 1971; July, 1976, pp. 673-677; January, 1979, pp. 34-51.

Wisconsin Studies in Contemporary Literature, autumn, 1967.

OBITUARIES:

PERIODICALS

Los Angeles Times, December 16, 1995, p. A26.

New York Times, December 15, 1995, p. B7.

Washington Post, December 15, 1995, p. D4.*

M-P

MacDONALD, Suse 1940-

PERSONAL: Given name rhymes with "news"; born March 3, 1940, in Evanston, IL; daughter of Stewart Y. (a professor) and Constance R. McMullen; married Stuart G. MacDonald (an architect), July 14, 1962; children: Alison Heath, Ripley Graeme. *Education:* Attended Chatham College, 1958-60; University of Iowa, B.A., 1962; also attended Radcliffe College, Art Institute, and New England School of Art and Design.

ADDRESSES: *Home*—Box 88, South Londonderry, VT 05155. *Office*—Box 25, South Londonderry, VT 05155. *Agent*—Phyllis Wender, 3 East 48th St., New York, NY 10017.

CAREER: United Press International, New York City, executive secretary to the picture editor, 1964; Caru Studios, New York City, textbook illustrator, 1964-69; MacDonald & Swan Construction, South Londonderry, VT, architectural designer, 1969-76; freelance advertising artist, 1982-85; author and illustrator, 1986—.

MEMBER: Society of Children's Book Writers and Illustrators, Authors Guild, Graphic Artists' Guild.

AWARDS, HONORS: "Editor's choice" citation, *Booklist,* "best books of the year" citation, *School Library Journal*, "pick of the lists" citation, American Booksellers Association, all 1986, Golden Kite Award, Society of Children's Book Writers, and Caldecott Honor Award, American Library Association, both 1987, all for *Alphabatics;* Gold Medal for preschool book, National Parenting Publication Awards, for *Nanta's Lion: A Search-and-Find Adventure.*

WRITINGS:

Alphabatics (children's picture book; Junior Literary Guild selection), Bradbury (New York City), 1986.
(With Bill Oakes) *Numblers* (children's picture book), Dial (New York City), 1988.
(With Oakes) *Puzzlers,* Dial, 1989.
(With Oakes) *Once upon Another,* Dial, 1990.
Space Spinners, Dial, 1991.
(Illustrator) Hank de Zutter, *Who Says a Dog Goes Bow-Wow?,* Doubleday (New York City), 1993.
Sea Shapes, Harcourt (San Diego, CA), 1994.
Nanta's Lion: A Search-and-Find Adventure, Morrow (New York City), 1995.
Peck, Slither and Slide, Harcourt, 1997.
Elephants on Board, Harcourt, 1999.

SIDELIGHTS: Suse MacDonald's children's books use bright, imaginative illustrations to illustrate simple stories and concepts for preschoolers. Her first book, *Alphabatics,* is also one of her most successful, having been honored with the prestigious Caldecott Award and numerous other accolades. Aimed at children between two and five years old, it uses two-page spreads to transform letters into images. In *Puzzlers,* which was coauthored with Bill Oakes, colorful collages of numbers introduce ideas of size and direction, such as widest, "backward," "first," and so on. A *Publishers Weekly* reviewer praised the illustrations and declared that "the fun-filled presentation . . . will teach children in an encouraging way."

MacDonald and Oakes collaborated again on *Once upon Another,* which features two stories, one reading from front to back, the other from back to front. The stories are retold versions of favorite old fables, "The Tortoise and the Hare" and "The Lion and the Mouse," and the characters are represented by abstract forms created from torn paper. The book is "brilliant in color, conceptions, and design," approved a *Kirkus Reviews* writer, who also called it "a feast for the eye." Collages were featured again in Hank de Zutter's *Who Says a Dog Goes Bow-wow?,* illustrated by MacDonald. This book presents sixteen animals and tells how the sounds each makes are interpreted in various languages. A *Publishers Weekly* reviewer observed that the book encourages global thinking and praised MacDonald's "expressive menagerie" depicted in "bursts of color."

In *Sea Shapes* MacDonald transformed basic shapes such as diamonds, ovals, and spirals into a variety of sea creatures. A left-hand page shows the transformation of a diamond into multiple fish scales, for instance, and the right-hand page shows the fish in its natural environment. The book also includes a glossary providing information about the creatures and their habitats. According to a *Horn Book* reviewer, "Ocean animals and simple shapes become a very elegant combination" in the book.

MacDonald's 1995 book, *Nanta's Lion: A Search-and-Find Adventure,* features a Masai girl searching for the lion that has been hunting her village's cattle. Nanta is unsuccessful, but attentive readers will find an image of the elusive lion in the book's final spread, built up gradually by the die-cut pages in what a *Publishers Weekly* reviewer deemed a "snazzy surprise ending."

Another animal-oriented book, *Peck, Slither and Slide,* encourages readers to guess which creature is pecking, slithering, or sliding. In comments to *CA,* MacDonald described it as "a playful concept book about animal behavior, action verbs, and visual discovery." The author rounded out the book with notes about the animals' size, habitat, and way of life. MacDonald described *Elephants on Board* as "a playful tale about a dozen elephants' trip to the circus. When their bus breaks down they decide that nearby mammoth construction equipment can get them there on time. A ride is found but not in the way they expect."

MacDonald once told *CA:* "After college I married, and my husband and I settled in New York City. I wanted to get a job using my artistic talents, but several years passed before I landed a position at Caru Studios, where I made illustrations for textbooks. I stayed there for five years.

"Then my husband and I moved back to the family farm in Weston, Vermont, and took over a construction company. We worked together in the construction business for ten years and raised two children. While both kids were young, we spent a lot of time at the farm pond, and I found myself searching, as I had when I was a child, among the reeds and beneath the surface to find out what lived there. I began making drawings and thinking once again about illustrating books.

"When our second child entered first grade, I decided to pursue that interest. I quit my job and went back to school. I drove back and forth between Vermont and Boston for four years, attending classes at Radcliffe, the Art Institute, the New England School of Art and Design, and other schools in the city. I took courses in all sorts of things, including illustration, silkscreening, paper making, sketching, drawing, design, topography, and writing. It is hard to pinpoint the time when I decided that children's book illustration was the field in which I wanted to concentrate my energies. My interests just seemed to lean in that direction.

"Eventually I enrolled in Marion Perry's classes in children's book writing and illustration at Radcliffe. It was then that I really became involved in children's books. I wrote and illustrated several stories, including 'Matt the Fat Cat,' a tale which my young son had written.

"After completing my studies, I bought an old house in South Londonderry, Vermont, in partnership with two other artists. We spent six months renovating the building and setting up six artist's studios, one for each of us and three which we rent. I put together a portfolio and began to look for work, in both advertising and the children's book field. My first assignments were paper sculpture for advertising. These kept me going financially as I began to make the rounds of the children's book publishers.

"*Alphabatics* is the result of an idea which I had for a long time. The idea emerged from the wealth of information which I gathered while taking topography in art school. In that course, we worked exclusively with letter forms, shrinking and expanding them and manipulating their shapes in various ways.

I was intrigued by the process and felt there were possibilities in it for a book. It was several years, however, before I put my ideas down on paper. Once I did, the first publisher I showed it to liked the idea, and I was on my way.

"Selling that book, which was my first, was very exciting. I love the picture book format and feel it offers challenging opportunities for creative illustration."

BIOGRAPHICAL/CRITICAL SOURCES:

PERIODICALS

Booklist, May 15, 1993, p. 1693; September 1, 1994, p. 46; April 15, 1995, p. 1506.
Horn Book, January-February, 1990, p. 55; November-December, 1994, p. 722.
Kirkus Reviews, July 15, 1990, p. 1005.
Publishers Weekly, August 25, 1989, p. 63; August 10, 1990, p. 444; November 1, 1991, p. 80; January 25, 1993, p. 86-87; April 24, 1995, p. 71; March 31, 1997.
School Arts, April, 1990, p. 61.
School Library Journal, October, 1989, p. 91; November, 1990, p. 96; October, 1991, p. 100; August, 1993, p. 156; November, 1994, p. 84; May, 1995, p. 86.

*   *   *

MACINTYRE, Ben 1963-

PERSONAL: Born in 1963.

CAREER: Journalist and author. Worked as foreign affairs reporter for England's *Sunday Correspondent,* New York bureau chief of London *Times,* and Paris bureau chief of London *Times.*

WRITINGS:

Forgotten Fatherland: The Search for Elisabeth Nietzsche, Farrar, Straus (New York City), 1992.
The Napoleon of Crime: The Life and Times of Adam Worth, Master Thief, Farrar, Straus, 1997.

Contributor to periodicals, including the *New York Times Book Review.*

SIDELIGHTS: Journalist Ben Macintyre has written biographies of two controversial, flamboyant figures: Elisabeth Nietzsche, the sister of philosopher Friedrich Nietzsche and the founder of a racially-pure community in the jungles of Paraguay, and Adam Worth, a legendary criminal mastermind of the 1890s.

Macintyre's first book, *Forgotten Fatherland: The Search for Elisabeth Nietzsche,* details the life of German philosopher Friedrich Nietzsche's sister Elisabeth and the ways in which she affected the life and writings of her brother. As Macintyre explains in the book, Elisabeth not only destroyed Nietzsche's relationship with Lou Andreas Salome, a woman he proposed marriage to, but she herself married a rabid anti-Semite, Bernhard Forster. The Forsters traveled to Paraguay in 1886 to form an idealistic, "pure" Aryan community, but when it failed and Forster committed suicide, Elisabeth returned to Germany to take care of her brother, who by that time was seriously mentally ill.

Macintyre notes in *Forgotten Fatherland* that though Friedrich Nietzsche had already published several works of philosophy, he was not yet famous. Under Elisabeth's care—and with her revising his works so that they appeared to embrace fascism and anti-Semitism when originally they did not—Nietzsche's prestige began to increase. After his death, but still within the lifetime and influence of Elisabeth, his philosophy was adopted and used by Adolf Hitler and the Nazi regime. Indeed, when Elisabeth died at the age of eighty-nine in 1935, Hitler gave her a state funeral and wept over her casket. As Macintyre told Jon Elsen in the *New York Times Book Review,* Elisabeth "did a brilliant job of making [Nietzsche] famous and at the same time making him infamous. She overlaid him with her own views—but she did it in a very stylish way."

In addition to relating these events in *Forgotten Fatherland,* Macintyre also tells of his own journey to the remains of the Paraguayan colony that Elisabeth and her husband founded. There, Simon Collier reported in the *New York Times Book Review,* "a handful of descendants of the original families still survived, still scraped a modest living from the poor soil, still spoke German with a thick Saxon accent and still preserved a residual notion of Aryan supremacy." They also displayed the effects of severe inbreeding. George Steiner, reviewing *Forgotten Fatherland* in the *New Yorker,* praised Macintyre for linking these two aspects of Elisabeth Nietzsche's story together, calling it "a sparkling idea" that "yields vivid travel writing and information of a ghostly but fascinating sort."

In his second book, *The Napoleon of Crime: The Life and Times of Adam Worth, Master Thief,* Macintyre offered a biography of the man who served as the real-life model for Professor Moriarty—the fictional archenemy of detective Sherlock Holmes. Adam Worth was the son of German Jewish immigrants who came to America around 1850. Worth began his adult life honestly enough, working as a clerk in a store. His criminal activities began after he enlisted with the Union Army at the outbreak of the Civil War. He fought and was wounded at the Battle of Bull Run, then found a way to be declared dead— freeing him to reenlist many times under assumed names, deserting each time after he collected the thousand dollar enlistment bounty. When the war ended and this means of income was closed to him, Worth drifted north to New York City, where he became a pickpocket. He was arrested and imprisoned in Sing Sing, but escaped by tugboat to return to Manhattan. He changed his vocation to that of burglar and eventually formed a partnership with Mother Mandelbaum, a shrewd, tough woman known as the best fence for stolen goods in New York.

Worth's exploits gradually became more daring and ambitious. He and a partner eventually pulled off a million-dollar bank robbery in Boston, then headed to London. In Liverpool, Worth met the woman who would be the love of his life, Kitty Farrell. She was a waitress at the time, but soon joined Worth and his partner, "Piano Charley" Bullard. Worth and Bullard expanded their operations across England and Europe, meanwhile establishing themselves under assumed names as wealthy, respectable gentlemen. Despite his countless crimes, Worth was in some ways a decent man, disdaining violence, never carrying a gun, and going to great lengths and expense to protect and care for his international gang. His most daring crime was the theft of Thomas Gainsborough's famed portrait of Georgiana, the Duchess of Devonshire. He intended to use it to ransom his brother from prison, but shortly after he got the painting, his sibling was released on a technicality. Worth developed a strange obsession with the portrait, in part because it reminded him of Kitty, who had deserted him and broken his heart. He never sold the painting, but he sometimes slept with it under his pillow and took it with him when he traveled.

Reviewing *The Napoleon of Crime* in the *New York Times,* John Mortimer comments: "The drug culture has imposed a deadening uniformity on robbery. . . . Criminals, on the whole, seem to have become as brutal and unintelligent as the films and television programs that are made about them. How refreshing it is, therefore, to look back at a more enlightened age, and to a master thief who hated violence and was impeccably loyal to his employees. . . . All praise then to Ben Macintyre. . . . [He has produced] a hilarious and highly readable account of a time when there was still a certain amount of honor among thieves." A *Los Angeles Times Book Review* reviewer, Allen Barra, comments that "Macintyre's detective work in unearthing the details of his subject's crimes is as exemplary as that of Worth's lifelong nemesis, William Pinkerton of the Pinkerton Detective Agency." Mike Phillips asserted in the *New Statesman,* "Macintyre . . . treats Worth as a brilliant, flawed human being, driven by the greed and moral ambiguity that shaped the mores of his time. In spite of the accumulation of detail and the sheer breadth of the book's reach he maintains a firm grip on his narrative and, in the end, his portrait of Worth as a tragic figure is almost persuasive." Richard Bernstein concluded in the *New York Times* that *The Napoleon of Crime* is "a brisk, lively, colorful biography of an amazing criminal."

BIOGRAPHICAL/CRITICAL SOURCES:

PERIODICALS

Atlantic Monthly, September, 1997, p. 117.
Booklist, August, 1997, p. 1857.
Economist, November 15, 1997, p. 12.
Insight on the News, January 12, 1998, p. 36.
Kirkus Reviews, May 15, 1997, p. 778.
Library Journal, June 15, 1997, p. 84.
Los Angeles Times, September 24, 1992, p. E2.
Los Angeles Times Book Review, August 31, 1997, p. 9.
New Republic, November 9, 1992, p. 50.
New Statesman, August 1, 1997, p. 48.
New Yorker, October 19, 1992, pp. 122-26; August 11, 1997, p. 76.
New York Times, August 27, 1997, p. C13.
New York Times Book Review, October 4, 1992, p. 9; August 24, 1997, p. 10.
Observer, June 15, 1997, p. 16.
People, October 27, 1997, p. 33.
Publishers Weekly, May 26, 1997, p. 72.
Smithsonian, October, 1997, p. 152.
Times (London), April 9, 1992, p. 4.
Washington Post, August 13, 1997, p. C2.

Washington Post Book World, September 27, 1992, p. 5.

* * *

MALABAILA, Damiano
See LEVI, Primo

* * *

MANNING, Rosemary (Joy) 1911-1988
   (Sarah Davys, Mary Voyle)

PERSONAL: Born December 9, 1911, in Weymouth, Dorset, England; died April 15, 1988, of pancreatic cancer, in Tunbridge Wells, Kent, England. *Education:* Attended Poltimore College, Devon, 1924-30; University of London, B.A. in classics, 1931. *Avocational interests:* Music, books, the country.

CAREER: Writer. Worked as shop assistant and secretary, 1933-37; school teacher in Sussex, 1938-42, and in St. George's, Ascot, 1942-43; joint headmistress of school in Hertfordshire, 1943-50, and of St. Christopher's School, Hampstead, 1950-72.

WRITINGS:

NOVELS

(Under pseudonym Mary Voyle) *Remaining a Stranger,* Heinemann (London), 1953.
(Under pseudonym Mary Voyle) *A Change of Direction,* Heinemann, 1955.
The Shape of Innocence, Doubleday (New York City), 1960, published in England as *Look, Stranger,* J. Cape (London), 1960.
The Chinese Garden, J. Cape, 1962, Farrar, Straus (New York City), 1964, reprinted, Brilliance Books, 1984.
Man on a Tower, J. Cape, 1965.
Open the Door, J. Cape, 1983.

JUVENILE

(Editor) *The Shepherds' Play* [and] *Noah and the Flood: Two Miracle Plays Arranged for Young People,* Grant, 1955.
Arripay, illustrated by Victor Ambrus, Constable, 1963, Farrar, Straus, 1964.

Boney Was a Warrior, Hamish Hamilton, 1966.
Heraldry, illustrated by Janet Price, A. & C. Black, 1966.
(Editor) William Blake, *A Grain of Sand: Poems for Young Readers,* engravings by Blake, F. Watts, 1967.
The Rocking Horse, illustrated by Lynette Hemmant, Hamish Hamilton, 1970.
(Condensor) Charles Dickens, *Great Expectations,* illustrated by Gareth Floyd, Collins, 1970.
Rosemary Manning's Book of Railways and Railwaymen, Kestrel Books (London), 1977.

"SUSAN AND R. DRAGON" SERIES

Green Smoke, illustrated by Constance Marshall, Doubleday, 1957, reprinted, 1982.
Dragon in Danger, illustrated by Marshall, Doubleday, 1959, reprinted, 1982.
The Dragon's Quest, illustrated by Marshall, Doubleday, 1961.
Dragon in the Harbour, illustrated by Peter Rush, Kestrel Books, 1980.

OTHER

From Holst to Britten: A Study of Modern Choral Music, Workers' Music Association (London), 1949.
(Under pseudonym Sarah Davys) *A Time and a Time: An Autobiography* (autobiography of Manning), Boyars (New York City), 1971, new edition with introduction (under name Rosemary Manning), 1986.
A Corridor of Mirrors (autobiography), Women's Press (London), 1987.

Also author of *Down by the Riverside,* 1983. Contributor of short stories to *Cornhill, Cosmopolitan, Transatlantic Review, Homes and Gardens, Horizon,* and *Mademoiselle;* contributor of book reviews to newspapers.

SIDELIGHTS: The fiction of Rosemary Manning is distinguished, according to Andrew Sinclair in the *Times Literary Supplement,* by "her rare grace, her spare plotting, [and] her excellent interweaving of legends and private lives." Predominantly set in the west country of England, Manning's novels reflect the author's interest in history and folklore, and have been particularly noted for stylistic originality. Of *The Chinese Garden,* which deals with corruption in an all-girls boarding school, Haskel Frankel commented in the *New York Herald Tribune Books* that

Manning "is a stylist writing of our century but calling to mind an earlier time." Frankel added that the novel displays "something of the misty, undefined evil that pervades [Henry James's] 'The Turn of the Screw' . . . [and] something of the controlled violence of [Emily Bronte's] 'Wuthering Heights,'" yet he concedes that Manning's style is very much her own. A *Times Literary Supplement* contributor similarly remarked on Manning's 1965 novel *Man on a Tower:* "It is not often that one is confronted with a novel which is peculiar to itself and whose peculiarity is completely acceptable. . . . Rosemary Manning is a novelist of unusual interest. She combines realism with stylization and can produce without effort the nuances of atmosphere whether scenic or moral—it is impossible to compare her with anyone else but most rewarding to read her."

Manning was also a noted author of books for young people, including the "Susan and R. Dragon" series which features an amiable 1500-year-old Cornish dragon and the young girl who befriends him. Regarding the fourth book in the series, *Dragon in the Harbour,* Judith Elkin wrote in the *Times Literary Supplement:* "This is a pleasant, lively story, again establishing the dragon as a real character: gregarious, moral, at times short-tempered and always hungry. This fantasy element in an everyday setting and interspersed with a mystery, makes a light-hearted and very readable story for younger children." Manning's interest in history was also evident in her books for young people. *Arripay,* set in fifteenth-century England at the time of the Hundred Years War with France, is the compassionate story of a fisherman's son who must choose between pursuing the pious lifestyle of a monk or the adventurous, potentially wealthy, world of a pirate. A reviewer for the *Times Literary Supplement* remarked that "Rosemary Manning tells the story of one of those unfortunates who are born out of their time," praising her characterization of the young man, in addition to her descriptions of natural landscapes, for their "most extraordinary luminous quality."

Manning embarked on a different direction with her autobiography *A Time and a Time,* first published under the pseudonym Sarah Davys, and later reissued under Manning's own name. Written after a suicide attempt, *A Time and a Time* traces significant cornerstones of Manning's life: important childhood influences, her long career as a headmistress and writer, and various lesbian love affairs. A reviewer for the *Times Literary Supplement* wrote that the emphasis in *A Time and a Time* is on internal exploration: "It is

the chronicle of an inner life and therefore of an emotional search, chiefly through homosexual loves: much that is part of most people's lives is noticeably absent or blurred." The reviewer added that although the book displays "tendencies to pose, to evade, to settle for 'fine writing' . . . it penetrates deeply into the nature of a particular kind of loneliness, and the painful page-to-page struggle for honesty compels respect."

Manning's second autobiography, *A Corridor of Mirrors,* was published in 1987 and further explores themes of love and loss as well as examining her inspiration as a writer and as a woman. Regarding *A Corridor of Mirrors,* Michele Roberts wrote in the *New Statesman* that an important relationship exists between outer events and inner experience: "Weaving against [a] strand of 'history' and constantly interrupting it is another thread: paragraphs, chapters, that chart the painful and joyous ebb and flow of desire that resulted in love affairs with women and the writing of books. . . . These two strands, fighting and intertwining, make for wonderful, helterskelter reading, a sense of being in conversation with the author." Manuel Stimpson added in the *Times Literary Supplement* that Manning's new autobiography explores "her past, her family, her friends, and herself with fresh understanding. . . . One senses that her views of what she has written about may yet undergo further changes." Stimpson concluded that this aspect of *A Corridor of Mirrors* "enhances the book, making clear as few autobiographies have done that we are never finished with our past."

"Rosemary Manning," wrote Lis Whitelaw in *Gay and Lesbian Literature,* "always claimed, in *A Corridor of Mirrors* and elsewhere, that she did not write *as* a lesbian and that the habit of secrecy that she cultivated for much of her life did not affect her writing. She was convinced that the freedom to write openly about gay sexuality would not produce better writing. What this argument fails to acknowledge, however, is that she always wrote out of her pain and frequent loneliness, and that much of that pain and loneliness was a direct consequence of her lesbian identity."

BIOGRAPHICAL/CRITICAL SOURCES:

BOOKS

Gay and Lesbian Literature, Volume 2, St. James Press (Detroit), 1998.

Grier, Barbara, *The Lesbian in Literature,* Naiad Press (Tallahassee), 1981.

Hobby, Elaine and Chris White, editors, *What Lesbians Do in Books,* Women's Press, 1991, pp. 134-54.

PERIODICALS

City Limits, April 16-22, 1982.
New Statesman, June 8, 1962; June 24, 1983; July 31, 1987.
New York Herald Tribune Books, September 1, 1963.
Times (London), June 23, 1983.
Times Educational Supplement, January 28, 1983.
Times Literary Supplement, November 25, 1960; November 28, 1963; January 28, 1965; November 24, 1966; May 25, 1967; May 14, 1971; December 2, 1977; November 21, 1980; July 15, 1983; September 25-October 1, 1987.*.

*   *   *

MARKLIN, Megan
See HARRINGTON, William

*   *   *

MARTIN, Malachi
(Michael Serafian)

PERSONAL: Born in Kerry, Ireland; came to the United States, 1965, naturalized citizen, 1970. *Education:* Attended Oxford University and Hebrew University of Jerusalem; earned Ph.D. from University of Louvain.

CAREER: Writer. Roman Catholic priest of Society of Jesus (Jesuits), until 1964, laicized, 1964; professor at Pontifical Biblical Institute in Rome; associate of Cardinal Augustine Bea and Pope John XXIII; worked as waiter, taxi driver, longshoreman, painter, and public relations firm employee, beginning 1965; editor of *Encyclopaedia Britannica,* New York City; co-founder of Collector's Funding (antiques firm).

AWARDS, HONORS: Awarded Guggenheim fellowship twice.

WRITINGS:

(Under pseudonym Michael Serafian) *The Pilgrim,* Farrar, Straus (New York City), 1964.
The Encounter: Religions in Crisis, Farrar, Straus, 1969, reprinted, Dial Press (New York City), 1983.
Three Popes and the Cardinal, Farrar, Straus, 1972.
Jesus Now, Dutton (New York City), 1973.
The New Castle: Reaching for the Ultimate, Dutton, 1974.
Hostage to the Devil, Reader's Digest Press (New York City), 1976, reprinted as *Hostage to the Devil: The Possession and Exorcism of Five Living Americans,* Perennial Library (New York City), 1987.
The Final Conclave, Stein & Day (New York City), 1978.
King of Kings: A Novel, Simon & Schuster (New York City), 1980.
The Decline and Fall of the Roman Church, Putnam (New York City), 1981.
There Is Still Love, Macmillan (New York City), 1984.
Rich Church, Poor Church, Putnam, 1984.
Vatican: A Novel, Harper (New York City), 1986.
The Jesuits: The Society of Jesus and the Betrayal of the Roman Catholic Church, Simon & Schuster, 1987.
The Keys of This Blood: The Struggle for World Domination between Pope John Paul II, Mikhail Gorbachev, and the Capitalist West, Simon & Schuster, 1990.
Windswept House: A Vatican Novel, Doubleday (Garden City, NY), 1996.

Also author of *The Scribal Character of the Dead Sea Scrolls.* Former columnist for *National Review.* Contributor to periodicals, including *Harper's* and *New York Daily News.*

WORK IN PROGRESS: A Guide Book to the End Times.

SIDELIGHTS: Former Jesuit priest and Vatican insider Malachi Martin has used his talents as a writer to call attention to serious issues facing the Roman Catholic Church in recent years. Martin's books—both fiction and nonfiction—suggest that deep conspiracies are afoot which aim to fit Catholicism into an ecumenical New World Order. Himself a student of ancient apocryphal writings, Martin peppers his novels especially with at least the possibility of Luciferian victories over the powers of the godly in the modern church. Conservative and traditionalist, he is decidedly opposed to modern Catholic Church organizational tactics and, upon occasion, critical of papal decisions reaching as far back as Vatican II. Since Martin left the Jesuits in 1964, he has expressed his convictions in books which have received a wide variety of responses from critics in the United States. To quote *New York Times Book Review* contributor Paul Hofman, the author finds the Roman Catholic Church "pluralistic, permissive, ecumenical and evolutionary, with a rebellious, decadent clergy, an ignorant and recalcitrant body of bishops and a confused and divided assembly of believers."

In *The Encounter,* Martin analyzes the historical development of the three major religions, Judaism, Christianity, and Islam, concluding that they have become virtually irrelevant to modern man because their institutionalization had suffocated the spark of life which had glowed during their early "priceless moments." Melvin Maddocks explained the gist of Martin's argument: "He describes how, in all three cases, the truth-in-the-desert—the vision that transcended history—hardened into a dogma and grew gross as a worldly power among worldly powers. . . . All orthodoxies, whether political or religious, tend to play the same game, which Dr. Martin calls 'dominance.' At some point, he assumes, the second, third, or fortieth generation of a religion losees sight of that vision-in-the-desert and become machineries for their own self-perpetuation. . . . The self-perpetuation of that 'wealth, power, and influence,' he believes, has become of profound insignificance to modern man. The phenomenon of change—radical, breath taking change—has undermined authority, making strange and difficult the common religious premises of 'final revelation,' 'permanent truth,' and 'ethical absolutes.'"

Several critics questioned Martin's characterization of "modern man" as a being "intent on encountering himself in the raw, not through the colored glasses of ancient mythologies or modern ideological presuppositions." Michael J. Rush protested: "His depiction of modern man is degrading, superficial and, I dare say, false. . . . The members of the new generation may not be engaged in a search for the traditional God of Judaism, Christianity, and Islam, but neither are they settling for a purely scientific or mechanical explanation for man's wealth of capacities." Eugene Fontinell added: "There is the flavor of an outmoded positivism in the assertion that 'Western man's sociology is completely value-free.'" While other critics

found fault with Martin's "bog of historical minutiae," historical speculation, and "glibly stated reasoning," Maddocks emphasized the spirit of the work, declaring: "What gives Dr. Martin's book its special force is the evident agony with which he has conducted his investigation. He is as sorrowfully angry as he is erudite, and his book, consequently, turns out to be a spiritual autobiography as well as a work of scholarship."

Three Popes and a Cardinal revealed many of Martin's views on the Roman Catholic Church and the "high places" in Rome to which he enjoyed intimate access during Vatican II. Robert McAfee Brown observed: "His book is by turns brash, tender, impudent, caring, arrogant, brilliant and muddled. It is inspired by a passionate love of man and an equally passionate hatred of individual men. It implies a latent and wistful hope for what modern Catholicism might have become, and therefore expresses a patent repugnance for what it has in fact become." Most critics, including Brown, did not share Martin's pessimism about the Vatican Council or his belief that the church was fast approaching its demise.

An interview with Martin further illuminated his views on the church. "That organization (the Catholic Church and other high churches) is going to fade away because it's an organization created by men who were power brokers and still are," he maintained. "They tied it to an economic system and they tied it to political big deals, and now that's all over. It's good that it's happening because dignity, rings, hand kissing and satin slippers and Latin have nothing to do with the spirit whatever."

In *Jesus Now,* Martin continued his attack on the subordination of religious truth to the world's power structures. D. A. Boileau noted: "You find first a destroying of the images of Jesus, as lived in the Church and the world. Martin is hacking idols, laying bare the good conscience of Catholics, Protestants, and orthodoxes, the infantileness or dishonesty of revolutionaries, gay people, and charismatics. . . . Martin is rejecting the narrow search of the historical Jesus and is bringing some incisive correctives and criticisms."

Martin's book *The Final Conclave* elaborated upon this theme of the church's involvement in the world's power struggle, making some startling claims about the internal politics of the Vatican. He declared:

"The Church was allied with Western European governments when those governments exercised power and influence over the rest of the world. Now that influence, some Cardinals believe, is gone. They believe that new governments in France and Italy may be led by Communists. Important Churchmen are convinced that Latin America will go the way of Southeast Asia. These Cardinals believe the Church must ally itself with the next world empire, which will be Communist-dominated. . . . I see two great institutions in danger, the Roman Catholic Church and the United States. The electioneering now going on for a new Pope involves five factions, at least one of which clearly favors a Rome-Moscow axis and wants to see a new Pope elected who will support such an alliance. A Pope cannot be impeached. Once he is elected, he and the faction he represents will use the might and power of the Church not to minister to souls but to effect an alliance that will isolate the United States and put its institutions in great jeopardy. It was my duty as a Catholic and an American to reveal the secret negotiations now going on. Silence would have been the highest treason."

Martin continues to follow his "duty as a Catholic" by exposing the church's intentions as international economic and political trends accelerate. He explained his fears in an interview with *Paranoia: The Conspiracy Reader.* "For the moment, Lucifer the biggest archangel, the leader of the revolt against God, has a big in with certain Vatican officials," he said. "Enthronement doesn't mean that he rules. It means that [certain Vatican officials] did their best to put him there. The ideal would be to have their man as Pope. In that case then Satan would be enthroned." Martin sees evidence of the church's disintegration evident in the "reforms" of Vatican II, in the nonconformist behavior of certain factions of the Jesuits, in Pope John Paul II's numerous international travels, and certainly in the behavior and agenda of certain important Cardinals and bishops within the church. "There is an unspoken alliance today between powers inside the Vatican and leaders of major international humanist organizations who would change the Roman Catholic Church from a sacred institution to one whose primary function is to act as a stabilizing social force in the world," he warned in *U.S. News & World Report.* "They see the church as the only global structure able to do this."

Martin has fictionalized his predictions in the novel *Windswept House,* a story of Vatican politics that follows two American brothers as they uncover Satan-worship and international intrigue in Rome. A

Publishers Weekly reviewer wrote of *Windswept House:* "Martin's concern is what he sees as the erosion of the Church's moral authority, both from within and without. . . . Martin attributes this erosion to a global conspiracy among world powers both East and West, fueled by Satanic influence and by the failure of John XXIII to act upon the Third Prophecy of the Fatima Letter in 1960." In *Paranoia: The Conspiracy Reader,* Uri Dowbenko maintained that when perusing *Windswept House,* "the reader is put in the position of concluding that the New World Order is a done deal, that a One World Government is here and now and, as they say, it's all over but the crying." Dowbenko added that the book is "a controversial and provocative story. It delves into the depths of treachery, intrigue and Machiavellian politics at the highest levels of the Roman Church." A *Kirkus Reviews* correspondent found *Windswept House* to be "a mammoth meditation on the troubled state of today's Catholic Church. . . . Slowly, indeed, Martin's passions—and his agony over the dire straits of his faith—build into a deeply felt moral crisis."

BIOGRAPHICAL/CRITICAL SOURCES:

BOOKS

The Author Speaks: Selected "PW" Interviews, 1967-1976, R. R. Bowker (New York City), 1977, pp. 370-73.

PERIODICALS

Baltimore News-American, October 20, 1974.
Christian Century, June 24, 1970.
Christian Science Monitor, March 26, 1970.
Commonwealth, May 29, 1970.
Detroit News, June 19, 1996.
Kirkus Reviews, May 1, 1996.
National Catholic Reporter, November 19, 1993, p. 31.
National Review, November 9, 1973.
New York Times, March 9, 1970; April 11, 1972.
New York Times Book Review, April 19, 1970; April 5, 1981, p. 14; February 2, 1986, p. 16; April 5, 1987, p. 15.
Paranoia: The Conspiracy Reader, winter, 1997-98, pp. 16-21.
People, November 25, 1996, pp. 38-39.
Publishers Weekly, May 13, 1996, pp. 55-56.
Saturday Review, February 28, 1970; April 8, 1972.
This Week in Bible Prophecy, April 18, 1996.
U.S. News & World Report, June 10, 1996, p. 66.*

MARTIN, Ruth
  See RAYNER, Claire (Berenice)

*   *   *

MAXIM, John R. 1937-

PERSONAL: Born February 18, 1937, in New York, NY; son of Hiram Julian (an investigator) and Mary A. (a business manager; maiden name, Mitchell) Maxim; married first wife, August 1, 1964 (divorced, 1978); married Christine Giles Sterling (a nurse), August 16, 1980; children: Jeffrey, Christopher, Vickie Lewis. *Education:* Fordham University, B.A., 1958. *Politics:* Republican. *Religion:* Roman Catholic.

ADDRESSES: Home—139 South Compo Rd., Westport, CT 06880. *Agent*—Howard Morhaim, 501 Fifth Ave., New York, NY 10017.

CAREER: Procter & Gamble, Cincinnati, OH, product manager, 1962-66; McCann Erickson, New York City, vice-president, 1966-70; Marschalk Co., New York City, senior vice-president, 1970-77, Davidoff Advertising Agency, Fairfield, CT, senior vice-president in charge of marketing, 1978-85; Maxim Associates (consulting firm) Westport, CT, president, 1985—. Marketing specialist for luxury travel. Director of United Appeal and Boy Scouts of America.

MEMBER: Authors Guild, Greenwich Racquet Club, Riverside Yacht Club, Fairfield County Ad Club.

AWARDS, HONORS: Numerous awards for advertising excellence.

WRITINGS:

NOVELS

Platforms, Putnam (New York City), 1981.
Abel/Baker/Charlie, Houghton (Boston), 1983.
Time Out of Mind, Houghton, 1985.
The Bannerman Solution, Bantam (New York City), 1989.
The Bannerman Effect, Bantam, 1990.
Bannerman's Law, Bantam, 1991.
A Matter of Honor, Bantam, 1993.
The Shadow Box, Avon Books (New York City), 1996.
Haven, Avon Books, 1997.

OTHER

(With Leatrice Gilbert Fountain) *Dark Star* (biography), St. Martin's (New York City), 1985.

SIDELIGHTS: John R. Maxim has written a number of mysteries and thrillers, including four novels featuring Paul Bannerman, an espionage investigator whose cases take him throughout the world. Maxim's other fast-paced espionage adventures concern Israeli agents, drug smugglers, former KGB officials and Arab terrorists.

In *The Shadow Box,* Wall Street investment banker Michael Fallon finds himself entangled with a ring of prescription drug counterfeiters who, to protect their trade, begin killing those who may know too much about their operation. The story, writes J. D. Reed in *People* magazine, "gives readers a hard look at a little-known but lucrative area of international crime." Calling the novel a "crackerjack thriller," the critic for *Publishers Weekly* notes: "It's a complicated storyline that Maxim plays out with skill, boosting the narration with fluid writing and well-drawn characters." George Needham in *Booklist* judges *The Shadow Box* as "a thoroughly entertaining novel, an effective thriller yet reminiscent in its breeziness of the best of Donald Westlake."

Haven tells of a plot by Arab terrorists to steal American nuclear weapons. Former Israeli agent Elizabeth Stride and East German terrorist Martin Kessler, working to rekindle their love affair from years before, must work together to thwart the scheme. "Maxim has created vivid characters who have a witty take on their mythic reputations," according to the *Publishers Weekly* reviewer. Maxim, writes Roland C. Person in the *Library Journal,* "constructs a complex plot, juggles numerous characters, and pulls it all off with a cinematic, breathless pace."

Maxim told *CA:* "I'm your basic type who always dreamed of being a writer but never believed hard enough and got derailed by the need to make a living the corporate way. I had a midlife fish or cut-bait crisis, took a year off, wrote my first novel, and went back to work when it didn't make me rich. I have now written four books—three novels and a biography of John Gilbert—in six years by starting at four A.M. then going to the office at nine. Otherwise, I have traveled very broadly as a consultant to two cruise companies and the Orient Express, have started my own consulting firm, continue to ski in

Switzerland every January, and sail and play tennis as much as possible."

BIOGRAPHICAL/CRITICAL SOURCES:

PERIODICALS

Booklist, July, 1996, p. 1808.
Library Journal, August, 1997, p. 133.
New York Times Book Review, February 9, 1986, p. 11.
People Weekly, October 28, 1996, p. 40.
Publishers Weekly, July 12, 1993, p. 74; July 22, 1996, p. 227; August 4, 1997, p. 63.

*   *   *

MAYER, Bernadette 1945-

PERSONAL: Born May 12, 1945, in Brooklyn, NY; daughter of Theodore A. (an electrician) and Marie (Stumpf) Mayer; companion of Lewis Warsh (a poet and publisher); children: Marie, Sophia, Max. *Education:* New School for Social Research, B.A., 1967; also attended Barnard College, Columbia University, and College of New Rochelle.

ADDRESSES: Home—New York, NY.

CAREER: Poet. Teacher at schools and workshops, including St. Mark's Poetry Project, New York City, and at the New School for Social Research, New York City.

AWARDS, HONORS: Poets Foundation grant, 1967; National Institute of Arts and Letters grant, 1971; Creative Artists Public Service Program grant in fiction, 1976.

WRITINGS:

Ceremony Latin, Angel Hair (New York City), 1964.
Story, 0 to 9 Books (New York City), 1968.
Moving, Angel Hair, 1971.
(With Anne Waldman) *The Basketball Article,* Angel Hair, 1975.
Memory (performance art, exhibited in New York City, 1972), North Atlantic (Plainville, VT), 1975.
Studying Hunger, Serendipity (Berkeley, CA), 1976.
Poetry, Kulchur Foundation (New York City), 1976.
Erudition ex Memoria, Angel Hair, 1977.
The Golden Book of Words, Angel Hair (Lenox, MA), 1978.

Midwinter Day, Turtle Island Foundation (Berkeley), 1982.
Incidents Reports Sonnets, Archipelago (New York City), 1984.
Utopia, United Artists Books (New York City), 1984.
Mutual Aid, Mademoiselle de la Mole Press (New York City), 1985.
Sonnets, Tender Buttons (New York City), 1989.
(With Dale Worsley) *The Art of Science Writing,* Teachers & Writers (New York City), 1989.
The Formal Field of Kissing, Catchword Papers (New York City), 1990.
A Bernadette Mayer Reader, New Directions (New York City), 1992.
The Desire of Mothers to Please Others in Letters, Hard Press (Stockbridge, MS), 1994.
Proper Name and Other Stories, New Directions, 1996.

Contributor to anthologies, including *Anthology of New York Poets,* edited by Ron Padgett and David Shapiro, Random House, 1970; *Another World,* edited by Anne Waldman, Bobbs-Merrill, 1971; *Young American Poets 2,* edited by Paul Carroll, Follett, 1972; *Individuals,* edited by Alan Sondheim, Dutton, 1975; *None of the Above,* edited by Michael Lally, Crossing Press, 1976; and *A Code of Signals: Recent Writings in Poetics,* edited by Michael Palmer, North Atlantic, 1983. Contributor of poetry to *Ice, Tzarad, 0 to 9, Lines,* and other publications.

SIDELIGHTS: Basing much of her work on the environment in and around her home in New York City, poet and teacher Bernadette Mayer has created a body of work characterized by what *Dictionary of Literary Biography* essayist Peter Baker calls "a startling inclusivity by which the poet tries to re-create the innumerable objects, events, memories, and dreams that range into the field of an alert consciousness." Beginning her career as a performance artist with the 1972 exhibit *Memory,* Mayer has been considered one of the catalysts of the so-called "Language" movement in poetry through her association with poets Charles Bernstein, Peter Seaton, and Nick Piombino. However, Mayer herself has eschewed such categorization, and her work, experimental in nature, continues to defy easy classification.

Memory, which was exhibited at New York's 98 Greene Street Gallery, was comprised of over 1,000 photographs—one roll of film for every day during the month of July, 1971—arranged on walls in rows and accompanied by seven hours of energetic, almost spontaneous narration. Published in an abridged print version in 1975, the exhibit gained its creator instant fame within Manhattan's Artistic enclave; in the *Village Voice* A. D. Coleman called the installation "a unique and deeply exciting document" and noted that Mayer's exhibit "fall[s] outside the countaries of what is generally considered to be photographic art."

Mayer's reputation as an experimental artist was made with *Memory,* and future works would build upon that reputation. Her 1975 work *Studying Hunger* would be a prose version of *Memory,* consisting as it does of over 300 pages of journal entries documenting one month in the poet's life. Only one fifth of the work was actually published in book form. Mayer's work during the latter half of the 1970s was, by contrast to *Memory* and *Studying Hunger,* more conventional in form, comprised by poems written earlier in her career and those she had written quickly, in response to particular inspirations, rather than planned and constructed over long periods of time. These poems' conventionality caused some critics to condemn Mayer for abandoning the experimentalist "cause," while others considered such works to be more accessible to the average reader. In fact, in contrast to the many volumes she has published through small presses, poems in Mayer's collections *Poetry* and *The Golden Book of Words,* first published between 1976 and 1978, would serve as the bulk of New Directions' *A Bernadette Mayer Reader,* which was released to relatively wide national distribution in 1992.

"The body of Mayer's work reveals her clear allegiance to certain practices of surrealism," maintains Baker, "as well as to the experimental techniques of [Gertrude] Stein, William Carlos Williams, and other writers in the American tradition." Both her conventional poems and her highly praised book-length poem *Midwinter Day*—a 119-page work composed during the course of a single day the poet spent in Lenox, Massachusetts in December of 1978—speak to Mayer's familiarity with the American literary tradition. Of *Midwinter Day,* which Baker notes is acclaimed by some as "one of the unacknowledged masterpieces of late-twentieth-century writing in English," reviewer Fanny Howe remarked in *American Book Review* that, "In a language made up of idiom and lyricism, which cancels the boundaries between prose and poetry, . . . Mayer's. . . . search for pattern woven out of small actions confirms the notion that seeing *what is* is a radical human gesture. Doctrine is irrelevant here to the moral—and solitary—courage displayed by this act of writing, and sharing of that writing."

More recent works by Mayer have been less monumental in their undertaking than *Memory* or *Midwinter Day.* Formated almost like a social studies textbook, *Utopia* addresses Mayer's social concerns, interleaving her verses with those of other poets to create a collaborative work. 1994's *The Desires of Mothers to Please Others in Letters* is a collection of prose poems written during the poet's third pregnancy. While the limited distribution of her work, except for the *Reader,* outside of New York City has caused Mayer to be relatively little studied by academics, her career as a teacher of experimental poetry techniques—particularly at New York's St. Mark's Poetry Project—and her efforts to extend the use of language "beyond poetic theory of any kind and closer to an honest . . . means of expressing the reality of the human mind," in the words of *Contemporary Women Poets* contributor Denise Wiloch, have made her instrumental in expanding the limits of poetry as a literary form.

BIOGRAPHICAL/CRITICAL SOURCES:

BOOKS

Contemporary Women Poets, St. James Press (Detroit), 1997.
Dictionary of Literary Biography, Volume 165: *American Poets since World War II, Fourth Series,* Gale (Detroit), 1996.

PERIODICALS

American Book Review, July, 1984, p. 16.
Kirkus Reviews, May 1, 1996, p. 639.
Library Journal, December 15, 1976, p. 2540.
Lingo, number 1, 1993.
Multicultural Review, June, 1993, pp. 62-63.
Poetry Project Newsletter, October/November, 1992.
Publishers Weekly, May 6, 1996, p. 74.
Review of Contemporary Fiction, fall, 1996, p. 198.
Village Voice, August 21, 1972.
Voice Literary Supplement, May, 1983, p. 5.*

*   *   *

McCONNELL, Frank D(eMay) 1942-

PERSONAL: Born May 20, 1942 in Louisville, KY; married, 1964; children: one. *Education:* University of Notre Dame, B.A., 1964; Yale University, M.A., 1965, Ph.D., 1968.

ADDRESSES: Office—Department of English, Northwestern University, Evanston, IL 60201.

CAREER: Cornell University, Ithaca, NY, assistant professor of English, 1967-71; Northwestern University, Evanston, IL, professor of English, 1971—.

WRITINGS:

MYSTERY NOVELS

Murder among Friends, Walker (New York City), 1983.
Blood Lake, Walker, 1987.
The Frog King, Walker, 1990.
Liar's Poker, Walker, 1993.

OTHER

The Confessional Imagination: A Reading of Wordsworth's Prelude, Johns Hopkins University Press (Baltimore), 1974.
The Spoken Seen: Film and the Romantic Imagination, Johns Hopkins University Press, 1975.
Four Postwar American Novelists: Bellow, Mailer, Barth, and Pynchon, University of Chicago Press (Chicago), 1977.
(Editor) *Byron's Poetry: Authoritative Texts, Letters, Journals, Criticism, Images of Byron,* Norton (New York City), 1978.
Storytelling and Mythmaking: Images from Film and Literature, Oxford University Press (New York City), 1979.
The Science Fiction of H. G. Wells, Oxford University Press, 1981.

Contributor to literature journals.

SIDELIGHTS: After publishing a number of volumes of literary criticism, Frank D. McConnell began writing mystery novels in 1983. His novels chronicle the cases of Bridget O'Toole, an ex-nun who has taken over her ailing father's detective agency, and Harry Garnish, the agency's chief detective. Together, the pair unravel mysterious circumstances involving colorful characters and far-flung locales.

Marilyn Stasio, writing in the *New York Times Book Review,* calls Garnish "a clever monologuist" and Bridget "a hugely fat but sweet-tempered nun." Sometimes their business relationship, Stasio finds, "plays like a stupid parody of Rex Stout's Nero Wolfe—Archie Goodwin sleuthing act." Their cases, Stasio believes, "are almost too weird to describe."

Speaking of *The Frog King,* Stasio explains that the "many bizarre characters . . . give this odyssey its oddball charm."

Liar's Poker is concerned with a client's wife who makes oddly generous donations to a religious center and is then found near death in a motel room with a young college student. Were members of the religious sect responsible? The investigation leads Garnish into a sexual encounter with a woman who may be trying to use him against his client's best interests. The critic for *Publishers Weekly* finds the novel to be "short on plot" but "long on moxie."

McConnell's volume of criticism, *Four Postwar American Novelists: Bellow, Mailer, Barth, and Pynchon,* was praised by D. J. Leigh in *Best Sellers.* Leigh observes, "McConnell combines the formal analysis of old Yale 'new critical' mentors . . . with sociophilosophical approaches of the new Yale gurus . . . to produce one of the finest critiques of contemporary fiction." The critic concludes that "few readers of these four novelists can afford to dismiss McConnell's excellent and provocative book."

BIOGRAPHICAL/CRITICAL SOURCES:

PERIODICALS

American Literature, January, 1978.
Best Sellers, October, 1977.
Encounter, February, 1977.
Journal of Aesthetics, winter, 1976.
New York Times Book Review, August 12, 1990.
Publishers Weekly, April 19, 1993, p. 52.
Times Literary Supplement, August 13, 1976.
Washington Post Book World, March 22, 1981.

*   *   *

McGAUGHEY, Neil 1951-

PERSONAL: Surname pronounced "McGoy"; born October 3, 1951, in Natchez, MS. *Ethnicity:* "Caucasian." *Education:* William Carey College, Hattiesburg, MS, graduate (summa cum laude), 1973. *Politics:* "Try to get along with everybody." *Religion:* "A personal and private matter." *Avocational interests:* Collecting first edition mystery novels.

ADDRESSES: Agent—Martha Kaplan, Martha Kaplan Agency, 110 West 86th St., New York, NY 10024.

CAREER: Clarion-Ledger, Jackson, MS, reviewer of mystery books, 1985-95. Vice president and board member, Mississippi Committee for Prevention of Child Abuse. Chairperson of 1996 Edgar Committee for Best Critical or Biographical Work, Mystery Writers of America.

MEMBER: Mystery Writers of America, Sisters in Crime.

WRITINGS:

"STOKES MORAN" MYSTERY NOVELS

Otherwise Known as Murder, Scribner (New York City), 1994.
And Then There Were Ten, Scribner, 1995.
The Best Money Murder Can Buy, Scribner, 1996.
A Corpse by Any Other Name, Scribner, 1997.

SIDELIGHTS: Neil McGaughey writes the "Stokes Moran" mystery series, which feature Kyle Malachi, who publishes mystery book reviews under the pseudonym Stokes Moran. Aimed at mystery afficionados, the Stokes Moran stories are "chock-full of allusions to famous mystery writers, classic whodunits, and the legend and lore of the genre," as Emily Melton notes in *Booklist.*

Otherwise Known as Murder introduces Kyle, who is offered a large sum of money to track down and interview reclusive mystery novelist Seymour Severe. Travelling to New Orleans, where Severe sets his novels, Kyle is drugged while in a gay bar and wakes up in bed with a corpse. "A mildly amusing and entertaining book," as Melton describes it, the story is labeled "arch and awkward" by the critic for *Publishers Weekly.*

And Then There Were Ten has Kyle helping to save a friend from potential blackmail. Years before, the friend appeared in a porno film with other actors who later became stars. The film has been stolen, and Kyle and his fiancee Lee Holland must track it down before careers are damaged. Melton calls the novel "a mildly entertaining story with enough mystery-related quips, quotes, and quirks to satisfy mystery afficionados."

Kyle is happily married in *The Best Murder Money Can Buy,* but is thrown into confusion when he meets a man claiming to be his long-lost twin brother. When the mystery twin turns up dead, Kyle takes over his identity to track down the killer. Applying

"techniques learned from fictional detectives and guided by his knowledge of plots from various past masters, Kyle eventually succeeds in his goal," according to the critic for *Publishers Weekly.* Melton finds that, "as usual, McGaughey's witty dialogue, inventive plotting, and solid prose add up to entertaining reading."

A peeved Kyle kills off his pseudonym Stokes Moran in *A Corpse by Any Other Name* by calling in an obituary to the *New York Times.* When an actual person with the same name turns up dead, Kyle must answer for his actions. Melton calls the story "more fluff than substance" offering "an inventive plot and some likable characters." The critic for *Publishers Weekly* believes "the whole serious-silly mix . . . works well as McGaughey delivers good mystery plotting with all the in-genre jokes."

BIOGRAPHICAL/CRITICAL SOURCES:

PERIODICALS

Armchair Detective, winter, 1995, p. 40.
Booklist, July, 1994, p. 1926; June 1, 1995, p. 1735; July, 1996, p. 1809; March 15, 1998, p. 1205.
Library Journal, June 1, 1995, p. 168; February 1, 1998, p. 116.
Publishers Weekly, June 13, 1994, p. 53; May 15, 1995, p. 58; June 10, 1996, p. 88; January 26, 1998, p. 73.

* * *

McGINNISS, Joe 1942-

PERSONAL: Born December 9, 1942, in New York, NY; son of Joseph Aloysius (a travel agent) and Mary (Leonard) McGinniss; married Christine Cooke, September 25, 1965 (divorced); married Nancy Doherty (an editor and photographer), November 20, 1976; children: (first marriage) Christine, Suzanne, Joe; (second marriage) Matthew, James. *Education:* Holy Cross College, B.S., 1964.

ADDRESSES: Agent—Morton L. Janklow, 598 Madison Ave., New York, NY 10022.

CAREER: Port Chester Daily Item, Port Chester, NY, reporter, 1964; *Worcester Telegram,* Worcester, MA, reporter, 1965; *Philadelphia Bulletin,* Philadelphia, PA, reporter, 1966; *Philadelphia Inquirer,* Philadelphia, columnist, 1967-68; freelance writer, 1968—. Lecturer in writing at Bennington College.

WRITINGS:

The Selling of the President, 1968, Trident (New York City), 1969, with an introduction by the author, 1988.

The Dream Team (novel), Random House (New York City), 1972.

Heroes, Viking (New York City), 1976.

Going to Extremes, Knopf (New York City), 1980.

Fatal Vision, Putnam (New York City), 1983.

Blind Faith, Putnam, 1988.

Cruel Doubt, Simon & Schuster (New York City), 1991.

The Last Brother: The Rise and Fall of Teddy Kennedy, Simon & Schuster, 1993.

Contributor of articles to *Harper's, Sports Illustrated, TV Guide,* and other periodicals.

ADAPTATIONS: The Selling of the President, 1968 was adapted for stage by Stuart Hample; *Fatal Vision* was filmed as a television miniseries that aired in 1984; *Blind Faith* was adapted as a television miniseries by National Broadcasting Company (NBC).

SIDELIGHTS: Joe McGinniss is a noted nonfiction author whose works are characterized by an intense personal involvement with the topics at hand. Since the late-1960s McGinniss, a former journalist, has concentrated on writing full-length books; his research has taken him to the upper reaches of Alaska as well as far and wide through the lower forty-eight states. Two of his titles—*The Selling of the President, 1968* and *Fatal Vision*—have been bestsellers in the nonfiction market and have proven controversial in both their subjects and their composition. These and others of the author's works, including *The Dream Team, Heroes,* and *Going to Extremes,* have been praised for their insights and cogency of expression. To quote *New York Times* contributor Jimmy Breslin, McGinniss's style produces "sentences that read so easily that one tends to forget he is reading."

McGinniss was born in New York City late in 1942. He grew up in Rye, New York, an imaginative youngster who was educated in parochial schools. In 1964 he received a bachelor of science degree from Holy Cross College and immediately went to work as

a reporter for the *Port Chester Daily Item.* Within months he landed a job in Worcester, Massachusetts on the *Worcester Telegram.* McGinniss worked as a general assignment reporter at both newspapers, but he aspired to sportswriting. He finally achieved that goal at the *Philadelphia Bulletin* in 1966 and was so successful that the rival *Philadelphia Inquirer* offered him a sports column. After only a year with the *Bulletin* he went to the *Inquirer,* not as a sports writer but as a general issues columnist—a coveted position, especially for a writer several years shy of thirty. According to *New Republic* reviewer John Osborne, McGinniss became known in Philadelphia as "something of a journalistic prodigy, a sharp-shooter with minimal regard for reportorial niceties and a special appeal to young readers." McGinniss aimed at the biggest issues—the escalation of the United States' involvement in the Vietnam War, the assassinations of Dr. Martin Luther King Jr. and Robert F. Kennedy, and the 1968 presidential primaries. The political climate of the late-1960s prepared him for his first book, *The Selling of the President, 1968.*

A chance conversation on a commuter train in 1967 led McGinniss to an astonishing subject. The journalist discovered that each presidential candidate, Hubert Humphrey and Richard Nixon, employed a team of advertising executives to create an "images" that would make the candidate more palatable to television viewers. McGinniss's commuter train contact was with the "Humphrey account," but McGinniss could not persuade that camp to reveal its secrets. Instead he turned to the Nixon campaign, where the media advisors accorded him an unusually intimate view of the marketing of candidate Nixon. Quitting his job at the *Inquirer,* McGinniss travelled with the Nixon team for five months. "My great advantage was that I wasn't considered press," he told *Life* magazine. "I was the guy writing a book."

Publication of *The Selling of the President, 1968* caused a sensation. The book was on the bestseller list for seven months, topping the list for four. McGinniss had the distinction of becoming the youngest author of nonfiction—excepting Anne Frank—ever to have penned such a blockbuster. Nixon's aides were shocked to discover that the innocuous young observer who had watched them at work had revealed their attempts to manipulate the electorate. Reviewers, on the other hand, have praised McGinniss for his revelations. *Christian Century* contributor Robert Miller writes: "Readers with illusions about the relationship of media and message in a large-scale political campaign will quickly be disillusioned by this book. McGinniss gives a behind-the-scenes look at a group of men and women using a very effective TV technique to help their client win the presidency of the U.S. At times this book will scare you." In the *New York Times,* Christopher Lehmann-Haupt calls the work "a series of smartly turned-out scenes from backstage at the 1968 Presidential turkey raffle" and adds that what McGinniss saw and heard "he has recorded artfully enough to simultaneously entertain us and make us fear for the future of the Republic."

National notoriety at age twenty-seven can be daunting. McGinniss's next two books, *The Dream Team* and *Heroes,* both explore the pleasures and perils of fame, premature and otherwise. In the novel *The Dream Team,* a bestselling author on tour promoting his book becomes sidetracked by horse racing, alcohol, and the attentions of a young television reporter. *Heroes,* a nonfiction work, consists of a series of interviews with prominent national figures from several walks of life; critics have contended that the book reveals as much about its author's emotional turmoil as it does about the men he interviewed. McGinniss invested much time and effort in the projects, and both were modest successes. Then, in 1975 he opted for a complete change of environment and subject matter. Journeying to Alaska, he spent a year documenting life in that beautiful but inhospitable state. The resulting book, *Going to Extremes,* offers a glimpse at the underside of Alaska's economic expansion. *New Republic* correspondent Dan Cryer observes that in *Going to Extremes,* McGinniss "has succeeded well in capturing an Alaska on the verge of selling its soul to big oil. . . . He is a first-rate reporter whose stories graphically convey the culture shock wracking present-day Alaska." In the *Nation,* Mark Kramer concludes that the book "is fine reading. It is thick with whole people, exotic landscapes, the nervous and constant curiosity of an adventurer who knows that the essence of place is more likely found while chatting in barrooms than while viewing the wondrous works of man and nature."

McGinniss's next project consumed more than four years of his life. *Fatal Vision,* his 1983 bestseller, gives a comprehensive account of the murder conviction of Dr. Jeffrey MacDonald, a man convicted of brutally slaying his pregnant wife and two young daughters. When McGinniss met MacDonald in 1979, the infamous surgeon was facing trial after a

series of legal delays and after having been exonerated in a shoddily conducted Army hearing. MacDonald staunchly maintained his innocence in the 1970 triple murder, but as McGinniss began to piece together the evidence he became more and more convinced of the doctor's guilt. According to Joan Barthel in the *New York Times Book Review,* McGinniss "becomes a genuinely sympathetic character in [*Fatal Vision*]. . . . He confronts recurring questions of guilt and innocence and the ambivalence of love. . . . These things happen when reporters become involved in people's lives and deaths, when a writing project evolves into a kind of selective, if unforeseen and not entirely voluntary, human bondage. It is this involvement, finally, that makes *Fatal Vision*—even beyond the fascination of the story it tells . . .—well worth reading."

Throughout his protracted legal battles to stay out of prison, MacDonald was convinced that McGinniss intended to portray him as an innocent victim of police harassment. When *Fatal Vision* was published, MacDonald—who already was earning a percentage of the profits—sued McGinniss for wooing his further cooperation even though the author believed him to be guilty. A community of fellow writers came to McGinniss's aid in a court case that many felt would determine every nonfiction author's prerogative to formulate independent conclusions. McGinniss maintained that he never led MacDonald to believe the book would exonerate him and that it took many months of research and conversations to reach any conclusion at all. In Lehmann-Haupt's opinion, this attitude is reflected in the book. McGinniss "makes it clear to the reader from the start that he was free to decide one way or another about Dr. MacDonald's claim of innocence, and he makes it clear, I think, that Dr. MacDonald knew he was taking his chances," the critic writes. "'Fatal Vision' smells of integrity, and that's one of the many things about it that make it irresistible to read, even if its vision of the human soul is somewhat bleak and frightening."

The celebrated court case ended with a deadlocked jury. MacDonald pursued a new trial, prompting McGinniss to agree to an out-of-court settlement without admission of liability. The author told the *Los Angeles Times* that he accepted the settlement—which he does not have to pay personally—because he wanted to reduce MacDonald's avenues for public attention. Also, he said, "I don't want to give MacDonald the satisfaction of taking me away from productive work again."

McGinniss's next work was another investigation of a brutal family murder. In 1990 Bonnie Von Stein and her husband were brutally attacked, beaten, and stabbed. Bonnie survived, but her husband did not. The family's great wealth led some to suspect Bonnie of killing her husband for money, but as it turned out, her son from a previous marriage had hired a classmate to murder both his mother and stepfather. Bonnie Von Stein herself asked McGinniss to write the book in order to help her understand her son's heinous deeds and all the other horrors she had endured. According to Linda Steiner in *Dictionary of Literary Biography,* "McGinniss managed to incorporate an analysis of several potentially confusing medical, legal, and ethical dilemmas into a highly readable narrative, *Cruel Doubt.* Indeed, he showed considerable sensitivity." Yet the author probably only exacerbated Bonnie Von Stein's mental and emotional torment by speculating that her daughter was also a conspirator in the crime.

McGinniss's next book brought him the greatest critical scorn he had yet endured in his career. *The Last Brother: The Rise and Fall of Teddy Kennedy* is, on the surface, a biography of Edward Kennedy, but it contained a great deal of unsavory material about the entire Kennedy clan. Commentators derided McGinniss's style, which included interjecting thoughts he imagined many of his subjects must have had and which were surmised without the cooperation of any Kennedy family member. "The prose is filled with melodrama and sarcasm," reports Steiner. "More ominously, noted historians William Manchester and Doris Kearns Goodwin claimed McGinniss stole from their published work."

Steiner observed that "although it is saturated with detail, much of [McGinniss's] writing is cliched and ponderous. Nonetheless, when judged by aesthetic criteria and formal structured, McGinniss's books include many vignettes that might be seen as generally successful pieces of literary journalism. . . . [His] interest in detecting reality is . . . similar to the views of scientists and conventional-minded journalists who believe that the consequences of the search itself of the achievement of 'truth' are irrelevant."

BIOGRAPHICAL/CRITICAL SOURCES:

BOOKS

Authors in the News, Volume 2, Gale (Detroit), 1976.

Connery, Thomas B., editor, *A Sourcebook of American Literary Journalism,* Greenwood Press (Westport, CT), 1993.

Contemporary Literary Criticism, Volume 32, Gale, 1985.

Dictionary of Literary Biography, Volume 185: *American Literary Journalists, 1945-1995,* Gale, 1997.

Lounsberry, Barbara, *The Art of Fact: Contemporary Artists of Nonfiction,* Greenwood Press, 1990.

McGinniss, Joe, *Heroes,* Viking, 1976.

Malcolm, Janet, *The Journalist and the Murderer,* Knopf, 1990.

Potter, Jerry Allen, and Fred Bost, *Fatal Justice: Reinvestigating the MacDonald Murders,* Norton (New York City), 1995.

Stull, James N., *Literary Selves. Autobiography and Contemporary American Nonfiction,* Greenwood Press, 1993.

PERIODICALS

Atlantic, July, 1976.

Boston Globe, January 11, 1989, pp. 65-66; August 8, 1993, pp. B1-B2.

Chicago Tribune, August 22, 1987; October 15, 1991, section 5, p. 1.

Christian Century, February 4, 1970.

Christian Science Monitor, November 13, 1969.

Commonweal, October 24, 1969.

Detroit News, May 30, 1972.

Globe and Mail (Toronto), November 17, 1984.

Harper's, October, 1983; August, 1985.

Life, October 10, 1969.

Listener, March 5, 1970.

Los Angeles Times, July 9, 1987; July 23, 1987; July 24, 1987; August 3, 1987; August 5, 1987; August 6, 1987; August 22, 1987; November 24, 1987; November 25, 1987; January 25, 1995, p. 13.

Nation, September 27, 1980; November 12, 1983.

National Review, November 18, 1969.

New Republic, October 11, 1969; November 15, 1980; October 24, 1983.

New Statesman, March 6, 1970; June 1, 1973.

Newsweek, September 29, 1969; October 13, 1969; April 12, 1971; September 22, 1980; September 12, 1983.

New Yorker, December 27, 1969; October 3, 1983.

New York Post, October 8, 1969.

New York Times, August 6, 1969; October 3, 1969; January 30, 1972; March 5, 1972; May 9, 1972; April 27, 1976; September 21, 1983; November 16, 1984; August 22, 1987; March 29, 1989, pp. B1-B2; July 27, 1993, pp. C13, C16.

New York Times Book Review, October 5, 1969; April 30, 1972; April 18, 1976; September 14, 1980; September 25, 1983.

Progressive, November, 1993, pp. 16-17.

Publishers Weekly, April 27, 1984; October 18, 1991, pp. 40-41.

Saturday Review, September, 1980.

Spectator, March 14, 1970.

Time, September 26, 1983.

Times (London), November 25, 1987.

Times Literary Supplement, November 20, 1969; May 25, 1973; August 17, 1984.

Village Voice, September 20, 1983.

Washington Post, December 2, 1980; October 20, 1983; August 21, 1987.

Washington Post Book World, April 18, 1976; September 14, 1980; December 2, 1980; August 28, 1983.

Writers Digest, March, 1976.*

* * *

McKALE, Donald M(arshall) 1943-

PERSONAL: Born October 24, 1943, in Clay Center, KS; son of Donald Vincent and Mildred (Wedd) McKale; married Janna Fredregill, June 4, 1966; children: Emily Anne, David Marshall. *Education:* Iowa State University, B.S., 1966; University of Missouri, M.A., 1967; Kent State University, Ph.D., 1970. *Religion:* Presbyterian. *Avocational interests:* Watching athletics on television, reading, spending time with the family, playing tennis and racquetball.

ADDRESSES: Home—116 Princess Lane, Clemson, SC 29631. *Office*—Department of History, Clemson University, Clemson, SC 29631.

CAREER: Georgia College, Milledgeville, assistant professor, 1970-74, associate professor, 1974-78, professor of history, 1978-79; Clemson University, Clemson, SC, professor of history, 1979—. Visiting associate professor of history, University of Nebraska, 1975-76.

MEMBER: American Historical Association, Conference Group on Central European History.

WRITINGS:

The Nazi Party Courts: Hitler's Management of Conflict in His Movement, 1921-1945, University Press of Kansas (Lawrence), 1974.

The Swastika outside Germany, Kent State University Press (Kent, OH), 1977.

Hitler: The Survival Myth, Stein & Day (New York City), 1981.

Curt Pruefer: German Diplomat from the Kaiser to Hitler, Kent State University Press, 1987.

(Editor and author of foreword) *Tradition: A History of the Presidency of Clemson University,* Mercer (Macon, GA), 1988.

(Editor and author of introduction) *Rewriting History: The Original and Revised World War II Diaries of Curt Pruefer, Nazi Diplomat,* Kent State University Press, 1988.

War by Revolution: Germany and Great Britain in the Middle East in the Era of World War I, Kent State University Press, 1998.

Contributor of articles and reviews to *Research Studies* (of Washington State University), *Jewish Social Studies, International Review of History and Political Science, Journal of European Studies, Choice,* and *Journal of Contemporary History.*

SIDELIGHTS: Donald M. McKale has written several works on the history of Nazi Germany which have shed new light on neglected areas. McKale's first book, *The Nazi Party Courts: Hitler's Management of Conflict in His Movement, 1921-1945,* is an in-depth study of the Nazi Party's internal court system where disputes between members were resolved. The courts also determined who was suitable for membership and who should be expelled. According to the *Choice* reviewer, the Nazi Party court system "contributed significantly to the transformation of Germany . . . into a terroristic police state." Calling the book a "compact and highly readable analysis," T. E. Willey in *Library Journal* concludes that *The Nazi Party Courts* is "an admirable monograph, essential."

In *The Swastika outside Germany,* McKale examined the overseas activities of Nazi organizations during the 1930s and 1940s, particularly the efforts made by the German government to influence Germans living in other countries. Based on the records of the German Foreign Ministry, McKale's study is "a carefully documented description of the origins and operations of the Auslands-Organisation (Foreign Organization) of the Nazi Party," as D. P. Jensen writes in *Library Journal.* The *Choice* reviewer describes the book as "a comprehensive study of a complex external dimension to Hitler's Third Reich."

McKale examines the persistent rumors of Hitler's survival following World War II in *Hitler: The Sur-*

vival Myth. Inspired by deliberate Soviet propaganda, wishful thinking by former Nazis, and media fantasies of resurgent Nazism, the myth of Hitler's survival spawned a number of both possible and highly unlikely scenarios. These scenarios included stories of Hitler living quietly with Eva Braun in South America or in a secret Antarctic Nazi base; there were even rumors about Hitler's alleged children living on in remote parts of the world. *Hitler: The Survival Myth* is "well written, scrupulously researched, exhaustively documented," writes John Yohalem in the *New York Times Book Review.* Yohalem finds that "McKale has covered all the rumors. . . . He presents the evidence for us to draw our own conclusions, and he does it with lucidity."

BIOGRAPHICAL/CRITICAL SOURCES:

PERIODICALS

Annals of the American Academy, March, 1975; September, 1978.
Booklist, April 15, 1978.
Choice, November, 1974; April, 1978; June, 1981.
Library Journal, July, 1974; April 15, 1978; February 1, 1981.
New York Times Book Review, February 22, 1981, p. 18.

*   *   *

McPHERSON, Sandra 1943-

PERSONAL: Born August 2, 1943, in San Jose, CA; daughter of Walter James (a physical education professor) and Frances (Gibson) McPherson; married Henry D. Carlile (an English professor and poet), July 22, 1966 (divorced, 1985); married Walter Pavlich, 1995; children: (first marriage) Phoebe. *Education:* Attended Westmont College, 1961-63; San Jose State College (now University), B.A., 1965; University of Washington, Seattle, graduate study, 1965-66.

ADDRESSES: Home—2052 Calaveras Ave., Davis, CA 95616-3021. *E-mail*—sjmcpherson@ucdavis.edu.

CAREER: Poet and educator. Honeywell, Inc., Seattle, WA, technical writer, 1966; University of Iowa, Writers' Workshop, Iowa City, member of faculty, 1974-76, 1978-80; University of California, Berkeley, visiting faculty member, 1981; member of faculty, Oregon Writers' Workshop, Pacific Northwest College of Art, 1981-85; University of California, Davis, professor of English, 1985—. Member, Forum on Individuality, White House Conference on Children, 1970. Has given poetry readings at universities and schools throughout the United States.

AWARDS, HONORS: Helen Bullis Prize, *Poetry Northwest,* 1968; Ingram Merrill Foundation grants, 1972, 1984; Bess Hokin prize for poetry, 1972; Emily Dickinson Prize, Poetry Society of America, 1973; National Endowment for the Arts grants, 1974-75, 1980, 1985; Blumenthal-Leviton-Blonder prize for poetry, 1975; Guggenheim fellowship, 1976-77; National Book Award nomination, 1979, for *The Year of Our Birth*; Northwest Booksellers Prize for *Radiation*; American Academy and Institute of Arts and Letters award, 1987; Eunice Tietjens Memorial Prize, *Poetry,* 1991.

WRITINGS:

POETRY

Elegies for the Hot Season, Indiana University Press (Bloomington), 1970.
Radiation, Ecco Press (New York City), 1973.
The Year of Our Birth, Ecco Press, 1978.
Sensing, Meadow Press (San Francisco), 1980.
Patron Happiness, Ecco Press, 1983.
Pheasant Flower, Owl Creek Press (Missoula, MT), 1985.
Floralia, illustrations by Claire Van Vliet, Janus Press (Portland, OR), 1985.
Responsibility for Blue, Trilobite Press (Denton, TX), 1985.
At the Grave of Hazel Hall, Ives Street Press (Sweden, ME), 1988.
Streamers, Ecco Press, 1988.
Designating Duet, Janus Press (West Burke, VT), 1989.
The God of Indeterminacy, University of Illinois Press, 1993.
Edge Effect: Trails and Portrayals, University Press of New England (Hanover, NH), 1996.
The Spaces between Birds: Mother/Daughter Poems, 1967-1995, University Press of New England, 1996.
Beauty in Use, Janus Press, 1997.

Contributor to anthologies, including *Best Poems of 1968,* Borestone Mountain Poetry Awards, 1969; *American Literary Anthology III,* Viking, 1970; *Rising Tides: Twentieth-Century American Women Po-*

ets, Washington Square Press, 1973; *No More Masks! No More Mythologies!,* Doubleday, 1973; *Modern Poetry of Western America,* Brigham Young University Press, 1975; and *The American Poetry Anthology: Poets under Forty,* Avon, 1975. Contributor of poetry to various periodicals, including *Nation, New Yorker, Poetry, New Republic, Field, Iowa Review, Harper's, Ironwood, Poetry Northwest,* and *Antaeus.*

OTHER

(Editor) *Journey from Essex: Poems for John Clare,* Graywolf Press (Port Townsend, WA), 1981.
(Editor with Bill Henderson and Laura Jensen), *The Pushcart Prize XIV: Best of the Small Presses, 1989-90,* Pushcart Press (Wainscott, NY), 1989.

SIDELIGHTS: Sandra McPherson weaves vivid images culled from nature into what *Contemporary Women Poets* contributor David Young characterizes as "rich, complex, and deeply satisfying poems." In collections that include the National Book Award-nominated *The Year of Our Birth,* 1988's *At the Grave of Hazel Hall,* and 1996's *Edge Effect: Trails and Portrayals,* McPherson has increasingly honed her unsentimental, insightful verse, imbuing it with images reflective of diverse folk arts and refining her expressions of a cultural perspective that is uniquely American.

Reviewing 1970's *Elegies for the Hot Season,* McPherson's first published collection of verse, Jonathan Galassi of *Poetry* notes a similarity to the late poet Sylvia Plath in the "stark, basic pictures that give shape to this poet's deepest insights." Valerie Trueblood, commenting on the work in *American Poetry Review,* believes "this is the world at its plainest and most sign-giving. . . . McPherson has a gift . . . for bringing the physical world close without blinking at it."

McPherson's characteristic unadorned presentation is continued in 1973's *Radiations,* a collection that "seemed to clear a space for itself among the books of the year," according to Trueblood, "and to sit in its own ring of light." There are two distinct kinds of poems in this collection, David Cavitch maintains in his review for the *New York Times Book Review.* The first, according to the critic, are poems that "express a sensitive young woman's decorous thoughts around the house," while in the others "McPherson connects her personal existence to large, contemporary metaphors, and her simple, homebody language acquires the overtones of fierce

truth, coolly delivered." Throughout each of McPherson's subsequent collections, readers follow "details of the poet's life," according to Young: "marriage, motherhood, eventual divorce, mental illness in a daughter, remarriage, relations with adoptive parents, and a midlife reunion with birth parents" each figure within the poet's "visionary outlook that never loses its rooting in ordinary experience."

The "poles" of the poet's imaginary world are "absence and presence," according to Margaret Gibson in *Library Journal* in a review of McPherson's *The Year of Our Birth,* "as she traces the process of consciousness in fragments of childhood and in moments which touch adult lives." Joyce Carol Oates, reviewing McPherson's 1978 collection for the *New Republic,* finds that despite "too many poems that read like facile exercises," *The Year of Our Birth* contains "beautifully rendered poems with the lucidity of parables." Noteworthy within the collection is the ten-part "Studies in the Imaginary," which Young praises for its "light touch and elusive control of statement," as well for as the poet's "expert handling of submerged drama and marshalled associations."

1996's *The Spaces between Birds: Mother/Daughter Poems, 1967-1995* encompasses the relationship between the poet and her daughter, Phoebe, who was born with a form of autism. The collection juxtaposes poems by McPherson with those of her daughter, creating an effect that *Poetry* reviewer Leslie Ullman notes creates "an implicit and thoroughly winning intimacy, a kind of duet," showing "the sympathetic connections between mother and daughter . . . [that] grounds itself in an energy that is powerfully feminine," and also expressing the poet's reaction to her daughter's erratic behavior: the "raw despair, the sense of entrapment, the shadow-side of intimacy made darkest in its moments of helplessness," in the words of Ullman. A *Publishers Weekly* critic, calling *The Spaces between Birds* "a flock of hard truths, joyfully told," praises McPherson as "a distinctive stylist and a compassionate voice whose work continues to enrich and reward readers."

The first of the two parts of *Edge Effect,* published the same year as *The Spaces between Birds,* returns the poet to the examinations of folk art forms that served as her focus in such volumes as *The God of Indeterminacy.* Here McPherson writes of the creative vision of those she dubs "outsider" artists, particularly the work of the impoverished and the dispossessed, as well as returning to her examination of quilt work. The poet's perspective, according to Ullman, is "not merely a celebration of the marginal, but the definition of a new aesthetic behind works done by those to whom the word 'aesthetic' would have little meaning." The second half of *Edge Effect* finds McPherson celebrating the landscape of the Pacific Northwest, relating to the natural beauty of the region's trails and shoreline using the same aesthetic criteria with which she observed the folk art of "outsider" artists. "In this context," Ullman explains in another *Poetry* review, "nature is re-seen in its small eccentricities and larger harmonies, like a homemade object . . . given presence by being placed in good light." With both *The Spaces between Birds* and *Edge Effect,* concludes Young, McPherson's "sympathy with the unsung creators of her own culture has proved to be profound and revelatory . . . Her creative energies seem undiminished."

BIOGRAPHICAL/CRITICAL SOURCES:

BOOKS

Contemporary Women Poets, St. James Press (Detroit), 1997.

PERIODICALS

American Poetry Review, July, 1978; August, 1994, pp. 26-27.
Booklist, March 15, 1996, p. 1236.
Library Journal, February 15, 1978; March 1, 1996, p. 81.
New Republic, December 9, 1978.
New York Times Book Review, November 17, 1974.
Parnassus, February, 1994, p. 174.
Poetry, August, 1971; May, 1975; March, 1997, pp. 341-44.
Publishers Weekly, February 26, 1996, p. 102.*

*   *   *

MCVEAN, James
   See LUARD, Nicholas

*   *   *

MEYER, June
   See JORDAN, June

MITCHELL, Greg 1947-

PERSONAL: Born December 7, 1947, in Niagara Falls, NY; son of Stanley (an accountant) and Edith (Munro) Mitchell. *Education:* St. Bonaventure University, B.A., 1970.

ADDRESSES: Home—85 East 10th St., New York, NY 10003.

CAREER: Niagara Falls Gazette, Niagara Falls, NY, reporter, 1968-69; *Zygote,* New York City, news editor, 1970; *Crawdaddy,* New York City, senior editor, 1971-76; *Politicks,* New York City, senior editor, 1977—. Former editor, *Nuclear Times.*

AWARDS, HONORS: New York State Publishers Association distinguished local reporting award, 1970, for ten-part series on police-black relations in Niagara Falls, NY.

WRITINGS:

Truth—and Consequences: Seven Who Would Not Be Silenced, Dembner Books (New York City), 1981.
(Editor) *Cats, Chocolate, Clowns, and Other Amusing, Interesting, and Useful Subjects Covered by Newsletters,* Dembner Books, 1982.
(With Pascal James Imperato) *Acceptable Risks,* Viking (New York City), 1985.
The Campaign of the Century: Upton Sinclair's Race for Governor of California and the Birth of Media Politics, Random House, 1992.
(Editor with Peter Knobler) *Very Seventies: A Cultural History of the 1970s,* Simon & Schuster (New York City), 1995.
(With Robert Jay Lifton) *Hiroshima in America: Fifty Years of Denial,* Putnam (New York City), 1995.
Tricky Dick and the Pink Lady, Random House, 1997.

Contributor to periodicals, including *Progressive.*

SIDELIGHTS: Greg Mitchell's primary interest as a writer and editor is American politics and culture in the decades since the Second World War. As an editor of such magazines as *Politicks* and *Nuclear Times,* and as a contributor to *Progressive,* Mitchell has focused on writing about recent political events from a decidedly left-wing perspective.

Mitchell's book *Hiroshima in America,* which he co-wrote with Robert Jay Lifton, contends that the

United States government deliberately concealed the human suffering at Hiroshima and Nagasaki in order to make nuclear weapons more palatable to the American public. As Mitchell explained in the *Progressive:* "From the start, Americans were not shown the human effects of the bomb, and nearly fifty years later the same impulses [are] at play. . . . There remains today a reluctance to face squarely what America did; there's a desire to excuse it, perhaps even wish it away." In *Hiroshima in America,* Mitchell calls the official American response to Hiroshima "the mother of coverups," suggesting that it was further aided by collective American guilt and denial.

"While *Hiroshima in America* sums up the historical controversies about the use of the bomb with admirable economy, it is not yet another book about why the bombs were used," noted Mike Moore in the *Bulletin of the Atomic Scientists.* "Rather, its main purpose is to explore the impact of the bombs' use on America over the past 50 years—the 'mythology Americans have constructed around Hiroshima, and its cost to ourselves and to the world.'" Moore praised the book as "an extended essay into the psychological consequences of the first use of atomic weapons . . . full of keen insight." *Progressive* reviewer Samuel H. Day called *Hiroshima in America* "indelible," especially for its use of first-hand accounts of the destruction. To quote Day, "the resurrection of those early voices of outrage gives aid and comfort to those of us for whom even one Hiroshima remains one too many."

Mitchell's *Tricky Dick and the Pink Lady* re-visits the 1950 senatorial campaign between Richard Nixon and Helen Gahagan Douglas. Mitchell demonstrates that Nixon used anti-Communist hysteria to discredit Douglas, calling her "pink right down to her underwear." An *Economist* reviewer declared that, in *Tricky Dick and the Pink Lady,* Mitchell "presents a fair, compelling and convincing account of a dark period of American history," and a *Library Journal* correspondent found the work an "evocative political morality tale . . . strongly recommended."

BIOGRAPHICAL/CRITICAL SOURCES:

PERIODICALS

Bulletin of the Atomic Scientists, July-August, 1995, pp. 73-74.
Economist, February 14, 1998, p. R9.
Entertainment Weekly, July 21, 1995, p. 58.

Library Journal, November 1, 1997, p. 104.
Progressive, August, 1995, pp. 22-27; January, 1996, pp. 40-41.
Publishers Weekly, February 20, 1995, p. 202; May 29, 1995, p. 74.

* * *

MONTGOMERY, Rutherford George 1894-1985 (Al Avery, Everitt Proctor)

PERSONAL: Born April 12, 1894, in Straubville, ND; died July 3, 1985; son of George Y. and Matilda (Proctor) Montgomery; married Eunice Opal Kirks, February 14, 1930; children: Earl, Polly Montgomery Hecathorn, Marylin Montgomery Fitch. *Education:* Studied at Colorado Agricultural College, Western State College of Colorado, and University of Nebraska. *Avocational interests:* Flying, outdoor life.

CAREER: Hot Springs Elementary School, Hot Springs, WY, teacher, 1915-17; Delta County High Schools, Cedaredge, CO, teacher and principal, 1921-24; Montrose County Junior High School, Montrose, CO, principal, 1924-28; State of Colorado, Gunnison county judge, 1931-36, budget commissioner, 1932-38; free-lance writer, primarily of youth books, 1939—. Ghost writer for Dick Tracy series, 1941-46; creative writing teacher, Los Gatos, CA, 1955-57; writer, Walt Disney Studios, Burbank, CA, 1958-62. *Military service:* U.S. Army Air Corps, 1917-19; became sergeant.

MEMBER: Society of Authors, Western Writers of America, Writers Guild of America West.

AWARDS, HONORS: Commonwealth Club of California juvenile silver medal, 1953, for *Wapiti the Elk; New York Herald Tribune* Children's Spring Book Festival award, 1956, and Boys' Clubs of America junior book award, 1957, both for *Beaver Water;* Western Writers of America Spur Award, for children's books, 1966.

WRITINGS:

Troopers Three, Doubleday (New York City), 1932.
Call of the West, Grosset, 1933.
Broken Fang, M. A. Donohue (Chicago), 1935, 2nd edition, Caxton (Caldwell, ID), 1939.

Carcajou, Caxton, 1936, reprinted, Houghton (Boston), 1967.
Yellow Eyes, Caxton, 1937.
Gray Wolf, Houghton, 1938.
High Country, Derrydale Press (New York City), 1938.
The Trail of the Buffalo, Houghton, 1939.
Timberlane Tales, McKay (Philadelphia), 1939.
Midnight, Henry Holt (New York City), 1940.
Star Ball of the Rangers, McKay, 1941.
Iceblink, Henry Holt, 1941.
Hurricane Yank, McKay, 1942.
Husky, Co-Pilot of the Pilgrim, Henry Holt, 1942.
Thumbs Up! McKay, 1942.
Ghost Town Adventure, Henry Holt 1942.
Trapers' Trail, Henry Holt, 1943.
War Wings, McKay, 1943.
Out of the Sun, McKay, 1943.
Warhawk Patrol, McKay, 1944.
Big Brownie, Henry Holt, 1944.
Thunderboats, Ho!, McKay, 1945.
Sea Raiders Ho!, McKay, 1945.
Rough Riders Ho!, McKay, 1946.
The Mystery of the Turquoise Frog, Messner (New York City), 1946.
Kildee House, Doubleday, 1949, reprinted, Walker (New York City), 1993.
The Mystery of the Crystal Canyon, Winston (Philadelphia), 1951.
The Capture of the Golden Stallion, Little, Brown (Boston), 1951.
Hill Ranch, Doubleday, 1951.
Mister Jim, Faber, 1952, World Publishing (Cleveland), 1957.
Wapiti, the Elk, Little, Brown, 1952.
White Mountaineer, Little, Brown, 1953.
Seecatch, a Story of a Fur Seal, Ginn (Boston), 1953.
McGonnigle's Lake, Doubleday, 1953.
The Golden Stallion's Revenge, Little, Brown, 1953.
The Golden Stallion's to the Rescue, Little, Brown, 1954.
Amikuk, World Publishing, 1955.
Black Powder Empire, Little, Brown, 1955.
The Golden Stallion's Victory, Little, Brown, 1956.
Beaver Water, World Publishing, 1956.
Claim Jumpers of Marble Canyon, Knopf (New York City), 1956.
Jets Away!, Dodd (New York City), 1957.
Mountain Man, World Publishing, 1957.
Tom Pittman, USAF, Duell, Sloan & Pearce (New York City), 1957.
Whitetail: The Story of a Prairie Dog, World Publishing, 1958.

The Silver Hills, World Publishing, 1958.
Kent Barstow, Special Agent, Duell, Sloan & Pearce 1958.
In Happy Hollow, Doubleday, 1958.
The Golden Stallion and the Wolf Dog, Little, Brown, 1958.
(With Natlee Kenoyer) *A Horse for Claudia and Dennis,* Duell, Sloan & Pearce, 1958.
Tim's Mountain, World Publishing, 1959.
(Editor) *A Saddlebag of Tales,* Dodd, 1959.
Missile Away: A Kent Barstow Adventure, Duell, Sloan & Pearce, 1959.
The Golden Stallion's Adventure at Redstone, Little, Brown, 1959.
(With Grover Heiman) *Jet Navigator, Strategic Air Command,* Dodd, 1959.
Mission Intruder: A Kent Barstow Adventure, Duell, Sloan & Pearce, 1960.
Walt Disney's Weecha: A Fact-Fiction Nature Story, Golden Press (New York City), 1960.
Walt Disney's The Odyssey of an Otter: A Fact-Fiction Nature Story, Golden Press, 1960.
Walt Disney's El Blanco: The Legend of the White Stallion, Golden Press, 1961.
Kent Barstow, Space Man, Duell, Sloan & Pearce, 1961.
King of the Castle: The Story of a Kangaroo Rat, World Publishing, 1961.
Klepty, Duell, Sloan & Pearce, 1961.
Walt Disney's Cougar: A Fact-Fiction Nature Story, Golden Press, 1961.
Sex Isn't Everything, Dodd, 1961.
The Golden Stallion, Grosset, 1962.
The Capture of the West Wind, Duell, Sloan & Pearce, 1962.
Snowman, Duell, Sloan & Pearce, 1962.
Monte, the Bear Who Became a Celebrity, Duell, Sloan & Pearce, 1962.
Crazy Kill Range, World Publishing, 1963.
The Defiant Heart, Duell, Sloan & Pearce, 1963.
Kent Barstow and the Commando Flight, Duell, Sloan & Pearce, 1963.
McNulty's Holiday, Duell, Sloan & Pearce, 1963.
Kent Barstow on a B-70 Mission, Duell, Sloan & Pearce, 1964.
Kent Barstow Aboard the Dyna Soar, Duell, Sloan & Pearce, 1964.
The Living Wilderness, Dodd, 1964.
Ghost Town Gold, World Publishing, 1965.
The Stubborn One, Duell, Sloan & Pearce, 1965.
Into the Groove, Dodd, 1966.
Thornbush Jungle, World Publishing, 1966.
The Golden Stallion and the Mysterious Feud, Little, Brown, 1967.

A Kinkajou on the Town, World Publishing, 1967.
Smoky Trail, Ward, Lock, 1967.
Dolphins as They Are, Duell, Sloan & Pearce, 1969.
Corey's Sea Monster, World Publishing, 1969.
Pekan the Shadow, Caxton, 1970.
Big Red, a Wild Stallion, Caxton, 1971.
Rufus, Caxton, 1973.

"A YANKEE FLIER" SERIES; UNDER PSEUDONYM AL AVERY

A Yankee Flier with the R.A.F., Grosset, 1941.
A Yankee Flier in the Far East, Grosset, 1942.
A Yankee Flier in the South Pacific, Grosset, 1943.
A Yankee Flier in North Africa, Grosset, 1943.
A Yankee Flier over Berlin, Grosset, 1944.
A Yankee Flier in Italy, Grosset, 1944.
A Yankee Flier on a Rescue Mission, Grosset, 1945.
A Yankee Flier in Normandy, Grosset, 1945.
A Yankee Flier under Secret Orders, Grosset, 1946.

UNDER PSEUDONYM EVERITT PROCTOR

The Cruise of the Jeannette, Westminster, 1944.
Thar She Blows, Westminster, 1945.
Men Against the Ice, Westminster, 1946.

OTHER

Also author of screen and television plays. Contributor of more than 500 short stories to magazines for girls and boys.

SIDELIGHTS: In a writing career that lasted four decades and included 100 books, Rutherford George Montgomery wrote stories for children about airplanes and pilots, about boys and girls who lived on the Western frontier, and about animals of particular interest to young readers. A reviewer for the *Chicago Sunday Tribune* once noted "Montgomery is a master at bringing the outdoors with all its sights and sounds and smells to his readers." In *Silver Hills,* which a *Christian Science Monitor* reviewer called "a well-written and colorful realistic story," Montgomery tells the story of Darcy Hardy, a fiery redhead who sets out to right the wrong done to her father by his associates in a silver mine near Virginia City. Reviewers commended Montgomery for his characterization, plot, and setting. A contributor to *Kirkus Reviews* found that "Darcy and her father are appealing and the narrative is well packed." And, according to R. E. Livsey in an article in the *Saturday Review,* "The author's picture of an exciting, violent frontier town, with its rough, sturdy inhabitants is

fresh and believable." Livsey continued, "It is especially interesting that he should tell the story of Virginia City, with its strikingly male life, through the eyes of a young gently bred girl." *Silver Hills,* like his Golden Stallion series and the majority of his other works, reflects the author's positive view of the frontier and the relationships established there among people and between people and animals. "The predominant note," observed Christine Bold in *Twentieth-Century Western Writers,* "is one of harmony, broken only temporarily and re-asserted at the end."

BIOGRAPHICAL/CRITICAL SOURCES:

BOOKS

Twentieth-Century Western Writers, second edition, St. James Press, 1991.

PERIODICALS

Booklist, November 15, 1958, p. 162.
Books, December 25, 1938, p. 9.
Chicago Sunday Tribune, November 11, 1951, p. 12; November 17, 1957, p. 120; May 10, 1959, p. 12.
Christian Science Monitor, September 9, 1943, p. 6; September 27, 1951, p. 13; May 8, 1958, p. 10.
Horn Book, September, 1951, p. 330.
Kirkus Reviews, August, 1951; September 1, 1956, p. 635; February 1, 1957, p. 85; July 15, 1957, p. 488; February 1, 1958, p. 78; June 1, 1958, p. 378; September 1, 1958, p. 661; March 1, 1959, p. 177.
Library Journal, December 15, 1943, p. 1052; October 15, 1951, p. 1716; December 1, 1951, p. 2017; March 15, 1957, p. 888; May 15, 1957, p. 1363; October 15, 1957, p. 2701; May 15, 1958, p. 1610; October 15, 1958, p. 3011.
New York Herald Tribune Book Review, May 12, 1957, p. 33; May 11, 1958, p. 24; September 7, 1958, p. 9; May 31, 1959, p. 10.
New York Times, October 14, 1951, p. 38; December 16, 1951; March 24, 1957, p. 42.
New York Times Book Review, June 25, 1967.
San Francisco Chronicle, May 12, 1957, p. 30; August 10, 1958, p. 23; May 17, 1959, p. 24.
Saturday Review, February 16, 1957, p. 53; September 21, 1957, p. 43; August 23, 1958, p. 35.
Wilson Library Bulletin, May, 1943, p. 76; July, 1958, p. 303; May, 1959, p. 266.*

MORSI, Pamela 1951-

PERSONAL: Born March 12, 1951, in Muskogee, OK; daughter of Vance Russell (an oil field laborer) and Zoe (a practical nurse; maiden name, Gilkey) Sylvester; married Farouk S. Morsi (an accountant), January 8, 1979 (died, 1996); children: Tamer, Leila. *Education:* Oklahoma State University, B.A., 1973; University of Missouri, M.A., 1977. *Politics:* Democrat. *Religion:* Baptist.

ADDRESSES: Office—P.O. Box 6249, San Antonio, TX 78209. *Agent*—Irene Goodman, Irene Goodman Literary Agency, 521 Fifth Ave., 17th Floor, New York, NY 10175.

CAREER: Muskogee Public Library, Muskogee, OK, library assistant, 1973-75; Ellis Library, Columbia, MO, library assistant, 1975-76; Oklahoma State University, Tulsa, librarian at School of Medicine, 1976-80; Roper Hospital, Charleston, SC, librarian, 1985-92; writer, 1992—.

MEMBER: Novelists, Inc., Romance Writers of America, Louisiana Romance Writers of America, SARA.

AWARDS, HONORS: Named best new author of historical romance by *RT,* 1991; Maggie Award from Georgia Romance Writers, 1992; RITA Award from Romance Writers of America, 1992, 1996; Reviewer's Choice Award from *RT,* 1992.

WRITINGS:

ROMANCE NOVELS

Heaven Sent, Bantam (New York City), 1991.
Courting Miss Hattie, Bantam, 1991.
Garters, Jove (New York City), 1992.
(With Jean Anne Caldwell, Ann Carberry, and Karen Lockwood) *Summer Magic,* Jove, 1993.
Wild Oats, Jove, 1993.
Runabout, Jove, 1994.
Marrying Stone, Jove, 1994.
The Love Charm, Avon (New York City), 1996.
Simple Jess, Jove, 1996.
No Ordinary Princess, Avon, 1997.
Sealed with a Kiss, Avon, 1998.

SIDELIGHTS: Pamela Morsi's romantic novels have attracted millions of readers with their "down-to-earth" characters and charm. As a child, Morsi was an avid reader, growing up in a small town with no

public library. Her desire to make books more accessible to children led her to choose a career as a librarian. That job helped her pay the bills for seventeen years, but she always harbored another ambition as well. She once told *CA:* "I wanted to be a writer almost since the moment I learned to read. I was given the admonition to 'write what you know.' That bit of advice almost derailed my career completely. I was very aware that, as a white-trash kid living on a dirt road in a half-horse town, I knew nothing.

"By 1988 I had risen up to middle class and had a successful professional career and a nice family. On my thirty-seventh birthday, I came home from work, rolled myself into a fetal position on the bed, and began to sob, 'I could have been a writer.' My husband was very sympathetic . . . for a while. After several weeks, however, he went out and bought me a computer, put it in the corner of our bedroom, and told me to 'write your damned book or shut up about it.' I wrote it." Morsi's first book, *Heaven Sent,* was quickly acquired by Bantam/Doubleday/Dell.

Her books have been described as having a 'working class' slant. Unlike many books in the romance genre, her heroes and heroines are not aristocratic, but rather shopkeepers, farmhands, and other ordinary folk. The author commented to *Romance Reader* interviewer Cathy Sova: "I strongly believe that everyone, rich and poor, every color and creed, every age and sexual preference, every level of physical attractiveness can fall in love. People like me do fall in love. And that love between decent hardworking folks who care about community and family is at least as interesting as the private life of Marla and the Donald. That's how I started out with a 'working class vision.'"

Morsi's work is also unique in that one of her main characters is a mentally handicapped man. The character, Jess, was introduced in *The Marrying Stone* as a secondary character. In that book, his limited intelligence and sweet nature served to offset the sophisticated hero, a Harvard musicologist. Morsi told Sova that when *Marrying Stone* was completed, "I knew that I wanted him to fulfill his ambitions of having his own gun, his own dog, and a woman. In order for that to happen, I had to give Jess his own story. The publisher was very resistant to this idea, believing that readers could not accept a hero who was so obviously imperfect." Yet the finished story, *Simple Jess,* proved the publishers wrong; it was as popular as any of Morsi's books. Morsi added to

Sova: "As a parent of a mentally handicapped daughter, I find a lot of mentally handicapped people in my life. Since my books in some ways reflect my life, it is only natural that all kinds of people show up in my stories."

BIOGRAPHICAL/CRITICAL SOURCES:

PERIODICALS

Romance Reader, August 31, 1997.

*   *   *

MORSON, Gary Saul 1948-

PERSONAL: Born April 19, 1948, in New York, NY; son of David M. (a physician) and Evelyn (a social worker; maiden name, Estrin) Morson; married Ewa Hauser, March 31, 1970 (divorced, 1976); married Miriam Jane Ackerman (a fund-raiser), July 7, 1983; children: Emily. *Education:* Yale University, B.A., 1969, M.Phil., 1973, Ph.D., 1974; attended Brasenose College, Oxford, 1969-70.

ADDRESSES: Home—215 Adler Dr., Libertyville, IL 60048. *Office*—Department of Slavic Languages, Northwestern University, Kresge Hall, Evanston, IL 60208-2206.

CAREER: University of Pennsylvania, Philadelphia, assistant professor, 1974-80, associate professor of Slavic languages, 1980-85; Northwestern University, Evanston, IL, professor of Slavic languages, 1986-90, Frances Hooper Professor of Arts and Humanities, 1990—

MEMBER: International Dostoevsky Society, Modern Language Association of America, Association of Literary Scholars and Critics (member of council), American Association of Teachers of Slavic and East European Languages, American Comparative Literature Association, Tolstoy Society (president, 1991—).

AWARDS, HONORS: Fellow of National Endowment for the Humanities, 1978, Howard Foundation, 1978-79, and National Humanities Center, 1978-79; American Association of Teachers of Slavic and East European Languages best scholarly book award, 1992, for *Mikhail Bakhtin: Creation of a Prosaics.*

WRITINGS:

The Boundaries of Genre: Dostoevsky's "Diary of a Writer" and the Traditions of Literary Utopia, University of Texas Press (Austin), 1981.

(Editor) *Literature and History: Theoretical Problems and Russian Case Studies,* Stanford University Press (Stanford, CA), 1986.

(Editor) *Bakhtin: Essays and Dialogues on His Work,* University of Chicago Press (Chicago), 1986.

Hidden in Plain View: Narrative and Creative Potentials in "War and Peace", Stanford University Press, 1987.

(Editor with Caryl Emerson) *Rethinking Bakhtin: Extensions and Challenges,* Northwestern University Press (Evanston, IL), 1989.

(With Emerson) *Mikhail Bakhtin: Creation of a Prosaics,* Stanford University Press, 1990.

(Author of introductory study) Fyodor Dostoevsky, *A Writer's Diary: Volume 1, 1873-1876,* Northwestern University Press, 1993.

Narrative and Freedom: The Shadows of Time, Yale University Press (New Haven), 1994.

(Editor with Elizabeth Cheresh Allen) *Freedom and Responsibility in Russian Literature: Essays in Honor of Robert Louis Jackson,* Northwestern University Press/Yale Center for International and Area Studies, 1995.

Editor of Russian Series, Northwestern University Press, 1986-92, and Yale University Press, 1992—; editor of Theory Series, Northwestern University Press, 1992—.

SIDELIGHTS: Gary Saul Morson is described as a "preeminent scholar of Russian literary theoretician Mikhail Bakhtin, and of Dostoyevsky and Tolstoy" by D. B. Johnson in *Choice.* Morson's works include *Narrative and Freedom: The Shadows of Time,* in which the author examines the literary dilemma posed by a plotted, fictional depiction of free will. "The author's thesis," Kathleen Parthe explains in *Society,* "is that the way we orient ourselves to the present moment, and the present moment to the past and future, has everything to do with the way we make moral choices." Morson examines the contradiction, Parthe notes, between a fictional character's "assertion of freedom" and "the author's already completed plan." "Morson's ethics of temporal freedom are soundly articulated," writes Steven Connor in the *Times Literary Supplement,* "and his argument represents a significant contribution to the growing literature within philosophy and cultural theory on the relations between time and value." Johnson calls the book "a richly textured, thought-provoking study that is an engaging blend of philosophy, literary theory, and criticism." Parthe calls *Narrative and Freedom* "a forceful and convincing discussion of some of the most significant questions that literature attempts, if not to answer, then at least to pose in thought-provoking ways."

BIOGRAPHICAL/CRITICAL SOURCES:

PERIODICALS

Choice, June, 1995, p. 1600.
Journal of the History of Ideas, January, 1995, p. 171.
Publishers Weekly, May 31, 1993, p. 33.
Slavic Review, winter, 1995, p. 1070.
Society, July-August, 1996, p. 88.
Times Literary Supplement, January 5, 1996, p. 24.

* * *

MURRAY, K(atherine) M(aud) Elisabeth 1909-1998

PERSONAL: Born December 3, 1909, in Cambridge, England; died February, 1998; daughter of Harold James R. (an inspector of schools) and Kate Maitland (Crosthwaite) Murray. *Education:* Somerville College, Oxford, B.A. (honors), 1931, B.Litt., 1933. *Religion:* Church of England.

CAREER: Ashburne Hall, Manchester, England, tutor and librarian, 1935-37; Oxford University, Somerville College, Oxford, England, Mary Somerville research fellow, 1937-38; Cambridge University, Girton College, Cambridge, England, assistant tutor and registrar, 1938-44, domestic bursar, 1942-44, junior bursar, 1944-48; Bishop Otter College of Education, Chichester, England, principal, 1948-70; writer, 1970-98. Chichester District Council, member, beginning 1973, vice-chairman of planning committee, beginning 1976.

MEMBER: Society of Antiquaries (fellow), Sussex Archaeological Society (chairman of council, 1964-77; president, beginning 1977).

AWARDS, HONORS: Mond student at British School of Archaeology in Jerusalem, 1933.

WRITINGS:

The Constitutional History of the Cinque Ports, Manchester University Press, 1935.
The Register of Daniel Rough, Common Clerk of Romney, Records Branch, Kent Archaeological Society, 1945.
Caught in the Web of Words: James Murray and the Oxford English Dictionary, Yale University Press (New Haven, CT), 1977.

Contributor to history and archaeology journals.

SIDELIGHTS: In *Caught in the Web of Words: James Murray and the Oxford English Dictionary,* K. M. Elisabeth Murray wrote a biography of her grandfather, James A. H. Murray, the editor of the original *Oxford English Dictionary.* Now considered one of the world's finest dictionaries, the *Oxford English Dictionary* provides quotes from history and literature to illustrate the earliest known examples of each word it defines. "The reading required to find quotes, keeping the volunteers motivated, finding volunteers who were competent, maintaining funding from Oxford, the number of slips with quotations that were created (eventually five million) and the physical handling of these slips was daunting," wrote Kathleen Bradford in *Liberty.* Drawing on old family letters, diaries and other documents, Murray created what J. M. Edelstein in the *New Republic* called "an extraordinarily detailed account of the triumphs and frustrations which were part of the history of the *Dictionary.*" Catherine von Schon in *Library Journal* concluded: "Murray has written a most interesting, detailed, and readable biography of her grandfather which happens also to include the story of the greatest dictionary of modern times."

Murray once told *CA:* "I am only an amateur archaeologist. I became interested at school in Colchester and during my time at Oxford, when I became president of the Oxford University Archaeological Society. I excavated on weekends at a Saxon site near Oxford and on vacations at Colchester (a Roman site). As a student of the British School of Archaeology in Jerusalem I joined the Samaria expedition for one season."

BIOGRAPHICAL/CRITICAL SOURCES:

PERIODICALS

America, April 29, 1978, p. 350.
American Scholar, spring, 1978, p. 283.

Best Sellers, November, 1977, p. 245.
Booklist, January 1, 1978, p. 721.
Books and Bookmen, December, 1977, p. 26.
Book World, November 27, 1977, p. E5.
Choice, March, 1978, p. 72.
Commonweal, January 20, 1978, p. 55.
Economist, September 24, 1977, p. 140.
Georgia Review, summer, 1978, p. 458.
Hudson Review, winter, 1979, p. 704.
Liberty, March, 1998, pp. 66-67.
Library Journal, November 15, 1977, p. 2338.
Listener, October 20, 1977, p. 514.
New Leader, December 5, 1977, p. 7.
New Republic, Novemebr 12, 1977, p. 33.
New Statesman, October 14, 1977, p. 510.
Newsweek, November 7, 1977, p. 98.
New Yorker, November 21, 1977, p. 222.
New York Review of Books, June 1, 1978, p. 30.
New York Times, October 19, 1977, p. 29.
New York Times Book Review, October 30, 1977, p. 13.
Observer, December 11, 1977, p. 29.
Publishers Weekly, September 12, 1977, p. 125.
Saturday Review, November 12, 1977, p. 30.
Sewanee Review, July, 1978, p. 72.
Time, December 26, 1977, p. 67.
Village Voice, Februayr 20, 1978, p. 87.
Virginia Quarterly Review, spring, 1978, p. 338.
Wall Street Journal, November 21, 1977, p. 26.
Yale Review, June, 1978, p. 578.

OBITUARIES:

PERIODICALS

Independent, February 25, 1998, p. 17.*

* * *

MUSKE, Carol
  See MUSKE-DUKES, Carol (Anne)

* * *

MUSKE-DUKES, Carol (Anne) 1945-
  (Carol Muske)

PERSONAL: Born December 17, 1945, in St. Paul, MN; daughter of William Howard (in real estate) and Elizabeth (Kuchera) Muske; married Edward Healton (a neurologist; divorced); married David C. Dukes (an actor), January 31, 1983; children: (second marriage) Annie Cameron, Shawn (stepchild). *Ethnicity:* "Caucasian." *Education:* Creighton University, B.A., 1967; San Francisco State College (now University), M.A., 1970. *Avocational interests:* Travel.

*ADDRESSES: Home—*Los Angeles, CA. *Office—*Department of English, University of Southern California, Los Angeles, CA 90089. *Email—*carolmd@mizar.usc.edu.

CAREER: Free Space (a creative writing program), Women's House of Detention, Riker's Island, NY, founder and director, 1972-73; Art Without Walls/Free Space (a writing/art program for women prisoners), New York City, director, 1974-82; University of Southern California, Los Angeles, lecturer in creative writing, 1985-89, associate professor, 1989-91, professor of English, 1991—. Instructor at New School for Social Research, New York University, Columbia University, University of California, Irvine, University of Virginia, University of Iowa. Jenny McKean Moore lecturer, George Washington University; lecturer to women's groups; poetry readings given around the country.

MEMBER: Authors Guild, Authors League of America, Poets and Writers, Poetry Society of America (member, board of governors), PEN, National Writers Union, National Organization for Women, Los Angeles Library Association (member of board of advisors).

AWARDS, HONORS: Dylan Thomas Poetry Award, New School for Social Research, 1973, for poem, "Swansong"; Pushcart Prizes, 1978, 1988-89, 1992-93; Alice Fay Di Castagnola Award, Poetry Society, 1979; fellowships from Guggenheim Foundation, 1981, National Endowment for the Arts, 1984, and Ingram Merrill Foundation, 1988.

WRITINGS:

POETRY; UNDER NAME CAROL MUSKE

Camouflage, University of Pittsburgh Press (Pittsburgh, PA), 1975.
Skylight, Doubleday (New York City), 1981.
Wyndmere, University of Pittsburgh Press, 1985.
Applause, University of Pittsburgh Press, 1989.
Red Trousseau, Viking/Penguin (New York City), 1993.
An Octave Above: New and Selected Poems, Penguin, 1997.

UNDER NAME CAROL MUSKE-DUKES

Dear Digby (novel), Viking, 1989.
Saving St. Germ (novel), Viking, 1993.
Women and Poetry: Truth, Autobiography, and the Shape of the Self (criticism), University of Michigan Press (Ann Arbor), 1997.

OTHER

Contributor to books, including *Eating the Menu,* edited by B. E. Taylor, W. C. Brown, 1974; *The American Poetry Anthology,* edited by Daniel Halpern, Avon, 1975; also *The Pushcart Prize Anthology, Poet's Choice,* and *Woman Poet.* Contributor to periodicals, including *Ms., Oui, New Yorker, Field, Esquire, American Poetry Review, New York Times, New York Times Book Review, Los Angeles Times Book Review, Yale Review,* and *Village Voice.* Assistant editor of *Antaeus,* 1972—.

WORK IN PROGRESS: Two Secrets (a novel), forthcoming; two plays and a guide to creative writing.

ADAPTATIONS: The novel *Dear Digby* has been optioned by Orion Pictures for a feature film; *Saving St. Germ* was optioned for film by actress Julia Ormond, 1997.

SIDELIGHTS: Carol Muske-Dukes, who publishes her poetry under the name Carol Muske, has developed a reputation as a careful writer who balances rhetorical precision with a unique manner of relating personal experience. Writing in *Contemporary Women Poets,* essayist Duane Ackerson notes of Muske-Dukes' verse that, "while well-anchored in daily life, [it] moves far beyond to become a meditation on philosophical concerns like the nature of time and the value of life. This carefully achieved scope contributes much of what is powerful and persuasive in her work." In addition to her poetry, Muske-Dukes is the author of two novels, including *Dear Digby* and *Saving St. Germ,* as well as a volume of poetry criticism titled *Women and Poetry: Truth, Autobiography, and the Shape of the Self.*

Camouflage, published in 1975 as Muske-Dukes' first book-length collection of verse and which shows the influence of such American poets as Gertrude Stein, has been followed by other volumes of poetry on an average of every five years. Holly Prado, reviewing the poems in Muske-Dukes' third collection, 1985's *Wyndmere,* in the *Los Angeles Times,* terms the work "honed and consciously crafted," and

points out that "she's discovered a way to work magic within the boundaries of technical achievement." For Prado, one of the ways Muske-Dukes works her "magic" is through a process of intimation with her audience: "Her contemplation of experience is personal yet moves further, into the spiritual and philosophical; then it belongs not only to the poet but to all of us." In a critique of 1989's *Applause,* Wayne Koestenbaum is equally impressed with Muske-Dukes' method of identification; "she reaches past anecdote," he writes in the *New York Times Book Review.* Although Koestenbaum suggests that her wordage gives "too little tonal pleasure," he admits that Muske-Dukes "tempers glib candor with a recognition that language is inevitably impeded and enriched by all that resists easy saying."

In *Red Trousseau,* published in 1993, the color red and what it represents serve as the theme weaving its way throughout the collection: from the red of fire and anger to that of blood, sexual passion, and robust good health. 1997's *An Octave above Thunder* provides an overview of Muske-Dukes' work, revealing what *Library Journal* contributor Fred Muratori calls "an expanding poetic consciousness, from 1970s Surrealism Lite . . . through feminism and political awareness, . . . to self-analysis and ambitious meditation."

Muske-Dukes published her first story at age eleven and had begun writing poetry at an even earlier age. "But I was fairly unconscious about the power of words and what it meant to have the power to use them until I came to New York in 1971," she once explained to *CA.* After becoming involved in several writing workshops, including the Free Space writing program that she founded at the women's prison on Riker's Island in 1972, she "began to hear the dialogue between craft and sentiment, form and feeling." Still she considers herself to be primarily a visual poet: "images come . . . easily to me, imagistic phrases litter my poems. I feel very close to painters, our processes are similar."

The difference between "seeing" and "hearing" her writing is one of the distinctions Muske-Dukes finds between her poetry and her prose. "The problem for me is 'hearing' what I write—that's why it was so refreshing for me to write [my first novel] I found a voice, I trusted it, I let it speak. Beyond time and how time happens in a poem or a story, the relationship between eye and ear forms the difference for me between poetry and prose. In prose, the reader listens, the reader is being told a story, she hears, *then* sees—in poems, the reader *sees* aurally, the eye and ear become one."

In her first published departure from poetry, the 1989 novel *Dear Digby,* Muske-Dukes examines sexual politics, voyeurism, and neurosis through the cynical eyes of Willis Jane Digby, an editor of reader mail to the feminist magazine *SIS.* "The social satire gets diluted by some of the more difficult aspects of the plot," claims Stephen McCauley in a review of the novel for the *New York Times Book Review.* The critic does insist, however, that Muske-Dukes "has written a novel full of sharp insights and surprising images. . . . She is particularly good at writing amusing hit-and-run portraits." Linsey Abrams, in an appraisal of *Dear Digby* for the *Los Angeles Times Book Review,* calls the author "a fine stylist. Her sculpted images and energetic prose make her storytelling vivid and compelling."

With the same precision she composes her poetry, Muske-Dukes extracts real meaning from the images created by the words in each of her novels, and her wide variety of subjects demonstrate her broad learning. Reviewing *Saving St. Germ,* her 1993 work of fiction, Tom De Haven comments in the *New York Times Book Review* that Muske-Dukes has created a protagonist "as likeable as she is off-putting, with habits, quirks and observations that startle you with their strangeness but always feel true." In her exploration of the world of a university biochemist hired to "do something flashy, fund-attracting" in contrast with her natural impulse to put on a white lab coat and putter about in the lab unbothered, Muske-Dukes creates what De Haven calls "a truly original work of fiction, something fresh—the exploration of a subculture that's baffling, often intimidating, to most of us, and usually ignored by American literary novelists."

"My primary motivation for writing is to keep myself sane," Muske-Dukes more recently told *CA.* "My reading influences my work. Family life influences my work. I don't watch TV or read newspapers regularly, but I swallow maybe two books (poetry, novels, nonfiction) per week, along with articles, criticism, etc.

"My writing process is completely random. I write whenever and wherever I can: stopped at red lights, in doctors' waiting rooms, at my computer, at 2:30 a.m. in or out of bed. I write constantly in my head. As many writers have said before me, I didn't chose my subjects, they chose me. I was 'given' a set of

themes early in life and they've obsessed me and continue to do so." Her advice to aspiring writers: "to read—and beyond that, don't take any advice. Especially from writers, they all lie."

BIOGRAPHICAL/CRITICAL SOURCES:

BOOKS

Contemporary Literary Criticism, Volume 90, Gale (Detroit), 1996.
Contemporary Women Poets, St. James Press (Detroit), 1997.
Modern American Women Poets, Dodd, 1984.

PERIODICALS

Chicago Tribune, May 23, 1989.
Choice, January, 1976, p. 1447.
Kirkus Reviews, December 1, 1992, p. 1462.
Library Journal, October 1, 1997, p. 86.
Los Angeles Times, April 6, 1989.
Los Angeles Times Book Review, December 1, 1985, p. 11; May 21, 1989, p. 3; September 15, 1991, p. 10.
New York Times Book Review, November 3, 1985, p. 13; April 16, 1989, p. 13; September 24, 1989, pp. 50-51; April 11, 1993, p. 18.
Poetry, December, 1985, pp. 163-64; April, 1994, pp. 39-53.
Washington Post, April 24, 1989.
Writer's Digest, February, 1996, p. 12.

*   *   *

NICHOLS, John (Treadwell) 1940-

PERSONAL: Born July 23, 1940, in Berkeley, CA; son of David G. (a psycho-linguist) and Monique (Robert) Nichols; divorced; children: Luke, Tania. *Education:* Hamilton College, B.A., 1962.

ADDRESSES: Home—Box 1165, Taos, NM 87571. *Agent*—Curtis Brown Ltd., 575 Madison Ave., New York, NY 10022.

CAREER: Writer. Has held various jobs, including that of blues singer in a Greenwich Village cafe, firefighter in the Chiricuahua Mountains of Arizona, and dishwasher in Hartford, CT; partner and artist in "Jest-No" greeting card business, 1962; English teacher in Barcelona, Spain, for three months.

AWARDS, HONORS: New Mexico Governor's Award, 1981.

WRITINGS:

The Sterile Cuckoo (novel), McKay (New York City), 1965.

The Wizard of Loneliness (novel), Putnam (New York City), 1966.

If Mountains Die (nonfiction), photographs by William Davis, Knopf (New York City), 1979.

A Ghost in the Music (novel; Quality Paperback Book Club selection), Holt (New York City), 1979.

The Last Beautiful Days of Autumn (nonfiction photo essay), Holt, 1982.

On the Mesa, Peregrine Smith (Salt Lake City, UT), 1986.

American Blood (novel), Holt, 1987.

A Fragile Beauty, Peregrine Smith, 1987.

The Sky's the Limit, Norton (New York City), 1990.

NEW MEXICO TRILOGY; NOVELS

The Milagro Beanfield War, Holt, 1974.

The Magic Journey (Quality Paperback Book Club selection), Holt, 1978.

The Nirvana Blues, Holt, 1981.

Also contributor of short stories to periodicals.

ADAPTATIONS: The Sterile Cuckoo, directed by Alan J. Pakula and starring Liza Minnelli, was released by Paramount in 1969; *The Milagro Beanfield War,* directed by Robert Redford, was released in 1988; *The Wizard of Loneliness,* directed by Jenny Bowen, was released in 1988.

SIDELIGHTS: John Nichols' New Mexico Trilogy (*The Milagro Beanfield War, The Magic Journey,* and *The Nirvana Blues*) traces the four-decade transformation of a small New Mexico town from a quiet, traditional society to its modern, commercial lifestyle. In the trilogy, Nichols is concerned with the destruction of traditional communities and cultures in the name of progress and, in particular, with the economic system that fosters such destruction.

"At the beginning of the trilogy," John McLellan writes in the *Washington Post,* "New Mexico was still a relatively unspoiled land, the possession of Indians and Mexicans who lived off the land. It was ripe for spoiling, and the story of that spoiling is a major concern of the trilogy." As Jeffrey Burke of

Harper's explains the story: "Speculators, developers, politicians—the usual crowd of cashers-in—have weaned the locals away from a land-based economy to the almighty greenback and introduced them to the marvels of installment plans, menial labor, and debt. By the time the older Pueblo get around to actively protesting, they've lost their children, their culture, [and] their farms to the maw of red-blooded, white-skinned capitalism."

In the face of this onslaught by Anglos and their social and economic imperatives, a small act of resistance ignites a clash of cultures. This is the story of *The Milagro Beanfield War.* Hispanic Joe Mondragon, a jack-of-all-trades, decides to tap into an irrigation canal so that he can raise some beans on a plot of his family's land. The only problem is that water is like gold in the West and this water belongs to the forces of Anglo progress. "The beanfield becomes a symbol of the plight of the Chicano in New Mexico—lost water rights, lost lands, and exploitation at the hands of outsiders," writes Carl R. Shirley in the *Dictionary of Literary Biography Yearbook.* In highlighting this plight, "Nichols draws upon the possibilities inherent in the genre to write a social novel different from most other socially oriented American novels," John E. Loftis maintains the *Rocky Mountain Review of Language and Literature.* "The central conflict in this novel is between two cultures, two ways of life, two views of reality: the Anglo and the Chicano."

To capture the conflict that swirls around the beanfield, Nichols "creates an original blend of myth and reality in his fictive world," notes Shirley. "The floodgates of the author's imagination are also opened," Shirley adds, "and the reader witnesses a phantasmagoria of colorful characters." The result is a novel that suggests to some reviewers a mix of John Steinbeck, William Faulkner, and Gabriel Garcia Marquez. For *National Observer* reviewer Larry L. King, however, *The Milagro Beanfield War* "is a big, gassy, convoluted book that adds up to a disappointment—one somehow failing to equal the sum of its many parts." And, Frederick Busch, writing in the *New York Times Book Review,* finds fault with Nichols's many colorful characters. "The characters, first of all, are stereotypes. . . . They don't exist in and of themselves, and they don't act because of inner necessity. . . . They seem instead to act for the sake of yet another amusing tale told by a decent, charming fellow-drinker during an afternoon in a quiet bar."

Loftis, in his review, takes account of criticism like that offered by Busch. He comments, "Busch makes several astute observations, but because of the ways in which he applies these observations to the novel, he condemns it for what seem to me wrong reasons." As he points out, "Wars, after all, are fought between social groups, not individuals, and Nichols chooses not to focus on an individual protagonist whose personality, values, and consciousness usually provide coherence and continuity to a novel." Instead, continues the critic, "The two cultures, Chicano and Anglo, and the values they represent are the protagonist and antagonist in *The Milagro Beanfield War;* they are forces too powerful to be controlled, too intertwined to be separated into clearly defined and formulated principles, and too random and haphazard in events to be represented by any one character." Loftis concludes, "Nichols' concerns as novelist are primarily social, and he has created an unusual kind of protagonist, and thus novel, to give artistic form to these concerns."

In *The Magic Journey,* the second novel of the trilogy, Nichols again explores the effect of progress on a small Chicano community, Chamisaville. The progress begins with a bang, transforming the sleepy town into a tangled mass of tourist traps. A school bus under repair explodes. The site soon yields hot springs. A shrine is set up to the Dynamite Virgin. Tourists come and spas, hotels, restaurants, and shops spring up to attend to their needs. As with his previous New Mexico novel, Nichols weaves together many elements, making *The Magic Journey* "a plausible history of exploitation, lush with eccentric characters, with myths, legends, ghosts, and revealing shards from the past four decades, all carried by a Dickensian narrative exuberance," Jeffrey Burke writes in *Harper's.* Jonathan Yardley finds in the *New York Times Book Review* that this "tale of how progress comes to the little Southwestern settlement of Chamisaville—transforming it into the 'playground of the Land of Enchantment' and displacing its true owners in the name of profit—is consistently diverting and occasionally amusing."

Nichols, in mixing humor into this social novel, goes too far—according to Burke—losing the delicate balance necessary for good satire. Burke writes, "Nichols's creative energy runs so often to comic invention, to caricature instead of character . . . that he entertains far more than he instructs. . . . The imbalance makes for ambivalence." Shirley sees greater balance in Nichols's storytelling, because he finds connections between this story and the culture

from which it emerges. "*The Magic Journey*'s characters are more in the tradition of Latin America than of the United States," Shirley maintains. "In Spanish-speaking countries, personal eccentricity is the norm rather than a deviation; unusual characters or even living caricatures are much more likely to be encountered, not only in literature but also on the streets. Nichols manifests a high degree of understanding of the people about whom he is writing and whose standard he has chosen to carry." In his own way, Nichols hopes to remind readers, in the words he quotes from President Woodrow Wilson, that "we are all caught in a great economic system which is heartless." "Nichols proposes," Bruce Cook of the *Washington Post* writes, "to change that system."

In *The Nirvana Blues,* third in the trilogy, an Anglo garbage man plans a drug deal to earn enough money to buy his own piece of New Mexico from the last Chicano in town. In this way, Nichols "practically shuts the door on any hope he has for the survival of Chicano culture and traditional lifestyle," observes Shirley. Here, as with the previous two novels, "Some of the many comic episodes are truly hilarious," Shirley notes, "but again, as in *The Milagro Beanfield War* and *The Magic Journey,* there is an underlying feeling of sadness and despair at the uncontrollable and inevitable circumstances that lead to the death of Eloy [the last Chicano] and his way of life. Nichols is laughing through his tears and causing his readers to do the same." For Lynn Z. Bloom, writing in *Western American Literature,* "Nichols's cautionary tale makes us yearn for heroes, saviors of the land, preservers of stability, natural beauty, integrity of human relationships."

Norbert Blei of the *Chicago Tribune Book World* concludes his evaluation of the New Mexico Trilogy with high praise. "It will be," he states, "one of the most significant contributions to American literature in some time. . . . Nichols has left us with a classic American trilogy."

Nichols has also written novels outside his "New Mexico Trilogy." These books are also marked by colorful characters and familiar locales and deal with larger social issues, but they focus tighter on more intimate issues such as family and love. Of these, the most highly regarded novel is his first, *The Sterile Cuckoo.* The novel's narrator, Jerry, offers an account of his sophomore year in college, during which time he learned little of academic value, but much of collegiate love. "Square at first sight for its evocation, through half-amused, half-boastful reminiscence, of frat-house drinking revels . . . at second glance, Nichols' book takes on a deeper dimension," Albert Goldman remarks in the *Nation*. "With astuteness and unfailing intuition, the young author has placed at the heart of his college recollections an absolutely unique yet broadly representative character named Pookie Adams. A comedienne, who has adopted the new humor as her personal life style, Pookie is the type of today's funny little old college girl." And, although Jerry is the narrator, this is Pookie's story. "Although Pookie often appears a fragile, childlike moppet encased in a gauzy pink cocoon of Disneyland fantasy . . . her actions and daydreams suggest pathological hatred," observes Goldman. And, the reviewer continues, "Spunky as her efforts are to exorcise fear with farce, their ultimate effect is to make her a 'sterile cuckoo,' cut off from life by the comic persona she originally adopted to protect her deeply damaged personality."

Granville Hicks values *The Sterile Cuckoo* "the best of many novels I have recently read about sex and the younger generation. For one thing," he writes in *Saturday Review,* "it presented a heroine who was both attractive and credible and for the most part unstereotyped. For another, I was impressed by the skill with which the author let the narrator expose himself as a heel." Other reviewers criticized the novel for a lack of realism and for being out of touch with its turbulent times. Richard A. Blessing addresses this issue in an article for the *Journal of Popular Culture*. "Critics of both the novel and the movie have scoffed at its lack of 'realism'. . . . A more discerning reading will show that the nightmare of violence in the atomic age is so pervasive in *The Sterile Cuckoo* that there is scarcely a page on which it is not present." He adds, "Let me suggest that Pookie and her friends are as aware of the horror of modern life as are their more recent counterparts at Columbia or Berkeley, but that their response to that horror is different, is more grotesque because the horror is more real and more grotesque to them." Blessing concludes, "Nichols has produced, I think, an important contribution to the popular literature of the '60s."

In this and other novels, critics have admired the versatility of Nichols' prose. John McLellan notes Nichols's "virtuoso style, the profusion of strange but believable characters, the skill with which small incidents are developed and the curious blend of humor and pathos, which are often found fighting for supremacy in a single phrase." Nichols "has all of Steinbeck's gifts," Norbert Blei states, "the same

overwhelming compassion for people, plus an even finer sense of humor, and the need to celebrate the cause and dignity of man." In a *Book Week* review of *The Sterile Cuckoo,* Patricia MacManus lists "an effervescent wit, a remarkable ear for dialogue, . . . a feeling for off-beat characterizations, and—oh, yes— the saving grace . . . of a rueful sense of the ludicrous" as being some of Nichols' writing assets. Speaking of his use of humor, Nichols once told *CA:* "I am a great believer in humor as a weapon and feel that while some of my work may be polemical, it's important that it is also funny and entertaining, and above all compassionate."

Nichols also explained to *CA* his motivations for writing and how they underwent a change beginning with his third novel: "Basically, my life, my literary focus, my ambitions, changed radically during the mid-1960s when I was active in the anti-Vietnam War movement. I came to view the world, and how it functions, from a mostly Marxist perspective, and most of what I've written since 1966 reflects this perspective. During the 1960s and early-1970s I wrote nearly a dozen novels, motivated by this new point of view, none of which saw the light of publishing day. Yet eventually I began to learn how to create an art that is both polemical and entertaining, and have managed in the past five years to guide a handful of new books into print.

"I am strongly committed, in my life and in my work, to bringing about changes in the nature of our society which I believe absolutely necessary to the well-being of us all. I'm tired of our destruction of human, spiritual, and natural resources, particularly among minorities and working class and third world peoples—both in our country and abroad. I hope some day to see a more equal distribution of wealth and opportunity in our nation and around the world, and an end to American imperialism. I have a great faith in the energy of our people, in the vitality of our myriad cultures. I have a tendency to believe that the survival or the destruction of our planet is in the hands of the U.S.A. That makes our nation one of the scariest and most exciting countries on Earth. I just wish that more of our artists and writers would accept social responsibility as an integral part of their credos, instead of wallowing in the cynical, self-centered nihilism that characterizes too much of what is popular and successful nowadays."

Norbert Blei of the *Chicago Tribune Book World* holds that "there used to be writers that cared about people. . . . Proletarian writers they were called. . . .

Nichols, now, seems almost alone upon this inherited terrain." Blei believes that Nichols' work "reminds us of the love and laughter, the courage it takes to be honest, caring human beings in an age when greed and self-fulfillment seem synonymous."

BIOGRAPHICAL/CRITICAL SOURCES:

BOOKS

Contemporary Authors Autobiography Series, Volume 2, Gale (Detroit), 1985.
Dictionary of Literary Biography Yearbook: 1982, Gale, 1983.
Twentieth-Century Western Writers, second edition, St. James Press (Detroit), 1991.
Wild, Peter, *John Nichols,* Boise State University (Boise, ID), 1986.

PERIODICALS

America, February 26, 1966.
Atlantic Monthly, March, 1965, p. 193.
Best Sellers, January 15, 1965; November, 1979, p. 283; September, 1981, p. 209.
Book Week, January 24, 1965; February 20, 1966.
Chicago Tribune Book World, October 7, 1979; August 16, 1981.
Christian Science Monitor, February 4, 1965.
Confluencia, October, 1978.
Harper's, April, 1965; March, 1966; August, 1978.
Journal of Popular Culture, summer, 1973, p. 124.
Kirkus Reviews, May 1, 1979, p. 562.
Nation, February 8, 1965, p. 142.
National Observer, November 16, 1974, p. 27.
New America, spring, 1979.
New York Herald Tribune, February 24, 1966, p. 21.
New York Times Book Review, January 17, 1965, p. 46; March 6, 1966, p. 52; October 27, 1974, p. 53; April 16, 1978, p. 15; June 10, 1979, p. 18; October 28, 1979.
Observer, May 15, 1977.
Publishers Weekly, June 11, 1982, p. 54.
Rocky Mountain Review of Language and Literature, Volume 38, number 4, 1984, p. 201.
Saturday Review, January 30, 1965, p. 26; February 26, 1966, p. 29.
Village Voice, June 30, 1979.
Washington Post, June 17, 1978; August 28, 1981.
Washington Post Book World, September 9, 1979; August 28, 1981.
Western American Literature, November, 1975, p. 249; winter, 1982-83, p. 372; spring, 1983, p. 54.

NIGHBERT, David F(ranklin) 1948-

PERSONAL: Born July 26, 1948, in Knoxville, TN; son of Herbert Cane (a wool presser) and Dorothy Jeanette (a secretary and homemaker; maiden name, Watson) Nighbert; married Stephanie Weems, 1972 (divorced, 1982). *Education:* Attended Maryville College, 1966-71, and University of Tennessee, 1971-72. *Politics:* "Liberal Democrat." *Religion:* "Former Southern Baptist, currently agnostic." *Avocational interests:* Reading, movies, pocket billiards.

ADDRESSES: Home—501 East 87th St., Apt. 9-D, New York, NY 10128. *Office*—Tower Video, 1977 Broadway, New York, NY 10023. *Agent*—Susan Ann Protter, 110 West 40th St., New York, NY 10018.

CAREER: Tower Records, New York City, assistant manager, 1989—. Worked at numerous jobs, including stock clerk, butcher's assistant, encyclopedia salesperson, construction laborer, actor, singer, and playwright.

WRITINGS:

SCIENCE FICTION

Timelapse, St. Martin's (New York City), 1988.
Clouds of Magellan, St. Martin's, 1991.

"BULL COCHRAN" MYSTERY SERIES

Strikezone, St. Martin's, 1989.
Squeezeplay, St. Martin's, 1992.
Shutout, St. Martin's, 1995.

SIDELIGHTS: David F. Nighbert has written both science-fiction novels and mysteries. In his first book, *Timelapse,* the cyborg Anton Stryker—a dead man revived as a superior, robotic individual—is bent on obtaining revenge against his killer, a villain planning wholesale destruction. A reviewer for *Commodore Computing International* describes *Timelapse* as a "well-written, fast moving" tale.

Clouds of Magellan, Nighbert's next science-fiction novel, is an action-packed sequel to *Timelapse.* Here the cyborg Stryker is trying to reach a giant alien artifact called the Wheel and finds himself stalked by his killer's henchman. A *Locus* reviewer recommends the book as being entertaining and "nicely written."

Nighbert's mysteries feature William "Bull" Cochran, a former minor-league pitcher who left the game when a bad pitch killed a batter. His first mystery, *Strikezone,* finds Cochran established in the moving business with Juice Hanzlik, his former catcher. When Hanzlik is murdered, Cochran undertakes an investigation into his late partner's affairs. A critic for *Kirkus Reviews* considers *Strikezone* "a powerful punch to the kidneys . . . with plot surprises that are actually surprising."

Shutout finds Cochran called in when his girlfriend's uncle commits suicide and her father is killed. "The investigation," writes Wes Lukowsky in *Booklist,* "leads . . . into the usual southern gothic family morass of illegitimacy, homosexuality, greed, blackmail, envy, and lust." The critic for *Publishers Weekly* calls the novel "an adroitly crafted series entry, written with care and attention to character, plot and setting."

Nighbert told *CA:* "It's often difficult to say where a story began, but with *Strikezone* I know exactly. It was a moonless night in the summer of 1978. I was with a friend in the living room of her beach house. We were sitting in the dark, the sliding glass door open to the breeze, when we noticed two sets of headlights on the beach facing each other across fifty yards of sand. The cars rolled forward, then sped up and headed straight for each other. As they passed we heard flat, cracking sounds. I thought it might be gunfire, but my friend thought I was being dramatic. The cars turned and charged a second time and again we heard the cracking sounds as they passed. This time I saw what I thought was a muzzle flash, and I was sure it was gunfire, but my friend still wasn't convinced. The third time neither car seemed inclined to give way. Only at the last second did one swerve, ending up jammed into the dunes. The driver tried to free his vehicle, but it was stuck. The other car turned and came back, stopping about twenty feet away. Then it revved and surged forward, slamming into the jammed car. Three times it did this. My friend and I were transfixed throughout, unable to move or take our eyes off the scene. Only when the jammed car finally caught fire did we come out of our daze and call the police.

"The other car was long gone by the time the police arrived. I answered the same questions over and over, while my own questions were left unanswered. There was nothing about the incident in the papers or on television, and the police wouldn't tell me what had happened. It's possible they didn't know. I won-der to this day what I witnessed. Whatever it was, it set my mind to working. There's no scene like this in *Strikezone,* but the book would probably never have been written without it."

BIOGRAPHICAL/CRITICAL SOURCES:

PERIODICALS

Analog Science Fiction/Science Fact, April, 1989, pp. 178-79.
Booklist, March 15, 1995, p. 1312.
Commodore Computing International, July, 1989.
Kirkus Reviews, June 15, 1989.
Locus, June 1991, p. 31.
Publishers Weekly, February 6, 1995, p. 79.
Woodland Hills News, (Los Angeles, CA; Simi Valley edition) June 30, 1991.

* * *

NYE, Naomi Shihab 1952-

PERSONAL: Born March 12, 1952, in St. Louis, MO; daughter of Aziz and Miriam Naomi (Allwardt) Shihab; married Michael Nye (a lawyer and photographer), September 2, 1978; children: Madison Cloudfeather (son). *Education:* Trinity University, B.A., 1974. *Politics:* Independent. *Religion:* Ecumenical. *Avocational interests:* Traveling, reading, cooking, exercising.

ADDRESSES: Home—806 South Main Ave., San Antonio, TX 78204.

CAREER: Freelance writer, editor, and speaker, 1974—. Visiting writer, University of Hawaii, 1991, University of Alaska, Fairbanks, 1994, and University of Texas at Austin, 1995, and others.

MEMBER: Academy of American Poets, Poets and Writers, Texas Institute of Letters, RAWI (association of Arab-American writers).

AWARDS, HONORS: Voertman Poetry Prize, Texas Institute of Letters, 1980, for *Different Ways to Pray,* and 1982, for *Hugging the Jukebox; Hugging the Jukebox* named a notable book of 1982, American Library Association (ALA); winner of four Pushcart Prizes; I. B. Lavan Award, Academy of American Poets, 1988; Charity Randall Prize for Spoken Poetry, with Galway Kinnell, International Poetry Forum, 1988; Jane Addams Children's Book award, 1994; Judy Lopez Memorial Award for children's literature and Texas Institute of Letters Best Book for Young Readers, both for *Habibi*; Paterson Poetry Prize for *The Tree Is Older than You Are*; numerous ALA notable book and best book citations.

WRITINGS:

POETRY

Different Ways to Pray, Breitenbush (Portland, OR), 1980.
Hugging the Jukebox, Dutton (New York City), 1982.
Yellow Glove, Breitenbush, 1986.
Invisible, Trilobite (Denton, TX), 1987.
Mint, State Street Press (Brockport, NY), 1991.
Red Suitcase, BOA Editions (Rochester, NY), 1994.
Words under the Words: Selected Poems, Far Corner Books (Portland, OR), 1995.
Fuel, BOA Editions, 1998.

Author of chapbooks *Tattooed Feet,* 1977, and *Eye-to-Eye,* 1978.

Contributor to *Texas Poets in Concert: A Quartet,* edited by Richard B. Sale, University of North Texas Press, 1990. Essay chosen for inclusion in *Best American Essays 1991,* edited by Joyce Carol Oates. Contributor of poems to periodicals, including *Atlantic Monthly, Georgia Review,* and *Hayden's Ferry Review.*

FICTION; FOR CHILDREN

Sitti's Secrets, illustrated by Nancy Carpenter, Macmillan (New York City), 1994.
Benito's Dream Bottle, illustrated by Yu Cha Pak, Simon & Schuster (New York City), 1995.
Lullaby Raft (also see below), illustrated by Vivienne Flesher, Simon & Schuster, 1997.

OTHER

(Editor) *This Same Sky: A Collection of Poems from around the World* (for children), Four Winds, 1992.
(Editor) *The Tree Is Older than You Are,* Simon & Schuster, 1995.
Never in a Hurry (essays), University of South Carolina Press (Columbia), 1996.
Habibi (novel), Simon & Schuster, 1996.

(Editor, with Paul Janeczco) *I Feel a Little Jumpy around You: A Book of Her Poems and His Poems Collected in Paris,* Simon & Schuster, 1996.
The Space between Our Footsteps: Poems and Paintings from the Middle East, Simon & Schuster, 1998.

Contributor of stories and essays to periodicals, including *Virginia Quarterly Review, Southwest Review, Georgia Review, Ploughshares, Manoa, Houston Chronicle,* and *Austin Chronicle.*

Recordings include *Rutabaga-Roo* (songs), Flying Cat (San Antonio), 1979; *Lullaby Raft,* Flying Cat, 1981; and *The Spoken Page* (poetry reading), International Poetry Forum (Pittsburgh), 1988.

SIDELIGHTS: Naomi Shihab Nye is known for award-winning poetry that lends a fresh perspective to ordinary events, people, and objects. "For me the primary source of poetry has always been local life, random characters met on the streets, our own ancestry sifting down to us through small essential daily tasks," Nye was quoted as saying by Jane L. Tanner in an essay published in the *Dictionary of Literary Biography.* Characterizing Nye's "prolific cannon" in *Contemporary Women Poets,* Paul Christensen noted that Nye "is building a reputation . . . as the voice of childhood in America, the voice of the girl at the age of daring exploration." Nye's poetry is also informed by her Palestinian-American background as well as other cultures. In her work, according to Tanner, "Nye observes the business of living and the continuity among all the world's inhabitants. . . . She is international in scope and internal in focus."

Nye was born in St. Louis, Missouri, to a Palestinian father and an American mother of German-Swiss descent. After spending much of her childhood in St. Louis, Nye moved with her family to Jerusalem, which was then part of Jordan. Nye attended a year of high school in Jordan before her family moved to San Antonio, Texas, where the poet continues to live with her husband and son. "My poems and stories often begin with the voices of our neighbors, mostly Mexican-American, always inventive and surprising," Nye wrote in a press release for Four Winds Press. "I never get tired of mixtures."

Nye's earliest published work consisted of a 1977 chapbook titled *Tattooed Feet;* another chapbook, *Eye-to-Eye,* followed in 1978. These early poems, written in free verse, often reflect the theme of a journey or quest. The opening poem in *Tattooed Feet,* "Pilgrimage," describes Via Dolorosa Street in Jerusalem; another verse is titled "Home." According to Tanner, "Nye finds grandeur in the mundane, even in minutiae, from the West Bank to Mexico to a car wash in Paris, Texas, 'perfectly ordered images / sophisticated enough to be called poetry.'" Tanner continued, "What is remarkable is Nye's ability to draw clear parallels between the ordinary and the sublime."

In her first full-length collection, 1980's *Different Ways to Pray,* Nye explores the differences as well as the shared experiences of localized cultures from California to Texas, from South America to Mexico. The poem "Madison Street" is set in America, where Nye comments, "I was not here when all this started / still there is some larger belonging." In another verse she focuses on cultural unity: "My grandmother's eyes say Allah is everywhere." And in "Grandfather's Heaven" a child declares: "Grandma liked me even though my daddy was a Moslem." As Tanner observed, "with her acceptance of different 'ways to pray' is also Nye's growing awareness that living in the world can sometimes be difficult." The quality of *Different Ways to Pray* was recognized by the Texas Institute of Letters, which awarded Nye the Voertman Poetry Prize in 1980.

Nye followed *Different Ways to Pray* with *On the Edge of the Sky,* a slim volume printed on handmade paper, and *Hugging the Jukebox,* a full-length collection that also won the Voertman Poetry Prize. In *Hugging the Jukebox* Nye continues to focus on the ordinary, on connections between diverse peoples, and on the perspectives of those in other lands. She writes: "we move forward, / confident we were born into a large family, / our brothers cover the earth." Nye creates poetry from everyday scenes in "The Trashpickers of San Antonio," where the trashpickers are "murmuring in a language soft as rags." Other poems in *Hugging the Jukebox* include the lullaby "Martita y Luisa," "Nelle," and the title verse, which is about a young boy who lives in the Caribbean with his grandparents. The boy in "Hugging the Jukebox" is enthusiastic about the jukebox he adopts, singing its songs in a way that "strings a hundred passionate sentences in a single line."

Reviewers generally praised *Hugging the Jukebox,* noting Nye's warmth and celebratory tone. Writing in the *Village Voice,* Mary Logue commented that in Nye's poems about mundane daily life, "sometimes the fabric is thin and the mundaneness of the action shows through. But, in an alchemical process of purification, Nye often pulls gold from the ordinary." Logue also observed that "when Nye chooses to push herself and write dramatically, she creates powerful poems." And according to *Library Journal* contributor David Kirby, the poet "seems to be in good, easy relation with the earth and its peoples." In Christensen's view, Nye "does not avoid the horrors of urban life, but she patches together the vision of simple nature struggling up through the cracks of the city."

Nye's next collection, *Yellow Glove,* was published in 1986. Unlike her earlier work, the poems in *Yellow Glove* present a more mature perspective tempered by tragedy and sorrow. In this collection Nye considers the Palestinian-Israeli conflict in "Blood," describes a cafe in combat-weary Beirut, bemoans "a world where no one saves anyone," and observes in "The Gardener" that "everything she planted gave up under the ground." "Still there arises out of these tragic phrases a message of hope," Tanner commented, "a realization that strength comes from facing adversity and that joy won from sorrow is priceless." *Georgia Review* contributor Philip Booth declared that Nye "knows more than most of us how many people(s) live; and she does justice to them, and to the need for change, by bringing home to readers both how variously and how similarly all people live."

In addition to her poetry collections, Nye has produced fiction for children, poetry and song recordings, and poetry translations. She has also produced a book of essays, *Never in a Hurry,* published in 1996, and edited several books of poems, including *This Same Sky: A Collection of Poems from around the World,* a book for young people that was published in 1992. An anthology of poetry in translation, *This Same Sky* represents the work of 129 poets from sixty-eight countries. In her introduction, Nye writes, "Whenever someone suggests 'how much is lost in translation!' I want to say, 'Perhaps—but how much is gained!'"

Reviewers praised *This Same Sky,* which also includes a country and poet index, a map, and suggestions for further reading. These extras, according to a *Horn Book* reviewer, give "additional luster to a book which should prove invaluable for intercultural education as well as for pure pleasure." Although contributor Lauralyn Persson noted in *School Library Journal* that some of the poems in the collection would be better appreciated by adults, the reviewer observed that the book is "brimming with much lovely material." And *Booklist* critic Hazel Rochman called *This Same Sky* "an extraordinary anthology, not only in its global range . . . but also in the quality of the selections and the immediacy of their appeal."

Sitti's Secrets, an illustrated narrative for children, was published in 1994, and concerns an Arab American child's relationship with her *Sitti* (Arabic for grandmother) who lives in a Palestinian village. The child, Mona, recalls visiting Sitti in Palestine: the surroundings, the culture, and how the two of them invented their own "sign" language to overcome the English-Arabic language barrier. And when Mona returns to the United States, she sustains the bond with her sitti through her active imagination. Mona also writes a letter to the President of the United States asking him for peace, and informing him that she knows he would like her sitti a great deal if he were to meet her. A reviewer for *Booklist* praised Nye for capturing the emotions of the "child who longs for a distant grandparent" as well as for writing a narrative that deals personally with Arabs and Arab Americans. A contributor to *Kirkus Reviews* asserted that Nye "deftly assembles particulars" of the relationship between grandmother and granddaughter and recounts "incidents with quiet eloquence."

In 1997 Nye published *Habibi,* her first young adult novel. Readers meet Liyana Abboud, an Arab-American teen who moves with her family to her Palestinian father's native country during the 1970s, only to discover that the violence in Jerusalem has not yet abated. As Liyana notes, "in Jerusalem, so much old anger floated around. . . . [that] the air felt stacked with weeping and raging and praying to God by all the different names." Autobiographical in its focus, *Habibi* was praised by Karen Leggett who noted in the *New York Times Book Review* that the novel, "filled with poetic images," magnifies through the lens of adolescence "the joys and anxieties of growing up even as it radically simplifies the complexities of the adult world. . . . Nye is meticulously sensitive to this rainbow of emotion." Appraising *Habibi* in *Horn Book,* contributor Jennifer M. Brabander agreed, stating that "the leisurely progression of the narrative matches the slow and stately pace of daily life" in Jerusalem, "and the text's poetic turns of phrase accurately reflect Liyana's passion for words and language."

Paraphrasing fellow poet William Stafford, Nye once told *CA:* "I believe poetry is as basic to our lives (as in 'getting back to basics') and to education as any-

thing else there could possibly be. I salute all the writers workshops for teachers and the writers-in-the-schools projects around the United States which have blossomed in the last twenty years. Student writing shows the positive effects. This is a particularly *American* phenomenon, and we should support and champion it whenever possible!"

BIOGRAPHICAL/CRITICAL SOURCES:

BOOKS

Contemporary Women Poets, St. James Press (Detroit), 1997.
Dictionary of Literary Biography, Volume 120: *American Poets since World War II,* Gale (Detroit), 1992.
Nye, Naomi Shihab, *Different Ways to Pray,* Breitenbush, 1980.
Nye, *Hugging the Jukebox,* Dutton, 1982.
Nye, *Yellow Glove,* Breitenbush, 1986.

PERIODICALS

Booklist, October 15, 1992, p. 425; March 15, 1994, p. 1374.
Bulletin of the Center for Children's Books, March, 1994, p. 228.
Georgia Review, spring, 1989.
Horn Book, March/April, 1993, p. 215; November/December, 1996, p. 755; November/December, 1997, p. 683.
Kirkus Reviews, February 15, 1994, p. 231; April 1, 1998.
Library Journal, August, 1982.
New York Times Book Review, November 16, 1997; November 23, 1997.
Publishers Weekly, May 13, 1996, p. 77; September 8, 1997, p. 77.
School Library Journal, December, 1992, p. 139; September, 1997; May, 1998.
Village Voice, January 18, 1983, p. 37.

*   *   *

ORBEN, Robert 1927-

PERSONAL: Born March 4, 1927, in New York, NY; son of Walter August and Marie (Neweceral) Orben; married Jean Louise Connelly, July 25, 1945. *Ethnicity:* "Human." *Religion:* Unitarian. *Avocational interests:* Travel, theater.

ADDRESSES: Home and office—3709 S. George Mason Dr., #205E, Falls Church, VA 22041-3700.

CAREER: Writer and consultant, 1946—; lecturer on humor in communications, 1977—. Comedy writer for Jack Paar, 1962-63, Red Skelton, 1964-70, and Dick Gregory; speechwriter for President Gerald Ford, 1974-76, director of White House speechwriting department, 1976-77. President of Comedy Center, Inc., Wilmington, DE, 1971-73. Public speaker on the subject of humor for business audiences and communications groups; conducts workshops and seminars on public speaking and speechwriting.

MEMBER: Writers Guild, National Press Club (Washington, DC).

AWARDS, HONORS: Recipient of the World Humor Award from the Workshop Library on World Humor, 1992.

WRITINGS:

(Editor) Dick Gregory, *From the Back of the Bus,* Dutton (New York City), 1962.
The Joke-Teller's Handbook, or 1,999 Belly Laughs, Doubleday (New York City), 1966, Crown, 1986.
The Ad-Libber's Handbook: 2000 New Laughs for Speakers, Doubleday, 1969, published as *2000 New Laughs for Speakers: The Ad-Libber's Handbook,* Gramercy (New York City), 1978.
The Encyclopedia of One-Liner Comedy, Doubleday, 1971, reprinted as *2000 Sure-Fire Jokes for Speakers and Writers: The Encyclopedia of One-Liner Comedy,* 1986.
2500 Jokes to Start 'Em Laughing, Doubleday, 1979.
2100 Laughs for All Occasions, Doubleday, 1983.
2400 Jokes to Brighten Your Speeches, Doubleday, 1984.
2000 Sure-Fire Jokes for Speakers: The Encyclopedia of One-Liner Comedy, Doubleday, 1986.

Also author of more than forty humor books in the "Orben Comedy Series," including *Ad Libs, Bits, Boffs and Banter, Belly Laughs, The Best of Current Comedy, Big Big Laughs, Blue Ribbon, Calendar Comedy, Caravan, Classified Comedy, Comedian's Gag File, Comedian's Professional Source-Book, Comedy Technique, The Emcee's Handbook, Emcee Blockbusters, The Encyclopedia of Patter, Fillers, Flip Lines, Gag Bonanza, Gag Showcase, If You Have to Be a Comic, Jackpot, Laugh Package, Magic Dotes, M.C. Bits, Patter Parade, Quickies,* *Rapid Fire Comedy, Screamline Comedy, Showstoppers, Sight Bits, Spotlight on Comedy,* and *The Working Comedian's Gag-File.*

Contributor to magazines. Editor of *Orben's Current Comedy,* 1958-89.

WORK IN PROGRESS: A book of speech humor; a book on public speaking.

SIDELIGHTS: For over fifty years, Robert Orben has provided comedy material for public speakers, entertainers, and leaders in business, politics, and community affairs through his books and his magazine, *Orben's Current Comedy.* The author began his career at the age of eighteen, when he saw a need for material for professional comedians and published *The Encyclopedia of Patter;* he progressed to writing for such show business luminaries as Red Skelton and Dick Gregory, and eventually branched out into advising political and business leaders, becoming a writer for President Gerald Ford. As Orben told Janine Ragan in *USA Today,* humor is useful to people in business and other traditionally "serious" occupations: "Laughter is an ideal tension breaker. An apt joke gives everybody involved enough time to draw back, rethink a position or reconsider an action." Orben also recognizes the importance of laughter to political candidates, commenting in *Time* that a sense of humor "is one of the attributes a good candidate must have." "Humor is one of the best forms of communication known to man," the author revealed to Marjorie Hunter in the *New York Times.* "It can soothe, heal and build. If you can put someone at ease," he concluded, "you have a friend."

Orben's *The Joke-Teller's Handbook, or 1,999 Belly Laughs, 2000 New Laughs for Speakers: The Ad-Libber's Handbook, 2500 Jokes to Start 'Em Laughing,* and *2400 Jokes to Brighten Your Speeches* are currently in reprint through Wilshire Book Company.

BIOGRAPHICAL/CRITICAL SOURCES:

PERIODICALS

Campaigns & Elections, Volume 10, number 2, August, 1989.
Investor's Business Daily, August 14, 1996.
Los Angeles Times, January 19, 1983.
New York Times, June 5, 1977; June 1, 1982.
Time, August 15, 1983.
USA Today, August 6, 1984.
U.S. News and World Report, December 17, 1979.

Wall Street Journal, January 26, 1995; January 24, 1997.

* * *

O'REILLY, Montagu
    See ANDREWS, Wayne

* * *

ORNISH, Dean 1953-

PERSONAL: Born July 16, 1953, in Dallas, TX; son of a dentist; married Shirley E. Brown (a nutritional expert and codirector of Ornish's research; divorced); married Mary Blackwell, June, 1998. *Education:* Attended Rice University; University of Texas at Austin, B.A. (summa cum laude), 1975; Baylor College of Medicine, M.D., 1980; completed internship and residency at Massachusetts General Hospital and Harvard Medical School.

ADDRESSES: Home—Sausalito, CA.   *Office*—900 Bridgeway, Suite 2, Sausalito, CA 94965. *Agent*—c/o Random House, Inc., 201 East 50th St., New York, NY 10022.

CAREER: University of California, San Francisco, School of Medicine, Division of General Internal Medicine, assistant clinical professor of medicine and attending physician, 1984—; University of California, San Francisco, founder, president and Bucksbaum Chair in Preventive Medicine of Preventive Medicine Research Institute, 1984—; Presbyterian Hospital, California Pacific Medical Center, San Francisco, medical staff and attending physician, 1984—. Saybrook Institute Graduate School and Research Center, scientific advisory council, 1987-91; National Institute for the Clinical Application of Behavioral Medicine, advisory council, 1989—; member of National Institutes of Health Planning Panel to Assess Unconventional Medical Practices, 1992. Lecturer.

MEMBER: Harris County Medical Society, American Medical Students Association (founding member), American Medical Association, American College of Physicians (associate), Massachusetts Medical Society, Suffolk County Medical Society, American Association for the Advancement of Science, New York

Academy of Sciences, American Heart Association, Society of Behavioral Medicine (fellow), American Heart Association, Phi Beta Kappa, Omicron Delta Kappa, Phi Kappa Phi.

AWARDS, HONORS: Judge's Award, Refocus National Photography Competition; Best of Show, Ninth Annual Juried Photography Exhibition; Moody C. Bettis Memorial Award for Excellence in Community Medicine; Franzheim Award, The Franzheim Synergy Trust; grants from National Institutes of Health; fellowships from Department of Internal Medicine at Baylor College of Medicine and The Franzheim Synergy Trust; U. S. Army Surgeon General Medal.

WRITINGS:

Stress, Diet, and Your Heart, foreword by Alexander Leaf, recipes by Martha Rose Shulman, Holt (New York City), 1982.
Dr. Dean Ornish's Program for Reversing Heart Disease: The Only System Scientifically Proven to Reverse Heart Disease without Drugs or Surgery, Random House (New York City), 1990.
Eat More, Weigh Less: Dr. Dean Ornish's Life Choice Program for Losing Weight Safely While Eating Abundantly, HarperCollins (New York City), 1993.
(With Janet Fletcher, Jean-Marc Fullsack, and Helen Roe) *Everyday Cooking with Dr. Dean Ornish: 150 Easy, Low-Fat, High-Flavor Recipes,* HarperCollins, 1996.
Love and Survival: The Scientific Basis for the Healing Power of Intimacy, HarperCollins, 1998.

Contributing editor of *American Journal of Health Promotion,* 1987—; member of advisory boards, including *The Harris County Physician,* 1975-76, *HeartCorps,* 1989-90, *Prevention,* 1989—, and *Yoga Journal,* 1989—. Contributor of articles, reviews, and photographs to periodicals, including *Advances, Hospital Practice, Lancet, Patient Care, World Review of Nutrition and Dietetics, Atherosclerosis Reviews,* and *Rolling Stone.*

SIDELIGHTS: Dr. Dean Ornish secured the medical community's attention in 1989 when he began issuing data showing that the atherosclerotic patients he had been treating without drugs or invasive surgery had reduced the overall blockages in their arteries. That attention became international in 1990 with the publication of Ornish's findings in *Lancet,* a British medical journal, and the issuance of the physician's best-selling book, *Dr. Dean Ornish's Program for Reversing Heart Disease: The Only System Scientifically Proven to Reverse Heart Disease without Drugs or Surgery.*

In this book as well as in the two others he has written, *Stress, Diet, and Your Heart* and *Eat More, Weigh Less: Dr. Dean Ornish's Life Choice Program for Losing Weight Safely While Eating Abundantly,* the author outlines his prescription for fighting heart disease. In addition, he presents the research that supports his ideas, providing readers with tips and recipes to help them make the comprehensive lifestyle changes he advocates. Among the alterations Ornish recommends to his patients and readers is the incorporation of stress-management techniques such as meditation, imagery, breathing, and yoga exercises into their lives. The doctor tells readers to make a habit of engaging in light aerobic exercise and adhering to a high-fiber, low-fat, low-salt, vegetarian diet. Smokers are warned to stop. Ornish also offers suggestions for healthier methods of coping with the emotional pain he believes everyone experiences in one form or another. According to *U.S. News & World Report* contributor Joanne Silberner, "The books can provide what many doctors don't have time for—inspiration and imparting nutritional knowledge."

Although Ornish's lifestyle recommendations are similar to those advocated by most cardiologists, his prescription for health is much stricter. For example, the American Heart Association recommends that atherosclerotic patients obtain only thirty percent of their calories from fat; Ornish wants fat to account for a mere ten percent of the calories his patients consume. Ornish's plan also differs in the results it has achieved. His research patients, all seriously ill at one time, have reduced their arterial blockages without the aid of pharmaceuticals or invasive surgical techniques. As quoted in the *New York Times,* Ornish defends his techniques, saying: "I don't understand why asking people to eat a well-balanced vegetarian diet is considered drastic while it is medically conservative to cut people open or put them on powerful cholesterol-lowering drugs the rest of their lives."

Founder and president of the Preventive Medicine Research Institute of the University of California at San Francisco, Ornish has pursued what other more mainstream medical practitioners deemed "radical" notions. These so-called radical ideas have included the belief that there is a link between the causes of

depression and heart disease and that bypasses and angioplasty only treat the symptoms, not the causes, of heart disease. Furthermore, he believes that having deeply intimate, loving relationships can be invaluable in preventing and treating heart disease. He explores this theme in detail in his 1998 publication, *Love and Survival: The Scientific Basis for the Healing Power of Intimacy.* "Ornish conceives love broadly, bringing in the love of God as well as of mate, family, and friends," notes Ray Olson in *Booklist.* The doctor believes that "spiritual heart disease is the real epidemic," as Stephen Goode and Rick Kozak quoted him as saying in *Insight on the News.* In other words, an unwillingness to open up, be vulnerable, and be committed are at the root of much of the epidemic of heart disease. "Love and intimacy can make a profound difference in the quality of our lives and even in the quantity of our lives in terms of how long we live," Ornish continued. "If we understand that something matters in a meaningful and a powerful way, as these do, then we find our own pathways toward them. It takes a certain amount of courage to be willing to do that, even more than changing one's diet, because you can only be intimate to the degree that you can dare to be vulnerable. If you make yourself vulnerable, you might get hurt."

Responding to criticisms of his work as unscientific and unquantifiable, Ornish mused, "In science we tend to believe what we can measure—and we can measure cholesterol, blood pressure, heart rate. But it's hard to measure or quantify love and intimacy, and so we have tended to split off emotional factors in medicine. . . . Instead we focus on that which can be quantified. . . .Some in research science behave like the old joke about the man who loses his wallet over in the dark alley but looks for it under the street lamp because the light is better there. So we tend to focus on cholesterol and blood pressure, even though they may not be the most meaningful aspects of our health."

In *Love and Intimacy,* Ornish offers both clinical and anecdotal evidence as well as research findings to support his theories. "This is intriguing and persuasive testimony that many may find squares with common sense," said Olson. In one study cited by the author, 4,700 residents of Alameda County, California, were monitored for ten years. At the outset of the study, participants made note of their principal sources of companionship, and estimated how much time they devoted to each one. Over the course of the study, participants reporting the least social contact died at a rate almost three times higher than those with the most. The source of that companionship seemed irrelevant. It might be a romantic partner, a friend, a parent or other relative, or a tightly-knit church or social group. "People with commitments to honor are less likely to abuse themselves," notes *Newsweek*'s Geoffrey Cowley in his review of Ornish's book. "They drink less, eat better and avoid needless risks. Companionship also lets us share feelings that would otherwise fester."

BIOGRAPHICAL/CRITICAL SOURCES:

PERIODICALS

Advances, spring, 1992.
American Journal of Cardiology, April 1, 1992.
Atlanta Constitution, November 2, 1990.
Booklist, March 15, 1983; February 1, 1998, p. 875.
Choices in Cardiology, January/February, 1991.
Esquire, July, 1989; June, 1990.
Hospital Practice, May 15, 1991.
In Health, December/January, 1992.
Insight on the News, March 30, 1998, p. 21.
Journal of the American Dietetic Association, February, 1991.
Lancet, July 21, 1990.
Los Angeles Times, November 15, 1988.
Newsweek, July 30, 1990; March 16, 1998, p. 54.
New York Times, July 21, 1990; December 29, 1991; July 21, 1993; July 28, 1993.
Patient Care, October 15, 1991.
People, March 16, 1998, p. 36.
Publishers Weekly, November 19, 1982.
Reader's Digest, February, 1991.
Time, October 29, 1990.
U.S. News & World Report, August 6, 1990.

*   *   *

PAIRO, Preston (A. III) 1958-

PERSONAL: Born April 17, 1958, in Maryland; son of Preston A., Jr. (an attorney) and Carol R. Pairo; married; wife's name, Moira Elizabeth (a tailor), May 5, 1985. *Education:* Loyola College, Baltimore, MD, B.S., 1979; University of Baltimore, J.D., 1983.

ADDRESSES: Office—Pairo & Pairo, 9050-A Frederick Rd., Ellicott City, MD 21042. *Agent*—

Agnes Birnbaum, 88 Bleecker St., No. 6-P, New York, NY 10012.

CAREER: Pairo & Pairo, Ellicott City, MD, attorney, 1983—.

WRITINGS:

NOVELS

The Captain Drowns, Maryland Locale, 1986.
Winner's Cut, Richardson & Stierman (New York City), 1986.
Razor Moon, Fawcett (New York City), 1988.
Haitian Red, Richardson & Stierman, 1988.
Midnight Razz, Dell (New York City), 1991.
Beach Money, Walker (New York City), 1991.
One Dead Judge, Walker, 1993.
Breach of Trust, St. Martin's (New York City), 1995.
Bright Eyes, Onyx Books, 1996.
The Angel's Crime, Onyx Books, 1998.

Contributor of about 200 short stories to magazines.

SIDELIGHTS: Preston Pairo has written a number of fast-paced mysteries and crime thrillers, many of them set in his native Maryland. A practicing attorney, and the tenth consecutive lawyer in his family, Pairo has created several attorney characters, including Dallas Henry, a part-time lawyer and motel owner on the Maryland shore, and Harry Walsh, a Baltimore lawyer.

In *One Dead Judge* Dallas Henry investigates the mysterious death of a retired judge in a hit-and-run accident. While a convention fills the resort town with lawyers, Henry must unravel the complicated circumstances surrounding the judge's death while convincing the police he is not the killer himself. The critic for *Publishers Weekly* finds the novel "a raunchy, warmhearted read only slightly spoiled by an excess of attorneys."

Harry Walsh is a Baltimore attorney commonly believed to be connected to the Mob because his father earned local crime boss Sam Giardino's eternal gratitude for taking a bullet meant for him. When Harry's brother is murdered in *Breach of Trust,* he goes to Giardino for assistance. "As the case unfolds," writes Wes Lukowsky in *Booklist,* "Harry is forced to reexamine his concepts of trust and commitment. . . . This is an excellent mystery with as many layers as an onion, a wonderfully introspective protagonist, and a surprising but honest conclusion."

Pairo told *CA:* "If only there was some wonderful, emotional tale to which I could attribute my interest in writing! I write stories that are fun for me to write and, hopefully, fun for readers to race through. My books usually take place at the beach, in Florida or the Caribbean. I'm not much on preaching social issues, nor am I a gut-wrencher or tear-jerker. If someone finishes one of my books and had a good time in the process, my goals have been met in full. Most likely, I should spend more time writing what the marketplace will buy, but that seems too wild and fickle a target to aim for, so I try to remain content with the enjoyment of writing and try to ignore the pain and suffering of publishing."

BIOGRAPHICAL/CRITICAL SOURCES:

PERIODICALS

Booklist, July, 1995, p. 1865.
New York Times Book Review, April 19, 1987, p. 22.
Publishers Weekly, January 18, 1993, p. 453.

*   *   *

PATTERSON, Peter
See TERSON, Peter

*   *   *

PLIMPTON, George (Ames) 1927-

PERSONAL: Born March 18, 1927, in New York, NY; son of Francis T. P. (a lawyer and former U.S. deputy representative to the United Nations) and Pauline (Ames) Plimpton; married Freddy Medora Espy (a photography studio assistant), March 28, 1968 (divorced, 1988); married Sarah Whitehead Dudley, 1991; children: (first marriage) Medora Ames, Taylor Ames, (second marriage) Olivia Hartley, Laura Dudley. *Education:* Harvard University, A.B., 1950; King's College, Cambridge, B.A., 1952, M.A., 1954. *Politics:* Democrat. *Religion:* Unitarian Universalist.

ADDRESSES: Home—541 East 72nd St., New York, NY 10021. *Office*—Paris Review, Inc., 45-39 171st Pl., Flushing, NY 11358. *Agent*—Russell & Volkening, 50 West 29th St., New York, NY 10001.

CAREER: Writer and editor. Editor of the Harvard *Lampoon,* c. 1948-50; *Paris Review,* principal editor, 1953—, publisher, with Doubleday & Co., of Paris Review Editions (books), 1965—. *Horizon,* associate editor, 1959-61; *Sports Illustrated,* contributing editor, 1967—; *Harper's,* associate editor, 1972—; *Food and Wine,* contributing editor, 1978; *Realities,* member of editorial advisory board, 1978. American Literature Anthology program, director, 1967—; National Foundation on the Arts and Humanities, chief editor of annual anthology of work from literary magazines; adviser on John F. Kennedy Oral History Project. Instructor at Barnard College, 1956-58; associate fellow, Trumbull College, Yale, 1967. Occasional actor in films; journalistic participant in sporting and musical events. Honorary commissioner of fireworks, New York City, 1973—. Trustee, National Art Museum of Sport, 1967—, WNET-TV, 1973—, Police Athletic League, 1976—, African Wildlife Leadership Foundation, 1980—, Guild Hall, East Hampton, 1980—. *Military service:* U.S. Army, 1945-48; became second lieutenant.

MEMBER: PEN, Pyrotechnics Guild International, American Pyrotechniques Association, NFL Alumni Association, Mayflower Descendants Society; clubs include Century Association, Racquet and Tennis, Brooks, Piping Rock, Dutch Treat, Coffee House, Devon Yacht, Travelers (Paris), Explorers.

AWARDS, HONORS: Distinguished achievement award, University of Southern California, 1967; Mark Twain Award, International Platform Association, 1982; l'Ordre des Arts et des Lettres, France, 1994; several honorary degrees, including Franklin Pierce College, 1968, Hobart Smith College, 1978, Stonehill College, 1982, University of Southern California, 1986, and Pine Manor College, 1988.

WRITINGS:

EDITOR

Writers at Work: The Paris Review Interviews, Viking (New York City), Volume 1, 1957, Volume 2, 1963, Volume 3, 1967, Volume 4, 1976, Volume 5, 1981, Volume 6, 1984, Volume 7, 1986, Volume 8, 1988, Volume 9, 1992.
(With Peter Ardery) *The American Literary Anthology,* number 1, Farrar, Straus (New York City),

1968, number 2, Random House (New York City), 1969, number 3, Viking, 1970.

Jean Stein, *American Journey: The Times of Robert Kennedy* (interviews), Harcourt (New York City), 1970.

Stein, *Edie: An American Biography,* Knopf (New York City), 1982, reprinted as *Edie: American Girl,* Grove Press (New York City), 1994.

(With Christopher Hemphill) Diana Vreeland, *D.V.,* Random House, 1984.

Fireworks: A History and Celebration, Doubleday (Garden City, NY), 1984.

Poets at Work: The Paris Review Interviews, Viking, 1989.

Women Writers at Work, Viking, 1989.

The Writer's Chapbook: A Compendium of Fact, Opinion, Wit, and Advice from the Twentieth-Century's Preeminent Writers, Viking, 1989.

The Best of Bad Hemingway: Choice Entries from the Harry's Bar & American Grill Imitation Hemingway Competition, Harcourt (San Diego), Volume 1, 1989, Volume 2, 1991.

The Paris Review Anthology, Norton (New York City), 1990.

SPORTS WRITING

Out of My League (baseball anecdotes), Harper (New York City), 1961.

Paper Lion (football anecdotes), Harper, 1966.

The Bogey Man (golf anecdotes), Harper, 1968.

(Editor and author of introduction) Pierre Etche-baster, *Pierre's Book: The Game of Court Tennis,* Barre Publishers (Barre, MA), 1971.

(With Alex Karras and John Gordy) *Mad Ducks and Bears: Football Revisited* (football anecdotes), Random House, 1973.

One for the Record: The Inside Story of Hank Aaron's Chase for the Home Run Record, Harper, 1974.

Shadow Box (boxing anecdotes), Putnam (New York City), 1977.

One More July: A Football Dialogue with Bill Curry, Harper, 1977.

Sports!, photographs by Neil Leifer, H. N. Abrams (New York City), 1978.

A Sports Bestiary (cartoons), illustrated by Arnold Roth, McGraw-Hill (New York City), 1982.

Open Net (hockey anecdotes), Norton, 1985.

The Curious Case of Sidd Finch (baseball novel), Macmillan (New York City), 1987.

The X Factor, Whittle Direct (Knoxville, TN), 1990, revised edition, Norton, 1995.

The Best of Plimpton, Atlantic Monthly Press (New York City), 1990.

The Official Olympics Triplecast Viewer's Guide, Barcelona commemorative edition, Pindar, 1992.

The Norton Book of Sports, Norton, 1992.

OTHER

The Rabbit's Umbrella (juvenile), Viking, 1955.

(With William Kronick) *Plimpton! Shoot-out at Rio Lobo* (script), American Broadcasting Company (ABC-TV), 1970.

Plimpton! The Man on the Flying Trapeze (script), ABC-TV, 1970.

(With Kronick) *Plimpton! Did You Hear the One About. . .?* (script), ABC-TV, 1971.

(With Kronick) *Plimpton! The Great Quarterback Sneak* (script), ABC-TV, 1971.

(With Kronick) *Plimpton! Adventure in Africa* (script), ABC-TV, 1972.

(Author of introduction) Bill Plympton, *Medium Rare: Cartoons,* Holt (New York City), 1978.

(Author of introduction) *Oakes Ames: Jottings of a Harvard Botanist, 1874-1950,* edited by Pauline Ames Plimpton, Harvard University Press (Cambridge, MA), 1980.

(Contributor) Bernard Oldsey, editor, *Ernest Hemingway, The Papers of a Writer,* Garland (New York City), 1981.

(With Jean Kennedy Smith) *Chronicles of Courage: Very Special Artists* (interviews), Random House, 1993.

Truman Capote: In Which Various Friends, Enemies, Acquaintances, and Detractors Recall His Turbulent Career, Doubleday, 1997.

ADAPTATIONS: Paper Lion, the story of Plimpton's experiences as a short-term member of the Detroit Lions football team, was filmed by United Artists in 1968. Alan Alda portrayed Plimpton, but the author himself also had a role—he played Bill Ford.

SIDELIGHTS: "Among literary journalists George Plimpton is so unusual that he marches not just to a different drummer but more nearly to a different orchestra," declares Sam G. Riley in *Dictionary of Literary Biography.* Authorities call George Plimpton a "professional amateur," for, although writing is his primary occupation, he has also pitched in a post-season All-Star game in Yankee Stadium; held the position of third-string rookie quarterback for the Detroit Lions in 1963, taking the field in one exhibition game (and later playing with the Baltimore Colts against the Lions); golfed in several Pro-Am tournaments; briefly appeared in a basketball game for the Boston Celtics; boxed with former light heavyweight champion Archie Moore; and served as a goalie for the Boston Bruins hockey team in 1977 and the Edmonton Oilers in 1985. He also fought in a bullfight staged by Ernest Hemingway in 1954, and worked as a trapeze artist, lion-tamer, and clown for the Clyde Beatty-Cole Brothers Circus.

In less athletic activities, Plimpton developed a stand-up comedy routine and performed it in Las Vegas. He served as a percussionist with the New York Philharmonic and as a guest conductor of the Cincinnati Symphony. He has also been seen in films, including as a bad guy shot by John Wayne in *Rio Lobo,* in Norman Mailer's *Beyond the Law,* and in the film version of his book *Paper Lion.* On television Plimpton has hosted specials and appeared in commercials, and since 1973 he has exercised his interest in pyrotechnics as honorary commissioner of fireworks for New York City. He has also devoted considerable energy to literary pursuits of the highest caliber, including editing the prestigious *Paris Review.*

"Plimpton's career as a literary journalist largely has been founded upon the appeal of contrast," muses Riley. "First, there is the internal element of contrast: on one hand, the serious editor of belles lettres, on the other, the purveyor of entertaining journalistic nonfiction and televised specials. Foremost is the contrast that he himself presents vis-a-vis the people he has competed against in his myriad adventures: the tweedy, genteel literary figure at play on the turf of rougher, more hardbitten types, the bon vivant amid serious athletes, and the amateur generalist head to head with professional specialists."

Reviewers consider *Paper Lion,* Plimpton's book about his football adventures with the Detroit Lions, a classic of sports writing. It "is the best book written about pro football—maybe about any sport—because he captured with absolute fidelity how the average fan might feel given the opportunity to try out for a professional football team," explains Hal Higdon in *Saturday Review.* The book attracted sports fans not only through its innovative concept—a writer actually taking the field with a professional team—but also through the author's command over language. "Practically everybody loves George's stuff because George writes with an affection for his fellow man, has a rare eye for the bizarre, and a nice sense of his own ineptitude," declares Trent Frayne in the Toronto *Globe and Mail.* "[Ernest]

Hemingway . . . [once] said, 'Plimpton is the dark side of the moon of Walter Mitty.'"

Many writers echo Hemingway's statement. However, although Plimpton's adventures superficially resemble those of James Thurber's famous character, there are many differences between the two. "In his participatory journalism [Plimpton] has been described wrongly as a Walter Mitty, and he is nothing of the sort. This is no daydreaming nebbish," declares Joe Flaherty in the *New York Times Book Review.* Plimpton's adventures are tangible rather than imaginary. Yet, while Mitty in his dreams is a fantastic success at everything he undertakes, Plimpton's efforts almost invariably result in failure and humiliation. "Plimpton has stock in setting himself up as a naif . . . many of us are familiar with his gangling, tweedy demeanor and Oxford accent. He plays the 'fancy pants' to our outhouse Americana," Flaherty asserts. "George Plimpton doesn't want to be known as an athlete," explains Cal Reynard in the *Arizona Daily Star.* "He figures his role in sports is that of the spectator, but he wants to get closer to the game than the stands."

After more than twenty years of writing nonfiction about sports, Plimpton published his first sports novel, *The Curious Case of Sidd Finch,* in 1987. Plimpton based the story on a *Sports Illustrated* article he had written for the 1985 April Fools Day issue about a former Harvard man-cum-Buddhist-monk, Siddhartha (Sidd) Finch, who can pitch a baseball faster than any other pitcher in the history of the game—about 150 MPH. Plimpton's article claimed that Finch was about to sign with the New York Mets, and speculated about the impact an unhittable pitcher would have on the game of baseball. *The Curious Case of Sidd Finch* expands on the article, telling how Finch, after much self-doubt, is persuaded to play for the Mets and, on his return to Shea Stadium, pitches what former major league pitcher Jim Brosnan, writing in the *Washington Post Book World,* calls "THE perfect game"; he strikes out the entire batting lineup of the St. Louis Cardinals in perfect order.

Reviewers have commented on *The Curious Case of Sidd Finch* with mixed feelings. Although Brosnan finds the novel "sort of like a shaggy-dog tale that once was a crisp one-liner," he continues, "*The Curious Case of Sidd Finch* is not the rollicking farce I'd hoped for, but it's worth a reading." Lee Green, writing in the *Los Angeles Times Book Review,* calls the book a "wonderfully wry and whimsical debut novel," while National League president and *New York Times Book Review* contributor A. Bartlett Giamatti states, "Mr. Plimpton's control is masterly," and adds, "[The baseball] culture is splendidly rendered with an experienced insider's knowledge, and the whole saga of Finch's brief, astonishing passage through big-league baseball is at once a parody of every player's as-told-to biography, a satire on professional sports, an extended (and intriguing) meditation on our national pastime and a touching variant on the novel of education as Sidd learns of the world."

Although his sports writing remains his best-known work, Plimpton has also written on a wide range of other subjects. His own upper-class roots provided him with a number of unique social connections, including a close relationship with the Kennedy family. He was a Harvard classmate of Robert Kennedy's, and was walking directly in front of the senator when he was assassinated in 1968. In *American Journey: The Times of Robert F. Kennedy,* he presented 347 interviews to form a picture of Robert Kennedy's life and the procession of his funeral train from New York to Washington.

Plimpton's own interest centers on the small literary magazine he has edited since 1953. James Warren explains in the *Chicago Tribune,* "It's the *Paris Review,* not the chronicles of his own sporting foibles . . . that constitutes the soul—and takes up much of the time—of Plimpton's life." The *Paris Review,* unlike many other literary magazines, focuses on creative writing rather than criticism. Many famous American writers—including Jack Kerouac, Philip Roth, Henry Miller, and John Updike—have published first efforts or complete works in its pages.

Plimpton's interviews with writers about the craft of writing are a major attraction of the journal. It was the *Paris Review,* explains Nona Balakian in the *New York Times,* that first "developed a new kind of extended and articulate interview that combined the Boswellian aim with an exploration of the ideas of major contemporary writers on the art of fiction and poetry." "The thing that makes these interviews different from most interviews," writes Mark Harris in Chicago's *Tribune Books,* "is that they go on long enough to get somewhere. If they do not arrive at the point I dreamily hoped for—creativity totally clarified with a supplementary manual on How To Write—they supply very good instruction nevertheless." The result, Balakian concludes, is "a height-

ened awareness of a writer's overall purpose and meaning."

Poets at Work and *Women Writers at Work,* both edited by Plimpton, consist of interviews that originally appeared in the *Paris Review. Poets at Work* includes conversations with T. S. Eliot, Marianne Moore, Anne Sexton, Allen Ginsberg, William Carlos Williams, James Dickey, and others. Poet Donald Hall describes the interviews in his introduction to the volume as "literary history as gossip." *Women Writers at Work* also contains interviews with Marianne Moore and Anne Sexton, along with Dorothy Parker, Rebecca West, Isak Dinesen, and ten other contemporary female writers. Summarizing the significance of both volumes, *Listener* contributor Peter Parker writes, "these interviews are a permanent and invaluable record of the working practices, opinions and observations of those who have reflected our century in their poetry and prose."

The Writer's Chapbook belongs to the same series, bringing together additional interviews from the *Paris Review* under the editorial supervision of Plimpton. This miscellaneous compendium offers insight into the writing profession through intimate and often offhanded conversations with established literary figures such as T. S. Eliot, W. H. Auden, and Ezra Pound. According to *New York Times Book Review* contributor David Kirby, "There is little fact and less advice in the 'Chapbook,' its subtitle notwithstanding, but there are plenty of opinions, most of them rather negative: poetry readings are nightmares, politics and writing don't mix, professors and critics (the terms are interchangeable) don't know what they are talking about."

The Paris Review Anthology, also edited by Plimpton, features selections from the journal since its establishment. "The overall tone of *The Paris Review* is high spirited, even mischievous," writes Kirby. The volume includes the quintessential *Paris Review* story "Night Flight to Stockholm" by Dallas Wiebe, which describes how an aspiring writer eventually wins the Noble Prize in Literature by sending dismembered parts of his body along with submissions to major literary journals. Kirby concludes, "*The Paris Review Anthology* is historically important as well, since it reminds readers how a new era in letters began."

Plimpton returned to sports and the competitive spirit with *The X Factor: A Quest for Excellence,* his investigation into the attributes possessed by winners.

After narrowly losing a game of horseshoes to President-elect George Bush, Plimpton set out to uncover the universal secret of success through conversations with various sports legends, coaches, and top executives. "Suffice to say that where Mr. Plimpton draws upon his X factor is in his prose style, in his unfailing ability to find the perfectly funny word or phrase," writes Christopher Lehmann-Haupt in the *New York Times*. "What also never lets him down is his capacity to get the most unlikely people to take part in his offbeat fantasies." In the end, Plimpton manages to get a rematch with President Bush.

With *The Norton Book of Sports* Plimpton provides an eclectic collection of stories by both sport writers and literary figures, including Mark Twain, Thomas Wolfe, James Joyce, and Robert Bly. *Tribune Books* contributor Robert Olen Butler writes, "George Plimpton has assembled this collection of commentary, fiction, reminiscence, poetry and journalism wonderfully well, filling us with that impression of sports which is always hard to explain, that behind the seeming triviality of these games there resides something profound."

The Best of Plimpton brings together examples of the author's writings over a period of thirty-five years. "While his contemporaries were off writing about war, sex and assorted other social upheavals, Plimpton was writing humorously and indelibly about taking poet Marianne Moore to the World Series, playing the triangle with the New York Philharmonic, boxing heavyweight Archie Moore," writes Malcolm Jones Jr. in *Newsweek*. "Plimpton's subject is passion, whether he finds it in the major leagues, in a man who catches grapes in his mouth or in a bespectacled boy playing football."

"Plimpton has enjoyed a career unlike that of any other literary figure—journalist, author, editor, or otherwise," concluded Riley. "His varied accomplishments render his career hard to sum up, but a quotation he himself used in *The Norton Book of Sports* from poet Donald Hall . . . says it fairly well: 'Half my poet friends think I am insane to waste my time writing about sports and to loiter in the company of professional athletes. The other half would murder to be in my place.'"

BIOGRAPHICAL/CRITICAL SOURCES:

BOOKS

Anderson, Elliott, and Mary Kinzie, editors, *The Little Magazine in America: A Modern Documen-*

tary History, Pushcart Press (New York City), 1978.
Authors in the News, Volume 1, Gale (Detroit), 1976.
Contemporary Literary Criticism, Volume 36, Gale, 1986.
Dictionary of Literary Biography, Volume 185: *American Literary Journalists, 1945-1995, First Series*, Gale, 1997.
Talese, Gay, *The Overreachers*, Harper, 1965.

PERIODICALS

America, February 20, 1993, p. 2.
Antioch Review, winter, 1990, p. 121.
Arizona Daily Star, March 24, 1974.
Belles Lettres, summer, 1990, p. 47.
Bloomsbury Review, March-April, 1990, p. 7.
Booklist, September 15, 1989, p. 136; October 1, 1990, p. 248.
Book Week, October 23, 1966.
Chicago Tribune, December 22, 1986; June 15-June 16, 1987.
Christian Science Monitor, December 5, 1968.
Commentary, October, 1967.
Commonweal, September 14, 1990, p. 523.
Detroit News, March 16, 1986.
Editor & Publisher, April 20, 1985, pp. 7-8.
Esquire, January, 1976, pp. 115-17, 142, 144, 146; November, 1985, p. 243.
Gentleman's Quarterly, October, 1989, pp. 183, 186.
Globe and Mail (Toronto), July 7, 1984; February 8, 1986; June 14, 1986.
Harper's Bazaar, November, 1973, pp. 103, 134-35, 142.
Kliatt, September, 1989, p. 25.
Library Journal, November 1, 1989, p. 91; March 1, 1990, p. 94; April 1, 1992, p. 124; March 1, 1995, p. 79.
Listener, October 26, 1989, p. 33.
Los Angeles Times, July 22, 1982; March 20, 1987.
Los Angeles Times Book Review, September 30, 1984; June 21, 1987.
Midwest Quarterly, spring, 1989, pp. 372-86.
Milwaukee Journal, November 12, 1974.
Nation, June 10, 1991, pp. 762-63.
Newsweek, January 14, 1991, p. 52.
New Yorker, November 12, 1966; June 27, 1994, p. 44.
New York Herald Tribune, April 23, 1961.
New York Review of Books, February 23, 1967; February 7, 1974.
New York Times, November 12, 1973; July 29, 1977; November 16, 1977; March 28, 1981; June 14,

1984; November 14, 1985; July 30, 1987; March 6, 1995.

New York Times Book Review, April 23, 1961; November 10, 1968; January 6, 1974; July 31, 1977; November 6, 1977; June 17, 1984; September 23, 1984; November 24, 1985; July 5, 1987; March 4, 1990, p. 11; July 2, 1995, p. 11.

Observer, June 23, 1991.

Playboy, December, 1990, p. 29; April, 1995, p. 34.

Saturday Review, December 10, 1966; August 14, 1971.

Spectator, October 14, 1978.

Sports Illustrated, September 13, 1965, p. 4; August 3, 1992, p. 6.

Time, April 7, 1967, p. 40; December 19, 1977; September 10, 1984; December 8, 1986; April 13, 1987, pp. 9-11; June 8, 1987.

Times Literary Supplement, December 1, 1978; January 21, 1983; December 21, 1984; August 2, 1985; September 5, 1986; March 20, 1987.

Tribune Books (Chicago), May 3, 1981; September 2, 1984; October 14, 1984; November 24, 1985; July 5, 1987; June 14, 1992, p. 6; December 6, 1992.

Village Voice, June 11, 1991, p. 30.

Wall Street Journal, August 28, 1984.

Washington Post, January 7, 1986.

Washington Post Book World, May 27, 1984; September 2, 1984; June 21, 1987; July 9, 1989; October 21, 1990; March 12, 1995.

Writers Digest, June, 1974, pp. 17-18.*

* * *

PROCTOR, Everitt
See MONTGOMERY, Rutherford George

R

RALEIGH, Michael 1947-

PERSONAL: Born April 8, 1947, in Chicago, IL; son of Bernard J. (a store manager) and Mary T. (a cashier; maiden name, McHugh) Raleigh; married Katherine Ann Powell (a teacher and homemaker), March 21, 1981; children: Sean, Peter, Caitlin. *Education:* De Paul University, A.B., 1969; Michigan State University, M.A., 1971. *Politics:* Democrat. *Religion:* Roman Catholic.

ADDRESSES: Home—1415 West Addison, Chicago, IL 60613. *Agent*—Jane Jordan Browne, Multimedia Product Development, Inc., 410 South Michigan Ave., Room 724, Chicago, IL 60605.

CAREER: Truman Community College, Chicago, IL, instructor in English, 1980—; part-time English teacher at De Paul University and Roosevelt University. Has worked variously as a bank teller, a librarian, a clerk, a microfiche camera operator, a charity fund raiser, a bartender, and a program manager for a federally funded social service agency.

MEMBER: International PEN, Mystery Writers of America, Private Eye Writers of America.

AWARDS, HONORS: Fellow of Illinois Arts Council, 1984, 1985, 1986, and 1989.

WRITINGS:

"PAUL WHELAN" MYSTERIES

Death in Uptown, St. Martin's (New York City), 1991.
A Body in Belmont Harbor, St. Martin's, 1993.
The Maxwell Street Blues, St. Martin's, 1994.
Killer on Argyle Street, St. Martin's, 1995.
The Riverview Murders, St. Martin's, 1997.

Contributor of poems and stories to magazines.

SIDELIGHTS: Michael Raleigh's hard-boiled detective character Paul Whelan dogs murderers in Chicago. A critic for *Publishers Weekly* describes Whelan as "a grungy, moral and pleasingly anachronistic shamus working the ethnically diverse, economically bruised neighborhoods of Chicago's Uptown district." Whelan's adventures contain, writes Wes Lukowsky in *Booklist,* "an agreeably low-key protagonist; plenty of vivid Chicago atmosphere; and a well-rounded portrayal of mean streets and the often very decent people forced to inhabit them."

In *The Maxwell Street Blues,* Whelan is called in when a street vendor goes missing. When the missing man is found shot dead, and other vendors start dying as well, Whelan must track down a killer with vengeance in mind. Marilyn Stasio in the *New York Times Book Review* notes that Whelan "manages to conduct a very thorough investigation by winning over grumpy bartenders, crabby waitresses and wary old men on benches. He likes these people—and that's good enough reason to like him."

Killer on Argyle Street involves a missing teenaged boy whose petty criminal friends have turned up dead. Whelan is brought in to find the missing boy, and soon finds himself in the middle of a violent family blood feud. "Raleigh has a thing for losers," Stasio remarks, "characterizing them with compassionate care that spills over into his affectionate studies of bartenders, waitresses, and the owners of a slew of delis, bodegas and restaurants. . . . Although this walk-and-talk book is awfully light on action, there's lots of life on these streets and plenty of curb traffic."

When an elderly man is murdered in *The Riverview Murders,* Whelan is hired to locate the man's business partner, who went missing some thirty years before. The *Publishers Weekly* critic believes that "Raleigh's latest tale demonstrates his knack for fashioning living, breathing characters out of his tough urban settings." Lukowsky calls the novel a "riveting private-eye yarn" and "a solid entry in an underappreciated, carefully crafted series."

Raleigh once told *CA:* "I waited a long time to see the publication of my first novel. Twenty-one years passed between the day I wrote and sent out my first short story and the day my book *Death in Uptown* appeared. If nothing else, that experience taught me patience and gave me a great deal of opportunity to think about the kind of writing I most wanted to produce.

"The idea of becoming a writer first occurred to me during college, but a wise creative writing teacher told me that it would be best to find some way of paying the rent and buying food while I was becoming one. I took his advice and spent most of the 1970s and 1980s writing in my free time while working at a succession of unrelated and often unpleasant jobs. I like to think that this period broadened my horizons a bit in terms of subject matter and interest.

"I started out writing poetry, sending my poems to magazines great and small. I succeeded in having half-a-dozen poems published, amassed a magnificent collection of rejection slips in most of the colors of the spectrum, and developed a good enough ear for verse to realize that mine was undistinguished at best. I then turned to the short story, producing tales that demonstrated the influence of a pair of great Chicago writers, Nelson Algren and a wonderful, but now largely ignored, novelist named James T. Farrell. My efforts earned me occasional publication in respectable little magazines and a fresh infusion of new blood into my burgeoning file of rejection slips. I also became, during this time, an admirer of Thornton Wilder and Graham Greene, novelists who seemed to feel, with justification, that a writer could be successful writing any type of book he wanted, about any subject and in any form.

"A novel can be defined as 'a long work of fiction that an author never gets around to starting.' For

years I told myself that I was soon going to start a novel, some kind of novel. What forced my hand was a growing frustration at the incredible length of time it can take a magazine to reject a single story and the realization that, for me at least, the short story held no promise of success in the foreseeable future.

"Between 1986 and 1990 I wrote three novels and started at least two others, whose unfinished remains lie moldering somewhere in my desk. Two of the novels that I completed were what might be called 'offbeat comedies,' and the third was an urban detective novel. In the course of marketing the first, I earned numerous rejections from both editors and agents, but I received enough encouragement to continue sending out my manuscripts. Eventually I found an agent who seemed to think that I was publishable, and it was with her invaluable assistance that my first detective novel was published in 1991.

"My primary interests as a writer lie in several areas. My first love is comedy, far and away the most satisfying type of writing to me, and I hope to continue to pursue this interest in a number of offbeat projects. My second area of interest is the mystery. My mystery novels feature Chicago detective Paul Whelan, an idiosyncratic man with unorthodox methods, acute instincts, and a quirky sense of humor, and his friend and occasional nemesis, the belligerent Al Bauman of the Chicago Police."

BIOGRAPHICAL/CRITICAL SOURCES:

PERIODICALS

Booklist, September 1, 1994, p. 27; September 15, 1995, p. 144; August, 1997, p. 1886.
New York Times Book Review, November 6, 1994; October 22, 1995.
Publishers Weekly, January 18, 1993, p. 452; August 1, 1994, p. 74; August 14, 1995, p. 74; May 12, 1997, p. 61.

*   *   *

RAYNER, Claire (Berenice) 1931-
    (Sheila Brandon, Berry Chetwynd, Ann Lynton, Ruth Martin, Isobel Saxe)

PERSONAL: Born January 22, 1931, in London, England; married Desmond Rayner (a literary agent, manager, and painter), June 23, 1957; children: Amanda, Adam, Jay. *Education:* Studied nursing at Royal Northern Hospital, London; studied midwifery at Guy's Hospital.

ADDRESSES: Home—Holly Wood House, Roxborough Ave., Harrow-on-the-Hill, Middlesex HA1 3BU, England. *Agent*—Desmond Rayner, Holly Wood House, Roxborough Ave., Harrow-on-the-Hill, Middlesex HA1 3BU, England; and Aaron M. Priest, Aaron M. Priest Literary Agency, 565 Fifth Ave., New York, NY 10017.

CAREER: Writer and broadcaster. Nurse and midwife at hospitals in London, including Royal Free Hospital and Whittington Hospital, 1954-60. Presenter of BBC-1 television series, *Claire Rayner's Casebook*, 1980-84; co-presenter of Thames Television program, *Kitchen Garden;* presenter of BBC-Wales radio program, *Contact;* creator of six videotapes, *In Company with Claire Rayner.* Has appeared frequently on British radio and television programs; makes weekly appearances on TV-AM program *Good Morning Britain.* Lecturer throughout the United Kingdom.

MEMBER: Freedom of the City of London.

AWARDS, HONORS: Named one of the women "most British women would regard as a role model" in a national survey, 1988; honorary fellowship, Polytechnic of North London; Best Specialist Columnist of the Year Award, *Publisher.*

WRITINGS:

NONFICTION

(Editor under pseudonym Ruth Martin) *Before the Baby—and After,* Hurst & Blackett (London), 1958.
Mothers and Midwives, Allen & Unwin (London), 1962.
What Happens in the Hospital, Hart-Davis (London), 1963.
The Calendar of Childhood: A Guide for All Mothers, Ebury Press (London), 1964.
Your Baby, Hamlyn (London), 1965.
Careers with Children, R. Hale (London), 1966.
Housework—The Easy Way, Transworld, 1967.
Shall I Be a Nurse?, Wheaton (Exeter), 1967.
Home Nursing and Family Health, Transworld, 1967.
101 Facts an Expectant Mother Should Know, Dickens Press (London), 1967.

Essentials of Outpatient Nursing, Arlington Books (London), 1967.
For Children: Equipping a Home for a Growing Family, Macdonald for Council of Industrial Design (London), 1967.
101 Key Facts of Practical Baby Care, Dickens Press (London), 1967.
(Under pseudonym Ann Lynton) *Mothercraft,* Corgi (London), 1967.
A Parent's Guide to Sex Education, Corgi, 1968, Dolphin Books (New York City), 1969.
People in Love: A Modern Guide to Sex in Marriage, Hamlyn, 1968, revised edition published as *About Sex,* Fontana Books (London), 1972.
Protecting Your Baby, Richardson Merrell, 1971.
Woman's Medical Dictionary, Corgi, 1971.
When to Call the Doctor—What to Do Whilst Waiting, Corgi, 1972.
The Shy Person's Book, Wolfe (London), 1973, McKay (New York City), 1974.
Childcare Made Simple, W. H. Allen (London), 1973, 2nd edition, Heinemann (London), 1983.
Where Do I Come From?: Answers to a Child's Questions about Sex, Arlington Books, 1974.
You Know More Than You Think You Do, MIND Council (London), 1975.
(Contributing editor) *The Rand McNally Atlas of the Body and Mind,* Rand McNally (Chicago), 1976, published in England as *The Mitchell Beazley Atlas of the Body and Mind,* Mitchell Beazley (London), 1976.
(With Keith Fordyce) *Kitchen Garden,* Independent Television Publications (London), 1976.
(With Keith Fordyce) *More Kitchen Garden,* Independent Television Publications, 1977.
Family Feelings: Understanding Your Child from Zero to Five, Arrow (London), 1977.
Claire Rayner Answers Your 100 Questions on Pregnancy, BBC Publications (London), 1977.
(With Keith Fordyce) *Claire and Keith's Kitchen Garden,* Arrow, 1978.
The Body Book (for children), G. Whizzard (London), 1978, Barron's (Woodbury, NY), 1980.
Related to Sex, Paddington Press (New York City), 1979.
(With Keith Fordyce) *Greenhouse Gardening,* Hamlyn, 1979.
Everything Your Doctor Would Tell You If He Had the Time, Putnam (New York City), 1980.
Claire Rayner's Lifeguide: A Commonsense Approach to Modern Living, New English Library (London), 1980.
Baby and Young Child Care: A Practical Guide for Parents of Children Aged Zero-Five Years,

Purnell (Maidenhead, Burkshire), 1981, published as *Child Care from Birth to Age Five,* H. P. Books, 1983.

Growing Pains and How to Avoid Them, Heinemann, 1984.

Claire Rayner's Marriage Guide: How to Make Yours Work, Macmillan, 1984.

The Getting Better Book (for children), Deutsch (London), 1985.

Woman, Hamlyn, 1986.

(Editor) *When I Grow Up: Children's Views on Aulthood,* Virgin Books (London), 1986.

Safe Sex, Sphere Books (London), 1987.

Claire Rayner Talking, Southdown Press, 1988.

The Don't Spoil Your Body Book (for children), illustrated by Tony King, Barron's (New York City), 1989.

Postscripts, M. Joseph (London), 1991.

Dangerous Things, Viking (New York City), 1993.

London Lodgings, M. Joseph, 1994, St. Martin's (New York City), 1995.

NOVELS

Shilling a Pound Pears, Hart-Davis, 1964.

The House on the Fen, Bantam (New York City), 1967.

Starch of Aprons, R. Hale, 1967, published as *The Hive,* Corgi, 1968.

Lady Mislaid, Corgi, 1968.

Death on the Table, Corgi, 1969.

The Meddlers, Simon & Schuster (New York City), 1970.

A Time to Heal, Simon & Schuster, 1972.

The Burning Summer, Allison & Busby (London), 1972.

Sisters, Hutchinson (London), 1978.

Reprise, Hutchinson, 1980.

The Running Years, Hutchinson, 1981, Delacorte (New York City), 1982.

Family Chorus, Hutchinson, 1984.

The Virus Man, Hutchinson, 1985.

Lunching at Laura's, Arrow, 1986.

Maddie, M. Joseph, 1988.

Clinical Judgements, M. Joseph, 1989, Viking, 1990.

"THE POPPY CHRONICLES" SERIES

Jubilee, Weidenfeld & Nicolson (London), 1987.
Flanders, Weidenfeld & Nicolson, 1988.
Flapper, Weidenfeld & Nicolson, 1989.
Blitz, Weidenfeld & Nicolson, 1990.

Festival, Weidenfeld & Nicolson, 1991.
Sixties, Weidenfeld & Nicolson, 1992.

"THE PERFORMERS" SERIES

Gower Street, Simon & Schuster, 1973.
The Haymarket, Simon & Schuster, 1974.
Paddington Green, Simon & Schuster, 1975.
Soho Square, Putnam, 1976.
Bedford Row, Putnam, 1977.
Long Acre, Cassell (London), 1978, published as *Covent Garden,* Putnam, 1978.
Charing Cross, Putnam, 1979.
The Strand, Putnam, 1980.
Chelsea Reach, Weidenfeld & Nicolson, 1982.
Shaftesbury Avenue, Weidenfeld & Nicolson, 1983.
Piccadilly, Weidenfeld & Nicolson, 1985.
Seven Dials, Weidenfeld & Nicolson, 1987.

NOVELS UNDER PSEUDONYM SHEILA BRANDON

The Final Year, Corgi, 1962.
Cottage Hospital, Corgi, 1963, reprinted under name Claire Rayner, Severn House, 1993.
Children's Ward, Corgi, 1964.
The Lonely One, Corgi, 1965.
The Doctors of Downlands, Corgi, 1968.
The Private Wing, Corgi, 1971.
Nurse in the Sun, Corgi, 1972.

UNDER THE PSEUDONYM RUTH MARTIN

Witchcraft and the Inquisition in Venice, 1550-1650, Blackwell (New York City), 1989.

OTHER

(Under pseudonym Isobel Saxe) *Desperate Remedies,* Corgi, 1968.

Woman's Own, regular columnist under house pseudonym Ruth Martin for nine years, under name Claire Rayner, 1975-88; regular columnist, *Woman,* 1988—; author of regular column, "Problem Page," for *Petticoat, Sun, Sunday Mirror,* and *Today.* Contributor to magazines and newspapers, including *Lancet, Medical World, Nursing Times, Nursing Mirror,* and *Design.* Many of Rayner's books have been translated.

SIDELIGHTS: Claire Rayner is a prolific and versatile writer equally well known for her nonfiction advice and how-to books as for her many works of fiction, including historical, romance, and suspense novels. Her fiction is praised for its accurate and realistic depiction of the ways in which large historical events and movements affect the private lives of Victorian and early twentieth-century characters.

Rayner's first series of novels, known as "The Performers," focuses on two families over the course of several generations in nineteenth-century England as they attempt to break into the upper echelons of society through success in the theater and in medicine. "The Victorian period—the background against which Rayner's characters act out their lives—is a rich period for any novelist and Rayner selects her material with care," observed Kate Thompson in *Romance and Historical Writers*. Although the author received some criticism for failing to make the movement of her fictional characters as interesting as the historical movements—such as the professionalization of medicine—which affect them, Thompson concluded: "'The Performers' series is an uncompromising and accurate portrayal of Victorian life, written with a compassion and sensitivity that never degenerates into sentimentality."

Rayner's second series of novels, "The Poppy Chronicles," draws upon the major historical events of the twentieth century, including the fight for women's suffrage and the two world wars, just as the "Performers" series drew upon the nineteenth century. The series follows Poppy, an illegitimate child, through her participation in the Suffragette movement, marriage and the trials of a blended family, into the moral dilemmas posed by the privations suffered by England's population during World War II and the Blitz. "As with 'The Performers' series, 'The Poppy Chronicles' do not always have happy endings," noted Thompson. "Again Rayner explores the full range of human emotions and behaviour."

According to Kate Waters in *School Library Journal*, Rayner is known in her homeland of England as "a medical Dear Abby" who dispenses medical advice as well as advice on sex, childrearing, marital problems, and a number of other popular topics. A columnist for several British publications, Rayner has also published many books on medical topics for the general reader.

BIOGRAPHICAL/CRITICAL SOURCES:

BOOKS

Twentieth-Century Romance and Historical Writers, 3rd edition, St. James Press (Detroit), 1994.

PERIODICALS

Best Sellers, August 1, 1970, p. 175; August 15, 1973, p. 229; November 1, 1974, p. 338; December, 1982, p. 337.

Booklist, March 1, 1976, p. 960; July 1, 1980, p. 1581; September 1, 1982, p. 30; March 1, 1984, p. 998; January 1, 1990, p. 893.

Books and Bookmen, May, 1970, p. 24; December, 1972, pp. 120, 124; March, 1974, p. 103.

Book World, December 4, 1983, p. 8.

British Book News, September, 1984, p. 561; October, 1986, p. 569.

Changing Times, August, 1983, p. 74.

Kirkus Reviews, May 1, 1970, p. 527; June 1, 1973, p. 620; August 1, 1974, p. 832; December 1, 1975, p. 1349; September 1, 1977, p. 952; September 1, 1978, p. 969; July 1, 1979, p. 760; August 15, 1980, p. 566; September 1, 1982, p. 1016; November 1, 1989, p. 1557.

Kliatt, fall, 1983, pp. 40, 42.

Library Journal, July, 1970, p. 2519; July, 1973, p. 2147; July, 1974, p. 1849; September 1, 1979, p. 1720; July, 1980, p. 1531; September 15, 1982, p. 1771.

Listener, November 9, 1978, p. 624.

New York Times Book Review, August 16, 1970, p. 30.

Observer, December 16, 1973, p. 32; May 22, 1988, p. 42.

Publishers Weekly, May 18, 1970, p. 33; June 18, 1973, p. 66; August 19, 1974, p. 76; December 1, 1975, p. 60; September 18, 1978, p. 160; June 25, 1979, p. 112; April 4, 1980, p. 68; September 3, 1982, p. 53; November 17, 1989, p. 43.

Punch, April 16, 1986, p. 52.

School Librarian, December, 1985, p. 367; November, 1989, p. 155.

School Library Journal, September, 1980, p. 101; November, 1984, p. 142; April, 1985, p. 100; April, 1989, p. 98; January, 1990, p. 117.

Times Educational Supplement, October 20, 1978, p. 42; December 26, 1980, p. 16; November 16, 1984, p. 26; November 14, 1986, p. 30; June 2, 1989, p. B15.

Times Literary Supplement, March 29, 1985, p. 354.

*   *   *

RENTON, Cam
See ARMSTRONG, Richard

RIFFE, Ernest
  See BERGMAN, (Ernst) Ingmar

*   *   *

RIGSBY, Howard 1909-1975
  (Mark Howard, Vechel Howard)

PERSONAL: Born November 12, 1909, in Denver, CO; died November 7, 1975; son of Vechel and Jean (Howard) Rigsby; married Margaret Eleanor Hunter, 1931 (divorced); children: Charity (Mrs. Richard Crane), Judith (Mrs. John MacCormack). *Education:* Studied at San Mateo Junior College, 1928-29, San Jose State College (now California State University at San Jose), 1930; University of Nevada, B.A., 1931.

CAREER: Freelance writer; reporter for *Nevada State Journal,* Reno, and *Herald Tribune,* Paris, in the 1930s; editor of *Argosy,* New York City, 1938. *Military service:* U.S. Army Signal Corps, 1942-46; became captain; received Army Commendation Ribbon.

MEMBER: Mystery Writers of America (member, national board of directors, 1959), Dramatists Guild, Writers Guild, Authors League of America.

AWARDS, HONORS: Lucinda was named one of *New York Times'* ten best mysteries of 1954; poetry prize, *Monterey Peninsula Herald,* 1964, for Kennedy eulogy, "Seven Gray Horses."

WRITINGS:

NOVELS

Kill and Tell (mystery), Morrow (New York City), 1951.
Murder for the Holidays (mystery), Morrow, 1951.
Range in Texas (western), Gold Medal (New York City), 1953.
As a Man Falls, Fawcett (New York City), 1954.
Lucinda (mystery), Gold Medal, 1954.
The Lone Gun (western), Fawcett, 1955.
The Reluctant Gun (western), Gold Medal, 1957.
The Avenger, Crowell (New York City), 1957, reissued as *Naked to My Pride,* Popular Library (New York City), 1958.
Clash of Shadows (mystery), Lippincott (Philadelphia), 1959.

(As Mark Howard) *A Time for Passion,* Dell (New York City), 1960.
The Tulip Tree, Doubleday (New York City), 1963.
Calliope Reef, Doubleday, 1967.

NOVELS; UNDER NAME VECHEL HOWARD

Sundown at Crazy Horse (western), Gold Medal, 1957, reissued as *The Last Sunset,* Muller (London), 1961.
Tall in the West (western), Gold Medal, 1958.
Murder on Iler Mind, Gold Medal, 1959.
Murder with Love, Gold Medal, 1959.
Stage to Painted Creek (western), Gold Medal, 1959.

OTHER

Voyage to Leandro (for children), Harper (New York City), 1939.

Author, with Dorothy Heyward, of the play, *South Pacific,* which ran on Broadway, 1943-44; writer of television scripts for *Rawhide* series. Short stories have appeared in *Saturday, Evening Post, McCall's, Ladies' Home Journal, Collier's American, Blue Book, Argosy,* and other magazines, sometimes under the pseudonym Mark Howard.

SIDELIGHTS: Howard Rigsby published various works of fiction (novels, plays, and short stories) within differ genres (western and mystery) and for different audiences (adults and children.) George Kelly wrote in *Twentieth-Century Western Writers* that "Rigsby, better known for his mystery fiction, . . . produced a small number of western novels notable for their excellence." Kelly, who maintained that Rigsby wrote many of his best westerns under the pseudonym Vechel Howard, cited *Sundown at Crazy Horse* as Rigsby's best western. And *Stage to Painted Creek* Kelly described as "taut storytelling at its best."

Kill and Tell, one of Rigsby's mysteries, was praised by Anthony Boucher in the *New York Times* for "well-sketched" characters and its "portrayal of a small California seacoast town." Of a later mystery, *Clash of Shadows,* Boucher once again praised Rigsby's choice of setting, but commented in the *New York Times Book Review* that "an overindulgence in flashbacks weakens the urgency of the situation; but the story is good reading." The novelist's penchant for flashbacks was also the focus of L. G. Offord's *San Francisco Chronicle* review of *Clash of Shadows.* Offord characterized the work as "a novel done in a series of suspenseful present menaces with flashbacks—skillfully arranged and mounting in intensity."

Rigsby's first published novel, *Voyage to Leandro,* was an adventure tale written for children. E. L. Buell remarked in the *New York Times* that *Voyage to Leandro* "is written with a dashing brilliance which can evoke either a sense of strange, almost macabre, horror, or the disillusion and discomfort of romance gone astray."

Rigsby wrote verse and westerns for recreation—he also read and played tennis—and once claimed he had no major interest outside of writing. Living in Mexico, Paris, and all over the United States, his exposure to a variety of settings influenced his work. His book, *Sundown at Crazy Horse,* was adapted as the Universal picture *The Last Sunset,* starring Kirk Douglas and Rock Hudson, in 1961. He wrote the book for two musicals, "neither of which quite made it to Broadway." The Heyward-Rigsby play *South Pacific,* followed the musical of the same name by six years.

BIOGRAPHICAL/CRITICAL SOURCES:

BOOKS

Twentieth-Century Western Writers, second edition, St. James Press (Chicago), 1991.

PERIODICALS

New York Times, December 10, 1939; November 18, 1951.
New York Times Book Review, November 15, 1959.
San Francisco Chronicle, December 20, 1959.*

*   *   *

RILEY, Carroll L(averne) 1923-

PERSONAL: Born April 18, 1923, in Summersville, MO; son of Benjamin Franklin (a farmer) and Minnie Belle (Smith) Riley; married Brent Locke (a writer), March 25, 1948; children: Janet Olyn (deceased), Benjamin Locke, Victoria Smith, Cynthia Winningham. *Education:* Southwest Missouri State, study in chemistry and the classics, 1940-41, 1945-46; University of New Mexico, B.A. (with honors), 1948, Ph.D., 1952; University of California, Los Angeles, M.A., 1950.

ADDRESSES: Home—1106 6th St., Las Vegas, NM 87701. *Office*—University Museum Laboratory of Anthropology, Museum of New Mexico, New Mexico Highlands University. *E-mail*—criley @nmhu.campus.mci.net.

CAREER: University of Colorado, Boulder, instructor in anthropology, 1953-54; University of North Carolina at Chapel Hill, assistant professor of anthropology, 1954-55; Southern Illinois University (SIU) at Carbondale, assistant professor, 1955-60, associate professor, 1960-67, professor, 1967-86, (concurrent) professor of anthropology, 1974-86, distinguished professor of anthropology, 1986-87, distinguished professor emeritus, 1987—, Department of Anthropology, co-director of graduate studies, 1970-72, director of graduate studies, 1978-79, 1983-84, 1985-87, acting chairperson, summers, 1964, 1966, 1970, and shorter periods, 1983-87, chairperson, 1979-82, University Museum and Art Galleries, curator of physical anthropology, 1955-61, curator of anthropology, 1970-72, and 1974—, director, 1972-74, associate director for academic programs and research, 1974-76; University Museum Laboratory of Anthropology, Museum of New Mexico, New Mexico Highlands University, research associate, 1987—, adjunct professor, 1989—; Smithsonian Institution, research collaborator, 1988—. Invited lecturer, various institutions of higher learning, U.S., Canada, Europe, and Latin America; lecturer, New Mexico Humanities Council, 1991-95, Smithsonian Associates Program, 1991—, Camino Real Project, 1992-93.

Has conducted field work in Ireland, the Mediterranean, Mexico, United States, and Venezuela. Consultant to Lands Division, U.S. Department of Justice, 1952-53, summer, 1955, fall, 1956, to NDEA (on various anthropology-oriented programs), throughout the 1960s, to southern Illinois city and regional museum programs, 1972-76, to Black Elk Productions (educational films on Native Americans), throughout the 1970s, to G. G. Palmer, director of Camino Real Museum project, 1995—; reviewer, undergraduate and graduate programs in anthropology, Western Washington State University, 1981. Member, board of directors, Illinois-Sao Paulo Partners (American-Brazilian States), 1973-74, and Archaeological Consulting and Mapping Services, Tucson, AZ, 1997—; Illinois Academy of Science, first chairperson, Anthropology Section, 1959-60, member, editorial board, 1979-81; member of planning conference, Columbus Quincentenary, National Museum of American History, Smithsonian Institution, 1987-92, and of Camino Real Project, 1989-92; commissioner and member of advisory board, XII Travelers Project, EL Paso, TX, 1989—. Member, board of directors, Central Carbondale (IL) Area Historic Association; member, gift committee, SIU Museum and Art Galleries Association, 1979-82, chairperson, 1981-82; member, Las Vegas (NM) Arts Council, 1984—, and Las Vegas (NM) Citizens' Committee for Historic Preservation, 1988—. *Military service:* U.S. Army Air Forces, 1942-45; became sergeant.

MEMBER: American Anthropological Association (fellow), American Association for the Advancement of Science (fellow), American Society for Ethnohistory, Association for the Study of Language in Prehistory, Society for American Archaeology, Explorers Club (fellow), Archaeological Society of New Mexico, Arizona Archaeological and Historical Society, Historical Society of New Mexico, Sigma Xi.

AWARDS, HONORS: Grants from Social Science Research Council, 1950-51, U.S. Public Health Service, 1956-57, 1958-59, 1960-61, 1961-62, 1962-63, American Philosophical Society, 1960, 1971, American Council of Learned Societies, 1965, (with C. H. Lange) National Endowment for the Humanities, 1967-68, 1968-69, (with C. H. Lange and E. M. Lange) 1981, National Foundation on the Arts and Humanities, 1967-68, 1968-69, and Illinois Arts Council, 1975-76, Seton Hall University Museum, 1983, SIU, 1984, SIU Foundation to Distinguished Professors, 1986-87, Conservation Analytical Laboratory of Smithsonian Institution, for involvement with *Pottery Production and Exchange, A.D. 1540-1890* project (studying the Hopi), 1988-2000, New Mexico Endowment for the Humanities, 1992-93, for *A Zuni Life,* with J. A. Jones and Virgil Wyaco; recipient of Kaplan Research Award, SIU Sigma XI Chapter in conjunction with SIU Foundation, 1965, for contributions to scientific research; recipient of Delta Award, Friends of the Morris Library, 1982, for scholarly contributions; recipient of Gaspar de Villagra Award, Historical Society of New Mexico, 1985; recipient of Governor's Award of Honor for Historic Preservation, State of New Mexico, 1985.

WRITINGS:

The Origins of Civilization, Southern Illinois University Press (Carbondale), 1969, updated paperback edition, Arcturus Books, 1972.
(With J. C. Kelley) *Pre-Columbian Contact with Nuclear America,* Mesoamerican Studies Number

4, Research Records of the University Museum, Southern Illinois University Press, 1969.
Cultural and Historical Dictionary of Saudi Arabia, Scarecrow, 1972.
Historical and Cultural Dictionary of Saudi Arabia, Scarecrow Press (Metuchen, NJ), 1972.
Salish and Chimakuam-Speaking Indians of the Puget Sound Basin of Washington, Clearwater Publishing (New York City), 1973.
Ethnological Field Investigation and Analysis of Historical Material Relative to Group Distribution and Utilization of Natural Resources among Puget Sound Indians in Washington, Clearwater Publishing, 1974.
The Mesoamerican Southwest: Readings in Archeology, Ethnohistory, and Ethnology, Dumbarton Oaks (Washington, DC), 1974.
Makah Indians of Western Washington: A Study of Group Distribution, Political Organization and Concepts of Land Use, Clearwater Publishing, 1976.
Sixteenth Century Trade in the Greater Southwest, Mesoamerican Studies, Number 10, Research Records of the University Museum, Southern Illinois University, 1976.
The Frontier People: The Greater Southwest in the Protohistoric Period, Southern Illinois University Center for Archaeological Investigations, 1982, revised and expanded edition, University of New Mexico Press (Albuquerque, NM), 1987.
Rio del Norte: People of the Upper Rio Grande from Earliest Times to the Pueblo Revolt, University of Utah Press (Salt Lake City), 1995.
(With C. H. Lange) *Bandelier, The Life and Adventures of Adolph F. Bandelier, American Archaeologist and Scientist,* University of Utah Press, 1996.
(Author of introductory section on Zuni history and culture) *A Zuni Life,* Virgil Wyaco (as told to Courtway Jones), University of New Mexico Press, 1998.

EDITOR

(And annotator with Charles H. Lange) *The Southwest Journals of Adolph Bandelier,* University of New Mexico Press), Volume 1: *1880-1882,* 1966, Volume 2: (with C. H. Lange) *1883-1884,* 1970, Volume 3: (with C. H. Lange and Elizabeth M. Lange) *1885-1888,* 1975, Volume 4: *1889-1892,* 1984.
(With W. W. Taylor) *American Historical Anthropology: Essays in Honor of Leslie Spier,* Southern Illinois University Press, 1967.

(Editor-in-chief, with J. C. Kelley, C. W. Pennington, and R. L. Rands) *Man across the Sea: Problems of Old World-New World Pre-Columbian Contacts,* University of Texas Press (Austin), 1971, third edition, 1976.
(With Basil C. Hedrick and J. C. Kelley) *The North Mexican Frontier,* Southern Illinois University Press, 1971.
(With Hedrick and J. C. Kelley) *The Mesoamerican Southwest: Readings in Archeology, Ethnohistory, and Ethnology,* Southern Illinois University Press, 1973.
(With Hedrick) *The Journey of the Vaca Party: A Translation of the "Joint Report" of Alvar Nunez Cabeza de Vaca and His Companions as Reproduced in Oviedo de Valdes, with the Spanish Text,* University Museum Studies, Series Number 2, Southern Illinois University, 1974, reprinted in *The Native American and Spanish Experience in the Greater Southwest,* edited by D. Snow, Garland Publishing (New York City), 1992.
(With Hedrick) *Documents Ancillary to the Vaca Journey,* University Museum Series, Number 5, Southern Illinois University, 1976.
(With Hedrick) *Across the Chichimec Sea: Papers in Honor of J. Charles Kelley,* Southern Illinois University Press, 1978.
(With Hedrick) *New Frontiers in the Archaeology and Ethnohistory of the Greater Southwest in the Protohistoric Period,* Transactions of the Illinois State Academy of Science, Volume 74, Number 4, 1980.
(With Curtis F. Schaafsma) *The Casas Grandes World,* University of Utah Press, 1998.

OTHER

Author of numerous papers presented at professional meetings.

Also author of several monographs. Contributor of articles and reviews to professional journals.

WORK IN PROGRESS: A Troubled Century: Native Americans and Spaniards in the Seventeenth Century Southwest.

SIDELIGHTS: Man across the Sea: Problems of Old World-New World Pre-Columbian Contacts was printed in Japanese translation by Soseiki Publisher (Tokyo, Japan), 1977, second edition, Hachiman Shoten (Tokyo, Japan), 1987.

RIPLEY, Michael David 1952-
(Mike Ripley; Duncan Torrens, a pseudonym)

PERSONAL: Born September 29, 1952, in Huddersfield, Yorkshire, England; son of Ronald and Ada Sylvia Ripley; married Alyson Jane White; children: Elizabeth Kate. *Education:* University of East Anglia, B.A. (with honors), 1974. *Politics:* Conservative. *Religion:* "None."

ADDRESSES: Home—73 Chapel Rd., West Bergholt, Essex CO6 3JA, England. *Office*—Brewers' Society, 42 Portman Sq., London W1H 0BB, England. *Agent*—David Higham Associates, 5-8 Lower John St., London W1R 4HA, England.

CAREER: University of Essex, Essex, England, public relations officer, 1975-78; Brewers' Society, London, England, senior public relations officer, 1978—.

MEMBER: Crime Writers Association, Dorothy L. Sayers Society, British Guild of Beer Writers, Mystery Writers of America.

AWARDS, HONORS: Last Laugh Award for most humorous crime novel from Crime Writers Association, 1989, for *Angel Touch,* and 1991, for *Angels in Arms.*

WRITINGS:

UNDER NAME MIKE RIPLEY; MYSTERY NOVELS

Just Another Angel, Collins (London), 1988.
Angel Touch, Collins, 1989.
Angel Hunt, Collins, 1990.
Angel Eyes, Collins, 1990.
Angel City, Collins, 1991, St. Martin's (New York City), 1995.
Angels in Arms, St. Martin's, 1992.
Angel Confidential, Collins, 1995.
Family of Angels, Collins, 1996.
(Editor with Maxim Jakubowski) *Fresh Blood,* Bloodlines (London), 1996.
That Angel Look, Dufour (Chester Springs, PA), 1997.
(Editor with Jakubowski) *Fresh Blood 2,* Dufour, 1997.

OTHER

Also author of scripts for *Lovejoy* television series. Brewing correspondent for *Encyclopaedia Britannica;* author of "Crimebeat" column for *Sunday Tele-*

graph, 1989—. Contributor of short stories to periodicals under name Mike Ripley and of articles to periodicals under pseudonym Duncan Torrens.

SIDELIGHTS: Mike Ripley's mystery adventures about London taxicab driver Fitzroy McLean Angel are witty, fast-paced romps set in London's underworld. Winner of two Last Laugh Awards from the Crime Writers Association, Ripley often combines humor with his mysteries.

Typical of the Angel series is *Angel City,* in which a homeless man hires Angel to help deliver mysterious packages at night. When his employer vanishes, Angel "wanders deep into the cold world of the city's homeless, talking to lost souls and encountering an occasional angel of mercy" in his search for the missing man, as the critic for *Publishers Weekly* notes. In *That Angel Look* the London cabbie finds himself involved with fashion designers and a dead photographer. David Pitt in *Booklist* calls the novel "a rousing success," while the critic for *Publishers Weekly* believes that, "with Angel as a guide, lowlife London has never been a more seductive proposition."

Ripley has also co-edited, with Maxim Jakubowski, two volumes of crime fiction by young writers. *Fresh Blood* and *Fresh Blood 2* present stories by up and coming writers whose work is on the edge. Marilyn Stasio in the *New York Times Book Review* calls *Fresh Blood* "a terrific introduction to these articulate and unpredictable voices." The critic for *Publishers Weekly* finds that *Fresh Blood 2* "offers reason to imagine that some of the talent on display will soon crack crime fiction's top rank."

Ripley told *CA:* "I have always written for newspapers for a living, beginning at age fifteen, but I only began to write fiction in 1984. My first comedy crime novel—*Just Another Angel*—was written for therapy, after three years of work on a serious, but still unpublished, thriller. The novel was accepted by my first choice publisher within ten days. It seems that being funny pays.

"Angel is not a detective, indeed he's not much of a hero at all. He is youngish, streetwise, self-contained. He has not dropped out of the rat race: he never joined it. The books are not whodunits but 'how-does-he-get-out-of-this?' adventures. Angel looks on England (and especially London) in the late-1980s as a contemporary, but an outsider by choice. Each book involves him in a different world: in *Just*

Another Angel, small-time gangsters; *Angel Touch,* the financial wheeler-dealing world; *Angel Hunt,* the world of animal-rights campaigners. . . . If a friend is in trouble, Angel will go to the wall for them—or find someone else to."

BIOGRAPHICAL/CRITICAL SOURCES:

PERIODICALS

Booklist, March 15, 1998, p. 1206.
New York Times Book Review, March 30, 1997.
Publishers Weekly, December 12, 1994, p. 53; February 2, 1998, p. 84; February 16, 1998, p. 207.

*   *   *

RIPLEY, Mike
    See RIPLEY, Michael David

*   *   *

ROBINS, Denise (Naomi) 1897-1985
    (Denise Chesterson, Ashley French, Harriet Gray, Hervey Hamilton, Julia Kane, Francesca Wright)

PERSONAL: Born February 1, 1897, in London, England; died after a long illness, May 1, 1985, in Haywards Heath (one source says London), England; daughter of Herman (a music critic and singing teacher) and Denise (a writer; maiden name, Cornwell) Klein; married Arthur Robins, June 18, 1918 (divorced, 1938); married O'Neill Pearson (an army officer), October 30, 1939; children: (first marriage) Eve Louise, Patricia Denise, Anne Eleanor. *Education:* Attended schools in Staten Island, NY, San Diego, CA, and London, England. *Politics:* Conservative. *Avocational interests:* Travel, music, collecting antiques and books, gardening, dogs.

CAREER: Dundee Courier, Dundee, Scotland, journalist, 1914-15; free-lance journalist, broadcaster, and novelist, 1915-85. Made many appearances on British Broadcasting Corp. (BBC-TV).

MEMBER: Romantic Novelists Association (cofounder, 1960; president, 1960-66), Men and Women of Today Club (past president).

WRITINGS:

ROMANCE NOVELS

The Marriage Bond, Hodder & Stoughton (London), 1924.

Sealed Lips, Hodder & Stoughton, 1924.

The Forbidden Bride, Newnes's Pocket Novels (London), 1926.

The Man Between, Newnes's Pocket Novels, 1926.

The Passionate Awakening, Newnes' Pocket Novels, 1926.

The Inevitable End, Mills & Boon (London), 1927.

Jonquil, Mills & Boon, 1927.

The Triumph of the Rat, Philip Allan & Co. (London), 1927.

Forbidden Love, Newnes Pocket Novels, 1927.

Desire Is Blind, Mills & Boon, 1928.

The Passionate Flame, Mills & Boon, 1928.

White Jade, Mills & Boon, 1928.

Women Who Seek, Mills & Boon, 1928.

The Dark Death, Mills & Boon, 1929.

The Enduring Flame, Mills & Boon, 1929, Ballantine (New York City), 1975.

Heavy Clay, Mills & Boon, 1929.

Love Was a Jest, Mills & Boon, 1929.

And All Because . . . , Mills & Boon, 1930, published as *Love's Victory,* G. H. Watt (New York City), 1933.

It Wasn't Love, Mills & Boon, 1930.

Swing of Youth, Mills & Boon, 1930.

Crowns, Pounds, and Guineas, Mills & Boon, 1931, published as *The Wild Bird,* G. H. Watt, 1932.

Fever of Love, Mills & Boon, 1931.

Lovers of Janine, Mills & Boon, 1931.

Second Best, Mills & Boon, 1931, G. H. Watt, 1933.

Blaze of Love, Mills & Boon, 1932.

The Boundary Line, G. H. Watt, 1932.

The Secret Hour, Mills & Boon, 1932.

There Are Limits, Mills & Boon, 1932, published as *No Sacrifice,* G. H. Watt, 1934.

Gay Defeat, Mills & Boon, 1933.

Life's a Game, Mills & Boon, 1933.

Men Are Only Human, Macaulay (New York City), 1933.

Shatter the Sky, Mills & Boon, 1933.

Strange Rapture, Mills & Boon, 1933.

Brief Ecstasy, Mills & Boon, 1934, Ballantine, 1976.

Never Give All, Macaulay, 1934.

Slave-Woman, Mills & Boon, 1934, Macaulay, 1935.

Sweet Love, Mills & Boon, 1934.

All This for Love, Mills & Boon, 1935.

Climb to the Stars, Nicholson & Watson (London), 1935.

How Great the Price, Mills & Boon, 1935.

Life and Love, Nicholson & Watson, 1935, Avon (New York City), 1978).

Ivor Novello's Murder in Mayfair (novelization of the play), Mills & Boon, 1935.

Love Game, Nicholson & Watson, 1936.

Those Who Love, Nicholson & Watson, 1936.

Were I Thy Bride, Nicholson & Watson, 1936, Pyramid (New York City), 1966, published as *Betrayal,* Hodder & Stoughton, 1976.

Kiss of Youth, Nicholson & Watson, 1937, Avon, 1976.

Set Me Free, Nicholson & Watson, 1937.

The Tiger in Men, Nicholson & Watson, 1937, reprinted, Avon, 1979.

The Woman's Side of It, Nicholson & Watson, 1937.

Restless Heart, Nicholson & Watson, 1938, Arcadia House (New York City), 1940.

Since We Love, Nicholson & Watson, 1938, Arcadia House, 1941.

You Have Chosen, Nicholson & Watson, 1938.

Dear Loyalty, Nicholson & Watson, 1939.

Gypsy Lover, Nicholson & Watson, 1939.

I, Too, Have Loved, Nicholson & Watson, 1939, Avon, 1979.

Officer's Wife, Nicholson & Watson, 1939.

Forget That I Remember, Arcadia House, 1940 (published in England as *Sweet Sorrow,* Nicholson & Watson, 1940).

Island of Flowers, Nicholson & Watson, 1940, Avon, 1977.

Little We Know, Hutchinson (London), 1940.

To Love Is to Live, Hutchinson, 1940.

If This Be Destiny, Hutchinson, 1941.

Love Is Enough, Hutchinson, 1941, reprinted, Arrow Books (London), 1966.

Set the Stars Alight, Hutchinson, 1941, new edition, Arrow Books, 1971.

Winged Love, Hutchinson, 1941, Avon, 1978.

This One Night, Hutchinson, 1942, Avon, 1975.

War Marriage, Hutchinson, 1942, published as *Let Me Love,* Hodder & Stoughton, 1979.

What Matters Most, Hutchinson, 1942.

The Changing Years, Hutchinson, 1943, Beagle (New York City), 1974.

Daughter Knows Best, Hutchinson, 1943.

Dust of Dreams, Hutchinson, 1943, Avon, 1976.

Escape to Love, Hutchinson, 1943, Avon, 1976.

This Spring of Love, Hutchinson, 1943.

War Changes Everything, Todd Publishing (London), 1943.

Give Me Back My Heart, Hutchinson, 1944, new edition, Arrow Books, 1971.

How to Forget, Hutchinson, 1944.

Never Look Back, Hutchinson, 1944.
Desert Rapture, Hutchinson, 1945, Avon, 1979.
Love So Young, Hutchinson, 1945.
All for You, Hutchinson, 1946, Ballantine, 1975.
Heart's Desire, William Foster (London), 1946.
Greater than All, Hutchinson, 1946.
Separation, William Foster, 1946.
The Story of Veronica, Hutchinson, 1946.
Forgive Me, My Love, Docker Hanley, 1947.
More than Love, Hutchinson, 1947.
Could I Forget, Hutchinson, 1948, Avon, 1976.
Khamsin, Hutchinson, 1948, Avon, 1978.
Love Me No More!, Hutchinson, 1948, new edition, Arrow Books, 1971.
The Hard Way, Hutchinson, 1949.
To Love Again, Hutchinson, 1949, Harlequin (Toronto), 1961.
The Uncertain Heart, Hutchinson, 1949, Avon, 1977.
The Feast Is Finished, Hutchinson, 1950, Avon, 1979.
Love Hath an Island, Hutchinson, 1950.
Heart of Paris, Hutchinson, 1951.
Infatuation, Hutchinson, 1951.
Only My Dreams, Hutchinson, 1951, Avon, 1976.
Second Marriage, Hutchinson, 1951, Avon, 1981.
Something to Love, Hutchinson, 1951.
The Other Love, Hutchinson, 1952.
Strange Meeting, Hutchinson, 1952.
The First Long Kiss, Hutchinson, 1953, Avon, 1976.
My True Love, Hutchinson, 1953, Avon, 1977.
The Long Shadow, Hutchinson, 1954, Avon, 1979.
Venetian Rhapsody, Hutchinson, 1954, Avon, 1979.
Bitter-Sweet, Hutchinson, 1955.
The Unshaken Loyalty, Hutchinson, 1955.
All That Matters, Hutchinson, 1956.
The Enchanted Island, Hutchinson, 1956, Avon, 1974.
Arrow in the Heart, Hodder & Stoughton, 1957.
The Noble One, Hodder & Stoughton, 1957.
The Seagull's Cry, Hutchinson, 1957, Avon, 1979.
Chateau of Flowers, Hodder & Stoughton, 1958.
The Untrodden Snow, Hodder & Stoughton, 1958.
Do Not Go, My Love, Hodder & Stoughton, 1959, Ballantine, 1974.
We Two Together, Hodder & Stoughton, 1959.
The Unlit Fire, Hodder & Stoughton, 1960.
I Should Have Known, Hodder & Stoughton, 1961.
A Promise Is for Ever, Hodder & Stoughton, 1961.
Put Back the Clock, Hodder & Stoughton, 1962, Pyramid, 1967.
Mad Is the Heart, Hodder & Stoughton, 1963.
Nightingale's Song, Hodder & Stoughton, 1963, Pyramid, 1966.
Reputation, Hodder & Stoughton, 1963.

Meet Me in Monte Carlo, Arrow Books, 1964, Avon, 1979.
Moment of Love, Hodder & Stoughton, 1964, Pyramid, 1966.
Loving and Giving, Hodder & Stoughton, 1965, Ballantine, 1975.
The Strong Heart, Hodder & Stoughton, 1965.
Lightning Strikes Twice, Hodder & Stoughton, 1966.
O Love! O Fire! Panther (London), 1966.
The Crash, Hodder & Stoughton, 1966.
House of the Seventh Cross, Coronet, 1967, published as *House by the Watch Tower,* Arcadia House, 1968.
Wait for Tomorrow, Hodder & Stoughton, 1967.
Laurence, My Love, Hodder & Stoughton, 1968.
Love and Desire and Hate, Hodder & Stoughton, 1969.
A Love Like Ours, Hodder & Stoughton, 1969, Ballantine, 1976.
Sweet Cassandra, Hodder & Stoughton, 1970.
Forbidden, Hodder & Stoughton, 1971.
The Other Side of Love, Hodder & Stoughton, 1973, Ballantine, 1975.
Twice Have I Loved, Hodder & Stoughton, 1973, Ballantine, 1975.
Dark Corridor, Hodder & Stoughton, 1974.
The Snow Must Return, Coronet Books, 1974.
Two Loves, Bantam, 1975.
Come Back, Yesterday, Hodder & Stoughton, 1976.
Fauna (omnibus, includes *The Flame and the Frost,*), Avon, 1978.
Love, Volumes IV-VII, Ballantine, 1980.

UNDER PSEUDONYM DENISE CHESTERTON

The Price of Folly, Merit (London), 1955.
Two Loves, Merit, 1955, published under name Denise Robins, Bantam, 1975.
When a Woman Loves, Merit, 1955.

UNDER PSEUDONYM ASHLEY FRENCH

Once Is Enough, Hutchinson, 1953, published under name Denise Robins, Panther Books, 1963.
The Bitter Core, Hutchinson, 1954, published under name Denise Robins, Panther Books, 1965.
The Breaking Point, Hutchinson, 1956, published under name Denise Robins, Panther Books, 1965, Bantam (New York City), 1975.

UNDER PSEUDONYM HARRIET GRAY

Gold for the Gay Masters, Rich & Cowan (London), 1954, Avon, 1956, published under name Denise Robins, Arrow Books, 1965.

Bride of Doom, Rich & Cowan, 1956, as *Bride of Violence,* Avon, 1957; published under name Denise Robins, Mayflower Books, 1966.

The Flame and the Frost, Rich & Cowan, 1957.

Dance in the Dust, R. Hale (London), 1959, published under name Denise Robins, Mayflower Books, 1973, Avon, 1978.

My Lady Destiny, R. Hale, 1961, published under name Denise Robins, Avon, 1978.

UNDER PSEUDONYM HERVEY HAMILTON

Family Holiday, Nicholson & Watson, 1937, published under name Denise Robins, Mayflower, 1978.

Figs in Frost, Macdonald & Co. (London), 1946.

UNDER PSEUDONYM JULIA KANE

Dark Secret Love, Hodder & Stoughton, 1962, published under name Denise Robins, Mayflower Books, 1967.

The Sin Was Mine, Hodder & Stoughton, 1964, published under name Denise Robins, Mayflower Books, 1967.

Time Runs Out, Hodder & Stoughton, 1965.

UNDER PSEUDONYM FRANCESCA WRIGHT

The Loves of Lucrezia, Rich & Cowan, 1953.

She-Devil: The Story of Jezebel, Corgi Books (London), 1970, published under name Denise Robins as *Jezebel,* Hodder & Stoughton, 1977.

OTHER

(With Roland Pertwee) *Heat Wave* (play; first produced in London at St. James Theatre, 1929), Dial Press, 1930.

Love Poems, and Others, Mills & Boon, 1930.

Heat Wave: The Story of the Play by Roland Pertwee, Mills & Boon, 1930.

One Night in Ceylon, and Others (stories), Mills & Boon, 1931.

(With Michael Pertwee) *Light the Candles: A Play in One Act* (adapted from Robins' short story of the same title), English Theatre Guild, 1957.

Light the Candles (stories), Hurst & Blackett, 1959.

(Editor) *The World of Romance* (stories), New English Library (London), 1964.

Stranger than Fiction: Denise Robins Tells Her Life Story, Hodder & Stoughton, 1965.

Contributor to *Nash's Magazine, Ideal Home, She, Woman's Weekly,* and to *Daily Express* and *Evening Standard.* Editor of correspondence page, *She* magazine, beginning 1954.

SIDELIGHTS: A best-selling author, Robins wrote more than 200 novels during her sixty-year career. Her first novel, *The Marriage Bond,* was published in 1924, and a half-century later, her novels of the 1930s and 1940s were being reprinted in new editions for modern audiences. Robins's books—at one time advertised on London buses as "Robins for Romance"—sold more than 100 million copies and were translated into fifteen languages.

Robins is notable as an author who, within the genre of romance, attempted nearly every type of romantic entanglement imaginable, according to Tessa Rose Chester in *Twentieth-Century Romance and Historical Writers.* Thus, several of her early books take on the still-sensitive topics of divorce and extra-marital affairs, while later works envision love affairs between women in their forties and younger men, and portray the pain of lost love as well as that of love revealed to be mere infatuation. Along with stock stories of love on the rebound, recounted in such works as *Put Back the Clock* and *The Crash,* and, in *Give Me Back My Heart,* of arranged marriages, Robins also ventured into more challenging territory in such works as *Figs in Frost* and *Once Is Enough,* in which a woman leaves her children with the husband she has divorced. Chester also noted an alteration in the author's sensibility as the decades of the twentieth century passed and Robins continued to write romances: "The character of each decade of the 20th century can . . . be seen over the range of her novels, especially in fashion details, the intrusion of World War II, the slowly changing attitudes toward divorce and infidelity, and the freedom of women in particular regarding careers and financial and moral independence."

Occasionally, Robins's quest for innovative plots for her romances yields an equally potent suspense plot, as in *Heat Wave,* a "strong and passionate drama," Chester averred. Other works noted for strong subplots include the historical romances Robins published under the pseudonym Harriet Gray, including *Gold for the Gay Masters, Bride of Doom,* and *The Flame and the Frost,* set during the nineteenth century and centering on a quadroon slave and her descendents. "The stories are well punctuated with dramatic climaxes, moving fast and furiously against a rich backcloth of elaborately painted characters and settings," Chester observed. Although Robins's romances have occasionally been faulted for focusing on the overblown emotions of beautiful, but shallow, characters, such works as *The Feast Is Finished,* in which a woman is torn between the unavailable man she truly loves and a desire not to hurt the man who truly loves her, garnered praise in *Publishers Weekly* as "a tightly written—and quite sad—love story, involving believable characters and emotions."

Robins once told *CA:* "With a few exceptions it is inevitable that a novelist who begins to write when young, and continues through a long literary career, must necessarily produce a change in his work when he is older. I know that my own novels show this clearly. As a young writer my style was purely romantic and sentimental. That sort of book may still interest a few faithful readers but might well bore those who no longer understand romantic love in its purest form." She continued: "I myself, have matured. The writer of today is no longer the young girl who published her first book in 1924. I think my latest novels are indicative of my maturity. My writing has improved. It is certainly more serious. I am still incurably romantic but I have also become more of a realist. I would find it impossible today to write only about innocence, humility, self-sacrifice, etc., and all the 'lilies and languors' of the almost impossible love of forty years ago. I am interested in modern youth. They give me their views, and I like to write about them. Their new world moves at a terrific pace so I find that I also like to write about it."

In Robins's opinion, "[young people's] attitude to life has changed mainly because of the new freedom allowed by parents and teachers—freedom of thought as well as movement. The things the girls in my original books used not to know about until they were at least 17 or 18, they now start learning in junior classes." She concluded: "I find that I enjoy writing about the modern girl. I can admire her, and the liking has increased over the years."

BIOGRAPHICAL/CRITICAL SOURCES:

BOOKS

Robins, Denise, *Stranger than Fiction: Denise Robins Tells Her Life Story,* Hodder & Stoughton, 1965.
Twentieth-Century Romance and Historical Writers, 3rd edition, St. James Press (Detroit), 1994.

PERIODICALS

Best Sellers, September 15, 1970, p. 238.
Books and Bookmen, July, 1965, p. 33; July, 1968; October, 1968, p. 42; April, 1969, p. 56; May, 1971, p. 50; March, 1973, p. 76.
Publishers Weekly, August 28, 1978, p. 392; May 28, 1979, p. 54.
Spectator, February 5, 1972, p. 197; September 14, 1974, p. 338.
Times Literary Supplement, March 25, 1965, p. 237.

OBITUARIES:

PERIODICALS

Baltimore Sun, May 8, 1985.
Chicago Tribune, May 4, 1985.
Detroit Free Press, May 3, 1985.
New York Daily News, May 3, 1985.
Times (London), May 3, 1985.*

*   *   *

RODGERS, Carolyn M(arie) 1945-

PERSONAL: Born December 14, 1945, in Chicago, IL; daughter of Clarence and Bazella (Colding) Rodgers. *Education:* Attended University of Illinois, 1960-61; Roosevelt University, B.A., 1981; University of Chicago, M.A. (English), 1984. *Religion:* African Methodist Episcopal.

ADDRESSES: Home—12750 South Sangamon, Chicago, IL 60643.

CAREER: Young Mens Christian Association (YMCA), Chicago, IL, social worker, 1963-68; Columbia College, lecturer in Afro-American literature, 1968-69; University of Washington, Seattle, instructor in Afro-American literature, summer, 1970; Albany State College, Albany, GA, writer-in-residence, 1972; Malcolm X College, Chicago, writer-in-residence, 1972; Indiana University, Bloomington, instructor in Afro-American literature, summer, 1973; Chicago State University, Chicago, English remediation tutor, 1981; Columbia College, instructor, 1989-91; Harold Washington College, faculty advisor to student newspaper and instructor in English, 1998—.

MEMBER: Organization of Black American Culture Writers Workshop, Gwendolyn Brooks Writers Workshop, Delta Sigma Theta.

AWARDS, HONORS: First Conrad Kent Rivers Memorial Fund Award, 1968; National Endowment for the Arts grant, 1970; Poet Laureate Award, Society of Midland Authors, 1970; National Book Award nomination, 1976, for *how i got ovah: New and Selected Poems*; Carnegie Award, 1979; PEN awards; Gwendolyn Brooks fellowship.

WRITINGS:

POETRY

Paper Soul, Third World Press (Chicago), 1968.
Songs of a Blackbird, Third World Press, 1969.
Two Love Raps, Third World Press, 1969.
Now Ain't That Love, Broadside Press (Detroit), 1970.
For H. W. Fuller, Broadside Press, 1970.
For Flip Wilson, Broadside Press, 1971.
Long Rap/Commonly Known as a Poetic Essay, Broadside Press, 1971.
how i got ovah: New and Selected Poems, Doubleday (New York City), 1975.
The Heart as Ever Green: Poems, Doubleday, 1978.
Translation: Poems, Eden Press (Chicago), 1980.
Finite Forms: Poems, Eden Press, 1985.
Morning Glory, Eden Press, 1989.
We're Only Human, Eden Press, 1994.
A Train Called Judah, Eden Press, 1996.
The Girl with Blue Hair, Eden Press, 1996.
Salt, Eden Press, 1998.

OTHER

(Editor) *Roots* (anthology), Indiana University Press (Bloomington), 1973.
A Little Lower than Angels (novel), Eden Press, 1984.

Contributor to anthologies, including *Black Arts,* edited by Ahmed Alhamsi and Harun K. Wangara, Broadside Press, 1969; *Brothers and Sisters,* edited by Arnold Adoff, Macmillan, 1970; *We Speak as Liberators,* edited by Orde Coombs, Dodd, 1970; *Natural Process,* edited by Ted Wilentz and Tom Weatherley, Hill & Wang, 1970; *Jump Bad,* edited by Gwendolyn Brooks, Broadside Press, 1971; *The Black Poets,* edited by Dudley Randall, Bantam, 1971; *Blackspirits,* edited by Woodie King, Random House, 1972; *Afro-American Writing,* edited by Ri-

chard A. Long and Eugenia W. Collier, New York University Press, 1972; *Nommo,* edited by William R. Robinson, Macmillan, 1972; *The Poetry of Black America,* edited by Adoff, Harper, 1973; *Understanding the New Black Poetry,* edited by Stephen Henderson, Morrow, 1973; *Black Sister,* Indiana University Press, 1983; *Confirmation Anthology,* edited by Amiri Baraka, Morrow, 1984; *Masterpieces of African-American Literature,* edited by Frank N. Magill, HarperCollins, 1992; *Father Songs,* edited by Gloria Wade-Gayles, Beacon Press, 1997; and *Honey, Hush,* edited by Daryl Cumber Dance, Norton, 1998.

Former reviewer for Chicago *Daily News* and columnist for Milwaukee *Courier.*

SIDELIGHTS: Carolyn M. Rodgers is known primarily for her association with the Chicago Organization of Black American Culture of the 1960s. Calling her "one of the most sensitive and complex poets to emerge from this movement and struggle with its contradictions," essayist Bettye J. Parker-Smith suggests in *Black Women Writers (1950-1980): A Critical Evaluation* that Rodgers has been "instrumental in helping create, and give a new definition or receptive power to, poetry as a Black art form." Among Rodgers' published poetry are the collections *Songs of a Blackbird, how i got ovah: New and Selected Poems,* and *The Heart as Ever Green.*

Although Rodgers' poetry has always concerned the search for self, it has evolved over several decades from a militant, sociological perspective to a more introspective one. Jean Davis indicates in a *Dictionary of Literary Biography* essay that while Rodgers has spent most of her career as a poet in her native Chicago, she has since gone on to gain national recognition for "her thematic concerns with feminist issues," in particular those issues that directly affect African American women in a transitional society. Angelene Jamison asserts in her essay for *Black Women Writers (1950-1980),* that like "most of the Black women poets . . . casually referred to only as by-products of the New Black Arts Movement," Rodgers still awaits the attention her work deserves, as well as her "appropriate place in literature."

Rodgers began writing "quasi seriously" as a response to the frustrations she experienced during her first year at college, going on to participate in the Organization of Black American Culture's Writers Workshop and becoming closely associated with the prolific black arts movement of the 1960s. The poet's spiritual and philosophical take on the problems of African Americans, and her effort to communicate with blacks on a unique level, suggest to Parker-Smith that Rodgers is "an exemplar of the 'revolutionary poet.'" Rodgers, who considers her work both art as well as polemic, has professed no distinctly defined political stance; rather, as she told Evans, she feels literature "functions as a type of catharsis or amen arena" in the lives of people. "I think it speaks not only to the political sensibility but to the heart, the mind, the spirit, and the soul of every man, woman, and child," the poet explained. Noting that Rodgers' poetry voices varied concerns, including "revolution, love, Black male-female relationships, religion, and the complexities of Black womanhood," Jamison declares that "through a skillfully uncluttered use of several literary devices, she convincingly reinterprets the love, pain, longings, struggles, victories, the day-to-day routines of Black people from the point of view of the Black woman. Gracefully courageous enough to explore long-hidden truths, about Black women particularly, her poetry shows honesty, warmth, and love for Black people."

Rodgers' first volume of poetry, 1968's *Paper Soul,* "reflects the duality of an individual struggling to reconcile complex realities, dilemmas, and contradictions," in the opinion of Davis, who recognizes a thematic shift in the poet's second volume of poetry, *Songs of a Blackbird.* Davis suggests that the former addresses "identity, religion, revolution, and love, or more accurately a woman's need for love," whereas the latter deals with "survival, street life, mother-daughter conflict, and love." Indicating that these poems are increasingly concerned with "the black woman poet as a major theme," Davis states that "questions of identity for the poet remain connected with relationships between black men and women but become more centrally located in the woman's ability to express herself."

While Rodgers' poetry of the late-1960s is characterized by Davis as "vivid and forceful," her early volumes were not unanimously praised. Rodgers' "poems, especially the early works, are efforts to break the silences, to break down the walls," according to *Contemporary Women Poets* essayist Janis Butler Holm, citing such works as "U Name This One," which describes life on Chicago's streets, "where pee wee cut lonnell fuh fuckin wid/ his sistuh and blood baptized the street/ at least twice ev'ry week and judy got/ kicked outa grammar school fuh bein pregnant/ and died tryin to ungrow the seed." Davis credits the poet's "use of speech patterns and

of lengthened prose-like lines" with sparking trepidation on the part of contemporary critics. Such stylistic measures were "an attempt at breaking away from the restrictions of conventional forms and modes, and most especially from those considered appropriate for women poets," according to Davis Inasmuch as language structure and theme were the general hallmarks of the black art movement during this period, Parker-Smith cites Rodgers' incorporation of obscenities and the pattern of black speech as especially courageous for a woman poet. Although acknowledging a certain inconsistency in the language of her early poetry, Davis believes that "Rodgers nonetheless had an eye for the contradictions of black experience, particularly the revolutionary or militant experience of the 1960s."

Parker-Smith describes what she perceives as two stages of Rodgers' work, what she refers to as the poet's "two distinct and clear baptisms." The poet's early work is "rough-hewn, folk-spirited, and held 'down at the river' amid water moccasins in the face of a glaring midday sun." Rodgers' poems in *Paper Soul, Two Love Raps,* and *Songs of a Blackbird* reveal "her impudence, through the use of her wit, obscenities, the argumentation in her love and revolution poems, and the pain and presence of her mother," according to Parker-Smith, who suggests that "the ribald outcry, the incongruity and cynicism that characterize the first period are links in Rodgers' chain of personal judgments—her attempts to come to grips with 'self'—and with the Black Arts Movement as a whole."

The poet's second phase finds her more mature, more sophisticated, her judgements more modulated. During this time, Rodgers moved from Chicago-based Third World Press to a larger commercial publishing house, as well as breaking from the Organization of Black American Culture. Considering *how i got ovah* and *The Heart as Ever Green: Poems* within the scope of this second phase, Parker-Smith finds that Rodgers closely examines "the revolution, its contradictions, and her relationship to it."

In Rodgers's *how i got ovah: New and Selected Poems,* written in the mid-1970s, the poet exhibits a heightened "clarity of expression and a respect for well-crafted language," according to Davis, who perceives "humor, sincerity, and love" in the autobiographical poems about "black revolution, feminism, religion, God, the black church, and the black family, especially the mother." Similarly, Hilda Njoki McElroy writes in *Black World:* "It is obvious that Carolyn Rodgers loves her craft and her people. *how i got ovah* is a result of this love match. It is an important literary contribution containing many aspects of human frailty/achievement, love/hate, positive/negative, funny/sad, beautiful/ugly which makes it deeeeep, very deeeeep." Suggesting that these poems "reveal Rodgers' transformation from a . . . militant Black woman to a woman intensely concerned with God, traditional values, and her private self," Davis adds that "although her messages often explore social conflict, they usually conclude with a sense of peace, hope, and a desire to search for life's real treasure—inner beauty."

Identity and potentiality continue to be central themes throughout Rodgers' work that have solidified in what Davis terms an "evolving feminism." "I see myself as becoming," Rodgers told Evans. Davis suggests that "determination to grow and to be is the most prevalent idea" in Rodgers's *The Heart as Ever Green,* where "the themes of human dignity, feminism, love, black consciousness, and Christianity are repeated throughout." Suggesting that the "level of honesty" in Rodgers' work correlates with the poet's own level of freedom, Jamison believes that "in a variety of idioms ranging from the street to the church, she writes about Black women with a kind of sensitivity and warmth that brings them out of the poems and into our own lives." Jamison adds that "clearly, her artistry brings these women to life, but it is her love for them that gives them their rightful place in literature. The love, the skill, indeed the vision, which she brings to her poetry must certainly help Black women rediscover and better understand themselves."

Although survival represents a dominant theme in her stories and poetry, Davis believes that Rodgers "interweaves the idea of adaptability and conveys the concomitant message of life's ever-changing avenues for black people whom she sees as her special audience." She quotes Rodgers' regarding her writing being "for whoever wants to read it. . . one poem doesn't do that. But I try to put as many as I can in a book. A poem for somebody young, religious people, the church people. Just people. Specifically, Black people. I would like for them to like me."

BIOGRAPHICAL/CRITICAL SOURCES:

BOOKS

Contemporary Women Poets, St. James Press (Detroit), 1997.
Dictionary of Literary Biography, Volume 41: *Afro-American Poets since 1955,* Gale (Detroit), 1985.
Evans, Mari, editor, *Black Women Writers (1950-1980): A Critical Evaluation,* Doubleday, 1984.

PERIODICALS

Black Scholar, March, 1981, p. 90.
Black World, August, 1970: February, 1976.
Booklist, September 1, 1978, p. 20.
Chicago Tribune, November 19, 1978.
Kirkus Reviews, April 15, 1978, p. 490.
Library Journal, August, 1978, p. 1516.
Negro Digest, September, 1968.
Publishers Weekly, April 24, 1978, p. 75.
Washington Post Book World, May 18, 1975.

S

SARRANTONIO, Al 1952-

PERSONAL: Born May 25, 1952, in Queens, NY; married; children: two sons. *Education:* Manhattan College, B.A., 1974.

ADDRESSES: Home—Putnam Valley, NY. *Agent*—Sharon Jarvis & Co., 260 Willard Ave., Staten Island, NY 10314.

CAREER: Doubleday & Co., Inc., New York City, editorial assistant, 1975-82; writer, 1982—.

MEMBER: Science Fiction Writers of America, Horror Writers of America.

AWARDS, HONORS: Shamus Award nominee for *Cold Night.*

WRITINGS:

NOVELS

The Worms, Doubleday (Garden City, NY), 1985.
Totentanz, Tor Books (New York City), 1985.
Campbell Wood, Doubleday, 1986.
The Boy with Penny Eyes, Tor Books, 1987.
Cold Night, Tor Books, 1987.
Moonbane, Bantam (New York City), 1989.
October, Bantam, 1990.
House Haunted, Bantam, 1991.
Skeletons, Bantam, 1992.
Summer Cool, Walker (New York City), 1993.
Kitt Peak, M. Evans (New York City), 1993.
Exile, New American Library (New York City), 1996.
Journey, New American Library, 1997.

Personal Agendas, Dell (New York City), 1997.
Return, New American Library, 1998.

OTHER

(Editor) *The Fireside Treasury of Great Humor,* Simon & Schuster (New York City), 1987.
(Editor) *The Fireside Treasury of New Humor,* Simon & Schuster, 1989.
(Editor) *The National Lampoon Treasury of Humor,* Simon & Schuster, 1991.
(Editor with Martin H. Greenberg) *100 Hair-Raising Little Horror Stories,* Barnes & Noble (New York City), 1993.

Also author of *West Texas,* M. Evans. Work represented in anthologies, including *The Year's Best Horror Stories,* Volumes XI and XII, *Great Ghost Stories, Laughing Space, Ghosts, Fears,* and *Shadows,* Volumes 4, 5, 6, and 8. Contributor of stories to *Heavy Metal, Twilight Zone, Isaac Asimov's Science Fiction Magazine, Night Cry* and *Mystery Scene.*

SIDELIGHTS: Al Sarrantonio has written two novels featuring private investigator Jack Blaine, a retired cop who operates in the Yonkers area of New York. In *Cold Night* and *Summer Cool,* Blaine investigates police chicanery. Blaine is eased from the police force in *Cold Night,* due to the machinations of corrupt officers. In *Summer Cool,* he is asked to find a cop who has abandoned his family, left town and seems to be murdering his drug dealing buddies. A critic for *Publishers Weekly* writes: "Drugs, betrayal and corruption at the highest levels figure in a story that stretches the bounds of credibility but provides a satisfying, even shocking, climax."

Sarrantonio has also written a number of horror thrillers, science fiction novels and short stories for magazines. Writing in the *St. James Guide to Horror, Ghost and Gothic Writers,* Don D'Ammassa cites Sarrantonio's novel *Totentanz* as "a powerful, controlled work, unusually so for a first novel. . . . *The Boy with Penny Eyes* is Sarrantonio's most restrained and successful horror novel. The boy of the title appears to be autistic, never shows joy or sorrow, never speaks, and the adults who shuffle him from one home to another despair of ever reaching him. But he isn't entirely unaware. His eyes are always moving, watching, searching for another child, the other half of his personality from whom he has been supernaturally severed. . . . The most interesting and in some ways the best-written of Sarrantonio's horror novels is *Skeletons,* which also contains a great deal of dark humour. Through some unexplained device, all of the skeletons on Earth have been restored to life, and each of them is determined to pursue his or her former career. . . . Despite the obvious satire, the mood of the novel is distinctly that of horror, because the armies of the undead intend to supplant the living and wrest from them control of the Earth. . . . This one's a bizarre twist on the *Night of the Living Dead* films."

D'Ammassa concludes: "In general Sarrantonio's short fiction seems more controlled and thoughtful than his novels, which often rely so much on physical action that the characters never achieve any depth. At the same time *The Boy with Penny Eyes* and *Skeletons* in particular indicate that Sarrantonio possesses the skills to be a successful novelist when he sets his mind to it."

BIOGRAPHICAL/CRITICAL SOURCES:

BOOKS

St. James Guide to Horror, Ghost and Gothic Writers, St. James Press (Detroit), 1998.

PERIODICALS

Publishers Weekly, July 12, 1993, p. 72.

* * *

SAXE, Isobel
  See RAYNER, Claire (Berenice)

SEELYE, John (Douglas) 1931-

PERSONAL: Surname is pronounced *See-lee;* born January 1, 1931, in Hartford, CT; son of Douglas Stuart (an engineer) and Maida (a secretary; maiden name, LeGeyt) Seelye; married Catherine Maybury (a textual editor), March 15, 1968 (died, 1982); married Alice Hunt Wilkerson, 1988. *Education:* Wesleyan University, Middletown, CT, B.A., 1953; Claremont College, M.A., 1956, Ph.D., 1961. *Politics:* "Lapsed Republican/disgruntled Democrat." *Religion:* "Old-time."

ADDRESSES: Home—439 Northeast Ninth Ave., Gainesville, FL 32601.

CAREER: University of California, Berkeley, associate professor of English, 1960-65; University of Connecticut, Storrs, associate professor, 1966-71, professor of English, 1971-74; University of North Carolina, Chapel Hill, professor of English, 1974-84; University of Florida, Gainesville, graduate research professor, 1984—. *Military service:* U.S. Naval Reserve, 1953-55; became lieutenant junior grade.

MEMBER: American Studies Association, American Antiquarian Society, Modern Language Association, Popular Culture Association, PEN Club, Hillsborough Historical Society (member of board of directors).

AWARDS, HONORS: Senior fellow, National Endowment for the Humanities, 1972, 1980, 1985; Guggenheim fellow, 1973; Mellon fellow, 1983.

WRITINGS:

The True Adventures of Huckleberry Finn, as Told by John Seelye, Northwestern University Press (Evanston, IL), 1970.
Melville: The Ironic Diagram, Northwestern University Press, 1970.
The Kid (novel), Viking (New York City), 1972.
Dirty Tricks; or, Nick Noxin's Natural Nobility (novel), Liveright (New York City), 1974.
Prophetic Waters: The River in Early American Life and Literature, Oxford University Press (New York City), 1977.
Mark Twain in the Movies: A Meditation with Pictures, Viking, 1977.
Rational Exultation: Erie Canal Celebration, American Antiquarian Society (Worcester, MA), 1985.
If at First You Don't Secede, Try, Try Again: Southern Literature from Fenimore Cooper to Faulkner, American Antiquarian Society, 1989.

Beautiful Machine: Rivers and the Republican Plan, 1755-1825, Oxford University Press, 1991.

Memory's Nation: The Place of Plymouth Rock, University of North Carolina Press (Chapel Hill), 1998.

Contributor to *Literature in Revolution,* Holt (New York City), 1972.

EDITOR

Arthur Gordon Pym, Benito Cereno, and Related Writings, Lippincott (Philadelphia, PA), 1967.

J. Ross Browne, *Etchings of a Whaling Cruise,* Harvard University Press (Cambridge, MA), 1968.

Mark Twain, *The Adventures of Tom Sawyer,* Penguin (New York City), 1985.

Twain, *The Adventures of Huckleberry Finn,* Penguin, 1986.

Owen Wister, *The Virginian,* Penguin, 1986.

Asa Sheldon, Yankee Drover, University Press of New England (Hanover, NH), 1988.

Twain, *Life on the Mississippi,* Oxford University Press, 1990.

Edgar Rice Burroughs, *Tarzan of the Apes,* Penguin, 1990.

(And author of introduction) Johann David Wyss, *The Swiss Family Robinson,* Oxford University Press, 1991.

Stories of the Old West: Tales of the Mining Camp, Cavalry Troop, and Cattle Ranch, Penguin (New York City), 1994.

Contributing editor, *New Republic,* 1972-79; member of editorial board, *American Literature,* 1974-78.

SIDELIGHTS: Whether reworking his country's literary traditions as a novelist or assessing its early myths as a critic, John Seelye has established himself as an original and imaginative writer. Michael Cleary explained in *Twentieth-Century Western Writers,* "Seelye's works examine the inter-relationships of classic American literature and the criticism which surrounds it. His unique method is to incorporate well-known literary characters, themes, and theories into works which have been labeled 'revisionist novels' and 'reactionary satires.'" In *The True Adventures of Huckleberry Finn* he dared rewrite Mark Twain's classic; in *The Kid* he took liberties with the Western novel in presenting his version of life in the Old West; in *Dirty Tricks* he framed the Richard Nixon saga within the outline of a Horatio Alger "strive and succeed" story. Later, in his highly ac-

claimed critical work, *Prophetic Waters,* Seelye studied the writings of America's settlers and suggested "a newer and older point of origin" for American literature.

Seelye's first major book was *The True Adventures of Huckleberry Finn.* The story "was mostly by Mr. Mark Twain," Seelye's Huck Finn explained. "Only there was some things which he stretched and some which he left out, so I went to work and done the best I could to fix it up. . . . I was glad to do it, seeing how the book had made so many crickits and liberians unhappy the way he had written it."

Among those critics "Huck" referred to are those who have found the book's ending too facile and its language less colorful than Huck's character would suggest. Cleary commented; "[The] novel 'corrects' the flaws of Twain's book by rewriting it according to the demands of disputatious critics. . . . Seelye's version escapes the Victorian prudery which bound Twain and has continued to resctict writers of the popular Western." In Seelye's revision, reported *Time,* "Jim drowns while trying to escape a band of bloodthirsty, reward-hungry rednecks, and Huck is so disgusted and depressed that he doesn't give a damn what happens next." *The True Adventures* also includes its share of language that would have compounded the scandal caused when the original book was published. Twain had agreed to "eliminate references to blasphemy, bad odors, dead cats, and to change the phrase 'in a sweat' to 'worrying,'" noted the *Time* reviewer. "John Seelye puts that sort of stuff back in, with additions that will surely get Huck Finn an X rating at the local library." Jean Stafford told readers of the *Washington Post Book World:* "Seelye's excisions, by and large, are so deft, his neoplasms so foxily insinuated . . . his imitation of Mark Twain's manner and language so sedulous, that the corpus (but for the ending) does not, at first glance, seem to have been tampered with at all."

The Kid is a western about two drifters who wander into a small town in Wyoming in 1887 and precipitate a series of gruesome conflicts and confrontations. This novel, more typical of the western genre than *The True Adventures,* is replete with saloon, villains, gunplay, multiple murders, frontier justice, and a surprise ending. Peter Dollard reported in *Library Journal,* "Seelye's West, beneath its comic and virile swagger, is squalid, fetid, and brutal. This [is a] remarkably effective novel." Cleary wrote: "In this unique novel, the literary puzzle is . . . complex, juxtaposing major literary themes and theories from a number of classic American novels and playing them against the formula of the Western. . . . *The Kid* breaks new ground in western fiction by evaluating the genre against the serious novels and criticism which have helped to shape its development. . . . [It] reads as an adventure, a tall tale, an allegory—and it manages to succeed on all levels. It is one of the most ingenious, ambitious, and important of the contemporary western novels."

After writing *The Kid,* Seelye published *Dirty Tricks.* In *The Kid,* Seelye had adapted the plot of Melville's *Billy Budd* to ends suggested by critic Leslie Fielder; in *Dirty Tricks,* a political satire, he imitated the Horatio Alger stories popular at the turn of the century. "He has produced an exceptionally faithful reproduction of the genre," reported Paul Showers in the *New York Times Book Review.* Unfortunately, the book "makes you think less about Richard Nixon than about grandpappy and great-grandpappy," added Showers. "What sort of people were they to fall for such stuff?" Jonathan Yardley also agreed, in *New Republic,* that the book did not quite fulfill its promise. "*Dirty Tricks* is entertaining and diverting," Yardley said, "but it is hard to laugh at (much less with) Richard Nixon. Indignation, outrage, pity, contempt—okay; but laughter, no thanks. That, of course, is not Seelye's fault; but quite inadvertently, he reminds us how unfunny Richard Nixon is."

In an interview with *CA,* Seelye described the evolution of *Dirty Tricks:* "What I started to do early on was a Horatio Alger-style biography of Richard Nixon: you know, the young man who starts out with nothing and then works his way to the top. When you write anything you want to know where you're going. . . . With *Dirty Tricks* I had a pretty obvious idea of Nixon as a kind of parodized Alger figure, but I didn't know how I was going to end it. I started after Nixon won the election in 1968, but I wasn't going anywhere with it. . . . Then along came Watergate, and I said, 'Ah, here's my ending—the Great Trial.'" In response to negative reviews of his novel, Seelye commented: "It wasn't quite the sensation I thought it was going to be; in fact, most people thought it was a very bad idea. . . . So it just wasn't very good timing, I guess. But it's one of my favorite books, of the things I've done."

In *Prophetic Waters,* Seelye examined the writings of the American explorers and settlers from the sixteenth to the early eighteenth century. He interprets

these writings not "as evidence that history happened in a certain way," pointed out Ormond Seavey in *Nation,* but as "a complex and interrelated drama in which the actors repeat one another's rituals of confrontation with the continent." Seelye searches for the symbolic or mythical elements in what these settlers wrote, said *Saturday Review* critic Charles Nicol. He concludes that "our first explorers and settlers persisted in seeing what they wanted to see rather than what lay in their paths."

Seelye's book was well received, particularly as an informative and original work. Nicol insisted "the originality of *Prophetic Waters* lies not in what Seelye has read but in how he has read it." H. J. Cloke commended it in an *America* review: "The narrative, on the whole, is illuminating. Seelye's thesis comprehends a wealth of material without being reductionist, and his sensitive readings of individual texts reveal his depth as a critic and scholar." Cloke noted, however, "Professor Seelye has a penchant for puns, word plays and riddling the names of our forefathers that would shame the Puritan versifiers and try the patience of the modern reader." But Seavey wrote: "[His] prose . . . tends toward the excessively lush. . . . [His] efforts to evoke the minds of these first observers remind us that they themselves were even more ecstatic than he is."

In addition to his fiction, Seelye has written a number of scholarly studies and other nonfiction. These include *Mark Twain in the Movies: A Meditation with Pictures.* Seelye told *CA* that the book deals with a side of Twain that many readers prefer to ignore: "an unpleasant part of Mark Twain. That rather cruel, mean, senile business began to come out at the end. I did nothing more than provide the photographs and the commentary." The book was not a critical success. Seelye added: "It barely got reviewed, mostly unfavorably. Apparently people really don't want to know *everything* about Mark Twain. They want to preserve that image of the fiery old man, and they're not really too curious about his darker side. I suppose in the long run that might be just as well."

Seelye summarized his work: "My fiction and nonfiction tend to merge: as in *Prophetic Waters,* I like to impose fictional frames on history, and I also like to use writing as a critical tool to better understand what's going on in our popular classics. . . . As far as my fiction writing is concerned, I'm glad to be in the South now. . . . The New South is full of very rich fiction, still waiting to be written."

BIOGRAPHICAL/CRITICAL SOURCES:

BOOKS

Contemporary Literary Criticism, Volume 7, Gale
     (Detroit, MI), 1977.
Twentieth-Century Western Writers, second edition,
     St. James Press (Detroit), 1991.

PERIODICALS

America, October 1, 1977.
American Literature, January, 1971; March, 1978.
Best Sellers, March 15, 1972.
Library Journal, October 1, 1971; February 1, 1972.
Nation, June 1, 1970; June 11, 1977.
New England Quarterly, September, 1977.
New Republic, January 26, 1974.
Newsweek, May 16, 1970; January 7, 1974.
New York Times Book Review, January 23, 1972;
     February 24, 1974.
Saturday Review, May 28, 1977.
Time, March 2, 1970.
Times Literary Supplement, February 3, 1978.
Washington Post Book World, May 10, 1970, p.4.

                    *   *   *

SERAFIAN, Michael
   See MARTIN, Malachi

                    *   *   *

SHAHN, Bernarda Bryson
   See BRYSON, Bernarda

                    *   *   *

SHEMIE, Bonnie (Jean Brenner) 1949-

PERSONAL: Born May 10, 1949, in Cleveland, OH;
daughter of William (an engineer) and Louise (a
nurse; maiden name, Lundgren) Brenner; married
Milo Shemie (an engineer), 1974; children: Khuther
William, Benjamin David, Daniel Naim. *Education:*
Allegheny College, B.A., 1971. *Religion:* Jewish.
Avocational interests: Skiing, hiking, canoeing.

ADDRESSES: Home—4474 De Maisonneuve W.,
Montreal, Quebec, H32 1L7, Canada. *Agent*—Tun-
dra Books, 481 University Ave., Suite 802, Toronto,
Ontario, M5G 2E9, Canada.

CAREER: Author and illustrator. Worked for various
advertising agencies in Montreal, Quebec, in graphic
design and illustration, 1973-76; freelance illustrator,
1976-85. Presenter at elementary schools, public libraries, Reading Association, and library and school
conferences. *Exhibitions:* Shemie's works have appeared in a number of group and solo shows since
1975.

AWARDS, HONORS: Choice Book citation, Canadian
Children's Book Centre, and Prix d'Excellence de
l'Association des Consommateurs de Quebec (for the
French edition), both 1991, for *Houses of Bark: Tipi,
Wigwam and Longhouse: Native Dwellings, Wood-
land Indians;* Choice Book citation, Canadian
Children's Book Centre, 1991, for *Houses of Snow,
Skin and Bones: Native Dwellings, the Far North;*
Canadian Materials Notable Book citation, Canadian
Library Association, 1992, for *Houses of Hide and
Earth: Native Dwellings, Plains Indians;* Our Choice
citation, Canadian Children's Book Centre, 1993, for
*Houses of Wood: Native Dwellings, the Northwest
Coast.*

WRITINGS:

SELF-ILLUSTRATED; FOR CHILDREN; PUBLISHED BY TUN-
     DRA BOOKS

*Houses of Snow, Skin and Bones: Native Dwellings,
     the Far North,* 1989.
*Houses of Bark: Tipi, Wigwam, and Longhouse:
     Native Dwellings, Woodland Indians,* 1990.
*Houses of Hide and Earth: Native Dwellings, Plains
     Indians,* 1991.
*Houses of Wood: Native Dwellings, the Northwest
     Coast,* 1992.
Mounds of Earth and Shell: The Southeast, 1993.
Houses of Adobe: The Southwest, 1995.
Houses of China, 1996.

WORK IN PROGRESS: A series of books about lost
cities.

SIDELIGHTS: Bonnie Shemie is the author and illustrator of a series of books for elementary-age children on the dwellings of Native Americans. The
series began with *Houses of Snow, Skin and Bones:
Native Dwellings, the Far North,* a detailed look at

the various types of homes built by the Inuit tribes of Alaska. In text that alternates between simple descriptions aimed at younger readers and more complex discussions intended for older children, the author places the building of homes in the context of the culture as a whole. "Shemie looks at these dwellings with admiration," noted Denise Wilms of *Booklist*. In a statement that would be echoed by reviewers of later volumes in the series, Noel McDermott in *Canadian Children's Literature* proclaimed the work "a well-written and beautifully illustrated book, in which carefully researched information is presented, clearly and accurately and without any tendency to eulogize or romanticize."

Houses of Bark: Tipi, Wigwam and Longhouse: Native Dwellings, Woodland Indians was received by commentators with similar enthusiasm. *Booklist* contributor Carolyn Phelan noted that "the softly textured artwork" creates "an appealing vision of tribal life in eastern North America." "Information given in the text is very well explained, with a deceptively simple conciseness," remarked a critic for *Junior Bookshelf* in a review of the first three books in the series. *Houses of Wood: Native Dwellings, the Northwest Coast,* the fourth book in the series, describes the dwellings built by the Indian groups who lived from northern California through British Columbia and into southern Alaska, where the region's massive trees were the most sensible resource for building materials. "Like its predecessors, *Houses of Wood* focuses on the homes while giving detailed information on other facets of the particular people's way of life," observed Patricia Fry in *Canadian Materials*. Although Annette Goldsmith, a reviewer for *Quill & Quire,* complained about the lack of table of contents and index to help guide readers through the information in the book, she also concluded: "The subject and length are sufficiently limited, however, and the book so interesting, that this should not deter readers."

In *Mounds of Earth and Shell: The Southeast,* Shemie turned from Native homes to explore the mysterious mounds that probably served as burial sites and ceremonial and sacred places in the southeastern United States, where a few of these mounds still remain. Shemie's illustrations demonstrate what the mounds looked like during the time they were in use and offer diagrams of several mounds showing the location of artifacts found in modern times. Like the other works in this series, *Mounds of Earth and Shell* features both "clear, involving text and strong, colourful illustra-

tions," according to *Quill & Quire* contributor Fred Boer. The book provides one of the few sources of information on the subject for children, noted Carolyn Phelan in her *Booklist* appraisal, calling *Mounds of Earth and Shell* an "attractive book."

Shemie's books for children on the architecture of Native Americans are equally admired for the author's clear presentation of useful information and the warmth and attractiveness of her precise drawings and color illustrations. "Shemie is that rare combination of writer/artist who is equally dedicated to intensive research and to art," remarked critic Patricia Fry in *Canadian Materials*. Works such as *Houses of Snow, Skin and Bones* and *Houses of Bark* have captured attention for the way in which the author integrates information about the construction of such dwellings with details about the lives of the people who built and lived in these homes. Shemie "places house-building within its cultural context," Goldsmith stated. In addition, critics have noted that the author's dual text, with simple explanations on pages with color illustrations alternating with more complex narratives on pages with line drawings, makes the books in this series useful and attractive to a broad range of students looking for information on the history of Native American dwellings.

Shemie told *CA:* "I was very fortunate. My work was noticed at a local exhibition by the editor and owner of Tundra Books, May Cutler. She coached and cajoled me into writing as well as illustrating my books. I work at home in the basement, in the winter surrounded by heaters and bicycles, where it is quiet and I can concentrate.

"My advice to young author/illustrators: there are many wonderful topics yet to be explored. Extraordinary things are produced by ordinary people like you and me."

BIOGRAPHICAL/CRITICAL SOURCES:

PERIODICALS

Booklist, December 15, 1989, pp. 835-36; January 15, 1991, p. 1058; January 1, 1994, pp. 825-26.
Bulletin of the Center for Children's Books, December, 1989, p. 96.
Canadian Children's Literature, No. 63, 1991, pp. 78-79.
Canadian Materials, January, 1991, p. 24; March, 1993, p. 57.

Junior Bookshelf, June, 1994, pp. 102-03; June, 1996, pp. 113-14.
Quill & Quire, October, 1992, pp. 36, 38; October, 1993, p. 43.
School Library Journal, February, 1997, p. 125.

* * *

SHEPHERD, Gordon
   See BROOK-SHEPHERD, (Frederick) Gordon

* * *

SKIDELSKY, Robert 1939-

PERSONAL: Surname is pronounced Ski-*del*-ski; born April 25, 1939, in Harbin, Manchuria; son of Boris J. and Galia (Sapelkin) Skidelsky; married Augusta Mary Clarissa Hope, 1970, children: two sons, one deceased. *Education:* Jesus College, Oxford, B.A., 1961; Nuffield College, Oxford, Ph.D., 1965. *Religion:* Church of England. *Avocational interests:* Music, especially opera and piano; tennis and table tennis, ballet, cinema, squash.

ADDRESSES: Home—Tilton House, Firle, East Sussex BN8 6LL, England. *Office*— Department of International Studies, University of Warwick, Coventry CV4 7AL, England. *Agent*—A. D. Peters & Co. Ltd., 10 Buckingham St., London WC2N 6BU, England.

CAREER: Oxford University, Nuffield College, Oxford, England, research fellow, 1965-68; British Academy, London, research fellow, 1968-70; Johns Hopkins University, School of Advanced International Studies, Washington, DC, visiting and associate professor, 1970-76; Polytechnic of North London, London, head of department of History, Philosophy, and European Studies, 1976-78; University of Warwick, Coventry, England, professor of international studies, 1978—; House of Lords, member, 1991—.Visiting professor, Columbia University, 1973. Charleston Trust, chair, 1987—; SDP, Policy Committee, 1988; Social Market Foundation, director, 1989.

MEMBER: Royal Over-Seas League, United Oxford & Cambridge University.

AWARDS, HONORS: Wolfson Prize for History in the United Kingdom.

WRITINGS:

Politicians and the Slump: The Labour Government of 1929-1931, Macmillan (London), 1967.
(Contributor) S. J. Woolf, editor, *European Fascism,* Weidenfeld & Nicolson (London), 1968, Random House (New York City), 1969, new edition, Weidenfeld & Nicolson, 1981.
English Progressive Schools, Penguin (Harmondsworth, West Drayton, Middx), 1969.
Oswald Mosley, Macmillan (London and New York City), 1975, U.S. edition published as *Sir Oswald Mosley,* second edition, 1980.
(Contributor) Milo Keynes, editor, *Essays on John Maynard Keynes,* Cambridge University Press (Cambridge), 1975.
John Maynard Keynes, Macmillan, Volume I: *Hopes Betrayed, 1883-1920,* 1983, Viking (New York City), 1986, Volume II: *The Economist as Savior, 1920-1937,* Viking, 1994.
Interests and Obsessions (selected essays), Macmillan, 1993.
Keynes and the United States, College of Liberal Arts, Harry Ransom Humanities Research Center, University of Texas at Austin (Austin), 1993.
The World After Communism: A Polemic for Our Times, Macmillan, 1995, published as *The Road to Serfdom: The Economic and Political Consequences of the End of Communism,* Penguin (New York City), 1996.
Keynes, Oxford University Press (Oxford and New York City), 1996.
(Contributor) *Three Great Economists,* Oxford University Press (Oxford and New York City), 1997.

EDITOR

(With Vernon Bogdanor) *The Age of Affluence, 1951-1964,* Macmillan (London), 1970.
The End of the Keynesian Era, Macmillan (London and New York City), 1977.
(And author of introduction with Michael Holroyd) William Gerhardie, *God's Fifth Column: A Biography of the Age, 1890-1940,* Simon & Schuster (New York City), 1981, republished Overlook Press (Woodstock, NY), 1991.
(And author of introduction) *Thatcherism,* Chatto & Windus (London), 1988, B. Blackwell (Oxford, UK and Cambridge, MA), 1990.

Russia's Stormy Path to Reform, Social Market Foundation (London), 1995.

Contributor to the *Times, Times Literary Supplement, New Society, Encounter, Spectator,* and other journals and newspapers.

SIDELIGHTS: A professor of political economy as well as a member of the House of Lords, Robert Skidelsky is the author and editor of numerous works on political and economic issues. His highly acclaimed biographical works on John Maynard Keynes are perhaps his most recognized publications. *John Maynard Keynes* is a voluminous biography which presents multiple facets of the man, his work, and his world. Volume I, *Hopes Betrayed 1883-1920,* "is authoritative, documented, and readable—indispensable for anyone who wants to understand the young Keynes and the moral and philosophical problems that exercised his mind," according to Noel Annan in the *New York Review of Books.* Volume II, *The Economist as Savior, 1920-1937* "examines Keynes' personal, intellectual, artistic, money-making and political life . . . to indicate a remarkable disparateness," writes Leonard Silk in *The New Leader.*

John Maynard Keynes: Hopes Betrayed 1883-1920 "is freshly and vigorously written," remarks *The Spectator*'s Norman Stone. Jose Harris, writing for the *London Review of Books,* describes *Hopes Betrayed 1883-1920* as "a study that can be recommended to a wide variety of readers. There are plenty of Bloomsbury tidbits and bawdy stories for those who like them, while, for intellectual and social historians, Skidelsky's Cambridge will be indispensable. For those who worry about the fate of civilisation, this is on more than one level a profoundly serious and thought-provoking book." Stone compliments the book's "discussion of the philosophical atmosphere of Cambridge around 1900" and less positively comments: "Homosexuality was a constant, unremitting theme in Keynes's early life, as Skidelsky makes abundantly (and perhaps excessively) clear." David Cannadine praises Skidelsky in *The New Republic* for writing a "most vivid and plausible picture" of the young Keynes and states: "[T]o deal with the Cambridge background, the cultural context, the emotional involvements, the economics and the individuals, requires an array of accomplishments and a degree of expositional skills that few historians can boast. It is a measure of Skidelsky's real achievement that he triumphantly surmounts these obstacles." On the other hand,

Cannadine faults Skidelsky for giving "insufficient attention to the impact that [Keynes] made on other people," arguing that "the essence of his personality is never fully captured, and the individual himself remains allusive." Cannadine concludes: "[I]t may be that Skidelsky has tried just a little too hard to integrate and homogenize what was, by his own admission, a highly compartmentalized existence."

John Maynard Keynes: The Economist as Savior, 1920-1937 is "comprehensive in explaining Keynes's role as a political and social figure" and "superbly discusses Keynes's major academic books" yet it "[assumes] readers know the technical meaning of economic terms" and "[fails] to present us with Keynes as a man of his times," according to Nicolas Sanchez in *America.* In his review in *The New Republic,* Alan Ryan writes that this volume "reads like the work of an old and intimate friend" and specifies: "It is admiring, but not uncritical; relaxed and unhurried, but incisive. . . . A splendidly open account. . . . Deeply pleasurable to read, evocative as well as instructive and a book that asks to be taken on several levels—as a portrait of Keynes first and foremost, but also as a portrait of a governing class; and an essay on the sociology of knowledge; and an account of an unlikely but wonderfully successful marriage; and an exploration of the money-making temperament."

Oswald Mosley, "a disciple of Keynes," notes *New Statesman*'s Stephen Koss, is the subject of another biography by Skidelsky. Mosley was an influential political and economic figure in British history and is associated with fascism. *Oswald Mosley* is "a patient and painstaking biography," according to Anthony Howard of the *New York Times Book Review.* According to Ross, *Oswald Mosley* "is not, in any sense, an official biography, although the author received valuable assistance and, one gathers, a degree of encouragement from his subject." Koss praises Skidelsky's presentation of Mosely's economic thought and considers the study "resourceful in its research, shrewd in its assessments of people and events and courageous in its readiness to censure or praise." A *New Yorker* reviewer recognizes the presence of both "sorrowful compassion for his subject" and "intellectual self-confidence," noting that the book "is loaded with donnish and quarrelsome asides." In the *Times Literary Supplement,* John Vincent argues that there is a lack of accessible hard evidence "about Mosley as a person or the BUF [British Union of Fascists] as an organization" and states that *Oswald Mosley* is "not a book about Mosley but a book about Mr. Skidelsky's interpretation of Mosley." Vincent remarks that "some may feel Mr. Skidelsky has given his readers a too favourable and selective an impression, not of Sir Oswald, but of the Fascism that Sir Oswald claimed to control."

Skidelsky's first book, *Politicians and the Slump: The Labour Government of 1929-31,* centers on British political history. At the time of it's publication in 1967, a reviewer for the *Times Literary Supplement* commented: "Mr. Skidelsky's book, as others have pointed out, is fortunate in its occurrence. The measures and problems of 1967 have a lot in common with those of 1931. "Writing in the *Spectator,* Jo Grimond praises the book and similarly describes it as "a tragedy written round the mismanagement of British government which still continues today." The book is noted in *Choice* as a "valuable," "useful supplement and to some extent a corrective to the more favorable treatment of this period by" a couple different publications. Grimond states: "Mr. Skidelsky's theme is that, in 1929, the division in British politics lay not between capitalism and socialism but between the conservatism of the Tory and Labour parties supported by the bureaucracy and business, on the one side, and the Liberal party and certain other progressive groups such as that led by Mosley, on the other side."

In 1996, almost three decades later, Skidelsky's economic and political lens has widened for his *Road to Serfdom: The Economic and Political Consequences of the End of Communism.* Herbert Stein's discussion in the *New York Times Book Review* is descriptively subtitled: "an economist sees Thatcherism, Reaganism and the fall of Communism as part of the same great historical movement." "Skidelsky," Stein argues, "has admirably organized a large body of information into a plausible story that is surely true in the main. It deserves attention. But it is not the whole truth," according to Stein, who faults the book for a few omissions and commissions of information. For example, Stein charges that Skidelsky "too readily attributes the ills from which we have obviously suffered . . . to collectivism, but says too little about the problems stored up for us for the future by the unwise undertaking of obligations in the 1960s and 1970s." Stein argues that "Skidelsky's discussion of the collapse of Communism and the sequel up to now is the most informative part of the book."

BIOGRAPHICAL/CRITICAL SOURCES:

BOOKS

Three Great Economists, Oxford University Press (New York City), 1997.

PERIODICALS

America, July 16, 1994.
Books, January, 1970.
Choice, November, 1969.
Encounter, June, 1975.
Financial Times, April 3, 1975.
Forbes, February 28, 1994.
Listener, November 30, 1967.
London Review of Books, December 1, 1983.
London Times, April 3, 1975.
National Review, March 21, 1994.
New Leader, December 27, 1993.
New Republic, June 23, 1986; April 18, 1994.
New Society, April 3, 1975.
New Statesman, March 21, 1975.
New Yorker, August 18, 1975.
New York Review of Books, July 19, 1984.
New York Times Book Review, May 11, 1975; February 25, 1996.
Publishers Weekly, December 6, 1993.
Spectator, December 15, 1967; December 20, 1969; December 10, 1983.
Time, June 9, 1975; May 16, 1986.
Times Educational Supplement, November 4, 1983.
Times Literary Supplement, December 14, 1967; April 16, 1970; April 4, 1975; April 3, 1981.*

*   *   *

SMITH, Brian R.   1939-

PERSONAL: Born May 29, 1939, in Montreal, Quebec, Canada; son of Elmer Hunt (an American government employee) and Jessie (a secretary and painter; maiden name, Millar) Smith; married Rosemary Spillane, May 21, 1961 (divorced May 1, 1980); married Audrey L. Caldwell (a medical secretary), October 11, 1980 (divorced, April 23, 1983); married Myrna M. Milani (a veterinarian and author), March 3, 1985 (divorced May 10, 1997); children: Adam David, Elizabeth Anne, Vanessa Concordia. *Ethnicity:* "British Canadian." *Education:* Northeastern University, B.S.M.E. (with honors), 1962; University of Pittsburgh, M.B.A., 1963;

attended Harpur College (now State University of New York at Binghamton), 1963-64.

ADDRESSES: Home and office—114 Monument Hill Rd., Springfield, VT 05156.   *E-mail*—bsmith@vermontel.com.

CAREER: International Business Machines (IBM) Corp., Endicott, NY, administrative assistant, 1963-64; B. R. Smith and Associates, Inc., Westmoreland, NH, president and government and business management consultant, beginning in 1967—. Registered engineer in Vermont and New Hampshire; Computer Control Corp., vice-president, beginning in 1968; MPB Corp., manager of marketing research and planning; New Hampshire Ball Bearings, Inc., product sales manager; Meditron Instrument Corp., co-founder and president, 1973-76; Veterinary Advisory Services of Denver, staff adviser. Fainshaw Press, co-owner and managing editor. Franklin Pierce College, Rindge, NH, faculty member and director of Division of Economics and Management, 1977-79, adjunct faculty member, beginning in 1980; teacher at colleges, including Southern Vermont College, Antioch College, Keene State College, Nathaniel Hawthorne College, Community College of Vermont, Lyndon State College, New Hampshire Technical College, and Norwich University. Producer of the television program *Beyond the Bottom Line,* first broadcast by Public Broadcasting System, August, 1981. Veterans Administration Medical Center, White River Junction, VT, volunteer, 1994-95; Vermont Anti-Hunger Corps, volunteer, 1995-96; New Hampshire Department of Employment Security, part-time employee. *Military service:* U.S. Army, Corps of Engineers, Engineer Strategic Studies Group, 1964-66; served in Vietnam; became captain.

WRITINGS:

The Small Computer in Small Business, Stephen Greene (Brattleboro, VT), 1981.
How to Prosper in Your Own Business, Stephen Greene, 1981.
The Country Consultant, Consultants News (Fitzwilliam, NH), 1982.
(With Robert Fritz) *The Power of Choice,* Fainshaw (Westmoreland, NH), 1982.
(With Daniel J. Austin) *Word Processing: A Guide for Small Business,* Stephen Greene, 1983.
Successful Marketing for Small Business, Stephen Greene, 1984.

Seed Money, Lewis Publishing, 1984, published as *Raising Seed Money for Your Own Business,* Viking-Penguin (New York City), 1984.
Soft Words for a Hard Technology, Prentice-Hall (Englewood Cliffs, NJ), 1984.
(With Myrna Milani) *A Primer of Rotational Physics,* Fainshaw, 1984.
(With Milani) *Rotational Physics: The Principles of Energy,* Fainshaw, 1985.
(With Tom West) *Buying Your Own Small Business,* Viking-Penguin, 1985.
(With West) *Buying a Franchise,* Viking-Penguin, 1986.
(Guest editor) *Computers in Veterinary Medicine,* W. B. Saunders (Philadelphia, PA), 1986.
(With Milani) *Beyond the Magic Circle: The Role of Intimacy in Business,* Fainshaw, 1989.
How to Become Successfully Self-Employed, Bob Adams (Brighton, MA), 1991.
(Co-author) *Business Management for the Veterinary Practitioner,* Chubb Communications, 1995.

Contributor of more than 200 articles to science and management periodicals.

WORK IN PROGRESS: Roads Taken.

SIDELIGHTS: Brian R. Smith told *CA:* "The early part of my professional career was devoted to learning the operating fundamentals of business—both large corporations and small entrepreneurial ventures. I focused my attention as much on the practical matters of manufacturing, marketing, and finance as on the issue of people in the working environment. Thus, my first several books deal heavily with practical information for business owners, corporate/institutional managers, entrepreneurs, and consultants. In the past several years, I have become more concerned with the people who work—whether these folks are self-employed or employees. In the years to come, I believe that major emphasis will be given to the nature of the human being, our place in our and other 'universes,' and the continuing history and lessons of our species. As a communicator—a writer, teacher, and speaker—I plan to have a major part in the new experiment that awaits us all."

Smith added: "I agree with Richard Bach (author of *Jonathan Livingston Seagull* and *Illusions*) that writing is somewhat difficult and a lot of work. I don't get great satisfaction from it and can't really say why I do it in the first place. Looking back, most of what I've written seems now to be rather flat and colorless. In the past I had no great inspiration; I merely felt there were things I'd learned that I needed to pass on. Co-authored books were entirely a different story. In those cases I always felt that others had more of the content to share, and my role was that of a scribe, rather than a true contributor.

"I am engaged in a new writing project, however, which is quite different from what I've done before. A few years ago, I swore I'd written my last sentence, except for letters and e-mail to friends and colleagues, but several folks told me that I had at least one more book left in me—one which had to be highly personal and quite intimate. Therefore, I've begun work on a book I hope to present to my youngest daughter on her sixteenth birthday. The working title is *Roads Taken.* I'm not sure it will ever be published, but it really doesn't matter."

BIOGRAPHICAL/CRITICAL SOURCES:

PERIODICALS

Free Enterprise, April, 1978.

*   *   *

SPEAR, Benjamin
  See HENISCH, Heinz K.

*   *   *

STERN, Richard Martin 1915-

PERSONAL: Born March 17, 1915, in Fresno, CA; son of Charles Frank (a banker) and True (Aiken) Stern; married Dorothy Helen Atherton, December 20, 1937; children: (adopted) Mary Elisabeth Emery (Mrs. Robert Michael Vinton). *Education:* Attended Harvard College (now Harvard University), 1933-36.

ADDRESSES: Home—Rte. 9, Box 55, Santa Fe, NM 87505. *Agent*—Brandt & Brandt, 1501 Broadway, New York, NY 10036.

CAREER: Writer. Hearst Corp., New York City, trainee, 1936-37; worked at Exhibitors Art and Design, San Francisco, CA, 1938, and Boothe Fruit Co., Modesto, CA, 1938-39; Lockheed Aircraft Corp., Burbank, CA, manufacturing engineer, 1940-45.

MEMBER: Authors Guild, Authors League of America, Mystery Writers of America (director, 1961-63, 1965-66, 1969-70; vice-president, 1962-63; president, 1971), Crime Writers Association, Press Club (London), Quien Sabe Club.

AWARDS, HONORS: Edgar Allan Poe Award for best first mystery novel, Mystery Writers of America, 1958, for *The Bright Road to Fear.*

WRITINGS:

The Bright Road to Fear, Ballantine (New York City), 1958.
Suspense: Four Short Novels, Ballantine, 1959.
The Search for Tabitha Carr, Scribner (New York City), 1960.
These Unlucky Deeds, Scribner, 1961, published as *Quidnunc County,* Eyre & Spottiswoode (London), 1961.
High Hazard, Scribner, 1962.
Cry Havoc, Scribner, 1963.
Right Hand Opposite, Scribner, 1964.
I Hide, We Seek, Scribner, 1965.
The Kessler Legacy, Scribner, 1967.
Merry Go Round, Scribner, 1969.
Brood of Eagles, World Publishing (Cleveland), 1969.
Manuscript for Murder, Scribner, 1970.
Murder in the Walls, Scribner, 1971.
You Don't Need an Enemy, Scribner, 1972.
Stanfield Harvest, World Publishing, 1972.
Death in the Snow, Scribner, 1973.
The Tower, McKay (New York City), 1973.
Power, McKay, 1974.
The Will, Doubleday (New York City), 1976.
Snowbound Six, Doubleday, 1977.
Flood, Doubleday, 1979.
The Big Bridge, Doubleday, 1982.
Wildfire, Secker & Warburg (London), 1985, Norton (New York City), 1986.
Tsunami, Norton, 1988.
Tangled Murders, Pocket Books (New York City), 1989.
(Contributor) *The Rigby File,* Hodder & Stoughton (London), 1989.
Missing Man, Pocket Books, 1990.
Interloper, Pocket Books, 1990.

Contributor of short stories to periodicals, including *Saturday Evening Post, Collier's, Cosmopolitan, Argosy, Good Housekeeping,* and *McCall's.* Member of editorial board, *Writer,* 1976—. Nine of Stern's novels have been published as *Reader's Digest* Condensed Books. A collection of Stern's manuscripts is housed at the Mugar Memorial Library at Boston University.

ADAPTATIONS: The Tower was filmed in 1974 by Twentieth Century-Fox Film Corp. as *The Towering Inferno.*

SIDELIGHTS: Richard Martin Stern has written both mysteries and disaster novels. He is considered to be, Dorothy B. Hughes notes in the *St. James Guide to Crime and Mystery Writers,* "one of the most inventive and respected writers of the American mystery." His disaster novel *The Tower,* the story of a fire in a skyscraper, formed the basis for the successful film *The Towering Inferno,* which launched a cycle of disaster films in the 1970s.

Stern began as a magazine writer in the 1950s, his stories appearing in a variety of leading periodicals of the time. Following the success of his first mystery novel, *The Bright Road to Fear,* which won an Edgar Allan Poe Award from the Mystery Writers of America, Stern wrote a series of mysteries throughout the 1960s. A world traveler, Stern incorporates places he has visited as backgrounds in his many novels. "His backgrounds," Hughes writes, "are as important as the story lines of his plots."

In the 1970s, Stern wrote *The Tower,* the story of a disastrous fire in a newly-constructed skyscraper. The novel's success as a book and film led him to write a number of other stories in the disaster genre. Speaking of *Wildfire,* a disaster novel about a horrendous forest fire in a national park, Hughes notes that "Stern, once again, writes a gripping suspenseful novel in which his characters are driven to a state of abject terror."

Summarizing Stern's work, Hughes finds that his "style is not influenced by fads and fancies. He writes the prose of an educated, intelligent man, who has a keen curiosity as to the whys of events, a curiosity only to be satisfied by solving the puzzles propounded."

Stern explains in an article for *Writer* magazine that a writer's "goal should be that long after the facts of the story have faded in memory, at least some of your characters in the tale will remain in the readers' minds, and if you have done your job well and made the story powerful enough, you can hope that the readers may find themselves wondering how they might have behaved under similar circumstances."

Stern once told *CA:* "To paraphrase John D. MacDonald, when you spend your life doing what you would rather do than anything else—write stories—and you are paid for it, that is a license to steal."

BIOGRAPHICAL/CRITICAL SOURCES:

BOOKS

St. James Guide to Crime and Mystery Writers, 4th edition, St. James Press (Detroit), 1996.

PERIODICALS

Armchair Detective, spring, 1990, p. 251.
Books and Bookmen, June, 1975.
New York Times, October 19, 1973.
New York Times Book Review, May 16, 1971; July 4, 1976.
Observer, February 8, 1970.
Publishers Weekly, December 15, 1989, p. 61.
Times Literary Supplement, March 5, 1970.
Washington Post Book World, May 20, 1973.
Writer, June, 1996, p. 7.

*   *   *

STEWART, Will
 See WILLIAMSON, John Stewart

*   *   *

STOCKLEY, Grif 1944-

PERSONAL: Born October 9, 1944, in Memphis, TN; son of Griffin J. (a farmer and in business) and Temple (Wall) Stockley; children: one daughter. *Education:* Southwestern at Memphis, B.A., 1965; University of Arkansas, J.D., 1972.

ADDRESSES: Office—Central Arkansas Legal Services, 209 West Capitol, Little Rock, AR 72201. *Agent*—Charlotte Gordon, 235 East 22nd St., New York, NY 10010.

CAREER: Writer. Peace Corps, rural community development organizer in Colombia, 1965-67; Central Arkansas Legal Services, Little Rock, AR, attorney, 1972—. University of Arkansas at Little Rock, adjunct professor, c. 1987-92, and visiting professor of law. *Military service:* Served in U.S. Army for two years during late 1960s.

WRITINGS:

Expert Testimony, Summit Books (New York City), 1991.
Probable Cause, Simon & Schuster (New York City), 1992.
Religious Conviction, Simon & Schuster, 1994.
Illegal Motion, Simon & Schuster, 1995.
Blind Judgment, Simon & Schuster, 1997.

SIDELIGHTS: Grif Stockley writes mysteries featuring Gideon Page, an Arkansas defense lawyer. Stockley writes "with wit, irony, and a good lawyer's intimate understanding of the daily life of the defense bar and the dynamics of trial," according to D. A. Ball in *Entertainment Weekly.*

Page's cases have involved a psychologist accused of murder when a patient's electroshock therapy turns deadly (*Probable Cause*), a minister's daughter on trial for killing her husband (*Religious Conviction*), and a white cheerleader who claims she was raped by a black athlete (*Illegal Motion*). In a review of *Religious Conviction,* a *Publishers Weekly* critic notes Stockley's "jauntily colloquial prose" and concludes: "He has produced a high-quality thriller with more on its mind than whodunit." Speaking of *Illegal Motion,* Wes Lukowsky in *Booklist* states: "Stockley, himself an Arkansas attorney, presents his story with compassion, humor, and the moral ambiguity of the real world. Right and wrong are seldom clear cut, and the likable Page ekes out a living shading the gray areas for whoever pays the bill."

Stockley once told *CA:* "Thus far, the fiction that I have been able to get published is derived from much of my own personal experience. The protagonist of both novels, Gideon Page, is a middle-aged attorney in a southern city, which all local readers identify correctly as Little Rock. The core of Gideon's personal relationships revolves around his teenaged daughter Sarah. Though my daughter is now about to leave her teens, Sarah is very much modeled on that relationship. Similarly, in *Expert Testimony* much of the action takes place at the Arkansas State Hospital. For many years I routinely represented clients at that facility. In *Probable Cause,* Gideon represents a psychologist who works at an institution for persons with developmental disabilities. I have had some legal experience in that venue as well. My main impe-

tus for writing mysteries comes from writer Scott Turow's success. After reading *Presumed Innocent,* I felt I was capable of writing a mystery with a southern flavor."

BIOGRAPHICAL/CRITICAL SOURCES:

PERIODICALS

Booklist, January 1, 1994, p. 808; August, 1995, p. 1932.
Entertainment Weekly, August 18, 1995, p. 51.
Publishers Weekly, December 20, 1993, p. 54; June 19, 1995, p. 53.
Time, January 11, 1993, p. 52.

* * *

**STURTZEL, Howard A(llison) 1894-1985
(Paul Annixter)**

PERSONAL: Born June 25, 1894, in Minneapolis, MN; died November, 1985; son of Edward John and Carrie E. (Pirkiss) Sturtzel; married Jane Levington Comfort (a writer), February 18, 1920. *Education:* Attended Fargo College and North Dakota Agricultural College (now North Dakota State University). *Avocational interests:* Reading, gardening, mountain climbing.

CAREER: Writer since age of nineteen.

WRITINGS:

UNDER PSEUDONYM PAUL ANNIXTER

Wilderness Ways, Penn, 1930.
Swiftwater, Wyn, 1950.
Brought to Cover (story collection), Wyn, 1951.
The Hunting Horn (story collection), Hill & Wang (New York City), 1957.
Pride of Lions (story collection), Hill & Wang, 1960.
Puck of the Dusk, Scribner (New York City), 1970.
The Best Nature Stories of Paul Annixter, Lawrence Hill, 1974.

WITH WIFE, JANET LEVINGTON STURTZEL, UNDER PSEUDONYMS PAUL ANNIXTER AND JANE ANNIXTER; PUBLISHED BY HOLIDAY HOUSE (NEW YORK CITY), EXCEPT AS INDICATED

The Runner, 1956.
Buffalo Chief, 1958.

Horns of Plenty, 1960.
Peace Comes to Castle Oak, Longmans, Green, 1961.
The Phantom Stallion, Golden Press (New York City), 1961.
Trouble at Paintrock, Golden Press, 1962.
Windigo, 1963.
Wagon Scout, 1965.
The Cat That Clumped, 1966.
The Great White, 1966.
Vikan the Mighty, 1969.
Ahmeek, 1970.
White Shell Horse, 1971.
Sea Otter, 1972.
Trumpeter: The Story of a Swan, 1973.
Wapootin, Coward, 1976.
Monkeys and Apes, F. Watts (New York City), 1976.
Brown Rats, Black Rats, Prentice-Hall (Englewood Cliffs, NJ), 1977.
The Year of the She-Grizzly, Coward, 1978.
The Last Monster, Harcourt (San Diego), 1980.

OTHER

Devil of the Woods (story collection), Hill & Wang, 1958.

Contributor of short stories to magazines.

SIDELIGHTS: Howard A. Sturtzel wrote many books and stories about wildlife and human adventures in nature—usually publishing them under the pseudonym Paul Annixter. He also collaborated on many such books with his wife Janet, who used the pseudonym Jane Annixter. "Whether the author writes about crocodiles, dogs, coons, opossums or wild boars, each story is well organized and interesting," approved H. S. Pearson in a *New York Times* review of the short-story collection *Brought to Cover.* J. H. Jackson, writing in the *San Francisco Chronicle,* concurred that "almost any man who has hunted, fished or lived at all in the outdoors will take pleasure in reading" all the stories in the book.

In the novel *Swiftwater,* the author told of the Calloways—father and son trappers, the last of their kind in the north woods of Maine. Both have a deep love for the creatures of the wild, and after many trials and tribulations, young Buck Calloway achieves his dream of establishing a bird sanctuary. *Library Journal* reviewer R. W. Henderson considered *Swiftwater* "a moving plea for conservation," while a *New York Herald Tribune Book Review* contributor assured readers that "Annixter's story brings you close to nature, to the stillness of the forest and

the miracle of the changing seasons. . . . [*Swiftwater*] has a winter morning magic."

In *Puck of the Dusk,* Sturtzel presented the life story of a bat, told in narrative form in vocabulary appropriate for younger readers. M. B. Mason, a reviewer for *Library Journal,* disapproved of the dark-colored pages that were intended to convey the feeling of nocturnal life, but Philip and Phylis Morrison took exception to that view in *Scientific American,* who praised the marriage of text and book design as resulting in "a book of extraordinary harmony" and contended that young readers "might well learn through it to understand and trust the darkness."

"As a very young man," Sturtzel once told *CA,* "I took up a timber claim in northern Minnesota. It was while proving up on the land that I began writing, mostly nature stories about the animals and elements I was up against. Published more than 500 short stories in the period prior to 1950, covering almost all American magazines from the *Saturday Evening Post* down to the pulps. In 1955, my wife and I began collaborating on nature novels for young people. . . . In the main our stories deal with some phase of human and animal interrelation, which offers to our minds a different and deeper sort of heart interest."

BIOGRAPHICAL/CRITICAL SOURCES:

PERIODICALS

Booklist, January 1, 1950; December 1, 1951; May 1, 1957; June 1, 1960.
Bookmark, April, 1950; March, 1960.
Books, November 16, 1930, p. 14.
Book Week, November 6, 1966; March 19, 1967.
Boston Transcript, November 22, 1930, p. 3.
Chicago Sunday Tribune, January 29, 1950, p. 5; October 7, 1951, p. 5.
Christian Science Monitor, February 27, 1971, p. 15.
Christian Spectator, March, 1971.
Cleveland Open Shelf, January, 1931, p. 5.
Horn Book, August, 1957.
Instructor, May, 1974.
Kirkus Reviews, November 1, 1949; July 15, 1951; March 1, 1957; January 1, 1960.
Library Journal, December 1, 1949; April 15, 1950; August, 1951; April 1, 1957; February 15, 1960; November 15, 1970.
New York Herald Tribune Book Review, February 12, 1950, p. 13.

New York Times, January 22, 1950, p. 26; December 16, 1951, p. 17.

New York Times Book Review, May 9, 1965; January 22, 1967.

San Francisco Chronicle, March 12, 1950, p. 19; October 16, 1951, p. 16; September 15, 1957, p. 22.

Saturday Review, December 19, 1931; September 19, 1970.

Saturday Review of Literature, February 11, 1950.

Scientific American, December, 1970.

Times Literary Supplement, November 26, 1931, p. 949.

Wilson Library Bulletin, December, 1930; February, 1950; May, 1957.*

* * *

SYMONS, (Hugh Brennan) Scott 1933-

PERSONAL: Born July 13, 1933, in Toronto, Ontario, Canada; son of Harry L. Symons; marriage ended. *Education:* University of Toronto, B.A., 1955; King's College, Cambridge, M.A.; Sorbonne, University of Paris, Diplome d'Etudes Superieures.

ADDRESSES: Home—Newfoundland, Canada. *Office*—University of Toronto, Toronto, Ontario, Canada.

CAREER: Writer. Journalist with the *Toronto Telegram,* Toronto, Ontario, 1957-58, *Quebec City Chronicle-Telegraph,* Quebec City, Quebec, 1958-59, and *La Presse,* Montreal, Quebec, 1960-61; University of Toronto, professor of fine arts, 1961-65. Worked as curator of Sigmund Samuel Canadiana Collection and Canadiana Gallery of Royal Ontario Museum, Toronto; taught contemporary art at University of Pennsylvania. Editorialist and reporter for various Canadian journals. Consultant to Smithsonian Institution.

AWARDS, HONORS: Beta Sigma Phi award for best first Canadian novel, 1968; senior arts grant from Canada Council, 1973.

WRITINGS:

NOVELS

Combat Journal of Place d'Armes, McClelland & Stewart (Toronto), 1967.

Civic Square, McClelland & Stewart, 1969.

Helmet of Flesh, New American Library (New York City), 1986.

OTHER

Heritage: A Romantic Look at Early Canadian Furniture, New York Graphic Society (Greenwich, CT), 1971.

Contributor to periodicals, including *Montreal Presse, Montreal Nouveau Journal, Toronto Telegram,* and *Quebec Chronicle Telegram.* A collection of Symon's unpublished diaries and correspondence is housed at the library of Trinity College, University of Toronto.

SIDELIGHTS: Scott Symons is not among the best known Canadian authors, but he has won the reputation of a formidable writer whose works provoke a strong response. According to *Dictionary of Literary Biography* contributor Charles Taylor, Symons "has attacked virtually every major aspect of modern Canada. Yet he has also found much to celebrate—including his country's British and French traditions, homosexual and heterosexual love, birds and flowers, and the mystery of the Eucharist—exploring these topics with a ferocious joy."

Symons has become something of a cult figure for many Canadian intellectuals and university students because of his work and his unconventional lifestyle. He was born in Toronto to a family of English, Irish, and German background. His cultured, socially respectable family was staunchly British, and Symons received an elite education at two private schools, the University of Toronto, King's College, and the Sorbonne. For a time, he seemed destined to become a leader of the Canadian cultural establishment. "But Symons grew increasingly distressed at the limitations of his society, concluding that it offered little scope for either reverence or passion," reported Taylor. "On one level, English-Canadians had become little more than second-rate Americans . . . succumbing to liberal doctrines of material progress. On another level, . . . they had become victims of a Calvinist rigidity and had (quite literally) lost their ability to touch."

In the mid-1960s, Symons gave up social respectability, job security, and his marriage to move to Montreal and pursue a writing career. His first novel, *Combat Journal of Place d'Armes,* was an autobiographical tale of a man who rejects his background and pursues his vision in old Montreal, finding joy both in Notre Dame Cathedral and in the arms of male prostitutes. Numerous critics disparaged the book, but *Place D'Armes* became an underground classic, and won the Beta Sigma Phi award for the best first novel by a Canadian author.

By the time *Place D'Armes* was in print, Symons had begun a six-year journey with a young male lover that ranged from Mexico to Newfoundland and the lumber camps of British Columbia. During this period, he completed his second novel, *Civic Square,* described by Taylor as "a prolix work in which the author ranges around his native Toronto, addresses the reader directly in lengthy letters, and describes his struggle to achieve psychic and physical harmony ('I want my balls and my brains working together') in a society ruled by 'Blandmen.'" *Civic Square* was enthusiastically received by some critics, but it was published only in a limited edition and was never available to the general reading public.

Symon's North American wanderings also yielded *Heritage,* in which he used photographs of early Canadian furniture to illustrate his point that Canadians "had potent and civilized traditions which they had largely betrayed," explains Taylor. "As usual, the prose is pungent, but the picture-book format compelled Symons to abandon the prolixity and self-indulgence of his novels."

In the 1970s, Symons returned to Mexico and on to Morocco. He also began work on the first volume of a proposed trilogy. That book, *Helmet of Flesh,* was published in 1986. Like his other novels, it features an autobiographical protagonist who tests himself against society. *Helmet of Flesh* "celebrates the "incarnational mode of being' which he found in North Africa: a world of touch and passion, of harmony between mind and body," confides Taylor. The critic went on to say that *Helmet of Flesh* was received as a book that "shows enormous growth in maturity and craftsmanship and is a work of considerable stature."

BIOGRAPHICAL/CRITICAL SOURCES:

BOOKS

Dictionary of Literary Biography, Volume 53: *Canadian Writers Since 1960, First Series,* Gale (Detroit), 1986.
Gibson, Graeme, *Eleven Canadian Novelists,* Anasi (Toronto), 1973, pp. 301-324.
Taylor, Charles, *Six Journeys: A Canadian Pattern,* Anasi, 1977, pp. 191-243.

PERIODICALS

Canadian Forum, May, 1967.

T-V

TARN, Nathaniel 1928-

PERSONAL: Born June 30, 1928, in Paris, France; son of Mendel Myer (some sources say Marcel) and Yvonne Cecile Leah (Suchar) Tarn; married Patricia Renate Cramer, 1956 (marriage ended); married Janet Rodney, 1982; children: (first marriage) Andrea, Marc. *Ethnicity:* "Earth." *Education:* Cambridge University, B.A. (with honors), 1948, M.A., 1952; graduate study at Sorbonne, University of Paris, 1949-51; University of Chicago, M.A., 1952, Ph.D., 1957; additional graduate study at London School of Economics and Political Science.

ADDRESSES: Home—P. O. Box 871, Tesuque, NM 87574. *Email*—kandahar@worldnet.att.net.

CAREER: Writer. Anthropologist in Guatemala, Burma, and other countries, 1952-79; Jonathan Cape Ltd. (publishers), London, founder and director of Cape Goliard Press and editor of Cape Editions, 1967-69; Rutgers University, Rutgers College, New Brunswick, NJ, professor of comparative literature, 1970-84, professor emeritus, 1984—. Lecturer at colleges and universities, including University of Chicago and University of London, 1952-67; visiting professor at State University of New York at Buffalo and Princeton University, 1969-70.

AWARDS, HONORS: Guinness Prize for poetry, 1963; Wenner Gren Foundation fellowship in anthropology and literature, 1979-81; Commonwealth of Pennsylvania fellowship in poetry, 1983; Rockefeller Foundation fellowship, Bellagio, Italy, 1988.

WRITINGS:

Old Savage/Young City (poems), J. Cape (London), 1964, Random House (New York City), 1965.

(With Richard Murphy and Jon Silkin) *Penguin Modern Poets No. Seven: Richard Murphy, Jon Silkin, Nathaniel Tarn,* Penguin, 1965.

(Translator) Pablo Neruda, *The Heights of Macchu Picchu,* J. Cape (London), 1966, Farrar, Straus (New York City), 1967.

Where Babylon Ends (poems), J. Cape, 1967, Grossman, 1968.

(Editor and co-translator) *Con Cuba: An Anthology of Cuban Poetry of the Last Sixty Years,* Grossman, 1969.

The Beautiful Contradictions (poems), J. Cape, 1969, Random House, 1970.

October (poems), Trigram Press (London), 1969.

(Translator) Victor Segalen, *Stelae,* Unicorn Press (Santa Barbara, CA), 1969.

The Silence (poems), M'Arte (Milano), 1970.

(Editor) Pablo Neruda, *Selected Poems,* J. Cape, 1970, Delacorte (New York City), 1972.

A Nowhere for Vallejo (poems), Random House, 1971.

Lyrics for the Bride of God; Section: The Artemision (poems; also see below), Tree Books (Berkeley, CA), 1973.

The Persephones, Christopher's Books (Santa Barbara, CA), 1974.

Lyrics for the Bride of God (poems), New Directions (New York City), 1975.

Narrative of This Fall, Black Sparrow Press (Los Angeles), 1975.

The House of Leaves (poems), Black Sparrow Press (Santa Barbara, CA), 1976.

The Microcosm, Membrane Press (Milwaukee, WI), 1977.

Birdscapes with Seaside, Black Sparrow Press, 1978.

(With wife, Janet Rodney) *From Alaska: The Ground of Our Great Admiration of Nature,* Permanent Press (New York City), 1978.

(With Rodney) *The Forest: In Part* (poems), Perishable Press (Mt. Horeb, WI), 1978.

(With Rodney) *Atitlan/Alashka,* Brillig (Boulder, CO), 1979.

The Land Songs: Further Annotations from Baja California (poems), Blue Guitar Books (London), 1979.

Weekends in Mexico (poems), Oxus Press (London), 1982.

The Desert Mothers (poems), Salt-Works Press, 1984.

At the Western Gates (poems), Tooth of Time Press (Santa Fe, NM), 1985.

Palenque: Selected Poems (poems), Oasis Press (London), 1986.

Seeing America First (poems), Coffee House Press (Minneapolis, MN), 1989.

(Translator) Pablo Neruda, *Four Odes, One Song,* Labyrinth Editions (Honolulu, HI), 1990.

Views from the Weaving Mountains: Selected Essays in Poetics and Anthropology, University of New Mexico Press (Albuquerque), 1991.

Flying the Body: Poems, 1991-92, Arundel Press (Los Angeles), 1993.

(Editor) Natasha Tarn, *Multitude of One,* Grenfell Press (New York City), 1993.

(With Martin Prechtel) *Scandals in the House of Birds: Shamans and Priests on Lake Atitlan,* Marsilio Publishers (New York City), 1998.

Author and reader of *Nathaniel Tarn Reading His Poems with Comment in the Recording Laboratory, March 23, 1971,* and of *Robin Skelton and Nathaniel Tarn Reading and Discussing Their Poems in the Coolidge Auditorium, March 22, 1971.* Contributor to many anthologies in the United States, including *Talking Poetry,* edited by Lee Bartlett, University of New Mexico Press, 1987; *American Poetry since 1950,* edited by E. Weinberger, Marsilio (New York City), 1996; and *Poems for the Millenium,* edited by J. Rothenberg, University of California Press (Berkeley), 1998. Contributor to anthologies in France, Italy, Russia, China, Mexico, Spain, and the Netherlands, including *Poeti Inglesi del 900,* edited by Roberto Sanesi, *Anthologie de la Poesie Americaine,* edited by Jacques Roubaud, and *Levenstekens en Doodsinjalen,* edited by Hans Ten Berge. Contributor to periodicals, including *Times Literary Supplement, Observer, New York Times, Credences, Temblor,* and *Sagetrieb.* Contributing editor, *Conjunc-*

tions, PO&SIE (Paris), *Courrier du Centre International de Poesie* (Brussels), and *Modern Poetry in Translation* (London).

WORK IN PROGRESS: "*Architextures,* a book of prose poems; *Auto-Anthropology,* to be a thematic study of the object Tarn treated as an anthropological entity; a second volume on Atitlan; a selected poems; two volumes of poems."

SIDELIGHTS: Nathaniel Tarn's multi-cultural interests are seen in his early work as an anthropologist and continue in his work as an internationally acclaimed translator, poet, and critic. For his views on "the state of the art of poetry in this complex society," which is, as he told *CA,* "a most complex business," he recommends the essay "Dr. Jekyll, the Anthropologist, Emerges and Marches into the Notebooks of Mr. Hyde, the Poet" in the literary journal *Conjunctions.* His contribution to *American Poetry,* the essay "Child as Father to the Man," he says, also gives insight into his writings.

Important influences on his poetry among moderns include Ezra Pound, William Carlos Williams, Hugh MacDiarmid, Charles Olson, Robert Duncan, and Jack Spicer. In addition, poets from many countries—Andre Breton, Guillame Apollinaire, Arthur Rimbaud, Fernando Pessoa, and Rainer Maria Rilke—have shaped his poetic vision. Tarn's characteristic writing style is eclectic, having the inclusiveness and open forms of his masters. His poems refer to the myths, philosophies, political concerns, plant and animal life, and landscapes known to people from many nations and time periods. In *The Beautiful Contradictions,* Tarn states his personal objective: "It is up to me to call into being everything that is." Like Whitman's style, Tarn's style "is a very original mixture of the high and the low, the deliberately elevated and the humorously familiar," observes a *Times Literary Supplement* reviewer. Writing about *Lyrics for the Bride of God* in *Harper's Bookletter,* Hayden Carruth remarks that "Tarn has attempted . . . a poem in the grand modern matter, after Pound's *Cantos* or Williams' *Paterson* and . . . he has largely succeeded." Of the same book, a *Choice* critic, notes that in this work, too, Tarn sounds "distinctly like Whitman, a Whitman writing about America in the 1970's. But his style is strikingly different and idiosyncratic, and his poems dazzle with a kaleidoscope of bright images."

A number of critics respond negatively to Tarn's long sentences and catalogues. As a *Times Literary*

Supplement reviewer puts it in a review of *The Beautiful Contradictions,* "This is the poetry of a man who has come through a tremendous foreign reading list and lived to get it all mixed up for us." Other critics, however, respond more favorably. Of a later book, *The House of Leaves, Times Literary Supplement* contributor D. M. Thomas comments, "There was always a sense of continental ambition in [Tarn's] work, poems that seemed to wish the pages wider. To read his new collection is a little like flying over America: A Whitmanesque grandiloquence. . . , repetition upon repetition, accretion upon accretion. . . . Much of it is beautiful and true."

For a summary of previous stages in Tarn's development as a poet, *American Book Review* contributor Rochelle Ratner recommends *Atitlan/Alashka:* "Each previous book that Tarn published has been such a complete vision in itself that we tend to think it is his *only* vision. *Atitlan* not only shows the scope of Tarn's field, it shows the fusion of his various periods." Theodore Enslin remarks in the same issue of the *American Book Review* that in addition to showing the width of Tarn's range, this collection also shows "how an omnivorous appetite is controlled by a discriminating intelligence, at the same time that the rush of highly colored and charged language fills the landscape with both form and that form's detail." In *At the Western Gates,* published in 1986, Tarn adds new resonance to his images while giving "free play to all the senses," observes a *Voice Literary Supplement* reviewer, who concludes, "with a prophetic sense of sure direction, his new poems move beyond their surface splendor into the depths beneath."

Of the later book *At the Western Gates, Artspace* contributor Gene Frumkin comments, "while these poems are shorter and sing more, on the whole, than Tarn's usual pattern of work, the desert does make its appearance; neither positive nor negative in itself, it brings to the poetry a doubleness, an ambiguity which, as it develops, gives us a sure sign of this poet's mastery. Tarn is thoughtful, religiously, and he is a man whose concern lies with the total culture of any place; the songs of his birds and of his whales are the up and down of a cosmos, his encompassing effort to construct lyricism not only as music but as the music of mind's flow through the mystery of nature." Tarn's next book, *The Desert Mothers,* presents longer poems again, but Frumkin relates that the ideas the poems develop are more significant than their length.

Tarn told *CA* that reviews often overemphasize his style, which he sees "as only one facet of the work as if there were no other facets. This concerns the 'rambling,' 'long sentences,' 'grandiloquent,' 'omnivorous' aspect. I believe that, if one looks at the books, there is an alternation between this aspect and another which is far tighter and more controlled. Also between lines, spread and compression. Among controlled, short-lined, simple works, I would place *October;* much of *The House of Leaves;* much of *A Nowhere for Vallejo;* and almost all of *At the Western Gates.* The poems in *Seeing America First* are extremely compressed: seventy poems, each one of which has the exact same number of spaces in each line *when typed* so that the poems are perfectly rectangular, justified on each side, looking *like* prose poems, but *not* prose poems. One cannot be less rambling than that!"

Explaining why he works in both shorter and longer forms, Tarn added, "The complexity/simplicity alternation responds to a belief I have that the fundamental contradiction in the poem's role in society is exasperated today more than at any other time in 'modernist/postmodernist' history. For the craft to progress, the poem has to improve on a long tradition of complexity, difficulty, even obscurity if it is to 'make it new' as Pound prescribed. On the other hand, the whole tradition has of late made it more and more difficult for poetry to find any kind of readership except among other poets. One of the ways of dealing with this is to write (at least) two kinds of poetry so as to give the work as a whole the optimal chance of reaching one or more publics."

Discussing his work in an entry for the *Contemporary Authors Autobiography Series (CAAS),* Tarn cited "a lifelong interest in religions and symbolic systems—primarily, but not exclusively, Classical, Judaeo-Christian, Mayan and Buddhist—has been a very powerful motivating force. A strong sense of the interrelationships of man and *polis* and a dark view of man's inhumanity to man have also provided the 'matter' of much poetry." Looking back over the years, he remembered: "In childhood and youth a passionate involvement with nature—especially ornithological and vegetal—occasioned many poems. Over the years, this has to some extent given way to an inextinguishable romance with culture in the form of great human works in any medium (the arts, architecture, technology) and a theoretical interest in the interplay between natural and civil ecology and conservation: that some can even discuss these apart from each other seems to me an impossible aberration."

Tarn also discussed his concern about the declining status of the poet and poetry in "our increasingly illiterate culture. At a very banal level, almost all of us poets of my age sense some kind of great difference between the life we used to have and the one we lead now. I dare say I was more fortunate than many in my beginnings, but I treasured the sense of having a publishing house, an editor, the occasional lunch, the pretense that one's vocation was of use to the world." Tarn noted that even as late as the 1960s, there was "extraordinary interest in poetry; the possibility of substantial and extremely well-attended readings; the sense of a potential (probably illusory) for significant political action. . . . All that began to give way—the very day, I believe, when the Vietnam War ended. Only the very smallest number of 'known,' 'famed,' 'noted,' 'awarded' bards now enjoys such luxuries. The world of publishing, sold out to corporatism, is deliquescing beyond all recognition. The culture overproduces 'poets' in the 'creative writing' schools while at the same time underproducing readers throughout the educational system at all levels."

BIOGRAPHICAL/CRITICAL SOURCES:

BOOKS

Bartlett, Lee, *Nathaniel Tarn, A Descriptive Bibliography,* McFarland, 1987.
Bartlett, editor, *Talking Poetry: Conversations in the Workshop with Contemporary Poets,* University of New Mexico Press, 1987.
Bartlett, *The Sun is but a Morning Star: Essays on Western American Literature,* University of New Mexico Press, 1989.
Contemporary Authors Autobiography Series, Volume 16, Gale (Detroit), 1992.
Fisch, Harold, *The Dual Image,* [London], 1971.
McQuade, Molly, *An Unsentimental Education: Writers and Chicago,* University of Chicago Press, 1995.
Tarn, Nathaniel, *The Beautiful Contradictions,* J. Cape, 1969, Random House, 1970.

PERIODICALS

American Book Review, Volume 2, number 5, 1980.
American Poetry Review, Volume 1, number 2, 1984.
Artspace, Volume 5, number 1, 1985-86.
Boundary 2, Volume 4, number 1, 1975.
Choice, November, 1975; April, 1977.

Conjunctions, Number 6, 1984.
Credences, Number 4, 1977.
Harper's Bookletter, October 13, 1975.
Judaism, fall, 1965.
Library Journal, June 15, 1965; April 15, 1971.
New York Times Book Review, September 25, 1966; May 21, 1967; May 7, 1972; September 7, 1975.
Poetry, June, 1968.
Saturday Review, October 9, 1965; December 13, 1968.
Spectator, January 1, 1965.
Sulfur, Number 14, 1985/86.
Times (London), April 6, 1968; June 7, 1969.
Times Literary Supplement, January 7, 1965; October 12, 1967; August 7, 1969; April 9, 1970; August 4, 1972; May 20, 1977.
Voice Literary Supplement, February, 1986.

* * *

TAYLOR, Eleanor Ross 1920-

PERSONAL: Born June 30, 1920, in North Carolina; daughter of Fred E. and Jennie (Lilly) Ross; married Peter Taylor (a writer), June 4, 1943; children: Katherine, Peter. *Education:* University of North Carolina at Greensboro, B.A., 1940; additional study at Vanderbilt University, 1942-43.

ADDRESSES: Home—1841 Wayside Pl., Charlottesville, VA 22903.

CAREER: High school teacher of English in North Carolina schools, 1940-42, 1944-45; worked in various public libraries in North Carolina and Tennessee, 1943-44; University of North Carolina, Greensboro, reserve librarian, 1945-46; University of Virginia, Charlottesville, teacher of poetry writing, 1977.

AWARDS, HONORS: National Book Award nomination, 1960, for *Wilderness of Ladies;* D. Litt. from University of North Carolina at Greensboro, 1976.

WRITINGS:

Wilderness of Ladies (poetry), McDowell, Obolensky, 1960.
Welcome Eumenides (poetry), Braziller (New York City), 1972.

New and Selected Poems, Wright (Winston-Salem, NC), 1983.

Days Going/Days Coming Back, University of Utah Press (Salt Lake City), 1991.

Contributor of poems to journals, including *Sewanee Review* and *Southern Poetry Review.* Poetry editor, *Shenandoah* magazine, 1977.

SIDELIGHTS: Eleanor Ross Taylor's poems spring from her experiences as a Southerner and as a woman. Her first book, *Wilderness of Ladies,* attracted a small but loyal band of admirers, including Randall Jarrell. Adrienne Rich observes that many of the poems in this collection of verse "speak of the underground life of women, the Southern white Protestant woman in particular, the woman-writer, the woman in the family, coping, hoarding, preserving, observing, keeping up appearances, seeing through the myths and hypocrisies, nursing the sick, conspiring with sister-women, possessed of a will to survive and to see others survive."

Twelve years elapsed between the publication of *Wilderness of Ladies* and *Welcome Eumenides.* In the ensuing years the women's liberation movement had gained ground, which helped to create a larger audience for Taylor's poetry. *Welcome Eumenides* received accolades from a number of critics. Erica Jong finds Taylor's depictions of women striking: "In her poems about women, she often seems to be concerned with the stripping away of outward roles that hide a woman's true identity even from herself." But Taylor's poems were not extolled merely because they were topical; commentators also admired her poetic techniques. A reviewer for *Virginia Quarterly Review* notes that "there is an intense reality in her images, a firmness and strength in her style." Taylor's poems "set their own standard for honesty and wit, for rueful downrightness, for sparkle and restraint few other poets reach," Robert Mazzocco writes.

Rich lavishes praise on Ross and *Welcome Eumenides* in the *New York Times Book Review.* "What I find compelling in the poems of Eleanor Taylor, besides the authority and originality of her language, is the underlying sense of how the conflicts of imaginative and intelligent women have driven them on, lashed them into genius or madness, how the home-nursing, the household administration, the patience and skill in relationships acquired at such expense in a family-centered life, became an essential part of the strength

of a woman . . . but at a tremendous price." Rich finds the title poem to be the most compelling of a strong collection. It is written in the voice of Florence Nightingale and refers to the heroic nurse's days in the Crimean War. Rich calls it "densely woven and refrained" and declares that "Taylor has brought together the waste of women in society and the waste of men in ward and twisted them inseparably."

Taylor's *New and Selected Poems* contained two poems described by a *Virginia Quarterly Review* writer and Alan Williamson in *Boston Review* as her very best: "The Ribbon to Norwood" and "Rachel Plummer's Dream." The *Virginia Quarterly Review* contributor comments that "Mrs. Taylor's ambitious poetry, always rather cryptic, has become even more elliptical of late. . . . So unrelenting are the demands of her poetry on the reader's imagination that to read it as it must be read is to feel oneself a poet." Williamson names "Rachel Plummer's Dream," which tells of a pioneer woman kidnapped by Indians, as "perhaps the best of the many contemporary poem-parables about woman as survivor and self-discoverer, because it is the strangest and the least predictable."

Seeking to describe Taylor's verse and the poet herself, Mazzocco arrives at this explanation: "Taylor is a little like a Southern belle who has uncharacteristically read all the big books, thought all the gray thoughts, who is a bit fearful perhaps of expressing grief or depth of the cruel chemical wit of which she is capable, yet who, against 'cyclonic gust and chilly rain,' expresses them forthrightly anyway."

BIOGRAPHICAL/CRITICAL SOURCES:

BOOKS

Contemporary Literary Criticism, Gale (Detroit), Volume 5, 1976.

PERIODICALS

Boston Review, August, 1986, p. 12.
Choice, March, 1973, p. 99.
Library Journal, April 15, 1972., p. 1442.
New York Review of Books, April 3, 1975.
New York Times Book Review, July 2, 1972, p. 3.
Parnassus, fall/winter, 1974, pp. 77-88.
Virginia Quarterly Review, autumn, 1972; winter, 1985, p. 26.

TAYLOR, Elizabeth 1912-1975

PERSONAL: Born July 3, 1912, in Reading, Berkshire, England; died of cancer, November 19, 1975; daughter of Oliver and Elsie (Fewtrell) Coles; married John William Kendall Taylor (in confectionary business), March 11, 1936; children: Renny (son), Joanna (Mrs. David Routledge). *Education:* Attended the Abbey School, Reading. *Politics:* Labour. *Religion:* None. *Avocational interests:* Travel in Greece.

CAREER: Writer. Worked as a governess and in a library.

MEMBER: PEN, Society of Authors.

WRITINGS:

At Mrs. Lippincote's, P. Davies, 1945, Knopf (New York City), 1946.
Palladian, P. Davies, 1946, Knopf, 1947, reprinted, Virago (New York City), 1985.
A View of the Harbour, Knopf, 1949, reprinted with a new afterword by Robert Liddell, Virago, 1987.
A Wreath of Roses, Knopf, 1949, reprinted, Penguin (New York City), 1987.
A Game of Hide-and-Seek, Knopf, 1951, reprinted, Virago, 1986.
The Sleeping Beauty, Viking (New York City), 1953, reprinted with a new introduction by Susannah Clapp, Dial (New York City), 1983.
Hester Lilly: Twelve Short Stories, Viking, 1954 (published in England as *Hester Lilly and Other Stories,* P. Davies, 1954, reprinted with anew introduction by A. L. Barker, Virago, 1990).
Angel, Viking, 1957.
The Blush and Other Stories, P. Davies, 1958, Viking, 1959, reprinted with a new introduction by Paul Bailey, Virago, 1987.
In a Summer Season, Viking, 1961.
The Soul of Kindness, Viking, 1964, reprinted with a new introduction by Paul Bailey, Virago (London), 1983.
A Dedicated Man and Other Stories, Viking, 1965.
Mossy Trotter (for children), Harcourt, 1967.
The Wedding Group, Viking, 1968.
(Contributor) J. Burnley, editor, *Penguin Modern Stories 6,* Penguin, 1970.
Mrs. Palfrey at the Claremont, Viking, 1971, reprinted with a new introduction by Paul Bailey, Dial, 1983.
The Devastating Boys and Other Stories, Viking, 1972.

Blaming, Viking, 1976.
Dangerous Calm: The Selected Stories of Elizabeth Taylor, Virago (London), 1995.

Contributor of short stories to *Harper's, New Yorker,* and *Vogue.*

ADAPTATIONS: "A Dedicated Man" and *Mrs. Palfrey at the Claremont* were both adapted for television.

SIDELIGHTS: Shortly before Elizabeth Taylor's death, a *Times Literary Supplement* critic called her one of "the four or five most distinguished living practitioners of the art of the short story in the English-speaking world." Other reviewers wrote similarly of Taylor's talents as a short story writer and a novelist. In the *New York Times Book Review* Martin Levin referred to the author as "a pastel stylist," and a *Harper's* reviewer noted, "Taylor couldn't write an inelegant sentence if she tried and her prose is a delight." In *Library Journal,* Elizabeth Thalman once listed the "literary qualities that have won . . . Taylor a devoted following." According to Thalman these were "irony, humor, artful structuring and stylistic grace." Despite such consistent praise, however, Taylor remains relatively obscure. *Dictionary of Literary Biography* contributor K. M. Stemmler theorized that this is because of the quiet nature of the author's life and work.

As a young woman, Taylor worked as a governess and a librarian; after her marriage, she settled into the predictable routine she most preferred. "I dislike much travel or change of environment, and prefer the days . . . to come round almost the same, week after week," she was quoted as saying in the *New York Herald Tribune Book Review.* Her writing reflects this attitude, usually focusing on the routine details of everyday life. This fondness for exploring domestic life and relationships has led some reviewers to compare her to Jane Austen.

Yet Stemmler commented: "While Taylor may have been influenced by Austen's depiction of characters' relationships or even Austen's style, Taylor's work deals more directly with the ironies of relationships." The critic found that themes of isolation and class differences recur frequently in the author's work. She further noted: "Despite the polite descriptions reviewers gave of Taylor's work, she was, however subtly, constantly addressing issues of sexuality and sexual tensions between characters."

A common criticism of Taylor's work is that her characters are insufficiently developed. A *Times Literary Supplement* reviewer, for example, wrote that in *The Wedding Group* "Taylor . . . left too much unsaid, too many superb opportunities to expand a scene or a character only half explored." And Joyce Carol Oates, writing in the *Washington Past Book World,* remarked: "The people [Taylor] deals with in her fiction are not people, but characters. They are imagined as interior creations, existing within the confines of their particular stories."

Despite such negative criticism, Guy Davenport noted in *National Review* that Taylor's readers "realize that [they] are in the hands of a real novelist, the kind of analytical and unfoolable mind that invented the novel in the first place." And Stemmler noted: "Instead of presenting characters to the reader, Taylor has a way of bringing the reader to the characters. Thus, an examination of the characters' experiences becomes an examination of the reader's life. . . . Taylor seems intrigued by characters' desires to create or control their own environment and the subsequent failure that accompanies such desires." Summing up the author's work, Alice McCahill wrote in *Best Sellers* that her novels all show "the same keen understanding of people, the ability to share that understanding with her readers, a sense of humor, and a gift and feeling for words."

BIOGRAPHICAL/CRITICAL SOURCES:

BOOKS

Brophy, Brigid, *Don't Never Forget,* Holt (New York City), 1966, pp. 162-64.
Contemporary Literary Criticism, Gale (Detroit), Volume 2, 1974, Volume 4, 1975, Volume 29, 1984.
Dictionary of Literary Biography, Volume 139: *British Short-Fiction Writers, 1945-1980,* Gale, 1994.
Leclercq, Florence, *Elizabeth Taylor,* Twayne (Boston), 1985.
Liddell, Robert, *Elizabeth and Ivy,* Owen (London), 1986.
Pym, Barbara, *A Very Private Eye,* Random House (New York City), 1984.

PERIODICALS

Best Sellers, April 1, 1968.
Encounter, September, 1972.
Harper's, August, 1964.
Isis, January 28, 1959.
Library Journal, February 1, 1968.
National Review, April 23, 1968.
New Republic, November 2, 1953, p. 25; August 22, 1964.
New Statesman, August 27, 1971; August 10, 1973, 192-93.
New York Herald Tribune Book Review, October 11, 1953.
New York Times Book Review, March 31, 1968; April 23, 1972; March 29, 1987.
Review of English Literature, April, 1960.
Spectator, June 14, 1957, pp. 784, 786.
Times Literary Supplement, September 24, 1964; May 9, 1968; August 27, 1971; June 9, 1972; July 1, 1983; November 29, 1985; December 19, 1986; September 18-24, 1987.
Washington Post Book World, April 30, 1972; August 21, 1983, pp. 1-2.
Wilson Library Bulletin, April, 1948, p. 580.

OBITUARIES:

PERIODICALS

London Times, November 21, 1975.*

*   *   *

TERSON, Peter 1932-
(Peter Patterson)

PERSONAL: Birth-given name Peter Patterson; known professionally as Peter Terson; born February 24, 1932, in Tyne, England; son of Peter (a joiner) and Jane (a playwright) Patterson; married Sheila Bailey, May 25, 1955; children: Bruce, Neil, Janie. *Education:* Attended Newcastle-upon-Tyne Technical College and Redland Training College, Bristol, 1952-54.

ADDRESSES: Home—87 Middlebridge St., Romsey, Hampshire, England. *Agent*—Lemon, Unna, and Durbridge, 24 Pottery Lane, Holland Park, London W11 4LZ, England.

CAREER: Worked as draftsman; schoolteacher of physical education, 1953-65; playwright, 1965—. Resident playwright, Victoria Theatre, Stoke-on-Trent, England, 1966-67; writer for National Youth Theatre, 1966. *Military service:* Royal Air Force, 1950-52.

AWARDS, HONORS: Arts Council bursary, 1966; John Whitney Award, 1967; Writers Guild of Great Britain award, 1971; Radio Scriptwriter award, 1972; promising playwright's award from Lord Goodman.

WRITINGS:

UNDER NAME PETER TERSON; PLAYS

A Night to Make the Angels Weep (first produced in Stoke-on-Trent, England, at Victoria Theatre, 1964; produced in London, 1971), published in *New English Dramatists Eleven,* Penguin (London), 1967.

The Mighty Reservoy (first produced in Stoke-on-Trent at Victoria Theatre, 1964; produced in London, 1967), published in *New English Dramatists Fourteen,* Penguin, 1970.

The Rat Run, first produced in Stoke-on-Trent, 1965.

All Honour Mr. Todd, first produced in Stoke-on-Trent at Victoria Theatre, 1966.

I'm in Charge of These Ruins, first produced in Stoke-on-Trent at Victoria Theatre, 1966.

(With others) *Sing an Arful Story,* first produced in Stoke-on-Trent, 1966.

Jock-on-the-Go (adaptation of story, *Jock-at-a-Venture,* by Arnold Bennett), first produced in Stoke-on-Trent, 1966.

Holder Dying, first produced in part in Stoke-on-Trent, 1966.

Zigger Zagger (first produced in London, 1967), published in *Zigger Zagger and Mooney and His Caravans* (also see below), Penguin (Harmondsworth, England), 1970.

(With Joyce Cheeseman) *Clayhanger* (adaptation of the novel Bennett), first produced in Stoke-on-Trent, 1967.

The Ballad of the Artificial Mash, first produced in Stoke-on-Trent at Victoria Theatre, 1967.

The Apprentices (first produced in London, 1968), Penguin, 1970.

The Adventures of Gervase Beckett; or, The Man Who Changed Places (first produced in Stoke-on-Trent, 1969), Eyre Methuean (London), 1973.

Fuzz, first produced in London, 1969.

Inside-Outside, first produced in Nottingham, England, 1970.

The Affair at Bennett's Hill, Worcestershire, first produced in Stoke-on-Trent, 1970.

Spring-Heeled Jack (first produced in London, 1970), published in *Plays and Players,* November, 1970.

The 1861 Whitby Lifeboat Disaster, first produced in Stoke-on-Trent, 1970, produced in London, 1971.

The Knotty: A Musical Documentary, Methuen (London), 1970.

(With Mike Butler) *The Samaritan,* (first produced in Stoke-on-Trent, 1971, produced in London, 1971), published in *Plays and Players,* July, 1971.

Cadium Firty, first produced in London, 1971.

Good Lads at Heart, first produced in London, 1971, produced in New York at Brooklyn Academy of Music Opera House, 1979.

Slip Road Wedding, first produced in Newcastle-upon-Tyne, England, 1971, produced in London, 1971.

Prisoners of the War, first produced in Newcastle-upon-Tyne, 1971.

But Fred, Freud Is Dead (first produced in Stoke-on-Trent, 1972), published in *Plays and Players,* March, 1972.

Moby Dick, first produced in Stoke-on-Trent, 1972.

The Most Cheerful Man, first produced in London, 1973.

Geordie's March, first produced in London, 1973.

The Trip to Florence, first produced in London, 1974.

Lost Yer Tongue?, first produced in Newcastle-upon-Tyne, 1974.

Vince Lays the Carpet, and Fred Erects the Tent, first produced in Stoke-on-Trent, 1975.

The Ballad of Ben Bagot, published in *Prompt Two,* edited by Alan Durband, Hutchinson, 1976.

(With Paul Joyce) *Love Us and Leave Us,* first produced in London, 1976.

The Bread and Butter Trade, first produced in London, 1976.

Twilight Joker, first produced in Brighton, 1977, produced in London, 1978.

Pinvin Careless and His Lines of Force, produced in Stoke-on-Trent, 1977.

Family Ties: Wrong First Time; Never Right, Yet Again (produced in London, 1977), published in *Act 2,* edited by David Self and Ray Speakman, Hutchinson (London), 1979.

Forest Lodge, produced in Salisbury, 1977.

Tolly of the Black Boy, produced in Edinburgh, 1977.

Rattling the Railings (produced in London, 1978), French (London), 1979.

The Banger, produced in Nottingham, 1978.

Cul de Sac, first produced in Chichester, 1978, produced in London, 1979.

England, My Own, produced in London, 1978.

Soldier Boy, produced in London, 1978.
VE Night, produced in Chicester, 1979.
The Limes, and I Kid You Not, produced in London, 1979.
The Pied Piper (adaptation of the poem by Robert Browning; musical; produced in Stoke-on Trent, 1980), French, 1982.
The Ticket, produced in London, 1980.
The Night John, produced in London, 1980.
We Were All Heroes, produced in Andover, Hampshire, 1981.
Aesop's Fables (musical; produced in Stoke-on-Trent, 1983), French, 1986.
Strippers (produced in Newcastle-upon-Tyne, 1984; produced in London, 1985), Amber Lane Press (Oxford), 1985.
Hotel Dorado, produced in Newcastle-upon-Tyne, 1985.
The Weeping Madonna, published in *New Plays 1: Contemporary One-Act Plays,* Oxford University Press (Oxford, England), 1988.

Also author of *Dobson's Drie Bobs, The Launching of the Esso Northumbria,* and *I Would Prefer Not To* (adaptation of the novella *Bartleby* by Herman Melville).

TELEVISION PLAYS

Mooney and His Caravans (first broadcast in 1966; produced on stage in London, 1968), published in *Zigger Zagger and Mooney and His Caravans.*
The Heroism of Thomas Chadwick, 1967.
The Last Train Through the Harecastle Tunnel, 1969.
The Gregorian Chant, 1972.
The Dividing Fence, 1972.
Shakespeare—or Bust, 1973.
Three for the Fancy, 1973.
Dancing in the Dark, 1974.
The Rough and the Smooth, 1975.
(With Joyce) *The Jolly Swagman,* 1976.
The Ballad of Ben Bagot, 1977.
The Reluctant Chosen, 1979.
Put Out to Grass, 1979.
Atlantis, 1983.

Author of the *Salvation Army* series.

RADIO PLAYS

The Fishing Party, 1971.
Play Soft, Then Attack, 1978.
The First Flame, 1980.
The Rundle Gibbet, 1981.

The Overnight Man, 1982.
The Romany Trip (documentary), 1983.
The Top Sail at Imberley, 1983.
Madam Main Course, 1983.
Poole Harbour, 1984.
Letters to the Otter, 1985.
When Youth and Pleasure Meet, 1986.
The Mumper, 1988.
Blind Down the Thames, 1988.
Stones, Tops, and Tarns, 1989.
Tales My Father Taught Me, 1990.

OTHER

The Offcuts Voyage, Oxford University Press, 1988.

Editor of *New Plays 1,* 1988, *New Plays 2,* 1989, and *New Plays 3,* 1990, Oxford University Press.

SIDELIGHTS: Peter Terson had already launched a career as a physical education teacher when the birth of his first child revived an interest in writing that had been dormant for years. Finding that he was often up in the middle of the night after caring for his infant son, Terson began work on a novel; he eventually abandoned the project in favor of writing plays, a decision based on his interest in writing dialogue. His first two plays were optioned by the BBC but never produced because they were judged to need too much work to adapt them for broadcast. Terson was encouraged by the sales, however, and continued to write in his spare time for the next seven years.

During much of this period Terson lived in the Vale of Evesham, a rural, fruit-growing area in central England. His early plays are set in Evesham and contain a sinister undercurrent: progress and civilization threaten nature and alienate humankind. Terson sent samples of his work to Peter Cheeseman, director of the Victoria Theatre in Stoke-on-Trent, an in-the-round theatre committed to regionalism. Cheeseman was impressed with Terson's work and *A Night to Make the Angels Weep* was performed at the Victoria in 1964. Other Terson plays set in the Vale of Evesham and sharing the theme of rural tradition opposing the forces of change include *The Mighty Reservoy, Mooney and His Caravans, All Honour Mr. Todd,* and *I'm in Charge of These Ruins,* As a collection the plays constitute a cycle, emphasizing themes in a quiet, dialogue-centered fashion.

Typical of Terson's writing during this period is *Mooney and His Caravans,* The story centers on a married couple, Charley and Mave, who are so determined to escape city life that they are willing to submit themselves to repeated degradation in a rural trailer-park community run like a concentration camp by the evil, cunning Mooney. Humiliated and stripped of all pretense, with Mave carrying Mooney's baby, the couple rediscovers their love for each other and returns to the city. Although deciding that the play was not one of Terson's best, *Observer* critic Ronald Bryden writes: "I wish all disciples of Artaud who preach the death of language in drama could compare that blurred vision with Peter Terson's comedy."

Terson was named resident playwright of the Victoria Theatre in 1966, and was also invited to write a play for the National Youth Theatre by its director, Michael Croft. Terson's acceptance of the offer required a major change in his writing style; whereas the productions at the Victoria Theatre were small in scale and represented regional, rural interests, the London-based National Youth presented large, showy productions, staged by schoolchildren and young adults, and dealt with themes that appealed to urban youth. Terson responded to the challenge with *Zigger Zagger,* a look at almost fanatical adoration of and identification with professional soccer teams as seen through the eyes of Harry Philton, a school dropout seeking his niche in a society in decline. Harry bounces from job to job, falling into unhappy relationships and a dead-end career.

"The perception of [soccer] as substitute religion," writes *New Statesman* critic Brian Glanville, "of the fan as aimless victim of an industrialised society, is hardly original, but Mr. Terson tricks it out with fine vigour and invention." The play was considered by some critics to be too simplistic, but Philip French, in a later *New Statesman* review, writes that he felt the play possessed "a coherence and consistency in its over-simplification, and important questions are asked in a way too rarely done in the theatre." Bryden, again writing in *Observer,* praises Terson as being "that rare thing, a poet of the theatre."

Terson gave up his post as resident playwright at the Victoria Theatre in 1967 and began to devote more time to working with the National Youth Theatre, evolving the themes he had developed in *Zigger Zagger. The Apprentices* is an elaboration on those themes in a more naturalistic fashion; the hopes and dreams of a working class youth are stripped away one by one until he finds himself trapped in a colorless, meaningless world with no future. *Listener*

critic D.A.N. Jones writes: "Terson presents aspects of that huge body of individuals known as the working class, from his own angle, in a strong and serious way. I wish he had rivals, with different angles."

Terson's ability to tailor a play to fit a particular cast and director has led some observers to classify him as a "primitive" to describe his unsophisticated natural talents and observations of human nature. However, the versatility required to be able to write for both the small, in-the-round Victoria Theatre and the National Youth Theatre with its large company of amateur players is considerable. In order to fully utilize the potential of the National Youth Theatre Terson would start with a basic outline and, working with cast and director Croft, work out staging details and dialogue.

An example of the success of this technique was observed by *New York Times* critic Richard Eder when *Good Lads at Heart* played in New York City in 1979. The play, which examines the life and relationships of eighteen boys in reform school, presented the difficult task of adequately developing each of the characters. Eder writes: "The play, written by Peter Terson for the group, is descriptive and instructive. Mr. Terson has not created a notable play but he has created a very useful one; and one that beautifully fits the nature and abilities of the performers."

In an essay about Terson in *Dictionary of Literary Biography,* Gillette Elvgren compares the playwright to such luminaries as Arnold Wesker, John Osborne, and Harold Pinter, who also came from Britain's working class. "But unlike some works of these playwrights," observes Elvgren, "his own plays continue to reflect and draw sustenance from this heritage. Through their language and characters, his dramas depict man's isolation from the land and from his work. . . . Terson imbues his characters with a kind of colloquial relevance (and oftentimes delightful eccentricity) that never loses touch with the sources of work and class from which the writer sprang. Terson's particular and unique strengths as a playwright stem from this ability."

Elvgren comments that the violent climaxes of many of Terson's early plays recalled the youthful work of Anton Chekov, in that it is "somewhat arbitrary and contrived." He muses that television and radio were excellent media for showcasing the strengths of Terson's work, naming *The Last Train Through the*

Harcastle Tunnel, The Fishing Party, and *The Gregorian Chant* as "humorous, ironic works that do not demand the sustained dramatic intensity of an evening in the theater." He finds these works to be "poetic and mood statements which bring to life the workers who people the rural villages of the Midlands and the industrial back streets of the Northern cities."

Terson has been underrated by many commentators, according to John Elsom in *Contemporary Dramatists.* Referring to the common description of the writer as a "primitive" talent, Elsom surmises that the term was "intended to mean that his technique is artless, his observation fresh and original, and his naturally prolific talent untainted by too much sophistication." Yet the critic decides that "this somewhat backhanded tribute . . . belittles his ability." He theorizes that the theater establishment has a difficult time fully accepting Terson's work because it does not include "popular West End comedies" or "middle-class families in the grip of emotional dilemmas." Instead, he writes about "problems which . . . seem to him more important. He is a highly skilled writer with a particular insight into Northern working-class societies and whose plays have, at best, a richness of imagination and an infectious humour." Elsom concludes: "Terson's plays have a much greater variety and range than is often supposed. . . . His influence in British regional theatre has been considerable, and more than any other contemporary dramatist he carries forward the ideas of social drama."

BIOGRAPHICAL/CRITICAL SOURCES:

BOOKS

Contemporary Dramatists, St. James Press (Detroit), 1993.
Dictionary of Literary Biography, Volume 13: *British Dramatists since World War II,* Gale (Detroit), 1982.

PERIODICALS

Drama, winter, 1968.
Evening Sentinel, October 4, 1967, p. 6.
London Magazine, June, 1968.
New Statesman, September 29, 1967; March 22, 1968; August 28, 1968; May 15, 1970.
New York Times, March 28, 1979.
Observer, September 3, 1967; May 19, 1968; August 25, 1968.

Plays and Players, September, 1970; October, 1970; November, 1970; March, 1972.
Punch, March 20, 1968; September 2, 1970.
Spectator, September 2, 1967; September 6, 1969.
Stage, August 27, 1970; September 17, 1970; December 3, 1970; August 5, 1971; September 30, 1971.
Times Literary Supplement, April 23, 1970.
Variety, October 6, 1971.

*   *   *

TORRENS, Duncan
  See RIPLEY, Michael David

*   *   *

TURTON, James
  See CRACE, Jim

*   *   *

UNO, Chiyo 1897-1996

PERSONAL: Born in 1897, near Hiroshima, Japan; died June 10, 1996, in Tokyo, Japan; married a banker (divorced); married second husband, Ozaki Shiro (a novelist; divorced); companion of Togo Seiji (a painter) for five years; married and divorced two additional times. *Ethnicity:* Japanese.

CAREER: Writer. Worked variously as an elementary school teacher's assistant, a waiter, and a kimono designer. Founder of *Sutairu* (Style), a Japanese fashion magazine, in 1936.

AWARDS, HONORS: First prize, for a short story, 1921; bestowed with the Third Order of the Sacred Treasure by the emperor of Japan; named a "person of cultural merit," 1989; has also been awarded the Joryu Bungaku Sho (Women's Literature Prize) twice, the Noma Hiroshi Prize, and the Art Academy Prize.

WRITINGS:

Iro zange, [Japan], 1935, published in the United States as *Confessions of Love,* translation by

Phyllis Birnbaum, University of Hawaii Press (Honolulu), 1989.

Kimono tokuhon, [Japan], 1957.

Onna no nikki, [Japan], 1960.

Kaze no oto, [Japan], 1969.

Shitashii naka (essays), [Japan], 1970.

Teiketsu (short stories), [Japan], 1970.

Kofuku (short stories), [Japan], 1972.

Watakushi no bungakuteki kaisoki (reminiscences), [Japan], 1972.

Aru hitori no onna no hanashi, [Japan], 1972, published with another story as *Aru hitori no onna no hanashi; Ame no oto,* Bungei Shunju (Tokyo), 1983; published in the United States as *The Story of a Single Woman,* translation by Rebecca L. Copeland, P. Owen (London), 1992.

Koi wa tanoshii ka (essays), [Japan], 1974.

Am no oto, [Japan], 1974, published with another story as *Aru hitori no onna no hanashi; Ame no oto,* Bungei Shunju, 1983.

Yaeyama no yuki (short stories), [Japan], 1975.

Usuzumi no sakura, [Japan], 1975.

Mama no hanashi, [Japan], 1976.

(With Tsuneko Nakazato) *Ofuku shokan,* [Japan], 1976.

Mizunishi shoin no musume (short stories), [Japan], 1977.

Ikite yuku watakushi (autobiography), Mainichi Shinbunsha (Tokyo), 1983.

Aru otoko no danmen (short stories), Kodansha (Tokyo), 1984.

The Sound of the Wind: The Life and Works of Uno Chiyo (includes the novellas *The Puppet Maker, The Sound of the Wind,* and *This Powder Box*), translation by Copeland, University of Hawaii Press, 1992.

Watanabe Masahiko hen, Nihon Tosho Senta (Tokyo), 1995.

The original version of *The Puppet Maker* was published in 1942, *This Powder Box* first appeared in 1967, and *The Sound of the Wind* saw print in 1969. Also author of stories and novellas, including *Ohan.* Contributor to periodicals.

ADAPTATIONS: A program for Japanese television was created and aired based on Uno's autobiography, *Ikite yuku watakushi.*

SIDELIGHTS: Uno Chiyo was an influential fiction writer whose novels, short stories, and novellas often took her own romantic adventures as their subject matter. "Like Jean Rhys . . . and Anais Nin . . . in

Europe, she wrote of sex with candour and style," according to a writer for the *Economist.* In *Confessions of Love,* a novel first published in 1935, Uno fictionalized the character of her real-life lover, the painter Togo Seiji, whose failed co-suicide with his former lover had scandalized the nation, and formed the basis of Uno's plot. In *The Story of a Single Woman,* Uno retells her own life story, from her childhood in a village near Hiroshima to the moment in 1930 when she decides to move in with the painter whose failed suicide reminds the protagonist of her own father's death. "Part of the fascination of Uno's writing is founded on just such an interplay of auto-biographical/biographical fact with the contrary demands of fiction and art," observed Marilyn Jeanne Miller in a *World Literature Today* review of the English translation of *Confessions of Love.*

Uno's childhood, the subject of her novellas *The Sound of the Wind* and *The Story of a Single Woman,* was dominated by her father, who assured her that men did not like women with complexions as dark as hers, and whose too great love for mistresses and gambling was overlooked by his forgiving wife. The dramatic death of her father, depicted in *The Story of a Single Woman* with him crawling across the snow, fending off would-be helpers, and coughing up blood, combined with "her teenage discovery of the dramatic changes to be wrought with white face powder," set her free from her past, according to Ruth Pavey of *New Statesman and Society.* "Emboldened by her mask and the elegant clothes she was good at contriving, she embarked on her dual, entwined career as *femme fatale* and writer," Pavey continued.

The Story of a Single Woman is told by a seventy-year-old narrator who looks back upon the tumultuous love affairs of her life. Uno's own experiences form the basis of the novel although, as Celeste Loughman noted in *World Literature Today,* "Uno alters biographical facts to make her point." Loughman found: "Most of the details follow closely the events of Uno's life, but the conclusion is a reminder that the work is fiction after all." In the novel, the narrator leaves her lover to begin anew; Uno stayed with hers for another five years. Loughman wondered: "The ending might be Uno speculating on what might have happened on the road not taken."

Uno's early career as an elementary school assistant teacher was cut short when an affair she openly conducted with another teacher was used as an excuse to dismiss her. She left provincial Hiroshima for Tokyo, then in the throes of "*ero-guro-nansensu* (eroticism, grotesquerie and nonsense)," the wild era of the 1920s, according to Julian Loose in the *Times Literary Supplement*. A writer for the *Economist* compared Tokyo of that time with "the notorious nightlife of Weimar Germany." There she waited tables in a cafe frequented by the literati, and began writing her own stories, featuring daring women whose mask-like makeup, passion for love affairs, and freedom to come and go as they please matched her own. "No one is as fortunate as a woman writer," Uno wrote after the demise of her second marriage, according to Loose. "No sooner does she break up with a man than she can write about it all without the slightest sense of shame."

In 1936, Uno started *Sutairu* with one of her husbands, and the publication has been described as Japan's first fashion magazine. With time out for World War II, Uno devoted a large part of her energies to the world of magazine publishing over the next two decades. During her long career, she also published numerous serialized stories in newspapers, and a column offering romantic advice to lovelorn women. "However breezily she may have started as a writer," Pavey remarked, referring to the author's claim that she became a writer in an effort to earn more money than earlier careers had allowed, "the fine, fleeting lightness of her mature style, with its appearance of guileless candour, is as much suggestive of painstaking craft, skillfully disguised, as of naivety." Although critics disagree about the lasting importance of Uno's writings, the author is commonly regarded as one of the founders of modern Japanese literature. Loose asserted: "Indomitable and unapologetic, her song of herself helped make possible the bold, independent voices of a new generation of Japanese women writers."

"I never forced myself to do anything I didn't want to do," claimed Uno in a 1987 interview as quoted in the *New York Times* obituary. "I've lived my life just the way I wanted to." Indeed, remarked critic Loose in the *Times Literary Supplement*, "She not only lived a life of reckless freedom, she wrote about it, bringing a new zest and fresh perspective to the Japanese genre of autobiographical fiction." Although critics disagree about the ultimate merit of her essentially autobiographical, intensely personal, often romantic works of fiction, Uno's standing among influential twentieth-century Japanese writers is unquestioned.

BIOGRAPHICAL/CRITICAL SOURCES:

BOOKS

Copeland, Rebecca L., *The Sound of the Wind: The Life and Works of Uno Chiyo,* University of Hawaii Press, 1992.

PERIODICALS

Belles Lettres, spring, 1990, p. 20.
Economist, June 22, 1996, p. 85.
New Statesman and Society, November 27, 1992, p. 43.
New York Times Book Review, September 20, 1992.
Times Literary Supplement, March 16, 1990, p. 293; December 4, 1994, p. 20.
World Literature Today, Volume 63, number 4, pp. 743-44; autumn, 1994, p. 889.

OBITUARIES:

PERIODICALS

New York Times, June 12, 1996, p. D23.*

* * *

VAILLAND, Roger (Francois) 1907-1965

PERSONAL: Born October 15, 1907, in Acy-en-Multien, France; son of George Francois (a surveyor and architect) and Genevieve (Morel) Vailland; died of lung cancer, May 11, 1965; married Andree Blavette Boule (a nightclub singer), May, 1936 (separated 1949); married Elisabeth Naldi, 1954. *Education:* Attended Lycee Louis-le-Grand in Paris, France, and the Sorbonne. *Politics:* Communist.

CAREER: Novelist, journalist, essayist, and dramatist. Co-founder of review *Le Grand Jeu*; *Paris-Soir*, Paris, France, foreign correspondent in the Balkans, the Near East, and Ethiopia, 1930-40; full-time writer, 1945-65. *Military service:* Served with French resistance movement derailing troop transport trains during World War II.

AWARDS, HONORS: Prix-Interallie, 1945, for *Drole de jeu*; Prix Goncourt, 1957, for *La Loi*.

WRITINGS:

FICTION; IN ENGLISH TRANSLATION

Drole de jeu, [Paris], 1946, translated by Gerald Hopkins as *Playing for Keeps,* Houghton (Boston), 1948, published as *Playing with Fire,* Chatto & Windus (London), 1948.

La Loi, Gallimard (Paris), 1957, translated by Peter Wiles as *The Law,* Knopf (New York City), 1958.

Les Mauvais Coups, Sagittaire, 1959, translated by Wiles as *Turn of the Wheel,* Knopf, 1962.

La Fete, Gallimard, 1960, translated by Wiles as *The Sovereigns,* J. Cape (London), 1960, published as *Fete,* Knopf, 1961.

(Author of adaptation with Roger Vadim and Claude Brule) *Les Liaisons dangereuses 1960: Un film de Roger Vadim* (screenplay), Julliard, 1960, translated by Bernard Shir-Cliff as *Roger Vadim's "Les Liaisons dangereuses,"* Ballantine (New York City), 1962.

La Truite, Gallimard, 1964, translated by Wiles as *The Trout,* Dutton (New York City), 1965, published as *The Young Trout,* Collins (London), 1965.

FICTION, IN FRENCH

Heloise et Abelard (three-act play), [Paris], 1947.

Bon pied, bon oeil, Correa (Paris), 1950.

Le Colonel Foster plaidera coupable (five-act play), Les Editeurs Francais Reunis, 1951.

Un Jeune homme seul, Correa, 1951.

Beau Masque, Gallimard, 1954.

Trois cent vingt-cinq mille francs, Correa, 1956, English Universities Press (London), 1975.

Monsieur Jean (three-act play), Gallimard, 1959.

NONFICTION, IN FRENCH

La Bataille d'Alsace: Novembre-decembre 1944, J. Haumont, 1945.

Quelques reflexions sur la singularite d'etre francais, J. Haumont, 1946.

(With Raymond Manevy) *Un Homme du peuple sous la revolution,* Correa, 1947.

Le Surrealisme contre la revolution, Editions sociales, 1948.

Boroboudour: Voyage a Bali, Java et autres iles (travel), Correa, 1951.

Choses vues en Egypte, Editions Defense de la Paix (Paris), 1952.

Experience du drame, Correa, 1953.

(Editor) *Laclos par lui-meme: Images et textes,* Editions du Seuil (Paris), 1953.

Eloge du cardinal de Bernis, Fasquelle, 1956.

(Editor) C. Suetonius Tranquillus, *Les Douze Cesars: Choises et commentees,* Editions Buchet-Chastel, 1962.

Le Regard froid: Reflexions, equisses, libelles, 1945-1962, B. Grasset, 1963.

La Reunion, Editions Rencontre, 1964.

Ecrits intimes, Gallimard, 1968.

Lettres a sa famille, Gallimard, 1972.

Le Saint empire, Editions de la Difference, 1979.

Chronique des annees folles a la Liberation, 1928-1945, Messidor/Editions sociales, 1984.

Chronique d'Hiroshima a Goldfinger, 1945-1965, Messidor/Editions sociales, 1984.

La Visirova, ou, Des Folies-Bergere jusqu'au trone (title means "Visirova or, From the Folies-Bergeres Right up to the Throne"), Editions Messidor, 1986.

Cortes, le conquerant de l'Eldorado, Messidor, 1992.

N'aimer que ce qui n'a pas de prix, Editions du Rocher (Monaco), 1995.

OTHER

Ouevres completes, Editions Rencontre (Lausanne), 1967-68, Volume 1: *Drole de jeu,* Volume 2: *Les Mauvais Coups; Bon pied, bon oeil,* Volume 3: *Un Jeune homme seul; Trois cent vingt-cinq mille francs,* Volume 4: *Heloise et Abelard; Le Colonel Foster plaidera coupable,* Volume 5: *Monsieur Jean; Experience du drame; Batailles pour l'humanite; Les Liaisons dangereuses 1960,* Volume 6: *Boroboudour; Choses vues en Egypte; La Reunion,* Volume 7: *Beau Masque,* Volume 8: *Le Regard froid; Le Surrealisme contre la revolution,* Volume 9: *Laclos par lui-meme; Les Douze Cesars; Sur "Manon Lescant,"* Volume 10: *Un Homme du peuple sous la revolution; Recits et reportages; Ecrits politiques,* Volume 11: *La Loi.*

Film scenarios include "Les Mauvais coups" and a television adaptation of his *Trois cent vingt-cinq mille francs.* Contributor to journals, including *Les Oeuvres libres, Paris-Soir,* and *Humanite.*

SIDELIGHTS: Roger Vailland earned international recognition during his lifetime for the crisp dialogue, economical prose style, and dry, ironic humor of his writings. His first novel, *Drole de jeu,* which was translated as *Playing for Keeps,* won the Prix-

Interallie in 1945. Vailland struggled with alcohol and drug addiction throughout much of his life, as well as with the contradictory lures of political commitment in the form of communist and the quirky jeu d'esprit of individualism. Such struggles are reflected in his writings, making his work difficult to define, according to J. E. Flower writing in the *Dictionary of Literary Biography,* and contributing to Vailland's failure to be "accorded a major role in the developments of French literature in the twentieth century."

Vailland had a comfortable, middle-class childhood in Rheims and elsewhere in France, including a year's stint in Paris, a period he later recounted in fictional form in his novel *Un Jeune homme seul.* He began writing poetry, and joined a group of rebellious teenagers who attempted to flout the conventional bourgeois society around them. They took drugs and began publishing a surrealist journal called *Le Grand Jeu (The Great Game).* The journal lasted only three issues but was significant enough to come to the attention of Andre Breton, who publicly accused Vailland of lacking political integrity.

Vailland often struggled to convince others of the sincerity of his political beliefs—an application to join the communist party submitted in the early 1940s never received a response, for example—and his ongoing battles with drug and alcohol addiction didn't help matters. In the 1930s the young author began contributing to articles to *Paris-Midi* and an early novel, *La Virisova ou des Folies-Bergeres jusqu'au trone* was serialized in *Paris-Soir.* In 1936 he married Andree Blavette, a nightclub singer, and completed another novel, *Un Homme du peuple sous la Revolution,* co-authored by Raymond Manevy. He underwent a detoxification program for drugs in 1938 but in 1939, when he attempted to enlist in the military at the outbreak of World War II, he was declared unfit for service. He worked as a journalist for *Paris-Soir* during the early years of the war, but like many French people at the time, Vailland was hardly worried about the threat from Germany, according to Flower. Then, in late 1942 or early 1943, after the invasion of the Southern Zone by the Germans, he joined the French Resistance. "This was a major break with the kind of self-indulgent, precarious life he had been leading hitherto," Flower remarked.

During this period Vailland wrote *Drole de jeu* (translated as *Playing for Keeps*), a novel of the Resistance that won the Prix Interallie in 1945. This is consid-

ered Vailland's first major work of fiction and contains elements seen in later works, such as a theatrical structure heavily dependent upon dialogue and a focus upon an ideal figure, often a thinly disguised autobiographical portrait, whose status as an amateur or individualist raises him above those around him. He continued to struggle with his addictions, underwent another detoxification in 1947, and separated from his wife. Vailland's self-doubts found expression in *Les Mauvais coups* (translated as *Turn of the Wheel*), in which the love-hate relationship between a married couple is complicated the appearance of another woman. "The novel contains a good deal of heavy sexual symbolism, and the whole pattern of conflicted emotions is supported by regular reference to the seasons and the natural world," Flower observed.

This was followed by *Bon pied, bon oeil,* an explicitly political novel through which, along with *Un Jeune homme seul,* Vailland expressed his intentions to become more politically active, and less consumed by private passions. Vailland met the woman who would become his second wife in 1949, and "her greater political commitment and sense of purpose appear to have given Vailland increased stability," wrote Flower. The author continued to contribute to journals and wrote a play, *Le Colonel Foster plaidera coupable,* which attacked the Western powers for their intervention in Korea and secured his membership in the communist party. Vailland's next two novels, *Beau Masque* and *Trois cent vingt-cinq mille francs,* "are both intentionally much more didactic and militant than any before or after," according to Flower, an expression of the author's commitment to the communist party. Not long after the triumphant publication of these works came the exposure of the evils of Stalinism by the new Soviet premier, Nikita Khrushchev, however. "Vailland was physically ill for two days and his whole attitude to life shaken," Flower remarked. He became increasingly critical of the communist party and officially withdrew three years later.

His next work, *La Loi,* which won the Prix Goncourt and for which he is best known, is seen as a deliberate departure from the novels that immediately preceded it. Set in Italy, the story centers on Don Cesare, who rules the small village of Manacore, and whose life mirrors in significant ways the one readers have found in Vailland's own diaries, Flower noted. "The novel also explores some familiar themes: social manipulation, family tensions, the maternal relationship between a young man,

Francesco, and an older woman, Donna Lucrezia. There are some fine descriptions, and features of the natural world are used to give depth to a provincialism of the most deep-rooted kind," Flower continued.

Vailland's shift away from the political and toward the personal appears complete with subsequent publications, including a play, *Monsieur Jean,* in which the hero is killed by a falling portrait of Stalin. The author's diaries reflect his far greater interest in gaining self-control than in political events during this period, Flower noted. Two other novels, *La Fete* and *La Truite* (published as *The Young Trout*), both of which portray human activities in a ritualistic, highly artificial manner were published during this time. He became terminally ill with lung cancer during the writing of *La Truite* and died in May 1965. "To summarize the qualities of Vailland's work is not easy," wrote Flower. "Its mixture of several constant themes and shifting objectives, as well as its preoccupation with technical mastery and sharply observed detail, can result at best in writing that is forceful and persuasive. But the writing can also appear self-indulgent and artificial." His individualism, always at war with his political commitment, helped him avoid the pitfalls of the worst in politically motivated fiction, but Vailland is nonetheless likely to remain a marginal figure in postwar literature.

BIOGRAPHICAL/CRITICAL SOURCES:

BOOKS

Ballet, Rene, Elisabeth Vailland, and Henri Bourbon, *Roger Vailland,* P. Seghers, 1973.

Courriere, Yves, *Roger Vailland, ou, Un libertin au regard froid,* Plon (Paris), 1991.
Dictionary of Literary Biography, Volume 83: *French Novelists since 1960,* Gale (Detroit), 1989.
Flower, John Ernest, *Roger Vailland: The Man and His Masks,* Hodder & Stoughton (London), 1975.
McNatt, Jo Ann, *The Novels of Roger Vailland: The Amateur and the Professional,* P. Lang (New York), 1986.
Pornon, Francis, *Un Homme seul: sur les pas de Roger Vailland,* Editions Paroles d'aube (Venissieux), 1995.
Tusseau, Jean Pierre, *Roger Vailland: un ecrivain au service du peuple,* Debresse (Paris), 1976.

PERIODICALS

National Review, December, 1946.
New Republic, May 7, 1951.
New York Times, September 28, 1958.
Reporter, November 13, 1958; November 12, 1959.
Times Literary Supplement, September 28, 1967.

OBITUARIES:

New York Times, May 13, 1965.
Newsweek, May 24, 1965.
Publishers Weekly, May 31, 1965.
Times Literary Supplement, September 28, 1967.*

* * *

VOYLE, Mary
See MANNING, Rosemary (Joy)

W-Z

WEBB, Stephen S(aunders) 1937-

PERSONAL: Born May 25, 1937, in Syracuse, NY; married, 1959; children: two. *Education:* Williams College, B.A., 1959; University of Wisconsin (now University of Wisconsin—Madison), M.S., 1961, Ph.D., 1965.

ADDRESSES: Office—Department of History, Syracuse University, Maxwell Hall, Syracuse, NY 13210.

CAREER: St. Lawrence University, Canton, NY, assistant professor of history, 1964-65; College of William and Mary, Williamsburg, VA, assistant professor of history, 1965-68; Syracuse University, Syracuse, NY, associate professor, 1968-79, professor of history, 1979—, chair, master of social science degree program, 1974-80. Institute of Early American History and Culture, fellow, 1965-68, associate, 1977—; Columbia University seminar on early American history and culture, associate, 1968—, chair, 1976-77; Charles Warren Center, Harvard University, fellow, 1971-72, 1974-75.

AWARDS, HONORS: National Endowment for the Humanities fellow, 1971-72.

WRITINGS:

Government in Britain and America, Harper (New York City), 1978.
The Governors-General: The English Army and the Definition of the Empire, 1569-1681, University of North Carolina Press (Chapel Hill), 1979.
1676: The End of American Independence, Knopf (New York City), 1984.

Lord Churchill's Coup: The Anglo-American Empire and the Glorious Revolution Reconsidered, Knopf, 1995.

Contributor to history journals.

SIDELIGHTS: Stephen S. Webb is a historian specializing in the period in which North America was under British colonial rule. He has won praise for chronicling this period vividly and engagingly, but he also has generated controversy. In three books—*The Governors-General: The English Army and the Definition of Empire, 1569-1681, 1676: The End of American Independence,* and *Lord Churchill's Coup: The Anglo-American Empire and the Glorious Revolution Reconsidered*—Webb has argued that military interests, rather than commercial or ideological ones, were key to shaping British policy in the American colonies during the seventeenth century. This view runs contrary to that held by numerous other historians.

Assessing *The Governors-General* for the *New York Review of Books,* Edmund S. Morgan noted that Webb takes issue with the assertion of Charles McLean Andrews, "the most magisterial colonial historian of this century," that during the early colonial period Britain focused on commercial development of North America, and that a switch to emphasis on military objectives came in the late eighteenth century, precipitating the American Revolution. "According to Webb, England already had a military imperial policy and also a military domestic policy for more than a century before the American Revolution," Morgan related. Webb's book contends that by assigning military officers known as governors-general and forces of soldiers to the colonies, in a

422

system that Webb refers to as "garrison government," the British crown attempted to curtail the power of wealthy landowners and business interests, thereby maintaining British control of the colonies and setting the stage for empire-building. Webb also makes the case that garrison government protected ordinary citizens against oppression by the upper class.

Several critics questioned Webb's thesis. Morgan argued that colonial officials, in their effort to govern effectively, did not try to quash the power of local elites, but instead usually sought their cooperation. The available military forces were too small to allow the governors-general to impose their will on the gentry, he added. Clive Holmes, writing in *American Historical Review,* thought Webb set up "a false dichotomy" between military and commercial concerns; often, Holmes asserted, one served the interests of the other. In Webb's book, Holmes observed, "evidence that might suggest the commercial thrust behind imperial expansion is simply passed over." William R. Johnson, in an essay for the *William and Mary Quarterly,* complained that Webb "ignores the way in which soldier executives sought as greedily as any moneygrubbing merchant to profit from their colonial posts." He added that "commercial prosperity, a search for revenue, the pursuit of individual advancement, and the quest for legitimacy—these, rather than the individual ambitions of army officers serving out their later years in America, shaped late seventeenth-century Anglo-colonial development and led the way toward a centralized and more uniformly administered imperial policy." In a response written for the same publication, Webb countered that Johnson had underestimated the size and power of the military forces in the colonies, and that his work was not intended to discount Andrews' view of the significance of commerce in colonial America, but rather to place it in the context of imperialism. "The new, larger, imperial view nowhere denies the importance of either the pecuniary or the parochial in Anglo-American history," Webb insisted.

Some critics admired certain aspects of the work. Holmes, even while unconvinced by all of Webb's contentions, called the author's achievement "very considerable" and added that "his challenges have ensured that no future historian of the first empire can invoke commercial interests as the sole motivation for its growth." And Morgan allowed that despite his reservations, *The Governors-General* "is clearly a work to be taken seriously. But it is not too early to say that it will require more demonstration than the author has thus far given us to establish his daring and original thesis."

Webb further develops that thesis in *1676*. In this book he holds that colonists had enjoyed a great degree of independence until that year, when events gave Britain the opportunity to consolidate its power over its subjects in North America. These events were Bacon's Rebellion, a revolt against the governor of Virginia; King Philip's War, an uprising by Indians in New England against colonial settlements there; and the alliance of the Iroquois tribe with the British. In a critique for the journal *History: Reviews of New Books,* Richard P. Gildrie summed up Webb's claims by saying that "some are true, others dubious, but virtually all provocative." *New York Times Book Review* contributor William S. McFeely was bothered by what he called "the undemocratic premise that lies at the core of the work." McFeely explained that Webb "has given us a great deal of evidence of the death and destruction that 17th-century Americans inflicted on one another, but his suggestion that their independent ways were the cause of the discord and that the submission to empire was its cure is not persuasive." In the *Journal of American History,* Douglas Edward Leach applauded Webb for putting forth a "complex and exciting thesis," but objected to "his tendency to make sweeping and often exaggerated generalizations." Still, he opined that the book was well worth reading and likely to inspire much lively discussion among devotees of history.

In *Lord Churchill's Coup,* Webb offers a revisionist look at the Glorious Revolution of 1688-89, which saw King James II driven from England's throne and, so the traditional interpretation goes, political and religious freedom restored to the nation. These events, noted Derek Hirst in the *New York Times Book Review,* "were thought to enshrine individual rights and local liberties, to assert parliamentary limitations on government." But Webb contends that the Glorious Revolution was primarily an assertion by military men of their own power and that of the Church of England. Webb sees Lord John Churchill, a general and former ally of the king's, as the revolution's chief instigator. "Webb argues that [Churchill] objected to the king's absolutist policies, to his attempts to return England to the Catholic faith, and to his willingness to win French support by making concessions that undermined English interests in America," Johann P. Somerville stated in *Reviews in American History.* Churchill, according to Webb, sparked the revolution by aligning himself with William of Orange, the Dutch ruler who invaded England, married James's daughter Mary, and became King William III of England.

Somerville thought Webb overstated Churchill's role in the revolution; Churchill, he said, "was far from being the first influential person" to switch his allegiance from James to William. The reviewer also took issue with the idea that the military imposed its will on the political leaders of England. "Rather," Somerville declared, "a small, primitive, and underdeveloped army did the bidding of a powerful and sophisticated political machine." Hirst held that Webb emphasized the military's influence at the expense of other significant forces at work in England at this time, including philosophers, scientists, and the growing urban population. "Only by ignoring the capacity of this society to act through informal means is Mr. Webb able to insist on the overriding importance of the army," Hirst submitted. *Canadian Historical Review* contributor Marc Egnal had a similar criticism. "Webb ignores the makeup of the crowds that sometimes march on the stage, and has little to say about the role of social classes," Egnal stated. "He also denigrates the importance of mercantilist policies and economic motives. Webb's narrow focus perhaps makes his account more exciting, but ultimately creates a weaker explanation." Some of the reviewers, though, lauded the book's style. "Webb does not wholly vindicate his thesis," Somerville wrote. "But this is nevertheless a well-argued, lucid, readable, and entertaining book." Egnal pronounced *Lord Churchill's Coup* "a glowing exception" to the generalization that books by professional historians are dull, and praised Webb's narrative skills and his portraits of Churchill and other key figures. "But despite its genuine strengths," he added, "Webb's book remains more an engaging than a convincing account of the origins and aftermath of the Glorious Revolution."

BIOGRAPHICAL/CRITICAL SOURCES:

PERIODICALS

American Historical Review, June, 1981, pp. 589-90; June, 1985, pp. 751-52.
Canadian Historical Review, June, 1997, p. 321.
History: Reviews of New Books, January, 1985, p. 60.
Journal of American History, June, 1985, pp. 127-28.

New York Review of Books, December 4, 1980, pp. 47-48.
New York Times Book Review, June 24, 1984, p. 13; November 26, 1995, p. 20.
Reviews in American History, September, 1996, pp. 389-94.
Times Literary Supplement, December 27, 1985, p. 1491.
William and Mary Quarterly, July, 1986, pp. 408-30, 431-459; October, 1996, pp. 809-10.*

—Sketch by Trudy Ring

*   *   *

WESCOTT, Glenway 1901-1987

PERSONAL: Born April 11, 1901, in Kewaskum, WI; died of a stroke, February 22, 1987, in Rosemont, NJ; son of Bruce Peters (a farmer) and Josephine (Gordon) Wescott. *Education:* Attended University of Chicago, 1917-19.

CAREER: Writer.

MEMBER: Authors Guild of the Authors League of America (member of council), National Institute of Arts and Letters (president, 1959-62), American Academy of Arts and Letters.

AWARDS, HONORS: Harper Prize, 1927, for *The Grandmothers: A Family Portrait;* D.Litt., Rutgers University, 1963.

WRITINGS:

The Bitterns: A Book of Twelve Poems, Monroe Wheeler (Evanston, IL), 1920.
The Apple of the Eye (novel), Dial (New York City), 1924.
Natives of Rock: XX Poems, 1921-1922, Francisco Bianco (New York City), 1925.
. . . Like a Lover (stories), Monroe Wheeler (Macon, France), 1926.
The Grandmothers: A Family Portrait (novel), Harper (New York City), 1927.
Good-bye, Wisconsin (stories), Harper, 1928, reprinted, Books for Libraries Press, 1970.
The Babe's Bed (novella), Harrison (Paris), 1930.
(Translator) Prosper Merimee, *Carmine,* Harrison, 1931.
Fear and Trembling (essays), Harper, 1932.

A Calendar of Saints for Unbelievers, Harrison (Paris), 1932, Harper, 1933, reprinted, Leete's Island Books, 1976.

The Pilgrim Hawk: A Love Story, Harper, 1940.

(Contributor) Margaret Mayorga, editor, *The Best One-Act Plays of 1940,* Dodd, 1941.

Apartment in Athens (novel), Harper, 1945, reprinted, Greenwood Press, 1972, published as *Household in Athens,* Hamish Hamilton (London), 1945.

(Editor and author of introduction) *The Maugham Reader,* Doubleday (New York City), 1950.

(Editor and author of introduction) *Short Novels of Colette,* Dial (New York City), 1951.

(Adaptor) *Twelve Fables of Aesop,* Museum of Modern Art (New York City), 1954.

Images of Truth: Remembrances and Criticism, Harper, 1962.

The Best of All Possible Worlds: Journals, Letters, and Remembrances, 1914-1937, Farrar, Straus (New York City), 1975.

Continual Lessons: The Journals of Glenway Wescott, 1937-1955, edited by Robert Phelps and Jerry Rosco, Farrar, Straus, 1990.

A Visit to Priapus, Jerry Rosco (New York City), 1995.

Also author of *Elizabeth Madox Roberts: A Personal Note,* 1930, and of *The Dream of Audubon,* a ballet libretto. Contributor to *Signatures, Life and Letters Today, Harper's, Dial, Bookman, Hound and Horn, New Republic, Atlantic Monthly, Poetry, Chicago Review, Southern Review, New York Times, Grand Street, Partisan Review,* and other publications. Collections of Wescott's manuscripts are housed at the Beinecke Library of Yale University and the New York Public Library.

SIDELIGHTS: Glenway Wescott made his reputation in the 1920s with the novel *The Grandmothers: A Family Portrait* and the story collection *Good-Bye, Wisconsin.* Both are autobiographical works set in Wescott's native Wisconsin. The critically acclaimed novel *The Pilgrim Hawk: A Love Story* appeared in 1940, and the best-selling *Apartment in Athens* in 1945. But for the last forty years of his life Wescott was to publish no new fiction. The reason for his long silence is still a matter of speculation among critics.

Wescott was first known as an Imagist poet, publishing his first collection of poems at the age of nineteen. But it was as a writer of fiction that he earned critical recognition. In *The Apple of the Eye, The*

Grandmothers, and *Good-Bye, Wisconsin,* Wescott fashioned his memories of his rural Wisconsin childhood into fiction. "Wescott," Bruce Bawer explained in the *New Criterion,* "was elaborately, almost compulsively, exploring his roots." In each of these works, Sy M. Kahn wrote in the *Dictionary of Literary Biography,* "Wescott employs a central young narrator. . . . Nostalgically and elegiacally, each of these narrators imaginatively recreates the American past, as symbolized in rural characters from Wisconsin, and in so doing he reveals the involvement, and, ultimately, the rebellion of his own mind and sensibility."

The Apple of the Eye, Wescott's first novel, was published when the author was twenty-three years old. "Though it has many of the shortcomings of youthful first works," William Rueckert of the *Dictionary of Literary Biography* commented, "it is an impressive, quite original first novel." It tells the story of Dan Strane, a Wisconsin teenager who comes to a bitter awareness of the puritanical restrictions of his rural upbringing and takes steps to free himself from them. Bawer described the novel as "a peculiar hodge-podge" and believed that Wescott's "metaphors and similes . . . feel particularly forced and overdone." Writing in his *Glenway Wescott: The Paradox of Voice,* Ira Johnson admitted that *The Apple of the Eye* possessed "a limited though powerful and rhetorical narrative voice. [But] two serious flaws are evident: the novel's didacticism, due to Wescott's conception of *image* and *truth,* and the disparity between the omniscient narrator and the rest of the work."

Wescott's second novel, *The Grandmothers,* "established him as one of the major American novelists of his generation," Bawer wrote. A series of short narratives based on the pictures in a family album, *The Grandmothers* recounts many actual events in Wescott's family history. As Kahn explained, "Wescott first conceived *The Grandmothers* as a history of his own family rather than a work of fiction, but as the work grew, it compelled his imagination to transcend memory, and the work was transmuted from a personal memoir to a skillful and successful novel."

Critics of the time praised *The Grandmothers* as a major work of uniquely American fiction. Burton Rascoe of *Bookman,* for example, called it "a novel not only with its roots in the American soil, but it is a novel of those roots and of that soil. It is a novel that gives a new significance to American life." In similar terms, C. P. Fadiman of the *Nation* believed that "Wescott's very beautiful and moving chronicle is possibly the first artistically satisfying rendition of the soul of an American pioneer community and its descendants."

The care with which Wescott prepared the novel, and the depth of his concern for the people he portrays, are qualities highlighted by several commentators. The *Atlantic*'s M. E. Chase believed that the novel "stands out as a book which has been conceived in deep and quiet perceptions and born in pride, care, and patience." Reviewing the book for the *New York Times,* J. Carter called it "a fine piece of work, conceived and matured in all seriousness and thoroughness of workmanship." Allan Nevins of the *Saturday Review of Literature* emphasized the emotional quality of Wescott's narrative. "It is," Nevins wrote, "the ebullient freshness and force, the tenderness as well as the keenness of the insight into human motives and ideals and frailties, and the sincerity of the author's reverence for what he calls 'ghosts of the little local history' . . . , which give the uneven, inchoate narrative the inspiration it unquestionably has." Bawer maintained that "there is something wonderfully mature about [*The Grandmothers*], about its quiet recognition that we are all the products of our families, and that the better we understand them the better we can understand—and create—ourselves."

A year after the appearance of *The Grandmothers,* Wescott published a collection of stories entitled *Good-Bye, Wisconsin,* which again explores the scenes and events of his own childhood. The opening piece, an essay explaining the book's subject matter, "is not a piece of objective social analysis," Johnson wrote, "but an attack, which presents in terms of his personal vision the reasons why Wescott finds the Middle West and America a place that in countless ways prevents the development of the self." As Rueckert explained: "The stories of *Good-Bye, Wisconsin* tell over and over again the sad lives of those who have been victims of the Midwest and found it impossible to flourish there."

By the time *Good-Bye, Wisconsin* was published, Wescott had already left the United States to live in France. He was to spend eight years there. But despite his distance from his native region, Wescott continued to write of Wisconsin. "Wescott was an expatriate, living in France," as Walter Allen explained in his *The Modern Novel in Britain and the United States,* "but, on the evidence of his fiction,

still unable to escape from Wisconsin, his native state, which seems at times almost as much a state of mind as a place." His *The Babe's Bed,* a short novella-length work published in a limited edition, is set in Wisconsin although, as Rueckert argued, "the story is not really an examination of the region at all; instead, it expresses for the first time Wescott's self-doubts about himself as a fiction writer."

Because of his growing self-doubts, Wescott did not publish any fiction for ten years. His reputation suffered during this time, partly because his two nonfiction books of this period— *Fear and Trembling* and *A Calendar of Saints for Unbelievers*—were failures. But with the 1940 novel *The Pilgrim Hawk,* Wescott regained critical acceptance while finally moving beyond his Wisconsin background.

The Pilgrim Hawk is an autobiographical work set in 1920s France. It revolves around a group of people who spend a day together in the countryside: the narrator Alwyn Tower, who is an American novelist, his cousin Alexandra Henry, and two of Alexandra's friends, Larry and Madeleine Cullen. The Cullens have brought a pet falcon with them and it becomes the central metaphor of the novel. Subtitled *A Love Story,* the book ultimately concerns the Cullens' marriage and the reaction of Alwyn, an old bachelor, to it. The falcon's captivity is seen by Alwyn as a symbol for the marriage. But when at novel's end the falcon is released, soars high into the air exuberantly, only to return again, Alwyn discerns a new depth to the marriage relationship.

A "haunting, poetic, compressed story of love and art, freedom and captivity," as a London *Times* writer described the novel, *The Pilgrim Hawk* was widely acclaimed. Wescott, A. L. Graham of *Library Journal* wrote, "has created a strange, tense atmosphere, while telling the story with delicacy and charm." Writing in *Books,* Rose Feld called *The Pilgrim Hawk* "a tightly bound little tale that has depths and flights far beyond the surface of the human entanglements it covers." Rueckert called the novel Wescott's "one authentic masterpiece," while Johnson found it "the culmination of his career as a fiction writer." Bawer believed *The Pilgrim Hawk* to be perhaps Wescott's "most nearly perfect work— taut, subtle, and exquisitely ordered."

In 1945 Wescott published *Apartment in Athens,* a novel quite different from his earlier efforts. It concerns a family in occupied Greece during the Second World War who must allow a German soldier to stay at their apartment. The tensions between the family and their unwanted guest are described "with the minimal amount of fictional distortion. It is the attempt of an essentially romantic, lyric, naturally symbolic novelist to write realistic fiction," as Rueckert explained.

"It was," Kahn wrote of *Apartment in Athens,* "a popular success but is considerably below the artistic achievement of his two most distinguished works, *The Grandmothers* and *The Pilgrim Hawk.*" But Edmund Wilson disagreed. Writing in his *Classics and Commercials,* Wilson believed that "the cramped physical and moral conditions, the readjustments in the relationships of the family, the whole distortion of the social organism by the unassimilated presence of the foreigner—all this is most successfully created."

After the success of *Apartment in Athens* in 1945, Wescott was to publish no more fiction. *Images of Truth: Remembrances and Criticism,* a collection of his nonfiction, appeared in 1962;*The Best of All Possible Worlds: Journals, Letters, and Remembrances, 1914-1937* was published in 1975. But Wescott's fiction remained unpublished. He claimed to have finished manuscripts with which he was unsatisfied stored in trunks. "Any explanation," Rueckert wrote, "of Wescott's diminishing career is probably psychological and personal." Bawer speculated after Wescott's death in 1987 that one reason for the long silence may have been Wescott's homosexuality; he had lived since his teens with Monroe Wheeler. An autobiographical writer, Wescott had already successfully written about his childhood and coming of age. "But few readers, at that time anyway, would have regarded [a] sensitive and candid novel based upon Wescott's adult domestic life," Bawer commented, "with anything other than horror."

Whatever the reasons for Wescott's forty years of silence, he holds, Rueckert claimed, "a significant, if minor place in the literary history of our time." And *The Pilgrim Hawk,* Rueckert believed, "will remain one of [our] finest short novels." Wescott's "major distinction in American Literature," according to Jerry Rosco in *Gay and Lesbian Literature,* "is as a lyrical prose stylist of unsurpassed skill, intelligence, and subtlety. As an author he is associated with the Midwest regional writers, the Paris expatriate writers of the 1920s, and the New York literary scene. And as a public figure, he is a mainstream author whose place in gay literature is part of his legacy." "To

read the body of work that [Wescott] has left behind," Bawer commented, "is not only to marvel at its charm and polish but to admire its probity and seriousness of purpose. . . . That Glenway Wescott has fallen into near-obscurity is a measure less of his own failings than of the misbegotten values of the literary culture that has allowed him to fall." The London *Times* commentator believed that despite his years of silence, Wescott "did enough to be remembered so long as fiction is read."

BIOGRAPHICAL/CRITICAL SOURCES:

BOOKS

Allan, Walter, *The Modern Novel in Britain and the United States,* Dutton, 1965.

Contemporary Literary Criticism, Volume 13, Gale (Detroit), 1980.

Contemporary Novelists, 4th edition, St. Martin's, 1986.

Cowley, Malcolm, *The Exile's Return,* Viking, 1951.

Dictionary of Literary Biography, Gale, Volume 4: *American Writers in Paris, 1920-1939,* 1980, Volume 9: *American Novelists, 1910-1945,* 1981.

French, Warren, editor, *The Twenties: Fiction, Poetry, Drama,* Everett/Edwards, 1975.

Gay and Lesbian Literature, Volume 2, St. James Press (Detroit), 1998.

Hicks, Granville, *The Great Tradition: An Interpretation of American Literature since the Civil War,* Macmillan, 1933.

Johnson, Ira, *Glenway Wescott: The Paradox of Voice,* Kennikat, 1971.

Moss, Howard, *Writing against Time,* Morrow, 1969.

Phelps, Robert, and Jerry Rosco, *Continual Lessons: The Journals of Glenway Wescott, 1937-1955,* Farrar, Straus, 1990.

Rueckert, William H., *Glenway Wescott,* Twayne, 1965.

Wilson, Edmund, *Classics and Commercials,* Farrar, Straus, 1950.

Zabel, Morton Dauwen, *Craft and Character: Texts, Method and Vocation in Modern Fiction,* Viking, 1957.

PERIODICALS

Accent, Volume 7, 1945, pp. 44-53.

Advocate, February 12, 1991, p. 79.

Atlantic, October, 1927.

Bay Area Reporter, January 10, 1991, p. 31.

Body Politic, July, 1986, pp. 32-33.
Bookman, September, 1927; October, 1928; April, 1931, pp. 142-145.
Books, September 23, 1928; December 8, 1940.
Bulletin of Bibliography, Number 22, 1956; September-December, 1958.
Chicago Review, winter, 1990, pp. 113-129.
Chicago Tribune, April 7, 1991.
College English, March, 1957.
Commonweal, October 12, 1962.
Critique: Studies in Modern Fiction, June, 1965, pp. 5-12.
Dial, December, 1924; November, 1927.
Guide (Boston), January, 1991, pp. 96-99.
James White Review, summer, 1986, p. 11; summer, 1991, p. 12.
Lambda Book Report, May/June, 1991, p. 34.
Library Journal, November 1, 1940.
Literary Review, winter, 1988, pp. 133-142.
Nation, October 12, 1927; December 21, 1940.
New Republic, December 9, 1940.
New Yorker, September 29, 1962; April 29, 1991, p. 104.
New York Times, August 28, 1927; December 1, 1940.
New York Times Book Review, October 21, 1962.
Outweek, January 30, 1991, pp. 52-53.
Papers on English Language and Literature, summer, 1965.
Saturday Review, October 6, 1962.
Saturday Review of Literature, September 24, 1927; November 30, 1940.
Studies in Short Fiction, spring, 1994, p. 187.
Time, September 28, 1962.
Washington Post Book World, May 25, 1986; January 13, 1991, p. 5.

OBITUARIES:

BOOKS

PERIODICALS

International Herald Tribune, March 2, 1987.
New York Times, February 24, 1987.
Times (London), February 27, 1987.
Times (Trenton), February 24, 1987.
Trentonian, February 24, 1987.*

*   *   *

WILLIAMSON, Jack
  See WILLIAMSON, John Stewart

WILLIAMSON, John Stewart 1908-
  (Jack Williamson; Will Stewart, a pseudonym)

PERSONAL: Born April 29, 1908, in Bisbee, Arizona Territory (now the state of Arizona); son of Asa Lee (a rancher and teacher) and Lucy Betty (a former teacher; maiden name, Hunt) Williamson; married Blanche Slaten Harp (a merchant), August 15, 1947; children: (stepchildren) Keigm Harp, Adele Harp Lovorn. *Education:* Home schooled until he was twelve, then attended high school in Richland, NM; attended West Texas State Teachers College (now West Texas State University), 1928-30, and University of New Mexico, 1932-33; Eastern New Mexico University, B.A. (summa cum laude) and M.A., 1957; University of Colorado at Boulder, Ph.D., 1964. *Politics:* Democrat. *Religion:* Methodist.

ADDRESSES: Home—Box 761, Portales, NM 88130. *Agent*—Eleanor Wood, Spectrum Literary Agency, 432 Park Ave. S., Rm. 1205, New York, NY 10016.

CAREER: Fantasy and science fiction writer, 1928—; *News Tribune,* Portales, NM, wire editor, 1947; creator of comic strip "Beyond Mars" for New York *Sunday News,* 1953-56; New Mexico Military Institute, Roswell, instructor in English, 1957-59; University of Colorado at Boulder, instructor in English, 1960; Eastern New Mexico University, Portales, associate professor, 1960-69, professor, 1969-77, currently Distinguished Research Professor in English. Guest of honor, Thirty-fifth World Science Fiction Convention, Miami, 1977, and at numerous regional conventions.

MEMBER: Science Fiction Writers of America (president, 1978-80), National Council of Teachers of English, Masons, Rotary Club.

AWARDS, HONORS: First Fandom Science Fiction Hall of Fame Award, 1968; Pilgrim Award, Science Fiction Research Association, 1973; Grand Master Award for lifetime achievement, Science Fiction Writers of America, 1976; Hugo Award, 1985, for *Wonder's Child: My Life in Science Fiction.*

WRITINGS:

SCIENCE FICTION NOVELS; UNDER NAME JACK WILLIAMSON

(With Miles J. Breuer) *The Girl from Mars,* Stellar, 1929.

The Legion of Space (also see below), illustrated by A. J. Donnell, Fantasy Press, 1947.

Darker than You Think, Fantasy Press, 1948.

The Humanoids (originally published in *Astounding* as *And Searching Mind*), Simon & Schuster, 1949.

One against the Legion (also see below), Fantasy Press, 1950, published with novella *Nowhere Near,* Pyramid, 1967.

The Green Girl, Avon, 1950.

The Cometeers (also see below), illustrated by Ed Cartier, Fantasy Press, 1950.

Dragon's Island, Simon & Schuster, 1951, published as *The Not-Men,* Belmont, 1968.

The Legend of Time, Fantasy Press, 1952, published as *The Legion of Time* and *After Worlds End,* two volumes, Digit, 1961.

Dome around America, Ace, 1955.

(With James E. Gunn) *Star Bridge,* Gnome Press, 1955.

The Trial of Terra, Ace, 1962.

Golden Blood, Lancer, 1964.

The Reign of Wizardry, Lancer, 1964.

Bright New Universe, Ace, 1967.

Trapped in Space (juvenile), illustrated by Robert Amundsen, Doubleday, 1968.

The Moon Children, Putnam, 1972.

The Power of Blackness, Berkley, 1976.

Brother to Demons, Brother to God, Bobbs-Merrill, 1979.

The Humanoid Touch (sequel to *The Humanoids*), Holt, 1980.

Three from the Legion (contains *The Legion of Space, The Cometeers,* and *One against the Legion*), Doubleday, 1981.

(With Breuer) *The Birth of a New Republic: Jack Williamson—The Collector's Edition,* Volume II, P.D.A. Enterprises, 1981.

Manseed, Ballantine, 1982.

The Queen of the Legion, Pocket Books, 1983.

Lifeburst, Ballantine, 1984.

Firebird, Bluejay, 1986.

(With Frederik Pohl) *Land's End,* T. Doherty, 1988.

Mazeway, Ballantine, 1990.

(With Pohl) *The Singers of Time,* Doubleday, 1991.

Beachhead, Tor (New York), 1992.

Demon Moon, Tor, 1994.

The Black Sun, Tor, 1997.

"JIM EDEN" SERIES; UNDER NAME JACK WILLIAMSON; WITH FREDERIK POHL

Undersea Quest, Gnome Press, 1954.

Undersea Fleet, Gnome Press, 1956.

Undersea City, Gnome Press, 1958.

"STARCHILD" TRILOGY; UNDER NAME JACK WILLIAMSON; WITH POHL

The Reefs of Space (also see below), Ballantine, 1964.

Starchild (also see below), Ballantine, 1965.

Rogue Star (also see below), Ballantine, 1969.

The Starchild Trilogy (contains *The Reefs of Space, Starchild,* and *Rogue Star*), Doubleday, 1977.

"CUCKOO'S SAGA"; UNDER NAME JACK WILLIAMSON; WITH POHL

Farthest Star (also see below), Ballantine, 1975.

Wall around a Star (also see below), Ballantine, 1983.

The Saga of Cuckoo (contains *Farthest Star* and *Wall around a Star*), Doubleday, 1983.

SHORT STORY COLLECTIONS; UNDER NAME JACK WILLIAMSON

Lady in Danger, Utopian, 1945.

(With Murray Leinster and John Wyndham) *Three Stories,* Doubleday, 1967, published as *A Sense of Wonder: Three Science Fiction Stories,* edited by Sam Moskowitz, Sidgwick & Jackson (London), 1967.

The Pandora Effect, Ace, 1969.

People Machines, Ace, 1971.

The Early Williamson, Doubleday, 1975.

Dreadful Sleep, Weinberg (Chicago), 1977.

The Best of Jack Williamson, introduction by Pohl, Ballantine, 1978.

The Alien Intelligence: Jack Williamson—The Collector's Edition, Volume I, P.D.A. Enterprises, 1980.

(With others) *Medea: Harlan's World,* edited by Harlan Ellison, illustrated by Kelly Freas, cartography by Diane Duane, Bantam, 1985.

SCIENCE-FICTION NOVELS; UNDER PSEUDONYM WILL STEWART

Seetee Shock (originally published serially), Simon & Schuster, 1950, reprinted under name Jack Williamson, Lancer, 1968.

Seetee Ship (originally published serially), Gnome Press, 1951, reprinted under name Jack Williamson, Lancer, 1968.

OTHER; UNDER NAME JACK WILLIAMSON

Teaching Science Fiction (nonfiction), privately printed, 1973.

(Editor) *Teaching Science Fiction: Education for Tomorrow* (essays), Owlswick, 1980.

Wonder's Child: My Life in Science Fiction (autobiography), Bluejay, 1985.

But Not Warriors: A Novel (World War II), Lynx, 1989.

Contributor of stories, under name Jack Williamson, to science-fiction anthologies, including *Of Worlds Beyond,* edited by Lloyd Arthur Eshbach, Fantasy Press, 1947; *The Mirror of Infinity,* edited by Robert Silverberg, Harper, 1970; *The Science Fiction Hall of Fame,* edited by Ben Bova, Doubleday, 1973; *Before the Golden Age,* edited by Isaac Asimov, Doubleday, 1974; *Science Fiction: Today and Tomorrow,* edited by Reginald Bretnor, Harper, 1974; and *The Best Science Fiction of the Year, Number Six,* edited by Terry Carr, Holt, 1977. Contributor of short stories to periodicals, including *Amazing Stories, Science Wonder Stories, Air Wonder Stories, Astounding Stories, Wonder Stories, Weird Tales, Astounding Science Fiction, Argosy,* and others.

SIDELIGHTS: Science-fiction writer Jack Williamson was born in Arizona Territory, moved to Mexico, then Texas, and then, by covered wagon, to a homestead in eastern New Mexico. "We lived on isolated farms and ranches, far from anybody, and when I was young I knew very few other kids; so I lived to a great extent in my imagination. . . . Life would have been absolutely empty without imagination," Williamson was quoted as saying to Rosemary Herbert in *Publishers Weekly.* Because his family's ranch failed to prosper, Williamson was unable to pursue his ambition of becoming a scientist. However, by employing both his imagination and his interest for science, he has become a pivotal author in the genre of science fiction.

While he was living in the desert land of New Mexico, Williamson discovered Hugo Gernsback's new magazine, *Amazing Stories.* "Here were space craft taking off from other worlds, travel in time and all sorts of wonderful inventions!," quotes Herbert. Williamson decided to take a chance writing in the genre and sold his first story, "The Metal Man," to *Amazing Stories* in 1928. Thirteen of his first twenty-one published stories were spectacular enough to gain covers in the early science-fiction magazines, often appearing in installments. Williamson says he generally earned his living writing for these magazines for as little as a half-cent per word.

"If science-fiction writing is an art that can be taught, there is probably no one in the world better qualified to teach it than Jack Williamson," remarks Sam Moskowitz in *Seekers of Tomorrow: Masters of Science Fiction.* "[Williamson is] an author who pioneered superior characterization in a field almost barren of it, realism in the presentation of human motivation previously unknown, scientific rationalization of supernatural concepts for story purposes, and exploitation of the untapped story potentials of antimatter." As an academic, Williamson also legitimized science fiction as a field deserving of literary attention. In recognition of his contributions, he received the Grand Master Award for lifetime achievement from the Science Fiction Writers of America in 1976.

Williamson initially attracted attention in the science-fiction genre as a master of the space opera. *The Legion of Space* (1934), the first book of what was to become a series, put Williamson on equal ground with such science-fiction writers as John W. Campbell and Edward E. "Doc" Smith. Set in the thirtieth century, *The Legion of Space*'s authenticity rests on the development of the memorable comic figure Giles Habibula. Alfred D. Stewart writes in the *Dictionary of Literary Biography:* "Developed in Dickensian fashion through distinctive traits of speech and character, [Habibula] is modeled on Shakespeare's Falstaff; he is a born thief who whines about his ills and threats to his personal safety throughout the series." In his second book in the series, *The Cometeers,* Williamson introduces another interesting character, Orco. During the course of the story, Orco discovers, to his distress, that he is not a true human. While the characterization in these early stories was found to be rather striking by reviewers, Moskowitz claims that Williamson's true expertise at characterization came in the stories that followed. "Realism was present in the characterization as well as in the plotting of [his later] stories. Giles Habibula had been a milestone, but Garth Hammond, aptly labeled 'a hero whose heart is purest brass,' in [the short story 'Crucible of Power'], was a giant step towards believability in science fiction. Hammond was the man who made the first trip to Mars and built a power station near the sun for sheer selfish, self-seeking gain. . . . There had never been anything as blunt as this in science fiction before. . . . After [Williamson] showed the way, not-completely-sympathetic and more three-dimensional people began to appear" in science fiction.

Reviewers label Williamson's early writing, such as the "Legion of Space" novels, fantasy literature.

Stewart stresses that such novels were "vehicles for cosmic plotting and pseudo-scientific devices, not for the examination of man's possibilities. Williamson's [eventual] fascination with [Charles] Darwin, H. G. Wells, and evolution led him, in his best thought-out and best written books, to deal with real possibilities for man, not exaggerated romantic vagaries." Williamson's writing, beginning in the 'forties, became more grounded in logical scientific explanations. He wrote his "Seetee" series in the early part of the decade under the pseudonym Will Stewart; to some they are considered the best expositions on the subject of antimatter ever written. (The concept of antimatter, or contra-terrene, is the condition in which positive and negative charges are reversed from that typical on earth.) In *Seetee Ship,* the earth has become morally and politically stagnant, and scientists, known as "asterites," strive to legalize the use of antimatter as a means of reestablishing freedom and progress for mankind. But the asterites and the Establishment are at odds. In the sequel, *Seetee Shock,* the conflict has expanded—the asterites are convinced the power of antimatter should be available to all inhabitants on all planets. When the novel's hero, Nick Jenkins, manages to turn on a special transmitter, the Fifth Freedom results, destroying governments and establishing freedom for all in the universe.

Williamson's most famous novel, *The Humanoids,* also strives for human freedom, but the outcome is disastrous. The humanoids are small robots who have as their goal the protection and happiness of man. However, Stewart says, "As Williamson remarked in a talk at the 1977 World Science-Fiction Convention, 'Their built-in benevolence goes too far. Alert to the potential harm in nearly every human activity, they don't let people drive cars, ride bicycles, smoke, drink or engage in unsupervised sex. Doing everything for everybody, they forbid all free action. Their world becomes a luxurious but nightmarish prison of total frustration.'" Eventually man must regain his freedom and does so by developing psychic powers. A contributor to the *New York Herald Tribune Book Review* believes *The Humanoids* "deals, essentially, with the conflict that began when the wheel and the lever were invented: the battle between men and machines." Does advanced technology cause man to progress or regress? Williamson questions. Thirty years later Williamson wrote the sequel to *The Humanoids,* titled *The Humanoid Touch,* which some reviewers found disappointing. "Williamson is able to offer only a partial answer to the humanoid challenge—a utopia the hero escapes

to, where the psychic and biological sciences have achieved ultimate perfection," notes a critic in *Publishers Weekly.*

Several of Williamson's other works focus on genetic engineering, advanced human evolution, and a number of additional evolutionary possibilities. Four distinct species of man exist in *Brother to Demons, Brother to Gods:* premen, trumen, mumen, and stargods. Because of the varying abilities and moralities of these four species, a power struggle arises and the only hope for universal peace is the evolution of "ultiman," a being of perfect love and power. According to Stewart, "*Brother to Demons, Brother to Gods* focuses in the end on humanity's stupendous potential." *Fireways,* set in the contemporary world, also explores the positive and negative possibilities inherent in genetic engineering. Scientists at a top-secret lab create a completely new life form, a tiny pink "worm" that is capable of communicating telepathically with humans. However, in the course of their experimentation, they also manage to unleash a genetic plague that destroys an entire town. Along the way the CIA, the KGB, the Pentagon, and religious fanatics all get into the act. Thomas Pearson, reviewing the book for *Voice of Youth Advocates,* finds it "face-paced, well-plotted," and "thoughtful," and equates it to "the medical thrillers written by Robin Cook and Michael Crichton."

Throughout his eighties Williamson not only continued to produce a variety of science-fiction novels at a steady pace, but novels that were for the most part well received. In *Mazeway,* set against a far-future interstellar backdrop, young Ben Dain attempts to save a dying Earth by convincing the Eldren, an ancient and powerful alien race, that humans are worthy of their attention. A reviewer for *Kliatt* calls it a "well-done tale" with "unusual and wonderfully depicted aliens, subverted robots, death, and mystery." Joel Singer in *Voice of Youth Advocates* feels the book is "well thought out and plotted," but suffers from a disjointed writing style from one chapter to the next. In *Beachhead,* Williamson returns to the near-future with a book exploring the human exploration and colonization of Mars. The adversities the pioneers must confront—a deadly virus, a mutiny, a crash landing—are played against a parallel plot involving the financial machinations and intrigues within the multinational consortium backing the mission. Dan Chow, writing in *Locus,* praises Williamson's scientific research and observes that "*Beachhead* shows a freshness and vigor which would be remarkable in a writer generations younger." In *Demon Moon,* Williamson harkens back to his pulp origins with a tale of a world infested by wolves, wyverns, and dragons that is reminiscent of his classic *Darker than You Think.* According to Russell Letson in *Locus,* the book "creates a surface of high-fantasy motifs whose rationalizations turn out to be science fictional." Letson feels that the world Williamson creates is both "fantastic and real enough to push back when poked." Tom Easton in *Analog* credits *Demon Moon* as a successful thriller, but finds it lacking in originality and too derivative of other work in the field. In *Black Sun,* a ravaged Earth sends out ninety-nine star ships in an attempt to seed the galaxy with humanity and ensure the survival of the species. The book deals with the travails of the last ship to leave Earth: its landing on a frozen planet, its incompetent and crazed captain, and the strange discoveries of past habitation on the planet as the crew members attempt to explore their new world and survive. According to a reviewer in *Publishers Weekly,* Williamson "mixes quantum physics with a decidedly old-fashioned pulp-adventure plot" but "[w]hat's important here . . . is that essential SF attribute, the sense of wonder, which Williamson once again generates in spades by skillfully evoking an unknown alien planet and the inhuman intelligences who once populated it."

Stewart believes "the future of science fiction is now as unlimited as the future of science itself, and Jack Williamson is one of the pioneer writers who made it so." Yet more than a pioneer, Williamson has remained a significant voice in the field. Moskowitz credits him as "one of the most adaptable science fiction writers alive." Chow notes that "Williamson continues to astonish. This man simply cannot be underestimated or dismissed as a relic of prehistory. Many are the authors, decades younger, who have fallen by the wayside. Yet Williamson goes on, by the evidence, as fresh as ever."

Williamson told *CA:* "Though retired from actual teaching, I'm still a full-time science-fiction writer, happy that ideas still happen, that I enjoy making them into stories, that editors and readers still seem interested—sometimes, anyhow.

"With so many old and dear friends gone, I have probably been writing science fiction longer than anybody else who is still writing science fiction. Unlike those who dislike the label 'science fiction' on their work, I've always been proud of it. Though some apologists claim too much for the genre, I think some of our claims are justified. It's a way of think-

ing and feeling about change, about the impacts of science and technology on our minds and our lives—impacts that keep coming harder and faster. Some of the things that some science-fiction writers do, at least some of the time, are akin to what some scientists do. For one small example, newspaper reporters who interview me these days give me credit for coining the phrase 'genetic engineering'—for a novel, *Dragon's Island,* first published in 1951, a couple of years before Watson and Crick broke the genetic code and touched off the current exciting transformation of imagined possibility into hard science.

"Since I discovered science fiction—back in 1926, before it had been named science fiction—it has been half my life. For the first twenty years and more; writing it paid barely enough to let me keep writing it, but in recent decades the rewards in recognition as well as in royalties have been more generous than I had ever dared expect. Looking back on a life of being reasonably well rewarded for doing exactly what I wanted to do, I feel pretty lucky. Pretty optimistic, too, about the ability of homo sapiens to keep on surviving crises as it has always survived them, and about my own ability to survive a little longer as a science fiction writer."

Williamson's work has been translated into numerous languages. A collection of his work can be found at Eastern New Mexico University in Portales, New Mexico.

BIOGRAPHICAL/CRITICAL SOURCES:

BOOKS

Clareson, Thomas D., editor, *Voices for the Future: Essays on Major Science-Fiction Writers,* Volume 1, Bowling Green University, 1976.

Contemporary Literary Criticism, Volume 29, Gale (Detroit), 1984.

Dictionary of Literary Biography, Volume 8: *Twentieth-Century American Science-Fiction Writers,* Gale, 1981.

Hauptmann, Richard A., *The Work of Jack Williamson: An Annotated Bibliography and Literary Guide,* edited by Boden Clark, Borgo Press (San Bernardino, CA), 1997.

McCaffrey, Larry, *Jack Williamson: An Interview,* Northhouse & Northouse (Dallas), 1988.

Moskowitz, Sam, *Seekers of Tomorrow: Masters of Science Fiction,* World Publishing, 1966.

Myers, Robert E., editor, *Jack Williamson: A Primary and Secondary Bibliography,* G. K. Hall, 1980.

Williamson, Jack, *Wonder's Child: My Life in Science Fiction* (autobiography), Bluejay, 1985.

Zelany, Roger, editor, *The Williamson Effect,* Tor, 1996.

PERIODICALS

Amazing Stories, October, 1964.
Analog, mid-December, 1994, p. 165.
Kliatt, January, 1991, p. 25.
Library Journal, February 15, 1997, p. 164.
Locus, July, 1992, p. 29; May, 1994, pp. 27-28.
Los Angeles Times, October 21, 1980.
New York Herald Tribune Book Review, October 9, 1949.
Publishers Weekly, September 12, 1980; May 23, 1986; January, 20, 1997, p. 399.
Science Fiction Horizons, number 1, 1964.
Tribune Books (Chicago), August 30, 1992, p. 6.
Voice of Youth Advocates, December, 1986, p. 242; October, 1990, pp. 233-34.
Washington Post Book World, September 30, 1984; September 28, 1986.

*　*　*

WINANT, Fran 1943-

PERSONAL: Born October 28, 1943, in New York, NY. *Education:* Fordham University, B.A., 1975.

ADDRESSES: Office—Violet Press, P.O. Box 398, New York, NY 10009.

CAREER: Co-founder of Gay Liberation Front, 1969; co-founder of RadicaLesbians, 1970; co-founder of Violet Press, early 1970s.

MEMBER: Poetry Society of America.

AWARDS, HONORS: Isaacson Poetry Award from New School for Social Research, 1968; New York State Arts Council CAPS grant, 1978; National Endowment for the Arts fellowship, 1989-90.

WRITINGS:

Looking at Women, Violet Press (New York City), 1971.

Dyke Jacket, Violet Press, 1976.
Goddess of Lesbian Dreams, Violet Press, 1980.

PLAYS

Closer Since the Shooting (one-act), first produced in New York at Judson Poets' Theatre, February 8, 1969.
Play 1, 2, 3, 4 (one-act), first produced in New York at Cubiculo Theatre, June 13, 1969.

OTHER

(Editor with Judy Grepperd) *We Are All Lesbians,* Violet Press, 1975.

Work appears in anthologies, including *The Lesbian Reader,* Amazon Press (Oakland, CA), 1975; *Lesbian Poetry: An Anthology,* Persephone Press (Watertown, MA), 1981; *The Penguin Book of Homosexual Verse,* Penguin (New York City), 1983; *Out of the Closets: Voices of Gay Liberation,* New York University Press (New York City), 1992; *Lesbian Quotations,* Alyson Publications (Boston), 1993; *Queer Dog: Homo/Pup/Poems,* Cleis Press (San Francisco), 1998.

SIDELIGHTS: Fran Winant was one of the founders of the Gay Liberation Front in 1969. "Winant holds a unique vantage point from which to comment on the movement's unfolding," writes Melissa Tedrowe in *Gay and Lesbian Literature.* Winant went on in 1970 to found RadicaLesbians, a spin-off group from Gay Liberation Front which launched "some of the first all-women dances and poetry readings," Tedrowe notes. With her then-partner Judy Grepperd, Winant also opened a food co-op called the Lesbian Food Conspiracy at this time.

Winant's writings grow from her involvement with the gay movement in America. Her poetry—collected in *Looking at Women, Dyke Jacket* and *Goddess of Lesbian Dreams*—has been published by Violet Press, a publishing house set up by Winant and Grepperd. Among Winant's most noteworthy poems, according to Tedrowe, is "Christopher St. Liberation Day, June 28, 1970"—a poem which "captures the intensity and promise of that first march," as Tedrowe writes. Winant's poems have appeared in a number of anthologies devoted to the works of gay and lesbian writers.

Winant has also created works in the field of painting. Tedrowe explains that Winant's painting "frequently celebrates the beauty and spirit of her dog, Cindy." Winant has exhibited her work at "A Lesbian Show," the first exclusively lesbian art show at an established gallery.

BIOGRAPHICAL/CRITICAL SOURCES:

BOOKS

Cooper, Emmanuel, *The Sexual Perspective: Homosexuality and Art in the Last 100 Years in the West,* Routledge (New York City), 1994.
Gay and Lesbian Literature, Volume 2, St. James Press (Detroit), 1998.
Ornstein, Gloria and Irene Diamond, *Reweaving the World: The Emergence of Ecofeminism,* Sierra Club Books (San Francisco), 1990.

PERIODICALS

Art Journal, winter, 1997.
Arts Magazine, October, 1982.
Heresies Magazine, fall, 1977.
Outweek, June 26, 1989.
Soho News, February 2, 1977; September, 1980.
Villager, November, 1982.
Village Voice, March 8, 1977; September, 1980; November 13, 1990.

* * *

WINGS, Mary 1949-

PERSONAL: Born April 14, 1949, in Chicago, IL; daughter of John (a furniture fabricator) and Betty (a painter; maiden name, Lee) Geller. *Religion:* "Raised Bahai." *Avocational interests:* Set design, cartooning.

ADDRESSES: Home and office—168 1/2 Precita Ave., San Francisco, CA 94110. *Agent*—Charlotte Sheedy, 611 Broadway, Suite 428, New York, NY 10012.

CAREER: Writer, sculptor, film maker. Worked as school bus driver, banjo player in feminist musical group, and teacher of mystery writing; graphic designer, Institute for Policy Studies, Amsterdam. San Francisco International Lesbian and Gay Film Festival, member of board of directors of Frameline, 1989—.

MEMBER: Mystery Writers of America, Sisters in Crime, San Francisco Gay and Lesbian History Project.

AWARDS, HONORS: Best Novel of the Year Award, *City Limits Magazine* (London), 1986, for *She Came Too Late;* California Arts Council grant; Raymond Chandler Fulbright Award nomination for detective spy fiction, 1993; Lambda Book Award, 1994, for best lesbian mystery novel.

WRITINGS:

MYSTERY NOVELS

She Came Too Late, Women's Press (London), 1986, Crossing Press (Freedom, CA), 1987.
She Came in a Flash, Women's Press, 1988, Dutton (New York City), 1989.
Divine Victim, Women's Press, 1992, Dutton, 1993.
She Came by the Book, Women's Press, 1995, Berkley (New York City), 1996.
She Came to the Castro, Berkley, 1997.

COMIC BOOKS

Come out Comix, Portland Women's Resource Center (Portland, OR), 1974.
Dyke Shorts, Last Gasp (San Francisco), 1980.
Are Your Highs Getting You Down?, Substance Abuse Groups of the Pacific Center (Berkeley, CA), 1981.

OTHER

Contributor of stories and articles to books, including *Daring to Dissent: Lesbian Culture from Margin to Mainstream,* Cassel, 1994; and *Reader, I Murdered Him, Too,* Women's Press, 1995. Contributor of stories and articles to periodicals, including *Out/Look* and *New Statesman & Society.* Illustrator and designer of *Making a Show of It: A Guide to Concert Promotion* by Ginny Berson, Redwood Records, 1980. Producer, with Eric Garber, of the screenplay *Greta Garbo: A Woman of Affairs.*

WORK IN PROGRESS: Too Thin to Be Believed.

SIDELIGHTS: American-born Mary Wings penned her first two novels while living and working in the Netherlands. Wings told the *St. James Guide to Crime & Mystery Writers* that "listening to a foreign language you are just learning, made my typewriter . . . look like a mechanical gate to home. . . . Writing about the sunny skies and crazy people who inhabit the U.S. brought me comfort, brought me home." Most of Wings' novels are written in the hard-boiled, *noir* style of 1940s and 1950s detective fiction; in contrast, her settings are contemporary and her ongoing protagonist, Emma Victor, is female and lesbian. According to Lynne Maxwell, writing in *Gay and Lesbian Literature,* Wings' novels represent more than well-wrought entertainments. Maxwell feels that Wings "came on the literary scene just in time to successfully chronicle lesbian cultural history in the late 20th century."

She Came Too Late, the first book in the Victor series, is set in Boston and draws on Wings' own experience working as a counselor on a women's crisis line. After failing to respond quickly enough to a caller's plea for help, Emma sets out to solve the woman's murder. The novel also details the evolution of a serious lesbian relationship for Emma. Adrian Muller, in the *St. James Guide to Crime & Mystery Writers,* notes that the plot of the book "touches on various politics—sexual, social, and workplace—but Wings manages to avoid turning her novel into a politically correct sermon by taking potshots at all areas of society." Maxwell states that *She Came Too Late* "celebrates lesbian friendship even as it explores the difficulties of initiating and continuing lesbian romantic relationships."

In Emma's second outing, *She Came in a Flash,* the setting changes to San Francisco where Emma is working as a public relations director for a women's benefit concert. A friend's sister is murdered after joining a religious cult. Emma goes undercover to join the cult herself and solve the crime. Maxwell feels that "Wings provides acute insight into the lesbian community, this time in its California incarnation, replete with New Age fascinations."

Wings' third novel, written after her return to the United States in 1988, was a marked departure from the Victor series. The award-winning *Divine Victim* is a gothic thriller set in Montana, where a lesbian couple must inhabit a house for one year to claim the inheritance left to one of the women by her aunt. Muller sees the book as derivative of Daphne Du Maurier's *Rebecca.* "Filled with mystical dreams, teasing recollections, and Catholic symbolism," Muller states, "the novel is a gripping thriller that can't be put down until its conclusion." Maxwell observes that Wings' background in graphic art and her firsthand knowledge of Europe figure prominently in the characterization and flashbacks in *Divine Victim.*

In the fourth and fifth books in the Emma Victor series, *She Came by the Book* and *She Came to the*

Castro, Emma has become a private detective working in San Francisco. The former novels deals with a death by poison at the inaugural gala for the Lesbian and Gay Archive and Emma's subsequent search for a series of photographs taken at the party. Pam Lambert, in *People Weekly,* states: "Author Wings, a San Francisco resident, knows the territory intimately—as well as how to spin a snappy tale with more twists than Lombard Street." *She Came to the Castro* broadens Emma's investigative range in a case involving political blackmail and a global conspiracy. A reviewer for *Publishers Weekly* notes that "[t]he tale barrels alone amicably, and Wings' light touch is refreshing—except for the occasional turns toward comicbook hysteria."

Maxwell believes that what distinguishes Wings' novels are their narrative voice, which "always rings true, creating from language a truly rounded character." She also stresses that Wings' "wit and psychological acumen" have allowed the novelist to transcend an exclusively lesbian niche to become a prominent mystery writer for a wider audience.

BIOGRAPHICAL/CRITICAL SOURCES:

BOOKS

Pederson, Jay P., editor, *St. James Guide to Crime & Mystery Writers,* 4th edition, St. James Press (Detroit), 1996.
Pendergast, Tom, and Sara Pendergast, editors, *Gay & Lesbian Literature,* Volume 2, St. James Press, 1998.

PERIODICALS

Entertainment Weekly, March 29, 1996, p. 56.
People Weekly, April 29, 1996, p. 36.
Publishers Weekly, February 19, 1996, p. 207; January 13, 1997, p. 57.

* * *

WOLFE, Thomas Kennerly, Jr. 1930-
(Tom Wolfe)

PERSONAL: Born March 2, 1931, in Richmond, VA; son of Thomas Kennerly (a scientist and business executive) and Helen (Hughes) Wolfe; married Sheila Berger (art director of *Harper's* magazine),

1978; children: Alexandra, Thomas. *Education:* Washington and Lee University, B.A. (cum laude), 1951; Yale University, Ph.D., 1957. *Avocational interests:* Window shopping.

ADDRESSES: Home—New York, NY. *Office*—c/o Farrar Straus & Giroux, Inc., 19 Union Sq. W., New York, NY 10003-3007. *Agent*—International Creative Management, 40 West 57th St., New York, NY 10019.

CAREER: Writer, journalist, social commentator, and artist. *Springfield Union,* Springfield, MA, reporter, 1956-59; *Washington Post,* Washington, DC, reporter and Latin American correspondent, 1959-62; *New York Herald Tribune,* New York City, reporter and writer for *New York* Sunday magazine (now *New York* magazine), 1962-66; *New York World Journal Tribune,* New York City, writer, 1966-67; *New York* magazine, New York City, contributing editor, 1968-76; *Esquire* magazine, New York City, contributing editor, 1977—; *Harper's* magazine, New York City, contributing artist, 1978-81. Has exhibited drawings in one-man shows at Maynard Walker Gallery, 1965, and Tunnel Gallery, 1974.

AWARDS, HONORS: Washington Newspaper Guild awards for foreign news reporting and for humor, both 1961; Society of Magazine Writers award for excellence, 1970; D.F.A., Minneapolis College of Art, 1971; Frank Luther Mott research award, 1973; D.Litt., Washington and Lee University, 1974; named Virginia Laureate for literature, 1977; American Book Award and National Book Critics Circle Award, both 1980, for *The Right Stuff;* Harold D. Vursell Memorial Award for excellence in literature, American Institute of Arts and Letters, 1980; Columbia Journalism Award, 1980; citation for art history from National Sculpture Society, 1980; L.H.D. from Virginia Commonwealth University, 1983, and Southampton College, 1984; John Dos Passos Award, 1984; Gari Melchers Medal, 1986; Benjamin Pierce Cheney Medal from Eastern Washington University, 1986; Washington Irving Medal for literary excellence from Nicholas Society, 1986; D.F.A., School of Visual Arts, 1987; L.H.D, Randolph-Macon College, Manhattanville College, 1988, and Longwood College, 1989; D.Litt., St. Andrews Presbyterian College, and John Hopkins University, 1990, University of Richmond, 1993; St. Louis Literary award, Quinnipiac College, 1990, presidential award, 1993.

WRITINGS:

UNDER NAME TOM WOLFE

(Self-illustrated) *The Kandy-Kolored Tangerine-Flake Streamline Baby* (essays), Farrar, Straus (New York City), 1965.

(Contributor) Alan Rinzler, editor, *The New York Spy,* David White (Port Washington, NY), 1967.

The Electric Kool-Aid Acid Test, Farrar, Straus, 1968.

The Pump House Gang (essays), Farrar, Straus, 1968, published as *The Mid-Atlantic Man and Other New Breeds in England and America,* Weidenfeld & Nicolson (London), 1969.

Radical Chic and Mau Mauing the Flak Catchers (essays), Farrar, Straus, 1970.

(Editor with E. W. Johnson, and contributor) *The New Journalism* (anthology), Harper (New York City), 1973.

(Self-illustrated) *The Painted Word,* Farrar, Straus, 1975.

(Self-illustrated) *Mauve Gloves & Madmen, Clutter & Vine, and Other Short Stories* (essays), Farrar, Straus, 1976.

(Contributor) Susan Feldman, editor, *Marie Cosindas, Color Photographs,* New York Graphic Society (New York City), 1978.

The Right Stuff (also see below), Farrar, Straus, 1979.

(Self-illustrated) *In Our Time* (essays), Farrar, Straus, 1980.

From Bauhaus to Our House, Farrar, Straus, 1981.

(Self-illustrated) *The Purple Decades: A Reader* (collection), Farrar, Straus, 1982.

The Bonfire of the Vanities (novel; also see below), Farrar, Straus, 1987.

Two Complete Books (contains *The Right Stuff* and *The Bonfire of the Vanities*), Wings (Belfast, ME), 1994.

A Man in Full (novel), Farrar, Straus, 1998.

Contributor of numerous articles to periodicals. Cofounder of literary quarterly *Shenandoah.*

ADAPTATIONS: The Right Stuff was adapted for a film of the same title, Warner Bros., 1983; *Bonfire of the Vanities,* directed by Brian DePalma and starring Tom Hanks, Melanie Griffith, and Bruce Willis, was filmed and released in 1990.

SIDELIGHTS: "Those of you who are not aware of Tom Wolfe should—really—do your best to acquaint yourselves with him," writes William F. Buckley in the *National Review.* "He is probably the most skilful writer in America. I mean by that he can do more things with words than anyone else." Satirist, caricaturist, social critic, coiner of phrases ("Radical Chic," "The Me Decade"), Wolfe has become known as a leading chronicler of American trends. His painstaking research and detailed accounts have made him a widely respected reporter; at the same time, his unorthodox style and frequently unpopular opinions have resulted in a great deal of controversy. Leslie Bennetts of the *Philadelphia Bulletin* calls him "a professional rogue," who has "needled and knifed at the mighty of every description, exposing in print the follies and foibles of superstars from Leonard Bernstein to the Hell's Angels. Gleefully ripping off every shred of disguise from anyone's pretensions, Wolfe has performed his dissections in *New York* Magazine, *Esquire,* and *Rolling Stone,* not to mention his earlier years on the *New York Herald Tribune* and the *Washington Post.*"

Considering Wolfe's body of work, Richard A. Kallan declares in *Dictionary of Literary Biography:* "Wolfe's writings have produced penetrating social and cultural insights, raised intriguing journalistic questions, and suggested the vast potential of nonfictional writing when exercised by a stylistically inventive, perceptive author committed to investigative reporting. For these accomplishments, Tom Wolfe ranks as one of the premier literary journalists in America."

Wolfe is generally recognized as one of the leaders in the branch of writing known as "New Journalism." Bennetts says that while Wolfe did not invent the movement, "he at least became its stentorian spokesman and most flamboyant practitioner." *Fort Lauderdale Sun-Sentinel* writer Margo Harakas believes that there is "only a handful of standouts among [New Journalists]—Jimmy Breslin, Gay Talese, Hunter Thompson, and of course, Wolfe, with his explosive punctuation, name brand detailing, and kaleidoscopic descriptions." In a *Writer's Digest* article, Wolfe defines New Journalism as "the use by people writing nonfiction of techniques which heretofore had been thought of as confined to the novel or to the short story, to create in one form both the kind of objective reality of journalism and the subjective reality that people have always gone to the novel for." The techniques employed in New Journalism, then, include a number of devices borrowed from traditional fiction writing: extensive dialogue; shifting point of view; scene-by-scene construction; detailed descriptions of setting, clothes, and other physical features; complex character development; and, depending on the reporter and on the subject, varying degrees of innovation in the use of language and punctuation.

Wolfe's association with New Journalism began in 1963, when he wrote his first magazine article, a piece on custom automobiles. He had become intrigued with the strange subculture of West Coast car customizers and was beginning to see these individuals as folk artists worthy of serious study. He convinced *Esquire* magazine to send him to California, where he researched the story, interviewed a number of subjects, and, says Harakas, "racked up a $750 tab at the Beverly Wilshire Hotel (picked up by *Esquire,* of course)." Then, having returned to New York to write the article, he found that standard journalistic techniques, those he had employed so successfully during his years of newspaper work, could not adequately describe the bizarre people and machines he had encountered in California.

Stymied, he put off writing the story until, finally, he called Byron Dobell, his editor at *Esquire,* and admitted that he was unable to finish the project. Dobell told him to type up his notes so that the magazine could get another writer to do the job. In the introduction to *The Kandy-Kolored Tangerine-Flake Streamline Baby,* Wolfe writes: "About 8 o'clock that night I started typing the notes out in the form of a memorandum that began, 'Dear Byron.' I started typing away, starting right with the first time I saw any custom cars in California." In an attempt to provide every possible detail for the writer who was to finish the piece, he wrote in a stream-of-consciousness style, including even some of his most garbled notes and random thoughts. "I wrapped up the memorandum about 6:15 A.M., and by this time it was 49 pages long. I took it over to *Esquire* as soon as they opened up, about 9:30 A.M. About 4 P.M. I got a call from Byron Dobell. He told me they were striking out the 'Dear Byron' at the top of the memorandum and running the rest of it in the magazine."

It is the style developed during the writing of the custom car article—his unique blend of "pop" language and creative punctuation—that for many years remained Wolfe's trademark. He was a pioneer in the use of what several reviewers refer to as an "aural" style of writing, a technique intended to make the reader come as close as possible to experiencing an event first-hand. Wilfrid Sheed, in the *New York Times Book Review,* says that Wolfe tries to find "a language proper to each subject, a special sound to convey its uniqueness"; and *Newsweek*'s Jack Kroll feels that Wolfe is "a genuine poet" among journalists, who is able "to get under the skin of a phenomenon and transmit its metabolic rhythm. . . . He creates the most vivid, most pertinent possible dimension of his subject." F. N. Jones, in a *Library Journal* article, describes Wolfe's prose as "free-flowing colorful Joycean, quote-slang, repetitive, cult or class jargon with literary and other reverberations."

Wolfe's style, combined with solid reporting and a highly critical eye, quickly gained a large audience for his magazine pieces. When his first book, *The Kandy-Kolored Tangerine-Flake Streamline Baby,* a collection of twenty-two of his best essays, was published in 1965, William James Smith wrote in *Commonweal:* "Two years ago [Tom Wolfe] was unknown and today those who are not mocking him are doing their level best to emulate him. Magazine editors are currently flooded with Zonk! articles written, putatively, in the manner of Wolfe and, by common account, uniformly impossible. . . . None of his parodists—and even fewer of his emulators—has successfully captured much of the flavor of Wolfe. . . . They miss the spark of personality that is more arresting than the funny punctuation. Wolfe has it, that magical quality that marks prose as distinctively one's own."

In *The Kandy-Kolored Tangerine-Flake Streamline Baby* Wolfe analyzes, caricaturizes, and satirizes a number of early-'60s American trends and pop culture heroes. His essays zero in on the city of Las Vegas, the Peppermint Lounge, demolition derbies, fashion, art galleries, doormen, nannies, and such personalities as Murray the K, Phil Spector, Baby Jane Holzer, and Muhammed Ali (then Cassius Clay). "He knows everything," writes Kurt Vonnegut in the *New York Times Book Review.* "I do not mean he *thinks* he knows everything. He is loaded with facile junk, as all personal journalists have to be—otherwise, how can they write so amusingly and fast?. . . . Verdict: Excellent book by a genius who will do anything to get attention."

What Wolfe has done, according to *Commonweal*'s Smith, "is simply to describe the brave new world of the 'unconscious avant-garde' who are shaping our future, but he has described this world with a vividness and accuracy that makes it something more than real." In a *New Republic* article, Joseph Epstein expresses the opinion that "Wolfe is perhaps most

fatiguing when writing about the lower classes. Here he becomes Dr. Wolfe, Department of American Studies, and what he finds attractive about the lower orders, as has many an intellectual slummer before him, is their vitality. At bottom, what is involved here is worship of the Noble Savage. . . . Wolfe is much better when he writes about New York City. Here he drops his studied spontaneity, eases up on the rococo, slips his doctorate, and takes on the tone of the reasonably feeling New Yorker who has not yet been knocked insensate by the clatter of that city." A *Newsweek* writer concludes that "partly, Wolfe belongs to the old noble breed of poet-journalists, like Ben Hecht, and partly he belongs to a new breed of supereducated hip sensibilities like Jonathan Miller and Terry Southern, who see the complete human comedy in everything from a hair-do to a holocaust. Vulgar? A bit. Sentimental? A tick. But this is the nature of journalism, with its crackling short waves transmitting the living moment."

In *The Electric Kool-Aid Acid Test,* Wolfe applies his distinctive brand of journalism to novelist Ken Kesey and his "Merry Pranksters," a West Coast group dedicated to LSD and the pursuit of the psychedelic experience. Joel Lieber of the *Nation* says that in this book Wolfe "has come as close as seems possible, with words, at re-creating the entire mental atmosphere of a scene in which one's understanding is based on feeling rather than verbalization. . . . [The book] is nonfiction told as experimental fiction; it is a genuine feat and a landmark in reporting style." Lawrence Dietz, in a *National Review* article, calls *The Electric Kool-Aid Acid Test* "the best work Wolfe has done, and certainly the most profound and insightful book that has been written about the psychedelic life. . . . [He] has elicited a history of the spread of LSD from 1960 (when Kesey and others got their first jolts in lab experiments) to 1967, when practically any kid with five dollars could buy some kind of trip or other." Dietz feels that Wolfe displays "a willingness to let accuracy take the place of the hysterical imprecations that have passed for reportage in most magazine articles and books" on this subject.

Kallan notes that *The Electric Kool-Aid Acid Test* demonstrates "a frequent characteristic of Wolfe's style," namely, "a repetition of a single metaphor to synthesize his thesis. Through [the book]. . . , Wolfe notes Kesey's battle cry, "You're either on the bus or off the bus.'. . . . The bus, as the reader soon realizes, symbolized the entire trip, the quest for personal growth and self-discovery. To say one is either on the bus or off the bus is to say he is either committed to the search for identity or he is not. There is no middle ground, no partial enthusiasm—one is completely dedicated or he is off the "bus.'"

Wolfe's 1970 book, *Radical Chic and Mau Mauing the Flak Catchers,* was made up of two lengthy essays. The first, "Radical Chic," elicited by far the most critical commentary; it deals with a fund-raising party given by Leonard Bernstein in his Park Avenue apartment on January 14, 1970, to raise money for the Black Panthers. Wolfe was at the party, and he became aware of the incongruity of the scene, distinguished, according to Melvin Maddocks of the *Christian Science Monitor,* by "white liberals nibbling caviar while signing checks for the revolution with their free hand." Thomas R. Edwards writes in the *New York Times Book Review:* "For Wolfe, the scene in the Bernsteins' living room demonstrates his pet sociological thesis, here called *nostalgie de la boue,* the aristocrat's hankering for a proletarian primitivism. He shows us cultivated parvenu Jews, torn between cherished new 'right wing' lifestyles and the 'left wing' politics of their own oppressive history, ludicrously confused about how to take the black revolution. Though there's a touch of ugliness in his determination to let us know, without seeming to do so, that certain socialites with gentile names weren't born that way, 'Radical Chic' is sometimes brilliant and telling in its dramatization of this case."

A *Times Literary Supplement* reviewer says that Wolfe "both defends and exonerates the Bernsteins, that is—their motives were sound, liberal, serious, responsible—while cocking an almighty snook at 'the essential double-track mentality of Radical Chic—*nostalgie de la boue* and high protocol' that can entertain Afro hair-styles with Roquefort cheese savouries in a Park Avenue duplex. . . . The slogan 'Mr. Parlour Panther,' in the end, is inevitably unfurled to flutter in the ironic breeze. Such is this dazzling piece of trapeze work by the most practised social stuntman of them all."

Many readers were not happy with *Radical Chic and Mau Mauing the Flak Catchers.* As William F. Buckley explains in the *National Review,* "[Wolfe] has written a very, very controversial book, for which he has been publicly excommunicated from the company of the orthodox by the bishops who preside over the *New York Review of Books.*" Buckley continues: "What Mr. Wolfe did in this book was MAKE FUN of Bernstein et al., and if you have never been told, you MUST NOT MAKE FUN of

Bernstein et al., when what hangs in the balance is Bernstein's moral prestige plus the integrity of Black Protest; learn the lesson now." Edwards feels that Wolfe "humiliates and degrades everyone concerned, his pre-potent but child-like and shiftless blacks no less than his gutless, time-serving, sexually-fearful white bureaucrats." Timothy Foote, in a *Time* article, notes: "When a *Time* reporter recently asked a minister of the Panther Party's shadow government about the truthfulness of Wolfe's *Radical Chic* account, the reply was ominous: 'You mean that dirty, blatant, lying, racist dog who wrote that fascist disgusting thing in *New York* magazine?'" Yet, despite the objections to the book, Foote insists, the fact remains that "it is generally so accurate that even some of the irate guests at the Bernsteins later wondered how Wolfe—who in fact used shorthand—managed to smuggle a tape recorder onto the premises."

Christopher Lehmann-Haupt of the *New York Times,* noting that "Radical Chic" first appeared as a magazine article, writes: "When the news got out that it would be published as a book eventually, one began to prepare a mental review of it. One had certain questions—the usual Tom Wolfe questions: Where exactly was Wolfe located when all those things occurred? Just how did he learn Leonard Bernstein's innermost fantasies? At exactly what points did Wolfe's imagination impinge on his inferences, and his inferences on his facts?. . . Still, one was prepared to forget those questions. The vision of the Beautiful People dos-a-dosing with black revolutionaries while white servants passed out 'little Roquefort cheese morsels rolled in crushed nuts' was too outrageous. Shivers of malice ran up and down one's spine. Wolfe's anatomy of radical chic would have to be celebrated." The book, Lehmann-Haupt concludes, "represents Wolfe at his best, worst, and most. It has his uncanny eye for life-styles; his obsessive lists of brand names and artifacts; his wicked, frequently cruel, cartoon of people's physical traits; his perfect mimicry of speech patterns. Once again, Wolfe proves himself the complete chameleon, capable of turning any color. He understands the human animal like no sociologist around."

The Painted Word was another of Wolfe's more controversial works. T. O'Hara, in a *Best Sellers* review, sums up the book's thesis: "About 10,000 people constitute the present art world. Artists, doing what they must to survive, obey orders and follow the gospel as written by the monarchs." Among these monarchs, in Wolfe's opinion, are three of our most influential and well-respected art critics: Clement

Greenberg, Harold Rosenberg, and Leo Steinberg (the "kings of cultureburg," he calls them). In a *Time* article, Robert Hughes says that "the New York art world, especially in its present decay, is the easiest target a pop sociologist could ask for. Most of it is a wallow of egotism, social climbing and power brokerage, and the only thing that makes it tolerable is the occasional reward of experiencing a good work of art in all its richness, complexity and difficulty. Take the art from the art world, as Wolfe does, and the matrix becomes fit for caricature. Since Wolfe is unable to show any intelligent response to painting, caricature is what we get. . . . Wolfe seems to know virtually nothing about the history of art, American or European."

New York Times art critic John Russell, writing in the *New York Times Book Review,* states: "If someone who is tone-deaf goes to Carnegie Hall every night of the year, he is, of course, entitled to his opinion of what he has listened to, just as a eunuch is entitled to his opinion of sex. But in the one case, as in the other, we on our side are entitled to discount what they say. Given the range, the variety and the degree of accomplishment represented by the names on Mr. Wolfe's list [including artists such as Pollock, de Kooning, Warhol, Newman, Rauschenberg, and Stella], we are entitled to think that if he got no visual reward from any of them, . . . the fault may not lie with the art."

As Ruth Berenson of the *National Review* points out, however, response to the book is generally dependent on the extent to which an individual is involved in the world of modern art. She maintains that *The Painted Word* "will delight those who have long harbored dark suspicions that modern art beginning with Picasso is a put-on, a gigantic hoax perpetrated on a gullible public by a mysterious cabal of artists, critics, dealers, and collectors aided and abetted by *Time* and *Newsweek*. Those who take modern art somewhat more seriously will be disappointed."

In *From Bauhaus to Our House,* published in 1981, Wolfe does to modern architecture what he did to modern art in *The Painted Word,* and the response has been similar: Readers close to the subject tend to resent the intrusion by an "outsider," while those with a more detached point of view often appreciate the author's fresh perspective. *New York Times* architecture critic Paul Goldberger, in a *New York Times Book Review* article, writes: "Mr. Wolfe wants to argue that ideology has gotten in the way of common sense. Beginning half a century ago with the origins

of the International Style in Europe, he attempts to trace the development of that style, which for many, including Mr. Wolfe, is a virtual synonym for modern architecture. . . . We are told how the International Style became a 'compound'—a select, private, cult-like group of ideologues [including Walter Gropius, Mies van der Rohe, Marcel Breuer, and Josef Albers] whose great mission, as Mr. Wolfe sees it, was to foist modern design upon an unwilling world. . . . The problem, I think . . . is that Tom Wolfe has no eye. He has a wonderful ear, and he listens hard and long, but he does not seem to see. . . . He does precisely what he warns us against; he has listened to the words, not looked at the architecture."

In a *Washington Post Book World* review, *Post* architecture critic Benjamin Forgey says that *Bauhaus* "is a case of crying Wolfe for one more time. *Bauhaus* is distinguished by the same total loathing of modern culture that motivated *The Painted Word*. . . . Wolfe's explanation is that modernism has been a conspiracy. In place of the New York critics who foisted abstract art upon us, we have the European giants of architecture . . . and their abject American followers. In Wolfe's view the motivation was pretty much the same, too. They were all playing the hypocritical bohemian game of spitting on the bourgeois." Forgey feels that "there is some truth in this, but it makes for a thin book and a narrow, limited history of architecture in the 20th century."

On the other hand, *New York Times* literary critic Lehmann-Haupt makes the point that even many architects have been unhappy with the structures created by proponents of the Bauhaus school. This style of architecture (distinguished by what is often referred to as a "glass box" appearance) was, for instance, denigrated by architect Peter Blake in his 1977 book, *Form Follows Fiasco*. According to Lehmann-Haupt, Blake "anathematized modern architecture for being sterile, functionless and ugly"; thus Wolfe "has not really come up with anything very startling when he laments the irony that four-fifths of the way into the American Century, when what we ought to be expressing with our building is 'exuberance, power, empire, grandeur, or even high spirits and playfulness,' what we still see inflicted upon us is the anti-bourgeois, socialist, pro-worker ideas that arose from 'the smoking rubble of Europe after the Great War.' But the explication of this notion is done with such verve and hilarity by Mr. Wolfe that its substance almost doesn't seem to matter. . . . It flows with natural rhetorical rhythm. . . . And often enough it is to laugh right out loud." John Brooks, in a review for Chicago's *Tribune Books,* calls the book "a readable polemic on how in our architecture over the past few decades things have gone very much as they have in the other visual arts—a triumph of conformity over true innovation, of timidity over uninhibited expression, of irony over straightfor- wardness, of posing over real accomplishment. . . . *From Bauhaus to Our House* is lucidly and for the most part gracefully written."

In 1979 Wolfe published the book that many critics consider his finest: *The Right Stuff,* an award-win- ning study of the early years of the U.S. space pro- gram. At one point in the book Wolfe attempts to define the "ineffable quality" from which the title is taken: "It obviously involved bravery. But it was not bravery in the simple sense of being willing to risk your life . . . any fool could do that. . . . No, the idea . . . seemed to be that a man should have the ability to go up in a hurtling piece of machinery and put his hide on the line and then have the moxie, the reflexes, the experience, the coolness, to pull it back in the last yawning moment—and then to go up again *the next day,* and the next day, and every next day."

The main characters in the book are, of course, the first U.S. astronaut team: Scott Carpenter, Gordon Cooper, John Glenn, Gus Replace, Wally Schirra, Alan Shepard, and Deke Slayton. Wolfe assiduously chronicles their early careers as test pilots, their private lives, their selection for the astronaut pro- gram and the subsequent medical processing and training. But, as *Commonweal*'s Thomas Powers points out, *The Right Stuff* "is not a history; it is far too thin in dates, facts and source citations to serve any such pulse. It is a work of literature which must stand or fall as a coherent text, and its subject is not the Mercury program itself but the impulse behind it, the unreflecting competitiveness which drove the original astronauts to the quite extraordinary lengths Wolfe describes so vividly." That the author goes beyond mere reportage of historical fact is confirmed by Mort Sheinman in a *Chicago Tribune* article: "Wolfe tells us what it's like to go 'shooting straight through the top of the sky,' to be 'in a king's soli- tude, unique and inviolate, above the dome of the world.' He describes what happens when someone is immolated by airplane fuel, and he talks about the nightmares and hallucinations experienced by the wives. . . . [*The Right Stuff*] is a dazzling piece of work, something that reveals much about the nature of bravery and celebrity and—yes—patriotism."

Time writer R. Z. Sheppard says that the book "is crammed with inside poop and racy incident that 19 years ago was ignored by what [Wolfe] terms the 'proper Victorian gents' of the press. The fast cars, booze, astro groupies, the envies and injuries of the military caste system were not part of what Ameri- cans would have considered the right stuff. Wolfe lays it all out in brilliantly stated Op Lit scenes: the tacky cocktail lounges of Cocoa Beach where one could hear the *Horst Wessel Song* sung by ex-rocket scientists of the Third Reich; Vice President Lyndon Johnson furiously cooling his heels outside the Glenn house because Annie Glenn would not let him in during her husband's countdown; Alan Shepard los- ing a struggle with his full bladder moments before lift-off; the overeager press terrifying Ham the chimp after his proficient flight; the astronauts surrounded by thousands of cheering Texans waving hunks of raw meat during an honorary barbecue in the Hous- ton Coliseum."

Christopher Lehmann-Haupt of the *New York Times* writes: "What fun it is to watch Mr. Wolfe put the antiseptic space program into the traces of his inimi- table verbal cadenzas. It's a little like hearing the story of Jesus of Nazareth through the lips of the Chicago nightclub comedian Lord Buckley." Lehmann-Haupt says that in this book Wolfe under- takes "the restoration of the zits and rogue cilia of hair to the face of the American space program" and reveals a good deal of the gossip that was denied the public by a hero-worshipping press in the early 'six- ties, gossip "about how the test-pilot fraternity looked down on the early astronauts for being trained monkeys in a capsule ('spam in a can') instead of pilots in control of their craft; about the real feelings of the original seven for one another and the tension that arose between the upright John Glenn and some of the others over their after-hours behavior, particu- larly with the 'juicy little girls' who materialized wherever they trained; and about what National Aeronautical and Space Administration engineers re- ally felt about the flight of Gus Grissom and Scott Carpenter and the possibility that they had secretly panicked."

Former test pilot and astronaut Michael Collins (a member of the Gemini 10 flight and command mod- ule pilot on the Apollo 11 moon flight), writes in a *Washington Post Book World* review: "I lived at Edwards [Air Force Base, site of the Air Force Flight Test Center], for four years, and, improbable as some of Tom's tales seem, I know he's telling it like it was. He is the first gifted writer to explore the relationship between test pilots and astronauts—the obvious similarities and the subtle differences. He's obviously done a lot of homework—too much in some cases. Some of this stuff could only be interesting to Al Shepard's mother. While the first part of the book is a paean to guts, to the 'right stuff,' it is followed by a chronology—but one that might have profited from a little tighter editing. But it's still light-years ahead of the endless drivel [Norman] Mailer has put out about the Apollo program, and in places the Wolfe genius really shines." Collins feels that at times Wolfe allows himself to get too close to his subject: "He's almost one of the boys—and there's too much to admire and not enough to eviscerate." As a result "*The Right Stuff* is not vintage, psychedelic Tom Wolfe, but if you . . . have ever been curious about what the space program was really all about in those halcyon Kennedy and Mercury years, then this is your book."

In a review of *The Right Stuff* for the *Lone Star Book Review*, Martha Heimberg says that, for the most part, "Wolfe's reporting, while being marvelously entertaining writing, has also represented a telling and trustworthy point of view. His is one of those finely critical intelligences that can detect the slightest pretention or falsification in an official posture or social pose. And, when he does, he goes after the hypocrisy—whether large or small, left or right—with all the zeal of the dedicated reformer." Like Collins, Heimberg feels that *The Right Stuff* "represents a departure for the satirist whose observant eye and caustic pen have impaled on the page a wide range of American social phenomena" in that Wolfe "clearly likes his subjects—none are treated as grist for the satirist's mill, but put down with as great a skill and detail as an observer could possibly muster." She concludes that "the book represents a tremendous accomplishment and a new direction for a writer who figures among the top stylists of his generation."

By the mid-1980s Wolfe had a new ambition for his writing. As he told the *New York Times:* "I was curious, having spouted off so much about fiction and nonfiction, and having said that the novelists weren't doing a good job, to see what would happen if I tried it. Also, I guess I subconsciously had the suspicion that maybe, what if all this to-do I've made about nonfiction is because I really, secretly think I can't do a novel. So I said, well, I've got to prove this to myself." The result was *The Bonfire of the Vanities,* a novel that exposes the greed and hate seething in modern New York City. In the book, a

smug Wall Streeter named Sherman McCoy is reduced to a political pawn when he is implicated in the hit-and-run traffic death of a young black man. *Washington Post Book World*'s Jonathan Yardley calls *Bonfire* "a superb human comedy and the first novel ever to get contemporary New York, in all its arrogance and shame and heterogeneity and insularity, exactly right." After his novel became a major bestseller, Wolfe issued what he called a "literary manifesto" in *Harper's* magazine. He urged fellow novelists to abandon the esoteric literary experiments that have characterized fiction for much of the twentieth century and use realism to chronicle the bizarre and astounding world around them. The author's peers reacted with both praise and condemnation. "Ever the provocateur," reported *Time,* "Wolfe is enjoying the controversy."

Although there can be no question that Wolfe has achieved a reputation as a superb stylist and skillful reporter, no discussion of Wolfe would be complete without some mention of his famous wardrobe. *Philadelphia Bulletin* writer Leslie Bennetts tells of an encounter with the author when he lectured at Villanova University: "The legendary sartorial splendors were there, of course: the gorgeous three-piece creamy white suit he has been renowned for . . . (how many must he have, do you suppose, to appear in spotless vanilla every day: rows upon rows of them hanging in shadowed closets, a veritable army of Gatsby ghosts waiting to emerge?). Not to mention the navy suede shoes, dark as midnight, or the jaunty matching suede hat, or the sweeping midnight cashmere coat of the exact same hue, or the crisp matching tie on which perched a golden half-moon pin to complement the glittering gold watch chain that swung gracefully from the milky vest. Or the navy silk handkerchief peeking out from the white suit pocket, or the white silk handkerchief peeking out from the navy coat pocket."

Wolfe told Bennetts that he began wearing the white suits in 1962: "That was when I had a white suit made, started wearing it in January, and found it annoyed people tremendously. Even slight departures in dress at that time really spun people out. So I liked it. It's kind of a harmless form of aggression, I guess." But Wolfe's mode of dress has also been an important part of his journalism, serving as a device to distance him from his subject. He told Susan Forrest of the *Fort Lauderdale News:* "A writer can find out more if he doesn't pretend to be hip. . . . If people see you are an outsider, they will come up and tell you things. If you're trying to be hip, you can't ask a lot of naive questions." This technique has been effective for Wolfe in interviewing stock car racers, Hell's Angels, and— particularly—astronauts. He feels that at least part of the success of *The Right Stuff* is due to the fact that he did not try to get too close to that inner circle. Wolfe told Janet Maslin of the *New York Times Book Review:* "I looked like Ruggles of Red Gap to them, I'm sure. . . . But I've long since given up on the idea of going into a situation trying to act like part of it. . . . Besides, it was useless for me to try to fit into the world of pilots, because I didn't know a thing about flying. I also sensed that pilots, like people in the psychedelic life, really dislike people who presume a familiarity with the Lodge."

A writer for *Time* calls Wolfe's form of dress "a splendiferous advertisement for his individuality. The game requires a lot of reverse spin and body English but it boils down to antichic chic. Exclaims Wolfe proudly: 'I own no summer house, no car, I wear tank tops when I swim, long white pants when I play tennis, and I'm probably the last man in America to still do the Royal Canadian Air Force exercises.'"

"Whatever his future literary offerings, Wolfe thus far has delivered a bursting portfolio of provocative observations and thoughts," muses Kallan. "When students of American culture look back on the last third of the twentieth century, Wolfe may well be the person toward whom they turn. More than any other fiction or nonfiction writer, he has recorded in detail the popular mentality of the period. For this reason his essays seem certain to be restudied. Already, signs of reevaluation and discussion of his work are evident: once criticism focused on Wolfe's writing style and his school of journalism, but now it looks more to the meaning and implications of his message."

BIOGRAPHICAL/CRITICAL SOURCES:

BOOKS

Authors in the News, Volume 2, Gale (Detroit), 1976.

Bellamy, Joe David, editor, *The New Fiction: Interviews with Innovative American Writers,* University of Illinois Press (Champaign, IL), 1974.

Bestsellers 89, Issue 1, Gale, 1989.

Connery, Thomas B., editor, *A Sourcebook of American Literary Journalism: Representative Writers in an Emerging Genre,* Greenwood Press (Westport, CT), 1992.

Contemporary Literary Criticism, Gale, Volume 1, 1973, Volume 2, 1974, Volume 9, 1978, Volume 15, 1980, Volume 35, 1985, Volume 51, 1989.

Dennis, Everette E., *The Magic Writing Machine: Student Probes of the New Journalism,* School of Journalism, University of Oregon (Eugene, OR), 1971.

Dictionary of Literary Biography, Volume 185: *American Literary Journalists, 1945-1995, First Series,* Gale, 1997.

Fact and Fiction: The New Journalism and the Nonfiction Novel, University of North Carolina Press (Chapel Hill), 1977.

Hellmann, John, *Fables of Fact: The New Journalism as New Fiction,* University of Illinois Press (Urbana), 1981.

Literary Selves: Autobiography and Contemporary American Nonfiction, Greenwood Press, 1993.

Lounsberry, *The Art of Fact: Contemporary Artists of Nonfiction,* Greenwood Press, 1990.

McKeen, William, *Tom Wolfe,* Prentice Hall (Englewood Cliffs, NJ), 1995.

Scura, Dorothy, editor, *Conversations with Tom Wolfe,* University Press of Mississippi (Jackson), 1990.

Shomette, Doug, editor, *the Critical Response to Tom Wolfe,* Greenwood Press, 1992.

PERIODICALS

America, February 5, 1977; April 2, 1988.

American Journalism Review, October, 1994, pp. 40-46.

American Journal of Sociology, November 1983, pp. 739-41.

American Libraries, July-August, 1990, p. 644.

Atlantic, October, 1979; December, 1987.

Best Sellers, August, 1975.

Books and Art, September 28, 1979.

Books in Canada, April, 1988.

Business Week, November 23, 1987.

Chicago Tribune, September 9, 1979; September 15, 1979; January 16, 1983; November 4, 1987.

Christian Science Monitor, November 17, 1970; November 3, 1987.

Columbia Journalism Review, winter, 1966, pp. 29-34; July/August, 1972, pp. 45-47.

Commentary, March, 1971; May, 1977; February, 1980; February, 1988.

Commonweal, September 17, 1965; December 20, 1968; March 3, 1978; October 12, 1979; February 26, 1988.

Communication Monographs, number 46, 1979, pp. 52-62.

Critical Studies in Mass Communication, March, 1984, pp. 51-65.

Detroit News, October 14, 1979; November 9, 1980.

Economist, December 22, 1990, p. 120.

Encounter, September, 1977.

Fort Lauderdale News, April 22, 1975.

Fort Lauderdale Sentinel, April 22, 1975.

Globe and Mail (Toronto), December 5, 1987.

Guardian Weekly, February 21, 1988.

Harper's, February, 1971; November, 1989; January, 1990.

Journal of American Culture, summer, 1990, pp. 39-50; fall, 1991.

Journal of Popular Culture, summer, 1974, pp. 71-79; summer, 1975; fall, 1984, pp. 111-15.

Library Journal, August, 1968; February 15, 1995, p. 199.

Listener, February 11, 1988.

London Review of Books, February 18, 1988.

Lone Star Book Review, November, 1979.

Los Angeles Times, October 19, 1979; November 22, 1987; October 12, 1989.

Los Angeles Times Book Review, November 2, 1980; October 25, 1981; October 17, 1982; January 23, 1983; October 25, 1987.

Nation, March 5, 1977; November 3, 1977; January 28, 1991, p. 100.

National Review, August 27, 1968; January 26, 1971; August 1, 1975; February 19, 1977; December 18, 1987.

New Leader, January 31, 1977.

New Republic, July 14, 1965; December 19, 1970; November 23, 1987.

New Statesman, February 12, 1988.

Newsweek, June 28, 1965; August 26, 1968; June 9, 1975; September 17, 1979; October 26, 1987.

New York, September 21, 1981; March 21, 1988; January 7, 1991, p. 64.

New Yorker, February 1, 1988.

New York Review of Books, August 26, 1965, pp. 3-5; February 3, 1966, pp. 18-24; December 17, 1970; June 26, 1975; January 20, 1977; October 28, 1979; November 4, 1982; February 4, 1988.

New York Times, November 25, 1970; May 27, 1975; November 26, 1976; September 14, 1979; October 9, 1981; December 20, 1981; October 13, 1987; October 22, 1987; November 21, 1987; December 31, 1987; January 3, 1988; March 11, 1988.

New York Times Book Review, June 27, 1965, pp. 4, 38; August 18, 1968; November 29, 1970; December 3, 1972; June 15, 1975; December 26, 1976; October 28, 1979; October 11, 1981; October 10, 1982; November 1, 1987.

Observer (London), February 7, 1988.

Partisan Review, number 3, 1969, pp. 535-44; number 2, 1974.

People, December 24, 1979; November 23, 1987.

Philadelphia Bulletin, February 10, 1975.

Punch, February 12, 1988.

Rolling Stone, August 21, 1980; November 5-December 10, 1987.

Saturday Review, September 15, 1979; April, 1981.

Spectator, February 13, 1988.

Time, September 6, 1968; December 21, 1970; June 23, 1975; December 27, 1976; September 29, 1979; November 9, 1987; February 13, 1989; November 27, 1989.

Times (London), February 11, 1988; February 13, 1989; April 22, 1989.

Times Literary Supplement, October 1, 1971; November 30, 1979; November 26, 1980; March 18, 1988.

Tribune Books (Chicago), December 7, 1980; October 25, 1981; January 16, 1983; August 2, 1987; October 18, 1987.

U.S. News and World Report, November 23, 1987; December 25, 1989, p. 117.

Village Voice, September 10, 1979.

Wall Street Journal, October 29, 1987.

Washington Monthly, March, 1988.

Washington Post, September 4, 1979; October 23, 1980; March 27, 1988; October 17, 1989.

Washington Post Book World, September 9, 1979; November 23, 1980; November 15, 1981; November 7, 1982; October 25, 1987.

Writer's Digest, January, 1970.*

*   *   *

WOLFE, Tom
See WOLFE, Thomas Kennerly, Jr.

*   *   *

WOLVERTON, Terry 1954-

PERSONAL: Born August 23, 1954, in Cocoa Beach, FL; companion of Susan Silton (a visual artist).

Education: Attended University of Detroit, 1972-73, University of Toronto, 1973-74, and Sagaris Institute, 1975; Thomas Jefferson College, B.A., 1977; Feminist Studio Workshop, Certificate, 1978.

ADDRESSES: Home—Los Angeles, CA. *Agent*—Robert Drake, Drake Literary Agency, 314 South Iseminger St., Philadelphia, PA 19107-6904.

CAREER: Woman's Building, Los Angeles, CA, calendar editor, 1977-81, administrative assistant, 1981-84, member of board of directors, 1982-86, development director, 1984-88, executive director, 1988-89; Consult'Her (management consulting firm), principal, 1982—. Adult education instructor in and around Los Angeles, CA. Los Angeles Artists Organizations, founder, 1986; California Confederation of the Arts, member of Public Policy Committee, 1986-88; Fringe Festival Los Angeles, member of board of directors, 1987-88; Los Angeles Poetry Festival, member of advisory board, 1990—. Lesbian Art Project, cofounder, 1977, codirector, 1977-80; Incest Awareness Project, co-organizer, 1979-81; White Women's Anti-Racism Consciousness Raising, founder, 1980; ArtTable, member, 1987-89; First Impressions Performance, member of advisory committee, 1991-94.

MEMBER: PEN Center U.S.A. West.

AWARDS, HONORS: Award from Gay and Lesbian Academic Union, 1981; Merit Award from JVC Tokyo Video Festival, 1981, for *Me and My Shadow;* artist in residence, California Arts Council, 1984-96; Lesbian Rights Award from Southern California Women for Understanding, 1986; grant from Los Angeles Cultural Affairs Department, 1990-91; Vesta Award in Literature, Woman's Building, 1991; first place winner, *Sheila-Na-Gig* Annual Poetry Contest, 1994; Movers and Shakers Award for women writers, from Southern California Library for Social Research, 1995.

WRITINGS:

Blue Moon (poems and prose), Women's Graphic Center (Los Angeles, CA), 1977.
In Silence Secrets Turn to Lies/Secrets Shared Become Sacred Truth (performance text), produced in Los Angeles, at Woman's Building, 1979.
(With Vicki Stolsen) *Ya Got Class, Real Class* (performance text), produced in Los Angeles, at Los Angeles Contemporary Exhibitions, 1980.

Medium: Memory/Muse (performance text), produced in Long Beach, CA, at Long Beach Museum of Art, 1983.
Familiar (performance text), produced in Venice, CA, at Social and Public Art Resource Center, 1984.
Me and My Shadow (performance text), produced in New York City, at ABC No Rio, 1984.
(With Catherine Stifter) *dis-a-buse: to free from a misconception or delusion* (performance text), produced at Woman's Building, 1986.
A Merry Little Christmas (three-act play), staged reading produced in Los Angeles, at Celebration Theater, 1987.
(Editor with Benjamin Weissman) *Harbinger: Poetry and Fiction by Los Angeles Writers,* Los Angeles Festival and Beyond Baroque (Los Angeles), 1990.
(Editor with Robert Drake) *Indivisible: New Short Fiction by West Coast Gay and Lesbian Writers,* Plume (New York), 1991.
(Editor) *Blood Whispers: L.A. Writers on AIDS,* Silverton Books (Los Angeles), Volume I, 1991, Volume II, 1994.
Black Slip (poems), Clothespin Fever Press (San Diego, CA), 1992.
(Editor) Brenda L. Underhill, *Creating Visibility: Providing Lesbian-Sensitive and Lesbian-Specific Alcoholism Recovery Services,* Alcoholism Center for Women (Los Angeles), 1993.
(Editor with Drake) *Hers: Brilliant New Fiction by Lesbian Writers,* Faber (Boston), 1995.
(Editor with Drake) *His: Brilliant New Fiction by Gay Writers,* Faber, 1995.
Bailey's Beads (novel), Faber, 1996.
(Editor with Drake) *His 2: Brilliant New Fiction by Gay Writers,* Faber, 1997.
(Editor with Drake) *Hers 2: Brilliant New Fiction by Lesbian Writers,* Faber, 1997.

Author of exhibition catalogs. Work represented in anthologies, including *Grand Passion: The Poets of Los Angeles and Beyond,* Red Wind Books, 1995; *The Femme Mystique,* edited by Leslea Newman, Alyson (Boston, MA), 1995; and *The Best Lesbian Erotica 1995,* edited by Tristan Taormina and Heather Lewis, Cleis (Pittsburgh, PA), 1996. Contributor of articles, stories, and poems to magazines, including *Caprice, Modern Words, Evergreen Chronicles, American Writing, Los Angeles Weekly,* and *California Quarterly.*

SIDELIGHTS: Terry Wolverton has co-edited several popular collections of gay and lesbian writing.

"Wolverton," writes Patti Capel Swartz in *Gay and Lesbian Literature,* "has been a primary force in creating visibility for artists and writers, and in forging cohesion and creativity within the feminist lesbian, gay, bi-sexual and trans communities."

Together with Robert Drake, Wolverton has co-edited the collections *His, His 2, Hers* and *Hers 2.* Speaking of *His,* a collection of fiction by a number of gay writers, the critic for *Publishers Weekly* finds the book to be "rich, imaginative and diverse. . . . These stories evince a wide range of characters and locales that hold the reader's interest." In a review of *Hers,* a collection of fiction by lesbian writers, Whitney Scott in *Booklist* concludes: "This is a thought-provoking compilation worthy of non-lesbian readers' attention."

"Wolverton's work and politics," writes Swartz, "are inseparable. Her life reflects her work, and her work her life. She has never turned away from looking at the issues of the communities in which she works. . . . Wolverton's work demonstrates a full and diverse spectrum of living and being. Her work, in every form, demonstrates the full range of her humanity."

BIOGRAPHICAL/CRITICAL SOURCES:

BOOKS

Gay and Lesbian Literature, Volume 2, St. James Press (Detroit), 1998.

PERIODICALS

Artweek, August 10, 1985.
Baltimore Alternative, September, 1996.
Booklist, August, 1995, p. 1929; September 1, 1996, p. 66.
High Performance, spring/summer, 1988.
Lambda Book Report, September/October, 1995, p. 27; September/October, 1996, p. 23; November, 1997, pp. 8-9.
Library Journal, June 1, 1997, p. 153; June 15, 1997, p. 100.
Los Angeles Herald Examiner, December 30, 1987.
Outlines, September, 1996.
Outnow!, October 15, 1996.
Pasadena Weekly, October 7, 1994.
Publishers Weekly, July 3, 1995, p. 57; August 14, 1995, p. 77; July 15, 1996, p. 56.

WRIGHT, Francesca
See ROBINS, Denise (Naomi)

* * *

ZIMMERMAN, Bruce 1952-

PERSONAL: Born June 11, 1952, in Sacramento, CA; son of Warren (an air force officer) and Lorraine (LaGue) Zimmerman; married Bettina Foy Benson, September 24, 1977; children: Quinn, Cort. *Education:* Attended San Francisco State University, 1975-78.

ADDRESSES: Home—1824 Vamo Dr., Sarasota, FL 34231. *Agent*—A. L. Hart, Jr., Fox Chase Agency, Public Ledger Building, Philadelphia, PA 19106.

CAREER: Journalist in San Miguel de Allende, Mexico, 1983-88; writer.

MEMBER: International Association of Crime Writers, International PEN, Authors Guild, Mystery Writers of America.

AWARDS, HONORS: National short story award from Nissan Corp., 1979, for "An Open Door"; Edgar Allan Poe Award nomination, Mystery Writers of America, 1989, for *Blood Under the Bridge.*

WRITINGS:

"QUINN PARKER" MYSTERY SERIES

Blood Under the Bridge, Harper (New York City), 1989.
Thicker than Water, HarperCollins (New York City), 1992.
Full-Bodied Red, HarperCollins, 1993.
Crimson Green, HarperCollins, 1994.

OTHER

Also author of short stories, including "An Open Door," and of "Bay Rum," a feature film optioned by Burt Reynolds Productions, 1989.

SIDELIGHTS: Bruce Zimmerman lives in the San Francisco Bay Area, which is also the setting for his "Quinn Parker" mystery series. Parker is a therapist specializing in phobias, particularly fears of heights, oceans, and flying. In his debut, *Blood under the*

Bridge, Parker both investigates and becomes the prime suspect in the murder of a former girlfriend. Marilyn Stasio, a reviewer for the *New York Times Book Review,* allows that Zimmerman was trafficking in "some pretty tired conventions here," but finds that the author "consistently makes something tricky out of these formula pieces." Referring to the Bay Area setting, Stasio notes, "Other detectives might have staked out this territory, but Mr. Zimmerman's likable hero makes a fresh claim." Reviewing *Thicker than Water,* another Quinn Parker adventure, Stasio credits the author with maintaining "a light, amusing touch that keeps the twisty plot and unpredictable characters in brisk motion."

Full-Bodied Red is the third mystery featuring Parker, this one set in the wine country of California. The plot concerns a young patient of Parker's who is the heir to a large vineyard. The heir's stepfather attacks Parker, and is subsequently found dead; once again, the therapist is a prime suspect in the very crime he is trying to solve. A *Publishers Weekly* writer calls the novel "a smooth, literate puzzle with a couple of surprises" in its web of blackmail, family secrets, and suspicious deaths. *Crimson Green,* the fourth entry in the series, is set on the tony golf courses of the West Coast. A pro golfer is gunned down just as he is about to capture a badly-needed title. Parker, caddying for a friend, plunges into the investigation. A *Publishers Weekly* reviewer credits Zimmerman with being "adept" at writing action scenes, and further notes that the author "provides enough male bonding here for a series of beer commercials."

BIOGRAPHICAL/CRITICAL SOURCES:

PERIODICALS

Booklist, August, 1994, p. 2029.
New York Times Book Review, July 9, 1989, section 7, p. 24; June 30, 1991.
Publishers Weekly, April 5, 1993, p. 67; August 8, 1994, p. 392.